A history of Eastern Europe

Eastern Europe has been divided from the West by much more than the relatively ephemeral experience of communist rule and Soviet domination, and the major problems and challenges confronting post-communist Eastern Europe are as much political, social and cultural as they are economic.

In *A history of Eastern Europe: Crisis and change*, Robert Bideleux and Ian Jeffries examine the problems that have bedevilled this troubled region during its imperial past, in the interwar period, under fascism, under communism and since 1989. The book provides a thematic historical survey and analysis of the formative processes of political, social and economic change which have played the paramount roles in shaping the development of the region. This is the most ambitious and wide-ranging history of the 'lands between', the lands which have lain between Germany, Italy and the Tsarist and Soviet empires.

While mainly concentrating on the modern era and on the effects of ethnic nationalism, fascism and communism, the book also offers original, striking and revisionist coverage of:

- ancient and medieval times
- the Hussite Revolution, the Renaissance, the Reformation and the Counter-Revolution
- the legacies of Byzantium, the Ottoman Empire and the Habsburg Empire
- the rise and decline of the Polish-Lithuanian Commonwealth
- the impact of the region's powerful Russian and Germanic neighbours
- rival concepts of 'Central' and 'Eastern Europe'
- the 1920s land reforms and the 1930s Depression
- democratization and the 'Return to Europe'

Robert Bideleux is Director of the Centre of Russian and East European Studies and Senior Lecturer in Politics at the University of Wales Swansea. **Ian Jeffries** is a member of the Centre and a lecturer in the Department of Economics, the University of Wales Swansea.

A history of Eastern Europe

Crisis and change

Robert Bideleux and Ian Jeffries

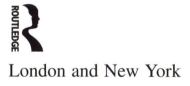

London and New York

For our parents

First published 1998
by Routledge
11 New Fetter Lane, London EC4P 4EE

Simultaneously published in the USA and Canada
by Routledge
29 West 35th Street, New York, NY 10001

© 1998 Robert Bideleux and Ian Jeffries

Typeset in Times by Keystroke, Jacaranda Lodge, Wolverhampton
Printed in Great Britain by T.J. International Ltd, Padstow, Cornwall

British Library Cataloguing in Publication Data
A catalogue record for this book is available from the British Library

Library of Congress Cataloguing in Publication Data
Bideleux, Robert.
    A history of eastern Europe : crisis and change / Robert Bideleux
and Ian Jeffries.
        p.   cm.
    Includes bibliographical references and index.
    1. Europe, Eastern—History. I. Jeffries, Ian. II. Title.
DJK38.B53   1997
947—dc21   97–12358
                                                          CIP

ISBN 0–415–16111–8
        0–415–16112–6 (pbk)

Contents

Maps

Preface

The central purpose of this book is to provide a thematic historical survey and analysis of the formative processes of political, social and economic change which (in our judgement) have played the paramount roles in shaping the development of East Central and South-eastern Europe: regions which in recent times have had the great misfortune of lying between the former Tsarist and Soviet empires, on the one side, and Germany and Italy, on the other.

The book is the result of nearly a decade of fruitful collaboration between two authors who have shared a long-standing interest in East Central and South-eastern Europe, a staunch belief in civic values and tolerance, and a strong commitment to interdisciplinary approaches to academic study. It was originally envisaged that this thematic historical survey and analysis of the region as a whole would be complemented by separate chapters on the evolution of its individual states during the twentieth century, all within a single volume. A natural division of labour recommended itself from the outset: Robert Bideleux would mainly provide the thematic and historical perspectives, analyses and narratives, while Ian Jeffries would mainly provide more detailed accounts and analyses of recent economic and political changes in individual countries. However, as we became more and more aware of the bearing of the imperial past and of the inter-war years on the complex problems of the post-communist present, the project far outgrew the confines of a single book. Hence we have had to reorganize our material into two volumes, the first of which has been largely written by Robert Bideleux, albeit with indispensable inputs from Ian Jeffries at every stage. This should be seen as the first part of a joint two-volume project. The second book, which is well under way, will provide more detailed treatment of individual states during the twentieth century, paying particular attention to their transition to democracy and the market economy during the 1990s. Nevertheless, we believe that the present work can be read as a coherent and self-contained thematic survey and interpretation of the political, social and economic evolution of East Central and South-eastern Europe from late antiquity to the mid-1990s.

Even in a book of this magnitude, it is impossible to cover every conceivable angle. One has to be judiciously selective. We took an early decision to minimize the space devoted to the more ephemeral forms of military and diplomatic activity, partly because these have already received abundant attention from military and diplomatic historians, but mainly because we believe that in the long run the huffing and puffing of soldiers and diplomats has been of less consequence than the interaction of broader and more persistent political, social, cultural and economic processes. Of course we have endeavoured to outline and discuss major military and diplomatic actions and events which have had enduring effects on Eastern Europe, especially the Mongol incursions (1240–41, 1259, 1287), the medieval Crusades, the Thirty Years' War (1618–48), the devastating Ottoman and Swedish invasions, the successive partitions of Poland (1772, 1793, 1795), the Congress of Vienna (1815), the Berlin Congress of 1878, the two world wars, the peace settlements of 1919–20 and the notorious 'percentages agreement' between Churchill and Stalin in October 1944. On the whole, however, we find ourselves in agreement with the well-known British historian of Poland, Norman Davies: 'Very few, if any, of the diplomatic memoranda concerning Poland's future ever exerted a decisive influence on the course of events. Many of them . . . remained a dead letter . . . Others were simply ignored. The most important of them did nothing but express the pious aspirations of their authors or confirm the details of political settlements already accomplished . . . At . . . critical moments, matters were decided not at the conference table, but by the situation on the ground and by the men who held the reins of practical power. At moments of less importance, diplomatic action counted for even less . . . The Polish nation grew from infancy to maturity regardless of the diplomats, and it owes them no debt of gratitude' (Davies 1982: 15).

Similarly, we have had to keep to a minimum the attention devoted to significant external actors, e.g. Bismarck. Although figures such as Bismarck loom very large in the writings of some diplomatic historians, we would humbly submit that the Iron Chancellor had rather less impact on the history of *Zwischeneuropa* than did several other 'off stage' actors, among whom Marx, Lenin, Stalin, Khrushchev, Brezhnev, Gorbachev, Christ, Calvin, Mussolini, Hitler and Ghengis Khan most readily spring to mind! But one has to draw a line somewhere.

Much more regrettable is the fact that we have had to confine ourselves to passing references to many important cultural and intellectual developments. To have given them proper coverage would have doubled or trebled the size of the book. However, we have managed to pay some attention to such crucial matters as the impact of Christianity, the Renaissance, the Reformation, the Counter-Reformation, the Enlightenment, nationalism and Marxism, albeit in highly summarized form. Half a loaf is better than none!

Over the past twenty-five years or more, we have digested large quantities of English-language secondary sources on East European history, politics, society, culture and economic development, much of it written by East Europeans. Far from there being a shortage of such material, there is enough to occupy several lifetimes. While we fully acknowledge the great importance of more specialized and narrowly focused research monographs and articles based upon foreign-language and primary sources, we contend that there is also a crucial role for grand syntheses drawing on a much wider range of secondary sources. We could not have devoured and digested nearly as many ideas, interpretations and findings as we have done (across a very wide front) if we had been reading such material in foreign languages, even though we are conversant with several European languages ranging from Portuguese to Russian. We also decided early on to omit the accents from East European names and words, since these unfamiliar signs tend to leave most Western readers even less certain about pronunciation.

It is also necessary to say a few preliminary words about the extent and nomenclature of the region(s) covered by this book. The naming and demarcation of European regions will always be fraught with political and cultural controversy and loaded with implicit and/or contentious claims and connotations. Fortunately, there is fairly widespread agreement that South-eastern Europe is synonymous with the Balkan peninsula and that

East Central Europe comprises Poland, Hungary, the Czech Republic and Slovakia. However, there have been long disputes as to where exactly the northern Balkans end and where East Central Europe begins. In terms of physical geography and ethnicity, for example, Slovenia, Croatia and Transylvania are usually included in the Balkans (i.e. South-eastern Europe). Yet for centuries Slovenia was an integral and strongly assimilated part of the Austrian Habsburg domains (longer, indeed, than Bohemia and Moravia), while for similarly long stretches of history Croatia and Transylvania were key components of the kingdom of Hungary. Moreover, all these areas have long been part of Western (Catholic) Christendom rather than the Eastern Orthodox world. Should they therefore be included in East Central Europe? It is not just a matter of geography. Nor is it merely an academic question. It directly influences international perceptions of their standing in the European 'pecking order'. It will even affect the speed with which Slovenia, Croatia and Romania may be admitted into the European Union (EU) and/or NATO. Since this book is more attuned to historical than to geographical criteria, we consider that these areas were in many respects borderlands of East Central Europe up to the First World War, but that after that their destinies were primarily determined by their inclusion in the new or expanded Balkan states. Yet we do not accept that this should automatically consign Slovenia, Croatia or Romania to lower positions in the queue for EU and/or NATO membership. Notwithstanding the very negative images generated by the Ceausescu and Iliescu regimes, the 1991–95 Yugoslav conflict and the widespread poverty and corruption in the Balkans, it is clear that the alleged 'superiority' of East Central Europe has been exaggerated by those who conveniently forget that the latter has been a crucible of racial hatreds, National Socialism and the Kafkaesque state during the twentieth century. It is untenable simply to contrast Balkan vices with sanitized and idealized visions of East Central European virtue.

Unfortunately, the English language lacks an appropriate and widely acceptable collective name for these two regions. In German they have been aptly named *Zwischeneuropa* ('in-between Europe'). This has the advantage of encapsulating their fundamental predicament, that of 'living between East and West, or between Germany and Russia, or, in early modern times, between Turks and Habsburgs' (Burke 1985: 2). But there is no similarly apt English name. The nearest equivalent is 'the lands between', but it has never passed into common usage.

Of course we realize that it has become fashionable to refer to these regions as Central Europe. But, for reasons set out more fully in the Introduction, we have resisted the temptation to follow suit. For most citizens of the European Union, the term 'Central Europe' primarily applies to Germany and Austria (the former 'Central Powers'). It still has connotations of *Mitteleuropa* and of Austrian and German imperialism. Moreover, the inclusion of 'the land between' within an expanded conception of Central Europe implicitly (often deliberately) overstates the degree to which they have been part of the European mainstream ('at the heart of Europe'). It overlooks the major extent to which they have been part of the European 'periphery' in medieval times and again since the later seventeenth century. Even more crucially, it (implicitly) understates the magnitude of the political and cultural reorientations as well as the economic and social changes which these post-communist states will have to undergo if they really want to consummate their 'return to Europe'.

Therefore, *faute de mieux*, we have continued to refer to these regions as Eastern Europe, the name by which they were generally known during the 1945–89 East–West partition of Europe. This is done, not in order to impugn or belittle their 'Europeanness', but rather to distinguish them from both Central Europe (Germany and Austria) and the former Soviet Republics, including the three Baltic states (of Estonia, Latvia and Lithuania). We have no wish to slight the peoples of *Zwischeneuropa*, whose European credentials are amply endorsed in this book. Nor do we wish to give any offence to the Baltic states, which understandably demand to be treated on a par with Poland, the Czech Republic and Hungary. Admittedly, some books on Eastern Europe have dealt with the Baltic states alongside Poland, Hungary and former Czechoslovakia, i.e. as part of East Central Europe, on the grounds that they formally achieved independent statehood within the eastern zone of Europe from 1918 to 1940 and that their forebears were (to varying degrees) united with Poland from the sixteenth to the eighteenth centuries (see, for example, Rothschild 1974 and Crampton 1994). However, we have two overriding reasons for excluding the Baltic states and their forebears from the present book. Firstly, the territories which have emerged as the Baltic states from 1918 to 1914 and again since 1990 were from the eighteenth century to 1991 (with relatively brief interruptions) integral parts of the Tsarist and Soviet empires rather than 'the lands between'. Thus it would make little sense to include them in a work dealing specifically with the latter. Secondly, since the late eighteenth century the political, social, cultural and economic affairs of the territories that have become the Baltic states have been much more strongly intertwined with those of Russia, the Soviet Union and Scandinavia than with those of Poland, the Czech Lands or Hungary.

We would like to thank Dr Eleanor Breuning, Dr Gareth Pritchard, Professor George Blazyca and Professor Jack Morrison for their copious and constructive comments on the manuscript, which prompted many corrections and clarifications. In recent years Robert Bideleux has also benefited from many stimulating discussions with Dr Bruce Haddock. We take full responsibility for any remaining errors and controversial or questionable judgements, especially as we have not shied away from controversy. When necessary, we have been prepared to challenge or even reject the conventional wisdom.

We also greatly appreciate the support and assistance we have received from Heather McCallum at Routledge. Our desk editor, Ian Critchley, was a big help during the final stages of the production of the book. Finally, Robert Bideleux would like to offer heart-felt thanks to Ian Jeffries for maintaining both his faith in the project and the patience of Job while the book outgrew its much more modest original intentions, as well as to Alison, Chantal and Kieran Bideleux for their forbearance over the past few years. Dr Alison Bideleux also provided much appreciated books and comments on the Byzantine Empire and on certain aspects of the Renaissance. Without these the volume might have been somewhat shorter, but it would also have been much the poorer. We hope that the prolonged gestation period has resulted in a deeper, sounder and more probing book.

MAPS

We gratefully acknowledge permission to reproduce Maps 6, 15, 31 and 42 from *A Concise Historical Atlas of Eastern Europe* by Dennis P. Hupchick and Harold E. Cox, copyright © D. Hupchick and H. Cox (St. Martin's Press, Incorporated, and Macmillan Ltd 1996).

Abbreviations

CEFTA	Central European Free Trade Area
CIS	Commonwealth of Independent States
CMEA	Council of Mutual Economic Assistance (Comecon)
COCOM	Co-ordinating Committee for Multilateral Trade Controls
CSCE	Conference on Security and Co-operation in Europe
EBRD	European Bank for Reconstruction and Development
EC	European Community
ECSC	European Coal and Steel Community
EEC	European Economic Community
EEN	Eastern Europe Newsletter
EFTA	European Free Trade Association
EPU	European Payments Union
EU	European Union
FT	*Financial Times*
GATT	General Agreement on Tariffs and Trade
G7	Group of Seven
G24	Group of Twenty-Four
IHT	*International Herald Tribune*
IMF	International Monetary Fund
KOR	Committee for Workers' Defence
NATO	North Atlantic Treaty Organization
OECD	Organization for Economic Co-operation and Development
OEEC	Organization for European Economic Co-operation
OPEC	Organization of Petroleum Exporting Countries
OSCE	Organization for Security and Co-operation in Europe
PHARE	Pologne, Hongrie: activité pour la restructuration économique
TACIS	Technical Assistance to the Commonwealth of Independent States
TEMPUS	Trans-European Mobility Scheme for University Studies
WEU	Western European Union
WTO	World Trade Organization

Introduction
Crisis and change in East Central and South-eastern Europe

This book offers a largely thematic historical survey and analysis of the processes of political, social, cultural and economic change that have shaped the lands which lie between Germany, Italy and the former Tsarist and Soviet empires. German writers used to refer to this area as *Zwischeneuropa*. Unfortunately, this apt term has no such neat equivalent in English. The closest approximation is 'the lands between', as used in the titles of several major books and articles on the region (e.g. Palmer 1970 and Croan 1989). It has the virtue of encapsulating the region's essential misfortune in modern times, that of being sandwiched between overwhelmingly powerful empires: Germanic on the one side and Ottoman, Tsarist or Soviet on the other. In the words of the Czechoslovak dissident Milan Simecka: 'We live in the awareness that our unhappy situation on the borders of two civilizations absolves us from the outset from any responsibility for the nation's fate. Try as we may, there is nothing we can do to help ourselves' (Simecka 1985: 159). Indeed, as relatively small and vulnerable 'latecomers' to a Europe of sovereign nation-states, the peoples of East Central and South-eastern Europe acquired their modern national identities, territories and statehood at least partly through the grace and favour of Europe's Great Powers. Acute awareness of this uncomfortable predicament has helped to perpetuate widespread 'national insecurity'. It has also encouraged fatalistic assumptions that the peoples of the region would usually be acted upon, rather than act, and that external powers would make territorial dispositions to suit themselves, as indeed they did (most notably through the peace treaties of 1648, 1713, 1815, 1878 and 1918–19, the successive partitions of Poland in 1772, 1793 and 1795, the dismemberment of Czechoslovakia in 1938–39 and the Yalta and Potsdam agreements of 1945). These were self-fulfilling expectations.

More than this, the medieval and early modern history of these marchlands was blighted by persistent warfare against marauders and interlopers from both East and West: Avars, Huns, Magyars, Bulgars, Mongols and Turks from Asia; German colonists, Venetian traders and Catholic Crusaders from the West. Indeed, the battle lines between Roman Catholicism and Byzantine Orthodoxy and, to a lesser degree, between Christianity and Islam shuttled back and forth across the Balkans and East Central Europe. Viewed in an even longer perspective, the peoples of *Zwischeneuropa* acted as 'a buffer between the West and Asia, allowing the Western nations to develop in comparative security their own civilization, while the fury of the Asiatic whirlwinds spent itself on their backs. And throughout these centuries their powerful neighbours in the West exploited their weakness to encroach on their territory and ruin their economic life' (Seton-Watson 1945: 21–2). Moreover, successive strata of conquerors, colonists and indigenous peoples have settled in the area. Many of them have at one time or another built up states of their own at the expense of their neighbours, and 'the rise and fall of these short-lived states has left many disputed frontier regions and several inextricably mixed populations' (pp. 11, 74). The onslaughts from the West were generally motivated by a desire to conquer, to colonize or to convert, whereas the major Asiatic incursions seem to have been precipitated by occurrences on the distant northern frontiers of China. When Central Asian nomadic peoples made periodic (and usually unsuccessful) attempts to overrun the opulent Chinese 'middle kingdom', their leaders were sometimes deflected westwards across the open Eurasian steppes in search of fresh pastures and plunder to support their tribal hordes.

Thus Eastern Europeans have often faced hazards on two fronts, as well as cultural and colonial penetration from both East and West. The eminent Polish writer Witold Gombrowicz once mused: 'What is Poland? A country between East and West, where Europe somehow all but comes to an end, a transitional country where East and West mutually weaken each other. But . . . our country is a little bit of a parody of the East and of the West. . . . Our "superficiality", our "carefreeness" are essentially aspects of an irresponsible infantile relationship to culture and life, our lack of faith in reality. The origin of this may be that we are neither properly Europe or Asia' (quoted by Kiss 1987: 130, 135–6).

Besides setting out the structure of the book, this introduction examines the important debate as to whether 'the lands between' should be considered to be 'Central' or 'Eastern' Europe. In the process, we explain why we continue to use the term 'Eastern Europe' (contrary to the wishes of many of the region's inhabitants) and why we distinguish the value-laden political and cultural use of the terms 'Eastern' and 'Western' from the more neutral geographical terms 'eastern' and 'western'. Next, in further justification of our preferred usage, we offer a preliminary historical overview of the causes and consequences of Europe's East–West divergences. Finally, we outline our views on the uses and abuses of history as a means of illuminating the present and on the ways in which the present inevitably influences perceptions of the past.

THE STRUCTURE OF THE BOOK

Part I The 'Balkanization' of South-eastern Europe

Part I endeavours to explain how South-eastern Europe, which was in many respects the cradle of European civilization and has in the past comprised some of Europe's strongest and most highly developed states, became 'Balkanized', a byword for acutely debilitating fragmentation, inter-ethnic conflict, underdevelopment and loss of political and economic autonomy. In particular, we join the ranks of those who challenge the widely accepted view that the main responsibility for Balkan decline and disunity can be laid at the door of the 'alien' and sometimes stultifying and oppressive Ottoman Empire, a view still propagated in the Balkan media, schools, universities and 'official' or nationalist history books. The latter tend to be more concerned with national myth-making, the 'justification' of territorial claims and the nursing of ancient grievances than with the search for historical truth. Or, to put it another way, their conceptions of 'truth' are quite shamelessly self-interested. This is not to deny that similar practices are employed in many other parts of the world, only to alert readers to the pernicious and often anachronistic uses and abuses of history by modern nationalist as well as communist historians. Thus modern 'national' histories of Serbia and Bulgaria, for example, have unfortunately tended to portray the medieval Serbian and Bulgarian kingdoms as embryonic nation-states whose glorious national development was brutally cut short by alien conquerors and subsequently stifled by several centuries of Ottoman imperial rule. Furthermore, they have often taken the maximum territorial extensions of those far from 'national' medieval kingdoms as being indicative of the 'natural' or 'historic' boundaries of their countries (and during the twentieth century historical 'memories' of these aggressive medieval polities have metamorphosed into modern nationalist programmes of territorial aggrandisement and 'ethnic cleansing'). In reality, however, there were already various symptoms or portents of decline and political, cultural and economic fragmentation in the Balkans *before* the Ottomans appeared on the scene. Indeed, these problems contributed to the ease with which the Ottomans subjugated the Balkans, and some of them were initially alleviated to varying degrees by Ottoman rule. The early Ottoman rulers can be seen as having tried to make the best of a bad job. Admittedly, the so-called Pax Ottomanica did not last for very long and, eventually, the sclerotic tendencies of the Ottoman system thwarted many efforts to modernize the Balkan economies and education systems, impairing their capacity to adapt or to meet the challenges of a changing world. The Ottomans can also be accused of perpetuating or failing to resolve many of the problems that they inherited in their Balkan domains, even if those problems were not of their own making. In that respect, however, they were no more 'culpable' than their Christian predecessors.

Nevertheless, by greatly delaying the development of independent nation-states, liberalism and the rule of law, the dogged persistence of the Ottoman imperial polity was also conducive to the emergence of exclusive and illiberal 'ethnic' conceptions and definitions of 'the nation', rather than more inclusive and liberal ones. 'Ethnic' nationalism elevates the rights of collectivities above those of individuals, even those of the individual members of ethnic majorities. The terrible 'ethnic purification' or 'ethnic cleansing' undertaken in parts of the Balkans during and immediately after the two World Wars and again in the first half of the 1990s can be seen as the logical culmination of the exclusive and illiberal conceptions and definitions of nationhood that developed mainly as a result of the late survival of supranational imperial polities in the region and the weak development of the rule of law. The 'activist' forms of nationalism and radicalism fostered by the French Revolution had a similarly intolerant and even murderous potential, especially in the hands of a Robespierre or a Saint-Just. But in Western Europe, fortunately, this was counteracted and held in check by the relatively strong development of the rule of law, the separation of powers, liberalism and concepts of limited government. Western European political communities have been governed and held together by common bodies of law, with a clear distinction between the public and private domains and strong constitutional restraints on the acquisition and use of power within specific historically determined jurisdictions and territories. By contrast, 'activist' forms of politics substitute ideology and a shared sense of mission or purpose for law as the basis of the political community, have scant regard for constitutional restraints on the acquisition and use of power, subordinate individuals to an all-embracing and all-intrusive political order and refuse to regard existing frontiers and jurisdictions as inviolable (O'Sullivan 1983: 35–7). Unfortunately, there have been fewer checks and safeguards against illiberal 'activist' doctrines, movements and states in eastern than in western Europe. Consequently, it is sometimes argued that this, rather than the prevalence of illiberal 'ethnic' nationalism, has been the most crucial respect in which eastern Europe has differed from western Europe in modern times. However, if limited government and the rule of law were adequate safeguards against ethnic excesses, it would be difficult to explain the triumph of Nazism in Weimar Germany, a country that prided itself on having a *Rechtsstaat* (in contrast to the Balkans and the Russian domains). It was precisely the fact that the German nation and national state were conceived and defined in ethnic rather than historic territorial terms that led successive generations of pan-German nationalists (culminating in Nazism) to try to unite all Germans in a single German superstate, with ultimately disastrous consequences for both Europe and Germany. Thus the triumph of Nazism among the Germans (who, like the peoples of eastern Europe, defined themselves as an 'ethnic' nation) seems to confirm that the prevalence of 'ethnic' nationalism was more important than any weakness of legal and constitutional safeguards in explaining the widespread occurrence of 'ethnic' excesses in twentieth-century Central and Eastern Europe.

The Serbs and the Croats have not been the only ones in the Balkans to have committed 'ethnic' atrocities at one time or another during the twentieth century. Nor has such barbarism been confined to so-called 'Christian' peoples. In adjacent Asia Minor, Moslem Turks have engaged in similar barbarities against Christian Armenians and Greeks and against Moslem Kurds. Yet, rather than pointing the finger of blame at particular religious and ethnic groups who have committed such atrocities at various times and places, we consider that the root cause of this terrible malady has been the 'ethnic' conception and definition of nationhood which arose largely as a result of the predominance of supranational imperial polities in the Balkans and Asia Minor up to the end of the First World War. In this respect the peoples of the Balkans and Anatolia have been to a large extent victims of circumstance, or prisoners of potentially lethal 'received ideas'. They are not, in our view, inherently more vicious or more incapable of living at peace with their neighbours than are the peoples of western Europe. (One could easily cite numerous barbarities committed by western Europeans, not least against Jews, Gypsies, Moslems, Catalans, Basques, Asians, blacks and the Irish.) The 'surgical' creation of several 'ethnically purified' or 'ethnically cleansed' nation-states in the Balkans has been the painful and tragic outcome of the prevalence of exclusive 'ethnic' conceptions of the nation and of the principle of national self-determination (both of which put a high premium on 'ethnic homogeneity' or 'ethnic purity') and of the attendant weakness of liberal values and legal constraints on 'ethnic' excesses. Indeed, in a region where nations are defined in narrowly ethnic terms, the enunciation of the principle of national self-determination is an open invitation to inter-ethnic conflict and 'ethnic cleansing', and the potential for inter-ethnic conflict and human tragedy in the Balkans and Anatolia will continue to be quite horrific until their various peoples either abandon 'ethnic' nationalism or are finally 'resettled' into ethnically 'cleansed' or 'purified' nation-states, carved out of the former ethnic patchworks. (A similarly barbaric logic was responsible for the 'ethnic purification' of Germany, Austria, the Czech Lands, Slovakia, Poland and Hungary during and immediately after the Second World War.) Even that would not be a real solution, however, because inter-ethnic hatreds could still persist between ethnically 'homogenized' states and antisemitism has continued to flourish in countries whose former Jewish minorities have been almost completely eradicated. Furthermore, 'ethnic purification' would leave a country morally, culturally and technologically stunted and impoverished. Lasting and self-renewing cultural, material and spiritual strengths are to be found in ethnic and cultural diversity, most visibly in the case of the United States, rather than in homogeneity. The only sure escape from the problems caused by 'ethnic nationalism' is to be found in the renunciation of 'ethnic nationalism' in favour of more liberal and inclusive 'civic' forms of identity, allegiance and community, and this should be made an explicit prerequisite for membership of collectivities such as the EU and NATO, which exist to defend liberal 'civic' values.

Part II East Central Europe prior to the Habsburg ascendancy

The main aim of Part II is to examine the various reasons for the rise and decline of the medieval and early modern kingdoms of Poland, Hungary and Bohemia, each of which had at least half a millennium of independent existence before eventually succumbing to imperial control. In addition to outlining their major problems and achievements and the main traditions, values and orientations which they bequeathed to posterity, we pay particular attention to the power, privileges and internal divisions of the East Central European nobilities, the impact of Christianization, the Hussite Revolution and the strengths and weaknesses of the East Central European Renaissance and Reformation.

Part III East Central Europe during the Habsburg ascendancy

Part III, which examines the rise and fall of the Habsburg Monarchy, has three closely interrelated aims: (i) to assess the long-term impact and legacies of the Habsburg Empire in East Central Europe; (ii) to analyse some of the associated divergences between much of the region and western Europe; and (iii) to examine the reasons why most of East Central Europe remained under supranational imperial control during the eighteenth and nineteenth centuries, while the West was steadily evolving towards a system of national states. In the process we endeavour to explain why most of the region fell so far behind most of the national or proto-national states of western Europe as regards urbanization, industrialization, agricultural development and science and technology during the seventeenth and eighteenth centuries. This paves the way for an assessment of the Revolutions of 1848, an analysis of the impressive economic and cultural revivals in Hungary, German Austria and the Czech Lands during the later nineteenth century and a discussion of the precocious development of so-called 'finance capitalism' and 'monopoly capitalism' during the final decades of the Habsburg Empire. (We emphasize that Lenin added remarkably little to Hilferding's path-breaking ideas on the subject.) We also examine the reasons for (and the explosive consequences of) the fact that the development of East Central European nationalism *preceded* the emergence of nation-states, in marked contrast to the western European experience.

Our account of the legacies of the Habsburg Empire highlights the fundamental causes and the catastrophic consequences of the almost 'racial' chasm that opened up between the Austro-Germans and the Austro-Slavs from 1848 onward. The resultant political blind spots, mutual misunderstandings and mutual mistrust encouraged erstwhile Austro-German 'liberals' to sell out to Habsburg neo-absolutism, impaired the potential for healthy social and political co-operation and poisoned the wells of liberalism and democracy for a long time to come. It also sowed the seeds of the racial crimes committed against the Jews, Gypsies and Slavs of Central and Eastern Europe by the Nazis and their many Austrian and Bohemian German collaborators between 1938 and 1945.

We emphasize the dire consequences of the development of (pan-) German 'ethnic' nationalism as a major political force in East Central Europe from 1848 to 1945 not in order to incite Germanophobia but simply to stress the terrible (and not always premeditated) effects of 'ethnic' nationalism in a multi-ethnic region. The results should be seen as an illustration of the general dangers posed by insidious 'ethnic' nationalism, rather than as a peculiar product of 'the German national character' (as so many Germanophobes have seen it). On a smaller scale (but only because this has involved much smaller nations), Magyar, Croatian and Serbian 'ethnic' nationalism has displayed similarly lethal tendencies, while Bulgarian, Romanian, Albanian, Greek, Turkish, Polish, and Slovak 'ethnic' nationalisms have not been altogether free of them. Conversely, while the Jews have undeniably been the biggest victims of the growth of 'ethnic' nationalism, exclusivism and 'purification' or 'cleansing' in Central and Eastern Europe, that ought not to be allowed to obscure its devastating effects upon the Gypsies and Slavs. (To avoid double standards, one should also regret the ethnic exclusivism and messianism of some sections of the Jewish and Slavic communities, while acknowledging that such phenomena have partly been defensive reactions.)

At the same time, we point out that in modern times each East European nation has tended to portray its own treatment of ethnic minorities as exemplary. Such attitudes were increasingly reflected in press reports, school textbooks and political pronouncements. Anyone who said otherwise was liable to be regarded as a slanderer or a traitor, as someone who was consciously or unconsciously aiding foreign or irredentist conspiracies to besmirch and subvert the nation's integrity (whether moral or territorial). These attitudes generally coexisted with widespread policies of forcible assimilation of ethnic minorities, which contributed to a general lowering of standards of conduct and culture both through a form of 'moral brutalization' of the perpetrators and by turning the school system into 'a kind of chauvinistic nursery' that stunted the mental development of its pupils (Jaszi 1929: 330, 340–1).

In dealing with the external relations of the Habsburg Empire we emphasize that the alliance with Germany after 1879, preceded by the termination (during the Crimean War of 1853–56) of the long-standing policy of co-operation with Russia in the Balkans, divided Europe into two mutually hostile power blocs that were launched upon a collision course which eventually engulfed Europe in the First World War, which in turn precipitated the disintegration of Europe's eastern empires. We attach major importance to the problems and miscalculations of the Habsburg Monarchy and its tangled relations with Serbia in bringing about this fateful course of events. Serbia was attacked primarily because it embodied a national principle which, if it had been accepted as the basis of legitimate claims to sovereign statehood for the Serbs and other ethnic groups in the Habsburg Empire, could soon have destroyed the latter. If Austria-Hungary had acted more astutely and less heavy-handedly, it is quite conceivable that most South Slavs would have preferred to remain under Habsburg rule, as part of a Triple rather than a Dual Monarchy. Partitioned Poland (1795–1918) is treated in Part II (Chapter 5, pp. 161–88) for convenience.

Part IV Eastern Europe between the two world wars

Part IV offers explanations for the failure of various (often half-hearted) attempts to establish independent and democratic nation-states and viable national market economies in East Central and South-eastern Europe between the two world wars. While giving due weight to external factors beyond East European control, our main emphasis is on the intrinsic defects of the 1919–20 peace settlements and of the underlying 'ethnic' concepts and definitions of nationhood and national self-determination, largely resulting from the late establishment of nation-states in the region and the consequent prevalence of intolerant and exclusive 'ethnic' nationalism over inclusive 'civic' nationalism. We broadly concur with Sir Lewis Namier's contention that healthy constitutional development is most likely to occur within civic polities which take existing states and territories as their starting point, instead of trying to make states and territories correspond exclusively to particular ethnic groups. 'Self-determination . . . contests frontiers, negates the existing state and its inner development, and by [fostering] civil and international strife is apt to stultify constitutional growth' (Namier 1946: 26–7). If only the Eastern European right had generally shared Namier's profound rejection of ethnic nationalism it would have become a much more peaceful, prosperous and stable region. In our view, the Western powers have learned little from the mistakes they made in Eastern Europe after the First World War. After 1989 they initially sponsored the principle of national self-determination (and hence the ethnically defined nation-state) almost as blindly as they did before the Second World War, with similarly tragic consequences (particularly in former Yugoslavia). We go on to discuss the origins and the severe impact of the 1930s Depression. This undermined any remaining hopes for the development of liberal capitalism, liberal democracy and progressive social reform in inter-war Eastern Europe. It also exacerbated inter-ethnic tensions and tendencies towards economic nationalism, authoritarianism and fascism. We offer a radical reappraisal of the nature of the agrarian problems of inter-war Eastern Europe and of the impact of the 1920s land reforms.

Part IV also examines rival interpretations of the nature and significance of fascism in East Central and South-eastern Europe. We emphasize that the prevalence of 'integral' and 'ethnic' nationalism favoured authoritarianism, étatism, economic nationalism and collective rather than individual rights and obligations. Indeed, East European nationalism was often proto-fascist and this predisposed its adherents to fascist or quasi-fascist solutions for national and international political, economic and ethnic problems. Fascism also demonstrated the hazards of taking national self-determination to its logical conclusion. We also pay particular attention to official communist interpretations of fascism and of the struggle between communism and fascism, arguing that they were not as oversimplified as they are usually alleged to have been and that they played a pivotal role in communist thinking on how to expand communist power and influence in Europe through the armed overthrow and military defeat of fascism.

Part V In the shadow of Yalta: Eastern Europe since the Second World War

Finally, Part V provides an interpretation of the rise and fall of communist rule in Eastern Europe. It is widely accepted that the success or failure of the East European communist regimes came to depend on the maintenance of sustained economic growth and rising consumption levels. These were objectives that none of them could easily attain on their own, in an autarkic fashion. Therefore they would ultimately depend on how successfully they could escape or surmount the (initially self-imposed) austerities and constraints of 'boxed in' self-reliance and central planning by promoting transnational and/or supranational economic co-operation, division of labour and integration within the Council of Mutual Economic Assistance (CMEA or Comecon), which also offered increased (preferential) access to the vast markets and mineral resources of the Soviet Union. Thus the failure of Comecon to promote a high degree of integration between its members ultimately contributed to the downfall of the East European communist regimes. We also analyse some of the social and political factors that also contributed to the collapse of communist rule and the significance of the Revolutions of 1989. The book concludes with an appraisal of the major problems and dilemmas that have had to be confronted during the transitions to democracy and market economies and the repossession of untrammelled national sovereignty by the East European states.

MORE THAN A NAME: THE CONTROVERSIES OVER 'CENTRAL' AND 'EASTERN' EUROPE

Many natives of 'the lands between' violently object to the Western habit of referring to their region as 'Eastern Europe'. In an influential essay published in French in 1983, and in English in 1984, the Czech writer Milan Kundera proclaimed Hungary, Czechoslovakia and Poland as (in spirit at least) part of the West. 'What does Europe mean to a Hungarian, a Czech, a Pole?' he asked. 'For a thousand years their nations have belonged to the part of Europe rooted in Roman Christianity. They have participated in every period of its history. For them, the word "Europe" does not represent a phenomenon of geography, but a spiritual notion synonymous with the word "West". The moment Hungary is no longer European – that is, no longer Western – it is driven from its own destiny, beyond its own history: it loses the essence of its identity.' In Kundera's view, geographical Europe (extending from the Atlantic to the Ural mountains) had long been 'divided into two halves which evolved separately: one tied to ancient Rome and the Catholic Church, the other anchored in Byzantium and the Orthodox Church'. After the Second World War, however, 'the border between the two Europes shifted several hundred kilometres to the west, and several nations that had always considered themselves to be Western woke up to discover that they were now in the East (Kundera 1984: 33).

From Kundera's standpoint, Roman Catholic Poland, Hungary and Czechoslovakia constituted 'the eastern border of the West' rather than the western border of the East. (Perhaps deliberately, he omits to mention Catholic Slovenia and Croatia.) In his view the East meant, above all, Russia and 'nothing could be more foreign to Central Europe and its passion for variety than Russia: uniform, standardizing, centralizing' (p. 33). Indeed, 'on the eastern border of the West – more than anywhere else – Russia is seen not just as one more European power but as a singular civilization, an *other* civilization . . . Russia knows another (greater) dimension of disaster, another image of space (a space so immense entire nations are swallowed up in it), another sense of time (slow and patient), another way of laughing, living, and dying. That is why the countries in Central Europe feel that the change in their destiny that occurred after 1945 is not merely a political catastrophe: it is also an attack on their civilization' (p. 34).

Kundera was especially alert to the dangers of pan-Slavism: 'The Czechs . . . loved to brandish naively their "Slavic ideology" as a defence against German aggressiveness. The Russians, on the other hand, enjoyed making use of it to justify their own imperial ambitions. "The Russians like to label everything Russian as Slavic, so that later they can label everything Slavic as Russian," the great Czech writer Karel Havlicek declared in 1844, trying to warn his compatriots against their silly and ignorant enthusiasm for Russia.' Kundera emphasized that for a thousand years the Czechs 'never had any direct contact with Russia. In spite of their linguistic kinship, the Czechs and the Russians have never shared a common *world*: neither a common history nor a common culture.' Moreover, the relationship between the Poles and the Russians 'has never been less than a struggle of life and death. Joseph Conrad . . . wrote that "nothing could be more alien to what is called in the literary world the "Slavic spirit" than the Polish temperament with its chivalric devotion to moral constraints and its exaggerated respect for individual rights"' (p. 34).

Since the publication of this famous essay on 'The tragedy of Central Europe' there has been growing insistence on calling the area 'Central' rather than 'Eastern' Europe. This is much more than a semantic quibble. It goes to the heart of the region's self-image and aspirations. The debates about 'Central' and 'Eastern' Europe are a form of soul-searching about what the peoples and states of the region are or should be. Moreover, the campaign to bring back 'Central' Europe has become an integral part of 'the long revolution against Yalta', i.e. against the Allies' decision to partition Europe into Soviet and Western spheres of influence in 1945 (Feher 1988). It therefore merits serious consideration, even if it raises more problems than it solves. 'Yalta created a geopolitical entity, "Eastern Europe", which as a polity or a community of destiny had never before existed' (p. 20).

Writing on the eve of the East European Revolutions of 1989, the Czechoslovak dissident Miroslav Kusy declared that 'Eastern Europe' was merely 'a political power-bloc of the Comecon and Warsaw Pact states' and that any sense of 'East Europeanness' that its inhabitants may have had was 'tantamount to the feelings shared by an eagle and a lion living alongside each other in a zoo' (Kusy 1989: 93). In the opinion of Jacques Rupnik, 'From Prague to Budapest, from Cracow to Zagreb, the rediscovery of Central Europe will remain one of the major intellectual and political developments of the 1980s and will no doubt be a vital ingredient in the reshaping of the political map of Europe in the post-Yalta era' (Rupnik 1990: 250). 'The project of Central Europe has been gradually filling the historical and political vacuum created by the deconstruction of Eastern Europe' (Feher 1989: 415).

This 'rediscovery of Central Europe' has already had a major impact on the way in which the history of the region is perceived. Thus, according to the Polish-American historian Piotr Wandycz, 'Bohemia (later Czechoslovakia), Hungary and Poland did belong to the Western civilization. Christianity and all that it stood for had come to them from Rome or, to put it differently, the Western impact was the dominant and lasting one.' Thus the peoples of East Central Europe 'became part of the West' and 'were shaped by and experienced all the great historical currents: Renaissance, Reformation, Enlightenment, the French and Industrial Revolutions. They differed drastically from the East.' Bordering on Russia and the Ottoman domains, these marchlands 'regarded themselves, and were regarded by others, as the bulwark of Christendom . . . Their eastern frontiers marked the frontiers of Europe' (Wandycz 1992: 3).

Similarly, the Hungarian academic Peter Hanak has argued that 'Central Europe' was 'the Eastern zone of the West' rather than 'the Western "rim" of the East'. Thus the Austro-Hungarian Empire was 'the eastern frontier of liberal constitutional rule up to the First World War. This political system (in spite of its limitations and transgressions) carried forward and upheld the heritage of European humanism, enlightenment and liberalism. . . . The Monarchy (including Hungary) . . . stood in the middle between fully fledged parliamentary democracy in the West and autocracy in the East. This is precisely the meaning of the term: Central Europe.' In his view, 'the fact that the peoples of this region . . . have often been at loggerheads, riven by conflicts and hatreds, is no argument against the historical existence of the entity. On the contrary, this is proof of its existence: it is neighbours who are mostly cursed by anger, hatred and strife. The historical existence of such an entity does not necessarily imply the perception of regional identity' (Hanak 1989: 57, 68–9).

It is often claimed that, as a result of their location on the exposed eastern frontiers of Western Christendom, defending Western civilization against Asiatic and/or Russian 'barbarism', the Poles, the Czechs and the Hungarians could see the more clearly what Europe was and thus became more fervently Western than the West. It can indeed be argued that 'Europeanness' was most highly prized, not by those who took it for granted, but by those who lived in greatest fear of losing it. 'Central Europe longed to be a condensed version of Europe itself in all its cultural variety, a small arch-European Europe' (Kundera 1984: 33). Hugh Seton-Watson maintained that 'nowhere in the world is there so widespread a belief in the reality, and the importance, of a European cultural community as in the countries lying between the EEC territory and the Soviet Union' (Seton-Watson 1985: 14).

Indeed, this region played a pivotal role in defining and popularizing the very idea of Europe in Renaissance times. Until the fifteenth century the concept of Europe was 'a neutral geographical expression'. It fell to Polish, Hungarian, Bohemian and Austrian publicists, who feared that Europe was under mortal threat from the steadily advancing Ottoman 'menace', to proclaim that they and their Catholic rulers were defending 'not merely European territory but specifically European values against Moslem aggression' (Coles 1968: 148). John Paul II, 'the Polish Pope', declared in June 1991: 'We do not have to enter Europe, because we helped to create it and we did so with greater effort than those who claim a monopoly of Europeanism' (quoted by Kumar 1992: 460). This belief is very important to the East Central European intelligentsias. It has helped their countries to persevere with exceedingly arduous processes of economic and institutional reform since 1989. It has also informed their drive to reintegration into the European 'mainstream', currently epitomized by the EU and NATO.

In 1993, in response to the question 'Why should the post-communist countries of Europe seek membership of NATO?', the Czech President Vaclav Havel declared that there were three main reasons why his own country should do so: 'First, the Czech Republic lies in the very centre of Europe, which has traditionally been a crossroads of different spiritual trends and geopolitical interests.' The Czechs have learned from bitter experience that 'we must take an active interest in what goes on in the rest of Europe. Such matters always affect us more than they do many other countries. That is why we have a heightened sense of obligation to Europe.' But the Czechs do not want 'to take without giving. We want an active role in the defence of European peace and democracy. Too often, we have had direct experience of where indifference to the fate of others can lead, and we are determined not to succumb to that kind of indifference.' Secondly, Czechs 'share the values on which NATO was founded and which it exists to defend. We are not just endorsing such values from the outside; over the centuries we have made our own contribution to their creation and cultivation. Why then should we not take part in defending them?' Thirdly, the Czechs have 'vivid memories of the Munich crisis in 1938 when, without consulting us, part of our country was bargained away to Hitler. Munich meant not only the failure of the Western democracies to confront the Nazi evil – a failure for which the West had to pay dearly – but the collapse of the European collective security of the time. This experience tells us how important it is for a country so exposed to be firmly involved – in its own interests and the general interest – in a working system of collective security.' More generally, the Czech Republic, Hungary, Poland, Slovakia and Slovenia 'clearly belong to the Western sphere of European civilization. They . . . are simply declaring an affinity with an institution they belong to intrinsically, where they see their own security interests best served and where they can actively participate' (*IHT*, 20 October 1993, p. 4).

Nevertheless, in glossing over the many cultural, economic and historical divergences between western and East Central Europe (at least since the seventeenth century, if not before then), and in claiming that their homelands have long been Western in spirit, the new champions of 'Central Europe' seem seriously to underestimate the scale of the economic, political and cultural 'adjustments' that have yet to be made if they are really to 'join' and to be fully accepted as part of the West. No one can dispute either the European 'credentials' of East Central Europe or the fact that it is very different from Russia, but that does not in itself make it Western. One of the primary tasks of this book is to offer hard-headed analyses of some of the historic differences between western Europe on the one hand and East Central Europe and the Balkans on the other. These emerged long before the advent of communist rule and the Cold War partition of Europe and they will long outlive the legacies of that more recent, vividly remembered but relatively ephemeral experience. The differences cannot be expunged overnight. If the governments and citizens of the countries in question are lulled into thinking that their region is already Western, they will be less likely to accept either the magnitude or the necessity of those painful 'adjustments'. Their so-called 'return to Europe' will not succeed if it is based upon wishful thinking and self-delusion; and that would be a tragedy for the the whole of Europe, not just 'Central Europe'. This is not a trivial issue. It is a matter of great practical as well as academic importance.

In any case, the name 'Central Europe' has widely differing meanings and connotations for Poles, Czechs, Slovaks, Hungarians, Croats, Slovenes, Austrians, Germans, Ukrainians, Belorussians, Lithuanians, Gypsies and Jews, let alone the British, the French, the Russians and the Italians. Does Kundera's 'Central Europe' include the millions of former Ukrainian, Belorussian and Lithuanian inhabitants of inter-war Poland, Hungary and Czechoslovakia? After all, they and their ancestors participated in many of the same formative historical processes and cultural experiences as did the Poles, the Czechs and the Magyars. For centuries they were all part of the same 'middle European' world. On the other hand, would it be either fair or rational to treat Ukrainians and Belorussians differently from their Russian 'cousins'? Equally, is it either fair or rational to regard East Central Europe as more 'Western' than the Balkans? The areas that became Poland, Slovakia and the Czech Lands had never been part of the Roman Empire, whereas the Balkans (most of which Kundera implicitly excludes from his concept of the

'Roman' West) were part of it for centuries. It is virtually impossible to find and employ consistent criteria and lines of demarcation in these matters. Indeed, on a deeper level, those who call European culture 'Western' are actually prejudging 'one of the most difficult and controversial questions of European history' (Halecki 1950: 11). For, if one adopts a less Eurocentric standpoint, Europe can be seen as a small rocky promontory sticking out of the colossal Asian land mass, whence many of Europe's ideas, religions, products and technologies have originated, as indeed did such peoples as the Bulgars and the Magyars.

For most people, however, the term 'Central Europe' means Germany, above all, as well as Austria, Hungary, the Czech Republic, Slovakia and possibly Poland, Slovenia and Croatia. From its inception, indeed, the concept of 'Central Europe' (alias *Mitteleuropa*) was redolent of pan-Germanism, of German and Austrian imperialism, and of German economic and cultural hegemony over East Central Europe and the Balkans. The geographer Joseph Partsch, in his book *Mitteleuropa* (published in 1904), proclaimed that 'All of Central Europe belongs, knowingly or unknowingly, to the sphere of German civilization' (quoted by Schwarz 1989: 145). Friedrich Naumann's best-selling *Mitteleuropa* (published in Berlin in 1915) intermixed German imperialist rhetoric with hymns of praise to nature, mountaineering, travel, the Danube and Central European art and with imperial condescension towards non-German cultures: 'Central Europe will be German in its core, will use German . . . as a matter of course, but must show indulgence and flexibility towards the other languages involved, for only then can harmony prevail' (p. 101). Nevertheless, in Naumann's view, 'Central Europe came about through Prussian victories' (pp. 57–8) (quoted by Schwarz 1989: 147). Similarly, in an essay published in Vienna in 1930, Albrecht Haushofer declared that 'Central Europe . . . owes its creation to the Germans. It would not exist without them' (quoted by Schwarz 1989: 146). It was in this context that Tomas Garrigue Masaryk, the founder and first President of Czechoslovakia, coined the name 'East Central Europe' during the First World War, in opposition to German use of the term *Mitteleuropa* 'as a justification for imperial Germany's expansionist plans' (Garton Ash 1986: 210). Masaryk defined East Central Europe as 'the lands between East and West, more particularly between the Germans and the Russians' (Kumar 1992: 446), which is also our own preferred usage.

More seriously, Kundera's idealization of 'Central Europe' as a bearer and custodian of Western values is not easily reconciled with its other role as a crucible of extremely illiberal ideas, projects and doctrines, culminating in Nazism, mass genocide and Auschwitz. In the words of the Croatian writer Miroslav Krleza, 'Central Europe doesn't represent for me, on the aesthetic level, a separate universe . . . Naumann's beloved theory of the unity of Mitteleuropa has been variously used either as a political pretext (pan-German or Austro-imperialism . . .), or as a nostalgic longing for the past' (Matvejevic 1989: 183–4). However, at least some of those who have championed the revival of the concept of 'Central Europe' since the 1980s may have been consciously or unconsciously wanting to substitute German for Russian influence in Eastern Europe in the hope that Germany will regenerate the region and reintegrate it into the European 'mainstream', in much the same way that earlier adherents of pan-Slavism had looked to Russia for 'a fraternal hand' in the liberation of Eastern Europe from German, Austro-Hungarian or Ottoman tutelage. If so, they have been playing dangerous and somewhat opportunistic games that could backfire on them.

Russia's political and cultural traditions undoubtedly appear monolithic, exclusive and intolerant of nonconformity and dissent, in comparison with the greater pluralism (if not always tolerance) of western and East Central Europe. In the opinion of the Hungarian philosopher Mihaly Vajda, 'in Russia one cannot find the main features of the civilization we call European . . . The leading value of Europe is *freedom* . . . the freedom of the individual limited only by that of others' (Vajda 1986: 168). Nevertheless, it was not legitimate to hold the Soviet Union wholly responsible for the suppression of East Central European traditions of pluralism and observance of the rule of law. It would be nice to believe that 'Central Europe' was a bed of roses until the Russians arrived. But, as remarked by the Czechoslovak dissident Milan Simecka, it was not Soviet Russia but Nazi Germany that 'tore up by the roots that certain decency of political and cultural standards which the Central European nations managed to preserve more or less intact up to 1937 . . . At the moment the tragedy of Central Europe began to unfold, Eastern influences were negligible . . . The cancer which finally put paid to what had gone before was nurtured on Western European history and fed on the decaying legacy of Western European intellectual movements' (Simecka 1985: 158–9). In 1987, with impeccable intellectual honesty, Simecka added that after the Second World War 'the Central European nations were neither as politically mature, nor quite as innocent as Kundera would have us think . . . with everyone trying to grab as much as they could for themselves. . . . The "leading value" in those days was the "national interest", so-called, not internal freedom' (Simecka 1987: 179). Indeed, 'one of the reasons why the influence of the "other civilization" [Russia] was so effective was because, to a certain extent, we provided it with fertile soil' (p. 180). The Kafkaesque world prefigured the communist states. Timothy Garton Ash has similarly pointed out that 'specifically *Central* European traditions . . . at least facilitated the establishment of communist regimes in Hungary and Czechoslovakia . . . A super-bureaucratic statism and formalistic legalism taken to absurd (and sometimes already inhuman) extremes were, after all, particularly characteristic of Central Europe before 1914.' He asks, rhetorically, 'What was really more characteristic of historic Central Europe: cosmopolitan tolerance, or nationalism and racism?' (Garton Ash 1986: 195). In the words of President Havel 'We are struggling not only against the heritage of communism, but also against the many problems that have cursed our history in the more distant past' (Havel 1994a: 163).

Those who have professed to believe in the actual or potential unity and cohesion of 'Central Europe' have probably underrated the force of the predominantly centrifugal tendencies of its constituent peoples. The notion that a specific set of shared values binds those countries together would be more convincing if such values were not largely confined to small groups of intellectuals. In the vision of 'Central Europe' propounded above all by Vaclav Havel, the Hungarian writer Gyorgy Konrad and the Polish historian and dissident Adam Michnik during the 1980s, citizens, relying on their own initiative and moral resources, would create their own democratic institutions and autonomous associations ('civil society') in order to compensate for the failure of the state to encourage and to nourish them, under regimes that were committed to the suppression of all independent political and cultural activity (Glenny 1990: 186). Thus Gyorgy Konrad argued that in contrast to the West, where civil society controlled the state, Central Europe was characterized by the independence or separation of civil society from the state. Central Europe was a region in which civil society had had to reject and distance itself from the state, increasingly replacing official state values, ideologies and structures with its own autonomous ones. 'On no account were we West Europeans, but we are not East Europeans either' (Konrad 1984: 91–114). East Central European dissidents developed a common set of values emphasizing social self-organization and self-defence, non-violence, the priority of the individual over the state and society and the primacy of individual human rights (Garton Ash 1986: 197–204). 'Truth and certain elementary values such as respect for human rights, civil society, the indivisibility of freedom and the rule of law – these were the notions that bound us together and made it worth our while to enter again and again into the unequal struggle with the powers that be' (Havel 1994a: 215). The starting point of such struggles was 'neither the will to power nor an ideological vision of the world, but rather a moral stance', intended to promote 'a climate of solidarity, creativity, co-operation, tolerance and deepening responsibility' (pp. 216–17).

After the collapse of communist rule and Soviet hegemony in 1989, however, the memory of East Central European dissident collaboration against a common oppressor quickly faded and (with the notable exception of Vaclav Havel) the former dissident intellectuals who gained high office in the new post-communist regimes soon fell from grace, while 'Central European' ideals foundered amid growing inter-state rivalries and competition for Western investment, economic assistance and political favour. The break-up of Czechoslovakia (the Czech Republic and Slovakia became independent countries on 1 January 1993) was a major setback for the concept of East Central Europe as a cohesive entity based upon shared values, beliefs, experiences and aspirations. (However, if it had been put to a referendum, it is clear that the 'velvet divorce' would not have gone through. A majority of both Czechs and Slovaks were opposed to it.) Yet even Kundera acknowledged that 'Central Europe is not a state; it is a culture or a fate. Its borders are imaginary and must be drawn and redrawn with each new historical situation' (Kundera 1984: 35). In 1986 the Hungarian writer Gyorgy Konrad, another leading champion of 'Central Europe', similarly acknowledged that it was not a reality but a project or an aspiration: 'What is revolutionary about the idea of Central Europe is precisely the fact that today it is only a dream. By contrast with the political reality of Eastern Europe and Western Europe, Central Europe exists only as a cultural counterhypothesis. . . . If there is no Central Europe, there is no Europe. . . . If we don't cling to the utopia of Central Europe we must give up the game. . . . Being Central European does not mean having a nationality, but rather an outlook on the world' (Konrad 1986: 113–16).

In the opinion of Pedrag Matvejevic, a professor at the University of Zagreb, 'Central Europe, or what actually remains of it, is engaged in the laborious process of recovering from the losses it has suffered . . . Central Europe is abandoning itself to sweet memories, struggling with difficulty against its own provincialism, and often proving itself ill-equipped to rejuvenate its old traditions' (Matvejevic 1989: 190). Kundera appears almost to agree: 'the nations of Central Europe have used up their strength in the struggle to survive' (Kundera 1984: 34). As argued by Garton Ash (1986: 212): 'If the term 'Central Europe' is to acquire some positive substance, then the discussion will have to move forward from the declamatory, the sentimental and the incantational to a dispassionate and rigorous examination both of the real legacy of historic Central Europe – which is as much one of divisions as of unities – and of the true conditions of present-day East Central Europe.'

This book can be seen as a modest contribution to the first of these two tasks. There is no doubting the existence of East Central Europe as a fairly distinct cultural and historical region, essentially comprising the easterly territories of the former Habsburg Empire and clearly distinguishable from Germany, Italy and Switzerland as well as from the southern and eastern Balkans and Russia. But we see more justification for treating East Central Europe as the most Westernized part of the East than for regarding it as the most easterly part of the West, as will be explained more fully below. We take this view out of concern, respect and affection rather than low regard for the region. If such a stance still offends those East Central Europeans who insist that they and their ancestors have long felt themselves to be part of 'the West', we can only demur that it is a very difficult judgement. It is based neither on ignorance nor on ill-will, and it is not nearly as disparaging and offensive as many of the statements made by the champions of 'Central Europe' about the Eastern Orthodox peoples and cultures of the Balkans and Russia. More important, as mentioned above, it would be a disservice to East Central Europeans if the ardent desire to (re)integrate into the European mainstream were allowed to obscure the magnitude of the social and cultural as well as economic adjustments they have yet to make.

GRADATIONS OF DIFFERENCE: A PRELIMINARY OVERVIEW OF EAST–WEST DIVERGENCE

Above and beyond these present-day objections to the (re)designation of 'East Central Europe' as 'Central Europe', and to the notion that its inhabitants have long been 'Western' at heart, this book also endeavours to analyse and explain the historic divergence of East Central Europe and the Balkans from western Europe and, less explicitly, from each other. The most important differences have concerned their divergent forms and conceptions of Christianity, 'feudalism', absolutism and nationhood, their contrasting responses to the late medieval and early modern 'crises of feudalism', the relatively late emergence and retention of serfdom in many parts of eastern Europe, the long survival of imperial polities in most of the region, the consequent late establishment of independent nation-states throughout the region, and the development of asymmetrical 'periphery–core' relations between eastern and western Europe. However, while it is often necessary or convenient to draw broad-brush distinctions between 'eastern Europe' and 'western Europe', we are fully aware that 'western Europe' has never been a unified or monolithic entity either. We try consistently to use the term as a geographical expression, referring to the western 'half' of the continent, rather than in a more loaded political sense. We also recognize that, like 'Eastern Europe', 'Western Europe' became a formal political and economic entity only in the wake of the Yalta and Potsdam agreements of 1945, and that it did not achieve institutional expression until the establishment of the Council of Europe, the OEEC, the ECSC, the WEU and the EEC during the late 1940s or the 1950s. Indeed, culturally as well as geographically, Greece belongs to eastern Europe, even though it was incorporated into 'Western Europe' for political and strategic reasons during the Cold War (Bideleux 1996: 129–32). Scandinavia clearly constitutes a distinct sub-region of its own, as does south-western Europe (Portugal, Spain and Italy). But it is not possible to delve into these differences within the confines of the present work. Detailed comparisons with Russia will similarly have to wait for another book, one that could carefully differentiate the sense from the torrents of nonsense that have been spouted on that topic. In particular, out of an understandable desire to differentiate their own 'homelands' as sharply as possible from the Eastern Orthodox world, writers such as Kundera (1984), Szucs (1988), Hanak (1989) and Wandycz (1992) have rather exaggerated the 'otherness', oppression, uniformity, centralization, peasant poverty, economic stagnation and absence of private initiative and enterprise in what they term 'the East', especially imperial Russia. In point of fact, late Tsarist Russia experienced a sizeable economic boom. It was buoyed up by significant advances in peasant agriculture, rising popular literacy, expectations and consumption levels, growing regional and occupational specialization, Western-style class differentiation, foreign direct investment and the emergence of millions of small and some 'big time' capitalist entrepreneurs. The Tsarist empire was never as static, monolithic or centrally controlled as the over-used notion of a Russian 'oriental despotism' would seem to suggest. (These views are developed at greater length in Bideleux 1987: 11–18, 1990, 1994.)

The East–West division of Europe has its roots partly in the East–West partitions of the Roman Empire in 285 and 395 AD and in the growing divergence and eventual schism between Eastern Orthodox and Western (Roman) Catholic Christianity, as explained in Part I. The fifth-century disintegration of the Western Roman Empire paved the way for the eventual evolution of western Europe through fragmented, warring and decentralized feudal polities to the precocious development of both agrarian and urban capitalism in the interstices of feudal society. This subsequently set the scene for the emergence of proto-national monarchies, proto-industrial economies and embryonic 'civic' nation-states. In the East, by contrast, outwardly splendid but ultimately stultifying imperial polities remained dominant until 1918. The Eastern Roman Empire (Byzantium) survived until the fifteenth century, only to be succeeded by the Ottoman Empire from 1453 until the end of the First World War. Meanwhile most of East Central Europe (initially excluding Poland–Lithuania and the Ottoman-ruled territories) gradually fell under Habsburg imperial control, especially after the death of the joint King of Hungary and Bohemia at the battle of Mohacs in 1526 and the failure of the two major Ottoman sieges of Vienna in 1529 and 1683.

The extreme fragmentation of western European polities from the sixth to the eighth centuries AD (the so-called Dark Ages) facilitated the emergence of unusually decentralized societies within which power was dispersed downwards to relatively autonomous landed nobilities, ecclesiastical lords and burghers. In an influential essay on the origins of Europe's deep-seated East–West divisions, the Hungarian philosopher Jeno Szucs has emphasized the seminal importance of the ways in which they made possible an enduring separation of 'state' and 'society' in western Europe (Szucs 1988: 298–9). It also allowed the Roman Catholic Church to escape from 'caesaropapism' and the tutelage of the state and to assert the autonomy of its spiritual authority and domain (pp. 299–300). This was in marked contrast to the position of the Eastern Orthodox Church, which was to remain the generally compliant and obsequious servant of the Byzantine state and its successors in south-eastern Europe and Russia. Moreover, the separation of the temporal and spiritual spheres in western Europe eventually made it possible to extricate politics from religious ethics and theology and facilitated the development of secular political thought and secular conceptions of authority. 'The West's separation of the sacred and the secular, the ideological and political spheres, was uniquely fruitful, and without it the future "freedoms", the theoretical emancipation of "society", the future nation-states, the Renaissance and the Reformation alike could never have ensued' (Szucs 1988: 300). Indeed, in the words of the Hungarian philosopher Mihaly Vajda, 'The really important feature of West European development from the Middle Ages onwards was the gradual separation of state and society. Out of West European political and social disintegration and fragmentation there arose new urban communities within which the attitudes and behaviour of individuals were shaped less and less by tradition ... And – most importantly – relations among various social groups were settled increasingly by contract' (Vajda 1988: 341).

Such processes were to be experienced hardly at all in the medieval Balkans and Russia and only in truncated forms in East Central Europe. Thus eastern Europe at least partly missed out on some of the most formative experiences of the West. While it is commonly accepted that the Protestant parts of Europe attached much greater importance to mass education and allowed a greater latitude for debate, enquiry and dissent than did the states that remained Roman Catholic, it is less widely appreciated that, for all its authoritarianism, bigotry and fear of popular education, the Roman Catholic Church continued to attach much more importance to scholarship and to the education of its own clergy and the ruling classes than did the Eastern Orthodox Church, which tolerated quite abysmal levels of ignorance and blind prejudice among clergy and laity alike. Similarly, the enduring rearguard resistance of the Roman Catholic Church to extensions of temporal authority over spiritual matters (even in communist Poland and Hungary in more recent times) has always sharply contrasted with the slavish subservience of the Eastern Orthodox Church to temporal rulers, be they Byzantine, Bulgar, Serb, Tsarist or communist. This greater independence of the Roman Catholic Church from the temporal ruler was not necessarily inherent in Roman Catholicism. It has been more plausibly argued that the political disintegration and chaos into which western Europe was plunged by the so-called 'barbarian' invasions and the collapse of the Western Roman Empire allowed the Roman Catholic Church to assert and consolidate its independence from western Europe's temporal rulers, whereas the Eastern Orthodox Church remained in a kind of Babylonian captivity under the Byzantine Empire and its Ottoman, Tsarist and communist successors. During the ninth century Charlemagne temporarily re-established an imperial polity in western Europe, 'utilizing the last reserves of the Frankish institutions' as well as the last vestiges of Roman imperial tradition. 'But these reserves had already been exhausted, and the temporary edifice was destroyed once and for all by a new element that arose from below – vassalage' (Szucs 1988: 300). Subsequent attempts to relaunch an all-embracing Holy Roman Empire merely succeeded in delaying the emergence of a unified German state until the late nineteenth century.

Fortunately, the forms of vassalage that emerged in medieval western Europe were able to preserve or regain the considerable autonomy that had been won by the nobility, the Church and the towns during the so-called Dark Ages and established reciprocal and quasi-contractual relations between rulers and their vassals (Szucs 1988: 300–1). Between about 1050 and 1300 the western European 'feudal' economies enjoyed a period of dynamic expansion, attended by the rise of towns, cities and city-states, major technical and organizational advances in agriculture, industry, finance and commerce, substantial increases in living standards and in the size and social status of nobilities and urban patriciates, and significant extensions of the rights and liberties of the more prosperous strata. In contrast to the experience of Eastern Orthodox Christendom and the great Asiatic despotisms, moreover, western European vassals were rarely required to engage in total self-abasement to their overlords. They were normally allowed to hold their heads erect and clasp the hand of their liege lord instead of having to grovel at his feet. Indeed, a cardinal feature of western European feudalism was that it began to enshrine a basic concept of 'human dignity as a constitutive element in its political relations' (p. 302). Furthermore, political fragmentation, decentralization and the consequent multiplicity of small jurisdictions (each with its own feudal courts and customary laws) offered fertile soil for the development of the rule of law and of a relatively autonomous Christian lay culture, morality and scale of values which rulers, for the most part, felt bound to respect (pp. 302–3). Thus administrative, military, fiscal and judicial functions came to be separated from the personal authority of the ruler and were distributed between various layers of feudal society. Hence the growing autonomy of the nobility, the Church, the towns and the law courts fostered the development of 'civil society', 'civil liberties' and contractual market relations in western Europe. This extended freedoms downward, accelerating the conversion of servile obligations into cash nexuses and the gradual dissolution of serfdom (pp. 305–6).

The concept of 'civil society' (*societas civilis*) came into use in the mid-thirteenth century to refer to this growth of autonomous institutions and activities. The West gradually accepted the notion that rulers (even supposedly 'absolute' rulers) had to respect and operate within the laws of the realm and were thus responsible or even subservient to 'society' seen as an abstract legal entity (Szucs 1988: 308). In the West, significantly, it was increasingly assumed that 'civil society' should control the ruler and/or the state, whereas the much weaker forms of 'civil society' that have emerged (if at all) in eastern Europe (including East Central Europe) have usually been seen as acting in opposition to the ruler/state. In other words, while the West assumed an increasingly co-operative and consensual relationship between 'civil society' and the ruler/state, the East assumed a rather more combative and antagonistic relationship between its relatively stunted 'civil society' and its generally stronger rulers and states.

To be sure, there were times when it seemed as if East Central Europe was being assimilated into the emerging 'modernity' of Western Christendom. From the tenth to the sixteenth centuries, it is variously argued, the cultural and economic 'distance' between East Central and Western Europe was considerably reduced (see Topolski 1981: 375–9; Szucs 1988: 331; Janos 1982: 30–1; Berend 1986: 331–2; Wandycz 1992: 6; and Part II, below). Adherence to the Western branch of Christianity, combined with a massive influx of German colonists, traders, priests, lawyers and administrators, brought East Central Europe into ever-closer communion with western European cultures, partly making up for the fact that most of the area (unlike South-eastern Europe) did not previously have a Germano-Roman heritage. It hastened the development of written languages, theological and scientific learning and scholarship, jurisprudence, commerce, agricultural and mining techniques, more formal and regular methods of administration, and towns as seats of temporal and ecclesiastical administration, commerce, learning and civic culture.

During the fourteenth, fifteenth and sixteenth centuries, monarchical prerogatives were increasingly circumscribed and eroded in Poland, Hungary, Bohemia and Moravia, which experienced significant development of commerce, crafts, mining, towns and autonomous decentralized activity (civil society). Consequently the region's educated elites participated vigorously in the European humanist intellectual currents which engendered the Renaissance, the Reformation, the early stages of the Scientific

Revolution and the revival of Roman law. Indeed, while the sixteenth century was an epoch of religious bigotry and strife in western Europe, Poland, Bohemia, Moravia and Transylvania became havens of religious toleration. In addition, heavy ploughs and the three-field system had been introduced into East Central European agriculture by the fourteenth century (Topolski 1981: 376; Wandycz 1992: 30), and German and East Central European ore mining was greatly stimulated by the discovery of the *seiger* process for separating silver from copper ore, with the result that the minting of metallic money quintupled between 1460 and 1530 (Anderson 1979: 22). Major cosmopolitan universities were established in Prague in 1348, in Vienna in 1365, in Krakow in 1400 and in Vilnius in 1579. (Universities were also established in Pecs in 1361 and at Pozsony/Bratislava in 1465, but these did not survive for long.) The first printing presses were established in the 1450s in Bohemia and in the 1470s in Poland and Hungary, compared with the 1460s in Italy and the 1470s in both England and France. Vernacular writing proliferated in East Central Europe from the thirteenth century onward. Translations of the Bible into the vernacular appeared first of all in Germany and Italy, then in Bohemia and Hungary, and only after that in England and France (Wandycz 1992: 36–7). The first vernacular printed books were published in 1513 in the case of Poland and in 1541 in that of Hungary. During the sixteenth century about 8,000 titles were published in Poland, compared with some 10,000 in England (pp. 50–1). R.J.W. Evans has suggested that during the sixteenth century the Danubian lands 'belonged . . . more nearly to Western Europe than at any time before or since' (Evans 1979: xxii). By 1500 around 25 per cent of the population lived in towns in Moravia, about 20 per cent did so in Bohemia and in Poland proper (excluding the vast Grand Duchy of Lithuania) and about 15 per cent of the population was urban in Hungary, although such proportions were still far below the 50 per cent levels estimated for the Low Countries and northern Italy in the same period (Wandycz 1992: 60). In spite of the existence of considerable evidence to the contrary, moreover, Mihaly Vajda claims that the 'autonomies' that struck root in East Central Europe between 1000 and 1500 'did not wither away . . . In East Central Europe the estates remained vigorously alive . . . The consciousness and attitudes of individualism were alive and well, the desire for autonomy ever-present' (Vajda 1988: 343).

Nevertheless, Wandycz concedes that the apparent Westernization of East Central Europe at that time remained somewhat 'shallow' and 'superficial' (Wandycz 1992: 6). The Hungarian economic historian Ivan Berend also emphasizes that these centuries did not witness the establishment of 'feudalism in the Western sense'. The forms of feudalism may have been introduced, but 'the substance of feudalism was never integrated into the social fabric of East European life' (Berend 1986: 331). According to Anderson (1979: 243), 'The frontier character of Eastern social formations rendered it extremely difficult for dynastic rulers to enforce liege obedience from military settlers and landowners, in an unbounded milieu where armed adventurers and anarchic velleities were often at a premium. The result was that vertical feudal solidarity was much weaker than in the West. There were few organic ties binding the various aristocracies together.' The region's towns were mostly 'alien' German and Jewish enclaves. They were not strong enough to challenge or counterbalance the power of either the landed nobility or the ruler. Nor were they sufficiently integrated with their Slavic or Hungarian hinterlands to be able to reshape society in the way that the rise of towns, cities and city-states did in western Europe. 'Commodity production, and with it the money economy, had not penetrated to the extent that it had in the West' (Gunst 1989: 66). Many western European towns soon developed beyond their initial roles as military, ecclesiastical or administrative strongholds into centres of commerce and production. By contrast, sixteenth-century eastern European 'towns' usually remained little more than administrative centres, way stations, collection points, garrisons or chartered villages (pp. 57–9). They were seats of consumption rather than production. It was only their size (and sometimes their legal status) that gave them an urban appearance. With the possible exceptions of Bohemia and Moravia, eastern European townspeople failed to match either the degree of independence and political representation or the range of civil liberties won by their western European counterparts. The consequences of all this were to be laid bare by the differing responses of eastern and western Europe to their respective late medieval 'crises of feudalism'.

Between about 1300 and 1450 many parts of western Europe were convulsed by Malthusian crises (reflected in famines, epidemics, drastic declines in population and widespread social and political unrest), whereas the economies of East Central Europe and Russia underwent dynamic expansion. The western European economic crises and Malthusian constraints on economic and population growth were eventually overcome through the expansion of interregional and overseas commerce (permitting increased economic specialization and the introduction or development of new products), advances in agricultural, industrial and maritime organization and technology, territorial consolidation, and alliances between proto-national monarchies and nascent bourgeoisies (facilitating monarchical assaults on feudal privilege and particularism). 'European feudalism – far from constituting an exclusively agrarian economy – was the *first* mode of production in history to accord an autonomous structural base to urban production and exchange' (Anderson 1979: 21). There was also an influx of precious and semi-precious metals (initially from Germany and East Central Europe and later from the New World) which increased the money supply and price levels, facilitated trade with Asia, encouraged the commercialization of agriculture and accelerated the dissolution of serfdom, mainly between 1450 and 1620. However, the overcoming of the economic crises in western Europe roughly coincided with the onset of similar crises during the later sixteenth and early seventeenth centuries in East Central Europe. These too were manifested in famines, epidemics, dramatic demographic declines and widespread urban and rural unrest. Malthusian factors were compounded by the effects of recurrent Ottoman military depredations and the devastating Thirty Years' War (1618–48). In contrast to western Europe, moreover, these crises mainly resulted in considerable de-urbanization and the conclusion of reactionary alliances between actual or aspiring absolute monarchs and the big landowners, to the detriment of most peasants and townspeople. The major exception was the Polish–Lithuanian Commonwealth, where the exceedingly large and already powerful landed nobility contrived to strengthen themselves still further at the expense of the monarchy and central government as well as the peasantry and townspeople, by virtually monopolizing political power. The earlier western European crises had in the long run enhanced the economic importance and political leverage of the commercial classes and the towns (especially in the nascent capitalist 'core' economies of north-western Europe, led by the Netherlands and England) and hastened the dissolution of serfdom. Over most of eastern Europe, however, the crises of the sixteenth and seventeenth centuries downgraded the political and economic position of towns and townspeople and resulted in major extensions and intensifications of serfdom, prolonging its existence until the mid-nineteenth century. Indeed, the legislative strengthening of eastern European serfdom had already begun in the 1490s in Hungary, Poland, Brandenburg, Mecklenburg, Prussia, Bohemia and Russia, during the preceding economic upswing. Mounting labour shortages (relative to rapidly expanding cultivated areas and mining operations) and rising prices and living costs, combined with the fact that most landowners lacked sufficient finance to take full advantage of the expanding urban and export markets for eastern European grain, cattle, timber and metal ores, evoked concerted action to restrict the rights and mobility of the peasantry, who could then be subjected to increased compulsory dues in kind and labour obligations. A fundamental East–West divergence began within Europe in this period: 'While western Europe was evolving capitalist conditions, the region east of the Elbe sharply deviated from that experience . . . Serfs were again bound to the soil . . . and feudal dues paid in crops and labour . . . gradually replaced the customary money rent. This change began at about the end of the fifteenth century . . . The two halves of Europe clearly split . . . The division of labour that took place in the modern world economy then forming reduced the countries of Eastern Europe to the role of suppliers of cereals and livestock' (Berend 1986: 334–5).

Thus the 'Western model' of early modern society was based upon the elimination of serfdom, whereas 'the Eastern was based on prolonging it' (Szucs 1988: 312). Ironically, by expanding demand for eastern European primary commodity exports, the western European economic recovery further entrenched the position of this so-called 'second serfdom' in eastern Europe, 'causing the great estates cultivated by forced labour to become the typical Eastern partner in the East–West division of labour that developed' (p. 313). In the opinion of the influential Marxist agrarian historian Robert Brenner, 'the peasantry of the East was much less well-positioned to resist the seigneurial reaction than was its Western counterpart, basically because the lords had led and dominated the process of colonization by which North-eastern Europe had been settled' and the region was therefore subjected to 'an extraordinarily tight form of feudal property relations' under the so-called 'second serfdom' (Brenner 1989: 44). The significance of this system went far beyond the narrowly economic sphere. It established a profound difference between eastern and western European society. 'This difference had important cultural and moral dimensions, affecting not only the serfs, whom it degraded, but their owners, many of whom were corrupted by the almost absolute power they wielded over them,' and the heritage of serfdom has influenced 'popular and elite attitudes down to the present day' (Longworth 1994: 298). However, it should be noted that serfdom was much more prevalent in East Central Europe than in the Balkans, whose inhabitants were in this important respect less deeply scarred than their more northerly neighbours.

From the sixteenth century onwards, Immanuel Wallerstein has argued, East Central Europe was incorporated into a peripheral and dependent role in an emerging 'capitalist world economy' whose core was situated in north-western Europe, especially the Netherlands and England. Seen in this perspective, the intensification and extension of serfdom in early modern East Central Europe was not a 'pre-capitalist' or 'feudal' phenomenon but a specific product and manifestation of emergent capitalism. It was analogous to the coercive 'cash crop labour systems' implanted in the Americas, where servile forced labour similarly became a commodity to be bought and sold in economies that were likewise reoriented towards the production of primary commodities for profit and for export to the north-western European core states, which allegedly appropriated most of the 'surplus value' generated by the 'world economy' as a whole and held the underdeveloped peripheries in subordinate 'dependent' roles (Wallerstein 1974a, b).

It is certainly true that the sixteenth century saw the beginnings of qualitatively significant exports of grain, timber and livestock from the Baltic hinterland to north-western Europe and that these exports emanated from large landed estates employing serf labour. However, Piotr Wandycz rightly points out that the so-called 'second serfdom' which arose in early modern eastern Europe 'took a long time in crystallizing and was less the product of the agrarian boom than of the tightening market that followed' during the seventeenth century (Wandycz 1992: 59). One must also beware of the temptation to exaggerate the role of external market forces in the extension and intensification of eastern European serfdom. Only a tiny proportion of eastern Europe's grain output was exported to western Europe during the sixteenth century and such exports were largely confined to areas with easy riverine access to the major Baltic ports, e.g. along the Vistula to Gdansk (Danzig). Grain exports from relatively landlocked Austria, Bohemia, Moravia and Hungary were at that time either negligible or non-existent. Even in the case of Poland grain exports amounted to only about 12 per cent of total grain output, according to Wandycz (p. 58), and they may not have exceeded 2.5 per cent of total grain output, in the opinion of Jerzy Topolski (1981: 391). Grain exports from the Baltic region to western Europe were still 'marginal in relation to total demand and supply' (p. 392). Indeed, Hungarian, Russian and Romanian grain exports did not really 'take off' until the construction of railway networks in the second half of the nineteenth century, even if southern Poland, Hungary, Wallachia and Moldavia were already participating actively in the trans-European cattle trade (p. 397). For logistical reasons, sixteeenth-century East Central European agricultural trade was largely geared to local urban markets (p. 396). Wallerstein's influential thesis that sixteenth-century Baltic grain and timber exports to the nascent urban industrial 'core' economies of north-western Europe restructured the East Central European economies and reduced them to a dependent peripheral status in the emerging 'capitalist world economy' has therefore jumped the gun by two or three centuries. Jacek Kochanowicz concludes, as we do, that the affinities between the East Central European economies and their retardation relative to those of the West were more attributable to internal factors, especially to similarities of social structure, than to external ones (Kochanowicz 1989: 119). Moreover, as Daniel Chirot has argued, the further growth of eastern European economic dependence on the West from the seventeenth to the nineteenth centuries produced neither the uniformly negative and stultifying effects postulated by Marxist 'dependency' theorists nor the uniformly positive stimuli and 'demonstration effects' postulated by 'modernization' (alias 'Westernization') theorists (Chirot 1989: 8–10).

In any case, the more promising economic and cultural trends in East Central Europe during the Renaissance period were nipped in the bud by the combined effects of the Ottoman onslaughts, the partly religious warfare of the seventeenth century, the expansion of intolerant absolutist empires, the attendant reinforcement of seigneurial privilege and agrarian serfdom, the decline of towns and the persecution and/or emigration of religious dissenters, freethinkers and (within the Habsburg Empire) Jews. The emigrants included substantial numbers of merchants, nobles and craftsmen. These mainly took refuge in Protestant Germany, Scandinavia, Britain and the Netherlands, whose economic and intellectual gains were to be East Central Europe's loss. The Habsburg domains in East Central Europe were increasingly held together by rigidly enforced *Kaisertreue* (loyalty to the emperor), by Counter-Reformation Catholicism and 'not least by a certain sense of insecurity which made them cling to the spiritual legacy of Rome with exaggerated tenacity' (Adam Zamoyski, *The Times*, 30 November 1995, p. 38).

Admittedly, various manifestations of 'absolutism' also emerged in early modern western Europe. But here, as the British Marxist historian Perry Anderson has argued, 'the very term "absolutism" was a misnomer', for no Western monarchy ever exercised 'absolute power over its subjects, in the sense of an untrammelled despotism' (Anderson 1979: 49). Thus Jean Bodin, the leading sixteenth-century theoretical exponent of French 'absolutism', took for granted the existence of strict limitations on the powers of the 'absolute' monarch: 'It is not within the competence of any prince in the world to levy taxes at will on his people, or to seize the goods of another arbitrarily' the reason being that 'since the sovereign prince has no power to transgress the laws of nature, which God – whose image he is on earth – has ordained, he cannot take the property of another without a just and reasonable cause' (quoted on p. 50). One finds similar assumptions in the writings of other leading Western theoreticians of absolutism (e.g. Hobbes and Grotius), as noted by Szucs (1988: 320). Anderson has provided a penetrating and persuasive formulation of the essential differences between the Western and Eastern manifestations of 'absolutism'. The absolutist state in the West was 'the redeployed political apparatus of a feudal class which had accepted the commutation of [seigneurial] dues. It was a *compensation for the disappearance of serfdom*, in the context of an increasingly urban economy which it did not completely control and to which it had to adapt.' The absolutist state in the East, by contrast, was '*a device for the consolidation of serfdom*, in a landscape scoured of autonomous urban life or resistance. The manorial reaction in the East meant that a new world had to be implanted from above, by main force. The dose of violence pumped into social relations was correspondingly far greater.' The maturation of absolutist states in the East during the seventeenth century 'dealt a death-blow to the possibility of a revival of urban independence in the East. The new monarchies – Hohenzollern, Habsburg and Romanov – unshakeably assured the political supremacy of the nobility over the towns ... In the Czech Lands, the Thirty Years' War finished off the pride and growth of the Bohemian and Moravian cities' (Anderson 1979: 195, 205; italics in the original).

Ironically, the Polish nobility successfully warded off any 'absolutist' ambitions on the part of their own monarchs, only to be defeated by Russian, Prussian and Austrian absolutism (alias 'the Partitioning Powers') in 1772, 1793 and 1795. The structure and outward forms of 'absolutism' were even more strongly shaped by the requirements of war in seventeenth- and eighteenth-century eastern Europe than they had been in sixteenth- and seventeenth-century western Europe. The eastern European nobilities were to a large extent service nobilities and they regularly wore uniform to emphasize that they represented the strong arm of the state. In Russia and in the Austrian domains of the Habsburg Monarchy, as well as in Prussia, 'The entire State thus acquired a military trim. The whole social system was placed at the service of militarism' (p. 213). The harshness and the militarism of the eastern European 'absolutist' states were also a response to seigneurial fears of the ever-present danger of peasant revolts against the rigours and degradation of serfdom (p. 212). Anderson concludes that 'in Eastern Europe, the social power of the nobility was unqualified by any ascendant bourgeoisie such as marked Western Europe: seigneurial domination was unfettered. Eastern Absolutism thus more patently and unequivocally displayed its class composition than [did] its Western counterpart. Built upon serfdom, the feudal cast of its State structure was more blunt and manifest' (p. 430).

The resultant political and social rigidities severely cramped East Central European development during the seventeenth and eighteenth centuries. Towns and the embryonic urban merchant classes went into temporary decline, partly as a result of the above-mentioned religious persecution, emigration and devastating warfare and partly because the major noble producers of exportable grain, timber and livestock surpluses established direct relations with western European merchants and financiers, bypassing the often ethnically 'alien' Baltic towns and middlemen. In the case of Poland, moreover, laws passed as early as 1496 by the ascendant nobility prohibited burghers and merchants from owning land, travelling abroad or engaging in foreign trade. 'Polish merchants therefore remained primarily local middlemen. They did not specialize to any great extent and, more importantly, banking did not become an important part of their operations, as was happening among the larger Western European merchants . . . Polish towns and burghers were unable to become autonomous social or political forces. They were unable to forge national bonds among themselves, or to act as a uniting force. Nor were they available for use by the kings against the encroachment of noble power' (Kochanowicz 1989: 112, 114).

In the case of the more landlocked Habsburg Empire the landed nobility increasingly acquired and exploited restrictive local monopolies of activities such as grain milling and the selling of wines and spirits (Gunst 1989: 71). The proportion of its population living in towns had fallen to 8 per cent by 1735 and was still only 8.6 per cent in 1840 (Hanak 1989: 63). Levels of urbanization were even lower in the southern and eastern Balkans. In the famous words of the first manifesto of the Russian Social Democratic Workers' Party (written in 1898), 'The further east in Europe one proceeds, the weaker, the more cowardly and the baser in the political sense becomes the bourgeoisie and the greater are the cultural and political tasks that devolve upon the proletariat.' It would indeed fall to the communists finally to eliminate the residual power and wealth of the big landowners in many parts of Eastern Europe in the aftermath of the Second World War.

These disadvantages, combined with the growth of western European colonial commerce and the displacement of the world's major trade routes away from the Mediterranean and the Baltic towards Europe's Atlantic seaboard, caused both East Central Europe and the Balkans to fall far behind maritime western Europe, which developed increasingly secular and urban 'civic' societies with much greater freedom of thought, occupation and commerce. The subsequent north-western European Industrial Revolution, coupled with the growing specialization of Eastern Europe in less sophisticated and generally less remunerative primary products, widened Europe's East–West disparity in *per capita* national income from around two to one to about three to one within the space of some fifty years (Berend 1986: 339). This fundamental economic disparity would widen still further during the twentieth century and will persist well into the twenty-first century, even on the most optimistic assumptions. However, if the East European states continue to be dogged by the kinds of crisis that they have repeatedly experienced in modern times, it will be an even longer haul.

Of course the development of Eastern Europe has not been impeded solely by man-made political, cultural and institutional factors. Much of the region is quite landlocked by comparison with western Europe, which is much better served by navigable rivers and its coastal waters. Much of western Europe also has a moister and more temperate climate, a longer growing season and less mountainous terrain than does most of eastern Europe, and it has been less prone to soil erosion. Natural advantages of this sort made it easier for western European centres of trade and craft industry to link up with one another commercially. Such a trade network was established as early as the 1180s, according to the French medieval historian Georges Duby, who calls this one of the 'main turning points in European economic history' (Duby 1974: 257–70). At the opposite pole, 'No such network of commercial centers connected Balkan and Byzantine territory by that date or afterwards . . . The Balkan lack of coastal access or navigable rivers combined with the Ottoman wheat monopoly, designed to provision Constantinople at artificially low prices, to keep other urban grain markets from becoming integrated into a "national market". It typically cost more than the purchase price to transport 100 kilograms of wheat just 100 kilometres. Bulk trade could hardly flourish under these conditions' (Lampe 1989: 180, 184). This in turn helps to explain the relatively low population densities and the comparative scarcity of large towns and cities in eastern Europe, and that (together with the restrictive effects of the 'second serfdom') further limited commercial opportunities and the size of markets. With a population of around 22 million in 1700, the whole of Eastern Europe had about as many inhabitants as France at that time, while the only really significant urban markets within the region during the early eighteenth century were Constantinople (400,000), Vienna (120,000), Prague (50,000) and Warsaw (30,000) (Okey 1982: 21, 32).

THE CURSE OF 'ETHNIC' NATIONALISM

If the outcome of the western European 'crisis of feudalism' generally hastened the formation and consolidation of proto-national states, it is equally clear that the outcome of the corresponding eastern European crises facilitated the emergence and consolidation of 'absolutist' multinational imperial polities which managed to retain control of most of Eastern Europe until 1918. The crucial consequence of this particular East–West divergence was that in western Europe modern nationalist doctrines would develop *after* (or, in some cases, even as a result of) the establishment of nation-states, whereas in eastern Europe the advent of modern nationalism would come *before* the creation of nation-states. This in turn meant that, whereas western European nations would generally be conceived and defined in inclusive 'civic' terms (as the people of particular states and territories), in eastern Europe nations were destined to be conceived and defined in more exclusive cultural or 'ethnic' terms, since they neither derived from nor corresponded to the existing multinational imperial states within which they were lodged. This seemingly innocuous divergence has been responsible for the most fundamental and damaging differences between Western and Eastern polities and societies in the twentieth century. 'Between the wars, nationalism was the curse of eastern Europe – a political curse, in that national grievances, real or unreal, provided pretexts for oppressive rule and strong points for Nazi domination – and an economic curse, in that the national tariff walls were an obstacle to development' (Warriner 1950: 64).

If exclusive and frequently illiberal 'ethnic' nationalism has not been the 'original sin' or the 'root of all evil' in twentieth-century eastern European politics, it has come pretty close to that. It has poisoned the wells of liberalism and democracy in the region for as long as independent nation-states have existed there. It has also distorted and impeded the rule of law, equality of opportunity and the neutral operation of market economies. Inter-ethnic tensions, jealousies and conflicts have thrown up major road-blocks on the tortuous paths to pluralistic liberal democracy and market systems, even where they have not resulted in outright war. Conversely, the failure of liberalism and the rule of law to put down deeply entrenched roots in East European societies has made it all the more difficult to curb or constrain 'ethnic' excesses. 'The dominant nationality in each country indiscriminately looks upon the state as its very own, however undemocratic it may be' (Vajda 1988: 344). In eastern Europe, experiments in democracy have tended to degenerate into 'intolerant majoritarianism', trampling under foot the rights of minorities – and, ultimately, those of the majorities as well. Moreover, so long as it is believed that each ethnic group has 'freehold rights' over a particular patch of land, there will always remain the potential for violent inter-ethnic conflict in some benighted part of this war-scarred region.

The belated initiation and the even later completion of the nation-building and state-building processes and the prominence of 'ethnic' or 'integral' nationalism in twentieth-century eastern Europe is thus mainly to be explained by centuries of sharply contrasting political, social and economic conditions and structures. As will be made plain in Parts I–III, we do not believe in the frequently alleged existence of innate differences in the 'ethnic make-up' and 'temper' of the two halves of Europe. That kind of stereotyping borders on racial prejudice and racism. The distinctive political and cultural complexions of the eastern European nations were, in our view, not innate but structurally determined. Regrettably, the structures and contexts within which eastern European nationalism emerged did not reinforce but came into conflict with the development of tolerance and mutual respect. In the West civil society has mainly 'defended pluralism and its autonomy against the encroachments of the state', but in Eastern Europe it has tended to become 'the mainstay of a national identity that was often endangered by the foreign ruler or foreign state' and was thus 'the principal defender of nationhood'. This engendered 'a certain uniformism and intolerance in the name of a common stand against the non-national or anti-national forces', i.e. the 'mentality of the besieged fortress' (Wandycz 1992: 8). Before Bohemia, Hungary and Poland fell under the control of alien absolutist empires, multicultural and multi-ethnic 'political nations' did indeed begin to emerge in East Central Europe. 'It was the interruption of statehood . . . that vitiated the process of nation forming along Western lines. The result was an evolution toward a different concept of nationhood, colored by the romantic outlook, conceived in terms of ethnicity and cultural–linguistic criteria' (p. 7).

After centuries under the 'imperial heel' (partly in the so-called 'prison-house of nations') the long submerged or subjugated peoples of Eastern Europe were finally 'liberated' in the wake of several Balkan wars, culminating in the First World War. Even after the disintegration of Europe's eastern empires, however, eastern and western Europe still constituted contrasting civilizations, as portrayed in Francois Delaisy's influential book *Les Deux Europes* (published in 1924), in Henry Tiltman's still fascinating *Peasant Europe* (published in 1934) and in David Mitrany's brilliant polemic against urban neo-mercantilism entitled *Marx against the Peasant* (published in 1951).

Miklos Duray, an outspoken member of the Hungarian minority in Slovakia during the 1980s, has argued that, quite apart from their distinctive social and economic structures, the political systems and cultures of the 'successor states' that emerged out of the disintegration of the Habsburg, Tsarist, Hohenzollern and Ottoman Empires were fatally scarred by 'the absolutization of the national idea', i.e. by an intolerant majoritarianism or 'totalitarian nationalism' that erected new barriers and aroused new conflicts between nations (Duray 1989: 98–9). 'Within the political designs of the new states which emerged victorious on the historical stage, there was room only for their own power interests, for the interests of the ruling nation. There was no room for the national and cultural interests of the defeated nations . . . nor was there any provision for protecting the interests and identity of the national minorities . . . It was in this respect that Eastern Central Europe most clearly divorced itself from the West' (pp. 101–2), long before the advent of either Soviet hegemony or communist dictatorship. This fateful blemish played a crucial role in alienating inter-war Eastern Europe from Western values and civilization (which is not to say that the West was a model of perfection, simply that it was different in certain crucial respects). Similarly, following the demise of the Nazi 'New Order' in 1945, 'The situation positively invited unrestrained behaviour because the concept of ethnic totality, no less alien to modern European traditions than Hitlerite or Stalinist ideas, had become the rule' (p. 104). Duray deeply regretted that the seven decades since 1918 had seen 'no great improvement in conditions for a settlement between neighbouring countries in Eastern Central Europe, despite the fact that the countries of the area share such a similar past' (p. 110). The potential consequences are quite serious: 'Political pluralism emerged in Western Europe particularly as a means of resolving social, political and ideological conflicts . . . Such a concept of pluralism is absent from the traditional political culture of the Eastern Central European countries. It can even be said to run counter to our traditions' (pp. 112–13).

Such a situation is not readily conducive to 'the politics of interests, characterized by pragmatic calculation, bargaining and compromise'. Instead 'we find the predominance of values which are inherently non-negotiable and absolute'. What is more, ' The leading role of intellectuals in transitional politics is also a factor promoting the primacy of value-based politics, and the background of many politically active intellectuals in the embattled anti-communist underground opposition can also be adduced to explain the unwillingness to compromise which is a striking feature of post-communist politics' (Batt 1994a: 37). This does not augur well for the long-term success or durability of the current attempts to build pluralistic liberal democracies and liberal market economies in Eastern Europe. This is not to deny that some countries in the region appear to have made remarkably rapid progress in those directions. Yet the very rapidity of the transition raises doubts as to how deep and enduring the changes really can have been. It has rarely (if ever) been possible to acquire a truly democratic system and a functioning market economy 'off the peg', in the way that one does when one purchases a ready-made suit. The pluralism and the liberal democracies and market economies of the West are the products of centuries of struggle and hard-won incremental gains. It is much easier to reproduce their outward forms than their inner life and substance. It is doubtful whether such tortuous processes can be telescoped into just one or two decades in Eastern Europe, especially when it offers such inauspicious soil for pluralism and for political, religious and ethnic tolerance.

We fear that it is going to be much harder for East Europeans to overcome the deep-rooted 'home grown' legacies of exclusive and illiberal 'ethnic' nationalism than to throw off the largely alien and externally imposed ideological heritage of Marxism–Leninism. Indeed, President Havel has argued that 'While the Western democracies have had decades to create a civil society, to build internationally integrated structures, and to learn the arts of peaceful international coexistence and cooperation, the countries ruled by communism could not go through this creative process' (Havel 1994a: 223). Unfortunately, communist rule was 'far from being simply the dictatorship of one group of people over another. It was a genuinely totalitarian system, that is, it permeated every aspect of life and deformed everything it touched, including all the natural ways people had evolved of living together.' The communist regimes fostered 'a specific structure of values and models of behaviour . . . When communist power and its ideology collapsed, this structure collapsed along with it. But people couldn't simply absorb and internalize a new structure immediately, one that would correspond to the elementary principles of civic society and democracy.' The transition period is fraught with danger: 'In a situation where one system has collapsed and a new one does not yet exist, many people feel empty and frustrated. This condition is fertile ground for radicalism of all kinds, for the hunt for scapegoats, and for the need to hide behind the anonymity of the group, be it socially or ethnically based. It encourages hatred of the world, self-affirmation at all costs, the feeling that everything is now permitted and the unparalleled flourishing of selfishness . . . It gives rise . . . to political extremism, to the most primitive cult of consumerism, to a carpetbagging morality . . . the eruption of so many different kinds of old-fashioned patriotism, revivalist messianism, conservatism and expressions of hatred' (pp. 221–2).

At the same time, we also recognize the difficulties that Eastern Europeans will face in shaking off all the legacies of communist rule. It has not been possible to round up a handful of chief villains and to subject them to latter-day Nuremberg trials. The communist regimes lasted much longer than the Nazi regime and, in consequence, there was much more universal complicity in communist wrongdoing. Corruption, illegality and reliance on the black market were matters of daily survival, and many people refrained from speaking up on behalf of those falsely accused of wrongdoing (or sometimes even informed on their neighbours) in order to protect a son, a daughter, a parent or a close friend. In his New Year's Day address on 1 January 1990 President Havel said of the effects of communist rule: 'We have to accept this legacy as a sin we committeed against ourselves. If we accept it as such, we will understand that it is up to us all, and up to us alone, to do something about it. We cannot blame the previous rulers for everything, not only because it would be untrue, but also because it would blunt the duty that each of us faces today: namely, the obligation to act independently, freely, reasonably and quickly' (Havel 1994a: 15). It will take East Europeans a long time to burn this legacy out of their souls. Not all are as high-minded as Havel, and they do not always welcome his voicing of home truths.

CRISIS AND CHANGE

The development of Eastern Europe never has been and never will be just a 'staggered' and 'inferior' repetition of the development of the West. It has always had, and will continue to have, an agenda and a dynamic of its own. In Eastern Europe, to a much greater extent than in the West, fundamental changes in political, social and economic structures or systems have tended to occur only as a result of convulsive or cataclysmic crises, such as those that shook Eastern Europe during the Revolutions of 1848–49, in the wake of the Austro-Prussian War of 1866 and the stock-market crash of 1873, after the Balkan Wars of 1876–78 and 1912–13, amid the political upheavals of 1905–08, during and after the two World Wars, during the 1930s Depression, after the death of Stalin in

1953, during the attempted reforms of 1956 and 1968 and during the disintegration of the communist systems between 1989 and 1991. The striking frequency and magnitude of these crises, along with the consequent preponderance of erratic, eruptive or convulsive patterns of change, helps to justify the title of this book. Crises have repeatedly destabilized the precarious foundations and structures of East European regimes and societies, thereby creating opportunities for radical and/or reactionary change. Gradual, evolutionary or incremental change on the Western pattern has not been wholly absent, of course, but it has been much less prominent than in western Europe. (Significantly, whereas the major benchmarks in western European history tend to be 'success dates', such as 1492, 1945 and 1957, many of the major landmarks in eastern European history are the dates of alleged historical catastrophes, such as 1453, 1526, 1620 and 1914.) Moreover, the somewhat belated appearance of railways, big cities, large-scale industrialization, cyclical booms and slumps, population explosions, the uprooting of millions of people from the countryside to the towns, mass education, mass nationalism, political parties and trade unions during the nineteenth century greatly increased the region's social and political instability and turbulence and accelerated the pace of change. Societies in flux tend to experience acute political, social and cultural disorientation and despair, producing much pain and suffering as well as explosions of literary, intellectual, musical and artistic creativity and innovation. Indeed, in a region characterized by sporadic and eruptive patterns of change, political stabilization probably required wholesale social 'engineering' more than piecemeal 'constitutional tinkering' (Longworth 1994: 114). The region has repeatedly experienced periods of feverish social and/or political reform, such as the reforms of Emperor Joseph II during the 1780s, the Revolutions of 1848–49, the immediate aftermaths of the two World Wars and the period since 1989, interspersed with long periods of political immobilism or even retreat. During the twentieth century, however, crises have tended to 'break down the already precarious structure of mass society' and thus to increase the chances of success 'for anti-democratic mass movements' (Kornhauser 1960: 113).

In these particular respects the region's modern social and political dynamics have been quite amenable to the forms of 'revolution from above' favoured by communist, fascist and authoritarian nationalist regimes. Nevertheless, this does not mean that we should automatically accept Alexander Gerschenkron's influential thesis that, as a result of the 'relative backwardness' of pre-1914 eastern Europe, the state had to play a much larger developmental role there than it did in the industrialization of western Europe (Gerschenkron 1962: 5–30, 353–64). His superficially persuasive argument is that the initial poverty of these predominantly agrarian economies, the increasing economies of scale and capital intensity of many industrial technologies, and the increasingly important 'linkages' and 'complementarities' between various industrial sectors and infrastructural investment (especially in railways) were constantly expanding the capital requirements of industrialization and the critical minimum effort needed to launch it as a self-reinforcing and sustainable process. In his account, these expanding financial requirements could be met only by the state and/or specialized investment banks, in most cases partly by attracting and harnessing inflows of Western loan capital and foreign direct investment. In such 'backward' economies, increased state enterprise, contracts, investment subsidies and other developmental expenditure had to be financed mainly by increased taxation of the preponderant agricultural sector. This 'fiscal squeeze' would reduce effective demand for industrial and agricultural consumer goods, thereby increasing the importance of state contracts, investment subsidies and other forms of protectionism in sustaining demand for industrial products (especially producer goods), while forcing the primary sector to expand its exports, which would in turn help to service the foreign debt and finance much-needed imports of Western machinery and equipment.

Gerschenkron's critics have, however, shown that he implicitly underrated the important role played by the state and sometimes even by banks in the early stages of western European industrialization. The forms of state intervention and bank finance used in Western industrialization may have been different, but they were often none the less crucial. Thus the state made some decisive contributions to the economic success of eighteenth-century England, not least through its increasingly liberal trade policies, the Enclosure Acts, the Acts of Union with Scotland and Ireland and the promotion of British maritime supremacy and colonial power, while banks played a leading role in the Industrial Revolution in Scotland (Cameron 1966: 60–99). Moreover, the economic roles of the state, investment banks and foreign direct investment and the capital intensity of certain industries increased almost everywhere in the late nineteenth and early twentieth centuries. These trends were not peculiar to Europe's so-called 'backward economies' or 'late industrializers'. They had more to do with the arms race and the growth of defence expenditure and of military-industrial complexes than with the needs of civilian economic development (let alone public welfare provision, which remained modest until the 1940s). Indeed, while parts of pre-1914 eastern Europe did develop some large-scale and capital-intensive industries (e.g. oil, steel and chemicals) for military reasons or where specific natural resource endowments warranted it, in most areas industrialization continued to be based mainly on a gradually expanding production of low-technology and labour-intensive consumer goods such as textiles, processed foods and drinks (Bideleux 1987: 15, 17, 55–6, 259–61). It was not until the First World War and the subsequent emergence of autarkic and etatist communist and fascist regimes that the eastern European economies began to conform more closely to the Gerschenkronian model, albeit primarily for military and doctrinal reasons. It is anachronistic to try to project these patterns backwards on to the pre-1914 period, as Gerschenkron did. Moreover, it was certainly not necessary or inevitable for economic development to be directly funded and controlled by the state in the *dirigiste* or 'neo-mercantilist' manner in Europe's less developed economies. The 1980s and 1990s have witnessed a massive worldwide retreat from corporatism and collectivism and, on the doctrinal level, a 'neo-liberal' counter-revolution against the 'neo-mercantilism' of the preceding decades, not least among the so-called 'developing countries'. The demise of command planning can obviously be seen as part of this new trend.

THE PAST IN THE PRESENT AND THE PRESENT IN THE PAST

The Polish writer and Nobel Prize winner Czeslaw Milosz remarked in 1986 that the most striking feature of East Central European consciousness was 'its awareness of history, both as the past and as the present' (Milosz 1986: 117). Such an observation is even more applicable to the Balkans, where events that occurred 500 or even 2,500 years ago are often debated as if they had happened yesterday. Post-communist Eastern Europe is undergoing not merely a 'return to Europe' but also a 'return to history', not least through the raking up of old animosities, rivalries, territorial grievances and geopolitical ambitions. It has experienced not 'the end' but a 'rebirth' of history (Glenny 1990: 183).

On the other hand, George Schöpflin has cautioned against the propensity to regard the post-communist states 'as societies that have been taken out of the deep freeze, in which the attitudes and prejudices that were current before the communist takeover have remained miraculously conserved and are now rampant. A moment's thought will show how silly this proposition is. It implies that forty to seventy years of massive upheaval, the extension of the power of the state to encompass the whole of society, far-reaching industrialization, major demographic change, the introduction of mass education and the impact of the mass media have all left these societies unaffected. It does not need much reflection to see how implausible the deep freeze scenario is in the light of these changes' (Schöpflin 1994: 130). He is of course correct, up to a point. Attitudes and prejudices concerning social and moral issues such as marriage in church, teenage sex, abortion and the position of women have indeed undergone a major transformation.

Nevertheless, considering all that Eastern Europeans have been through under fascist and communist rule, it is remarkable that so many grievances and attitudes on national, ethnic and geopolitical issues have changed so little. As argued by President Havel in 1993, 'many of the nations suppressed by communism had never enjoyed freedom, not even before its advent'. Thus they had not had 'a chance to resolve many of the basic questions of their existence as countries. Consequently thousands of unsolved problems have now suddenly burst forth into the light of day, problems left unsolved by history, problems we had wrongly supposed were long forgotten. It is truly astonishing to discover how, after decades of falsified history and ideological manipulation and massaging, nothing has been forgotten. Nations are now remembering their ancient achievements and their ancient suffering, their . . . ancient statehood and their former borders, their traditional animosities and affinities – in short, they are suddenly recalling a history that, until recently, had been carefully concealed or misrepresented' (Havel 1994a: 223). Collective hatred has a terrible 'power to draw other people into its vortex' (p. 103). Furthermore, Tony Judt has lamented that in post-communist East Europe 'liberal intellectuals who would have people forget past conflicts or put aside bad memories are accused of reimposing censorship or allowing past crimes to go unpunished' and of reverting to the communist practice of blanking out 'whatever was inconvenient about local history', whereas 'journalists, politicians or teachers who make a point of recalling every real or fabricated slight inflicted upon the nation by others, or who seek to restore glorious icons of the national story, present themselves as engaged in the recovery and recognition of a real, "healthy" past once again available to all. Just how much this matters can be seen in the "battle for history" being played out in Croatia and Serbia today' (*The Times Literary Supplement*, 11 February 1994, p. 4). However, while Judt goes on to suggest that too much dwelling on the past induces 'self-pity', paranoia and 'gloomy pessimism', and that 'the best way to avoid repeating the past may be to forget about it', we consider that to be a cop-out. The same mistakes have been made again and again by politicians and peoples who wilfully ignore the lessons of the past and, instead of trying to come to terms with painful home truths, reinvent the past to suit themselves. The only way to overcome such attitudes to the past is to challenge them head-on. Otherwise East Europe's tragic history will repeat itself *ad infinitum*.

In the opinion of Milan Kundera, the successive 'Central European' revolts against communist rule and Soviet domination expressed essentially conservative strivings 'to restore the past' (Kundera 1984: 38). The traumatic experience of communist dictatorship and Soviet domination was but a brief episode in the history of Eastern Europe, which has been marked by various political, cultural and economic influences that lasted far longer than the communist experiment, even if that is still the most vivid memory. To a large extent, it is those older, deeper and temporarily suppressed influences that have been reasserting themselves most strongly since 1989. Therefore, even to begin to understand Eastern Europe in the 1990s, one has to try to understand its history and the turbulent or conflicting emotions that this arouses among its inhabitants. At the same time, however, one has to bear in mind that the ever-changing present is constantly shifting our perspectives on the past. Our current vantage point is not something fixed. In the words of the eminent philosopher of history R.G. Collingwood, 'Every present has a past of its own, and any imaginative reconstruction of the past aims at reconstructing the past of this present' (Collingwood 1946: 247). Hence the process of writing history is never complete and 'every generation must rewrite history in its own way; every new historian, not content with giving new answers to old questions, must revise the questions themselves'. Indeed, the historian is 'part of the process he is studying . . . and can see it only from the point of view which at this present moment he occupies within it' (p. 248). These observations are particularly pertinent to any reappraisal of East European history at the present time. The Revolutions of 1989 and their aftermath have not only presented old questions in a new light. They have also raised questions about the past of the new present. This book attempts to cast fresh light on many old questions and to pose (and even answer!) some new questions.

Most historians quite rightly insist that the past has to be studied for its own sake. They point out that it is dangerous, distorting and anachronistic to try to impose present-day categories, concepts, concerns and ways of seeing things on the past, or to allow only present-day concepts and concerns to dictate the questions we ask about the past. Nevertheless, there is no escaping the fact that current concerns and perceptions inevitably influence and inform any historian's enquiries into the past, including the choice of questions, subject matter and methods. It is therefore safer and wiser to recognise this inescapable fact (as well as its wider implications) than to try to ignore it by pretending that it need not apply or does not exist. As Collingwood argued in his 1926 'Lectures on the philosophy of history', 'To speak of the past as presenting a definite pattern implies not only that it has a necessary structure, but that this structure culminates in or centres around the present . . . All history is an attempt to understand the present by reconstructing its determining conditions . . . The present world, as we apprehend it in perception, is the starting point of history: history attempts to explain this present world by tracing its origins . . . All history is therefore universal history in that it is an attempt to give an account, as complete as possible, of the present world; but because the present world is inexhaustible in its content, the account can never be complete . . . Every history is in fact an historical monograph, a discussion of a limited historical problem . . . But a genuine and competent historical monograph is really a universal history . . . in the sense that its writer has been driven to write it by the way in which the world now presents itself to him' (Collingwood 1994: 418–21).

In the former communist states the need for each generation of historians to rewrite history in the light of a new present took on added significance, as historians were generally expected to toe the prevailing party line. Moreover, when communist rule collapsed, historians began to rewrite history yet again, both in order to exorcise the ghosts of the communist past and sometimes (regrettably) to rehabilitate the ghosts of an earlier ethnic nationalist past! However, the intrusion of the present into the past need not always be detrimental. The present can frequently help to shed new light on the past, just as the past has often illuminated the present. This is not to deny that wilful and insensitive attempts to project the present on to the past do indeed result in bad history. Nevertheless, new developments in the present have often suggested fruitful new ways of looking at the past and have even revolutionized our understanding of various historical processes and events. Thus the experience of living through two supranational ideological conflicts and two devastating World Wars transformed the way in which historians studied and conceptualized the Thirty Years' War that racked Germany and East Central Europe from 1618 to 1648 (see, for example, Polisensky 1974: 16–17, 257–65). The more recent emergence of the Third World and 'dependency theory' radically altered historical perceptions of the shifts in the patterns of international trade and specialization that occurred in the sixteenth and seventeenth centuries, including the relationship between eastern and western Europe at that time (see, for example, Wallerstein 1974a, b). Similarly, the development of national income accounting since the 1930s has revolutionized the way in which historians now study nineteenth-century economic development, not least by precipitating ingenious retrospective estimations of *per capita* levels and rates of growth of national income.

Historians must endeavour to understand the past on its own terms. But the objects of their enquiries, the questions they ask, the way their questions are framed and the sources and methods they favour will necessarily be influenced and informed by the present, and may be none the worse for it. The two poles are not necessarily mutually exclusive. Ideally, they should be mutually supportive. That was the spirit in which we approached the writing of this book. To shut your eyes to the past is to be blind to both the present and the future.

Some historians will baulk at the very wide scope of our enquiries, protesting that a project of such proportions cannot have been based upon primary research. We make no apology for the fact that our survey has necessarily been based upon a large number of secondary sources, many written by East Europeans, others by Westerners. There is an absolutely indispensable role for more specialized articles and monographs. Nevertheless, as Collingwood warned back in 1928, 'the professional historian tries in vain to reach the universal by adding particular to particular', while 'the general public . . . suspects, not without reason, that the absorption of historians in points of detail is not merely distracting their attention from . . . larger problems, but is depriving them of the power to deal with such problems at all' (Collingwood 1994: 455). From time to time, therefore, amid the inexorable proliferation of new specialist writing on all aspects of East European history, some writers have to attempt the grand synthesis. If this larger challenge or requirement is not taken up by historians, it will be met by 'the writings of journalists and novelists and clergymen, who, just because they are novices in history, have never taken a vow to refrain from dealing with interesting questions' (p. 455). In the Balkans and East Central Europe, unfortunately, this task has mainly fallen not even to benign and respectable 'novelists and clergymen' but to crude propagandists and ethnic hate-mongers who exploit, falsify and distort history for their own nefarious purposes. It is therefore all the more necessary for disinterested and liberal-minded historians to try to expose the many distortions and falsehoods and to offer sober, honest and impartial interpretations of the past in order to foster a wider and sounder understanding of where Eastern Europeans have come from and where they may be going. This is also needed in order to break down many popular misconceptions, to heal past wounds and to facilitate reconciliation between old antagonists.

Part I

The 'Balkanization' of South-eastern Europe

From ancient times to the First World War

Introduction: the process of 'Balkanization'

The Balkan peninsula and the adjacent Aegean and Ionian islands were the cradle of European civilization. In late Roman and early medieval times they were again among the most 'civilized' and economically developed areas in Europe. By the late nineteenth century, however, north-western Europe was calling the shots and the newly independent Balkan states were among the most conflict-prone and (not unrelatedly) least developed countries in Europe.

This part of the book explains how such a drastic reversal of fortune came about, i.e. how the Balkans became 'Balkanized'. Specialists on the Roman, Byzantine and Ottoman Empires may blench at how much of the story has had to be omitted and some will no doubt disagree with our interpretation of the more contentious issues. But it is necessary to provide some sort of historical backdrop, albeit briefly and selectively, in order to shed light on the deep historical roots of recent problems and conflicts in this unhappy region. To this end, moreover, Part I contains a number of extended quotations from the writings of eminent historians of the Balkans. These will give the reader an idea of the ethnocentric manner in which Balkan history tends to be written. Western historians of the Balkans sometimes succumb to anti-Turkish or anti-Islamic bias, while historians from the Balkans are inclined to be tendentious, frequently presenting very partisan views in the guise of 'the truth'. The latter often have an axe to grind, old scores to settle or territorial claims to advance. Indeed, events that occurred centuries ago are frequently treated as if they happened yesterday. They are still 'live issues' that continue to arouse strong hatred, resentment, jealousy or national pride. Current conflicts are intensified by overheated memories of classical and medieval heroes, atrocities, acts of valour, battles and imperial grandeur. This sometimes ludicrous, sometimes tragic, ever-present obsession with the past continues to inflame relations between, for example, the peoples of the former Yugoslavia, between the Greeks and their neighbours (especially over the issue of Macedonia), between Romanians and Hungarians (especially over the Hungarian minority in Transylvania) and between Albanians and their neighbours (especially over Kosovo, Epirus and western Macedonia). History and the misuse of history in pursuit of pernicious nationalist goals have pervaded Balkan politics and state-building from the late nineteenth century to the present day. On 10 December 1992, for example, over 1 million Greeks (about a third of the population of Athens) took part in mass protests against the proposed use of the name 'Macedonia' by the former Yugoslav republic. Likewise on 31 March 1994 over a million Greeks demonstrated in Salonika in support of their country's economic sanctions against the Former Yugoslav Republic of Macedonia. The Greek state has even prosecuted and imprisoned some of its own citizens for daring to publicize the Slav Macedonian case and the existence of a significant Slav minority in northern Greece. There is no such thing as a Macedonian nation or nationality in the eyes of most Greeks and anyone who says otherwise is a traitor. It is impossible to begin to explain such attitudes and the recent conflicts in the Balkans without recourse to long historical perspectives. But, even then, one is merely scratching the surface of complex and intractable problems and passions. As emphasized in David Owen's account of his experiences as an international negotiator during the South Slav conflict between 1992 and 1995, 'Nothing is simple in the Balkans. History pervades everything . . . It is not sufficient to explain away the frequently broken promises, the unobserved cease-fires, merely as the actions of lying individuals. They were also the product of South Slavic history' (Owen 1996: 1–2). Moreover, Noel Malcolm has also noted that during the early 1990s the major perpetrators of violence in former Yugoslavia tried not only to ruin their enemies' future but also to expunge the evidence and destroy the cultural and architectural heritage of their enemies' past (Malcolm 1994: xxiii). This kind of 'historical vandalism' is an extreme expression of the same urges that have prompted Greeks to kick over the traces of Slav settlement in Greece, Romanians to try to bulldoze the vestiges of Hungarian settlement in Romania, and Bulgarians to reclassify or drive away the remnants of Turkish settlement in Bulgaria. In the Balkans history is a battleground on which, or in whose name, innumerable atrocities have been committed by nationalist and religious as well as communist fanatics.

South-eastern Europe was known to the Ottoman Turks as 'Rumelia', to eighteenth-century Europeans as 'Turkey-in-Europe', to medieval Christendom as 'Romanie' and to the classical world as Illyricum, Macedonia and Thrace (Stoianovich 1967: 4). During the nineteenth century the term 'Balkans' (derived from the Turkish word for mountains) was aptly applied to the region. This in turn gave rise to the term 'Balkanization', referring to the problems afflicting the newly independent Balkan states. Campbell (1963: 397) usefully characterized the latter as 'a group of small, unstable and weak states, each based on the idea of nationality, in an area in which nation and state did not and could not coincide; all with conflicting territorial claims and with ethnic minorities that had to be assimilated or repressed; driven into unstable and changing alignments among themselves; seeking support from outside powers . . . and in turn being used by those powers for the latter's strategic advantage'. The ensuing 'international anarchy', as Campbell trenchantly observed, 'found its logical outcome in two great periods of war, from 1912 to 1922 and from 1939 to 1945'. In such a region 'nationalism, which in a generally liberal and democratic form had inspired the Balkan peoples in the long struggle for freedom and independence, finally helped to open the gates to Hitler' and during the Second World War 'continued to consume the nations themselves in the fires of hatred and massacre' (p. 398). Campbell also expressed the view that, if non-communist regimes had been re-established in the Balkans after the Second World War 'either through the return of old politicians from exile or through the emergence of new nationalist leaders, it is difficult to see how bitter and destructive national conflicts could have been avoided' since 'the nationalist forces . . . gave every evidence of lacking the capacity to rise above the conflicts of the past' (p. 399). Communist rule to varying degrees constrained inter-ethnic strife, but Campbell's well founded fear has been tragically borne out by events in the early 1990s. How did the Balkans reach such a sorry state?

According to most Balkan historians, the explanations are mainly to be found in the baleful impact of four to five centuries of Ottoman overlordship (from the fourteenth or fifteenth century to the nineteenth or early twentieth). Thus the well respected Balkan historian Peter Sugar has boldly proclaimed that 'South-eastern Europe became "Balkanized" under Ottoman rule' (Sugar 1977: 287). In his view, 'Ottoman conquest destroyed the larger units represented by the [former] states of South-eastern Europe' and in their place created 'a multitude of theoretically self-contained units which were small enough to be powerless but large enough to be functionally useful' (p. 279). However, 'The result was a very strict, over-organized socio-economic structure that soon ossified and was, at the same time, amazingly lenient. This licence prevented the enserfment of the South-eastern European peasantry and allowed the population, both urban and rural, to organize on a small communal basis under the leadership of its own elected officials . . . and facilitated their [later] rebirth in the form of modern nations' (pp. 279–80). He also argues that 'the most important change that Ottoman rule brought to South-eastern Europe was the large-scale demographic transformation of the area', including the northward displacement of the Serbs, Romanian migrations into the Banat and the Crisana, and Albanian migrations into Kosovo, Epirus and Macedonia. These migrations produced 'a mosaic of hopelessly interwoven population patterns' (p. 283). Consequently, 'Ottoman social organization and the migratory patterns created by the forces that the Ottomans had set in motion were responsible for the appearance of South-eastern Europe's major modern international problem: large areas inhabited by ethnically mixed populations' (p. 284).

In a similar but more blatantly anti-Turkish vein, Wayne Vucinich has claimed that 'Ottoman rule had a devastating effect on the cultural life of most of the conquered nations. In the Balkans, for example, learning virtually dried up, and art deteriorated from the exquisite medieval masterpieces to simple primitive creations. Once on a cultural level with the rest of Europe, the Balkan peoples had fallen far behind by the nineteenth century. There were several reasons for this. The Ottoman regime obliterated many of the spiritual and material resources of the subject peoples. Medieval states were eradicated, scions of conquered nobility killed off, churches and monasteries demolished, lands devastated, settlements destroyed, and large segments of the population dispersed. The Christian communities, deprived of their own resources for development, were given no comparable substitute. Moreover, they were isolated from cities and the mainstream of civilization, and restricted to a rural and pastoral life. As a result of long Turkish rule, the Balkan peoples became "the most backward" in Europe. Like the Turks themselves, they were bypassed by the Renaissance' (Vucinich 1965: 68–9).

In order to avoid such monocausal and ethnocentric explanations of the 'Balkanization' of South-eastern Europe and to place the Ottoman impact in proper historical perspective, due consideration must be given to the interplay of various cultural, demographic, economic and natural-environmental factors, the wider international or geographical context and the impact of other imperial powers. It then becomes clear that much that has been attributed to the 'Ottoman impact' was already in existence or incipient or merely inherited and perpetuated (rather than initiated) by Ottoman rule. The Ottoman conquest presented the Balkan peoples with a convenient and superficially persuasive *scapegoat*, which has helped divert attention from the ways in which their own cultures, institutions, rulers and histories must share the 'blame' for their deteriorating predicament and, indeed, for the ease with which the Ottomans subjugated the Balkans for several centuries. During the twentieth century it has also provided a pretext for Bulgarian, Serbian and Greek oppression of Turkish, Albanian and other Moslem minorities.

It is probably fairer to emphasize the roles of location, accessibility and terrain in enticing and facilitating wave upon wave of inward migration and conquest, rather than to blame 'Balkanization' on any one of the successive conquering and colonizing peoples who have intruded upon the region. Here the ethnic 'tectonic plates' of Europe and Asia have grated over the centuries and such an area was bound to be unsettled at times of conflict. Settled imperial rule, whether Greek, Roman, Ottoman or communist, in fact offered a chance of socio-economic development. Kostanick (1963: 2) points out that the Balkan peninsula is 'a jumble of mountainous valleys and cul-de-sacs that unquestionably produce local isolation' for its ethnically diverse inhabitants, who have therefore clustered into numerous little pockets. Yet a network of major river valleys (such as the Morava–Vardar corridor and the Sava and Maritsa valleys) connects the eastern Mediterranean with the Danube basin, the Dardanelles, the Bosphorus and Asia Minor, providing easy access for foreign invaders and colonists from both East and West to this strategic crossroads between Europe and Asia.

Stavrianos (1958: 12) emphasizes that the location and the accessibility of the peninsula encouraged frequent and prolonged invasions. 'The struggle against these invasions . . . hindered the process of racial assimilation which has been the characteristic development in Western Europe. The complex terrain is also an important factor. If the peninsula had been a plateau instead of a highly mountainous and diversified region, it is probable that the various races would have amalgamated to a considerable degree. A common Balkan ethnic strain might have evolved.' Contrary to Sugar's claim (1977: 287) that 'South-eastern Europe became "Balkanized" under Ottoman rule', it can be affirmed that 'By the fifteenth century the Slavs were in firm possession of a broad belt from the Adriatic to the Black Seas. The dispossessed Illyrians were concentrated in present-day Albania and the scattered Thraco-Dacians were reappearing as the nomadic Vlachs of the central highlands and as the Romanians of the newly-emerging trans-Danubian states, Moldavia and Wallachia. This ethnic distribution that took place in the Byzantine period has persisted with slight changes to the present' (Stavrianos 1958: 32).

The above-mentioned migrations which occurred under Ottoman rule marginally altered the ethnic distribution and, in the twentieth century, have fuelled conflicting territorial claims to Kosovo. But they did not greatly increase the overall complexity of the ethnic patchwork in the Balkans. The Ottoman system was essentially a response to (rather than the cause of) the ethnic complexity of South-eastern Europe. Even if the Ottoman Empire had never existed, therefore, the later spread of the ideas of nationalism, national self-determination and the nation-state would have had explosive consequences in the Balkans. It should be pointed out that monocausal ethnocentric emphasis on the Ottoman impact also encourages unfair neglect of some underlying natural-environmental, geopolitical and economic factors in the deteriorating fortunes of the Balkan peninsula. These were largely beyond the control of either the Ottoman or earlier empires.

Jonathan Eyal has questioned the very notion of 'Balkanization', which rests on the perception of the Balkans as an unusually fractious and conflict-prone region. 'While the region has suffered more than its share of violence, much of it was engineered by competing alliances hatched out in the West, rather than by local animosities. Nor is it true that the Balkans are still torn by "tribal warfare": former Yugoslavia always excepted, there is no other Balkan country in which ethnic minorities represent more than 10 per cent of the population. Nor is land up for grabs elsewhere. "Balkanization" is a Western nightmare, not an Eastern reality' (*The Independent*, 10 November 1993, p. 18).

Eyal's argument merits serious consideration, but it does not stand up to close scrutiny. Ethnic minorities are clustered in small or large pockets all over the Balkans (including parts of Romania, Greece and Bulgaria) and they have been strongly resistant to cultural assimilation. Moreover, to suggest that the problems are largely confined to the former Yugoslavia is dangerously misleading. The conflicts over Bosnia and, *a fortiori*, over Macedonia, Kosovo and Transylvania, have the potential to engulf adjacent states (and indeed the whole of the Balkans) in a more general conflagration. To say that much of the violent conflict has been 'engineered by competing alliances hatched in the West' is merely another way of saying that the ethnic geography of the Balkans encourages external interference in (internal) Balkan affairs.

The West European nations are probably composed of just as many different ethnic and linguistic 'strains' as those of the Balkans. France comprises Frankish, Norman, Gallic, Iberian and Ligurian 'strains' (among others) and Italy has long been an ethnic 'melting pot'. Britain, Belgium, the Netherlands, Switzerland and Spain clearly incorporate diverse ethnic and linguistic groups. The essential difference between the Balkans and Western Europe lies not in the number of component linguistic and ethnic 'strains', but rather in the particular circumstances which made possible the extensive fusion or unification of diverse 'strains' into relatively discrete and homogeneous units in Western Europe and the equally extensive perpetuation of separate ethnic identities and allegiances in the Balkans. Indeed, 'the unique feature of Balkan ethnic evolution is that virtually all the races that have actually settled there, as distinguished from those that have simply marched through, have been able to preserve their identity to the present' (Stavrianos 1958: 13). Thus they did not evolve and amalgamate into more clearly delineated nation-states. This was largely a consequence both of the distinctive physical geography of the Balkans and of the relatively late survival of multicultural and multi-ethnic imperial polities in Eastern Europe. These two factors have helped to preserve linguistic and ethnic diversity.

1 South-eastern Europe before the Ottomans

SOUTH-EASTERN EUROPE IN ANCIENT TIMES

The first major European civilization was that of ancient Greece. Heavily influenced by the Minoan civilization in Crete (*c*. 3400–1100 BC), an advanced 'Bronze Age' Hellenic civilization (that of the Achaeans) developed around Mycenae, Tiryns, Pylos, Athens and Thebes from *c*. 1600 BC. Mainland Greece entered a period of decline from *c*. 1100 BC, however, in the wake of the destructive Dorian invasions. The Dorians, who spoke the Doric dialect of the Greek language, were better armed but less 'civilized' than their Achaean cousins, many of whom migrated to Greek colonies in coastal Asia Minor. From *c*. 480 BC, however, 'classical' Greek civilization flourished around the emerging mercantile city-states of Athens, Sparta, Thebes, Argos and Corinth, in Attica and the Peloponnesus. Guided by philosophers and historians in place of priests and prophets, 'classical' Greece developed new ethics, literature, drama, art and architecture, based upon secularism and humanism. It was the age of Aeschylus, Sophocles, Euripides, Aristophanes, Herodotus, Thucydides, Plato and Aristotle. At the same time additional Greek colonies were founded along the Black Sea, the Adriatic, Ionian and Aegean coasts and up the river Danube, increasing Hellenic influence on other inhabitants of the Balkan peninsula, especially the Thracians (in present-day Bulgaria and Romania), the Illyrians (in what eventually became Yugoslavia) and the Macedonians (who were either Hellenes or semi-Hellenized Illyrians). But the Greek city-states dissipated their strength in chronic internecine warfare and were duly conquered by Philip II of Macedon (who reigned 395–336 BC) and his famous warrior son Alexander the Great (336–323 BC), whose far-flung and short-lived empire extended from Egypt through Asia Minor, Syria and Mesopotamia (Iraq) to Persia and the Punjab.

Soon afterwards, however, the illustrious Balkan peninsula attracted the attention of Rome. Following protracted power struggles and warfare, the expanding Roman Empire conquered Illyria (present-day Albania, Bosnia and Croatia) in 167 BC, Macedonia in 146 BC, the Achaean League of Greek cities in 150 BC and Dacia (present-day Romania) in 106 AD. In Dacia Roman rule lasted only from 106 to 275 AD, but this imperial outpost became so thoroughly 'Romanized' that the modern descendants of the native Dacians (Thracians) and Roman colonists refer to themselves as Romanians and speak a Romance language which is closely related to Italian.

Although the Romans came as conquerors, they had a very high regard for the older Greek civilization, which they sought to preserve and assimilate. Greek was granted equal status with Latin as one of the two official languages of imperial administration, the law courts, commerce and learning. It was no accident that the New Testament was written and disseminated in Greek rather than Latin. The civilization which developed in the Balkans in Roman times was Greek, with a preponderance of Hellenic influences in the south and east (including Asia Minor) and of Latin influences in the north and west. Graeco-Roman civilization, which had been concentrated in a few coastal areas, was gradually disseminated more widely. Indeed, the construction of remarkable Roman military and commercial highways across the peninsula effectively linked the major new towns in the interior, including Singidunum (Belgrade), Serdica (Sofia), Philippopolis (Plovdiv), Naissus (Nis) and Hadrianopolis (Adrianople/Edirne), with major ports such as Dyrrachium (Durres), Thessaloniki (Salonika), Byzantium (Istanbul), Tomis (Constanta), Odessos (Varna), Mesembria (Nesebur), Epetion (Split) and Trogurium (Trogir). These flourishing Balkan towns boasted impressive temples, villas, palaces, baths, aqueducts and sewage systems (and their 'Roman remains' eventually became important tourist attractions in more recent times). The Roman impact was greatest in the prosperous province of Illyricum (Illyria). Here irrigated agriculture, viticulture, textile manufacture and the mining of gold, silver, iron and lead flourished. Several Illyrian soldiers of humble origin even rose to the rank of Emperor (Claudius, Aurelian, Probus, Diocletian and Maximian). The language became Latinized (and Italian is still widely understood along the Adriatic coast, where it was later to be reinforced by Venetian influences). The indigenous Illyrian dialects were to survive (with heavy Latin, Greek, Slav and Turkic overlays) only in mountainous and relatively impenetrable Albania.

EAST–WEST DIVERGENCE AND THE RISE OF BYZANTIUM

Between the second and fourth centuries AD the centre of gravity of the Roman Empire gradually shifted from the western to the eastern Mediterranean. Commerce and banking were more highly developed in the eastern Mediterranean, through which passed the great trade routes carrying the produce of Asia to European markets. The eastern provinces also had to be fortified, both militarily and economically, in order to fend off growing threats from the 'barbarian' marauders from north central Europe and the Eurasian steppes and from a burgeoning Persian Empire. Mining, metalworking, arms production, textiles, leatherwork, sheep-rearing, food-processing, fishing and communications were developed in the Balkans and Asia Minor, which together formed 'a self-sufficient unit which never had to cope with difficulties of supply' (Haussig 1971: 31–4).

The escalating frontier warfare fostered the emergence of able 'self-made' frontier commanders, often of humble Balkan origin, as the new imperial 'strong men'. Political power slowly slipped from the civilian Roman Senate and senatorial aristocracy in Italy to the ascendant frontier commanders, who became the new Roman emperors and provincial governors. These professional soldiers and military 'usurpers' doubled the size of the Roman army to about 600,000 men and broke the unwieldy legions down into smaller and more mobile detachments backed up by heavy cavalry, especially under the emperor Diocletian (284–305 AD). In these respects the Balkan and Danubian provinces, which now 'participated fully in the Roman empire for the first time . . . suddenly became seedbeds of talent' (Brown 1971: 24–5, 41).

Eastern Mediterranean agriculture became relatively productive and responsive, reflecting the stimuli of military requirements and the high social mobility and fluidity of 'frontier' regions. As a result there was a prevalence of independent self-motivated peasant farmers or, conversely, a relative absence of deeply entrenched and oppressive landed aristocracies. In Italy, by contrast, agricultural productivity and incentives were gradually depressed by the growing concentration of land holdings in the hands of the increasingly oppressive and close-knit senatorial aristocracy (latifundists), who also increasingly resisted imperial demands for taxes and military service. The famed Roman military and administrative efficiency atrophied in Italy, while a new breed of soldier-administrator was emerging in the Balkans. Falling productivity and growing dependence on (expensive) imported food and raw materials increased Italian prices and the cost of living, depressing both the position of the labouring classes and the competitiveness of Italian industries. Italy thus lost its lead in ceramics to Germany, in wine production to Gaul and North Africa and in metal goods, armaments, textiles, leatherwork and glassware to the eastern Mediterranean, which lured away many of Italy's skilled workers and craftsmen (Haussig 1971: 26–8).

It eventually became clear that Rome was no longer in a position to control its far-flung empire. Emperor Diocletian (of humble Balkan origin, the reader will recall) decided to divide the unwieldy realm between himself and three of his Balkan colleagues in 295 AD. But, shortly after Diocletian's retirement in 305 AD to his remarkable palace in Split (Salonae) on the Dalmatian coast, the empire was forcibly reunited by Emperor Constantine I (312–337 AD), who defeated his co-rulers in battle in 312 AD and 323–24 AD respectively. He later attributed his decisive victory in 312 AD to divine intervention (Grant 1978: 300–8).

In 312 AD Emperor Constantine was ostensibly 'converted' to Christianity. As recently as 257–59 AD and 302–10 AD the empire's Christian inhabitants had been subjected to systematic official persecution. From 260 to 302 AD, however, Christianity profited from a prolonged period of toleration, renewed by official edicts of religious toleration in 311 and 313 AD, although as yet no more than 10 per cent of the imperial population were Christian (Woodhouse 1977: 22). Christians barely outnumbered Jews, who constituted 8 per cent of the imperial population, according to Haussig (1971: 45). It would appear that Constantine was influenced by the ideas of 'Christian Apologists' such as Lactantius and Eusebius, who argued that Christianity had found a *modus vivendi* with Roman civilization and that it could be the salvation (in more than one sense) of the beleaguered Roman Empire (Brown 1971: 84, 86). Constantine certainly sought to use Christianity to bolster his imperial authority and to re-establish the empire on new foundations, although Christianity did not actually become the official religion until 380 AD, under Emperor Theodosius I (379–95 AD). Constantine sought to blend Graeco-Roman paganism, philosophy and emperor worship with Christianity rather than root out the non-Christian elements in imperial culture.

In 324 AD Constantine laid the foundations of a new imperial capital, a 'new Rome', on the site of the small Greek trading colony of Byzantium, established in 660 BC in a strategic position on the Bosphorus. Here he grouped around himself a new civilian ruling class, reversing the previous trend towards military rule. Thus the Roman Empire 'found its way to a new identity, as the empire of Constantinople' (Brown 1971: 88, 138). Constantinople became the crucible of a new civilization, an amalgam of Christian, Eastern, Hellenistic and Roman elements.

In 395 AD, following the death of Theodosius I, the Roman Empire underwent a lasting East–West division, consolidating 'Greek' predominance in the strengthened eastern empire and 'Latin' predominance in the disintegrating western empire. Faced with concurrent threats of invasion from north central Europe and the Eurasian steppes, the eastern empire offered the so-called 'barbarian' invaders bribes ('subsidies') and other inducements to refrain from further raids and attacks. It also enlisted some 'barbarians' into the imperial service and, in 400 AD, treacherously massacred the 'barbarian' Goths who had been invited to reside in Constantinople. These 'civilized' stratagems successfully deflected the 'barbarian' invasions away from the Balkans and Asia Minor and into Italy, Spain and Gaul. The Vandals prepared to invade Gaul and Spain in 406–09 AD, while the Visigoths invaded Italy in 402 AD. They set about the sack of Rome in 410 AD, after the rich and vain Roman senators had refused to buy them off (much as they had increasingly refused to furnish the taxes and recruits needed to keep the Roman armies effective). The western imperial government retreated to Ravenna, but the western empire never recovered from the blows to its power and prestige before the last western Roman emperor was finally deposed by 'barbarians' in 476 AD. Thus, while the Balkans were to remain under imperial rule for a further 1,400 years, the western empire fragmented into a multiplicity of 'barbarian' states. These would eventually evolve into more or less discrete, homogeneous nation-states, long before anyone dreamed of establishing such states in the Balkans. Moreover the 'barbarians'' destruction of the imperial polity in the former domains of the western Roman empire during the fifth century further strengthened the position of the already emerging latifundia and landed aristocracies. This aided the subsequent development of decentralized 'feudal' polities, economies and societies, out of which capitalism would later emerge. Thus the 'barbarian' destruction of the western Roman empire helped to set the stage for the future emergence of Western feudalism, capitalism and nation-states. In the Balkans, by contrast, the long survival of an imperial polity would help to perpetuate the legal, administrative, cultural, military and economic achievements of the eastern Roman empire (eventually contributing to the early stages of the Renaissance), but at the price of long-term retardation of the development of nation-states and decentralized feudal (and subsequently capitalist) economies and societies. The historic significance of this political, cultural and socio-economic 'parting of the ways', formalized in 395 AD, can hardly be overstated. It partly explains why the illustrious civilization preserved by the eastern Roman empire ('Byzantium') eventually lost out to a more dynamic, decentralized West, which fostered the precocious development of feudalism, capitalism and nation-states.

THE BYZANTINE ERA

The Greek-dominated (yet cosmopolitan and neo-Roman) Byzantine Empire lasted from 395 to 1204 AD, with a 'brief' *reprise* from 1261 to 1453. A thousand years of Byzantine domination and influence were to have a much deeper and more enduring impact on the Balkans than did the four to five centuries of Ottoman overlordship. Despite the widespread survival of Turkish cuisine, coffee houses, bazaars, mosques and minarets, the art, architecture, customs, values, beliefs and physical appearance of Balkan villages and towns owe much more to the Byzantine heritage than to the Ottomans and Islam. As Stavrianos (1958: 32) points out: 'The modern culture of the Balkans . . . had evolved by the fifteenth century through a process of Byzantinization. For the South Slavs, and the Albanians and Rumanians for that matter, Byzantium was . . . the great educator, the

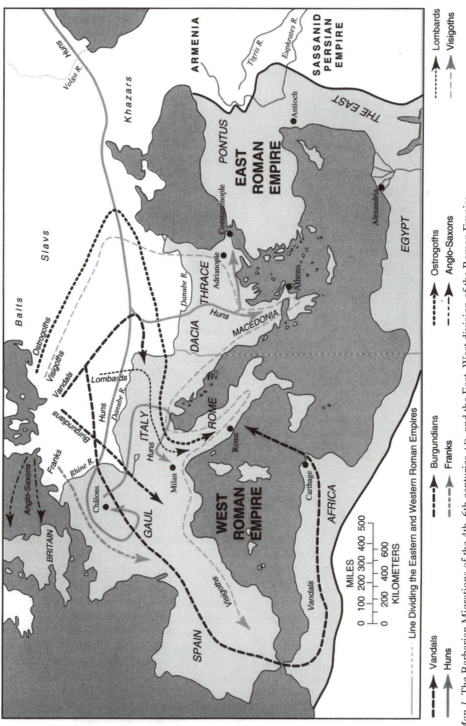

Map 1 The Barbarian Migrations of the 4th–6th centuries AD, and the East–West division of the Roman Empire

great initiator, the source of both religion and civilization. Her missionaries spread the gospel among the barbarians, and with it they brought Byzantine legal ideas, literature, art, trade, and everything else that constitutes a distinctive civilization.'

The modern Balkan states were to inherit 'a native culture which was basically Byzantine but modified by centuries of Muslim domination' (Jelavich and Jelavich 1963: xv). Byzantium's subjects were 'enthusiastic "Romans". They called themselves *Rhomaioi* for the next thousand years; and in the medieval Near East the Byzantine Empire was known as *Rum*, "Rome", and Christians as "Romans", *Rumi*.' Yet they exhibited little veneration for Rome as such. They expressed their imperial loyalties 'not through the brittle protocol of senatorial or civic institutions, but directly – by falling on their knees before statues and icons of the emperor' (Brown 1971: 42). Thus they practised a Christianized form of pagan Roman emperor worship.

Significantly, the Greeks still refer to themselves as 'Romioi' today and Byzantine Christianity absorbed even more pagan and 'Eastern' influences than did Western Christianity. Indeed, Christianity originated as one among many eastern cults. From Syro-Iranian and Egyptian civilization Byzantine Christianity assimilated the cult of icons or the veneration of images, monasticism and the veneration of Mary as the Mother of God (the Theokotos), as a concession to eastern and Egyptian cults of the Great Mother goddess (Artemis, Cybele, Isis). Nike, the pagan goddess of Victory, provided the prototype for Christian depictions of angels. The widespread cult of the sun god (and of the emperor as a sun god) engendered Christian depictions of Christ and the apostles as sun gods emitting an aura or nimbus (rays of light) and of Christ as an emperor or sun king. It also led to the decision to celebrate Christmas on 25 December, the 'birthday' (feast day) of the sun god (Haussig 1971: 36–8, 43). Inevitably much of this found its way into Western Christianity too, but it was stronger in Byzantium. Thus the Roman cult of the emperor as a god, 'linking the cult of the sun god with the imperial cult', was 'reconciled' with the adoption of Christianity by fostering a new cult of the Christian Byzantine Emperor as the head of the Byzantine Church and as the focus of imperial loyalty and obedience. 'He who denied the doctrine pronounced by the Emperor was a traitor to the Empire and had sinned against the person of the Emperor' (p. 40). Soon the basilica and the simple domed edifice, both of which had previously been associated with pagan emperor worship and used as mausoleums for members of the imperial family, were promoted as the standard forms of church architecture. Likewise, the higher clergy were dressed up in imperial robes to emphasize that they were the emperor's servants and representatives, while churches were decorated with imperial portraits constantly to remind worshippers of their omnipresent, omnipotent, divinely 'anointed' ruler. Moreover, the formal adoption of Christianity as the official state religion and as a basis of imperial cohesion and authority obliged the Byzantine state to try to uphold, impose or strive for Christian unity and 'orthodoxy' ('right belief').

Thus the official Byzantine Church came to see itself as 'the Orthodox Church', while other Christian tendencies and denominations were regarded as 'heterodox' and potentially heretical and subversive 'deviations'. Nevertheless, protracted imperial endeavours to find and impose doctrinal compromises (or 'diplomatic' formulas) on the Coptic (Egyptian), Syrian, Nestorian and Armenian Churches, in a vain quest for Christian and imperial unity, had the opposite effect of hardening positions and antagonisms. The Nestorians were forced to take refuge in the Persian Empire, while the Roman papacy and the older patriarchates of Antioch, Alexandria and Jerusalem were antagonized by imperial assertions of the primacy of the new 'upstart' patriarchate of Constantinople, which was under direct imperial control and therefore lacked their supposed 'spiritual integrity'. (Over the centuries more than one in three Constantinople patriarchs were to be dismissed by the emperor, according to Soisson: 1977: 112.) This encouraged both the (western) Roman Catholic Church and the (eastern) 'monophysite' Armenian, Coptic, Syrian and Nestorian Churches repeatedly to challenge and repudiate the religious authority of Constantinople. The more Constantinople tried to conciliate and accommodate the 'monophysite' Churches (which, prefiguring Islam, insisted on the 'oneness' of God), the more it alienated the western Church and the papacy. 'Thus there came about the separation of the Byzantine Church from the Christian Churches in the East and West, and this separation must be regarded as the formative influence in the rise of Byzantine civilization' (Haussig 1971: 44–5).

These fundamental divisions within the Christian world were steadily to deepen in the centuries preceding the final rift or 'schism' between the Roman Catholic and the Byzantine Orthodox Churches in 1054. They were even more important and significant than the later cleavage within Western Christianity, between the Roman Catholic and Protestant Churches. They solidified and gave a sharper doctrinal edge to an enduring East–West divide within European civilization. This, much more than the relatively recent, superficial and short-lived impact of communism and the Cold War, is what has most fundamentally differentiated East from West, Eastern Orthodox Serbs from Roman Catholic (i.e. 'Westernized') Croats and Slovenes, Bulgarians and Romanians from Austro-Germans and Czechs, and Russians and Ukrainians from West Europeans. (Indeed, the jagged frontier between Serbia and Croatia almost corresponds to the boundaries drawn between the eastern and western Roman empires in 295 and 395 AD.) This serves notice that it will require much more than the end of communism and the Cold War to unite Europe.

The resilience and longevity of the Byzantine empire were to rest, in large measure, on its Graeco-Roman heritage, on the almost impregnable nodal position of the imperial metropolis and on its control of the Bosphorus. With an 'eminently defensible' site, a superb natural harbour and a commanding position on the only sea lanes between the Mediterranean and the Black Sea, and on the best land route between Europe and south-west Asia, Constantinople was destined to become the natural 'confluence' between East and West, between Roman law, administration and military technology, Greek philosophy, paganism and the three great monotheistic religions (Judaism, Christianity and Islam). Before long the city expanded to around 500,000 inhabitants (Woodhouse 1977: 21, 34). 'Constantinople combined the pride of a city-state and the high morale of an outpost with the resources of a vast Near Eastern empire' (Brown 1971: 137).

Although its survival was to be repeatedly endangered by external military threats, Constantinople would fall into enemy hands on only two occasions, in 1204 and 1453. So long as the city itself survived intact, the Byzantine Empire would remain capable of remarkable recoveries, such as those that were to occur after the formidable Arab, Avar, Slav and Bulgar invasions of the Byzantine dominions between the seventh and the eleventh centuries. Constantinople was the economic heart of the Byzantine Empire, whose industries, commerce, movable wealth and hundreds of thousands of merchants and craftsmen were to remain heavily concentrated within its great walls (Andreades 1948: 70). Even if much of its hinterland were to fall into enemy hands, the city could still derive revenue, wealth and naval-mercantile power from its control of the Bosphorus. In this respect, the Byzantine Empire went into terminal decline only when (in desperation) it surrendered control of its trade, customs revenues and shipping to the rising Italian naval-mercantile city-states from 1082 onwards, as this move gradually stifled the empire's powers of recuperation. But, even when its revenues, trade and shipping fell under alien control, Constantinople remained the great emporium of the eastern Mediterranean (Haussig 1971: 313).

After the devastating fifth-century 'barbarian' invasions, a fairly unified Roman Empire was briefly re-established by the Byzantine emperor Justinian I (527–65 AD), who greatly increased the efficiency (and oppressiveness) of the central administration and tax collection. He spent his greatly augmented revenues (together with the accumulated fiscal surpluses of some thrifty predecessors) on massive construction projects, including the refortification of the empire's exposed northern (Danubian) frontiers and on blandishments or 'subsidies' to its potential enemies (Woodhouse 1977: 33). He also instigated an ambitious codification of Roman law. Justinian's legal codes eroded slavery, strengthened serfdom, reduced sexual inequalities in the laws of succession and inheritance, permitted divorce, outlawed rape and castration, introduced some safeguards against arbitrary detention, imprisonment and crucifixion, brought Christianity into the law and made Church property inalienable, thereby accelerating the (already excessive) enrichment of the monasteries (Soisson 1977: 41–5). Viewed in a longer perspective, however, Justinian contributed to a 'hardening' of East–West divergences.

Citizens and senators of Constantinople rose against their dynamic, big-spending, autocratic emperor during the 'Nika' ('Vanquish') riots of 532 AD, in which half the city went up in flames. Steeled by his wife Theodora, a former circus prostitute, Justinian simply redoubled his efforts. He embarked on even more imposing, grandiose construction projects, including the reconstruction of the great cathedral of Hagia (St) Sophia. He also launched some impromptu 'diversionary' wars, which resulted in unexpectedly large and rapid conquests, namely North Africa in 533–34 AD, Italy in 537–40 AD and southern Spain in 554 AD. But Byzantine imperialism had overreached itself, leaving its Balkan and Anatolian heartlands dangerously exposed, overstretched, overtaxed, overcentralized and underprovided. Starting in the 540s AD, Slav and (Turkic) Avars and Bulgars invaded and colonized the territories which now make up Serbia, Croatia, Bosnia-Hercegovina, Macedonia, mainland Greece, Bulgaria and southern Romania, displacing large numbers of Greeks, Illyrians (Albanians) and 'Latinized' or 'Romanized' Dacians and Vlachs (Romanians) and dramatically altering the ethnic geography of the Balkans. Armenians rebelled against Byzantine overlordship in eastern Anatolia and a new Persian Empire overran Syria.

The Byzantine and Persian Empires were to be locked in mortal combat from 540 to 629 AD, weakening Byzantine control over most of Justinian's Italian, Spanish and North African conquests. Persia was finally defeated by Byzantium in 629 AD. But the struggle left both sides too drained and weakened to resist the meteoric rise of the Arab Moslem Empire between 634 and 647 AD. The Persian Empire was easily conquered by the Arab Moslem Empire in 637–41 AD and most of its subjects subsequently accepted Islam. Similarly, Byzantium lost Syria, Palestine and Egypt to the Arab Moslem Empire in 636–42 AD. This quickly led to the Arab Moslem conquest of North Africa, although Byzantine Carthage held out until 699 AD. The Byzantines also managed to repel two massive Arab assaults on Constantinople in 677–78 and 717–18 AD respectively, before stemming the tide of the Arabs' north-westward expansion in 738 AD.

In the meantime, however, the Slavs and the (Turkic) Bulgars had been able to consolidate their territorial advances into the Balkans. The Slav and Bulgar tribal confederations which were established in the Balkans in the mid-seventh century were 'not yet states in the true sense . . . They were temporary . . . and lacked a standing military force, an administration or a strictly defined state territory.' But the onset of class differentiation soon called into existence 'organs of government and coercion to protect the interests of the now wealthy tribal aristocracy and to ward off possible attacks' (Hristov 1985: 26). In 681 AD, while it was still under severe threat from the Arabs, Byzantium was obliged to concede diplomatic recognition to the embryonic Bulgar–Slav state, in what was to become Bulgaria.

Theocratic legacies

In the course of the protracted struggle between Byzantium and Persia (540–629 AD) and the explosive expansion of the Arab Moslem Empire along the southern shores of the Mediterranean (637–47 AD), the Byzantine Empire took on 'the solidarity and splendid isolation that marked it out throughout the Middle Ages'. Henceforth Byzantium saw itself as the Christian fortress of the Near East. 'Byzantines regarded themselves no longer as citizens of a world empire, but as a Chosen People ringed by hostile, pagan nations . . . In such a closed society, treason was equated with unbelief. The hardening of boundaries reflects an inner rigidity' (Brown 1971: 172, 174). Balkan Orthodox Christianity would still bear the marks of this rigid 'beleaguered outpost' mentality in the nineteenth and twentieth centuries (most obviously among the Serbs, as recently as the early 1990s).

Moreover, Byzantium came to see itself 'no longer as a society in which Christianity was merely the dominant religion, but as a totally Christian society'. Paganism was suppressed and the non-Christian became a social outcast (Brown 1971: 174). Indeed, the adoption of Christianity as the official imperial religion in 380 AD had already resulted in greater exclusiveness and intolerance towards non-Christians. 'The Christian Church differed from other oriental cults, which it resembled in so many ways, through its intolerance' (p. 65). The ensuing restrictions on the building of synagogues and on the right of Jews to hold public office, to marry non-Jews and to appear in court had culminated in the abolition of the Jewish patriarchate (425 AD), in Christian boycotts of Jewish traders and doctors and in Christian pogroms (assaults) on Jews, Jewish properties and synagogues. 'The Byzantine Empire did not succeed in integrating the Jews into the Christian Roman state. The Jews remained an alien body within the Byzantine Empire' (Haussig 1971: 47).

Since the 380s AD there had also been a steady growth of Christian monasticism. Monastic orders became the 'shock troops' of Christianity, asserting Christianity as the imperial religion and assaulting pagans, Jews and heretics, egged on by emperors who shared their prejudices (Brown 1971: 104). From the fifth century onwards much of the wealth which would previously have been channelled into public and private construction and investment flowed into the coffers of the Church and monasteries 'for the remission of sins' or to cover the costs of acquittal at the Last Judgement (p. 108). By 527 AD there were at least 100 monasteries in and around Constantinople alone (Woodhouse 1977: 26).

Before long, as Byzantine monks and missionaries propagated Orthodox Christianity among the other inhabitants of the southern and eastern Balkans (and Roman Catholic rivals did the same in the north-western Balkans), the Balkans as a whole became littered with monasteries. Bulgaria, for example, came to have 150 (Hristov 1985: 70). Many of them were massive and quite a few are still standing or even in full operation to this day. In this way a significant part of the Balkans' wealth and manpower would be siphoned off by a partly parasitic social group who would 'sterilize' much of that wealth in the form of beautiful but 'non-productive' monastic and ecclesiastical buildings and magnificent religious ornamentation.

The powerful impact of Christian monasticism in the Balkans, however, was not wholly negative. 'The monasteries harnessed the chronic underemployment of the towns and villages' by mobilizing thousands of zealous monastic retainers and staffing hospitals, soup kitchens, almshouses and nursing, ambulance, burial and carrying services (Brown 1971: 110). In addition, Byzantine monks and missionaries were to play a seminal role in the creation of South Slav written languages and literature. Cyril and Methodius, two Byzantine monks allegedly of South Slavic extraction, initiated the process of translating Byzantine religious writings from the Greek into Slavonic languages. So that they could begin this pioneering work, Cyril devised the first Slavonic alphabet or script (the 'Glagolitic' script) around 855 AD. In 862 AD, at the invitation of Prince Rostislav, the two brothers were sent to Moravia on a mission to counteract growing Germanic and Roman Catholic influence in that region. (In those days major powers used 'religious advisers' as instruments of foreign policy, rather in the way that 'political advisers' were attached to Third World governments by major world powers during the Cold War.) But the arrival of Cyril and Methodius in Moravia aroused strong German and Roman Catholic opposition to their mission. So they were obliged to travel to Rome to defend their use of a Slavonic language and script for evangelical and liturgical purposes in violation of the principle that the divinely ordained Christian languages were Hebrew, Latin and Greek.

In 885 AD, after both Cyril and Methodius had died, their Orthodox disciples were forcibly hounded out of Moravia by Germanic Roman Catholics. But the fugitives were given sanctuary by Prince Boris of Bulgaria, who had already decided (for reasons of state) to adopt Byzantine Orthodox Christianity as his country's official religion and to foster a Slavonic written language, both as a means of absorbing and competing with the magnificent and imposing cultural attainments of Byzantium and as a means of enhancing Bulgaria's wider international standing. In Bulgaria the disciples of Cyril and Methodius resumed the work of translating Byzantine religious literature into 'Old Bulgarian' (alias 'Church Slavonic') and for the purpose they adapted the Glagolitic and Greek alphabets to create the so-called 'Cyrillic' script (in honour of Cyril). With relatively minor modifications it was to become the template upon which the written national languages of other Eastern Orthodox Slavs, such as the Serbs, the Ukrainians and Russians, were gradually to be hammered out under the (far from disinterested) guidance of Eastern Orthodox clergy. This was to foster enduring linguistic and 'spiritual' bonds (as well as rivalries) between Bulgarians, Macedonians, Serbs, Montenegrins, Russians, Belorussians and Ukrainians, all of whom still use archaic 'Church Slavonic' (or 'Old Bulgarian') for some ecclesiastical or liturgical purposes. More immediately, as was (even) acknowledged in a semi-official Marxist history of Bulgaria published under communist rule, 'Christianity also brought the Bulgarians closer to the culturally most

advanced European nations and enabled them to attain a higher level of development'
(Hristov 1985: 33–40). Orthodox clergy and Christianity were to fulfil similar functions
for Serbia and Montenegro (and for Kiev Rus, the first Russo-Ukrainian state).

There was, however, a 'down' side to all this, the reverse side of the same coin. During
the tenth century, as observed in the case of Bulgaria by Hristov (1985: 44), 'more and
more peasants began losing their land and became bound to the estates of the secular and
church feudals'. But the official Church preached that the world had been ordered that
way by God. 'The church also claimed that their wealth should not arouse envy,
discontent or resistance, because nothing in the world ever happened against God's Will'
(p. 44). It is indeed hard to deny the emphasis in official Christianity (here, as elsewhere)
on divinely ordained roles and hierarchies, on uncritical and uncomplaining obedience to
social 'superiors' and on 'rendering unto Caesar that which is Caesar's'. Since less than
one-third of the Balkan population ever became Moslem, fatalistic and hierarchical
'official' Christianity should be seen as a more plausible source of the alleged 'Balkan
fatalism' which Vucinich (1963: 90–1, 1965: 69) prefers to attribute to the influence of
Islamic fatalism ('kismet') under Ottoman rule.

In any event the Byzantine and neo-Byzantine Balkans experienced the triumph of an
intolerant 'middlebrow' Christian culture, shared by both rulers and ruled (Brown 1971:
181). Its characteristic manifestations were Christian hagiographies ('lives of the saints'),
icons, Orthodox church music (unaccompanied devotional chants and liturgies) and
cults around 'holy relics' (pp. 181–3). These have remained immediately recognizable
hallmarks of Balkan culture ever since. In the same centuries the more centralized
autocracy bequeathed by Emperor Justinian I (527–65 AD) also 'fatally weakened' the
independence of the imperial bureaucracy, the provincial cities and the scholar gentry,
the traditional social pillars of secular classical education and culture (p. 180). Thus the
alleged cultural 'decline' or 'retrogression' of the Balkans, in the sense of a narrowing of
minds and horizons and a retreat from secular humanism and learning, began long before
the arrival of the Turks. Indeed, the great challenge posed by the seventh-century Arab
Moslem Empire 'completed the Christianization of the public life' of Byzantine cities,
submerging 'the last vestige of a secular culture' (pp. 186–7). In the new religious culture
'a man was defined by his religion . . . He did not owe allegiance to a state; he belonged
to a religious community . . . The arrival of the Arabs merely cut the last threads that had
bound the provincials of the Near East to the Roman Empire . . . This was the final
victory of the idea of the religious community over the classical idea of the state' (Brown
1971: 186–7).

These changes clearly prefigure the '*millet* system' of the Ottoman Empire, which was
based upon segregation into autonomous religious communities (rather than social
classes or ethnic groups). They can only have retarded the development of modern
concepts of citizenship, civil rights and statehood in the Balkans. They help to explain
some of the primitive 'atavistic' qualities of modern Balkan politics, which have deep
structural and historical roots and cannot be glibly blamed on the effects of Ottoman rule,
even if many writers still find it convenient to do so.

The strategic interface between Islam and Western Christendom

The Arab conquest of Syria, Palestine, North Africa, Spain, the Balearic Islands, Corsica,
Sardinia, Sicily, Crete, Cyprus and Armenia ended exclusive European control of the

Mediterranean. It also disrupted Europe's traditional lines of trade and communication with Asia, causing a contraction of European and Mediterranean commerce from the seventh century to the ninth. In response, from the late seventh century to the tenth, Byzantium used its continuing naval power in the eastern Mediterranean to prevent goods from the East (spices, medicinal herbs, dyes, myrrh, precious stones, silks, cottons, fine fabrics, sugar) from being shipped directly from Syrian and Egyptian ports to Western Europe. Instead, it redirected them through Byzantine ports (especially Constantinople), where they were subjected to high customs duties, shipping charges and profit mark-ups, before being re-exported to Western and Central Europe, mainly through Italian (especially Venetian) distribution agents. This sowed the seeds of Venetian maritime-commercial power, which would eventually rival and undermine that of Byzantium.

Byzantium also continued to dominate trade with the East via the Black Sea, including grain, furs, metals and amber from the Black Sea littoral. Furthermore, control of European trade with the East helped Byzantium to protect and foster its own industries and crafts. The Byzantine state 'virtually stopped its eastern import trade from bringing Syrian or Egyptian goods into the empire. Only raw materials were allowed to be imported. In this way its own industries and sales were safeguarded' (Haussig 1971: 172–3). Byzantine luxury and craft industries reached their peak between the ninth and eleventh centuries, producing fine fabrics, silks, carpets, paper, ceramics, leather goods, carvings, icons and metalwork (especially goblets, ewers, enamels and bronzes). Two monks had smuggled some silkworm eggs from Persia to Byzantium as early as 550 AD and the silks of the Byzantine Empire became famous throughout medieval Europe. Byzantium had also discovered from Persia the secret of how to make luxury paper from rags, while from the Arabs it had learned how to make and use decorative ceramic tiles and faience (majolica) (p. 169).

In the ninth and tenth centuries, however, the Arabs managed to break through the Byzantine blockade and to turn the tables on Byzantium by capturing strategic Mediterranean islands and control of the Straits of Messina and then imposing a naval blockade on the Adriatic and the Aegean Seas. In any case, high-cost Byzantine exports and re-exports were gradually being priced out of European markets. This was the result of excessive Byzantine customs tolls, shipping fees and mark-ups as well as over-restrictive guild regulations. All this encouraged the rising Italian maritime-commercial powers (led by Venice) to trade directly with the Arab world, bypassing Byzantium and contributing to its incipient commercial and industrial decline (Haussig 1971: 306–7). In spite of the commercial and military 'stand-off', however, there was still a degree of mutual respect, commerce and cultural cross-fertilization between Byzantium and the Moslem states. 'Mosques were built in Constantinople, just as Christian churches remained open in Muslim territory. Rarely were either attacked or desecrated . . . Christianity and Islam were both more intolerant of their own heretics within than either was of the other' (Woodhouse 1977: 44). Arab mathematics, science, astronomy and medicine, mediated through Byzantium, were still to play seminal roles in the European Renaissance.

The decline of Byzantium

All the while, however, the underlying economic strength of the Byzantine Empire was being sapped by its over-regulated, restrictive and protected economic system, by excessive taxation of the peasantry and townspeople and by a steadily increasing concentration of land, power and wealth in the hands of the essentially parasitic monasteries and big private landowners (who were gradually enserfing much of the labour force). Until the tenth century the imperial administration regulated prices, wages, rents, interest rates and the activities of industrial and commercial guilds. It also imposed compulsory loans and periodically debased the coinage, reducing confidence in the currency and in financial rewards. The erratic but inexorable contraction of the imperial territory and population, caused by Arab, Bulgar, Turkish and Slav territorial encroachments, led to the erosion of official salaries and the growth of official corruption and extortion, the sale of offices and increasing reliance on tax-farmers (Haussig 1971: 178). 'Officials regarded their office as a means of amassing as much wealth as possible. Responsibility towards the state and integrity were non-existent' (p. 177).

Official corruption, extortion and nepotism thus became endemic in the Balkans long before the establishment of the Ottoman Empire, although Balkan historians such as Sugar (1977: 288) and Vucinich (1963: 89–90, 1965: 120) still see fit to blame the Ottoman regime for patterns of official corruption and extortion which it merely inherited and perpetuated. The contraction of the imperial tax base and the growing reliance on corrupt and extortionate tax-farmers placed a crushing burden on the peasantry and led to the growth of debt-servitude, foreclosures and the usurpation of peasant land by rich tax-farmers, provincial administrators and a rising class of 'feudal' frontier barons who gained the upper hand in imperial affairs after the tenth century (Haussig 1971: 184–5, 304–8). 'From the eleventh century the Byzantine administration was no longer capable of defending the small landowners', and taxation, which was 'increasingly indulgent towards the monasteries and the powerful classes, became of necessity more and more oppressive for the mass of the people' (Andreades 1948: 69). The peasantry, the 'backbone' of the Byzantine state, 'were systematically destroyed by tax legislation which denied them the possibility of working on an economic basis' (Haussig 1971: 185). The life of the Balkan peasant was increasingly dominated by fear and dread of the tax collector, the imperial administrator, the big landowner, the moneylender and the foreign marauder (Baynes and Moss 1948: xxix).

Territorial contraction brought about not merely a tightening of imperial finances and increasing concentration of land and wealth in fewer hands, but also a narrowing of commercial and cultural horizons. Shorn of the bulk of its western and Asiatic territories, the Byzantine world became less cosmopolitan, more inward-looking and more narrowly and homogeneously Greek and Orthodox in its culture and attitudes. In losing its former breadth it became culturally and spiritually impoverished (Baynes and Moss 1948: 13).

From the tenth century, moreover, Byzantine state regulation of prices, wages, rents, guilds and grain marketing broke down. This reduced the role of the state in the economy, 'freeing' it from restrictive and distorting state tutelage. Yet it also reduced the capacity of the Byzantine state to protect Byzantine industries through tariffs and import restrictions. 'No longer was any attempt made to protect the home market by tariffs, or by limiting exports and imports.' Instead 'the Empire resorted to bartering its sovereign rights in return for military aid from other powers'. Byzantium thus surrendered its economic independence to foreign commercial powers and 'ceased to be a great economic power' (Haussig 1971: 310). The silk industry was lost to Italy when the Normans captured Corinth and Thebes in 1147 and transported both silkworms and workers to Sicily, which was then under Norman rule (Haussig 1971: 309). Moreover, shipping firms gradually relocated from Byzantium to Italian cities to escape the excessive taxation (p. 313). The Byzantines thus abandoned the proactive principle of 'carrying their wares to foreign ports' in favour of passively 'waiting for the foreign purchaser to come to them' (Andreades 1948: 67). By the twelfth century 'Byzantine trade was no longer predominantly concerned with luxury goods, as it had been . . . between the sixth and tenth centuries' (Haussig 1971: 313). Instead, Constantinople became merely an entrepôt for the foodstuffs (such as grain, olive oil and sunflower oil) and raw materials (such as wool and flax) required by expanding West European cities and textile industries.

In 1054 there occurred the final rift or 'schism' between the Roman Catholic and Eastern Orthodox Churches. Beyond the never-resolved battle for primacy between Rome and Constantinople, between Pope and Patriarch and between Western and Eastern Christendom, there were ever-widening linguistic, semantic, doctrinal, liturgical and organizational differences between the two Churches, for example over the Roman Catholic doctrines of the 'double procession of the Holy Spirit', the celibacy of priests and the use of unleavened bread. There were also divergent attitudes to icons, relics, Mary and the relationship between the believer and God (reflected in differences in church furniture and layout) and differences in the fingers and movements to be used in making the sign of the cross. In 1050 a papal synod banned the use of Orthodox rites in Italy. The Orthodox Patriarch retaliated by banning the use of Catholic rites in Constantinople and by closing the Catholic churches there when they refused to comply. Finally, the papal legate sent to negotiate with Constantinople in 1054 'excommunicated' the Orthodox Church (Woodhouse 1977: 65; Haussig 1971: 315).

In 1071 Byzantium was dealt two lethal blows. It lost Bari, its last Italian stronghold, to the Normans. And at the battle of Manzikert it was decisively defeated by the rising power of the Seljuk Turks, who proceeded to take control of Asia Minor, depriving Byzantium of a major source of revenue and recruits. Henceforth Byzantium would desperately cast around for new expedients and allies in a vain endeavour to arrest its ineluctable decline.

In 1082, in return for an empty promise of Venetian naval assistance against the Normans and the Turks, Byzantium granted Venetians free access to the main Byzantine ports, along with control of the main harbour facilities (including warehouses) and of key public offices. But Venice proved a fickle ally and did little to halt the encroachments of either the Normans or the Turks. The treaty of 1082 became a slowly tightening 'noose around the neck of the Byzantine Empire . . . condemning her to slow death by strangulation' (Haussig 1971: 318). In an attempt to escape this predicament Byzantium made similar concessions to Pisa and Genoa (Venice's arch-rivals) and then, in 1171, arrested all Venetians on Byzantine soil and confiscated their warehouses. But it had to back down when, in retaliation, Venice flexed its muscles and seized the island of Chios, valued for its production of mastic. Thus the infamous Ottoman 'capitulations', which conferred humiliating 'unequal' trading privileges on Western powers in the later Turkish Empire, were clearly prefigured in Byzantium and were not a peculiarly Ottoman invention and sign of weakness.

The victories of the Seljuk Turks, especially at Manzikert (1071), raised the spectre of a Moslem–Turkish threat to 'Christendom'. This prompted Pope Gregory VII (1073–85) to promote the idea of a glorious Christian crusade (or holy war) to 'liberate' the 'Holy Lands' (Palestine and Syria) and eliminate the Turkish 'menace', to ensure the security of

Map 2 Eastern Europe, mid-eleventh century

both Byzantine Orthodox and Roman Catholic Europe. But Byzantium was to be irretrievably wounded by the Crusades, even though they were originally intended to 'save' it from the 'infidel' threat.

It fell to Pope Urban II (1088–99) to launch the First Crusade in 1095. The Pope appealed for a few thousand Christian volunteers, but both he and the Byzantine emperor Alexius I (1081–1118) were somewhat alarmed by the nature and magnitude of the response. Huge, disorderly and predatory armies of Frankish and Norman warriors, ruffians and adventurers were motivated as much by an appetite for plunder, profiteering and territorial gain as by pious concern for either the 'liberty' of the Holy Lands or the security of Byzantium and Christendom.

The First Crusade (1095–99) captured Nicaea (the Seljuk capital) in 1097, Antioch in 1098 and Jerusalem in 1099. But, having accomplished their declared mission, the crusaders turned to further plunder, territorial aggrandisement and fighting among themselves, allowing the Turks to counter-attack successfully from 1112 onwards. The inconclusive Second Crusade (1147–48) and the Third Crusade (1188–92) were followed by a catastrophic Fourth Crusade (1201–04), during which the increasingly powerful Venetian Republic diverted the lawless and unscrupulous crusaders away from the Holy Lands and against Byzantium. Indeed, Emperor Alexius III (1195–1203), who had been driven to conclude a humiliating peace and accommodation with the Turks in 1197 (in order to protect his rear), was a renegade and a traitor to the Christian cause in the eyes of many Catholic crusaders. Having forced him to abandon the Byzantine throne to his pliant younger brother in 1203, they captured, looted and vandalized Constantinople itself in 1204, massacring many of its Orthodox Christian, Moslem and Jewish inhabitants and desecrating many of its Orthodox churches and cathedrals. They divided most of the imperial possessions among themselves and, amid the battered remnants of Byzantium, they proclaimed a Catholic 'Latin Empire' under Count Baldwin of Flanders and a Venetian Catholic patriarch, subservient to both Venice and the Pope. After this long-remembered bout of Roman Catholic treachery, plunder, desecration and massacres, many Orthodox Christians concluded that they would rather submit to Moslem rule. This was to be a major reason why so many Orthodox Christians later rejected the humiliating and hegemonic terms on which a few Western Catholic rulers offered Byzantium token assistance against the Ottoman Turks in 1439–53 and 'accepted the Turkish conquest . . . as a merciful release from Latin domination' (Woodhouse 1977: 98). Indeed, the Ottomans were to treat Orthodox Christians and the Orthodox Church with rather more respect (on the whole) than the Catholic crusaders did, and the contrast would continue to colour the attitudes of Orthodox Christians (especially Serbs) towards their Catholic neighbours in Italy, Croatia, Slovenia, Austria and Hungary for centuries to come. Some of the crusaders were in a sense forerunners of the rowdy north-west European 'lager louts' who descend on the Balkan beaches each summer!

The Byzantine Empire did not die in 1204, however. Within a year 'Emperor' Baldwin had been defeated and captured by the Bulgars, who resented the crusaders' attempts to foist a Roman Catholic 'Latin Empire' on the Balkans, while Byzantine exiles and refugees rallied to a rival Orthodox Christian empire launched in Nicaea in Anatolia by Theodore Laskaris (1204–22). His successors, in alliance with the Bulgars and Genoa (which was seeking to outmanoeuvre its arch-rival Venice), gradually brought the southern Balkans back under Orthodox Christian control and, in 1261, recaptured Constantinople. The restored Byzantine state, however, 'was but the pitiful remains of an empire' (Diehl 1948: 37). In return for crucial naval assistance in the recapture of Constantinople, Genoa had been granted possession of strategic east Mediterranean islands, the Golden Horn (the prime position in Constantinople) and the right to collect 85 per cent of the customs revenue from sea traffic through the Bosphorus.

The Balkan economy and the stagnating civilizations of the eastern Mediterranean suffered further disruption and destabilization in the wake of renewed crusades in 1212, 1217–21, 1229, 1239, 1249, 1290 and 1343. These Catholic 'holy wars' served only to deepen and harden religious divisions and antagonisms, both between Roman Catholic and Eastern Orthodox Christendom and between the Christian and Moslem worlds, without achieving any lasting 'liberation' of the 'Holy Lands'. The crusades brought down the curtain on over 2,000 years of fruitful interaction and cross-fertilization between the civilizations of the Balkans and the Middle East, which had been at the heart of the eastern Mediterranean's extraordinary cultural ferment and creativity over so many centuries. Under the deadening impact of the crusades, the creative interface was replaced by a military stand-off between mutually antagonistic 'armed camps', not unlike the recently ended Cold War between the former communist bloc and the West. The main effects of the crusades were 'drastically to weaken the superior civilization they encountered and to undermine its moral standards', causing the Moslem world to turn in on itself and become 'over-sensitive, defensive, intolerant, sterile – attitudes that grew steadily worse as worldwide evolution, a process from which the Muslim world felt excluded, continued' (Mansfield 1992: 21–2). Aside from the Middle East, the main loser from this embattled and stultifying cultural introversion and defensiveness was to be South-eastern Europe, both because it was about to succumb to several centuries of Turkish Moslem rule and because it had previously enjoyed such mutually profitable relations with the Middle East.

THE RISE AND DECLINE OF THE FIRST SOUTH SLAV STATES

The multifaceted decline and tribulations of Byzantium left the Balkans with a power vacuum which was to be filled first of all by short-lived Bulgarian and Serbian empires and only later by the Ottoman Turks. The establishment of the first Bulgarian empire was masterminded by Prince (Khan) Boris (852–89 AD) and his illustrious Byzantine-educated, Greek-speaking son, Tsar Simeon (893–927 AD). (The title Tsar is cognate with Caesar.) Simeon vigorously promoted the new Slavic literary culture and an 'autocephalous' (self-governing) Bulgarian Orthodox Church. In 926 AD he established a Bulgarian Orthodox patriarchate at Preslav, his showy new capital city. He also conquered most of Macedonia, Serbia, Albania, Wallachia (Vlachia) and Thrace. 'He had it in his power to unite the South Slavs under his rule and to form a great Balkan Slavic empire. Instead he fell victim to the dream of Constantinople' (Stavrianos 1958: 26). He donned the imperial purple (the purple robes of a Roman or Byzantine emperor), pronounced himself 'Tsar of the Bulgars and Autocrat of the Romans' (i.e. Byzantine Orthodox Christians) and squandered his hard-won resources on grandiose construction projects and several major attempts to capture Constantinople, the last of which was cut short by his untimely death in 927 AD.

Simeon's son Peter (927–69 AD) made peace with Byzantium, married a Byzantine princess and gained recognition both of the Bulgarian Orthodox patriarchate and of himself as Tsar of the Bulgarians. But his dominions were repeatedly ravaged by Magyar and Pecheneg marauders and in 968–69 AD Preslav was capture by Kiev Rus. The Byzantine forces sent to 'liberate' Bulgaria from Russian rule brought most of it back under Byzantine control in 970–71 AD, although a Bulgarian 'rump' state survived in Macedonia until 1019. The last bastions of Bulgarian resistance were savagely subjugated by the Byzantine emperor 'Basil the Bulgar slayer' between 1014 and 1019. In 1014 around 14,000 Bulgarian warriors were taken prisoner and then blinded, so as to shock their kith and kin into submission to Byzantium.

The reimposition of Byzantine rule led to the abolition of the Bulgarian Orthodox patriarchate and the Hellenization of the Orthodox clergy, although the Bulgarian Slavonic liturgy and literature somehow survived ('miraculously', according to nationalist mythology), while Bulgaria's big landowners ('boyars') mostly collaborated and enriched themselves at their peasants' expense. But a tax-dodgers' rebellion, begun by a group of Bulgarian boyars at Trnovo in 1185, evoked Byzantium's reluctant recognition in 1187 of a new Bulgarian kingdom centred on Trnovo and ruled by the Asen family. Taking advantage of the conflicts and chaos precipitated by the Third Crusade (1187–92) and by the capture of Constantinople in 1204 (during the Fourth Crusade), Bulgaria's new rulers rapidly expanded their domains. In 1205 they defeated and captured Count Baldwin of Flanders, the first 'Latin' emperor, who had rashly attempted to subjugate Bulgaria in 1204. By 1231 the Russophil Tsar Ivan Asen II (1218–41) had gained control of Macedonia, Albania, Serbia, southern Wallachia and northern Greece, establishing a second Bulgarian empire embracing most of the Balkan peninsula. He emulated Simeon (893–927 AD) by proclaiming himself 'Tsar and Autocrat of the Bulgarians and Romans' and by restoring an autocephalous Bulgarian Orthodox Church and patriarchate in 1235. Beginning in 1237 and 1242, however, this second Bulgarian empire was hit by a devastating succession of Mongol/Tartar invasions. After 1241 it rapidly disintegrated under the combined weight of internal and external attacks. The quarrelsome self-serving boyars were unwilling either to accept a strong central administration and standing army or to unite against external foes. As always, they preferred to enhance their own local power and autonomy at the expense of the state and the peasantry.

In 1277 the downtrodden and repeatedly plundered Bulgarian peasantry rallied around Ivailo, a humble swineherd, who drove out the Tartars, married a widowed Bulgarian Tsarina and had himself crowned as Tsar. In seeking boyar and ecclesiastical support against the Tartars and Byzantium, however, Ivailo betrayed the peasantry, who thereupon deserted their 'peasant Tsar'. In 1280, while negotiating with the Tartar Khan Nogai, he was murdered by his Tartar hosts. With him died any immediate hope of a 'liberated' Bulgaria.

In 1330 Bulgaria was subjugated by a nascent Serbian Balkan empire established by the Serb rulers Stefan Urosh III (1321–31) and Stefan Dushan (1331–55). The latter's empire embraced Serbia, Montenegro, Macedonia, Bulgaria, Albania and northern Greece. Like Bulgaria's Tsar Simeon (893–927 AD) before him, however, Stefan Dushan threw away the chance of welding the South Slavs into a coherent and durable Balkan Slav state. Had either of them concentrated on such a realistic and feasible goal, the Balkans could easily have developed into a much less fractious and vulnerable region. Even the inhabitants of Albania and northern Greece could have been gradually Slavicized through migration, intermarriage and cultural assimilation, for there was at that time a common religion (Eastern Orthodox Christianity), and ethnic identities and allegiances were then more fluid than 'fixed'. But neither Simeon nor Stefan Dushan could resist the lure of Constantinople and the overweening imperial pretensions of a neo-Byzantine autocracy. In 1346, with lavish (Byzantine) pomp and ceremony, Stefan Dushan established an autocephalous Serbian Orthodox Church and patriarchate and had himself crowned as Tsar of the Serbs and Romans (Byzantines), a title which he soon expanded to 'Tsar and Autocrat of the Serbs, Romans, Bulgarians and Albanians' (Darby 1968: 98). In 1355, however, just as he was launching his long-planned conquest of Constantinople in alliance with the powerful maritime republics of Ragusa (Dubrovnik) and Venice, Stefan Dushan died of a fever. Thereupon his far from unified state began to disintegrate almost as rapidly as it had been assembled, as 'this imposing structure proved to be a phantom empire . . . The adoption of a Byzantine style masked, without eliminating, the centrifugal social tendencies represented by unruly . . . and self-interested magnates' (many of whom later 'defected' to the Ottomans during the decisive military showdown between the South Slavs and the Turks at the battle of Kosovo Plain in 1389) (Coles 1968: 22).

In retrospect, Bulgarian and Serbian nationalists and 'national' historians have naturally tended to see the medieval Bulgarian and Serbian kingdoms as nascent or embryonic nation-states whose 'glorious' national development was rudely cut short by foreign conquerors and subsequently stifled by several centuries of Ottoman Turkish rule. They have also been inclined to treat the maximum extension of their medieval kingdoms as 'the natural historical boundaries for their nations' (Jelavich 1983a: 27). Historical memories of these aggressive medieval kingdoms have translated into modern nationalist political programmes of territorial aggrandisement, causing immense bloodshed in the twentieth century.

In reality, however, these unstable and loose-knit medieval kingdoms were prone to internal disintegration even before they succumbed to foreign conquerors, and their territorial boundaries bore little correspondence to ethnic boundaries. More fundamentally, these states can be seen less as close forerunners or prototypes of the modern Bulgarian and Serbian nation-states than as attempts by Bulgarian and Serbian 'upstarts' to create Orthodox Balkan empires modelled on Byzantium and capable of usurping its imperial power, status and mission. National identities were still inchoate and fluid. They were much weaker than the widely shared identification with Orthodox Christianity and a Byzantine (or neo-Byzantine) civilization. Byzantium was always regarded by its rulers as 'the foremost civilization of the time'. That view was very much shared by its neighbours, who repeatedly aspired, not to destroy Byzantium, but 'to occupy the imperial city and to claim for themselves the prestige and position of the Byzantine emperor' (Jelavich 1983a: 12). Significantly, Byzantium served as a role model not only for other Orthodox Christian states but also for the Ottoman Turks, who were to inherit and reconstitute (rather than destroy) the Byzantine *imperium* in the Balkans. 'Balkan rulers wished to be Byzantine autocrats. They copied the court ceremonie[1] and they used Byzantine architectural styles for their buildings . . . Most important, the empire's high level of civilization provided patterns for government and culture' (p. 13).

From 1205 until 1355 it had seemed a racing certainty that one or other of the nascent South Slav empires would in due course conquer Byzantium and 'enter upon the Byzantine inheritance'; such a state might well have constituted an effective 'bulwark' against Ottoman expansion into Europe (Coles 1968: 21). But history is never acted out in accordance with a preordained script. The rapid disintegration of the Serbian empire after Stefan Dushan's death in 1355, followed by the momentous defeats suffered by Balkan Christian forces at the hands of the Ottomans in 1371 and 1389, allowed the Turks suddenly to erupt into the power vacuum created in the Balkans by the decline and contraction of both Byzantium and the South Slav states.

2   The rise of the Ottoman Empire

Europeans were caught almost completely off-guard by the remarkably rapid rise of the Ottoman 'menace' (as contemporaries perceived it). But Europe's capacity to resist the Ottoman advance was further reduced by such factors as the deep divisions between and within Roman Catholic and Eastern Orthodox Christendom, the deadly rivalries between Venice, Genoa, Ragusa and Constantinople, and the devastating effects of the Black Death. Bubonic plague spread westwards from Constantinople in 1347, decimating and terrorizing whole populations for several decades. (Bubonic plague persisted in the Balkans and Anatolia until the nineteenth century and has occasionally resurfaced in twentieth-century Russia and Kazakhstan.)

Successive waves of Turkic nomadic pastoralists, warriors and marauders had been fanning out from Central Asia into Anatolia, the Black Sea region and the Middle East since the eighth or ninth century, partly in a perpetual quest for fresh pastures and hunting grounds and partly in response to pressure on their eastern and northern flanks from the Mongols. The Seljuk Turks in particular had cleared the way for large-scale Turkic colonization and Islamicization of Anatolia since the eleventh century, gradually displacing northwards the formerly dominant Armenians and Byzantine Greeks. Indeed, Anatolia became a favourite stomping ground for large numbers of Moslem Turkish freebooters and frontiersmen known as 'ghazis' ('fighters against non-Moslems', from the Arabic word for 'raid').

THE HOUSE OF OSMAN

The Ottomans were named after Osman, who was born around 1258 and founded a small independent state in northern Anatolia in 1299 or 1300. Osman's father, Ertugrul, was a Turkic Moslem frontier warrior who had been awarded a small fief near Sogut during the thirteenth-century decline and fragmentation of the Seljuk Empire. Osman's gradual extension of his father's domains at the expense of both Byzantium and rival Turkic potentates culminated in his conquest of the city of Brusa (Bursa) on the southern shores of the Sea of Marmara in 1326. This strategically located city became the capital of the nascent Osmanli or 'Ottoman' state. The neighbouring Balkan and Anatolian states were preoccupied with more immediate threats, such as the Mongol and Tatar marauders who periodically 'erupted' from Asia. So they took little notice of the emergence of the Ottomans. Osman's son Orkhan (1326–59) captured the last important Byzantine cities in northern Anatolia, Nicaea (Iznik) in 1329 and Nicomedia (Izmit) in 1337.

Military success attracted growing numbers of Turkic and Moslem ghazis, adventurers and freebooters into the service of the House of Osman, whose followers were not members of a particular tribe or clan, but rather a mixture of many kinds of Turkic and Turkicized peoples who chose to follow Osman or subsequent rulers (Sultans) of the Osmanli state (Sugar 1977: 12–13). Nor were the Ottoman Sultans 'purely' Turkish. Orkhan (1326–59), Murad I (1359–89), Bayezid I (1389–1402), Murad II (1421–44) and Mehmed II (1451–81) married Christian European princesses in order to seal dynastic alliances with various South-east European rulers, while the remarkable Sultan Bayezid I was actually the son, grandson and husband of Christian South-east European princesses (pp. 15–16, 21).

The major challenge confronting the early Ottoman Sultans was how to harness and provide fulfilling outlets for the energies, appetites and religious fervour of their most numerous followers, the ghazis. 'The ever-increasing numbers of Islamic warriors who were attracted to the expanding Osmanli frontier state had to be kept occupied in some manner. The obvious solution lay across the Straits, where infidel Balkan kingdoms . . . promised rich spoils for the ghazis and new glory for the faith' (Stavrianos 1958: 36).

Ironically, having ended a thousand years of Byzantine power in Asia Minor in 1337, Ottoman Turks first entered the Balkans in 1345 as mercenaries (about 6,000 in all) in the service of an able Byzantine official and usurper named John Cantacuzene. They were to assist him in his successful seizure of the Byzantine imperial throne, completed in 1347. Having strengthened this 'unholy alliance' by marrying off his daughter Theodora to Sultan Orkhan (1326–59), Emperor Cantacuzene invited another 20,000 Ottoman mercenaries to the Balkans in 1349 to help him fight off Serbian encroachments on Byzantine territory. These first forays into South-eastern Europe whetted Ottoman Turkish appetites for new conquests and booty, with the result that the Ottomans returned (uninvited!) in 1352 and 1354 to capture Tzympe (Cimpe) and Gallipoli respectively. From their new strategic bridgeheads on the northern (European) shores of the Dardanelles and the Sea of Marmara, the Ottoman Turks found it remarkably easy to expand into the power vacuum created by the accelerating decline and contraction of the Serbian and Byzantine empires. By 1365 the Ottomans had consolidated their hold on eastern Thrace (including Plovdiv) and had transferred their capital from Bursa (Brusa) to Adrianople (Edirne) in the south-eastern Balkans. This area, roughly corresponding to the present-day Turkish toehold in Europe (together with Constantinople, after it fell to the Turks in 1453), was to be the only part of the Balkans that was ever intensively colonized by the Turks.

CHRISTIAN DISARRAY AND DEFEATS

The first major Catholic and Orthodox Christian forces despatched to arrest the Ottoman advance into South-eastern Europe were cut to shreds near Adrianople (Edirne) in 1364. A similar fate befell the Orthodox South Slav armies sent down the Maritsa valley to head off the Turks in 1371. These traumatic Christian defeats effectively left the way open for the Turks to advance into the very heart of the Balkans. They were able to capture Bitolj (Monastir) in 1380, Sofia in 1385, Nis in 1386, Salonika (Thessaloniki) in 1387 and Kolarovgrad (Shumen), Provadija (Pravadi) and Novi Pazar in 1388. On 15 (28) June 1389, according to Balkan Orthodox (especially Serbian) nationalist historiography, the Ottomans decisively defeated a grand coalition of Serb, Bulgarian, Albanian, Bosnian and Wallachian Orthodox Christian forces on Kosovo Plain, shattering the last remnants of the defunct Serbian empire. However, more detached historians tell a somewhat different story. 'Though Serbian myth and poetry have presented this battle as a cataclysmic defeat in which the flower of Balkan chivalry perished . . . the truth is a little less dramatic. Losses were heavy on both sides' (Malcolm 1994: 20). At the close of battle, the remnants of the Orthodox Christian forces withdrew. But then the Ottoman forces withdrew as well, because they lacked the numbers and strength to continue their 'offensive against the Balkan Christians' and because a Serb who had ostensibly deserted to the Ottoman side had managed to assassinate Sultan Murad I, with the result that Murad's eldest son, Bayezid (who commanded the Ottoman forces), felt obliged to pull back his remaining troops in order to make sure of his own succession to the sultanate. 'Thus, since the Turks also withdrew, one can conclude the battle was a draw' (Fine 1987: 410). Indeed, since the Serb and Bosnian forces had seemingly held off an Ottoman assault, they initially claimed that they had 'won' and they were hailed as saviours of Christendom. However, whereas the Serbs had lost a large part of their forces in holding the Turks to a temporary draw, the Ottomans still had thousands of fresh troops in reserve and were able to complete their conquest of the Orthodox Serb lands (other than Bosnian-ruled Hum and parts of Zeta/Montenegro) by 1392. Thus, although the Serbs may not have formally lost the battle of Kosovo in 1389, 'they lost the war because they were no longer able to resist the Turks effectively' (pp. 411–18).

A significant factor in these Ottoman victories was the regularity with which some Balkan Orthodox Christians either fought on the Ottoman side or else went over to the Ottomans in the crucial hour of battle. This partly reflected the fact that the declining and shrinking Orthodox Christian states commanded very little residual loyalty, support or credibility. Thus the 'rats' were deserting the 'sinking ships' in time-honoured fashion. It was also the result of a clever Ottoman policy of forcing many of the weak and vulnerable Christian princes and boyars lying in their path to acknowledge Ottoman overlordship (suzerainty), and contribute men, money and supplies ('tribute') to the Ottoman war machine, in return for lenient treatment, partial assimilation into the Ottoman aristocracy and retention of their land holdings and privileged social positions. Many Orthodox Christian princes, boyars and soldiers of fortune were to make a successful career out of 'loyal' service to the Ottoman state, perpetuating a long tradition of 'collaboration' with the dominant imperial or occupying power in the Balkans (continuing into the periods of Nazi and Soviet domination in the twentieth century). They were opportunists, hitching their fortunes to the rising star in their firmament. Some even 'converted' to Islam in order to enhance (or at least safeguard) their prospects under Ottoman domination. This was possibly a major factor in the emergence of the only sizeable non-Turkish Moslem communities in the Balkans, specifically in Bosnia, Hercegovina, Albania, Kosovo and western Macedonia (about which more will be said shortly).

Furthermore, many Christian traders and artisans were initially to prefer the 'order', stability, firmness and certainty offered by the Ottomans in their prime (during the so-called 'Pax Ottomanica') to the anarchy, instability, uncertainty, depredations and excessive taxation characteristic of the twilight years of the Balkan Christian states, on the eve of the Ottoman conquest. In addition, many Balkan peasants had suffered terribly from the anarchy, instability, insecurity and excessive 'feudal' and fiscal exactions of the warring, declining and disintegrating Balkan Christian states and from the intensification and territorial extension of serfdom. These peasants either saw the new Ottoman overlords as no worse than their Christian oppressors or even greeted them as potential 'liberators' from seigneurial and fiscal oppression and from the harmful consequences of anarchy, instability and constant warfare.

THE INCIPIENT ISLAMICIZATION OF BOSNIA AND HUM

There has also been a highly influential theory that many or even most of the inhabitants of Bosnia and Hum (Hercegovina) were adherents of a radical, heretical and violently persecuted Christian sect known as the Bogomils, founded in tenth-century Bulgarian Macedonia by a priest called Father Bogomil. Upholding a Manichaean dualist conception of the world as divided between the forces of Good (the spirit, light, God) and Evil (matter, darkness, the Devil), the Bogomils denounced the oppressiveness, extravagance, decadence and high living of the wealthy monasteries, the Church hierarchy and the (pseudo-) Christian ruling classes. In Bogomil eyes, wealth, luxury and material possessions were intrinsically evil. The Bogomils were to go further than any other section of Balkan society in welcoming the Ottoman Turks as 'liberators' who could finally free them from centuries of religious and political repression at the hands of the Christian 'Establishment' (both Orthodox and Catholic). To make sure of Ottoman protection against their former persecutors, the mainly Bogomil inhabitants of Bosnia, Hercegovina and parts of Macedonia even converted en masse to Islam, eventually creating a Moslem majority in Ottoman-ruled Bosnia-Hercegovina. This was the origin of the so-called 'Bosnian Moslems', who are mostly descended from Serbs who converted to Islam in order to escape 'official' Christian persecution of the 'Bogomil heresy'. They were to remain staunch supporters of Ottoman rule in the Balkans right up to the late nineteenth century, to the subsequent consternation of their Orthodox and Catholic neighbours.

The Bogomil theory has certain attractions. It seemingly offers a colourful and dramatic explanation of the conversion of a substantial section of Bosnia's population to Islam during the period of Ottoman rule. It presents the conversion, not as a mundane and protracted process but as a sudden 'mass conversion of Bogomils who, having held out for centuries against the competition and/or persecution of the Catholic and Orthodox Churches, finally preferred to transfer their allegiance to Islam'. The theory has therefore found particular favour among modern Bosnian Moslems. 'Instead of being seen as mere renegades from Catholicism or Orthodoxy (to which, at various times, Croats and Serbs have suggested that they should 'return'), they could now be regarded as descendants of the membership of an authentically and peculiarly Bosnian Church; and their turning to Islam could be described not as an act of weakness, but as a final gesture of defiance against their Christian persecutors' (Malcolm 1994: 29).

Latterly, however, this intriguing and still influential theory has been largely discredited by Fine (1976) and Malcolm (1994). Medieval Bosnia was formally under the ecclesiastical jurisdiction of the Western (Catholic) Church, and its rulers were at least outwardly Catholic. Twelfth- and thirteenth-century allegations of the emergence of widespread heresy in Bosnia (upon which the 'Bogomil' theory of Bosnia's conversion to Islam is based) emanated largely from outside Bosnia, chiefly from Hungary, Zeta (Montenegro), Spalato (Split) and Ragusa (Dubrovnik), each of which was advancing claims on Bosnian territory and/or seeking excuses to interfere in Bosnia's internal affairs (Malcolm 1994: 15, 31–2). By the fifteenth century the papacy and the Franciscans (who were engaged in a campaign to 'recatholicize' Bosnia) had joined in the allegations of heresy in this mountainous and remote country (pp. 23, 41). Nevertheless, 'the Bosnian Church was not identified as Bogomil at the time . . . and the only apparent instance of a medieval source referring to "Bogomils" in Bosnia was almost certainly a forgery' (p. 31).

According to Malcolm (1994: 33–9), the Bosnian Church was influenced not by Bogomilism but by the monastic precepts and practices of the Byzantine Orthodox Church, and these (rather than a heretical theology) were what its leaders were required to renounce at a synod held in Bolino Polje in April 1203. Moreover, true Bogomils were puritanically opposed to the wealth, power and high living of the established Churches and their temporal patrons, whereas the Bosnian Church seems to have accepted wealth, power and royal patronage without qualms. In any case, the separate Bosnian Church (distinct from both the Western/Catholic and the Eastern/Orthodox Churches) was 'largely defunct even before the Turkish conquest' of Bosnia in 1463 and therefore could not have played a major role in the area's subsequent Islamicization (pp. 41–2, 56).

This still leaves unanswered the perennial question of how Moslems became a majority of the population in Ottoman Bosnia. The process seems to have been a gradual one. Ottoman tax registers indicate that Moslems made up less than 10 per cent of the population in central and eastern Bosnia in 1468–69. In 1485 the *sandzak* of Bosnia still contained about 155,000 Christians and only 22,000 Moslems. But by the 1520s the Christian population had fallen to around 98,000, while the Moslem population had risen to 84,000. By the late sixteenth or early seventeenth century, Moslems were in a majority (Malcolm 1994: 52–3). There is no evidence of 'massive forcible conversion' to Islam or of 'mass resettlement . . . of Muslims from outside Bosnia' during the first century of Ottoman overlordship (p. 54). It was not necessary for Bosnian landowners to adopt Islam in order to be allowed to retain their land holdings (p. 64). Nor did Bosnians have to become Moslems in order to prosper, for the Ottoman domains were peppered with rich non-Moslem merchants (p. 65). However, there was a steady exodus of Catholics escaping actual or anticipated persecution (pp. 52–6). On the other hand, the more favoured Orthodox Church actually gained new adherents, monasteries and churches, but its ecclesiastical infrastructure was initially almost non-existent in Bosnia and it was therefore not strong enough to resist the country's Islamicization (pp. 57, 70–1). It should also be borne in mind that, in Bosnia's mainly remote and under-priested rural areas, 'Christianity (in whatever form) had probably become little more than a set of folk practices and ceremonies . . . The shift from folk Christianity to folk Islam was not very great; many of the same practices could continue, albeit with slightly different words or names . . . Many of the same festivals and holy days were celebrated by both religions' (p. 58). Bosnian Moslems continued to venerate the Virgin Mary, Christian saints and icons, and often retained Christian names and patronymics (pp. 59–60).

Conversion to Islam did confer some practical and career advantages. Christians could not bring lawsuits against Moslems or give testimony against Moslems in Moslem courts (Malcolm 1994: 66). It became increasingly necessary to be a Moslem in order to become an Ottoman official (p. 65). The spread of Islam was also related to the growth of new, largely Moslem towns such as Sarajevo and Mostar: 'Slaves who converted to Islam could apply for freedom . . . Converted and freed slaves were especially likely to end up in the expanding towns' (p. 66–7).

FLUCTUATING FORTUNES, 1389–1444

The Ottoman conquests were generally facilitated by the weakness of their Balkan opponents, who fielded armies numbering 'usually only hundreds rather than thousands' of troops and who not only refused to co-operate with one another but also fought among themselves (Fine 1987: 604). The smaller Balkan states, especially Bosnia, were more afraid of the Hungarians than of the Ottomans. Indeed, 'Orthodox Christians who knew of Ottoman religious tolerance often came to prefer the Turks to the intolerant Hungarians, who were likely to force Catholicism upon them' (p. 608). Moreover, the characteristic gradualness of the process of establishing Ottoman control (beginning with vassalage or suzerainty and the co-optation of Christian talent) also 'contributed greatly to the long-range success of the Ottomans' (p. 610), not least by reducing the likely resistance of the Balkan peoples (p. 607). Nevertheless, 'many Ottomans and Balkan Christians would have explained Ottoman success more simply, seeing it as resulting from the will of God, be it divine favour towards the Ottomans or divine anger at the Christians for their sins. This belief surely contributed to Ottoman success, for it gave . . . their troops confidence, an intangible but important factor in the winning of battles' (pp. 610–11).

During the 1390s, in the wake of the legendary battle of Kosovo Plain (1389), almost all the Orthodox Christian areas of the Balkans fell under Ottoman domination. The Orthodox rulers or princes of Serbia, Bulgaria, Macedonia, Bosnia, Albania and mainland Greece mostly became vassals of the Sultan and 'the Byzantine Empire was reduced to the great city and its immediate surroundings' (Sugar 1977: 21–3). Indeed, only Constantinople, Ragusa (Dubrovnik), Montenegro, the mainly Italian-controlled Greek archipelagoes and the Roman Catholic north-west corner, which could count on assistance from Catholic powers in Western and East Central Europe, were in a position to resist further Ottoman encroachments. These latter were also constrained by lengthening supply lines. Yet, when several Catholic powers mobilized a new crusade to 'roll back' the Turkish advance, the Catholic armies were decimated by the Turks at Nicopolis in 1396, with almost indecent encouragement and support from Orthodox Serbs.

In 1395, having almost encircled the imperial city, Sultan Bayezid I began an eight-year siege of Constantinople. Yet the Ottomans still lacked both the fire-power and the naval strength to break its great walls and its maritime lifeline to the outside world (as was again to be the case during the second Ottoman siege of Constantinople in 1422).

Then in 1402, like a bolt from the blue, the Samarkand-based Tatar/Turkic empire of Timur the Lame ('Tamarlane') exploded out of Central Asia into Anatolia. At the decisive battle of Ankara in July 1402, Timur defeated and captured Sultan Bayezid I (whose Turkic forces deserted to Timur's Tatar/Turkic side, while the Balkan Christian vassals remained loyal to the Sultan) and temporarily weakened the Ottomans' Anatolian power base before withdrawing to Central Asia in 1403 just as suddenly as he had arrived.

During the subsequent respite, prolonged by an eleven-year power struggle between Bayezid's four sons lasting from 1402 to 1413, most of the Balkan Christian princes regained their political independence and Byzantium regained some lost territories. 'Thus, the final outcome of the question of who would become the master of the Balkans was by no means a foregone conclusion' (Sugar 1977: 28).

The core territories of the House of Osman were reunited in 1413 under Sultan Mehmed I (1413–21). Turkish colonists and ghazis, Moslem Slavs, many Christian peasants and various Moslem and Christian commercial interests favoured the restoration of a Balkan 'Pax Ottomanica'. Indeed, Ottoman possessions and the power of the ghazis had survived more or less intact in the south-eastern Balkans, as Timur had not ventured that far. So the reborn Ottoman Empire sprang from a south-eastern Balkan power base, from which the Ottomans proceeded to conquer (or reconquer) the southern and eastern Balkans, numerous Mediterranean islands, Hungary, Anatolia, Transcaucasia and most of the Arab Moslem world over the next two centuries. In the 1420s, however, Venice still held a string of strategic islands and ports all around the Balkan peninsula, while the Balkan Christian princes were turning to Hungary for protection, and the second Ottoman siege of Constantinople in 1422 failed like the first (Sugar 1977: 28–9; Stavrianos 1958: 50–2).

THE COLLAPSE OF BALKAN CHRISTENDOM

Hungarian forces, led by the famous general Janos Hunyadi (aptly described by Stavrianos as a 'Christian ghazi'), won some major victories over the Ottomans up to 1443. But then the tide finally turned. Sultan Murad II (1421–51) roundly defeated a 'Christian coalition' of Hungarians, Venetians and Balkan princes in 1444 at Varna and in 1448 at the (less famous but more decisive) second battle of Kosovo Plain. Sultan Mehmed II (1451–81) followed up his father's great victories with the third and final siege of Constantinople in 1453. This time the Ottomans were in a position to close the Bosphorus to Byzantine shipping and to deploy cannons and bombards big enough to blast holes through the city walls, which had withstood twenty previous sieges. The city's population had dwindled to less than 75,000, of whom only 5,000 were equipped to fight. They were vastly outnumbered by the 150,000-strong Ottoman siege army (Stavrianos 1958: 55–6). For the Ottomans the conquest of Constantinople had become a strategic imperative. 'The existence of a Christian citadel . . . in the middle of the Sultan's lands in a very strategic position was a threat . . . So long as there was a Christian emperor and a patriarch independent of Ottoman power, the Sultan's Christian subjects . . . had to be considered as potentially revolutionary elements' (Sugar 1977: 65–6).

The Ottoman conquest of Constantinople eliminated the major strategic bridgehead which could have been used in any future Christian counter-offensive against Ottoman power in the Balkans. For the Ottomans, however, the capture of Constantinople involved much more than military and prudential considerations. For Constantinople was still a great entrepôt, situated at the centre of several major trade and communication networks which, despite the gradual decline and contraction of the Byzantine Empire, stood ready to be reactivated by any burgeoning imperial power that was strong enough to capture the imperial city and inherit its imperial mantle. This was the main reason why so many rising and aspiring imperial powers had attempted to capture Constantinople (including the Arab, Bulgarian, Serbian and Seljuk empires) and why imperial Russia would later try repeatedly to take Constantinople from the Ottomans. Its strategic position and nodal situation on the interface between southern Europe and south-west Asia made it the ideal location for the capital of an empire extending (or aspiring to extend) into both continents. Furthermore, the capture of Constantinople completed the transformation of the Ottomans from 'an oriental "horde" operating within a fairly fluid zone of operation . . . into one of the great historic imperialisms' (Coles 1968: 26). By conferring control of the narrow sea passage between the Mediterranean and the Black Sea it also furnished the Ottomans with vast new 'reservoirs' of food, raw materials and manpower, for the (mainly Greek and Genoese) Black Sea traders 'plied a rich trade with Europe' in cereals, horses, metals, fish, timber and slaves, which were now diverted to Ottoman use (p. 27). This also weakened Italian maritime-commercial dominance of the eastern Mediterranean, which had partly depended on privileged access to Byzantium and the Black Sea region.

Following the fall of Constantinople the rest of the Christian Orthodox Balkans quickly fell into the Ottomans' lap. In addition to Bulgaria, which had already been subjugated as part of the encirclement of Constantinople, they conquered Serbia (minus Belgrade) and mainland Greece in 1456–59, Bosnia in 1463, Albania in 1467–79, Hercegovina in 1482–83, Montenegro in 1499 and Belgrade in 1521. Wallachia and Moldavia submitted to Ottoman overlordship in 1476 and 1512 respectively. Only Montenegro, Wallachia and Moldavia retained a large measure of autonomy, albeit as vassals of the Sultan. Then, having briefly occupied central Hungary in 1526 and 1528, the Ottomans more lastingly conquered Hungarian-ruled Croatia and Transylvania (as well as Hungary proper) from the 1540s until the 1690s. On the Balkan mainland only Austrian-ruled Slovenia, the resilient maritime-commercial Republic of Ragusa and the Venetian-ruled Dalmatian and Albanian ports remained effectively outside Ottoman control, although even Venice and Ragusa at times accepted (nominal) Ottoman suzerainty in return for privileged commercial access to Ottoman ports. In addition many Aegean and Adriatic islands remained either under Venetian control or became havens for Greek and South Slav pirates. But the islanders soon found the rule of the Catholic, mercenary and exploitative Venetian Republic to be 'more oppressive than that of the Turks' and 'on balance . . . preferred the Turks to the Venetians as masters' (Woodhouse 1977: 108, 113). The Venetians taxed the islanders much more heavily than the Ottomans probably would have done, denied them any local self-government (in contrast to Ottoman preservation of Christian local autonomy), strictly controlled their trade (preventing either diversification or competition with Venetian traders) and encouraged Catholic priests to proselytize among Orthodox Christians (while deterring Orthodox priests from proselytizing among Catholics). Corfu, for example, was virtually transformed into a single-crop colonial plantation economy. Olives and olive oil were produced for export, with results that are still visible today; the island is in effect one huge olive grove with crumbling Venetian towns and forts.

THE LATE MEDIEVAL BALKANS UNDER OTTOMAN RULE

In 1453, when the Moslem Sultan Mehmed II captured Constantinople, the citadel of Eastern Orthodox Christendom, he did not proceed to destroy it, as he could so easily have done (or as Christian crusaders would almost certainly have done if they had captured the citadel of Islam). The looting and pillage by victorious troops was brought under control within a few days and was far less destructive and traumatic than the sack of Constantinople by Crusaders in 1204. Moreover, according to the Greek historian George Arnakis (1963: 127), 'Ottoman policy, for the most part, was not hostile to the Orthodox Church. The reason is obvious. It was essential to keep the Orthodox subjects of the Sultan from uniting with the Catholic Church, which was associated with the struggle to drive Islam out of Europe.'

Thus the Ottomans never attempted any 'forced' or large-scale Islamicization of the Balkans. Balkan Orthodox Christians were on the whole more valuable to the Ottomans as Christians than they would have been as either forced or voluntary converts to Islam. The Ottomans found it useful to win over a small number of Balkan Christians to Islam as allies and collaborators. But Islam prescribed that Moslems had to be liable to fewer and lower taxes than non-Moslems. The Ottomans, therefore, relied disproportionately on their Christian subjects for revenue. In addition, the Ottomans often forcibly recruited soldiers from the Christian populations of the Balkans to fight their Moslem rivals in Anatolia and in the Arab world. Islamic doctrine condemns 'aggressive' (i.e. un-provoked) warfare between Moslem states. According to the Koran, Moslems may fight only in self-defence or in retaliation. Thus the Ottoman conquests in the Moslem world were, initially at least, heavily reliant on the use of Christian recruits from the Balkans. Christians have often been 'scandalized' by the fact that most of these recruits were (involuntarily) dragooned into Ottoman service. Ottoman military recruitment and conduct were indeed frequently ruthless and brutal. On the other hand, it should also be emphasized that the large number of young Christian boys who were enslaved, Islamicized and reared in the elite Ottoman forces were destined to become the most privileged and powerful soldier-administrators of the Ottoman Empire, even though they remained the obedient 'slaves' of the Sultan. Indeed, according to Stavrianos (1958: 501), only five of the forty-nine grand vezirs (chief ministers) who served the Ottomans between 1453 and 1623 were of Turkish extraction. A majority were of Christian European origin (including at least eleven Slavs, eleven Albanians, six Greeks, one Armenian, one Georgian and one Italian). It is also significant that the Ottomans began their momentous conquest of the Arab world only in 1516–17, *after* they had conquered most of the Balkans. The Ottoman Empire was to be based not only on the commonly perceived Moslem conquest of South-eastern Europe but also on a less widely recognized *Balkan* conquest of the major Arab peoples.

As stated earlier, nationalist historians of the Balkan 'nations' and 'proto-nations' paint much blacker pictures of the impact of the Ottoman conquest on South-eastern Europe, none more so than the authors of some of the semi-official pseudo-Marxist 'national' histories published under communist rule. Even though Marxists were supposed to eschew nationalism and ethnocentrism, they often outdid non-Marxist nationalist historians, as part of an endeavour to prove the 'patriotic credentials' of the authors and of their com-munist masters. (This has undoubtedly facilitated the metamorphosis of many former Balkan communists into rabid nationalists, in all too successful attempts to hang on to power, positions and privileges. Indeed, in the case of Serbia an entire communist regime 'metamorphosed' into an equally aggressive and authoritarian nationalist one during the late 1980s and early 1990s.) Hristov is a typical example of this phenomenon: 'Bulgaria's fall under Turkish rule ushered in the grimmest period in the history of the Bulgarian people, a period of almost 500 years of foreign domination. During it, the very existence of the Bulgarians as a nationality was threatened as a result of . . . the brutal oppression and exploitation to which they were subjected by the Turkish conquerors . . . Bulgaria's conquest by the Turks was accompanied by the destruction of whole towns and villages and by an extermination, enslavement and eviction of the population. Hitherto prospering towns and villages were reduced to ruins and the land was turned into a desert. The population of whole regions was forced to seek refuge in the mountains . . . Heavy taxes, duties and fees were also imposed . . . The Turkish conquest led to a decline of crafts and trade . . . Many craftsmen and merchants perished . . . others were sold into slavery . . . The Turkish authorities . . . resorted to violence, bribery and lies to force the Bulgarian population to give up Christianity' (Hristov 1985: 63–5). However, this is a better description of the initial impact of *communist* rule in Bulgaria, as indeed is Hristov's additional comment that 'Many churches and monasteries . . . were destroyed . . . and for a long time it was forbidden to restore the demolished churches . . . The Bulgarian feudal class . . . was annihilated' (p. 65). It is ironic that the Turks were so strongly condemned by communists for (allegedly) pursuing policies which so closely foreshadowed those of the communist regimes after the Second World War.

In most countries, over periods of 500 years, some villages and towns are depopulated and fall into ruin, while others expand or even arise from nothing. But this is a normal response to economic and social change. It is not necessarily evidence of violent destruction and pillage. Significant numbers of Balkan Christians were undoubtedly killed or dispossessed by the Turks for their role in resisting the Ottoman conquest. Yet it should be remembered that for centuries before the Ottomans entered the arena Catholic and Orthodox Christians had been busily killing and forcibly converting each other (as well as non-Christians) in and around the Balkans. There is little evidence that the level of carnage and coercion significantly increased either during or after the establishment of Ottoman rule in the Balkans. On the contrary, it is often argued that the initial 'Pax Ottomanica' represented a marked improvement on the preceding disorder, depredations and internecine conflicts between Christian states (Stavrianos 1958: 99–100, 112–14; Woodhouse 1977: 101, 104, 108).

In the Balkans, on the whole, the early Ottoman rulers adopted 'a chivalrous and tolerant attitude towards the mainly Christian inhabitants of the lands they conquered. Some of these Christians converted to Islam, but even those who did not frequently welcomed the firm justice of Ottoman rule in contrast to the anarchic misgovernment of the decadent Byzantine Empire' (Mansfield 1992: 23). The Balkan Christian princes and nobility were gradually reduced in number, but that came about not so much through 'forced' Turkicization and Islamicization as through 'voluntary' prudential or opportunistic assimilation into the landed seigneurial class of the Ottoman Empire. This often involved voluntary 'conversion' to Islam and/or the adoption of Turkish names, dress, manners and life styles. Mehmed II, however, was determined that the Ottoman Empire would be more than an Islamic and Turkish sultanate. It would also be the heir and successor of Byzantium, the Eastern Roman Empire. The Ottoman Sultans purposefully preserved Constantinople, added to its architectural splendours, repopulated it and made it the capital of their expanding *imperium*. The city's population recovered from under 100,000 in 1453 to between 500,000 and 800,000 in 1600, making it by far the largest city in Europe (Coles 1968: 47). 'Many citizens who had fled before and after the siege returned on the promise of protection to their property and religion' (Stavrianos 1958: 60). Moslem doctrine specifically required (as it still does) political and religious toleration of Christians and Jews as 'peoples of the Book' (the Bible) and as fellow believers in the One God, so long as they did not engage in violent resistance or treachery against Islam (in which case they could legitimately be 'punished'). Moreover, because of their preoccupation with military, territorial and Islamic matters, the Ottoman rulers were willing from the outset to leave much of their empire's important commercial, administrative, political, diplomatic and ecclesiastical business in largely unsupervised Christian hands.

Sultan Mehmed II, who numbered two Christian princesses among his many wives, personally selected a new Christian Patriarch of Constantinople in 1453 (the previous incumbent having fled to Rome in 1451). The new Patriarch, known as Gennadius, was the popular anti-Catholic monk and theologian who had orchestrated Byzantine opposition to the unpopular (and unratified) terms of a reunion of the Churches, negotiated at the Council of Florence in 1439. Gennadius and his followers preferred to submit to the Sultan rather than to accept the vague and elusive support which the Pope and some Catholic states had been prepared to offer in return for abject Byzantine submission to the papacy and Roman Catholicism. That would have been more than most Orthodox Christians could stomach. (It also encouraged the Russians to establish their own Orthodox patriarchate in due course.) Moreover, the Ottomans soon silenced (or drove into exile) the few remaining advocates of the ill-fated reunion of the Churches. It suited the Ottomans to keep the major Christian Churches divided and at each others' throats (though they scarcely needed any encouragement!). Few Orthodox Christians could ever have accepted the arrogantly supremacist Roman Catholic terms for a reunion of the Churches. 'The essence of Orthodox belief was that with the confluence at Constantinople of Roman and Christian theories of terrestrial and celestial empire, the world had achieved its final order . . . Not only . . . was all future improvement or innovation impossible, but also error was unthinkable' (Woodhouse 1977: 30). For Orthodox Christians, Orthodoxy represented a kind of perfection. Any deviation from it was heterodox. Therefore the Orthodox Church could neither submit nor make any concessions to Roman Catholicism and the papacy, whose doctrines were (from the Orthodox standpoint) not just false, but nefarious. The Orthodox Church was (and remains) a profoundly conservative force, fiercely resistant not only to Roman Catholicism but also to the Renaissance, the Reformation and the Scientific Revolution. The fact that the latter had so little impact or resonance in the Ottoman dominions in the Balkans is usually attributed to various alleged effects of Ottoman rule. But the influence of the Orthodox Church and its Byzantine heritage was much more to blame, precisely because it was so much more central to Balkan civilization. Indeed, because late medieval Balkan Orthodox Christendom was convinced that it had combined all that was best in classical Graeco-Roman civilization with the highest and truest form of Christianity, it complacently (and misguidedly) felt no need of a Renaissance or a Reformation or a Scientific Revolution. Through all their afflictions, Balkan Orthodox Christians consoled or deluded themselves that they had already attained unsurpassable religious and cultural perfection.

With Ottoman support, the Constantinople patriarchate was able to arrest the Venetian-backed Roman Catholic 'proselytizing offensive' down the Balkan Adriatic coast, which penetrated as far south as Albania. It was also able to reassert its primacy among Orthodox patriarchates and to reduce the autonomy of the South Slav, Romanian and Albanian Orthodox Churches. These considerable setbacks to the development of separate South Slav, Albanian and Romanian national identities persisted until the re-emergence of autocephalous 'national' Orthodox Churches in the newly independent Balkan states during the nineteenth and early twentieth centuries. Yet 'in the eyes of the Turks, there was no essential difference between Greek and non-Greek Orthodox Christians' (Arnakis 1963: 127), just as most Europeans saw (and perhaps still see) the various Middle Eastern peoples simply as 'Moslems', as a single, largely undifferentiated mass. The Ottomans, therefore, saw no legitimate 'ethnic' or 'proto-national' objection to the extension of the Constantinople patriarchate's jurisdiction over all Balkan Orthodox Christians, or to the (implicit) dominance of Greeks over Albanians, Romanians and South Slavs. Nevertheless, the new Russian Orthodox patriarchate in Moscow remained outside the jurisdiction of the Ottomans and Constantinople. So, when Moscow declared itself to be 'the Third Rome', in succession to Byzantium, it gradually emerged as a rival source of support, religious authority and spiritual leadership for many Balkan Orthodox Christians after the fifteenth century. This continues to be the case today.

For the Ottomans, however, the Constantinople patriarchate was the one that mattered. Mehmed II in person installed the new Patriarch Gennadius 'with full Byzantine ritual and enhanced powers' (Woodhouse 1977: 95). In so doing he signalled his determination to inherit the Byzantine imperial mantle, to respect the customs and sensibilities of his Orthodox Christian subjects and to rule his Balkan domains indirectly, through the Constantinople patriarchate (p. 95). As part of this investiture Mehmed II gave Gennadius an imperial charter, or *berat*, granting the Orthodox Church and the Constantinople patriarchate considerably wider powers, prerogatives and privileges than they had previously been permitted under the Byzantine emperors. The *berat* recognized the Ecumenical Patriarch as the head of the Orthodox *millet* (religious community) and as a high-ranking *pasha* and *vezir* (official) of the Ottoman Empire, 'responsible for all the behaviour and loyalty of all the Sultan's Orthodox subjects' (Sugar 1977: 46). The *berat* gave him and his Synod 'the authority to settle all matters of doctrine, to control and discipline all members of the church, to manage all church property and to levy dues on laity and clergy alike' (Stavrianos 1958: 104). The Orthodox Church and its clergy were exempted from Ottoman taxation and were granted ecclesiastical autonomy (p. 60), but they were in addition given a conspicuous role in 'the assessing and collecting of taxes due to the state' (Sugar 1977: 46). (This sometimes made them unpopular.) The *berat* also promised freedom of conscience and worship. 'Orthodox Christians were free to keep sacred books and icons in their homes and to attend church services unmolested' (Stavrianos 1958: 104). Finally, the *berat* granted the Orthodox Church extensive jurisdiction over civil and family matters, including marriage, divorce and inheritance, since Ottoman family and civil laws were obviously not readily applicable to Christian populations (although Christian imperialists have often overlooked the fact that the reverse is equally true: Christian family and civil laws have not been readily applicable to Moslem populations!).

In due course Orthodox ecclesiastical courts and magistrates came to handle not only family matters but almost all civil litigation between Christians, while 'Orthodox bishops functioned in their dioceses virtually as prefects over the Christian population' (p. 104). In parallel to the Ottoman bureaucracy the Orthodox Church acquired numerous administrative and legal functions (in addition to traditional ecclesiastical ones) and came to see itself as 'a state within a state . . . as the *de facto* ruler and protector of the Christians' (Sugar 1977: 46–7). The Orthodox Church naturally saw itself as the mediator between Orthodox Christians and the Ottoman state and as the sole arbiter and interpreter of Christian interests and aspirations (although many Balkan Christians and nationalists *later* came to see the Church merely as a privileged, servile, venal and corrupt 'collaborator' with an alien 'enemy power' and 'oppressor'). Moreover, some of the Church's civil powers and functions were shared with local (elected) communal authorities in most Balkan villages, for the Ottomans permitted considerable local autonomy. 'Provided the taxes were paid, the Turks did not care what their subjects did with themselves. Local administration, trade and education were entirely their own affair' (Woodhouse 1977: 103–4).

Under Ottoman rule, admittedly, Orthodox Christians were denied civil and religious equality with Moslems and were subject to various disabilities and forms of discrimination: 'Non-Moslems were forbidden to ride horses or to bear arms. They were required to wear a particular costume to distinguish them from the true believers. Their dwellings could not be loftier than those of the Moslems. They could not repair their churches or ring their bells except by special permission . . . They were required to pay a special capitation tax . . . in place of military service. And until the seventeenth century the Orthodox Christians paid the tribute in children, from which Jews and Armenians were exempted' (Stavrianos 1958: 105).

In the eighteenth and nineteenth centuries, when Ottoman discipline and control gradually broke down, the religious toleration and safeguards established by the *berat* given to Gennadius in 1453 were sometimes violated. Then Christians (especially Armenians) became victims of 'outbursts of Moslem fanaticism or arbitrary actions by provincial officials' (Stavrianos 1958: 105), including illegal seizure of Church property and harassment of (sometimes dissident) clergy (p. 105) as well as the genocide perpetrated against Armenian Christians between 1894 and 1918. Nevertheless 'the position of the non-conformist was much more favourable in the Ottoman Empire than in Christian Europe' (p. 90). Indeed, Balkan Christians 'never experienced the persecution that the Moslems and the Jews suffered in Spain' (p. 107) or that the Jews were later to suffer in (Christian) Tsarist Russia and Nazi Germany – except, that is, at the hands of fellow Balkan Christians (for example, in 1941–45 and the early 1990s). The most eloquent testimony to early Ottoman religious toleration came when around 100,000 Sephardic Jews (including merchants, skilled craftsmen and professional men) hounded out of Christian Spain were welcomed into the Ottoman Empire in the late fifteenth and early sixteenth centuries. Spain's economic and cultural loss was the Ottomans' gain, as the Jews went on to play a crucial role in Ottoman commerce, crafts and city life (p. 90). This toleration, 'far ahead' of contemporaneous Christian practice, was 'enlightened statesmanship' (p. 60). As in the case of the Jews, Mehmed II sought to encourage 'his Orthodox subjects to regard him as their benefactor and protector' (p. 90). Indeed, there was much less doctrinal meddling and political interference in Church affairs under the Moslem Sultans than there had been under the overbearing and meddlesome Christian emperors, while Ottoman conquests in the Balkans and the Near East helped to reassert the (hitherto waning) authority of the Constantinople patriarchate over the various Orthodox Churches within Ottoman jurisdiction.

THE ORIGINS AND IMPACT OF THE *MILLET* SYSTEM

The *berat* given to Gennadius in 1453 played a catalytic role in the process by which the Ottoman Empire came to be organized on the basis of *religious* (not ethnic) communities and identities, with a separate religious and civil jurisdiction and legal system for each of the empire's major religious communities (*millets*). This so-called '*millet* system', which is often portrayed as a rigid system of social and religious segregation or 'apartheid', has been the subject of intense historical controversy, comparable to the heated debates over the effects of the caste system in India and of (racial) apartheid in South Africa. It is all too easy to portray the '*millet* system' as the root of all evil in the Balkans and the Near

East or to make it a convenient scapegoat, deflecting 'blame' away from other equally culpable institutions, attitudes, mentalities and policies.

The '*millet* system' has its defenders as well as its detractors. Moreover the word 'system', suggesting something carefully worked out, is somewhat misleading, as the '*millet* system' was never that. It evolved fortuitously, out of a series of *ad hoc* responses to complex situations and problems, and (like South African apartheid) it was always riddled with anomalies and misfits. Furthermore, as stated above, it should be strongly emphasized that the Ottomans merely reinforced and formalized the long-standing primacy of religion (rather than ethnicity) as the principal badge of identity and as the prime focus of community allegiance in the Balkans and the Near East. Yet, while it is important not to exaggerate the specifically Ottoman impact on the Balkans and the Near East, it is necessary to recognize that Ottoman adherence to Islam did complicate matters. It resulted in extensions of the powers and responsibilities of the Christian and Jewish *millets* in ways that would not otherwise have occurred and, in consequence, it increased the elements of rigidity in the '*millet* system' as a whole. In a real sense it extended the remit of religion, with damaging consequences down to the present day.

In Anatolia the absolute foundation stone of Ottoman authority, legitimacy and administration was the Islamic legal code (the *sharia*). It was administered, interpreted and subjected to continuous 'creative adaptation' to changing circumstances by learned Moslem religious scholars-cum-legal experts (the *ulema*, including *muftis*/jurists and *kadis*/judges). The *sharia* was increasingly supplemented by local customary laws (for which the Ottomans showed considerable respect) and by royal decrees (*kanuns*) on matters not covered or inadequately covered by Islamic doctrine (which had originated in very different circumstances several centuries earlier). Yet, since Islam has never recognized any fundamental distinction between the sacred and the secular, Islam remained the ultimate source of all authority and legitimacy in Moslem society. Islam was thus to remain much more dominant and all-pervasive in most Moslem states than Christianity was in the increasingly secular Christian states. Therefore the Ottoman Empire (like many other Moslem states before and since) was slow to develop more secular, universalistic conceptions of law, authority, citizenship and the rights and duties of citizens, which could have encompassed its non-Moslem subjects in a more unified, integrated polity. The Moslem system of legal administration and authority (which underpinned Ottoman rule first in Anatolia and later in the south-eastern Balkans, Bosnia, Albania and the Arab world) was capable of being applied only to predominantly Moslem populations. That did not give rise to many difficulties so long as non-Moslems constituted a dispersed minority of the Sultan's subjects. But it posed major problems for the Ottomans once they had conquered substantial Christian populations in the Balkans and Armenia. However, since the Ottomans subscribed to the Moslem view that authority, law and legitimacy could derive only from divine or religious sanction, they decided to accept and develop different (religiously inspired) legal systems and jurisdictions for *each* of the major religious communities (*millets*) under their rule. Just as Moslems were already subject to Moslem juridical administration and laws, so (from 1453 onwards) the Orthodox Christians were subject to the juridical administration of the Orthodox Church and its Constantinople patriarchate; Armenian Christians were to be subject to the juridical administration of the Gregorian (Armenian) Church and its Armenian Catholicos, and the Jewish religious community (the 'Yahuda *millet*') was to be subject to its own separate religious/juridical administration, with its own elected head (the *Haham basi*). Similar arrangements were later adopted for the much smaller Roman Catholic and Protestant communities, primarily comprising (and catering for) the 'expatriate' foreign merchants resident in the Ottoman Empire. In this way the Christian clergy became a mirror image of the *ulema*, exercising an authority over Christians comparable to that which the legal and theological experts of Islam wielded over Moslems. Conversely, the Sultan imitated Christian practice by organizing a regular hierarchy among the *ulema* and subjecting them to more rigorous government control than any previous Moslem ruler had done (Coles 1968: 30–1).

Almost all societies have largely hereditary forms of social and/or ethnic stratification and class differentiation which erect social barriers to equality of opportunity, social and occupational mobility and the economically optimal division of labour and deployment of talent. But these social structures are usually sufficiently fluid to permit considerable flexibility and social and occupational mobility. The barriers and restrictions have been greatest (and most irksome, frustrating, demoralizing or dispiriting) in systems which have most strictly enforced hereditary status and social, racial or religious segregation. Examples include American slavery, Russian serfdom, South African apartheid, India's caste system and the Ottoman '*millet* system'. Such systems could not but restrict social and occupational mobility, individual motivation, flexibility and overall economic performance (especially productivity), even if the harm is difficult or even impossible to quantify. The Ottoman '*millet* system' clearly comes into this category, even though there was considerable mobility and flexibility *within* each *millet* and despite the fact that the sytem was a not unreasonable *ad hoc* response to the complexities which the Ottomans inherited.

It has been argued that, in the end, 'The Ottoman Empire was enfeebled by its own deliberate policy of isolating from each other the several distinct component cultures. It failed to instill in its diverse subjects a sense of belonging. After the sixteenth century the inherent weaknesses of the Ottoman state stood forth fully revealed, and the empire entered a period of ineluctable decline' (Vucinich 1965: 3). This view is reinforced by Coles (1968: 73): 'The Ottoman Empire . . . was an impressive administrative artifact; but, held apart by religion, its components could never blend into a coherent whole. Such a system of arbitrarily contrived cohabitation was never likely to grow into an organic society. Any faltering or decline in the efficiency of the military establishment by means of which the Turks policed and defended their European empire was bound to reveal its essential disharmony and impermanence.'

On the other hand, it is also possible to take a much more positive view of the role of the Ottoman '*millet* system' in the Balkans. In the opinion of Stavrianos (1958: 114) the Ottomans 'unwittingly strengthened the group solidarity of their subjects' by granting them 'a large measure of communal autonomy' and by enforcing 'regulations separating Moslems from non-Moslems', allowing them 'to practise their faiths and to conduct their communal affairs with a minimum of intervention and taxation' and 'with a degree of peace and security that previously had been conspicuously absent'. Indeed, as is hinted by Stavrianos (1963: 195), the organization of the Ottoman Balkans on the basis of religious (rather than ethnic) affiliation made it possible to unite most of the Ottomans' Balkan subjects into a single Orthodox *millet* and to unite almost all the rest (Turks and most Albanians and Bosnians) into a single Moslem *millet*. Whatever the economic drawbacks, these relatively tidy arrangements based on religious affiliation were far less conducive to inter-communal strife (whether religious or ethnic) than the later organization of the Balkans on the basis of a multiplicity of intermingled and ill-defined 'national' groupings in the wake of the decline of Ottoman control from the late eighteenth century onwards. Over most of the world secularization and the consequent decline of religion ('theocracy') as a politically acceptable basis of social organization have allowed nationalism to fill the political vacuum created by the decline of religious authority ('divine sanction'). But in the Balkans, paradoxically, religion has acquired a more explosive and destructive power in the current 'age of nationalism' than it had in the preceding 'age of theocracy', when religion was more of a unifying force. The contrast has arisen partly because Balkan religions have become suffused and transformed by nationalism.

Furthermore, as argued by the Turkophil and Turcologist Stanford Shaw, geography and historical circumstances had fragmented the Balkans, Anatolia and the Arab lands into an unusually large number of separate (but intermingled) religious, ethnic, social and economic groups with 'little in common aside from a mutual need for some unifying force to provide security and regulate the economic factors on which the livelihood of all depended' (Shaw 1962: 617). These paramount needs forced the diverse groups 'to accept the rule of vast political empires – often the creation of one of them'. But successive empires were forced to accommodate the indelible diversities by maintaining 'communal and local groupings, while throwing . . . only a veneer of unity over the surviving internal disunity'. The Ottomans, by organizing these diverse groups into *millets* and guilds and, 'by writing down and making into law what had previously been . . . customary', gave their Balkan and Middle Eastern subjects a 'means by which they could preserve their traditional institutions and practices under the veneer of a common loyalty to the Sultan' (p. 617). Thus, in their heyday, the Ottomans upheld a political and economic order in which Turks, Arabs, Balkan Christians, Armenians and Jews could peacefully and profitably live and work side-by-side and freely trade with each other to their mutual benefit.

Instead of attempting to impose an Islamic and Turkic uniformity on their various Balkan, Middle Eastern and North African subjects, the Ottomans tolerated and protected religious and cultural diversity and a corresponding diversity of dress, *mores* and social conduct. The differing 'regulations of residence, clothing and social conduct' applied to members of the various *millets* were not 'products of malice or prejudice', but a method of regulating contact between 'persons of different religions, classes and ranks' so as to minimize friction or conflict: 'Each individual had a place in life determined by his class, rank, position and religion. Within the bounds (*hadd*) of this place, he was absolute . . . The whole purpose of the regulations called "discrimination" in the West was to reduce the possibility of friction and to supply visual signs of each person's *hadd*, so that others would know it, treat him in accordance with it and avoid infringing it, at least inadvertently' (Shaw 1962: 619). The rationale was that the only way such diverse and intermingled peoples could live, work and trade together in peace, harmony and prosperity was not by attempting to promote religious and racial assimilation into a common culture and identity (as that was fraught with the danger of endemic religious and racial warfare), but by respecting, protecting and institutionalizing religious, racial and cultural differences.

In reply to Shaw's strong defence of the Ottoman '*millet* system' Vucinich alludes to 'severe constraints' upon the 'freedom' of the members of a *millet* and to the 'economic emasculation' to which *millets* were subjected. 'The *millet* embraced neither a unified territory, nor a homogeneous ethnic group . . . It consisted of widely separated communities, isolated from each other, which enjoyed different social, political and economic privileges and were weakly linked through ecclesiastical administration . . . The *millet* system meant isolation . . . and isolation meant stagnation . . . While the *millet* system . . . enabled the Balkan peoples to preserve their traditions and ethnic individuality, it simultaneously retarded their social development. The rebuilding of their states was [to be] an enormous problem for the Balkan peoples' (Vucinich 1963: 87–8).

The obvious rejoinders to these criticisms are: (1) the '*millet* system' was never intended to prepare the Balkan peoples for independent nation-statehood; (2) the various (inappropriate) attempts (from 1804 to the early 1990s) to carve out nation-states from this ethnic patchwork have resulted in massive bloodshed; (3) the perpetuation of a political order based on religious (*millet*) rather than 'national' (ethnic) affiliations might have avoided the colossal human tragedies which occurred in the Balkans in 1912–18, 1941–45 and the early 1990s. Some (undoubtedly irksome) restrictions and some possible loss of economic efficiency (narrowly defined) would seem to have been a small price to pay for the greater peace and harmony (and hence prosperity) possible under the '*millet* system'. In the Balkan context, tragically, the Western (or Wilsonian) concept of a political order based on 'national' states is a recipe for human catastrophe.

TOWN VERSUS VILLAGE

The biggest change which can be unambiguously attributed to the long-term effects of Ottoman rule in the Balkans was the widespread 'ruralization' or 'pastoralization' of the Christian population (just as the biggest change wrought by communist rule was to be the reverse migration of most Balkan Christians from the countryside to the towns). In large measure it occurred because many urban opponents of Ottoman rule fled to the highlands or were taken captive (often as slaves) or took refuge in the kingdom of Hungary (which included Croatia, the Banat and Transylvania), while many of those who 'collaborated' with the Ottomans were gradually assimilated into the ascendant Moslem military, merchant, tax-collecting, administrative and land holding classes, who tended to congregate for mutual protection in the major Turkish garrison towns. Moreover 'Turks settled in the plains and river basins of the eastern and central Balkans and in the towns of the entire peninsula. Many Slavs abandoned the lowlands to settle in the uplands, where they Slavicized the Vlachs but adopted their pastoral habits' (Stoianovich 1967: 116).

The Ottomans repopulated, renovated and expanded many of the older Balkan towns, such as Adrianople, Monastir (Bitolj), Sofia, Belgrade, Salonika, Skoplje (Uskub), Janina, Mostar, Banja Luka, Hercegnovi, Athens and Philippopolis (Plovdiv). They also established major new towns, including Sarajevo, Travnik, Elbasan, Tirana and Novi Pazar, especially during the sixteenth-century commercial revival (Stoianovich 1960: 242–3; Vucinich 1962: 614). Thereafter, as urban populations became 'predominantly Moslem' and as rural populations became 'predominantly Christian', towns came to be seen as the abode of Moslem rulers, landlords, tax collectors, middlemen and agents of coercion, whereas villages came to symbolize 'the home of the oppressed and exploited Christian peasant, tax payer and food-producer', at least in the eyes of the Balkan Christians (Vucinich 1962: 603). 'The two societal components came to represent a struggle between two ways of life, which deepened and expanded as time went on . . .

After the Ottoman Empire expired, the village–city conflict continued, even though the city lost its Turkish character. This unbridged chasm is one of the major present-day problems' (p. 603). (The accuracy of this observation was to be tragically reconfirmed in the early 1990s, when many of the violent conflicts in former Yugoslavia were, at least initially, not just between Orthodox Serbs, Catholic Croats and Bosnian Moslems, but also between villagers and townspeople – often cutting across the religious and ethnic divide. The outstanding example was the siege of multi-ethnic, cosmopolitan Sarajevo by predominantly rural Bosnian Serbs.)

A further consequence of this town–country antagonism was that throughout the Ottoman period 'peasants were the backbone of the insurrectionary movements against Turkish rule' (Vucinich 1962: 603). Peasants rather than townspeople kept alive oral traditions, Christianity, Christian art and music, epic poetry, folk memories of 'medieval independence and glory, Balkan machismo and "true patriotism"'. Thus the nineteenth-century national revolutions sprang from 'the village and not from the city' (p. 603). It was only in the eighteenth century that South Slavs started to drift into the towns in any number and only in the nineteenth century that they developed their own national bourgeoisies. 'Until then . . . peasants were looked upon as "the real representatives" of the nation' (p. 614).

THE BALKAN CULTURAL 'RETARDATION' DEBATE

The Ottomans have also been accused of retarding the economic and cultural development of their Balkan Christian subjects by neglecting and restricting their educational development: 'The Ottoman Turks were unable to develop a dynamic civilization through an integration of the cultures of the conquered peoples . . . the Ottoman Empire was regulated by "an anti-literate elite" . . . The state did not provide for the enlightenment of the people of non-Moslem *millets*, but discouraged every form of learning . . . To be sure, Greeks, Armenians, Tsintsars and Jews who lived in the major cities were exposed to learning, could study abroad and could buy favours . . . But the rest of the population was driven into the hills and mountains, relegated to the status of peasantry, and cut off from cultural centres' (Vucinich 1962: 610, 635).

Setting aside the habitual exaggeration of the extent to which Balkan Christians were 'driven' into the hills and mountains, such accusations are based upon an anachronistic twentieth-century view of the powers and responsibilities of the state. Most states refused to accept direct responsibility for providing either education or other forms of social investment until the nineteenth century and some did not do so until the twentieth. Indeed, many states viewed mass education with misgivings, fearing that it would equip and encourage people to question and challenge religious and monarchical authority and the political and social *status quo*. Ottoman neglect of direct state provision of education was not untypical of the early modern period the world over. The only major exception occurred in the Germanic and Scandinavian states, influenced by Martin Luther's Protestant doctrine that every (male) Christian should be equipped to read the Bible for himself and to pursue his true 'vocation' in 'this life' to the best of his ability. That was the main reason why Lutheran and Calvinist countries pioneered state provision of mass education, long before the onset of large-scale capitalist industrialization. The extensive literature on the so-called 'Protestant ethic' and the rise of capitalism has tended to miss and to obscure this much more important and distinct advantage of the Lutheran and

Calvinist peoples. But in most countries, at least until the nineteenth century, education was limited to what could be provided by private charitable and (especially) religious institutions. In the Ottoman Empire, therefore, the Moslem *millet* was at least as uneducated and illiterate as the Christian *millets*. As in most states, underprivileged religious groups did not automatically experience educational disadvantage. (In fact discrimination has often spurred a quest for education in order to overcome social disadvantage. Jews came to be among the best-educated religious groups in antisemitic Christian Europe, Parsees became the best-educated Indians, Chinese religious minorities became the best-educated religious groups in South East Asia, Protestant minorities were more educated than their Catholic counterparts in Catholic Christendom and Nonconformists became more educated than Anglicans in England.) Consequently, even if Balkan Orthodox Christians were as educationally and culturally 'retarded' as most critics of Ottoman rule contend, it was due more to the continuing intellectual impoverishment and obscurantism of Orthodox Christianity and the Orthodox Church (which began long before the Ottoman era) than to undeniable Ottoman neglect (and occasional restriction) of educational provision – for Moslems and Jews as well as for Christians. Vucinich (1962: 609) tries to parry widespread criticism of the (Balkan) Orthodox Church by arguing that it 'kept touch with the outside world (the papacy, Venice, Austria and Russia) and facilitated the passage of a small amount of European influence through the Ottoman Curtain' and by blaming the Ottomans for the Church's undeniable decline: 'The long period of restrictive existence and close association with the Ottoman government had . . . a negative effect on the development of the Orthodox Church. Once a source of spiritual strength and intellectual power, the Church began to ossify.' It was 'forced to concern itself primarily with the physical preservation of its members. Theology and learning acquired a secondary importance and in these fields the Church stagnated' (Vucinich 1962: 609–10).

But these superficially plausible arguments do not hold much water. Most Orthodox Christians were at least as uneducated, illiterate and culturally impoverished under the politically independent Orthodox Christian regime in Tsarist Russia as they were under the 'Ottoman yoke' in the Balkans. Moreover, the Ottomans did not impose restrictions on the printing of books in non-Ottoman languages. 'So whatever harmful effects the absence of Ottoman printing may have had, it applied only to the Ottoman reading public, and cannot be used as an excuse for the non-Muslims' failure to take full advantage of the opportunities left to them . . . The question that remains is why Christian *millets* did not develop within the conditions of autonomy left to them. Whatever iron curtain the Ottomans may have erected between themselves and the European Enlightenment . . . much of the Balkan cultural backwardness in Ottoman times came as a result of the extraordinary influence of their own ecclesiastics' (Shaw 1962: 622). Indeed, Stavrianos maintains that: 'The church itself was profoundly hostile to the West.' Patriarch Gennadius and his successors 'opposed the West as the home of Catholicism and Protestantism and as the birthplace of the Renaissance. They rejected everything the Renaissance stood for.' More to the point, Balkan Orthodoxy opposed the West 'not only because it was heretical, but also because it was becoming modern. The inevitable result . . . was the intellectual isolation and stagnation of the Balkan peoples . . . Their intellectual horizon did not extend beyond the concepts of faith and local community affairs. Living in a static and self-contained Orthodox theocracy, they remained oblivious to the new learning, scientific advances and burgeoning of the arts that were transforming and revivifying the Western world' (Stavrianos 1958: 111). 'The iron curtain that cut off the Balkan Christians cannot be exclusively attributed to the Ottoman conquest. The profound anti-Westernism of the Orthodox Church was also responsible' (Stavrianos 1963: 186).

Despite the many accusations levelled against Ottoman rule in the Balkans, Stavrianos (1958: 107–8) plays down the magnitude of the Ottoman impact: 'The Turks had little influence on Balkan culture. One reason was that they were separated from their subjects by religious and social barriers. Another was that the Turks resided mostly in the towns . . . The superficiality of Turkish influence allowed the Balkan peoples to develop their cultures freely.' This was partly because 'the Turkish people were a minority in their empire and, furthermore, a minority whose energies were concentrated . . . upon war and conquest' (p. 91). Indeed, as late as June 1914 there were only about 2 million Turks resident in the Balkans, 1 million in and around Constantinople and another million scattered over other parts (p. 97). Moreover, for most of the time the Ottomans had 'less trouble ruling their Christian subjects . . . than their Moslem subjects' (p. 112). Ottoman institutions later 'deteriorated and became corrupt and oppressive. But in doing so Ottoman rule became less dangerous for the Balkan peoples. It did not threaten their national identities and cohesiveness. Its inefficiency and flabbiness eliminated the possibility of denationalization' (p. 113). In these respects Ottoman overlordship was less of a threat to existing cultural identities in the Balkans than was subsequent Tsarist and Germanic imperialism to those in East Central Europe.

3   The seeds of Ottoman decline

The Ottoman Empire had its heyday in the sixteenth century, during which it not only conquered most of the Arab Moslem world, most of Hungary (including Croatia and Transylvania), Azerbaijan, Georgia and numerous Mediterranean islands but also inflicted heavy naval defeats on Venice, Genoa and Spain. In 1521 the capture of Belgrade, the major fortress at the confluence of the middle Danube and several important tributaries, opened the way to the conquest of Hungary (1526–44) and an unsuccessful siege of Vienna (1529) by Sultan Suleiman 'the Magnificent' (1520–66). The Austrian Habsburgs refused to renounce their rival claim to the Hungarian throne (vacant since the decisive Ottoman victory over the Hungarians at the battle of Mohacs in 1526). But in Austria the Ottomans encountered an opponent displaying a more tenacious 'will and capacity to resist' and, with over-extended supply lines, the Ottomans were 'campaigning at the limit of their operational capacity' (Coles 1968: 82–7, 103). Indeed, from the 1530s onwards the Austrians encouraged and assisted Orthodox Serb refugees from Ottoman-ruled Serbia to settle in a semi-autonomous 'Military Frontier' zone (known as the 'Vojna Krajina' in Serbo-Croat) along the shifting border between the Habsburg and Ottoman dominions (and also, not unrelatedly, between Catholic and Orthodox Europe). Over several centuries this contributed to the growth of belligerent Serb populations in Croatia and Vojvodina (then part of southern Hungary). That was how the so-called 'Krajina' ('Frontier') region of Croatia came to be populated largely by Serbs. It was also the origin of the gradual Serbianization of Vojvodina, which has continued to unnerve and alienate the remaining Hungarian inhabitants, who now feel that they are an underprivileged Catholic minority discriminated against in 'their' province.

OTTOMAN STRENGTHS AND LIMITATIONS

In its prime the vigour and dynamism of the Ottoman Empire and the numerical superiority and valour of its armed forces continually expanded its frontiers and the opportunities for plunder, promotion and personal enrichment. Thus careers 'wide open to talent projected a succession of outstandingly able men to the summit of power' (Coles 1968: 54–5). The Ottomans were still strong enough to mount a sixty-day second siege of Vienna (again unsuccessful) in 1683. Their European territory reached its maximum extent as late as 1676 (p. 160), while their Arab Moslem dominions in Asia and North Africa went on expanding (albeit fitfully) during the eighteenth century. Moreover, so long as the empire seemed invincible the Balkans gave the Ottomans no real trouble.

Indeed, as part of a successfully expanding empire, the Balkan population enjoyed a period of relative peace and harmony and incurred comparatively low fiscal and 'feudal' exactions. Nevertheless, the seeds of decline had already been sown. 'Ottoman militarism was combined with a contempt for industry and commerce. The consequence was that when the empire was still in its heyday it was already being overtaken in material strength by the more innovative . . . economies of the Christian European states' (Mansfield 1992: 32). Within the Ottoman Empire industry and trade 'were left to the non-Muslim conquered subjects . . . Thus the stigma of the infidel became attached to the professions which the infidels followed, and remained so after many of the craftsmen had become Muslim . . . Christians, bankers, merchants and craftsmen were all involved in the general contempt which made the Ottoman Muslim impervious to ideas or inventions of Christian origin and unwilling to bend his own thoughts to the problems of artisans and vile mechanics' (Lewis 1961: 35).

Until the early sixteenth century, however, the Ottomans had remained quite receptive to new foreign ideas, products and technologies (from the Orient as well as from Europe). They had been quick to assimilate European advances in the design, production and deployment of artillery, smaller firearms and ships. As already mentioned, several Sultans had married (or were sons or grandsons of) Christian princesses. They were in close contact with Europe and their dominions were almost as 'European' as they were 'Asiatic'. Sultan Mehmed II even discussed theology with Patriarch Gennadius and invited him to write a tract explaining Christianity (Stavrianos 1958: 60). Indeed, the secret of the early Ottomans' success lay in 'their remarkable powers of assimilation . . . for, having no identity beyond that of a fighting force loyal to a particular commander, nothing was alien to them except peace' (Coles 1968: 71). Nor were they wholly unaffected by the enquiring humanistic spirit of the Renaissance (Stavrianos 1958: 131–2).

Their successors, nevertheless, were to be much less receptive and open-minded, partly as a result of the Ottoman conquest of the Arab Moslem heartlands in 1516–17. This increased the weight and influence of the conservative Moslem *ulema* and other specifically Moslem interests in what became an increasingly Islamic empire. Significantly, the Ottomans' conquests in the Middle East and North Africa were primarily precipitated by a determination to suppress a heterodox Shia rebellion in Anatolia in 1514. That prompted a punitive Ottoman offensive against the new Shia empire established in Persia and Mesopotamia (Iraq) by Ismail Safavi, the leader of a Shia sect and founder of Persia's Safavid dynasty (1500–1736). This in turn initiated over 200 years of intermittent warfare between the Ottomans and Persia. The Ottomans then conquered Mamluk Syria, Palestine, Egypt and western Arabia in 1516–17 in order to pre-empt a potential alliance between Egypt's Mamluk Sultan and Safavid Persia, while the subsequent Ottoman conquest of North Africa (excluding Morocco) forestalled the growth of the Shia state established by the Sadi Sharifs in Morocco in 1511 (incidentally bringing the Ottomans into protracted naval conflict with Christian Spain, which had finally been freed from the last vestiges of Moslem rule in 1492).

Therefore, in so far as the Ottoman Sultans won any support among their new Arab Moslem subjects, it was mainly as conservative upholders of Sunni Moslem orthodoxy (and conformity) against Shia Moslem heterodoxy and subversion. Furthermore, as a result of the Turkish conquest of the Arab Moslem heartlands in 1516–17, the Ottoman Sultan naturally became the 'Protector of the Holy Places' of Islam (Mecca, Medina,

Jerusalem and Hebron) and the 'Caliph of Islam', although only the last few Sultans made full use of the latter title in (unsuccessful) attempts to reverse or arrest the disintegration of their (by then) enfeebled empire. But their new custodial role in the Islamic world would restrict the Ottomans' future room to manoeuvre in such matters as institutional reform, education, censorship, the assimilation of Western ideas and knowledge, external relations and treatment of non-Moslems. Thus the Ottomans were able to accept Western-style weapons and ships, as these could be employed in the service of Islam against 'infidels'. But 'printing and clocks could not be accepted, for they served no such purpose, and might flaw the social fabric of Islam' (Lewis 1961: 41). This increasing 'Islamicization' of the Ottoman Empire inevitably reinforced the 'wide and unbridgeable gulf between the Ottomans and their Christian subjects' (Coles 1968: 73). Despite their laudable tolerance towards Orthodox Christians, the Ottomans could never accept them as equal partners and there was no mutual bond based upon shared beliefs and objectives.

Following the violent suppression of open manifestations of Shia heterodoxy in 1514–28, 'most Shia sympathizers on Ottoman territory reverted to their traditional ruse of outward conformity to Sunni practices' (Coles 1968: 67). The Ottomans mainly contented themselves with strengthening the hierarchical organization of the *ulema*, upholding strict Sunni Moslem orthodoxy and mobilizing Sunni Moslem support for further warfare against Shia Persia and Roman Catholic Europe. Unfortunately, such responses 'froze the intellectual life of the Ottoman Empire'. Instead of confronting the challenges to Sunni Islam intellectually, Turkish Moslems found it expedient 'to fall back on officially approved conformity and occasional persecution' (p. 68). At first this facade of Moslem unity and conformity in the Ottoman Empire contrasted favourably with the religious ferment, disunity and sectarian strife of Reformation Europe. In the long run, however, the contrast was to work in Europe's favour. The heated debates and 'mutual vituperation' between (and within) the Christian Churches and sects occasionally engendered a level and form of intellectual discourse and enquiry which had no parallel in the Ottoman Empire. Moreover, Ottoman rejection of any departure from 'strictly traditional' Sunni Moslem ideas, idioms and precepts would allow Europe to 'outstrip' the Turks and the Arabs in field after field (p. 68). The central Islamic lands became trapped in 'a revived and intolerant orthodoxy whose champions were increasingly impervious to external stimuli' (p. 62).

The early sixteenth-century convulsions in the Moslem world thus caused the Ottomans to abandon their former eclecticism in favour of a 'particularly rigid and exclusive Sunni orthodoxy' (Coles 1968: 72). A hitherto 'restless and fluid society' was soon subjected to 'the discipline of a conservative system of Moslem instruction and belief' (p. 74). Flushed with military success and 'sublime smugness *vis-à-vis* both heretics and unbelievers', the Ottomans 'increasingly neglected those elements in the intellectual heritage of Islam which might have enabled them to keep pace with . . . Europe' (p. 75).

Ottoman failure to meet internal and external cultural and intellectual challenges with anything more than 'strident reaffirmation' of Sunni orthodoxy encouraged Sunni Moslems to feel that 'uncritical acceptance of religious truth was the only safe and convenient intellectual posture. But, in the absence of controversy, intellectual vigour faded . . . This stagnation was a high price to pay for the suppression of heresy' (Coles 1968: 75). For most Moslems, Europe became 'an outer darkness of barbarism and unbelief, from which the sunlit world of Islam had nothing to learn and little to fear' (Lewis 1961: 34). Dazzled by the initially impressive military might of the Ottoman Empire, they clung too long to 'the dangerous but comfortable illusion of the immeasurable and immutable superiority of their own civilization' (p. 35). In addition, the Moslem doctrine of 'successive revelation' (the belief that God was revealed *fully* and *finally* only to the Prophet Mohammed, superseding previous revelations to the Jewish and Christian prophets) encouraged Moslems to discount Western thought and civilization as the product of earlier (and therefore imperfect and incomplete) Christian revelations (p. 40).

In various ways, therefore, Ottoman adherence to and enforcement of rigid Sunni Moslem orthodoxy had a stultifying effect on the empire. Coles (1968: 117) argues that its subjects were 'imprisoned within a social and political system which lacked the capacity for sustained development; whose values were fundamentally uncritical and uncreative; and whose elites found it impossible to advance beyond . . . violent and voluptuous parasitism'. As argued by Stavrianos (1958: 90), 'Ottoman culture was far from being scanty or inferior', yet 'it cannot be placed in the first rank of civilizations. It lacked the originality of a truly great civilization.'

THE WANING OF THE OTTOMAN EMPIRE

The scope and structure of this book preclude a full account of the resultant military, economic and cultural decline and territorial contraction of the Ottoman Empire. They also make it difficult to do justice to the rich literature and debates on the causes and consequences of these momentous processes. It will, therefore, be possible only to highlight some of the landmarks, determinants and repercussions and to sample some additional explanations.

Following the failure of the second Ottoman siege of Vienna in 1683 the Austrian Habsburgs launched a counter-offensive. They and their allies advanced deep into Ottoman territory in Hungary and Greece and on the Black Sea coast. The Ottomans were decisively defeated at the second battle of Mohacs in 1687 and at Zenta in 1697. Thereupon Hungary, Croatia and Transylvania were to come under Austrian Habsburg control. The ensuing peace treaty of Karlowitz (1699) was the first that the Ottoman Empire had ever had to sign as the defeated party, ceding extensive territories, long under Ottoman rule and regarded as part of the House of Islam, to the infidel enemy (Lewis 1961: 36). 'The Treaty of Karlowitz marked a final, decisive turning point in the military balance between Europe and the Islamic world . . . After Karlowitz the Turkish empire found itself on the defensive, seldom able to equal the strength of any European power' (Coles 1968: 195). The Austrian Empire had emerged as the dominant power in East Central Europe and was poised to encroach upon the Ottomans' Balkan dominions. Europe would never again be threatened by the Turkish menace. On the contrary, Europe henceforth faced 'the so-called Eastern Question, created by the recession of Ottoman power'. This gradually produced a power vacuum in the Near East 'and one of the basic problems of European diplomacy until the end of World War I was how to fill this vacuum' (Stavrianos 1958: 177). Ironically this growing European concern signalled the gradual acceptance of Turkey as a *European* power, albeit as 'the sick man of Europe'.

Austria completed its conquest of Hungary and captured most of Serbia (including Belgrade) and parts of Bosnia and Wallachia in 1716–17. These gains were ratified by the

Treaty of Passarowitz (Pozarevec) in 1718. But the Ottomans would have incurred even greater territorial losses in 1697–99 and 1716–18 if there had not been continuing quarrels and divisions among the European powers. These enabled the Ottomans to recover some ground in the Balkans in 1736–39 and subsequently to be 'left in peace' for three decades. From 1768 onwards, however, that peace was to be repeatedly broken by the emergence of an even greater threat to the Ottoman Empire, namely the rapid extension of imperial Russia's power and influence into the Balkans, the Black Sea region and Transcaucasia. This was combined with growing Russian support for fellow Orthodox Slav Christians in Montenegro, Serbia and Bulgaria and, more erratically, for Greek, Romanian and Georgian Orthodox and Armenian 'Gregorian' Christians (that is, so long as they remained under Ottoman rule; thereafter Russian 'concern' waned). The Turks were to be repeatedly defeated by the Russians on all three fronts from 1768 to 1919. Thus Russia gained control of most of the Black Sea steppes in 1768–74, the Crimea, the Kuban and the Black Sea itself in 1782–83, the rest of the Black Sea steppes in 1787–92, (independent) northern Azerbaijan in 1806–28, eastern Moldavia ('Bessarabia') in 1806–12 and most of Caucasian Armenia in 1827–28. In addition Russia gained a kind of commercial 'most favoured nation' status and a virtual 'protectorate' over Orthodox Christians throughout the Ottoman Empire in 1774. This encouraged Russian imperialists to dream of 'recapturing' Constantinople for Orthodox Christendom, especially in the 1780s and 1870s and again in 1915. More positively Russo-British military intervention secured Greek independence from Turkey in the late 1820s, while Russia's major victories over the Turks in 1876–78 gained full independence for Serbia, Montenegro and Romania and virtual independence for Bulgaria from 1878 onwards. But how did this sorry story of Ottoman decline and retreat come about?

Competing explanations of the Ottoman decline

Many historians have argued that the factors or processes which had initially sustained or contributed to Ottoman power and territorial expansion ceased to operate once the empire stopped expanding or reached the (notional) 'natural limits' of its expansion, and finally operated in reverse when the empire began to contract. 'The Ottoman systems of military organization, civil administration, taxation and land tenure were all geared to the needs of a society expanding by conquest and colonization into the lands of the infidel. They ceased to correspond to the different stresses of a frontier that was stationary or in retreat' (Lewis 1961: 27). Similarly, according to Woodhouse (1977: 114), 'The Turkish system was wholly unsuited to a settled way of life. Its merits were those of a machine for waging permanent war and maintaining permanent expansion. Only such a condition could provide the supply of slaves needed to man the administration and the forces and the booty and tax revenue necessary to support them . . . Both at the centre and at the periphery the system began to break down as the momentum of conquest became exhausted.' Therefore, since lengthening lines of supply, chains of command and channels of communication meant that the empire could not continue to expand indefinitely, 'it contained within it the seeds of its own decay' (p. 100). Eventually a vicious circle was set in motion: 'Inefficiency bred oppression, and oppression inefficiency' (p. 115).

Jones (1981: 185) gives the familiar theme a different twist: 'The Ottoman state was a plunder machine which needed booty or land to fuel itself, to pay its way, to reward its officer class . . . With military expansion brought to a halt, the state came under severe stress. Revenues sank and the army and navy could not be properly maintained, which in turn reduced military options. The system turned to prey on itself.' Moreover, while the zone of depredation shifted from the empire's borderlines to its core territories, the strain imposed upon Ottoman institutions by the cessation of territorial expansion and the decline in booty income engendered mounting political instability and disorder (Coles 1968: 170).

Kennedy (1989: 13) argues that by the late sixteenth century 'the empire was showing signs of strategical overextension, with a large army stationed in central Europe, an expensive navy operation in the Mediterranean, troops engaged in North Africa, the Aegean, Cyprus and the Red Sea, and the reinforcements needed to hold the Crimea against a rising Russian power. Even in the Near East . . . the Sultan could maintain his dominions only by crushing Shi'ite dissidents by force.' Responsibility for over-extending the Ottoman Empire surely fell primarily on Sultan Suleiman 'the Magnificent' (1520–66), the last 'great' Sultan. Although his apologists can argue that circumstances compelled him to act resolutely, he could have responded with greater caution and restraint. 'The structure of the empire was highly centralized, and therefore became increasingly difficult to operate as its territory grew' (Woodhouse 1977: 100). By the seventeenth century it had become 'too large to be administered by so centralized a government as the Sultanate necessarily was' (p. 114). Central control broke down, leading to widespread anarchy and local usurpation of political power. Yet any move formally to devolve power to the empire's constituent territories could only have accelerated the incipient imperial disintegration.

Imperial over-extension also became a burdensome economic drain. 'Ottoman imperialism, unlike that of the Spanish, Dutch and English, did not bring much in the way of economic benefit' (Kennedy 1989: 13). Islamic doctrine inhibited Ottoman fiscal exactions in the Arab Moslem domains. There were initial 'spoils of war' from the conquest of Hungary, but Ottoman pillage devastated and depopulated the Hungarian economy (Sugar 1977: 284; Coles 1968: 87). This drastically reduced its capacity to provide longer-term revenue. But economic development was impaired, above all, by the voracious demands and ambitions of the army. 'The agricultural surplus over subsistence needs that is the first prerequisite of modern growth was mortgaged to maintaining the large military establishment needed to expand the empire' (Lampe and Jackson 1982: 22). Thus by 1600 the share of military expenses in central government expenditure had risen from a modest 10 per cent to about 50 per cent (p. 26). This bears out the claim made by Vucinich (1962: 635) that the Ottoman system was more concerned with 'warfare' than with 'welfare'.

In western and central Europe the growth of bureaucracy and representative government was diminishing the importance and influence of monarchs. But the Ottoman state, essentially a war machine, remained unusually dependent on the calibre of its Sultans. 'For two and a half centuries a remarkable succession of ten outstanding rulers led the empire from victory to victory' (Stavrianos 1958: 118). But their successors included an astonishing number of 'incompetents, degenerates and misfits' (Lewis 1961: 23). This striking contrast has often been attributed to major changes in Ottoman customs. It had long been the practice for each incoming Sultan to have all his brothers and half-brothers murdered. (Ottoman polygamy ensured that they were numerous.) This ruthlessness reduced the risk of contested successions, political instability, civil war and biological in-breeding while ensuring that there were regular infusions of 'new blood' to replace the 'spillages'. From the early seventeenth century onwards, however, this barbaric custom was replaced by the confinement of all royal princes, with the exception of the sons of the reigning Sultan, to the royal harem under the watchful eye of royal eunuchs. 'Inevitably, they became mental and moral cripples' (Stavrianos 1958: 118). The harm thus inflicted on the dynasty was compounded by a change in the succession law in 1617. Henceforth the throne was to pass to the eldest male member of the royal family. 'This meant that future Sultans were to be drawn . . . from the brothers, uncles and cousins, who had passed their lives in . . . degenerating seclusion . . . It was only natural that they should continue to depend on the peculiar companions of their boyhood. These . . . now became imperial favourites, using the puppet sultans as tools . . . Ottoman history henceforth was the history of endless strife between various individuals and cliques' (pp. 118–19). Confinement of royal princes to the royal harem remained Ottoman practice until the nineteenth century, by which time it was too late to repair the harmful consequences of this infamous custom.

Histories of the Ottoman Empire have traditionally made great play with an alleged transformation of the land holding system and rural social structure of the Balkan provinces between *c.* 1600 and *c.* 1800 as a major explanation of imperial decline. When the empire was first established almost all land became (in law) the property of the Ottoman Sultans, who parcelled it out on temporary (i.e. conditional) tenure to their vassals and 'sipahi' (cavalry officers) in the form of 'timars' (often translated as 'military fiefs') in return for continuing loyal service. As late as the 1528 census 87 per cent of Ottoman territory was the property of the Sultan (Lampe and Jackson 1982: 24). Much of the rest belonged to religious bodies, so there was hardly any hereditary private ownership of land. The 'sipahi' could demand about three days' labour *per year* from peasants resident in their 'timars' (as against the two or three days *per week* demanded by Balkan lords in the late medieval Christian states). They were also allowed to collect 10–20 per cent of the harvest (towards the upkeep of their cavalry horses in the service of the Sultan) and to collect certain taxes (primarily the poll tax on adult non-Moslem males, levied in lieu of military service). This was the initial (successful) socio-economic basis of the Ottoman 'war machine'. Indeed, 'the force and extent of command from above was too powerful during the sixteenth century to permit local notables to carve out feudal and other customary rights for themselves' (Lampe and Jackson 1982: 23).

According to the conventional wisdom, this system underwent very detrimental changes after *c.* 1600. First, the 'sipahi' became militarily obsolete and superfluous. Consequently, Ottoman territorial expansion slowed down and from the 1690s went into reverse. This encouraged the militarily obsolete 'sipahi', along with other Ottoman servitors, to turn away from the (arrested) acquisition of new 'timars' for themselves and their sons through conquest to the conversion of their existing 'timars' and other land holdings into hereditary privately owned estates ('chifliks'). They turned from preying upon the Sultan's external foes to preying upon his unfortunate subjects. The attractions of private land holding were greatly enhanced by the rising urban and European demand for food, raw cotton and tobacco, accompanied by rocketing grain and land prices. Consequently, landholders renounced their former military traditions and vocation in favour of increasingly ruthless and mercenary 'exploitation' of the land and its cultivators. It was aided by the accompanying decline of central control, which not only reduced the state's capacity to restrain 'feudal' and fiscal excesses and extortion and private usurpation of state and/or peasant land, but even encouraged state officials to 'get in on the act' and pocket most of the proceeds, to the detriment of both the Ottoman treasury and the increasingly impoverished peasantry. Gradually many 'chiflik' holders emerged as rich and powerful magnates. They increasingly usurped provincial authority, becoming virtual kings of their own domains and a law unto themselves, contributing to the growing anarchy, lawlessness, banditry, insecurity and protection-racketeering in the Ottoman dominions during the eighteenth century.

According to more recent agrarian research, however, the growth and significance of the 'chiflik' system have been greatly exaggerated. It was largely absent from Serbia, Montenegro and Romania; in Bulgaria it 'covered just 20 per cent of the cultivated land in the regions where it was most widespread and as little as 5 per cent elsewhere' (Lampe and Jackson 1982: 34–7); no more than 10 per cent of Bulgarian peasants were subject to the 'chiflik' system; and the typical 'chiflik' in southern Bulgaria, north-eastern Greece and Macedonia, where the terrain was most suitable for arable farming, was little more than fifteen to thirty acres (6–12 ha) (pp. 34–7). Thus the typical 'chiflik' was no bigger than the average Russian peasant holding and most Balkan peasants remained relatively free of specifically 'seigneurial' or 'feudal' forms of oppression in the eighteenth and nineteenth centuries. The growing power and income of provincial 'notables' and prominent officials stemmed not so much from changes in land holding as from fiscal extortion, protection rackets, bribery and embezzlement, facilitated by the decline in central control over provincial servitors and tax collection and the ensuing growth of Ottoman reliance on tax-farmers (p. 37).

The effects in terms of depriving the state and the peasantry of income were probably just as detrimental as those of the alleged changes in land holding and rural social structure would have been. But the root causes of the economic and fiscal damage were not the ones traditionally alleged. On the contrary, far from *facilitating* the establishment and consolidation of private property in land, the ensuing conditions of anarchy, insecurity and lawlessness actually *impeded* the development of private property and enterprise, contributing to the increasing economic 'backwardness' of the Balkans *vis-à-vis* Western and Central Europe. A mitigating 'social advantage' was that when the Balkan countries gained independent statehood in the nineteenth and twentieth centuries they did not inherit strongly entrenched landed aristocracies and they were therefore able to develop relatively egalitarian societies. On the other hand, the conditions just described also contributed to the deeply entrenched traditions of corruption, extortion, embezzlement, bribery, protection-racketeering and lawlessness which continue to afflict public life in the Balkans to this day (see, for example, Sugar 1977: 287–8). (After 1989 the former communist 'nomenklatura' in effect often helped themselves to state property. Controls had to be introduced to regulate changes in ownership.)

Furthermore, according to Lampe and Jackson (1982: 37–8, 48–9), the total population of the Ottoman Balkans was catastrophically reduced from at least 8 million in 1600 to less than 3 million by 1750. This was the result of growing anarchy, lawlessness, insecurity, impoverishment, epidemics and the attendant mass migration of peasants from fertile but exposed lowlands to the relative safety of remote but infertile highlands and of neighbouring states. If they have been accurately assessed, migration and depopulation of such proportions can only have caused a crippling contraction of the economic and fiscal base of the Ottoman state, severely reducing its capacity to wage war against the increasingly powerful Habsburg and Tsarist empires. Unfortunately, it is not clear to what extent these population estimates were directly or indirectly influenced by (or derived from) apocalyptic Balkan nationalist and/or communist portrayals of the impact of Ottoman rule on the peninsula. In other words, were they based on sober and detached calculations by disinterested parties? There has been insufficient discussion or evaluation of the sources and methods used in reaching these pivotal population estimates or of how much credence they can be given.

The seventeenth-century reversal of Ottoman military fortunes was attributable to exogenous as well as endogenous factors. Above all, the Thirty Years' War (1618–48) had familiarized East Central Europe with new forms of military organization and technology, especially the use of light, mobile, powerful and accurate Swedish and Dutch artillery in support of highly trained, well equipped, mobile, versatile and strongly disciplined professional infantry. This combination (comparable to the development of the *Blitzkrieg* during the Second World War) could defeat even the most massive cavalry charge. This rendered the Ottoman 'sipahi' largely redundant or obsolete. Likewise, the Ottomans' massive and unwieldy cannons and bombards, ideal for laying siege to heavily fortified towns, were insufficiently mobile, accurate or versatile in support of infantry attacks. Moreover, the main body of Ottoman infantry, the infamous janissaries ('yeni-cheris' or 'new troops') were degenerating into increasingly corrupt and conservative part-time soldiers with extensive 'business interests'. This happened because the increasingly cash-strapped Ottoman rulers had imprudently permitted the janissaries to engage in privileged business 'sidelines' in order to supplement their rapidly depreciating state stipends. The result was that the janissaries' 'business interests', including many monopolies and extortion or protection rackets, began to come before their military responsibilities (Lewis 1961: 30; Coles 1968: 186–91; Stavrianos 1958: 121–3).

In addition, the new techniques of warfare were fearfully expensive. In real terms the cost of waging war rose at least sixfold between 1500 and 1650. This escalation of military costs naturally favoured the emergence of the four major European 'land powers' with strong tax-collecting bureaucracies (first France, later Austria, then Russia and finally Prussia/Germany), as they alone were fully able to meet the escalating cost. Weaker states, such as Poland, Hungary, Bohemia and the Italian city-states, were slowly swallowed up by these emerging 'superstates'. But, as indicated earlier, the Ottomans had never developed very effective revenue-raising machinery, partly because they had all too successfully relied on plunder and pillage from the fourteenth century to the sixteenth. They failed to perceive the advantages of higher regular taxation until the seventeenth century, by which time powerful vested interests were either opposed to such taxes or determined to pocket the proceeds for their own personal enrichment. 'Plunder . . . was no longer available in sufficiently large quantities or regular instalments to sustain the laborious enterprise of recruiting, training, paying, feeding and equipping a large army . . . The systematic rape of frontier areas enabled sixteenth-century Ottoman forces to live adequately off the land. This was no longer a possibility for seventeenth-century armies, which were often three or four times as large and operating in . . . depopulated countryside' (Coles 1968: 188, 191). The new warfare also depended on the emergence of sophisticated and expensive new munitions industries and supply systems, which the Ottoman Empire was slow to develop. The artisans of Constantinople were 'skilled and numerous, but hidebound and suspicious of innovation'. Moreover, their restrictive craft guilds were also affiliated to the janissaries, 'whose jealous determination to preserve their traditional military techniques led them to reject all suggestions in military technology'. By contrast, the Austrian Habsburgs could call on the metallurgical skills of Central Europe and were 'well placed to procure the elaborate and constantly changing equipment required for effective warfare' (p. 191).

Another, not unrelated, shortcoming of the seventeenth-century Ottoman state was its failure to emulate the French, Dutch and British by forging close alliances with rich merchants and bankers (Coles 1968: 190). The Austrian Habsburgs (and later the Prussian Hohenzollerns) did so as part of their crucial operations to meet the fast-growing financial requirements of the state (imparting new impetus to the development of capitalism), but the Ottomans did not. The Ottoman Empire had some rich merchants and bankers, but 'they were never able to play anything like the financial, economic and political role of their European counterparts', mainly because most of them 'were Christians or Jews – tolerated but second-class subjects of the Muslim state' (Lewis 1961: 31). Despite their wealth they were 'socially segregated; they could obtain political power only by stealth, and exercise it only by intrigue'. Consequently they were not able to establish political conditions more favourable to commerce; nor could they build a solid and stable foundation of banking and credit to bail the Ottoman state out of 'its perennial financial straits' (p. 32).

These deficiencies contributed to the gradual transformation of the Ottoman Empire and the Balkan 'successor states' into financial and commercial 'dependencies' or 'appendages' of Europe's advanced capitalist states. They became increasingly passive providers of food and raw materials to Western and Central European towns and industries and of outlets for Western and Central European manufactured goods and capital. By the nineteenth century, moreover, the Ottoman Empire had become what would now be called a 'Third World debtor state', constantly in danger of having to default on its increasingly onerous foreign debt and debt-service payments (as it actually did in 1875). This was to have the usual deleterious and demoralizing effect on investors' and business confidence, encouraging Balkan and 'foreign' capitalists alike to concentrate on short-term and/or speculative commodity and property dealings rather than longer-term productive and infrastructural ventures.

Mansfield (1992: 27) argues that the root problem of the Ottoman Empire was that the institutions it created (while initially effective) 'could not be developed and transformed to meet changing needs and circumstances'. Until the nineteenth century key institutions such as the janissaries, the *ulema*, the sultanate, the royal household, the 'Ruling Institution' and the '*millet*' system, all proved remarkably resistant to reform. 'Attempts to reform and revive the empire actually contributed to its break-up and decline' (p. 27). The Ottomans were indeed prisoners of their past. They eventually perceived the need for military, institutional and economic reforms, but the vested interests threatened by reform (and on whom the Ottomans were to some extent dependent for social, political or religious support) insisted that what was needed was stricter observance of past precedents and practices. In contrast to the Tsarist empire under Peter the Great (1689– 1725) and the more intelligent of his successors (Elizabeth, Catherine II, Alexander II), the Ottomans never managed to remodel themselves on supposedly Western patterns, because they were more constrained by their (hitherto 'successful') religion, because they could look back on a greater imperial past from which it was harder to escape and because 'no Peter the Great came to the Ottoman throne who was willing . . . to use the autocratic powers of his office for revolutionary purposes' (Coles 1968: 185, 172). Moreover, according to Mansfield (1992: 39), increasing Western penetration of the Ottoman

Empire had 'little effect on the minds and beliefs of Muslims . . . Secure in the knowledge of the superiority of Islam, they showed no interest in the ways of non-Muslim peoples.' This was in marked contrast to the first Moslem empires 'which had not hesitated to benefit from the wisdom and knowledge of other civilizations'. The only serious attempts to copy Western and Central European advances were in the military and naval fields, including mathematics, navigation and cartography, but the effect was 'entirely superficial'.

Until the nineteenth century the Ottomans continued to cling to the crumbling pillars of an outmoded social order which was well past its 'sell-by date'. Furthermore, when the Ottoman state attempted to reform itself in the nineteenth century, it was more concerned with promoting stronger, more efficient and (increasingly) authoritarian government than with stimulating independent local initiative and enterprise. In failing to foster an 'enterprise culture', and by attempting to maintain a 'paternal' state, it was still unable to emulate the successes of its major European rivals. State tutelage can be only as effective as the state that exercises it.

Natural, environmental and locational factors

In order to gain a fuller and more balanced understanding of the reasons for the military, economic and cultural 'decline' and 'retardation' of the Ottoman Empire and the Balkans (relative to Western and Central Europe), it is also necessary to look beyond narrowly institutional and cultural factors. Under Ottoman rule the predominantly Moslem and the predominantly Orthodox Christian areas of the Balkans undoubtedly lagged behind the economic, educational and cultural development of Western and Central Europe. But it does not follow that Ottoman rule was solely responsible. The predominantly Roman Catholic areas of the Balkans, which were mostly under Austro-Hungarian rule, also lagged behind Western and Central Europe in most respects, although they did develop more vigorously than the Moslem and Orthodox Christian areas. Moreover, as already mentioned, the Orthodox Christians of Russia also lagged far behind Western and Central Europe, albeit under the strong and independent Orthodox Christian Tsarist regime. Comparisons of this sort suggest that the 'decline' and 'retardation' of the Balkans also involved natural and environmental and/or locational factors which were largely beyond the control of any state or government and which went beyond cultural contrasts, important though those were. Strongly partisan historians of the Balkans (understandably) neglect or play down the role of the 'politically neutral' factors, which partly exonerate the major human actors among whom the partisans prefer to apportion 'blame'. However, inasmuch as Balkan economic 'decline' and 'retardation' were partly attributable to centuries of environmental or ecological damage caused by over-grazing, deforestation and soil erosion on Balkan hillsides, millions of Balkan peasants and landowners must have played a part (albeit inadvertently) in an ecological vicious circle.

The mainly hilly or mountainous Balkan terrain was often considered unsuitable for cultivation. Balkan landowners and hill farmers, therefore, kept relatively large numbers of sheep and goats (and, to a lesser extent, pigs, donkeys and mules). These animals, however, tend to close-crop grass and nibble at any foliage, young shoots and little saplings, sometimes denuding hillsides of their natural vegetation cover, while their hooves loosen soil and small stones. This in turn makes it easier for soil to be washed away by the (sometimes torrential) Mediterranean rainfall and for the shortened grass to be scorched dry by the fierce summer sunshine, while the reduction in soil and vegetation cover also increases the loss of rainwater through evaporation and 'run-off'. The ensuing desiccation of soils and vegetation in summer increases the risk of forest and bush fires and deforestation, while the latter further reduces soil retention, moisture retention and humidity and may lead to a drier climate. As a result, formerly lush and/or forested hillsides and mountainsides are indeed rendered suitable only for sheep, goats, donkeys and mules. So the ecological damage steadily intensifies until the increasingly barren and desiccated terrain can no longer support even those hardy animals. They are then moved on in search of fresh pastures, on which the vicious circle can start all over again.

These appear to have been the major mechanisms by which the Balkans (like most of Mediterranean Europe) have suffered from centuries of ecological damage, transforming vast tracts of formerly lush, humid and fertile terrain into barren scrubland on which not even sheep, goats, donkeys and mules can thrive. The effects have also been aggravated by over 2,000 years of uncontrolled felling of trees for fuel and timber-built dwellings, boats and ships. In the Balkans, as elsewhere in Mediterranean Europe, only quite draconian conservationist regimes could have averted the ecological devastation caused (largely inadvertently) by millions of landowners and hill farmers over the centuries. However, it is unlikely that either the Ottomans or Byzantium or any of the other polities which have ruled the region could have enforced the necessary restraint, even if they had fully understood the need for it.

In any case the long-term result was the gradual impoverishment of Balkan hill farming. This set the stage for the widespread depopulation of the degraded uplands through mass emigration in recent times and reduced potential rural investment in education, infrastructure and market integration. Moreover, the negative consequences were not confined to the uplands, although until recently that was where much of the population lived. Agricultural impoverishment also limited the potential rural tax base of the Balkan states, reduced rural demand for the products of Balkan towns and craft industry and, on the supply side, restricted the potential resource base of Balkan processing industries reliant upon agricultural raw materials.

The often marshy Balkan lowlands, on the other hand, were particularly prone to plague, malaria, scarlet fever, diphtheria and other epidemic diseases. (The impressive drainage, aqueducts and other 'waterworks' of Roman times had long since fallen into disrepair and decay.) This, combined with long periods of endemic disorder and warfare, was what had encouraged much of the Balkan population to migrate to less fertile (but safer and healthier) high ground. In addition, the fact that Ottoman taxation, like Byzantine taxation before it, fell much more heavily on arable land than on pasture also encouraged peasant farmers to take to the hills and mountains, where taxes were harder to collect. But these responses merely added to the population pressure, overgrazing and ecological damage on the uplands.

Furthermore, the Mediterranean climate, thin soils and rugged terrain of most parts of the Balkans were inherently less suited to the new root crops (turnips, swedes, beet and potatoes), grasses, clovers, crop rotation, heavier ploughs, bigger horses, larger carts and elaborate mixed farming systems which lay at the heart of the north-west European agricultural revolution than were the more temperate climate, deeper soils and gently undulating hills and plains of most parts of north-western Europe. Some significant new crops (e.g. maize, cotton and tobacco) were widely adopted by Balkan farmers in the seventeenth and eighteenth centuries. Yet, unlike the new crops adopted in north-western Europe, they did not (and probably could not) 'revolutionize' Balkan agriculture. The real Balkan agricultural revolution had to wait until the widespread development of irrigation, flood control, drainage, mechanization, tractors, paved roads, fast transport, horticulture and rural mass education between 1950 and 1980 (both in the communist Balkans and in Greece).

In addition, the eastern Mediterranean was the part of the world worst affected by the great shift or relocation of international trade routes away from the Black, Red and Mediterranean Seas, following the rise of the Atlantic economies, the West European development of transoceanic sailing ships and the West European voyages of discovery to the 'New World' and around Africa to India and the Far East. The Portuguese rounded the Cape of Good Hope in 1497, reached Calicut in India in 1498, seized Goa in 1510 and captured Malacca (the key to control of the Moluccas 'spice islands') in 1511. The Portuguese thus succeeded in 'outflanking' the traditional trade routes through the eastern Mediterranean and across Syria, Egypt, Asia Minor and Persia to the East. They also became a scourge of Moslem traders in the Red Sea, the Gulf and the Indian Ocean, while their forts and garrisons established Portuguese dominion over southern Arabia and the Gulf region. Nevertheless, despite the arrival of these Portuguese predators and 'interlopers', the lucrative overland Near Eastern spice trade between Europe, India and the South East Asian 'spice islands' enjoyed a strong revival following the Ottoman conquests in Syria, Palestine, Arabia and Egypt in 1516–17. Spices travelled much better on the overland caravan routes than on the long, dank, storm-tossed ocean voyage around the Cape of Good Hope.

After the sixteenth century, however, the spice trade and associated tolls and revenues steadily declined in the wake of the north-west European 'fodder revolution'. Over much of northern Europe new root crops and farming practices gradually made fresh meat available throughout the year, with the result that 'spices were no longer so essential to mask the taint of over-ripe meat' (Jones 1981: 179). In addition, from the seventeenth century onward, 'the establishment of Dutch and British power in Asia and the transference of the routes of world trade to the open oceans deprived Turkey of the greater part of her foreign commerce and left her, together with the countries over which she ruled, in a stagnant backwater through which the life-giving stream of world trade no longer flowed' (Lewis 1961: 28).

The consequences were incalculable. The eastern Mediterranean and the Black Sea regions, which had once been the hub of intercontinental trade, suffered much more than a quantitative contraction of commerce, shipping and entrepôt activities. They also largely missed out on the development of the Atlantic economy and the 'New World', together with the crucial stimuli and additional resources which the latter conferred (almost exclusively) on Western Europe. As E.L. Jones has emphasized, the storehouse of natural resources in the 'New World' was 'broken into once and for all' by West Europeans, who appropriated most of the benefits (in terms of additional resources and markets) in ways and on a scale that other parts of the 'Old World' have never been able to repeat. Indeed, the development options and possibilities of Western Europe were transformed by the additional fisheries, metal ores and forest products, natural fibres and food crops and the expanding opportunities for commerce and capital accumulation which were made available by West European penetration and conquest of the

'New World' and, to a lesser extent, Asia (Jones 1981: 81–4). The Atlantic seaboard location and the adventurous and systematically exploratory and innovative maritime orientation of the West European states gave them 'relatively cheap access to the rich, graspable resources of the Americas and the oceans and to large external markets' (pp. 227, 79–80).

This helped most of the West European states to sustain larger non-agricultural populations engaged in the expanding non-agricultural sectors of their economies. Thus Mediterranean Europe (including the Balkans) ceded its former position as the most urbanized macro-region of Europe to the rising Atlantic powers. In addition, transoceanic navigation provided a powerful stimulus to the development of mathematics, astronomy, optics, clocks, cartography, time-keeping and physics, which in turn made possible many of the advances of the seventeenth-century West European 'Scientific Revolution' and the emergence of a more secular scientific culture (see Cipolla 1970). These changes greatly assisted Western Europe to steal a march both on the Mediterranean world and on virtually landlocked East Central Europe in the Scientific, Commercial and later Industrial Revolutions. The types of shipping (including slave-powered galleys) and the techniques of navigation which were still in use on the Mediterranean and Black Seas were not readily adaptable to transoceanic trade.

During the seventeenth century the Balkans experienced demographic as well as economic contraction and, in view of the heavy Ottoman dependence on Balkan commerce and revenue, this must have contributed significantly to the economic decline of the Ottoman Empire as a whole. Moreover, even though Balkan commerce (and population) began to grow again in the eighteenth century, the revival was based merely upon the export of primary commodities. The increasingly passive dependence of the Balkans on the exchange of primary exports for industrial imports culminated in the Anglo-Ottoman Trade Treaty of 1838, which gave Britain and other European powers the right to trade throughout the Ottoman domains, subject only to minor anchorage fees and a 3 per cent *ad valorem* tariff on imports. This opened the door to foreign economic domination of the Ottoman Empire, largely eliminated two of the main sources of Ottoman state income (revenue from import duties and revenue from state monopolies) and effectively debarred the state from protecting Ottoman industries against foreign competition. 'As European manufactures flooded in, the traditional handicrafts and textile industries suffered' and, although merchants and bankers profited from the countervailing growth of foreign demand for raw materials and of urban demand for food, 'much of the newly created wealth accrued to foreigners' (Mansfield 1992: 57, 65–6, 69).

The eastern Mediterranean was to remain a commercial backwater until the opening of the Suez Canal in 1869. This contributed to a revival of the commercial fortunes and importance of the Balkans and the Near East in the twentieth century. Indeed, rapidly increasing quantities of Middle Eastern oil would be shipped to Europe through the Suez Canal and the eastern Mediterranean from the First World War until the Arab-Israeli War of 1967 and again after the reopening of the canal in the 1980s. Conversely, the expansion of Middle Eastern imports from Europe gave rise to a growing transit traffic through the Balkans from the 1960s until the eruption of hostilities in the Balkans (and in the Gulf region) in the early 1990s. How long it will be before the Balkan States can regain the commercial importance that they achieved during the 1970s and 1980s is, sadly, unclear.

It is clear, however, that the relative decline in Balkan and Ottoman economic fortunes from the seventeenth to the nineteenth centuries was in large measure due to forces outside Ottoman control. Thus it cannot be attributed entirely to cultural and institutional factors, let alone the actual or alleged deficiencies of Ottoman rule.

4   The decay of the Ottoman Empire and the emergence of Balkan 'national' states

The innumerable military humiliations suffered by the Ottomans from 1687 onwards also contributed to the weakening of central imperial authority over the provinces. As emphasized by Lewis (1961: 37), however, it was not among the Balkan Christians but among the Sultan's Moslem subjects in North Africa, Anatolia, Albania, Syria, Lebanon, Kurdistan and the Arabian peninsula that 'provincial independence first appeared and went furthest'. In Egypt, Syria, Albania, Anatolia, Baghdad and Basra ambitious provincial governors, military commanders or adventurous pashas, mainly members of the ruling Ottoman or Mamluk (Arabic for slave) military classes, took advantage of 'the remoteness and weakness of the Sultan's authority to intercept larger shares of the revenues of their provinces and to transform them into virtually independent principalities'.

These Moslem rebels and usurpers were not, for the most part, popular or proto-nationalist leaders. But in remote desert or mountainous areas such as Albania, Arabia, Libya, Lebanon, Kurdistan and the Anatolian interior, Moslem potentates with strong local roots and some popular support did emerge. Either way, however, the Ottomans' loss of authority and prestige and their increasingly apparent incapacity to defeat 'infidel' foes made a strong impression on many Moslem rebels and opportunists. For the Sultan's non-Moslem subjects in the Balkans and Armenia, conversely, the long series of military humiliations was a cumulative demonstration of Ottoman vulnerability, eroding the initial mystique of Ottoman invincibility and emboldening Christian 'upstarts' to begin openly challenging Ottoman authority.

To twentieth-century minds, conditioned to thinking in 'national' terms, the surprise is not that Balkan Orthodox Christians eventually rebelled against Ottoman rule, but that most of them accepted it for so long. A major reason for the apparent 'delay' was that nationalism did not become a potent factor in Ottoman imperial disintegration until the nineteenth century. Before then few Bulgarians, Serbs, Albanians, Greeks, Armenians, Kurds, Arabs or even Turks had developed a sense of cultural or ethnic identity that was *national* (in the modern sense of belonging to a clearly defined and accepted 'nation'), rather than religious or parochial. That was the principal reason why most of the Sultans' Christian subjects accepted Ottoman overlordship until the nineteenth century. Until then the many local rebellions were inspired by personal ambition, opportunism or specific economic or social or political grievances, rather than by more broadly based national or proto-national sentiments capable of transcending parochialism.

But when it finally emerged in the wake of the French Revolution and the Napoleonic Wars, under a combination of Western, East Central European and even Russian influences, the rise of nationalism had an even more explosive impact in the Balkans than in Western Europe. The Ottoman Empire was not a cohesive state enjoying the active allegiance of most of its subjects, but rather an agglomeration of disparate semi-autonomous groups. This inevitably reduced their willingness and capacity to resist foreign territorial encroachments, commercial penetration and military aggression. 'Since nationalism did not serve as a cement to hold the empire together, it functioned instead as a centrifugal force which eventually tore the empire apart. The absence of Ottoman nationalism left an ideological vacuum which was filled by the several Balkan, Arab and even Turkish nationalisms' (Stavrianos 1958: 130–1). Stanford Shaw emphasizes that 'National sentiment simply did not fit in with the order of society conceived of by even the most enlightened Ottomans of the time. They did not understand that nationalism had made impossible the maintenance of a *millet* system which had worked for centuries, no matter how much autonomy was to be given to each *millet*.' Increased autonomy for the separate '*millets*' could only accelerate imperial disintegration. From the 1870s to 1913, however, centralizing 'Young Ottomans' and 'Young Turk' reformers took the opposite tack. They tried to reconcile the Balkan provinces to reductions in local autonomy 'by advocating an "Ottomanization" of the population, an end to the *millet* system and its replacement by a common citizenship for all subjects of the Sultan regardless of religion, race and class', but this was 'entirely rejected by Balkan nationalists' (Shaw 1963: 74). Thus the Ottoman Empire and Balkan nationalism were irreconcilable forces. There was no way of satisfying the aspirations of both.

Furthermore, under the impact of the growth of commerce with Europe and increasing anarchy and insecurity in the Ottoman provinces during the eighteenth century, each community or collectivity 'strove desperately to improve its own position, generally at the expense of other collectivities' (Stoianovich 1963: 625). The inability of the Ottoman state to resolve these conflicts eventually resulted in the revolutionary transition from an imperial social order based upon a rigid hierarchy of legally defined and strictly segregated social estates and religious communities to new societies based upon more fluid social classes and national states (p. 625).

Stoianovich argues that a key factor in the 'spiritual and political awakening and cultural redirection of the Balkan peoples' was the growth of native merchant classes. Even though they comprised considerably less than 10 per cent of the population, 'they were the human catalysts that joined the Balkan peoples to Europe' both commercially and ideologically (Stoianovich 1960: 235). They financed 'the founding of schools and the dissemination of books in their respective national languages among their compatriots. They were also receptive to the ideas of the Enlightenment.' Some sought national independence 'even at the cost of social revolution' (p. 306). The eighteenth-century expansion of Western and Central European towns, populations and industry had expanded demand for Balkan primary exports of grain, hides, meat, wine, tobacco, vegetable oils, wax, raw silk, raw cotton, wool and timber, raising commodity prices and encouraging the production of cash crops for export (p. 255). Maize and cotton cultivation expanded particularly rapidly. Growing European demand for Ottoman (and particularly Balkan) primary products, combined with the declining capacity of the enfeebled Ottoman state to provide effective stimuli, support and protection for Ottoman (and especially Balkan) industries, transformed the Ottoman Empire (including most of the Balkans) into an exporter of food and raw materials and into an importer of 'European manufactured, processed, "colonial" and luxury goods, principally sugar, coffee, textiles, expensive Russian furs and Central European hardware and glassware' (p. 259). Even though these patterns of foreign trade contributed to a form of de-industrialization of the Balkans via the stagnation of many traditional craft industries, they nevertheless expanded the commercial opportunities for Balkan merchants, both as exporters and as importers. Indeed, 'Balkan merchants benefited from the change even more than European merchants' (p. 259). This was because European traders' ignorance of market conditions in the Balkans 'gave Balkan merchants . . . the opportunity to obtain control of most of the overland carrying trade, part of the maritime carrying trade and virtually the entire commerce of the Balkan interior. The commercial sector of the Balkan economy expanded, while the overall Balkan economy declined' (p. 263).

At first this expanding Balkan commerce was dominated by Greeks, Jews and Armenians. But by the late eighteenth century they had been joined by thrusting Serbian, Bulgarian, Macedonian, Bosnian and Albanian livestock dealers and muleteers and by Croatian and Albanian maritime traders, shipowners and seamen operating from the rugged Adriatic coast and islands, often as pirates (Stoianovich 1960: 269, 281, 283). 'The technique of their commerce was based on wile rather than science' (p. 297). Starting in the late eighteenth century, however, Ottoman/Moslem landlords and officials attempted to choke off this expansion of Balkan Christian mercantile power, which was (correctly) perceived as posing a serious threat to Ottoman/Moslem social and political ascendancy (p. 306–7). Perceiving their own interests to be threatened or poorly served by this Ottoman/Moslem ascendancy and reaction, 'Greek and Serbian merchants closed ranks temporarily with the peasantry and furnished the leadership of the Serbian (1804–15) and Greek (1821–29) wars of national liberation. By and large, however, both Greek and Serbian merchants favoured only limited social revolution. They desired to transfer property from the Turks and Moslems to themselves and, after that, to establish existing property on a secure basis' (p. 312).

Stoianovich (1962: 631–2) also emphasizes that the increasing insecurity of life and property under Ottoman rule (particularly among non-Moslems) also revived (or reversed the former decline of) the extended family and the importance of kinship and clan associations such as the South Slav 'zadruga', especially in remote, rugged, highland and frontier areas. This situation also strongly contributed to the growth of banditry and piracy in the Balkans and in the Adriatic, Ionian and Aegean islands. Visitors to these islands and adjacent mainland areas are constantly reminded of the extent to which they were used for piracy and of the fact that quite a few Adriatic and Aegean ports practically owed their existence to piracy. Thus in the early nineteenth-century Ottoman Balkans 'perhaps 10 per cent of the Christian population, at least in . . . the frontier areas, was organized militarily for the purpose of transforming or abolishing rather than defending the empire' (p. 632). These became the seedbeds of the Serbian and Greek national rebellions, which developed into Serbian and Greek wars of 'national liberation'. Moreover, when confronted with the task of bringing various Balkan clan, kinship, bandit, pirate, pastoral and trading associations under more unified and purposeful leadership and control, merchant, clan and bandit leaders engaged 'intellectuals' and publicists to propagate unifying nationalist ideologies and build up nationalist movements and organizations. These 'intellectuals' were among the early products of the new schools sponsored by Balkan merchants and/or had been educated abroad. There they had come into contact with the ideas of the European Enlightenment, the French Revolution and the Napoleonic empire. Although they were far from numerous, they exerted an influence out of all proportion to their number. They managed to give the Balkan revolts 'a new ideological goal: the reorganization of society upon a class and national rather than a corporate and imperial basis . . . In this manner, the Balkan revolutions were fatefully linked to the French, or Western, Revolution' (p. 632). Above all they absorbed and propagated the idea of the national state as a body of individuals with equal rights and obligations before the law and divided into social classes on the basis of economic status and wealth, rather than rigidly segregated into social estates and religious communities prescribed and regulated by a supranational and theocratic imperial order.

Simultaneously, moreover, the gradual secularization of West European culture and ideas under the impact of the Renaissance, the Scientific Revolution and the Enlightenment paved the way for a sea-change in the receptivity of Eastern Orthodox Christians to Western influences. 'So long as Western civilization was essentially Catholic or Protestant, it was unacceptable to Orthodox peoples. When it became primarily scientific and secular, it became acceptable, and even desirable, to a constantly growing proportion of the population' (Stavrianos 1963: 188). The eighteenth-century Enlightenment and the attendant growth of trade and contact with the West aroused demands for a reorientation towards Europe and 'pointed to a world beyond the horizons of the Orthodox East as a possible model for the future'. At the same time, however, this growing consciousness of 'alternatives beyond the world of Orthodox culture' planted anxieties and posed dilemmas which were to trouble modern Balkan consciences and fuel new (internal) ideological divisions and conflicts among the Balkan Orthodox peoples during the nineteenth and twentieth centuries (Kitromiledes 1995: 5).

Unfortunately the Balkan national revolutions could not occur in one clean sweep, permitting a quick and tidy reconstruction of Balkan societies on a uniform or consistent basis. Instead the revolutions proceeded erratically and sporadically during the whole period from 1804 to 1918 (and beyond), gradually embracing one locality after another and repeatedly exacerbating the political and religious/ethnic fragmentation ('Balkanization') of South-eastern Europe. These protracted, piecemeal and exceedingly disruptive processes were partly caused by external factors. These included great-power rivalries and interventions, Austrian territorial expansion into the northern and western Balkans, the residual (albeit waning) power and influence of the Ottoman Empire and the attempts of several European powers (including Britain) to prop up the 'Sick Man of Europe' (with the aim of blocking Russian imperial ambitions in the Balkans and of preserving an overall 'balance of power' in Europe). But they also reflected the variegated ethnic geography, ethnic consciousness and social and economic conditions in the Balkans. Only once, during the Balkan War of 1912, did the major Balkan nations manage to unite against a common external foe, namely the Ottoman Empire. But that momentary unity was quickly followed by a 'fratricidal' Second Balkan War between the victorious Balkan states during 1913 and by an even more cataclysmic 'Third Balkan War' between 1914 and 1918, which engulfed Europe and precipitated the final dissolution of the Ottoman, Tsarist and Habsburg Empires.

Not only were the Balkan provinces of the Ottoman Empire diverse and disunited, but they also became 'ripe' for 'national revolutions' at widely separated junctures. Owing to its close proximity to and economic dependence on Constantinople (Istanbul), Bulgaria was not ready for revolution until the 1870s. Moreover, the more divided, hesitant or even pro-Ottoman Moslem areas of Albania, Kosovo, Bosnia and western Macedonia were not really 'ripe' for 'national' self-rule until well into the twentieth century. (Albania had 'national' statehood thrust upon it in 1913, more as a result of great-power rivalries than in response to native demands for national self-determination.) In some respects, therefore, 'Balkanization' (including the wide scope for external interference in Balkan affairs) was an inescapable consequence of the (inevitably) erratic, protracted and fragmentary unfolding of the Balkan 'national revolutions'. Discrete, relatively compact and homogeneous nation-states were (and still are) almost impossible to achieve in this exceptionally variegated, strife-torn peninsula.

Nevertheless, against seemingly impossible odds, the Serbian and Greek revolutions 'effected the almost complete transfer of property and property rights . . . to the new political classes and to the peasantry . . . [and] . . . generated a current in favour of a new social order guaranteeing security of property and founded upon the principles of freedom of contact, equality before the law, and social mobility on the basis of free political and economic competition' (Stoianovich 1963: 312). Although this new social order had to be 'fought for over and over again . . . many institutions resembling those that had been introduced in Western Europe . . . were rapidly brought into being' (Stoianovich 1967: 152–3). By engaging in struggles 'against domestic as well as foreign tyranny', the nascent Balkan nations gradually succeeded in obtaining 'recognition of the principle of equality before the law' and the abolition of the former social hierarchy based upon hereditary legally defined social status (p. 162).

All the same, as Stoianovich (1967: 153) points out, the Balkan national revolutions remained 'unfinished revolutions' in the sense that they never fully established social structures that would have allowed them fully to consolidate and consummate the formal/ legal changes by fostering 'middle elements' that were 'sufficiently large, homogeneous and independent . . . to be able to manage the abnormal social strains created by the two world wars, a world economic crisis, communist revolution, fascist counter-revolution, economic change, technological backwardness, a "population explosion" and conflict between a multiplicity of cultural and political traditions'. Indeed, many of the problems that arose after the 1860s stemmed from 'the fact that equality before the law does not abolish economic inequality . . . [and yet] . . . the latter inequalities were exacerbated by a "population explosion" which left the peasantries with less and less land as they became more and more equal' (p. 162).

The Balkan 'population explosion' exacerbated existing social, economic and ecological strains. In the case of Serbia population density increased sixfold between 1800 and 1910 (Stoianovich 1967: 164), while that of Romania (Wallachia and Moldavia) rose fivefold between 1815 and 1912 (Stavrianos 1963: 200). By the 1900s the population was growing by about 1.5 per cent per annum in each of the Balkan states; this was double the rate for the Austro-Hungarian Empire and 50 per cent faster than the population growth of either Britain or Germany (Lampe and Jackson 1982: 164). Consequently, in the case of Serbia, the forested area shrank by two-thirds between 1815 and 1900 and the *per capita* availability of meat, milk and beasts of burden fell by two-thirds over the period 1859–1905, forcing Serbs to switch to a more cereal-based diet (Stoianovich 1967: 89, 165). Such changes, which also occurred in the other Balkan states, were closely interlinked with the resettlement of the long depopulated Balkan lowlands. But ecological damage continued apace, especially in upland areas.

Nevertheless, because the Balkans had comparatively low population densities to begin with, the Balkan states never became overpopulated in the Malthusian sense of being unable to feed their burgeoning populations. On the contrary, except in the case of Greece, *per capita* production of grain and potatoes remained comparatively high (Bideleux 1987: 250, table 11). Thus the Balkan states became 'overpopulated' only in the sense that they could not provide a livelihood for all their inhabitants, especially in rural areas, where there was a growing pool of surplus labour. 'More people were engaged in agriculture than were needed for the prevailing type of cultivation' (Stavrianos 1963: 200). This problem was exacerbated by the growing 'fragmentation' of peasant land holdings as they were passed on from generation to generation. Moreover, the smallness of Balkan industrial sectors (which employed less than 10 per cent of the work force and contributed less than 10 per cent of national income in each of the Balkan states) meant that it was not possible to absorb surplus rural labour into industrial employment to any major extent before the First World War or even in the inter-war period. In addition, although agriculture was far from becoming mechanized, there were numerous small improvements in modest agricultural equipment and implements (such as spades, hoes, scythes, sickles, carts, wheelbarrows, horseshoes and iron buckets). These improvements, together with the fact that farming was becoming more commercialized, cost-conscious and productive, also helped to render growing proportions of the farm population underemployed or even superfluous.

In each of the Balkan states, therefore, there was increasing social discontent, both among the peasantry and among those who drifted to the towns in a (frequently fruitless) quest for employment. 'The common dissatisfaction of Bulgarian, Serbian and Greek peasants appears to have been a shortage of money rather than food or other necessities; money not to pay taxes but to buy more manufactures and especially to buy more land, as a rational response to population pressure' (Lampe and Jackson 1982: 193). In Romania rural discontent erupted into a widespread peasant revolt in 1907, in which over 10,000 people perished. In Bulgaria peasant discontent was channelled into growing support for the radical Bulgarian Agrarian National Union from 1900 until the early 1920s, when its leader, Stamboliski, established a violent but short-lived 'peasant dictatorship'.

Another consequence of the Balkan 'population explosion' was the growing stream of emigration from the Balkans to Western and Central Europe and, above all, to the 'New World'. Between 1876 and 1915 over 319,000 Greeks, 92,000 Romanians, 80,000 Bulgarians and 1,380 Serbs emigrated to other continents. Thus about 10 per cent of the population of Greece had emigrated by 1912 (Lampe and Jackson 1982: 195–6), while as many as one-third of Montenegrin males did so (Stavrianos 1963: 206). Emigration was the Balkan safety valve. It also generated reverse flows of return migrants and remittances, which in turn helped to fund trade deficits (particularly in Greece), new businesses and capital formation. On the other hand, emigration left behind unfavourable demographic structures. Those who emigrated were the bolder spirits, the potential entrepreneurs and able-bodied young males who had been nurtured and educated at Balkan expense.

Sugar (1977: 282–3) argues that it was not when the Ottomans were still in full control, but during the nineteenth century (when most of the region was gradually 'liberated' from Ottoman rule), that the really striking 'gaps' or disparities in terms of levels of development opened up between the Balkans and north-western and central Europe. There is a lot to be said for such a view. Essentially, the contrasts in *per capita* levels of income and output widened dramatically as a result of the Industrial Revolution in north-west and central Europe in the late eighteenth and nineteenth centuries. 'Intellectually, economically, and even politically, the "Balkans" lagged further behind "civilized" Europe and appeared much more "backward" in 1880 than they had in 1780.' Despite all the allegations of Ottoman neglect, restrictions, repression and retardation of Balkan economic, educational, cultural and political development, until the nineteenth century most European countries were 'only slightly better off than those ruled from Istanbul'.

Considerations of this kind need not completely 'exonerate' the Ottomans, however. It is still entirely possible that some of the effects of Ottoman rule (or indeed the Balkan Wars and other damaging consequences of unsuccessful Ottoman attempts to hold on to the Balkans) contributed to Balkan inability or 'failure' to master or fully assimilate the economic and technical advances which occurred in north-western and central Europe in the late eighteenth and nineteenth centuries. For the latter clearly built upon prior developments or 'preconditions' which were conspicuously absent in the Balkans. Thus the Ottomans can still be accused of having 'failed' to prepare the ground for nineteenth-century technological advance, industrialization, education and democratization. Indeed, the Ottomans' successors were 'greatly handicapped' by the meagre Ottoman infrastructural legacy and 'the Ottoman period must be held responsible for bequeathing a totally inadequate, medieval manufacturing sector to the economies of the empire's successor states' (Sugar 1977: 285).

The Balkans, in common with Portugal, Spain and the Italian states (which soon lost their early lead in transoceanic navigation and commerce to England, Holland and France), were also handicapped by relatively low levels of educational provision (compared with north-western and central Europe) and by relatively authoritarian and theocratic governance. They were weighed down by powerful, oversized, parasitic and obscurantist ecclesiastical hierarchies and monastic domains. Moreover, their relatively rugged, mountainous terrain made inland transport and communications comparatively slow and expensive. They were short of navigable inland waterways, while the cost of constructing roads and railways over difficult terrain was to remain high, retarding market integration and the commercialization of the interior. For the most part they also lacked the fortuitous combinations of coal and metal ore deposits which were to give rise to so many centres of heavy industry in north-western and central Europe.

If the Balkans fell further behind north-western and central Europe, however, they nevertheless pulled further ahead of other territories or former territories of the Ottoman Empire. 'Around 1800 the Balkans were in most respects no better off than most of the Middle East. Grain yields may have been slightly higher. Transport was probably no better: more carts were used and more rivers were navigable, but the terrain was muddier and rougher and camel transport was not available. In some areas, notably Bulgaria, handicrafts were more widespread, but the region lacked the high crafts of Istanbul, Cairo, Aleppo, and Isfahan. Literacy was probably slightly, though surely not much higher, but urbanization was far lower' (Issawi 1989: 16–18).

And yet by 1914 the Balkans had, on most counts, moved decisively ahead of the Middle East, mainly because 'the Balkans obtained independence much earlier and, although Balkan governments were far from being models of stability and enlightenment, they were more responsive to national needs. They helped the economy by building infrastructure and extending credit and by bringing some industrialization before World War I.' Furthermore 'an enormous majority of peasants came to own their land and, since for a long time population density was light, their plots were adequate'. Ownership of the land they cultivated gave peasant farmers a powerful incentive to become more productive. Moreover, except in Romania, this tended to defuse the violent potential of class conflict. 'Only Romania had a large – and parasitic – landlord class and a very deprived peasantry, in spite of the agrarian reform law of 1864.' Thus the rapacious exploitation and oppression of vulnerable peasants by exceptionally corrupt and ruthless landlords and intermediaries ('arendasi') is widely judged to have been the main underlying cause of the great Romanian peasant revolt of 1907. But in this respect Romania is seen as the exception that proved the rule. In addition, the Balkan populations became 'distinctly more educated' than their Middle Eastern counterparts. 'By 1910 some 35 per cent to 40 per cent of children aged five to fourteen were attending primary school, and secondary enrollments were also high.' The result was that Balkan literacy rates surged ahead of those of Egypt, Turkey and the rest of the Middle East. The Balkans also have an 'important natural advantage over the Middle East: higher and more regular rainfall, resulting in more forests, more water power and more navigable rivers' (Issawi 1989: 16–18). This emphasis on the positive results of the fact that independent 'national' states emerged earlier in the Balkans than in the Middle East is quite compatible with our previous contention that the Ottoman conquest was not the chief cause of the relative retardation of the Balkans in comparison with the West, which had begun long before the Ottomans appeared on the scene. In the Balkans Ottoman overlordship had in essence perpetuated the Byzantine Orthodox and imperial heritage. Nevertheless, the termination of many centuries of imperial rule was in some respects a 'liberating' experience, even if it also opened some new cans of worms.

The leaders of the newly 'independent' Balkan peoples generally made some attempt to mould nation-states on Western patterns, even though the new countries actually comprised quite variegated populations. But the new polities were soon bedevilled by warring factions, with the result that weak and unstable regimes, lacking either democratic or truly 'national' legitimacy, resorted to repression, patronage, nepotism and cronyism to hold on to power. Governments 'made' elections rather than the other way around. As economies faltered and the rule of law lapsed, humble citizens rapidly lost faith in the new states and in the probity, efficacy and evenhandedness of governments and continued to put more trust in local clienteles and kinship associations to protect their interests.

The Balkan regimes proclaimed the need for 'progress', 'order' and 'Europeanization', encouraged European investment in Balkan railways, banks and industry, defended the interests of the propertied classes and sought to educate and 'Westernize' their compatriots, believing that industrialization and agricultural advance would automatically result from closer association with Europe's advanced capitalist powers. According to Stoianovich (1963: 320–2), 'The only elements of the bourgeois rational society which seeped down to the peasant . . . were the power of the state to recruit, punish and tax.' But Stavrianos takes a more positive view of the consequences: 'The diffusion of the money economy . . . increased village contacts with the outside world and thereby affected the traditional pattern of village life. The peasant sensed that literacy was essential under the new order . . . Hence he readily accepted elementary schooling for his children whenever it was made available . . . The younger generation was soon questioning the assumptions and attitudes upon which peasant life had been based . . . A new spirit of individualism and a desire for self-advancement undermined the solidarity of village life and even of the family . . . Tea, coffee, sugar and other commodities lost their character as luxury goods and passed into more common use. Town-made lamps replaced home-made candles, and the more prosperous peasants also bought furniture and household utensils. Iron ploughs became more common, though the poorer peasants continued to use the home-made iron-shod variety. A few householders began to buy ready-made clothing . . . In some peasant homes even a few books began to appear' (Stavrianos 1963: 204).

These seemingly modest changes represented a radical break with the self-sufficiency of earlier decades and the end of the closed, introverted village world of medieval and early modern times. The down side of all this was that the spread of the money economy subjected Balkan peasants to the sometimes violent fluctuations of national and inter-national markets. This increased rural economic inequalities, class differentiation and social (including ethnic) conflicts and antagonisms. Different ethnic groups which had often coexisted in relative peace and harmony for centuries were increasingly pitted against one another by market forces and by the scramble to create 'national' states and extend 'national' territories. Peasant 'land hunger' had *national* significance, as it still has in the Balkans today.

The newly independent Balkan states rapidly developed sizeable capital cities, standing armies, bureaucracies, railways and other trappings of modern statehood. Between 1878 and 1910, for example, the population of Bucharest expanded from 177,000 to 193,000, while that of Sofia rose from 20,000 to 103,000 and that of Belgrade from 30,000 to 90,000 (Lampe 1975: 72). Between 1885 and 1913 the value of foreign trade and budget receipts more than doubled in real terms in each of the Balkan states (except Greece), while *per capita* taxation roughly doubled (Spulber 1963: 348–9). Between 1870 and 1911 the railway network expanded as follows: Romania, from 248 km to 3,479 km; Bulgaria, from 224 km to 1,934 km; Serbia, from zero to 949 km; Greece, from 12 km to 1,573 km (Mitchell 1978: 317–18). However, even in the 1920s the railway density per 1,000 km^2 remained much less than in Western and Central Europe: Albania, 0 km; Greece, 22 km; Bosnia-Hercegovina, 25 km; Bulgaria, 28 km; Serbia, 29 km; Wallachia and Moldavia, 32 km; Croatia, 53 km; Transylvania, 55 km; Slovenia, 69 km; Italy, 67 km; France, 97; Germany, 123 km; Belgium, 370 km (Stoianovich 1967: 96). The underdevelopment of Balkan railways is sometimes attributed partly to the mountainous terrain, but we have not noticed any corresponding shortage of railways in mountainous Austria and Switzerland!

Stoianovich argues that nineteenth-century Balkan industrialization was stunted by the liberal Anglo-Ottoman trade treaty of 1838 and by the terms on which the new Balkan states gained great-power recognition in 1878. In his view 'the highly industrialized countries' set out to impede Balkan industrialization 'by trying to preserve intact the provisions of the Congress of Berlin (1878), which denied Serbia, Bulgaria and Romania the right to establish protective tariffs' (Stoianovich 1967: 97). Elsewhere he claims that 'The Balkan states could not protect themselves against the competition of European manufacturers, either because existing treaties forbade them to erect protective tariffs . . . or because the bulk of their exports was earmarked for one or two European countries which could deprive them of a market if they tried to assert their economic independence. The . . . pursuit of a more coherent economic programme was therefore delayed until the end of the century' (Stoianovich 1963: 319).

But the consequences were not quite as clear-cut as Stoianovich suggests. Some Balkan industrial development did take place in low-technology activities (such as food processing, textiles, tobacco processing, brewing and building materials), while Romania had developed the world's fifth largest oil industry by 1914. These were activities in which the Balkans enjoyed comparative cost advantages, thanks to the plentiful local availability of suitable raw materials and cheap labour. Free trade meant that the requisite industrial plant and equipment could be imported relatively cheaply from well established low-cost foreign suppliers. Until well into the twentieth century the Balkan states lacked the capital, educational and technical resource base on which to build up sophisticated engineering and metallurgical industries. In such circumstances industrial protectionism would have been more likely to protect inefficient producers and the excess profits of local monopolists than to evoke dynamic entrepreneurship and successful innovation.

Nevertheless, partly as a result of the stunted or retarded development of private enterprise, private capital and the middle classes, the forms of industrial capital which belatedly emerged in the newly 'independent' Balkan states were heavily dependent on state 'favours' and patronage, in the guise of selective protectionism, subsidies, lucrative contracts, tax exemptions, monopolies and privileged franchises. This provided fertile ground for the luxuriant growth of corruption. This context was reinforced by extensive state ownership of public utilities, mines, forests, foundries, munition plants and manufacturing enterprises. 'Far from being an autonomous force, [Balkan] capitalism was dependent upon the largesse of government bureaus and ministries . . . The capitalist class was dependent on the state; the state was dependent upon foreign capital' (Stoianovich 1963: 336). Balkan capitalists were thus about as 'independent' as Balkan states.

In the Balkans, as in many developing countries in the Third World, the capitalist state was to be much more than a referee among competing interests and the provider of a minimum of law and order and public services. It was to be the ultimate patron, directing and controlling (as well as responding to) social and economic forces and pressures. That role, rather than democratic processes and 'mandates', was to provide the main sources of its power and legitimacy. It would also in part serve the interests of foreign capital or foreign 'imperialism'. Moreover, each of the Balkan states became heavily (and vulnerably) dependent on a narrow range of primary exports (usually just two or three) to the main Western and Central European powers. The hazards of such dependence were to be brought home most painfully and fatefully in the 1930s.

Indeed, the Balkan states are semi-dependent states whose fate is determined directly or indirectly by the great powers. Since the decline of Byzantium South-eastern Europe has been repeatedly subject to 'great-power' intervention. The emergence of independent Balkan states between 1827 (Greece) and 1920 (Albania) owed as much to 'great-power' rivalries and intervention in the region as it did to internal developments. The so-called Eastern Question, which ran like a red thread through European diplomacy from 1718 to 1918, was essentially the question of how the European powers should carve up the Balkan territories of the declining Ottoman Empire (Stavrianos 1963: 199). Greek independence was secured by Anglo-Russian military intervention in the Greek War of Independence during the 1820s. Serbia, Montenegro, Romania and Bulgaria gained their independence through Russia's victory in the Russo-Turkish War of 1877–78, although the precise outcomes were modified and ratified by the other European powers at the 1878 Congress of Berlin (to the detriment of Bulgaria, which was forced to cede territory and settle for mere autonomy for the time being). Finally, Albania would probably have been carved up between Italy, Greece, Montenegro and Serbia but for the great powers' insistence on the creation of a separate Albanian state in 1912–13 and (again) in 1920. Charles and Barbara Jelavich (1963: xiv–xv) argue that 'Tsarist Russia, more than any other country, was responsible for the physical liberation of the Balkan peoples.' Indeed, Russia invaded parts of the Balkans in 1769–74, 1787–92, 1798–1812, 1829–34, 1848–51 and 1877–79. It was widely assumed that these Russian military interventions, together with pan-Slavic cultural and Orthodox religious ties, would eventually bring the Balkans under Russian domination. However, once they had been liberated from Ottoman rule, the new Balkan states soon discovered that Russia had little more to offer (apart from cultural goods, particularly music and literature, and some subsequent protection against potential Turkish, Austrian or Italian attacks). Thus it was primarily to Western and Central Europe that the new states turned for models, assistance, trade, investment and inspiration (until, that is, the Russians returned in force in 1944–45 to impose Soviet tutelage and communist rule).

Most of the Orthodox Christian populations of the Balkans gained and consolidated independent statehood and so-called 'self-government' between 1878 and 1914. The rest, along with most of the Roman Catholic and Moslem populations of the Balkans, had to wait until the final collapse of the Habsburg, Tsarist and Ottoman Empires at the end of the First World War. Except for Romania, the emerging 'national' states and cultures were quite aggressively demotic and strikingly free of aristocratic influence. Their preponderantly peasant cultures faced little competition from 'higher' aristocratic cultures. In contrast to 're-emergent' Poland and Hungary, the native nobilities and Christian aristocratic cultures which had begun to flourish in the Balkans in medieval times had largely disappeared in the course of four to five centuries of Moslem-Turkish domination. Only the Churches and the oral traditions of the Balkan peasantry had preserved the tattered remnants of the medieval Balkan Christian cultures.

The new, largely 'self-made' Balkan elites, including state officials, entrepreneurs, politicians, military officers and members of the liberal professions, were relatively 'open' to both money and talent. Perhaps because the new Balkan 'national' states contained relatively few proud descendants of ancient aristocratic families and no long-entrenched upper classes who could claim to have been the doughty custodians of national 'honour' and identity, they inherited no aristocratic models of deportment and deference, no established 'rules of the game' to regulate their unseemly scrambles for office (and for the spoils of office) and few effective checks or restraints on the misuse of public office or the misappropriation of public funds to line the pockets of public office-holders and their proverbial 'friends and relations'. Everything was 'up for grabs' in this 'survival of the fattest' environment. The 'mercenary' approach to public office-holding was a legacy of centuries of indirect rule of the Balkans through Byzantine, Ottoman and other intermediaries, who were fully expected to use the spoils of office to recoup the expenses and repay the political debts incurred during their ascent to public office.

It is the custom to blame this state of affairs squarely on the legacy of Ottoman rule. Thus Sugar argues that, as a result of the considerable local autonomy granted to both Moslem and non-Moslem '*millets*' in areas directly under Ottoman rule, relatively large numbers of individuals acquired some political and administrative experience and that it was these former communal office-holders who 'took over political leadership with relative ease prior to or just after the establishment of the various independent Southeast European states'. Political and administrative problems were to arise, not from lack of experience, but from the fact that self-serving and nepotistic Balkan office-holders and oligarchs had learned the tricks and techniques of political chicanery and corruption only too well. 'It was the Ottoman legacy and training that was reflected in their actions. This aspect of the Ottoman past was the most damaging of all the legacies bequeathed to the peoples of South-eastern Europe by their former masters.' Therefore 'the Ottoman political legacy must be considered the greatest problem faced by peoples who, once again, had become masters of their own destiny' (Sugar 1977: 286–8). Similarly, according to Vucinich (1965: 120), 'The Ottoman social system fostered many undesirable habits (e.g. the bribe, or *bakhshish*, distrust of government and so forth) . . . The notion persists that it is perfectly permissible to cheat and steal from the government, a problem with which none of the successor states has been able to cope altogether successfully.'

Such maladies have undoubtedly afflicted political life in the new Balkan 'national' states ever since, but it is as misleading as it is unjust to 'blame' this legacy squarely on the Ottomans. Rather, the gradual decline and retreat of Ottoman control permitted the re-emergence of age-old patterns of corruption, nepotism, lawlessness, extortion, protection-racketeering and self-serving administration in the Balkans. These were experienced not just in those areas that had been under Ottoman rule but throughout the Balkans, suggesting deeper and more pervasive causes. They had been conspicuous in the medieval Danubian and South Slav states and during the protracted decline of Byzantium. The re-emergence of such patterns in modern times is a reminder that, while 'Western' history gives every appearance of moving in a sort of linear progression, that of the Balkans seems to move in never-ending cycles.

Part II

East Central Europe prior to the Habsburg ascendancy

Introduction: the disputed 'roots' of East Central Europe

The Austrian Habsburgs were unable to write on a blank sheet of paper in East Central Europe. Before most of the region fell under the sway of the Austrian Habsburg Empire it experienced the turbulent rise of the medieval Czech, Polish and Magyar kingdoms, each of which lasted at least 500 years and left behind enduring social, cultural, political and economic legacies. Poland was by far the largest, the most enduring and the most influential of these three kingdoms. For a long time it offered the region a potent 'Commonwealth' alternative to Austrian Habsburg domination. It even became a major European power from the fifteenth to the late seventeenth centuries, without ever degenerating into a dynastic absolutist imperialism. Sadly, that contributed to its eventual undoing.

To say that the origins of these East Central European kingdoms are shrouded in myth and conjecture would be something of an understatement. Until the ninth or tenth century AD East Central Europe was essentially pagan and therefore lacked a literate Christian clergy capable of keeping written records or chronicles. Hence, through most of the first millennium AD, historians of East Central Europe can base their claims and judgements only on patchy and ambiguous archaeological evidence, odd fragments of 'popular' or 'national' folk tales and heroic but highly subjective guesswork. These difficulties are often openly admitted. Thus the historian Laszlo Makkai says of his Magyar fore-bears (who migrated from the Volga steppes to the Carpathian basin during the ninth century): 'Conflicting information from the available sources has inspired a variety of theories about the Hungarian migration . . . All that is certain is that the majority of the Hungarians did not leave the Volga before the second half of the ninth century' (Makkai 1975a: 21).

More problematically, there has been long-standing disagreement as to whether the Slavic ancestors of the Czech nation first settled in Bohemia and Moravia at some point in the sixth century AD (and whence they came) or whether the Czechs are in fact descended from allegedly Slavic 'Lusatians', whose presence in Bohemia can supposedly be traced back to the Bronze Age, i.e. 1400–1000 BC (Bradley 1971: 1–3, for the former view; Kavka 1960: 12–15, for the latter view). Later still, there is a dearth of documentary information on the fortunes of the Slavic inhabitants of Bohemia and Moravia during the 171-year span from 659 to 830 AD, which is rather a large gap (Kavka 1960: 15–18; Bradley 1971: 2–3).

In the case of Poland the earliest surviving documentary records are even later. They date from 965–66 AD, when the Polish ruler Mieszko I (who died in 992 AD) married a Czech princess, renounced paganism and was baptized into the Christian faith (Davies

1981: 3–4). Even after the establishment of a Polish Church in 1000 AD, the eleventh and twelfth centuries remain 'largely obscured by the deficiencies of the sources. Secular society was overwhelmingly illiterate' (p. 78). Moreover, while it is quite conceivable that somewhere in the Odra (Oder) basin or the Vistula basin there once lived people(s) who spoke a language or group of related languages from which modern Polish has since developed, it is impossible to trace the emergence of Polish 'in the absence of any linguistic records prior to the thirteenth century' (p. 47).

Feeding on patchy, fragmentary and ambiguous archaeological and philological evidence, the prehistory of East Central Europe has been a battleground between contending 'national' schools of history, archaeology, philology and ethnography. Each has explicitly or implicitly advanced or supported rival territorial claims by arguing that its own kinsmen were the 'original', 'native' or 'indigenous' inhabitants of particular areas and that the rival claimants were merely 'aliens', 'foreigners', 'transients' or 'interlopers' with no rights of possession or permanent settlement, even though many had lived there for centuries. Indeed, there is a great deal of truth in the definition of a nation as 'a group of persons united by a common error about their ancestry and a common dislike of their neighbours' (Deutsch 1969: 3).

Detached or disinterested Western specialists on East Central Europe have rightly emphasized the lack of information and consensus concerning the 'original' homeland(s) of the migratory Slavic peoples prior to the seventh century AD, and concerning the nature and timing of the processes by which they separated into Western, Eastern and Southern Slav linguistic and ethnic groupings (Davies 1981: 38–47). Therefore, despite the Poles' fervent belief in the *macierz* (motherland), 'it is impossible to identify any fixed territorial base which has been permanently, exclusively and inalienably Polish. Its territory, like the settlement patterns, cultural alignment and ethnic mix of its population, has been subject to continual transformations' (p. 24). It is likely that the Slavs were merely 'the latest among many Indo-European groups who have settled on the territory of present-day Poland' (pp. 43–4). Much the same can be said for Bohemia, Moravia and Slovakia (Bradley 1971: 1–2).

If populations were in an endemic state of movement and flux in most of Europe through much of the first millennium AD, it seems highly improbable that God had already led the ancestors of the Poles, the Czechs and the Slovaks to proto-national 'homelands' over which they could justly maintain permanent and exclusive jurisdiction for ever after, against all comers and prior occupants. (However, Hungarians do not even attempt to claim that present-day Hungary has been their national 'homeland' since time immemorial, because there is no denying the relatively late arrival of their Magyar forebears from Asia.)

Instead of labouring to project specious modern ethnic, national and territorial concepts and claims on to pre-modern multicultural societies within which modern ethnic and national identities had not yet crystallized (often in misguided attempts to ascribe the origins of modern ethnic and national conflicts to a pre-modern past), it would be much safer and wiser to emphasize that the peoples of East Central Europe are all 'mongrels' and that continual attempts to 'discover' or invent ethnically or even biologically pure pedigrees in pursuit of modern national, racial and territorial claims are just playing with fire. Our attitude to such matters is close to that of Paul Ignotus: 'The Hungarian nation . . . is supposed to be distinguished by its Asiatic race and language. All that has been said about its race is rubbish; language alone is the distinctive reality. Europe consists of racially impure nations, but Hungary tops the list for racial impurities. If the various Slav national groups to her north and south, the Austro-Germans to her west, and the Romanians to her east are all mixtures, Hungary is simply a mixture of these mixtures' (Ignotus 1972: 21).

We are not in any way suggesting that the uncertain 'mongrel' origins of the peoples of East Central Europe make them fundamentally different from those of southern, western or northern Europe. All Europeans share diverse and relatively obscure racial and ethnic origins (which ought to make them all 'Europeans' *first* and 'nationals' *second*). The real differences are that (i) there is less 'hard' information about East Central Europe than about the southern and western parts of the continent during the first millennium AD; (ii) this has rendered it easier for East Central European nationalists to make wild ethnic, racial and territorial claims with regard to that period; and (iii) this has contributed to the emergence of relatively narrow and exclusive ethnic and racial conceptions of the nation in East Central Europe.

Finally, it should be emphasized that the emergence of the medieval Polish, Czech and Magyar kingdoms substantially antedated modern conceptions of exclusive territorial jurisdiction and statehood. 'Political power radiated from a few centres of authority, whose spheres of influence constantly waxed and waned and very frequently overlapped.' The seats of royal power around which royal authority could be directly enforced were usually separated by vast expanses of ill-defined border country controlled by marcher lords who were to varying degrees a law unto themselves. In East Central Europe, where distances were far greater and more difficult to traverse than in western Europe, such conditions persisted until the middle of the seventeenth century in the kingdom of Bohemia and until the end of the eighteenth century in Poland and Hungary (Davies 1981: 33).

5 The vicissitudes of Poland

In modern times Poland has been renowned for the openness and vulnerability of its frontiers. On the broad North European Plain quite minor shifts in the balance of power have frequently resulted in remarkably large territorial changes. Here 'states could expand or contract faster and further than anywhere else in Europe' (Davies 1981: 23). Indeed, the scale and frequency of Poland's territorial shifts have made it the archetypal European state. This prompted the philosopher Michael Oakeshott to remark: 'The history of modern Europe is the history of Poland, only a little more so' (Oakeshott 1975: 186).

Poland has been especially easy to penetrate from the east and from the west and therefore has often furnished natural 'corridors' for successive waves of interlopers from the vast Eurasian steppes and forests into central and southern Europe and for successive Germanic thrusts towards the east, from the medieval German Catholic Crusaders and colonizers to Hitler's invasion of the Soviet Union in 1941–44.

Nevertheless, Poland's frontiers have never been completely open or exposed. To the south the Carpathian mountains for a long time constituted 'a barrier as lofty and effective as the Bavarian Alps or the French Pyrenees' (p. 34), while in medieval and early modern times the Baltic Sea and the glacial deposits, lagoons and morainic lakes that line the Baltic shore afforded some natural defences against external predators, although they simultaneously impaired Polish access to the sea. Moreover, before the advent of modern drainage and large-scale deforestation, the existence of extensive swamps and marshlands (notably the Pripet marshes) and primordial forests afforded some natural protection against marauders coming from the east and the west. Thus, at least until the tenth century AD, the territories that were to become ethnically Polish existed in relative isolation from the rest of Europe. Probably for the same reason, the typical pattern of settlement was 'not one of the large tribal centres, but of clusters of homesteads and small villages separated from each other by expanses of virgin land, each a self-sufficient unit' (Zamoyski 1987: 9).

Inclement climate, great distances and poor communications generally combined to isolate scattered communities from one another and foster the rugged rural individualism which was later extolled by so many Polish writers and poets. It has also been argued that this concatenation of natural conditions and human settlement patterns made it more difficult for rulers to construct successful power bases than was the case either in western Europe, 'where settlement was denser and connections between localities were closer', or in Muscovite Russia, 'where the localities readily submitted to the centre in the interests of protection and mutual supply' (Davies 1981: 50–2).

Nevertheless, Davies rightly warns that the historical experience of medieval and early modern Poland teaches one to beware of pushing geographical determinism too far. It has often been assumed that modes of political and societal development are in some sense predetermined by particular (God-given) geographical conditions and contexts, which are presumed to have engendered particular forms of state and society in the manner of the so-called 'river valley despotisms' or the short-lived empires of nomadic tribalists on the Eurasian and Mongolian steppes. Vast expanses, open frontiers and a harsh environment have often been adduced as explanations for the strongly autocratic, centralized and patrimonial characteristics of the Tsarist state. Yet diametrically opposite state characteristics were manifest in medieval and early modern Poland in geographical conditions that were not so very different from those in Russia. Indeed, in terms of climate, terrain and degree of access to the sea, late medieval Poland occupied an intermediate position between Russia and western Europe. Yet, instead of developing intermediate forms of polity and society, Poland became much more decentralized and anarchic than either (Davies 1981: 53).

Unfortunately, geographical determinism has been almost as rife among non-Marxist historians and historical geographers of Russia and East Central Europe as economic determinism has been in the cruder forms of Marxist historiography. Yet the 'once tempting idea that geographical conditions in the Polish lands nurtured Democracy as surely as Muscovy nurtured Autocracy does not find support in detailed research'. Geographical and economic conditions posed particular questions, options, constraints and problems, but *people* decided how to respond to them. 'The Polish state, like every other political organism, was created not by predetermined forces, but by men' (Davies 1981: 60). Feminists will complain that this formulation neglects the role of the other sex. Yet, prior to the 1990s, Polish men denied Polish women any active role in the creation of the Polish state. On the other hand, female rulers of Russia actively contributed to the destruction of the eighteenth-century Polish-Lithuanian state, but perhaps that should be less a source of pride than of shame!

The medieval Polish state, like that of Lithuania, was brought into being by warriors whose ability to conquer large areas of sparsely populated plain was not backed up by an aptitude for the construction of resilient, effective and enduring institutions and power structures (Davies 1981: 59). The highly decentralized administrations, finances, defences and power structures of the various medieval and early modern Polish and Lithuanian states and unions proved capable of warding off the relatively diffuse and/or ephemeral threats posed by the (Germanic) Holy Roman Empire, the Mongols, the Teutonic Knights, Riurik Muscovy, the Turks and the Crimean Tatars. But they were no match for the much more sustained, concentrated and formidable threats posed by the subsequent emergence of Romanov Russia and Hohenzollern Brandenburg-Prussia, with the occasional connivance of the Austrian Habsburgs. Indeed, the latter were slow to recognize that the 'upstart' Romanovs and Hohenzollerns would eventually imperil the Habsburg ascendancy in East Central and South-eastern Europe, much as the Polish-Lithuanian Commonwealth failed to foresee that its costly wars against the Turks, the Crimean Tatars and the Swedes would facilitate the aggrandizement of Habsburg Austria, Romanov Russia and Hohenzollern Brandenburg-Prussia.

THE ORIGINS OF 'POLAND'

Slavs of one sort or another probably first settled between the rivers Odra and Vistula during the seventh and eighth centuries AD (Davies 1981: 27). However, in view of the innumerable human migrations through and into this region and the resultant richness of its ethnic mix, 'it is quite impossible to isolate anything resembling an ethnic core or, at the distance of a thousand years, to distinguish Slavonic from non-Slavonic racial elements' (Davies 1981: 46).

Archaeologists have found evidence of human habitation in the current territory of Poland in the Iron Age (after 600 BC), in the Bronze Age (1800–400 BC) and even as far back as 180000 BC (in the Ojcow caves near Krakow). Primitive agriculture can be traced back to about 2500 BC and it appears that so-called Lusatians (named after the eastern German district in which they were first identified) inhabited this area between roughly 1300 and 400 BC. They built wooden forts, including a famous island fortress at Biskupin in eastern Pomerania some time around 550 BC and traded with Scandinavia and the Danube basin. The area was invaded by Scythian nomads from around 500 BC, but there is also archaeological evidence of Celtic settlement from around 400 BC and of Germanic incursions from the first century AD. The northern and eastern sections of modern Poland were also extensively settled by Baltic tribes (forebears of the modern Latvians and Lithuanians) (Davies 1981: 41, 44, xxxix).

The fact that Roman coins and artefacts have been widely discovered (sometimes in large quantities) in the lands between the Baltic and the Vistula suggests that Roman expeditionary forces and traders may have made forays into these territories (Geremek 1982: 14). Nevertheless, writers such as Tacitus clearly regarded the area as *terra incognita*. His remarks on the so-called 'Venedii' could just as credibly refer to Germanic as to Slavic inhabitants of the area (Davies 1981: 45). Therefore it is probably 'unwise to put the Slavonic tag on any archaeological finds prior to AD 500' within the post-1945 territory of Poland (p. 44).

The so-called 'autochthonous school' of Polish archaeology, philology and ethnography has postulated a direct line of ethnic descent from the (Bronze Age) Lusatians through the obscure Venedii of Roman times to the unambiguously Polish/ Slavic tribes of the tenth century, but this conjecture is contested by the older 'Prussian school', which treated the very same area as the 'ancestral homeland' of the *Früostgermanen* (the early East Germans) (Davies 1981: 39, 282). Moreover, some Slavonic archaeologists have questioned the alleged Lusatian and Venedian 'roots' of the proto-Slavs. Instead, they argue that the Slavs originated in the northern Carpathian region (where they intermingled with Baltic, German, Illyrian, Thracian and Iranian peoples) and that the Slav *diaspora* did not begin until the sixth century AD, when the Slavs were scattered by the impact of the invading Huns and Avars, nomadic warriors from Asia (pp. 40–3). There are no references to *Polanie* (Polanians or 'people of the open plain') before the tenth century AD. Even then these references are only to a single Slavic tribe inhabiting one section of the Warta-Vistula basin. But it was their ascent to pre-eminence and their ruler's (not unrelated) adoption of Christianity in 965–66 AD that gave birth to the concept of *Polska* (Poland), derived from the Polish word *pole* (meaning a field or open flat terrain).

Whatever their origins, the relative isolation of the *Polanie* from the outside world came to a fairly abrupt end when Otto I of Saxony subordinated the Premyslide ruler of

Bohemia in 950 and crushingly defeated the Magyars in 955. Otto was crowned Holy Roman Emperor in 962 and, in the same year, persuaded the Pope to raise the bishopric of Magdeburg to the status of a missionary diocese charged with bringing the Western Slavs into the Catholic fold, whether by hook or by crook!

It should also be noted, however, that Christianity had first arrived in Poland (the Krakow region) from the short-lived Moravian Empire in the ninth century, as a result of the proselytizing activities of the famous Byzantine monks named Cyril and Methodius. Thus the fact that the Poles first took their Christianity from Moravia and Bohemia, rather than from Germans or Italians, explains why much of the religious vocabulary of the Polish language has derived 'from Czech and Slavonic forms, not from German and Latin ones' (Davies 1981: 69). Indeed, it has even been questioned whether the Poles and the Czechs should be viewed as two wholly separate peoples at that time. Converted to the Western form of Christianity over a century before the Poles, 'the Czechs acted as the principal filter through which knowledge of the Western world reached Poland . . . It was through the Czech language that they received practically the whole of their political, religious and social vocabulary' (p. 85). Religious, political and cultural affinities between the two countries remained quite strong for several centuries, at least until the Czech Lands fell fully under Habsburg control as a result of the Thirty Years' War (1618–48).

THE IMPACT OF CHRISTIANIZATION

The decision of the Polanian ruler Mieszko I (963–92) to adopt Western Catholic rather than Eastern Orthodox Christianity in 965–66 AD was probably part and parcel of an alliance with the Roman Catholic rulers of Bohemia, designed to pre-empt or ward off the expansionist ambitions of the Catholic and aggressively proselytizing Germanic states. 'Mieszko I decided for co-operation with the Latin West, but with independence from Germany and under the protection of the papacy' (Halecki 1957: 2). However, other Polish historians question whether this new alignment really was 'the result of a conscious choice; indeed, it is not known whether the elites of the Piast state even saw the issue in terms of a distinct choice' (Geremek 1982: 16). Certainly, it is improbable that Mieszko I could have foreseen or fully appreciated the momentous consequences of the new alignment, which were still in the forefront of Polish spiritual, cultural and political life a thousand years later. It opened the doors to Latin Christian culture, to the establishment of a Polish Church and ecclesiastical province within Western (Catholic) Christendom, and to the commencement of Polish literacy, learning, formal administration and recorded history, imparting a sense of the country's past and of its present and future place in the world. Indeed, it has been suggested that it was not just Poland that adopted the Western (Catholic) form of Christianity, but also the West and the Catholic Church that adopted Poland (Davies 1981: 291). The *geopolitical* consequences of this sometimes fraught link have rumbled on into the twentieth century (especially since the election of a Polish Pope in 1978). It has long constituted the main basis of Poland's claim to be part of the West and to be entitled to Western assistance and protection whenever Poland's predominantly Catholic values and culture have seemed to be under external threat, just as Poland has always been willing to fight for the defence of Western Christendom (even in the latter's increasingly secularized form). But the West, ironically, has been inclined to view such matters in a more detached, self-interested and calculating manner, far removed from Polish idealism and self-sacrifice. In this respect, above all, Poland has never been truly Western (and is all the better for it!).

In 991 Mieszko I requested that his domains be put under direct papal protection. And in 1000 AD, during the reign of his son Boleslaw I Chrobry (992–1025) and just one week before the parallel inauguration of an analogous Hungarian Church, an autonomous Polish (Catholic) Church was established under the jurisdiction of the new Polish archbishopric and diocese of Gniezno, with the personal support and participation of the Saxon Emperor Otto III. Other Polish (Catholic) bishoprics were subsequently established at Krakow, Vratislaw (Wroclaw), Kolobrzeg (Kolberg) and, somewhat later, at Plock (1050), Wloclawek and Lubusz (1128), Wolin (1140), Lwow (1367) and Halicz (1375). Monasticism developed in Poland from the eleventh century onwards; by the twelfth century the country had an extensive parochial network.

In 1000 AD Emperor Otto III had in effect accepted the Polish ruler 'into the Ottonian family of kings' on a (formally) equal footing with Italy, Gaul and the Germanic states, as part of his imperial *Ostpolitik* (Geremek 1982: 18). Indeed, the adoption of Western (Catholic) Christianity conferred a distinctive ideological stamp and Christianizing mission on the Piast dynasty, which dominated Polish affairs from the tenth century to the fourteenth. The spread of Christianity 'created a demand for educated personnel capable of conducting missionary work and filling Church offices. Such people, initially at least, were supplied by Western monastic and ecclesiastical centres' (Geremek 1982: 19). At the same time, however, Polish clergy increasingly journeyed to Western centres, visiting monasteries and other educational and religious institutions. They brought home 'holy books, treatises and encyclopaedic works, the intellectual tools which enabled them to perform their spiritual functions and introduce their knowledge of Western practices, artistic forms and ideas into their own dioceses' (p. 20). The development of the Polish Church was even responsible for the introduction of new economic activities, such as glass-making and the manufacture of parchment, and it became the biggest employer of builders, glaziers, painters and scribes (Fedorowicz 1982: 153). Even after Poland officially became Catholic, however, it remained geographically remote from the main centres of Latin Western civilization and subject to rival influences from the East – initially from Byzantium, later from Lithuania and Muscovy, and later still from the Turks and the Crimean Tatars (with whom some members of the Polish nobility intermarried).

During the eleventh and twelfth centuries the Church became increasingly rich and powerful, mainly through the receipt of huge grants and bequests of land (together with the peasants inhabiting them). By the thirteenth century the Church had also won legal autonomy for its clergy, fiscal immunity for its landed estates and the right to choose its own bishops and abbots (Zientara 1982: 44).

Unfortunately, the energies released and the social changes set in motion by the adoption of Catholic Christianity by the Piast dynasty also accelerated the emergence of a landed nobility with ambitions of its own. That in turn contributed to the growth of internecine strife and, from 1138 to 1320, the political fragmentation of the Piast realm into a number of rival dukedoms (Fedorowicz 1982: 11). However, this occurred mainly because the rulers of medieval Poland (like those of Kievan Russia) drew no clear distinction between the public and the private property of the ruling dynasty. The royal family simply viewed the state and crown property as family possessions which, on the ruler's death, were generally shared out between the surviving male relatives. This was the source of fierce family feuds and fratricidal tendencies. Moreover, 'the need for each Piast duke to secure as much support as he could in the deepening political chaos meant that he would be more likely to offer generous rewards to his noble supporters in return for their loyalty and service, and these rewards were often grants of land together with the peasants inhabiting them' (p. 29). This contributed to the growth of magnate property and serfdom as well as political fragmentation.

FURTHER INFLUENCES FROM WESTERN CHRISTENDOM

The historian Benedykt Zientara has argued that medieval Western influence came to Poland in two fairly distinct waves. The first wave, the tenth-century adoption of Western (Catholic) Christianity and the resultant influx of foreign clergy, knights and merchants, mainly affected the upper strata of Polish society. The second wave, involving the adoption of so-called German law (*Ius Teutonicum*) and a much larger influx of German, Jewish, Flemish and Dutch peasants, artisans, traders, soldiers and other immigrants during the thirteenth and fourteenth centuries, affected the population as a whole (Zientara 1982: 31). German law assured settlers of personal freedom and hereditary land rights in return for the payment of fixed rents in cash or kind. It was used by both rulers and private landowners to accelerate the colonization of Poland's sparsely populated provinces. It was initially applied only to German, Flemish or Dutch colonists, but it was soon extended to all comers, including Poles from the more densely populated western provinces (p. 36).

Rural colonization developed hand in hand with increased immigration into existing towns and cities and the planning and construction of entirely new ones. Polish dukes and other big landowners began to employ foreign merchants as *locatores* (agents) with the power to organize settlement. 'They developed into active colonial entrepreneurs, travelling to Germany to recruit settlers, mediating between the newcomers and the princes, Church officials and other landowners, and laying out . . . the new settlements' (p. 37). The new urban settlements were planned and populated in much the same way and became separate judicial units administered in accordance with German law and municipal charters modelled on German town charters, outside the jurisdiction of ducal officials (pp. 37–8). Wroclaw, Poznan and Krakow were similarly 'incorporated' as German cities in 1242, 1253 and 1257, respectively, and they rapidly acquired German or Germanized burgher classes (Davies 1981: 78).

It was within this context of increasing 'incorporation' of towns and cities that the Prince of Krakow promulgated a famous General Charter of Jewish Liberties in 1264. It granted Jews exemption from slavery and serfdom, and freedom to practise their religion unmolested, to travel around Poland and to engage in trade (Davies 1981: 79). This gradually turned Poland into a safe haven for Western Christendom's increasingly persecuted Jews, who came to dominate Poland's mercantile/intermediary occupations (possibly the greatest poisoned chalice of all time).

Consequently, in spite of the damaging political fragmentation (1138–1320) and devastating Mongol and Lithuanian incursions and depredations, the thirteenth and fourteenth centuries saw a major development of towns, rural colonization, immigration, market integration, water, power and commercial production of grain, flax, hemp, wool, meat, minerals (lead, silver, bog iron and salt) and urban handicrafts (Zientara 1982: 38–9). The expansion of mining and metal production increased the minting and circulation of metallic currencies, accelerating the monetization of the economy (Davies 1981: 80).

In all, during the thirteenth and fourteenth centuries, approximately 250,000 Germans settled in a country with only about 1,500,000 native inhabitants. 'Assimilation was greatly facilitated by the extension of German law to the Polish population, thus putting an end to the privileged status of the newcomers.' Moreover, 'mixed marriages became common. Germans adopted Polish or Slavonic names . . . while Poles often took fashionable German names' (Zientara 1982: 40–1). The Polish language became suffused with German loan words. 'Even ideas with Polish equivalents came to be expressed with borrowed German words.' Germans introduced not only their own terminology but 'also their customs, which grew into Polish society to such an extent that they are now considered of Slavic origin' (p. 41).

In the face of this large-scale immigration and the wholesale Germanization of many towns, Poland's increasingly rich and powerful Catholic Church played a pivotal role in the maintenance of the Polish language and Polish autonomy, not least by sustaining Polish ecclesiastical unity and native control of ecclesiastical appointments. The Polish Church synod held at Leczyca in 1285 required all Church schools to teach the faithful the fundamentals of their faith, their prayers and their liturgy in the Polish language, while placing prohibitions on the appointment of teachers and clergy who were not fluent in Polish – even at parish level (pp. 44–6). In addition, the Church profited from the period of disintegration by further augmenting its revenues, properties, privileges and autonomy, although its inordinate wealth and immunities also brought it increasingly into conflict with Poland's temporal rulers (Davies 1981: 70).

FROM FRAGMENTATION TO UNIFICATION

Poland was fortunate that its period of political fragmentation (1138–1320) coincided with an era in which Bohemia, Hungary and the Holy Roman Empire were often similarly disunited. Yet in 1241, 1259 and 1287 the Polish lands were ravaged by Mongol invasions. Southern and eastern Poland were substantially depopulated (Zamoyski 1987: 28). Luckily for Poles, however, the prime target of the Mongol forays was not the Polish but the Hungarian plains. Moreover, the Poles were spared the longer-term subjugation and despoliation (the 'Mongol yoke') which befell their Lithuanian and especially their Russo-Ukrainian neighbours, who found themselves largely cut off from the rest of Europe for more than a century after 1241.

A more enduring threat to the well-being of the Polish Lands arose in the form of the chivalric Order of Teutonic Knights (originally established in Palestine on the pattern of the Knights Templar). In 1126 the ruler of Mazovia had rashly turned to this 'underemployed' crusading order for help in subduing his northern neighbours, the still pagan inhabitants of Prussia. The Grand Master astutely secured papal and imperial backing for the mission, along with a promise that (if successful) the Teutonic Order would gain jurisdiction over the conquered Prussian territory. Lured by the prospect of glory, land and booty, the Order attracted soldiers of fortune from many parts of Western Christendom, not merely from Germany. Aided by superior financial, commercial and logistical support, which included Hanseatic money and shipping services and a network of newly built and well fortified trading towns (notably Thorn/Torun, Elbing/Elblag, Kulm, Marienwerder, Braunsberg, Heilsberg and Königsberg, now Kaliningrad), the

Teutonic Order had completed its subjugation of the pagan Prussians by 1288. But it gained its richest prize in 1308, when the Polish authorities in the burgeoning port of Gdansk (Danzig) rashly appealed to the Teutonic Order for assistance in suppressing a local Pomeranian rebellion. The knights not only acceded to the request but also took possession of the city until 1454, severing Poland's major direct riverine access to the sea.

However, the debilitating onslaughts of the Mongols and the Teutonic Order awakened demands for the reunification of the Piast domains. The Polish Church lent powerful support to the unification movement. From 1300 to 1306, in the desperate hope that the kings of a neighbouring state might manage to impose the unity that native rulers had thus far been unable to achieve, the Polish crown was given to the last Premyslid kings of Bohemia, Vaclav II (1278–1305) and Vaclav III (1305–06). But even they proved incapable of bringing the Polish domains under unitary rule, and the once proud Premyslide dynasty expired with a whimper in 1306. Yet all was not lost. The power vacuum left by the sudden and ignominious demise of Bohemia's Premyslide dynasty was quickly filled by a militarily and politically accomplished Piast duke, Wladyslaw Lokietek, who largely reunified the Polish Lands and was crowned King of Poland (with the Pope's blessing) in 1320. The kingdom's fortunes were further enhanced by his son and successor Kazimiercz III (Casimir the Great, 1333–70). His first steps were to conclude a vital truce with the Teutonic Order in 1333 and to cement closer ties with the kingdoms of Hungary and Bohemia at a sumptuous gathering in the Hungarian castle of Visegrad in 1335. There, in return for Polish recognition of Bohemian claims to parts of Silesia, he persuaded Bohemia's King Jan (1310–42) to renounce his kingdom's claim to the Polish crown (deriving from the Premyslides' brief tenure of the Polish throne from 1300 to 1306).

Having thus secured his northern and western flanks, Kazimiercz III went on to subjugate Halicz (Galicia, including Lwow) and Volhynia during the 1340s and Podolia in 1366. The kingdom of Poland, which occupied 106,000 km^2 at the time of his accession in 1333, had grown to 260,000 km^2 by the time of his death in 1370 (Zamoyski 1987: 40). During his reign, moreover, fifty stone fortresses had been built and twenty-seven towns had been encircled with stone walls. (There is a saying that Kazimiercz III inherited a Poland built of wood and left it built of stone.) In addition, he promulgated a two-volume codification of Polish law in 1347. Commerce and urban life flourished and Poland's first university was established at Krakow in 1346.

DYNASTIC CRISES AND THE ORIGINS OF THE POLISH UNION WITH LITHUANIA (1386)

For all his constructive achievements, however, Kazimiercz III was unable to avert the extinction of the Piast dynasty on his death in 1370. Even though he married three times and sired several legitimate offspring, he left no legitimate and clear-cut male heir. He was therefore succeeded by his nephew, Louis of Anjou, who was also King Lajos of Hungary (1360–82) and an aspirant to the crown of the Angevin kingdom of Naples and Sicily. In order to buy off actual and potential opposition to his tenure of the Polish throne, this foreign absentee monarch (who was known as Ludwik in Polish) made large land grants and extended the prerogatives and privileges of Poland's nobility, clergy and towns by means of the Statute of Kosice (promulgated in 1374). In particular, this limited the fiscal and service obligations of the nobility, strengthened the fiscal privileges and autonomy of the Church and enhanced the liberties of townspeople.

Like his Piast predecessor, however, Ludwik (Louis) 'failed' to father a legitimate male heir. Hence his death in 1382 precipitated another succession crisis and a brief civil war between rival factions. In the end his younger daughter Jadwiga was crowned Queen of Poland in 1384 and her fiancé, Wilhelm von Habsburg, turned up in Krakow to claim his bride-to-be. But, fearful of falling under Habsburg control, the Polish nobility hounded the young Habsburg prince out of the city and Jadwiga's engagement was annulled. In February 1386 this helpless eleven-year-old girl was forced to marry a man more than three times her age: Jogaila, the Grand Duke of Lithuania. The Polish nobility, which had assumed the role of king-maker, used its newly acquired power to strengthen its already considerable prerogatives and privileges and to transform Poland into an elective monarchy. Nobles elected Jogaila (in Polish, Jagiello) their king at a grand assembly held in 1386 at Lublin. This noble assembly also approved a personal union between the Christian kingdom of Poland and the then still pagan Grand Duchy of Lithuania (at that time Europe's largest state) in order to ward off Teutonic and Habsburg expansion. A momentous Lithuanian victory over the Mongol/Tatar Golden Horde in 1362 had enabled Lithuania to occupy Kiev and most of the Ukraine, as far south as the Black Sea coast (Samsonowicz 1982: 54).

For his part, by accepting the Western (Catholic) form of Christianity from Poland, Jogaila led his grand duchy firmly into the fold of European civilization and neutralized the formal pretext for the Teutonic Order's crusading designs on Lithuania (for which it had gained papal backing in 1339). Moreover, since Lithuanian is directly related to the Slavonic languages, and since an old form of Byelorussian (not Lithuanian) was the official language of the grand duchy, the Lithuanian nobility probably felt some degree of cultural kinship with their Polish counterparts. In addition, while Polish nobles and colonizers lusted after the 'vacant' open spaces of the vast Lithuanian Grand Duchy, the Lithuanian nobility envied and hankered after the greater education, polish and privileges of the Polish nobility. Indeed, the Lithuanian nobility gradually became thoroughly 'polonized', while the Polish nobility increasingly preferred Latin and other western languages, with the ironic result that Polish eventually became more widely used among the Lithuanian than among the Polish nobility in the future Polish-Lithuanian Commonwealth (Davies 1982: 20–1).

The disconsolate young Queen Jadwiga died in 1399, aged twenty-four. Her personal wealth was bequeathed to the university in Krakow, which was then relaunched as the Jagiellonian University in her memory. Her death also precipitated the renegotiation of the terms of the personal union between Poland and Lithuania, to put it on a more lasting footing. In 1401 and 1413, respectively, the Polish and Lithuanian nobilities agreed that 'nothing should be decided in future without mutual consultation' and that matters of mutual concern (including the election of future monarchs) 'should be settled in joint assemblies of the nobility' (Davies 1981: 118–19). In 1425, moreover, Jogaila conceded the principle of *Neminem captivabimus nisi iure victum*, granting the nobility security against arbitrary arrest and the arbitrary seizure of property. This was the Polish-Lithuanian equivalent of the English principle of *Habeas corpus*, and it would later set Poland-Lithuania completely apart from the Russia of Ivan the Terrible (1533–84).

THE EMERGENCE OF POLAND-LITHUANIA AS A MAJOR EUROPEAN POWER

In spite of the strengthening bonds between Poland and Lithuania, the Teutonic Order was not tamed overnight. It managed to seize the island of Götland in 1398, the Neumark of Brandenburg in 1402 and Samogatia in 1404. But in 1410, at the battle of Grunwald (near the Prussian village of Tannenberg), a polyglot army of Poles, Lithuanians, Czechs, Balts, Ruthenes, Tatars and Wallachians ambushed and inflicted a famous defeat on a force of 27,000 Teutonic Knights, of whom nearly half (including the Grand Master) were killed and 14,000 taken prisoner. Modern nationalist historians have often presented this as a historic victory of the Slav nations over the German nation, which later won its revenge at the famous battle of Tannenberg in August 1914. In reality it was nothing of the sort. The victors in 1410 were a motley assortment of Slavs and non-Slavs, while the defeated Teutonic Knights were drawn from various parts of western and central Europe (not just Germany), and neither side considered the contest in modern nationalist terms at the time (Davies 1981: 120–3).

The resultant Treaty of Thorn (1411) was remarkably lenient, for the victors contented themselves with a modest restoration of free trade on the river Vistula. It is conceivable that Jogaila thought it prudent to allow the Teutonic Order to remain in existence in order to keep the Poles 'on side'. The Order suffered a more decisive setback in 1454, when the cities of Gdansk (Danzig), Elblag (Elbing) and Torun (Thorn) renounced their erstwhile allegiance to the Teutonic state and asked to be taken under the protection of the Polish king. This set off a thirteen-year Polish-Teutonic war, culminating in partition of the Teutonic domains in 1466. Western Prussia became an autonomous province within the kingdom of Poland, while East Prussia and Livonia became separate Teutonic fiefdoms under Polish suzerainty.

The rise of Gdansk (Danzig)

In 1466 Gdansk (Danzig) became the chief city of the new Polish province of Royal Prussia, and as the natural outlet for Poland's burgeoning grain, mineral and timber exports via the rivers Vistula and Bug it rocketed to pre-eminence among Poland's cities for the next three centuries. By 1600, with 50,000 inhabitants, it was five times the size of Warsaw (and more than three times the size of either Krakow or Poznan, its closest rivals), and 'Danzig patricians were no less wealthy than the great magnates, many of whom were deeply in debt to them' (Davies 1981: 271–2, 286). By 1500 about 800 ships were calling at Gdansk every year (Zamoyski 1987: 55) and in 1642 no fewer than 2,052 did so (Davies 1981: 258). Its major trade links were with the Netherlands, England, Scotland, Portugal, Spain and northern Italy (p. 260), and by 1650 about fifty Dutch and twenty English or Scottish trading companies maintained residents there (p. 258). Gdansk was virtually a state within a state, enjoying self-government, raising its own taxes, minting its own currency and maintaining its own militia, fortifications and warships. This cosmopolitan port city was a hive of activity, prosperity and culture ('common enough in Italy or the Netherlands, but unique in Poland'). It was also 'a shop window on European life' (p. 272), rather as the future St Petersburg would be for Russia.

The power play of the monarchy and the nobility

The dynastic union between Poland and Lithuania, followed by their victories over the Teutonic Order, catapulted the Jagiellonian realm into the ranks of the European powers. With the establishment of Jagiellon kings on the thrones of Hungary (1440–44, 1490–1526) and Bohemia (1471–1526), the Jagiellons ruled about one-third of mainland Europe (Zamoyski 1987: 50) and seemed to have gained the upper hand over the Habsburgs in the contest for supremacy over East Central Europe. Moreover, whereas Polish magnates had increased their power and wealth at the expense of the monarchy during the thirteenth and fourteenth centuries, the Jagiellon Grand Duke Kazimiercz IV managed to get himself elected and crowned King of Poland in 1446–47 'without giving much to the magnates' (Fedorowicz 1982: 92). In order to win over the nobility at the start of the Thirteen Years' War against the Teutonic Order (1454–66), Kazimiercz IV was admittedly obliged to issue the Statute of Nieszawa (1454), which stipulated that no new taxes could be levied nor armies raised without the consent of the noble-dominated provincial assemblies (*sejmiki*), whose meetings were regularized during the fifteenth century. In the process, however, the concentration of power in the hands of the magnate oligarchy was reduced and Kazimiercz IV was subsequently able to mobilize the provincial nobility (the 'gentry') as a counterweight to the magnates, much as some western European monarchs mobilized, enfranchised and increasingly relied upon the towns as a means of reducing their dependence upon the landed aristocracy (p. 93).

In 1526, however, the childless Jagiellon King of Hungary and Bohemia was defeated and killed by the Ottoman Turks at the battle of Mohacs. The Hungarian and Bohemian crowns thereupon passed to Ferdinand of Habsburg, who had married the sister of the deceased King Lajos/Ludvik (who was himself married to a Habsburg). But the implicit shift of power from the Jagiellons to the Austrian Habsburgs did not take effect immediately, since Bohemia retained considerable autonomy under Habsburg rule until 1620, while most of Hungary fell under the control of the Turks and/or their Transylvanian vassals until the 1680s.

In the meantime, Poland-Lithuania was able to enter its heyday – economically, culturally, spiritually and even politically. Indeed, Andrzej Wyczanski has argued that the alleged decline in the power of the fifteenth- and sixteenth-century Polish-Lithuanian monarchy has been greatly exaggerated. At least until 1573, in his view, the power of the monarch tended to increase rather than diminish, precisely because several kings successfully mobilized and deployed the middle ranks of the nobility (the 'gentry') against the power of the magnates. In this perspective, the major concessions granted to the nobility as a whole in 1374, 1425, 1454, 1505 and 1562–69 can be seen not as 'a weakening of royal authority' but as 'attempts at strengthening that authority by gaining the support of the gentry' against the magnates (Wyczanski 1982: 97). Thus 'the extension of the social basis of political power with the inclusion of the politically aware and active ranks of the gentry resulted in significant progress in the state's centralization and greater efficiency of administration'. Moreover, 'despite the gentry's wider participation in power, the monarch's competence and actual influence increased; this was accompanied by a corresponding erosion of the magnates' influence' (p. 148).

Even if he has slightly overstated his case, Wyczanski's thesis is a useful antidote to the frequent and easy temptation to project back on to the fifteenth- and sixteenth-century Polish-Lithuanian monarchy some of the problems of political impotence and paralysis which increasingly afflicted it from the mid-seventeenth century to the late eighteenth, and thus to perceive the gradual decline and eventual extinction of the Polish-Lithuanian realm as an ineluctable and predetermined process. Indeed, 'a span of over four hundred years seems to be rather too lengthy to be subsumed under one formula which imparts a single characteristic to the entire period. This demands an assumption of changelessness in existing conditions and institutions which is demonstrable nonsense' (Wyczanski 1982: 96).

The crucial point is that many European monarchical states (including Tsarist Russia, Habsburg Austria and Hohenzollern Brandenburg-Prussia) repeatedly recovered from what at the time probably looked like irreversible catastrophes, comparable to those suffered by seventeenth- and early eighteenth-century Poland-Lithuania. One must not assume that, because Poland-Lithuania suffered a number of severe setbacks and dynastic crises, it was therefore locked into an irreversible process of 'decline', just as one must not assume that Habsburg Austria, Tsarist Russia and Hohenzollern Brandenburg-Prussia were always 'rising'. They too experienced the dramatic seesawing of international power politics. Indeed, the extinction of particular dynasties was a problem that afflicted almost all Europe's monarchical states (albeit some more frequently than others). In any such state, moreover, a period of crisis has nearly always been one in which the nobility has temporarily been able to increase its prerogatives and privileges and to influence the selection or election of a new monarch and (potential) dynasty. Yet, once ensconced in power, the new ruler has usually been able to restore the hereditary basis of the monarchy, to suppress the elective principle and to reverse many or even most of the gains made by the nobility during the interregnum.

The pivotal question

The fundamental unresolved question concerning late medieval and early modern Poland-Lithuania is, in our view, how and why the Polish and Lithuanian nobilities were so unusually successful in permanently entrenching the elective principle and the major privileges and prerogatives gained during successive crises, even to the point of jeopardizing the very survival of their state (and hence of their own 'national' autonomy). This pivotal question is not always posed, let alone answered. We believe that the most satisfactory answers are to be found, not in the internal political and social dynamics of Poland and Lithuania considered as two separate entities, but in the additional dimensions and complications arising from the struggle to maintain a union between the two. Thus the requirements of the potent desire to cement and sustain the union helped to transform what would normally have been just a temporary acquisition of excessive and highly decentralized noble prerogatives and privileges and the even more temporary election of monarchs into formal and binding constitutional arrangements and agreements. Even more remarkably, these survived. That occurred not merely because the nobilities in question were strongly opposed to the establishment of a strong and centralized monarchy, military capability and state apparatus; most European nobilities were similarly inclined, yet they were usually unable to prevent the restoration or establishment of absolute monarchies elsewhere in Europe. The crucial additional ingredient in the preservation of extensive noble prerogatives and privileges and an elective monarchy in Poland-Lithuania was the inevitable fear that centralization and a strong monarchy could also have been used to establish the supremacy not only of the monarchy over the nobility but of one proto-national community over the other. A strong central authority could have ended the marriage between the two equal partners, whose survival seemed to be in the best interests of both sides (even though its procedures eventually exposed Poland-Lithuania to mounting external danger and interference).

THE BIRTH OF THE POLISH-LITHUANIAN COMMONWEALTH (REPUBLIC), 1569–76

The realm of the Jagiellons was, like the Habsburg Empire, an agglomeration of territories with widely differing populations, customs and forms of governance. 'The force holding this structure together was neither a feudal bond, nor a bureaucratic system, nor a military hegemony, but a broad consensus whose physical embodiment was the Jagiellon dynasty itself.' During the 1560s, therefore, the imminent extinction of that dynasty raised the fraught question of whether the Polish-Lithuanian union could 'continue to exist in its present form' (Zamoyski 1987: 92). Fearful of the predatory expansionism of Tsar Ivan the Terrible (1533–84), as well as of the incipient internal political crisis, Poland's Sejm and Senate met in joint session with their Lithuanian counterparts at Lublin in 1569 in order to sanction a new Act of Union (known to posterity as the Union of Lublin). It was agreed that the two Sejms and the two Senates would henceforth meet as one in the small but centrally located city of Warsaw, which became the capital of the new union. This *Rzeczpospolita Obojga Narodow* (Commonwealth, or Republic, of the Two Nations) was to constitute a single polity, with a unified market and a single currency. Lithuanian nobles were gradually to acquire much the same rights and status as their Polish counterparts (in theory at least). However, some Lithuanian magnates were less than thrilled at the prospect, fearing that their own dominance and privileges were being diluted and that the once mighty Grand Duchy of Lithuania was increasingly becoming the junior partner in this marriage of convenience. They tried to stonewall until, by way of retribution and/or coercion, Zygmunt II formally transferred Lithuania's Ukrainian provinces (Podlasie, Volhynia and Kiev) to the kingdom of Poland (Davies 1981: 152–3).

Zygmunt II (and with him the Jagiellon dynasty) died in 1572 and over 40,000 Polish and Lithuanian nobles attended a vast Convocation Sejm to elect a new king in 1573. (They met on a large field outside Warsaw.) Regrettably, they chose Henri de Valois, who (together with his brother King Charles IX of France) had enthusiastically participated in the notorious St Bartholomew's Eve massacre of some 20,000 *Huguenots* (French Protestants) on 24 August 1572, not long before his election to the Polish-Lithuanian throne. However, this unfortunate choice is rendered more comprehensible by a glance at the leading rival contenders – Tsar Ivan the Terrible, Prince Ernest of Habsburg, King Johan III of Sweden and a Transylvanian soldier of fortune named Stefan (Istvan) Bathory. The Habsburgs, like Muscovy and Sweden, were hoping for a dynastic annexation of Poland-Lithuania (at that time the largest state in Europe), whereas France was trying to construct an anti-Habsburg coalition. The Polish-Lithuanian nobility naturally opted for the candidate whom they thought they could most easily control, in order to safeguard the union, their own privileges and the Commonwealth's independence. Indeed, before confirming the election of Henri de Valois, they made him swear to uphold and abide by a new quasi-constitutional document. This came to be known as the *Acta Henriciana* and every subsequent monarch-elect similarly had to swear to uphold and abide by it before being confirmed as king.

The *Acta Henriciana* explicitly required the king (i) to maintain and respect the elective nature of the Polish-Lithuanian monarchy; (ii) to convoke the Sejm at least once every two years, in accordance with the terms laid down in the Union of Lublin; (iii) to respect the principle of religious toleration enshrined in the celebrated Statute of Toleration, passed by the Confederation of Warsaw in 1573; (iv) to obtain the Sejm's approval of any imposition of new taxes, declaration of war or summons of the nobility to military service (*levée-en-masse*); and (v) to recognize the nobility's right to resist, disobey or even withdraw their allegiance from the king if he broke any of these solemnly binding promises (Fedorowicz 1982: 110; Davies 1981: 334).

In the event Henri de Valois was quickly dismayed by the apparent poverty and monotony of the Polish countryside, bored by the seemingly interminable courtly deliberations in Latin and/or Polish (which he did not understand), put off by his courtiers' excessive drinking and agitated by news that his elder brother King Charles IX was seriously ill. When the latter died (childless) in May 1574 Henri rushed back home to become the new King of France, and, having refused to accept his younger brother as a viceroy, the Polish-Lithuanian nobility found themselves having to elect a new king in 1575. This time, with their restive and virtually leaderless Commonwealth under attack by Ivan the Terrible in Livonia and by Crimean Tatars in the Ukraine, the nobility chose the well educated and widely travelled Transylvanian Stefan (Istvan) Bathory, whose military prowess had already resulted in his election to the position of Prince of Transylvania in 1571 (Davies 1981: 416–23). However, besides having to accept the *Acta Henriciana* before his coronation in 1576, Bathory was also required to swear a *Pacta Conventa* (Covenant) with regard to his conduct of foreign policy and his management of crown finances, thereby setting another precedent for future royal elections (pp. 334–5). Nevertheless, despite these constitutional restraints, 'the king retained important powers and considerable room for manoeuvre', which an astute and energetic monarch such as Bathory (1576–86) could deploy to great effect. He was monarch of one of the largest states in Europe. 'As the incumbent of the Crown estates, he directly managed one-sixth of the land and population, disposing of economic and military resources greater than those of the greatest of the magnates.' He still wielded considerable powers of patronage, including the control of appointments to executive office, to lifelong tenancies of lucrative crown properties and monopolies and to many important judicial and ecclesiastical offices. 'In legislative matters he continued to issue edicts in all spheres not reserved by privilege to the Sejm; in military matters, he acted as the nominal Commander-in-Chief to whom all soldiers addressed their oath of allegiance.' He also acted as the 'protector of the lesser nobles against the magnates, and of the weaker estates . . . against the nobility'. In matters of foreign policy he had to persuade the resident senators to follow his lead, but he was not obliged to heed their every wish. Finally, it was the king who convened and dismissed the Sejm, directed the agenda of its debates and signed its resolutions into statutory law. 'The king may well have been the servant of the noble Republic, but he was no puppet' (p. 336).

URBANIZATION, RENAISSANCE AND REFORMATION

Economically and in other respects there was a significant narrowing of the gap between Poland and the southern and western regions of Europe from the fourteenth to the sixteenth centuries. A still relatively remote and sparsely populated Poland largely escaped the ravages of the Black Death and the associated disasters and crises which had convulsed western Europe during the fourteenth century. Instead, Poland entered an economic and demographic upswing which persisted into the sixteenth century (Zamoyski 1987: 59). Freer navigation was established on Poland's major rivers (the Vistula, the Bug, the Odra and the San). Roads were improved, packhorses gave way to wheeled transport, and a more unified market began to emerge. This, coupled with a 300 per cent rise in Poland's primary commodity prices during the sixteenth century, stimulated mining, agricultural production and the grain trade (Davies 1981: 128–9).

By 1500 'towns', defined here as settlements with 500 or more people, made up about 15 per cent of the population of the kingdom of Poland (excluding the Grand Duchy of Lithuania). Gdansk was Poland's largest city, with about 30,000 inhabitants, followed by Krakow (18,000), Lwow (8,000), Torun/Thorn (8,000), Elblag/Elbing (8,000), Poznan (6,000–7,000), Lublin (6,000–7,000) and Warsaw (6,000–7,000). Another eighty 'urban' settlements had 2,000–3,000 inhabitants and the other 513 had 500–2,000 each (Bogucka 1982: 138).

By 1600 'towns' with 500 or more inhabitants comprised 25 per cent of the population of the kingdom of Poland. Gdansk was still the largest, with about 70,000 inhabitants, followed by Krakow (28,000), Warsaw (20,000–30,000), Poznan (20,000), Lwow (20,000) Elblag/Elbing (15,000), Torun/Thorn (12,000), Sandomiercz (4,000–5,000), Kazimiercz Dolny (4,000–5,000) and Gniezno (4,000–5,000). However, the vast majority of the 900 'urban' settlements at that time still only comprised 500–2,000 inhabitants each (p. 139).

This growth of towns went hand-in-hand with the growth of the Jewish population, which numbered 450,000 or 4.5 per cent of the total population of the Polish-Lithuanian Commonwealth by 1648. Substantial numbers of Jewish refugees came to Poland from Spain after 1492 and from Portugal after 1496. As the Jews increased in number, however, they could no longer be restricted either to commercial and financial occupations or even to the towns. They broke the former Christian monopoly of handicrafts, founded their own craft guilds, 'left their traditional urban refuges, and penetrated into every nook and cranny of the rural areas. In the service of the nobility, they played an important pioneering role in the development of the south-eastern lands, especially in the Ukraine' (Davies 1981: 440). Like the Christian burgher communities, the Jews developed their own institutions of self-government, culminating in the creation of their own judicial and legislative Council of the Four Lands in 1580.

The Polish-Lithuanian Renaissance

The sixteenth-century European inflation and 'price revolution' (which increased grain prices much more than those of manufactures) also greatly improved Poland's external terms of trade. This made it easier for the landed classes to increase their expenditure on education and foreign study-travel – especially to Italy, where Polish students generally made up a quarter of the student body at the University of Padua between 1501 and 1605 (Zamoyski 1987: 108). But education had already developed considerably during the fourteenth and fifteenth centuries, albeit from very low base levels. By 1500 over 80 per cent of the 6,000 parishes in Wielkopolska and Malopolska had schools (Zamoyski 1987: 119) and most nobles had attained some degree of literacy (Wyrobisz 1982: 157). Moreover, during the reign of Kazimiercz IV (1446–92) approximately 15,000 students received an education at the revamped Jagiellonian University in Krakow. Among those admitted in 1491 was a certain Mikolaj Kopernik, alias Copernicus (1473–1543), whose *De Revolutionibus Orbium Coelestium* (1543) would radically transform not only mankind's view of the universe and of man's position within it, but even mankind's conception of itself. This was a seminal Polish contribution to the European Renaissance, the Scientific Revolution and the subsequent Enlightenment. Furthermore, in contrast to the fierce opposition which some of the ideas of Galileo, Giordano Bruno and Leonardo da Vinci encountered from the ecclesiastical and temporal authorities in sixteenth-century Italy, in Poland there was 'little or no resistance to the progress of new ideas, and the Church encouraged their dissemination' (Zamoyski 1987: 68). Poland offered humanist scholars a relatively clean slate on which to write. Perhaps the seemingly disadvantageous fact that Poland was less developed than areas such as Italy and France also meant that, at least in some respects, it had less accumulated ideological baggage to obstruct the path of radical new ideas. Indeed, humanism seems to have struck a chord with the fifteenth- and sixteenth-century Polish and Lithuanian nobilities, which rather self-consciously attempted to model their political institutions and concepts on those of the ancient Roman Republic, while aping the manners of their Italian contemporaries.

During the reigns of Zygmunt I (1506–48) and Zygmunt II (1548–72) there were substantial inflows of Italian artists and architects who transformed the appearance of Polish palaces, castles and country mansions. Poland was not only producing significant native painters, such as Marcin Czarny and Mikolaj Haberschrak, but also making its mark in the composition of church music (Zamoyski 1987: 66–7). Aided by 'the strong ferment of Catholic humanism' and the development of printing, the Renaissance 'struck deep roots in Poland' (Davies 1986: 294). The first Polish printing press had been established in Krakow in 1473 and the first book in Polish was published in 1513. The publication of significant numbers of books in Polish from the 1520s onwards fostered increased uniformity of spelling and grammar, transforming this language into a lucid, harmonious and efficient vehicle of expression. These literary and linguistic developments also helped to accelerate the Polonization of the Lithuanian, Byelorussian and Ukrainian nobilities. 'However, this proved in the end to be a mixed blessing' (Maczak 1992: 194), not least because it increased the cultural distance (and, increasingly, antagonism) between landlords and peasants and because diminished dependence on Latin and increased use of Polish eventually reduced Poland-Lithuania's contacts with southern and western Europe.

Humanism prepared the ground not only for the Renaissance but also for the Reformation. 'This is scarcely surprising, given the international character of humanism as an intellectual movement founded on Latin as a language of universal learning. We could even speak of a "humanist international", a body of like-minded scholars joined in a common campaign to reform European intellectual, cultural and religious life . . . The humanists were also responsible for harnessing the printing press to the cause of religious reform' (Scribner 1994: 217–18).

The Reformation in Poland-Lithuania

Within Poland-Lithuania Lutheranism was perceived as a specifically German religious doctrine and movement. It gained numerous adherents from the 1520s onwards among the predominantly German burghers, especially in the Baltic ports and the towns of

Silesia and Wielkopolska, reinforcing their sense of 'ethnic separateness' (Tazbir 1994: 168). But, by the same token, it failed to make much headway in towns such as Lwow or Przemysl which lacked a substantial German population. In effect, each major ethnic group now had its own distinctive creed(s).

The Lutheran Reformation delivered the *coup de grâce* to the Teutonic Order. In 1525, after the increasingly disconsolate Teutonic Knights had suddenly converted *en masse* to the doctrines of Martin Luther (who had promulgated his Ninety-five Theses in 1517), the Grand Master Albrecht von Hohenzollern decided to cut his losses by persuading King Zygmunt I (1506–48) to turn East Prussia into a secular fiefdom of the Polish crown and to invest him as its hereditary duke (Davies 1981: 143, 295). The erstwhile Teutonic state of Livonia, comprising much of what is now Latvia and Estonia, was similarly converted into a secular Polish fiefdom under a hereditary duke in 1561 in order to forestall the possibility that it might fall into the hands of the steadily advancing Russians, while the major port city of Riga was incorporated into the kingdom of Poland with the same local autonomy and privileges as Gdansk (pp. 146–7).

By the 1540s Calvinism was attracting increasingly powerful and influential converts and patronage among the magnates and the middle ranks of nobility, who went on to finance the establishment of several important and intellectually dynamic Calvinist academies and publishing houses as well as a Calvinist ecclesiastical infrastructure. Calvinism thus became rather fashionable in the wealthy, cosmopolitan and sophisticated sections of the nobility (who sometimes also 'persuaded' or put pressure on the inhabitants of their landed estates and adjacent townships to accept the creed of their local lords and masters). These Protestants formed a majority in the Sejm's Chamber of Deputies (the lower house) and among the lay members of the Senate (the upper house) by the 1560s, but this was not necessarily representative of the religious inclinations of the nobility as a whole (Zamoyski 1987: 81). Prominent Catholics often backed Protestant deputies in the Sejm in the expectation that the latter would staunchly defend the political prerogatives and privileges of the nobility against the absolutist pretensions of Catholic kings, i.e. for political rather than religious reasons. By 1569 Protestants comprised an estimated 20 per cent of the nobility (Tazbir 1994: 170) and approximately 15 per cent of the population as a whole, although nearly one-third of the latter were Lutheran German townspeople (Davies 1981: 183, 162).

The most interesting and distinctive Protestants in sixteenth-century Poland-Lithuania were the so-called Polish Brethren (alias Socinians or Arians), who comprised 2–3 per cent of the population by 1569. Their numbers were boosted by the expulsion of the so-called Czech Brethren from Bohemia to Poland-Lithuania in 1548–50. (They made up about 2 per cent of the population by 1569.) In common with other Unitarians, they dismissed the Holy Trinity and the alleged divinity of Christ in favour of an emphasis on the oneness of God and a literal or strictly rationalist ('no nonsense') interpretation of the Bible. This explains their pacifism, their egalitarianism and their perception of Christ as a divinely inspired man and teacher. They extolled freedom of thought and conscience (Davies 1981: 184–9). German Protestant sects, such as the Menonites, the Anabaptists and 'the Quakerish Schwenfeldians', also attracted approximately 4–5 per cent of the population by 1569, but their followings were largely confined to predominantly German towns (pp. 162, 190).

Protestant ideas probably appeared less 'shocking' or 'alarming' to Catholics in Poland-Lithuania than they did in predominantly Catholic countries, partly because

Polish and Lithuanian Catholics had already had to accept (and establish a *modus vivendi* with) a large Eastern Orthodox population which, like the Protestants, rejected the celibacy of parish priests, used the vernacular in the liturgy and accepted communion in both forms (the bread and the wine). Indeed, whereas in Germany and northern and western Europe the Reformation shattered a long-standing Christian unity, in Poland-Lithuania Christianity was already multi-denominational long before the start of the Reformation (Tazbir 1994: 168). Eastern Orthodox Christians already comprised approximately 40 per cent of the population and Armenian (Gregorian) Christians another 1 per cent or 2 per cent by the late fifteenth century. In Poland-Lithuania, moreover, the conduct of the Roman Catholic Church was constrained by the fact that it had never occupied the kind of unchallenged position that it had enjoyed in medieval southern and western Europe. Catholics comprised only 45–47 per cent of the population in 1569 and the Catholic Church had to contend with competition from Eastern Orthodox, Gregorian and Protestant forms of Christianity (Davies 1981: 162, 166, 172). Royal edicts against 'heresy' were increasingly thwarted by the independent-minded nobility and Sejm, who refused to enforce them. 'In a state which possessed no strong central executive authority, and where the ecclesiastical courts could not enforce their rulings, religious uniformity could not be imposed' (p. 199). In 1555 apostasy from the Catholic faith was in effect legalized for the nobility by a royal decree suspending the jurisdiction of ecclesiastical courts over lay courts, which also made it difficult to punish apostasy in the rest of the population. The legal jurisdiction of ecclesiastical courts was virtually annulled altogether in 1562–63 (Tazbir 1994: 169; Zamoyski 1987: 84).

In Poland-Lithuania the Reformation was received more as an interesting foreign ideology than as a protest against the moral and spiritual shortcomings of the Catholic Church. Certainly, it reinforced long-standing campaigns 'to abolish ecclesiastical jurisdiction over the laity, to achieve a just reform of the tithe and to compel the clergy to contribute to the defence of the realm' (Tazbir 1994: 170). But it was mainly an adjunct to 'the struggle for noble privilege' and 'a means of exerting pressure on the Catholic clergy, rather than a movement for radical reform of the Church' (p. 178). According to Adam Zamoyski (1987: 87), 'The Reformation in Poland was not at bottom a spiritual movement. It was a sally by the articulate classes who made use of the liberating challenge of Luther to further a process of intellectual and political emancipation which had started long before.'

This emphasis on political rather than strictly religious motives for supporting the Reformation in Poland is consistent with Janusz Tazbir's claim that, unlike their western European counterparts, Polish Calvinists continued to venerate certain 'national' saints and the Virgin Mary, to regard Mary as the 'patron of the entire "nation" of the nobility', and to celebrate Christmas and Easter in much the same manner as Catholics (Tazbir 1994: 212–13).

Religious toleration

The sixteenth-century Polish-Lithuanian nobility actively resisted the form of religious persecution which plagued southern and western Europe at the time. When the Bishop of Poznan tried to have four 'heretics' burnt at the stake in 1554 and 1555 the accused were rescued by armed posses of nobles, many of whom were practising Catholics. As one of them then pointed out, 'It is not a question of religion, it is a question of liberty' (Zamoyski 1987: 84).

Most remarkably of all, the Confederation of Warsaw which elected Henri de Valois as King of Poland-Lithuania in 1573 also passed a Statute of Toleration which stated: 'Whereas in our Commonwealth there is no small disagreement in the matter of the Christian faith, and in order to prevent that any harmful contention should arise from this, as we see clearly taking place in other kingdoms, we swear to each other, in our name and in that of our descendants for ever more, on our honour, our faith, our love and our conscience, that albeit we are *dissidentes in religione*, we will all keep the peace between ourselves, and that we will not, for the sake of our various faiths and differences of church, either shed blood or confiscate property, deny favour, imprison, or banish and . . . we will not aid or abet any power or office which strives to this' (quoted in Zamoyski 1987: 90–1).

This Statute of Toleration did not propose sanctions against those who attacked Protestant churches, homes, shops, funerals or cemeteries. Nor did it prevent the closure of Protestant churches and the expulsion of Protestants from Krakow in 1591, from Poznan in 1611 or from Lublin in 1627 (Tazbir 1994: 174). Nevertheless it was a potent inspiration and the Commonwealth's greatest contribution to the Renaissance spirit of toleration and universalism which ought to have pervaded late sixteenth-century Europe – instead of the mounting religious fractiousness and intolerance unleashed by the German, western and southern European Reformations and Counter-Reformations. Roman Catholicism remained the official (state) religion, yet the statute encompassed almost all Christian denominations (including Orthodox Christians and the Polish Brethren). It was an astonishing 'agreement to disagree', way ahead of its time.

This rare triumph of noble caste solidarity over religious fractiousness and intolerance was broadly observed and upheld by the subsequent rulers of Poland-Lithuania, even if there were some illegal lynchings and executions during periods of acute crisis (such as the 1650s and the 1700s). According to a Calvinist account of the Polish-Lithuanian Counter-Reformation, there were only twelve executions or sectarian killings of Protestants in Poland-Lithuania between 1550 and 1650, compared with over 500 in England and nearly 900 in the Netherlands over the same period (Zamoyski 1987: 91). Indeed, for all their alleged religious ardour, Poles have committed far fewer atrocities against 'their own people' than many other European nations have done. They have usually pulled back from the brink of violent internal conflict, even if they have (regrettably) not avoided frequent persecution of Jewish and Ukrainian minorities and violent conflict with their neighbours. The basic motivation has undoubtedly been a strong desire for ethnic 'self-preservation', but there has also been something more than that – something admirable.

Ecumenicism and the Uniate Church

During the middle years of the sixteenth century there were 'repeated attempts to devise a form of Confession acceptable to all' (Davies 1981: 183), with the aim of keeping the peace in a multicultural society. In 1555 a majority of deputies in the lower house of the Sejm even went so far as to demand the establishment of an ecumenical (interdenominational) Church of Poland which would perform its rites in the vernacular, allow priests to marry, offer communion in both forms (the bread and the wine) and vest ultimate control of the Church in a Polish-Lithuanian synod free of papal interference. King Zygmunt II (1548–72), who took an active interest in Protestantism and ecclesiastical reform while remaining a Catholic monarch, referred the matter to Rome, having famously stated: 'I am not the king of your conscience.' In other words, he regarded religion as a private and personal matter and he upheld freedom of thought and conscience. But such an outlook was incomprehensible to the Pope, who merely reprimanded the king for 'allowing his subjects to formulate such heretical demands' (Zamoyski 1987: 86).

The Commonwealth's ecumenicism also contributed to the creation of the Uniate Church in 1595–96, although the Church was unfortunately blighted from birth. A hybrid Church, it was Eastern Orthodox in its rites and customs (it retained the Slavonic Orthodox liturgy and the marriage of priests), but it owed allegiance to the Pope and the Vatican Curia rather than to the Orthodox Patriarch in Constantinople. Its establishment was partly a result of Polish Catholic attempts to render the Commonwealth's Eastern Orthodox inhabitants (who comprised about 40 per cent of the population) less susceptible to Muscovite Russian influence and to bind them more closely to the politically dominant Catholics (who made up 45–47 per cent of the population). It also arose out of various attempts by many Orthodox Christian clergy and nobility in the Ukraine (and to a lesser extent Byelorussia) to draw closer to the Roman Catholic Church and the Polish nobility in the wake of the fall of Constantinople to the Ottomans in 1453 and the subsequent northward offensives of the Turks and the Crimean Tatars. Moreover, the fall of Constantinople had encouraged Muscovite Russia to aspire to the leadership of all Eastern Orthodox peoples. This was the origin of Muscovite claims that Moscow was 'the Third Rome' (after Rome-Italy and Rome-Constantinople) and the chrysalis of a 'rising' world power and world civilization. In Polish-Lithuanian eyes, however, the pretensions of 'upstart' Muscovite rulers to the title of 'Tsar and Autocrat of all the Russias' was sheer effrontery, since many of the lands to which the Tsars laid claim 'belonged to the Republic and had never belonged to Muscovy' (Davies 1981: 387).

In 1588, during 'a pastoral visit to his flock in the Commonwealth', the Orthodox Patriarch of Constantinople seems to have authorized the Orthodox Bishop of Luck to open negotiations with the Catholic Bishop of Luck in the hope of attaining greater mutual recognition and local co-operation between their respective dioceses (Zamoyski 1987: 160). The following year, however, a fully fledged Orthodox patriarchate was established in Moscow, further inflating the latter's territorial and pastoral pretensions to the Ukraine and Byelorussia. This prompted some of the Commonwealth's Orthodox bishops (with active Jesuit encouragement) to send a letter to the Pope in 1595, asking him to admit the Orthodox Christians of the Ukraine and Byelorussia to the Roman Catholic Church without requiring them to renounce their Eastern Orthodox/Slavic customs and liturgy. The Jesuits put pressure on the Pope to assent to this arrangement, in the belief that it would open the way to increased Polonization of the Orthodox Christians of the Ukraine and Byelorussia and facilitate their future conversion to Roman Catholicism. The Pope was thus persuaded to issue a bull purportedly ending the schism between the Orthodox and the Catholic Churches in the Commonwealth. But the manoeuvre immediately backfired, because many of the Orthodox clergy and laity felt indignant that they had not been consulted and that they had been 'sold out' to the Roman Catholic Church by some high-handed and/or corrupt bishops and nobles, under pressure from the Jesuits. Therefore the joint synod which assembled in Brzesc (Brest) on

8 October 1596 to consummate the establishment of the so-called Uniate Church was racked by acrimony and dissension. Many Orthodox Christians (including several bishops) refused to accept the Union of Brest and the day ended with the rival Churches excommunicating one another!

Within the Commonwealth those Orthodox Christians who accepted the Union of Brest and the Uniate Church came to be known as the *unici* (uniates), while those who refused to do so were denounced as *dysunici* ('disuniates') and *dissidentes* (dissidents). For thirty-seven years the latter were harassed and deprived of any official recognition and status. However, treating the Orthodox Christians of the Ukraine and Byelorussia as dissidents and schismatics merely encouraged them to look east, to the burgeoning Russian Orthodox Church. The realization that this was happening eventually persuaded the Commonwealth's Catholic authorities to relent and rehabilitate the Orthodox hierarchy in 1633 (Davies 1981: 175).

All in all, this clumsy attempt to unite the Commonwealth's principal Churches increased rather than reduced its religious divisions and antagonisms. It also contributed to the emergence of wider antagonisms between Orthodox Eastern Slavs (Russians, Ukrainians and Byelorussians) and Poles which have survived into modern times. Polish Catholics have long tended to regard any compatriot attracted to Eastern Orthodoxy, to Eastern Slavic culture or (more recently) to Marxism-Leninism as a 'dissident' and as an irredeemable 'traitor' to Poland and its national religion.

The situation also encouraged the formerly Orthodox nobles in the Ukraine and Byelorussia to embrace full-blown Catholicism rather than the hybrid Uniate Church. Indeed, in breach of the founding agreements, the Commonwealth never granted the Uniates the same status and representation as Catholics, and Uniate numbers were steadily eroded by desertions to Eastern Orthodoxy and Roman Catholicism. Moreover, both Uniate and Eastern Orthodoxy became increasingly identified as banners and rallying points for peasant antagonism towards the increasingly Catholicized and Polonized nobility, especially in the borderlands of the Ukraine and Byelorussia. This was to be most evident during the tumultuous years between 1648 and 1668, but there were also significant 'after shocks' amid the warfare and unrest that occurred during the 1700s, 1733–35 and 1792–94, during the Polish uprisings of 1830–31, 1846 and 1863, during the First World War and its aftermath, and during the 1930s Depression. These social-cum-religious antagonisms contributed to significant revivals of Eastern Orthodoxy in the Ukraine and Byelorussia during the seventeenth and eighteenth centuries. However, most of the areas inhabited by Eastern Orthodox Christians were lost to Russia during the second half of the seventeenth century, with the result that Uniates still constituted about 33 per cent of the Commonwealth's population in 1772, compared with the Catholics' 43 per cent, the Eastern Orthodox Christians' 10 per cent, the Jews' 8 per cent and the Protestants' 4 per cent (Davies 1981: 162). The Uniates who came under Russian rule were even more badly treated by successive Russian regimes than Eastern Orthodox Christians had been by the Polish-Lithuanian Commonwealth. Many Russian bigots and nationalists regarded them as traitors and apostates. Indeed, it is unfortunate that the Union of Brest was ever initiated, since it has brought nothing but bitterness and grief.

THE HEYDAY OF THE *RZECZPOSPOLITA*, 1576–1648

King Stefan Bathory (1576–86) rapidly reformed the Polish-Lithuanian army and judiciary and brusquely brought to heel the overmighty magnates, the fractious Dnieper Cossacks and the city of Gdansk (which had come out in support of the Austrian Habsburgs). Crown revenues were almost doubled between 1576–77 and 1585–86 and there was retrenchment at court, while Gdansk, the Church and various vassals were deftly induced to make substantial 'voluntary' donations to the royal coffers. 'A ruler who was trusted by his subjects was able to mobilize unseen resources' (Davies 1981: 425–8). As a result Bathory had the wherewithal to roll back the Russian advance into Livonia and 'to carry the fight into enemy territory' by subduing Polotsk and laying siege to Pskov, with the loss of over 300,000 Russian lives. He thereby induced Ivan the Terrible to renounce his claims to Livonia, Polotsk, Velizh and Ushviata and to sue for peace in 1581–82 (pp. 429–31).

Bathory's brief but robust reign clearly demonstrated that an able and energetic ruler of the Polish-Lithuanian Commonwealth could still mobilize and deploy considerable strength and that, if the nobility had consistently selected its monarchs on the basis of proven ability and executive prowess, the elective monarchy could have been at least as effective as a hereditary one (perhaps more so, since it would have been less susceptible to the hazards of dynastic in-breeding). It could have functioned rather in the manner of the presidency of France's Fifth Republic, which has sometimes been likened to an elective monarchy. For the most part, however, the Commonwealth's nobles were less concerned with the common weal than with short-term tactical considerations and with safeguarding their own sectional interests, prerogatives and privileges. They therefore tended to elect relative nonentities.

Stefan Bathory left behind no obvious heir when he died in December 1586. His nephew was merely an 'also ran' in the royal election of 1587, which was essentially a contest between Sigismund Vasa, the Polish-speaking son and heir apparent of Sweden's King Johan III Vasa (who was married to a staunchly Catholic Jagiellon princess from Poland), and Archduke Maximilian of Habsburg, the brother of the Habsburg Emperor Rudolf II. In 1587, as Habsburg Spain was preparing to launch a great naval armada against England, the Habsburg 'mafia' seemed poised for supremacy over Europe. But many Polish-Lithuanian nobles were fearful of allowing their Commonwealth to fall into the Catholic absolutist clutches of the Austrian Habsburgs. Therefore magnates led by Vice-chancellor Jan Zamoyski pre-emptively engineered the election of the twenty-one-year-old Vasa prince as King Zygmunt III of Poland-Lithuania. They also defeated a Habsburg attempt to gain the Polish-Lithuanian throne by force. Ironically, the Catholic absolutist aspirations of Zygmunt III Vasa soon proved to be every bit as strong as those of the defeated candidate, but by then it was too late for Zamoyski to undo his mistake. The Commonwealth was saddled with a monarch who was congenitally at odds with its constitution.

Thus began a fateful new chapter in Polish-Lithuanian history: eighty-one years of Vasa rule (1587–1668) and a consequent embroilment in Swedish affairs for which the Commonwealth was to pay an unexpectedly high price in due course. Moreover, Zygmunt III soon alienated his original Polish-Lithuanian supporters by marrying a Habsburg archduchess, by proving highly susceptible to Jesuit and Habsburg influence, and by (mis)using his Polish-Lithuanian throne as a power base for several abortive attempts to roll back the Protestant Reformation and ensconce Catholic absolutist ('divine right') rule in both the Commonwealth and Sweden. At least that was the light in which his opponents and detractors saw him. In his own conscience he was undoubtedly acting in accordance with God's wishes and commands. Therefore, no matter how often he was forced to apologize and back down in public, he remained unrepentant at heart. But this in turn meant that the Polish and Lithuanian nobilities could never trust him to respect and uphold their cherished liberties, institutions and procedures. Indeed, his various attempts to establish a Catholic absolutist ('divine right') monarchy were inherently incompatible with the ethos of his noble subjects, while his all-or-nothing mindset prevented him from seeing the ways in which he could have deployed his still considerable monarchical powers and resources to greater effect. The upshot was 'a succession of fruitless and damaging collisions with the institutions of the Common-wealth' (Zamoyski 1987: 136).

Zygmunt III's reign (1587–1632) coincided with the Commonwealth's 'golden age' and was the longest in Polish-Lithuanian history. Yet, paradoxically, even on his deathbed Zygmunt remained less interested in the Commonwealth *per se* than in using its considerable power and influence in the Baltic region to contain the Reformation and bring his native Sweden back into the Catholic fold. In the process, however, he not only squandered some of the resources and opportunities provided by that 'golden age' but also sowed the seeds of the catastrophes which befell the Commonwealth during the reign of his second son, Jan Kazimiercz Vasa (1648–68). Zygmunt nevertheless deserves some credit for having helped to keep the Commonwealth out of the destructive and sectarian Thirty Years' War (1618–48).

Despite the eventual failure, one ought not to see Zygmunt III's aspiration to reverse the Swedish Reformation as doomed from the start. After all, the Bohemian and Hungarian Reformations *were* eventually reversed 'from above', in spite of having gained majority support. The Swedish Reformation had initially been fostered by Zygmunt III's grandfather, the usurper Gustav Vasa, not so much from deep religious conviction as out of a desire to consolidate his own insecure rule and Sweden's recently regained independence from Denmark. Until the 1560s, however, Swedish Protestantism gained little support outside the predominantly German population of Stockholm; and even then its future was 'far from secure' (Grell 1994: 113).

With his parents' approval, the future Zygmunt III had been brought up by Jesuit tutors who instilled in him an ardent desire to replace the Swedish Reformation and limited monarchy with Catholic absolutist 'divine right' rule. Fearing as much, the Swedish aristocracy made its crown prince sign a written undertaking to uphold and respect the established positions and prerogatives of the Swedish Diet and the semi-reformed Church of Sweden before he sailed away to take up the Polish-Lithuanian crown in 1587. Yet in 1589 he made an abortive attempt to cede that crown to the Habsburgs in return for Austrian money and help in reclaiming Sweden for Catholicism and in transferring Livonia and other south-eastern Baltic territories from Polish to Swedish rule. He was severely taken to task by the Sejm for this blatant breach of faith, which cannot have endeared him to the Swedish nobility either (Davies 1981: 436; Zamoyski 1987: 132).

When his father Johan III died in 1592, Zygmunt III returned to Sweden to claim his inheritance. But he met with sullen hostility and insults from the Swedish aristocracy and, fearing that he might be deposed from his Commonwealth throne *in absentia*, he sailed back to Poland-Lithuania in 1594, leaving behind Duke Karl of Söddermannland (his Protestant uncle) as regent in Sweden. Zygmunt III made another attempt to establish himself as king in Sweden in 1598, but that equally bruising encounter encouraged the hostile Diet to depose him from the Swedish throne in 1599. This action signalled the start of the open hostilities between an increasingly Protestant Sweden and an increasingly Catholic Commonwealth, which were to drag on intermittently until 1709. The stakes were raised in 1604, when Zygmunt III's uncle (the former regent) was elected King Karl IX of Sweden. This man was the founder of the Protestant line of Vasas, who were to succeed in transforming Sweden into one of Europe's great powers and in turning the tables on their Catholic cousins in Poland-Lithuania, both by championing the Protestant cause in East Central Europe and by repeatedly annexing the Baltic's south-eastern shores.

The opening shots in this protracted battle for supremacy in the Baltic region were fired in the 1600s and in the 1620s, when first Livonia and later Pomerania repeatedly changed hands. These conflicts were inflamed by the religious factor, as the predominantly Protestant merchants and patriciates of the major south-eastern Baltic ports (other than Protestant Elblag and Gdansk) gradually switched their allegiance to Protestant Sweden. However, a treaty signed at Stumdorf (Stumska Wies) in 1635 temporarily suspended the Catholic Vasas' claim to the Swedish throne (it was not finally renounced until 1660) and restored the Prussian and Pomeranian ports to the Commonwealth, while confirming Sweden's hold on Livonia. But this was merely the calm before the Swedish storm that was to devastate the Polish-Lithuanian Commonwealth during the late 1650s.

Meanwhile, different storms were brewing on the eastern front. The extinction of the long-standing Riurik dynasty in 1598, coming not long after the death of Tsar Ivan the Terrible in 1584, had plunged Russia into a period of political disintegration, poor harvests, pestilence and social unrest aptly known as the Time of Troubles. These tribulations, allied to dark suspicions concerning the means by which Tsar Boris Godunov (1598–1605) had gained his crown, threw up a number of pretenders to the Muscovite throne. Two of these so-called 'false Dmitris', both claiming to be the reputedly murdered yet 'miraculously saved' younger son of Ivan the Terrible, managed to enlist Polish-Lithuanian and Jesuit support for their bids for the Russian throne. The first of these Pretenders managed to enter Moscow and gain the Tsarist crown virtually unopposed in 1605 (at the very time when Tsar Boris Godunov died). But the following year he was overthrown and killed during an uprising orchestrated by a prominent Russian magnate, Vasily Shuisky, who thereupon had himself elected Tsar (1606–10).

Another 'false Dmitri' emerged in 1607 and (like his predecessor) garnered support from sections of the Polish-Lithuanian nobility with designs upon large tracts of Muscovite territory. The stakes were raised in 1609, when Tsar Shuisky and King Karl IX of Sweden concluded a military pact directed against Poland-Lithuania. This was a red rag to the Catholic bull. Zygmunt III immediately obtained papal and Jesuit support for a Catholic crusade against this 'unholy alliance' of Orthodox Russians and Protestant Swedes. He laid siege to the disputed city of Smolensk (which surrendered in 1611) while the pretender advanced on Moscow. When the main Muscovite army was crushed by the invading Poles and Lithuanians at Klushino in 1610, the Muscovite nobility deposed Shuisky and transferred their allegiance to Zygmunt's son Wladyslaw, whom they elected Tsar (1610–13). However, Zygmunt III's over-zealous insistence that Muscovy had to become Catholic provoked a rash of Russian anti-Catholic rebellions and the election of a new Russian Orthodox Tsar, Mikhail Romanov (1613–45). The Romanovs and the Russian Orthodox Church quickly rallied the Russians against the Catholic interlopers.

Without fully realizing how much was at stake, Poland-Lithuania had muffed a unique opportunity to dismember its most dangerous foe. However, according to Norman Davies (1981: 455), historical perceptions have been distorted by the power of the Russian plays and operas dealing with this period: 'The idea that the Republic of Poland-Lithuania, with its modest military resources and creaking finances, could ever have contemplated "occupying" or "subjugating" the vastnesses of Russia is preposterous . . . The Poles were only able to intervene at all because powerful factions among the Muscovite boyars [aristocrats] were pressing them to do so.' This may be true, but there is a big difference between 'occupying' or 'subjugating' Russia and fostering its potential for fragmentation. Poland-Lithuania failed to wrest maximum long-term advantage from Muscovy's temporarily prostrate condition, with the result that the Russians were soon able to tip the scales of territorial power in their own favour between 1654 and 1668.

In the eyes of contemporaries, however, the years between 1635 and 1648 appeared to herald the dawn of a new era of peace and prosperity for the Commonwealth. The aggressive proclivities of the Austrian Habsburgs, the Protestant Vasas and the Hohenzollerns were being absorbed elsewhere and Muscovy was engaged in internal recovery and reconstruction, with the result that Poland-Lithuania seemed to be under no immediate threat. When Zygmunt III died in 1632 he was smoothly succeeded by his eldest son, Wladyslaw IV (1632–48), who was in the comfortable position of being able to 'mediate on behalf of other states caught up in the Thirty Years' War' (Zamoyski 1987: 158).

Nevertheless, a colossal crisis was brewing. In 1640 and 1644 Podolia and Volynia were ravaged by marauding Crimean Tatars, who made off with thousands of captives. These raids prompted King Wladyslaw IV to plan a major military campaign against the Crimean Tatars and their Ottoman overlords in alliance with Muscovy and the Dnieper Cossacks, who were promised substantial shares of the spoils. However, the Sejm did not trust Wladyslaw IV and managed to obstruct his preparations in 1647–48, whereupon the already armed and mobilized Dnieper Cossacks ran amok under their unsavoury and opportunistic military leader Bogdan Chmielnicki (Khmelnitsky), who now made common cause with the Crimean Tatars *against* the Polish-Lithuanian Commonwealth. This Cossack rebellion, combined with several disastrously bungled attempts to bring the Cossacks to heel, ignited a massive explosion of peasant unrest in the Ukraine. At that time the Ukraine was home to a large number of runaway serfs, religious dissenters and peasants hostile to the southward spread of Polish-Lithuanian landlordism, serfdom and rack-renting Jewish 'middlemen'. To a far greater extent than anyone could have foreseen in 1648, the Cossack-cum-peasant rebellion was to have deadly consequences. These abruptly terminated the 'golden age' of the *Rzeczpospolita* and heralded its long and calamitous decline (1648–1795). Numerous weaknesses and portents of decline can of course be detected before 1648, but until that year the *Rzeczpospolita* was to all appearances riding high.

CATALYSTS OF DECLINE

In May 1648 Wladyslaw IV, the only person who could easily have placated the mutinous Cossacks, suddenly died. His younger brother, Jan Kazimiercz, was immediately sworn in as the new king during a hastily arranged cease-fire. But the truce was soon broken by the Ukraine's most powerful magnate, Prince Jarema Wisniowiecki, whose attempts to repress the rebel Cossacks misfired. This merely added fuel to the flames of rebellion, with the result that the conflict spluttered on for several more years. In 1654, moreover, Khmelnitsky placed his Cossacks under Muscovite 'protection'. Thereupon, taking advantage of the wounds inflicted upon Poland-Lithuania by the Russian-backed rebels in the Ukraine, King Karl X of Sweden (1654–60) suddenly occupied Pomerania in 1655 and proceeded to lay waste Warsaw, Krakow and many other Polish towns and cities. This orgy of killing and destruction brought relatively minor gains to Sweden, yet it had an intensity approaching that of the Nazi and Soviet devastation of Poland during the Second World War. It also further reduced the Commonwealth's capacity to resist its other foes. The malnourished, ravaged and disease-stricken population of Poland-Lithuania contracted by a quarter between 1648 and 1660, and some towns took over a century to regain their 1640s population level (Bogucka 1982: 140–1).

In addition, Polish Jews became a prime target of popular fury, especially in the south and east, where Jewish middlemen had increasingly become revenue collectors (and debt collectors) on behalf of the aristocracy, the crown and even the Catholic Church. Both the origins and the magnitude of the Jewish intermediaries' wealth aroused widespread popular antisemitism. This erupted into murderous pogroms between 1648 and 1656, during which time the Jewish population fell by nearly 100,000, through the combined effects of destruction, destitution and flight (Davies 1981: 467). The Jewish community subsequently retreated into itself and into the infamous ghettoes. 'The masses of Polish Jewry lived in desperate poverty, in an increasingly hostile environment.' This assisted the rabbinate gradually to reassert 'a medieval grip' over the orthodox Jewish community, yet simultaneously encouraged the growth of Hasidism, a mystical and ecstatic Jewish cult which attracted the growing number of impoverished Jewish slum dwellers and social outcasts. Even the semi-autonomous Jewish 'state within a state' was eventually dissolved in 1764, as a result of several decades of large-scale financial irregularity and embezzlement, which had brought the Commonwealth's Jewish financiers to the verge of bankruptcy (Zamoyski 1987: 214). Yet this failed to forestall another wave of pogroms in 1768, not to mention the even greater antisemitic crimes of more recent times.

It has been suggested that in 1655 a majority of the Commonwealth's population would have been 'quite prepared to accept' Karl X as king, but this Swede 'was only interested in keeping Pomerania and Livonia, and treated the rest of Poland as occupied territory. He and his generals immediately began exporting everything they could lay hands on . . . Protestant Swedes also took to burning down churches, having first emptied them of everything portable' (Zamoyski 1987: 169–70).

Incensed by the invaders' indiscriminate slaughter and pillage, and by the bigoted burning and desecration of Catholic churches and shrines, the Poles succeeded in rallying their scattered and decimated forces in order to fight off the Swedish vultures. The Catholic defenders of the fortified monastery of Jasna Gora near Czestochowa were allegedly assisted by the miraculous intervention of the Black Madonna (a portait of which still graces the abbey church to this day). It was here that the Swedes suffered their first reverse. By boosting the morale of the Commonwealth's troops, news of this event symbolically turned the tide and encouraged King Jan Kazimiercz to return from exile.

Ever since then the Black Madonna of Jasna Gora has remained the most prominent focus of Polish patriotism and Catholicism, contributing to successive Catholic revivals and the nationwide cult of the Virgin Mary.

Besides Jasna Gora, centres such as Gdansk and Lwow also managed to ward off the Swedish juggernaut, while countries such as the Netherlands and Denmark came to the Commonwealth's assistance (reasoning that their enemy's enemy was their friend!). After Khmelnitsky's death in 1657, moreover, the Cossacks vacillated between allegiance to Russia and allegiance to the Commonwealth and increasingly fought among themselves. However, one seemingly minor consequence of the Commonwealth's tribulations was eventually to prove lethal. In 1656 and 1657 the Hohenzollern ruler of Brandenburg and Prussia deftly played off the Swedes and the Poles against one another so as to obtain full sovereignty over his fiefdoms, which were soon to emerge from obscurity as the kingdom of Brandenburg-Prussia (and as the new incubator of Germanic imperialism).

Jan Kazimiercz abdicated in 1668 (mourning the death of his wife) and lived out his last years in France, where he died childless in 1672. Thus ended the Commonwealth's Vasa dynasty. However, while the Commonwealth's relative decline had undoubtedly begun by the 1650s, the process was not yet irreversible. The Commonwealth's capacity for regeneration proved to be remarkable. Its resources, if fully mobilized and well directed, were still considerable. Moreover, its territorial vastness and diversity meant that the processes of decline took place neither uniformly nor within a given time span, but erratically and unevenly over a long period. These factors were reinforced by the Commonwealth's political, religious and cultural eclecticism, which encouraged the fruitful coexistence of diverse and discrepant tendencies (Zamoyski 1987: 190–2).

The continually seesawing contest for supremacy in East Central Europe had started with 'a struggle between the Habsburgs and the Jagiellons over the crucial axis of Silesia, Bohemia and Hungary'. The early Jagiellons had gained the upper hand during the fifteenth century, but neither the later Jagiellons nor the Catholic Vasas managed to capitalize on their initial advantages (pp. 72–3). The Commonwealth became over-reliant on its powers of attraction, partly because the ruling oligarchies of Danzig, Prussia, Livonia, Ruthenia and Saxony were initially content to place themselves under its unobtrusive protective umbrella. Habsburg aggrandisement, by contrast, relied on a combination of dynastic alliances, diplomacy and shrewd marriages, backed up by a military establishment and industrial/financial support whose development was greatly accelerated by the Thirty Years' War (1618–48) and innumerable wars against the Turks (1520s–1690s).

It was doubly unfortunate for the Commonwealth that its own state structures 'gelled at a time when internal prosperity was at its height and the external threat was small. The decentralized traditions of defence, finance and executive power were perpetuated in line with previous conditions, and not in expectation of increased pressures' (Davies 1981: 58). The military prowess of the Polish-Lithuanian cavalry from the early fifteenth century to the late seventeenth was based on the spectacularly high mobility, surprise tactics and weight-effective weaponry made possible by the interbreeding of Tatar and European horses, the use of light Tatar saddles and reliance on the hybrid curved sabre modified from Tatar models by the Magyars and the Poles to give a 'uniquely high ratio of cutting-power to effort expended' (Zamoyski 1987: 154–6). These weapons, equestrian skills and surprise tactics allowed the Commonwealth to develop an economy of strength which was eventually to prove fatal (Majewski 1982: 182–3, 186, 189). 'Victory was repeatedly achieved at low cost and with little apparent effort, and this had a pernicious effect' (Zamoyski 1987: 156). While most of the monarchies in late sixteenth-century Europe typically spent 60–70 per cent of their revenue on military items, the figure for Poland was nearer 20 per cent (p. 103). The Commonwealth briefly built up a navy between the 1560s and the 1640s. (It even inflicted a defeat on the Swedish navy in 1627.) But the *szlachta* and the Sejm liked paying for a navy even less than paying for a large standing army, with the result that after the crisis of the 1650s the navy was allowed to run down and the Commonwealth became unduly dependent on Dutch and English maritime power (p. 156). Moreover, the Sejm repeatedly voted down proposals for a larger standing army (i) for reasons of cost and (ii) from fear that it could be used to suppress the 'liberties' of the *szlachta* and establish an absolute monarchy (p. 103). The Commonwealth even failed to develop a regular diplomatic corps and a central chancellery capable of devising and pursuing a coherent foreign policy (p. 175).

In 1669, in defiance of Habsburg and Bourbon candidatures for the Polish-Lithuanian throne, the nobility elected the rich but feckless Ukrainian magnate Michal Korybut Wisniowiecki as their new king (1669–73). Within four years he had died from eating too many gherkins, while parts of his seemingly moribund kingdom were being invaded by the Ottomans. In this hour of need, however, the Commonwealth was saved by the military prowess of the magnate Jan Sobieski, who unexpectedly annihilated the invading Turkish forces. He was thereupon elected king (1673–96) by the grateful nobility.

Unfortunately, instead of drastically augmenting the Commonwealth's permanent and professional establishment, its tax base and its arms production, this most illustrious warrior king still preferred to rely on the courage, dedication, *esprit de corps*, equestrian skills, mobility, light oriental sabres and tactical prowess of amateur noble volunteers and cavalrymen like himself. This sufficed in the short term. But in the long run it was to prove no match for the large professional armies, bureaucracies, tax revenues and armament industries that were being built up by the Commonwealth's neighbours, who were increasingly to outspend and outgun the chivalrous republic. 'Sobieski led by his own private example, dispensing his personal fortune in the service of the state . . . Sobieski was able to inspire the Republic to unparalleled efforts, in short bursts. But he left the outdated machine virtually exhausted . . . At the end of the reign, unpaid soldiery constituted a generalized plague in many provinces' (Davies 1981: 478).

When the Ottomans besieged Vienna in 1683 the Austrian Habsburgs readily entrusted the defence of their own domain and of Catholic Christendom to Sobieski, who had successfully harried the Turks during the 1670s. However, even though the Polish king covered himself with glory during the relief of Vienna (autumn 1683) and in the subsequent counter-offensive against the Turks, his celebrated victories benefited his own Commonwealth much less than the emergent Austrian Habsburg Empire and contributed to the eclipse of the former by the latter. Moreover, the attendant diversion of Polish-Lithuanian military resources towards the Danubian basin left the Commonwealth incapable of forestalling the final abandonment of the entire Ukraine to Russia in 1686. 'This . . . step, which more than any other marked the transformation of . . . Muscovy into "great Russia" and tipped the scales of power in Eastern Europe in Moscow's favour, was taken almost casually . . . The eventual recovery of Podolia at the Peace of Karlowitz in 1699 was small compensation' (Davies 1981: 487).

Poles have naturally tended to look back with pride at a Polish monarch 'whose deeds reverberated to their credit throughout Europe'. Yet his military valour and prowess and the political constraints to which he was subject in domestic affairs cannot wholly absolve him from responsibility for the ultimately disastrous consequences (for Poland-Lithuania) of his heavy involvement from 1683 to 1691 in anti-Turkish wars which he entered of his own volition and which squandered the Commonwealth's fiscal and military resources to the benefit of its regional rivals (Davies 1981: 491). Unfortunately for Poland-Lithuania, this great 'defender of Catholic Christendom' manifested none of the state-building drive and ambition of his Russian, Prussian, Austrian and French contemporaries. His military exploits served merely to accelerate (and conceal) the underlying decline of his realm. 'He lived to the end of his days more in the style of a wealthy nobleman . . . than a monarch . . . He was a warrior, with all the instincts and limitations of his trade' (p. 489). His death in 1696 stripped away the camouflage, leaving the Commonwealth's exhaustion and decline more plainly visible to Europe.

Thus by the end of the seventeenth century Poland-Lithuania occupied an increasingly anomalous position in a part of the world where absolutism was ascendant and only the Commonwealth refused to 'centralize political power within its sprawling domains'. This factor on its own would probably have sufficed to precipitate the Commonwealth's (imminent) political and military demise once its absolutist neighbours had become strong enough to dismember it 'with impunity' (Fedorowicz 1982: 2), even if other factors had not simultaneously contributed to its more deep-seated economic and cultural decline.

The war-weary, bankrupt and increasingly anarchic Commonwealth was largely at the mercy of its more powerful neighbours during the royal election of 1697, in which Sobieski's son Jacub (favoured by the Habsburgs) lost out to Friedrich-August of Saxony (alias August II, 1697–1733), who was backed by Tsar Peter the Great. In principle, the Catholic Saxon king had good reason to share the Commonwealth's fear of the waxing power of the Swedish Vasas and the Hohenzollerns, and this personal union between Saxony and the noble *Rzeczpospolita* therefore made sense as a new defensive alliance against the new Protestant powers. Yet in reality this vainglorious and over-sexed Saxon monarch (who fathered some 300 children) merely precipitated a protracted and destructive military contest between Sweden and Russia. Much of it was to be fought out in the Polish-Lithuanian domains, which were to take 280 years (1710–1990) fully to overcome the direct and indirect consequences.

August II rashly started the Great Northern War (1700–21) by attacking Swedish Livonia (including Riga) in the vain hope of bolstering his lacklustre status in the eyes of his new Polish-Lithuanian subjects and of the other European powers (who clearly perceived that his potency did not extend beyond the bedchamber). This act of folly provoked a devastating Swedish occupation of various parts of Poland-Lithuania from 1702 to 1709 and of Saxony from 1706 to 1709. Indeed, the Swedes were invited into Lithuania by a dissident Lithuanian magnate in 1702. This prompted other sections of the Lithuanian nobility to appeal for Russian military intervention *against* the Swedes. August II regained his Saxon and Polish-Lithuanian thrones only as a result of the defeat of Karl XII of Sweden by Peter the Great in 1709 at the momentous battle of Poltava, which finally extinguished Swedish power on the south-eastern shores of the Baltic Sea (and helped to launch the chastened Swedes on the long process of becoming the 'good Europeans' that they are today!). In the meantime, the Commonwealth's territories had changed hands several times and, as a result of the war and the attendant economic disruption, its population contracted by a quarter (Leslie 1971: 6). For a time Karl XII even sponsored a rival claimant to the Polish-Lithuanian throne (Stanislaw Lesczynski, the young *woewod* [palatine] of Poznan), while in 1701 the Hohenzollern Elector of Brandenbug and Duke of Prussia seized the opportunity to proclaim himself 'King Frederick I of Prussia' and to unite his separate domains under a single crown.

After his historic victory at Poltava in 1709 Peter the Great could easily have annexed large swathes of Polish-Lithuanian territory to Russia. However, he opted for indirect control of the Commonwealth through King August II, who owed his restoration wholly to Russian military intervention. Peter presumably regarded the Commonwealth either as too big a fish to swallow in one gulp or as too severely ravaged by seven years of fighting to be worth annexing. In 1715, still smarting at the armed reimposition of unpopular and discredited Saxon rule, a so-called 'confederation' of Polish-Lithuanian nobles and magnates vowed 'to expel the Saxons lock, stock and barrel'. But their plans were thwarted by renewed Russian military intervention and arbitration between 1715 and 1717 (Davies 1981: 499–500). In 1716 Russian officials persuaded August II to withdraw his Saxon troops from the Commonwealth permanently in return for the Polish-Lithuanian nobility's 'silent consent' to statutory limitations on the size of the Commonwealth's armed forces (roughly 20,000 combatants) and tax revenue (pp. 500–2). This humiliating agreement was underwritten by Russia, which also undertook to guarantee the much-devalued 'liberties' of the Polish-Lithuanian nobility and of Orthodox Christians. However, the *débâcle* was not merely a consequence of Russian tutelage. 'The "Golden Freedom" which most of the noble citizens were taught to regard as the glory of their Republic had lost its meaning in a land where nine-tenths of the population lived in poverty and servitude' (p. 513).

These new arrangements were rubber-stamped by a special one-day 'silent' session of the Sejm, which met surrounded by Russian troops on 30 January 1717. Thus began the centuries of Russian domination of Poland (1709–1989, with brief interruptions from 1806 to 1814 and from 1915 to 1945), employing an array of techniques anticipating those employed by the Soviet Union from 1945 to the 1980s. Indeed, the Commonwealth had lost something more fundamental than territory: its self-respect. 'The Polish political classes, appalled by the realization of their subjugation, flitted easily from abject indifference to desperate rebellion, defending their remaining privileges with a truculence that always seemed to invite the impending disaster' (Davies 1981: 500–1).

The emasculation of the central authorities and the Sejm left the Commonwealth to an even greater extent than before under the devolved control of the magnates, while the official armed forces were severely underfunded and were increasingly left to fend for themselves as best they could by means of billeting, pilfering and extortion rackets. These conditions encouraged the uncontrolled proliferation of private (baronial) armies which increasingly took the law into their own hands, with the paradoxical result that 'the most militarized society in Europe was unable to defend itself' (Davies 1981: 502–4). Indeed, by 1763 the Commonwealth's official armed forces were outnumbered eleven to one by those of Prussia, seventeen to one by those of Austria and twenty-eight to one by those of Russia (p. 504). These states were increasingly able to use the Commonwealth as a punchbag and 'as a battleground on which to settle their differences inexpensively'. The Commonwealth's emasculation suited its neighbours and 'whenever the Poles took steps to put their house in order both Russia and Prussia took counter-steps to see that nothing changed' (p. 513). In 1719 August II succeeded in regaining a modicum of autonomy by signing a treaty of alliance with Austria, England and Hanover (Gierowski 1982: 234), but the benefits did not endure beyond the end of his reign.

August II died in 1733. With French backing, and in defiance of Russia's wishes, the Polish-Lithuanian nobility elected the native nobleman Stanislaw Lesczynski (previously sponsored by Sweden's Karl XII in the 1700s) as their new king. But Russia insisted on the holding of a second (rigged) election, in order to install its preferred Saxon candidate, August III (son of August II), who had promised to cede Livonia to Russia once elected. The city of Gdansk, which raised an army in support of Lesczynski, was punitively occupied by Russian forces in 1734.

In the course of his thirty-year 'reign' (1734–64) August III spent only two years in Poland-Lithuania and only one Sejm succeeded in passing any legislation at all! 'The country seemed to run itself solely on the momentum of its own inertia . . . It was to the courts of the leading families and not to the royal court . . . that foreign powers sent envoys' (Zamoyski 1987: 212). Indeed, it is often argued that, since magnates with private armies increasingly controlled the lesser nobility and the law courts, and were not held in check by the enfeebled central institutions and authorities, the plight of the peasantry deteriorated still further, although there have also been opinions to the contrary (pp. 212–14).

Nevertheless, the Commonwealth's decline was not solely precipitated by political and military miscalculations and misfortunes, even if these were what most strongly distinguished Poland-Lithuania from neighbouring Russia, Prussia and Austria. The excessive size and privileges of the nobility, the excessive concentration of power and wealth in the hands of the magnates, the renewed spread and intensification of serfdom, and the decline of the Vistula grain trade, of the urban sector and of Polish Protestantism also played important roles, albeit with effects that were not so very dissimilar from those experienced in Hungary, Bohemia and Austria.

THE EXCESSIVE SIZE, PRIVILEGES AND SOCIAL STRATIFICATION OF THE NOBILITY

The nobility comprised 6.6 per cent of the Commonwealth's population in 1569, rising to about 9 per cent by 1700 (Davies 1981: 215). By 1569 the nobility owned approximately 60 per cent of the Commonwealth's territory, as against 25 per cent in Church ownership and 15 per cent still owned by the crown. In practice, however, many crown and ecclesiastical properties were controlled by secular magnates (p. 218). However, while some magnates owned mini-kingdoms, most nobles were materially not much better-off than the peasantry. 'In the Republic as a whole, well over half the nobility did not possess land' (pp. 228–9). Nevertheless, to be a member of the *szlachta* (the middling and lesser nobility) was rather 'like being a Roman Citizen'. The *szlachta* constituted the political nation, whereas the rest of the population (the *plebs*) 'did not count politically' (Zamoyski 1987: 92). While the magnates endeavoured to establish a narrow oligarchy, the rest of the nobility (the *szlachta*) fought for their own predominance within the political nation (p. 93).

The principal landmarks in the growth of the privileges of the nobility should be seen in chronological sequence:

1374. Noble demesnes were exempted from the land tax.

1425. Polish nobles were granted security from arbitrary arrest and/or seizure of property. This was extended to the Lithuanian nobility in 1434.

1454. Troops and new taxes were henceforth to be raised only with the consent of the provincial *sejmiki*.

1496. The mobility of agricultural tenants was formally restricted.

1501. Peasants were constitutionally tied to the land and to the will of their lord.

1505. Henceforth no major innovation was to be introduced without the Sejm's consent, and 'mixed marriages' between commoners and nobles were to be restricted.

1518. Peasants lost the right to appeal to crown law courts against their lord.

1520. The Sejm increased the statutory labour rent (*corvée*) for all agricultural tenants from twelve to fifty-two days per annum.

1565. Native burghers were debarred from engaging in foreign trade and foreign travel.

1573. Nobles were granted exclusive rights to exploit the timber and mineral resources on their land.

1576. Control of ennoblement was removed from the king, except the granting of wartime military honours. Royal ennoblements did not exceed 2,000 between 1569 and 1696, virtually turning the nobility into a closed caste. By 1600 only rich Gdansk patricians could hope to gain admission to the nobility (Davies 1981: 237; Maczak 1982: 127).

1611. Commoners were debarred from buying landed estates.

A great deal of significance has been attached to the infamous *liberum veto*, the right of just one dissenting deputy to prevent a legislative, financial or procedural decision of the Sejm from taking effect. It reflected the high premium on achieving unanimity or consensus in a society where the political executive could govern only with the overwhelming assent of the political nation. 'Laws and decisions which were passed in the face of opposition could not have been properly enforced' (Davies 1981: 339). The first occasion on which the time-honoured principle of unanimity was mischievously invoked as a technicality in order to paralyze the conduct of the Sejm's legitimate business was on 9 March 1652, during the crisis in the Ukraine (Zamoyski 1987: 183). However, the damaging effects of the *liberum veto* have been somewhat exaggerated. Its misuse was more a symptom than a cause of the Commonwealth's political problems. After 1652, indeed, it was not misused again until 1666 and 1668. It was only under August II (1697–1733) and August III (1734–63) that it was systematically abused in order to paralyze the passage of legislation and the conduct of state business, mainly by Sejm deputies acting in the pay and on the instructions of mischievous magnates and/or predatory powers (particularly Russia). 'By posing as champions of the "Golden Freedom" . . . they could ensure that the Republic remained incapable of organizing itself or offering resistance' (Davies 1981: 347). The final attempt to (mis)use the *liberum veto* 'was registered in 1763 by a deputy in Russian pay, who was laughed out of the Sejm. The power of veto had existed for well over a hundred years before it was used, and it continued to exist for thirty [years] after it was last invoked' (Zamoyski 1987: 207).

More persistently damaging was the right of 'Confederation', involving an association of nobles sworn to pursue a particular cause or grievance until 'justice' was achieved, and expressing the nobility's right to resist unjust laws and/or to withdraw allegiance from a king who violated his coronation oath to respect and uphold the laws of the realm. In principle, Confederation was not an act of rebellion but a constitutional process undertaken for the common good and in the name of the law. During the seventeenth and eighteenth centuries, however, it was increasingly invoked for nefarious purposes, often at the instigation of a foreign power (especially Russia). Armed Confederations were formed as early as 1302, 1382–84 and 1439, but major ones also emerged in the 1560s, 1573, 1606–08, 1656, 1672, 1704, 1715, 1733, 1767, 1768–72 and 1793 (Davies 1981: 339). Although they usually claimed to be defending the 'Golden Freedom', their cumulative effects were even more debilitating than France's relatively short-lived *frondes*, to which they bore more than a passing resemblance.

During the first half of the seventeenth century the fiscal revenues accruing to the Polish-Lithuanian state were merely about one-tenth of those accruing to the French state, partly because the Commonwealth's large Jewish community enjoyed fiscal autonomy and the commercial city of Gdansk had 'long benefited from extensive immunities (which is why it was so consistently patriotic in the face of foreign invasion and the threat of incorporation into a less accommodating state)'. But the main reason was that the nobility and the clergy were largely exempt from taxation, at least until the introduction of a 'relatively insignificant' poll tax in 1662 (Zamoyski 1987: 130). In sum, the main concentrations of income and wealth were grossly under-taxed, with the result that the taxes which were exacted fell mainly on those less able to afford them, to an even greater extent than was usual in early modern Europe.

As emphasized by Fedorowicz (1982: 5–8), during the seventeenth and eighteenth centuries the Polish-Lithuanian nobility maintained a political, social and economic hegemony 'such as existed in no other European country'. This dominant social estate 'overwhelmed and eliminated all alternative loci of power and shaped the . . . state in its own image to suit its own needs . . . In any healthy society, competing loci of power and influence tend to balance each other in a creative tension which offers that society the opportunity of flexible response to any crisis.' Conversely, 'a political monopoly of any sort is simply a recipe for sterile conservatism'. The all-pervasive hegemony of the Commonwealth nobility inhibited the development of a bourgeois ethos and bourgeois values even in the towns. Paradoxically the last noble *leveé en masse* occurred in 1667, and yet the less the nobility served in the republic's armed forces 'the more they believed in the myth of their chivalric role. The less they participated in government, the more indispensable they believed themselves to be' (Zamoyski 1987: 182, 221). However, it is not unusual for self-importance to be inversely related to intrinsic worth!

Furthermore, the ease with which the nobility contrived to promote and protect its perceived sectional interests through the Commonwealth's political and social institutions had an enervating effect. 'At no point in this divinely ordained process of gathering in the good things due to them did the *szlachta* need to make an investment or calculate with market forces: notions of thrift, risk, investment and the value of money were ignored' (Zamoyski 1987: 57). This left the Commonwealth's propertied classes rather poorly prepared for the psychological shift to a European world increasingly based upon markets, entrepreneurship, innovation and industry (in both senses of the word). Yet these same social groups, having brought the Commonwealth to the brink of ruin, were later to initiate energetic programmes of renewal and reform. History rarely adheres to a predictable, preordained script.

THE 'SECOND SERFDOM' AND THE RISE AND DECLINE OF THE VISTULA/BALTIC GRAIN TRADE

The expansion of the corporate privileges of the nobility coincided with the rise of the Vistula/Baltic grain trade and the renewed spread and intensification of serfdom, although the directions and relative magnitudes of the causal connections have long been the subject of heated debate. There is, however, little doubt that serfdom as such antedated the meteoric rise of the Vistula/Baltic grain trade during the fifteenth and sixteenth centuries. It therefore seems likely that the latter merely accelerated (rather than caused) the spread and intensification of serfdom in early modern Poland-Lithuania. Indeed, substantial increases in the external demand for and price of grain exerted increased pressure 'on the one element in the rural economy, labour, which was capable of more intensive exploitation. In order to meet the demand, noble landowners exacted more work and harsher conditions from their peasants' (Davies 1981: 280).

However, since the renewed spread and intensification of serfdom were not confined to regions which actively participated in the booming Baltic grain trade, they cannot have been the only major influence. Many commercial backwaters also succumbed to the so-called 'second serfdom'. Changes in seigneurial and governmental mentalities and ideologies also contributed. Nor can these retrograde social and economic trends be simply attributed to the growing power of the nobility and the increasing weakness of the central state in Poland-Lithuania, for serfdom was also being intensified and extended in early modern Russia, where the central state was becoming even stronger than the nobility, other than during periods of acute crisis such as the 'Time of Troubles' (1598–1613) and the 'Khovanschina' (1682–89). Many Marxists have argued that this is 'a distinction without a difference', on the grounds that the central and eastern European despotisms were just as expressive of and subservient to the class interests of the landed nobility as was the Polish-Lithuanian 'nobles' republic'. In our view, however, the interests, ambitions and responsibilities of the state, which represented a different mix of social, economic and political considerations, often overrode and/or conflicted with those of the landed nobility, even where the latter remained the most influential class; and it is therefore misguided and misleading to treat them as if they were identical. Thus while the relatively decentralized and market-driven spread and intensification of serfdom in Poland-Lithuania appear to have gone hand-in-hand with the growth of local seigneurial power and autonomy and the gradual emasculation of the state, we cannot ignore the fact that the strengthening and extension of serfdom in neighbouring Russia were undertaken at least partly in order to bind every social group (not just the serfs) to the service and overall control of an all-powerful Tsarist state. There were additional variations in the political and economic causes and consequences of the 'second serfdom' in Hungary, Bohemia and Brandenburg-Prussia (among others), further emphasizing that there was no simple correlation between state weakness, seigneurial power and the renewed spread and intensification of serfdom during the early modern era.

The faltering of Polish-Lithuanian grain exports from the 1620s onwards, combined with the dire consequences of the Swedish invasions (1655–60 and 1702–9) and anti-Turkish wars (1672–76 and 1683–91), introduced further complications. 'Faced with ruin, landowners looked not for long-range solutions but for drastic measures to deal with their pressing obligations . . . Losing his surplus production, the peasant also lost his chance for economic independence . . . He now limited himself to subsistence farming and fell ever more into dependence on the manor' (Kaminski 1975: 262). The 'second serfdom' was therefore fostered 'both by the rise of the Vistula trade and also, paradoxically, by its decline . . . Having toiled . . . to build the prosperity of the Republic's Golden Age, the serfs were now to be driven even harder to mitigate the effects of its misfortunes' (Davies 1981: 285, 290). This prompts Davies to remark, 'How much more fortunate was England, whose sheep nibbled their way through Feudalism at an early date'! (p. 296).

However, in spite of increased restrictions on peasant mobility, the transfer of legal jurisdiction over the peasantry from the central state to the local landed nobility and the resultant inability of the peasantry to obtain legal protection and redress against oppressive landlords through the law courts, research thus far indicates that the Commonwealth's peasants 'never lost their legal entity. A peasant could appear in court as plaintiff and defendant, he had full rights of ownership of moveable property, and in some cases he could buy, sell and bequeath land' (Kaminski 1975: 267). In these respects, if not others, their status remained somewhat higher than that of Russia's serfs. However, the smaller landlords' attempts to save themselves at the peasants' expense 'could not work for long', with the result that their estates diminished in size and number, while land holdings became increasingly concentrated in the hands of the magnates (p. 263).

The Vistula/Baltic grain trade never fully recovered from the devastation inflicted on the Commonwealth between 1648 and 1666 by Cossack rebels in the south and by foreign invasions from the north and east. In 1655 alone, for example, Gdansk lost about one-fifth of its inhabitants through the effects of plague and siege (Davies 1981: 288). The Commonwealth's foreign trade was further disrupted by the anti-Turkish wars of 1672–76 and 1683–91 and, altogether more seriously, by the renewed Swedish onslaughts of 1702–09. 'The decline of the Vistula trade after 1648 coincided with the decline of the power and prosperity of the Republic as a whole.' Even though some historians deny that the former contributed to the latter, 'the coincidence is more than a little striking' (p. 287). To make matters worse, external trade remained 'predominantly in foreign hands, which meant that a large part of the profit was made outside the country', and the great reduction in grain exports was not offset by any significant increase in manufactured exports, which were limited to 'a few low-quality finished products such as beer, rope and cloth' (Zamoyski 1987: 175).

However, it is clear that the Vistula grain trade had already started to decline before 1648. It seems to have peaked in 1618–19. After that the economic life of the whole of East Central and northern Europe was disturbed by the Thirty Years' War (1618–48), even though the Commonwealth contrived to keep out of it. By the 1640s Dutch merchants operating from Gdansk were experiencing difficulty in filling their ships with adequate supplies of Polish grain. Furthermore, once the established trading relations had been ruptured by the catastrophes of the 1650s and the 1700s, they proved difficult to restore. The confidence of foreign merchants and Polish producers was badly shaken and, once western European customers had been forced to seek out suppliers elsewhere, it was hard to win them back again when the hostilities abated (Davies 1981: 288–9). In addition, it is often argued that the productivity of Poland's landed estates had hit a ceiling by 1600, after which the landlords' main recourse was to work their peasants harder and harder in vain attempts to offset falling productivity with ever-increasing inputs of forced labour (p. 285). Significantly, the Polish-Lithuanian Commonwealth had neither the fiscal resources nor the concerted political resolve needed to overcome these limitations through state initiatives to reclaim heathland, upgrade agricultural techniques, improve the waterways and modernize the Baltic ports in the manner adopted by the adjacent kingdom of Prussia (p. 290).

At this same time advances in agricultural and drainage techniques were raising agricultural productivity in north-western Europe, while new sources of low-cost grain were being opened up in southern Europe, Russia and Brandenburg-Prussia, causing a further long-term erosion of the Commonwealth's comparative advantage in grain production and a deterioration in its terms of trade. In particular, the Polish-Lithuanian Baltic ports and hinterland faced mounting competition from Riga, Königsberg, Stettin, Lübek, Rostock and, in the eighteenth century, St Petersburg. By then the limitations of the Vistula as a natural waterway were also becoming apparent. Since dykes were never built along its flood-prone middle reaches, it was unsuited to the more modern forms of river traffic that were beginning to develop elsewhere in Europe (Davies 1981: 291). The *coup de grâce* was to be the loss of Gdansk to the kingdom of Prussia in 1772.

URBAN DECLINE

As a result of the catastrophes of 1655–60 and 1702–09, the Commonwealth's urban population fell by 60–70 per cent, to little more than 10 per cent of the total, and it was still below 20 per cent of the total in the mid-eighteenth century (Bogucka 1982: 140). Nevertheless, according to Norman Davies (1981: 293), 'cities have never been particularly prominent in Polish civilization. Their origins in the Middle Ages had such strong German connections that for long historians considered them to be mere colonial excrescences on the essentially rural Polish scene. The . . . prosperity in the sixteenth and early seventeenth centuries passed so quickly that they left few lasting traditions.' Such reservations apply *a fortiori* to Lithuania.

The privileges which successive Polish-Lithuanian kings had granted to the nobility had never been fully extended either to the Jewish or to the non-Jewish townspeople (burghers). The mainly German or Jewish leaders of the urban communities had rarely sought direct representation in the Sejm, preferring instead to deal with the king or to ask the local *woewoda* (palatine) to act on their behalf (Zamoyski 1987: 102). In the long term, this proved an unreliable and imprudent tactic. The potential emergence of the towns was also impeded by their failure to foster either common institutions or regular communication and alliances among themselves (Fedorowicz 1982: 115). Lacking either institutional bonds or political and cultural solidarity, the towns were thus unavailable 'for use by the kings against the encroachment of noble power' (Kochanowicz 1989: 114). In 1565, moreover, the noble-dominated Sejm passed a law prohibiting native burghers from travelling abroad to engage in trade, with the result that the latter fell increasingly under the control of foreign merchants and financiers and the agents of the landed nobility, to the great detriment of the towns and of the economy as a whole (Malowist 1959: 186–7). The 'economic policy of the nobles' also contributed to the decline of the towns by 'intensifying the export of foodstuffs and primary products and favouring the import of manufactures . . . which was harmful to the industrial production of the country' (p. 188). Thus the decline of the Commonwealth's urban sector cannot be blamed entirely on the barbarities of Swedish invaders. It was partly self-inflicted.

THE BATTLE FOR HEARTS AND SOULS: THE CATHOLIC COUNTER-REFORMATION

Starting in the later sixteenth century, the Catholic Counter-Reformation contributed to the Commonwealth's decline by reducing its cultural pluralism and vigour, its tolerance of diversity, its receptiveness to foreign (especially Western) influences and ideas, and the importance given to elementary schooling and humanist learning and enquiry. Whatever its religious merits, it resulted in cultural and intellectual impoverishment and a narrowing of mental horizons.

During the sixteenth century the Catholic Church retained control of its great wealth and extensive ecclesiastical infrastructure, despite the widespread 'defections' to Protestantism. It still had the wherewithal to mount a potent counter-offensive against the Reformers. The Jesuits, who were the shock troops of the Catholic Counter-Reformation, were introduced into the Commonwealth in 1564–65 on the initiative of Cardinal Stanislaw Hosius. Piotr Skarga (1536–1612), who rose to become the confessor and personal adviser of the militantly Catholic King Zygmunt III Vasa (1588–1632), argued that Poland-Lithuania would have to be 'reconquered for Rome, not by force . . . but by virtuous example, teaching, discussion . . . and persuasion' (Zamoyski 1987: 89–90). Skarga and other Jesuits 'ranged themselves behind the Crown, particularly after the accession of their ally Zygmunt III in 1588', believing that the decisive impediment to Catholic absolutism in Poland-Lithuania lay not so much in the existence of sizeable non-Catholic elements in the population as in the increasingly libertarian civil values and *esprit de corps* of the Catholic and non-Catholic nobility. 'The constitution of the Commonwealth stood in the way of the Counter-Reformation and the *szlachta* were the guardians of the constitution' (p. 147). That was one reason why Zygmunt III made repeated (albeit abortive) attempts to subvert the constitution and establish 'divine right' rule.

By 1642 forty-seven Jesuit colleges had been established in the Commonwealth (Davies 1981: 168). The most famous of them, the Jesuit College in Vilnius, was raised to university status by King Stefan Bathory in 1589. Jesuit schools and colleges churned out thousands of young nobles imbued with 'a ready-made set of religious, social and political principles' opposed to the humanism of the fifteenth and early sixteenth centuries, which had created such fertile ground for Protestantism. The Jesuits also published 'no less than 344 separate books . . . in Poland' between 1564 and 1600 (Zamoyski 1987: 147). They fostered the notions that 'to be Polish was to be Catholic' and that the various forms of Protestantism, Orthodoxy, Armenian Christianity and Judaism were essentially 'foreign'. (Yet Catholicism had also originated as a 'foreign' import, just as did these other denominations.) Thus, while it was accepted that foreigners and ethnic minorities could legitimately practise so-called 'foreign' religions, 'Poles who were Protestant began to be viewed as eccentric, even suspicious' (p. 149). It was but a short step from this to the conception of Poland-Lithuania as a bulwark of Catholic Christendom against the Turkish, Tatar and Russian hordes, in the struggles against whom so much of the Commonwealth's energy and resources were to be used up to the ultimate benefit of its regional rivals.

As a result of the Counter-Reformation and the profoundly traumatic experiences of 1648–60 and 1702–9, many Poles came to believe that 'fellow-countrymen outside the national church were untrustworthy and even wicked and that connivance at dissent imperilled their own salvation' (Reddaway *et al.* 1941: 95). This mentality also contributed to the emergence of the so-called Sarmatian outlook, 'produced by cross-pollination between Catholic high Baroque and Ottoman culture', which spread among the *szlachta* and was 'radically inimical to the bourgeois ethic of thrift, investment, self-improvement and discipline' (Zamoyski 1987: 204). The Sarmatian ethos became a gospel of mediocrity and complacency, an optimistic yet fatalistic belief that God would provide and ensure the Commonwealth's survival, just as surely as day follows night (p. 181). 'Xenophobia, bigotry and sheer ignorance combined to create an attitude which extolled anarchy and substituted drink for thought' (p. 221). By the end of the seventeenth century Jesuit education largely 'confined itself to inculcating into its pupils a religious, social and political catechism and teaching them enough Latin and Rhetoric to enable them to drone on for hours at political meetings' (p. 181). The retreat from genuine outward-looking, universalist Latin humanism compounded the Commowealth's growing cultural and intellectual isolation.

Nevertheless, the influence of the Jesuit Order should not be overstated. Up to the time of its dissolution in 1773 the Jesuits never controlled more than seventy of the republic's 1,200 religious houses and their influence should be seen as running in parallel with the expansion of other (less Machiavellian) contemplative, teaching and mendicant orders (Davies 1981: 168). Indeed, the number of monasteries rocketed from 220 in 1572 to 565 in 1648, while the foundation of Benedictine and Carmelite monasteries marked the beginning of a mystical tradition in Polish religious life (Zamoyski 1987: 145). Whether this was more 'cause' than 'effect' is open to question, but the gentle cult of the Virgin Mary became especially strong in Poland-Lithuania, where over a thousand Marian shrines were flourishing by the seventeenth century, each with its own 'miraculous' icon of the Mother of God (Davies 1981: 171).

As a result of inadvertent (probably male chauvinist) Protestant neglect of the spiritual needs and aspirations of women, the wives of the Protestant nobility often remained open or covert adherents of the Catholic faith and continued to raise their offspring of both sexes as Catholics (Zamoyski 1987: 90). This contributed to a decline of about two-thirds in the number of Protestant chapels between 1569 and 1600 and, as Calvinism became less fashionable in high society, the Protestants soon lost their majority in the Senate. Nevertheless, the waning of Polish Protestantism was also closely related to the pervasive 'change in the intellectual climate attendant upon the loss of the humanist vision', not only in Poland but across most of Catholic Europe, as the rationalism and pragmatic humanism of the early sixteenth century gave way to an 'agonizing search for absolutes' (p. 145).

The Reformation was further weakened by humanist intellectuals turning away from Protestantism, 'disillusioned by the intolerance of its leaders, its confessional fragmentation, and its increasingly arid intellectual debates reminiscent of the controversies of Scholasticism' (Tazbir 1994: 178). The Commonwealth's Protestants also failed to make many converts among the peasants. The Reformation appears to have had an in-built 'urban bias', partly because towns offered 'concentrations of population, nodes of communication and significant locations for intellectuals and important churchmen'. It made relatively little headway among agrarian populations, not just in Poland but also in France, Italy, Portugal and Spain, where it came up against 'the belief system and cultural presuppositions deeply rooted in the way of life of peasant producers . . . The process of desacralizing, deritualizing and demystifying was one which would have administered a traumatic shock to European rural culture and . . . was only possible under . . . limited conditions' (Scribner 1994: 221–2). Religious reform nevertheless managed to overcome such barriers in rural Bohemia, where it became 'closely associated with national identity, regardless of urban or rural context', and in rural Hungary, where its leading advocates immersed themselves in village and small-town life and were thus able 'to address the needs of Hungarian popular culture' (p. 223). In Poland-Lithuania, however, Lutheranism remained too closely identified with the sectional interests of German burghers, while Calvinism became too bound up with the concerns and aspirations of certain sections of the nobility. In north-western Europe the dynamics of the Renaissance and the Reformation were in some respects related to the rise of urban civilization and the drive to establish urban hegemony over the countryside (pp. 219–21), often in alliance with Renaissance and/or Protestant rulers (p. 2). Viewed in this light, the lesser number and size of East Central European towns (and their actual contraction during the late sixteenth and much of the seventeenth centuries), combined with the frequent alliance of East Central European rulers with members of the nobility (even though many of these were then Protestant) rather than with the towns, contributed to the eventual defeat of the East Central European Renaissance and Reformations.

The contraction of Protestantism among the Commonwealth's nobles was accelerated by the great favour which the long-reigning Zygmunt III (1588–1632) consistently showed towards Catholics in the exercise of his still considerable royal patronage (Zamoyski 1987: 145). The number of non-Catholics in the Senate plummeted from forty-one in 1587 to five by 1632 (Tazbir 1982: 204). The Protestant communities also contracted sharply as a result of the devastating Swedish Protestant invasions of the Commonwealth during the 1650s and the 1700s. The Swedes urged the Commonwealth's Protestants to transfer their allegiance to Sweden, and quite a few did so. This elicited savage retribution from the Catholic side, obliging many Polish and Lithuanian Protestants to return to Catholicism 'as proof of their patriotism' (Davies 1981: 198).

Nevertheless, the eventual victory of the Catholics was not predetermined by the 'Polonization' of Catholicism, since this did not precede the Protestants' major setbacks, but it did help to consolidate and deepen the Catholics' victory. An analogous role was played by the Commonwealth's geopolitical situation, for its enemies during the Reformation period were 'almost exclusively non-Catholic countries', whereas it rarely fell out with Catholic states. This reinforced a view of the Commonwealth as 'defender of the Catholic faith' which was hard to reconcile with its former emphasis on religious toleration (Tazbir 1994: 178–9).

In 1638, after two Protestant students had desecrated a Catholic roadside shrine, the Sejm ordered the closure of the prestigious Unitarian academy at Rakow, along with its printing press (Tazbir 1994: 175). The other illustrious Unitarian academy at Leszno, whose rector from 1628 to 1656 was the famous Czech philosopher and pedagogue Jan Amos Komensky (alias Comenius), was sacked and burnt by Polish troops at the start of the Swedish invasion of 1655–60 because it refused to hand over its Swedish garrison (Davies 1981: 189). In 1658 the Unitarians were even banished from the Commonwealth for refusing to take up arms to defend their country in a time of great peril (Zamoyski 1987: 144). The pacifist Quakers were similarly forced to emigrate from the Gdansk region in 1660. In 1668, moreover, the Sejm ordained that no Catholic could apostatize to another faith (on pain of exile), while in 1673 non-Catholics were debarred from entry into the ranks of the nobility, and in 1733 the Sejm barred non-Catholics from holding public office or serving in the Sejm (pp. 145, 221).

All the same, in Poland-Lithuania non-Catholics were rarely sentenced to death for their religious beliefs. They were more commonly sent into exile or given token fines. Moreover, the reductions in the political rights of non-Catholic nobles in the late seventeenth and early eighteenth centuries were reversed in 1768 and 1773, long before equivalent concessions were granted to Catholics in Protestant Britain (1829) or Sweden (1849) (Tazbir 1994: 179). Polish Catholicism continued to be characterized not so much by 'external militancy' as by 'extreme inward piety' (Davies 1981: 170). Significantly, the Crusades had never attracted many Polish participants; the Islamic threat was 'too close and too well known to hold much glamour'. Moreover, medieval Poland had repeatedly been threatened by Teutonic Crusaders who had spent more time fighting fellow Catholics than in 'converting the heathen' (p. 165). Polish Catholicism was to develop not so much an aggressive crusading spirit as a martyr complex, seeing Poland as 'the Christ among nations'. Anyway, given the non-existence of a powerful monarchy or central state on whose support it could call, in Poland-Lithuania the Catholic Church was unable to employ the same draconian methods of conversion or reconversion that were used to such effect in Spain, Italy and neighbouring Bohemia (p. 170).

Nevertheless, during the late seventeenth and early eighteenth centuries the Polish-Lithuanian Counter-Reformation did largely succeed in terminating the hitherto fruitful participation of Protestants (especially nobles) in the political and cultural life of the Commonwealth. But 'it paid dearly for this success', since the resultant diminution of the Commonweath's political pluralism and cultural diversity 'brought about intellectual stagnation in the camp of the victors' (Tazbir 1982: 216–17).

CRUEL TWISTS OF FATE, OR HOW THE COMMONWEALTH'S BELATED RECOVERY MERELY HASTENED ITS DEATH

In 1771, on the eve of the first Partition (1772), the Commonwealth was still one of the largest states in Europe. With 730,000 km² of territory, it was larger than either France or Spain (albeit smaller than the Tsarist and Habsburg Empires) and it had a population of about 11 million, exceeded only by that of France, Russia and the Habsburg Empire (Wandycz 1974: 3). Moreover, for fifty-five years (1735–90) the Commonwealth managed to keep out of protracted European wars. Its magnates even began to promote some rudimentary industrial development, despite (or, more probably, because of) the stagnation of its staple grain and timber exports and, after the first Partition in 1772, the loss of unrestricted access to the Baltic via the lower Vistula and Gdansk. The new industries mainly consisted of labour-intensive 'low-tech' manorial enterprises located on landed estates which used servile labour to produce items such as cloth, clothing, footwear, furnishings, vodka, glassware, pottery, porcelain, ironware, utensils, swords, carriages and even rifles for 'captive' or sheltered internal markets. There were also significant peasant handicraft industries located in 'industrial villages', while the central authorities built some larger-scale textile and armament manufactories in and around Warsaw, whose population had rocketed from 30,000 in 1760 to 150,000 by 1792. In addition, the wealthy bishopric of Krakow established what was eventually to become Poland's heavy industrial heartland (Zamoyski 1987: 238–9). Ironically, the Common-wealth's non-participation in major European wars and the irksome limitations on the size of its armed forces fortuitously freed resources for other purposes and contributed to a significant economic and demographic recovery. Between 1750 and 1790 the

Commonwealth's population expanded on average by about 1.2 per cent per annum, faster than that of either France or even England (Grochulska 1982: 247). Yet, in spite of these promising economic and demographic up-turns, the social structure of the eighteenth-century Commonwealth was not altered fundamentally. In 1770, on the eve of the first Partition, the nobility comprised 8–10 per cent of the population, Jews (mostly urban) about 10 per cent and non-Jewish burghers about 7 per cent. Most people were still peasants, of whom about 64 per cent lived on land controlled by the nobility, around 19 per cent on crown estates and approximately 17 per cent on Church land. The nobility controlled about 78 per cent of all land, the crown 13 per cent and the Catholic Church 9 per cent (Wandycz 1974: 5–6).

Following the death of August III in 1764, the Commonwealth's Russian overlords rigged the royal election in favour of Stanislaw Poniatowski, a former lover of Russia's Empress Catherine the Great (1762–96). Once crowned as King Stanislaw-August (1764–95), however, the new Polish ruler refused to play a meek and compliant role. He had an intelligent and educated mind of his own, which was no doubt partly what had attracted the German Grand Duchess Catherine to him in the first place, before she became Russia's Tsarina in 1761 (initially as the wife of Tsar Peter III, who was murdered, allegedly with her connivance, in 1762). Even the 'confederated' Sejm which elected Stanislaw-August enacted several 'progressive' reforms, including provision for majority voting in the provincial *sejmiki*, customs duties and the establishment of new fiscal and military commissions to enhance the Commonwealth's tax-collecting and defence capabilities. In 1765 he established a new academy, while in 1766 Chancellor Andrzej Zamoyski proposed constitutional reforms involving abolition of the *liberum veto*. Alarmed by the Commonwealth's attempts to reform itself, Russia and Prussia jointly threatened to invade if the reforms were not repealed and the 'confederated' Sejm not dissolved forthwith. They also decided to stir up trouble for the Commonwealth by jointly demanding that Eastern Orthodox and Lutheran Christians should have the same right to hold office as Catholics, even though neither Russia nor Prussia accorded a similar right to their own religious minorities! Russian troops then moved in to support two rebel 'confederations': a Lutheran one at Torun (Thorn) and an Eastern Orthodox one at Luck. In October 1767 the offending Sejm was hastily reconvened and, surrounded by Tsarist troops, forced to accede to Russia's demands. These included reaffirmations of the *liberum veto*, the right of 'confederation', elective monarchy, the noble monopoly of land ownership and public office, and 'the landowner's power of life and death over his peasants' (Zamoyski 1987: 225–6).

During the late 1760s, in any case, the Polish-Lithuanian political classes were becoming polarized into mutually antagonistic armed camps and the new ('upstart') king seemed powerless to prevent it. The 'scandalous' means by which he had attained the throne, along with his generally conciliatory and accommodating stance (including his acquiescence in the Sejm's weak-kneed capitulation to Russian pressure), provoked hot-headed demands for his dethronement and exile. In February 1768, at the town of Bar in Podolia, a confederation of Polish and Lithuanian magnates and their noble 'hangers on' began a 'war of independence' which Russia's famous general Suvurov took nearly four years to defeat. This was despite the fact that in 1768 the 'confederates' were attacked in the rear by insurgent Orthodox Christian peasants and Cossacks, who between them murdered some 200,000 Polish Catholics and Jews before they were themselves 'suppressed with matching severity' (Davies 1981: 519). Indeed, by the early 1770s the

Commonwealth as a whole was a boiling cauldron of social, political and religious unrest. However, the Russo-Turkish War of 1768–74 tied up many of the Tsarist troops who might otherwise have been used to 'pacify' this unruly republic. Empress Catherine therefore became increasingly receptive to Prussian proposals for the partition of Poland-Lithuania between Russia, Prussia and Austria.

However, it was the Habsburgs who set the dastardly ball rolling by unilaterally annexing Spisz in 1769 and Nowy Torg in 1770. The first trilateral Partition of Poland-Lithuania was then agreed in 1771 and implemented in 1772 (despite strong protests from more liberal-minded countries such as Britain, the Netherlands and Denmark). The Commonwealth was deprived of 35 per cent of its population and 29 per cent of its former territory. Russia not only consolidated its grip on Livonia and Courland (latterly reapportioned between Estonia and Latvia), but also annexed the (ethnically mainly Belorussian) provinces of Polotsk, Witebsk, Mscislaw and Homel, amounting to 12.68 per cent of the Commonwealth's former territory and 1,300,000 of its erstwhile inhabitants. Austria annexed several southern provinces, totalling some 11.17 per cent of the Commonwealth's former territory and 2,130,000 of its erstwhile inhabitants. Prussia ('modestly') helped itself to a small but invaluable chunk of Baltic littoral, comprising 'only' 4.94 per cent of the Commonwealth's former territory and 'a mere 580,000' of its erstwhile inhabitants (Davies 1981: 521–2). However, this not only joined up the hitherto separate parts of the kingdom of Brandenburg-Prussia but also gave it a stranglehold on the Commonwealth's main artery: its riverine access to Gdansk and the Baltic Sea. Indeed, Prussia was quick to impose 'draconian duties' and tolls on Polish grain shipped down the Vistula for export to other parts of Europe (Zamoyski 1987: 229).

Norman Davies has emphasized that the 'special sense of outrage which attended the fate of the Polish Republic was partly due to the fact that European princes had eaten a fellow European. But it was also due to the particular moment. Poland was partitioned on the eve of the birth of Nationalism and Liberalism, and thus became a symbol of all those people for whom self-determination and the consent of the governed provide the guiding principles of political life' (Davies 1981: 525). Indeed, few people could fail to feel sickened by the spectacle of three supposedly 'enlightened' rulers cynically haggling over the pickings 'before committing an act of cannibalism which cut across every concept of legality, morality and honour held at the time' (Zamoyski 1987: 4). It is therefore scarcely surprising that the Commonwealth's fate eventually became a *cause célèbre* among liberal-minded Europeans.

Nevertheless, one must guard against falling into the traps of special pleading, double standards and the temptation to idealize and romanticize the so-called 'political nation' of the Polish-Lithuanian Commonwealth. The moral issues were not quite as clear-cut as some of its champions would have us believe. After all, the vast majority of the Commonwealth's inhabitants, especially the non-Polish and non-Lithuanian peasantries, had been denied any form of self-determination and had been governed without consent, even before the Partitions. They had lived under the oppressive dominance of Polish and Lithuanian nobles ('the political nation'), many of whom were dyed-in-the-wool serf owners, and it is very doubtful whether the Commonwealth could have survived the introduction of genuine 'self-determination' and 'government by consent'. Moreover, most of the Polish and Lithuanian landed nobility continued to enjoy extensive local powers and prerogatives under their new overlords (especially in so-called 'Galicia', the area which came under Habsburg rule), to a considerably greater degree than was the case with many other subordinated ethnic groups in nineteenth-century eastern Europe. Therefore, the widespread view that the fate of the privileged 'political nation' of the Polish-Lithuanian Commonwealth was *especially* deserving of sympathy and solicitude because it was a 'great' and 'historic' nation (i.e. which had long been ranked among the oppressors rather than the oppressed) is one that we find hard to swallow! We doubt whether the Commonwealth's downtrodden peasants shed many tears over the slight diminution in the power and status of their privileged, haughty and often cruel, callous or repressive 'masters', who received a kind of come-uppance and a relatively small taste of their own medicine at the hands of the partitioning powers. Neither Polish nor non-Polish peasants showed much inclination to support the subsequent attempts of the Polish and Lithuanian nobilities to recover their former political independence, most notably during the abortive 'nationalistic' noble uprisings of 1830–31 and 1863–64 in the territories that fell under Tsarist rule. It is also appropriate to highlight the fact that many Polish and some Western writers on Polish history habitually refer to 'the Partition of Poland' and to the terrible fate of 'the Poles' in such a way as to imply that the fate and the feelings of Lithuania and the Lithuanians were of less account or on a lower level than those of Poland and the Poles. The participation of Lithuanian nobles in the so-called 'Polish uprisings' of 1830–31 and 1863–64 is often overlooked. Historically conscious Lithuanians feel slighted by the Polish *hauteur*, which has contributed to a marked cooling of relations between the Polish and Lithuanian political classes down to the present time.

Some ethnically Polish historians of Poland like to compare the status of the 'political nation' in the Polish-Lithuanian Commonwealth to that of Roman citizens in the Roman Empire (for example, Zamoyski 1987: 92–3). However, while one can find instructive positive parallels, there were also some darker ones. In both cases many of the human beings living under the same rule were either serfs or slaves with no rights of representation, redress or self-determination, and yet the privileged strata unquestioningly accepted such gross inequalities as part of the 'natural' and/or 'divinely ordained' social order. Moreover, one does not have to be Irish, black or Indonesian to perceive elements of myopia, self-deception or hypocrisy in British and Dutch 'liberal' outrage at the fate of the Polish-Lithuanian Commonwealth at the hands of the partitioning powers.

To our way of thinking, anyone who is fully committed to self-determination on an equal and liberal footing for all nations (and is genuinely outraged by the oppression of one nation by another) cannot legitimately regard some nations as 'greater' or 'nobler' or more 'elevated' than others. In particular, we see no acceptable grounds for placing either the Poles or the 'political nation' of the former Polish-Lithuanian Commonwealth on a higher 'moral pedestal' than the other subjugated peoples of eastern Europe, least of all those who continued to be downtrodden by the Polish nobility. Karl Marx was probably right to argue that the (social) emancipation of Europe was impossible without the (political) liberation of Poland, but he should also have spared a little thought for those Europeans whose overriding wish was to be freed from oppression by the Poles!

These reservations are not intended to excuse the successive Partitions of the Polish-Lithuanian Commonwealth, which violated the codes of conduct of their day as well as our own. Particularly shocking was the element of 'gang rape' in the callous and calculated way that the partitioning powers set about their victim. Equally disgusting was the ingratitude and perfidy of the Habsburgs, who, less than a century before their participation in the first Partition, had relied on the Polish-Lithuanian Commonwealth to save Vienna and their Austrian domains from falling into the clutches of the Turks in 1683.

Surprisingly soon after the first Partition the situation in the truncated Commonwealth stabilized, at least until the death of Frederick the Great in 1786. The political classes became increasingly polarized between the so-called 'Russian party', comprising those who accepted the *status quo* as a basis for more or less willing collaboration with Catherine the Great's Russia, and the 'patriotic party', made up of those who sought to strengthen the Commonwealth in the hope of eventually overturning an ignominious and vexatious *status quo*. Catherine could count on the active support of some of the leading magnates, whose privileges and prerogatives she had promised to maintain; many (perhaps most) of the Commonwealth's Orthodox and Lutheran Christians, whose positions she had promised to protect; and a substantial number of Sejm deputies and Catholic bishops (some of whom were in Russian pay). According to Davies (1981: 525–7), 'the most demoralizing aspect of the whole business was . . . the spectacle of a large number of Poles who willingly served the interests of the partitioning powers. After fifty years of fractional politics and "Russian protection", there was no shortage of citizens who made their careers by working . . . on behalf of foreign paymasters . . . Many . . . monopolized the leading military commands . . . and belonged to the most wealthy magnatial families . . . Men who dared to risk their lives and careers by protesting . . . were few and far between . . . In the Sejm of 1773, at the first Partition, only two honest men could be found.'

However, while it is indeed possible to cite the names of numerous magnatial 'collaborators' and various Sejm deputies, military commanders, high officials and Catholic bishops who owed their wealth and/or position to such 'collaboration', the Commonwealth was far from being a passive victim. It may have been powerless to hold off its assailants, but that should not be mistaken for either complicity or consent. The 'Russian party' did not include all the leading magnates and Catholic clergy. Nor did the Sejm always meekly comply with Russian demands, except on the (not infrequent) occasions when it had to conduct its business at the point of a Russian bayonet (and even then it sometimes dragged its feet). Many patriotic Poles and Lithuanians were of course stunned or caught off-guard by the first Partition, which was a *fait accompli* by the time they had fully grasped the enormity, the cynicism and the surgical precision of the amputations which had been inflicted on the Commonwealth. Nevertheless, the initial numbness, paralysis and sense of shock gradually gave way to anger and bitter contempt. As in post-Stalinist Poland, 'patriots' began to satirize their predicament and then discovered or invented social and intellectual 'spaces' within which they sought to exercise and assert an inner spiritual freedom, in defiance of the seemingly all-powerful Russian overlords.

The 'patriotic party', which enjoyed the advantage of occupying the moral high ground, came to rely on the support of (i) a steadily increasing leaven of outspoken 'patriots' in the middle and lower ranks of the nobility; (ii) a nascent, increasingly articulate and politically conscious 'national intelligentsia' recruited mainly but not exclusively from the nobility; and (iii) a cautious, vain, hedonistic, yet unusually astute and dedicated king, who fostered a ferment of 'enlightened' political debate and cultural regeneration. A significant number of 'enlightened' magnates, including Ignacy and Stanislaw Potocki, Andrzej Zamoyski, Stanislaw Malochowski, Adam Kazimiercz Czartoryski, Stansilaw Lubomirski, Michal Kazimiercz Oginski and Karol Radziwill, 'devoted their fortunes and their influence to the same cause, while less exalted figures, including many of the clergy, worked assiduously to put plans into action' (Zamoyski 1987: 237, 245–6).

The Commonwealth's incipient political and cultural rebirth was assisted by external factors. The contemporaneous European Enlightenment provided many useful models of political and social criticism and satire and fuelled the ferment of ideas, while the American Revolution supplied further sources of constitutional and military experience and inspiration. Indeed, the Commonwealth's future military hero, Tadeusz Kosciuszko (1746–1817), received royal approbation for his participation in the War of American Independence (in which he achieved the rank of brigadier-general), before he embarked on a radical reorganization of the Polish-Lithuanian armed forces in 1789 – year one of the French Revolution, which was yet another potent example and inspiration. Just as important, Catherine the Great and the Tsarist establishment were deeply distracted by the powerful peasant, Cossack and Volga Tatar rebellion of 1773–75 (about which some standard histories of Poland-Lithuania are curiously silent). This rebellion mobilized an area larger than France under the Cossack leader Yemelyan Pugachëv, who claimed to be Catherine's murdered husband Peter III and proclaimed the abolition of serfdom and Tsarist military service in the areas he controlled. The gargantuan task of suppressing this uprising obliged the Tsarist state to lower its guard (and reduce its troop levels) in the Commonwealth and opened an unexpected window of opportunity for Polish-Lithuanian political revival and reform.

In 1773 the same king and Sejm that had 'approved' the first Partition established a Commission on National Education, which was unprecedentedly given the task of reorganizing all schools, universities and colleges (including those run by the Churches) into a single country-wide education system. The commission was headed by a team of enlightened aristocrats, including Ignacy Potocki, Adam Kazimiercz Czartoryski, Andrzej Zamoyski, Joachim Chreptowicz and Bishop Ignacy Massalski. It was endowed with part of the wealth of the Jesuit Order (which was dissolved at the Pope's behest in 1773) and it 'laid down curricula, chose and published textbooks, and supervised standards and teachers', as part of 'a war on obscurantism . . . whose aim was the social and political regeneration of the state, based upon the re-education of society'. In 1778, furthermore, Chancellor Andrzej Zamoyski published a new Code of Laws which reasserted royal prerogatives, made state officials accountable to the Sejm, subjected the clergy and Church finances to state supervision, and increased the rights of the cities and the peasantry. But in 1789 its ratification by the Sejm was blocked by a 'combination of clerical bigotry and Prussian intrigue' (Zamoyski 1987: 230).

Stanislaw-August had already established a weekly periodical called *The Monitor* (modelled on Addison's *The Spectator*) and a new National Theatre in 1765. But during the late 1770s and the 1780s there was a veritable explosion of new satirical periodicals and plays. By 1792 one in forty-five inhabitants was a subscriber (and one in twenty a reader) of at least one of the new periodicals. The hundreds of newly written plays were largely imitative of genres established by playwrights such as Molière, Voltaire and Sheridan (Zamoyski 1987: 231). The reformers also dressed ostentatiously in French styles, quoted the *philosophes* and preached temperance, in the course of their campaigns against the atavistic dress, narrow 'know-nothing' outlook and alcoholic haze of the Sarmatian nobility.

The king also lavishly patronized painting, music and architecture by commissioning portraits and compositions, establishing five choirs and orchestras, attracting Paisiello and Cimarosa to Warsaw as court composers, and building (among other things) one of Europe's most elegant and refined palaces at Lazienki. Although all this ran up large debts, he 'believed passionately in the educational value of the arts' and argued that he was attempting to bequeath to posterity a cultural statement which would serve to inspire future generations and keep alive his vision of an intellectually and spiritually regenerated Commonwealth. In this mission he was undoubtedly successful (Zamoyski 1987: 240–4).

Stanislaw-August, who had come to the throne without either personal wealth or an illustrious lineage, was widely despised as a *parvenu* and as Catherine's ex-lover. He consequently had to rely on his intelligence, patience, tact and charm. As a former deputy in the Sejm he was familiar with its workings and mentalities. He was also very aware of 'the considerable influence and powers still at the disposal of the Crown' and he exploited them to the full in pursuit of his aims, which were 'not so much a policy as a vision'. Even more important, from his reading and travels across Europe he had gained 'an appreciation of the state as an institution, a concept hitherto absent from Polish political thought' (Zamoyski 1987: 236–7). His efforts to mobilize society through and in support of the state had a revolutionary impact on the nobility, who since the 1650s had come to accept (and even idealize) anarchy as a 'normal' condition. The Commonwealth had appeared to be held together by little more than the force of inertia.

The nascent intelligentsia was recruited mainly (but not exclusively) from the various rungs of the nobility. Yet it partly transcended class divisions and came to be united by a common educational background, outlook, mission to enlighten, and ethos of service to society, which it aimed to transform. This was a new Enlightenment version of older conceptions of the nobility as the political nation. It sought to transform the basis of the nobility's claim to lead the country from noble birth and descent to the more meritocratic criteria of educational ethos, training and mission. The ranks of the intelligentsia were rapidly expanded by the reformed schools, colleges and universities of the 1770s and 1780s, which churned out thousands of missionaries of Enlightenment and enemies of obscurantism (Zamoyski 1987: 237). However, the Polish-Lithuanian Enlightenment was primarily the work of some 700–800 people who published works that contributed to the intellectual and cultural ferment of the late eighteenth century (Grochulska 1982: 249).

Frederick the Great of Prussia, the chief instigator of the first Partition of Poland-Lithuania, died in 1786 and his successor was widely thought to be concerned at Russia's excessive aggrandizement and therefore more favourably disposed towards the Commonwealth's attempts to reform and rehabilitate itself. In a parallel bid to gain the goodwill of Catherine the Great, Stanislaw-August inveigled the empress to his royal palace at Karniow in 1787 and offered her his county's military support in the forthcoming Russo-Turkish War of 1787–91 (through which she hoped to acquire one or more Black Sea ports for Russia) in return for (i) permission to expand the Commonwealth's armed forces; (ii) Polish-Lithuanian participation in the anticipated commercial and territorial gains in the Black Sea region; and (iii) implicit rehabilitation of the full sovereignty and international standing of the truncated Commonwealth, by allowing it to participate in a formally equal partnership with Russia. (This would have prefigured the post-1956 'partnership' between Gomulka's Poland and Khrushchev's Soviet Union!) In the event, Catherine rejected the proposals. Confident that the Commonwealth's more avaricious magnates would support Russia's Black Sea exploits *unconditionally* (in the well founded expectation of private participation and gains), she saw no reason either to accept the king's offer or to condone the Commonwealth's reforms. It suited her to keep Poland-Lithuania in a hobbled and prostrate position and, in a private letter, she even remarked that 'truth to tell, there is no need or benefit for Russia in Poland becoming more active' (quoted by Davies 1981: 529).

Thereupon, in a vain attempt to curb Tsarist expansionism, Prussia concluded an alliance with Britain and the Netherlands and signalled that the Commonwealth could count on Prussia's approval if it were to deepen its reforms and reassert its sovereignty. With this apparent Prussian 'go-ahead', the Sejm which had been convoked in 1788 dared to embark on a more sweeping reform and rehabilitation programme. It immediately voted for increased defence expenditure and vested control of the army and foreign policy in commissions of the Sejm. In 1789, encouraged by the unexpected turn of events in France and by Russia's continuing embroilment in its war with the Turks (1787–91), the Sejm even instituted a (then radical) 10 per cent tax on income from noble land and a 20 per cent tax on income from Church land. It also appointed a commission to prepare a new written constitution and decided to prolong its own session for as long as necessary to see this constitutional reform through to completion (Zamoyski 1987: 246).

The draft constitution was finally unveiled on 3 May 1791. It retained the monarchy (which was expected to become hereditary, even though the king was a bachelor) and the privileged positions of the Catholic Church and the nobility. But it made the king's Ministers (redesignated Guardians of the Laws) accountable to the Sejm, it restored freedom of worship and it abolished the *liberum veto* and the right of confederation. Moreover, burghers were to be accorded 'the same rights and privileges' as the nobility, while peasants were promised 'the protection of the law and government of the country', and the standing army was to be expanded to 100,000 men (Davies 1981: 534). This new constitution was approved by the Sejm immediately and by the *sejmiki* in February 1792.

Russia signed a peace treaty with the Ottomans in January 1792, however, and by May that year Catherine was moving 96,000 Russian troops into the Commonwealth, ostensibly in response to appeals for 'help' from a Confederation convoked by members of the 'Russian party' at Torgowica in order to restore the Commonwealth's former 'Golden Freedom' (especially the *liberum veto*). Prussia, which had been invaded by revolutionary France in April 1792, was not in a position to respond to the Commonwealth's appeals for assistance (even if its ruler had been inclined to do so). By April 1792, moreover, the increasingly alarming course of the French Revolution had succeeded in uniting Europe's reactionary monarchies against the possibility of yet another revolutionary state – in their own 'back yard'. Commanded by Tadeusz Kosciuszko and Josef Poniatowski (the king's nephew), the Commonwealth's armies put up a brave fight, but the odds were overwhelmingly stacked against them. In August 1792, with the aim of averting a greater catastrophe, Stanislaw-August announced his government's capitulation to the Russian-backed Confederation of Torgowica and ordered the Commonwealth's troops to hold their fire. 'It was a shocking betrayal, executed for the most humane of motives. Faced by the Russians' threefold numerical superiority . . . he wanted to save his country unnecessary suffering. The Army dispersed. The commanding officers left hurriedly for exile. Warsaw was occupied without opposition' (Davies 1981: 536).

In August 1792, on the eve of a Prussian invasion of north-western Poland, Russia and Prussia agreed on a second Partition of the Commonwealth, which was implemented in early 1793. Russia absorbed the remnants of the Grand Duchy of Lithuania (250,000 km^2), while Prussia annexed not only Gdansk and Torun but also Wielkopolska and most of Malopolska, Poland's historic 'ethnic heartland' (580,000 km^2). Austria, which kept its hands clean on this occasion, got nothing. After three months of foot-dragging, this second Partition was eventually ratified in October 1793 by a Sejm whose members had been cowed and intimidated by Russian arrests, beatings, imprisonments and threats to sequestrate their property.

From March to November 1794, however, there was a nine-month Polish-Lithuanian insurrection against the Russian and Prussian occupation forces, whose presence (along with the virtual cessation of government) had contributed to economic collapse and the radicalization of the population. Having returned from exile, Kosciuszko proclaimed an Act of Insurrection in Krakow on 24 March 1794 and assumed dictatorial powers. On 4 April 4,000 Commonwealth troops and 2,000 peasants armed with scythes famously defeated a Russian army at Raclawice, encouraging the citizens of Warsaw and Vilnius (Wilno) to join the insurrection. In May the Supreme Council proclaimed the emancipation of the serfs, confiscated Church wealth, introduced an (unprecedented) graduated income tax and commandeered all factories. Desperately short of rifles, the insurrection employed novel combinations of artillery bombardment, cavalry charges and mass attacks by peasant scythemen! By 16 November, however, the insurrection had been brutally crushed by Russia, Prussia and (belatedly) Austria, which in 1795 carved up the last remnants of the Commonwealth between them. Russia again took the lion's share (120,000 km^2), but the 48,000 km^2 allocated to Prussia included Warsaw, while Austria grabbed 47,000 km^2 around Krakow (Davies 1981: 522). Overall, as a result of the three Partitions, Russia obtained 61 per cent of the former Commonwealth's territory and 45 per cent of its population (augmenting the Tsarist empire's territory and population by a mere 3 per cent and 16 per cent, respectively). Prussia obtained 20 per cent of the former Commonwealth's territory and 23 per cent of its population (expanding its own territory and population by a massive 50 per cent and 40 per cent, respectively). The Habsburg Empire acquired 19 per cent of the former Commonwealth's territory and 32 per cent of its population (expanding the Habsburg domains by 25 per cent and 17 per cent, respectively) (Skowronek 1982: 262–3).

In the final analysis, the insurrection of 1794 could have succeeded only if it had received major help from revolutionary France. But the latter left the Commonwealth to the tender mercies of its absolutist neighbours. 'Europe regarded the fall of the insurrection with indifference and accepted the liquidation of the Polish [-Lithuanian!] state without any greater protest. Ironically, Poland [-Lithuania] was extinguished in the end not because of anarchy but because it had become a force capable of revolutionizing central and eastern Europe' (Gierowski 1982: 237).

LIFE AFTER DEATH: THE PARTITIONED COMMONWEALTH, 1795–1918

Following the third Partition and the suppression of the last vestiges of the Kosciuszko rising, the prevailing mood in the partitioned Commonwealth was one of shock, apathy and fatalism, 'causing a temporary collapse of further political initiatives' (Skowronek 1982: 263).

The supplementary partition treaty signed by Russia, Prussia and Austria in January 1797 secretly incorporated the chilling stipulation that 'In view of the necessity to abolish everything which could revive the memory of the existence of the Kingdom of Poland . . . the high contracting parties are agreed and undertake never to include in their titles the name or designation of the Kingdom of Poland, which shall remain suppressed as from the present and for ever' (quoted by Davies 1981: 542). Significantly, as co-author of all the Partitions, the Tsarist regime claimed that it was merely recovering territories that had once been part of its ancient patrimony. In 1793 Catherine had even ordered the striking of a medal bearing the inscription: 'I have recovered what was torn away.' Nevertheless, this perception of her conduct was 'not shared by most of her contemporaries', while her immediate successors considered that the Partitions had been criminal acts and that 'only Russian *raison d'état* and exigencies of the balance of power' justified the retention of these 'annexed areas' (Wandycz 1974: 17). Yet Prussia similarly claimed that it had merely repossessed the lost patrimony of its Teutonic ancestors (Davies 1981: 81), while in 1772 Austria decided to call its share of the first Partition 'the Kingdom of Galicia and Lodomeria'. These names were Latinized versions of Halicz and Vladimir, two medieval dukedoms to which the Habsburgs had unearthed long-defunct Hungarian claims, although Halicz 'formed only a small part of the acquisition', while 'Vladimir lay outside the region', and neither was ever restored to the kingdom of Hungary! (Wandycz 1974: 11). Moreover, the additional territory which the Habsburgs annexed to Austria (not Hungary) in 1795 was christened New Galicia, cunningly exploiting their original sleight-of-hand to effect yet another! But the trick worked, for to this day historians generally refer to the areas annexed by Austria in 1772, 1795, 1815 and 1846 by the spurious name of Galicia.

These ruses and specious 'justifications' were meant to emphasize the apparent finality of the Partitions. Moreover, the fact that the partitioning powers professed to believe that the strength of their claim to their new territories went far beyond mere 'rights of conquest' helps to explain the policies pursued and the tenacity of their conduct. Indeed, it sometimes appears that the partitioning powers were indissolubly bound together in an almost Dostoyevskyan sense by their partnership in crime against the former Polish-Lithuanian Commonwealth. According to Zamoyski (1987: 5), these powers enlarged 'their imperial structures with materials taken from the Polish [-Lithuanian!] edifice which they had dismantled. They realized that any attempt at rebuilding Poland would strike at the very foundation of their new power'.

Nevertheless, it was by no means the end of the road for Polish and Lithuanian political, economic and cultural life. Refusing to die, the disembodied Commonwealth lived on in the consciousness of the political classes until 1939, when Hitler and Stalin finished off the job which Frederick the Great and Catherine the Great had begun. Thereafter, though Poland and Lithuania have subsequently been reborn (more than once!), the ideals of the Commonwealth were apparently damaged beyond repair. Since only one-fifth of the former Commonwealth came under Habsburg control, however, it seems appropriate to outline the aftermath of the Partitions here rather than in Part III. In common with the former partitioning powers, historians have never found neat and tidy ways of dealing with the partitioned Commonwealth, which has always stuck out like a sore thumb. (Our account of medieval and early modern East Central Europe is resumed in Chapter 6.)

The false dawns, 1797–1814

The solidarity of the partitioning powers was much weaker than has commonly been assumed. Sooner or later each of them proved willing to use (or curry favour with) the Poles in order to steal a march on the other two. 'The three courts intrigued against one another, and the possibility of reopening the Polish question appeared.' Thus the secret provision in the January 1797 partition treaty forswearing any further use of the word 'Poland' was really 'directed against plans any of the three courts might have for reviving Poland, as much as it was against the Poles' (Wandycz 1974: 25). Yet, in celebration of the death of his much-hated mother, Catherine the Great, Tsar Paul (1796–1801) freed Russia's most prominent Polish prisoners (including Kosciuszko, who returned to the United States on a promise never to take up arms against Russia again. He also spent long hours with deposed Stanislaw-August discussing a plan to resurrect the former Polish Commonwealth, and when the former Polish king died in 1798 'Paul gave him a state funeral and personally led the mourning' (Zamoyski 1987: 257). Indeed, the 'mad' Tsar's dedication to undoing his mother's 'achievements' contributed greatly to his own assassination by Russian nobles in 1801.

As early as October 1796, however, Napoleon Bonaparte's Polish aide-de-camp Jozef Sulkowski hinted that, if victorious in Italy, his master might be willing to lead French forces against Russia 'to force her to grant independence to Poland' (Wandycz 1974: 28). In December 1796, furthermore, Polish *émigrés* succeeded in persuading the somewhat nervous French government (the Directory) to allow General Henryk Dabrowski (who had distinguished himself in the Kosciuszko rising) to form an ancillary Polish Legion to fight under Napoleon against the Austrians in Italy, using a combination of *émigré* Polish officers like himself and Polish prisoners-of-war captured from the Austrian army (which had been recruiting heavily in Galicia). The small and ill-disciplined group of Polish *émigrés* who invaded Galicia from Ottoman-controlled Bukovina in July 1797 proved easy prey for the Austrians. But two additional Polish Legions were successfully formed to fight alongside the French under General Jozef Zajacek in Italy in 1798 and under General Karol Kniaziewicz on the Rhine in 1800. Polish hopes and morale were further raised by Kosciuszko's arrival in Paris from the United States in 1800 (Wandycz 1974: 26–30). The rousing marching song of the Polish Legions later became the national anthem.

Between 1797 and 1801 25,000–30,000 men served in the Polish Legions, which fought valiantly and with heavy losses in the battles of Trebia (1799), Marengo (1800) and Hohenlinden (1800). However, France managed to keep out of the wars with Austria and Prussia from 1801 to 1805, with the result that the Polish Legions were relegated to 'police duties' in Italy (instead of fighting the long-awaited war to liberate Poland-Lithuania). In 1802–03, ironically, they were sent (against their wishes) to suppress a slave rebellion in the French colony of Santo Domingo (Haiti), where many of them died of swamp fever in a fight not *for* but *against* freedom (Davies 1982: 296).

In 1800, moreover, there appeared an anonymous pamphlet entitled *Can the Poles Strike out to Independence?*. It was co-authored by Kosciuszko and his secretary Jozef Pawlikowski. They argued that the Poles could not count on the support of France or any other power and must therefore mobilize their own social and military resources (including the peasantry) for a demotic 'war of independence' under a charismatic commander with dictatorial powers, on the pattern of the 1794 Kosciuszko rising (Wandycz 1974: 32). This became the founding statement of the Polish insurrectionary tradition. Kosciuszko also warned his compatriots, 'Do not think that Bonaparte will restore Poland. He thinks only of himself . . . He is a tyrant whose only aim is to satisfy his own ambitions. I am sure that he will create nothing durable' (quoted by Davies 1982: 295).

Nevertheless, the Polish Legions had given Napoleon a significant demonstration of Polish military valour and potential, while the survivors constituted a valuable cadre of officers and men trained in Napoleonic warfare. These 'proved indispensable for the organization of the army of the future Duchy of Warsaw', which was to put Poland back on the map (Wandycz 1974: 32). Moreover, Polish contact with Napoleonic France helped to transform Polish nationalism into an ideology with an enlarged programmatic content, including an expanded conception of the political nation and of popular ('national') rights and obligations.

During the respite from war between 1801 and 1805 the Polish political torch passed from the *émigrés* in western Europe to a prominent Polish aristocrat in Russia. Sent to St Petersburg by the Czartoryski family as a virtual hostage and as a 'guarantee of good conduct' in 1795 (when he was twenty-five years old), Prince Adam Czartoryski had charmed his way into Grand Duke Alexander's inner circle of reformist and liberal-minded friends and advisers. Young Czartoryski had also engaged the sympathy of Russia's heir-apparent for the Polish cause, even before the assassination of Tsar Paul suddenly catapulted Alexander and his close advisers into positions of power in 1801. Czartoryski became Russia's Foreign Minister, a senator, a member of Alexander's council on education (charged with the expansion and modernization of education in Russia) and 'curator' of education within the former Grand Duchy of Lithuania, which Russia had acquired as a result of the Partitions. Czartoryski seemingly 'succeeded in reconciling in his own mind the greatness of Russia with the eventual rebirth of Poland'. He evidently hoped that the emergence of a modernized and liberalized Russia would eventually oblige the other partitioning powers to give up their sectors of Poland. 'A reconstituted Polish state in close alliance with Russia, possibly ruled by a Romanov, could satisfy both Polish and Russian interests' (Wandycz 1974: 34). At the height of Czartoryski's influence in Russian affairs, new universities were established at Kazan, Kharkhov and St Petersburg, while those at Vilnius (Wilno) and Tartu (Dorpat) were relaunched. Under Czartoryski's curatorship (1803–23) the University of Vilnius 'flourished as the premier centre of Polish literature and learning' (Davies 1981: 313), and it came to be undergirded by a network of 430 schools (Wandycz 1974: 95). However, Czartoryski also believed that, in order to outbid the destructive and destabilizing influence of the French Revolution and Bonapartism, Russia (in partnership with Britain) should strive to initiate a reconstruction of Europe into Christian confederations, including two broad Slavic unions in the East. This would allow every nation rights of self-expression and liberty within a framework conducive to peace, harmony and the containment of aggressive instincts and aspirations (Kukiel 1955: 30–6, 156–7).

In 1805, however, Napoleon was attacked by Austria and Russia, whose combined forces were soundly beaten at Austerlitz in December. In 1806, moreover, the creation of a French-dominated Confederation of the Rhine precipitated a Franco-Prussian war which resulted in Napoleon's lightning victories at Jena and Auerstadt and his occupation of Berlin in October. The way was now open for Polish uprisings and a revived Polish ('Northern') Legion to play prominent roles in the 'liberation' of Prussian Poland. After entering Berlin, Napoleon summoned Jozef Wybicki (an influential *émigré*) and General Dabrowski. The emperor urged them to seek Kosciuszko's support for a Polish insurrection against the extant Prussian authorities in Hohenzollern Poland, adding the taunt that it was now up to the Poles to demonstrate whether they were really 'worthy to be a nation once more'.

Nevertheless, few Poles were in any hurry to re-establish a Polish state under French patronage. Kosciuszko announced that he would co-operate with Napoleon only if three conditions could be met: the emancipation of the peasantry; the re-establishment of a Polish state extending from Gdansk to Riga, Odessa and the Carpathians; and the adoption of a political system modelled on that of Napoleon's arch-enemy, Great Britain! Moreover, Polish radicals and *émigrés* with French republican connections and/or unhappy memories of the earlier Polish Legions had every reason to mistrust Napoleon, who had avoided giving firm undertakings, while Polish estate holders with land holdings in areas still under Prussian, Austrian or Russian rule were initially afraid of putting themselves at risk by openly siding with the French. There were therefore no Polish insurrections in support of the French 'liberation' of Poznan and Warsaw in November and December 1806 (Wandycz 1974: 36–8).

Once French control of both Warsaw and Poznan was a *fait accompli*, however, large numbers of Polish Francophils quickly crawled out of the woodwork. 'Overcoming their initial distrust of Napoleon and his regime . . . radical groups in Poland declared in favour of co-operation with France. Napoleon's victories over the partitioning powers appealed to the popular imagination and surrounded him with a halo of heroism' (Wandycz 1974: 39). On the other hand, conservative Polish landowners soon saw that their fears of French 'radicalism' had been largely unnecessary. Even before becoming a monarch, Napoleon had reined-in revolutionary radicalism. Nor did he want to frighten the propertied classes of either Poland-Lithuania or the partitioning powers by inciting social revolution. 'The last thing that Napoleon wanted to do was to unite all three partitioning powers against France' (p. 37). Likewise, 'Napoleon did not want to base his Polish policy on the support of the masses' (p. 39). On the contrary, like most upstarts, opportunists and dictators, he was eager to strike a deal with the powers-that-be, if only they would accept him. He looked to Polish nobles and magnates for leadership and support. He gave the main portfolios in Warsaw's new Governing Commission to aristocrats. Prince Jozef Poniatowski (nephew of the last Polish king) was given command of the Polish army, which by 1807 had nearly 40,000 men under arms. 'The left had no representatives in the governmental structure' (p. 40). Kosciuszko's reluctance to return to Poland at this critical juncture deprived the 'progressives' of a charismatic and universally respected leader. It is not known whether he was motivated primarily by antipathy towards Napoleon, by his promises to the late Tsar Paul, by failing health (he died in 1817), or by a combination of all three.

However, the completion of Napoleon's conquest of Prussia (with Polish assistance) in June 1807 necessitated an 'answer' to the reopened Polish 'question'. Czartoryski strongly urged Tsar Alexander to resurrect a Polish realm under Russian patronage in order to forestall the emergence of yet another Bonapartist puppet state. At their famous meeting at Tilsit (aboard a raft on the river Niemen) Napoleon and Alexander offered each other the Polish crown, but at a price which neither would-be beneficiary was prepared to pay! In the end Gdansk was turned into a nominally independent 'free city' under French 'protection' and Russia took Bialystock, while the 2.6 million inhabitants of Wielkopolska and Mazovia were reconstituted as the Duchy of Warsaw. This was given the *Code Napoléon* and a French constitution which formally abolished serfdom, proclaimed the equality of all citizens before the law, recognized Roman Catholicism as the predominant religion and guaranteed freedom of worship. Nevertheless, the condition and economic security of many peasants actually deteriorated, while in 1808 the political rights of Jews were suspended for ten years on the specious grounds that they were 'as yet unassimilated' (Wandycz 1974: 46–7). The Polish-speaking king of Saxony (an ally of Napoleon) formally became the duchy's hereditary monarch, although he paid it just four visits. Legislative power was vested jointly in the monarch (or his nominees) and in a bicameral Sejm, comprising a nominated Senate and an elective Chamber of Deputies. Yet the duchy's official language was Polish and, in the eyes of many Poles, Poland was rising to fight another day. Indeed, from 1808 onwards men aged between twenty and twenty-eight became liable for up to six years' military service, mainly to fight in Napoleon's campaigns elsewhere in Europe. The army, which expanded from 30,000 men in 1808–09 to 100,000 in 1812, became the major drain on the duchy's human and fiscal resources.

In 1809 the duchy was invaded by Austria, which was again at war with Napoleon. Having held the Austrians to a draw, the duchy's military strategists (including Dabrowski and Poniatowski) shrewdly surrendered Warsaw to the Habsburgs but then proceeded to liberate Galicia. After the decisive defeat of Austria by Napoleon at Wagram in July 1809, the duchy was allowed to annexe so-called New Galicia (including Krakow), which expanded the duchy's territory to 155,430 km^2 and its population to 4.3 million inhabitants (Wandycz 1974: 43, 53). In 1810, worn down by his divided loyalties to Poland and Russia, Czartoryski finally requested indefinite 'leave of absence' from Tsar Alexander, who then assured him of his intention to restore a large Polish kingdom under Russian sponsorship. Word of this got back to an infuriated Napoleon, who accused Alexander of aggressive designs and duplicity. It was partly to forestall the Tsar's schemes (and perhaps to force him back into the French alliance system) that Napoleon assembled a voracious *grande armée* of 600,000 men in the impoverished Duchy of Warsaw during the spring of 1812, in preparation for his June invasion of Russia. Nearly 100,000 Polish soldiers took part in the campaign, which promised to 'liberate' large areas of Belorussia, Lithuania and Ukraine from Russian rule. However, Napoleon failed to capitalize fully on the nationalism of the Polish and Lithuanian nobilities by allowing them to form explicitly 'national' regiments, other than the 35,000 Poles under Poniatowski. Adding insult to injury, Napoleon entrusted Lithuania, Grodno and Minsk to a heavy-handed Dutch military governor with no knowledge of the local conditions and languages. There was no general mobilization of the Lithuanian nobility until December 1812 (Wandycz 1974: 59). But by then Napoleon was scuttling back towards Paris, passing through Warsaw without even a visit to his long-standing Polish mistress Maria Walewska, 'who was left to pursue him to Paris, and eventually to Elba' (Davies 1982: 304). After fighting the Russian army at Borodino in September 1812 (and witnessing the burning of Moscow in October), barely 20,000 Polish soldiers made it back to Poland. Warsaw fell to the Russians in February 1813. In March the duchy came under *de facto* Russian military rule for two years, while awaiting decisions on its long-term future at the Congress of Vienna in 1814–15.

All in all, the Napoleonic Wars had cruelly raised and dashed the hopes of the Polish and Lithuanian propertied classes. (The lower classes were still more acted upon than acting in their own right.) Kosciuszko's instinctive distrust of Napoleon had largely been vindicated. Napoleon had ruthlessly exploited the Polish 'patriots' for his own self-serving ends. In the process, nevertheless, Napoleon had helped to put Poland 'back on the map' in ways that might not have occurred without him. To that extent Kosciuszko made a costly error of judgement. The Poles would probably have registered larger and more enduring gains had he swallowed his misgivings and placed himself at the forefront of the renascent Polish state and the Polish forces which participated in Napoleon's campaigns, even if he was too unwell to play a more active role. All the same, however, the victorious partitioning powers made no renewed attempt permanently to eradicate the name of Poland from European history at the Congress of Vienna. Most of the erstwhile Duchy of Warsaw was incorporated into a new Kingdom of Poland in 1815, albeit under Tsar Alexander's sceptre. The Napoleonic Wars and the Duchy of Warsaw also bequeathed hopes and models of courage, devotion, action and statehood which repeatedly inspired successive generations of Poles (and, to a lesser degree, Lithuanians) right down to the Revolutions of 1989–91.

However, one must beware of the many romanticized and nationalistic accounts of the outlook and conduct of the Polish-Lithuanian nobility during the aftermath of the Partitions. Only a minority of the former *szlachta* managed to retain noble rank under the new imperial overlords. Countless thousands were downgraded to the status of commoners. The nobility as a whole lost much of its previous wealth and influence, most of its former political prerogatives, sinecures and representative institutions, and virtually all its hitherto customary management and/or exploitation of crown and ecclesiastical properties, although its seigneurial privileges remained largely intact. On discovering that they were now among the most 'superfluous people' in Europe, many demoralized and/or downgraded Polish-Lithuanian nobles threw themselves into a feckless and dissolute existence in 'downsized' Warsaw or Krakow, in various provincial backwaters, or in foreign resorts, spas, capitals and casinos, where some of them squandered or gambled away their remaining wealth. In addition, dispossessed, *déclassé* or impoverished nobles were particularly susceptible to the appeal of French Revolutionary ideas and/or Bonapartism, often out of sheer devilment, lust for revenge, opportunism or feelings of 'What the hell! What more have I got to lose?'. But this also intensified the alarm and anxiety felt by those who had somehow managed to hang on to at least part of their former exalted status and wealth, and rendered them all the more willing to collaborate and/or ingratiate themselves with the partitioning powers. This makes it rather less surprising that the (mainly Polish or Polonized) Lithuanian nobility presented an address to Catherine the Great in 1795 thanking her for taking over their country, while the city of Warsaw issued a declaration acclaiming Russia's Field-Marshal Suvorov as a 'liberator' (Wandycz 1974: 21). Unfortunately, once Polish-Lithuanian nobles and magnates were no longer even formally responsible for the well-being, security and good governance of the Commonwealth, some of them were encouraged to behave even more irresponsibly than before, while others recoiled in horror at the attitudes and conduct of their peers. This sorry predicament left Polish-Lithuanian nobles and magnates as deeply divided as ever.

After 1795 both Poles and Lithuanians were obliged gradually to come to terms with the deficiencies of the defunct Commonwealth and to nurture a new conception of the nation, embracing not just the nobility but the whole population. They had to learn ways of challenging and dispensing with the outmoded privileges and leadership roles of the seigneurial classes and how to induct other social groups into the struggle to regain national independence (Fedorowicz 1982: 260).

The fourth Partition, 1814–15

At the Congress of Vienna Tsar Alexander held out for the creation of an ethnically Polish kingdom, with himself as its hereditary constitutional monarch. However, since the predominantly Lithuanian, Belorussian and Ukrainian territories which Russia had acquired during the 1772, 1793 and 1795 Partitions were already being treated as integral parts of the Russian Empire (i.e. as Russia's 'western provinces'), the victorious Tsar expected the renascent Kingdom of Poland to be carved out of the former Prussian and Austrian shares of the partitioned Commonwealth, in effect substituting Tsarist for Napoleonic patronage of the erstwhile Duchy of Warsaw. The Prussians would have been prepared to go along with this if they could have been generously compensated with even more valuable territorial gains in Germany (Saxony as well as the Rhineland). However, Austria, Great Britain and France mistrusted the Tsar and were determined to minimize the westward expansion of Tsarism into Poland and of Prussia into Germany, partly for fear of upsetting the new balance of power in Europe.

For his part, Alexander was undoubtedly hurt and offended by his partners' reluctance to entrust almost the whole of Poland to his tender care. Ironically, this induced him to treat his new Polish subjects with uncharacteristic leniency and liberality, despite their active complicity in Napoleon's fateful invasion of Russia in 1812. 'Although bitter towards the Poles . . . the Tsar did not seek revenge.' He was 'genuinely interested in the liberal experiment' in his Polish Kingdom, which he 'visited almost annually and wanted to use . . . as an element to transform his empire' (Wandycz 1974: 61, 77). In the judgement of another Westernized Pole, 'Alexander was neither vengeful nor blind to the opportunities of the Polish question' (Zamoyski 1987: 265). This most complex of Russian monarchs was rather underrated at the time and has remained so.

In the end, the Congress agreed to transform the core areas of the Duchy of Warsaw into a Kingdom of Poland, of which the Tsar would be king. But Gdansk and most of Wielkopolska (renamed Posen or Poznania) were returned to Prussian rule, while Austria regained most of 'New Galicia' (minus Krakow, which became a nominally independent city-state). In Polish eyes the deal struck in Vienna 'amounted to a fourth Partition' (Halecki 1957: 9). However, as a result of the continuing diplomatic offensive and activity of Czartoryski, the Tsar's (probably genuine) desire to atone for the Partitions, and the patent inability of the other partitioning powers completely to 'stamp out' the indomitably Polish nation, the Vienna 'Final Act' contained a pledge that Poles would receive national representation and institutions 'in so far as compatible with the interests of the partitioning powers' (Article 1). It also called for 'the maintenance of free navigation, circulation of agrarian and industrial products and free transit' within and between the territories of the former Commonwealth (Article 14). For several decades after 1815, indeed, Poles continued to travel and communicate quite freely between the different parts of the former Commonwealth. 'Polish culture and learning continued to transcend political borders. None of the partitioning powers could conduct its Polish policy in isolation, and developments in one area, especially the Kingdom, affected the Polish situation everywhere' (Wandycz 1974: 62, 67). Therefore, when reading separate accounts of the different segments, one should keep in mind their perpetual interaction.

Nineteenth-century Poles dismissively referred to the new frontier lines as 'the Prussian cordon' or 'the Austrian cordon'. In spirit, the Commonwealth 'continued to exist in defiance of boundaries' (Zamoyski 1987: 267).

The 'Congress' Kingdom of Poland

With a territory of 127,000 km^2, the new Kingdom of Poland recognized by the Congress of Vienna in 1815 was somewhat smaller than its French-sponsored predecessor, the Duchy of Warsaw, but its population soared from 3.3 million in 1815 to over 13 million by 1913 (Davies 1982: 307). According to the 1897 census, 31.5 per cent of the population lived in towns and 72 per cent of the population was Polish (Wandycz 1974: 206; Leslie 1980: 40).

Tsar Alexander allowed Polish aristocrats who had fought against him (but who were now at his mercy) to retain their landed estates and, where applicable, military positions. He also allowed the so-called Congress Kingdom to keep its own Sejm, government, laws, courts, armed forces, national guard, education system and official language. There were no vindictive 'purges' comparable to those initiated by subsequent Russian rulers. Warsaw was even allowed to open its first university in 1816, and by 1821 the kingdom had over 1,000 primary schools, continuing the educational reforms initiated during the 1770s and 1780s. Nevertheless, Russian rulers 'often refused to recognize the noble status of the poorest, peasant-like *szlachta*'. Large numbers of the latter were resettled on the Black Sea steppes, which Russia was busily colonizing (Wandycz 1974: 18). By 1864, as a joint result of these rustications, successive economic crises and the punishments meted out to noble participants in the uprisings of 1830–31 and 1863–64, over half the erstwhile *szlachta* had lost its former noble rank within the Congress Kingdom (Davies 1982: 82).

The Constitutional Charter of November 1815, which was one of the most liberal-sounding constitutions of its time and which successive Tsar-kings were sworn to uphold, promised personal and religious freedom (including freedom from arbitrary arrest and punishment), proclaimed the inviolability of private property, recognized Roman Catholicism as the majority religion and provided for a bicameral Sejm comprising a nominated upper house (Senate) and an elected lower house whose members had to be landowners (Wandycz 1974: 74–5). At the opening of the 1818 session of the Sejm, however, the Tsar threw down the following (somewhat patronizing) challenge: 'The results of your labours will show me whether I shall be able to abide by my intention of expanding the concessions I have already made to you' (quoted by Zamoyski 1987: 266). As King of Poland, moreover, Alexander retained the power to appoint and dismiss Ministers and officials, to convoke or amend its legislation, to conduct foreign policy, to control the police, to bypass the Sejm on budgetary matters and to act as ultimate arbiter.

The Congress Kingdom's standing army of 30,000 men, which was 'capable of rapid expansion in wartime', used Polish as the sole language of command, wore Polish colours and uniforms and absorbed 40 per cent of public expenditure (Davies 1982: 311). 'Excellently trained and well administered, it was the pride of all Poles' (thus prefiguring the post-1918 and post-1945 Polish armies!). However, it was placed under the command of Alexander's brother, Grand Duke Konstantin, who was a typically Tsarist martinet and 'paradomaniac', even though his morganatic marriage to a Pole precluded any possibility of his acceding to the Russian throne and helped him to become genuinely and protectively enamoured of his adopted country. Moreover, in order to engender military dependence upon Russia, the Congress Kingdom was not allowed to establish armament factories (Wandycz 1974: 77–8).

In the immediate aftermath of the Napoleonic Wars numerous Polish landed estates throughout the former Commonwealth were very adversely affected by a slump in international grain prices, increased protection of some major western European markets against 'cheap' foreign grain (notably through the British corn laws passed in 1816), the loss of unimpeded access to Danzig and other Baltic ports, and Prussian state support for the Junker estates. These circumstances contributed to the financial 'ruin' of many marginal or heavily mortgaged Polish landowners, some of whom had to sell off or surrender their land holdings to creditors and/or more monied bankers, burghers or non-Poles (including Prussian Junkers in Poznania, Masuria and Pomerania).

This agrarian crisis, following hard on the heels of the deeply unsettling effects of the French Revolution and Bonapartist reformism and opportunism, again forced questions of agrarian reform into the forefront of public attention and debate. It even resulted in the initiation of a Prussian-style 'landless emancipation' of the serfs in nearby Estland in 1816, in Kurland in 1817, in Livonia in 1819 and in Prussian-ruled Poznania in 1823. These reforms helped to transform landed estates into large-scale capitalist enterprises employing landless or almost landless wage labourers. Such hard-nosed solutions were rejected as too risky and/or inhumane in the Congress Kingdom, in Russia's 'western provinces', in Russia proper and in the Habsburg Empire (including Galicia) at the time. Nevertheless, as Piotr Wandycz argues (1974: 67), the agrarian question 'demanded a solution on economic, social and humanitarian grounds, and it was pregnant with political meaning. Depending on the kind of solution adopted, the peasant could become either a loyal subject of the partitioning powers or a politically conscious member of the Polish nation. A struggle for the peasant's allegiance filled much of the history of the nineteenth century.' The Tsarist regime was to prove willing to go much further than either the rulers of Prussia or the Habsburg Empire in its endeavours to use agrarian reform as a means of winning over or at least 'neutralizing' the peasantry and thus depriving the rebellious Polish-Lithuanian nobility of potential peasant support for secessionist and autonomist movements.

From the 1820s onwards, however, much the most effective alleviations of the agricultural crisis in Prussia and the territories of the former Polish-Lithuanian Commonwealth stemmed from greatly expanded cultivation of potatoes, flax and sugar beet, increased and improved crop rotation and sheep breeding, intensive rearing of pigs on potatoes and surplus grain, vastly increased production of vodka (from potatoes and surplus grain), sausage, beer, sugar, linen and woollen textiles, and much reduced reliance on grain as the staple subsistence and cash crop. These developments led to correspondingly diminished reliance on helot labour to cultivate grain, which in turn made it easier to contemplate and accommodate the more widespread abolition of serfdom. By and large, the territories which were the first to abandon serfdom also pioneered the adoption of new cropping patterns and the development of distilling, brewing and food-processing.

Within the Congress Kingdom, to a far greater extent than in Prussian or Austrian Poland, the post-1814 agricultural crisis was also alleviated by the beginnings of more broadly based industrialization. From 1816 onwards the government and some forward-looking magnates of the Congress Kingdom successfully promoted coal, zinc and copper mining, zinc, copper and iron smelting, steel making and, less directly, distilling, brewing and the kingdom's mushrooming woollen and cotton textile industries. The latter were greatly assisted by the inclusion of the Congress Kingdom within the Russian imperial customs union. Direct access to the vast Russian market (from which Prussian, Austrian and Western competitors were increasingly excluded) not only gave the Congress Kingdom's native entrepreneurs a preferential position. It also encouraged Germanic and western European entrepreneurs, engineers and manufacturers of textiles and textile machinery to set up (or ally themselves with) firms in Congress Poland, both as part of a modern 'tariff-hopping' strategy and in order to take advantage of the ample availability of very cheap serf and ex-serf labour, which was largely surplus to local agricultural requirements. Moreover, some of the entrepreneurs, engineers and artisans involved in the hitherto burgeoning Poznanian textile industry, which now found itself severely squeezed by the more favoured and/or advanced textile producers of central and western Germany as a result of the Partitions, 'relocated' to the Congress Kingdom. Generally speaking, other than in distilling, brewing and food-processing, the industrialists or would-be industrialists of Poznania and Pomerania found it increasingly difficult to compete with the much stronger industries of Saxony, Silesia, Berlin and western Germany, while those of Austrian Poland were even less able to compete with the burgeoning industries of Bohemia and German Austria. The Congress Kingdom, by contrast, succeeded in becoming the most highly industrialized territory of the far less industrialized Russian Empire. It was able to meet many of the industrial requirements of St Petersburg, Moscow and the Tsarist state, including the supply of military uniforms for the Russian armies that held it in subjugation! The Congress Kingdom's preferential economic position was put in jeopardy by the liberalization of the Russian Empire's foreign trade during the 1850s and 1860s, which increasingly exposed the kingdom to industrial competition from the west, but the threat receded again when the Russian Empire's import tariffs were greatly increased during the 1880s and 1890s. The number of industrial workers in the Congress Kingdom rose to 75,000 in 1858, 150,000 in 1885 (when Poznania had only 28,000 and Galicia a mere 25,000) and 317,000 in 1913 (Wandycz 1974: 158, 202, 280).

Nevertheless, the narrowly economic advantages which the Congress Kingdom derived from being within the tariff walls of the Russian Empire were neither enough in themselves nor perceived with sufficient clarity (at least until the publication of Rosa Luxemburg's celebrated doctoral thesis *Die Industrielle Entwicklung Polens* in 1898) to persuade Polish patriots to give up the struggle against irksome and increasingly repressive Russian tutelage. Moreover, although Alexander I was in principle prepared to grant the Poles of the Congress Kingdom a degree of autonomy and some constitutional civil rights, even this least illiberal of Russian Tsars bristled when Poles had the 'effrontery' to insist on exercising their vaunted 'rights' at all assertively. The long honeymoon between Alexander I and his new Polish subjects ended in 1820, when a couple of liberal opposition deputies 'sought to expose the arbitrariness of the government and its attempts to muzzle the Sejm'. The shocked Tsar interpreted such criticism as 'an attack on the monarchy', deprived the critics of their seats in Sejm, dismissed the kingdom's liberal Commissioner of Education and Religion, enhanced the extra-constitutional powers of Grand Duke Konstantin and refrained from convoking another Sejm until 1825 (Wandycz 1974: 84). In 1823, in Russia's 'western provinces', there were several dismissals, arrests and deportations of freethinking Poles at the University of Wilno (Vilnius).

Russo-Polish relations rapidly deteriorated under Tsar Nicholas I (1825–55), who was deeply shaken at the very start of his reign by an abortive *coup d'état* by members of Russia's elite Guards regiments in St Petersburg on 14 December 1825. These so-called Decembrists had links with secret opposition groups in Warsaw, whose 'ringleaders' were (on the Tsar's instructions) brought to trial before a Senate tribunal in 1828. However, the Tsar and Grand Duke Konstantin accepted neither the Senators' ruling that 'membership of an unapproved society did not in itself constitute a treasonable act' nor the lenient sentences imposed. The Senators' proceedings were annulled and the accused were subsequently 'transported in chains to Siberia' (Davies 1982: 314). A classic pattern was emerging: 'having imposed a government and a Constitution on a satellite Poland, Russia could not countenance its legal functioning' (Zamoyski 1987: 269). In 1828, moreover, the Tsar initiated a vicious campaign of persecution and suppression against the Uniate Church in Russia's 'western provinces'. (It culminated in the 'return' of the Uniate hierarchy to the Eastern Orthodox 'fold' in 1839, amid continuing popular resistance.)

Polish anger at these flagrant violations of the Tsar's earlier manifesto promising to abide by the constitution and continue the policies of Alexander I contributed to the outbreak of a chaotic cadet officers' uprising in Warsaw on 29 November 1830. This so-called 'November rising' began amid a serious economic crisis and an alarming cholera epidemic, a few months after the final overthrow of France's Bourbon regime and the attainment of Belgian independence from the Netherlands. However, the ineptitude of the mutinous cadets (who accidentally killed some of their own people) enabled conservative members of the kingdom's government to regain the political initiative and exercise restraint. Out of a desire to avoid unnecessary bloodshed and burning of bridges, they allowed Grand Duke Konstantin to withdraw his Russian troops and officials safely from the Congress Kingdom to Russia (instead of holding them hostage) and tried to use the state of insurgency merely as a lever with which to extract constitutional guarantees and concessions from the Tsar. Unfortunately, Nicholas demanded unconditional capitulation and refused to negotiate, informing Grand Duke Konstantin that either Russia or Poland 'must now perish' (Davies 1982: 320). On 25 January 1831, while a Russian invasion force was assembling around Bialystok, the Sejm rashly voted to dethrone the Romanovs in the Congress Kingdom (emulating the recent Belgian dethronement of the house of Orange), thereby matching the Tsar's intransigence and transforming a hitherto restrained 'war of nerves' into a 'life or death' struggle for national independence. The move also alienated the other partitioning powers, who had been enjoying Russia's discomfiture. In February Prince Adam Czartoryski emerged as President of a Polish national government, which vainly scoured Europe for a new king while mobilizing over 57,000 Polish servicemen, who initially inflicted heavy defeats and casualties on much larger and more heavily armed (but cholera-stricken) Russian forces. However, the kingdom's military actions were poorly synchronized with those of over 20,000 Polish and Lithuanian rebels in Lithuania, Belorussia and the Ukraine (Wandycz 1974: 112–15). Moreover, the Polish leaders' reluctance to make a clean break with serfdom (for fear of alienating the mainstay of their own support, financial backing and officer class) inhibited them from fully mobilizing the peasantry, who could have turned their weapons against their 'masters'. By September 1831, therefore, the Congress

Kingdom could no longer hold off the sheer weight of the Russian steamroller, and Warsaw capitulated, while the Polish armies melted away and the political leaders fled abroad. For many Poles the cruellest cut came in 1832 when the Pope condemned the 'November rising' and lauded the Tsar for suppressing it.

This time Tsarist retribution was merciless. Nicholas I lacked the magnanimity of Alexander I. About 360 people were sentenced to death (though most of them had already escaped abroad), several thousand landed estates were confiscated, half the Catholic convents and monasteries were closed and over 50,000 Polish and Lithuanian nobles and officers were banished to the far nethers (Siberia, the Caucasus, beyond the Volga), some as convicts, others as low-ranking soldiers. The kingdom's constitution, Sejm, army and institutions of higher learning were abolished, as was the University of Wilno, while Russian replaced Polish as the official language (even in schools) in the 'western provinces'. The kingdom was in effect under Russian-administered martial law and its education system went to rack and ruin. In the later nineteenth century its adult literacy rates were lower than those of Russia.

Nearly 8,000 educated Poles became political *émigrés* after 1831, 'and for the next fifteen years the centre of Polish intellectual life and political activities shifted abroad, mainly to France' (Namier 1946: 43–4). Those who remained in their old homeland found outlets and/or solace in practical ('organic') work, which did at least yield economic dividends. The new-found apoliticism of the Polish and Lithuanian propertied classes was reinforced by a ferocious peasant revolt in Galicia in 1846, which resulted in the death of some 2,000 Polish landowners and encouraged the Tsarist regime to register and regulate peasant rights and obligations in the 'western provinces' as a means of currying favour with the serfs at their masters' expense.

Industry and trade resumed their earlier rapid expansion following the elimination of the temporary tariff barriers established between Russia and the Congress Kingdom from 1832 to 1851 and were further stimulated by the Crimean War (1853–56). But the political 'freeze' did not end until the death of Nicholas I in 1855. Polish attempts to use the Crimean War to reopen 'the Polish question' by military and diplomatic means came to naught. Nevertheless, Russia's humiliating defeats at British and French hands in the Crimea did contribute to a thaw by igniting popular unrest in many parts of the empire, by sapping Nicholas I's will to live, and by helping to convince Tsar Alexander II (1855–81) that the emancipation of the serfs in both Russia and the Congress Kingdom could not be postponed any longer. He would have to grasp the nettle. That firm conviction prompted Alexander II to invite the kingdom's newly established Agricultural Society to formulate far-reaching proposals for peasant emancipation and agrarian reform in 1858. Formed ostensibly to promote 'improving landlordism', the 4,000 members and seventy-seven district branches of the Agricultural Society actually functioned as a surrogate Sejm for the Polish landed nobility. Its president, Count Adam Zamoyski, became the unofficial 'spokesman of the Poles in the Kingdom' (Wandycz 1974: 156). By February 1861 large crowds were cheering the arrival of delegates to its meetings (not something one normally associates with agricultural societies!).

Well before this, however, Russia's Crimean defeats and the death of Nicholas I had already contributed to a widespread raising of hopes, spirits and expectations, to which the new Tsar virtually had to respond (regardless of his own 'honourable' convictions and inclinations). It would, however, prove difficult either to dampen or to satisfy these expectations of change. There is also much to be said for the Marxist thesis that the development of 'productive forces' in Russia and Poland had reached a point where it was both inhibited by and increasingly at odds with the prevailing 'social relations of production' (Bideleux 1994: 16–19).

In 1856 Alexander II announced his intention to initiate reforms in partnership with the propertied classes. He also appointed a (by Russian standards) liberal viceroy to the Congress Kingdom, amnestied the Poles who had been languishing in banishment since 1831, restored freedom of assembly, allowed the long-vacant archbishopric of Warsaw to be filled, and yet warned his Polish subjects not to indulge in impractical daydreams: 'Pas de rêveries, messieurs!' Long-forbidden subjects were freshly debated as hundreds of new societies blossomed. There were calls for Jewish emancipation and assimilation; the finest Russians (led by Alexander Herzen) promoted Russo-Polish reconciliation and co-operation in the interests of fraternal friendship, freedom and reform. It should always be remembered that, throughout the nineteenth century, there were deep friendships and alliances as well as awful antagonisms between Russians and Poles (Zamoyski 1987: 308).

By 1861, however, the 'thaw' and rekindled Polish nationalism were spawning demands and expectations which the Tsarist regime was unwilling (and probably unable) to assuage, and mass demonstrations to which the authorities overreacted, causing unnecessary fatalities and even the suppression of the Agricultural Society. The initial terms on which serfs were gradually to be emancipated (from 1861 onwards) fell far short of public expectations and became a bone of bitter contention. During 1861 and 1862 the singing of patriotic hymns at huge Catholic masses in the Congress Kingdom and in Russia's 'western provinces' gave expression to rising nationalist fervour, foreshadowing the 'singing revolutions' of the Polish and other Baltic peoples during the late Tsarist and late Soviet periods. The imposition of martial law in the 'western provinces' and the Congress Kingdom in October 1861 did not dampen opposition, but simply drove it underground. During 1862 and 1863, indeed, Polish 'patriots' developed an elaborate underground state with its own administration, secret army, diplomatic representation and intelligence network, in preparation for a concerted armed insurrection. What the Poles lacked in regular military forces, compared with 1830–31, they now made up for in superior morale, discipline and organization (prefiguring 1942–44). Sensing that something was afoot, yet unable to track it down, the Russian authorities and their Polish collaborators (led by the conservative reformer Count Alexander Wielopolski) cunningly announced their intention to draft 30,000 young Polish males into military service on 14 January 1863. However, this ruse was foiled by hastily bringing forward the start of the planned insurrection, which caught the authorities completely off-guard.

The insurgents of the 'January rising' had to avoid direct engagement with the 45,000 Russian troops stationed in the kingdom. Yet they managed to keep up hit-and-run attacks on Russian garrisons, encampments and officialdom from January 1863 to May 1864 (and even longer in some areas), forcing the Russians temporarily to evacuate three-quarters of the localities they had occupied (Wandycz 1974: 172–7). The rising spread deep into Lithuania, Belorussia and the Ukraine. It involved hundreds of Russian, Italian, German, French, British and Irish volunteers. While at any one time there were never more than 20,000 to 30,000 'insurgents in the field', approximately 200,000 people took part (p. 179). Remarkably, the actual identities of all but a few remained undetected and most of the 200,000 rebels 'simply melted away' at the end (Davies 1982: 363). However, as in 1831, while several European powers relished Russia's discomfiture, neither Prussia nor Austria could afford to let the rising succeed, and neither France nor Great Britain wanted to risk any military intervention on the insurgents' behalf.

To a far greater extent than Nicholas I, moreover, Alexander II was prepared to propitiate the peasantry by granting them additional land at their former masters' expense. However much the insurgents promised to accede to peasant aspirations or to prevent landowners from continuing to exact seigneurial dues from their former serfs, Alexander was willing to outbid them. Canny peasants probably twigged that, instead of putting their lives at risk by backing the insurgents' increasingly radical agrarian programme, they only needed to wait patiently to receive much the same agrarian gains (without risk!) from the Tsar. Indeed, the final terms on which the former serfs in Russia's 'western provinces' and the Congress Kingdom were emancipated in 1864 were among the most favourable in East Central Europe and the Russian Empire.

In the aftermath of the 1863 rising over 3,000 Polish and Lithuanian landed estates were confiscated. (Many were given to Tsarist officers or officials.) Approximately 400 people were executed after due legal process (the number summarily shot or hanged is harder to establish), while tens of thousands were deported to Siberia and other similarly inhospitable destinations. Warsaw became the capital of 'the Vistula Region' or 'the ten provinces', although the Congress Kingdom of Poland was not formally abolished until 1874. This territory was 'administered by Russians with Russian as the official language' (Wandycz 1974: 196) and in 1885 Russian also became the only language permitted in schools (Zamoyski 1987: 315). Neither 'the Vistula Region' nor 'the western provinces' was allowed the system of elected *zemstva* (provincial councils) established in Russia proper in 1864 or the elected municipal *dumi* (councils) introduced in the latter in 1870. Since they were also neither inclined nor encouraged to engage in Tsarist state service, the Tsar's Polish subjects again largely retreated from public political activity into 'organic work': the quiet construction of an economically and culturally renewed and strengthened Poland, an expanded industrial sector and a modernized infrastructure. In the longer term, however, this inevitably brought new players on to the political stage: an increasingly assertive bourgeoisie and 'bourgeois' political parties; several somewhat unassertive peasant parties; and politically awakened, partly Jewish and increasingly assertive industrial workers, trade unions and socialist parties. All these would eventually challenge the former political ascendancy of the magnates, the nobility and the *émigré* intelligentsia during the 1890s and the 1900s.

The assassination of Alexander II in 1881 and the accession of Alexander III changed the political climate very much for the worse. In the first place these events precipitated a wave of officially condoned pogroms against Jews in the Ukraine, Lithuania and, to a lesser degree, the former Congress Kingdom. The pogroms were both symptomatic of and conducive to a significant 'hardening' of official and even popular attitudes towards certain religious and ethnic groups (including Poles, Catholics and Armenians as well as Jews) and a deterioration of inter-ethnic and interdenominational relations in general. Polish, Lithuanian, Ukrainian and Belorussian national movements, which had been parting company since the 1863–64 uprising and the subsequent repression and mutual recriminations, also became increasingly antisemitic, partly because the development of capitalism seemed to be expanding the role of 'exploitative' Jewish middlemen and partly because growing urbanization was bringing ethnic Poles, Lithuanians, Ukrainians and Belorussians increasingly into competition with Jewish townspeople. The recurrent pogroms, which tended to be most violent in the Ukraine, Belorussia and Lithuania, also provoked an unsettling influx of Jewish refugees (so-called 'Litvaks') into the *relative* safety and civility of the former Congress Kingdom, where Jews already made up over 10 per cent of the population by 1881 (as was also the case in the 'western provinces'). Under Alexander III (1881–94) and Nicholas II (1894–1917), moreover, the Tsarist regime reverted to the repressive bigotry of Nicholas I, but applied it with the technology and ferocity of a more modern police state. For some people at least life in the western borderlands of the Russian Empire was becoming even nastier and more brutish than before, and this increasingly intemperate 'dog eat dog' climate was not alleviated by the rise of movements preaching class hatred. The growth of virulent nationalism was more often reinforced than dissipated or defused by the intensification of class antagonisms. When combined, they formed a particularly poisonous and explosive cocktail.

Modern Polish, Jewish and (later) Lithuanian nationalist movements oriented towards the emerging entrepreneurial and professional classes developed rapidly during the 1880s and 1890s and began to establish cross-border ties between different parts of the former Commonwealth. Similarly, in areas primarily inhabited by Poles, Jews and Lithuanians, small socialist groups oriented towards the wage-earning working class (as distinct from the peasantry) sprang up during the 1880s. After a major workers' strike in Lodz in 1892 they coalesced into larger movements and parties in 1893–96, well before their Russian and Ukrainian counterparts. However, these socialists eventually forged ties with sister movements in Russia, Germany and Austria as well as between the various components of the former Commonwealth. Yet, while some people interpreted such links as manifestations of a reassuring growth of 'proletarian internationalism', others saw them as an additional cause for alarm. When it came to the crucial test, moreover, these vaunted 'bonds' did not prevent (and rarely withstood) the outbreak of war in 1914.

In the former Congress Kingdom and in Russia's 'western provinces', even more than in Russia proper, the Russo-Japanese War of 1904–05 exacerbated already serious economic and social crises. These exploded into major anti-war and anti-Tsarist demonstrations, political as well as economic strikes and bloody clashes between workers and the Tsarist security forces (who were sometimes supported by the Polish propertied classes) from the autumn of 1904 to the summer of 1907, after which the fever temporarily subsided as the authorities resorted to increasingly draconian repression and divide-and-rule tactics. However, workers' unrest revived between 1912 and August 1914, whereupon the start of the First World War gave Tsarism a brief respite by allowing it to rally its Russian, Polish, Ukrainian, Jewish, Belorussian and Lithuanian subjects behind the war effort and to place would-be 'troublemakers' under military discipline.

The Prussian zones

The principal territories gained by the Hohenzollerns from the Polish-Lithuanian Commonwealth were West Prussia (1772–1807, 1815–1918), Mazovia and Bialystock (1795–1807), and, most important, Gdansk, Torun (Thorn) and Wielkopolska (1793–1807, 1815–1918). Prussian legal codes, administrative practices and personnel were introduced into these areas from 1795 onwards and elected provincial *sejmiki* were abolished, along with urban autonomy (Wandycz 1974: 14–15). The former crown estates and those belonging to insurrectionary nobles were first confiscated by the Prussian state and then sold to Germans (especially Junkers and bankers), ostensibly to raise revenue but perhaps also to Germanize these newly annexed territories. There were also substantial Polish populations in Prussian Pomerania, Masuria (in East Prussia) and Silesia, and in 1800 Poles comprised over 40 per cent of the population of the kingdom of Prussia. From 1807 to 1815, however, Prussia lost most of its Polish territory to the Duchy of Warsaw, while at the Congress of Vienna in 1814–15 the Hohenzollerns yielded Mazovia (including Warsaw) and Bialystock to victorious Russia, although they received ample compensation elsewhere (the Rhineland and part of Saxony).

During the late 1790s the Hohenzollern-ruled areas of Poland experienced a grain boom which mainly benefited the bigger landowners. But the boom collapsed during the 1800s, under the combined impact of British blockades and Napoleon's Continental System. As a result, much of the Polish *szlachta* had to sell off land to wealthier Germans.

In 1815 Wielkopolska was reconstituted as the semi-autonomous Grand Duchy of Posen, alias Poznania. Its area was just 29,000 km^2 and its population (80 per cent of which was Polish-speaking) was only 850,000 in 1815, rising to 2.15 million by 1911 (Davies 1982: 120; Leslie 1971: 21). It had its own *Landrat* (Diet), elected by the nobility, and Polish was the official language in education, administration and the courts. By contrast, Pomerania, Upper Silesia and East and West Prussia were governed and educated in German, as integral components of the kingdom of Prussia, with just a few concessions to the inchoate 'national' sensibilities of those inhabitants who spoke dialects of Polish as their mother tongue. However, many of the latter had an even weaker sense of 'Polishness' than did the mainly German-speaking inhabitants of Gdansk (Davies 1982: 112) and the Prussian monarchy was able to promote the concept of 'the loyal Polish-speaking Prussian' with some success so long as (i) the Prussian state remained more monarchical than (German) 'national' and (ii) the Polish-speakers of Pomerania, Masuria and Prussian Silesia retained essentially local identities and a stronger allegiance to the king than to the Polish 'nation'. By contrast the population of Poznania was classified as 60 per cent Polish, 34 per cent German and 6 per cent Jewish during the 1840s (Wandycz 1974: 139). By 1911, as a result of population shifts, the Jewish share had fallen to 1.2 per cent (p. 286) and that of the Germans to 30 per cent, while the Polish share had risen to 68 per cent (Leslie 1971: 21).

The subjugation of Prussia's Poles was aided by the circumstance that the exceptionally assiduous, efficient and law-governed Prussian civil service and armed forces were dominated by relatively educated and dutiful Protestant landowners (Junkers) whose power base lay mainly in areas with a substantial Polish population. It was doubly difficult for the relatively uneducated Poles to hold their own against a ruling class which presided over one of Europe's most developed education systems. This, besides producing such luminaries as Kant, Hegel, Fichte, Humboldt, Bunsen, Kleist and Lessing, acted as a cultural magnet and transformed Berlin and Königsberg into intellectual centres of the first order. 'Notwithstanding the authoritarian state, all political changes in Prussia were subjected to searching debate . . . In the absence of any comparable intellectual development in the Polish lands, many Poles were inevitably drawn into the world of German culture . . . Quite apart from official policy, therefore, many Poles in Prussia accepted that modernization went hand-in-hand with Germanization' (Davies 1982: 118–19). 'By 1848, 82 per cent of children were attending schools' (p. 123). Many influential Poznanian Poles concluded that their only course was to try to become even more efficient, orderly, educated and industrious than their Prussian Protestant overlords, in order to beat them at their own game! As one of them wrote in

1872, 'Learning, work, order and thrift, these are our new weapons . . . In this way you will save both yourself and Poland' (quoted in Wandycz 1974: 229).

There was a gradual dissolution of serfdom in most parts of Prussia between 1811 and 1853, although in Poznania the process was not initiated until 1823. But in Prussia, unlike the Congress Kingdom, Austria-Hungary and Russia, most of the former serfs were converted into landless agricultural labourers rather than independent peasant smallholders, while Junker dominance of the local law courts kept most of the agrarian population under landlord jurisdiction even after the dissolution of serfdom. For Prussia's Polish subjects the positive effects of formal personal emancipation were also offset by greatly increased burdens of taxation and compulsory military service (far in excess of anything imposed by the former Polish-Lithuanian Commonwealth).

After the abortive rising of 1830–31 in the Congress Kingdom, the Poznanian *Landrat* ceased to be convoked and some Poznanian Poles who had given Polish insurgents succour had their property confiscated, while over 250 Poznanian Poles were arrested during the Galician crisis of 1846. However, the latter group were set free following the outbreak of revolutionary unrest in Berlin on 20 March 1848 (Davies 1982: 12). Many of the German liberals, radicals and nationalists of 1848 were anti-Russian. Some considered that 'one of the first acts of a newly united Germany should be to make war upon Russia' and that 'Poland should be erected into an independent state to act as a buffer between Germany and Russia' (Leslie 1971: 19). In the *Neue Rheinische Zeitung* on 19 August 1848 Marx and Engels declared that 'The establishment of a democratic Poland is a primary condition for the establishment of a democratic Germany . . . She must receive at least the frontiers of 1772 and . . . a considerable stretch of coast' (quoted by Namier 1946: 51).

However, in a debate in the German National Assembly in July 1848 on the future of Poznania, a German from East Prussia helped to sway German liberal-nationalist opinion away from its former sympathy for the Polish cause. 'Are half a million Germans . . . to be relegated to the position of nationalized foreigners subject to another nation of lesser cultural content than themselves?' he asked. 'Our right is the right of the stronger, the right of conquest . . . Mere existence does not entitle a people to political independence, only the force to assert itself as a state' (quoted by Namier 1946: 88). This naked appeal to *force majeure* was to set the tone of German–Polish relations thereafter. By the end of April 1848, moreover, the Prussian army had already suppressed the Poznanian Polish militias and National Committee which had emerged in March. After 1848 Poznania lost the last vestiges of its formal autonomy, and was downgraded to a mere *Provinz* of the Prussian kingdom, as Germans veered from sympathy to hostility towards the Polish cause. This hardening of German attitudes seems even to have affected Engels, who wrote (to Marx) on 23 May 1851: 'The more I think about this business, the clearer it is to me that the Poles are *une nation foutue*, a serviceable instrument only until Russia herself is swept into the agrarian revolution. From that moment Poland loses all *raison d'être*. The Poles have never done anything in history except engage in brave, blatant foolery' (quoted by Namier 1946: 52). In contrast to Engels, however, Marx maintained his support for the Polish cause, instead of succumbing to German chauvinism and supremacism.

From 1850 to 1918 there were no comparable Prussian crises which Poles could have exploited to great advantage. However, the position of Prussia's Polish provinces was radically transformed by the creation of Bismarck's German Empire in 1871. From having been one of several provinces of the Hohenzollern kingdom, Poznania now became a virtual colony of the German state. 'The imperial union of the German lands established Germanity as the touchstone of respectability, in a way that never pertained before' (Davies 1982: 131). In 1872 German became the official language of instruction in all elementary schools (even in Poznania, where only religious education continued to be provided partly in Polish). In 1874 there was a ban on the use of Polish textbooks. In 1887 even the teaching of Polish as a 'foreign language' was discontinued in favour of English! Furthermore, teachers in state schools were no longer permitted to belong either to Polish or to Catholic organizations, while in 1876 German was made the exclusive language of administration, even in post offices, railway ticket offices and courts of law (Wandycz 1974: 235).

These measures coincided with Bismarck's infamous *Kulturkampf*, an attack on the alleged centrifugal and particularist tendencies of German as well as Polish Catholicism. The newly established German national state was determined to assert its temporal jurisdiction over the local branches of the Catholic Church, at a time when Pope Pius IX was challenging the authority and legitimacy of the new state by denouncing nationalism and encouraging ultramontanism. A series of German laws passed between 1872 and 1876 led to the expulsion of the Jesuits, the sequestration of Catholic Church properties, the severance of relations with the papacy and mass dismissals of Polish Catholic priests from teaching posts (mostly to be replaced by German Protestants). The conservative Polish Archbishop of Gniezno and Catholic Primate of Prussian Poland had initially been very willing to collaborate with the Prussian authorities against Polish nationalism, democracy and secular radicalism, supposedly to keep the universalist Catholic Church 'above' or 'out of' temporal politics (although it was nothing of the sort). But in 1874 he was arrested and imprisoned (for two years) for refusing to acquiesce in the subordination of the Catholic Church to the state. This former 'collaborator' suddenly became a 'national hero'. The German Archbishop of Cologne, two Polish bishops, most Polish deacons and over 100 Polish parish priests were also imprisoned, while many more were harassed or dismissed from their positions. These anti-Catholic campaigns were targeted at German as well as Polish clergy, but they bit deeper and lasted longer in Germany's Polish provinces, where they were inseparable from equally acrimonious linguistic and educational issues (Wandycz 1974: 228–34).

During the 1880s, moreover, German publicists, academics and politicians started drawing attention to the substantial exodus of Germans from the Polish provinces to the more industrialized, urbanized and prosperous parts of the German Empire. This flight from the east (known as the *Ostflucht*) aroused German fears that, in spite of the state-sponsored Germanization programme, 'Germandom' (*Deutschtum*) was losing ground to 'Slavdom' and that Germany's grip on these provinces was therefore becoming less secure. The German backlash began in 1885–86 with the controversial expulsion of approximately 26,000 Poles and Polish Jews who held Russian or Austrian rather than German citizenship, even though some of these families had lived in Prussia for several generations (Leslie 1980: 32). In 1886, sensing that his own political position was becoming less secure, Bismarck also played up and pandered to German xenophobia by calling for the creation of a commission to buy up Polish-owned land in the east and colonize it with German peasants (Wandycz 1974: 236). The resultant Colonization Commission, endowed with 100 million Marks, was backed not just by German imperialists but by National Liberals who saw peasant colonists as a useful counterweight to the excessive power of the Junkers in the 'eastern provinces' and also by Junkers who saw such colonists as a potential pool of cheap and/or dependent labour.

However, the main overall effect of the *Kulturkampf*, the Germanization programme and the Colonization Commission was to arouse, mobilize and even unite the Poles of Poznania, Pomerania, Masuria and Silesia in support of Polish nationalism, the Catholic Church, political struggle and cultural resistance, to an extent which they might never have achieved on their own, without German provocation. The Poles were goaded into strikingly successful political, economic, educational and cultural counter-offensives, which actually *reversed* Germanization on the ground, despite further escalations of Germany's 'eastern' imperialism and colonialism.

Following the establishment of the Pan-German Union in 1891, an association for the promotion of German interests in the 'eastern provinces' was launched in 1894. It was popularly known as the Hakata (after the initials of its founders, Hansemann, Kennemann and Tiedemann), before formally becoming the Deutscher Ostmarkverein in 1899. It enjoyed strong private, official and academic support and propagated a proto-Nazi *Lebensraum* programme and ideology. It systematically Germanized 'eastern' place names and public signs, fostered German cultural imperialism, and provided financial and other inducements for German farmers, officials, clergy and teachers to settle and work in the east. After Bismarck's fall in 1890, Kaiser Wilhelm II actively encouraged all this. Not only did he provide large benefactions, but his visits to East Prussia were even greeted by Prussian officials dressed up in the chain-mail, sallets and cloaks of the medieval Teutonic Knights. (On the other hand, it could be argued that this was little different from the pageantry of the investiture of English Princes of Wales!)

In response, the Polish and/or Catholic credit associations, agricultural co-operatives, mutual aid societies and land banks which had been launched in Prussia's 'eastern provinces' during the 1860s and 1870s were spurred to ever higher levels of activity. Polish farmers' *rolniki* ('circles'), whose membership rose tenfold between 1873 and 1914 (Wandycz 1974: 286), helped their members to undertake bulk purchases of seed, fertilizer, equipment and fuel, to secure more favourable terms for their produce, to buy additional land and to improve agricultural techniques and education (Davies 1982: 192). In Poznania, Pomerania and Upper Silesia the Union of Credit Associations expanded its membership from 26,533 in 1890 to 146,312 in 1913, while its deposits rose more than twentyfold. (The resultant 'squeezing out' of middlemen contributed to the large-scale Jewish emigration.) Moreover, the Land Purchase Bank which the Poles established in 1897 was soon able to offer higher dividends and easier credit terms than were its German rivals, thanks to its efficient and close-knit network of operations; between 1896 and 1904 there was a net 50,000 ha increase in Polish land ownership (Wandycz 1974: 286).

Thousands of German peasants were settled in Prussia's 'eastern provinces' by the Colonization Commission, but less than half of them were inward migrants from other parts of Germany, and they proved all too willing subsequently to resell the land they had acquired (often to Poles) in order to cash in on rising land prices (Leslie 1980: 35). Moreover, much of the money mobilized for the 'colonization' and Germanization of these 'eastern provinces' was diverted into the pockets of the Junkers, 'who made their patriotism a highly lucrative business' (Wandycz 1974: 237, 285–6). Indeed, it is unclear to what extent the latter was the programme's true purpose, with nationalist colonial rhetoric serving mainly as a smokescreen with which to deceive the German public (which was not so eager to subsidize profiteers and Junkers). Whatever the case, the programme failed to halt (let alone reverse) the long-term decline of Poznania's German population, which fell from 666,083 in 1861 to 637,000 in 1911, while its Polish population rose from 801,372 to 1,463,000 over the same period (Leslie 1971: 21).

In addition, Poles began to take full advantage of the ubiquitous schools, literacy, public libraries, reading rooms and museums provided by the German state, while increasingly reserving their own educational and cultural expenditure for extensive private tuition in Polish language, literature, history and Catholicism (Wandycz 1974: 232, 235, 283, 285). This started a tradition which helped to maintain Polish culture and morale during the periods of Nazi and communist rule. During the 1900s, moreover, Poles began to buy locally produced manufactures in preference to those from elsewhere, while the number of industrial workers in Poznania rose from 30,000 in 1875 to 162,000 in 1907 (p. 281). These trends led the German Ludwig Bernhard to conclude in 1910 that Prussia's Poles could be held up as a 'model of how a national minority can keep its independent existence and even strengthen it against a far stronger state authority'. Nevertheless, there was concern as to whether the Poles could have sustained this in the longer run, especially if the German state were to switch to 'a policy of unlimited oppression' (pp. 286–7). But we shall never know the answer to this question, because defeat in the First World War brought German hegemony to an abrupt end for most of the Prussian Poles.

Habsburg Galicia

In 1822 Galicia had a territory of 77,300 km^2 and a population of 4.8 million, which was approximately equal to the combined populations of Poznania and the Congress Kingdom (Davies 1982: 143, 120, 307). Indeed, its population density in 1822 (sixty-two people per square kilometre) was roughly *double* that of either Poznania (twenty-nine per square kilometre in 1815) or the Congress Kingdom (twenty-six per square kilometre in 1815), by our calculations. By 1910, however, Galicia's population of 7.3 million had been far surpassed by that of the Congress Kingdom (nearly 13 million), which by then had a population density exceeding that of either Galicia or Poznania. (The figures were approximately 101, ninety-four and seventy-four people per square kilometre, respectively, by our calculations.) Between 1870 and 1914 approximately 1.1 million people emigrated from Galicia and roughly 1.2 million departed from Prussian Poland, while 1.3 million left the Congress Kingdom (Wandycz 1974: 276). Relative to population, the rate of emigration was higher from Galicia than from the former Congress Kingdom, but that of Prussian Poland was the highest. The most important reasons for Galicia's comparatively slow population growth were its extreme poverty, the relative lack of opportunity and its high morbidity rates, all of which were reflected in comparatively high adult and infant mortality rates. It was a landlocked and relatively stagnant economic backwater. According to Wandycz (1974: 330), Galicia's *per capita* income in 1913 was only $38, as against $63 for the relatively industrialized Congress Kingdom and $113 for a still relatively agrarian Prussian Poland. In a book published in Lwow in 1887, entitled *Galician Misery in Figures*, Stanislaw Szczepanowski provided the following evidence: that Galicia's *per capita* agricultural production was two-thirds that of the Congress Kingdom and Hungary and less than half that of France; that its *per capita* food consumption was under half that of France and Great Britain and two-thirds that of Hungary; that the mortality rate was even higher in Galicia than in either Prussian Poland or the Congress Kingdom; that some 50,000 people were dying each year from malnutrition; and that conditions were worse than they had been in Ireland before the 1840s famine (Davies 1982: 145–6). A major cause of these problems was lack of education: 77 per cent of the population above school age were illiterate in 1880 (Leslie 1980: 15).

On the other hand, Austria was the only one of the three partitioning powers that was Roman Catholic (and therefore respected Polish Catholicism) and which, as a ramshackle multinational conglomeration, made a point of preserving the cultural and ethnic diversity of its subjects (partly in order to divide and rule) instead of trying to homogenize them. Galicia was also relatively unscathed by fighting, since it had not been involved in either the 1793 Partition or the 1794 uprising, and it had witnessed only light skirmishing in 1809 and 1813 (during the Napoleonic Wars). Northern Galicia was part of the Duchy of Warsaw from 1809 to 1815, yet Galicia never became a major battleground. After 1782, moreover, its peasants gained increased formal freedom to marry, change their occupation or leave the land. Habsburg rule also introduced legal restrictions on the acquisition of peasant land by non-peasants and on the labour dues which could be demanded by landlords. On the down side, taxation and military service obligations greatly increased, labour obligations persisted until the 1850s (albeit on a reduced scale) and, in this landlocked, undiversified and uncommercialized economy, peasants remained rather dependent on landlords and vulnerable to seigneurial pressure (Wandycz 1974: 13).

The main perceived drawbacks of Austrian rule in Galicia during the period from 1815 to 1861 were its absolutism and its neglect of the interests of this poor, remote and strategically unimportant province. 'Galicia was for Austria a province beyond the Carpathians, the loss of which could never have threatened the Empire with disruption' (Leslie 1980: 26).

As in Prussian Poland, the Congress Kingdom and Russia's 'western provinces', however, the lesser nobility rather lost out under Austrian rule. As Galicia's legal codes, administration and political institutions were 'Austrianized' from 1786 onwards, political *sejmiki* were replaced by a purely advisory Assembly of Estates dominated by magnates and the Catholic Church (Wandycz 1974: 12). By 1848 there were fewer than 2,000 registered (noble) landowning families in Galicia, and 300 of these were foreign (Davies 1982: 143). Moreover, by making the landlord class responsible for collecting taxes, administering the law and furnishing recruits for the Habsburg armed forces, Austrian rule exacerbated the peasant–landlord tensions which erupted into widespread violence in 1846 (Wandycz 1974: 13). The savagery of this revolt, which claimed thousands of lives on both sides, was compounded by inter-ethnic tensions. The landlord class was mainly Polish (or sometimes German), whereas the peasants were mainly Ruthenian (Ukrainian), especially in eastern Galicia. According to the 1822 census, 47.5 per cent of Galicia's population was Polish, 45.5 per cent was Ruthenian, 6 per cent was Jewish and 1 per cent was German (Wandycz 1974: 71). As a result of German and especially Jewish immigration, moreover, the ethnic composition became 45 per cent Polish, 41 per cent Ruthene, 11 per cent Jewish and 3 per cent German by 1880 (Davies 1982: 144). This was a potentially explosive mix. Indeed, the bloody peasant revolt of 1846 left Galicia's propertied classes deeply fearful of 'the masses', radicalism and anything that could re-ignite peasant hatred of the rich and powerful.

This helps to explain why there was so little social or educational change and reform, and no Galician revolution in 1848. Polish 'National Committees' were formed in Lwow (Galicia's capital) and in semi-autonomous Krakow in March 1848, and these petitioned the Habsburgs for Galician autonomy and emancipation of the serfs. But Krakow was subdued by Habsburg forces and bombardment in April 1848 (and forfeited its residual autonomy), while Lwow met a similar fate in November 1848.

In February 1861, in the wake of the humiliating eviction of the Habsburgs from Lombardy, Galicia was granted separate legal and administrative institutions, stopping short of autonomy. In December 1867, after even more humiliating Habsburg defeats in Germany and Venetia, Galicia was also granted an elective legislature (*sejm krajowy*) and a viceregal executive based in both Lwow and Krakow. At first less than 10 per cent of the population were enfranchised and the system of electoral *curia* (colleges) was weighted heavily in favour of Galicia's predominantly Polish landlords. However, there were mass demonstrations in Lwow in 1868 demanding further concessions. In response, the Polish language was given equal status with German in schools and law courts in 1868, in administration in 1869 and in the Jagiellonian University (in Krakow) in 1870. Galicia also gained an Academy of Sciences in 1872 and an Education Board to establish a comprehensive system of elementary schooling in 1873 (Davies 1982: 150–1). After 1867 Galicia's Catholic Poles were in effect admitted into the exalted ranks of the 'master races' of the Habsburg Empire, alongside the Austrian Germans and the Magyars, although this also added fuel to the rising flames of resentment among the empire's underprivileged peoples.

Between the 1870s and the First World War, while Prussian Poland was being subjected to aggressive Germanization and Russia's 'western provinces' and the former Congress Kingdom were incurring equally aggressive Russification policies, Krakow and Lwow emerged as the cultural and intellectual capitals of Poland. They produced books, journals, newspapers, plays and *belles lettres* which transcended the Partition and spiritually reunified the Poles (Davies 1982: 155), while the University of Lwow (established in 1817) and the Jagiellonian University gained strong international reputations in medicine, physics and history. Galician Poles were even permitted to celebrate the tercentenary of the Union of Lublin (1569), to erect a statue to their 'national bard' Adam Mickiewicz in Krakow in 1898, and to build a monument commemorating the six-hundredth anniversary of the battle of Grunwald (1410). Galician Poles even rose to the ranks of Austrian Prime Minister (Kazimiercz Badeni), Austrian Finance Minister (Juljan Dunajewski) and Habsburg Foreign Minister (Count Agenor Goluchowski). Galicia's peasants, on the other hand, remained among the poorest and most downtrodden in Europe.

In Galicia (as elsewhere) the 1900s witnessed mounting peasant and proletarian unrest. In eastern Galicia it was reinforced by inter-ethnic tension between the predominantly Polish (and Catholic) propertied classes and the mainly Ruthene (and Orthodox or Uniate) lower classes. Major peasant strikes in eastern Galicia in 1902–03 resulted in the appointment of a conciliatory and reform-minded Viceroy, Count Andrzej Potocki, who put forward agrarian concessions designed to divide the malcontents by propitiating the more prosperous peasant proprietors. Nevertheless, the savage Tsarist repression of workers' demonstrations in Warsaw and St Petersburg in late 1904 and early 1905 encouraged workers in Lwow and Krakow to stage mass demonstrations in solidarity with their Polish and Russian 'comrades'.

The continued growth of trade unions, the strike movement and both socialist and nationalist unrest during 1905 encouraged radicals to demand, and the Austrian government to consider granting, universal direct suffrage. In October 1905, however, the representatives of Galicia's frightened propertied classes helped to vote down proposals for electoral reform in the Austrian *Reichsrat* (parliament), whereupon the increasingly polarized towns of Galicia, German Austria and Bohemia were convulsed by even greater political unrest and confrontations. On 28 November 1905 the Austrian government decided to meet half-way the seemingly revolutionary demand for universal direct suffrage, but was consequently voted out of office by representatives of the recalcitrant Austrian-German and Galician propertied classes three months later. In the end, however, the Austrian Emperor Franz Joseph resolved the crisis by intervening in favour of adult male suffrage. Fresh elections to the Austrian *Reichsrat* were held on that basis in 1907, with the result that Galicia's (Ruthene as well as Polish) nationalist, peasantist, Christian Democrat and socialist parties gained greatly increased political representation at the expense of the aristocratic ruling classes.

Much the same pattern was repeated in (unreformed) elections to the Galician Diet in February 1908, except that several Polish parties entered an electoral pact and trounced their Ruthene rivals. The latter felt aggrieved at this and, when a student belonging to the Ukrainian Social Democratic Party took it upon himself to assassinate Viceroy Potocki in April 1908, the Ruthene press and party leaders refused to condemn the murder, whereupon the more rabid Polish nationalists called for draconian reprisals against the Ruthene community.

In fact Potocki had been trying to broker a power-sharing deal between Galicia's Polish and Ruthene politicians, partly in a *bona fide* attempt to defuse conflict and avert further bloodshed, but also in order to play off one group against the other and thus retain power and institutions in the hands of the conservative aristocracy. This policy was perpetuated by the new Viceroy, the loyalist historian and educationalist Michal Bobrzynski, who was prepared to grant the Ruthenes greater educational and cultural autonomy (including a university of their own in Lwow) in return for their acceptance of a 'junior partner' role in an autonomous and unitary Galicia governed by Polish aristocrats. The conservative 'rainbow coalition' which he assembled gained sweeping electoral endorsement in 1911. But in 1913 his compromise electoral reform deal, which would have fobbed off the Ruthenes with a mere 27 per cent of the seats in the Diet, was anathematized by Galicia's reactionary Catholic bishops and intransigent Polish nationalists. They denounced Bobrzynski as a 'traitor' and successfully bayed for his resignation. Faced with the threat of a concerted Ruthene campaign of non-co-operation and obstruction, however, the new Viceroy secured the Diet's approval of a somewhat 'watered down' version of Bobrzynski's political deal and successfully held fresh elections on that basis. Nevertheless, the stage had been set for a further 'war of attrition' between Ruthenes and Poles which a resurrected Poland would win by *force majeure* during the inter-war period, only to have the tables turned against it by the clumsy might of the Soviet Union in September 1939.

Spiritual sustenance

The Polish Catholic Church is generally regarded as a stalwart custodian and symbol of Polish national identity. During the Partition period, however, the role of the Church was ambiguous. It often provided spiritual strength and solace, and many of its clergy were active politically and educationally. Nevertheless, the dominant inclination of the Church hierarchy was to 'render unto Caesar that which is Caesar's'. It accorded a much higher priority to the preservation of the Church as a supranational Catholic institution and ministry than to the preservation of the Polish national culture and identity. Indeed, Catholic bishops and the Pope not infrequently sided with the state authorities *against* Polish nationalists, even in Prussian Poland and in the Congress Kingdom.

During the seemingly interminable Partition period the Polish sense of national identity and community was sustained, expanded and 'democratized' primarily by the vigorous development of Poland's language, literature and music. Poles were fortunate that, in contrast to modern Czech, Slovak, Ukrainian, Lithuanian, Latvian, Finnish, Estonian, Hungarian, Romanian and Serbo-Croat, whose vocabulary, grammar and syntax were not fully fashioned and standardized until the mid or late nineteenth century, Polish was already 'a fully competent all-purpose instrument long before the Partitions' (Davies 1982: 227).

The major figures in the development of Polish literature (and hence language) during the Partition period included Adam Mickiewicz (1798–1855), Juliusz Slowacki (1809–49), Zygmunt Krasinski (1812–59) and Henryk Sienkiewicz (1846–1916). However, Poland's most famous writer, Josef Korzienowski (1857–1924) 'defected' to the English language (and changed his name to Joseph Conrad). The principal carriers of the torch of Polish music, apart from Frederyk Chopin (1810–49), were Stanislaw Moniuszko (1819–72), Henryk Wieniawski (1835–80), Ignacy Paderewski (1860–1914) and Karol Szymanowski (1882–1937).

Among these literary and musical figures, Adam Mickiewicz occupied a special position. Poles looked to him as a 'spiritual leader', verging on 'oracular high priest' (Zamoyski 1987: 295). In his *Books of the Polish Nation and of the Polish Pilgrims* (1832) Mickiewicz popularized the idea that Poland was 'the Christ among nations'. It had been crucified in the cause of righteousness, but its crucifixion would expiate the sins of the world. That, in turn, would hasten its own resurrection. 'Poland will re-arise and free all the nations of Europe from bondage,' he declared (quoted by Namier 1946: 48). The political and spiritual significance of Polish national literature is further borne out by Russian estimates that by 1901 one-third of the population of the Congress Kingdom was involved in various forms of clandestine ('underground') education, based upon such writings (Davies 1982: 235). This was a form of national defiance tinged with worship.

The road to resurrection

After 1815 some Polish patriots came to the conclusion that they could not depend on (or even hope for) active support from their foreign sympathizers, and that they would therefore have to rely on their own efforts (whether through national insurrection or collaboration with one or more of the partitioning powers). Yet others came to believe that their own efforts to resurrect or liberate Poland *without* external support were in vain and therefore settled for 'organic work' and/or collaboration until such time as more propitious external circumstances might emerge. But it took many Poles a long time to learn the bitter lesson that, however much their nation might be 'reborn' spiritually, culturally or materially, they could neither liberate themselves nor be liberated by sympathetic foreign powers so long as the three partitioning powers did not fall out among themselves. It was not until Germany and Austria decided to go to war against Russia in the summer of 1914 that the political resurrection of Poland became a serious possibility. Indeed, other than in the context of a general European war, active intervention in support of the Polish cause was deemed contrary to the interests of the western European powers because it could have upset the European balance of power and because what they fundamentally desired was European peace, if only for commercial reasons, while (as in 1939) taking up the Polish cause had to involve war.

Nevertheless, the various Polish landed elites had been able to maintain their own ascendancy and that of the partitioning powers through varying degrees of collaboration with their foreign overlords and by co-opting (and even intermarrying with) segments of the rising Polish and Jewish bourgeoisies. Nevertheless, this fragile ascendancy was increasingly under challenge from emergent mass movements (whether nationalist, socialist or peasantist) and could hold only so long as the partitioning powers did not actively fall out among themselves. There had been serious possibilities of conflict between Austria and Russia, not only during the Crimean War of 1853–56, but also in the wake of the Russo-Turkish War of 1877–78 and during the Balkan crisis of 1908. But in each of these instances warfare between the partitioning powers was successfully averted. There had also been a serious risk of war between Austria and Prussia during the Revolutions of 1848, as part of their continuing competition for supremacy in the Germanic world, and they actually came to blows over the same issue in 1866. In the event, however, war was avoided in 1848 and was kept within strict temporal and geographical limits in 1866, with the result that the stability of the Partitions was not threatened. Furthermore, Austria and Prussia acted with restraint during the risings which occurred in the Congress Kingdom and Russia's 'western provinces' in 1830–31 and 1863–64, just as Russia refrained from attempting to profit from the Galician revolt of 1846. In each of these cases the other partitioning powers were content to gloat from the sidelines while providing very limited co-operation in tracking down 'suspects'.

The inability and/or unwillingness of the partitioning powers to pull back from the brink in July and August 1914 finally presented the chance that some Poles had been awaiting for so long. Yet, paradoxically, most Poles probably did not fully appreciate this until the closing stages of the First World War. Most of the Poles elected to the parliaments of the partitioning powers had 'loyally' voted for war credits and continued to support the respective 'war efforts'. By 1916 the armies of the partitioning powers contained 2 million Poles, including 4 per cent of the population of the Congress Kingdom, 15 per cent of the Prussian Poles and 16 per cent of the Galician Poles. In the course of the war, moreover, 450,000 Poles perished and nearly 1 million were wounded while fighting for the partitioning powers (Davies 1982: 382). As part of its 'scorched earth' tactics, moreover, the retreating Tsarist forces had also forcibly evacuated about 800,000 people from the Congress Kingdom deep into Russia (Leslie 1980: 115), where the Poles were abysmally treated.

The person who most vigorously exploited the opportunities opened up by the outbreak of the First World War was Josef Pilsudski (1867–1935), the future *generalissimo* and self-appointed custodian of Polish independence. This Polonized and impoverished Lithuanian noble, who had been banished to Siberia from 1887 to 1892, understandably regarded Tsarist Russia (more than Germany) as the major threat to the survival of the Polish nation and dreamed of resurrecting a tolerant multinational commonwealth of Poles, Lithuanians, Jews, Baltic Germans, Ukrainians and Belorussians, which would be large enough and strong enough to hold off Russia's 'Asiatic despotism' and 'barbarism'. Furthermore, those who shared Pilsudski's anti-Russian orientation generally feared that, in the words of a Polish proverb, 'while to the Germans we stand to lose our bodies, to the Russians we stand to lose our souls'. However, when Pilsudski resumed his budding political career in 1892 it was as a leading figure in the Polish Socialist Party (PPS), which was founded near Wilno in 1893. He served as the editor of its main journal, *Robotnik* (The Worker), from 1894 to 1900, and he gave the PPS a strong nationalist orientation, without rejecting its socialism and internationalism. Indeed, he had concluded that, since the propertied classes of the former Commonwealth were for the most part collaborating with the partitioning powers, any hope of resurrecting it would primarily depend on the combined struggles of the multicultural proletariat, peasantry and intelligentsia for social justice. The PPS sought national equality and brotherhood for Poles, Lithuanians, Jews, Germans, Ukrainians and Belorussians, in opposition to Tsarist oppression, discrimination and despotism. Although Pilsudski was arrested by the Tsarist police in 1900. he soon escaped and continued his machinations against Tsarism from abroad. He even went to Japan to investigate the potential for joint operations against Tsarism during the Russo-Japanese War of 1904–05. His mind was evidently turning to military and paramilitary activities.

After the defeat of the 1905 Revolution in Russian and Congress Poland, Pilsudski moved to Galicia. Here he established a semi-clandestine military force (known as the Union of Active Struggle) in response to what he correctly saw as the growing prospect of military conflict between the partitioning powers in the wake of the Austrian annexation of Bosnia-Hercegovina in 1908 (which set Austria and Russia on a collision course in the Balkans). Pilsudski initially envisaged that, in the event of war between the partitioning powers, his paramilitary units would move into Congress Poland and (in co-operation with the Austrian military but under his own command) foment a new Polish rising against Tsarism, which would in turn pave the way for the resurrection of a Polish-Lithuanian state. However, he changed tack when he realized the extent to which his chief political rivals, the 'National Democrats' (NDs), led by Roman Dmowski (1864–1939), were prepared to collaborate with Tsarist Russia against Germany and Austria. In diametric contrast to Pilsudski, Dmowski regarded German rather than Russian imperialism as the major threat to the survival of the Polish nation and, because he valued ethnic homogeneity above multi-ethnic grandeur, he was not anxious to 'recover' Lithuania, Belorussia and western Ukraine, nor to include either their peoples or the Jews in a reconstituted Polish state. He was therefore willing to collaborate with Russia against Germany and Austria, and he appeared to accept that the barbarities which Tsarism perpetrated against its non-Russian subjects were not very different from those that he (as the apostle of an 'ethnically pure' Poland) would have liked to perpetrate against Poland's 'alien' minorities (especially the Jews), given half a chance. He was a shockingly cold and calculating 'scientific' exponent of the infernal logic of ethnic egotism and ethnic 'purification' (alias 'cleansing'). Pilsudski's growing vanity, militarism and megalomania were far less disturbing than Dmowski's surgical mentality. Amid the heightened hopes and the military preparations prompted by the Balkan Wars of 1912–13, Pilsudski decided that the role of his 7,000 *Strzelcy* (Riflemen) would be to 'agitate by means of war' and to show his compatriots that they could achieve success through their own military prowess in the service of one or more of the warring parties (Wandycz 1974: 327–8), as they had done during the Napoleonic Wars. Pilsudski's forces recruited 'leaders with pretensions to military ability' (including Wladyslaw Sikorski, Edward Smigly-Rydz and Marian Kukiel), whose elevation 'owed nothing to their military education but everything to their conspiratorial past'. This would bequeath to post-1918 Poland 'an officer corps of dubious quality, but with a keen sense of its own importance in the body politic' (Leslie 1980: 109).

On 6 August 1914, five days after Germany declared war on Russia, Pilsudski led his new 'Polish Legions' into the former Congress Kingdom. He put out a proclamation from a (fictitious) Polish National Government in Warsaw which had supposedly called upon Poles to rise up and allegedly appointed him as the Supreme Commander (donning the mantle of Kosciuszko). However, these operations met with a cool reception from Poles who feared being tainted by association with the rebels, or who had turned their backs on the discredited insurrectionary tradition, and from property owners, who regarded Pilsudski either as an agent of the Central Powers (who had already razed the town of Kalisz) or as a dangerous socialist, revolutionary and dreamer (Wandycz 1974: 331–2). Nevertheless, the fact that Pilsudski had assembled Polish military forces which were to acquit themselves reasonably well in combat and managed to maintain a semi-autonomous existence placed Pilsudski in pole position for the power struggle in Poland at the end of the First World War. The defeated German military and political establishment chose to hand over the large areas which they still controlled to their erstwhile collaborator Pilsudski rather than to the Bolsheviks or to those Poles (including Dmowski) who had collaborated with the Entente. Sadly, the independence to which so many Poles had aspired for so long was to prove 'something of a disappointment' (Zamoyski 1987: 340), not only because they could no longer conveniently blame every problem and defect on the partitioning powers, but also because their long-suppressed ambitions and grievances now exploded and collided with one another.

6 The rise and decline of the kingdom of Hungary

THE EMERGENCE OF HUNGARY

The territory of present-day Hungary entered documented history in 9 BC, when its predominantly Celtic inhabitants were subjugated by the Romans. The low-lying Hungarian plain was still marshy and sparsely populated, but the hilly western region (Transdanubia, including Lake Balaton and present-day Pecs and Budapest) became the Roman province of Pannonia. The principal Roman town was Aquincum, whose substantial remains (including two amphitheatres and several public baths) have latterly been excavated and are to be found in District III of modern Budapest. Additional Roman remains have been unearthed in Pecs, Sopron and Szombathely. Archaeologists have established that Roman Pannonia had an economy based upon grain cultivation, stock-breeding (especially horses), viticulture, fruit growing and crafts such as stone-cutting, carriage building and pottery.

The Roman Empire's north-eastern border extended as far as the Danube, along which the Romans established watchtowers and encampments to ward off marauding 'barbarians'. Likewise, mountainous Transylvania (now Romanian, but for centuries Hungarian) became part of the Roman province of Dacia. When the Romans retreated in the face of escalating 'barbarian' assaults, however, Hungary was overrun by wave after wave of horse-borne nomadic warriors from the European steppes: the Huns during the fifth century; the Avars during the seventh century; the Magyars during the ninth century. These fearsome invasions induced many of the earlier (mainly Celtic) inhabitants to seek safer havens elsewhere in Europe. During the interlude between the dominion of the Huns and that of the Avars, however, there were significant migrations of Germanic, Daco-Romanian and Slavic settlers, who were subsequently subjugated and compelled to pay tribute by the marauding Avars and Magyars. The Avars were, however, subdued by the Franks towards the end of the eighth century.

In the dim and distant past the principal forebears of the Magyars may have originated as far east as Xinjiang or Inner Mongolia (in present-day China). Graves in a cemetery 50 km (thirty miles) east of Urumchi (the capital of Xinjiang) have been found to contain weapons and artefacts similar to those buried in Hungarian cemeteries dating from the ninth and tenth centuries. The burial methods and the writing systems on the graves are also similar. The cemetery in Xinjiang was discovered by the Hungarian explorer Aurel Stein and has been excavated by Hungarian archaeologists since 1986. It has also been discovered that the Ugars, an ethnic group living near the cemetery, know folk songs which perfectly fit the pentatonic scale which Bela Bartok found to be the basis of

Magyar folk music and that they have shamanist traditions resembling those of pre-Christian Hungary (John Pomfret, *The Guardian*, 8 February 1995, p. 8). Nevertheless, it is widely accepted that for centuries the Magyars' principal forebears lived in the wooded Ural–Volga region (in what is now Russia) and that during the fourth or fifth centuries AD these former hunters, gatherers and fishermen began to wander and mingle with the nomadic Bulgar-Turkic horsemen of the Volga steppes, from whom they learned formidable equestrian, stock-breeding and marauding skills. For a time they became part of the so-called Onogur tribal federation, from which the German name *Ungar* ('Hungarian', in English) probably derives. From the Bulgar-Turkic peoples of the Volga basin they also acquired new agricultural techniques and the runic Turkish alphabet, adapting it to the requirements of their Finno-Ungrian language.

Magyar is often said to be most closely related to the languages spoken by the Vogul and Ostiak tribes in Siberia and more distantly related to Finnish and Estonian, both of which also exhibited notable 'borrowings' from Turkish. About 10 per cent of Magyar words derive from Turkish. But how significant is this in practice? How far would a present-day Hungarian and a Vogul be able to understand one another? 'About as much as an Englishman and a Russian.' Moreover, the Asiatic origin of the Magyar language does not give modern Hungarians a feeling of being Asiatic, but rather one of 'having no relatives at all', or of 'being related to everybody' (Ignotus 1972: 21).

Between the 840s and the 890s, however, most of the Magyars' forebears appear to have been driven from the Volga basin by Pecheneg warrior nomads and, after brief sojourns on the Don, the Dnieper and the Dnestr, to have overrun the Carpathian basin (which they had previously raided) between 896 and 900 AD. The approximately 400,000 invaders, called Magyars after the name of their leading tribe, easily overwhelmed the area's mainly Slavic but also Germanic, Avar and Daco-Romanian inhabitants, whom they outnumbered roughly two to one.

The bellicose Magyar horsemen and warriors conquered not only the Carpathian basin, but also Transdanubia, parts of Transylvania and, in 907, the Ostmark (Austria). In addition, they undertook numerous plundering raids into Italy until 926, into Germany until 955 and into the Balkans until the 960s. Some of their raids even extended across France into northern Spain. In 904 Arpad (the *gyula* or deputy chief of the Magyar tribe) seized power and initiated the Arpad dynasty, which soon greatly enriched itself and then went on to rule Hungary until 1301.

German, Italian and Balkan rulers were terrorized into paying regular tribute to the Magyars, but the victims were gradually driven to unite against the marauders. Germanic armies inflicted severe defeats on the Magyars in 933 and 955 (restoring the Ostmark to Germanic control), and the Byzantine Empire had succeeded in fortifying its Danubian frontier more effectively by the 970s. Meanwhile the emergence of Kievan Russia limited the scope for marauding activities on the Black Sea steppes and curtailed the Magyars' contacts with the Turkic inhabitants of the Don and Volga basins.

ASSIMILATION INTO CATHOLIC CHRISTENDOM

Perceiving that the Magyars were gradually becoming 'encircled' by Christian states (including newly Christianized Bohemia and Poland), the Arpad ruler named Geza (970–97) performed an about-face. He reined in the Magyar warrior clan chiefs, forcibly subordinated them to his own *ispans* ('sheriffs') and an army of retainers recruited from abroad, and appropriated two-thirds of the land. In 973 he also sought to become the ally of the Germanic Emperor Otto I and asked him to send (Catholic) Christian missionaries into Hungary. Priests arrived, Geza and his family were expeditiously baptized into the Catholic faith and he married off three of his daughters to Christian rulers or crown princes. Legend has it that on Christmas Day in 1000 AD Geza's son Vajk, who had adopted the Christian name Istvan (Stephen), was crowned King of Hungary (1000–38) with a crown provided by the Pope (known henceforth as the crown of St Istvan/Stephen) and with the full approval of the (Catholic) Germanic Emperor Otto III (983–1002).

King Istvan took two-thirds of the population under direct royal jurisdiction, organized his realm into *megye* (counties) administered by his own appointees, founded and made lavish land grants to numerous monasteries and bishoprics, enforced the regular payment of tithes, and instigated the construction of many churches. Although the principal beneficiary was the Catholic Church, he and his successors also built and endowed a number of Eastern Orthodox monasteries and churches which ministered to the spiritual needs of an Orthodox religious minority (including some of the marriage partners of the ruling family) and provided an insurance policy against undue Germanic-Catholic dominance (at least until the thirteenth century).

Istvan and his immediate successors also made extensive land grants to their military retainers, who also acquired considerable numbers of serfs and even slaves to work their landed estates. 'In contrast to the feudal system of western Europe, smaller landowners were not liegemen of the great landlords, but those of the king himself, calling themselves "servitors of the king" and opposing the great landlords' (Halasz 1960: 51).

These changes were not well received by the predominantly pagan Magyar warriors and clan chiefs. The first few Arpad kings therefore relied heavily on foreign Christian soldiers, clergy and functionaries to govern the country, against sullen Magyar opposition. Pagan resistance leaders were 'punished with a savagery that was meant to serve as a deterrent' (Makkai 1975b: 36). Nevertheless, the adoption of Catholic Christianity 'introduced the Hungarian people into the community of European culture, accelerated the shift to agriculture, and protected the country from German aggression' (Halasz 1960: 49). Seen in a longer perspective, Hungary was entering a civilization wherein Latin was the lingua franca of the educated elite and within which the humanist outlook, ethos and values and Roman concepts of law, property and contract would come to prevail during the Renaissance and the Enlightenment. In these respects at least Hungary would become rather more Westernized than the Eastern Orthodox areas of the Balkans and Russia.

In the short term, however, the adoption and/or imposition of Christianity generated a great deal of violence and conflict. Moreover, the fact that King Istvan was predeceased by his only son gave rise to a contested succession. This encouraged several subsequent claimants to the Hungarian throne to fan the flames of pagan discontent. Some even appealed to the Germanic Emperors for military assistance. The latter proved all too eager to intervene and succeeded in establishing a short-lived imperial suzerainty over Hungary, although the fact that the latter was officially Catholic deprived the Germanic rulers of any pretext for launching a full-blown Christianizing conquest or crusade (in the manner of the Teutonic Knights in pagan Prussia and Lithuania). Interestingly, the major Magyar pagan rebellion of 1046 was suppressed with Kievan (Russian) military assistance, but the last Magyar pagan rising (in 1061) was crushed without recourse to foreign support.

The outbreak of armed conflict within the Germanic world and between Emperor Henry IV (1056–1106) and the papacy eventually gave Hungary a respite from Germanic imperial interference. The Hungarian kingdom was largely consolidated under Laszlo I (1077–95), who, with support and encouragement from (Italianate) Dalmatian port cities such as Trau, Zara (Zadar) and Spalato (Split), invaded Croatia, Slavonia and Dalmatia between 1089 and 1091. This brought the kingdom of Hungary into direct competition with the papacy, the Byzantine Empire and the Venetian Republic, which harboured designs of their own on Dalmatia and Croatia. King Laszlo I soon lost the Dalmatian port cities to Venice. But his successor Koloman (1095–1116) recaptured inland Dalmatia in 1097 (while Venice was preoccupied by the First Crusade) and was crowned King of Croatia and Dalmatia in 1102.

Croat historians have tended to portray this link as a limited 'union of crowns' or 'personal union' between the separate kingdoms of Hungary and Croatia (like the ones between Poland and Lithuania from 1386 to 1569 or between England and Scotland from 1604 to 1707), whereas many Magyar nationalist historians have preferred to see it as a form of annexation, incorporating Croatia (including Dalmatia and Slavonia) into a Greater Hungary and establishing permanent rights of Magyar overlordship in Croatia. Either way, however, Hungarian domination of Croatia was to continue on and off for another eight centuries, with the result that since 1918 Croats and Hungarians have often found it difficult to go their own completely separate ways or to view one another (and events in each other's countries) with detachment. Moreover, most of the Dalmatian coastal regions and port cities voluntarily placed themselves under Hungarian suzerainty in 1102 and 1105, respectively, as protection against the rapacious Venetians. At times Hungarian dominion also extended over medieval Bosnia and Serbia, although the latter were shortly to fall under Ottoman Turkish control.

Between 1115 and 1420 there were twenty-one wars between Venice and Hungary, with the result that some Dalmatian towns changed hands or shifted allegiance repeatedly, although most of the Dalmatian port cities remained mainly under Hungarian suzerainty. Thus Spalato (Split) reverted to Venice in 1327, but returned to Hungarian suzerainty in 1358, while Ragusa (Dubrovnik) accepted Venetian suzerainty from 1205 to 1358, but then reverted to Hungary. Only Zara (Zadar) remained mainly under Venetian control. By 1420, however, all the major Dalmatian port cities (other than Ragusa) were back under Venetian dominion, as a result of the major upheavals which were occurring in East Central Europe at that time.

Meanwhile the wealth and power of Hungary's secular and ecclesiastical landowners were steadily increasing, eventually encouraging them to challenge the power of the monarch. By 1200 the kingdom of Hungary had expanded to 220,000 km^2 (affording many opportunities for the granting or acquisition of substantial land holdings) and its population had increased to approximately 2 million, yielding a density of about nine people per square kilometre (Makkai 1975b: 51). 'Stock breeding, a legacy of the nomadic past, continued to be the Hungarians' chief source of livelihood' (p. 37) and during the eleventh century 'cattle were still the principal means of payment' (p. 40). But there was increased cultivation of wheat, barley, rye and oats (largely in place of the traditional but less valuable millet), and watermills and heavier ox-drawn ploughs were developed during the eleventh and twelfth centuries (pp. 37, 40, 50), while large numbers of sheep and pigs were reared in addition to the more traditional horses and cattle (p. 38). This helped to increase soil fertility and crop yields (p. 50) and encouraged the replacement of alternating periods of cultivation and fallow by more productive three-field systems (Halasz 1960: 51). Furthermore, the needs of the royal family, the big landlords and the Church, combined with an influx of German, Wallonian, Flemish, French and Italian merchants and colonists, stimulated the emergence of handicrafts, mining and viticulture, particularly among the non-Magyar population. Viticulture, which dated back to Roman times in Transdanubia, spread northwards and eastwards and was upgraded by French immigrants in the Tokai, Eger and Nagyvarad districts, whose wines were subsequently to become famous across Europe.

The growing availability of craft wares and agricultural surpluses, the development of copper, silver and gold mines, the increased minting of metallic money and the proliferation of bazaars and trade fairs resulted in and from the increased commercialization of the economy, the widespread commutation of agricultural labour services into obligations in cash and kind, and the development of towns from the twelfth to the fifteenth centuries. Already, by the end of the twelfth century, customs duties, tolls, mining royalties, taxes paid in cash and the profits of the royal mint were contributing as much as half of the crown revenues, greatly reducing the relative importance of revenue from the crown lands. 'This made it all the easier for the king to give large areas of his demesne to the land-hungry barons and lesser lords' (Makkai 1975b: 51–4).

Royal land grants were further increased by the succession struggles that occurred after the death of King Bela III (1172–96), between his sons Emeric (1196–1204) and Andras II (1205–35). These two brothers not only fought one another. They also allowed themselves to get drawn into the Crusades in 1200–04 and in 1217–18, respectively, with very damaging results. While they fought each other or were absent on costly and unsuccessful crusading missions instigated by the papacy (any gains accrued mainly to the Venetians and/or their western European allies), Hungary's servitor and baronial factions fought among themselves, took possession of large tracts of crown land and protested against taxation and the farming out of tax collection, coin minting and monopolies to rich Moslem and Jewish moneylenders and merchants.

In 1222 a severely weakened King Andras II was obliged to issue a Golden Bull (named after the gold seal attached to it) curtailing the powers of the monarchy and the Church, permitting the payment of ecclesiastical tithes in kind rather than in cash, regulating the Church's salt monopoly, exempting royal servitors from taxation, promising royal protection against harassment by magnates, and granting the nobility (especially royal servitors) a right of armed resistance in the event of the monarch breaking these pledges. This Golden Bull naturally infuriated Church leaders. In 1231 they persuaded the king to issue a revised version which omitted the clauses prejudicial to the Church's interests, expanded the jurisdiction of ecclesiastical courts and replaced the nobles' right of resistance with recognition of the Church's right to excommunicate the king for any breach of his new pledges. Andras II was in fact excommunicated the following year for attempting to regulate the Church's salt monopoly and for continuing to farm out tax collection and monopolies to Moslem and Jewish middlemen.

Hungary was still weakened by internal conflict when it was devastatingly invaded by Mongol marauders in 1241 and 1242. The whole area east of the Danube quickly fell into the hands of the invaders, since few of its forts and castles were able to offer effective resistance. In order to terrorize the population, large numbers of defenceless civilians were massacred, while others were carried off as slaves. Many of those who sought refuge in the forests, marshes or highlands died of hunger and disease. During the winter of 1241–42 the Mongols crossed the frozen Danube in order to invade Transdanubia. But by then the inhabitants of that region knew what to expect and the attackers encountered more effective resistance, before their sudden withdrawal in the summer of 1242 in order to elect a new leader (saving Hungary from the 'Mongol yoke' that befell Russia and Lithuania).

Paradoxically, by making labour more scarce, the dramatic drop in Hungary's population resulting from the Mongol invasion shifted the balance of power between peasants and landlords in the peasants' favour. Magnates in need of labour were prepared to grant protection to runaway serfs, while landlords who had an adequate supply of labour were obliged to reduce their demands for labour services and for dues in cash and kind and to grant movement and land holding in order to discourage their serfs from seeking new masters and/or the freedom of the wild frontier regions (Makkai 1975b: 70–1). Moreover, the widespread devastation resulting from the Mongol onslaughts forced the contending factions within Hungary temporarily to draw closer together and permit a fresh start.

King Bela IV (1235–70) fostered post-Mongol reconstruction and recovery (i) by making large new land grants to the magnates on condition that they built new stone castles in place of the traditional earthen forts and wooded stockades, (ii) by attracting German and western European immigrants into newly chartered (autonomous) 'royal' towns and (iii) by encouraging the construction of new fortified towns (including a new walled city in Buda, the nucleus of present-day Budapest). The resultant influx of German settlers, capital and technology gave a new impetus to the development of ore mining and smelting in the hills and mountains that ring the Carpathian basin.

In the later thirteenth century, however, there was renewed instability and internal conflict, largely stemming from royal endeavours to re-establish the power of the monarchy by employing the 'rough' services of pagan Cuman warrior nomads (originally from the Eurasian steppes) to subdue the overweening magnates. Before becoming king, Istvan V (1270–72) even married the daughter of the Cuman chief. Their half Cuman son and successor, Laszlo IV (1272–90), stoutly resisted the demands of the Church and the nobility for his Cuman kinsmen to be forcibly settled and converted to Christianity. Instead, he renounced his Christian queen (who ended her days in a nunnery) and went to live among the Cumans, having taken a pagan Cuman wife. In 1280 Hungary's Christian establishment succeeded in forcibly subduing the Cumans. But King Laszlo 'the Cuman' took his revenge in 1285 by inviting in the Mongols (now joined by the Cumans) to devastate large areas of Christian Hungary and establish the ascendancy of his Cuman entourage (including his pagan queen). In 1290, finally, Laszlo IV was murdered by Cuman assassins in the pay of the magnates. His successor, Andras III (1290–1301), Hungary's last Arpad monarch, presided helplessly over a country that was in reality controlled by feuding magnates who helped themselves (largely uninvited) to crown and Church property, state offices and ecclesiastical benefices.

THE ANJOU DYNASTY, 1308–82

The baronial anarchy, excesses and depredations of the subsequent interregnum (1301–08) elicited a powerful backlash among the higher clergy and the lower nobility, who generally supported endeavours to restore a strong monarchy by conferring the Hungarian crown on a scion of the ambitious Anjou dynasty, to whom the Arpads had been related by marriage. In 1308, finally, a papal legate managed to broker the accession of Prince Charles Robert of Anjou (son of the Angevin King of Naples and Sicily, Robert Martel), known as King Karoly I (1308–42).

Between 1308 and 1321, with the backing of the papacy, the Hungarian Church and large sections of the nobility, the new Angevin king gradually subdued the overmighty barons, repossessed most of the crown property which they had obtained by illicit means during the preceding period of baronial anarchy, and made fresh land grants to the 'loyalist' nobles who had assisted the establishment of the new dynasty. Quite fortuitously, the new dynasty was buoyed up by a sudden surge in Hungary's gold and silver production, which spawned whole new mining towns and for a time made the kingdom Europe's leading gold producer. In 1325 it was made obligatory to sell any gold or silver mined in Hungary to the royal mint at prices which were very favourable to the crown, although a new mining code gave the owners of ore-bearing land a guaranteed share of the proceeds as an incentive to develop mineral extraction further.

Under Charles of Anjou Hungary also cultivated new trade links with southern German towns and city-states (especially Nuremberg). This led to the development of new trade routes from Poland, Bohemia and the Germanic states through Hungary to the Balkans, the Adriatic and the Black Sea, outflanking Vienna and Venice and drawing Hungary closer to its northern and western neighbours. Eventually the ascendancy of southern German merchants and financiers over the Hungarian economy (especially mining) was to develop into a stranglehold. But in the short term, at least, the expansion of royal revenue from trade, customs duties, mining, minting and monopolies (the so-called *regalia*) rendered the crown less dependent on income from land, especially its own (Makkai 1975b: 73–5).

In 1335 King Charles (Karoly) entertained the rulers of Poland and Bohemia for several days at his fine royal palace in Visegrad. His lavish hospitality cemented an East Central European coalition against the Habsburgs and, among other things, allowed him to regain border territories which Hungary had lost to the Habsburgs under his predecessors and during the period of baronial anarchy. He also gained rights of succession for his son in Poland.

Charles's son and successor Lajos I (alias Louis of Anjou, 1342–82) was born and bred to be an empire builder. Angevin ambition and ascendancy pulled him in that direction. Yet he wasted a great deal of money and effort on three unsuccessful attempts to usurp the throne of his Neapolitan relatives (in 1347–48, 1350 and 1378–80). Nevertheless, he successfully fought off the Venetian Republic (which was vying for ascendancy in the Mediterranean) and re-established Hungarian hegemony over Croatia, Slavonia and the Dalmatian coast, while in 1370 he inherited the Polish throne (following the death of the last Piast king, Kazimiercz the Great). However, Louis (Lajos I) found his fractious Polish domains more of a hindrance than a help to his undying Adriatic and Neapolitan ambitions. He hardly set foot in Poland and preferred to summon Polish magnates to his opulent Hungarian palaces and to rule Poland from afar (through regents). Moreover, by the Statute of Kosice (1374), he conceded far-reaching privileges and prerogatives to the Polish nobility. He even failed to ensure the inheritance of the Polish throne by his elder daughter Maria and her husband Sigismund of Luxemburg (the younger son of King Karel of Bohemia, alias Holy Roman Emperor Karl IV). Instead, after a brief civil war (1382–84), Poland's Church and nobility conferred the Polish crown on his ten-year-old daughter Hedwig (Jadwiga) in 1384, and she was then forced to renounce her Habsburg fiancé and marry Grand Duke Jogaila of Lithuania. Poland thus deflected the ambitions of the Anjou, Luxemburg and Habsburg dynasties and hitched its fortunes to those of Jagiellon Lithuania.

THE LUXEMBURG CONNECTION, 1387–1437

The succession to Louis of Anjou was contested in Hungary as well. Following a protracted internal power struggle, the Hungarian throne was seized by the new King of Naples and Sicily in 1385 (reversing the former claims of the Hungarian Angevins on the Neapolitan throne). But within weeks he was murdered by a leading Magyar magnate, Miklos Garai. Garai and other magnates allied themselves with Sigismund of Luxemburg (husband of Maria of Anjou), who with their backing became King Zsigmund of Hungary for the next half-century (1387–1437). In addition, the latter was elected Holy Roman Emperor in 1410, and he also had himself crowned King of Bohemia in 1420 (in succession to his brother Vaclav). This ambitious Luxemburger thus gained at least nominal authority over Hungary, Bohemia and the Germanic Empire. In spite of this outwardly impressive accumulation of royal titles, however, his unusually long reign was not very successful.

The advancing Ottoman Turks gained control of almost all the Orthodox Christian areas of the Balkans in 1389, and the attempts of a Hungarian-led coalition of Catholic forces to halt the Ottoman juggernaut were decisively defeated at the battle of Nicopolis in 1396. Hungary enjoyed a respite from the 'Turkish menace' between 1402 and 1413 only because Timur the Lame suddenly devastated and shattered the unity of the crucial Ottoman domains in Asia Minor. But those territories were reunited under Sultan Mehmed I in 1413, and a Hungarian army was heavily defeated by the Ottomans in central Bosnia in 1414 (Malcolm 1994: 21). From 1416 until 1456 Ottoman forces were directly to threaten Hungary's southern borderlands. By then, however, Sigismund had become Holy Roman Emperor and was preoccupied with other matters, including efforts to reunite the Catholic Church (which was split between rival Popes from 1378 to 1417) and attempts to extirpate heresy. However, the condemnation and burning of the Czech Church reformer Jan Hus in 1415 (for alleged heresy) helped to precipitate the Czech Hussite Revolution (1419–34), which in turn fostered dissent and unrest in Hungary's western and southern borderlands during the 1420s and 1430s (Halasz 1960: 55; Makkai 1975b: 88). Sigismund spent the last seventeen years of his life trying to subjugate the Czechs. Consequently, he was not in a position to counter either the resurgent 'Turkish threat' or the renewed expansionism of the Venetians, to whom he abandoned Dalmatia in 1420 (after more than three centuries of Hungarian hegemony in that region).

There were a few more positive developments on the domestic front, however. Sigismund moved his royal seat to Buda, Hungary's largest city. During his reign Italians became prominent in civil, military and ecclesiastical administration and in court circles, which also attracted a number of Italian architects, artists and humanists (including the Florentine architect Manetto Ammantini, the painter Masolino da Panicale, an associate of Masaccio, and the humanists Branda Castiglione, Giuliano Cesarini, Pier Paolo Vergerio and Filippo Scolari). This influx paved the way for the ascendancy of Italian artistic styles, ideas and humanism in Hungary under King Matyas Hunyadi (1458–90) (Bialostocki 1985: 155; Klaniczay 1992: 164). In 1405 Sigismund also increased the autonomy of 'royal' towns, exempted urban merchants from the payment of tolls and confirmed the peasants' freedom of movement into the towns (Makkai 1975b: 87). Nevertheless, he 'ceded not only most of the royal estates to the barons, but also the actual administration of the country' (p. 93), and the serious peasant unrest in parts of Transylvania in 1437 met with the usual ruthless repression (p. 89).

THE HUNYADI ERA, 1443–90

In 1437 Sigismund was succeeded by his son-in-law, the Holy Roman Emperor Albrecht of Habsburg. But the latter's life was cut short by plague in 1439, thus removing Hungary from the Habsburg grasp for the time being. At that juncture, with Transylvania being ravaged by the Turks, a substantial section of the Magyar nobility turned to the valiant young Jagiellon king of Poland-Lithuania, Wladyslaw III, who became King Ulaszlo of Hungary (1440–44) and defeated the supporters of the rival Habsburg candidature.

Janos Hunyadi, defender of Christendom

Ulaszlo's brief reign witnessed the meteoric rise of Janos Hunyadi, a remarkable soldier of fortune from Transylvania. There has been much speculation concerning the paternity of this legendary figure, Hungary's foremost 'national hero'. On the face of it, his father was a Wallachian (Romanian) knight who was awarded the Transylvanian fortress of Vajda-Hunyad for his services to King Sigismund and henceforth went under the name of Hunyadi. But contemporaries suspected that Janos Hunyadi was really the illegitimate son of King Sigismund, in whose company he spent his youth. In his early adulthood Janos Hunyadi distinguished himself as a *condottiere* (mercenary) in Italy and in fighting against the Turks. Consequently, Kings Albrecht and Ulaszlo (Wladyslaw) gave him important military-governorships in Transylvania, which had become the prime battleground between Hungary and the Turks. He (mis)used his position to acquire the kingdom's largest land holdings (over 5 million acres/2 million ha) but then employed his vast wealth in order to field his own private armies against the Turks. This gave him the freedom to apply and develop his own innovative or unorthodox strategies and tactics. He initially relied on defensive or insidious guerilla warfare in collaboration with Bohemian (Hussite), Magyar, Wallachian, Serb and Albanian peasants and insurgents, even deploying mobile artillery wagons in the manner of the Bohemian Hussites. He inflicted surprise defeats on much larger Turkish forces in 1442 and 1443, contributing to a temporary 'liberation' of Serbia, Bosnia, northern Albania and parts of Bulgaria and Wallachia in 1443. Some writers attribute Janos Hunyadi's successes to 'an unshakeable belief that the God of the Christians had chosen him . . . to excel in wealth and power and to defeat the pagan Turks', combined with unusual reliance on 'well-trained mercenaries and masses of fanatical volunteers' in place of knightly cavalry and traditional feudal levies. 'He was one of the first to realize the supreme value of regular military forces in war, but at the same time he did not underestimate appeals to idealism; one of his chief propagandists was the Franciscan friar Giovanni de Capistrano, promoter of religious fervour among the overwhelmingly plebeian troops whom Hunyadi led against the Moslems when most of the Hungarian noblemen had deserted' (Ignotus 1972: 29). Others argue that Hunyadi turned the war against the Turks 'into the cause of the people' and that 'he did not behave as a conqueror or a missionary in the Balkans; he did not voice claims for Hungarian supremacy, but stressed the necessity of joining forces, of concerted efforts and common defence' (Halasz 1960: 60). In reality these various aspects of his persona and strategy were mutually reinforcing, and each played a part in his triumphs.

Desirous of a 'slice of the action' and a share of the glory, Polish forces led by King Wladyslaw (Ulaszlo) in person rashly launched a more conventional offensive in 1444, but they were crushed by the Turks at Varna and the king died in battle. After a brief but unedifying power struggle between leading Magyar magnates and the Habsburgs in 1445, the Diet decided to vest executive authority in Janos Hunyadi as military regent of Hungary in 1446, pending the return of the Habsburgs. (This was the historical precedent for the Horthy regency of 1920–44.) The Diet was unwilling to grant Hunyadi regal status; it still expected him to participate in the Diet's sessions on the same footing as other magnates, not as a would-be king. Moreover, Hunyadi's standing temporarily declined when his forces were defeated by the Turks at the second battle of Kosovo Plain in 1448, albeit mainly as a result of the treacherous conduct of a Serbian warlord (who changed sides and briefly held Hunyadi prisoner) and the fatal prevarication of Hunyadi's Albanian allies. This serious setback hastened moves to install Ladislas of Habsburg (son of Emperor Albrecht) as King Laszlo V of Hungary (1452–57). However, when the fall of Constantinople to the Turks in 1453 opened the way for full-scale Ottoman assaults on Hungary, the kingdom once again turned to Hunyadi for salvation, and he rose to the challenge. In 1456 he not only broke a great Turkish siege of the fortified city of Nandorfehervar (latterly Belgrade) but routed Turkish forces which outnumbered his own by more than three to one. Although he himself subsequently succumbed to a plague epidemic which decimated his armies, this legendary victory kept the Turks away from Hungary for another seventy years (until 1526).

The death of Hunyadi in 1456 encouraged jealous rival magnates to attempt to oust and kill off the rich and powerful Hunyadi 'clan'. During the resultant power struggle (in which one of Hunyadi's sons was killed), young King Ladislas (Laszlo) took refuge in Prague, where he unexpectedly died in 1457. Thus Hungary once again escaped from the Habsburgs' grasp. With the throne vacant, in January 1458 the Hungarian Diet conferred the crown of St Istvan on Janos Hunyadi's fifteen-year-old son Matyas (1458–90) and appointed his uncle Mikaly Szilagyi as regent. Thus began Hungary's most illustrious reign, the Indian summer of the kingdom's independence.

Matyas Hunyadi (1458–90) and the Hungarian Renaissance

King Matyas soon imprisoned his conspiratorial and meddlesome uncle and refused to release him until he undertook to lead a campaign against the Ottomans, who captured and beheaded him (Ignotus 1972: 30). Thus the Turks unwittingly helped to free the young king from avuncular and baronial tutelage. In 1463 the Ottomans occupied Bosnia (which was under Hungarian suzerainty) and executed the Catholic King of Bosnia, having first induced him to surrender by promising his safety (Malcolm 1994: 24). This Ottoman offensive and act of treachery encouraged Matyas to issue a call to arms. He concluded agreements with the Pope and the (Habsburg) Holy Roman Emperor and recaptured northern Bosnia (including Jajce), which became a Hungarian dependency and 'banate' (ruled by a 'ban' or viceroy) in 1464. However, Hungarian attempts to advance farther south were easily defeated by the Turks, teaching Matyas that his modest military and fiscal resources 'only sufficed for defence' rather than the great counter-offensive envisaged by Janos Hunyadi (Makkai 1975b: 102).

Matyas therefore resumed King Charles of Anjou's policy of subduing the overmighty magnates, taking back some of the royal properties and revenues which had fallen under their control and clamping down on embezzlement. By the end of his reign Matyas had managed to quintuple the overall royal revenue, although even that 'was barely sufficient for the strengthening of the achievements of centralized rule' on which he now embarked (Makkai 1975b: 102). In order to reduce his dependence upon and exposure to the leading magnates and their private armies, while also reinforcing the kingdom's defences, Matyas strengthened the fortifications along Hungary's southern frontiers and built up a permanent 30,000-strong professional army (the so-called 'Black Army'), mainly composed of foreign (especially Czech and German) mercenaries.

To this end, Matyas imposed taxes on the peasantry, but he simultaneously aided them against predatory landlords. 'Despite their heavy burdens, the people looked on King Matyas as their protector, and with good reason. A veritable cycle of legends grew up around . . . how the king went about the country redressing injustices' (Halasz 1960: 60–1). Indeed, the re-enserfment of the peasantry started later in Hungary than in other parts of East Central Europe. Legally the peasantry were not made 'totally subject to their lords' until 1515. Moreover, although there were temporary limitations on the peasants' freedom of movement under Matyas and in 1515, this particular freedom was reasserted by the Hungarian Diet of 1547 (as on several subsequent occasions) and was not legally terminated until 1608 (Kiraly 1975: 269).

There were baronial attempts to dethrone Matyas Hunyadi in 1467 and 1471. He therefore relied increasingly on professional officials recruited from the towns and even the peasantry rather than the magnates and lower nobility. After 1471, moreover, Diets were called only rarely, as Matyas preferred to rule by royal decree. A law of 1468 spoke of 'the absolute power [*absoluta potestas*] due to the king' (Makkai 1975b: 107–8). In 1486 he called a Diet which increased county autonomy and the privileges of the nobility as a whole, as a counterweight to the power of the magnates (p. 109).

Matyas himself was one of Europe's most educated monarchs, a true 'Renaissance prince'. He corresponded with eminent humanists and built up one of Europe's finest libraries, the Biblioteca Corvina. It employed legions of scribes, humanists, bookbinders and illuminators and became 'one of the major seats of learning in Central Europe, with its enormous quantities of ancient literary works and humanist writings' (Klaniczay 1992: 167). The library, which was named after the raven (*corvus*) in the Hunyadi family crest, was destroyed during the sixteenth-century Ottoman invasions. Other fine libraries were established by some higher clergy and magnates.

Hungary's first printing press went into operation in 1472–73, although the first book written in Hungarian (as against Latin) was not printed until 1533 (in Krakow!). Matyas was one of the first monarchs to use print and even posters as an instrument of political propaganda. He and the most prominent Hungarian humanists fostered the idea of Hungary as a prime custodian of European Christian and humanist values against the 'Turkish menace', thus contributing to the birth of the idea of Europe. During his reign, moreover, large numbers of foreign (mainly Italian) artists, architects and humanists were attracted to live and work in Hungary, including Galeotto Marzio, Antonio Bonfini, Bartolomeo Fonzeo, Aurelio Brandolino Lippo and Francesco Bandini (Klaniczay 1992: 166–7). Under Matyas 'Hungary became the first European country to adopt the Renaissance to any great extent' (Bialostocki 1985: 155). Indeed, for a short time it was 'the most important centre of humanism and Renaissance art' north of the

Alps (Makkai 1975b: 112). Hungary was also producing distinguished humanists of its own, most notably the chancellor Janos Vitez and his nephew Janus Pannonius ('the first great Hungarian poet'), who became Bishop of Pecs. During the fifteenth century over 5,000 people from Hungary attended foreign universities, principally in Italy, Paris and (increasingly) Krakow and Vienna. In 1465, moreover, a university known as the Academia Istropolitana was established in Pozsony/Bratislava in Slovakia (Ister being the Greek name for the Danube). It had faculties of arts, theology, medicine and law, although all except the law faculty were transferred to Buda after 1490 (Mikus 1977: 18).

Latent economic weaknesses

In the short term Matyas was assisted by a boom in Hungarian foreign trade, which yielded a fivefold increase in royal revenue from customs duties between 1450 and 1480 (Makkai 1975b: 105). Foreign (mainly German) merchants supplied textiles, metal products, spices and luxury goods in exchange for Hungarian gold, copper, cattle and wine. Unfortunately, 'Hungarian merchants considered it a quicker and safer investment to take part in foreign trade or to buy land than to engage in the development of domestic industry' (p. 104). As a result, Hungary became increasingly reliant on imported manufactures, and the hitherto impressive growth of Hungary's towns and craft industries ceased or even went into reverse during the late fifteenth century (p. 105).

Nevertheless, it would be unfair to blame Hungary's incipient urban-industrial decline on the behaviour or alleged defects and failings of its merchants. It is insufficiently understood that the ease with which Hungary was able to export significant quantities of fairly remunerative primary products blunted any commercial stimulus or incentive to develop manufacturing activities. In the terminology of modern economic historians, this was more a case of 'market failure' than of 'entrepreneurial failure'. There was serious mismatch between Hungary's long-term developmental needs (which included the development of manufacturing and arms production) and the essentially short-term signals and commercial incentives provided by market forces (which encouraged specialization in primary products and investment in land). In other words, Hungary's particular resource endowments, its comparative cost advantages and the market situation and incentives which its merchants faced were conducive to the development of primary rather than secondary economic activities. In addition, it was all too easy to allow Hungary's burgeoning foreign trade to be handled increasingly by foreign merchants, who had more capital, better connections and deeper knowledge of west European markets and requirements. Most entrepreneurs usually adopt the line of least resistance, and it would have taken great prescience, exceptional strength of mind, considerable capital resources and a willingness to 'buck the market' for Hungary's merchants to have acted differently.

The development of Hungarian manufacturing production and towns was also inhibited by the country's unfavourable geopolitical position. From the early fifteenth century to the late seventeenth it constituted the principal battleground between Western Christendom and the Ottoman Empire. The resultant hazards raised risk premia and made it commercially rational to invest mainly in land and short-term (often speculative) ventures rather than in manufacturing and towns. For these and other reasons, Hungary was one of the European countries least well placed to share in the economic, technological, cultural and military benefits and stimuli provided by the 'voyages of discovery' and the opening up of the New World.

All in all, therefore, some of the selfsame factors that helped Matyas to achieve his short-term objectives impeded or worked against the attainment of his longer-term aim of transforming Hungary into one of Europe's most highly developed powers. Even his efforts to strengthen the legal and municipal autonomy of towns were of little avail as a means of arresting Hungary's urban-industrial decline.

Partly with the intention of establishing 'control over the whole Central and East European trade' and recapturing the profits that were allegedly being 'taken out of the country by foreign merchants' (Makkai 1975b: 106), but also in the hope of establishing 'a strong state on the Danube capable of driving out the Turks from Europe' (Halasz 1960: 62), Matyas Hunyadi invaded Bohemia in 1468. In spite of being defeated and taken prisoner in 1469, he returned to the attack in 1470 and (with the support of Catholic nobles in Moravia and Silesia) had himself crowned King of Bohemia. However, these manoeuvres were strongly resisted by Hussite elements among the Czech nobility. In 1471 they offered the Bohemian throne to Prince Wladyslaw Jagiello (brother of the King of Poland), who had promised to establish religious toleration if he became king. The resultant seven-year war between the two contestants (1471–78) culminated in an agreed partition of the Czech Lands: Wladyslaw retained Bohemia proper, while Matyas took over the Moravian and Silesian territories. These acquisitions paved the way for Matyas to occupy eastern Austria in 1485, whereupon he made Vienna the capital of his kingdom in a bid for the title of Holy Roman Emperor. But this ambition was thwarted in 1486, when the Electors chose Maximilian of Habsburg as Emperor-elect. Matyas nevertheless remained in control of Vienna and eastern Austria until 1490.

It is quite conceivable that Matyas had hankered after the imperial crown all along and that his emphasis on the need to unite East Central Europe against the Turks was just a pretext or means to an end. He was certainly more keen to be recognized as Europe's leading Renaissance prince than to fight the infidel. 'Unlike his father, he had no intention of launching a major offensive war against the Turks, but wanted to stabilize the existing situation' (Halasz 1960: 62). The humanist Antonio Bonfini later stated that Matyas 'strove to transform Pannonia into a second Italy' (Klaniczay 1992: 167). Ironically, the wish was fulfilled but not in the sense that Matyas intended: Hungary (like Italy) was shortly to succumb to Habsburg domination.

THE ROAD TO DISASTER, 1490–1526: HUNGARY UNDER JAGIELLON RULE

The death of Matyas Hunyadi in 1490, combined with the fractious and 'unpatriotic' conduct of the nobility, plunged the kingdom into precipitous decline. Nevertheless, it did not immediately fall under Habsburg domination. Rather than risk the accession of either a Habsburg or another strong native king, the Magyar nobility chose to confer the vacant Hungarian throne on Wladyslaw (Vladislav), Bohemia's weak Jagiellon ruler, who now also became King Ulaszlo II of Hungary. (Matyas Hunyadi's son Janos, having been fobbed off with the title of King of Bosnia, died fighting the Turks in 1504.) Moreover, King Ulaszlo II (1490–1516) parried Habsburg designs on his Hungarian throne, both by repelling a Habsburg invasion of Hungary and by restoring Vienna and eastern Austria to

Habsburg control. He then curried favour with the Magyar aristocracy (to whose support he owed his Hungarian throne) by despatching Matyas Hunyadi's Black Army against the Turks without proper supplies or logistical support; when the battered and starving troops turned to plunder, he allowed Hungary's magnates to finish them off. 'After this most modern army of its time had been destroyed, the barons made the Diet force the king to grant regular pay to the baronial armies' (Makkai 1975b: 114). Ulaszlo II also permitted the magnates and higher clergy to usurp royal power and revenue for their own purposes. The king became increasingly dependent on the modest revenue of his Bohemian realm, on Habsburg goodwill and on usurious loans from south German financiers, especially the Fuggers, who also acquired control of Hungary's major copper and silver mines during the 1490s and 1500s. Efforts to bring these mines back under Hungarian (royal) control during the early 1520s closed off the supply of Fugger capital. The resultant deterioration in mining conditions precipitated a bloodily suppressed miners' uprising in April 1526, further weakening the kingdom at an absolutely crucial moment (p. 118). Hungary's urban sector atrophied as the cash-strapped king granted royal towns to the magnates, who in turn downgraded many townspeople as well as peasants to an increasingly restricted and dependent role. This encouraged a widespread retreat from trade and specialization, into local economic autarky.

In 1514 Hungary's Roman Catholic archbishop decided to divert the growing restiveness of the peasantry and the poorer nobles, clergy and townspeople into a people's Crusade against the gradually advancing Turks. However, the scale and fervour of the popular response prompted the frightened barons and the archbishop to halt further recruitment and to dispatch this 'people's army' against the Turks without appropriate weapons, money or sustenance, whereupon the would-be Crusaders angrily attacked the castles and wealthy monasteries of the magnates and the higher clergy. But, despite a few initial victories, these poorly armed popular uprisings were crushed with great brutality and were followed by savage baronial reprisals. The Diet which assembled in October 1514 enacted death sentences on the leaders of the rebel armies, restricted peasant mobility and ordered every serf to render one day's labour service per week to his lord and master. That same year the repressive 'new order' was hallowed by the infamous *Tripartitum opus iuris consuetudinarii inclyti regni Hungariae* (Tripartite Book of Customary Law of the Illustrious Kingdom of Hungary), published by the new palatine (lord chancellor), Istvan Werboczi. His *magnum opus*, which also codified the supposedly equal rights and privileges of the magnates and the more numerous lesser nobility (*una eademque nobilitas*), became 'not only a universally accepted law-book, but also the bible of the nobility' (Makkai 1975b: 117).

However, while the crisis of 1514 was indeed an important milestone in the re-enserfment of the peasantry, one should not underestimate the gradual and erratic character of this process. Hungarian Diets reaffirmed the serfs' right of movement in 1547 and on several subsequent occasions, with the result that the process of re-enserfment was not completed until the seventeenth century, if at all (Kiraly 1975: 269–71).

When the ignominious King Ulaszlo (Wladyslaw) II died in 1516 he was succeeded by his ten-year-old son Lajos (Ludvik) II in both Hungary and Bohemia. Not surprisingly, this mere stripling was unable to halt even deeper division, tension and paralysis. The situation facilitated Ottoman encroachments on the kingdom's southern frontiers, notably the loss of Nandorfehevar (Belgrade) to the Turks in 1521. But the magnates' belated appeals for Catholic Christian solidarity against the infidel fell on deaf ears. Even if foreign help had materialized, it would probably have been insufficient (or too late) to avert the annihilation of King Lajos II and approximately 25,000 poorly armed Hungarians by about 75,000 well armed Turks at the battle of Mohacs on 29 August 1526, after which the Ottomans allegedly carried off 200,000 Christians captive (Makkai 1975b: 117–18; Malcolm 1994: 66). According to Lazlo Makkai (1975c: 121–2), 'Mohacs was more than a defeat; it was in fact one of the greatest disasters in Hungarian history.' If 'blame' must be apportioned, it lay with both the magnates and the weak Jagiellon kings, who together had wantonly destroyed Matyas Hunyadi's Black Army as well as the 'people's army' of 1514.

THE DIVIDED KINGDOM, 1526–1687

The Ottomans briefly occupied Buda during the autumn of 1526. Nevertheless, since their supply lines were now dangerously extended and they feared a counter-attack by a still intact baronial army under Janos Zapolyai (who had arrived at the battle of Mohacs rather late in the day), the Turks limited themselves to the taking of captives and booty and then withdrew. Hungary thus remained free to fight back and to elect a new king.

In the ensuing elections Hungary's aristocratic *frondeurs* chose the magnate and former palatine Janos Zapolyai (1526–40). However, their 'centralist' rivals and opponents summoned a 'counter-Diet' and elected King Ferdinand of Habsburg (1526–64), whose father had concluded mutual succession and intermarriage pacts with King Ulaszlo II in 1505 and 1515 respectively. Thus at this critical juncture Hungary was gripped by a power struggle between two rival kings. In order to assist 'their man' (and thereby secure their own financial and mining interests) the Fuggers financed a Habsburg military occupation of Hungary. However, although Janos Zapolyai was forced into exile, this led him to persuade the Ottomans to launch a counter-offensive against Habsburg Hungary and Austria in 1529. The Habsburgs overcame the ensuing Turkish siege of Vienna, but the Ottomans helped to bring all except north-western Hungary under Zapolyai rule during the 1530s. In 1540 Janos Zapolyai's death precipitated another Habsburg attempt to take over the whole of Hungary, but in 1541 the Ottomans recaptured Buda and instituted a more lasting three-way partition of Hungary. North-western Hungary (Transdanubia and Slovakia) remained under Habsburg rule. Central Hungary (roughly the area between the Tisza and the Danube) came under direct Turkish control. But the territories east of the Tisza (the so-called Partium and Transylvania) were treated as an autonomous principality, albeit under indirect Ottoman suzerainty. This tripartite division endured with temporary lapses until the Habsburg 'reconquest' of Hungary, which followed the defeat of the Ottomans' second siege of Vienna in 1683.

Partitioned Hungary was afflicted by endemic marauding and social unrest and by several protracted wars of attrition between the Ottomans and the Habsburgs. In consequence, several fortified 'military frontier zones' were established, the economy regressed, many towns shrank, whole regions were quite extensively depopulated and the baronial oligarchy, which became a law unto itself, repeatedly expanded its land holdings, its serf holdings and its local prerogatives at the expense of the royal domain, the Catholic Church, the peasantry and the townspeople. By the 1550s Hungary's copper, silver and gold mines had lost their former importance, partly as a result of internal strife, but also because Europe was being flooded by cheaper and more plentiful copper, silver and gold from overseas. This increase in the money supply and the resultant sixteenth-century inflation increased Hungary's dependence on temporarily lucrative cattle and wine exports and on (relatively cheaper) imported manufactures, exacerbating the contraction of Hungarian towns and craft industries (Makkai 1875c: 136).

Deprived of careful arable husbandry (and increasingly denuded of protective tree cover), large tracts of the Hungarian Plain degenerated into noxious swamps and shifting sands. This gave rise to the so-called *puszta*, a Hungarian word meaning 'bare' or 'deserted' or 'desertified' in its adjectival form. Moreover, the proportion of the population speaking Magyar as their mother tongue slumped from over 80 per cent to less than 45 per cent of the total, partly as a result of Slavic and Romanian immigration into Hungary's depopulated areas (Ignotus 1972: 34). The sapping of Hungary's economic strength and the exacerbation of its social and cultural divisions must have prolonged partition and facilitated the country's subjugation by the Habsburgs.

REFORMATION, COUNTER-REFORMATION AND RECONQUEST

The turbulent sixteenth century was a period of cultural and religious ferment. Humanist writing and scholarship (along with Renaissance architecture and art) moved out of the narrow confines of the royal court and the higher clergy into the wider circles of the landed nobility and educated townspeople. 'Under the influence of Erasmus, the cult of the national language began . . . The first Church reformers also came from the ranks of the followers of Erasmus' (Makkai 1975c: 140).

The Reformation in Hungary

The Hungarian Reformation was a remarkable phenomenon. By 1600 nine-tenths of this hitherto overwhelmingly Catholic country had become Protestant (Klaniczay 1992: 172). The re-Catholicization of the Magyars during the seventeenth and eighteenth centuries (against seemingly insuperable odds) was pivotal to the establishment of Habsburg dominance. Yet the eventual triumph of the Catholic Counter-Reformation was to be mercifully incomplete. Down to the early twentieth century, most of the 'progressive' currents in Hungarian education, science, politics and economic development continued to flow from the Protestant communities.

Even before the battle of Mohacs, Martin Luther's ideas were making waves at the royal court of Lajos II and in the Erasmian circle of his Habsburg consort, Queen Maria. But after 1526 they attracted much wider attention. The legislation against Lutheranism promulgated between 1523 and 1525 became a dead letter after the death of Lajos II at Mohacs (Peter 1994: 158). Moreover, the presentation of a mutually agreed Confession of Faith (the so-called Augsburg Confession) by German Protestant rulers at Augsburg in 1530 helped to undermine the imperial proscription on Lutheranism and opened the floodgates of religious reform in both Germany and East Central Europe. Hungary's local authorities started allowing evangelical congregations to take over existing church buildings during the 1530s (p. 159).

After 1530, moreover, many hitherto conformist clergy began openly to display evangelical convictions and disaffection with the Catholic Church. They found shelter with Protestant lay patrons and 'became the most fervent propagators of the new faith'

(Peter 1994: 160). Two practical attractions must have been that Protestant clergy had greater freedom to preach, write and conduct services in the vernacular rather than Latin and were permitted to marry.

The anarchic conditions resulting from the tripartite division of Hungary during the 1540s made it increasingly difficult for either the rulers or the Catholic Church to stem (let alone turn) the 'reforming' tide, while the absence of systematic persecution of Protestants turned Hungary into a relatively safe haven for Protestant refugees from Bohemia and the southern German states. Swiss Protestant ideas rapidly gained ground at the expense of both Lutheranism and Catholicism between the 1540s and the 1570s, under the potent leadership of Marton Kalmancsehi Santa, Istvan Szegedi Kis and Peter Melius Juhasz. These men founded and built up the predominantly Calvinist 'Reformed Church', which by the 1560s was Hungary's largest religious denomination.

During the 1560s, under the influence of the maverick evangelist Ferenc David, a major Unitarian Church was established in eastern Hungary (Peter 1994: 161). In Transylvania Unitarianism briefly became an established and officially recognized religion, on an equal footing with Calvinism, Lutheranism and Catholicism (although the Eastern Orthodoxy of the region's Romanian peasants was merely tolerated). But Istvan Bathory, who ruled Transylvania from 1570 to 1586, allowed in the Jesuits and restricted Unitarianism, although the (unintended) effect was merely to reinforce the preponderance of Calvinism (Makkai 1975c: 142).

Alongside politically moderate forms of Protestantism, radical Anabaptism gained a popular following in Hungary during the troubled 1520s. However, it has yet to be established whether Hungarian Anabaptism drew its main inspiration from much older Hussite influences. Either way, Hungarian Anabaptism evoked severe repression from the landed nobility during the 1530s (Peter 1994: 160). A partly Protestant-inspired peasant uprising against both the Turks and landlordism in the Tisza region in 1570 met with a similar response (Makkai 1975c: 141). Anabaptists subsequently 'retreated into defensive communities of zealots who lived a simple peasant life of self-help and discipline' (Evans 1979: 10). Sabbatarian communities survived in Transylvania until the late nineteenth century.

Interestingly, while in Poland and Lithuania ethnic diversity seemed to hinder the diffusion of Protestant ideas, in Hungary 'a no less complex linguistic-ethnic mix . . . did not prevent large numbers turning to Protestant belief' (Scribner 1994: 216). Overall, Lutheran ideas prevailed among Hungary's German-speaking townspeople and in Slovakia, while Unitarianism was largely confined to Transylvania. But Calvinist (and to a lesser extent Anabaptist) ideas attracted numerous Magyar adherents in all three sectors of partitioned Hungary. Moreover, while it is sometimes argued that the eventual preponderance of Calvinism over Lutheranism reflected a Magyar reaction against the Germanic provenance of Lutheranism, in actual fact large numbers of Magyars continued to be attracted to the Germanic universities of Wittenberg, Heidelberg and Basel, which rather goes against allegations of anti-German sentiment. It has been more plausibly argued that Lutheranism 'made a deep impression on Central Europe, but it never secured dogmatic harmony in any one territory, let alone the kind of overall *rapport* between territories which would have assured it of political dominance' (Evans 1979: 8–9). In addition, Lutheranism offered nothing comparable to the Calvinist concepts of 'predestination' and 'the elect', which had an obvious appeal to the *amour-propre* of the nobilities of Poland, Lithuania, Bohemia and France as well as Hungary.

The main beneficiaries of the Reformation in East Central Europe were the nobilities and townspeople, who gained 'an access of confidence and strength' in their dealings with the region's Catholic rulers (Evans 1979: 5). A majority of Hungary's landed nobles embraced Protestantism, perhaps partly as a way of restricting monarchical and ecclesiastical power and laying hands on crown and Church property. Nobles were mainly attracted to Calvinism, but the towns, whose prosperous and industrious inhabitants tended to be German, more readily embraced Lutheranism. They appreciated its Germanic orientation, provenance and success ethic and its emphasis on education, vocation, work and sobriety.

The Reformation gave the Hungarian Renaissance a second wind. Protestants established numerous schools and printing presses. They preached, held services and printed books in the vernacular. The first Magyar grammar was published by the Protestant Matyas Devai Biro in 1538. The first complete printed Hungarian translation of the New Testament was published by Protestants in 1541. The Calvinist colleges established in Debrecen, Sarospatak and Marosvasarhely, together with the Unitarian college in Koloszvar, became Hungary's most renowned centres of learning. These trends were reinforced by the relative stability engendered by a longish truce between the Habsburgs and the Ottomans (1568–91) and an even longer period of reciprocal recognition and mutual accommodation between the Habsburgs and the principality of Transylvania (1570–1604). 'Under Protestant dominance, for thirty years after about 1570, a golden age of vernacular culture came into being.' During that time printed books were published in all the vernaculars spoken in Hungary. This had never happened before, and it did not recur 'for another hundred years' (Peter 1994: 163).

Much of the literature produced by Hungary's Protestants was critical of the Habsburgs and the moral and political failings of the formerly Catholic aristocracy as well as the Catholic Church. 'The poems of Andras Szkarosi Horvat, the plays of Mihaly Sztarai and the tales of Gaspar Heltai admonished both the Roman Catholic Church and the feudal lords for oppressing the people' (Makkai 1975c: 142).

The first complete translation of the Bible into Magyar, published at Vizsoly in 1590, had a major impact on the further development of the Magyar language. Nevertheless, Hungary was a partial exception to the regular claim that Protestant insistence on the laity reading the Bible for themselves (and being equipped to do so) was the driving force behind the development of vernacular languages and literary cultures during the Reformation. The fact that the first complete Magyar translation of the Bible was not published until 1590 indicates that in Hungary the Reformation 'did not put the Bible directly into the hands of the common people . . . Indeed, one eminent Calvinist bishop complained that the Reformation had done little to change the "total absence of culture" among the lower classes' (Peter 1994: 165). Thus there is a case to be made that (in spite of its formal numerical triumph) the Reformation was unable to put down such deep roots in Hungary as in countries with a stronger urban sector and a larger and more educated Bible-reading public. This would help to explain the otherwise puzzling ease with which the country was recatholicized during the seventeen and eighteenth centuries.

However, even if the Magyars were not immediately endowed with a printed complete vernacular translation of the Bible (a task whose magnitude should not be underestimated), 'they were none the less provided with a rich abundance of reading matter, largely supplied by Protestant authors'. Indeed, nearly half the printed works published in Hungary between 1570 and 1600 were produced in 'popular editions', and 75 per cent of these were published in Magyar rather than in Latin (Peter 1994: 165–6).

It has even been argued that the intellectual vigour and freedom of sixteenth-century East Central Europe did not draw strength from Protestantism *per se*. After all, many Protestants were bigots and Bible-thumpers of the first order. Their outlook was often infected by anti-intellectualism, belligerence, prejudice and internecine strife, even though they did put a much higher premium on both popular and higher education than did the Catholic Church at the time. Rather, intellectual life was enriched by the fact that 'the broadened theological spectrum brought, of necessity, a basic widening of horizons' (Evans 1979: 12). The Protestant Churches of East Central Europe were eventually weakened by their failure to attain any semblance of doctrinal unity, but 'Renaissance culture profited rather than suffered from its absence' (p. 6). Indeed, heated theological debates occurred not so much between Catholics and Protestants as 'between particular reformist trends' (Klaniczay 1992: 172). Yet the reformers rarely burdened the less educated laity with their theological disputations, which mostly remained 'locked up in unwieldy Latin tomes' (Peter 1994: 164), and Protestant Transylvania became renowned throughout Europe for its religious toleration.

Katalin Peter has emphasized that the Catholic Church was at first extraordinarily passive in the face of the Protestant advance. In Hungary Catholicism 'withdrew without defending itself'. No Catholic printing press was established to compete with the Protestant publishing offensive until 1578, by which time there were seven active Protestant presses. 'Catholics were not prohibited by their faith from writing popular verse, but they did not do so throughout the sixteenth century . . . There remained in the old Church a stiffness, along with an inability to identify with the common people' (Peter 1994: 162–3). By the 1570s 'between 80 and 85 per cent of the Christian population were Protestant' (p. 161).

In sharp contrast to northern Germany and England, however, 'Hungary became a Protestant country without a nudge from its rulers. There was no royal Act of Supremacy or anything similar proclaiming the Reformation' (Peter 1994: 161). More than that, western Hungary became Protestant in the face of consistent (albeit ineffectual) royal support for the Catholic Church. Indeed, even after 90 per cent of the faithful had defected to the Protestant camp and only between 300 and 350 Catholic parishes remained, 'the entire hierarchy of the Roman Church was preserved'. Catholic bishops were 'even appointed to those sees which had fallen under Ottoman rule'; nor did they lose their seats in the Diet, 'despite near-total Protestant predominance among . . . the inhabitants of Royal [western] Hungary' (p. 162). This meant that, when Hungary's Catholics finally bestirred themselves to mount a more vigorous Counter-Reformation during the seventeenth and eighteenth centuries, the mighty infrastructure of the Catholic Church was still at their disposal. They were slow to join the fight, but they had not thrown away their weapons.

If Hungarian Protestantism did enjoy significant patronage (or even some forcible imposition 'from above'), it came neither from monarchs nor from the towns but from Protestant (usually Calvinist) landowners who rather anticipated the famous principle of *cuius regio, eius religio* by expecting the inhabitants of their domains to adopt the religion of their 'lords and masters'. Moreover, if the landed nobility did play a major role in the conversion of the inhabitants of their domains to Protestantism, this development could be similarly reversed by the gradual return of most of their descendants to Catholicism during the seventeenth and eighteenth centuries.

From the 1620s onward the Catholic Church and its powerful lay patrons turned their attention 'back to the people', taking on the Protestants at their own game (Peter 1994: 167). Few of the first Catholic Counter-Reformers were popular, 'but each had some political *points d'appui*: they enjoyed a measure of official support and could profit from Protestant excesses' (Evans 1979: 43). Many East Central Europeans came to be troubled by the Reformation's fissiparity. 'Protestantism was well established; but where could it lead?' (p. 39). Not a few saw Protestantism as divisive, acrimonious and a threat to the established order (pp. 109–11). The Counter-Reformation was able to make telling use of the official status, the still considerable wealth and the majestic ecclesiastical infrastructure of the Catholic Church. 'Counter-reformers needed to breathe life into the shell of an army top-heavy with reluctant officers' (p. 42). However, there was 'a real devotional resurgence within Catholicism' in seventeenth-century Hungary (p. 250). The Pauline and Benedictine Orders, the cult of the Virgin Mary, the cult of St Istvan (Hungary's first Christian king), increased use of the vernacular, the educational and publishing activities of the Jesuits and the university which they founded in 1635 at Tyrnau spearheaded the Catholic revival (pp. 252–7). The Roman Catholic Church and the Habsburgs, who had often been at loggerheads, closed ranks for this pivotal counter-offensive. Furthermore, the Magyar aristocracy increasingly needed the support of the Habsburgs and the Catholic Church in order to fend off challenges to aristocratic power, wealth and privilege. There was an underlying 'community of interest . . . between dynasty, aristocracy and Catholic Church' (p. 240). But these realignments did not take place overnight. There was still a Protestant majority within the nobility after the consummation of the Habsburg 'reconquest' of Hungary in 1711, even though the Protestants were now on the defensive (Makkai 1975d: 187–9).

The inglorious *dénouement*

The truce between the Habsburgs and the Ottomans had broken down in 1591. Towards the end of the ensuing fifteen-year war of attrition (1591–1606), there was an acrimonious deterioration in relations between the Habsburgs and Hungary's ruling classes, who rued and resented the seemingly endless prolongation of this costly and inconclusive conflict, the thankless subordinate roles in which it placed them, and the fact that some of the Habsburg generals behaved more like rapacious anti-Protestant *conquistadores* than like respectful Christian allies.

Matters came to a head in 1604, when disillusioned Hungarian nobles led by Istvan Bocskai and Gabor Bethlen organized an anti-Habsburg uprising of peasant refugees, military frontiersmen and disaffected Magyar soldiers and mercenaries. With discreet Turkish assistance, Bocskai's rebel army expelled the Habsburgs, whereupon he was elected Prince of Transylvania and the Ottomans offered to make him King of Hungary (under their own protection, of course). However, many Hungarian nobles feared the power and barely restrained radicalism of Bocskai's unruly rebel forces, known as *hajdu*, or 'heyducks', even more than they disliked the Habsburgs. Bocskai therefore felt obliged to open negotiations with the Habsburgs.

The resultant Treaty of Vienna (1606) promised religious toleration and aristocratic autonomy in north-western Hungary (which now reverted to Habsburg control) and recognized the independence of the principality of Transylvania, while the *hajdu* were granted the status of autonomous military frontiersmen. This 'new deal' was accepted by the Ottomans in return for Habsburg territorial concessions. In practice, however, this new accommodation between the Habsburgs, the Ottomans and the Hungarian landed nobility was to be achieved at the expense of the peasantry, who were brought under the full legal jurisdiction of the landed nobility in 1608, and of the towns, which had fully succumbed to the political tutelage of the landed nobility by the 1650s (Makkai 1975c: 147–9).

Gabor Bathory, the sole surviving male descendant of the illustrious Istvan Bathory, became Prince of Transylvania in 1608. But the Habsburgs mounted an abortive military intervention against him in 1611 (in blatant violation of the 1606 Treaty of Vienna), and he had difficulty in controlling the *hajdu*, before he was assassinated in 1613. Nevertheless, Transylvania prospered and gained much greater freedom of manoeuvre under his anti-Habsburg successor Gabor Bethlen (1613–29). Bethlen attracted Czech and German Protestant craftsmen, merchants, miners and mining engineers to the principality, fostered industrial development, gave strong support to the towns, reduced the burdens on the peasantry, intervened against the Habsburgs during the first decade of the Thirty Years' War (1618–48) and brought half of Hungary under Transylvanian rule. Unfortunately, his Protestant allies never gave him the military and economic support that would have allowed him to reunite Hungary and liberate it from Ottoman domination, even though he took considerable military risks in order to assist his allies.

After Bethlen's death in 1629 further Habsburg military incursions were beaten off by the *hajdu*, acting in concert with Gyorgy Rakoczi (Hungary's richest Protestant magnate), who became the next Prince of Transylvania (1631–48). He extended religious tolerance to the peasantry and also intervened against the Habsburgs. But he intensified the exploitation of serfs and, according to Makkai (1975c: 157), 'His participation in the Thirty Years' War had nothing to do with . . . the reunion of Hungary, his main concern being the safety and further enrichment of his family estates.' He was succeeded by his son, Gyorgy Rakoczi II (1648–60), whose attempts to become King of Hungary by playing off the Habsburgs against the Ottomans led them to engage in debilitating military campaigns against one another in Transylvania and adjacent territories between 1658 and 1664. These conflicts ended in stalemate and the restoration of the *status quo ante*. But Transylvania was left stranded under a puppet ruler, Mihaly Apafi (1661–90), who was kept on a very tight leash by the Turks.

Meanwhile, Hungary's landed nobility was becoming more and more deeply divided – economically, politically, culturally and even in matters of religion. Many nobles (especially Catholics) decided that the only hope of 'liberating' Hungary from the 'Turkish yoke' lay in ever closer alliance with the Habsburgs, even if it meant accepting Habsburg tutelage. But other nobles (especially Protestants) concluded that the Habsburgs were much more intent on their own imperial aggrandizement than on genuinely liberating Hungary from Ottoman suzerainty, and some began to recruit peasant soldiers, *hajdu*, military frontiersmen, fugitive serfs and Magyar refugees (from the Balkans) into rebel guerrilla forces known as the *kuruc* movement. The word *kuruc*, which dates back to the medieval Crusades, is derived from the Latin word for cross (*crux*) and from the Turkish word for a rebel (*khurudsch*). After the revolt of Hungary's peasant Crusaders in 1514 the term *kuruc* was regularly applied to peasant rebels and 'freedom fighters', irrespective of whether they were fighting the Ottomans, the

Habsburgs or serf-owning Magyar landlords. Indeed, high-born Magyar opponents of Habsburg domination increasingly adopted the name *kuruc* in the hope of attracting greater support for the anti-Habsburg cause, whilst posing as Robin Hoods. Thus Count Imre Thokoly, a parvenu aristocrat whose recent ancestors had been peasants and cattle dealers, succeeded in establishing a relatively egalitarian *kuruc* principality in the highlands of northern Hungary from 1678 to 1686 (partly with financial assistance from France's King Louis XIV, who was competing with the Habsburgs for dominion over continental Europe). 'The majority of the Hungarian ruling class, however, were more afraid of the *kuruc* movement than of Habsburg oppression and held aloof' (Makkai 1975c: 167).

The stalemate in the long struggle between the Ottomans and the Habsburgs for control of Hungary was finally broken in 1683, when the Turks overreached themselves by laying siege to Vienna. International armies commanded on the Habsburgs' behalf by the Polish warrior king Jan Sobieski and by Duke Charles of Lorraine not only lifted the siege but launched a counter-offensive which 'liberated' Buda in 1686, Transylvania in 1687 and Belgrade in 1688. The Ottomans recaptured Belgrade in 1690 and defeated a Habsburg army at Lugos in eastern Hungary in 1695, only to be decisively defeated by the Habsburgs at the battle of Zenta in 1697. The whole of Hungary (including Transylvania, with the sole exception of the Temesvar/Timisoara region) was permanently ceded to the Habsburgs by the Ottomans under the Treaty of Karlocza (Karlowitz) in 1699.

For the Magyars, however, the results of the Habsburg 'liberation' of Hungary were more conducive to bitterness and discontent than to jubilation. As on previous occasions the Habsburg military commanders came and behaved more like bigoted and corrupt Catholic *conquistadores* than as liberators. The military forces which ran the country until 1695 indulged in looting, terror, persecution of Protestants, rape and extortion (Makkai 1975c: 169–70). Hungary was subjected to unaccustomed levels of taxation, partly to repay the cost of its own 'liberation'. In 1687 the Hungarian Diet was obliged to renounce ('in gratitude') its former right to (s)elect the King of Hungary, since the Habsburgs were henceforth to be the country's hereditary rulers. It also annulled the clause in the Golden Bull recognizing the right to resist unlawful or unconstitutional acts of government. Moreover, instead of reuniting the kingdom of Hungary, the Habsburgs chose to perpetuate the separate legal status and 'autonomy' of Transylvania and the military frontier regions, under governors appointed by and responsible to Vienna. The Habsburgs also established a commission which was to restore land to families who had fled from war zones or Turkish occupation zones only on presentation of written proof of ownership, even though many of the documents in question had been lost or abandoned in flight, and on payment of administrative and legal charges which the claimants could often ill afford. Consequently, much 'unclaimed' land reverted to the Habsburg treasury. Some of it was awarded to native Catholic ('loyalist') aristocrats, but much of it went to the Germanic and/or Catholic generals, military contractors and soldiers of fortune who had taken part in the 'war of liberation'. According to Robert Kann (1974: 73–4), 'The Hungarian nation had to pay the bill after the reconquest. By this conquest land was redistributed through imperial commissions. Former owners, suspected of disloyalty or religious nonconformism, lost their estates, which were given to foreigners, mostly German nobles. Worse was in store for many burghers in northern cities who lost their property and, after submission to torture, their lives.'

From 1703 to 1711, not surprisingly, there was widespread anti-Habsburg insurgency and unrest in Hungary, Croatia-Slavonia and Transylvania, involving Protestants, Magyar nationalists, Croatian separatists and, above all, *kuruc* armies led by Ferenc Rakoczi, who was elected to the position of Prince of Transyvlania in 1704 and presided over the creation of a siege economy and a highly militarized '*kuruc* state' (Makkai 1975d: 173–5). These anti-Habsburg rebels, fighting variously for autonomy or full independence or social emanicipation, sought to take full advantage of the fact that the bulk of the Habsburg armed forces were tied down in the War of the Spanish Succession (1701–14) in western Europe. In 1711, however, as the warfare in both western Europe and Hungary took a heavy toll, the Hungarian propertied classes sought a compromise peace with the hard-pressed Habsburgs. The ensuing Treaty of Szatmar (1711), negotiated against Prince Rakoczi's wishes and during his absence on a 'begging mission' in Peter the Great's Russia, established a highly decentralized *comitat* (county) system of aristocratic self-administration, aristocratic 'liberties' (including freedom of conscience and exemption of landowners from direct taxation) and a separate legal system and legal code. This was the origin of Hungary's special (some say anomalous or privileged) status within the Habsburg Empire.

As in 'reconquered' Bohemia, Hungary's magnates owed their new positions, privileges and possessions to their Habsburg patrons and protectors, to whom they initially became passive and compliant servitors rather than authentic and independent representatives and spokesmen of the Hungarian 'nation'. In contrast to Bohemia, however, this 'reconquest' did not lead to the wholesale Germanization of the towns and of the aristocracy. Indeed, the implanted foreign aristocrats gradually 'went native' and became doughty champions and custodians of an aristocratic Magyar 'nation' and Magyar autonomy, even though they remained wary of biting too savagely the hand that ultimately protected their position and privileges. Unlike the impecunious Magyar 'lesser nobility' (which comprised nearly 5 per cent of the population), the aristocracy was always afraid to sever totally its links with the Habsburgs. For their part, the Habsburgs had inherited the burned-out shell of a kingdom of Hungary which had been temporarily drained of its economic and spiritual lifeblood by decades of war, plunder, tribute, infrastructural neglect and internal strife. But, instead of seeking to expedite Hungary's recovery and reconstruction by promoting tolerance and reconciliation, the Habsburgs chose to fan the flames of bigotry and conflict by championing a Catholic Counter-Reformation in a predominantly Protestant country. This occurred at the very time when most European states were starting to turn away from religious intolerance and strife and were entering the age of the Enlightenment. There was even a reversal of roles, as Hungarian religious toleration succumbed to bigotry and absolutism while most of western Europe retreated from debilitating sectarian strife. Yet, in the final analysis, it is clear that the kingdom of Hungary was most fatally weakened by the frequent reluctance of major components of the landed nobility to put any sense of duty or allegiance to the kingdom as a whole before the defence of sectional interests, prerogatives and privileges. This, together with the kingdom's unhelpful religious divisions (rather than the more recent inter-ethnic ones), enabled the Habsburgs increasingly to divide-and-rule Hungary's noble and aristocratic factions, which, had they been more united in the kingdom's defence, should have been strong enough to fend off the Habsburg threat.

7 The kingdom of Bohemia and the Hussite heritage

BOHEMIA BEFORE AND AFTER THE ARRIVAL OF CHRISTIANITY

As a result of their virtuosic cultural and economic vigour over many centuries and their strategic location at the true heart of Europe, Bohemia and Moravia have had an importance in European history out of all proportion to their size. Moreover, with their relatively diverse natural resources, temperate climate, verdant vegetation and hospitable terrain, virtually encircled by a protective ring of ore-bearing mountains, the Czech Lands have been inhabited for about 200,000 years. Major settlements can be traced back to about 70,000 BC, and the smelting of local metal ores (beginning with copper) dates from before 2000 BC.

Between *c.* 500 and 100 BC the Czech Lands were mainly inhabited by Celtic tribes. The Romans used to refer to one of these tribes as the Boii (whence the name 'Bohemia'). But the area was also settled by (allegedly Slavic) Lusatians, of whom traces can be found as far back as the Bronze Age, furnishing the basis of Czech nationalist claims that the Slavs are the country's oldest surviving inhabitants. Around 1000 BC, moreover, the Celtic tribes appear to have been displaced westwards by Germanic warriors from the north European plain. The latter engaged in sporadic frontier wars with the Romans until late in the second century AD. But during the fourth century they in turn began to be displaced westwards by marauding Huns and, in the sixth and seventh centuries, by Avars, none of whom appears to have put down deep roots in either Bohemia or Moravia. Nevertheless, the major inflows of Slavic settlers (whom most Czechs regard as their 'lineal ancestors') probably did not occur until the sixth and seventh centuries. The Czech nation derives its name from the Cechi, the most prominent of these Slavic tribes. These settlers were at first enslaved by the Avars. But around 624 AD a wily merchant adventurer known as Samo successfully led a Slavic rising against the Avars and became the ruler of a Slavic tribal confederation centred on Moravia until his death about 658 AD.

The Slavs of Bohemia and Moravia then mysteriously disappear from the historical record until the emergence of a Moravian Slavic state about 830 AD under Mojmir I, who also conquered western Slovakia. (This was to be one of the few prolonged connections between the Czech Lands and Slovakia prior to the twentieth century.) Following Mojmir's death in 846, Moravia was invaded by Frankish Germans, who installed a client named Rostislav on the Moravian throne. Whether in order to escape from Frankish tutelage or to fend off Germanic/Catholic encroachments on his new domains, in 863 AD Rostislav asked two Byzantine monks called Cyril and Methodius to start baptising the leading families of Moravia (and later Bohemia) into Byzantine Orthodox Christianity.

Moravia had already cultivated commercial and cultural connections with Byzantium and (since 855) these two linguistically gifted monks had been engaged in the momentous tasks of devising a Slavonic alphabet (the Glagolitic script) and of translating parts of the Orthodox liturgy into their first *written* Slavonic language (latterly made famous in the West by Leos Janacek's stirring Glagolitic Mass). However, the rapid religious and cultural inroads achieved by these remarkable brothers from Salonika provoked a violent Germanic/Catholic counter-offensive. In 870 the unfortunate Rostislav was overthrown, imprisoned and blinded by his noxious nephew Svatopluk, with Germanic Catholic assistance. In 885, after both Cyril and Methodius had died (partly from exhaustion), Prince Svatopluk enforced a papal ban on the old Slavonic liturgy, while the Eastern Orthodox clergy and linguistic disciples of Cyril and Methodius were hounded out of the Czech Lands. Following Svatopluk's death in 894, however, the Czechs of Bohemia broke away from the so-called Moravian Empire, which finally collapsed under the weight of Magyar attacks in 906 AD, while the Czech Premyslide dynasty emerged in Bohemia. According to Czech national myth, this dynasty (which survived for over 400 years, until 1306) originated with a sturdy Bohemian ploughman named Premysl who married Princess Libuse, the valiant daughter of a ninth-century ruler of Bohemia, and 'lived happily ever after'. (The story has been immortalized by Bedrich Smetana's archetypal Czech nationalist opera *Libuse*.)

Bohemia's conversion to Catholicism was greatly accelerated by the pious life and premature death of the avid and well educated Czech proselytizer and church builder Duke Vaclav I (921–29). This 'good King Wenceslas' (of Christmas carol fame) was assassinated by his jealous younger brother in 929. The deceased duke was swiftly canonized by the Catholic Church, which also propagated pious legends about him (and named innumerable churches after him) throughout Western Christendom. Moreover, St Vaclav became the patron saint of the Bohemian state, and his image subsequently graced medieval Czech coins, seals and flags and the Bohemian crown. Although he himself had coyly declined the Germanic Catholic Emperor's offer of a royal crown, one was eventually conferred on Duke Vladislav II by the Imperial Diet at Regensburg in 1158 (in recompense for military assistance rendered to Emperor Frederick Barbarossa), and the royal title became hereditary in 1198 and permanent in 1212. This consummated the absorption of Bohemia into Catholic Christendom, under a Catholic see of its own (established in Prague in 973). As in the cases of Poland and Hungary, this stimulated the development of a literate clergy and ruling class, the use of Latin and an influx of Western European ideas, books, influences and learning. Meanwhile, the Bohemian Church was rapidly enriched by royal and private benefactors and bequests, and prominent royal clients, retainers and allies became assimilated into an ascendant serf-owning landed nobility between the tenth and twelfth centuries AD (Kavka 1960: 27–8).

THE THIRTEENTH-CENTURY APOGEE OF THE PREMYSLIDE DYNASTY

The status of the new kingdom of Bohemia rose substantially in the thirteenth century, during which the Premyslide kings took pride of place within the college of seven Electors of the Holy Roman Empire (i.e. among the rulers who elected the Holy Roman Emperor). The kingdom also underwent significant economic development. In agriculture iron ploughs and implements came into more widespread use, livestock herds increased and there was a general adoption of three-field rotation systems. Furthermore, German immigrants were lured in by the granting of hereditary and relatively unencumbered ('emphyteutic') leaseholds, which could be bought, sold or bequeathed (under so-called 'German law'). The areas of settlement and cultivation were greatly expanded by burning off and clearing large tracts of virgin forest, which was the main project for which German colonists were wanted in the first place. 'The expansion of agricultural output and the opportunities for marketing its produce eventually made it possible to substitute feudal money rents for forced labour and payments in kind' (Kavka 1960: 33). Indeed, the influence of 'German law' extended far beyond the border regions colonized by German immigrants. It helped to transform the agrarian relations between Czech landlords and peasants, as the latter also became much freer and economically more secure than before (Blum 1957: 814–17). Nevertheless, Czech landed nobles continued to exact small amounts of forced labour (*robota*) from the Czech peasantry, mainly for the construction and maintenance of roads, drainage ditches and, most interestingly, large fishponds. The latter were established in order to breed fish (especially carp) for sale on the emerging urban market and in neighbouring countries (Wright 1975: 241, 244).

The thirteenth-century expansion of commercial agriculture encouraged and facilitated the growth of craft industries and towns, since landlords and peasant smallholders were increasingly willing and able to exchange farm produce for manufactures. Furthermore, the growth of craft industries and towns attracted and was fostered by inflows of German merchants and craftsmen. Germans dominated the towns and craft guilds that expanded and proliferated under their royal or baronial castellans. German immigration and the growth of predominantly German towns was also brought about by the meteoric development of large silver mines at Jihlava and Kutna Hora, which turned the kingdom of Bohemia into the biggest producer of silver in Europe by 1300. Moreover, the monetization and commercialization of Bohemia's economy were to be greatly assisted by the minting of a silver currency which was in plentiful supply and readily acceptable in domestic and international transactions (Kavka 1960: 34–5).

These developments were to a large degree fortuitous. Yet the last Premislide kings were astute enough to encourage and to take full advantage of them, partly in order to enhance their wealth and international standing, partly to strengthen the ascendancy of the monarchy over Czech landed nobles, who consequently criticized and resented the growth of German influences, towns and urban autonomy (which in effect reduced the potential influence of the Czech nobility and placed German-speaking patriciates in control of most towns and the poorer or less skilled Czech traders and craftsmen).

In 1255 King Premysl Otakar II (1253–78) personally led a Catholic crusade against the pagan Prussians and founded the town of Königsberg (now Russia's Kaliningrad enclave), partly as a means of exerting territorial pressure on Poland. During the 1250s he also acquired the dukedoms of Austria, Styria, Carinthia and Carniola. This, along with the extinction of the Hohenstaufen dynasty of Holy Roman Emperors in 1254, encouraged him to make a concerted bid for the imperial crown. This king was particularly renowned for his military prowess, his promotion of towns and silver mining and, to the chagrin of the Czech landed nobility, his heavy reliance on Germans. In the end, however, his imperial ambitions were thwarted by a coalition of German princes led by Rudolf of Habsburg, a south-west German duke who was elected Holy Roman Emperor in 1273. In 1276 Emperor Rudolph invaded Austria (which became a hereditary Habsburg possession) and in 1278 he decisively defeated the Bohemian king, who died in battle. For the next five years Bohemia was ransacked by the deceased king's brother-in-law, the Margrave of Brandenburg, while Moravia had its first taste of Habsburg rule. (These unhappy experiences eventually inspired Smetana's opera *The Brandenburgers in Bohemia*.)

Nevertheless, the kingdom of Bohemia was subsequently reunited under Vaclav II (1282–1305). He gradually established Bohemian suzerainty over southern Silesia and the Krakow region and was even crowned King of Poland in 1300. However, this capable man died suddenly at the age of thirty-four in 1305. He was succeeded by his (childless) sixteen-year-old son Vaclav III (1305–06), who was mysteriously assassinated the following year whilst preparing to assert his royal authority over a deeply divided Poland. Thus the only native Bohemian dynasty came to an abrupt end, just when it seemed to be at the peak of its power. Moreover, the very success with which the Premyslide kings had maintained their absolute ascendancy over the Czech landed nobility meant that there was no other Czech family ready and waiting to step into the breach. This is an obvious down side of the extreme concentration of power in the hands of one family.

THE PRIME OF LUXEMBURG BOHEMIA

Between 1306 and 1310 there was a domestic and international power struggle for the vacant Bohemian throne, during which time Poland (not surprisingly) slipped the leash. But in 1310 the ten-year-old son of the recently elected Holy Roman Emperor (Heinrich von Luxemburg, 1308–14) was married to the younger sister of the late Vaclav II and was installed as King Jan of Bohemia (1310–42), founder of an illustrious Luxemburg dynasty (1310–1437). The Luxemburgs were evidently attracted by Bohemia's sizeable revenues and mineral wealth. These were consistently deployed to enhance the glitter and standing of their various 'family domains' in late medieval Europe, in much the same way that the Habsburgs were later to exploit the much greater revenues and mineral resources of the Fuggers, the Welsers and (especially) Spanish America in the pursuit of even larger dynastic ambitions.

King Jan managed to gain acceptance among the Czech landed nobility by repeatedly promising to respect and augment the privileges and prerogatives which had been asserted or acquired during the turmoil of 1306–10. These included the rights to hold Diets, collect taxes and monopolize the principal public offices. In any case the king was frequently abroad for long periods in pursuit of chivalric glory and the military and dynastic ambitions of the Luxemburg family. These prolonged absences resulted in territorial acquisitions for Bohemia (including the Cheb/Eger district and most of Lusatia and Silesia) and the king's premature death in a cavalry charge at the Anglo-French battle of Crécy in August 1346. Jan largely left the running of domestic affairs to his (somewhat older) Czech wife, whom he did not love, to the Czech magnates and higher clergy (who began to meet regularly to discuss affairs of state) and (from 1333 onwards) to his Francophil son Karel (who became Margrave of Moravia – a position analogous to that of the Prince of Wales – and Regent of Bohemia). The reign also saw continued development of agriculture, trade, crafts, towns and mining and, as a result of Karel's friendship with Pope Clement VI (his former tutor), the promotion of Prague's episcopal see to the status of archbishopric in 1344 (Betts 1970: 217–18, 223).

When Karel (Charles) inherited the Bohemian throne in 1346, he already had extensive international connections and experience of government. This, combined with his

Bohemian riches and his late father's chivalric reputation, secured his election as Holy Roman Emperor (1346–78). Unlike his father, and despite his predominantly French upbringing, however, Karel spoke Czech and 'identified himself with Bohemia, whose position he saw would provide an advantageous foundation for empire building, one much more reliable than divided and ungovernable Germany' (Betts 1970: 222). He therefore sought to enhance his own monarchical power and Bohemia's international standing still further by promoting educational, cultural, economic, legal and ecclesiastical reforms.

In 1348, with the co-operation of his ally Pope Clement VI, Karel founded the first university ever in the Holy Roman Empire and East Central Europe. The University of Prague was intended to be a genuinely universal and cosmopolitan institution, in which Czech and Polish would stand alongside Latin, Italian and German as languages of instruction; and it soon had around 7,000 students in a city with about 40,000 inhabitants (Bradley 1971: 38).

In 1350 Karel made Prague the capital city of the Holy Roman Empire, a status which it retained for fifty years. At about this time he initiated the construction of a Prague 'New Town', whose population eventually exceeded that of the 'Old Town'. He also rebuilt the royal castle of Hradcany and numerous fortresses, churches and monasteries, erected a new stone bridge across the river Vltava (the Charles Bridge, which still links the two halves of the capital), and launched the construction of the cathedral of St Vitus. This Francophil naturally brought foreign architects and artists to embellish Prague with 'masterpieces of the late Gothic style. His court and, especially, his chancery became centres of art and learning' (Kaminsky 1967: 7). Prague thus developed into a magnificent and truly European city which attracted merchants, nobles, clergy, architects and students from the Germanic world, France, Italy, Poland and Hungary.

During the 1350s King Karel also tamed the more unruly Czech magnates. He outlawed baronial banditry and had one of the wayward magnates publicly hanged, whereupon law and order descended on the countryside and the king's highways became relatively safe for traders. In the agricultural sector he actively promoted viticulture, fruit farming and commercial carp ponds. In addition, he established special tribunals to adjudicate disputes between landlords and peasants. Commerce and the craft industry were also stimulated by Karel's public works programmes, currency reform and incipient codification of customary law, as well as by the overall enhancement of law and order. Economic policy was less haphazard than it had been under Karel's predecessors (Bradley 1971: 35–6).

King Karel's activism was to have momentous consequences in the religious sphere, as became apparent soon after his death in 1378. Some of his initiatives seem quite innocuous at first glance, yet he inadvertently stirred up several hornets' nests, contributing to the religious, social and political convulsions for which Bohemia was to become well known during the fifteenth, sixteenth and seventeenth centuries. For a start, in the sardonic words of Kaminsky (1967: 8), 'To make Prague not only great but holy, he sent far and wide for relics, none of which were too improbable for his taste; Prague thus became the repository for a fabulous collection of such treasures as the Virgin's milk, one of Jesus' diapers, and a nail of the Cross. Indulgences were granted to persons visiting the shrines.' More important, but in the same spirit of conscientious yet prosaic piety, King Karel took up the cause of ecclesiastical reform.

THE WRITING ON THE WALL

In Bohemia (as in many other parts of Europe) the Catholic Church was evidently in need of reform, partly because the accumulation of ecclesiastical riches had palpably become an end in itself. By the fourteenth century the Church owned over one-third of the land in the kingdom of Bohemia (Kavka 1960: 45). Senior clergy and the mendicant orders were allegedly enriching themselves through various scams and abuses, including simony, pluralism and the charging of extortionate burial fees (Kaminsky 1967: 11, 20; Betts 1947: 375, 379). Moreover, the expansion of Bohemia's economy and revenues, combined with the proliferation of its holy relics and shrines, a burgeoning traffic in indulgences and the increasing habit of making the confirmation of ecclesiastical appointments subject to financial payments to the papacy, was turning the kingdom of Bohemia into a prime target for papal exploitation and ecclesiastical abuses. The situation was exacerbated by the papal financial difficulties arising from the 'Babylonian captivity' of the Avignon Popes (1309–77), the subsequent papal schism (1378–1414) and the economic and demographic crises that afflicted many parts of Catholic Christendom during the fourteenth century (especially the Black Death of 1348–50), which generally made it harder to collect papal revenues.

With his readiness to propitiate the Popes and to promote the traffic in indulgences, mainly for the sake of his own greater power and glory, King Karel was in a sense part of the problem which he sought to remedy. Nevertheless, through his friendship with Clement VI, who was Pope from 1342 to 1352, he secured the appointment of Arnost of Pardubic ('a zealous reformer of clerical abuses') as the first Archbishop of Prague (Betts 1970; 223). In an endeavour to raise the moral, spiritual and pastoral standards of the Catholic clergy, King Karel and Archbishop Arnost 'encouraged intensive teaching by evangelicals', brought 'famous foreign preachers' to Prague and even sent such men out to the provinces so that the whole country could 'benefit from their admonitions' (Bradley 1971: 39).

Most important, Karel persuaded the Austrian preacher Konrad Waldhauser to settle in Prague in 1363. From then until the latter's death in 1369, Prague's Germanic citizens were regularly chastised for their avarice, pride, opulence and religious pusillanimity. Waldhauser also lashed out at the vices and inadequacies of the mendicant orders and even the regular clergy, 'who sought their own profit instead of attending to the care of the souls entrusted to them' (Kaminsky 1967: 9). In addition, Waldhauser greatly influenced the up-and-coming generations of Czech religious reformers, especially Jan Milic of Kromeriz and Matej of Janov.

Having served (successively) as registrar, corrector and notary in King Karel's chancery between 1358 and 1362, Jan Milic suddenly decided in 1363 to renounce the life of comfort and official status and to become an impecunious preacher. From 1364 until his death in 1374 Milic proclaimed that there were many signs that the long-awaited Day of Judgement was approaching and that Christendom was woefully unprepared for the anticipated Second Coming of Christ. He therefore urged Christians to take Holy Communion frequently and *sub utraque specie* ('under both kinds', i.e. both the bread and the wine) in order to be ready at all times for the Second Coming and the Last Judgement, in accordance with Christ's bidding at the Last Supper. Before long the main body of adherents of the Czech reform movement became known either as the Utraquists, on account of their insistence that lay Christians as well as the clergy should regularly partake of Holy Communion *sub utraque specie*, or as the Calixtines, because the Communion chalice (*calix*) became their most distinctive and appealing symbol and clarion call. In Roman Catholic custom (since the twelfth century) the taking of Communion wine had been reserved for the clergy. Milic emphasized that this was contrary to Christ's explicit teaching and that, in God's eyes, lay Christians and their clergy ought to have been (indeed were) on a more equal footing.

In 1366, moreover, Jan Milic proclaimed that Karel, Holy Roman Emperor and King of Bohemia, was the Antichrist. 'The late-medieval mind, oppressed by the sense that the old order was breaking up, escaping from any control by religious and moral norms that still claimed validity, often expressed its conviction of total crisis in apocalyptic terms, chiefly the imagery associated with the figure of the Antichrist. Totally evil, destined to appear in the Last Days to wage war on Christ, the Antichrist represented not merely this or that lapse from the Christian norm, but the union of all the forces of perdition, including those in high places who were supposed to guard the Christian order but did not do so' (Kaminsky 1967: 10). Yet, however much this may have resonated or coincided with the popular eschatological imagery and beliefs of the time, many could have pointed to more 'deserving' candidates for the role of Antichrist than King Karel, who reacted with remarkable restraint. Indeed, it is significant that Milic suffered nothing more than a brief punitive confinement for making such an extreme claim against so powerful a personage, and that the preacher did not persevere with this particular claim. In 1367, moreover, Milic was permitted to travel to Rome to present his views on the crisis of Christendom to the Pope; when Milic was imprisoned by the Roman Inquisition on account of his criticisms of the Catholic clergy, King Karel even intervened to secure his release.

After his return to Prague, Milic was able to continue to preach unmolested from 1369 until his death in 1374. 'He attracted a band of preachers who joined him in his poor life, dependent on alms, constantly working among the people. Increasing numbers of the laity also adhered to his movement.' Furthermore, when Milic launched a mission to rescue and reform the city's prostitutes, the king 'gave him possession of one of Prague's leading brothels . . . Milic acquired enough money to buy some of the adjacent properties and received others as gifts.' He was therefore able to set up a community, which he named Jerusalem, devoted primarily 'to the housing and upkeep of the harlots he had converted'. However, 'his band of preachers also lived there . . . The clergy, of course, were scandalized' (Kaminsky 1967: 12). Yet it is apparent from his submissions to the Pope that Milic was more concerned with the 'evils' festering within the Church than with the oft lamented 'sins in the secular order', such as pride, vanity, false witness, fornication, aggression, oppression of the poor and disobedience to the Church. Few people took much notice of denunciations of the latter, since these were seen as ineluctable consequences of the fall of man. What really hit home were his condemnations of the lapses and failings of the Church. Milic denounced not only simony but 'the prelates' luxury and concubinage, their wealth and pluralism, their practice of usury . . . He also followed Waldhauser in denouncing the privileges of the mendicant orders, who . . . sold indulgences and used their special status to accumulate riches.' Nevertheless, he repeatedly affirmed his allegiance to the papacy and his fervent desire that the Pope would act 'to restore the purity of the Church, preferably by calling a general council in Rome'. His stance 'implied not subversion but restoration of ecclesiastical authority' (p. 11).

Jan Milic of Kromeriz was thus the true 'father' of the incipient Czech Reformation (Kavka 1994: 131). Nevertheless, 'Jerusalem' did not long survive his death in 1374, and the practice of frequent lay Communion *sub utraque specie* was condemned by the 'masters' of the University of Prague in 1388, whereupon a Church synod decreed that the laity could take Communion only once a month (Kaminsky 1967: 14, 18). But in 1391 the movement which Milic had launched found a new focus in the Bethlehem Chapel, which emphasized zealous preaching of the Gospel to one and all (p. 23) with the assistance of the first Czech translation of the scriptures, which had become available as early as the 1370s (Kavka 1994: 132).

However, Milic had not endeavoured to develop and substantiate a coherent system of thought and belief. His ideas and activities had emerged as spontaneous *ad hoc* responses to particular problems. The task of hammering and moulding his precepts into a coherent corpus of religious dogmas was mainly taken up by Matej of Janov (*c.* 1350–93), a Czech noble who had fallen under the influence of Milic in 1372 but studied at the University of Paris from 1373 to 1381. If Milic was the doughty and charismatic St Peter of the inchoate Czech Reformation, Matej of Janov was its more cerebral St Paul, who expounded and propagated the message in more elaborate and systematic written forms. In Paris, moreover, Janov came across criticisms of ecclesiastical abuses, opulence and laxity written by William of St Amour during the previous century and incorporated them into his own *Regulae Veteris et Novi Testamenti*. Janov strove to square the circle: 'to combine the ideal of pietism with that of the hierarchical Church. His fervour, his erudition, the broad range of his thought, which dealt with the local problem in European terms and defined the current situation in terms of the whole of Christian history – these traits would later make his *Regulae* an inexhaustible source of inspiration', especially for the more radical Czech religious reformers (Kaminsky 1967: 14–15, 22–3). Janov called for 'a restoration of the Church by a return to its apostolic origins and a consistent observance of the *"Rules of the Old and New Testaments"* . . . discarding all that could not be supported by the evidence of Scripture', although he tempered this strict biblicism with a 'belief in ongoing revelation by the Holy Spirit' (Kavka 1994: 132). His central message was that the lives of the clergy should be reformed and the true faith preached to the laity, who should be united with Christ through frequent Communion *sub utraque specie*, under the leadership of 'the holy people, the community of the saints within the ecclesiastical establishment' (Kaminsky 1967: 21). On his own admission, however, Janov remained profoundly torn between 'the two ways': (i) the 'systematic vanity' and moral hypocrisy of the careerist clergy, 'the great, the famous, the learned, those clothed in every appearance of holiness and wisdom . . . who say that they stand salubriously in Christ, serving him indeed with much diligence and endeavour, but in other respects show no mercy or charity'; and (ii) the true way of Jesus, exemplified by Jan Milic and his ilk, who renounced worldly vanities and wealth in favour of strenuous and selfless service to the poor and the needy (p. 17). This underlying tension must have been all the greater if, in Kaminsky's mordant words, the 'wealth, prestige and worldly brilliance that Milic voluntarily renounced' were to Janov merely 'the unattainable goals of a lifetime of inept careerism' (p. 16).

During the 1380s and 1390s the debates and contests between Bohemia's religious reformers and conservatives became increasingly entangled with a struggle between Czech and German 'masters' for control of the University of Prague. In the process, the latter's originally universalist and cosmopolitan ideals were submerged by waves of acrimony, intolerance and xenophobia which King Karel's lineal successor Vaclav IV (1378–1419) endeavoured to exploit to his own political advantage (but was ultimately unable to control).

The new reign began promisingly enough. 'Vaclav encouraged public building, patronized the arts, and . . . expanded the university . . . Czech literature flourished under him' (Bradley 1971: 40). But he allegedly became more interested in hunting and drinking than in discharging his royal (Bohemian) and imperial duties (Betts 1970: 225). Admittedly, his position was not made easier by his younger brothers Sigismund (Zikmund) and Jan or his cousin Jost, all of whom repeatedly intrigued against him in alliance with the Czech nobility. Jost was Margrave of Moravia (and subsequently Elector of Brandenburg). Jan ruled Lusatia. And Sigismund, whom Karel had betrothed to the infant daughter of Hungary's King Lajos I in 1372, eventually became King of Hungary (1387–1437), Holy Roman Emperor (1410–37) and King of Bohemia, having ceded Brandenburg to Jost. Vaclav IV was constantly having to look over his shoulder for fear of being dethroned by these scheming relatives. Although Karel had set in motion Vaclav's election to the position of Holy Roman Emperor in 1376, Vaclav did not attempt to have himself invested with the imperial crown until 1402, by which time the imperial title had been lost to Elector Ruprecht of the Palatinate (1400–10), with the result that Prague ceased to be the imperial capital. Moreover, Vaclav's belated attempt to assert his claim to the imperial crown resulted in his being temporarily taken prisoner by Sigismund, who (abortively) attempted to usurp the Bohemian throne. Perforce, the last sixteen years of Vaclav's reign (1403–19) witnessed a return to 'more or less despotic' rule (Betts 1970: 224–5). The king continued to steer clear of costly and disruptive military engagements, for which he earned some appreciation. But whenever any serious power challenge arose, he invariably wilted. Vaclav IV proved incapable of acting decisively when resolute action was required (Bradley 1971: 40–1). Futhermore, his recurrent attempts to increase royal control over Bohemia's Church and 'to tap its wealth' for his own purposes were stoutly resisted by Archbishops Jan of Jenstejn (1379–95) and Zbynek of Hasenburk (1395–1411) (Betts 1970: 226).

The struggle against German domination of the University of Prague began in earnest in 1384–85. Archbishop Jan of Jenstejn tried to defuse the conflict by proposing a form of power-sharing: certain university positions were to be preserved for Czechs, while others were to be held by Germans. 'Even this solution, which could be implemented only as the existing collegiate masters slowly died off, must have worked as a long-term source of irritation,' exacerbated by 'the self-generating ardours of academic factionalism' (Kaminsky 1967: 60). Moreover, the militant Czech professors began to realize that the university was a potent pulpit, as they mobilized support within the student body, among townspeople and in the country at large (Bradley 1971: 38). The dangerously xenophobic atmosphere flared up again in 1389, when Prague mobs 'lynched some 3,000 Jews and the whole city lapsed into chaos' (p. 40). In 1403, however, the still dominant Germans hit back at their Czech antagonists by accusing them of being adherents and pedlars of the radical ideas of the dissident Oxford philospher and theologian John Wyclif (*c.* 1330–84), whose major religious tracts (written between 1374 and 1384) argued that lay Christians should be able to read and interpret the Bible for themselves and in their own language, downplayed the differences between lay Christians and the clergy, denounced ecclesiastical wealth and luxury, denied papal supremacy and rejected the doctrine of transubstantiation (the belief that the bread and the wine, respectively, become the body and the blood of Christ during Holy Communion). Wyclif's religious teachings had already been condemned as 'heretical' by English bishops in 1382 and 1392. But in 1403 the mainly German congregation of the University of Prague 'raised the stakes' by condemning as 'heretical' a specially prepared list of forty-five purportedly Wyclifite 'articles' (tenets) which came to be known as the 'Forty-five Articles'.

JAN HUS AND THE FIRST REFORMATION

Wyclif's ideas were indeed being studied by like-minded Czechs. Contacts between England and Bohemia had increased considerably after 1382, when King Richard II (1377–99) married the sister of Vaclav IV; and the Czech reception of Wyclifism became a focus of conflict between Czechs and Germans in the University of Prague during the 1390s (Kaminsky 1967: 23–4). According to Betts (1947: 387), 'Czech scholars were ready to pick any bone with their German colleagues, and . . . they found in . . . Wyclif a potent force with which to attack the specific moral and political problems of their own day and their own country.' Wyclif's thought particularly influenced the Czech preacher and professor Jan Hus (*c.* 1371–1415), but Kaminsky emphasizes that Hus was 'only one of the Czechs who, in the 1390s, earned money by copying Wyclif's works and in the process drank in his doctrines' (Kaminsky 1967: 24). Jeronym Prazsky (Jerome of Prague), who did a great deal to publicize Wyclif's ideas in Poland, Hungary and Austria as well as in Bohemia (and was to be burnt as a 'heretic' a year after Hus), was 'the most pugnacious leader of the Wyclifites' (p. 62). Thus during the 1390s the Czech professors subsumed the cause of religious reform and the banner of Wylcif into their 'struggle with the German masters over power and place in the university. The result was the transformation of the Milician movement into what would soon become the movement led by Hus' (pp. 34–5). However, Hus did not simply appropriate Wyclif's ideas. The impact of the latter on the Hussite movement should be viewed, not as cause and effect, but in terms of parallel perceptions of (and responses to) the problems of fourteenth-century Catholic Christendom (pp. 24–5). 'Hus did copy whole pages and passages of Wyclif into his own works', but that would hardly have happened had not 'the heritage of the Bohemian religious movement' *predisposed* him to do so (p. 36). Plagiarism and originality were viewed differently in those days. The cult of originality had not developed and plagiarism was quite commonplace, even in Oxford! According to Betts (1947: 390), the passages that Hus copied from Wyclif are 'not so much evidence of Hus's lack of originality . . . as evidence that the disease from which Bohemia was suffering was general'. Furthermore, Kaminsky points out that Hus copied 'not slavishly but freely and creatively, disposing over the whole Wyclifite corpus with consummate skill . . . and converting the very difficult, often chaotic works of Wyclif into powerful, effective books' (Kaminsky 1967: 36).

Indeed, receptivity to foreign ideas is usually dependent not only on the intrinsic merits of the ideas in question but also on the responsiveness, creativity and adaptability of the receiver, whose importance in the propagation of ideas is often underrated. It is very significant that Wyclif's ideas, as assimilated into the Hussite movement, strongly contributed to the emergence of a country-wide religious reformation which also had substantial repercussions in adjacent Hungary and Poland (Betts 1947: 382–3), whereas in their original forms and setting they merely caused a few ripples on the English millpond. It seems that Bohemia not only provided more fertile soil but also grafted Wyclif's ideas on to various indigenous plants and developed them into more transformative hybrids.

Hus embraced Wyclif's premise that the 'law of Christ' (*lex Christi*) offered an 'absolutely self-sufficient' foundation for the administration of the Church and for all Christian thought and conduct. 'This law is embodied in Scripture, which is superior to all other sources of faith, especially to the traditions relied on by the Roman Church; by means of Scripture, and using our own reason, we can learn God's truth' (Kavka 1994: 132). Hus accepted Wyclif's view that, since the reign of Constantine (312–37 AD), the Church had succumbed to 'the lure of wealth and power and betrayed its mission' (p. 133). For Hus, as for Wyclif, the early Church served as a slogan representing 'everything good' that the medieval Church lacked, whereas 'all who were loyal to the papal and Roman establishment' came to be associated with 'the figure of Antichrist' (Kaminsky 1967: 40). Both Wyclif and Hus wanted the Pope to eschew 'the domination and power involved in jurisdiction' (p. 39). In *De ecclesia* (1413) Hus declared that 'no one is truly the vicar of Christ . . . unless he follow him in every way of life' (Kaminsky 1967: 53). Hus expected the clergy as a whole to renounce wealth and dominion, to lead and influence by example, and to live on alms. He thought the very existence of ecclesiastical wealth tended to divert the clergy from their religious mission and into a preoccupation with the getting of benefices and thus constituted a grave danger. 'Dogs fight over a bone. Take away the bone and the dogs stop fighting' (Kavka 1960: 46). Like Wyclif, Hus expected the powerful (including senior churchmen) to forfeit respect and authority if they fell into a state of mortal sin. Indeed, 'everyone had the right, even the duty, to defy orders that were contrary to binding principles of justice, which were to be judged by a person's own reason' (Kavka 1994: 132–3).

Nevertheless, Hus also diverged from Wyclif in certain fundamentals. He did not support Wyclif's rejection of the doctrine of transubstantiation, nor did he fully share Wyclif's willingness to trust secular rulers to effect a thorough reformation of the Church 'from above'. Like Milic and Janov, Hus believed that a reformation of the Church had to be effected mainly from within and 'from below', on the initiative of the community of truly committed Christian clergy and laity. To that end he favoured a return to the election of priests and prelates by the Christian community (on the model of the early Church), in place of appointments 'from above' (Kavka 1994: 133).

The power struggle and doctrinal disputes between the Czech religious reformers and the Prague Germans acquired more than local significance in 1408, when Ludolf Meistermann (a German theologian from Prague University) went to Rome to press charges of heresy against the prominent Czech Wyclifite, Stanislav of Znojmo. Pope Gregory XII referred the allegations to a French cardinal, who not only agreed that some of Wyclif's ideas were indeed 'heresy' but also ruled that they were not to be debated and that Catholics possessing Wyclif's 'heretical' works (or transcripts thereof) should turn them in forthwith (Kaminsky 1967: 60). Archbishop Zbynik, hitherto sympathetic to the religious reformers, now pressed the Czech members of Prague University into formally condemning the above-mentioned Forty-five Articles 'in their heretical, erroneous or scandalous senses' (p. 61).

Unfortunately the conflict between Czechs and Germans in Prague became fatally entangled with the politics of the Holy Roman Empire and the so-called 'papal schism' of 1378–1417 (between rival Popes in Rome and Avignon). When a number of influential

Catholic cardinals renounced their allegiance to the Roman Pope in May 1408, Vaclav IV grabbed at what appeared to be a God-sent opportunity to reverse the loss of his imperial title (which had been sanctioned by the Roman Pope in 1400), whereas Archbishop Zbynek and the Prague Germans preferred to reaffirm their allegiance to Rome. This brought the Germans into open confrontation with their king, who by force of circumstance (rather than religious conviction) temporarily found himself in the same political camp as the Czech religious reformers, who in turn began to regard Vaclav as a potentially helpful patron. This unholy alliance was consummated in January 1409, when (against the express wishes of Archbishop Zbynek and the Prague Germans) Vaclav publicly supported the Catholic cardinals who had masterminded a Church council at Pisa in an abortive attempt to reunite Catholic Christendom under a new Pope, Alexander V (1409–10), who was intended to stand above the existing papal rivals. The Czech members of Prague University responded by volubly supporting their king. He then reformed the university's constitution in such a way as to give the Czech 'masters' (all of whom were simultaneously priests of various kinds) a three-quarters majority on the governing council, which duly applauded the king's support for the Council of Pisa.

In February 1409 the leading Hussite legal scholar Jan Jesenic wrote a defence of the king's stance which cunningly combined support for Wyclifism and Vaclav's imperial aspirations with a seminal statement of Bohemian patriotism. It opened with a declaration that Vaclav, the 'Ever august King of the Romans and King of Bohemia, has dominion over the realm of Bohemia by divine grace. Therefore, according to the Law of God, the law of the canons and imperial law, it pertains primarily . . . to him to dispose over his realm and to provide for his subjects.' Thus the king had every right to restructure the university, which had been created to serve the needs of his realm; its German inhabitants (the 'foreigners') would just have to like it or lump it (Kaminsky 1967: 68). In the summer of 1409 Jesenic went even further (arguably, too far): 'Just as the Jews conspired against Christ and lyingly accused him before Pilate with false witnesses,' he claimed, so the German masters 'have conspired not only against Christ but against the whole realm of Bohemia and our University of Prague. Not only have they lyingly accused her before the prince of the realm . . . but they have treacherously defamed her to the best of their ability in various kingdoms and provinces . . . They say: the Czechs [*Boemi*] are heretics, are in error and deserving of death' (quoted on pp. 69–70). The Czechs were here perceived as a national community loyal to their king and to the law of God: 'a holy nation, as Jerome of Prague has said, comparable in its relationship with its king to Israel in its relationship with God' (pp. 70, 88). Some Czechs were thus beginning to see themselves as a chosen people. Sentiments such as these prefigured the pressure for proto-national religious autonomy which either accompanied or resulted from the sixteenth-century Protestant Reformations.

In the autumn of 1409, having belatedly decided to recognize and appeal to Pope Alexander V, Archbishop Zbynek complained that 'under the leadership of the Wyclifites, the clergy have been brought to total disobedience' by claims 'that ecclesiastical censures are nothing and that to rule the clergy pertains to the secular, not the episcopal power. In this way they have attracted many of the magnates to their erroneous opinions.' Indeed, they had induced the king to 'seize the temporal property of the clergy' (quoted by Kaminsky 1967: 71). In fact the king had already started confiscating clerical property during his earlier jurisdictional disputes with Bohemia's senior churchmen. But his new alliance with the reformers significantly accelerated the process and encouraged other secular landowners to follow his example. In retaliation, Pope Alexander instructed Archbishop Zbynek to investigate Wyclif's works, 'to prohibit the erroneous doctrines in them, and to prohibit preaching in private chapels – this last a point directed against Hus's pulpit in Bethlehem Chapel'. But Zbynek (over)reacted in 1410 by initiating the 'burning of Wyclif's books which had been requisitioned from members of the university'. The Czech religious reformers resorted to legal challenges in the canonical courts (i) alleging that Zbynek had exceeded his authority and had violated the papal privileges conferred on members of the University of Prague and (ii) pointing out that 'the preaching of the Word of God was enjoined by God's law, the Gospel, and hence could not be prohibited' (p. 72).

Hus defiantly publicized these legal challenges from his pulpit in Bethlehem Chapel and incited his 'flock' to support him. Following the death of Pope Alexander V in May 1410, however, the new Roman Pope John XXIII (1410–17) endorsed Archbishop Zbynek's actions, excommunicated the appellants and summoned Hus to defend himself in Rome. When Hus failed to turn up, he too was excommunicated, in February 1411. This prompted Czech church congregations and street demonstrators in Prague to sing and chant denunciations of the Pope and the Church hierarchy, whom they urged Vaclav to punish. The king duly confiscated some more clerical estates, including those of Archbishop Zbynek, who in turn 'excommunicated the royal officials and . . . imposed an interdict in Prague, which King Wenceslas simply commanded to be disobeyed' (Kaminsky 1967: 73–4). In July 1411 Zbynek appeared to capitulate, conceding that all excommunications and interdicts could be withdrawn and that the matters in dispute should be settled by royal arbitration, yet in September he died while fleeing to Hungary.

In May 1412, however, Vaclav changed sides. In return for a share of the proceeds, the king decided to support a large sale of papal indulgences to finance a papal war against Naples. Even some non-Hussites were scandalized, and the conflict rapidly escalated. In June 1412 Hus held a public disputation on the matter, at which Czech reformers overwhelmingly endorsed his strong condemnation of the sale of indulgences and denounced the Pope as Antichrist (Kaminsky 1967: 80). Hus complained that the Church treated all religious ceremonies as goods which they sold to the faithful: 'One pays for confession, for mass . . . for indulgences, for churching a woman, for a blessing, for burial, for funeral services and prayers' (Macek 1958: 15–16). In August the king not only condemned the above-mentioned Forty-five Articles and forbade his subjects either to speak against the sale of indulgences or to refer to the Pope as Antichrist, but even ordered the execution of three young Czechs who had continued to protest against 'the preaching of indulgences' (p. 81). And in September 1412 the excommunication of Jan Hus was enforced, prompting him to take refuge in the country houses and castles of the Czech nobility (among whom he continued to disseminate his ideas). He also took the opportunity to write his two masterpieces of 'applied Wyclifism', *On Simony* (1413, in Czech) and *De ecclesia* (1413, in Latin). But in 1413 King Vaclav had yet another change of heart. Fearful of the destabilizing consequences of unresolved religious dissension, he sought a mutual accommodation between the warring camps. He failed, however, since neither side was prepared to give ground on the substantive doctrinal differences (Kaminsky 1967: 92–5).

Under pressure from Vaclav's brother Sigismund (who in 1410 had been elected to the position of Holy Roman Emperor in addition to being King of Hungary), a vast Church council was convened at Constance from 1414 to 1417. The council's main task was to re-establish the unity and authority of the Church, which had been impaired by 'the scandalous spectacle of three contending Popes' (Kavka 1960: 47). But the council also summoned Jan Hus to defend himself against charges of heresy. Having received guarantees concerning his personal safety from Emperor Sigismund (who had an interest in resolving religious tensions in his brother's kingdom, which he hoped eventually to inherit), Hus welcomed the opportunity to expound and defend his views in front of senior Catholic churchmen, in the naive belief that they would give him a fair and honest hearing. After all, Hus was aiming not to subvert or to break with the Roman Catholic Church but to rejuvenate it. 'The Hussite idea was conceived in Latin, not Czech, and it was an idea of what the European Church should be' (Kaminsky 1967: 222). Thus 'when the chips were down' Hus was 'not prepared to repudiate the actual Church as the body of Antichrist' (p. 53). At the very least, he sought recognition of a reformed Bohemian Church *within* the Roman communion. Czech radicals were ready to forgo such recognition, but others were not. Indeed, so long as it was withheld 'even the most fundamental reformation in Bohemia would seem to be built on the sands of . . . schism' (pp. 222–3). 'The ideology of Hus encouraged others to revolt, but it led him to . . . submission and martyrdom' (p. 55). He 'staked everything on a public hearing' at the Council of Constance, in the hope of securing the future of Europe's first Reformation (whether as the start of a general European Reformation or as a more local 'Reformation in one country').

In breach of the promises he had received, Hus was interned soon after his arrival in Constance on 4 November 1414 and was eventually put on trial for daring to criticize corrupt ecclesiastical practices and to disagree with high-and-mighty prelates who had not come to Constance in order to engage in difficult doctrinal disputes with an upstart professor from Prague. Moreover, Hus was often put in the position of having to defend not his actual views but those attributed to the Czech religious reformers *en bloc* by their enemies, who erroneously tended to assume that the ideas of Hus and Wyclif were identical. (This confusion was increased by their reluctance actually to read the supposedly 'heretical' writings of either!) Confronted with the famous list of Forty-five Articles, 'Hus responded to most of the articles, "*non tenui nec non teneo*" – "I have not held it and I do not hold it" – and in most cases he was precisely or substantially correct' (Kaminsky 1967: 53).

At Constance Hus admittedly tried to tone down the significance and content of some of his earlier deeds and pronouncements. There is little doubt that 'his powerful preaching against the vices of the clergy' had helped to 'whip up the hatred of the people, who for their part tended to see things in the sharpest possible way'. The effect of his preaching had been 'inflammatory' and had helped to bring people into the streets from 1408 onwards. 'It was thanks above all to Hus's preaching and leadership that the . . . Wyclifite party enjoyed the ecclesiastical support of the people, most of whom could hardly have understood the doctrinal complexities in question' (Kaminsky 1967: 40). Moreover, Wyclif's ecclesiology had implicitly denied 'the actual Roman Church its title to institutional holiness, and hence . . . its final authority . . . Hus here followed Wyclif without significant variation' (p. 38). Hus had at least *appeared* to argue that the Pope was 'Antichrist' (p. 40), that the papal *curia* was 'the synagogue of Satan' (p. 53) and that prelates who exemplified 'not virtue but sin and vice' were 'enemies of Jesus Christ' (p. 38). He was therefore condemned and burned to death at Constance on 6 July 1415.

Nevertheless, in seeking to remove any unnecessary barriers to an accommodation with the rest of Catholic Christendom (if only to secure the future position of Bohemia's reformed Churches and clergy), Hus did not want to be 'encumbered by either his own or his followers' doctrinal excesses of former years' (Kaminsky 1967: 53). In any case, many of the doctrines which Hus actually or allegedly propounded 'were not heretical at all'. Even his denial of the absolute authority of the Pope was not very different from the implicit stance of the Council of Constance, which was the climax of the Catholic 'conciliar movement'. 'Hus was not a great or adventurous theologian.' His prominence mainly derived from the potency of his prose and his preaching, especially when criticizing clerical malpractices. 'He did, to be sure, take up the ideas of John Wyclif, but always with the necessary additions or subtractions to make them conformable to orthodoxy' (p. 35). 'He never ceased . . . to maintain that his programme was orthodox' (p. 5). His aim, like that of so many Christian reformers, was to restore the Church to its original purity rather than to reject, subvert or split it. When accused of preaching that the Pope was Antichrist, he replied that he had merely stated that a Pope 'who sold benefices, who was arrogant, greedy and otherwise contrary to Christ in way of life, was Antichrist' (p. 40). When accused of holding the view that 'To enrich the clergy is against the rule of Christ', he replied that 'clerics may legitimately have riches so long as they do not abuse them' (p. 54).

Unlike the more radical reformers who emphasized individual interpretation of the Bible, individual fulfilment of God's law and individual routes to salvation, Hus was more concerned to bring the condition and the administration of the Catholic Church as a whole into line with the teachings of the Gospels and St Paul (Kaminsky 1967: 79). This was not only the reason why Hus went to Constance but also the main reason why Hus, the 'eponymous hero' of the 'Hussite' Utraquist movement, did not endorse the call for frequent lay Communion *sub utraque specie* until 21 June 1415, just two weeks before his death (p. 134). The more radical Czech reformers had long insisted that this practice was not only prudent and desirable (in order to keep the practitioner perpetually prepared for the Second Coming), and consistent with the practice of the early Church, but also indispensable to individual salvation. They cited John 6:53 ('Except ye eat the flesh of the Son of man and drink his blood, ye have no life in you') and Matthew 26:27–8 ('And he took the cup and gave thanks, and gave it to them, saying, Drink ye all of it; for this is my blood of the new testament, which is shed for many for the remission of sins'). By contrast, Hus never argued that the taking of Communion wine (the chalice) was a prerequisite of salvation (Kaminsky 1967: 127). Hus seems to have accepted the Catholic doctrine that lay Christians need only receive the bread, because (i) the 'real presence' of Christ is integral to both the bread and the wine, (ii) John 6:53 can be interpreted in a more spiritual sense, and (iii) Christ's twelve disciples were prototypes of the clergy, not the laity (p. 11).

Until almost the end, therefore, Hus considered that the Czech reformers' growing insistence on the chalice for lay Christians was merely erecting an unnecessary additional barrier to a strongly desired accommodation with the Catholic Church. In different circumstances a compromise might have emerged, since lay Communion *sub utraque specie* had been common practice in the Catholic Church until the twelfth century (and has remained so in the Eastern Orthodox Church). However, the Council of Constance had been convened expressly to re-establish the unity and authority of the Catholic Church, not to accommodate diversity. On 15 June 1415, therefore, lay Communion *sub utraque specie* was emphatically condemned 'in the name of the whole Church' (Kaminsky 1967: 6). This intransigence signalled to the Czech reformers (including Hus) that 'the Council was not interested in an accommodation' (p. 222). (There are intriguing parallels between the shattering of Hus's hopes and illusions concerning the Catholic Church in June 1415, the collapse of President Benes's hopes and illusions *vis-à-vis* the Western powers in September 1938, and the crushing of Alexander Dubcek's hopes and illusions regarding the Soviet Union in August 1968. Czech leaders have had a history of being cruelly let down by foreign powers in whom they have had faith; the Czechs have rarely been left free to pursue the path of their choice for long.)

When Hus realized that the Council of Constance had thus precluded any possibility of an accommodation with the Czech reformers, he belatedly endorsed lay Communion *sub utraque specie*, not out of a conversion to the idea that it was a prerequisite of salvation but for the sake of greater doctrinal unity within the reform movement and increased consistency with his own calls for a return to the practices of the early Church. He now realized that, if the reform movement was to survive, the reformers would have to close ranks in support of Utraquism. On 21 June 1415 Hus wrote to the only other prominent Czech religious reformer still unconvinced of the need for lay Christians to partake of the Communion wine, urging him: 'Do not oppose the sacrament of the cup of the Lord which the Lord instituted through Himself and His apostle. For no scripture is opposed to it, but only a custom which I suppose has grown up by negligence. We ought not to follow custom, but Christ's example . . . I beseech you for God's sake to attack [the radical Utraquist] Master Jakoubek no longer, lest a schism occurs among the faithful that would delight the devil' (Hus 1972: 181–2).

In the final analysis Jan Hus was burned at the stake not because the prelates at Constance had been able to establish the heretical nature of his views (in their eyes he was guilty until proved innocent) but because he had steadfastly refused to 'recant' views which he did not hold (Kavka 1960: 47), or at least not in the blatantly subversive forms that were ascribed to him. Moreover, having been convened in order to re-establish the unity and authority of the Catholic Church, the council was not prepared to listen to unpalatable truths about the malpractices of the clergy from the likes of Jan Hus or his colleague Jeronym Prazsky, who was similarly burned as a heretic at the council's command on 30 May 1416. Corrupt institutions have often found it expedient to 'silence' internal critics rather than heed their criticisms, and the fifteenth-century Catholic Church was no exception. Indeed, the burning of Jan Hus and Jeronym Prazsky as 'heretics' helped to confine Europe's first Reformation to the Czech Lands and to delay the onset of a wider European Reformation by a century (until 1517, to be precise).

Back in Bohemia, however, the imprisonment, trial and burning of Jan Hus (in breach of the guarantees of his safety) and the council's intransigent condemnation of Utraquism precipitated popular protests and disorder and even incensed the increasingly Utraquist Czech nobility. There were innumerable written complaints and petitions against the way Hus had been treated, not only from the Czech Lands but also from the Polish nobility (Betts 1947: 381–2). In September 1415, above all, 452 Czech nobles attached their seals to eight copies of a letter proclaiming (in the name of the kingdom of Bohemia and the margravate of Moravia) that Jan Hus had lived 'piously and gently in Christ' and that his teachings had been Catholic and free from heresy. At Constance, it stated, 'Hus confessed to no crime, nor was he legitimately and properly convicted of any, nor were any errors or heresies . . . demonstrated against him.' Those who claimed that Bohemia and

Moravia were teeming with doctrinal error were declared to be foul liars and traitors. Finally it warned that the signatories would appeal to a future Pope and that, in the meantime, they would 'defend and protect, to the point of shedding our blood, the Law of our Lord Jesus Christ and its devout, humble and constant preachers, disregarding all human statutes to the contrary' (quoted by Kaminsky 1967: 143). During the same month many Hussite nobles formed a Hussite League whose founding pact stated: 'We shall command that on all our domains and properties the Word of God be freely preached and heard . . . We have also agreed to enjoin all our clergy whom we have under us not to accept any excommunications from anyone except those bishops under whom we live in Bohemia and Moravia . . . But if any of the bishops under whom we live should seek to oppress us or our clergy by improper excommunications or by force . . . we shall not obey them . . . And if anyone should seek to oppress us with any other, foreign excommunications, and should invoke the secular arm in connection with the issuing of them, we ought and wish to be of assistance to each other . . . so that we may not be oppressed' (quoted on pp. 144–5). This was in effect a call for the Bohemian (Czech) Church to free itself from the jurisdiction of Europe's Roman Catholic Church and to become a self-governing body under the protection of the Hussite nobility, who promised to defend it against potential royal and/or episcopal oppression as well as foreign interference. At the same time the University of Prague reaffirmed its support for the late Jan Hus (p. 159).

The immediate response of Bohemia's Catholic prelates, nobles and some royal officials (especially those who were German) was to harass and to threaten to excommunicate 'the itinerant preachers who were stirring the people up with attacks on the orthodox clergy and preaching without the permission of anyone' and the many lay Christians who, in defiance of the council's ban, continued to take Communion *sub utraque specie*. In October 1415 a Catholic League was launched in opposition to the Hussite League (Kaminsky 1967: 147, 157). King Vaclav IV 'was neither for nor against the reform' (p. 223), and Prague's Archbishop Konrad of Vechty (a German) was disinclined either to rock the boat or to bite the hand that fed him. But in November 1415, under pressure from the Council of Constance and the Czech zealot Bishop Zelezny, the archbishop ordered Prague's Catholic clergy to punish the defiant Czechs by refusing to administer any of the sacraments (other than baptism). This 'interdict' backfired: 'With . . . the churches silent and empty, the priests and preachers of the Hussite party could move in and take over' (pp. 158–60). Moreover, since the Catholic clergy were reneging on their religious duties, Hussite nobles, preachers, professors and burghers stepped up the ongoing 'secularization' of ecclesiastical estates, which had accounted for 'perhaps a third of the cultivable land' (p. 149), and deprived many Catholic priests of their benefices (p. 156). During the winter of 1415–16 'a sizeable portion of the Bohemian church organization thus passed into Hussite hands' (p. 161). In February 1416 the Council of Constance retaliated by summoning the 452 Czech nobles whose seals had been appended to the defiant letter of protest against the burning of Jan Hus in September 1415 'to appear before it for judgement' (p. 149). Their failure to show up (whether from fear or defiance) contributed to the decision of the Council of Constance to have Jeronym Prazsky (who had rather rashly come to Constance) burned as a heretic on 30 May 1416. The council also ordered the closure of Prague University (which had originally been a papal foundation) but the university continued to function and to hold defiant meetings (Bradley 1971: 47). Indeed, the heavy-handed actions of the Catholic hierarchy had merely helped to unite Czech religious dissidents behind Utraquism, with the result that 'by the end of 1416 the lay chalice was accepted by all who stood for the cause of Hus', although (like Hus) most of the masters of Prague University 'still shrank from the radical position that Utraquist Communion was necessary to salvation' (Kaminsky 1967: 161).

The feverish tension, excitement and confrontation contributed to the rapid collapse of royal as well as ecclesiastical authority from 1416 to 1418. Hussite and Catholic nobles, peasants and townspeople increasingly took matters (and property) into their own hands. In 1418, however, the new Pope elected by the Council of Constance in November 1417 ordered Vaclav IV to make more effort to reassert royal and Roman Catholic control of Bohemia and even to force the Hussites publicly to approve the condemnation and burning of Jan Hus (Kaminsky 1967: 266). In February 1419, after additional pressure and even threats from Emperor Sigismund (who by then was fully expecting to inherit the childless Vaclav's throne), the king finally launched a concerted campaign to restrict Utraquism severely and to restore former ecclesiastical properties and benefices to their previous Catholic incumbents. From February to June 1419 the Hussites of Prague seemed meekly to submit 'to a barely tolerated existence in a few churches' (p. 269). They retained 'nothing but a portion of the Catholic church-structure'. There was no independent Hussite Church which 'could have maintained itself in competition with a re-Catholicized establishment' (p. 268). It appeared that the Catholics were regaining control over Prague's religious life (p. 272). Catholic church services were finally resumed (p. 268).

Partly in response to these new restrictions and setbacks, in early 1419 Utraquists (and many more radical Christians) began regularly to congregate in remote places, mainly on hilltops, where they received lay Communion 'under both kinds' and listened to fiery (and often millenarian) preaching in an atmosphere of supercharged enthusiasm. This was the beginning of the radical 'Taborite' movement, named after one of the most influential of these religious encampments, located on a hill in southern Bohemia which was then given the biblical name of Mount Tabor. But these hilltop congregations were not merely a means of evading the royal restrictions on lay Communion 'under both kinds' in Prague and other major towns. Early Christian tradition identified Mount Tabor as the refuge in Galilee to which Christ and his disciples withdrew to get away from their persecutors and to pray and contemplate in peace and safety, and from which the disciples launched the early Christian Church soon after Christ's crucifixion (Kaminsky 1967: 282). Appropriately, it was from the new Mount Tabor that Bohemia's radical Christians would relaunch the Hussite movement and turn the tables on Vaclav IV and the Catholic Church in July 1419 (pp. 277–8).

It has long been argued that radical Taborite sectarianism was rooted in older Waldensian traditions which were revived under the impact of the Hussite Revolution (Thompson 1933: 23–42; Kavka 1994: 133–5). The Waldensian sect had been launched about 1176 by a rich merchant, Pierre Valdo of Lyons. Its doctrines reduced and simplified the Christian sacraments (especially for the clergy), encouraged vernacular worship and the use of unordained priests, and repudiated secular power, property, the veneration of saints, relics and images, the sale of indulgences and the Catholic concept of purgatory. Having spread through parts of medieval France, Spain, Italy and Germany, it was flourishing in German settlements in southern Bohemia by the 1320s (so much so that the Bishop of Prague had been obliged to spend eleven years at the papal court in Avignon defending himself and his clergy against charges of laxity and lack of vigilance)

(Bradley 1971: 29–30). But although there is circumstantial evidence that 'by 1415 there were Waldensian groups in south Bohemia who were doctrinally, socially and emotionally apt not only to receive the Hussite message but to . . . extend it and make it the ideology of a revolutionary sectarian movement', we cannot be sure that this is what actually happened, for 'there is no documentary evidence of *Czech* Waldensianism before 1415' (Kaminsky 1967: 178). Thus the origins of popular radical sectarianism in Bohemia before 1419 (the first year for which more information is available) have remained a matter of conjecture and counter-conjecture. The one certainty is that it grew dramatically from late 1415 onwards, engendering serious fears and dangers that the Hussite Revolution could founder on a fatal and/or insurmountable split between moderate Hussites (including most of the Czech nobles, burghers and professors) and the mainly less well-heeled radical sectarians. The Hussite leaders had to work hard to avert this (pp. 161–79).

After some characteristic hesitation, Vaclav IV went back on to the offensive on 6 July 1419. He installed new (anti-Hussite) magistrates (town councillors) in the New Town area of Prague. They forcibly removed parish schools from Hussite control and restored them to the Catholic Church, prohibited mass processions and imprisoned some lay Christians for the offence of taking Communion 'under both kinds'. On 22 July, however, tens of thousands of Czechs attended a 'nationwide congregation' at Mount Tabor, probably in preparation for action to bring Prague back under Hussite control and possibly to make contingency plans for the election of a new (Hussite) archbishop and/or king (Kaminsky 1967: 289–91). On 30 July a mass procession of radical Utraquists surrounded the town hall of Prague's New Town and evicted the anti-Hussite magistrates and other Catholics who were attending a meeting there, throwing about thirteen of them out of a high window to their death and killing several others as well. (This started an enduring Czech tradition of throwing political opponents out of a high window, known euphemistically as 'defenestration'.) Shortly afterwards new magistrates, Hussite 'men of substance' (not impoverished radicals), were elected. They were duly confirmed in office by Vaclav IV, who grudgingly accepted what was in effect a Hussite *coup* reversing the Catholic gains of the previous months. But the Hussite victory was almost immediately put in jeopardy by the death of King Vaclav from an apoplectic stroke on 16 August 1419 (pp. 294–6).

In order to increase their unity, the Hussites and the religious radicals hurriedly promulgated a joint programme, the so-called Four Articles of Prague: (i) unimpeded preaching of the Gospel to everyone; (ii) Communion 'under both kinds' for all Christians; (iii) the clergy to be divested of all worldly power and wealth; and (iv) public punishment of mortal sins, irrespective of a culprit's class or status (Kavka 1994: 152). 'Among the sins to be punished by persons appointed to do so were, in addition to theft, drunkenness and gambling, the exaction of feudal rents and an increase in interest and taxes. This was a plain attack on certain forms of feudal oppression . . . It cannot be said that the Four Prague Articles were a revolutionary programme aiming at the destruction of the feudal social order. Rather, in agreement with the class demands of the Hussite burgher opposition, they endeavoured to reform feudal society. While for the burghers the Four Prague Articles represented a programme of maximum demands, the poor considered them only as the starting point for realizing the revolutionary chiliast programme contained in the Taborite articles' (Macek 1958: 46–7).

THE HUSSITE WARS, 1419–34

Following the death of Vaclav IV on 16 August 1419, Prague radicals 'attacked various churches and monasteries, destroyed the brothels and kept the city in turmoil . . . In the provinces, too, radical Hussites attacked, smashed and burned monasteries' (Kaminsky 1967: 298). The storm centres of radical sectarianism shifted for a time from Mount Tabor in southern Bohemia to Plzen in western Bohemia (p. 299). However, since he was preoccupied at the time with Hungary's conflicts with the Turks and the Venetians, Sigismund instructed the Bohemian nobility to uphold the peace and the old religious *status quo* until the convocation of a Bohemian Synod and Diet, 'whose decisions would be referred to the Pope' (p. 303).

The more moderate or conservative Hussites (including most of the Hussite nobles, officials, patricians and masters of Prague University), who had hitherto advocated co-operation with temporal rulers as a means of reforming the Church and divesting it of undue power and wealth, concluded that they had little option but to submit to Sigismund's instructions and hope for the best. On 16 October 1419, therefore, there emerged 'a union of Catholics and conservative Hussites'. This evidently involved agreement to disagree about the meaning and practice of Holy Communion and to 'coexist in peace until Sigismund could come, take over the realm and procure a papal reconsideration of Utraquism' (Kaminsky 1967: 301–2). Even the magistrates of Prague's Old Town formally submitted to royal authority. The Catholics and the conservative Hussites contended that, while Sigismund had agreed to respect 'the rights and liberties of all estates', he nevertheless insisted on obedience, an immediate cessation of 'church-smashing' and 'unauthorized congregations', and the full rehabilitation of the monks, nuns and Catholic burghers who had been driven away by the previous violence. In addition, 'usurpations of royal authority by the magistrates of Prague were to be stopped' (p. 304). During October many Taborite radicals rumbustiously withdrew from Prague, 'smashing images in churches and monasteries' as they went, and the royalist union hired 'German and other non-Czech mercenaries to maintain order' (p. 306).

In retaliation, on 25 October 1419 Prague radicals led by the professional soldier Jan Zizka attacked and captured the royal fortress of Vysehrad, while in early November there were renewed inflows of provincial Taborites into the capital to reinforce the metropolitan radicals. Contingents from western Bohemia (including Plzen) managed to reach Prague without a fight, but those from the south (from Usti) were ambushed by royalist nobles near Zivhost and suffered heavy casualities. On hearing of this battle, which marked the start of the Hussite Wars, the Prague radicals expelled the royalists from Prague's Old Town and Prague Castle (Kaminsky 1967: 307). On 13 November, however, Prague's petrified magistrates struck another deal with the royalists: the moderate Hussite leadership would surrender the Vysehrad fortress and endeavour to prevent any further destruction of images, churches and monasteries, if the royalists would tolerate Utraquism and uphold 'the freedom of the Law of God in Prague and throughout Bohemia' (p. 308).

Nevertheless, Catholics and royalists took advantage of this 'Prague truce' to hunt down Hussites and Taborites in the provinces. Many Taborites then congregated in 'five cities of refuge' (Plzen, Zatec, Louny, Slany and Klatovy), in accordance with adventist prophecies that at the Second Coming of Christ 'the evil would perish and be exterminated, while the good would be preserved in five cities' (Kaminsky 1867:

310–12). Meanwhile Sigismund did not leave Hungary until early December 1419 (p. 313). Moreover, instead of making straight for Prague, he ordered the Bohemian Estates to attend a Christmas Diet in Brno (in Moravia). There he exacted oaths of obedience, promises that Hussite barricades and fortifications would be dismantled, and guarantees of the safety of the Catholics who would return to Prague (p. 362). However, the abject submission of the Prague patricians, the masters of Prague University and the Hussite nobility to the Emperor-king in December 1419 'inaugurated a period of reactionary resurgence' as Catholic priests, officials and burghers ('mostly Germans') returned to Prague boasting of 'a rosy future' under Sigismund, who 'replaced Hussite castellans and burgraves throughout Bohemia with Catholics' (pp. 314–15). Before long, royalist barons were 'rounding up' Hussites and Taborites 'for shipment to the Germans who operated the Kutna Hora extermination centre' (p. 326). The moderate Hussites of Prague then helplessly looked on with a profound sense of unease and depression which was 'no doubt intensified by the realization that they were silent partners in the extermination of their brethren'. But their rather lame response was to emphasize 'the Christian duty of patient submission', since 'the just man who dies not consenting to evil' would be rewarded in the hereafter (p. 363). This was cold comfort to the many Hussites and Taborites who were equally concerned with survival in the here and now. Indeed, but for Sigismund's monumental blunders, 'it is hard to see how Hussitism could have escaped liquidation, if only Sigismund had moved directly from Brno to Prague: secure in the capital, served by the burgraves of castles and towns throughout the realm, he could have crushed the centres of radical rebellion one by one' (p. 362).

Under increasingly savage persecution, Taborite radicals rapidly turned from New Testament piety, pacifism and withdrawal to Old Testament wrath, belligerence and appeals for divine retribution against Catholics, Germans and royalists (Kaminsky 1967: 320–2). 'Great masses of people were concentrated in the Taborite towns . . . lacking any regular means of support, and imbued with the conviction that everything outside their communities was foredoomed to total destruction. Such a situation could hardly fail to generate violence of the most hysterical kind, to say nothing of the plundering . . . necessary if the "elect" were not to starve to death' (p. 323). Even the Hussite masters of Prague University eventually felt constrained to acknowledge a Christian right of self-defence (pp. 326–7). But there was also 'religious violence, orgiastic and ritualistic as well as practical in character, for its purpose was to purge the world in preparation for . . . Christ's secret coming' (p. 347). In March 1420 the hard-pressed Taborite radicals of Pisek, Usti and Plzen congregated in the disused fortress of Hradiste. The fortress rapidly became the new 'city of Tabor, to which Hussites from all over the realm now came', and communal funds were initiated 'as the foundation of a new economic order, that of communism' (p. 335). The inhabitants were organized into four self-supporting demotic armies (one of which was commanded by Zizka), each carrying out fortification work day and night (p. 336). The armies set about imposing Taborite hegemony over as much of south Bohemia as possible. In the process 'towns, fortresses, monasteries and villages of the enemy were conquered; victims were slaughtered, booty was often burnt, quarter was rarely given. It was the total warfare called for by chiliast military doctrine' (p. 367). Many nearby villages ceased to exist as their inhabitants were drawn into Tabor (p. 336). Taborites took to heart Matthew 19:29 ('And every one that hath forsaken houses, or brethren, or sisters, or father, or mother, or wife, or children, or lands, for my name's sake, shall receive an hundredfold, and inherit everlasting life.') (p. 316). 'But the special feature of Tabor, that which distinguished it from all the sectarian heresies that influenced it, was its existence as a *society* – founded by adventism, animated by chiliasm, but actually supplying basic human needs in a practical effective manner, just as other societies did' (p. 360).

In the critical early stages Tabor's chances of survival were greatly enhanced by the fact that Sigismund was still preoccupied with his preparations for a great military campaign against the Turks. Instead of moving on immediately from Brno to Prague, he proceeded to the Silesian city of Wroclaw, where he had convoked an imperial Diet in order to drum up 'international' support for his projected crusade against the Ottomans. In January 1420, moreover, he implicitly abandoned his shrewd initial policy of keeping the moderate/conservative Hussites 'on side' by pursuing a gradualist strategy of suppressing the Hussite and Taborite rebels by slow strangulation. Instead, he impatiently made it known that, unless all Bohemia's religious dissenters immediately submitted to his authority, he would punish the Hussite community as a whole by force of arms, presumably so that he could then devote his undivided attention and resources to fighting the Moslem 'infidel'. In February 1420 he sent letters to barons, officials, prelates and magistrates all over Bohemia, warning them that anyone who refused either to renounce 'Wyclifism' or to ostracize and hunt down the Taborite congregations would be put to death (Kaminsky 1967: 332). In March 1420 Sigismund not only persuaded the Pope to sanction a Catholic crusade against 'Wyclifites, Hussites and other heretics' but also authorized the execution of the Prague merchant Jan Krasa (in Wroclaw) for refusing to accept a series of articles condemning Hus, Jeronym and Utraquism (p. 364). As a result of Sigismund's impatient obduracy, 'every Hussite would now have to resist, unless he was prepared to accept the articles that Krasa had refused; moreover, every patriotic Czech would feel at least some inclination to fight off the invading hordes of largely German crusaders' (p. 365). Against all the odds, Sigismund's 'stupidity' (p. 362) succeeded (where others had failed!) in rallying the whole of the Hussite camp around the defence of the Four Articles of Prague (p. 366–9).

The Hussite Union established in Prague in April 1420 formalized a (temporary) united front between the metropolitan Hussites and the provincial Taborites. Prague itself came under the control of eight military commanders, who were given 'full authority to take all measures necessary for the defence of the Hussite cause' (Kaminsky 1967: 368). The second manifesto of the Hussite Union (issued on 20 April 1420) reaffirmed the Four Articles of Prague and declared Sigismund to be not the king but the 'cruel enemy of the Bohemian realm and nationality'. He was charged with responsibility for the burning of Hus, the execution of Krasa, the establishment of the Kutna Hora extermination camp, the appeal for a Catholic crusade against Bohemia, and, above all, the defamation of the Bohemian nation with accusations of heresy (p. 370). Even the conservative Hussite leaders 'recognized that the repudiation of Sigismund made it necessary to find a new king', and in April and July 1420 they made tentative advances to Jogaila (Jagiello) of Poland-Lithuania (1386–1436).

In Prague on 27 May 1420, however, radical Hussites and Taborites carried out a 'radical *coup*', whereupon the city magistrates who had previously submitted to Sigismund were deposed and more radical replacements were elected (Kaminsky 1967: 372). The radicals were helped by 'the obvious fact that the right had shown itself entirely incapable of leadership in the most urgent of all matters, defence of the Hussite realm'. The *coup* was followed by a house-to-house visitation of non-Utraquists, who were given the choice of either accepting Communion *sub utraque specie* or exile (p. 374). Puritanical radicals also engaged in attacks on 'Sunday drinking' and on ostentation and unnecessary ornamentation, including 'decorative moustaches' and 'the usual superfluous millinery of the patrician female' (p. 372). Yet in May and June 1420 Prague sent negotiators to Sigismund. 'Had he been willing to promise protection for Utraquism and a generally gracious disposition towards his Hussite subjects, he would have been received with open arms.' Instead, this would-be king 'insisted on total, unconditional submission, dismantling of all defences, and disarmament' (p. 371), while Catholics continued to insist on a renunciation of Utraquism. Indeed, 'it was finally the refusal of the Catholics to debate this point further that frustrated the whole effort' (p. 375).

Sigismund finally arrived in Prague with an army of around 100,000 Catholic mercenaries and crusaders in June 1420. He occupied the castle, had himself crowned by Archbishop Konrad in the cathedral (across the river from the city) and laid siege to the Old and New Towns. But on 14 July, at Vitkov Hill, Sigismund's army was routed by Taborite forces under Jan Zizka. Sigismund returned to Prague with another large army in November 1420, yet it too was routed by Zizka's remarkable Taborites. Hussite and Taborite forces fought off further invasions of Bohemia by Sigismund and his German/imperial allies in 1421, 1422, 1423–24, 1426, 1427 and 1431. All eight invasions helped divert the Czech religious dissenters from their own internal differences of opinion, quarrels and power struggles, which might otherwise have torn the kingdom apart. Czech victories were attributable not only to strength of religious conviction but also to the military wizardry and innovations of Jan Zizka, who pioneered the use of light artillery in open battle. Hitherto, Europeans had used artillery merely as siege weapons. Zizka deftly deployed field guns (howitzers) mounted on fortified wagons which (when the need arose) were rapidly chained together to form almost impregnable circular wagon-forts (*laager*), from within which his gunners and infantry riflemen could freely fire at the relatively vulnerable enemy cavalry and attacking infantry. He also made skilful use of terrain, mobility and surprise tactics. After his death (from plague) in 1424, Taborite armies were led with similar élan by the charismatic soldier priest Prokop the Shaven. (Prokop was a highly educated man from a Prague patrician family. He was nicknamed 'the Shaven' because, in contrast to other Taborite priests, he chose not to grow a beard: Macek 1958: 66.) Their famed invincibility 'struck such terror in the hearts of the crusaders that . . . at Tachov (1427) and Domazlice (1431) the latter no sooner heard the rumble of the approaching wagons and the singing of the Hussite battle hymn "Ye Warriors of God" than they took to flight' (Kavka 1960: 50). Not content with the defence of Bohemia and Moravia, these Czech warriors 'believed that they had a divine mission to take the Word of God to other lands, and their terrible wagon armies rolled destructively through Silesia, Thuringia, Saxony, Bavaria, even in 1433 right through Poland to the mouth of the Vistula' (Betts 1970: 228).

Notwithstanding their military prowess, the Czech religious dissenters were far from united. In August 1420 the Taborites demanded stricter enforcement of the Four Articles of Prague. They sought the suppression of any remaining ecclesiastical wealth, simony, images and relics, the subjection of the writings of the masters of Prague University to close scrutiny and censorship by Christian zealots, and the purging and public punishment of sins such as fornication, adultery, prostitution, usury, fraud, commercial trickery, trafficking in stolen goods, swearing, the sale and consumption of alcoholic drinks, clerical misdemeanours and the wearing of fancy clothes (Kaminsky 1967:

376–7). If the moderate Hussites had fully acceded to Taborite demands Bohemia would have become a Christian forerunner of the present-day Iranian Islamic Republic, a society dominated by bigoted, puritanical and interfering religious zealots. 'The basic unit . . . would have been the congregation . . . Priests would interest themselves in governmental policy, and secular magistrates would provide support for the clergy and also enforce religious discipline' (p. 436). Another crucial division between Taborites and moderate Hussites opened up in September 1420, when the Taborites decisively broke with the Roman Catholic Church by electing their own bishop (i.e. one not consecrated by the Pope, in accordance with the so-called apostolic succession) and by giving their elected clergy much the same rights and status as lay Christians, in line with the Waldensian emphasis on the priesthood of all believers. 'Taborite Hussitism anticipated the Reformation of the sixteenth century in the reinstitution of the direct relationship between Christ and the lay person' (Kavka 1994: 134–5).

For the moderates who stood closer to Hus's own vision and teaching, the 'great dream of a Church regenerated first in Bohemia, then in the world' always remained the 'authentic message of Hussitism' (Kaminsky 1967: 435). They were not mere fainthearts. They still believed in the apostolic succession, i.e. in the anointing of priests by bishops who had been consecrated either by the Pope or by prelates consecrated by him (p. 383). But they were also fearful of the egalitarian (and potentially destabilizing) implications of the election of bishops and other clergy. For political and social as well as religious reasons, they had no desire to burn their bridges with Rome. They even tried to legitimate the Hussite Church and re-establish episcopal authority through Archbishop Konrad, who in fact joined the Hussites on 21 April 1421 (p. 437).

In 1421, nevertheless, the still noble-dominated Bohemian Diet refused to ratify Sigismund's coronation, declared him deposed and formally offered the Bohemian crown to Jogaila (Jagiello) of Poland-Lithuania, provided that he agreed to accept and uphold the Four Articles of Prague. He politely declined this 'poisoned chalice', yet offered his ineffectual nephew Zygmunt Korybutowicz as regent. However, the latter proved unacceptable to the radical Czech dissenters (who demanded a native Czech ruler) and they finally drove him back to Poland-Lithuania in 1427. For want of a generally acceptable king, therefore, the noble-dominated Bohemian Diet became the 'sovereign' power in the land from 1420 to 1436 (and again from 1439 to 1453). It even 'appointed and controlled the consistory of priests and masters of the university which governed the Hussite Church right down to 1620' (Betts 1970: 228). By 1422, indeed, moderate Hussites had regained the upper hand in Prague (Kavka 1960: 50). From then until the final showdown in 1434, Prague and Tabor were rival power centres, each propagating its own religious, political and social programme and seeking to extend its dominion in the realm (Kaminsky 1967: 461).

RIVAL INTERPRETATIONS OF THE HUSSITE REFORMATION AND ITS WIDER SIGNIFICANCE

According to various Marxist historians (above all Josef Macek), religious conflict was largely an expression of (or even a cloak for) class struggle, material objectives and class interests, and a response to an alleged 'crisis of feudalism' during the transition to a monetized economy in fourteenth- and fifteenth-century Europe. In this interpretation religion provided much of the language and imagery in which class struggle and class interests were imprisoned and articulated before the development of the more secular terminologies and ideologies of modern times. According to Macek, the Catholic Church was 'the ideological bulwark and defender of the feudal social order'. Therefore 'whoever attacked the Church was not only a heretic . . . but also a rebel against the bulwark of the feudal social order and against feudalism as such . . . It follows from this that every anti-feudal movement had to take on a religious form . . . The pulpit played a foremost part in confirming the revolutionary ideas and challenges. Only from the pulpit, in those days, could a scholar and thinker speak to the people and explain the causes of existing abuses, only in this way could he enlighten and lead the populace' (Macek 1958: 21). Thus it was no accident that the ideological leadership of the Hussite Revolution was provided by 'preachers who themselves suffered at the hands of the rich and dissolute Church hierarchy and were close to the sufferings of the common people' (p. 19). These are the main planks of Macek's argument that 'the Hussite revolutionary movement was also part of a general crisis of feudalism' (p. 11) and that it was 'the most powerful and effective attack upon feudalism up to that time'. 'It differed from all previous revolutionary struggles not only in duration [1419–37], but also in the wealth and elaboration of its programme and thus in its momentous international repercussions' (p. 13). Seen in this light, 'The Hussite movement created the conditions for the rise of the bourgeois revolutions which ultimately destroyed the rule of feudalism. Before the feudal system could be undermined in any country, its sacred central organization of the feudal lords – the Church – had to be attacked . . . In this sense the Hussite movement holds an important place in world history as the forerunner of the German Reformation' (p. 94).

Paradoxically, not even Czech nationalist historians have made quite such far-reaching claims concerning the 'world historical' significance of the events that took place in the 'small faraway country about which we know little' (Neville Chamberlain) between 1419 and 1437! The Hussite Reformation was, admittedly, Bohemia's biggest and most seminal contribution to European history and the most important forerunner of the German Reformation. Macek has also helped to explain why religious disputes which some secular Western minds now find incomprehensible or even trivial were in fact matters of life and death (and salvation and perdition) for late medieval Europeans. At a time of almost universal religious belief, when law and authority still rested on religious sanction, any questioning of the established Church and/or its doctrines involved a threat to stability, security, authority and obedience. In our view, however, the religious disputes and conflicts which occurred during the Hussite Reformation cannot be reduced simply to questions of class interest, economic calculation and social conflict. Moreover, for reasons which are set out below, it is by no means certain that the Hussite Reformation really did hasten the 'bourgeois revolutions'. It may have enhanced the power and influence of the burghers and the lesser nobility in the short term. But in the long run it fatally weakened their potential ally, the monarchy, and it greatly strengthened the baronial oligarchy. It also gave rise to serious commercial, economic, social and cultural setbacks which, on balance, delayed the 'bourgeois revolution' in Bohemia, not least through the disruptive and debilitating effects of protracted warfare and domestic conflict.

Through a somewhat uncritical (even hypocritical) reliance on Roman Catholic sources which ascribed the secularization of Bohemian and Moravian ecclesiastical property to human avarice, wickedness and lack of scruple, Macek and other Marxists (who do not normally have much truck with the Catholics) have portrayed the moderate Hussites as an emergent propertied class which cynically exploited religious ideas and conflicts for its own material and political benefit. However, while the secularization of ecclesiastical property undoubtedly assisted the emergence of new or expanded groups of private landowners, and while it would be churlish to deny that Hussite doctrine justifying the secularization of Church property must have attracted at least some of the nobles who founded the Hussite League in September 1415, the balance of religious and political opinion within the Bohemian and Moravian nobilities was not entirely explicable in terms of material self-interest and economic calculation. After all, 'any particular baron might have sought his material advantage on either side; indeed, those who stood by Catholicism were recompensed by Church property, either given to them in pledge of payment or simply taken over by them in the general turmoil. By the end of the Hussite Wars both parties of the nobility had proved to be the winners' (Kaminsky 1967: 151). Moreover, against any conclusion that this merely proves that *both* sides were primarily motivated by material self-interest and economic calculation, it should be remembered that barons whose political, social and economic interests were closely intertwined with those of the Church and the monarchy played a leading role in organizing the major letter of protest against the burning of Hus, in forming the Hussite League and in challenging the authority of the Chuch, King Vaclav and Emperor Sigismund, and that in so doing they were willing to put their lives, property and status at risk (pp. 143–5, 149–50). Conversely, many nobles who stood to gain from the secularization of Church property nevertheless remained loyal to the Church, King Vaclav and Emperor Sigismund. Kaminsky cogently concludes that 'no man's motives are pure, the complex of idealism and self-interest in any man's mind is perfectly impenetrable, and every great work of historical construction moves along by enlisting *all* the sources of energy available in the human material, which is of course tainted by sin' (p. 155).

Turning to Czech radical sectarianism, Macek contended that this too was an ideological manifestation of the class struggle, which was more important than the doctrinal labels and definitions (unreliably) applied to it by its enemies. In Macek's view, Taborite ideology expressed from the outset (spring 1419) the class hatred and rebelliousness of those exploited under feudalism. The chiliastic tendencies were not a response to the sieges and warfare of the early 1420s but were present from the start and were authentic expressions of the attitude of the oppressed towards their oppressors. In response to Macek's influential claims, Kaminsky has argued that, while there was an important 'element of actual and class war in the Taborite congregations, which like all mass movements drew largely on the numerous poor, it would be wrong to think of Tabor as essentially but a higher form of class warfare' (Kaminsky 1967: 283). The mere presence of large numbers of poor people at Tabor does not in itself establish that they controlled it (p. 288). In Kaminsky's view, the evidence is 'so scanty' and the exceptions are 'so important as to make the class interpretation more a matter of *a priori* construction than of scholarly inference. To put the point more precisely, there is no evidence at all to show that preexisting class interests *generated* the ideas in question' (pp. 397–8). Kaminsky even quotes a statement by Macek that 'we presuppose the immanent existence of class hatred and rebellion in the thinking of the exploited under feudalism' (p. 288). Unfortunately, Kaminsky himself sometimes lapses into similarly dogmatic *a priori* reasoning in making his case against Macek. 'There are always more poor people than well-off ones, but the latter are usually the ones who lead and prevail.' The poor 'could hardly have taken control away from the educated priests and preachers, the military men and the propertied peasants' (p. 288). The engagement of the Taborite movement in religious and political projects and debates of country-wide importance, able even to influence the course of events in Prague, is in Kaminsky's view *prima facie* evidence that men of substance – the educated preachers, priests, professors, propertied peasants and military men – must have called the shots (p. 289). Nevertheless, Kaminsky has persuasively argued that the Taborite congregations which emerged in 1419–20 were mass movements with a character determined less by the social provenance of their members, who were drawn from all social classes, than by the situations in which they found themselves. 'These new social formations had no ties to the established society' (p. 341). Tabor was 'a religious congregation that had taken on social existence, and as such was a new social formation'. It had 'its own irreducible pattern, its own laws of development, its own specific reality generating its own ideology' (p. 283). Although its ideology of total war was 'no doubt intensified . . . by the class hatred of the poor, their eagerness to settle accounts with the nobility', it was mainly preoccupied with matters of religion and with the struggle for survival in this world and in the hereafter (p. 393).

In locating the Hussite Revolution within the wider (European) context of a 'crisis of feudalism', however, Macek seems to be on stronger and more generally accepted ground. According to Kaminsky (1967: 1), 'the Hussite movement was both a reformation and a revolution, in fact *the* revolution of the late Middle Ages'. Moreover, in the words of an eminent British historian of the Hussite era, 'The Czech reform movement cannot be rightly appreciated unless it is looked at as part of a social, moral and political revolution affecting the whole continent' (Betts 1947: 373). Indeed, notwithstanding the pride of the Czech nationalist historian Frantisek Palacky in the particularity of the Hussite Reformation, the Czechs were experiencing (in an unusually acute form) religious, political, social and economic crises and changes which were afflicting many parts of Catholic Christendom (p. 377). 'The moral code that had been effective for the preservation of a purely agricultural society was proving inadequate to solve the new moral problems presented by an economy of buying and selling' (p. 383). There was widespread scrutiny of established precepts as more than a few critics called into question clerical luxury, ecclesiastical corruption, the sale of indulgences, the ritualistic performance of outward acts of penance and absolution, and the miraculous potential of holy relics and images (pp. 384–5). But only in Bohemia did it result in convulsive, far-reaching and enduring reformation and schism before the sixteenth century. This was attributable in part to the blatancy with which Bohemia's flourishing economy was being 'milked' by Church and crown, in part to the concurrence of its quest for religious reform with the struggle against heavy-handed and perfidious overlords, and in part to the potency of its religious and military leaders.

While the Hussite Revolution cannot be reduced to socio-economic or class conflict, it was undoubtedly an important factor. 'The artisans and working classes in the towns wished to overthrow the power of the wealthy patricians, to secure some influence on municipal administration, and to improve their own economic condition. The villeins on the land cherished the hope of escaping from their irksome duties and obligations. The lowest ranks of the clergy were desirous of ending the humiliating inequality of their social and economic position compared with that of the wealthy prelates, canons and rectors of great parishes' (Krofta 1936: 84). In the short term, many peasants and plebeians benefited from their important role in the Hussite and Taborite movements and from the abolition of tithes and other formerly compulsory payments to the Catholic Church. Furthermore, Czech religious reformers from Jan Milic onwards had emphasized the equality of all Christians in the sight of God and had tended to denounce oppression and demand a more just social order. In contrast to earlier European radicals who had tended to confine their religious and social radicalism to the realm of theory or to limit its application to those who renounced the world, the Czech reformers endeavoured to translate their ideals into practice within society as a whole. 'They broadened the medieval concept of freedom as a personal privilege to be acquired by rank or service or money into a universal moral principle . . . They sought, however haltingly, to bring society into line with the teachings of the New Testament, as they understood them, and with their conception of the life of the early Church' (Brock 1957: 22). Moreover, partly out of a religious desire to make the vernacular Bible and liturgy increasingly accessible to the laity, they promoted popular literacy and vernacular education, for girls as well as boys (Kavka 1960: 52).

In contrast to the rest of East Central Europe, burghers obtained substantial representation in the Bohemian Diet, while the Catholic Church forfeited most of its formerly vast property and power. Czechs also made gains at German expense. Many Germans left Bohemia altogether, both as a result of their loss of control of Prague University to the Czechs in 1409 and as a result of the expropriation of ecclesiastical property and the urban upheavals of 1419–21. The Czechs thus regained majority status in Prague and several other towns (until the 1620s) and Czech became even more established as the language of administration, education, scholarship and worship (Krofta 1936: 85–6; Kavka 1960: 53). During the Hussite wars, moreover, 'there grew the consciousness of national solidarity: the Hussite fight became a patriotic struggle . . . It is heart-felt patriotism that we find in . . . the songs and poems of the time. This led in turn to the growth of an individual Czech national culture' (Macek 1958: 96).

These gains had their down side, however. Patriotism easily degenerated into aggression and xenophobia. Religious and social unrest and recurrent warfare proved disruptive, draining and debilitating, especially to those who had 'no reserves to sustain them through the times of peril and destruction . . . Some peasants had left their lands to join the "warriors of God", and some had been driven from their lands and villages by marauding armies . . . There were more mouths to feed than hands to feed them' (Wright 1975: 242–3). In addition, the substantial increases in the land holdings and power of the nobility, in combination with incipient labour shortages, encouraged land owners to exact more onerous seigneurial dues from the peasantry. Many peasants tried to oppose this, but their resistance eventually evoked increased legal restraints on peasant freedoms in 1487, 1497 and 1500. However, the fact that these measures so closely coincided with the imposition of similar restrictions in other parts of East Central Europe and in Russia suggests that they were also the result of socio-economic and demographic trends which were not confined to the Czech Lands. (See pp. 21, 147, 199.)

Furthermore, as a result of the exodus of Germans, chronic instability, frequent warfare, increased use of the vernacular and diminished use of Latin and German, the University of Prague ceased to be a major cosmopolitan institution of learning. Prague became a more 'parochial' city, while the Czech Lands became somewhat isolated and impoverished, culturally and intellectually, at least until the early sixteenth century. According to Krofta (1936: 87), 'By retarding, and for some time entirely preventing, the influx of new currents of thought from the civilized West, Hussitism checked the development of the Czech nation in more than one branch of culture.' Large parts of Bohemia's artistic and architectural heritage fell victim to the iconoclasm of Hussite and Taborite bigots, who destroyed countless churches, monasteries, paintings and statues. Even more damagingly, violent conflict, Hussite and Taborite philistinism and the loss of royal and ecclesiastical patronage kept artists, architects and craftsmen from the production of new works of art and architecture, obliging many to change occupation and/or emigrate. This temporarily denuded Bohemia of indigenous artistic and architectural traditions and talent (p. 86). On the cultural front, according to Kavka (1960: 52–3), Hussite Bohemia made significant advances only in vernacular education, literature and music (especially hymns and chorales).

The Hussite and Taborite movements and the matching fanaticism and bigotry of their Catholic opponents also engendered stultifying intolerance, a preoccupation with religion and a narrowing of cultural horizons. These legacies 'erected barriers against the cultural and artistic transformations emanating from the Italian Renaissance' (Macek 1992: 215). They concentrated attention on 'the ethical and religious conception of the world and man, and thereby impeded the spread of the classical legacy'. They also delayed the emergence of secular art (pp. 210–11). Whereas the University of Krakow fostered the spread of Renaissance humanism in late fifteenth-century Poland, the University of Prague 'carried on teaching the obsolete curriculum of the Middle Ages' (p. 199). Only about 8 per cent of the publications printed in Bohemia between 1480 and 1526 'could be classified as Renaissance literature' (p. 206), while the eventual revival of artistic activity in Bohemia was not a home-grown phenomenon but an alien 'transplantation' from Italy (p. 212). This was not entirely the fault of the Czechs, however, since successive Catholic crusades against Bohemia (1420–31) and a papal prohibition on foreign merchants from entering Bohemia (1420–95) largely 'sealed off the Czech Lands from the sources of the Italian Renaissance' (pp. 198–9).

THE EBB TIDE OF THE HUSSITE REFORMATION

By the early 1430s the exhaustion, disruption, in-fighting and instability of the realm had heightened the readiness of the Hussite and Taborite leaders to settle their differences with the Catholic Church, with Sigismund, with each other and with neighbouring principalities and kingdoms (Krofta 1936: 74–5). Even the Taborites were suffering from 'the demoralization caused by continued warfare and the watering down of the original idealism by the increasing desire for the acquisition of wealth and plunder' (Brock 1957: 14). However, Marxist historians have especially emphasized the role of class interests in the desire of the Hussite nobility and burghers to reach an accommodation. 'Since the burghers, particularly in Prague, and the Hussite nobility had substantially achieved their objectives (expulsion of the German patricians with confiscation of their property, secularization of Church property and burgher representation in the Diet), they showed more and more readiness to come to terms with Sigismund and the Church' (Kavka 1960: 50). Nevertheless, it should not be forgotten that, for purely religious as well as social and political reasons, moderate Hussites (including Hus himself) had always desired a mutually acceptable settlement rather than an irreparable rupture with the Catholic Church and that (like Wyclif) they had long expected the monarch to be an ally in (rather than an obstacle to) reform of the Church.

In any case, the rout of some 130,000 Catholic crusaders by Czech forces in August 1431 (leading to the slaughter of thousands of crusaders during their headlong retreat) had finally persuaded the Roman Catholic hierarchy that Bohemia could not be brought to heel by force of arms and that more cunning methods would have to be employed. In October 1431, therefore, the Hussites were invited to send envoys to another Church council which had been in session in Basel since March 1431. This was potentially the great long-awaited opportunity to press home the Hussite case for reform of the Roman Catholic Church, and in 1432, after much heated debate, the Diet decided in principle to accept (Spinka 1968: 313). Yet even the conservative Hussites were wary of being ensnared and put on trial for heresy by the Church council. Moreover, Czech radicals contended that the negotiations should be conducted by laymen as well as churchmen, at a neutral venue and in accordance with ground rules agreed in advance. Of course the Church council expected the Hussites to accept whatever terms and judgements the prelates deigned to offer, but the Czech reformers refused to let the council be both judge and jury in its own court. At a preliminary meeting of representatives of the two sides in Cheb (Eger) in May 1432, the Czech reformers agreed to proceed only on the basis that the sole 'judge' in the matters under dispute would be the Law of God (as expressed in the Scriptures and the practices of Christ, the Apostles and the Early Church), while the judgements of any Church councils were to be accepted only in so far as they could be shown to be in accord with God's law (Krofta 1936: 80–1). 'What the Church had denied Hus it now had to grant the Hussites: it was forced to negotiate on the basis of "equal among equals" and to defend its own doctrines by argument' (Kavka 1960: 51). 'For the first and last time in history, the Roman Church recognized the principle of an authority higher than itself' (Kavka 1994: 135).

The fifteen Czech delegates to the Church council comprised a broad cross-section of religious opinion, including Prokop the Shaven and the Taborite 'bishop' Mikulas of Pelhrimov. Yet Prokop decided to keep up the pressure for a settlement by rejecting the council's plea for a truce while negotiations took place, and in early 1433 Taborite forces (allied with Poland-Lithuania against the Teutonic Knights) mounted an offensive through Lusatia and Silesia to Prussia and the mouth of the Vistula (Krofta 1936: 81). At Basel from January to April 1433 the Czech reformers took their stand on the Four Articles of Prague and the Law of God, while Catholic hard-liners fulminated against them and demanded their submission to the council's authority. Unable to break the deadlock, the Czech delegation went home, whereupon the council sent a delegation to Prague to test the water and negotiate directly with the Bohemian Diet and the Hussite nobility in May and June 1433. The delegates from Basel finally recognized that nothing less than the council's acceptance of lay Communion under both kinds and a diluted version of the Four Articles of Prague would satisfy even the conservative Hussites. However, while undertaking to persuade the council to make these minimum concessions, they also decided to pursue a divide-and-rule strategy by concluding a secret agreement with conservative Utraquist nobles to crush the radical Taborites by force of arms at the first opportunity (Krofta 1936: 81). The requisite concessions were approved by the Council of Basel in August 1433 (after fierce debate and assurances that these were only temporary expedients designed to bring Bohemia back into the fold – and then into line). The concessions became the basis of the *Compactata* (agreements) which were willingly approved by moderate and conservative Utraquists and grudgingly accepted as a basis for further negotiation by prominent Taborites on 30 November 1433 (Krofta 1936: 81; Spinka 1968: 315–16).

Desirous of a rapid restoration of 'normal conditions' to their country, conservative Utraquist nobles began to act upon their secret alliance with the Catholic camp in the spring of 1434. They seized control of Prague's Old Town and, at Lipany on 30 May 1434, using the military tactics and the technology pioneered by Zizka, they decimated a large Taborite army (led by Prokop the Shaven) which came to assist the beleaguered Prague radicals. Over 13,000 Taborites (including Prokop himself) were killed. Thus Taborite power and the myth of Taborite invincibility were finally shattered not by foreign crusaders but by Utraquist and Catholic compatriots, in an act of fratricide that mortally wounded the Hussite Reformation (Krofta 1936: 82; Spinka 1968: 317–18). The Utraquists did not lose out immediately, yet their influence was now largely confined to Bohemia and their negotiating hand had been seriously weakened. They were to prove incapable of sustaining their demand for universal Communion *sub utraque specie* in Bohemia when the Catholic Church began to renege on the *Compactata*. Moreover, although the Bohemian Diet and the Hussite clergy jointly elected an Utraquist Archbishop of Prague and two Utraquist bishops in October 1435, these prelates were recognized neither by the Pope nor by the Council of Basel. The Utraquist Church was thus denied apostolic legitimacy and the capacity to perpetuate itself by consecrating its own clergy.

But in 1436, desiring finally to ascend his elusive Bohemian throne, 'Sigismund promised that in property matters the *status quo* would remain, namely, the secularization of Church property and the confiscation of that of the German patriciate' (Kavka 1960: 51). He also proclaimed his own recognition of the *Compactata* and the duly elected Utraquist prelates (as well as his intention to press for their recognition by the Catholic Church), although he simultaneously reassured the Council of Basel that he did not intend to be bound by such commitments (Krofta 1936: 83, 88; Spinka 1968: 318). Since he had never felt bound even by his most solemn commitments, the council had no reason to disbelieve him!

In August 1436 Sigismund finally entered Prague as the acknowledged King of Bohemia. Once installed, however, he lost little time in reneging on the commitments he had made in order to (re)gain this throne. The Utraquist clergy began to be deprived of churches and positions of influence. Since the Hussites had never been formally constituted and recognized as a *separate* Church (precisely because their leaders had repeatedly sought recognition as a legitimate *part of* the Catholic Church), it proved all too easy for the Emperor-king to turn the clock back by replacing the Hussite incumbents of the Bohemian Church with Catholics. Even the Utraquist Archbishop of Prague, Jan of Rokycana, had to take refuge in Hussite strongholds in eastern Bohemia. In 1437, moreover, the Council of Basel declared that lay Communion under both kinds had never been ordained by Christ and that it was solely for the Roman Catholic Church (rather than autonomous groups and individuals) to determine whether, to whom and how it should be administered (Krofta 1936: 88).

In the face of mounting protests against his inveterate duplicity, however, Sigismund decided to leave Prague in November 1437. But he died on 9 December (during his escape to Hungary), after only sixteenth months on his hard-won Bohemian throne. Moreover, since he lacked any direct male heir, the Luxemburg dynasty came to an abrupt end, with its achievements now hanging in the balance. Yet he had amply demonstrated the fragility of the erstwhile Hussite ascendancy.

Sigismund's designated heir to the Bohemian throne was his son-in-law Albrecht II, Duke of Austria, who also became Holy Roman Emperor and King of Hungary and enjoyed the support of Bohemia's Catholics and conservative Utraquists. However, the Hussite majority in the Bohemian Diet preferred to offer the Czech crown to Grand Duke Kazimierz Jagiellon of Lithuania (brother of King Wladyslaw III of Poland), on condition that he agreed to uphold Utraquism and the *Compactata*. This incipient conflict was unexpectedly resolved by the premature death of Albrecht from plague in October 1439, while he was returning from an unsuccessful expedition against the advancing Turks (Krofta 1936: 89; Makkai 1975b: 95). This helped Bohemia (like Hungary) to escape from the Austrian Habsburgs' grasp for the time being.

The Bohemian Diet now appropriated the right to select Bohemia's next ruler and 'hawked' the Czech crown around half of Europe. But Catholic princes (including the Jagiellons) were 'hesitant to take on a heretical and schismatic country', while Bohemia's crown revenues and domains had become so greatly usurped and depleted that 'no one was willing to assume the financial burden of being King of Bohemia' (Betts 1970: 233). However, Albrecht's wife was pregnant when he died, and in 1440 she gave birth to a son known in Czech history as Ladislav 'the Posthumous'. In 1443 the Bohemian Diet decided *faute de mieux* to recognize Ladislav as the legitimate heir to the throne, as did the Hungarian Diet *vis-à-vis* Hungary in 1445. Some magnates were attracted by the prospect that the child king would be unable to exercise or assert any royal prerogatives for several years to come. But until 1453 it proved impossible to get young Ladislav released from the 'custody' of his guardian, the Habsburg Emperor Frederick III (1440–93), who had become interested in acquiring Hungary and to a lesser extent Bohemia for himself. In the meantime, in Bohemia as in Hungary, real power devolved on the landed nobility and the noble-dominated Diet, and this encouraged the emergence of native baronial aspirants to the throne.

During the early 1440s each of Bohemia's twelve counties formed an autonomous noble-dominated militia which sustained 'law and order' and other governmental functions in its own interests on its own 'patch', while Prague remained under the control of the alliance of well-heeled Catholics and conservative Utraquists which had solidified since 1434. Before long, however, there emerged various regional 'unions' of the nobility. In association with Archbishop Jan of Rokycana, who forcefully promoted religious consensus and political unity within the Hussite camp, the political and military union established by Hussite nobles in eastern Bohemia established its ascendancy. In 1444 it persuaded the Bohemian Diet to approve an 'official' compendium of Hussite beliefs and practices, including the following: the maintenance of the 'real presence of Christ' in Holy Communion; purgatory; invocation of the saints; penance; the seven sacraments; fasting; the use of vestments; and the preservation of ancient Church rituals. This doctrinal moderation implicitly condemned sectarian radicalism (Krofta 1936: 90). The Hussite Reformation was in retreat.

THE PODEBRADY ERA, 1448–71

In 1448 Jiri of Podebrady, the able twenty-eight-year-old leader of the Hussite noble union of eastern Bohemia, was strong enough to occupy Prague and put an end to

Catholic and conservative Utraquist control of the capital city. In October 1451 Emperor Frederick III, who was seeking Czech support against the Turks and for his ambitions in Hungary, agreed to the appointment of Jiri of Podebrady as 'governor' (regent) of Bohemia on Ladislav's behalf. In 1452 this title was confirmed by the Diet. In August that year Podebrady led a large army to Tabor and secured its submission (without a fight) to his own authority and to an adjudication in favour of the 'official' moderate Hussite doctrines authorized by the Diet in 1444. Those Taborites who refused to submit (including 'bishop' Mikulas of Pelhimov) spent the rest of their lives in castle dungeons. The subjugation of Tabor was completed in 1453 (Krofta 1936: 92).

In 1452, as a possible remedy for the chronic shortage of duly consecrated Hussite priests, there were also negotiations for the potential admission of the Hussites to the apostolic and (to some extent) patristic Eastern Orthodox Church, which had never departed from Communion *sub utraque specie* for lay Christians. Early in 1452 a Hussite 'convert' to the Eastern Orthodox Church arrived in Bohemia with a letter 'inviting the Czechs to join that Church and promising to provide them with clergy and bishops'. For its part, Byzantium was desperately seeking Christian allies and assistance against the Turks, who were then preparing to capture Constantinople. But potentially insurmountable difficulties arose when the Byzantines also sought union with the Roman Catholic Church (which had repeatedly condemned Utraquism), and the fall of Constantinople in May 1454 finally put paid to attempts to effect a 'union between the Hussites and the Eastern Church' (Krofta 1936: 94). This failure was all the more unfortunate in view of Byzantium's role in bringing Christianity to Bohemia in the first place. It also obliged the Hussites to continue their attempts to minimize their doctrinal differences from Roman Catholicism, if only to make it easier to persuade sympathetic, obliging or 'flexible' Italian Polish or Hungarian bishops to disobey their Church by ordaining a few Hussite priests.

In 1453 Emperor Frederick III finally released Ladislav 'the Posthumous', who agreed to accept the *Compactata*, to seek papal recognition of Archbishop Rokycana and to extend Podebrady's 'governorship' of Bohemia for another six years, in order to secure acceptance as King of Bohemia. But later that year the thirteen-year-old Habsburg was also recognized as King of Hungary, which was then under increased threat from the Turks following the fall of Constantinople. For this and other reasons Ladislav was absent from Bohemia from November 1454 to September 1457, leaving Podebrady in virtually undisputed control of the Czech kingdom. However, in order to escape the vicious power struggle which followed the death of Janos Hunyadi in August 1456, King Ladislav returned from Hungary to Bohemia in the autumn of 1457, bringing young Matyas Hunyadi with him as a hostage. While imprisoned in Prague, Matyas Hunyadi became engaged to the daughter of Jiri of Podebrady, who secured Hunyadi's release. In November 1457, moreover, Ladislav was struck down by plague. (It was the second time that plague had frustrated Habsburg designs on Hungary and Bohemia.) Furthermore, the Hungarian Diet's decision to elect Matyas Hunyadi to the Hungarian throne in January 1458 was emulated in the Bohemian Diet's election of Podebrady to the Bohemian throne in March 1458. In addition, Podebrady supported his daughter's marriage to Matyas Hunyadi and, in return, asked his new son-in-law to 'lay on' two Hungarian bishops to officiate at (and thus legitimize) Bohemia's coronation ceremony. As the price of their co-operation, however, the Hungarian bishops required Podebrady and his consort to take an oath 'to the effect that they would uphold obedience to the Papal See and, in agreement with Rome, lead their subjects away from all error'. Many Catholics took this to be an act of outright submission to the Catholic Church. But the next day Podebrady secretly swore to preserve 'all the liberties' of his realm. He remained a lifelong Hussite and defender of the *Compactata* (Krofta 1936: 96–7, 102).

Podebrady was invested with the regalia in 1459 by Emperor Frederick III, who was seeking his support both in Hungary and in imperial affairs. Even Pope Calixtus III (1455–58) had been prepared to recognize Podebrady for the sake of greater unity against the Turks. This helped the new king to quell resistance to his accession in Moravia (1459–60) and in Silesia (1459–60). During the early 1460s, moreover, Podebrady championed the creation of a league of Christian rulers (to resist the Turks, reform the Holy Roman Empire and submit religious, political and territorial disputes to a court of international arbitration). This project attracted international support. It even contributed to the conclusion of Bohemian alliances with the rulers of France, Poland-Lithuania and Austria (Krofta 1936: 97–9). At the same time, perhaps in order to show off his abhorrence of radical 'heretical' sectarianism, Podebrady took repressive action against the fast-growing Unity of Brethren, which had emerged during the late 1450s and was influenced by the radical Janovite, Taborite and Waldensian traditions and, above all, the pacifist writings of Petr Chelcicky (*c*. 1390–1460).

In 1462, with the approval of the Bohemian Diet, Podebrady made fresh overtures to Rome, seeking recognition and reconciliation on the basis of the *Compactata*. Pope Pius II (1458–64) replied by totally condemning lay Communion *sub utraque specie*, by repudiating the *Compactata* and by declaring that he could not recognize Podebrady as King of Bohemia until he had 'eradicated all error from his kingdom'. In response Podebrady imprisoned a papal envoy and proclaimed that the Podebrady family would be prepared to fight to the last for Utraquism. The Pope retaliated by taking the Catholic Silesian town of Wroclaw under papal protection in 1463 and by summoning Podebrady to Rome to face charges of heresy in 1464. This encouraged Czech Catholics to form a rebel League of Zelena Hora in 1465 (Krofta 1936: 98–9). Pope Paul II (1464–71) 'raised the stakes' even higher by declaring Podebrady to be guilty of confirmed heresy and by relieving his subjects of their duty of obedience towards him.

In 1468 the League of Zelena Hora received military support from Matyas Hunyadi, whose relations with Podebrady had soured since the death of his first wife (Podebrady's daughter) in 1464. Bohemia was thereby embroiled in a ten-year war with Hungary (1468–78). Podebrady initially lost Moravia, yet in 1469 he succeeded in capturing Hunyadi and the invader's armies. But Podebrady too trustingly set his son-in-law free in return for a solemn promise to reconcile the papacy to Bohemia on the basis of the *Compactata*. Instead, Hunyadi perfidiously persuaded the League of Zelena Hora to recognize himself as the new King of Bohemia, and the war resumed. Thereupon, with the approval of the Bohemian Diet, Podebrady obtained Polish-Lithuanian support by offering the succession to his Bohemian throne to the Jagiellon Crown Prince Wladyslaw in place of his own son, who had not gained widespread favour. Consequently, two months after Podebrady's death in March 1471, a Bohemian Diet unanimously elected this Jagiellon prince to be King Vladislav II of Bohemia (1471–1516).

Podebrady is sometimes seen as the Oliver Cromwell of the Hussite Reformation. He has even been accredited with teaching his contemporaries 'to distinguish between religion and politics' in such a way as to pave the way for 'the modern view of relations between Church and State' (Krofta 1936: 102). However, while he was undoubtedly a man of considerable talent and some valuable qualities, he ultimately failed in his endeavours to stabilize his realm by reconciling it with the papacy on the basis of the *Compactata*.

THE JAGIELLONS AND THE CONSOLIDATION OF BOHEMIA'S BARONIAL OLIGARCHY, 1471–1526

The accession of Vladislav II to the Bohemian throne in 1471 (in defiance of Matyas Hunyadi's rival pitch for it) was not conducive to a quick conclusion of the war between Bohemia and Hungary. As additional complications, the papacy backed the Hunyadi bid for the Bohemian crown and excommunicated Vladislav II, who was in turn offered the Hungarian throne by disaffected sections of the Magyar nobility. The subsequent military and political stalemate fostered a belief that the contest could be concluded only by temporary partition of the territories of the Bohemian crown between the rival claimants. Negotiations began in 1475 and culminated in the Treaty of Olomouc (1478), under which Matyas Hunyadi kept Moravia, Silesia and the Lusatias (Upper and Lower), while Vladislav retained Bohemia proper, and both rulers assumed the title of King of Bohemia!

This unstable and therefore hazardous outcome was resolved in 1490 by the death of Matyas Hunyadi (who had meanwhile been sharpening his claws on Austria). The Magyar magnates, who were generally averse to strong and wilful rulers, awarded the vacant Hungarian throne to Vladislav (as Ulaszlo II of Hungary) in preference to Matyas Hunyadi's son Janos (who became King of Bosnia and perished while fighting the Turks). Vladislav (Ulaszlo) II pleased his baronial sponsors by beating off a Habsburg invasion of Hungary, by restoring Vienna and eastern Austria to Habsburg control, by reuniting the territories of the Bohemian crown, and by consigning Hungary's powerful 'Black Army' to destruction by the Turks and by Magyar barons (who regarded it as an instrument of royal absolutism). Indeed, Vladislav's instinctive reaction to whatever his backers and advisers proposed was to say 'Oh, very well,' earning him the nickname of 'King Very Well'.

Even though Vladislav II agreed to uphold the *Compactata* and to seek papal recognition of the Utraquist wing of the Bohemian Church, the accession of a formally Roman Catholic monarch in 1478 led to a resurgence of Catholic power, influence and activity in the Czech Lands. Bohemia's Catholic consistory, which had taken refuge in Plzen from 1467 to 1478, now returned to Prague and, in alliance with Catholic nobles, Germans and monastic orders, set about winning people of all ranks back to Catholicism. This attempted 'counter-reformation' generated mounting tensions which finally erupted into violent conflict in 1483. Prague's Utraquists again formed a Hussite League which temporarily drove their Catholic opponents (and various 'defectors from Utraquism') out of the city. In 1485, however, the two sides reached an historic agreement (at Kutna Hora) to maintain (i) the Compactata, (ii) the existing 'share-out' of churches and (iii) the right of individual lay Christians to choose to take Communion either under one kind or both kinds in each others' churches, for a period of thirty-two years. This was done in order to avert the danger of a return to civil war and/or foreign military intervention (Krofta 1936: 109–11). Remarkably, the Treaty of Toleration (Kutna Hora) was repeatedly renewed until the suppression of Utraquism by the Habsburgs in 1627 (Brock 1957: 19). Freedom of worship was established 'even for those of servile status' (Kavka 1994: 136), despite the gradual deterioration of the socio-economic position of many peasants from 1487 onwards (Wright 1975: 242–3).

Under this protective shield, paradoxically, the Utraquists experienced an acute loss of élan. The resultant spiritual vacuum was partly filled by the 'separatist' Unity of Brethren, whose support had formerly been confined mainly to the former Taborite districts of southern Bohemia. The Unity of Brethren now retreated from earlier renunciations of worldly power, positions and wealth and spread to Prague and towns in northern Bohemia. It boasted between 300 and 400 'congregations' by 1500, although by then it too had fallen under the influence of wealthy, learned and powerful patrons who relaxed its former asceticism (Krofta 1936: 112). In 1503, however, the Catholic and Utraquist 'establishments' entered into an unholy alliance to persuade Vladislav II to proscribe the Unity of Brethren, who were subjected to a wave of more violent persecution in 1508. This not only served notice that the 1485 Treaty of Toleration (Kutna Hora) applied only to relations between Catholics and Utraquists, but also induced many Brethren to take refuge in more tolerant Moravia and Poland-Lithuania (Bradley 1971: 63–4). With this notable exception, however, the rest of Vladislav's forty-five-year reign in Bohemia was distinguished by a relative absence of religious strife and by freedom from foreign invasions and from involvement in either civil war or foreign wars. By the 1520s, moreover, less than 10 per cent of the population were Roman Catholic, although Catholics constituted somewhat higher percentages of the population in Moravia, Silesia and the Lusatias (Kavka 1960: 61).

After 1490 Vladislav II chose to reside in Buda (in Hungary) and rarely visited his Czech domains. This significantly reinforced baronial domination of the Bohemian and Moravian Diets and the ongoing accumulation of power, property and privileges in the hands of the major Bohemian and Moravian landowners, to the detriment of the peasantry, the lesser nobility, the Church and the towns. 'All high offices were held by members of a handful of the most powerful families. The big nobles launched an attack on the political status of the burghers and tried to expel them from the Diets. While their efforts proved unsuccessful, the burghers had to give up many economic advantages' (Kavka 1960: 56). Large landowners also established more and more carp ponds and breweries on their estates, expanded sheep-breeding, and moved into silver and tin mining, especially after the discovery of huge silver deposits (even larger than those of Kutna Hora) at Jachymov during the 1500s. These developments inexorably tipped the scales of power and wealth even more in the landowners' favour and facilitated the displacement of peasants from the most profitable land, the restriction of peasant mobility and the augmentation of seigneurial dues. At the same time, there was growing production of textiles (such as hats and linen cloth) under the rural 'putting out' system. This involved the exploitation of the underemployed labour of peasants in their own homes by commercial middlemen – to the detriment of the towns, whose craft industries stagnated (pp. 57, 61–2).

This baronial ascendancy was augmented yet again in 1516 by the accession of Vladislav's ten-year-old son Ludvik, who simultaneously became King Lajos II of Hungary and (like his father) preferred to reside in Buda. He visited Bohemia only once (for his coronation in 1522), before being mortally wounded while fighting the Turks at the fateful battle of Mohacs in 1526 (Bradley 1971: 62). It would be misleading, however, to attribute the baronial ascendancy mainly to the weakness, negligence and absenteeism of the Jagiellon kings of Bohemia. In retrospect, and in apparent contradiction of some Marxist claims that the Hussite Revolution hastened the rise of a powerful bourgeoisie, it is clear that one of the major unintended (and unexpected) consequences of the Hussite Reformation and its aftermath was the halting of earlier trends towards the consolidation of a proto-national monarchical regime, which, in alliance with the towns and the lesser nobility, might have been strong enough to curb the growth of the power, property and privileges of the landed nobles. In the event, the larger landowners of Bohemia and Moravia were greatly strengthened and enriched by (i) the secularization of Church lands, (ii) the erosion and eventual breakdown of royal authority between 1408 and 1420, and (iii) the long spans (1420–36, 1439–53 and 1490–1526) during which the territories of the Bohemian crown were in practice ruled by their noble-dominated Diets, in the physical absence of the putative king (whether his name was Sigismund, Ladislav, Vladislav II or Ludvik). The development of the Bohemian polity was thus deflected from the incipient 'Western European' trajectory of the thirteenth and fourteenth centuries. It switched to a more typically 'East Central European' trajectory in which the largely unchecked growth of baronial power, property and privilege gradually emasculated central ('royal') government (and the development of towns and independent small or medium-sized farmers) and eventually left the country incapable of fending off 'foreign' absolutism (Habsburg absolutism in the cases of Bohemia and Hungary; Tsarist, Hohenzollern and Habsburg absolutism in the case of Poland-Lithuania). By 1526, however, the baronial ascendancy was so strongly established in Bohemia and Hungary that it took the Habsburgs nearly a century fully to assert their authority and control over Bohemia and more than three centuries to do so in Hungary. Viewed in this light, the superficial perceptions that Bohemia and Hungary fully succumbed to 'foreign' absolutism much earlier and much more easily than did Poland-Lithuania are somewhat misleading. In reality the baronial power which had emasculated central ('royal') government in Bohemia and Hungary, eventually rendering both these realms rather susceptible to Habsburg domination, also became the major post-1526 bulwark against full-blown Habsburg absolutism (until the 1620s in Bohemia and until the 1850s in Hungary).

THE TRANSITION TO HABSBURG RULE, 1526–64

In 1526 the Bohemian Diet nevertheless voted to confer the vacant Bohemian throne on Ferdinand of Habsburg (1526–64). He was already the ruler of Austria, was about to become the nominal King of Hungary and, as the so-called 'King of the Germans', was next in line for the imperial crown (which he eventually inherited from his brother, Emperor Charles V, in 1556). The Bohemian Diet turned to Ferdinand at least partly because he belonged to an ascendant European dynasty which looked capable of rehabilitating Bohemia internationally and of protecting it against the steadily advancing 'Turkish menace'. As the figurehead of an increasingly stable, efficient and systematic royal administration in Austria, moreover, Ferdinand held out the prospect of an end to the arbitrary, erratic and semi-anarchic rule which Bohemia had experienced between 1471 and 1526 under the Jagiellons (Bradley 1971: 67–8). On the other hand, there was every likelihood that Ferdinand, as ruler of Austria and parts of Hungary and as 'adjutant' on imperial matters to Charles V, would be yet another absentee monarch. But for many of Bohemia's magnates that was probably part of the attraction. If they thought that would make him a 'soft touch', however, they seriously miscalculated.

Eventually, Ferdinand bullied and cajoled the Bohemian Diet into surrendering its vaunted right freely to elect the king of Bohemia. Ferdinand claimed the Bohemian throne not by dint of having been personally *elected* to it, but by virtue of the (implicitly binding) mutual succession and intermarriage pacts concluded in 1505 and 1515 between Emperor Maximilian I (1493–1519) and Vladislav (Ulaszlo) II, at least partly out of fear of the 'Turkish threat'. The succession to the Bohemian throne was supposed to remain in the possession of Ferdinand's lineal descendants, and the Bohemian Diet would therefore merely 'confirm' (rather than 'elect') the future kings of Bohemia. Not surprisingly, however, the permanence and the validity of this concession (obtained under duress) were to be repeatedly contested by later Bohemian Diets, when they were required to 'confirm' some distinctly unappetizing Habsburg heirs to the Bohemian throne.

In 1527, moreover, Ferdinand began to create powerful new institutions through which to reduce territorial and especially urban autonomy and to foster more co-ordination of policies throughout his various realms: the Secret Council (*Geheimer Rat*), with extensive jurisdiction over both foreign and domestic policies; the Court Chamber (*Hofkammer*), responsible for the collection and management of crown revenues; and the Court War Council (*Hofkriegsrat*), which served as a supreme 'ministry of defence for the German and Austro-Bohemian-Hungarian Habsburg lands' (Kann 1974: 30). Such measures were only partly a response to the exigencies of warfare against the Turks. They also expressed a strong desire to control for control's sake and to muzzle dissent.

In 1546–47, partly in reaction to Ferdinand's restrictive centralizing measures, Bohemian Utraquist and Protestant nobles and townspeople staged a major armed uprising in support of the German Protestant Union and against the Habsburgs' inchoate Catholic absolutism and 'strong-arm' attempts to stamp out the Reformation which was sweeping through their realms. Ferdinand's forceful yet controlled suppression of this uprising paved the way for further measures to restrict municipal and rural (local) autonomy in both Bohemia and Moravia by systematically subordinating lower bodies to higher ones (with a new supreme Court of Appeal at their apex). These actions were accompanied by more severe restriction and repression of religious nonconformity, driving many Brethren to take refuge in Moravia and Poland-Lithuania, and the surrender of the Diet's role in the confirmation of ecclesiastical appointments (whether Catholic or Utraquist). In 1562 Ferdinand appointed a Roman Catholic to the position of Archbishop of Prague and then dismissed the Utraquist consistory and appointed a new one of his own choosing in an abortive attempt to force the Utraquists to submit to the new archbishop (Bradley 1971: 69–71). By the time of Ferdinand's death in 1564 the kingdom of Bohemia was rather more centralized than it had been in 1526.

In spite of these political shenanigans, however, the kingdom of Bohemia did not immediately become part of a Habsburg Empire, any more than earlier dynastic unions with the larger kingdom of Hungary had made it part of a Hungarian empire (or than having a Jagiellon king had made it part of the Polish-Lithuanian Commonwealth). Even the elevation of King Ferdinand to the position of Holy Roman Emperor in 1556 did not in itself reduce Bohemia to the status of a Habsburg 'colonial possession'. On the contrary, the Habsburg Emperor and aesthete Rudolf II (1576–1612) would emulate Emperor Karel of Luxemburg (1347–78) by making the magnificent city of Prague his imperial capital, culturally and intellectually as well as politically. Not until the utterly devastating conquest and subjugation of Bohemia by the Habsburgs during the 1620s can it be said that Bohemia truly became a quasi-colonial possession of an emerging Habsburg Empire. After 1526, nevertheless, the politics of the kingdom of Bohemia were inextricably bound up with those of the Austrian Habsburg crown lands.

UNFINISHED BUSINESS: THE SECOND REFORMATION

During the early 1520s, not surprisingly, the kingdom of Bohemia began to be influenced by the doctrines of the German Protestant reformer Martin Luther, who occasionally wrote to prominent Utraquists and the 'citizens of Prague'. Moreover, although Luther's Catholic opponents warned him against treading the same path as 'the heretic Hus', he publicly acknowledged the importance of Hus's teaching. Indeed, the Hussite Reformation had established a precedent and a role model which Europe's Protestant reformers 'could not but take into account', and lay Communion *sub utraque specie* was in due course adopted by 'practically all the reformed churches' (Kavka 1994: 140). During the 1520s, significantly, there were two new editions of *De ecclesia* (1413), Hus's major work, written in Latin for a cosmopolitan European readership (rather than in Czech for a local one).

However, the sixteenth-century Protestant Reformation differed from the earlier Hussite Reformation in several major respects. The main emphasis of the religious reformers in fourteenth- and fifteenth-century Bohemia was on the perceived need to reform and simplify the institutions and practices of the Church in an endeavour to bring them closer to the perceived spirit, teachings and morality of the Gospels, the Sermon on the Mount, the Last Supper and the early Church. Thus the Hussites discounted the role of icons, relics and indulgences, but they developed no doctrine of justification (salvation) by faith. They simply urged Christians *collectively* to try to live like Christ and in strict accordance with his received teachings. The later Protestant Reformation, by contrast, placed much greater emphasis on matters of theology, on the Letters of St Paul, on rejection of the Catholic concept of purgatory (and all that went with it) and, above all, on *individual* justification (salvation) by *faith*.

On the other hand, both Reformations featured radical Waldensian, millenarian and eschatological currents, belief in the 'priesthood of all believers' and in the ultimate authority of the Holy Scriptures, advocacy of the vernacular and popular education, and various versions of predestination (conceptions of 'the elect'). These do not seem to have been major areas of contrast. Both clearly perceived that administrative reforms on their own could not remedy spiritual barrenness, and that 'good works' had to be supplemented by the gift of 'grace'. But for the Czech Utraquists 'grace' had to be attained primarily by means of the frequent collective, miraculous, sacramental renewal of both clergy and laity through active participation in Communion under both kinds, whereas for the later Protestant reformers it was to be attained primarily by means of spiritual rebirth through faith and commitment to the Lord. For Utraquists, in other words, neither faith nor 'good works' would suffice; grace and salvation could be ensured only by frequent sacramental consumption of both the bread and the wine, whose significance was miraculous and mystical as well as spiritual. In contrast to Protestantism, therefore, Utraquist grace and salvation were not primarily a matter of getting one's theology right, but rather of proper and frequent administration of the Eucharist as a full and inclusive re-enactment of the Last Supper, in strict accordance with Christ's command. It was in this respect that Czech Utraquism differed most fundamentally from Protestantism as well as Catholicism (Betts 1931: 347–50).

Rather than simply reinforcing the legacies of the Hussite Reformation, Lutheran (and later Calvinist) influences introduced further elements of diversity, complexity, fragmentation and friction into the religious, political and cultural mosaic of the Czech Lands.

Ironically, in view of their earlier hostility to Hussitism and all its works, the groups which were most immediately receptive to Lutheran ideas were the German communities of Silesia and the Lusatias, the predominantly German towns of Moravia, and the largely German-inhabited northern borderlands of Bohemia and Moravia (Kavka 1994: 141). The Germans, who had always been 'the backbone of the Catholic Church' in the Czech Lands, now went over in droves to Lutheranism (Bradley 1971: 64). In part, these Germans proved responsive to Lutheran ideas precisely because they had been largely bypassed by the (manifestly Czech) Hussite Reformation, but also because Luther was a German who often addressed fellow Germans in their own tongue. As with the German minorities in Poland-Lithuania and in Hungary, Lutheranism helped to strengthen their specifically German identity. It became a badge of 'Germandom' to a far greater extent than Luther perhaps had ever intended.

In addition, many Moravian, Silesian and Lusatian Czechs had remained Roman Catholic, and their lands had not undergone nearly as much secularization of Church property and suppression of ecclesiastical corruption and abuses as Bohemia had. They had tended to regard Hussitism, Utraquism and Taborite sectarianism as quintessentially Bohemian rather than as pan-Czech phenomena. Under Lutheran influence, however, some of them belatedly accepted that their Catholic ecclesiastical institutions and clergy stood in need of reform.

By contrast, the Utraquist Czechs of Bohemia were not widely attracted by Lutheranism at first. After all, they had already been through a momentous Reformation of their own, their feelings towards which were of great pride and/or attachment. Church land had already been secularized and the most glaring ecclesiastical corruption and abuses had already been quashed. 'Since the main tasks of the Reformation had already been fulfilled . . . the socio-religious motivation from which the German and Swiss Reformations arose was absent . . . The dissatisfaction of the poorer classes in the population, especially the peasants, which was at the root of the German Peasants' War and the radical currents of the Reformation in general, had already found a vent in sects of the Taborite–Waldensian kind.' Furthermore, 'post-revolutionary fatigue' and the allegedly 'more shallow character of religious life in the Utraquist Church' had arguably left the Hussite burghers, clergy and nobility somewhat 'insensitive to those distressing questions about whether salvation was assured, to which the Reformation of the sixteenth century provided a welcome answer' (Kavka 1994: 141). At a more basic level, earlier German enmity towards the Hussite Reformation made many Czechs initially look askance at a Reformation masterminded and propagated by Germans. Thus, when (under Lutheran influence) the Utraquist general assembly approved a series of 'doctrinal and administrative innovations' in 1524, conservative Utraquists in Prague reacted 'against this foreign corruption' of their established faith and practices. 'Rioting and lynching forced the Utraquist leaders to abandon their reforms,' and many Utraquists 'joined the Catholics in demanding the suppression of the German faith' (Bradley 1971: 64). Thus, even in Bohemia, the Habsburgs were not alone in their struggle against Lutheranism and related forms of religious nonconformity. Indeed, although the wording of King Ferdinand's coronation oath committed him to 'encourage and protect' Bohemia's two recognized churches, Catholic and Utraquist, that still left him free to step up the persecution of the unauthorized denominations and sects, such as the Unity of Brethren, Lollards, Anabaptists and Lutherans (p. 70).

Before long, however, the Czech Utraquists began formally to split into 'old' and 'new' branches. 'The new Utraquists were openly Protestant and evangelical' (Bradley 1971: 70). Indeed, by referring to their Hussite precursors as 'evangelicals', the new Utraquists and the Unity of Brethren postulated 'a continuity of tradition, a clear progression from Hus and Jerome of Prague, through the Bohemian Brethren to Lutheranism' (Tazbir 1994: 171). Moreover, the gravitation of the 'reborn' Unity of Brethren towards Lutheranism (and later Calvinism) had been heralded by the teachings of Lukas of Prague between 1495 and his death in 1528. 'The reform of the Church on the principle of "the law of Christ", as determined by Wyclif, Hus and most determinedly by the Taborites, appeared to Lukas merely as a means, not an end . . . According to Lukas, faith, as the only way to redemption, is required by God more than works. He thus anticipated Luther's teachings . . . Unlike Luther, however, Lukas did not reject works, holding them as the inseparable supplement to faith and its telltale signs' (Kavka 1994: 138–9).

Spurred on by competition from the Brethren and by the fresh vitality of Lutheranism, which also offered an end to the Hussites' sense of beleaguered isolation in Europe, Czech Utraquism similarly gravitated towards the Protestant 'camp'. In 1546–47 some 'old' as well as 'new' Utraquists rose up in support of the German Protestant Union's defiance of King Ferdinand's brother, Emperor Charles V, and 'dared to send a small military contingent to the Duke of Saxony, the leader of the Protestant nobles in Germany' (Bradley 1971: 70). Ferdinand himself was more concerned with the Ottoman than with the Protestant threat to the Habsburg realms and to the security of Christendom. He was therefore more 'ready to compromise with the Protestants, even on such issues as the celibacy of priests and lay Communion under both kinds (Kann 1974: 36–7). 'Ferdinand, superior in intelligence . . . and at the same time less prejudiced' nevertheless 'deferred to the Emperor . . . in his overall policies' (p. 29). In the long run, however, this ambivalent stance would gradually unite most Protestants, Utraquists and Brethren in opposition to the Habsburgs and the Catholic Church.

BOHEMIA'S INDIAN SUMMER

The kingdom of Bohemia was not severely oppressed during the reigns of Maximilian II (1564–77), Rudolf II (1577–1611) and Matthias (1611–17). Maximilian II was at first preoccupied with the Habsburg struggle to 'liberate' Hungary from the Turks. Although he initially refused formally to lift his father's prohibitions against Lutheranism and the Unity of Brethren in Bohemia, he refrained from implementing the Counter-Reformatory programme formulated by the Church Council of Trent (1545–47, 1551–52, 1562–63). Interestingly, he was rumoured to be a closet Lutheran, and he felt able to permit the 'free exercise of the Lutheran faith for nobles and their subjects' in Austria in 1568 (Evans 1979: 6). In Bohemia 'he preferred to leave the Czechs alone so long as they paid their taxes and provided troops for the Turkish wars' (Bradley 1971: 73).

This encouraged the Bohemian Lutherans, Utraquists and Brethren to reach an agreement on a unified corpus of beliefs and practices, the so-called Czech Confession of 1575. In characteristic fashion, the Bohemian Diet entrusted the final drafting to a commission comprising six magnates, six lesser nobles and six burghers. Roughly half the text was based upon the so-called Augsburg Confession (agreed between German Protestant rulers in 1530). Another third was borrowed from the Confession adopted by the Unity of Brethren in 1567. The remainder (perhaps the most important part) consisted of the Four Articles of Prague (1419), Hussite synodal resolutions dating from 1421, and potent passages from Czech hymns and from the writings of Hus. It was cunningly couched in such a way as to present the sixteenth-century Reformation merely as a continuation and a 'completion' of its Hussite predecessor, as was the accompanying ecclesiastical ordinance. Confronted by an expectant coalition of Protestants, Brethren and Utraquists at a stormy session of the Bohemian Diet in 1575, 'Maximilian II, on behalf of himself and his successor Rudolf II, authorized the Czech Confession and Ordinance only orally and as valid only for the aristocracy. The nobility did not protest in any way about the exclusion of the royal towns . . . This was a consequence of the principle *cuius regio, eius religio* gaining ground in Bohemia . . . Even so, with this regulation of ecclesiastical affairs the Czech Kingdom ranked among those countries with the most extensive religious freedom. The Czech Confession provided a successful way of overcoming antagonisms' (Kavka 1994: 146).

Even though this outcome was dependent on Catholic and royal acquiescence in and voluntary observance of a non-binding gentlemen's agreement (rather than a legally binding consitutional document), it was regarded as a victory for toleration and for the non-Catholic majority. Late sixteenth-century Bohemia prospered, relations between Czechs and Germans became quite cordial and, until 1599, Bohemian Protestants and Catholics even began to pride themselves on their mutual tolerance. This, according to Polisensky (1974: 85), was 'the main precept of Bohemian politics, which informed the country's government throughout the sixteenth century: negotiation, based on respect for the demands of each party, as the best guarantee for ensuring concord . . . This principle, expressing itself in religious issues as the tolerance of other confessions, penetrated deeply into the personal relationships within the families of the nobility. In many cases members of the same house, even the same family, belonged to different churches and this religious diversity was no hindrance in either private life or public activity.' These admirable precepts gave birth to a tradition of mutual respect and accommodation which resurfaced in successive Czech 'national revivals' during the nineteenth and twentieth centuries. Even the *petka* system of mutual consultation and power-sharing between the five major political parties in inter-war Czechoslovakia has been regarded as a return to the modes of coexistence between Czechs, Germans, Catholics and Protestants which first emerged in sixteenth-century Bohemia.

Under Rudolf II, moreover, Prague became once again the political, commercial and cultural capital of the Holy Roman Empire and the hub of East Central Europe. Bohemia's nodal position, the buoyancy of its mining, agriculture and textiles, and the temporary abatement of the Ottoman–Habsburg struggle for control of Hungary from 1568 to 1592 allowed Rudolf to indulge in extravagant patronage of art, architecture and music. He brought in numerous Dutch, German and Swiss artists and architects, as well as a few Italians, in order to give Prague a Late Mannerist 'facelift'. But there was also a fine flowering of vernacular styles of art and architecture, not least among the numerous castles and palaces built by rich magnates who vied with each other in aping the Emperor. At the same time, Prague became one of the musical capitals of Europe, thanks to Rudolf's patronage of orchestras, choirs and polyphonic music. Last but not least, he built up a major art collection, including works by Leonardo da Vinci, Raphael, Tintoretto, Titian, Brueghel, Dürer, Holbein and Cranach. Intellectually, Rudolf's Prague was home to the Czech founder of meridian astronomy, Tadeas Hajek of Hajek, the German mathematician and astronomer Johannes Kepler and the Danish astronomer Tycho Brahe, while in medicine Jan Jessenius pioneered dissection at Prague University.

INTO THE ABYSS: THE CRUSHING OF BOHEMIA

Beneath Bohemia's new outward appearance of calm and opulence the Counter-Reformation began to stir. The Jesuits had 'set up shop' in Prague and in Olomouc in 1566 in order to educate future generations of Catholic zealots. The Catholic revival gathered pace from the 1570s onward, when new seminaries were founded, more Catholic priests were 'planted' and Catholic monasteries were reactivated (Evans 1979: 46–7; Kavka 1994: 144). As in Poland and Hungary, the Catholic Counter-Reformation in Bohemia and Moravia took a leaf out of the Protestants' book by encouraging the use of the vernacular in popular worship, by requiring parish priests to be fluent in the vernacular, and by promoting the printing of hagiographic and devotional literature written in the vernacular (Evans 1979: 229–30).

Catholic Counter-Reformers had already triumphed in northern Italy and Bavaria during the 1560s and 1570s, but the tide really turned against Protestantism during the 1590s. 'Its fissiparity had been made evident to all.' Furthermore, the resumption of war between the Habsburgs and the Ottomans between 1591 and 1606 'meant disillusion, insolvency and disorder' (Evans 1979: 39). Moreover, although Rudolf II agreed to respect the Czech Confession of 1575, he became more and more preoccupied with patronage of the arts and architecture and less and less interested in the actual government of Bohemia. From 1599 onwards he unwisely allowed militant Catholics to monopolize Bohemia's key administrative and judicial offices and to discriminate actively in favour of Catholics and the Catholic Church. Not unrelatedly, an increasing proportion of aristocrats were converting or reconverting to Catholicism (about a quarter in the early seventeenth century) in order to improve their career prospects at court (Kavka 1994: 147).

Non-Catholic Germans as well as Czechs began to feel that their liberties were under threat, and they launched a counter-attack against the Catholics. This counter-offensive found an opportunistic ally in Rudolf's power-hungry younger brother Matthias, who had unsuccessfully fought the Turks in Hungary from 1593 to 1606 and subsequently served (or at least posed) as the champion of the Hungarian, Moravian and Bohemian Protestants (Kann 1974: 41–3). In 1608, while threatening to lead a Protestant rebellion, Matthias became ruler of Hungary and Moravia and *de facto* head of the Austrian Habsburg dynasty, partly because Rudolf II was becoming mentally deranged.

In 1609, in competition with Matthias and under pressure from Bohemian Protestants and Utraquists, Rudolf promulgated a legal guarantee of religious liberties in Bohemia, this time for peasants and townspeople as well as the nobility. In 1610, however, Bohemia was invaded by Archduke Leopold, Rudolf's cousin and Bishop of Passau. Since the Protestants and Utraquists now refused to assist the Emperor (whom they suspected of collusion with Leopold), the hapless Rudolf had to appeal to Matthias for help in forcing Leopold to withdraw. Rudolf was then obliged to abdicate in favour of Matthias, who became King of Bohemia in 1611 and Emperor (on Rudolf's death) in 1612.

As Emperor (1612–19) and as king of both Bohemia (1611–17) and Hungary (1608–18) Matthias was prepared to respect Protestant and Utraquist liberties in return for support against the anti-Habsburg rulers of Transylvania and their Ottoman overlords (with whom the Habsburgs were still competing for control of Hungary, in peace as in war). But Bohemia's increasingly militant Catholics (now mainly Czechs) had other ideas, and this precipitated a deadly but protracted power struggle between Catholics and non-Catholics for control of the kingdom.

In March 1618, alarmed by the forced closure of two Protestant churches and by the imminent accession of a more bigoted and absolutist Habsburg Emperor, Ferdinand II (1619–37), who had already been crowned King of Bohemia in 1617, Czech and Bohemian German Protestant leaders called a session of the Bohemian Diet to protest strongly against Catholic violations of the religious liberties decreed by Rudolf II in 1609. On 23 May 1618, in defiance of Emperor Matthias's prohibition of 'any futher meetings', the Diet met again to list its religious and political grievances. This document maintained that the Diet was opposed not to Emperor Matthias but to the conduct of his Catholic chief officials in Prague. 'Had this thesis been accepted in Vienna, it would have been possible to resolve the conflict, but the Court wholeheartedly took the side of its [Bohemian] representatives' (Polisensky 1974: 103). It was not simply a clash between Protestantism and Catholicism. It was really a confrontation between absolutism buttressed by religious bigotry, on the one side, and 'the policy of Bohemia, which was founded on the recognition of free religious and political expression and . . . the principle of negotiation and compromise rather than dictation', on the other (p. 104). Indeed, the defiant stand taken by Bohemia's non-Catholic majority was initially supported by many Bohemian Catholics, including some Catholic magnates (e.g. Divis Cernin of Chudenice, Hrzan of Harasov and Jan Slavata of Chlum), even though the Catholics were mainly gravitating towards the Habsburgs (p. 106). It should also be emphasized that, in contrast to the Hussite Revolution and the clashes that scarred Bohemia between 1848 and 1948, this was in no sense a conflict between Czechs and Germans, even though it has occasionally been portrayed in (anachronistic) nationalist terminology. The Bohemian Germans played a prominent and honourable role in this nascent Bohemian rebellion against incipient Habsburg Catholic absolutism, and 'no serious racial tension can be found between Czechs and Germans in Bohemia either before or after 1620' (Evans 1979: 231).

On 23 May 1618, egged on by Count Matthias Thurn, Vaclav Bodovec, Albrecht Jan Smiricky and other radical members of the Bohemian Diet, Prague Protestants and Utraquists stormed Prague Castle. There the leading Catholic royalist officials, Jaroslav Borita of Martinic and Vilem Slavata of Chlum, were thrown out of a castle window (echoing the infamous 'defenestration' of royalist magistrates in Prague in July 1419). However, the unfortunates survived this indignity and fled to Vienna in order to urge the Habsburgs to crush the incipient Bohemian rebellion. Meanwhile, the Bohemian Diet elected a thirty-six-man Directorate (twelve magnates, twelve lesser nobles and twelve burghers) to take up the reins of power. It also appointed the Bohemian Germans, Count Matthias Thurn and Georg von Hohenlohe, as commanders of the rebel armed forces, which were initially made up of volunteers and mercenaries.

In July 1618 King Ferdinand II ordered the arrest and confinement of Cardinal Khlesl, who was trying to broker a peaceful and mutually acceptable outcome to the confrontation, and set in motion a Habsburg invasion of southern Bohemia. In

Ferdinand's bigoted absolutist mind Protestantism was nothing more or less than religious heresy and political subversion, while 'the Catholic monarch, prostrate before God, must become all-powerful over his own subjects'. The legalistic view, 'that Protestants had never acquired real public rights, was now underscored by a theocratic one, that Protestants could not belong within society at all' (Evans 1979: 68). At first, however, the Habsburgs repeatedly underestimated the strength of their opponents' support and resolve, with the result that the modest initial Habsburg interventions in Bohemia in July and August 1618 were easily defeated. However, Moravia (along with Silesia and the Lusatias) had not only declared its neutrality in June 1618, for fear of getting drawn into an unwanted armed conflict not of its making, but also granted Habsburg armies free passage across Moravian territory, thereby enabling the Habsburgs to attack Bohemia from behind. In addition, Ferdinand II was well placed to call upon military, moral and monetary solidarity and support from other Catholic rulers (especially Maximilian of Bavaria and Philip III of Spain), whereas the major German Protestant rulers were rather reluctant to give active assistance to Bohemia and even gave their backing to the election of Ferdinand II to the imperial throne when Matthias died in March 1619. Indeed, the story of the Czechs from 1618 to 1620, as in the 1420s, 1848, 1938 and 1968, was of the habitual (but not necessarily ill-founded) reluctance of those who supposedly shared their beliefs and/or values to rally to their support. The Czechs have nearly always found themselves deserted by their 'friends' just when they most needed them.

Exposed to the danger of attack from several sides, in August 1618 the Bohemian Diet decided to draft every fifth townsman and every tenth male peasant into hastily expanded armies. In addition, the Diet had to raise new taxes and loans to finance, arm, train and equip these new conscript armies and their small core of professional soldiers. While major arms consignments were purchased from Nuremberg, 'local production of arms, both light and heavy, flourished in many workshops in Prague and other large towns . . . At the same time as mobilizing their own troops, the Directors . . . took steps to disarm Catholics who were known to be strong supporters of Ferdinand II' (Polisensky 1974: 109). However, the cost of this siege economy soon proved onerous and debilitating, especially as only the most niggardly financial and military assistance was forthcoming from the Netherlands, England and the German Protestant Union (pp. 109, 115, 172).

Shortly after the death of Emperor Matthias on 20 March 1619, however, Silesia, the Lusatias and Upper Austria decided to join the Bohemian opposition to Ferdinand II. This major shift in the balance of power, combined with the impending succession of a Jesuit-educated absolutist bigot to the imperial throne, finally persuaded even Moravia to go over to the Bohemian cause in May 1619. These new accessions of strength enabled Count Thurn quickly to repel the main Habsburg armies and to lay siege to Vienna. This in turn encouraged the Diets of Upper and Lower Austria to demand full freedom of religion in Upper and Lower Austria (Kann 1974: 50).

In July 1619, since there seemed to be little point in (or support for) attempting to reach an accommodation with Ferdinand II, the Bohemian Diet decided to confiscate the remaining properties of the Bohemian crown, of the Catholic Church and of those Catholics who were actively supporting Bohemia's foes. The chief targets of these expropriations were the Jesuit Order and the Catholic monasteries, and the sale of sequestered estates provided the wherewithal to finance the war effort (Polisensky 1974:

109–10. However, with the assistance of Bohemian military deficiencies and an invasion of Upper Austria by Maximilian of Bavaria (the leader of the Catholic League), Habsburg forces were able not only to stand their ground around Vienna and Budejovice (Budweis), but also to launch counter-strikes into Bohemia. Nevertheless, by August the forces of the Directorate were in a position to consolidate its authority and control over the Czech territories. 'The crucial need was to stabilize the situation (and thus to yoke together more closely the different Bohemian lands) by resolving the problem of a new head of state and laying the foundation of a constitution in which real power should lie with the body of Estates' (pp. 112–13). On 23 July 1619, therefore, the Bohemian Diet adopted a new constitution which 'established the relation between monarch and Estates and laid the basis for peaceful evolution by granting religious freedom to all confessions, the Roman Catholic among them' (p. 114). On 26 August 1619, moreover, the Diet formally deposed Ferdinand II from the Bohemian throne and elected in his place Frederick, Elector of the Palatinate and head of the German Protestant Union. However, Frederick was a very unfortunate choice. First, together with the Protestant Electors of Saxony and Brandenburg, he actually voted for the election of Ferdinand II to the imperial title, thus helping to confer greater legitimacy and authority on Bohemia's chief foe. Second, Frederick sowed dissension and discontent by dismissing many of the incumbent Bohemian officials (whether Czech, German, Protestant, Utraquist or Catholic) and replacing them with foreigners (mainly German Protestants from other countries). Third, he proved to be a very ineffectual king. Nevertheless, in late 1619 rebel Bohemia gained more active support from Protestant Transylvania and from the Diets of Upper and Lower Austria, which sought to exert concerted pressure on the Austrian Habsburgs to make religious and political concessions all round. But, just when Bohemian and Transylvanian forces were poised for a combined assault on Vienna, the Transylvanian Protestant forces were diverted by problems at home and the offensive fizzled out. In February 1620 the Protestant ruler of Transylvania, Gabor Bethlen, concluded a truce with Ferdinand II and Bohemia found itself rather isolated once more.

There was inconclusive skirmishing between Bohemia and its Catholic absolutist foes from February to August 1620. But thereafter Bohemia came under concerted attack from Bavarian, Austrian Habsburg and (more treacherously) Protestant Saxon forces. Ferdinand II had succeeded in tempting the Protestant Elector of Saxony to attack Bohemia in the expectation of gaining the Lusatias. As the pincers closed Bohemia found itself virtually abandoned to its fate by Moravia, Transylvania, Denmark and the German Protestant princes. 'The diplomatic abandonment of Bohemia by England, Holland and France (who were by the summer seeking mainly to defend the Palatinate on the Rhine) meant that help from this quarter shrank to an insignificant trickle' (Polisensky 1974: 115).

The tawdry *dénouement* was a two-hour battle on the so-called White Mountain, a hill not far from Prague. The pusillanimous King Frederick simply fled, thereby sowing panic, disillusionment and confusion in the Bohemian armies and administration and handing the Habsburgs a walkover victory. 'The two-year war had already brought economic exhaustion and left the army short of equipment and supplies' (Polisensky 1974: 116). However, 'the personal incompetence, indeed cowardice, of Frederick and his government turned defeat into calamity . . . Only the flight of the . . . King from his capital and the collapse of the government led to the loss of the city and confirmed the Imperialists' triumph' (p. 119).

The absence of any major counterpart to the 1420s Taborite movement and the demotic armies of Jan Zizka and Prokop the Shaven also contributed to the speed with which the Bohemian rebellion of 1618–20 was defeated. The Directorate was 'not able to stir the subject masses into sufficient activity', partly because it failed to promote 'radical improvements' in the peasants' plight and thereby strengthen the forces at its disposal 'both physically and morally'. Yet one cannot simply blame the defeat of the rebellion on the failure of the leading members of the Bohemian Diet to transcend the inhibitions and limitations of their class. The Directorate had 'little practical opportunity in the anxious years of 1619–20 to turn economic and social life into new channels, and the situation of the Bohemian peasants (far better than that of their German or Polish neighbours) did not call for any sudden fundamental reforms', according to Polisensky (1974: 118). Moreover, even though there was continued popular resistance to the invading Bavarian and Saxon armies in 1621 (especially at Tabor), there was nothing comparable to the chiliastic fervour of the early Taborites or the military genius of Jan Zizka and Prokop the Shaven waiting in the wings. In addition, Emperor Ferdinand II was from the outset rather more resolute than Emperor Sigismund had ever been. The peasant revolts which occurred in eastern Bohemia and in Moravia in 1621 and 1622 were ruthlessly suppressed.

After the battle of the White Mountain the victors lost little time in using pillage, expropriation and financial scams to settle political scores and recoup the cost of conquering the Czech Lands. By November 1620 commissions were being established to identify the names and the assets of the nobles and burghers who had actively resisted the Habsburgs, in preparation for punitive expropriation. In 1621 these commissions began to confiscate the properties of those Czechs and Bohemian Germans who had gone into hiding and/or exile, while twenty-seven alleged ringleaders of the rebellion were publicly executed in Prague's Old Town Square and the properties of their families were also confiscated (Polisensky 1974: 138; Kavka 1960: 65). During 1621–22, moreover, Bavarian and Saxon as well as Austrian troops were 'given free rein to plunder the estates and townhouses of their defeated opponents' and to extort 'large sums of money and massive payments in kind' (Polisensky 1974: 142). In 1622 there was a major onslaught on those members of the Diet who had not actively resisted the Directorate during the Bohemian rebellion. Within eighteen months the confiscation commissions had 'destroyed the material foundations of 680 noble families (with a further 250 in Moravia) and innumerable burghers' (p. 138). In 1623 many landowners were compelled to sell their estates at give-away prices, for no other reason than that they were not Catholic. Overall, during the 1620s over half of Bohemia's landed estates changed hands (Evans 1979: 197). This massive redivision of property 'represented a revolution within the ruling classes' (Polisensky 1974: 146). After 1623, following foreign protests, the assault on the nobles abated somewhat. But attacks on the burghers escalated. Many burghers (even Catholics) who had allegedly collaborated with the Directorate incurred heavy fines and expropriation. Those who were driven into exile tended to lose any remaining possessions to the pro-Habsburg vultures (p. 139).

These events took a heavy toll on the economy. In 1622, moreover, a nefarious consortium advanced 6 million gulden to Ferdinand II 'in return for a year's profits from the Bohemian mint', and it made a fortune for itself 'by hectically minting debased coins for a year'. By 1624 the currency had lost nine-tenths of its former value and real property prices had collapsed, precipitating 'wholesale economic decline' (Polisensky 1974:

139–41). From the 1620s onward, what is more, peasant land tenure became more uncertain, for many of the records of the peasants' rights had been 'lost, destroyed or deliberately mislaid' by scheming landlords. 'Peasant lands were increasingly incorporated into the dominical lands; or well-cultivated, fertile peasant land might be exchanged under duress for poor dominical land ... Demands for *robota* [labour services] increased rapidly ... and came to consume, in some cases, more than half of the peasants' number of workdays per annum' (Wright 1975: 248). Bohemian peasants already needed seigneurial permission to marry, to change occupation and to move to another locality well before 1620, but after 1620 such permission became more expensive to obtain and was more frequently refused (pp. 246–7).

While the property, power and privileges of many magnates increased, the elimination of much of the lesser nobility was 'a high priority for the confiscatory commissions', since Vienna saw that estate as the main source of trouble. This curtailed a traditional source of administrators, soldiers, scholars, political activism and social dynamism. It also fatally weakened the 'old and accepted social network' of interrelated noble families whose role before 1620 had been 'to mitigate the tensions of class and nationality' (Polisensky 1974: 146–7). There was to be an increasingly unbridgeable gulf between the magnates and the rest of the population.

On the religious front Calvinist preachers were expelled in 1621, Lutheran and Utraquist preachers were expelled in 1622, and all non-Catholic clergy were banished from Bohemia and Moravia in 1624 (Polisensky 1974: 144). Moreover, the constitutional changes which were imposed on Bohemia and Moravia in 1627 (over the heads of their Diets, which had not met since 1620) made all non-Catholic faiths (other than Judaism) illegal and restored the Catholic clergy to the status of first estate of the realm. They also made the Bohemian crown hereditary in the house of Habsburg, made the sovereign the sole author of legislation, gave the sovereign control of the patents of nobility, made all public officials swear allegiance to the sovereign alone (no longer to the 'commonwealth of Bohemia'), raised the German language to parity with Czech, and reduced Bohemia and Moravia practically to the status of mere provinces (Evans 1979: 198–9; Kann 1974: 51). In Bohemia in 1627 and in Moravia in 1628, furthermore, clergy, nobles and burghers were given six months' notice either to 'revert' to Catholicism or to leave the country. Several thousands opted for the latter, including the eminent pedagogue and 'senior' of the Unity of Brethren, Jan Amos Komensky (alias Comenius, 1592–1670), who was one of the pioneers of modern polytechnical co-education (with an emphasis on the gradual acquisition of knowledge and understanding and the avoidance of rote learning and corporal coercion).

In 1629, moreover, Ferdinand II issued an Edict of Restitution, which ordered the restoration (restitution) of all the property taken from the Catholic Church. This virtually completed the establishment of a Catholic absolutist theocracy which gradually re-Catholicized Bohemia and Moravia and treated the two centuries between the start of the Hussite Revolution and the battle of the White Mountain as an aberration in Czech history. For Hussitism, Utraquism and Protestantism it substituted an artificially resuscitated native Roman Catholic tradition based upon the (somewhat sentimental) idealization of St Vaclav (Good King Wenceslas), *Bohemia Sancta* and the Virgin Mary, whose cult was expressed in hundreds of local votive pictures and sanctuaries (Evans 1979: 223–4). Owing to a chronic shortage of Catholic priests, however, re-Catholicization was heavily concentrated in the towns, where it worked hand-in-glove with re-Germanization. Many Czech peasants experienced not so much persecution or forcible re-Catholicization as religious neglect, although they were generally expected to mimic the Catholicization of their 'masters'. Over half of Bohemia's 'livings' were vacant during the 1640s, and in 1635 Moravia's 636 parishes had only 257 resident clergy, most of whom belonged to monastic orders (p. 123). Lutheranism and Calvinism did not regain legal recognition by the state until 1781, and the indigenous Czech Churches had to wait even longer – until the ordinances of 1848 and 1861, which granted limited freedom of religion and ecclesiastical autonomy within a somewhat stultifying Catholic imperium (Kavka 1994: 151).

The Thirty Years' War, which had been initiated by the Habsburg suppression of the Bohemian rebellion of 1618–20, veered away from Czech soil between 1621 and 1626, only to come back again as a result of the (partly self-interested) championship of the Protestant cause by Denmark (1626–30), Saxony (1631–32) and Sweden (1630–48). By the end of this kaleidoscopic and immensely destructive conflict, which has been brilliantly analysed by J.V. Polisensky (1974), the population had fallen by between a quarter (Bradley 1971: 71) and a half (Kavka 1960: 71), while the (re)enserfment of the Czech peasantry proceeded apace (Wright 1975: 246–8). Bohemia was pulverized. Most of the non-Catholic nobility emigrated or perished, as did many (perhaps most) of the non-Catholic townspeople. Local autonomies faded away yet 'the main beneficiary was not the crown but the great latifundium, freed from the meddling of towns and petty nobility' (Evans 1979: 213).

By 1650 foreign Catholic nobles, parvenus and soldiers of fortune (*condottieri*), whose services the Habsburgs rewarded with grants of land (mainly for lack of cash), 'owned' about two-fifths of Bohemia's peasants. Yet 'they exercised little power in their adopted country'. Catholic members of the severely depleted 'old nobility' continued to provide political leadership (Evans 1979: 201–4). This ruling oligarchy was largely made up of native Bohemian and Moravian magnates bearing such names as Kinsky, Slavata, Martinic, Cernin, Waldstein (alias Wallenstein), Vojtech, Vrbna, Lobkovic, Kolovrat, Kounice (alias Kaunitz) and Sedlnicky. They were the major 'winners'. Indeed, by 1650 62 per cent of the Bohemian and Moravian peasantry 'belonged' to just eighty-five noble families (pp. 205–10, 93). Together with the forcibly 'restored' Catholic Church, they now constituted the main bulwark of Habsburg Catholic absolutism.

THE HUSSITE HERITAGE: FROM HUS TO HAVEL

What then survived of the Hussite heritage? Perhaps the most enduring legacy of Jan Hus and his fellow reformers was not specific religious or reforming currents so much as a tradition of moral honesty and courage which has tended to expose the obverse moral shortcomings of the European communities and political configurations to which the Czechs have been either aspiring or forced to belong. The apparent power and tenacity of this Hussite legacy are all the more remarkable given that the Czechs were re-Catholicized during the late seventeenth and eighteenth centuries. Just as Milic, Hus and many of their Czech contemporaries cumulatively exposed the unwillingness (even inability) of the medieval Catholic Church to live up to its professed values, beliefs and ideals, so did later figures such as Frantisek Palacky and Tomas Masaryk unmask the unwillingness of the Habsburg Monarchy to live up to its law-abiding and universalist pretensions. Likewise, the dignified restraint of the Czechs when they were betrayed by the governments of Britain and France in 1938 helped to reveal the full extent of the 'leading' Western European democracies' reluctance to stand up for their professed values and ideals. In 1968 the infectious idealism of Alexander Dubcek (a Slovak) and his Czech and Slovak contemporaries exposed the completeness of the failure of the other self-proclaimed communist regimes even to begin to live up to their supposed ideals. Since the last years of communist rule Vaclav Havel has shone his moral searchlight on the elements of hypocrisy in both Soviet and Western dealings with other parts of the world (especially Eastern Europe). The shining examples of Milic, Matej of Janov, Hus and others of the same mettle have seemingly encouraged generations of Czechs to 'speak truth unto power', and to revere, admire and take pride in (rather than to disparage, belittle or sneer at) those who do. Indeed, ever since 1420 the Czech people have repeatedly incurred the 'displeasure' of major European powers, not because the Czechs (other than the Taborites) have been willing or even able to pose significant threats of a military and/or economic nature, but precisely because such powers have often felt acutely discomfited or even threatened by the honesty and unpretentious moral superiority of Czechs, from Hus to Havel.

Part III

East Central Europe during the Habsburg ascendancy

Introduction: the importance of being Austria

No other major European dynasty has survived as long as the Austrian Habsburgs (1273–1918) or left so deep an imprint on European history. In most states governments and dynasties have come and gone, but territories have remained much the same (in the short term, at least). In the Habsburg Empire, by contrast, territories came and went, but the dynasty endured until 1918. Moreover, much that has happened in East Central Europe since then has been a consequence of the collapse of the Habsburg Empire in 1918. Imperial political and economic union, security and order gave way to political and economic fragmentation, insecurity, disorder, instability, irredentism, revanchism, beggar-my-neighbour protectionism and international discord. Before long, however, the power vacuum left by the demise of the Habsburg Empire was filled by Nazi Germany. In a sense, Hitler was 'Austria's revenge' for the long succession of military and diplomatic humiliations inflicted upon Austria between 1859 and 1918. 'Hitler had learnt everything he knew in Austria – his nationalism from Schönerer, his antisemitism and appeal to the "little man" from Lueger. He brought into German politics a demagogy peculiarly Viennese' (Taylor 1976: 258). Hitler's peculiar hatred of South Slavs, Czechs, Gypsies and Jews was much more Austrian than German in inspiration.

Moreover, following the defeat and East–West partition of Germany in 1945, the continuing post-Habsburg power vacuum in East Central Europe was rather more durably and constructively filled by a large westward extension of the Soviet Russian empire, albeit at great social, cultural and political cost. This lasted seven times as long as Hitler's 'New Order' and it achieved much more, yet it became an oppressive and stultifying straitjacket on the peoples of East Central Europe. The collapse of Soviet power and communist rule in East Central Europe has, however, reopened old wounds and restored the post-Habsburg power vacuum in the region. The chances are that it will again be filled either by a resurgent 'united' German economic power or by a resurgent Russian military power, unless the void is quickly filled by a strong confederal union of East Central European peoples and/or an expeditious eastward extension of the European Union. Unfortunately, the fact that, in the long run, the latter would be by far the most advantageous options for both Western and East Central Europeans alike in no way guarantees that the formidable immediate obstacles to their realization can be overcome. Not every problem has a solution, and states often fail to act in their own or their citizens' best interests, as the history of post-Habsburg East Central Europe has repeatedly demonstrated. Indeed, the disintegration of the Habsburg Empire in 1918 neither resolved nor helped to resolve the problems of East Central Europe, which had contributed so much to its downfall. The increased political and economic fragmentation merely made the problems more acute, acrimonious and intractable.

In a much-quoted 'open letter' refusing an invitation to take part in the German provisional parliament (*Vorparlament*), which met in Frankfurt during the revolutionary upheavals of 1848, the eminent Czech nationalist and historian Frantisek Palacky warned that 'along the frontiers of the Russian Empire there live many nations widely differing in origin, in language, in history and morals – Slavs, Wallachians [Romanians], Magyars and Germans . . . Turks and Albanians – none of whom is sufficiently powerful to bid successful defiance to the superior neighbour on the East [Russia] for all time. They could do so only if a close and firm tie bound them all together as one. The vital artery of this necessary union of nations is the Danube. The focus of power of such a union must never be diverted far from this river, if the union is to be effective and remain so. Assuredly, if the Austrian state had not [already] existed for ages, it would have been a behest for us in the interests of Europe and indeed of humanity to endeavour to create it' (Palacky 1948: 306). Playing upon European (especially German) Russophobia, Palacky pointed out that the vast and almost impregnable Russian state was expanding 'decade by decade' and that its seemingly unstoppable expansion was threatening to establish 'a universal monarchy, that is to say, an infinite and inexpressible evil . . . such as I, though heart and soul a Slav, would none the less profoundly regret from the standpoint of humanity'. Palacky denied that he was anti-Russian: 'On the contrary, I observe with pleasure and sympathy every step forward which that great nation makes within its natural borders along the path of civilization.' Nevertheless, 'the bare possibility of a universal Russian monarchy has no more determined opponent or foe than myself – not because that monarchy would be Russian but because it would be universal' (p. 305). In Palacky's view, however, the Austrian Empire could become a fully effective bulwark against external threats to this region only if it assumed a federalized form. In its own long-term interests, Austria would have to accept 'the fundamental rule . . . that all the nationalities and all the religions under her sceptre should enjoy complete equality of rights and respect . . . Nature knows neither dominant nor underyoked nations. If the bond which unites a number of diverse nations in a single political entity is to be firm and enduring, no nation can have cause to fear that the union will cost it any of the things which it holds most dear. On the contrary, each must have the certain hope that in the central authority it will find defence and protection against possible violation by neighbours of the principles of equality' (p. 306).

Palacky's influential compatriot and fellow nationalist, Karel Havlicek, expressed a similar view in 1848: 'Complete independence for the Czechs at this time, when only tremendous empires are being formed in Europe, would be very unfortunate. We could not be anything but a very weak state, dependent upon other states, and our national existence would be constantly imperilled. On the other hand, in a close union with the other Slavs in Austria, we would enjoy a large measure of independence . . . and, at the same time, considerable advantages from the association with a powerful state. All we can do is to co-operate frankly and sincerely in building and maintaining the Austrian empire' (quoted by Kann 1950a: 166).

Palacky provided further clarification of this so-called 'Austro-Slav' position in 1864: 'We Bohemians certainly wish sincerely for the preservation and unity of Austria. Considering that by our own efforts we could scarcely create an independent sovereign state, we can preserve our historico-political entity, our particular nationality and culture and, finally, our economic life nowhere and in no better way than we can in Austria. That means in a free Austria, organized on the basis of autonomy and equality. We have no hopes and no political perspectives beyond Austria' (quoted by Kann 1950b: 138).

The view that the Austrian Empire was a 'European necessity' received additional backing from Lord Palmerston, the long-serving nineteenth-century British Foreign Secretary and Prime Minister. In 1848 he told the House of Commons that 'Austria is a most important element in the balance of European power. Austria stands in the centre of Europe, a barrier against encroachment on the one side and against invasion on the other. The political independence and the liberties of Europe are bound up, in my opinion, with the maintenance and integrity of Austria as a great European Power; and therefore anything which tends . . . to weaken Austria, but still more to reduce her from the position of a first-rate Power . . . must be a great calamity to Europe and one which every Englishman ought to deprecate and try to prevent' (quoted in Bourne 1979: 296).

Even Karl Marx (in 1860) conceded that 'the circumstance which legitimates the existence of Austria since the middle of the eighteenth century is its resistance to the advance of Russia in Eastern Europe' (quoted by Jaszi 1929: 9). Otto Bauer, the leading theoretician of Austrian Marxism, similarly declared that 'So long as Russian Czardom remained intact, the existence of the Austro-Hungarian Empire was a historical necessity. Had it been overthrown, the Slav states that would have emerged from it would inevitably have become vassal states of Russia. Its downfall would therefore have established the domination of Czardom over Europe . . . The victory of the Russian Revolution drove forward the national revolution of the Czechs, the Poles and the Yugoslavs . . . The defeat of the German Empire assured the victory of the revolution. So long as the German Empire remained intact, the Slav peoples . . . could not desire the downfall of the [Habsburg] Monarchy. Only when the power of the German Empire . . . was broken by superior forces could the revolution of the Czechs, the South Slavs and the Poles be crowned with complete victory' (Bauer 1925: 72–3).

Thus it was only with the defeat and demise of the Russian and German empires that the peoples of East Central Europe became convinced that it was 'safe' to establish independent nation-states in place of the Austro-Hungarian Empire. Unfortunately for them, however, the power of Germany and Russia soon revived in even more threatening forms than before. It might have been safer to have remained under Habsburg protection! Significantly, in a memorandum dated 27 June 1848, the Russian Foreign Minister Count Charles von Nesselrode concurred with the widespread insistence on the pivotal importance of the Austrian Empire: 'The void which its disappearance would create would be so enormous and the difficulty of filling it so great, that it ought to continue for a long time yet, given the lack of anything to put in its place' (quoted by Sked 1989: 18).

During the Cold War era a chorus of American and *émigré* scholars lamented the disintegration of the Austro-Hungarian Empire at the end of the First World War and the loss of the opportunity to transform it into a federal, multinational buffer state separating Germany and Russia. In the judgement of George Kennan (1979: 423), a prominent American diplomat, diplomatic historian and adviser on Russian and East European affairs in the Cold War period, 'The Austro-Hungarian Empire still looks better as a solution to the tangled problems of that part of the world than anything that has succeeded it.' Its demise engendered a motley assortment of small, vulnerable and far from homogeneous nation-states and a power vacuum which was bound to be filled by Germany and/or Russia. In the event the void was filled first by Nazi Germany, engulfing Europe in the Second World War and the Holocaust, and then, in the wake of the defeat of Hitler, by the westward extension of Soviet power into the Balkans and East Central Europe. Seen in this light, the illiberal (and sometimes oppressive) efforts of conservative statesmen such as Prince Clemens Metternich, Prince Felix Schwarzenberg and Emperor Franz Joseph to preserve the imperial *status quo* in nineteenth-century East Central Europe look less like the unthinking knee-jerk responses of dyed-in-the-wool reactionaries than like quixotic or altruistic endeavours to hold back the potentially violent and destructive tides of radical and nationalist revolution. Metternich, for example, saw the empire as 'a system in which a variety of nationalities coexisted within a monarchical framework based on social hierarchy and the rule of law. Placed at the centre of the continent, it was also a "European necessity", the very pivot of the balance of power' (Sked 1989: 16). Some American 'Cold Warriors' came to see Metternich 'as some sort of nineteenth-century John Foster Dulles, stemming the tide of red revolution' (p. 26). Indeed, like many latter-day conservatives and 'Cold Warriors', Metternich was barely capable of differentiating liberalism from revolutionary nationalism and socialism (p. 25). Nevertheless, the eventual failure of the Austro-Hungarian dam to hold back the tides of nationalist and socialist revolution really did open the way to the massive upheavals, destruction and loss of life during Europe's 'Second Thirty Years' War', lasting from 1914 to 1945. (The first having lasted from 1618 to 1648.)

The twilight years of the Austro-Hungarian Empire witnessed a proliferation of liberal, Austro-Slav and Austro-Marxist schemes to reconstitute the imperial polity on new, democratic, multinational 'federal' foundations. Their exponents recognized 'the feebleness, the dead weight of bureaucracy, the conflict of national claims; yet all looked forward to a "solution". This solution, universally expected, was Federalism, the attractive name for diverse schemes' (Taylor 1976: 224). Because everyone recoiled in alarm at the prospect of the endemic conflict and economic collapse which could follow in the wake of imperial disintegration, there was a great thirst for 'solutions' and a great willingness to believe in them. 'Solutions' were all too easy to devise on paper. The problem was how to get one generally accepted (p. 225).

These 'eleventh-hour' schemes for a federal multinational empire presupposed that Vienna and the Habsburgs would continue to provide overall co-ordination of central government, especially economic policy, foreign policy and military affairs. However, the Habsburgs and the vast majority of Austrian Germans seemed to prefer an ever closer partnership with the burgeoning German Empire to any form of power-sharing with their Slav subjects, towards whom they displayed either patronizing condescension or (more commonly) haughty contempt.

Austro-Slavs, Austrian Marxists and Austrian liberals looked to Vienna and the Habsburgs for federal 'solutions' to the empire's 'nationality problems'. Yet to do so was 'to fail to understand the nature of the Monarchy' (Taylor 1976: 226). The Habsburgs generally 'strove to keep their dominions apart, not to bring them together'; they were afraid to unite them 'even in subjection' (pp. 12–13). With the possible exception of Joseph II (1780–90), the Habsburg emperors saw their subjects as the servants of the dynasty rather than the other way round. Furthermore, according to Justus Freimund's treatise *Österreichs Zukunft* (1867), 'Federalism is incompatible with the concept of a powerful monarchy. Federalism is possible only in a republic like Switzerland.' Austria could not tolerate freedom, as 'a free Austria is only a bridge to complete disintegration'.

Yet, since the march of history was towards greater freedom, 'world history has passed judgement upon Austria and condemned her to fall' (quoted by Kann 1950b: 140). Kann challenges Freimund's dogmatic assertion that federalism is incompatible with monarchy. Nevertheless, he concludes that 'if the union of eastern central European peoples on a federal democratic basis should ever be achieved, it would have little in common with the set-up in the Habsburg Empire' (p. 290).

Any thoroughgoing democratic federalism, granting genuine autonomy to all ethnic and/or territorial subdivisions, was indeed incompatible with (or, at any rate, unacceptable to) this particular monarchy. According to Sugar (1963: 2–4): 'The Habsburgs . . . followed a purely dynastic policy of protecting their *Hausmacht* (patrimonial rights), emphasizing *Kaisertreue* (loyalty to the emperor and his family) and promoting a sort of dynastic patriotism. *Kaisertreue* held the empire together until the end of World War I and made most national groups seek, almost to the last . . . a solution for their grievances within the state rather than in secession. This indicates not so much the success of the ruling family's policy as the inability of its subjects to find another principle on which even a substantial part of them could agree.' Moreover, Fischer-Galati (1963: 32) argues that '*Kaisertreue* precluded democratic reform and the reorganization of the Empire on the basis of ethnic or individual sovereignty.'

In any case, it is doubtful whether any far-reaching federal reorganization of the Habsburg Empire could have resolved or defused its 'nationalities problem' for long, even if it had been possible to implement (or impose) such a 'solution'. The granting of substantial autonomy to the major ethnic groups and/or territorial subdivisions would probably have whetted their appetite for full independence while reducing the capacity of the central authorities to hold the ring. However much the imperial territory were to be subdivided, some subdivisions would still have contained insecure, vulnerable and/or discontented ethnic minorities, some of whom would have sought 'union' with (or the 'protection' of) their co-nationals in neighbouring states and regions. Moreover, the constituent nationalities and territories of the Habsburg Empire remained extremely disparate in terms of levels of economic development, class configurations, educational attainments, geopolitical orientations and levels of national consciousness. To regard them as mutually compatible components of a viable, harmonious federation or confederation required wishful thinking of the first order; but optimism and blind faith are not sufficient bases on which to build viable state structures (Sugar 1967: 119). 'Men thought to alter the European position of the Habsburg Monarchy by changing its internal structure; in reality a change in its internal structure could only come about after a change, or rather a catastrophe, in its European position' (Taylor 1976: 225).

An East Central European federal or confederal union would have been riven by precisely the same inter-ethnic frictions, jealousies, rivalries and cultural fault lines that had helped to destroy the Habsburg Empire in 1918. Indeed, it is arguable that the supranational Habsburg *Hausmacht* and *Kaisertreue* were more capable of holding the ring and papering over the cracks than any East Central European federation or confederation would have been, precisely because the dynasty constituted a strong *supranational* arbiter and focus of allegiance, standing above and policing inter-ethnic squabbles. The very existence of a large supranational empire limited the enormous scope for violent conflict (either within an ethnically structured multinational federation or between ethnically based states) in East Central Europe. 'The Monarchy had not been a "solution"; it had rested on scepticism of the possibility of a "solution" and had therefore sought to conserve, though without faith, institutions which had long lost moral sanction' (Taylor 1976: 252). With respect to *intentions*, it may be true that 'the Habsburg Monarchy was not a device for enabling a number of nationalities to live together' (p. 132). But, objectively speaking, that was one of the vital functions it performed. In that sense the dissolution of the Monarchy in 1918 was a historic 'mistake', even if it was seemingly unavoidable at the time. Against such a view, Adam Zamoyski has recently argued that 'most of the problems of Central Europe were created by Habsburg rule, whose vicious logic required that all subject peoples should be required to hate each other' (*The Times*, 30 November 1995, p. 38). However, while the divide-and-rule tactics of the Habsburg Empire undoubtedly sowed the seeds of many subsequent conflicts in the so-called 'successor states', it would be churlish to deny that (for its own 'reasons of state') it kept such conflicts within certain bounds so long as the Habsburgs remained in control.

THE ETHNIC AND TERRITORIAL CONFIGURATION OF THE HABSBURG EMPIRE

In 1910 this sprawling, mountainous, ramshackle empire extended over 257,478 square miles, making it Europe's second largest state (only Tsarist Russia was larger). Its 50 million inhabitants comprised thirteen significant 'nationalities' or national groupings. No one group (except the Slavs as a whole) was dominant in numerical terms, as the following division shows: Germans, 22 per cent; Magyars (Hungarians), 18 per cent; Czechs, 12 per cent; Poles, 10 per cent; Ruthenes/Ukrainians, 8 per cent; Romanians, 6 per cent; Jews, 5–6 per cent; Croats, 5 per cent; Serbs, 4 per cent; Slovaks, 4 per cent; Slovenes, 3 per cent; Italians, 2 per cent; Bosnian Moslems, 1 per cent. These official census statistics have been rounded. They have also been adjusted slightly to allow for the Jews. The Jews were not an officially recognized 'nationality', so they were mostly lumped in with the Germans and Magyars. But their numbers can be roughly surmised from the census returns on religious affiliations. Here the dominance of Roman Catholicism stands out clearly: Roman Catholics (including 'Uniates' or Ukrainian Catholics of the Orthodox rite), 77 per cent; Protestants, 9 per cent; Jews, 4 per cent; and Moslems, 1 per cent (Kann 1974: 606–8). Significant numbers of Jews had converted to Christianity or, especially if they were Marxists, had become atheists. Therefore Jews must have made up rather more than 4 per cent of the population. Jews were exceptionally prominent in the business community and in the liberal professions, especially law, medicine and the press. In both Austria and Hungary they contributed powerfully to the development of capitalism, liberalism, Marxism, intellectual life in general and publishing, although their glittering successes in these fields made them a favourite target of Austrian reactionaries, racists and malcontents, sowing the seeds of Hitler's Holocaust. The two largest national groupings, the Germans in the west and the Magyars (Hungarians) in the east, were substantially outnumbered by their Slav subjects (Czechs, Slovaks, Poles, Ruthenes, Croats, Serbs, Slovenes and Bosnian Moslems), who altogether made up 46 per cent of the Empire's population.

The 'Austrian' half of the empire comprised an untidy agglomeration of disparate territories which had been fully subjugated and brought under direct Viennese rule by the Austrian Habsburgs over a span of several centuries. At the heart of these Austrian 'Crown lands' (*Kronländer*) lay German Austria (*Deutsch Österreich*: the 'German

Eastern Realm'). This included semi-industrial Lower Austria (capital: Vienna), agrarian Upper Austria (capital: Linz), semi-industrial Styria (capital: Graz) and the Alpine, extensively forested and predominantly pastoral Western Lands (the Tyrol, Salzburg, Vorarlberg and Carinthia). The nobility, the officials and the burghers of German Austria dominated the western-cum-northern half of the empire in partnership with the Roman Catholic Church, the military, the mostly German-speaking estate owners and burghers of the kingdom of Bohemia (comprising the Czech Lands, or Bohemia, Moravia and parts of Silesia), and the Polish aristocracy and clergy of Galicia and Bukovina. These last two provinces made up 'Austrian Poland', annexed by the Habsburgs when the former Commonwealth of Poland-Lithuania was 'partitioned' between Russia, Prussia and Austria in the late eighteenth century.

The regions subject to the most direct forms of Austro-German rule were the following: the predominantly Slovene provinces of Carniola, Gorz (Gorizia) and Istria (including the important predominantly Italian-speaking port of Trieste), which were annexed in the fourteenth century; the largely Croatian province of Dalmatia, annexed in 1797; and the partly Serbian, partly Croatian but predominantly Bosnian/Moslem provinces of Bosnia and Hercegovina. The latter came under Austrian military occupation in 1878 and were formally annexed in 1908, triggering the chain of events that were to lead to the outbreak of the First World War. There had also been long periods of Austrian rule in Lombardy (1714–1859), Venetia (1797–1866), Tuscany (1736–1801) and the Southern Netherlands (1714–94), but these regions lie outside the scope of this book. Moreover, despite their considerable resources and potential and the importance attached to them by the Habsburgs, the power base and centre of gravity of the empire remained in the Austrian 'crown lands' and, from 1526 to 1918, in the kingdoms of Bohemia (including Moravia) and Hungary (including Croatia, Slovakia and Transylvania). The Habsburgs ruled the eastern half of the empire in partnership with the wealthy Magyar aristocracy of the constitutionally quite separate and much more unified kingdom of Hungary. The latter constituted a natural physical unit. The fertile, saucer-shaped Hungarian plain, through which flowed the river Danube and its major tributary, the Tisza, was almost encircled by the rim of mainly forested and/or pastoral highlands which comprised the greater part of Slovakia, Ruthenia, Transylvania, Banat and Croatia-Slavonia.

From 1711 to 1848 the Habsburg kingdom of Hungary had a distinct, highly decentralized and aristocratic *comitat* ('county') system of administration, which made for weak central government but conferred considerable autonomy. This helped Hungary to preserve a separate legal, administrative and cultural tradition and identity. It was largely exempt from the sporadic Habsburg drives for greater political and administrative centralization and uniformity, which were virtually confined to the western ('Austrian') half of the empire. But from 1848 to 1860, in retribution for the Magyar nobility's enthusiastic participation in an abortive Hungarian 'national revolution' under Lajos Kossuth in 1848–49, Hungary was subjected to a punitive spell of Austrian 'direct rule', during which the Habsburgs made considerable use of military tribunals and repression to 'pacify' the unruly kingdom. (Feelings ran high, as each side lost around 50,000 lives in the Austro-Hungarian conflict of 1848–40; Deak 1979: 329.) Yet from 1867 to 1918, in the wake of a humiliating and debilitating succession of Habsburg/Austrian military defeats in both Italy (1859 and 1866) and Germany (1864 and 1866), the empire was transformed into a so-called 'Dual Monarchy'. Under this regime, the Magyar aristocracy

Map 3 Eastern Europe, 1815

and lesser nobility were allowed to establish a dynamic and repressive central government of their own within the kingdom of Hungary, in place of the earlier decentralized *comitat* system of local aristocratic administrative autonomy. This heralded an enhanced partnership between the Habsburgs and Hungary's landlord class and the commencement of aggressive programmes of repression and cultural assimilation ('Magyarization') of their hapless Slovak, Ruthene and Romanian subjects. (Jewish assimilation in this era was still largely voluntary, motivated by hunger for social and economic advancement – as indeed it was for some Slovaks and Romanians as well.)

From the 1870s to the 1890s, perhaps as a consequence of the natural coherence of the kingdom of Hungary as a physical and economic unit and the very secure political and cultural hegemony of the Magyar 'Establishment' over its non-Magyar subjects (whose national awakenings had barely begun), 'Magyarization' seemed to progress very effectively. In reality, however, the Magyar 'Establishment' was merely alienating and antagonizing hitherto 'loyal' or submissive subjects and fanning the embers of embittered and vengeful Slovak, Romanian and Ruthenian/Ukrainian nationalisms, which were to find expression in fast-growing Slovak, Romanian and Ruthene/Ukrainian autonomist and separatist movements between 1900 and 1920. Relations between Magyars and non-Magyars were to become locked into cycles of repression and mutual estrangement, culminating in the extremely violent 'revolutionary disintegration' of the kingdom of Hungary between 1918 and 1920, when it lost two-thirds of its former territory.

Until the coming of the railways the Habsburg Empire remained essentially a loose assemblage of localized, autarkic manorial and village economies, remotely presided over by a weakly developed state which was buttressed by the Roman Catholic Church, the landed nobility and administrative/garrison towns. Only gradually did the coming of railways, the expansion of trade in grain and timber, the growth of industrial villages and towns and the development of capitalism erode local isolation and autarky and increase the influence and power of the state and the national market. Almost to the end, according to A.J.P. Taylor (1976: 10), 'The Habsburg lands were a collection of entailed estates, not a state; and the Habsburgs were landlords, not rulers . . . They could compound with anything, except with the demand to be free of landlords; this demand was their ruin.'

It has been argued that even the core territories of the empire lacked economic and geographical coherence: 'Bohemia was connected through her rivers with the economy of Germany; Galicia and the Bukovina were cut off from the rest of the Monarchy by mountains; Vorarlberg was connected to the textile-producing regions of Switzerland and Swabia; the Monarchy lacked any river route to her main Adriatic ports; the Danube was extremely difficult to navigate; and two-thirds of the Monarchy was covered by hills and mountains' (Sked 1989: 198). This difficult terrain made the cost of railway and canal construction much higher than in western Europe, impeding imperial integration.

By contrast, Kann (1967: 30) refers to 'the community of interests of the peoples of the Danubian area from the time when Bohemia, Hungary, Croatia and the hereditary [Austrian] German lands were united together in 1526–27 down to . . . 1918'. Likewise, Jaszi (1929: 38) wrote that 'Though this Empire as a whole did not have a unified national and geographical basis, still important popular forces were at work to form a vague feeling of solidarity in the nucleus of the Empire among Austria, Bohemia, Hungary and Croatia.' These core territories came to share a common (or at any rate overlapping) visual, cultural and culinary heritage, whether in music, in literature or in the distinctive atmosphere, architecture and cuisine of East Central European towns. For many observers this shared heritage largely defines East Central European civilization.

The unifying 'main artery' of the empire was the Danube. Both before the river became fully navigable and even after the advent of railways, the Danube river basin was the natural line of communication linking Bavaria, Linz, Vienna, Bratislava (the capital of Slovakia), Budapest (the capital of Hungary), Szeged (on the Tisza, a major tributary into the Hungarian plain), Slavonia, Zagreb (the Croatian capital, on the Sava, another tributary) and, beyond the empire, Belgrade (capital of Serbia), Wallachia (Romania) and the Black Sea. From 1784 onwards the Ottoman Empire began to allow international river traffic to have access to Belgrade, Wallachia and the Black Sea, whereupon the Magyars began to straighten their sections of the Danube. From the later nineteenth century, river improvements on the Hungarian plain and in Romania began to be combined with flood control, drainage and irrigation schemes as grain cultivation and exports expanded. The Danube Steamboat Navigation Company was established in 1831 and by the 1870s it was operating 140 steamers up and down the river.

The 1878 Congress of Berlin assigned Austria-Hungary the prime responsibility for making improvements to the treacherous Iron Gates gorge, running between the Carpathians and the Balkans. Channels were cut through the cataracts on this section of the river in 1895–99. Between 1901 and 1913 river traffic through the Iron Gates doubled. (It mainly comprised Romanian oil and agricultural products, which were exported upstream to East Central Europe and Germany, and some coal and industrial products, shipped downstream to the Black Sea states from Central Europe.) By 1913 Danube river freight amounted to some 13 million tonnes per annum, although this was still far below the 60 million tonnes per annum carried on the Rhine in western Europe. It was singularly unfortunate that the Danube flowed not towards but away from Europe's main centres of trade, industry and population. Thankfully, such physical constraints have since been reduced to virtual insignificance by the development of more modern forms of mass transport and communications, with the result that the region's predominant orientation and *choice* of partners can be determined on the basis of political and commercial considerations. Until recently, however, the region has rarely had much choice in the matter.

8　The rise of the Habsburg Empire

The historical roots, ethos and 'mission' of the Austrian Empire can be traced back to the *Ostmark* (Eastern March; hence the name *Österreich*, or Eastern Realm, Latinized into Austria). It was founded in 803 AD by Emperor Charlemagne as a fortified eastern outpost of Roman Catholic (Western) Christendom and of the new (Franco-German) Holy Roman Empire, of which he had been crowned Emperor by the Pope in 800 AD. From 803 to 1918 the enduring purpose and overriding 'mission' of the Ostmark was to stand guard over the Danubian gateway into Catholic Christendom and ward off Slav, 'infidel' and 'barbarian' incursions from the East. Throughout its long history the Austrian realm had the somewhat rigid, hard-edged, embattled spirit and mentality of a beleaguered 'frontier state'. It continued to see itself as a bastion of specifically 'Germanic' Catholic values in a sea of hostile Slavs, long after its Czech, Slovak, Slovene, Croat and Polish neighbours had been converted to Catholicism. This nurtured a strong sense of internal as well as external 'threat'. Indeed, the military and militarism of the Austrian realm eventually became 'far more . . . an instrument for maintaining inner cohesion than of a defence against foreign aggressors' (Jaszi 1929: 137).

Austria, like Prussia, emerged on the basis of successive eastward migrations of belligerent German colonists into what had been the historic 'homelands' of the Slavs. The Germans who migrated north-eastwards (including the infamous Teutonic Knights) created the nucleus of the future Prussian state, while German settlers in Bohemia, Moravia, Hungary, Transylvania, Croatia and Slovenia became the allies and 'shock troops' of the nascent Austrian state and diffused Germanic Catholic urban civilization, education, architecture and farming practices among the Slavs, Magyars and Romanians of East Central Europe and the northern Balkans.

Between 976 and 1246 the Ostmark was consolidated and extended into Styria and Carniola by the Babenburg dynasty. However, the House of Babenburg came to an abrupt end in 1246, when the reigning duke died in battle with neighbouring Hungary. In 1251, however, the vacant Babenburg fiefs were seized, not by the King of Hungary but by King Premysl Otakar II of Bohemia, a rival contender for the imperial crown of the Holy Roman Empire. But in 1273 the princes of this largely Germanic imperial confederation decided to elect Rudolf of Habsburg, a magnate with extensive possessions in south-western Germany, to the imperial throne. In 1276 and 1278 he inflicted decisive defeats on Bohemia, and in 1282 he established his descendants as the hereditary rulers of the Austrian crown lands (a position which the Habsburgs retained until 1918). From 1306 to 1307 a Habsburg occupied the Bohemian throne and from 1437 to 1439 the Habsburg emperor Albrecht II occupied both the Hungarian and the Bohemian thrones in the first of several attempts to bring Hungary and/or Bohemia under Austrian-German rule. The Habsburgs also acquired Carinthia in 1335, Tyrol in 1363, Istria in 1374, Vorarlberg in 1375, Trieste in 1382, Gorizia in 1500 and Friuli in 1511. From 1438 to 1740, moreover, only Habsburgs were to be elected to the imperial throne, which became in effect a Habsburg family heirloom. Vienna, which became the Austrian capital in 1146, was raised to the status of a bishopric in 1469.

Following the Ottoman capture of Constantinople in 1453, the strategically exposed and vulnerable kingdom of Hungary endeavoured to expand and strengthen itself at Austria's expense. The Hungarian king Matyas Hunyadi even captured Vienna in 1485. After his death in 1490, however, the increasingly disunited and beleaguered Hungarian realm turned to Austria for a defensive dynastic alliance, sealed by the intermarriage of the respective royal families. This was to become the basis on which the Austrian Habsburgs would lay claim to the vacant Hungarian throne in 1526, when the last independent King of Hungary was routed by the Ottoman Turks at the battle of Mohacs and died during his flight. Moreover, since this same King of Hungary was simultaneously King of Bohemia, the Habsburgs also gained possession of the suddenly vacant Bohemian throne. This action needed and gained the formal approval of the noble-dominated Bohemian Diet, which now looked to the Austrian Habsburgs to give Bohemia the unity, military protection and 'strong government' that it urgently required in the face of the growing 'Turkish menace'. However, the Ottoman Sultan Suleiman the Magnificent had not defeated Hungary in 1526 only then to let it fall under the sway of the more organized and tenacious Austrian Habsburgs. By late 1527 the Austrian king (and future Emperor) Ferdinand I had forced most of the Magyar aristocracy to accept his claim to the Hungarian throne and to pay increased dues (ostensibly 'tithes') to finance new defences against the Turks. In 1529, therefore, Suleiman reinvaded Hungary and, in an attempt to deter or pre-empt future Austrian Habsburg counter-offensives, laid siege to Vienna. But this stretched Ottoman military resources, techniques and supply lines beyond their limits and capabilities; with the support of Martin Luther and Lutheran as well as Catholic German princes, the Habsburgs stood their ground and eventually forced the Sultan to pull back his forces and lift the siege. Nevertheless, these were only the opening shots in an enormously taxing and protracted struggle between the Ottomans and the Austrian Habsburgs for control of Hungary, culminating in a second unsuccessful Ottoman siege of Vienna in 1683 and the subsequent Ottoman retreat from most parts of Hungary between 1683 and 1699. This contest was to become one of the two main crucibles within which Austrian absolutism, militarism and obscurantism were to be forged. The other was the Thirty Years' War within East Central Europe from 1618 to 1648.

Indeed, whether they themselves were conscious of it or not, the Habsburgs appeared to be engaged in a bid for the mastery of Europe. Emperor Maximilian I (1493–1519), who was greatly enriched by his own 'dynastic' marriage to the heiress of Burgundy (including the Low Countries) in 1477, also married his son to the daughter of the co-rulers of Castile and Aragon (Spain) in 1496 and his grandson to the daughter of the King of Hungary and Bohemia in 1506. These 'dynastic' marriages paved the way for a truly phenomenal expansion of the Habsburg dominions and an even greater expansion of Habsburg revenue from silver mining in central Europe and Spanish America as well as from Dutch, Belgian and Spanish maritime commerce in Europe, the Americas and Asia.

Emperor Charles V (1519–56) came into this extraordinary inheritance just as the Protestant Reformation was getting under way in central and northern Europe and as the Ottoman Turkish threat to Catholic Europe was reaching its peak. As ruler of Burgundy, the Low Countries, Spain, Spanish America, parts of Italy and the Holy Roman Empire, he naturally saw himself as the supreme arbiter and divinely anointed custodian of Roman Catholic Christendom, mirroring the position of Sultan Suleiman the Magnificent in the Moslem world at that time. Charles V saw Protestant 'heresy' as a fundamental challenge to his imperial authority and legitimacy, as well as to the religious unity of his vast dominions. But in the course of his indefatigable warfare against both external (Ottoman) and internal (Protestant) enemies, he frittered away the vast revenue from the silver mines of Spanish America, bankrupted the major Central European finance houses (the Fuggers and the Welsers, who had derived their fortune from mining and metallurgy), ruined Europe's richest entrepôt (the port city of Antwerp) and drove thousands of economically valuable Protestant merchants, artisans and financiers into exile from his increasingly bigoted Roman Catholic dominions.

After the eventual abdication of Charles V, who had seemingly dissipated so much of the Habsburgs' strength and riches to so little avail, Emperor Ferdinand I (1556–64) and his successors continued to consolidate and defend the East Central European territories of the Austrian-German Habsburgs. They agreed to relinquish the Low Countries, Italy and Spanish America to the Spanish Habsburgs, who proceeded to squander the rest of their 'silver' revenue on ill-fated and/or misconceived military exploits, such as the Spanish Armada (which was largely destroyed by Sir Francis Drake in 1588) and their attempted suppression of the revolt of the Dutch Netherlands from 1566 to 1648.

Meanwhile, from 1478 to 1573, there was a long succession of peasant revolts in Croatia and Slovenia, partly precipitated by Ottoman Turkish raids and territorial encroachments and partly by Protestant influences. Austrian Habsburg reprisals against the rebellious peasantry and the establishment of a fortified 'Military Frontier' (*Vojna Krajina*) to slow down and eventually repel the Ottoman advance in the northern and western Balkans gradually resulted in increased German and Catholic colonization, proselytism, influence and control in those areas (extending as far south as northern Albania and as far east as the Vojvodina, the Banat and Transylvania).

Notwithstanding the Habsburgs' staunch adherence to Roman Catholicism (which was crucial to their legitimacy, authority and self-regard), Protestantism attracted a considerable East Central European following after the 1520s. By the 1580s Protestants of various hues were clearly in a majority not only in the kingdom of Bohemia but also in Hungary. Even in Lower Austria (including Vienna), the Catholic Church experienced a slump in church attendance, fee income, donations and recruitment to the priesthood. Indeed, Protestant leaders extracted pledges of religious toleration from their Habsburg rulers in 1568 in Lower Austria, in 1575 and 1609 in Bohemia, and in 1608 in Moravia and north-western Hungary, at moments when the Habsburgs urgently needed Protestant as well as Catholic support for their titanic struggle against the Moslem Turks in Hungary and the Balkans.

Starting in 1599, however, the Habsburgs increasingly allowed militant Catholic royalists to monopolize Bohemia's key administrative and juridical positions, and to discriminate actively in favour of Catholics and Catholicism to the detriment of the non-Catholic majority. Czech and German Protestant nobles and burghers, along with many Utraquists and liberal Czech and German Catholics, felt that their existing liberties and Bohemian autonomy and tolerance were being increasingly threatened or compromised by a dangerous Catholic absolutist cabal.

THE THIRTY YEARS' WAR (1618–48) AND ITS LEGACIES

The ensuing armed conflict between Bohemia and the Habsburgs emboldened the Bohemian Diet formally to terminate Habsburg rule in Bohemia in August 1619 and then to confer the Bohemian throne on Frederick, Elector of the Palatinate and Germany's leading Protestant prince, thereby 'internationalizing' the conflict. However, with help from Maximilian of Bavaria, the Spanish Habsburgs and the (Protestant) Elector of Saxony, the Austrian Habsburgs crushed the Bohemian insurgents at the fateful battle of the White Mountain (near Prague) in November 1620. In the violent aftermath of this decisive battle, which heralded further decades of conflict and nearly three centuries of subjugation, Bohemia's population declined by at least a quarter, while over half the land passed into the hands of Catholic loyalist magnates and soldiers of fortune. They took over Bohemia's administration, suppressed traditional Bohemian rights and liberties, intensified serfdom and greatly increased levels of taxation. Whether motivated by bad consciences at having abandoned their Bohemian brethren to a terrible fate, or by fear of the ensuing augmentation of Habsburg power and dominance in Europe, rising Protestant powers such as Holland (1621), Denmark (1626) and Sweden (1630) belatedly took up arms in the name of the Protestant/anti-Habsburg 'cause'. Yet this merely escalated and prolonged this devastating European war, whose legacy of destruction was to be felt for almost a century after its formal termination by the Peace of Westphalia in 1648. East Central Europe, above all Bohemia, bore the brunt of the resultant devastation and carnage.

The Thirty Years' War also forced East Central Europe to develop and/or assimilate new methods of warfare based upon the use of well trained, flexible and mobile professional infantry, supported by light, accurate, mobile and powerful Dutch and Swedish artillery. These were enormously expensive but extremely effective. In central and eastern Europe, only strong centralized states with powerful, innovative bureaucracies and systems of public finance could afford them. The belligerents were unable to base their war effort on old-fashioned plunder and 'spoils of war', because the battlegrounds soon became too devastated and drained of movable resources to sustain that kind of warfare. This circumstance favoured the rising Austrian Empire to the detriment of its smaller or weaker or less centralized neighbours, much as it subsequently favoured the rise of the Russian and Prussian empires. Moreover, with the mining, metallurgical and technical resources of East Central Europe at their command, the Austrian Habsburgs were relatively well placed to meet the rapidly rising industrial and technical demands of the new forms of warfare. These factors not only helped the Habsburgs to strengthen their grip on East Central Europe, but also steadily tipped the military balance against the Ottomans in the protracted struggle for control of Hungary and the Balkans (Coles 1968: 186–91). The Austrian Habsburgs would have emerged even stronger if they had not simultaneously persecuted and driven into exile so many Protestant, Jewish and freethinking merchants, artisans and financiers. Indeed, it is not unfair to claim that 'the Habsburgs were distinguished by neither heroism nor intelligence; but their tenacity was unequalled, their ambition unbounded and their luck phenomenal' (p. 118).

The results of the Thirty Years' War included the 'atomization' of the German-speaking world into more than 300 states (most of them under the dominance of Habsburg Austria for the next century and a half) and the triumph of absolutism and bigotry over freethinking and tolerance in the greater part of East Central Europe. The ascent of Ferdinand II to the role of crusading Emperor (1619–37) made him 'master in his own house' and 'acquired a momentum which would allow his intelligent and more flexible heir to consolidate the achievement once peace was established'. Indeed, by the 1640s Ferdinand III (1637–57) enjoyed the immeasurable advantage that his regime 'now represented the only possible embodiment of order in Central Europe' and therefore had to be accepted by 'all who sought peace and recovery' (Evans 1979: 76). After 1648 the East Central European Counter-Reformation could proceed 'with greater intensity' and 'on a firmer base' (p. 117). 'Ecclesiastical and civil authorities combined to create a new kind of unity' (p. 140). Nevertheless, the Peace of Westphalia (1648) also marked the end of the 'wars of religion' which had racked Europe since the early sixteenth century. Henceforth wars would be fought for purely selfish dynastic, commercial and geopolitical rather than ideological reasons until the return to much more disruptive ideological warfare after the French Revolution (and again in the twentieth century). The exceptions were the continuing wars against Islam, although even these became increasingly secular, non-ideological power struggles for control of Hungary and the Balkans. In post-1648 Europe, other than in the Balkans, religious affiliation became a purely internal matter for each state rather than a pretext for warfare and for interference in each other's internal affairs. Indeed, the Peace of Westphalia bequeathed a new European state system which was supposedly based upon the exclusive jurisdiction of each state within its own territory, although in reality the major powers continued to violate the sovereignty of their weaker neighbours when they saw fit to do so. (The most extreme example was the successive Partitions of Poland-Lithuania between Russia, Prussia and Austria in the late eighteenth century.)

CULTURAL AND ECONOMIC RETARDATION

The triumphalism of Austrian absolutism and Counter-Reformation Catholicism, which was soon to be further reinforced by the Habsburg triumph over the Turks in Hungary between 1686 and 1699, engendered a deepening intellectual and cultural 'freeze' in East Central Europe in the late seventeenth and early eighteenth centuries. Thousands of Protestants, Jews and freethinkers (i.e. all 'heretics') were harassed, persecuted and driven into exile, many of them taking refuge in Protestant England, Scotland, Holland, Scandinavia and northern Germany. East Central Europe's loss was north-western Europe's gain, as the intellectual, scientific, technological and financial leadership of Europe shifted north-westwards, intersecting with the north-west European 'commercial revolution' and dramatic developments in the Atlantic economy. The latter gave rise to additional stimuli from 'new' non-European products such as cotton, silk, indigo, potatoes, tobacco, sugar, cocoa, coffee and tea. These in turn gave rise to new commercial, industrial, agricultural and scientific possibilities, including the vile profits of the Atlantic slave trade and major developments in shipping, shipbuilding, navigation and hence mathematics, optics, horology and physics (the principal thrusts of the Scientific Revolution). Such possibilities were largely closed off to the relatively hidebound and landlocked Habsburg Empire from the 1620s until the belated but vigorous development of the Enlightenment, 'enlightened despotism' and inland commerce in central and eastern Europe in the later eighteenth century.

By facilitating the commercial and scientific revolutions in north-western Europe, while strengthening absolutism, the Counter-Reformation and the ascendancy of big landowners and serf owners in central and eastern Europe, the effects of the Thirty Years' War (1618–48) and the Habsburg 'reconquest' of Hungary (1686–99) had powerfully contributed to a widening gap and a temporary 'parting of the ways' between north-western and East Central Europe. While north-western Europe had actively (albeit inadvertently) fostered capitalism and an increasingly secular, scientific and rationalist civilization, East Central Europe had experienced increased bigotry, obscurantism and 'refeudalization', including the intensification of serfdom and the concentration of land holdings in fewer (and less progressive) hands. In various regions of East Central Europe the effects were 'incalculably deleterious, setting back the development of communities by nearly a century and burdening them with a shortsighted, incompetent upstart nobility which could only prosper at the expense of the peasantry'. The most tragic setbacks occurred in formerly liberal and progressive Bohemia, where 'refeudalization . . . delayed any further development and fettered all economic initiative. It also changed the whole character of the state.' Henceforth the antagonism between Czechs and Germans would grow in intensity, as Germans came to dominate Bohemia and as the empire's administration fell into 'the hands of the new "Austrian" nobility which had made its fortune through confiscations' (Polisensky 1974: 263–4). Ironically, in so far as Catholic magnates made economic gains from the dispossession of Protestants, Utraquists and anti-Habsburg Catholics, they also compromised their integrity and independence. Until well into the nineteenth century, therefore, the 'decapitated' kingdom of Bohemia was to be short of effective and independent champions of its particular interests.

Meanwhile, an emerging East–West division of labour within Europe was encouraging East Central Europeans to specialize in the production and export of primary products by large estates employing serf labour in exchange for north-west European manufactured goods produced by wage labour. This placed East Central Europe in a subordinate, inferior, semi-colonial role *vis-à-vis* north-western Europe (p. 260). Overall, these were among the most important causes of the economic, technological and cultural retardation of East Central Europe relative to north-western Europe during the seventeenth and early eighteenth centuries.

From the 1640s to the 1740s, at the height of the 'feudal reaction', East Central Europe experienced steadily rising rents and dues, the erosion of peasant rights and land holdings, the extension of manorial cultivation and the intensification of serfdom, especially under Leopold I (1658–1705). Big landowners (including the Catholic Church and the royal family) became more actively involved in the administration of their estates and in the production and marketing of timber, linen and woollen textiles, hard liquor and minerals (such as iron, copper, coal and salt) as well as grain. They increasingly bypassed urban middlemen and fostered rural industries which could undercut urban crafts and guilds. They often employed Jews as their commercial agents. In response, non-Jewish burghers became more restrictive, defensive and antisemitic, thereby exacerbating the relative decline of towns. Big landowners also increasingly employed Jews as stewards or bailiffs ('front men') in their dealings with the peasantry, thereby contributing to the growth of peasant antisemitism. The lesser nobility, on the other hand, became more and more dependent on employment in the army, the bureaucracy and the Roman Catholic Church. But it faced mounting competition from able and well-heeled commoners. This fuelled demands for special educational provision for the sons of the lesser nobility.

FROM 'RECONQUEST' AND MERCANTILISM TO ENLIGHTENED DESPOTISM, 1686–1790

The spectacular failure of the second (and final) Turkish siege of Vienna in 1683 opened the way for a successful Austrian counter-offensive. This accomplished a Habsburg 'reconquest' of the Hungarian plain, Croatia-Slavonia and Transylvania between 1686 and 1699. The 'reconquest' was accompanied by pillage, by the widespread persecution of Hungarian Protestants (who had been relatively safe under Turkish suzerainty) and by a massive redistribution of land into the hands of an 'implanted' Catholic loyalist aristocracy and Catholic soldiers of fortune who had taken part in the 'glorious crusade' against the Turks. This persecution and rapacity gave rise to widespread anti-Habsburg insurgency in Hungary, Croatia, Slavonia and Transylvania from 1703 to 1711. The rebels took full advantage of the fact that most of the Austrian Habsburg armed forces were tied down in the War of the Spanish Succession (1701–14) in western Europe. The Austrian Habsburgs failed in their very costly bid for the vacant Spanish throne. But, in concert with England and Holland, they gained the Southern Netherlands and valuable Italian territories (Tuscany, Lombardy, Parma and Sardinia) and defeated King Louis XIV's bid for Bourbon hegemony over western Europe. In 1711, as the warfare in both western Europe and Hungary took a heavy toll, the Magyar propertied classes agreed to a compromise peace with the hard-pressed Austrian Habsburgs. The resultant Treaty of Szatmar (1711) gave Hungary a highly decentralized system of aristocratic self-administration, aristocratic 'liberties' (including freedom of conscience and exemption of landowners from direct taxation) and a separate legal system. It served as the basis of aristocratic 'loyalist' collaboration with the Austrian Habsburgs from 1711 to 1847 and of Hungary's special status within the Austrian Habsburg Empire.

Emperors Joseph I (1705–11) and Karl VI (1711–40) were somewhat less bigoted, more pragmatic and more conciliatory than their immediate predecessors. The relatively peaceful, mercantilist reign of Karl VI was also notable for the promotion of manorial and cottage industries (especially linen and woollen textiles), large-scale state-subsidized 'manufactories' (non-mechanized factories), mining, metallurgy and luxury craft industries (including porcelain, glassware, silk, lace, leather goods and clothes). These mainly developed in and around Vienna and in Bohemia-Moravia, with ancillary centres of mining and heavy industry in Styria and Silesia. Trade with the eastern Mediterranean and the Ottoman domains was encouraged by the proclamation of free trade in the Adriatic in 1717, by the 1718 peace treaty with Turkey (which also permanently ceded the 'Banat of Temesvar' to Austrian Habsburg control), by the development of Trieste and Fiume (Rijeka) as 'free ports', by the construction of highways from these ports to Vienna, and by the 'busting' of Venetian monopolies and trade privileges in the Adriatic and in the eastern Mediterranean/Ottoman domains. An exotic new world was opening up to the East Central Europeans.

From 1740 to 1780 the Habsburg Empire benefited from the 'enlightened despotism' of Maria Theresa, a shrewd 'Erastian' or 'Reform' Catholic who strongly encouraged the use of Church wealth for state and philanthropic purposes, including the beginnings of mass education in German Austria and in Bohemia-Moravia (in direct competition with the German/Lutheran states) and the more extensive provision of hospices and poor relief. However, despite Karl VI's extraordinary efforts to secure Bohemian (1720), Croatian (1721), Hungarian (1722), Transylvanian (1723), Belgian (1724), Lombard (1725) and the German princes' recognition of his daughter's claim to the whole

Habsburg inheritance (through a legal device known to historians as the Pragmatic Sanction), the succession of Maria Theresa was contested by Charles Albert of Bavaria, who was 'elected' to the imperial throne (1742–45). During the War of the Austrian Succession (1740–48) Maria Theresa eventually succeeded in getting her husband, Francis of Lorraine, elected Emperor in 1745, although real power remained in her own hands and (as a 'sweetener') she had to cede mineral-rich Lower Silesia to King Frederick ('the Great') of Prussia. (Here she unwittingly helped to set in motion a process of Prussian aggrandizement which would eventually lead to German unification and the overshadowing of the Habsburg Empire by Germany in the late nineteenth century.)

From 1749 to 1756, in the aftermath of the War of the Austrian Succession, there was a great burst of reform and centralization in Austria proper and in Bohemia-Moravia (but not in Hungary, Croatia or Transylvania). It was designed to expand the revenue base of the state sufficiently to support a standing army of 108,000 men. It was mainly implemented by parvenu bureaucrats under the guidance of Chancellor Friedrich Haugwitz in the teeth of strong opposition from the older nobility and the provincial Diets or Estates. The latter were increasingly confined to the local administration of central taxation and recruitment policies. In emulation of Prussia, moreover, a land register was established to serve as the basis of more systematic taxation of the (hitherto undertaxed) wealth of the landed nobility and for legal checks on any further erosion of peasant land holdings by big landowners. The latter marked the start of a paternalistic policy of 'peasant protection' which helped to arrest (and eventually reverse) the relative decline of independent peasant agriculture in East Central Europe, with important political, social and economic consequences for the later rise (or resurgence) of a number of submerged and downtrodden 'peasant nations' during the nineteenth and twentieth centuries.

The Seven Years' War (1756–63), which pitted the Habsburg Empire, France and Russia against Britain, Hanover and Prussia, was followed by a prolonged period of retrenchment, reform and relative peace (1763–92). The overriding aims were to expand the Habsburg revenue base sufficiently to support a standing army of 300,000 men, whilst endeavouring to avoid costly and disruptive military engagements so as to provide a breathing space for steady economic growth. Unable to compete successfully in the emerging capitalist 'world economy', the Habsburg Empire settled for an East–West division of labour within its own relatively autarkic territory and economic domain. This led to a customs union of Austria proper with Bohemia, Moravia and Habsburg Silesia in 1775 and to a substantial expansion of interregional trade and specialization. That in turn stimulated river improvements, canal construction, a network of hard-surfaced highways (over 700 km by 1800), market integration, further expansion of cottage and manorial industries, the proliferation of water-powered mills and factories (there were at least 280 'manufactories' in Austria by 1790) and the revival of towns as centres of trade and industry. These changes, combined with the resultant acceleration in population growth, helped to bring about extensions of the cultivated area, the diffusion of new crops (e.g. maize and potatoes), the introduction of new cropping systems and livestock breeds (e.g. Merino sheep), the loosening and erosion of serfdom, rising real incomes, the emergence of new forms of textile and clothing production (especially cotton) and advances in flour-milling, baking, brewing, wine-making and distilling. The increased emission and use of paper money (induced by growing state expenditure on the army, arms production, education and infrastructure and by the ensuing budget deficits) also increased financial liquidity and the commercialization and expansion of the economy. By 1789 'conditions over much of the Habsburg Empire were ripe for the introduction of factory industry: capital, skills and enterprise were available, and the institutional framework was reasonably favourable' (Gross 1973: 247). By then German Austria, Slovenia and the Czech Lands had become net exporters of manufactures. In 1782–83 finished goods made up 66 per cent of their exports and only 16 per cent of their imports (Good 1984: 25).

The most dramatic economic and social transformations occurred in Bohemia, Moravia and Habsburg Silesia. The emasculation of political ambition and activity in the Czech Lands since the Thirty Years' War (1618–48) had gradually encouraged both nobles and burghers to seek solace or to find alternative outlets for their energies, education and talents in the development of urban and rural textile, food-processing, brewing, distilling, woodworking, glassware and metallurgical industries, capitalizing on their relatively diverse and plentiful agricultural, mineral, timber and water resources and nodal situation. The increasing commercialization of agriculture as well as industry and the accelerating development of cottage, manorial and urban craft/manufacturing industries hastened the dissolution of serfdom, laid the economic and social foundations of a Czech 'national renaissance' and initiated the transformation of the Czech Lands into the industrial hub of the Habsburg Empire.

All these economic and social changes broke down social barriers, increased social 'mixing' (including intermarriage between persons of different classes, religions and nationalities) and enhanced social, geographical and occupational mobility. This allowed more and more people to find and pursue their 'true vocation' (the activity in which they could excel or perform their best), instead of remaining trapped within the confines of the social, religious, ethnic and occupational groups into which they had been born. This increased social fluidity, by promoting the fuller and more productive utilization of human resources, was a crucial stimulus to modern economic growth and to the movement away from relatively rigid and restrictive social, ethnic and religious hierarchies and mental horizons. Potentially the biggest beneficiaries of these changes were those groups which had hitherto been most restricted, i.e. serfs and Jews. Their gradual emancipation made possible new flowerings of hitherto suppressed talents.

In 1765 Joseph II, Maria Theresa's austere but 'enlightened' son, inherited the imperial crown (on the death of his father). He became a very active promoter of reform, although ultimate power and authority still remained with his mother. His reign (1765–90) saw the emergence of a reforming alliance of the Habsburgs with the lesser nobility, the burgher class, the peasantry and 'Erastian' or 'Reform' Catholics, against the overprivileged Church and aristocracy, but only in the 'Austrian' half of the empire. In 1767 statutory limitations on the labour-service obligations of the peasantry were enacted in German Austria. A Czech peasant revolt prompted similar changes in the Czech Lands in 1775. Regular taxation of the massive riches of the Catholic Church was instituted in 1769. And in 1773, with papal consent, the Habsburgs dissolved the wealthy and overweening Jesuit Order and its large network of schools and academies for the offspring of the upper classes, paving the way for a rapid expansion of more utilitarian state education, based upon an extensive network of elementary and secondary schools (*Normalschulen* and *Realschulen*). These soon placed German Austria and the Czech Lands in the forefront of European educational development, almost on a par with Protestant north Germany, Switzerland, Holland and Scandinavia and far ahead of

France, Britain, southern Europe and Russia. This educational system laid the foundations of a brilliant cultural and intellectual renaissance of the Habsburg Empire from the late eighteenth century to the early twentieth. It eventually produced such major figures as the psychologist Sigmund Freud, the writers Franz Kafka, Karel Capek, Jaroslav Hasek, Arthur Schnitzler and Hugo von Hofmannsthal, the philosophers Ernst Mach and Tomas Masaryk, the Marxists Otto Bauer, Rudolf Hilferding and Georg Lukacs, the economists Karl Menger, Eugen von Böhm-Bawerk, Ludwig von Mises, Friedrich von Hayek and Joseph Schumpeter, the painters Gustav Klimt and Oskar Kokoschka and, last but not least, the composers Franz Schubert, Hugo Wolf, Anton Bruckner, Gustav Mahler, Arnold Schönberg, Alban Berg, Bedrich Smetana, Antonin Dvorak, Leos Janacek, Bela Bartok and Zoltan Kodaly.

Indeed, contrary to popular belief, the Habsburg Empire did not go into long-term 'decline' during the nineteenth century, other than in a purely military and territorial sense. As a great power it was eventually eclipsed by the emerging German Empire. It also lost territory to the processes of German and Italian unification. But economically, culturally and intellectually the Habsburg Empire continued to develop vigorously right up to the First World War. By 1913 the *per capita* national income of German Austria was only about 10 per cent below that of Germany and roughly on a par with that of France (Good 1984: 241).

The death of Maria Theresa in 1780 ushered in a hyperactive final decade of reform under Joseph II, now freed from his cautious mother's apron strings. In 1781 he abolished personal serfdom and many compulsory peasant dues ('banalities') in German Austria and the Czech Lands. In the same year he issued a Patent of Toleration for Lutherans, Calvinists and Orthodox Christians, but not for sectarians or Jews. (He felt that the time was not yet ripe either for 'Jewish emancipation' or for the 'unleashing' of evangelical Christians.) He also relaxed censorship in order to mobilize public opinion and evoke a ferment in favour of reform. But he was too authoritarian, impatient, impulsive and convinced of his own 'rightness' to act on a basis of formal accountability. Any notion that he should have to account for his actions or introduce elements of democracy was anathema to this benign yet idiosyncratic autocrat (unfairly portrayed as an oaf in Milos Forman's celebrated film *Amadeus*).

In 1782 Joseph II ordered the dissolution of around 700 'contemplative' monasteries and convents and outlawed mendicancy (begging) by monks, while permitting the continued existence of about 1,400 monasteries and convents which ostensibly supported or provided 'really useful' trades, charity and health care. In 1784 he instituted a total ban on the importation of most manufactures, so as to protect Austro-Czech industries and foster greater imperial *Autarkie* (self-sufficiency). This also encouraged Swiss, German, British and French firms to establish subsidiaries in Austria. In 1785 he suspended Hungary's aristocratic 'liberties' (i.e. privileges) and local self-administration and imposed an Austrian-controlled central administration, with a view to extending his radical reforms to Hungary while sweeping aside Magyar aristocratic and ecclesiastical opposition to his programme. His major aims in Hungary were to establish more effective and equitable taxation, to abolish personal serfdom and to unify the Hungarian market.

The reign of Joseph II was also characterized by active promotion of the German language and German culture. The German Society popularized the works of German writers. In 1772 the company of French actors was replaced by Germans at the court theatre, which Joseph II reorganized into the Deutsches Nationaltheater in 1776. In 1782, at the Emperor's command, it commissioned and staged the first major German-language opera, Mozart's *Die Entführung aus dem Serail*. (Even more significantly, one of Vienna's suburban theatres commissioned and staged Mozart's *Die Zauberflöte* in 1791.) More controversially, Joseph II ordered the imposition of German (in place of Latin) as the official language of administration in Hungary in 1784, but this decree was reversed after his death in 1790. German nevertheless strengthened its hold as the lingua franca of officialdom and 'high culture' in East Central Europe.

In the revolutionary year of 1789, finally, Joseph II introduced a uniform 12 per cent tax on the gross yield of both noble and peasant land (as recorded in official registers), combined with a statutory limitation of the seigneurial and ecclesiastical dues payable by the peasantry to just 18 per cent of the gross yield of their land, in both German Austria and the Czech Lands. After tax, therefore, peasants in these areas were henceforth to retain a statutory 70 per cent of the gross yield of their land (as an incentive to produce and sell more), while state revenues would increase at the expense of the nobility and the Catholic Church.

Overall, according to A.J.P. Taylor (1976: 19), Joseph II's reforms were 'an astonishing achievement'. Interfering in everything, he amounted to a one-man revolution. But this apparent strength was also his major weakness. His revolutionary policies lacked 'the support of a revolutionary class'. Paradoxically, his aims could have been achieved in full only by a real revolution, yet that would also have destroyed the Habsburg Monarchy. On a more sceptical note, Kann (1974: 184) has characterized the achievements of Joseph II as 'the system of the enlightened police state: everything for the people; nothing by the people . . . It was rigid and uncompromising.' At its core was 'the notion that only one man can rule and govern and that all those entrusted with the manifold tasks of government should receive their authority from him'. Sadly, this was to become one of the most enduring legacies of Joseph II (often affectionately or ironically described as 'the people's emperor'), particularly for the fascist and communist rulers of East Central Europe in the twentieth century.

REVOLUTION AND REACTION, 1789–1848

The outbreak of the French Revolution in 1789 and the death of Joseph II in 1790 led to a substantial retreat from reform under his brother, Leopold II (1790–92), the erstwhile 'enlightened' ruler of Tuscany. As a sop to the empire's alarmed and agitated aristocracies, Leopold II immediately rescinded his brother's controversial land taxes and restored Hungary's aristocratic 'liberties' and self-administration (as 'guaranteed' by the Treaty of Szatmar in 1711). In 1791, in a vain attempt to counterbalance these concessions to 'Reaction', he introduced a police reform which established a right of *Habeas corpus* and citizens' right to information, while giving the police public health responsibilities (e.g. concerning quarantine regulations). He also increased the representation of peasants and burghers in the provincial Diets or Estates.

The retreat from reform turned into headlong flight during the long and reactionary reign of Emperor Franz II (1792–1835). Amid mounting unrest, his reign began with a purge of reformers from the central imperial administration, the reaffirmation of traditional seigneurial and ecclesiastical privileges and the substantial reversal of the enlightened reforms of Maria Theresa and Joseph II. The whole climate changed.

Revolutionary France declared war on an increasingly reactionary Habsburg Empire in April 1792. The Habsburgs unsuccessfully fought back against revolutionary France and the subsequent Bonapartist regime from April 1792 to October 1797, from March 1799 to July 1800, from September to December 1805 and from April to July 1809. The Habsburg war effort was severely constrained by the restored fiscal privileges and preferences of the landed nobility, the Catholic Church and the kingdom of Hungary and by far from 'meritocratic' military and social hierarchies. As a result of successive military defeats, the Habsburgs lost the southern Netherlands (which had already rebelled against Habsburg rule in 1789) and, temporarily, their Italian and South Slav possessions and some of their German and Alpine territories. (Napoleon even occupied Vienna itself in 1805.) In 1804, when Napoleon crowned himself Emperor of the French (with the Pope's blessing), the Habsburgs relaunched or reconstituted their remaining Austrian-German, Bohemian, Hungarian and Polish (Galician) dominions as 'the Austrian Empire' (not wishing to be upstaged by the 'Corsican upstart'). But in 1806, to forestall an Austrian attempt to unite the Germanic world against France, Napoleon obliged the newly established 'Confederation of the Rhine' to force Franz II to abdicate as Holy Roman Emperor and formally end the defunct (Germanic) Holy Roman Empire.

The succession of costly and unsuccessful wars, the ensuing losses of territory and revenue and the consequent soaring budget deficits (financed to a large extent by printing paper money) induced the Habsburgs to declare their state financially bankrupt in 1811. This 'state bankruptcy' shook the confidence of domestic and foreign investors and reduced the empire's international credit rating in subsequent decades. More generally the recurrent warfare, the disruption of established trade networks and the Continental System (Napoleon's attempted economic blockade of Britain) isolated the Austrian Empire from the new products and technologies of the British 'Industrial Revolution' and caused serious setbacks to the industrial development achieved in German Austria and the Czech Lands in the eighteenth century. A few industries (for instance, cotton textiles and sugar refining) may have benefited temporarily by being sheltered from British competition, but they either collapsed (sugar) or went into severe recession (cotton textiles) when the restoration of peace and freer trade exposed them to a 'cold blast' of foreign competition after 1815.

The age of Metternich, 1809–48

From 1809 to 1848 the conduct of Habsburg foreign policy fell into the capable but ultra-conservative hands of Count (from 1813 Prince) Clemens Metternich. In 1821 he also became court and state chancellor with wider responsibility for imperial affairs. Metternich knew (or quickly learned) how to play a very weak hand to maximum advantage. He would contrive to keep the brittle Habsburg Empire out of wars it could not win, to let others bear the brunt of its European battles and (when it was clear which way the wind was blowing) to become the chief peace broker of the victors. He would thus make Vienna the hub of European affairs from 1814 to 1848. Metternich understood that what remained of the Habsburg Empire could preserve the illusion of a 'great power' only if used very sparingly.

In Metternich's eyes the interests of Europe coincided with the interests of the Habsburg Empire. The Monarchy was a 'European necessity'. Therefore, what was good for the Habsburgs had to be good for Europe. From his ultra-conservative standpoint there could be no difference or conflict between the two. His most remarkable achievement (or good fortune) was that Europe's other powers were persuaded of this too, at least until the destabilizing rise of a unified Germany and a unified Italy upset these stabilizing assumptions from the 1860s onward. The upshot was that Metternich would not only guide the foreign policy of the Habsburg Empire but, through it, influence the destiny of Europe. Without Metternich, some have argued, nineteenth-century Europe could have developed along much more liberal lines. 'Metternich set the tone for a whole era' (Sked 1989: 8, 16, 24). Furthermore, Metternich would regain by diplomacy much of the territory and influence that his immediate predecessors lost by warfare and, under his guidance, the Habsburg Empire found itself a new European 'mission' and hence a new lease of life as a major bulwark against revolution (whether radical, liberal or national).

In March 1813, hard on the heels of Napoleon's disastrous invasion of Russia in 1812, Prussia declared war on France. At first 'Austria stood on the sidelines and offered only "armed mediation" between the warring parties' (Kann 1974: 226). However, when a badly shaken Napoleon yielded to Austria's sizeable territorial demands virtually without a fight ('the greatest mistake of his career'), Austria joined a 'grand alliance' of Russia, Sweden and Britain against France and went to war (despite soaring budget deficits and inflation) in August 1813. Napoleon was decisively defeated at the battle of Leipzig in October 1813. When he nevertheless rejected Metternich's conciliatory and shrewdly judged offer of recognition within the 'natural frontiers' of France (on the grounds that he, as 'the son of fortune', could ill afford to 'accept defeat' graciously in the way that 'legitimate rulers' had done) the grand coalition went on to depose Napoleon, occupy Paris and restore the French Bourbons in the spring of 1814. Partly as a result of the moderating influence and geographical calculations of Metternich, the peace terms imposed on France by the subsequent Congress of Vienna (September 1814–June 1815) were a 'model of restraint' (pp. 226–8).

Metternich skilfully headed off Russian and Prussian demands for the imposition of more punitive peace terms on France, because these could have opened the way for the establishment of a Russian-backed Prussian ascendancy in Germany in return for Prussian acceptance of complete Russian control of Poland (to the detriment of Austria on both counts). Hence Metternich entered a secret alliance with the British and the French delegations to resist the Russian and Prussian designs on Poland and Germany (p. 232), while also accepting the Russian Tsar's proposal of a conservative 'Holy Alliance' of Russia, Prussia and Austria to uphold the political and territorial *status quo* (particularly in central and eastern Europe). This was more in keeping with Metternich's preferred emphasis on 'legitimacy', on full restoration of the *status quo ante* wherever possible, on territorial 'compensation' where necessary and on the maintenance of a European 'balance of power' as the appropriate foundations for a (conservative) 'new European order' (p. 229).

Through the territorial settlements agreed at the Congress of Vienna in 1815 Metternich seemed to have secured a more compact and easily defended Austrian Empire. In compensation for the permanent loss of the economically valuable but strategically vulnerable southern Netherlands (Belgium), the Habsburgs secured most of northern and central Italy (Lombardy, the Veneto, Trentino, Tuscany, Modena, Piacenza and Parma) and a conservative/Catholic alliance with the papacy and the Papal States. In place of a sham/defunct 'Holy Roman Empire', which had been fragmented into over 300 states under the terms of the Treaty of Westphalia (1648), Prince Metternich secured a seemingly more coherent and effective 'German Confederation' of thirty-nine states (including British-ruled Hanover, Danish-ruled Holstein, Dutch-ruled Luxembourg, Bohemia and four city-states), under the authority of a bi-cameral *Bundestag* (or confederal Diet) in Frankfurt am Main and a permanent Austrian 'presidency'. It was originally established as an instrument of mutual defence against potential external threats, e.g. French revanchism or Russian imperialism. But in practice it soon became an instrument for maintaining the internal *status quo*, for blocking internal change, for great-power interference in the internal affairs of the smaller German states and for closer co-operation between political police and censors in a reactionary struggle against the (real or imagined) internal security threats posed by nascent German nationalism, liberalism and student radicalism, from 1817 to 1848.

In September 1819, under pressure from Metternich following the March assassination of the notable playwright August von Kotzebue by a German nationalist student (Karl Sand), the Frankfurt Bundestag unanimously approved a draconian set of decrees adopted by a congress of German states in Karlsbad in August 1819. Up to 1848 these notorious 'Karlsbad Decrees' (renewed for an indefinite period in 1824) subjected the 'Germanic world' (including Bohemia) to wide-ranging police powers, elaborate and irksome censorship, a purge and police surveillance of universities, the prohibition of all student societies, networks of police 'spies' and 'informers' and blacklists of suspect individuals, i.e. the paraphernalia of a modern *Polizeistaat* (police state). In 1820, moreover, Article 13 of the German Confederation was modified to concentrate all sovereign power in the hands of rulers and to curb the granting of 'constitutions' and the 'consultative' roles of representative bodies such as provincial Diets. And in 1832 and 1834, following the revolutions in various parts of Europe in 1830–31, these provisions and the supporting networks of police, censors, spies and informers were strengthened still further, leading to the suppression of several Diets and universities. It is thus scarcely surprising that Metternich, the architect of 'Reaction', should have become such a hero to American conservative Cold Warriors and diplomatic historians such as the young Henry Kissinger.

The Austrian Empire thus re-emerged as the dominant reactionary power in East Central Europe as well as in the Italian peninsula. This also strengthened its position in Dalmatia, Croatia, the Adriatic and the eastern Mediterranean. But appearances were deceptive. In the longer term the imposition of an alien, repressive and ultra-conservative Austrian hegemony in Italy aroused an Italian nationalist backlash which would culminate in successive wars of Italian unification (1848–49, 1859–60 and 1866, with a 'postscript' in 1915–18). It was not just that 'progressive' currents found themselves blocked, repressed and censored by the conservative–Catholic Austrian alliance with the papacy. The Austrians also patently failed to understand the venality and the sometimes prickly sensibilities of the wealthy Italian aristocrats who (for the most part) would have been willing to be 'co-opted' or 'bought off' by the Habsburgs, since they had a long-standing tradition of 'collaboration' with foreign rulers. Instead they found themselves 'slighted' and excluded from political power and court circles by haughty, aloof and often austere German-speaking viceroys, officers and officials who refused to recognize most Italian titles of nobility. The upshot was that the greater part of the Austrian army had to be stationed in northern and central Italy to keep the lid on this simmering cauldron of social and nationalist discontents. Austria's Italian possessions became more of a liability than an asset, not least because they diverted Habsburg attention from the (potentially) much more serious challenges to imperial power which were brewing in Germany and the Balkans.

The greatly reduced political fragmentation of the 'Germanic world' after 1815 made Austrian dominance far less complete and less secure than it had been in the seventeenth and eighteenth centuries. Medium-sized German states (e.g. Bavaria, Saxony and Hanover) could hope to gain greater freedom of manoeuvre for themselves by playing off Prussia against Austria. For its part Prussia used its acquisition of the Rhineland in 1815, its espousal of free trade from 1818 onwards and the development of the *Deutsche Zollverein* (German Customs Union) and a more integrated German economy from 1834 onwards to bind the more industrialized German states more closely to itself and to marginalize Austria. Indeed, Prussia could afford to pursue its German interests and ambitions more singlemindedly than Austria; and, for geographical reasons, almost any integrated German market and transport system had to involve Prussia and the Rhineland, but could (and increasingly did) bypass Austria. In implicit acknowledgement of Prussia's growing role and status as 'the other power' in Germany, Austria increasingly relied on Prussia to 'police' and 'protect' the German Confederation. 'In theory, Austria and Prussia were combined in the defence of Germany; in practice, Austria left the main task to Prussia and discovered, too late, the penalty of her adroitness' (Taylor 1976: 34).

Furthermore, expansion into the Balkans had set the Austrian Empire on a potential 'collision course' with the Russian Empire, which was busily expanding its 'fraternal' influence on Orthodox Serbia, Montenegro, Bulgaria and, less enduringly, on non-Slavic Romania and Greece. Indeed, Russia's acquisition of Bessarabia (present-day Moldova) in 1812 had brought her within reach of the river Danube. Almost any further expansion by Russia into the Balkans would have led to Russian control of the mouth and lower reaches of the Danube, the main artery of the Austrian Empire. Finally, by advancing into the Balkans the Habsburgs were storing up potentially explosive 'south Slav problems' for the future, just to add to their inflammable Magyar, Italian, German and Bohemian problems.

The quickening pace of economic and social change

Nevertheless, these slowly germinating problems remained under wraps until 1848. Despite (or perhaps because of) the repressive conservatism and stability of the Metternich era, the Austrian Empire achieved steady economic recovery during the 1820s and significant economic growth in the 1830s and early 1840s. For the period 1830–45, in the 'Austrian half' of the empire, it has been estimated that average annual growth rates were in the region of 2.5–3.3 per cent for aggregate industrial output, 7 per cent for mining output, 4–5 per cent for metallurgy, 4 per cent for engineering, 4 per cent for textiles (7 per cent for cotton) and 2 per cent for food-processing (5 per cent in the case of sugar refining). Crop production grew at an average annual rate of 1.2–1.4 per cent. In contrast, population growth was only 0.7 per cent per annum (Good 1984: 45–8, 69). On the same territory, the non-agricultural work force had grown to about 28 per cent of the total by 1850, but in Bohemia the proportion was 36 per cent (pp. 46–7). The very existence of an adequate statistical basis for such estimates is itself indicative of significant economic and administrative attainments in mid-nineteenth-century Austria, especially Bohemia.

The establishment of the Danube Steam Navigation Company in 1831 was a major milestone in the development of the Danube as the 'main artery' of the Habsburg Empire, since steam-powered vessels could easily navigate upstream as well as down. During the 1830s and early 1840s Hungary became a significant exporter of grain, wool, timber and flour up the Danube to Austria and Germany. This immediately stimulated the construction of Hungary's first large-scale flour mills and steam-powered sawmills, which in turn helped to stimulate the commercialization of Hungarian agriculture, with major extensions of grain cultivation and livestock rearing, significant drainage, irrigation and river improvement schemes and increased employment of wage labour in place of serfs. In German Austria and the Czech Lands, by contrast, the major developments in the 1830s and early 1840s were in food-processing, brewing, distilling, textiles, metallurgy, mining and machine-building, drawing upon greater supplies of capital and a more educated and technologically receptive work force. During the 1830s and 1840s there was a revival of the refining of beet sugar, in which the Austrian Empire (and especially the Czech Lands) was destined to become a world leader in both output and technology. Large-scale brewing of beer began to develop in Vienna, Prague and Plzen (the home of the famous Pilsener lager process). The growth of urban demand for food, drinks, clothing, timber and agricultural raw materials, transport improvements and the growth of interregional trade and specialization encouraged the growth of more productive and more market-oriented agriculture, land improvement, capital accumulation and the diffusion of new and more remunerative root and forage crops, crop rotation and livestock breeds in both halves of the Habsburg Empire. In 1836 the ocean-going Austrian Lloyd Steamship Company was established, operating services from Fiume and Trieste. Between 1835 and 1839 Austria's first steam-powered railways were built north and south of Vienna, using Austrian-made rails. Over 140 km of railway had been opened by 1839, 378 km by 1842 and 1,025 km by 1848, although only 46 km had as yet been opened in Hungary by 1846.

From 1815 to 1848, in East Central Europe as well as in western Europe, there occurred a steady drift of population away from the land and 'industrial' villages into large towns and cities. By 1850 Vienna had about 444,000 inhabitants (compared with 247,000 in 1800), Budapest had 178,000 (54,000 in 1800), Prague had 118,000 (75,000 in 1800) and Krakow had 50,000 (24,000 in 1800). The Revolutionary and Napoleonic Wars of 1792–1814 had unsettled thousands of rural communities and had mobilized and/or uprooted millions of people. Many of the millions of men who had fought in those wars (often in foreign lands) later found it difficult to settle back into their former homes, villages and occupations. Many had acquired the 'wander lust', while others were just plain restless, often perhaps without quite knowing why.

In addition, war, revolution, agrarian change and the continuing rise of capitalism were helping to burst the constricting bonds of serfdom and so-called 'feudalism', which still tied tens of millions of peasants to virtually hereditary domiciles, social positions and occupations. Compared with semi-industrial Britain, however, much lower proportions of the uprooted or displaced persons who drifted into the larger towns and cities on the Continent were being absorbed into regular paid employment. In continental Europe industrialization had not yet assumed such massive proportions as it had in Britain. Instead of being thoroughly incorporated into a relatively stable and settled urban proletariat or upper/lower middle class, as in Britain, the Continental 'flotsam and jetsam' remained relatively unincorporated 'lumpenproletarians' (if they were uneducated) or members of an unincorporated and insecure 'lumpen' intelligentsia or 'lumpen' bourgeoisie (if they were educated). Thus the increasingly overcrowded large towns and cities on the Continent were being swollen by tens of thousands of homeless and unemployed persons (vagrants, waifs and beggars), prostitutes, petty criminals, casual labourers, opportunists and fortune-hunters.

The Continent was suffering not so much from the development of industry as from insufficient expansion of industrial and commercial employment (despite impressive rises in industrial output). Indeed, the beginnings of mechanization (especially in textile production), falling transport costs, the advent of railways and the growing scale, concentration and productivity of continental European industry were undercutting and making redundant millions of urban as well as rural handicraftsmen (especially hand-loom weavers), who found it increasingly difficult to compete with the products of factory industry, whether domestic or imported. Some rural centres of handicraft industry achieved the transitions to large-scale mechanized production and became 'little Manchesters' (including parts of Bohemia, German Austria and the Rhineland). But their success merely exacerbated the plight of the majority of handicraft centres, many of which ultimately failed to adapt and survive, particularly during the 'hungry' 1840s (this was particularly the case in areas such as Silesia, Flanders, south-western Ireland and rural Hungary, which experienced rural 'de-industrialization' from the 1830s to the 1850s).

Yet because industrialization and the construction of railways not only destroyed old crafts but sometimes gave rise to new craft employment or gave some existing handicraft industries larger markets, the *overall* number of continental Europeans dependent on the land and/or handicraft industries did not decline dramatically in absolute terms, even though their share of the total population was falling. The crucial point is that these 'traditional' occupations were unable to absorb Europe's burgeoning population growth. In the main it was 'surplus' labour (surplus to the requirements of traditional activities) which increasingly drifted to the larger towns and cities, desperately seeking new ways of making a living, even if it meant engaging in petty crime, prostitution, begging or scavenging. Such phenomena are nowadays assumed to be more characteristic of Third World industrialization (which has also generally failed to generate sufficient paid employment). But it is pertinent to remember that continental Europe passed through a similar phase in the middle decades of the nineteenth century and that it constituted the basic socio-economic context of the 1848 Revolutions. Socially, the latter were arguably more the result of the *insufficient* development (rather than the development) of capitalism. Those who had either lost or not yet found a secure foothold in Europe's emerging urban industrial civilization often ended up in the ranks of the unincorporated 'lumpenproletariat' or the 'lumpen' bourgeoisie or the 'lumpen' intelligentsia (the would-be workers, entrepreneurs, professionals and intellectuals). They furnished many of the 'foot soldiers', 'rent-a-mobs' and malcontents who participated in the Revolutions of 1848.

Significantly, the 1840s also saw the beginnings of mass emigration from East Central Europe (and also from Ireland) to the Americas. Like the 'social misfits', malcontents, miscreants, rebels and revolutionaries of 1848, the emigrants were not only trying to escape from social injustice, political and religious intolerance and economic misfortune. They were also seeking (or hoping to build) new lives in a more just new world, with greater equality of opportunity for all. After the collapse of the 1848 Revolutions in East

Central Europe (as in Italy) more and more people turned their thoughts to emigration. The latter became a major social and political 'safety valve', helping to prevent any major recurrence of the revolutionary turmoil of 1848–49 in East Central Europe in the remaining years of the empire.

The Metternich regime

The Metternich regime had built dams to hold back the rising tide of nationalism, liberalism, radicalism and discontent. In 1848 these dams burst, partly because the political heartlands of continental Europe were all convulsed by powerful social and ideological currents (and the Austrian Empire could not be hermetically insulated from them) and partly because they went hand-in-hand with the mushrooming growth of new social classes. These new social classes, the bourgeoisie and the proletariat, could not easily be accommodated within the existing social hierarchies, rooted as these were in specifically pre-industrial economies and societies. Only countries which were in a real sense on the political periphery of continental Europe (Britain, Ireland, Scandinavia, Russia, Serbia, Greece, Albania, Spain and Portugal) failed to experience revolution in 1848.

Although the Austrian Empire under Metternich was a *Polizeistaat* in the sense that the state employed censorship, police spies and informers, interception of mail, arbitrary powers of arrest, travel restrictions and mandatory registration of residence, servants, hotel visitors and Jews, there was another (somewhat contradictory) side to the coin. Metternich professed to believe in a *Rechtsstaat*, a 'law-governed society'. The 'supranational' imperial government in Vienna (unlike its post-1867 Magyar counterpart in Budapest) did make some attempt to be 'neutral' or impartial in its treatment of the various 'nationalities', despite the troublesome growth of pan-German nationalism and the preponderance of Austrian Germans in the imperial administration. Metternich believed in 'pure' rather than 'constitutional' monarchy. But he did not support arbitrary monarchy, which he equated with 'oriental despotism'. He expected the monarch to take advice, to pursue 'orderly practices of government' and to uphold the laws, the justice, the social order and the Roman Catholic precepts upon which monarchical authority and legitimacy ultimately rested (and which the Monarchy would violate at its peril). Essentially, Metternich saw the Habsburg Empire as 'a system in which a variety of nationalities coexisted within a monarchical framework based on social hierarchy and the rule of law' (Sked 1989: 25, 16).

The nineteenth-century Habsburg bureaucracy was relatively competent, conscientious, impartial, professional, law-abiding and free from corruption – in comparison, that is, with the states located further south and east in Europe. This legacy (even more than the higher levels of education, technology and economic development) became the crucial advantage of the Czech Republic, Hungary and Slovenia over most other eastern European states during the post-1989 transition to democracy and the market. The legacy of a relatively 'law-governed' administrative tradition and society is what has placed them (along with Poland and the Baltic States) at the front of the queue for eventual membership of the European Union and has made them the preferred locations for Western companies and investment in central and eastern Europe. The rule of law is a prerequisite for the proper functioning of both democracy and market economies, especially in relation to international dealings and transactions. Market economies can, of course, operate without democracy. But, if they are to be fully consummated, both require the rule of law and a neutral or impartial state capable of consistently upholding and enforcing the rules and contracts on which they rest, as a basis for autonomous and pluralist political, social, cultural and economic activity.

Fortunately for German Austria, the Czech Lands, Austrian Poland, Hungary, northern Italy and Slovenia, Metternich's Austrian Empire largely rested on dynastic 'rights' and 'legitimacy', international treaties and international law. Consequently the 'rule of law' was essential to the empire's survival, even if it was never fully upheld and enforced. By nineteenth-century standards, the state kept relatively few political prisoners and made little (if any) use of torture. Foreign (even 'prohibited') literature circulated widely, while the police were in fact too few in number to exercise effective control during a crisis. Thus in Vienna in 1848 Metternich could rely only on a garrison of 14,000, a police force of 1,000 and a municipal guard of 14,000 (most of whom were bandsmen), while the Austrian Empire as a whole was arguably under-policed (Sked 1989: 44–52, 82–3).

9 An empire in crisis
East Central Europe and the Revolutions of 1848–49

THE INCIPIENT DESTABILIZATION OF EAST CENTRAL EUROPE

The political stability that East Central Europe lost in 1848 (with the fall of the Metternich regime) was not regained until 1948 (with the full imposition of Stalinist control), after a whole century of endemic instability and crisis. After 1848 Habsburg absolutism was always on the defensive. 'The dynastic idea was challenged and, once challenged, could never recover the unconscious security of the past. The "Austrian idea" became an idea like any other, competing for intellectual backing; and the dynasty survived not on its own strength, but by manoeuvring the forces of rival nations and classes' (Taylor 1976: 56–7). But, in the final analysis, 'the Habsburg Monarchy and nationalism were incompatible; no real peace was possible between them. Metternich saw this more clearly than many of his successors' (p. 40). This was at the heart of the subsequent endemic instability and crisis up to 1918 and even beyond, when the problem became one of what would take the Habsburg Empire's place. The Revolutions of 1848–49 also first posed and made some Europeans fully aware of the difficulty of accommodating a unified German polity in a Europe mainly made up of much smaller nations and states (or would-be states). Indeed, the Czech leaders of 1848 were the first people to be directly confronted by 'the German problem', which has loomed so large in European affairs ever since. For these and other reasons 1848 was an extraordinary 'defining moment' in the emergence of modern Europe, especially in the Habsburg domains.

It is extremely difficult to provide an adequate overview of the polycentric and kaleidoscopically interacting events of 1848–49. The Revolutions within the Austrian Empire 'took place in several theatres and on several levels. All were interrelated. This factor can never be fully shown in a historical presentation, which cannot tell all at the same time' (Kann 1974: 299). Moreover, there were major interactions and overlaps between internal and external events – for example, between the revolutions and the Austro-Prussian competition for predominance in the German-speaking world, or between the Austrian wars against Piedmont-Sardinia and the revolutions in Lombardy and Venetia. Besides, the revolutions in the Austrian Empire 'flared up in some places, then quietened down to move to other scenes, to break out again in the old places. There is no centre or continuity in the revolutionary events' (p. 300).

Nevertheless, despite the striking diversity of the territories that became embroiled in the Revolutions of 1848–49, 'the European Continent responded to the impulses and trends of the revolution with a remarkable uniformity', because there existed 'a basic unity and cohesion in the intellectual world of the European Continent, such as usually asserts itself in the peak periods of its spiritual development'. The Revolutions of 1848–49 were 'born at least as much of hopes as of discontents' and their 'common denominator was ideological'. It was for this reason, above all, that Sir Lewis Namier called these convulsions 'the revolution of the intellectuals – *la révolution des clercs*' (Namier 1946: 4). 'The Revolution of 1848 was universally expected, and it was super-national as none before or after; it ran through and enveloped the core of Europe' (p. 3). Indeed, it helped to define the emergent 'core of Europe' to a degree that even someone as prescient as Namier could not have foreseen. For the countries which actively participated in the Revolutions of 1848–49 have strongly desired to be at the heart of the late twentieth-century European integration process, whereas 'peripheral' or semi-detached countries such as Britain, Norway, Sweden and Russia, which were mere onlookers and bystanders during the 'revolution of the intellectuals', have remained on the margins of 'the European project'. In truth, the countries that were intellectually detached from the Revolutions of 1848–49 have tended to remain similarly 'disengaged' from many of the political and ideological currents, projects and concerns of Europe's 'core' countries ever since.

The Revolutions of 1848 were preceded by some local grain harvest failures and severe potato blight in 1845–47 and by industrial recession in 1847. These misfortunes contributed to the climate of heightened social tension and economic distress and added to the already menacing problems of vagrancy, banditry and urban unemployment. Between 1847 and 1850, moreover, many parts of eastern, central and even western Europe were convulsed by a massive cholera epidemic. The terrible gastric symptoms of that relatively unfamiliar disease and woeful ignorance about its nature and transmission, combined with the fact that the millions of victims were heavily concentrated among the lower orders (including vagrants, waifs, beggars and lumpenproletarians), fuelled false rumours that the disease was spread by physical contact with human 'vermin' and that the terrified upper classes were attempting to 'poison off' large segments of the dirty, 'dangerous', fast-growing and semi-criminalized lower orders. Such rumours further exacerbated the tensions and mutual distrust between social classes and between the rulers and the ruled. In the end, however, the Revolutions of 1848–49 were defeated because, except in Hungary, 'ultimate control of the state-machine, and still more of the armies of the Great powers on the European Continent, remained with the Conservatives' (Namier 1946: 31).

THE GALICIAN REVOLT OF 1846

In February 1846, as an ominous prologue to the Revolutions of 1848, an unsuccessful revolt of the Polish nationalist nobility in semi-autonomous Krakow sparked off a major rebellion of the exceptionally impoverished and downtrodden serfs of western and central Galicia against their Polish 'masters'. It has been hotly debated whether this serf rebellion was deviously incited by the Austrian authorities. Wandycz (1974: 134–5) claims that the Polish nationalist insurgents were 'massacred by peasant bands which had been mobilized and paid by the Austrian commander . . . The Galician administration, which had taken no preventive measures against the approaching revolution, fostered the peasants' antagonism toward the revolutionary nobles and connived at or in some cases engineered the peasant outbreaks.' On the other hand, Sked (1989: 63) asserts that 'the

Habsburg authorities – despite later charges of connivance – knew nothing about what was going on and were appalled at the results of the blood-lust'. Either way, the conflicting accounts agree that thousands of Polish landlords and estate managers were killed by their cruelly oppressed serfs before the *jacquerie* was brutally suppressed by Austrian troops. The lesson was not lost on the partitioning powers, who thus discovered the 'Achilles heel' of the Polish nationalist nobility. Indeed, Metternich wrote to Field Marshal Radetzky: 'An extraordinary event has just taken place . . . The attempt by the Polish Emigration to start another revolution in the former Polish territories has been . . . smashed by the Polish peasantry . . . A new era, therefore, has dawned' (p. 64). Moreover, the imperial powers had learned that they could turn the tables on (and literally cut the ground from under) recalcitrant or nationalistic nobilities by wooing and manipulating their maltreated peasants, whether by enacting 'populist' agrarian and electoral reforms or by 'mobilizing' peasant discontent against landlords. This was to be one of the most potent (albeit double-edged) swords in imperial hands from 1848 to 1918. After 1846, therefore, the Habsburgs could count on the calculated 'loyalism' of the shocked and chastened Galician nobility. Indeed, Austrian Poland produced a rather muted, subdued response to the Revolutions of 1848.

ITALY IGNITES, 1847–49

The opening shots in the Revolutions of 1848 were fired in Italy. In 1847, in Habsburg-ruled Lombardy and Venetia, democrats and 'patriots' put strong pressure on the leading 'moderates' to petition Emperor Ferdinand for self-government and civil liberties. Tension rose as the police attacked a peaceful demonstration in Milan in September 1847, encouraging northern Italian democrats and 'patriots' to back a ('no smoking') boycott of the (Habsburg) state tobacco monopoly. In retaliation, the Austrian authorities provoked violent clashes between the army (under the octogenarian Radetzky) and unarmed civilians on 3 January 1848, as 'justification' for the imposition of martial law. This merely confirmed popular perceptions of Habsburg hegemony as the overriding obstacle to the liberation and unification of Italy. Beyond the more academic expressions of anti-Habsburg sentiment, Verdi's *Nabucco* (1842) potently caught and expressed the growing public mood of eloquent protest against Italy's 'Babylonian captivity'. Indeed, the opera's moving 'chorus of the exiled Hebrew slaves' ('Va, pensiero') was not only the most inspired and inspiring expression of 'the soul of the nation', but also became a favourite anthem of many subsequent European 'national liberation' movements, including the 'singing revolutions' in eastern Europe. It was seconded by the similarly affecting 'chorus of Scottish exiles' from Verdi's *Macbeth* (1847), which was immediately taken up by the 'patriots' of 1848.

The embattled northern Italian 'patriots' and democrats were spurred on by the news of successful popular uprisings against Neapolitan Bourbon absolutism in Sicily (12–27 January 1848), the promulgation of liberal constitutions in the Kingdom of Naples and Sicily (29 January) and in Tuscany (11 February), the forced abdication of King Louis Philippe in France (24 February) and the forced resignation of Metternich in Vienna (13 March). On 18 March, finally, workers and craftsmen, led by young Italian 'patriots' and democrats, launched an anti-Habsburg uprising in Milan. But Milan's radical 'patriots' and democrats were insufficiently prepared, united or resolute to keep the upper hand and establish either a radical provisional government or a democratic republic.

Before the radicals could consolidate their initial ascendancy, Lombardy's propertied classes (who were terrified of both 'republican anarchy' and far-reaching 'social revolution') seized the initiative and appealed to the adjacent kingdom of Piedmont and Sardinia for military assistance against the Austrian army and (implicitly) against the radical 'patriots', democrats and populace. Radicals and republicans were fobbed off with empty assurances that the invading Piedmontese army (commanded by King Carlo Alberto in person) would not simply annex Lombardy but would accept the result of a plebiscite and that, once the Habsburgs were decisively defeated, Italy's constitution and destiny would be discussed and settled by the country as a whole.

In Venice, by contrast, aided by the fact that Habsburg troops were already being withdrawn in response to the crisis in Lombardy, radical democrats led by Daniele Manin seized power on 22 March 1848 and quickly proclaimed a new Venetian Republic. With the Habsburgs seemingly 'finished' in Italy, the 'client' rulers of Parma and Modena also capitulated within days.

Nevertheless, Piedmont's King Carlo Alberto and the Italian 'patriots' failed to press home their initial advantage. Their fatal delays, disorganization and tactical errors allowed Radetzky to regroup the Habsburg forces, defeat Piedmont-Sardinia (twice over, in July 1848 and March 1849), reconquer Austria's Italian possessions (summer 1849) and restore the *status quo ante*. (Radetzky's decisive victories are commemorated in the popular, chauvinistic 'Radetzky March' by Johann Strauss Senior, which still concludes the New Year's Day concert in Vienna every year.) The defeated north Italian revolutions had a wider and more important significance, however. They set an anti-Habsburg agenda for the Italian *Risorgimento* (Revival) in the 1850s and 1860s. They also intensified the Habsburgs' (ultimately ruinous and irrational) obsession with hanging on at all costs to their not so important or valuable Italian domains. This tied up Habsburg forces which could otherwise have been used to 'nip in the bud' the potentially more menacing revolts in German Austria, Bohemia and Hungary. Indeed, the various oppositional forces in the Habsburg Empire in 1848–49 were able to remain in the ascendant only so long as the bulk of the imperial army was pinned down in northern Italy. Some writers and politicians argued that the Habsburgs could not survive the loss of their Italian possessions, but in point of fact they did survive the loss of Lombardy in 1859 and of the Veneto in 1866. As a result of their strenuous and futile attempts to prevent the (probably inevitable) loss of their Italian possessions, which they succeeded only in postponing for a few years, they also fatally weakened their hold on Hungary and the German confederation. This was too great a price to pay for a sunny 'imperial back yard' in Italy.

THE END OF THE METTERNICH REGIME, MARCH 1848

News of the dramatic events in Italy in January 1848 and of the fall of the French monarchy on 24 February 1848 soon travelled by train, post and telegraph to many parts of the Habsburg Empire and the Germanic world. But these 'ripples' from France and Italy merely acted as a catalyst. Habsburg absolutism was already under increasing challenge in German Austria, Bohemia and Hungary *before* 1848, as was Prussian absolutism in northern Germany and the Rhineland.

By the end of February 1848 radical and nationalist students had taken to the streets in Buda and Pest. On 3 March 1848 Lajos Kossuth, leader of the radical nationalist Magyar nobility in the Hungarian Diet, called for the liberation of Hungary from Austrian tutelage and came to Vienna to incite rebellion at the very nerve-centre of the Habsburg Empire. On 11 March 1848 radical Czechs and Germans met in Prague to demand a restoration of the unity, civil liberties and self-government of the long defunct Kingdom of Bohemia (or, in other words, a revival of the pre-1620s Bohemian constitution and quasi-statehood). In early March, amid growing street demonstrations in Vienna and a run on the banks, the Habsburgs panicked and prepared to ditch Metternich, in the hope that it would calm the rapidly spreading unrest.

On 13 March 1848, egged on by those who resented or envied Metternich's position and power and by the search for a scapegoat, the Diet of Lower Austria (the Vienna region) openly demanded his resignation; the demand was immediately taken up by protesters on Vienna's streets. Since no one rallied to his defence, Metternich complied. Yet, instead of defusing the crisis, his resignation merely created a power vacuum and encouraged the malcontents to step up their agitation and demands. The Habsburgs temporarily lost control of events as power passed to the provinces and city streets, and the Austrian Empire came closer to disintegration in 1848–49 than at any other time before the First World War. The unrest in Vienna and the fall of Metternich caused imperial paralysis and a loss of direction and authority in what had become a very centrally directed polity, leaving the confused provincial authorities to flounder about without clear or practicable instructions. The Revolutions of 1848 laid bare the latent tensions and contradictions between and within the various peoples that made up the Habsburg Empire.

THE RESURGENCE OF HUNGARY, 1790–1849

The strongest challenge to the political and territorial integrity of the Habsburg Empire during the Revolutions of 1848–49 emanated from Hungary. The roots of this challenge have been (very illuminatingly) traced back to changes which came over Hungary in the late eighteenth and early nineteenth centuries (Janos 1982: 16–83). During the 1790s and 1800s, stimulated by the supply needs of the warring European armies and the disruption of agricultural production in Europe's major war zones, grain and wool prices had more than quadrupled. In response to these exceptional wartime conditions, Hungary's production and exports of grain and wool had dramatically increased (both in volume and, especially, in value). Magyar landowners had raised both the area and the methods of grain cultivation. The Magyar nobility had been able greatly to expand its consumption of Western-style foods, drinks, clothing, furnishings, glassware, silverware and even books and newspapers (including many imported products), and several wealthy aristocrats had begun to sponsor a new generation of 'improving landlords' and 'enlightened' gentlemen farmers, in emulation of British role models. Acting in conjunction with the ideas, attitudes and policies of the late eighteenth-century Enlightenment and 'enlightened despotism', these new circumstances and stimuli had initiated a 'cultural revolution' involving fundamental changes in the mentality, outlook, life style and aspirations of Hungary's increasingly educated and assertive nobility, who made up the top 5 per cent of the population (Deak 1979: 4).

The Magyar nobility was disproportionately large because it included anyone who could claim descent from the numerous family retainers, vassals and other feudal servitors of the medieval Arpad dynasty and, in addition, the descendants of the large numbers of warriors who had been ennobled in order to augment the recruitment of fighting men into the armies of the rival rulers of Hungary during the Turkish Wars of the sixteenth and seventeenth centuries. By the 1780s, 108 aristocratic families (the 'magnates') controlled about 40 per cent of all fiefs in twenty-seven counties of Hungary (including Croatia-Slavonia, but excluding Transylvania). Another 40 per cent of all fiefs belonged to a much more numerous section of the nobility known as the 'bene possessionati'. In the early nineteenth century the latter started to refer to themselves as the 'gentry', using either the actual English word or its Magyarized form (*dzsentri*). They began to ape the manners, ideas and life style of their English 'cousins'. But four-fifths of the nobility, who numbered around 389,000 people (including dependants) in 1787 and about 617,000 in 1839, were in no sense *seigneurs* or 'feudal lords'. They were mostly smallholders or minor state officials or the minions of rich magnates, and were distinguished from commoners only by their formal fiscal exemptions and legal immunities and their right of participation in local 'noble assemblies' and in elections to the lower house of the Hungarian Diet (Janos 1982: 17–19). The poorest nobles were commonly known as the 'sandalled' nobility because they could not afford fine boots. Until the early nineteenth century membership of the Magyar 'nobility' was virtually synonymous with membership of the Magyar political 'nation' (*natio*). In effect 'Magyar was a class term: it meant an owner of land exempt from the land-tax, or one who attended the county assemblies and took part in the elections to the Diet' (Taylor 1976: 26–7). Burghers also enjoyed local self-administration and token representation in the Hungarian Diet, but the burgher 'estate' largely consisted of Germans (and, from the 1840s, Jewish immigrants from Poland, Austria and Russia) rather than Magyars.

From 1792 to 1809, in repeated attempts to elicit increased Magyar 'contributions' of money and men to successive war efforts against France, the Austrian Emperor (Franz) had wooed and flattered the Magyar nobility/'nation'. During the sessions of the Hungarian Diet in 1809 he had even had to pose as a 'Hungarian patriot' in order to counter Napoleon's appeal for a Hungarian revolt against the Habsburgs (Taylor 1976: 44). But in 1811, when the Austrian state declared itself bankrupt, the Hungarian Diet had refused to accede to Habsburg attempts to devalue the Hungarian currency (to reduce it to parity with the greatly depreciated Austrian currency). The Diet was in the end prorogued by the infuriated Emperor, who refused to call another Hungarian Diet until 1825, violating his constitutional duty to convoke a Diet at least once every three years (Kann 1974: 237).

Furthermore, the termination of the Napoleonic Wars in 1814 was followed by a steep decline in the effective demand for and the prices of grain and wool. This brought financial ruin to large sections of the Magyar nobility who had borrowed heavily during the boom years of the 1790s and 1800s or who were living beyond their means. Many more experienced acute difficulty in adjusting to the straitened economic circumstances of the post-1814 decade and to an increasingly competitive commercial environment thereafter, having grown accustomed to greatly increased expenditure on 'status con-sumption'. (These difficulties of adjustment were perhaps reflected in the Magyar saying 'A gentleman is never in a hurry, never shows surprise and never repays his debts'!) Many items which had until recently been 'luxuries' reserved to the very rich had come to be seen as 'daily necessities', including tea, coffee, sugar, white bread, newspapers, books, perfumes, cosmetics and, above all, a regular change of clothing. The magnates were cushioned by the sheer size of their estates, but the smaller land holdings of the 'gentry' could less easily sustain their rising 'cash flow' requirements, while the landless or near-landless 'lesser nobility' stood little chance at all. Consequently the sons of the 'gentry', as well as the still rapidly proliferating 'lesser nobility', were hurled into an unseemly scramble for further education and state or professional employment. By 1846 Hungary had 33,000 'college graduates' and 'twice as many licensed attorneys *per capita* as the more developed western provinces of the . . . Empire' but only a fraction found employment commensurate with their qualifications, and 'most of the students lived in abject poverty, supporting themselves by manual labour and the collection of alms' (Janos 1982: 42–3). Thus the Magyar nobility became a seething cauldron of frustrated professional and social ambitions as well as of endemic economic anxiety and political discontent. There was growing realization that the problems could be resolved only by the creation of a Magyar state as a 'system of outdoor relief' for the unemployed sons of the Magyar nobility.

In the same period, not unrelatedly, the Magyar nobility became increasingly conscious of the extent to which Hungary had fallen behind the economic and cultural/technological development of north-western Europe. The gap had widened significantly since the fifteenth and sixteenth centuries. As a major producer and exporter of gold, silver, copper, cattle and grain, occupying a strategic position on the overland trade routes between the Baltic and the eastern Mediterranean, Renaissance Hungary had attracted large numbers of German merchants and artisans who had built up substantial craft industries and towns. Hungary's urban economy and culture had declined during the seventeenth and eighteenth centuries, however, as its gold and silver mines neared exhaustion and European trade gravitated towards the Atlantic.

Eighteenth-century Hungary was a landlocked commercial backwater, whose craft industries also suffered from Habsburg commercial discrimination in favour of the industrial interests of German Austria and Bohemia. By 1787 the population of the 'free royal cities' was only 6 per cent of the total (with up to 60 per cent of so-called 'townspeople' at least partly dependent on agriculture) and urban representation had been reduced to a single seat in the lower house of the Hungarian Diet (as against fifty-five for the 'noble' counties) (Janos 1982: 30–3). There was a serious growth of vagrancy and banditry, while agriculture was dominated by oppressive and inefficient systems of serfdom, and some districts regressed to a primitive barter economy. Nevertheless, 'the fertility of the land and the favourable ratio of land to population provided adequate nutrition for most' (p. 33), while tales of the country's religious tolerance and natural wealth and the availability of 'vacant' land attracted about a million (mainly German-speaking) immigrants between 1711 and 1780 and significant Jewish immigration thereafter.

Starting in the 1790s, however, statistical enquiries and the writings of foreign visitors began to quantify and to publicize the degree to which Hungary lagged behind Austria, the German states and north-western Europe. Many formerly 'hallowed' objects of Magyar pride and mythology, even the vaunted 'liberties' (i.e. privileges) of the Magyar aristocracy, began to be questioned or to be seen either as a hindrance to effective remedial action or as a source of ignorance, superstition, oppression, filth and shame. For instance, the Frenchman Marcel de Serres, in his *Voyage en Autriche* (published in Paris in 1814) wrote that 'The Hungarians are naturally indolent . . . Although Hungary is a naturally fertile country, the inhabitants have no idea how to extract the riches of the soil . . . Ignorant and superstitious, the Hungarians are bad agriculturalists and equally little attracted to trade' (cited by Janos 1982: 47–9).

While many Magyars took offence at such aspersions on their honour and self-image, others began to call for fundamental reforms. During the 1830s the leading reformer was a wealthy magnate, Count Istvan Szechenyi (1791–1860), widely revered as the 'father' of modern Hungary (even by his critics). An admirer of English trade and industry, and especially of 'improving landlordism' and the Whigs, Szechenyi advocated the liberalization of Hungary's restrictive land laws, the abolition of serfdom and the expansion of education and credit so as to facilitate the buying, selling and mortgaging of land in order to encourage both foreign and domestic investment in a commercial–agricultural revolution led by magnates like himself. In his view, the ensuing increases in agricultural productivity and incomes would adequately compensate the landlord class for the loss of serf labour and 'feudal' dues (persuading them to forgo their time-honoured tax exemptions) and raise popular purchasing power, expand the domestic market for both agricultural and industrial products and generate the farm surpluses needed to service the foreign debt and to feed and finance an expanding industrial sector. This 'virtuous circle' would, he hoped, transform the Magyars into 'one big happy family', headed by the magnates, of course. This aristocratic, neo-physiocratic 'agriculture first' strategy was primarily expounded in his two major works, *Hitel* (Credit, published in 1830) and *Verlag* (Enlightenment, published in 1832), which later became 'Bibles' of Hungarian liberal-conservative paternalism. According to this programme, mass education, civil equality before the law and hence the abolition of serfdom were needed to transform all adults into fully fledged, legally responsible economic actors and contractual partners in economic transactions. Furthermore, he advocated the substitution of Magyar for Latin as Hungary's official language on purely pragmatic grounds, in order to enable more people to participate in civic and economic life, and not out of a chauvinistic desire to submerge the vernacular languages of Hungary's large non-Magyar minorities. Indeed, he counselled against his compatriots' persistent attempts to impose the Magyar language on the Croat, Slovak, Romanian and Ruthene minorities. Ever a gradualist and 'loyalist' aristocrat, Szechenyi aimed to achieve his programme 'organically', in collaboration (not confrontation) with the Habsburgs and the non-Magyar minorities. He eschewed confrontation, radicalism and strident nationalism, in the belief that his projects (and, equally, his class) needed the support and stability that the multinational empire could provide.

Szechenyi led by example. He donated a year's income from his estates to found a Hungarian Academy (to rehabilitate Magyar culture). He established the 'National Casino' (as a debating society) and instigated river improvements, urban renewal and the building of a permanent bridge between Buda and Pest, while in the Diet he battled against the entail laws, designed to keep landed estates intact down the generations. He seemingly preferred voluntary to state action. But most of his peers were in no hurry to renounce their fiscal and feudal/seigneurial privileges. The Hungarian Diet would approve only a very watered-down manumission law (1826), permitting the liberation of serfs on an individual basis, at the serf owners' discretion. Not until after the Revolutions of 1848–49 did a chastened Magyar aristocracy accept the bulk of Szechenyi's programme, albeit partly as a post-revolutionary *fait accompli*.

In 1831 there was a peasant revolt in north-eastern Hungary, precipitated partly by the Polish uprising of 1830–31 in Russian Poland and partly by the terrifying cholera epidemics which swept across Poland, Russia and Austria as well as Hungary in 1831. Many peasants, regarding the pills they were told to swallow, the chemicals that were poured into public wells and the treatment administered in makeshift cholera clinics as a desperate attempt by the frightened ruling classes to poison the 'menacing' lower classes, started attacking officials, landowners, clergy and Jews in Hungary as elsewhere in Europe. The Hungarian peasant revolt was ruthlessly suppressed, with over 100 rebels being executed. After this, fear of peasant revolt polarized the Magyar 'political nation' into advocates of repression and advocates of reform (Deak 1979: 22). Indeed, until 1848 it robbed both the government and the nobility of the courage and political will needed to introduce social and agrarian reforms to relieve the plight of the peasants, most of whom were serfs.

During the 1840s, however, the political initiative had passed to more radical, impatient and stridently nationalistic Magyar 'gentry', headed by the demagogic Lutheran lawyer and journalist Lajos Kossuth (1802–94). One must beware of Austrian, Czech and Slovak claims that Kossuth was a Slovak 'convert' to Magyarism. His mother was German, but his father's Magyar line can be traced back to 1263 (Deak 1979: 9–10). (But no doubt some wag will ask, 'What about before that?') Kossuth flattered and won the hearts of the Magyar nobility by referring to them all as 'gentry' and by reassuring them that they, through all their provincial prejudices and xenophobia, were the true embodiment and custodians of the Magyar nation and 'national virtues'. As the indefatigable writer and producer of the hand-written *Parliamentary Reports* from 1833 to 1836, the popular *Municipal Reports* from 1837 to 1838 and the widely read *Pesti Hirlap* (Pest News) from 1841 to 1844, Kossuth played upon the hopes, prejudices and anxieties of the Magyar nobility. The 'gentry' would no longer acquiesce in the leadership of the 'loyalist' aristocracy in the Hungarian Diet. On the contrary, the ascendant radical nationalist increasingly dictated terms or 'laid down the law' to the magnates, the Habsburgs and the Viennese bureaucracy, who were increasingly thrown on to the defensive. Kossuth was not silenced by his three-year detention and trial from 1837 to 1840. On the contrary, he became a national *cause célèbre*, not least for the political skill with which he conducted his own defence (Deak 1979: 32–3).

In the economic sphere Kossuth rejected the decentralized, *laissez-faire*, 'agriculture first' (neo-physiocratic) development strategy favoured by Szechenyi. Instead, Kossuth advocated industrial subsidies and a more centralized and interventionist strategy of state-induced industrialization, drawing upon Friedrich List's *National System of Political Economy* (published in 1841; famous for its 'infant industry' argument for tariff protection). In 1843 Kossuth co-authored a memorandum attributing Hungary's relative backwardness to its 'colonial dependence' on Austria, to the scarcity of technical personnel and to 'the existence of social and political institutions diametrically opposed to industrial interests', and advocating the development of 'national industry' by all available means, including industrial subsidies and tax concessions. When it was rejected by the 'loyalist' aristocracy and the imperial authorities, Kossuth supported the first-ever Magyar boycott of imported industrial goods in 1844. In 1846, echoing Listian economic nationalism, Kossuth wrote that 'those who do not possess the independent levers of civilization are only a people or race, but cannot be treated as a nation. Among these levers the most significant are trade and manufacturing industries. Without them one can exist as a country, but not as a nation' (quoted in Janos 1982: 66–8).

More ominously, in 1840 the Diet declared Magyar to be the official language of the kingdom of Hungary, even though Magyars comprised only 37 per cent of the population (45 per cent if Croatia-Slavonia is excluded) (Janos 1982: 11). By disadvantaging non-

Magyars, including German-speaking imperial officials, the 1844 language law gave the Magyar nobility a near-monopoly of state employment in Hungary. Moreover, it imposed Magyar as the language of secondary education for non-Magyars (even in Croatia-Slavonia), as if Hungary was a unitary and culturally homogeneous kingdom (Kann 1974: 288). Indeed, Kossuth was openly demanding 'the unity of the lands of the Crown of King Istvan' (a euphemism for centralization, aggressive 'Magyarization' and the suppression of the residual autonomy and/or separate cultural identities of the Croats, Slovaks, Transylvanian Romanians and Carpathian Ruthenes). Of course, many non-Magyars voluntarily assimilated into the 'dominant' ethnic group through intermarriage and/or in the hope of more rapid social and occupational advancement. This applied *a fortiori* to the so-called 'Saxon Germans' of Transylvania (who managed to maintain their centuries-old privileged position by 'collaborating' with the Magyars) and to the Jews, who were granted a Bill of Rights in the burgher estate by the Hungarian Diet in 1840 (despite an initial royal veto in response to antisemitic lobbying from German townspeople).

Hungary was by no means free of the antisemitisim which was rife in Europe at the time. Not only was there residual Christian antisemitism, but German burghers (and later non-German migrants to the towns) often viewed Jews as unwelcome direct competitors in urban trades and professions, while the numerous antisemitic pronouncements of Count Istvan Szechenyi expressed the fear that 'if the Jews were emancipated and given the right to acquire land, the economically inexperienced and heavily indebted landed classes would lose their holdings to them' (Janos 1982: 80). This did to some extent occur in late nineteenth-century Romania, with the rise of the *arendasi* (agrarian 'middlemen', mostly Jewish traders and moneylenders, who ruthlessly exploited the peasantry). But most of the Magyar nobility (including Kossuth as well as most magnates) welcomed the Jews as 'useful' entrepreneurs and potential allies in the building of a Magyar nation and national economy. Most preferred the prospect of a politically passive, pliable and dependent Jewish bourgeoisie to that of a potentially recalcitrant, independent and politically assertive German-speaking bourgeoisie. Indeed, many of Hungary's Jews were vulnerable and malleable recent immigrants, eager to 'make good', assimilate, learn Magyar and loyally serve their host nation and noble protectors. Magyar landowners always remained much freer from antisemitism than did their Austria-German and Polish counterparts and they made some effort to 'shield' Jews from virulent urban antisemitism during the 1930s (although such efforts ended abruptly in 1940). Some intermarried with Jewish financiers. Many were also quick to see advantages in employing Jews as 'front men' in their often oppressive or disreputable dealings with the peasantry and farm servants. Unfortunately these 'mismarriages' of convenience, expediency and principle, combined with the prominent role played by Jews in the development of capitalism and the liberal professions in Hungary, contributed to the subsequent growth of peasant and anti-capitalist antisemitism, which in turn coloured the attitudes of migrants to the towns (including landless 'lesser nobles') when Jews came to dominate the urban trades and professions.

Between the early 1820s and the mid-1840s, as Deak argues (1979: 61), Hungary underwent a 'phenomenal' political, social and cultural transformation. In the early 1820s, with its Diet unconvoked, 'its agriculture medieval, its trade in crisis, its society old-fashioned and rigid' and the Magyar language 'unused except in colloquial speech', Hungary remained 'one of the more backward and less influential provinces' of the

Habsburg Empire. By the mid-1840s, however, 'the Diet was frequently in session . . . political parties had been constituted . . . newspapers poured out social criticism and political programmes; the country's internal administrative machinery had become almost entirely Magyar; Hungarian literature was thriving . . . the social structure had become less rigid' and serfdom was about to be abolished. Nevertheless, Deak warns, Hungary's resurgence was 'built on shaky foundations. Created not by a rising industrial bourgeoisie but by the landed nobility, Hungarian progress lacked solid economic backing' (pp. 61–2). Indeed, despite some 'modest successes' in agriculture, trade, transport and industry, 'Hungary's economy was falling behind the western parts of the Monarchy' (p. 62). The latter had ten times as many capitalist enterprises, employed fifteen times as many steam engines and produced six times as much pig and cast iron as did Hungary (p. 50). For a short time the Magyar leaders could conceal their economic weakness behind a 'facade of modernistic slogans and an excellent political organization', but this bluff could succeed 'only as long as neither the Court nor the Austro German (and Czech) ruling circles were able to adopt similar slogans and political organization' (p. 62). While recognizing that it would have been hard for the Magyar leadership to resist the seductive opportunities for national assertion which presented themselves in 1848, Deak soberly concludes that 'Szechenyi was right and Kossuth was wrong: Hungary ought not to have embarked on its great political venture without having first developed economic strength and a bourgeois society' (p. 62). The Hungarian Revolution of 1848 was premature and foolhardy, but nationalists are often blind to harsh realities. In 1847 Kossuth was finally elected to the Hungarian Diet, where he stepped up the Magyar nationalists' campaign to make Hungary 'their own'.

The 'awakening' of Croatia, Slovakia and Transylvania

During the 1840s, moreover, aggressive Magyar nationalism began to antagonize and politically 'awaken' some members of the Croat, Slovak, Ruthene and Transylvanian Romanian peoples or 'proto-nations'. This was to be the Magyar nationalists' biggest blunder, strongly contributing to the defeat of the Hungarian Revolution of 1848–49 and to the complete dismemberment of the 'thousand-year-old Kingdom of Hungary' in 1918–19. The initial Slovak, Ruthene and Transylvanian Romanian responses were, however, weakened by their lack of 'political and territorial organization' (Kann 1974: 287) as well as their relatively low levels of national-historical consciousness.

The nobility of autonomous Croatia reacted strongly from the onset, however. Ironically, Croatian nobles had hitherto been staunch allies of the Magyar nobility, united in joint defence of their local autonomy and class privileges against threats both 'from above' (the Habsburg Emperors and the imperial bureaucracy) and 'from below' (the downtrodden peasantry). Since 1591 the Croatian *Sabor* (Diet) had regularly sent delegates to take part in the deliberations of the Hungarian Diet. Having tasted direct rule from Vienna (1767–78), the Sabor resolved to return to indirect rule by Hungary in 1779. After the centralizing rule of Joseph II (1780–90), the Sabor voluntarily transferred the voting of taxes ('contributions') and control of the 'common affairs' of Croatia and Hungary to the Hungarian Diet (1790). The Sabor even resolved that Magyar should be taught in Croatian schools (1827) and that a knowledge of Magyar should be required of Croatian officials (1830). 'There had been no hostility between Hungarian and Croat nobles. Indeed Croat privileges owed their survival to the association with Hungary; in isolation the Croat nobles would have shared the fate of the Czechs' (Taylor 1976: 27). But the Croatian nobility strongly resented attempts to *impose* more far-reaching 'Magyarization' on Croatia. In addition to their long-standing alliance with the Magyar nobility, the Croatian nobility also had strong traditions of military service in the imperial armed forces and of loyalty to the Habsburg Emperor. 'Magyar nationalism pushed the Croat nobles into the arms of the Habsburgs' (p. 28). In 1847 the Sabor itself succumbed to linguistic nationalism and declared Serbo-Croat to be the official language of Croatia-Slavonia (in place of both Magyar and Latin). This put it in direct conflict with the Hungarian Diet.

In 1848–49 Croatian soldiers, headed by Baron Josip Jelacic, were to play a prominent role in the suppression of the Hungarian and Viennese Revolutions. Likewise, the subsequent Habsburg failure to 'reward' the Croat loyalism of 1848–49 either by fully restoring Croatian autonomy in the 1850s or by protecting Croatia against the renewal of aggressive 'Magyarism' from 1875 onwards would eventually drive away many Croats into a cultural and political *rapprochement* with their Orthodox South Slav 'cousins', the Serbs, from whom they had hitherto been separated by a religious chasm.

The Hungarian Revolution of 1848–49

In March 1848, following the resignation of Metternich, the Hungarian Diet renounced all Viennese authority and jurisdiction over Hungary and retained only a 'personal union' of the kingdom with the Habsburg Monarchy (including the presence of a Habsburg viceroy in Budapest). The Diet legislated for the establishment of a sovereign Magyar national state, to comprise all 'the lands of the Crown of St Istvan' (i.e. including Transylvania, Slovakia and Croatia). This state was to have its own army, foreign policy, budget, currency and government responsible to a fully fledged parliament elected on a uniform franchise limited to the 'top' 6.5 per cent of the population (about the same as in Great Britain at the time). Most remarkably, the instinctively conservative Diet also abolished serfdom, tithes, the tax exemptions of the nobility and the entailment of feudal estates. By arguing that, unless the 'gentry' took the lead in promoting radical reform, 'real' radicals would mobilize the restive and largely non-Magyar peasantry (mostly serfs) against the (largely Magyar) propertied classes, 'Kossuth, alone in Europe, persuaded his followers to outbid the radicals instead of seeking dynastic protection against them' (Taylor 1976: 59). It was a major feat, but more was to follow. Archduke Stefan, the Habsburg viceroy in Hungary, timidly surrendered his power to a Magyar government under Count Lajos Batthyany, with Kossuth as Minister of Finance, Count Istvan Szechenyi as Minister of Public Works, Ferenc Deak as Justice Minister and Jozsef Eötvös as Education Minister (i.e. a coalition of magnates and 'lesser' nobility).

On 11 April 1848 the 'March Laws' and associated changes were ratified by Emperor Ferdinand, formally legalizing the Hungarian Revolution and the creation of a separate Hungarian state (p. 63). Indeed, Istvan Deak called his major study of Hungary under Kossuth *The Lawful Revolution* (1979), on the grounds that these changes gained the requisite 'royal assent' and that the Magyars merely seized upon the fall of the (somewhat unconstitutional) Metternich regime as an opportunity to reassert the Hungarian right of self-government which was supposed to have been enshrined in the Treaty of Szatmar (1711) and reaffirmed by the terms on which the Hungarian and Transylvanian Diets approved the Pragmatic Sanction in 1722–23. In this sense the Hungarian Diet of

March–April 1848 was more truly 'reactionary' than 'revolutionary' (Sked 1989: 58–9). This is a useful reminder that the Magyar leaders were 'respectable' and socially conservative men of property, who did not see themselves as revolutionaries and who would have been terrified at the prospect of a 'real' (social) revolution directed against the propertied classes. In other ways, however, this view is as misleading as the recent tendency to overemphasize the outward or formal 'legalism' of the Nazi take-over in Germany in 1933. Both belittle (to an unacceptable degree) the revolutionary significance of the events, the magnitude of the changes and the gravity of the consequences.

The Transylvanian Diet, dominated by fearful Magyar and 'Saxon' German land-owners, voted for the full incorporation of Transylvania into a unitary Hungary, but alarm about the possible consequences helped to trigger rebellions among the largely Romanian peasants of Transylvania and among the Serbs of the Military Frontier regions. Most peasants were also disappointed that the agrarian reforms had not gone far enough and would leave many of them just as poor, dependent and vulnerable as before. Indeed, many a landowner was in no hurry to apply the reforms to his own estate(s) or became a law unto himself.

Croatian resentment of the huge concessions to the Magyars led Emperor Ferdinand to appoint the Croat officer, landowner and 'patriot' Josip Jelacic as *Ban* (Viceroy) of Croatia in March 1848. But in June, under Magyar pressure, Jelacic was seemingly dismissed, although he in fact continued to act on the Habsburgs' behalf. His formal reinstatement in September 1848 signalled the start of a Croatian military offensive against the Magyars. This soon escalated into all-out war between Hungary and Austria, and the deeply divided Batthyany government had to resign. The Hungarian parliament (elected in June 1848) handed power to a Committee of National Defence headed by Kossuth. He quickly organized and provisioned a remarkably successful 170,000–strong Magyar national army (known as the *honved* battalions), repressed the rebellions and dissent among the non-Magyar minorities, fought off the initial Croat and Austrian-German invasions of Hungary and consolidated his position as virtual dictator. In April 1849, at the peak of his apparent power and success, he proclaimed a republic and formally 'deposed' the Habsburgs in Hungary.

Kossuth's Hungarian Republic was probably doomed from the start, however. The odds were stacked against it. Lacking significant military-industrial capacity, Hungary was hopelessly outgunned. It had been seriously weakened by the rebellions and lack of support among its mostly peasant and/or non-Magyar inhabitants. Its mere existence threatened monarchical legitimacy, the European 'balance of power' and Russia's hold on Poland. (This virtually guaranteed that Russia would intervene militarily, as actually occurred in June–August 1849.) Even the 'liberal' governments of Britain and France tacitly welcomed its demise, because of the importance of the Habsburg Empire to the stability of East Central Europe, the containment of Russia and the European balance of power. Thus Kossuth's regime remained bereft of allies (other than Polish 'patriots', who were ultimately more of a liability than an asset). In the end the Magyars chose to surrender to Russian rather than Austrian *force majeure* in August 1849. But the Austrians bore the brunt of the campaign, incurring about 50,000 war deaths to the Russians' 543 (not counting 11,028 cholera victims). The Magyars also incurred about 50,000 war deaths (Sked 1989: 102). The blood-letting did not stop there. About 150 Magyars (including thirteen generals) were executed for their prominent role in the Hungarian Revolution and 1,765 were imprisoned, although Kossuth himself escaped into permanent exile. Hungary was then punitively subjected to a decade of centralized absolutist 'direct rule' from Vienna, i.e. by Austrian-German officials. But many of the reforms enacted by the Hungarian Revolution of 1848–49 (especially the abolition of serfdom and of the tax exemptions of the nobility) were maintained, if only as a further punishment for the mutinous Magyar gentry. Ironically, Austrian direct rule was even imposed on Croatia, Transylvania and the Military Frontier regions, which thus received as a 'reward' what the Magyars suffered as a punishment.

In defence of the leaders of the doomed Hungarian Revolution of 1848–49, Istvan Deak has written (slightly disingenuously): 'Kossuth and his companions did not seek to suppress the [non-Magyar] nationalities; they aimed to liberate them. The liberal reforms of 1848 were meant to benefit everyone in Hungary; they were to make citizens of subjects. On the other hand, the liberal revolution could not tolerate the survival of distinct corporations (privileged or unprivileged), estates, guilds, free towns and religious or national autonomies. Kossuth may have acted foolishly and brutally but, for better or worse, he behaved as a true liberal revolutionary, a comrade of the men of Paris, of the men of the Frankfurt Assembly' (Deak 1967: 308).

In our view, the Hungarian Revolution was afflicted by a fatal schizophrenia. On one level it was a liberal universalist revolution, bestowing rights and obligations without religious or ethnic discrimination or favour. But it was also a Magyar nationalist revolution in which non-Magyars could participate fully only if they accepted the primacy of the Magyar language and aspirations and the transformation of the formerly multicultural and cosmopolitan Hungarian state into an expressly Magyar state. Similar tensions between liberalism and nationalism have bedevilled every step towards liberal democracy in Eastern Europe ever since. But the first open manifestations of this perennial East European problem occurred in Hungary in 1848.

THE CZECH REVIVAL, 1820s–1840s, AND THE SLAV CONGRESS OF JUNE 1848

For Bohemia and Moravia 1848 was a moment of truth. It brought home to many Czechs the realization that, despite their irksome lack of political autonomy, they could at least defend and develop their own national language, culture, identity and economy within the polyglot Habsburg Empire, and that the preservation of this multinational state offered the best (and perhaps the only) safeguard against absorption and eventual submergence in a Greater Germany, as envisaged by the German liberals and nationalists of the Frankfurt *Vorparlament* of 1848–49 (and as achieved by Hitler in 1938–39).

Indeed, in the eyes of the Frankfurt and Bohemian Germans, the defunct Kingdom of Bohemia was just as much part of the Germanic world as was German Austria. That was why the German liberal-nationalist *Vorparlament* (Pre-parliament) in Frankfurt invited Frantisek Palacky, as the acknowledged Czech spokesman and leader, to take part in its deliberations. The invitation was sent in a fraternal rather than predatory or imperialistic spirit, but it nevertheless elicited Palacky's famous frosty reply of 11 April 1848: 'I am unable, gentlemen, to accept your invitation . . . The object of your assembly is to establish a federation of the German nation in place of the existing [con]federation of princes, to guide the German nation to real unity . . . and in this manner expand the power and strength of the German Reich. Although I respect such effort and the sentiments upon which it is based, I cannot, precisely for the reason that I respect it, participate in it . . . I am not a German . . . I am a Bohemian of Slavonic blood' (Palacky 1948: 303–4). Palacky maintained that the Czech nation had 'never regarded itself as pertaining to the German nation . . . The whole union of the Czech lands, first with the Holy Roman (German) Empire and then with the German confederation, was always a mere dynastic tie' (p. 304).

The second reason for Palacky's unwillingness to participate in the German *Vorparlament* was that its implicit purpose was 'to undermine Austria as an independent empire and indeed to make her impossible for all time', whereas from his standpoint the Habsburg Monarchy was 'an empire whose preservation, integrity and consolidation is, and must be, a great and important matter not only for my own nation but also for the whole of Europe, indeed, for humanity and civilization itself' (p. 305). Palacky saw the Austrian Empire as an indispensable 'bulwark' against otherwise unchecked Russian or German or Magyar dominion over large swathes of Eastern Europe and as a 'guardian of Europe against Asiatic elements of every possible type' (p. 306). Thus historical and geopolitical considerations obliged Palacky 'to turn, not to Frankfurt, but to Vienna, to seek there the centre which is fitted and predestined to ensure and defend the peace, the liberty and the rights of my nation. But *your* endeavours, gentlemen, seem now to me to be directed . . . not only towards ruinously undermining, but even utterly destroying, that centre to whose authority and strength I look for salvation . . . If Europe is to be saved, Vienna must not sink to the role of a provincial town. If there exist in Vienna people who ask to have Frankfurt as their capital, we can only cry: Lord, forgive them, for they know not what they ask!' (p. 307).

Palacky's open letter has been described as 'one of the great documents of the nineteenth century' (Taylor 1940: 70). It served notice that, in Czech eyes, Bohemia and Moravia belonged to the Slavic rather than the Germanic world and that the westernmost Slavs were no longer prepared passively to allow their fate to be decided by others. That in turn rudely awakened both Bohemian and Austrian Germans to the fact that they could not blithely assume that their interests would happily and 'fraternally' coincide with those of the Czechs and that the Czechs would follow their lead. This heralded the underlying antagonism between the Czechs and both Bohemian-German and Austrian-German liberals which would increasingly bedevil both Bohemian and Austrian/imperial politics from the 1860s until the very end of the Habsburg Empire. That antagonism prevented the creation of a harmonious liberal alliance capable of transcending narrow nationalist interests and dashed any real hope of liberalizing, democratizing or federalizing the Monarchy and of reconciling the Czechs and Germans in Bohemia. It portended great dangers, not just for the peoples immediately affected, but ultimately (in 1938–39) for Europe as a whole.

Since the early nineteenth century there had been a remarkable Czech linguistic and cultural 'renaissance'. It was a largely accidental by-product of the social, administrative and educational reforms of Emperor Joseph II (1765–90) and of the vigorous Czech economic development. In order to assist and encourage some of his (mainly German) imperial officials to learn Czech more effectively, Joseph II also sanctioned the establishment of university chairs in Czech language and philology. Contrary to official intentions, however, these chairs became 'research centres of nationalism' and helped to elevate Czech 'from the humble position of a means of communication for peasants to that of an academic discipline and literary instrument' (Bradley 1971: 113–14). Until then Czech had 'no fixed grammar and consisted only of spoken dialects'. The first comprehensive Czech grammar was published in 1809 by Father Josef Dobrovsky, director of the Hradiste seminary. He persuaded many of his fellow clergy and former pupils to produce sermons and poetry in 'formal Czech', using his grammar (p. 114). Josef Jungmann, prefect of the Academic Gymnasium in Prague, went on to publish an authoritative guide to Czech literary style. He also translated various foreign works into Czech, to show that Czech was a competent vehicle of cultural expression (p. 122) and to persuade the authorities to permit the teaching of Czech in secondary schools (Kann 1974: 385).

Before long the Czech language was developing rapidly as the major outward manifestation of Czech national identity and as the preferred means of mass literary communication of the new generations of Czech teachers, clergy, lawyers, writers, journalists, professors, doctors, engineers, scientists, architects, musicians, merchants and industrialists, who proved to be the main beneficiaries of Joseph II's social and educational reforms and the chief 'missionaries' of the Czech national renaissance. This Czech revival benefited from and contributed to the development of the Bohemian Society of Sciences (established in 1784), the Czech Association for the Encouragement of Industry (1833) and, above all, the journal and the Czech Publishing Committee (*Matica ceska*) of the Bohemian Museum, which were established in 1827 and 1830 respectively by Frantisek Palacky. In the 1820s and 1830s the Czech patriot V.M. Kramerius became a regular publisher of Czech 'revival' books and journals, including one prophetically entitled *Cechoslovak* (1820–25). Two 'revival' journals (*Ceska vcela* and *Kvety ceske*) survived from the 1830s to 1849, when they were shut down by the imperial authorities. An enduring Czech newspaper (*Prazske noviny*) emerged in the 1830s. 'The institutionalization of Czech cultural efforts had immediate and far-reaching effects . . . Czech literature really began to flourish and to create a large reading public' (Bradley 1971: 122–3). Aided by large-scale rural–urban migration the Czech intelligentsia began to reverse the seventeenth-century Germanization of Bohemia's towns and cities. Nevertheless, it is significant that, even in the later nineteenth century, some leading Czech writers, composers and intellectuals still found it easier or more advantageous to write in German (e.g. Franz Kafka and Bedrich Smetana).

The dominant role of the non-noble intelligentsia in the nineteenth-century Czech revival has been contrasted with the similarly hegemonic role of the nobility in the concurrent Magyar revival, in an attempt to explain the strongly cultural and apolitical orientation of the Czech renaissance. As remarked by Bradley (1971: 115), 'The Czechs, in contrast to the Hungarians, would not be *political* nationalists, for the Czech nobility refused to assume political leadership . . . Czech nationalism had to be cultural, for only Czech intellectuals were prepared to take up its cause. Thus, between 1780 and 1880, with a short interruption in 1848, Czech nationalism was expressed in poetry and prose, in books of research and in plays, in operas and music, in journals, newspapers, museums and national theatres, but hardly at all in social and political terms.'

In fact, this Czech–Magyar contrast is not as clear-cut as it superficially appears. Landless, impecunious but educated Magyar nobles were so thick on the ground that they in effect became the Magyar intelligentsia and led the national 'revival'. Lajos Kossuth, Jozsef Eötvös and Ferenc Deak were just as much members of the intelligentsia as of the nobility. The Magyar magnates were closer counterparts of the Bohemian nobility, not just in terms of wealth and privilege but also in their vacillating and ambivalent attitude towards nationalism and revolution (both groups tried to run with the hare and hunt with the hounds). Moreover, the notions that an intelligentsia cannot exercise political leadership and that intelligentsia nationalism had to be more cultural than political are refuted by the Russian as well as the Magyar example. Bradley (1971) is on stronger ground with regard to the significance he attaches to the role of historians in the Czech revival (pp. 114–16).

Well before the Bohemian Diet designated Frantisek Palacky (1798–1876) the 'official historian' of Bohemia in 1829, the historians G. Dobner, B. Piter, A. Voigt and M. Pelcl played a pivotal role in the Czech 'revival'. Significantly, Dobner, Piter and Voigt were Germans who, through their historian's enthusiasm for setting the historical record straight and for championing history's underdogs, became fervent 'converts' to the Czech national cause. In a sense this was just one of several illustrious examples of the pioneering role of eighteenth- and nineteenth-century German intellectuals in promoting 'rediscoveries' and 'revivals' of Slavic cultures, languages and history. But the Czech case was special. Living cheek-by-jowl with Germans (and before the forging of a modernized and standardized written Czech language) many Czech commoners had become as Germanized as the last remnants of the Czech nobility. 'History alone could convince them that they were a separate nation capable of pursuing a unique national existence' (Bradley 1971: 114).

This explains both the Czech nationalists' obsession with Czech history and the striking ascendancy of historians (especially Palacky) in the Czech national movement in the early and mid-nineteenth century. That in turn helps to account for the Czech national leadership's seemingly quixotic and anachronistic preoccupation, from the 1840s to the 1870s, with reclaiming the 'historic rights' of the (long defunct) Kingdom of Bohemia. They dreamed of restoring the former legislative and fiscal autonomy of the Bohemian Diet and of re-establishing the fine ideal of Bohemia as a tolerant multicultural home of both Czechs and Germans (and of Catholics and non-Catholics), peacefully coexisting, sharing power and prospering as they had done in the sixteenth century. It also partly explains Palacky's conciliatory attitude towards the Bohemian Germans and the German-dominated Bohemian Diet (and vice versa, at least until March 1848). This attitude is often glibly dismissed as 'conservative' and 'backward-looking', but that is misleading. It was really derived from a high-minded humanist desire to resurrect the 'Bohemian model' of tolerance, co-operation and power-sharing which had been so wantonly destroyed by the Habsburgs in the seventeenth century.

Palacky's 'historicism' and idealism might have provided a practical basis for a *modus vivendi* in Bohemia from 1848 onwards *if* the Czechs and the Bohemian Germans had been able to work out their own local constitutional, cultural and economic arrangements in isolation from the wider imperial and Germanic worlds. Many Bohemian Germans, including members of the rich aristocracy, had had their fill of austere, arrogant, restrictive and interfering Habsburg absolutism and were ready to make common cause with the conciliatory Czech leadership in the 1840s. When news of Metternich's fall reached Prague in mid-March 1848 it evoked profound feelings of hope, liberation and goodwill.

In mid-March 1848 the Bohemian Diet, dominated by Germans and great landowners, took the lead in demanding the restoration of the so-called *Staatrecht* (right of autonomy) of the erstwhile Kingdom of Bohemia, as it had done already in 1846 (Bradley 1971: 124; Taylor 1976: 50). This demand was less radical than it sounds, as it would have further enhanced the dominant position of the Bohemian German privileged class. The Diet elected a so-called National Committee which was quickly joined by the Czech national leadership. Together they sent a delegation to Vienna on 20 March 1848 to present their demands for a resurrection of Bohemian liberties and autonomy. These (like the more radical demands presented at the end of March) were nonchalantly shrugged off by the new imperial Prime Minister, Count Anton Kolovrat, himself a very rich Bohemian magnate. He merely offered linguistic parity for Czech and German in Bohemian schools and administration (which had already been achieved in practice). While in Vienna, however, the Czech spokesmen bumped into Slav petitioners from other parts of the empire. Together they came up with the idea of convoking an ('Austrian') Slav Congress. Contrary to common belief, it was intended to be more of an academic than a political gathering. Organized by linguists, writers and historians (including Palacky), it was summoned to discuss Slavonic philology, literature and (academic) theories of Slavonic unity. Profiting from the new freedom of speech and assembly, they invited about 150 Slavs of varying distinction to congregate in Prague in early June 1848 (Bradley 1971: 126). In the event, over 300 delegates from all the Slav nations except Bulgaria took part, turning it into a pan-Slav rather than a narrowly Austro-Slav congress (Macurek 1948: 329–30). Many of the participants decided to turn up in national costume.

On 8 April 1848, meanwhile, Bohemia had received a charter granting administrative autonomy as well as full equality of Czech with German. On 29 May the imperial governor of Bohemia, Count Leo Thun, reacted to the accelerating decline of Viennese authority by establishing a *de facto* 'provisional government', composed of moderate Czechs and Bohemian Germans. This initially gained Habsburg approval and, but for an unexpected turn of events in Prague, could conceivably have consummated the incipient restoration of Bohemian autonomy (Taylor 1976: 68).

The opening session of the Slav Congress in Prague on 2 June 1848 passed off largely without incident. Meeting in the 'eye' of the 1848 Revolutions, however, the congress could not avoid getting drawn into politics. It produced two major political documents. One, a loyal Address to the Emperor, detailed the autonomist demands of his Slav subjects and vehemently denounced pan-German and German liberal calls for a Greater Germany (including large chunks of the Austrian Empire). The other, a more radical Manifesto of the First Slavonic Congress to the Nations of Europe, contrasted the conquering martial traditions of 'the Latin and Germanic nations' with the allegedly pacific and libertarian traditions of the Slavs (conveniently overlooking Tsarist militarism and expansionism and the military exploits of the medieval Polish, Serb and Bulgarian kingdoms). 'We Slavs reject and hold in abhorrence all dominion based on main force [*force majeure*] and evasion of the law; we reject all privileges and prerogatives . . . We demand unconditional equality before the law, an equal measure of rights and duties for all.' The manifesto also announced that the Slavonic Congress had 'proposed to the Austrian Emperor, under whose constitutional rule the majority of us live, that the imperial state be converted into a federation of nations all enjoying equal rights'. At the very least, Slavs ought to gain 'the same rights . . . as the German and Magyar nations already enjoy'. In addition, the manifesto called for an end to the tripartite partition of Poland and the 'inhuman and violent' treatment of the various Slav inhabitants of the kingdom of Hungary. It asked the Austrian Germans, Prussia and Saxony to accord their Slav subjects greater dignity and respect. It demanded that the

Slavic subjects of the Ottoman Empire should 'be enabled to give free play to their national aspirations in state form'. Finally, it proposed 'that a general European Congress of Nations be summoned for the discussion of all international questions'. (The full text was published in English translation by William Beardmore in *The Slavonic Review* XXVI, 1948, pp. 303–13, from which these quotations are taken.)

Thus, while most of the prominent German and Magyar nationalists and liberals of 1848 continued to think in terms of *supremacy* and *overlordship* over the other peoples of East Central Europe and the northern Balkans, upheld most of the existing *privileges* of the propertied classes, subscribed to the idea of a *hierarchy* of nations, and scorned or sneered at the loftier aspirations of the first Slavonic Congress, the latter called for the 'liberty, fraternity and equality of all nations' and the liberty and equal rights of all individuals, irrespective of nationality. More's the pity that, faced with Magyar and Germanic repression and obduracy, the nascent Slavic national liberation movements did not continue to develop in this liberal cosmopolitan and egalitarian direction (inspired by the high-mindedness of men such as Giuseppe Mazzini and Frantisek Palacky) but soon succumbed to the fatal deformations of exclusive and intolerant 'ethnic' nationalism and Russian imperialist pan-Slavism during the late nineteenth and early twentieth centuries.

Further sessions of the Slavonic Congress were planned to discuss closer co-operation between the 'Austrian' Slavs. Since late May, however, Prague had been subject to heavy-handed policing by rather 'jumpy' imperial forces commanded by Prince Alfred Windischgrätz, who made provocative public pronouncements and positioned heavy artillery on the heights overlooking the city centre. Moreover, despite its largely apolitical orientation, the Czech 'revival' had engendered a highly charged cultural ferment which intensified the excited and expectant atmosphere in Bohemia in 1848. On 12 June, following a peaceful rally and Mass in the central (now St Wenceslas) square, scuffles broke out between students and the troops who were patrolling the streets. The military overreacted, barricades sprang up and Prague was engulfed in six days of bloody street fighting, which was brought to an end only by several hours of heavy artillery bombardment of the city centre on 17 June. Windischgrätz became the first 'hero' of the Counter-revolution (before Radetzky in August), although even the Frankfurt Assembly considered sending troops to assist in putting down the revolt (Taylor 1976: 70).

The Slav Congress was disbanded and Prague was placed under martial law (tying down troops who were more genuinely needed elsewhere). Convinced that the initial clashes (which his own heavy-handedness had provoked) were the work of Czech agitators and revolutionaries, Windischgrätz instigated a witch-hunt for the (non-existent) 'ringleaders', leading to the detention of ninety-four 'suspects'. Elections to an Austrian constituent assembly were held in July, while Prague was still under martial law. The Windischgrätz claimed that this made the elections much freer, although one duly elected Czech deputy was then arrested as an alleged 'insurrectionist'! To cap it all, the German 'liberal' majority in the Austrian constituent assembly refused even to discuss Czech proposals for limited Bohemian autonomy. 'Parliamentary rebuffs were felt as national discrimination, or even persecution' (Bradley 1971: 127). In May 1849, finally, there was another witch-hunt against Czech students and radicals (alleged 'conspirators'), many of whom were sentenced to long prison terms or driven into exile in western Europe. Other Czechs emigrated to the United States, forming the nucleus of a later significant community of Czech Americans. (One of these, the impecunious Antonin Dvorak, expressed his deepest yearnings for home in the 'New World' symphony. Ironically, it owed much more to the 'old' world than the 'new' yet was to inspire the distinctive sound-world of countless American 'westerns'.)

The events of 1848–49 severely strained relations between Czechs and Germans (both in Bohemia and in Austria generally) and made it clear that neither the Habsburgs nor the Austrian Germans had any wish to concede even limited political autonomy and liberties to Bohemia. Moreover, a whole generation of Czech nationalists was left deeply disillusioned with (treacherous) politics and literally shell-shocked by the bombardment of Prague. These Old Czechs, as they became known to the subsequent generation of so-called Young Czechs, retreated into the relative safety of economic, educational, cultural and scholarly activity, producing further flowerings of Czech industry, intellect and creativity. Led initially by the venerable Frantisek Palacky and later by his son-in-law Frantisek Rieger, the Old Czechs did not fully re-enter Austrian politics until forced to do so in 1879 by mounting pressure and criticism from the more radical and assertive Young Czechs.

In the meantime, however, the Old Czechs never gave up on one modest political goal. That was to capture control of the (increasingly insignificant) Bohemian Diet from the Bohemian German aristocracy. To this end they used the Czechs' increasing capital accumulation to buy landed estates, which would make them eligible for membership of the dominant landowners' curia (section) in the Diet. This process was unacceptably slow and expensive, however, so in 1879 they finally succumbed to a political deal with the Austrian Prime Minister, Count Eduard Taaffe. It gave them (largely cosmetic) language concessions in Bohemian administration, control of the (largely impotent) Bohemian Diet and (from 1882) their 'own' Czech University in Prague, separate from that of the Bohemian Germans. In return, they agreed to give active support to Taaffe's conservative coalition government in the Austrian parliament, which the Czechs had been boycotting since 1863. But, except for the university, the Czechs 'gains' soon proved to be pyrrhic victories. The Bohemian Germans simply copied the previous Czech obstructionist tactics in the Bohemian Diet (which was often paralysed or suspended) and staged (sometimes violent) mass demonstrations to demand purely German administration in parts of Bohemia where Germans were in the majority. There was intermittent, debilitating and deliberately dangerous inter-communal violence and political paralysis in Bohemia from the 1880s to 1919 (with worse to follow). It was eventually to poison and undermine the workings of the Austrian *Reichsrat* from 1893 onwards.

In one important respect, however, Czech nationalists came out of the shocks and failures of 1848–49 with their confidence increased. They now had a greater awareness of the extent to which their own problems and aspirations were shared by other 'Austrian' Slav peoples, for whom the well educated and economically successful Czechs could increasingly act as spokesmen, role models, legal advocates, moral crusaders and cultural leaders. Czech nationalists became increasingly pan-Slav in outlook and derived new strength from the belief that the Czechs were no longer just one small Slav nation dominated by powerful Germanic neighbours, but the most 'advanced' representatives of a huge 'awakening' civilization. In 1867 Palacky participated in the first Pan-Slav Congress in Moscow and appeared to endorse its programme. The increasingly Russophil Czechs developed significant links and sympathies with the Slovenes, the Croats and the Serbs, even if their relations with the Poles and the Slovaks were more ambivalent. (From an early stage there were tensions and rivalries between the Czechs and Poles, while Slovak nationalists soon came to fear and resent Czech 'superiority' and 'tutelage'.) The Czechs, next to the Austrian Germans, provided the largest numbers of administrators, academics, judges, lawyers, teachers, engineers and entrepreneurs in the Habsburg Empire. They built bridges, railways, public buildings, theatres and cathedrals, while Czech bankers and industrialists began to invest in the less developed imperial periphery, becoming (sometimes arrogant or insensitive) missionaries of Czech and/or Slavonic 'progress' and 'enlightenment'. The down side of all this was that Czech nationalism became noticeably less 'civic'/tolerant and more 'ethnic', exclusive and chauvinistic as the century wore on. Nevertheless, it remained rather more liberal than that of most of the other peoples of central and eastern Europe.

Ironically, the thorough subjugation of the Czech Lands and the contraction of the native Czech nobility during the seventeenth century had paved the way for the eventual re-emergence of the Czechs as a bourgeois demotic and highly industrialized nation in the late nineteenth century, whereas the preservation of the power and privileges of the Magyar 'political nation' (the nobility) delayed the emergence of a Magyar bourgeoisie, industrialization and a more demotic society in Hungary. Thus the Magyars' supposed advantages eventually proved to be a curse, whereas the Czechs' punishment ultimately proved a blessing in disguise.

In the aftermath of 1848, however, the Czech leaders felt trapped, with little room for manoeuvre. Czechs feared that if the grip of the Habsburgs were really to be broken, they could soon find themselves 'swallowed up' in a Greater Germany. On the other hand, if the Habsburgs were to stay in control, it would be on their own terms. Thus Bohemia's affairs could not be settled in isolation from the wider Germanic and imperial worlds. Moreover, increasingly alarmed at the growing economic and cultural success of the Czechs, many Bohemian Germans were fearful of any weakening of their political and economic dominance in Bohemia or their umbilical cord to Vienna, while some already dreamed of absorption into a Greater Germany (to be 'united' with other Germans and to ensure permanent German dominance of Bohemia). In the opinion of A.J.P. Taylor (1976: 143), 'At heart every German, from the Frankfurt liberals of 1848 to Hitler, regarded Bohemia as a German protectorate.' But this may be a bit extreme. The key point is that the aftermath of 1848–49 brought out the worst in the Austrian and Bohemian Germans and that the Czechs, owing to their central location and economic and cultural success, were to be among the prime targets (and eventual victims) of German supremacism.

THE VIENNESE REVOLUTIONS OF 1848

At the nerve centre of the Habsburg Empire, meanwhile, the fall of Metternich on 13 March 1848 had resulted in a succession of supposedly 'liberal' constitutionalist governments headed by Count Franz Anton Kolowrat (17 March–4 April), Count Karl Ficquelmont (4 April–3 May), Baron Franz von Pillersdorf (3 May–8 July) and Baron Johann von Wessenberg (19 July–20 November). None of them was able to assert much authority, either inside or outside Vienna. These Premiers, along with most of their colleagues, were too closely associated with the previous regime. As the state councillor with overall responsibility for Austria's finances and internal affairs from 1826 to early 1848, Kolowrat had been Metternich's chief rival and opponent, yet he could not wholly dissociate himself from the moral and political opprobrium into which the regime had fallen. Ficquelmont could not shake off the stigma of having been groomed by Metternich as his favoured successor. Pillersdorf was a long-serving state functionary who lacked the courage to live up to his 'liberal' pretensions and/or convictions. Wessenberg was a competent career diplomat but a political nonentity. All four proved too slow, hidebound and hesitant to deliver timely and satisfactory constitutional concessions and practical reforms. Their offerings were always too little and too late. Thus they repeatedly lost the political initiative to impatient and exasperated radicals, who temporarily succeeded in pushing many Austrian-German townspeople leftward and towards direct action. Consequently there were several successive waves of revolution in Vienna in 1848, each more radical than its precursor.

In mid-March 1848 there was a liberal-constitutionalist revolution, which was to a considerable extent engineered and stage-managed by fractious anti-Metternich elements within the ruling classes (including several Habsburg archdukes and Archduchess Sophie, the scheming mother of Franz Joseph). They manipulated public hostility towards Metternich for their own ends, as a means of extracting very limited constitutional concessions and changes of personnel (little more than a 'changing of the guard'). The most remarkable thing was that in the end Metternich, like so many of Europe's chief Ministers in early 1848, put up so little resistance. Almost nothing was done to avert the 13 March demonstrations and riots that toppled Metternich (Rath 1957: 55). There was no serious attempt to impose martial law. It was as if he, like several others, had lost the will (and faith in his capacity) to govern, and fatalistically acccepted that his allotted time was up. This averted a bloodbath. What is more, the Habsburgs proved only too willing to make a scapegoat of their most unpopular Minister, who was not as powerful as many people believed, while his old rivals and protégés were ready and waiting to step into his shoes. Indeed, some of the supposed 'liberals' were in fact closet conservatives who merely envied or resented Metternich's vaunted power and influence and wished to take his place.

The declared aims and concerns of the Austrian-German 'liberals' on the eve of their March 1848 revolution were remarkably limited. Since the 1830s a crescendo of 'liberal' criticism of the Metternich regime had found various means of expression via foreign publications, especially in books and newspapers which were published in the German states and illegally imported and circulated among the well educated propertied classes, in circumvention of the Austrian censors and police surveillance (Rath 1957: 10–11, 19–31). Oppositional literature was discussed and circulated by 'liberal' clubs, notably the Legal–Political Reading Club (established in 1842) and the Concordia Society (1840), which developed close links with the Lower Austrian Diet, the liberal nobility, some state functionaries and the Lower Austrian Manufacturers' Association (1840). During the 1830s and 1840s the lethargy which had previously characterized Austria's provincial Diets was replaced by 'intrepid, energetic activity' and 'liberal' demands (pp. 28–32). In Vienna, starting in the early 1840s, 'Witty attacks on the government circulated through the salons and coffee houses . . . Liberal passages were inserted into plays . . . and were acclaimed with great applause' (p. 20). Liberals reproached the Metternich regime for 'its incompetence, sterility and immobility' and its 'attitude towards religion and education, the stifling press censorship and the omnipresent police' (p. 8). Before 1848, however, 'none of the . . . "liberal" writers . . . expressed a desire for a constitution, a bill of rights, popular sovereignty or a genuine "liberal" parliament'

(p. 27). No one was demanding freedom from search, freedom of assembly, abolition of the monarchy or ministerial accountability to a directly elected parliament (p. 44). 'Except for Archduke Louis, no member of the imperial family was attacked . . . In all the oppositional literature, not once was a demand made for revolution' (Rath 1957: 27). Austria's 'liberal' opposition was calling only for religious toleration, the relaxation of censorship and police powers, freedom of trade(s), the abolition of monopolies, decentralization of government, consultative assemblies and more competent Ministers (Sked 1989: 53–5).

In 1848, like their counterparts elsewhere in Europe, Austrian 'liberals' wanted neither popular sovereignty nor universal rights of political participation. On the contrary, they desired a constitution which would enhance the rights and privileges of the 'respectable' propertied classes by guaranteeing them the prerogative of co-operating with the monarch in making laws and approving taxes and by prohibiting royal violations of their rights as property-owning, taxpaying and law-abiding subjects. Thus 'the moderate liberals of the March revolution . . . merely wanted a parliament of property-holders to check the Emperor's absolute powers and advise him on legislation' (Rath 1957: 3–4, 194). Austria's burgeoning middle class, believing that they had 'the brains, the know-how and the money' required by the state, deeply resented their continued exclusion from privilege and high society. 'They yearned to replace the absolutist state with a liberal monarchy over which they could exercise considerable control' (p. 16). Yet neither the *haute bourgeoisie*, which looked to the state for ennoblements and protection, nor the professional and functionary classes, which looked to the state for employment, pensions and subsidized education, were particularly revolutionary. But a major problem for these middle classes was that the expansion of higher education had far outstripped the state's capacity to provide white-collar employment for graduates. This gave rise to large numbers of unemployed graduates and disaffected students, creating an impoverished, alienated and radicalized intelligentsia (Sked 1989: 78–80). Such people would do their best to push the 1848 Revolutions further to the left, in Austria as in other parts of central and eastern Europe.

On 15 March 1848, having finally agreed to convoke a representative assembly which would negotiate a constitution, Emperor Ferdinand was cheered and 'serenaded' by immense crowds gathered in Joseph Square. That night there were great torchlit processions through the city, which was ablaze with lights. 'Thousands of people – Germans, Hungarians, Italians, Bohemians, Poles and Jews – jostled each other in brotherly harmony to celebrate the dawn of a new freedom. Total strangers embraced one another on the streets and joined in singing' (Rath 1957: 86–7). The carnival atmosphere continued the next day, when Kossuth successfully negotiated self-government for Hungary and was carried shoulder-high through the streets of Vienna. (The general euphoria prefigured the scenes of jubilation in Berlin and Prague in November and December 1989, when the communist dictatorships collapsed.) 'All classes of malcontents had worked together to bring on the revolution' (p. 88). Yet as soon as the propertied 'liberals' had gained what they wanted, they immediately initiated mass arrests of the lower-class radicals, rioters and demonstrators who had helped them to secure the resignation of Metternich and the promise of an assembly to draw up a constitution. By the night of 15 March the jails were already full to overflowing (p. 88). As far as the 'liberal' propertied classes were concerned, the March Revolution had served its purpose, and they began to fear that the 'moderate' political revolution which they had initiated might slip out of their control and lead to a more violent social revolution. So they threw their weight behind efforts to restore law and order. 'They now wanted peace and stability so that they could reconstruct society in accordance with their interpretation of the revolutionary idea and . . . take full advantage of the privileges they believed the revolution had assured them' (Rath 1957: 4, 88, 224). When the revolution lurched to the left on 15 and 29 May, moreover, large numbers of 'liberals' defected to the 'ultra-conservative' camp (p. 274).

However, the radical intelligentsia, university students and Vienna's 'underprivileged' classes felt increasingly cheated, slighted and alienated. They even felt 'betrayed' by the new government's acts of repression, by the lack of further reform, by the filling of government posts with stalwarts of the previous regime and by Emperor Ferdinand's decision to 'grant' (unilaterally) a very limited and elitist constitution (on 25 April) and a very restrictive electoral law (on 11 May), in contravention of his promises to convoke a representative body which would freely determine the constitution. Ferdinand also upset a widespread assumption and expectation that this body would be elected on a broad franchise, even though he had never promised that.

On 15 May 1848, amid mounting popular unrest and major political confrontations between the supposedly 'liberal' government and both the (student) Academic Legion and the (burgher) National Guard, the radical democrats, who believed in popular sovereignty, were victorious over the moderate liberals of the March Revolution. The radicals had won recognition of the principles of universal suffrage and popular sovereignty, in that the emperor and the government had been forced to agree to submit 'the emperor's constitution to a democratically elected parliament for alteration as it saw fit' (Rath 1957: 194).

On 17 May, ostensibly fearing for Ferdinand's safety, the royal family evacuated him and his wife to Innsbruck. For many conservatives and property-owners the news that the Habsburg emperor had been 'forced to flee' from his capital was a cause for alarm, but other people (including the government) felt let down, betrayed or even affronted. It certainly helped to polarize public opinion, while his subsequent reluctance to return to Vienna further reduced the popular esteem and affection which 'Ferdi the Benevolent' had hitherto enjoyed (despite many harsh or unkind judgements on the emperor's debilitating epilepsy).

A bungled government attempt to suppress the (student) Academic Legion on 25 May rallied National Guardsmen, workers and parts of the lower middle class to the students' defence. This led to the establishment of a more effective organ of 'people's power', a revolutionary Committee of Citizens, National Guards and Students, popularly known as the Security Committee (or Committee of Public Safety). From 26 May to 23 August the students and their proletarian and petty-bourgeois allies were 'the recognized leaders of Vienna. Their Security Committee watched over every move of the authorities and superintended the police and the military' (Rath 1957: 218). The government was implicitly reduced to the status of an interim 'caretaker administration', with rapidly dwindling authority over other parts of the Austrian Empire. By midsummer there were in effect separate governments for German Austria, Bohemia, Moravia, Galicia, Hungary, Croatia, Lombardy and Venetia, while Austrian-German allegiances were divided between the government, Vienna's Security Committee, the Court Camarilla at Innsbruck, the duly elected Austrian constituent assembly and the German National Assembly in Frankfurt.

The crucial task which Vienna's Security Committee had to set itself, in view of its radical (partly 'utopian socialist') ideology and its need of lower-class support, was to alleviate the mounting unemployment, dwindling food supplies, soaring living costs and deepening destitution of Vienna's lower classes. It therefore established a Labour Committee to expand the public works projects on the Prater and along the Danube and the Wien which the 'liberals' had initiated in March 1848 to relieve politically dangerous poverty and unemployment. But the projects soon brought themselves and the revolution into disrepute. 'Much of the work, the cost of which was borne by the city, was useless. More and more workers were occupied with the pointless earthworks in the Prater. They were poorly supervised and . . . workers were quick to learn that they could earn a day's wage by doing little more than report for work' (Rath 1957: 220). By early June these projects were employing over 20,000 people (over a fifth of Vienna's work force) and drawing workers away from cash-strapped private workshops and factories. Attempts to bring the escalating cost and abuses under control provoked mass protests on 15–17 June and 21–3 August. These were suppressed by National and Civic Guards, fatally fracturing the fragile unity of the radical coalition. The public works programme ultimately failed its intended beneficiaries and alienated its former well-wishers. Within Vienna this fairly comprehensive failure probably sealed the fate of the 1848 Revolution. Yet the experiment was probably doomed from the outset, given the disruptive effects of the revolution on markets, business confidence, revenue and labour discipline, the intermittent destruction of factories, machinery and property and Vienna's increasing inability either to assure or pay for essential supplies of food and raw materials, underlining the impossibility of ('utopian') 'socialism in one city'.

Austria's long-awaited constituent sssembly (elected on a broad but indirect franchise in June) finally opened on 22 July 1848. It fully exposed the inner contradictions of the Habsburg Empire. Its legitimacy and competence as an imperial institution were inevitably compromised by the fact that Hungary, Lombardy and Venetia were not (and did not want to be!) represented in it, while the Austrian and Bohemian Germans had already elected deputies to the German National Assembly in Frankfurt, which had opened on 18 May and was supposed to be negotiating either a federal or a confederal constitution for a 'united Germany' (including German Austria and, despite Czech objections, Bohemia). Moreover, almost half the Austrian Reichstag deputies were Slavs, who initially objected to the official assumption that parliamentary debate would be conducted exclusively in German. A substantial number of Slav deputies knew little or no German. Furthermore, 25 per cent of the deputies were peasants, rather than more educated and bilingual townspeople. However, since German was the only feasible lingua franca, the Slavs eventually relented on condition that all proceedings were translated into the mother tongues of the non-German deputies, severely slowing up the assembly's business. Another problem was the overrepresentation of the bourgeoisie (60 per cent of all deputies) and the corresponding underrepresentation of other social classes. This multi-ethnic assembly also wasted much of its time bickering over the order of business and the composition of committees (Rath 1957: 274–9).

The upshot of all this was the (perhaps inevitable) failure of the constituent assembly to seize the political initiative, live up to expectations or gain much public confidence and support. Moreover, the lesson that the multi-ethnic Austrian Empire was perhaps not really governable on the West European 'liberal' (constitutional monarchy) model lowered Austrian-German resistance to the restoration of Habsburg absolutism. This formally took place on 7 March 1849, when the Reichstag was forcibly dissolved by the new 'strong man' Prince Felix Schwarzenberg (who had been Prime Minister of Austria since 21 November 1948). Schwarzenberg's *coup d'état* evoked barely a whimper of protest, partly because the constituent assembly had already marginalized itself by withdrawing from Vienna to Kromeriz (Kremsier) in Moravia to escape the hazards of the violent Viennese uprising which began on 6 October 1848.

THE DISSOLUTION OF AUSTRIAN SERFDOM

The most important legislation enacted by the shortlived Austrian Reichstag was the Act of Peasant Emancipation, passed on 7 September 1848. It has long been regarded as 'the greatest achievement of the revolutions of 1848' (Taylor 1976: 72). Indeed, these revolutions occurred in predominantly peasant societies, whose only irresistible force was the peasants' desire to be free of the *Robot* (compulsory labour service to landlords) and other 'feudal dues'. This elemental force ran along different channels from urban radicalism. Moreover, 'the peasant revolt against the *Robot* made their lords revolutionary as well, or at least unreliable supporters of imperial authority'. Even the loyalty of the magnates was shaken once the implicit bargain between them and the Habsburgs was broken. The Monarchy had not kept the peasants down, so the landed classes looked around for new allies (p. 57). Indeed, since 1846 the Austrian and Hungarian ruling classes had been dreading recurrences of the kind of peasant Jacquerie that had ravaged Austrian Poland in February and March of that year.

Nevertheless, the Peasant Emancipation Act was little more than a formal endorsement and elaboration of an imperial manifesto of 11 April 1848, which promised to liberate the peasants 'from all services and dues incumbent on the land by 1 January 1849' (Rath 1957: 127). On 24 September 1848 about 20,000 people (including many peasants from surrounding areas) paraded through Vienna in celebration of the 'abolition of serfdom'. Many radical democrats blithely assumed that, since they had been instrumental in 'giving' the former serfs their freedom, the peasantry would in turn gratefully back them in their own (characteristically urban) radical demands (p. 316). But the urban radicals were to be bitterly disappointed, and this sense of disappointment (allied to mutual incomprehension and differing agendas) would later bedevil relations between peasant and urban radical movements, culminating in the fateful mutual suspicion, mistrust and recrimination between peasant and Marxist parties in Eastern Europe from the 1900s to the 1940s.

In the event many peasants felt disappointed with (or even cheated by) the limited scope and hard-nosed terms of the 1848 Emancipation Act and the persistence of some forms of 'feudal' dependence on big landowners. They especially resented the indignity and hardship of having to pay for some of their new 'freedoms' and the land allotted to them (particularly since their former 'masters' received partial compensation for loss of services, income and land), while the big landed estates remained largely intact and continued to account for nearly half of all farmland, instead of being broken up and distributed among the peasants and farm labourers who had worked them for centuries. Moreover, the failure to allot any land at all to cottars and farm 'servants'/labourers gave these groups more reason to feel anger rather than gratitude towards the constituent assembly radicals and 'liberals'. On the other hand, those peasants who *were* satisfied by the scope and terms of the Emancipation Act felt less gratitude to the constituent assembly than to the Habsburg emperor, for it was his manifesto of 11 April 1848 that first proclaimed the imminent abolition of serfdom and it was 'his' officials who had implemented it. The contented sections of the peasantry 'lost all interest in continuing the revolution' and favoured the restoration of law and order (p. 127). By late September most peasants were 'probably indifferent to the outcome of the revolution' (p. 316), since it had moved in directions and on to an agenda in which they could have little direct interest or role. Some, especially the 'loyalist' Austrian-German Catholic peasantry, were decidedly 'hostile to the radicals' (pp. 120, 316).

Either way, by delivering the *coup de grâce* against serfdom and temporarily defusing the agrarian question and the class struggle between the peasantry and the landed nobility, the Emancipation Act diminished the peasants' interest in continuing the revolution. Thenceforth the centre of gravity of imperial politics shifted from class struggle to inter-ethnic or 'national' struggles or, in other words, to a political terrain that was to be much more congenial to the right than to the left, to 'reaction' rather than 'revolution' or 'reform'. For several decades this gave East Central European politics a powerful 'shove' to the right. The latter successfully used nationalism and inter-ethnic conflicts to 'divide and rule', i.e. to deflect, defuse and defeat class struggles by playing the 'nationalities' off against each other.

Nevertheless, in Austria as in Hungary, the Peasant Emancipation Acts 'swept away the underpinnings upon which the economy of most noble landowners had rested'. The latter forfeited the goods, services and cash dues hitherto provided by 'their' peasants, as well as their former tax exemptions and part of their landed estates. 'Their indemnification fell short of compensating them for their material losses, and was further reduced by declines in the value of indemnification bonds' (Blum 1978: 425). Their difficulties were compounded by noble nonchalance, extravagance and lack of entrepreneurial expertise and business acumen. 'The high grain prices of the 1850s and 1860s enabled most of them to survive despite their inefficiency.' But when international grain prices fell in the face of growing competition from cheap American and Russian grain in the 1870s and 1880s, the Austro-Hungarian estate owners' financial losses multiplied. Many had to sell all or parts of their estates or lost them to creditors (p. 426). Moreover, the loss of their seigneural role 'stripped the concept of nobility of its essential meaning' (p. 419). For centuries the official pretext for the privileges and prerogatives of the landed nobility had rested on their supposed care and responsibility for the peasants in their charge, but the Emancipation Acts largely transferred these powers and functions to the state. Furthermore, the Emancipation Acts made everyone (at least nominally) equal before the law. There was to be one law for all subjects, holding out the prospect of 'equal civil, personal and property rights' for all, although many inequities persisted in practice (p. 440). For example, the mobility and civil rights of farm 'servants'/labourers were severely restricted in Hungary well into the twentieth century (p. 430). But 'these lingering relics of times past were destined to disappear' as the individual gained increased freedom to choose an occupation and a marriage partner, to move about at will, to sign contracts, to buy and sell goods and services and to do as he or (sometimes) she wished with his or (very rarely) her property. 'These freedoms greatly facilitated the acceleration in ... economic growth in the one-time servile lands ... after their emancipation' (pp. 440–1). At the same time, however, the Emancipation Acts gave a powerful new impetus to the undermining and dissolution of the time-honoured bases of power, authority, hierarchy, deference and obedience in East Central Europe, which culminated in the collapse of the Habsburg Empire in 1918. Since then the peoples of East Central Europe have been desperately seeking durable and generally acceptable new bases for social and political stability, legitimacy and authority. How successful they have been is still open to debate.

THE POLITICAL POLARIZATION OF VIENNA

Meanwhile, the fragile unity of the radical democratic coalition in Vienna had been ruptured when Civic and National Guards, who had hitherto formed part of that coalition, savagely suppressed workers' protests against wage cuts (on the public works projects) on 23 August 1848. This 'bloody act of treachery', as workers and radicals saw it, also temporarily reasserted the tenuous authority of the 'liberal' government which had ordered the wage cuts and the Guards' repression of the ensuing protests.

Faced with the gathering strength of the (regrouped) counter-revolutionary forces after 23 August (and not just in Vienna but also in Bohemia and northern Italy), there emerged a desperate (almost quixotic) 'last ditch' attempt by an increasingly beleaguered radical minority (drawn from the intelligentsia, the lower middle class, the students, the civil militias, the Vienna garrison and the working class) to save the increasingly imperilled 'revolutionary gains' by seizing control of Vienna from 6 to 31 October 1848.

There was no longer any 'middle ground' by October. Hence either the radicals had to triumph or the reactionaries would do so. It was 'make or break' time. The catalysts of Vienna's 'October Revolution' were the menacing 'pincer' movements of the Croatian royalist forces commanded by Jelacic, Bohemian royalist forces commanded by Windischgrätz, and the Habsburgs' northern Italian forces commanded by Radetzky, plus the 'liberal' government's attempt to make the politically divided grenadiers of the Vienna garrison join in the counter-revolutionary offensive against Kossuth's Hungary in early October 1848. A potent underlying factor in this October insurrection was, however, Vienna's accelerating economic collapse. By late September major segments of Vienna's lower middle and working classes were experiencing acute hardship, bordering on starvation (Rath 1957: 320). The insurrection began with a mutiny of Vienna's Richter battalion on the morning of 6 October, after it had been ordered to march against the Magyars. The mutineers were supported by radicals, students and disaffected workers and Guardsmen, who went on a rampage which culminated in the gruesome murder and mutilation of War Minister Latour later that day.

On 7 October Emperor Ferdinand, who had eventually returned to Vienna on 12 August, fled to Moravia, where he was soon followed (at a respectful distance) by most of the 'liberal' government, much of the constituent assembly and many senior bureaucrats, virtually abandoning Vienna to the rebels. Nevertheless, despite the unrest and near starvation in Vienna, 'there was little robbery or plundering'. This was testimony to 'the great respect of even the most extreme radicals for property rights'. However, no one knew what to do. 'Everyone was issuing orders simultaneously, but nobody wanted to obey anyone else . . . Courage was no substitute for leadership' (Rath 1957: 339). A last-minute Magyar attempt to relieve the rebels and break the Habsburg siege of Vienna on 30 October was easily defeated (pp. 356–7). The Viennese rebels were finally forced to surrender on 31 October by a combination of military encirclement, hunger and thirst. Many townspeople greeted the triumphant Habsburg forces as 'liberators', not only from the hunger and thirst but also from the reign of terror unleashed by some despairing rebels during the last days of the siege (pp. 351–3). Windischgrätz then imposed censorship and martial law, prohibited political clubs and public meetings, placed over 2,000 people in political detention and executed nine of the rebel leaders (pp. 363–4). His brother-in-law, Prince Felix Schwarzenberg, launched a new government of conservative 'loyalists' and renegade 'liberals' on 21 November, persuaded Emperor Ferdinand to abdicate in favour of his eighteen-year-old nephew Franz Joseph on 2 December and dissolved the constituent assembly on 7 March, with a soon broken promise that a new constitution drawn up by the new government would come into effect when the emergency ended (pp. 364–5). The counter-revolutionaries could now turn their full attention to Hungary, where the Magyar nationalist revolution was decisively defeated in August 1849, snuffing out the (forlorn) 'last hope' of the 1848 radicals.

THE FATEFUL FISSURE: GERMANS VERSUS SLAVS

The central reason why the 1848 Revolutions within German Austria and Bohemia neither developed to the same degree as their counterparts in Hungary and northern Italy nor achieved anything as tangible as the overthrow of the monarchy in France lay in the inability of the major protagonists in German Austria and Bohemia to unite around a common overarching goal, or to share a single clearly identifiable focus. Magyar and Italian radicals were in broad agreement on the paramount aim of self-government, whether it be within or without the Habsburg Monarchy, while in France there was almost unanimous applause at the abdication of King Louis Philippe. But the emergence of a (Pan) German National Assembly at Frankfurt in the spring of 1848 confronted most Austrian and Bohemian Germans with a difficult choice between Greater Germany and Greater Austria, between pan-Germanism and a supranational Habsburg Empire. Their unwillingness and inability to make a clear-cut choice between the two gave their political behaviour a fatal hesitancy and indecisiveness in 1848–49. This in turn allowed the Habsburg civil and military authorities to make the choice for them, in favour of Greater Austria and a forceful reassertion of Habsburg absolutism. Even the Czechs could not unreservedly back the goal of 'national' self-government once they had concluded that they needed a multicultural Greater Austria, within which they could preserve and develop their Czech culture and identity, if they were not to be swallowed up and smothered by a nationalistic Greater Germany.

   The Austrian Revolutions of 1848 also failed because they helped to polarize rather than harmonize national sentiments and aspirations within the Austro-Hungarian Empire. The various political factions in Vienna in 1848 were united in their hostility to the Czechs, even though the Czechs merely aspired to 'the same liberties the Viennese had gained during the March revolution' (Rath 1957: 145). The subsequent granting of autonomy and equality of Czech with German in Bohemia 'deeply angered' the Austrian Germans, who were aspiring to 'a German empire that was to embrace all the lands of the historic Holy Roman Empire. They could not comprehend how any sensible people could voluntarily decline to share the future in store for the German race' (p. 146). The Slav Congress in Prague held in June 1848 led many Austrian Germans to see the Slavs as traitors, ingrates and a threat to the survival of the Austrian Empire and of their own variously privileged positions within it (pp. 255, 258). 'Germans in Bohemia denounced the congress as high treason. After this display of Slavic unity they were . . . convinced that only a close union with Germany could save them from Slav domination' (p. 260).

Behind Slav solidarity Austrian and Bohemian Germans saw the spectre of Russian imperialism (p. 254). Moreover, when South Slavs started referring to Austrian Germans as 'oppressors' and criticized the primacy of German in Slovene and Croatian secondary schools, such 'impertinence' from an 'inferior race' drew Austrian-German counter-claims that only Germans and instruction in German could initiate South Slavs into 'the great cultural community of central Europe' (p. 257).

During the spring and early summer of 1848, with Hungary and Bohemia reasserting their autonomy, northern Italy in the throes of secession and a few Poles plotting against the partitioning powers, many Austrian Germans concluded that they had little to lose and much to gain from a 'united Germany'. They gave little thought to the effects that *Anschluss* (union) with other German states would have on the non-German nationalities of the Austrian Empire. Moreover, the 'vast majority of the Viennese' considered the revolutionary concessions gained in Germany to be 'their own' and the creation of the German National Assembly in Frankfurt to be the prelude to the establishment of their own constituent assembly and Reichstag. For many Austrian Germans 'the liberal reforms . . . in Austria were of secondary importance to those . . . in Germany. In this sense the Viennese Revolution of 1848 was as much a German as an Austrian revolution.' This was particularly true of the Viennese students and radicals, many of whom were 'ardent proponents of union with Germany'. They wanted Austria to merge with other German lands in order to create 'a single democratic state comprising all the German-speaking peoples in central Europe' (Rath 1957: 133, 251). Thus they could make common cause with Italian and Magyar radicals and nationalists against the Habsburgs because they fully expected and accepted the secession of northern Italy and Hungary. Yet Austrian-German radicals were also among the most militant, obdurate and inconsiderate German nationalists and chauvinists *vis-à-vis* the Czechs and the South Slavs, who did not relish the prospect of (even a democratic) Greater Germany (pp. 145–53, 255–66).

On the whole, 'Austro-Germans were incapable of understanding that, to non-Germans, "freedom" meant freedom from age-old German domination as well as from absolutism. Their feelings of superiority prevented them from admitting that the aspirations of subject nationalities for freedom were as natural and as honest as the longings of the Germans for political liberation' (Rath 1957: 267). These attitudes and blind spots go some way to explaining the subsequent deterioration in inter-ethnic relations within the Austrian half of the empire. They also sowed the seeds of the crimes committed against the Slavs of East Central Europe and the Balkans by Hitler, the Nazis and many Austrian and Bohemian Germans between 1938 and 1945. In relation to the Poles, the Czechs and the South Slavs, Sir Lewis Namier maintained, the German 'liberals' and nationalists of 1848 were 'in reality forerunners of Hitler' (Namier 1946: 33).

The 1848 Revolutions and the 'coming of age' of German nationalism thus confronted Austrian Germans with a fatal dilemma which would significantly contribute not only to the defeat of those revolutions but also to the collapse of the Austrian Empire in 1918 and to the demise of the 'first' Austrian Republic in 1938. As Germans, did they want to become full participants in a united German Reich? Or did they prefer to preserve and pursue their distinctively 'Austrian' identity, interests and statehood? The dilemma was not finally resolved until 1945–46, when 'Austrians' found it expedient to bury and forget their long-standing demand for *Anschluss* (union) with Germany, in a remarkable fit (or feat) of 'collective amnesia' and an attempt to dissociate themselves from the crimes of Nazi Germany, to which Hitler and countless other Austrians had actively and seminally contributed. The Revolutions of 1848 and the attendant 'flowering' of German national-ism posed an analogous dilemma for Bohemian Germans. This contributed to the defeat of those revolutions, the eventual disintegration of the Austrian Empire and the Nazi dismemberment of Czechoslovakia in 1938–39, to which the Bohemian (alias Sudeten) Germans also actively and seminally contributed (as they did to many other Nazi crimes). Their dilemma was resolved in the end only by the expulsion of over 3 million Bohemian/Sudeten Germans from the Czech Lands in 1945–46. The essential purpose of highlighting these long-term consequences of the emergence of (pan) German 'ethnic' nationalism as a major political force in East Central Europe from 1848 to 1945 is not to encourage (let alone to endorse) 'Germanophobia' but to emphasize the frequently horrific (and not always intended) effects of 'ethnic' nationalism in the multi-ethnic mosaic of central and eastern Europe. The ultimately devastating effect of the rise of (pan) German 'ethnic' nationalism was (to be precise) the most momentous manifestation of a more general problem, rather than a reflection on 'the German national character' (if any such thing exists). On a smaller scale (because they involve much smaller nations), Magyar, Croat and more recently Serbian 'ethnic' nationalisms have produced similar consequences, while Bulgarian, Romanian, Albanian, Greek, Turkish, Slovak and Polish 'ethnic' nationalisms have sometimes exhibited the potential to do so.

In 1848 even the Habsburgs were torn between their Germanic 'mission' and their Danubian 'destiny'. On 29 June 1848 the German National Assembly in Frankfurt resolved (by 436 votes to eighty-five) to nominate the popular Habsburg archduke Johann as 'imperial regent' of the (stillborn) 'united Germany'. Yet, on 22 July 1848, the same Habsburg archduke opened the Austrian constituent assembly in Vienna. He thus became the formal president of two rival constituent assemblies, relating to two quite different polities. Always with an eye to the main chance, the Habsburgs were in a sense hedging their bets. Indeed, court circles and Viennese radicals and 'liberals' shared a belief that the remodelling of the Habsburg Empire should be carried out 'in accordance with the wishes of the "master nations"'. Moreover, the 'liberals' and radicals assumed that the Habsburg Empire was 'a German state which would also play the chief part in a new liberal Germany, and they pressed as strongly for elections to the German national assembly in Frankfurt as for a constituent assembly in Austria' (Taylor 1976: 63).

However, Austria's privileged property-owning 'liberals' and conservatives were already questioning whether Austria would really be better placed as a border province of a united Greater Germany than as the metropolitan core of its own multinational Danubian empire. The Austrian 'liberal' government voiced its reservations in the *Wiener Zeitung* as early as 21 April 1848: 'Filled with the desire to have a close union with Germany, Austria will gladly seize any opportunity to prove its loyalty to the common German cause. However, it can never completely renounce the special interests of the different parts of its territory . . . It cannot approve any unqualified submission to the assembly of the German confederation or give up its independence in internal administration . . . In so far as this is irreconcilable with the nature of a confederation, Austria is not in a position to join one' (quoted by Rath 1957: 139–40). Metropolitan Vienna and Austria's propertied classes certainly had more to lose than to gain from a united Greater Germany, although it took them a little while to accept that they could not have their *Kuchen* and eat it. 'Very few Austro-Germans clearly understood that they would have to renounce their citizenship in the Austrian Monarchy if they were to become citizens of the German Empire' (p. 250).

RIVAL PERSPECTIVES ON 1848

1848 in Marxist perspective

According to a large body of Marxist scholarship, the 1848 Revolutions marked the decisive cathartic phase in the (terminal) 'crisis of feudalism'. Marxists saw in them the final victory of capitalism and the bourgeoisie over the previously dominant 'feudal' classes (the nobility and the clergy) and the transition from a society based on a relatively rigid hierarchy of social 'orders' (legal 'estates') to one based on a looser, more fluid and more mobile class structure. Most Marxist histories of central and eastern Europe treat history as a teleological, sequential progression through successive 'forms' of society and 'stages' of development, each having its own distinctive prevailing 'mode of production', 'social relations' and 'dominant class'. The prime movers or driving forces of this process are the 'the class struggle' and 'the growth of society's productive forces'. The passage from one historical 'stage' of development and 'form' of society to the next involves an all-pervasive 'crisis' of the outmoded, obsolescent and hitherto dominant 'social relations' and 'mode of production'. It also involves the emergence of a new, more dynamic and more productive dominant class and 'mode of production', along with new 'social relations' corresponding to the requirements of this next 'inevitable' stage in the sequence. The transition period can take the form of a revolution or 'accelerated evolution', when the sheer weight of the foregoing evolutionary quantitative change finally breaks down political barriers and social resistance and adds up to a decisive quantitative change. Revolutions mark a transition from a 'lower' to a 'higher' or more advanced 'mode of production' and 'form of society', in this instance from 'feudalism' to 'capitalism'. Revolution becomes 'necessary' when the prevailing system of 'social relations' falls behind the level of development of a society's 'productive forces' (especially its human resources) and, instead of assisting their development, becomes a 'brake' on their progressive advancement. The prevailing 'social relations' then serve not to stimulate but to discourage or even thwart useful economic activity. This in turn contributes to the growing social tensions, disaffection and frustration to which a revolution gives vent.

In the mid-nineteenth century the Habsburg Empire was a multinational peasant society dominated and held together by an absolute monarchy, an octopus-like state bureaucracy, a still relatively small commercial and industrial sector, a large standing army of mainly peasant conscripts, the Catholic Church and a privileged landed nobility. The established Church and the landed nobility were for the most part servants and guardians of the state. They derived much of their power and position from a long history of subservience to the monarchy and from their close links with the army and the bureaucracy. In the West social structures and class configurations largely determined the nature of the state. In the Habsburg Empire, by contrast, the absolutist state to a large extent determined the nature of the social hierarchy and 'social relations'. It regulated the functions, obligations and prerogatives of each legally defined 'social estate'. Everybody, from birth, was registered as belonging to a particular 'social estate' (the nobility, clergy, peasantry, etc.), although there was some (limited) upward social mobility through service to the state or through state-recognized entrepreneurial success. The resultant social hierarchy was relatively rigid and static. No 'social estate' successfully challenged the Habsburg Monarchy, which, by maintaining its ultimate patrimonial authority over resources and patronage and by treating all subjects (in their various capacities) as its servants, managed to prevent the consolidation of independent concentrations of power and wealth beyond its overall control. To the end, the Habsburg state remained the major source of favours, contracts, sinecures, permissions, protection, subsidies and hand-outs. The nobility (excluding the mutinous Magyars), the clergy, the professions and the business community generally refrained from biting the hand that fed them.

However, the hierarchy of 'social estates', expressing particular relationships to the state and only loosely related to each individual's economic status and functions, was gradually giving way to a more variegated and autonomous (i.e. free-standing) class structure, involving a closer correspondence between social and economic status and functions, partly as a result of the development of capitalism. The advancing commercialization of the economy was accompanied by a more gradual growth in the number, class consciousness and class aspirations of merchants, mine owners, industrialists, financiers, engineers, managers, lawyers, publishers, shopkeepers, artisans and urban workers. This in turn gave rise to major manifestations of class conflict in 1848–49. More significantly, perhaps, the development of capitalism had strongly contributed to the emergence of mutually competitive and increasingly assertive 'national bourgeoisies', particularly among the Austrian and Bohemian Germans, the Czechs and the Magyars, thus greatly exacerbating the 'nationality problems' of this multinational empire. By fostering commercialization, industrialization, transport, mobility, wider markets, cheap print and broader horizons, capitalism eroded parochialism and raised both national and class consciousness among ever wider social strata. It also gave rise to new social classes which were not easily accommodated within the prevailing 'feudal' social hierarchy of nobles, clergy, burghers and peasants, causing the existing social order to 'burst at the seams' in the late 1840s.

Many non-Marxists accept that there is much to be said for the weighty and influential Marxist perspectives on the significance of the 1848 Revolutions in East Central Europe, especially when it comes to the formal juridical aspects of the socio-economic changes brought about by (or in response to) these upheavals. The 1848 Revolutions and their aftermath certainly gave rise to increased trade liberalization, railway construction and market integration; a legislative 'clearing of the decks' for a more intensive and larger-scale development of capitalism; and the formal abolition of many 'last remnants' of serfdom and so-called 'feudalism'. Various state monopolies and guild restrictions on crafts (including protection for craftsmen) were relaxed or abolished, mining laws were liberalized, many state railways were privatized, limited liability was established and the formation of joint stock companies (including joint stock banks) was made easier. Financially the almost bankrupt Habsburg state became even more dependent upon (and 'in hock' to) 'liberal' Viennese and Bohemian capitalists. Moreover, the 'pure' rights of private property were strengthened even though (in terms of legal privilege and status) the landed nobility had been the biggest losers.

In the words of the Marxist historian Roman Rodolski, 'the true historical task of the Revolution of 1848–49 in Austria consisted in clearing the way for the capitalist mode of production, which had developed in Austria since the middle of the eighteenth century, and in sweeping away all impediments which stood in the way of its complete development' (quoted in Good 1984: 40). Similarly, the Hungarian Marxist historian Peter Hanak (1975: 113) claims that 'by abolishing feudalism, the Hungarian Revolution of 1848 helped to create the economic preconditions and the legal–political frame-work necessary for capitalistic development. This made it possible for Hungary to adapt her economy to the market possibilities offered by the Industrial Revolution in western and central Europe and to share in the agrarian boom of the period between 1850 and 1873.'

In apparent concurrence with these Marxist perspectives, an eminent non-Marxist historian has declared that 'The landed nobility had been the defeated party in 1849, defeated as emphatically as extreme radicalism . . . The new centralization deprived the nobility of all power in the localities; and the new absolutism trampled on historic rights as firmly as on popular sovereignty' (Taylor 1976: 97). Moreover, the Emancipation Acts reduced the landowners' power and incentive to keep 'a large peasant population tied to the soil: the smaller peasants sold their holdings to wealthier peasants and moved to the towns. A labour force was placed at the service of capitalism', while the 'ruined' owners of small or non-viable landed estates increasingly sought refuge in the rapidly expanding state bureaucracies, in the professions and even in business. 'Thus the gentry, historically the opponents of the centralized state, now identified themselves with it' (pp. 73, 185–6). This was especially true of Hungary, well into the twentieth century.

1848 in revisionist perspective

Nevertheless, when the focus is broadened away from the narrowly juridical aspects, the predominant Marxist perspectives become less convincing. In Hungary, for example, the 1848 Revolution and the abolition of serfdom, 'feudalism' and (temporarily) Habsburg absolutism were spearheaded not by the bourgeoisie but by the nobility, against the opposition of a large section of the bourgeoisie. History refuses to conform to preconceived historical schemes. As observed by a somewhat ironical Hungarian Marxist historian of Hungary: 'It is one of the anomalies of Hungarian social development that the change to bourgeois conditions depended so little on the class which should have been responsible . . . that is to say, the bourgeoisie itself.' On the contrary, 'when the time came for the actual change to bourgeois conditions, there was no bourgeois force capable of carrying out the task. The bourgeoisie of the royal towns in fact fought on the side of the court, defending feudalism against national independence as represented by the feudal nobility' (Bartha 1975: 239). Moreover, despite the formal abolition of serfdom (along with various seigneurial and ecclesiastical privileges and prerogatives) and the constant erosion of the power and significance of the 'feudal' provincial Diets and the hierarchy of 'social estates' after 1848, the fundamental structures of power and land ownership remained broadly unchanged. These structures continued to be dominated by the landed nobility, and many 'feudal survivals' persisted until 1918 (or even until 1945 in the case of Hungary). Thus there was more continuity than change in the agrarian and power structures of East Central Europe after 1848.

Furthermore, Marxist historians have been second to none in pointing out the *incompleteness* of the post-1848 'transformation' and of 'the transition from feudalism to capitalism'. They convincingly attribute it to the numerical and political weakness and ethnic fragmentation of the emerging bourgeoisies and the consequent fragility and pusillanimity of East Central European 'liberalism', which all the more easily incurred political defeats or succumbed to nationalism and capitulated to (or compromised with) absolute monarchy. As argued by Hanak (1975a: 115), 'the revolution that ended feudalism did not fundamentally alter the . . . social and ethnic structures and the national and class relationships which existed in East Central Europe. The numerically and economically stronger nations and classes, primarily the Austro-German bourgeoisie and the Austrian and Hungarian landowners, continued to maintain their predominance over other classes and peoples.' Within Hungary, he contends, the landed nobility 'continued to be the ruling class and provided the large majority of the political leadership'. Meagre industrial development and the primacy of agriculture contributed to 'the preservation of the old social structure and the continued dominance of the large estates'. Many estate owners 'became successful capitalists, but they did not become modern entrepreneurs'. They retained their traditional values, life style and social aloofness, adopting only 'the external trappings of the modern bourgeois world' (p. 125). Moreover, just as the more prosperous peasants failed to integrate either into the gentry or into the bourgeoisie, most farm labourers remained tied to the village and failed to merge with the urban proletariat (p. 126). Thus Hungary's rural sector failed to swell either the bourgeoisie or the proletariat to the degree anticipated by Marxist theory.

The Austrian Marxist historian Eduard März has emphasized the persistence in Austria (as in Hungary) of 'feudal values and life styles which impaired the building up of a capitalist ethic'. He infers that 'the dominance of a feudal-conservative and military class is a decisive drag on the unfolding of productive forces' (quoted in Good 1984: 95). Moreover, as argued by the non-Marxist historian A.J.P. Taylor (1976: 73), by the early twentieth century 'great estates predominated more than ever before'. Although the 'small gentry were truly ruined' by the dissolution of serfdom (a ruin reinforced by growing competition on international grain markets after 1873), the 'great estates' were able to draw upon greater capital reserves, economies of scale and access to credit. They could more easily invest in productive and/or labour-saving agricultural technology, including steam threshers, steam ploughs and mechanical harvesters, helping them to weather the loss of serf labour and the post-1873 decline in international grain prices. By buying up some of the 'distressed' gentry estates at knock-down prices they sometimes managed to reap significant capital gains and additional economies of scale. The magnates also had more diversified asset portfolios. Thus in Bohemia in 1880 they owned 500 of the 800 breweries, eighty of the 120 sugar factories and 300 of the 400 distilleries, while 'Hungarian magnates owned sawmills, paper-factories, coal-mines, hotels and spas' (pp. 73, 185–6).

Furthermore, as an American school of 'new economic historians' of nineteenth-century Austria-Hungary has persuasively argued (on the basis of new quantitative evidence and techniques), the dissolution of serfdom did not lead to a dramatic acceleration of overall economic growth and capital accumulation. There was merely a resumption of the development patterns and the gradually accelerating growth rates established between 1830 and 1845. Although Austria suffered serious economic reverses from 1859 to 1864 and from 1873 to 1879, there was 'a vigorous economic recovery in the 1880s. In neither depression was the Austrian economy permanently knocked off the long-term growth path established before 1848' (Good 1984: 87). In Hungary the average annual growth of industrial, mining and construction activity actually decelerated from 2.4 per cent during 1830–47 to 1.3 per cent during 1864–74, before surging to 6.1 per cent during 1874–83. It continued at 3.8 per cent during 1883–96, 1.8 per cent during 1896–1906 and 4.6 per cent during 1906–12 (Komlos 1981: 10).

Komlos has also calculated that on the eve of the 1848 Revolutions compulsory (serf) labour accounted for only 9 per cent of all labour time applied to arable land in Austria and 4.4 per cent in Hungary. Therefore, even if one (generously) assumes that 'free' labour was 50 per cent more productive than forced (serf) labour, the switch from the latter to the former merely resulted in a one-off gain in output equivalent to 2.4 per cent of GNP in Austria and 1.2 per cent of GNP in Hungary (Good 1984: 93). It is also argued that, since the state bonds received by landowners as indemnification for the dissolution of serfdom could be 'realized' as capital only by being sold to capitalists, capital merely changed hands. There may not have been any net addition to the overall supply of capital through the indemnification process. In any case the real value of the state bonds received as compensation rapidly fell as a result of the subsequent bout of inflation.

However, the methods of these 'new economic historians' take little account of the less quantifiable social, institutional and psychological effects of the dissolution of serfdom on economic performance, through the increases in social fluidity, in geographical and occupational mobility, in demand for and access to education, in commercialization of the rural sector and in commercial incentives, morale and work incentives. These can only have contributed to the well documented secular acceleration and diversification of economic development in both Austria and Hungary. Indeed, even if there was no dramatic acceleration of economic growth in the immediate aftermath of the 1848 Revolutions and the dissolution of serfdom, it is nevertheless possible that those momentous events really were 'necessary' if the previously established 'growth paths' were to be resumed and sustained as successfully as they were (up to the Balkan Wars of 1912–13). The economic and social crises of 1845–47 suggest that the development patterns initiated between 1830 and 1845 were encountering serious social and institutional impediments which had to be removed or circumvented if steady economic growth was eventually to be resumed and sustained. To that extent the Marxist perspectives may still be quite sound.

In so far as the 1848 Revolutions involved fully fledged class struggle, it was in the main between sections of the upper and middle classes (including the intelligentsia), although even here ideological and national differences often cut across class divisions. It is necessary to guard against the danger of seriously underestimating the inchoate nature of the urban lower classes at that time. It is all too easy to over-interpret and romanticize the 1848 Revolutions as heroic (albeit fumbling and faltering) attempts by the downtrodden lower classes to establish a more egalitarian democratic order. Exaggerated or romanticized interpretations of this sort were prevalent in the cruder Marxist histories of East Central Europe published by the former communist regimes, as part of their endeavour to (mis)use history to enhance (or exaggerate) their revolutionary 'pedigrees' and legitimacy. In fact, even at its most extreme, the Austrian Revolution of 1848 was largely the work of middle-class radical liberal and radical nationalist movements. 'The major issues were not "monarchism versus republicanism" or "capitalism versus socialism", as was to be true a half-century later.' There was relatively little 'class struggle' (in the Marxist sense) between the bourgeoisie and the proletariat. The main battles were 'between the nobility and upper middle classes on the one hand and the radical students and left-wing intelligentsia supported by the lower middle classes and the proletariat, on the other'. Wealthy 'liberals' and conservatives stood opposed to radicals who wanted to turn a limited 'liberal revolution' into a more far-reaching 'democratic' one (Rath 1957: 241). On occasion, however, the lower classes were 'used' by radicals as cannon fodder. Conversely, the wealthy 'liberals' and conservatives gradually gained or 'mobilized' the support of many not-so-wealthy shopkeepers, low-level officials and (in the provinces) Roman Catholic peasant proprietors. Without this 'popular' support the 'Counter-revolution' would not have triumphed as resoundingly as it did.

Nevertheless, the plight of Vienna's lower classes in the 1840s was indeed terrible and they were sometimes driven to 'direct action' by their deepening destitution and distress. 'The industrial revolution in Austria had brought in its train the usual miserable working conditions.' Into Vienna, in search of jobs, flooded the 'sons and daughters of impoverished peasants and destitute handicrafts workers'. The competition for work was intense. Industrial workers were thus obliged to 'work for a pittance' and accept a standard twelve-to-fourteen-hour day, even for the women and children who made up 60 per cent of the work force in the cotton and paper industries of Lower Austria in 1845 (Rath 1957: 13). Their plight was worsened by a lethal combination of soaring prices (after the bad harvests of 1846 and 1847), epidemics, economic recession and mounting unemployment. 'By 1847 10,000 factory workers had been dismissed from their jobs in Vienna alone. The suburbs . . . were filled with unemployed proletarians who were rapidly growing destitute.' Some turned to prostitution, others to petty pilfering and crime. These proletarians and lumpenproletarians were 'ready to join any movement that might bring them bread' (p. 14). Their uncontrolled violence, machine-breaking, looting of shops and arson attacks on factories in Vienna's industrial suburbs from 13 to 15 March 1848 as well as their angry and menacing marches into the city centre on 15 May, 26 May, 15–17 June, 21–3 August, 13 September and 6–7 October repeatedly terrified the shopkeepers and propertied classes, driving the 'liberals' among them firmly into the 'law and order' camp.

Workers did articulate distinctly working-class demands for higher wages, a ten-hour working day, restrictions on the number of apprentices assigned to any employer (and on the employment of children and females in factories), the establishment of fixed ratios between machine and manual work in industry, care for the sick and the disabled, workers' administration of funds for workers in need and more humane treatment of workers by employers and foremen (Rath 1957: 128–9). But it is nevertheless arguable that they had as yet 'no feeling of class consciousness in the Marxist sense' (p. 14). Rath refers to them as 'leaderless, ignorant, starving and seemingly impotent' (p. 88). When Karl Marx visited Vienna in late summer 1848, hoping to find fertile soil for his 'scientific' socialism, his ideas were brusquely rejected (p. 296). Marx and Engels later described the Viennese working class of 1848 as 'distrusted, disarmed, disorganized, hardly emerging from the intellectual bondage of the old regime, hardly awakening' (p. 240). Elsewhere, however, Rath concedes that 'the conflict on August 21 and 23 was a kind of limited class struggle that served to make the proletariat conscious of the fact that they formed a class of their own'. Workers battled with property-owning Civic and National Guardsmen. 'Seeing themselves deserted by all the middle-class groups in Vienna, the workers were forced to develop a feeling of class consciousness' (p. 296).

On 30 August 1848 the 'liberal' conservative *Wiener Zeitung* presciently warned that the quite savage repression of workers' protests against a government decision to cut wages on public works projects on 23 August 1848 'separated the workers, as such, from other classes. It has given them an idea – that of their own misfortune. It has bequeathed them a historical tradition . . . The workers have seen the contrast between their defenceless poverty and armed property. And at this moment there came into being a proletariat that formerly did not exist.' The Viennese students and middle-class radicals, who had repeatedly received support from the working-class suburbs in their critical moments of need, failed to give the workers reciprocal support when they needed it most. They just stood by, helplessly gawping at the carnage (Rath 1957: 293–7). Thus, even if the Viennese Revolution of 1848 was not the *result* of class conflict between proletarians and the propertied classes, it nevertheless *gave birth to* the proletarian class consciousness and class conflict in East Central Europe which would by the 1900s rival nationalism as the great internal threat to political stability and to the survival of the Habsburg Empire.

10 The empire strikes back: 1849–1914

FROM 'LIBERAL' COUNTER-REVOLUTION TO NEO-ABSOLUTISM

In the wake of the political defeat of the 1848 Revolutions, the chastened Austrian-German 'liberals' looked to the Habsburg state to carry out the economic 'anti-feudal' and unifying elements of the 'liberal' programme by autocratic means, much as Prussian German 'liberals' looked to the Hohenzollern state to do the same within the German *Zollverein* (Customs Union, established in the 1830s). The 'liberal' propertied classes had suffered a real scare in 1848. Having slightly lifted the lid of the 'Pandora's box' of democracy, they had seemingly lost control to 'radicals' who wanted to advance beyond limited, orderly and elitist 'democracy for the rich' towards a more egalitarian 'democracy for the masses', threatening the privileged position and prerogatives of the rich. On further reflection, therefore, 'repentant liberals' concluded that it would be far safer to rely on monarchical power and authority to implement vital parts of the 'liberal' programme in a more strictly controlled manner ('from above'). Thus many 'liberals' sold out to the dynasty in the belief that they could 'use' it to attain important 'liberal' objectives. These included: an imperial customs union; the construction of railways; the promotion of industry, banks and joint stock companies; the rule of law (the setting up of a *Rechtsstaat*); 'responsible' quasi-constitutional government; the further suppression of seigneurial privilege; the abolition of the hereditary rights of landlords in local jurisdiction/administration; the erosion of the powers of landlord-dominated provincial Diets; the creation of a more uniform and more unitary state; and the opening of official careers to (mainly bourgeois) 'talent'.

However, while considerable 'progress' was made on all these fronts from the 1850s to the 1870s, it was achieved at a high political price. Paradoxically, 'liberal progress' gave a new lease of life to a fundamentally illiberal Habsburg absolutism. The dynasty used an army of tamed and compliant 'liberals' to attain conservative dynastic aims, to create a larger, stronger and more modern dynastic power base, to centralize the state, to reduce the roles of local/feudal 'particularism' and the landed nobility, to greatly extend the power and competence of the imperial bureaucracy and to establish a Kafkaesque 'Big Brother' state in East Central Europe long before the arrival of communist dictatorship. (By the same token, however, it will take far more than the 'mere' elimination of communist dictatorship to rid the East Central European societies of their illiberal deformities, which long preceded the so-called 'Sovietization' of the region after the Second World War.) Ironically, once the Austrian-German 'liberals' had served the dynasty's purpose they were unceremoniously ditched by the Habsburgs at the end of the 1870s.

Emboldened by the apparent completeness of their political and military victories over the radical, 'liberal' and nationalist movements of 1848, the Schwarzenberg government and Emperor Franz Joseph were not content merely to restore the *status quo ante*. They had no wish to return to the immobilism, muddle and inertia of the Metternich era. They also tried to efface all memory of the humiliations and compromises of 1848. Instead of fully reinstating the aristocratic imperial councils, provincial Diets, local 'feudal' jurisdictions and the Hungarian *comitat* system, all of which had provided platforms for the 'liberals' of 1848, the victors decided to press home their 'total victory' by bringing to fruition Joseph II's dream of a Germanic *Gesamtstaat*. This envisaged a centralized and unitary empire ruled directly from Vienna by a highly professional German-speaking imperial bureaucracy, the military, imperial viceroys and other local and provincial plenipotentiaries. Overbearing German-speaking imperial officials and military commanders elbowed aside not only the 1848 'liberals' but federalist aristocratic conservatives as well.

The chief architect of this so-called 'neo-absolutism' was Schwarzenberg's first Justice Minister and subsequent Interior Minister, Alexander Bach, a renegade 'liberal' lawyer who had played a prominent role in the March 1848 'liberal' Revolution in Vienna before gravitating towards the 'law and order' camp in the summer. Even before the sudden death of Schwarzenberg in April 1852, Bach had emerged as the *éminence grise* of the neo-absolutist regime (although Emperor Franz Joseph allowed the office of Prime Minister formally to lapse, becoming in effect his own chief Minister). Under the so-called 'Bach System', professional middle-class German bureaucrats overrode traditional local autonomies and noble prerogatives and brushed aside historic claims and privileges with an almost Jacobin fanaticism. Hungary, they argued, had forfeited its former constitutional rights in 1848 by rebelling against Austria and by formally deposing the Habsburgs. Treated as a newly conquered country, Hungary was to be administered by officers and officials imported from Austria. Known as the 'Bach hussars', they were dressed up in ostentatious pseudo-Hungarian uniforms (braided tunics, swords and hats with feather cockades). Likewise, Croatia, Transylvania, Slovakia, Bohemia and Galicia were allowed even less autonomy than before. 'The Austrian Empire became, for the first and last time, a fully unitary state. There was a single system of administration, carried out by German officials on orders from Vienna; a single code of laws; a single system of taxation' (Taylor 1976: 85).

Furthermore, by dissolving many former monopolies, state ventures and guild restrictions, by liberalizing the mining laws, by reducing external tariffs and by abolishing the 'tariff wall' between Austria and Hungary, the neo-absolutist regime stimulated trade and economic growth. The Habsburg state also embarked on a railway building programme between 1851 and 1854 in order to boost and further integrate the post-revolutionary imperial economy. By 1854 70 per cent of the 1,433 km rail network was state-owned. But the state incurred budget deficits, exacerbated by the high costs of the 1848 Revolutions and the ensuing wars with Hungary and Piedmont, the expense of railway construction, the indemnification of ex-serf owners and the commercially disruptive effects of the 1853–56 Crimean War between Russia, on the one side, and Britain, France, Piedmont and the Ottoman Empire, on the other. In 1854–55, therefore, the state decided to privatize its railways and to leave further railway construction to private interests, albeit with state-guaranteed dividends and duty-free importation of rails and rolling stock. This largely involuntary *volte-face* was presented as a major sop or concession to the 'repentant liberals'. It also stimulated a large influx of foreign (especially French) investment in Austrian banks and railways.

This economic liberalization and market integration allowed Hungarian landowners to export grain, timber and livestock products more freely to Austria, undercutting many Austrian-German and Czech farmers and driving some of them off the land into the developing urban sector. It also turned Hungary into a freely accessible 'captive market' for Austrian-German and Bohemian textile and producer goods industries, to the detriment of Hungary's underdeveloped textile and craft industries and to the consternation of Magyar nationalists. But the burgeoning Hungarian flour-milling, sugar-refining, brewing, distilling, wine-making and leather goods industries (in which Hungary either had or soon achieved comparative cost advantages) actually benefited from unimpeded access to the expanding Austro-Bohemian market. Hungarian exports of flour and sugar increased dramatically as a result. In the longer term Hungarian economic development was also accelerated by growing inflows of foreign (especially Austrian-German and Jewish) capital and producer goods, which re-equipped Hungary's industries, expanded and modernized its infrastructure and eventually created some significant engineering enterprises (notably the Ganz works). There emerged a symbiotic relationship between the Austrian and Hungarian economies (Komlos 1981: 10–12).

All these developments enhanced the importance of Vienna as a commercial, financial and industrial centre, assisted the political stabilization of Habsburg neo-absolutism and temporarily revived Austrian claims to economic, cultural and political ascendancy in the Germanic world, winning the allegiance of many pan-German 'liberals' as well as nationalists. In December 1850 Prussia renounced its bid for a north German union and agreed to a restoration of the German Confederation under Austria's presidency. However, unlike 1860s Prussia, Austria could not afford to consummate its renewed ascendancy over Germany by brazenly and unreservedly mobilizing and appealing to German nationalism. Austria therefore repeatedly lost out to Bismarck's Prussia in the German wars of unification in 1864, 1866 and 1870.

Emperor Franz Joseph (1848–1914) necessarily played a pivotal role in the return to absolutism. Sworn in as Emperor in December 1848, after the court camarilla had finally decided that Emperor Ferdinand should abdicate, the new eighteen-year-old monarch did not consider himself bound by the promises and concessions which had been extracted from his 'Uncle Ferdi' under duress and in violation of 'divinely ordained' dynastic rights. Born plain 'Franz', he adopted the additional name 'Joseph' in an attempt to invoke the spirit (and claim the mantle) of 'people's Emperor' Joseph II. Eventually his adopted name came to signify a combination of obduracy and 'firmness' (like his great-uncle Franz) and 'reform from above' (like Joseph II). In his dull and dreary devotion to duty, the dynasty and the defence of the Habsburg patrimony, Franz Joseph became the archetypal Austrian bureaucrat, the epitome of imperial inertia and routine. 'It was a perpetual puzzle to him that he could not make his Empire work merely by sitting at his desk and signing documents for eight hours a day' (Taylor 1976: 78). He was 'an Emperor without ideas; this was his strength' (p. 175). His limited vision, his lack of fixed ideas and his ruthless opportunism were what enabled him to survive so long amid the eddying currents of the late nineteenth and early twentieth centuries. He saw himself as the servant of *all* his subjects. Yet he was not willing to surrender to them any control over the major instruments of state power and coercion, namely the armed forces, the imperial bureaucracy, the police and the decisions of war and peace.

Franz Joseph and his chief Ministers lacked a coherent, clear-sighted programme for the future. 'At the heart of the counter-revolution lay not strength and direction but dissension and confusion' (Sked 1989: 134). But the drift and disorientation were camouflaged (and the vacuum was filled) by a reassertion of absolutism and the powers of the Catholic Church. Imposing forms marked a lack of modern substance capable of meeting the needs of a rapidly industrializing and increasingly educated and sophisticated empire. The Monarchy became more and more outmoded and anachronistic as a political organization precisely because its economic, military and cultural strength continued to develop. The Concordat of 1855 gave the Roman Catholic Church an unprecedented degree of independence and control of education, censorship and family law. Non-Catholics were banned from teaching in Catholic/state schools and new restrictions were imposed on the Jews, while a 'spirit of intolerance paralysed intellectual life'. The Habsburg Empire was in effect subjected to another Catholic counter-revolution, enforced by police informers and spies (Kann 1974: 321–2). However, like the renewal of absolutism, this artificial revival of the Church was an attempt 'to defeat the modern spirit with weapons taken from a seventeenth-century museum'. Moreover, whereas before 1848 it had still been possible for dissidents to believe that the evils of absolutism could be remedied in a manner acceptable to the dynasty, the post-1848 counter-revolution appeared to rule out such grounds for hope or optimism. 'The new absolutism was without promise; this was its worst feature' (Taylor 1976: 89).

Nevertheless, the Bach System survived only until 1859. A stock exchange crisis in 1857 shook investors' confidence in the regime, which also committed fatal blunders in the foreign policy field. During the Crimean War the perfidious Habsburgs refused to reciprocate the significant 'moral' and military support that they had received from Tsar Nicholas I against the Hungarian Revolution in 1849 by siding with Russia against its British, French, Turkish and Piedmontese foes in the Black Sea region. On the contrary, in June 1854 the ungrateful Austrians sent Russia an ultimatum demanding the withdrawal of its occupying forces from Moldavia and Wallachia (nascent Romania). Russia's armies were withdrawn and Austrian troops took their place. Russia was thus cut off from the Balkans, leaving Austria as the dominant power in the region and in control of almost the entire length of the Danube. But it was a pyrrhic victory, for these moves left Austria without major allies. Russia attributed its own defeat to Austrian perfidy, while Britain and France concluded that the bloody and costly Crimean War could have been avoided altogether if Austria had actively supported them at the outset (instead of professing neutrality). In 1856 Austria was forced to withdraw its troops from Moldavia and Wallachia, which went on to become the virtually independent state of Romania under French patronage in the 1860s, temporarily negating the growth of Austrian influence in the Balkans.

Viewed in a longer perspective, Austria's ill-judged and undignified manoeuvres during the Crimean War marked the end of nearly a century of fruitful co-operation between the Tsarist and Habsburg Empires over the Balkans, Poland and Hungary and the beginning of mutual hostility and open rivalry in the Balkans. It would culminate in the First World War and the final disintegration of both imperial rivals. More immediately, however, by entering the Crimean War on the Anglo-French side, Piedmont obtained a promise of future French military assistance against Austria in northern Italy. This led to Franco-Piedmontese military victories over Austria in 1859, the Habsburgs' permanent loss of Lombardy and the formation of an anti-Austrian 'united' Italian state in 1860 and the Habsburgs' loss of Venetia in 1866.

These defeats and setbacks, coming on top of the economic hiccup of 1857 and the ever-growing unpopularity of bureaucratic centralism, deeply discredited the 'Bach bureaucracy' and forced Bach himself to resign in July 1959. To bolster his own weakened position and authority, Franz Joseph initially fell back upon a socially and politically conservative and quasi-federalist partnership between the crown and the loyalist aristocracies of the Habsburg Empire. The Polish aristocrat (and former viceroy of Galicia) Count Agenor Goluchowski became the new 'Minister of State'. In 1860 considerable powers were devolved to landlord-dominated provincial Diets, which were reconstituted for the purpose. The overwhelmingly conservative and ultra-loyal Galician Polish aristocracy gained substantial provincial autonomy for the first time, while Croatia, Transylvania, Bohemia and Moravia benefited to varying but more limited extents. In Hungary proper the aristocratic pre-1848 constitution of the Diet and the county system of local self-administration were restored, curtailing Austrian 'direct rule'. In October 1860 the so-called 'October Diploma' announced that most imperial legislation (excluding all military and foreign policy matters) would henceforth be submitted for inspection by the provincial Diets and an augmented imperial *Reichsrat*, whose additional members were being selected by Emperor Franz Joseph from the more 'respectable' members of the provincial Diets.

These changes did not begin to satisfy the Magyar nobility. Magyar nationalism had been roused to fever pitch by the excitement of Italian unification and the cult of the Italian nationalist 'freedom fighter' Garibaldi, whose army of 'red shirts' had been joined by some Magyar veterans of 1848–49. Kossuth courted Emperor Napoleon III and concluded a pact with Cavour, the Piedmontese Prime Minister and 'midwife' of Italian unification. Magyar public opinion was also galvanized by the violent death of a young Magyar demonstrator in Budapest and the suicide of Count Istvan Szechenyi in March and April 1860 respectively. The Magyar leaders were not seeking a restoration of the limited, decentralized, aristocratic autonomy of the Metternich era, nor did they want to be represented in an imperial parliament (not even in a real one). They boycotted the augmented imperial *Reichsrat* and demanded the restoration of their modern 'liberal' constitution of April 1848, including a fully fledged Hungarian government and parliament at Budapest. On the other hand, Austrian-German bureaucrats, the Viennese 'liberal' press and parts of the Austrian-German bourgeoisie were up in arms against the October Diploma because it threatened to undo the 'unifying' centralizing achievements of the 1850s and jeopardize Austrian-German dominance of the conduct of imperial affairs.

Faced with uncompromising Magyar nationalism and the realization that aristocratic federalism was a recipe for political paralysis which would weaken the Monarchy and alienate the Austrian-German imperial bureaucrats and bourgeoisie without in any way placating the Magyars, Emperor Franz Joseph backtracked. In December 1860 the conservative Polish aristocrat Goluchowski was dismissed. He was replaced by an Austrian-German 'liberal', Anton von Schmerling, whose chief task was to reaffirm 'centralism' and win back the wavering Austrian-German 'liberals', bureaucrats and bourgeoisie. Through the so-called February Patent of February 1861 the *Reichsrat* was upgraded to the status of a bicameral imperial quasi-parliament, with an upper house nominated by Franz Joseph and a 343-member lower house of representatives elected by the provincial Diets. The Diets (even the Hungarian one) were implicitly downgraded to the status of electoral colleges and organs of local government. Moreover, through so-called 'electoral geometry' (gerrymandering) as well as restrictive property qualifications and the division of the electorate into separate curia, representation in the provincial Diets and (more tellingly) in the *Reichsrat* was weighted heavily in favour of Germans.

These new arrangements were no more acceptable to the Habsburgs' non-German subjects than the October Diploma had been. The Magyar Diet decided to behave like a real Hungarian parliament, to persevere with the Magyar boycott of the imperial *Reichsrat* and to approve an address to the crown drafted by the 'liberal' landowner and lawyer Ferenc Deak, affirming the legality of the Hungarian constitutional laws passed in the spring of 1848. Continuing Magyar defiance led to the suspension of the Hungarian Diet and *comitat* system and to the return of the 'Bach hussars' and Austrian direct rule in Hungary from 1862 to 1865. Meanwhile, the Croatian Diet had resolved from the start to boycott the *Reichsrat* (and was then suspended), the Czechs followed suit from 1863 onwards and the Galician Poles did so from 1864.

All this added up to a *de facto* return to absolutism, which was barely mitigated by the existence of a very unrepresentative and widely boycotted *Reichsrat*. Even the privileged and overrepresented Austrian and Bohemian Germans felt dissatisfied, partly because the February Patent of 1861 contained none of the provisions essential to a constitutional system. It made no provision for freedom of the press, for immunity from arbitrary arrest (not even for members of the *Reichsrat*), for an independent judiciary or for the accountability of Ministers to the *Reichsrat*. Tax levels, military matters and foreign policy remained outside the control of the *Reichsrat*. The imperial government could even govern and issue regulations on the Emperor's authority when the *Reichsrat* was not in session (Taylor 1976: 107). What is more, the February Patent had been granted by the Emperor's grace and could be revoked at will. 'The *Reichsrat* had not attained its position by struggle; therefore, despite its parliamentary appearance, it was a body without power.' The fact that the Germans owed their majority in the *Reichsrat* to a restricted franchise and 'electoral geometry' made them dependent on government support, rather than the government dependent on their support (p. 114). Moreover, by noisily applauding the government's intransigence towards the Magyar Diet in August 1861, the *Reichsrat* Germans betrayed their former 'liberal' principles and became subservient allies of the Habsburgs (p. 112). They decided that this was the way to safeguard the vaunted imperial customs union, economic liberalization and Germanic hegemony, against the importunate demands and aspirations of more 'reactionary' and/or overtly nationalistic Magyar, Polish, Czech and Croat notables. In Taylor's judgement, 'the decision taken in 1861 was the doom of stability and peace in central Europe . . . The Germans received an artificial majority in a sham parliament; in return they abandoned their liberal principles . . . and committed themselves to support the dynasty whatever its policy' (p. 114).

Few believed that this virtual restoration of Habsburg absolutism would last long, resting as it did on a narrow base of Austrian and Bohemian-German support and the occasional show of force. Indeed, the ordinance restoring Austrian direct rule in Hungary in the autumn of 1861 was officially known as the *provisorium* (provisional regulation). The non-German subjects of the Habsburgs decided to sit it out. Violent struggle was 'off the agenda' after the repression they had suffered in 1849–50. Nor was it deemed necessary (Hanak 1975b: 311).

In the autumn of 1864 the *Reichsrat* Germans finally baulked at the imperial government's intransigence and opted for an accommodation with the Magyars. As in 1848, Magyar domination of Hungary would be a price that Austrian and Bohemian German 'liberals' and nationalists were willing to pay (at least temporarily) while they reinforced their own domination of the rest of the Monarchy. In late 1864 even Emperor Franz Joseph started putting out feelers to Ferenc Deak, who had emerged as the *de facto* Magyar leader in succession to Kossuth and Szechenyi.

In 1862, significantly, the exiled Kossuth had finally lost faith in either revolutionary war or Franco-Italian military intervention as the way to regain Magyar independence. In a complete *volte-face*, he now urged his Magyar compatriots to repair their relations with the Croats, the Serbs and the Romanians and, instead of scorning or oppressing them, promote an anti-Habsburg Danubian Confederation in which the Magyars could partici- pate as equal partners and as leaders (Jaszi 1929: 313). He declared that the Magyars should place themselves at the head of a multinational anti-Habsburg (and implicitly anti-Ottoman) Danubian liberation movement, if they were not to end up 'either in German bondage or torn asunder by the assaults of the awakening nationalities'.

Kossuth's noble vision and change of heart abruptly ended his practical political influence among the Magyars, although he remained a revered 'national hero' on account of his paramount role in 1848–49. 'Kossuth's prophetic warnings and his plan for confederation were rejected by the leading sections of the nobility, not because of their utopian nature, but because of their conciliatoriness, which came near to renouncing Hungarian supremacy and the territorial integrity of the country' (Hanak 1975b: 313). Indeed, any suggestion that the proud Magyar 'master race' should ally itself or associate on an equal footing with the 'backward' Slavic and Romanian 'peasant peoples' was anathema to the haughty Magyar nobility and strident Magyar nationalists. The latter groups now preferred to reach a deal with the Austrian Germans, whom they regarded as 'true equals' and 'natural partners' (despite the carnage and repression inflicted upon them by the Austrian Germans in the wake of the 1848 Revolutions), rather than to allow themselves to become associated with 'inferior' Balkan peoples. 'Better Vienna than Belgrade!' Kossuth's former followers declared (Taylor 1976: 122). Such attitudes not only help to explain why the Magyar leadership chose to seek an accommodation with their Austrian-German rather than with their Slav and Romanian neighbours. They have also provided enduring obstacles to almost all attempts to resolve the problem of their Magyar minorities in (and relations with) Romania, Serbia, Croatia and Slovakia. (To some extent they even lie behind the continuing Magyar nationalist assumption that the Magyars, as a 'superior' nation, merit *preferential* treatment from the West – at least on a par with Austria, the Czech Republic and Poland – and that they should be admitted to the EU and NATO long before their 'inferior' Balkan neighbours get so much as a look- in. In other words, essentially the same assumptions and sense of superiority lay behind Magyar expectations of a privileged position within the Habsburg Empire as have lain behind recent Magyar expectations of preferential treatment from the West in general and from the EU in particular.)

In 1863 and 1864 the Schmerling government faced mounting discontent, even within its 'natural' Austrian-German constituency. The disaffection was exacerbated by the fiscal and monetary 'squeeze' which followed the war of 1859. In early 1865 Schmerling finally felt obliged to reconvene the temporarily suspended Magyar and Croatian Diets. In an article published on 16 April 1865 Ferenc Deak disavowed any intention of weakening the essential foundations and integrity of the Habsburg Empire, within whose framework 'the basic laws of the Hungarian constitution should be given adequate scope'. In May he went on to acknowledge the existence of important matters of common concern to both Austria and Hungary. These reassurances cleared the way for the dismissal of Schmerling and his 'centralist' allies in July 1865 and the commencement of lengthy negotiations which would culminate in the May 1867 *Ausgleich* ('compromise') between the Magyars and their monarch, who came to Budapest in person to announce his intention of satisfying the *loyal* and *legitimate* aspirations of his Hungarian subjects (Hanak 1975b: 315; Taylor 1976: 122).

While internal considerations and dynamics were much more important than has usually been recognized by many ('general') European historians, it is also true that the *rapprochement* between the Magyars and their monarch was enormously reinforced and facilitated by the external humiliations inflicted upon the Habsburg Empire by Bismarck's Prussia between 1863 and 1866. The August 1863 meeting of the still Habsburg-dominated German Confederation was boycotted by the King of Prussia, without whom the other German rulers would transact no business. That autumn Prussia also slammed the door on Austrian membership of the thriving Prussian-dominated German *Zollverein* (customs union), threatening to marginalize Austria in German economic affairs. In 1864 a joint Prussian and Austrian invasion of the duchies of Schleswig and Holstein deprived Denmark of one-third of its territory. This showed many German princelings that they had a new Prussian 'boss' and initiated the forceful unification of most of Germany under the Prussian crown (completed by the Franco-Prussian War of 1870–71).

In early 1866 the Habsburgs prepared for an impending 'showdown' with Bismarck's Prussia. They appeared to have enlisted the support of most of the Catholic and some of the Lutheran German states against Prussian expansionism/'imperialism'. The Austrian Foreign Minister also reached a secret agreement with Napoleon III that, in the event of the anticipated Habsburg victory over Prussia, Austria would cede Venetia to France (which would in turn reap the honour and rewards of ceding it to Italy) and obtain territorial compensation in Silesia and the Rhineland at Prussia's expense, in consultation with France. But Bismarck outmanoeuvred the Habsburgs. In April 1866 he appealed to and allied himself with German 'liberalism' and nationalism in Prussia and elsewhere by proposing that the Diet of the German Confederation should henceforth be elected by adult male suffrage (as was the Prussian parliament). Then in June 1866, having bought Italy's support by promising her Venetia, Prussia rapidly invaded Hanover (a British appendage), Saxony, Kurhesse and Bohemia and, on 3–4 July 1866, decisively defeated the main Habsburg forces at Sadowa (Königsgrätz). Bismarck's quick-fire 'knockout blows' successfully averted a protracted and mutually destructive Austro-Prussian war and avoided any potentially costly French, British or Russian mediation between the two sides. Europe's other powers, along with Austria, simply yielded to Bismarck's *fait accompli*. The Treaty of Prague (23 August 1866) brought to an end centuries of Habsburg power and influence in Germany and Italy and eventually encouraged the Habsburgs to seek territorial compensation in the Balkans (with ultimately catastrophic consequences). It also imposed a small but humiliating indemnity on Austria and it sanctioned both the formation of a Prussian-dominated North German Confederation and Prussia's annexation of Hanover, Schleswig, Holstein, Nassau, Frankfurt and Kurhessen.

These peace terms were, nevertheless, nowhere near as harsh as they could have been. Bismarck stoutly resisted the King of Prussia's demands for extensive annexations of Habsburg territory (Kann 1974: 276). Bismarck strove to preserve the Austrian Empire as a defeated junior partner among the German states, not to destroy it. The continued existence of the Austrian Empire was a bulwark against the creation of a Greater Germany, which would have been more than Bismarck and the Prussian Junker class could have hoped to control for long and which might well have provoked the formation of anti-German coalitions among its fearful European neighbours. The Magyars, Czechs, Slovaks, Slovenes, Poles, Romanians, Russia, France, Italy and Britain vastly preferred the prolonged existence of the Habsburg Empire to the creation of a Greater Germany which would have dominated and destabilized Europe. Excluded from both Italy and Germany, the Austro-Hungarian Empire (as it became in 1867) still served as a useful barrier to either German or (alternatively) Russian hegemony over East Central Europe and the Balkans. Its prolonged existence conveniently put off having to address big questions which the European powers preferred not to have to answer (i.e. what to put in its place or the questions which have plagued East Central Europe and the northern Balkans since 1918). To his great credit as a European statesman, Bismarck recognized the need to 'preserve Austria as she was in 1866', although this strongly contributed to the element of 'suspended animation' in many areas of Austrian imperial politics from 1867 to 1918 (Taylor 1976: 127–9). In 1866, as in 1815, 'Austria was preserved to suit the convenience of others, not by her own strength' (p. 37). This signalled the beginning of the end of the Habsburg Empire as a military power, although it continued to develop economically and culturally right up to the First World War.

THE *AUSGLEICH* (COMPROMISE) OF 1867

The defeats and humiliations of 1859–66 finally induced Emperor Franz Joseph to seek far-reaching accommodations with the Austrian-German 'liberals' as well as with the Magyar nobility, who had displayed exemplary loyalty and restraint during the crisis of 1866, in marked contrast to those of 1848 and even 1859. Franz Joseph now needed their *active* support not only to ensure that he and the house of Habsburg survived the humiliating *débâcles* of 1859 and 1866, to which his extensive personal involvement in foreign and military affairs had conspicuously contributed, but also to try to recoup some of the Habsburgs' losses. In October 1866 he entrusted Habsburg foreign policy to the former Prime Minister of Saxony, Baron (later Count) Ferdinand Beust, who was (mistakenly) considered to be more of a match for Bismarck. His primary political task was to try to construct a new anti-Prussian coalition, internally as well as externally, to try to turn the clock back to its position in 1863, if not earlier still. To stand even the slightest chance of success, this 'revanchist' strategy would require a comprehensive internal reorganization of the Habsburg Empire, including a complete reconciliation and a power-sharing partnership with the Magyar nobility and the Austrian-German 'liberals' (Kann 1974: 276–7). The major flaw in this scenario was that these were the two groups who were least likely to welcome and enthusiastically support another war against Prussia. For, because they thought that they owed their big gains in 1867 to the defeat of Austria by Prussia in 1866, they similarly feared that those gains could be reversed after any future Austro-Hungarian victory over Prussia. Moreover, Austrian Germans would have been most reluctant to go to war against a unified German national state, even one dominated by the widely detested Prussians. What is more, the terms of the 1867 *Ausgleich* made it almost impossible to seek (let alone attain) an all-round resolution of the Monarchy's ultimately fatal 'nationality problems' and thus made it harder, not easier, for Austria to 'get even with' Prussia.

In effect the Austro-Hungarian 'compromise' of 1867 instituted a union of two equal semi-sovereign states: Austria and Hungary. They would share the same monarch, a customs union, a single currency, common finances, common foreign and defence policies, unified diplomatic representation, joint armed forces and an integrated military command structure centred on Vienna. German would remain the language of military command and the lingua franca of the empire, while the Emperor of Austria/King of Hungary would retain sole jurisdiction over foreign and military affairs. Hungary would be allowed to establish only token armed forces of its own and would have little say in imperial military affairs. 'The Hungarian parliament's authority in military matters was limited to fixing the number of recruits, to voting on the completion of the ranks, and to deciding where the troops were to be stationed. The dynasty had absolute control over all other military concerns . . . The army acted as an independent power, often behaved in a provocatively anti-Hungarian manner and deliberately insulted national feelings' (Hanak 1975a: 119). This was to become the major bone of contention between the Magyars and the Austrian imperial authorities, culminating in a very tense 'stand-off' in 1903–06 (which led to a brief suspension of the Hungarian parliament and constitution by the Austrian emperor and armed forces in early 1906).

Ministers continued to be appointed by and responsible to the Habsburg emperor/king rather than the Austrian and Hungarian parliaments. The few Ministers in common were to be responsible to the emperor/king and to a committee comprising equal numbers of delegates from the two respective parliaments. They alone could deliberate and advise the emperor/king on matters of common policy, thereby removing many aspects of high policy from effective parliamentary scrutiny and control. The so-called 'common finances' were those sustaining the common policies and institutions of the empire, notably defence and foreign policy. These joint expenses were to be apportioned between Austria and Hungary in accordance with a ratio to be agreed between the respective parliaments once every ten years, as part of a so-called 'economic compromise' (which also covered such matters as external tariffs and trade, monetary affairs, railway routes and the decennial renewal of the customs union). It was initially decided to divide the empire's 'common expenses' 70:30, imposing a heavier fiscal burden on Austria than on Hungary, but in 1907 the ratio was altered to a more equitable 63.6:36.4. The negotiations and posturing which accompanied the decennial renewal of the 'economic compromise' were sometimes very fraught.

It was significant that the 1867 'compromise' was concluded not between the assorted representative bodies and peoples of Austria and Hungary but bilaterally, between Emperor Franz Joseph and self-appointed Magyar negotiators, over the heads of the various nationalities and their (indirectly) elected representatives. Even the Austrian *Reichsrat*, which had hitherto been intended to develop into a body representing the Habsburg Empire as a whole, was presented with an immutable fait accompli, as was the Hungarian Diet. This merely emphasized that neither body was a fully fledged parliament and that neither could exercise any positive control over the affairs of the empire as a whole, as distinct from those of its two increasingly separate 'halves'. Instead the 'compromise' became something of a 'blocker's charter'. It allowed each side a veto on any fundamental alteration in the constitutional arrangements of the other and in the relationship between the two, thus obstructing any attempt to reach a more comprehensive settlement or accommodation with the non-German and non-Magyar subjects of the Habsburg emperor.

The *Ausgleich* helped to preserve the dominance of the two imperial 'master races': the Austro-Germans and the Magyars. Yet the fears and insecurity of the Magyars (concerning the fragility of their dominance and their incomplete autonomy within the kingdom of Hungary) meant that they were never willing to take the risk of granting equal rights and status to the other nationalities within 'their half' of the empire. They also viewed with apprehension the persistent pressure for greater ethnic equality and popular participation in quasi-parliamentary institutions in the 'Austrian half' of the empire. The nub of the problem, in the eyes of the imperial authorities as well as the Magyar leadership, was 'how to cut the Habsburg Monarchy in two while leaving it in one piece' (Sked 1989: 194). The essence of the solution was encapsulated in the (perhaps apocryphal) words of the main Magyar negotiator, Count Gyula Andrassy, to an Austro-German colleague: 'You look after your Slavs and we'll look after ours' (p. 190). 'Andrassy desired an Austria centralized, liberal and German, just as Hungary would be centralized, liberal and Magyar . . . The Germans and the Magyars were to be the "Peoples of state"; as for the others, Andrassy said, the Slavs are not fit to govern, they must be ruled' (Taylor 1976: 130).

Nevertheless, the Austro-Hungarian 'compromise' satisfied no one. 'The Germans of the Monarchy came to detest it and many Hungarians also wanted to alter it. The other races of the Monarchy – quite properly – felt cheated by it . . . The "compromise" of 1867 had surrendered them to the master races' (Sked 1989: 188–9). In 1895 the leader of Austria's right-wing Christian Social Party, Karl Lueger, told the *Reichsrat* that he considered the Dual Monarchy to be 'the greatest misfortune which my fatherland has ever had to suffer' (p. 189). The Austrian public came to resent the seemingly 'sinister and predominant role of Hungary within the Monarchy', because the Magyars regularly vetoed any change in the *status quo*, while 'Hungarian public opinion still considered Hungary to be oppressed', because autonomous Hungary was still not allowed to assert its full sovereignty, independence and freedom of manoeuvre (pp. 190–4).

It is also illuminating to view the 1867 'compromise' through a Marxist prism, as the 'closing act in the period of bourgeois revolutions'. Following the failure of the 'liberal' and nationalist revolutions of 1848–49 and of the neo-absolutist regime of 1849–66, the 'compromise' provided for 'an anti-democratic solution to the question of bourgeois transformation', i.e. the transition to capitalism. 'The Emperor, in order to save his Empire, gave his consent to moderate constitutional limitations on his unlimited power . . . The new system did not alter, indeed reinforced, national oppression . . . The system of big estates was not weakened but consolidated.' In this way the 'remnants of feudalism were preserved within the framework of capitalism', while the survivals of absolutism were 'wrapped in the forms of constitutionalism'. Thus the *Ausgleich* 'merely closed an era' without either accomplishing 'the bourgeois revolution' or solving its 'basic problems' (Hanak 1975b: 318–19). The consequent incompleteness of the transition was to be a major factor behind the mounting tensions and ambiguities of the so-called Dual Monarchy.

THE ASCENDANCY OF THE AUSTRIAN-GERMAN 'LIBERALS', 1867–79

Between 1867 and 1893 Austria enjoyed two long spans of stable constitutional government. The first was under the Austrian-German 'liberals' headed by Prince Karl Auersperg (1867–68) and his brother Prince Adolf Auersperg (1871–79). The second was under Count Eduard Taaffe's so-called 'Iron Ring' of German, Polish and Czech conservatives, Catholics and landowners, from 1879 to 1893.

The 'high tide' of liberal reform

To smooth the passage of the 1867 'compromise' through the *Reichsrat*, Emperor Franz Joseph accepted an impressive array of 'liberal' legislation and the enhancement of German 'liberal' hegemony in Austria. In the Austrian *Reichsrat* which convened in May 1867, German 'liberals' had a two-thirds majority (Kann 1974: 338), even though Germans made up only one-third of the population. Five 'constitutional laws' passed in December 1867 strengthened individual liberties and the prerogatives of parliament (p. 339). Laws passed in May 1868 and May 1869 established secular civil marriage, secular compulsory state education (restricting the role of the clergy to religious instruction) and the legal equality of all denominations. Interdenominational marriage was made easier and in August 1870 the 1855 Concordat with the Vatican was repudiated, along with the 1870 papal encyclical proclaiming papal 'infallibility'. State supervision of Church finances and administration was introduced in 1874. Austria remained in many respects a semi-absolutist 'police state', but there were some checks and balances and there was formal freedom of expression and equality before the law. According to Taylor (1976: 138), 'it was a police state exposed to public criticism and confined to civilized behaviour'. The Austrian after 1867 had 'more civic security than the German and was in the hands of more capable officials' than were either the French or the Italians.

The 1867–79 German 'liberal' ascendancy in Austria was substantially reinforced by a system of political representation which privileged property owners and taxpayers (in common with 'liberal' parliamentary systems elsewhere in nineteenth-century Europe). Within the Austrian half of the Monarchy Germans constituted one-third of the population but contributed two-thirds of all direct taxes. The Austrian-German 'liberals' denied that they were merely a new elite which had hi-jacked the Austrian state for its own nefarious purposes. Like most nineteenth-century 'liberals' elsewhere, they maintained that wealth was the chief qualification for political responsibility and that 'the prizes in the economic struggle went to those that "earned" them . . . They were not democrats . . . but they were not fanatics' (Whiteside 1967: 178–9, 184). On average a German paid twice as much tax as a Czech or an Italian, four and a half times as much as a Pole and seven times as much as a South Slav (Jaszi 1929: 278–9). Nevertheless, the German hegemony over Austria 'rested less on inordinate parliamentary strength than on an economically privileged status anchored in various educational and social advantages' (Kann 1974: 426). As late as 1914 80 per cent of the officials in fourteen central Ministries (including the three 'joint' Ministries), over half the students in higher education, over half the higher clergy and 78 per cent of the commissioned officers in the imperial armed forces were Germans (Whiteside 1967: 164–6; Zollner 1967: 222). Germans continued to dominate Austria's economic, cultural and intellectual life, despite the nineteenth-century Czech renaissance (Jaszi 1929: 279–80). According to Whiteside (1967: 168–9), who somewhat overstates his argument, the 'open character of the German community' made it easy for other nationals to assimilate into it. 'Intelligent, ambitious people were attracted to it.' Consequently 'German culture penetrated and influenced most of the Empire's peoples'. Capitalism reinforced the pre-eminence and integrative effect of Austrian-German culture. 'It is doubtful whether any other ethnic–cultural group in the region could have performed the political, economic and cultural task of building and holding together the Empire . . . At any rate it was the Germans who had the human and material resources to fill the political and economic vacuum in Eastern Europe.' These factors facilitated, but did not justify, Austrian hegemony.

The 1867–73 boom and the 1873 crash

Between 1867 and 1873 the Austrian-German 'liberals' were also buoyed up by an unprecedented economic boom, known to historians as the *Gründerzeit*. Fuelled by the additional paper money issued to finance the wars of 1864 and 1866 and by net inflows of foreign capital (mainly from France and Belgium), there were speculative booms in banking, real estate and construction, and the rail network more than doubled, with the result that by 1873 all the major towns and cities of German Austria, Bohemia and Hungary were linked to each other and to the outside world by rail. The railway mania in turn stimulated the growth of mining, metallurgy, engineering and grain production, while get-rich-quick company promoters launched numerous joint stock companies (including five joint stock banks). The heady *nouveau riche* atmosphere in Vienna at the time was perfectly caught (slightly after the event) by Johann Strauss Jnr's 'fizzing' operetta *Die Fledermaus* (1874).

The great Central European stock market 'crash' (*Krach*) of May 1873 brought the *Gründerzeit* to an abrupt end, less than a month after the triumphal opening of a big World Exhibition in Vienna. The confidence of (and in) Austrian-German 'liberalism' was severely shaken by the *Krach* and the ensuing six-year economic depression, which was accompanied by high interest rates, widespread bankruptcies, falling international grain prices and growing demands for social and commercial protectionism and increased state intervention in economic affairs. The *Krach* brought out into the open numerous corrupt or illicit or unsound financial dealings, some of them involving prominent 'liberal' politicians and tycoons. It also precipitated the growth of popular (anti-capitalist) antisemitism as well as a retreat from 'liberalism'. The *Krach* and the subsequent scandals focused the minds of millions on the evils and hypocrisy of a 'liberal' regime which, 'while theorizing about liberty and equality, challenged their very existence'. They responded to the denunciations uttered by 'nationalist democrats, social-minded Catholics and even feudal aristocrats'. By the end of the decade many were ready to support 'political movements that wanted to replace the existing liberal system with some kind of social community organized around nationality, religion, class or occupational estate' (Whiteside 1967: 180). Thus began the retreat from 'liberalism' into various forms of corporatism, several of which were to come to awful fruition in the twentieth century.

THE BALEFUL IMPLICATIONS OF THE HABSBURG OCCUPATION OF BOSNIA-HERCEGOVINA, 1878–1918

Emperor Franz Joseph, who had never been greatly enamoured of the Austrian-German 'liberals', finally dismissed them from office in 1879, after they had failed to applaud the Austrian military occupation of Bosnia-Hercegovina the previous year (sanctioned by the European great powers at the Berlin Congress of 1878). Franz Joseph was to be particularly 'sensitive' (i.e. insensitive!) over this issue because the occupation and eventual (1908) annexation of the region represented the only territorial gain he ever made. But it was one that would dangerously magnify and inflame 'the South Slav problem' within the Habsburg Empire in due course and introduce a new source of friction into relations between the Viennese imperial 'establishment' and the Magyar political elite. Many Magyars feared that any direct incorporation of additional South Slav territories and populations either into Austria or into the Monarchy as a whole would strengthen Slav demands for the conversion of the Dual Monarchy into a Triple Monarchy, thus giving the Slavs formal parity with the Magyars and jeopardizing the fragile equilibrium and exclusive bilateral basis of the 1867 'compromise'. For these reasons Magyar political leaders (not unlike the Austrian-German 'liberals') were wary of Habsburg territorial ambitions in the Balkans and refused to permit Bosnia and Hercegovina to be fully incorporated either into Austria or even into the Monarchy as a whole. (Any move of that sort would also have incensed many Russians and Serbs, as the unilateral annexation of Bosnia-Hercegovina by the Monarchy did in 1908.) Since the Viennese imperial 'establishment' was equally loath to allow them to be incorporated into Hungary (as some Magyar 'hawks' would have wished), Bosnia and Hercegovina were confined to a quasi-colonial status outside the formal framework of the Monarchy, 'protected' by the Habsburg armed forces and administered by officials from the joint Austro-Hungarian Ministry of Finance. This soon resulted in acute neglect, mounting impoverishment, festering social problems, heavy-handed repression and provocative high-profile support for the small Catholic (Croat) minority and the Catholic Church, in an 'unholy alliance' with the reactionary and oppressive Moslem landlord class and the conservative Moslem clergy, mainly to the detriment of the Orthodox Serbs. Right up to the end of Austrian rule, over 80 per cent of the population of Bosnia-Hercegovina remained illiterate. The most visible 'constructive' impact of Austrian rule was the building of grandiose Roman Catholic churches and cathedrals and showy 'imperial baroque' public buildings, especially in the capital, Sarajevo. Instead of blending in with the beautiful vernacular architecture they stood out like a sore thumb, becoming hated symbols of an overbearing and intrusive alien regime. Far more than they realized, the Austrians' divisive policies were stoking up inter-communal tensions and grievances for the future.

In the Monarchy's defence, it has been claimed that the new Austrian Catholic overlords were 'extremely energetic in their efforts to develop the Bosnian economy'. By 1907 they had constructed 1,022 km of railway, over 1,000 km of highway, bridges (121 of them), chemical plants, iron and steel works, cigarette and carpet factories, model farms, a model vineyard, a *shariat* school to train judges for the Moslem law courts, nearly 200 elementary schools, three high schools, a technical school, a teacher training college and an agricultural college, while also developing iron, copper and chrome mines as well as forestry (Malcolm 1994: 141–4). Free elementary education in state schools, in which members of each denomination were to receive separate religious instruction from their own clergy, was made compulsory in 1909 (pp. 143–4). By 1913 Bosnia's industrial work force exceeded 65,000 persons (p. 141) and 41,500 serfs had been able to buy their freedom since 1879, although more than 93,000 families remained in bondage (pp. 140–1).

Nevertheless, these vaunted achievements did more to confirm than to refute the essentially alien, incursive, disruptive and colonial character of Habsburg rule in Bosnia and Hercegovina. Many colonial regimes were boasting similar 'achievements' at the time. Moreover, whatever the material benefits, the fact remains that the delicate, centuries-old symbiosis and equilibrium between Bosnia's Moslems, Orthodox Christians and Catholics were fatefully disturbed by the sudden influx of Catholic officials, colonists, soldiers and clergy. It was reinforced by Catholic pressure on non-Catholics to convert to Catholicism when marrying a Catholic and to raise the children of such marriages as Catholics. The number of (predominantly Catholic) Austro-Hungarian immigrants resident in Bosnia rose from 16,500 in 1880 to 108,000 in 1910 (Malcolm 1994: 143). The Catholic population of Sarajevo soared from 800 in 1878 to 3,876 as early as 1884 (p. 144). While the Ottomans had latterly employed only 120 officials to rule Bosnia and Hercegovina, by 1910 the Habsburgs were employing 9,533 to do so (p. 138). Moreover, a combination of tax inducements and Catholic missionary and 'frontier' spirit encouraged nearly 10,000 Austro-Hungarian colonists to establish fifty-four 'agricultural colonies' in Bosnia, despite local Moslem and Orthodox resentment of such colonial intrusions (p. 143).

From 1882 to 1903 Benjamin Kallay, a former diplomat and the future author of a respected history of the Serbs, ran the civil administration of Bosnia-Hercegovina while also serving as the joint Finance Minister of Austria-Hungary. Kallay boldly endeavoured to foster a distinct Bosnian national identity that would unite the area's Moslem, Orthodox Christian and Catholic inhabitants and keep them separate from their Serbian and Croatian neighbours (pp. 147–8). Had it been possible to keep Bosnia-Hercegovina completely sealed off from the outside world, Malcolm argues, such a policy might have succeeded. It did not elicit positive responses from the tolerant, cosmopolitan, civic-minded Moslems of Sarajevo, who had long maintained civil relations with their Orthodox Christian, Catholic and Jewish neighbours. Moreover, in Bosnia and Hercegovina religious affiliations had not yet fully metamorphosed into separate national identities. Nevertheless, it proved impossible to prevent Serbian and Croatian nationalist ideas from spreading to the Orthodox and Catholic populations of Bosnia and Hercegovina 'through the very networks of priests, schoolteachers and educated newspaper readers which Austro-Hungarian policy had helped to bring into being' (pp. 148–9). What is more, government co-operation with the Moslem leadership in Sarajevo not only antagonized the more uncompromising Moslem leaders in Travnik and Mostar (who adopted intransigent positions 'in order to discredit their Sarajevan rivals') but also aroused suspicion and resentment among those Catholic and Orthodox Christians who thought they should now enjoy a monopoly of official favour and consolidation (pp. 145–7). At the same time, the Monarchy's increasingly aggressive, divisive and ham-fisted treatment of neighbouring Serbia and Croatia was fanning the flames of Serbian and Croatian nationalism and Yugoslavism. Thus the Monarchy's policy towards Bosnia and Hercegovina was doomed to failure by the inherent contradictions within its policies towards the South Slavs in general (p. 150). In this respect, as in so many others, the Habsburgs unwittingly sowed and watered some of the seeds of later tragedies in the South Slav lands. It is not surprising that the shots that triggered the First World War were fired in Bosnia.

THE ASCENDANCY OF THE CONSERVATIVE 'IRON RING' IN AUSTRIA, 1879–93

After their ejection from office the Austrian-German 'liberals' lost the elections of summer 1879 and were replaced by a conservative coalition of German, Polish and Czech Catholics and landowners cobbled together by Count Eduard Taaffe. He persuaded the 'Old Czech' leaders to abandon their boycott of the *Reichsrat* by promising them increased provincial autonomy and linguistic/cultural equality with the Germans within Bohemia. Similar blandishments were offered to the conservative Catholic and land-owning leaderships of Galicia and Slovenia. (Indeed, the Polish aristocracy had already been brought 'on side' by the granting of extensive administrative, educational and cultural autonomy to Galicia in 1868 and the creation of a Ministry of Galician Affairs in 1871.) Aided and abetted by Count Taaffe's masterly political manipulations, Austria's non-German majority stopped trying to disrupt the new constitutional system and instead competed for government favours and for jobs in the fast-expanding imperial and provincial bureaucracies. The governing coalition was held together by the Premier's promises of a new road or railway line here and a new school or university there. The leaders of the rival national parties, bargaining with the Prime Minister and bustling self-importantly along the corridors of the huge *Reichsrat* building, 'ceased to press for any fundamental change of system'. Thus Taaffe's political juggling act brought Austria a period of political stability, economic recovery and administrative devolution. 'For a decade the bitterness went out of public life . . . A new "Austrian" conception was born – an Austria of devoted state servants' (Taylor 1976: 157–8).

THE FATEFUL IMPLICATIONS OF THE 1879 DUAL ALLIANCE BETWEEN THE HABSBURG MONARCHY AND GERMANY

The new conservative trend was consolidated by the (initially secret) 'Dual Alliance' of October 1879, which fatefully locked the Habsburg and Hohenzollern empires together in mutual embrace. As far back as 1870 George Stratimirovich (a Serb member of the Hungarian parliament) had warned that, if it were to come about, 'this Austrian–Prussian alliance will certainly not secure the peace of Europe. On the contrary, the alliance of the Russian and French states which will become necessary [in response] is going to sow the seeds of a new world war and thus it is going to threaten our very existence' (quoted in Barany 1967: 249). While someone as astute as Bismarck was in charge of German foreign policy, this potentially disastrous division of continental Europe into two mutually hostile power blocs was averted by keeping Germany on good terms with Russia (as a sort of 'fail safe' mechanism). Bismarck engineered a precautionary three-year alliance of the three central and east European emperors in 1881 and its renewal for another three years in 1884. In a change of tack in 1887 Bismarck then negotiated a secret Reinsurance Treaty with Russia, pledging that Russia and Germany would remain benevolently neutral toward one another if either were attacked by a third power. In other words, despite the (essentially defensive) Dual Alliance between Germany and

Austria-Hungary, Germany would not be obliged to support a Habsburg attack on Russia. In return, Russia would decline to support France in a revanchist war against Germany. In addition, Bismarck repeatedly refused to give any blank-cheque support to the Habsburgs' expansionist ambitions in the Balkans. (Indeed, in 1876 Bismarck had told the German *Reichstag* that the Balkans were not worth the sacrifice of a single limb of a single Prussian soldier. Chancellor Kohl was saying precisely the opposite by 1995!) After Bismarck's fall from grace in 1890, however, the inexperienced and inept Kaiser Wilhelm II threw Bismarckian caution to the winds and allowed the Reinsurance Treaty with Russia to lapse. The almost immediate consequence was the conclusion of a Franco-Russian alliance (1894) and the perilous division of continental Europe into two mutually suspicious armed camps, fraught with dangers of titanic conflict.

The Dual Alliance of 1879 represented much more than a strategic or diplomatic move, even if its full significance could not have been apparent to the principal actors at the time. It was part of a more fundamental political realignment within the Germanic world. In Germany in 1878 Bismarck had ditched the predominantly Protestant north German National Liberals (the erstwhile champions of a Listian 'liberal' free-trading and *laissez-faire* Germany), in favour of a new alliance with the staunchly Catholic, protectionist, south German and pro-Austrian Centre Party. This realignment or reorientation marked a decisive shift from political, social and economic liberalism to corporatism, protectionism and conservative etatism and the emergence of the so-called Central Powers as a cohesive conservative military, political and economic power bloc in Central and Eastern Europe. The secret Habsburg–Hohenzollern 'Dual Alliance' of 1879 was soon followed by a secret treaty under which the feckless Obrenovich dynasty transformed Serbia into a *de facto* Habsburg protectorate. In 1882 the 'Dual Alliance' was expanded into a secret 'Triple Alliance' with Italy, while Romania entered secret defence pacts with both Austria-Hungary and Germany in 1883. These secret treaties facilitated closer economic ties, driven by the steady growth of German investment, banking, industrial subsidiaries and trade in Austria-Hungary, Italy, Serbia and Romania, and by growing exports of Romanian grain, timber and oil up the increasingly navigable Danube to Hungary, Austria and Germany.

THE DAMAGING CONSEQUENCES OF THE GROWTH OF GERMAN 'ETHNIC' NATIONALISM AND PAN-GERMANISM, 1879–1914

Count Taaffe's 'Iron Ring' was finally shattered on the rocks of resurgent inter-ethnic conflict in the early 1890s. The problem had its roots in smouldering Austrian and Bohemian German resentment of the abrupt termination of their former exclusive political supremacy in Austria in 1879. They tended to blame the decline of German predominance on the alleged treachery and timidity of their political 'masters', including the dynasty. In the seminal Linz Programme of 1882, a number of disaffected pan-German 'liberals' boldly called for the metamorphosis of Austria (including Bohemia-Moravia, but shorn of Galicia and Dalmatia) into an integral German state enveloped in an economic union and military alliance with the German empire and preserving only a dynastic tie ('personal union') with an otherwise independent kingdom of Hungary. The principal authors of this 'liberal' pan-German manifesto were the militant pan-German Georg von Schönerer, the lawyer Robert Pattai, the writer Engelbert Penerstorfer, the Austrian-Jewish physician (and future leader of the Austrian Social Democrats) Viktor

Adler and the eminent Austrian-Jewish historian Heinrich Friedjung. Like the pan-German 'liberals' of 1848, they looked to the wider 'German nation' to transform Austria into a unitary German state. In the final analysis true pan-Germans would have preferred an *Anschluss* (union) of Austria with Germany to the preservation of Austria-Hungary and, in this perspective, the Linz Programme can be seen as a 'liberal' trail-blazer for the Austrian Social Democratic and pan-German demands for *Anschluss* with Germany which were blocked by France in 1918–20 and 1929–31 (only to be accomplished by Hitler in 1938). Within two years, however, Schönerer finally broke with the 'liberals' and launched an overtly racist, antisemitic and anti-Catholic pan-German movement, the German National Association. While this failed to attract a mass following, it did achieve a sinister behind-the-scenes influence in organizations such as the *Deutscher Schulverein* (German Schools Association) and the *Turnvereine* (athletic clubs) patronized by Austrian-German officials and pan-German intellectuals. It also served as an incubator of proto-Nazi ideology.

Austrian and Bohemian Germans saw themselves as increasingly beleaguered groups fighting a losing battle to hold back 'the barbarians' and conserve their own exclusive control of all the best schools, universities, museums, galleries and theatres, as well as the provincial Diets and countless 'rotten boroughs'. Many 'disgusted' Austrian and Bohemian Germans did not know 'what the world was coming to' as their most hallowed institutions and preserves were gatecrashed, polluted and desecrated by 'inferior' non-German 'upstarts'. They therefore engaged in a tenacious rearguard action against what they perceived to be insidious, subversive and quite outrageous Slav encroachments on their exclusive privileged positions and glorious ('sacred') heritage as 'the people of the state'.

The fall of Count Taaffe's 'Iron Ring', 1893

In 1890 Germanic outrage bordered on apoplexy when a committee of moderate and conciliatory Czechs and Germans under Count Taaffe's chairmanship decided to redivide ethnically mixed provinces along ethnic lines in an attempt to defuse inter-ethnic tensions. This decision provoked precisely the opposite of what was intended, namely an explosion of German and Czech indignation and decisive defeats for Taaffe's moderate Czech and Bohemian supporters in the 1890 Bohemian elections, depriving Count Taaffe of much-needed parliamentary support. The Premier then backtracked in an attempt to placate the irate Bohemian Germans and win crucial parliamentary support from moderate Austrian Germans. But this ungainly manoeuvre also served to antagonize further the Czechs, who had hitherto been Count Taaffe's most reliable supporters.

In desperation Count Taaffe proposed to appeal over the heads of the 'bourgeois' nationalist and pan-German 'liberals' to the more conservative, deferential, loyalist and less nationalistic masses, by dramatically extending the franchise and the parliamentary representation of the lower classes. Such a stratagem might have worked in 1893. Active support for the querulous nationalist and 'liberal' movements still seemed to be largely confined to the professional and propertied classes, while divisive national and class consciousness still appeared to be relatively inchoate among the lower classes, especially non-Germans. Moreover, universal suffrage had demonstrably served the counter-revolution well in France and Germany, just as Proudhon had predicted it would. In Austria, if Count Taaffe had been allowed to introduce a wider franchise and greater parliamentary representation of the underprivileged classes in 1893, the 'bourgeois' nationalists and 'liberals' could well have lost out to the nascent 'mass party' of the right, the Catholic, 'loyalist' and antisemitic Christian Socials. Launched in 1887 by an erstwhile 'liberal' turned demagogue and antisemite, Karl Lueger, the Christian Social Party rapidly won mass support among conservative, Catholic, loyalist and mainly Austrian-German traders, shopkeepers, small farmers and minor officials who envied, resented and felt threatened, slighted or cheated by 'big business', Jewish middlemen, the partly Jewish *haute bourgeoisie*, the substantially Jewish-owned 'liberal' press and the partly Jewish 'liberal' contingent in the *Reichsrat*. By rapidly winning over most of the potential lower middle-class, German-speaking voters in both urban and rural Austria, the Christian Socials fatally fractured the Austrian bourgeoisie and robbed both Austrian 'liberalism' and pan-Germanism of their potential mass support and political clout. Indeed, by 1895 Lueger was outpolling the hitherto dominant 'liberals' in Vienna's mayoral elections, although Emperor Franz Joseph refused to allow such a disreputable demagogue to assume the mayoral office until after his fourth successive electoral triumph. (That was in 1897, whereupon Lueger remained Mayor of Vienna until 1910.)

However, the prospect of admitting the rude plebeian hordes into parliamentary politics alarmed not only Count Taaffe's 'bourgeois' nationalist and 'liberal' opponents but also his own conservative allies in the *Reichstag* and in government. After all, electoral reform could have opened the doors not only to the far from 'respectable' Christian Socials but also to the Marxist (and even more 'alarming') Austrian Social Democratic Party, launched in 1889 by the former 'liberal' Viktor Adler on an anti-capitalist, anti-militarist, anti-monarchist and anticlerical platform. Faced with united 'liberal', conservative and pan-German opposition to the Prime Minister's proposed electoral stratagem, Franz Joseph decided that he could no longer keep Count Taaffe in the premiership, although the emperor himself was to resort to a similar stratagem in 1907, when he imposed direct universal manhood suffrage for that year's *Reichsrat* elections in an attempt to undercut divisive nationalism by strengthening the 'supranational' Social Democrats and 'loyalist' Christian Socials.

The gradual breakdown of constitutional government in Austria, 1893–1914

From 1893 to 1895 Austria was governed by a 'grand coalition' under Prince Alfred Windisgrätz, but it too foundered on the rock of inter-ethnic conflict, this time between Germans and Slovenes in Styria. Austria was in the process of becoming ungovernable by parliamentary means. Ultimately it was held together only by an 'iron frame of bureaucracy', supplemented by a residual loyalty to the emperor.

The breakdown of a political system which had survived in either 'liberal' or conservative variants from 1867 to 1895 induced Franz Joseph to put his faith in a high-minded non-partisan 'strong man'. Such a man would endeavour to cut Austria's 'Gordian knots' and overcome its creeping political paralysis by imposing bold but judicious 'solutions' on Austria's most divisive, destabilizing and seemingly insoluble problems. For this herculean role the emperor shrewdly chose neither a German nor a Magyar but Count Kasimir Badeni, the 'loyalist' but reputably 'liberal' Polish governor of Galicia.

Badeni got off to a flying start in 1896 by introducing a system of graduated personal income tax and a widely applauded electoral compromise. This involved the addition of a fifth electoral curia which would elect seventy-two *Reichsrat* deputies (out of a new total of 425) on the basis of adult male suffrage, thereby introducing a modicum of working-class representation for the first time. But Badeni's boldest '*coup*' pertained to Bohemia. As part of the political 'deal' concluded between Count Taaffe and the Czech leadership in 1879, bilingualism had been imposed on Bohemia's officials of the 'outer service', i.e. those dealing directly with members of the public. But Bohemia's officials of the so-called 'inner service' (those dealing with other officials and with Vienna) had remained exclusively German-speaking. In April 1897, however, Badeni decreed that even officials of the 'inner service' in Bohemia had to be fluent in both Czech and German. Although seemingly even-handed, this would have given the Czechs a near-monopoly of official posts in Bohemia, because as a matter of course Czechs knew German as well as their mother tongue, whereas very few Bohemian Germans had learned Czech (or were willing to do so). Badeni's language decree detonated an explosion of Germanic fury, whipped up still further by Schönerer's German National Association. There were mass demonstrations and riots all over Austria, supported by angry meetings in many parts of Germany, forcing Badeni into retreat and (in November 1897) out of office. This 'Teutonic fury' was merely the culmination of the mounting inter-ethnic protests and violence which had scarred public life in Bohemia since the early 1880s (Bradley 1971: 135–8) and of the Germanic intransigence and 'negations' which, in the opinion of A.J.P. Taylor (1976: 183), 'did more than anything else to destroy the Habsburg Empire'. The Germans were not powerful enough to transform Austria into a German national state, yet they were strong enough to thwart any other 'solution' to its inter-ethnic conflicts. This was an apparently insoluble question.

After the failure of Badeni, Franz Joseph and his Ministers virtually gave up the quest for definitive solutions to Austria's so-called 'nationality problems'. This reinforced the emperor's innate pessimism, fatalism and sense of impending doom. As early as 1866 he had written to his mother: 'One just has to resist as long as possible, to do one's duty to the last and finally perish with honour' (quoted in Sked 1989: 229). This became a *Leitmotif* of his long reign. It was as if he expected his house and his empire to go down in flames sooner or later. He was preparing for *Götterdämmerung*. Austrian politics was to become merely a holding operation, intermittently marred by violent outbursts of defensive aggression. There was a terrifying sense of drift, of living on borrowed time and of Austria's rulers merely reacting defensively to uncontrollable malign forces and events in wholly unchartered waters.

For their part, the *Reichsrat* party leaders were increasingly incapable of forming (let alone maintaining) a constitutional government. They preferred to jostle for position and favours and to leave the responsibility for governing Austria to others. Hence the growing 'irresponsibility' of the *Reichsrat* party leaders 'encouraged, even compelled, the Emperor to keep the real authority in his own hands', although that both further encouraged and enabled the parliamentary party leaders to continue to evade their constitutional responsibilities (Taylor 1976: 170–2). It was a vicious circle. The actual business of government increasingly fell into the hands of 'faceless' state functionaries, selected by Franz Joseph from the higher ranks of the imperial bureaucracy. Meanwhile the *Reichsrat* lost almost all influence on policy matters and became little more than a forum in which the Prime Minister (now merely the top state functionary) could from time to time meet the parliamentary party leaders to hear grievances, strike bargains and grant favours (a new school here, a new road or railway route there), in order to keep them 'sweet' (pp. 198–9).

Ernst von Körber, Prime Minister from 1900 to 1904, made further abortive attempts to settle the 'language question' in Bohemia and to 'buy off' Czech and Slovene nationalist discontent through programmes of public works and railway construction (known as *politischer Kuhhandel*, 'political cow-trading', the Austrian equivalent of American 'pork barrel' politics). However, even he had to govern largely by emergency regulations and imperial decrees.

During the premiership of Paul von Gautsch (1904–06) the economy enjoyed a boom but there was a crisis in relations between Austria and Hungary, challenging the whole basis of the 1867 'compromise' and the Dual Monarchy. From 1903 to 1906 the Magyars refused to supply their quota of soldiers for service in the Austro-Hungarian army unless Magyar was made the official 'language of command' of the Magyar contingents, in effect creating a separate Magyar army under Magyar officers, since few non-Magyars could speak or write this very different language. Magyar unity on the issue did not seriously crack until the Habsburg authorities, having imposed military rule and suspended Hungary's parliament, threatened to introduce adult male suffrage for the election of a new parliament (in which the Magyars would thus forfeit their built-in majority).

Under Gautsch's successor, Max von Beck (1906–08), Austro-Hungarian relations were 'normalized' by the capitulation of most of the Magyar magnates and nobility and a peaceful revision and renewal of the pivotal 'compromise' (including the so-called 'economic compromise') in 1907. However, partly in reponse to the success of the 'sobering' threat to impose adult male suffrage on Hungary in 1906, Emperor Franz Joseph was encouraged to try to 'escape from the nationalist conflicts of middle-class politicians' by imposing direct adult male suffrage on a reluctant and rather apprehensive Austrian *Reichsrat* in 1907. The manoeuvre worked remarkably well. The 1907 *Reichsrat* elections, held under the new franchise, returned the Christian Socials and the (Marxist) Social Democrats as the two largest parties. It was 'a triumph for the imperial idea', for both parties wished to preserve the territorial integrity of the Habsburg Empire (albeit in a federalized form in the case of the Social Democrats) and Franz Joseph 'recovered greater freedom of action than he ever enjoyed since 1867' (Taylor 1976: 212). A budget was approved without recourse to emergency regulations and, most unusually, Beck even included some *Reichsrat* members in his government. But this 'honeymoon' period did not last long. By 1911 even the Social Democrats had begun to split along ethnic lines, while the demagogic and antisemitic Christian Social Party soon dropped any pretence of high-minded Roman Catholic universalism and brazenly championed Austrian-German supremacism and sectional interests.

Under Austria's last long-serving Prime Minister, Count Karl Stürgkh (1911–16), the Bohemian constitution was suspended (in 1913) amid resurgent inter-ethnic conflict in the Czech Lands, while the increasingly deadlocked and marginalized *Reichsrat* was itself prorogued from March 1914 (i.e. four months *before* the outbreak of the First World War) until after the assassination of Count Stürgkh by the socialist Friedrich Adler (son of Victor Adler) in October 1916 and the death of Franz Joseph in November 1916. It seems that the gradual breakdown of constitutional government in Austria was an unstoppable, albeit erratic, process. The multinational dynastic polity proved increasingly incapable of generating and sustaining the minimum degree of consensus and common allegiance necessary to bind it together and to make stable parliamentary government possible, despite the fact that this was a period of impressive economic advance and dazzling cultural and intellectual creativity. Among the most illustrious figures were Freud, Kafka, the poets Hofmannsthal and Rilke, composers such as Mahler, Schönberg, Berg, Dvorak, Janacek and Suk, artists such as Klimt and Kokoschka, the philosopher Mach, economists such as Menger, von Mises, Hayek and Schumpeter, and the Marxist theoreticians Hilferding and Bauer.

11 Capitalism and the seeds of social revolution in Austria and Hungary

THE ECONOMIC RESURGENCE OF AUSTRIA

Austria's economic resurgence during the 1880s and 1890s was stimulated and assisted by a number of factors: increased state expenditure on physical infrastructure (especially railways) and on armaments; growing industrial protectionism and cartelization; the creation of 'captive' export markets in Hungary and the Balkans; and strengthening economic ties with Germany (from which Austria's increasingly educated engineers, managers and work force readily assimilated the latest technologies, business methods and banking practices). Reflecting an earlier (more negative) view of nineteenth-century Austria's economic performance, Gross (1973: 229) once wrote that 'the long-run decline of Habsburg from the status of a first rank power must have hampered economic growth at least because of the persistent costly efforts to halt or at least disguise the process'. Yet between 1880 and 1913 Austria's industrial output grew by about 3.6 per cent per annum on average, i.e. at approximately the same rate as that of Germany between 1870 and 1913 (Rudolph 1976: 235). Austria's industrial output roughly doubled between 1880 and 1895 and roughly trebled between 1880 and 1913 (Good 1984: 258–9). Furthermore, Austria's real per capita GNP grew at an average annual rate of 1.32 per cent between 1870 and 1913, roughly on a par with Switzerland (1.32 per cent) and Norway (1.35 per cent) and well ahead of Spain (0.25 per cent), Italy (0.81 per cent), Holland (0.93 per cent), Britain (1.0 per cent), Belgium (1.05 per cent) and France (1.06 per cent) during the same period. Only a few European countries did significantly better: Germany (1.51 per cent), Hungary (1.7 per cent), Denmark (2.19 per cent) and Sweden (2.39 per cent) (pp. 239–40). By 1913 the per capita GNP of German Austria had drawn level with that of France and was only 10 per cent below that of Germany, while for Austria as a whole it was 38 per cent below that of France, 43 per cent below that of Germany, roughly on a par with Italy and about 44 per cent above that of Hungary (pp. 219–20, 241–2). (Note that we employ the specific term Gross National Product only when it is the one used by the source quoted.)

Between 1880 and 1913 the average annual growth rate of Austria's former 'leading sectors' (food-processing and textiles) eased off to 2.7 per cent and 3.1 per cent respectively (Rudolph 1976: 13). This was partly because the rate of growth of demand for their products was tailing off slightly as particular markets approached saturation point and partly because the initially explosive growth potential of the technological advances which had revolutionized these industries was nearing exhaustion. Nevertheless, German Austria and the Czech Lands were emerging as European technological leaders in several light industries, including sugar refining, brewing (Pilsener lager) and glass-making. The new 'leading sectors' were engineering and metallurgy, which grew on average by 9.5 per cent and 7 per cent per annum respectively (p. 13). These industries directly benefited from the high level of state expenditure on railway construction, the pan-European arms race, the relatively rapid development of engineering and metal-lurgical technologies and the increasing industrial concentration, protectionism and cartelization in the decades leading up to the First World War. Protectionism, the arms race and high infrastructural expenditure particularly promoted the heavy industries which were emerging in Styria and (above all) the Czech Lands. By 1910, with just 36 per cent of the population of the Austrian half of the empire, the Czech Lands were producing 58 per cent of its pig iron, over 80 per cent of its cast iron, 86 per cent of its anthracite (hard coal), 84 per cent of its lignite (brown coal), 75 per cent of its chemicals, 94 per cent of its refined sugar, 59 per cent of its beer and over 75 per cent of its textiles. In 1902 the Czech Lands provided over 56 per cent of the industrial work force and 68 per cent of Austria's mechanical horsepower (Rudolph 1976: 41). The introduction of the Gilchrist–Thomas process (1879) revolutionized the use of low-grade, highly phosphoric Bohemian and Moravian iron ores for steel making. The Skoda works (directed by Emil and Karl Skoda) had become the Monarchy's major producer of machinery and armaments by the 1900s.

Rudolph argues that the 'impressive growth' and industrial attainments of German Austria and the Czech Lands prior to the First World War were partly obscured or concealed by the presence of populous underdeveloped regions within the Austro-Hungarian Empire and customs union and that it is just as misleading to concentrate on per capita figures for the Monarchy as a whole as it would be to do so 'for the British Empire as a whole' (Rudolph 1976: 9–10). Instead, he argues, areas such as Hungary or Galicia should be viewed as 'enclave economies' and 'the development of the Austro-Hungarian Monarchy may be seen as that of an industrializing region, the Austrian–Czech Land complex, which by its political power, in collaboration with the landed interests of its economic hinterland, and by means of its economic power, its role as a financial centre and its cartels, was able to develop itself at the expense of the enclave areas' (p. 10). The main problem with this interpretation is that the supposedly deprived and abused Hungarian economy actually grew somewhat faster than its Austrian counterpart between 1870 and 1913 and, according to a whole cohort of distinguished Hungarian Marxist economic historians (including Berend, Ranki, Katus and Hanak), it gained much more than it lost through its so-called 'dependence' on Austria. It gained in terms of political and economic stability and coherence, attraction of foreign (especially Austrian) finance and entrepreneurship, and preferential access to a secure market for its primary exports. This was not a zero sum game: Austria's gain was not necessarily Hungary's loss, since there was often a reciprocal gain to Hungary. Indeed, between 1867 and 1914 foreign (mainly Austrian) investment made up around 40 per cent of total investment in Hungary and something approaching 80 per cent of Austrian foreign investment was destined for Hungary (Good 1984: 108). What is more, from the mid-1860s onwards periods of faster growth in Hungary tended to coincide with periods of slower growth in Austria and vice versa (Komlos 1981: 10–11). Average annual rates of growth in Austria and Hungary respectively were as follows: 3.9 per cent and 1.4 per cent, 1867–71; 2.4 per cent and 5.1 per cent, 1871–84; 2.8 per cent and 3.3 per cent, 1884–98; 3.8 per cent and 2.4 per cent, 1898–1907; 1.6 per cent and 5.3 per cent,

1907–13. 'The mechanism for this pattern is to be sought in the flow of capital between Austria and Hungary' (p. 12). In particular, the 1873 crash encouraged a migration of capital from Austria, where speculators had over-invested during the 1867–73 *Gründer-zeit*, to Hungary, which now seemed a safer bet. Conversely, as Austrian industrialization gradually regained momentum during the 1880s and 1890s, capital began to flow back to Austria and the Hungarian industrial boom of 1874–83 began to slow down. Finally, the industrial slow-down in Austria after 1907 was associated with a renewed outflow of capital from Austria into Hungary, where it financed another Hungarian industrial boom before the brief Austrian industrial revival of 1911–13 (reflecting sharply increased state spending on infrastructure and armaments, in apparent preparation for war).

The existence of various natural and man-made complementarities rendered the Austro-Hungarian economic relationship more mutually advantageous (symbiotic) than 'predatory' or 'exploitative'. By 1901 Hungary absorbed 35 per cent of Austria's exports and supplied 38 per cent of its imports, but Austria absorbed 72 per cent of Hungary's exports and supplied 79 per cent of its imports. In 1913 Hungary still accounted for 37 per cent of Austria's exports and 32 per cent of its imports, while Austria took 75 per cent of Hungary's exports and provided 72 per cent of its imports (Jenks 1967: 36). In 1913 Austria and Hungary exported only about 7 per cent of their combined GNP to markets outside the Monarchy. (Germany, by comparison, exported 14.6 per cent of its GNP, while the corresponding figure for France was 15.3 per cent.) In 1910, further-more, Austria-Hungary accounted for only 5.6 per cent of European exports, compared with 20.4 per cent for Germany, 13.4 per cent for France, 23.7 per cent for Britain and 8.9 per cent for Russia (Good 1984: 109). The relative smallness of Austria-Hungary's export sector and the relatively high level of imperial autarky both reflected and reinforced the strong dependence on internal inter-regional trade, especially (but not exclusively) between Austria and Hungary. This adds weight to the observation that 'while nationalistic passions ran high . . . few men went so far as to advocate the atomization of the Empire. Such restraint may have been motivated in part by a fear of Austria-Hungary's powerful neighbours to the north and east, who were known for their ruthless treatment of minorities; and it may have been caused, perhaps to even greater extent, by a widely shared realization that the customs union, for all its defects and imperfections, was an alternative preferable to the Balkanization of Central Europe' (März 1953: 135).

'FINANCE CAPITALISM' AND 'MONOPOLY CAPITALISM': HILFERDING AND THE LENINIST ROAD TO 'SOCIALISM'

Together with Germany and Switzerland, Austria was in the forefront of the development of European 'finance capitalism' and 'monopoly capitalism'. It was no accident that the first major treatise on cartels was written by the Austrian Friedrich Kleinwächter (1883) or that entrepreneurial bankers and the creation of bank credit were to be so central to Joseph Schumpeter's influential theory of capitalist economic development. Moreover, the seminal Marxist analysis of the transformation of competitive and pluralistic 'liberal capitalism' into monopolistic 'finance capital' was written by another Austrian, Rudolph Hilferding (1910), who was later to serve as a socialist Finance Minister in Germany in 1923 and in 1928–29. Lenin's more famous analysis of 'monopoly capitalism' in 1917–18 added remarkably little to Hilferding's seminal insights.

In Austria, as in Germany, the growth of protectionism and of state and bank involvement in railway construction, arms production and the development of the affiliated heavy industries created an environment conducive to industrial concentration, cartelization and collusive/monopolistic practices. In north-western Europe and the United States law courts and legislatures have generally regarded cartels and monopolistic arrangements in the private sector as illegal 'conspiracies in restraint of trade', detrimental to the 'public interest' and to the long-term health and vigour of a market economy. The Germanic world, by contrast, adopted much more permissive or even positively pro-cartel and pro-monopoly attitudes. The 'liberal' interlude in the German-speaking states during the 1850s and 1860s was only a temporary aberration on their part, reflecting the short-lived ideological ascendancy and example of a 'liberal' Britain which was then at the peak of its power, success and influence. Austria, like Germany and Switzerland, never wholly 'kicked the habit' of forming collusive industrial and trade associations. Hence seventy-four voluntary associations of manufacturers were established in Austria between 1839 and 1892, mainly to lobby for protective tariffs (Good 1984: 218).

The connections and mutual support between these associations facilitated collusion, amalgamations and the subsequent growth of price-fixing and market-sharing agreements, particularly in those industries which were gradually insulated against potentially disruptive foreign competition by the raising of protective tariffs (Gross 1973: 258–9). Austria's first cartel agreement was established by rail producers in 1878, in the wake of the post-1873 depression. By 1890 there were eighteen such agreements, over half of them in the mining and metallurgical sectors. Austria had fifty-seven cartel agreements by 1900, 120 by 1909 (including nineteen in mining and metallurgy, twelve in chemicals, twenty-seven in textiles, ten in glass-making and nine in food-processing) and 200 in 1912, by which time cartels had become the norm rather than the exception in Austrian industry (Good 1984: 219). 'As in Germany, the Austrian courts tended to view cartel arrangements as legally binding contracts', rather than as illegal conspiracies in restraint of competition; and in 1897, seven years after the passing of the famous American 'anti-trust' laws, the Austrian state became 'the first in Europe to anchor the formation of cartels in law' (pp. 235–6). In Austria cartels were extolled as the way to avoid the 'anarchy' of competition and to protect the small producer and safeguard industrial profit margins, firms, investments and jobs, thereby encouraging and facilitating investment in new technologies, scientific industries, rationalization and large industrial complexes and making the work force less likely to fear and oppose change. Economists of the German historical school argued that cartels were 'a mechanism for spreading the dislocations arising from capitalism out over time, to give the system a chance to absorb surplus labour and capital. This meant protecting the interests of the weak as well as the strong' (p. 235). Some argued that unrestrained competition would indiscriminately cripple, dissipate or destroy economic potential and that 'only a temperate and sometimes regulated competition' would allow new productive forces to come to full fruition, while another declared that cartels did not hold up necessary progress, but merely constituted a gentler transition. Such views evoked a positive response in Austria (pp. 235–6).

Cartelization in turn paved the way for multiple or interlocking directorships, for the representation of bankers on boards of directors in industry and for increased intermarriage of industrial and banking families. An Austrian industrialist would sometimes find it expedient to marry off his prettiest daughter to an eligible bank director twice her age. Moreover, after the great 'crash' of 1873, some of the banks which managed to survive had to foreclose on their more 'over-extended' industrial clients and thus acquired significant industrial assets. However, the chastening experience of the 1873 'crash' also discouraged bankers from investing heavily in industry again until 1895, when Austria's banks began to promote a second *Gründerzeit* (Good 1984: 209; Rudolph 1976: 102–3). By 1914 the major Austrian banks had 'firmly embedded themselves in a number of major industrial firms' and banks held about 73 per cent of the share capital of joint stock mining and milling companies, about 80 per cent of that of the joint stock sugar companies and almost 100 per cent of that of the joint stock metalworking, machine-building and armaments companies (Rudolph 1976: 118–20). Similarly, by 1913 the five largest Budapest banks accounted for 57 per cent of all Hungarian bank credit, held 47 per cent of the capital of Hungary's industrial firms and controlled 225 of Hungary's 250 largest companies, while in 1907 just twenty-five enterprises employed 25 per cent of Hungary's industrial work force (Good 1984: 108; Janos 1982: 151). The bank of the Austrian Rothschilds, the famous Creditanstalt, eventually came to control nearly one-third of Austria's industrial assets. That was the main reason why its collapse in 1931 was to have such devastating repercussions on the economies of central and eastern Europe.

However, despite their increasingly hegemonic position, Austrian banks did not for the most part play the actively entrepreneurial or risk-taking role postulated by Joseph Schumpeter and Alexander Gerschenkron, among others. Their role was typically passive or permissive rather than actively promotional and entrepreneurial. The banking system was the lubricant rather than the propulsive force of the capitalist machine. Bankers selected industrial clients whom they expected to be a safe bet, i.e. 'plump juicy firms with favourable prospects, firms with the difficulties and risks of their early years already completed' (Rudolph 1976: 104). With the passage of time ties deepened with these select firms 'rather than widening into promotional activity per se' (p. 103). In keeping with the more usual stereotype, Austrian bankers were cautious and risk-averse, as it was virtually their duty to be (pp. 184, 193–4). Thus the notion of 'the banks as entrepreneurs, initiating industrial development and tiding nascent firms through the dangerous years of their youth and adolescence must be largely discarded' in favour of one of 'cautious bankers who were for many years entirely averse to industrial promotion' (p. 191).

Economists, lawyers and policy-makers in the Western 'liberal tradition' have tended to look down their noses at the more mercantilist, protectionist and corporatist traditions of the German-speaking states. But the arguments put forward by the latter cannot be lightly dismissed in the face of the economic performance of those states (e.g. safeguarding profit margins, investments, firms and jobs; reducing the risks to industrialists, investors and employees; introducing new technologies and investing in new 'science-based' industries). The 'corporatism' and 'social protectionism' favoured by socially-minded Catholics (the Austrian Christian Socials and the German Centre Party) and by conservative paternalistic states arguably engendered more biddable and amenable working classes, more ready to accept industrial change linked with social safeguards. Commercial protectionism was meant to shield cartels and monopolies against foreign competitors ('interlopers') and, by boosting domestic profit margins, helped to finance export promotion, research and development, horizontal and vertical integration, the creation of large integrated industrial complexes and diversification into 'high-tech' science-based industries. 'Intermarriage' between industry and banking increased industrial access to bank funding, while bankers increasingly encouraged collusion, co-operation, cartels and amalgamations among their clients or even acted as industrial 'marriage brokers'. (Similar issues are posed today by doctrinaire Anglo-Saxon neoclassical advocacy of the liberalization of labour and capital as well as product markets, privatization and 'rolling back the state' in general, as against German and Scandinavian advocacy of more regulated and corporatist economic systems and more protective welfare states.)

Western 'liberal' and 'neo-liberal' criticisms of Central European corporatist, protectionist and mercantilist traditions carry a lot more conviction on the political front. Such traditions certainly made it much easier for Central European monarchies and dictatorships to offer economic and social protection and security as a substitute for fundamental civil and political liberties and may even have fostered a widespread willingness to barter away such liberties in return for the offer of protection and security (out of a 'fear of freedom'). Such a trade-off has been made with quite disturbing frequency in Central Europe.

Be that as it may. In 1907 the major Austrian banks came together in a banking cartel, largely to regulate the activities of the cartelized industries in which they had acquired such a large stake (Good 1984: 210). In 1914 this tendency towards cartelization and monopoly within Austrian 'finance capitalism' culminated in the creation of a so-called *Kontrollbank*. This was intended to serve as 'a central supervisory apparatus for the cartels, whose activity in reality extended to the guidance of syndicates, central sales bureaus and control bureaus and, in addition, to the mediation of trade between producers and merchants' (März, quoted in Rudolph 1976: 105).

In *Das Finanzcapital* (published in 1910) Hilferding went so far as to portray the bankers of the new era of 'finance capitalism' as essentially *parasitic* upon industry and agriculture and as the product (even the archetype) of the putative 'advanced senility' of capitalism, in contrast to the more dynamic, heroic, competitive, innovative, buccaneering capitalism of the 'liberal era' and earlier. For Hilferding the significance of the transformation of Austria's former 'liberal' capitalism into illiberal cartelized and monopolistic 'finance capitalism' was as much political as economic. 'Finance capitalism', in its maturity, 'is the highest stage of concentration of economic and political power in the hands of the capitalist oligarchy' (Hilferding 1981: 370). 'Finance capitalism' had ended the former separation of industrial, mercantile and banking capital, bringing them together 'under the common direction of high finance, in which the masters of industry and of the banks are united in a close personal association' (p. 301). This had fundamentally changed the relationship between the capitalist classes and the state. While capitalism was still an emergent and divided force the bourgeoisie had struggled against mercantilism, against the privileges and monopolies of large trading and colonial companies and of the closed craft guilds, and against 'the centralized and privilege-dispensing state'. Its struggle became a battle for economic freedom, which in turn developed into 'a broader struggle for individual liberty against the tutelege of the state' (p. 301). Until the 1860s, therefore, the issues that agitated the bourgeoisie were 'essentially constitutional', i.e. issues that 'affected all citizens alike, uniting them in a common struggle against reaction and the vestiges of feudal and absolutist-bureaucratic rule' (p. 337). But the development of cartels and 'finance capitalism' had fundamentally altered political alignments and the balance of forces. 'Cartelization . . . co-ordinates the political interests of capital and enables the whole weight of economic power to be exerted directly on the state' (p. 338). Moreover, 'the process of agglomeration in capitalist monopolies gives capital an interest in strengthening the power of the state. At the same time, capital acquires the power to dominate the state' (p. 337). Listian demands for *temporary* and *selective* protection of 'infant industries' gave way to organized lobbying for *permanent* protection of *established* industries, monopolies and cartels in order to help to make inflated profits on the home market, partly to subsidize exports and partly to finance higher investment (pp. 304–10.) 'Cartelization also strengthens the employers' position on the labour market and weakens that of trade unions' (p. 365), thereby inaugurating 'the ultimate phase of the class struggle between the bourgeoisie and the proletariat' (p. 367).

In Hilferding's view, however, the extraordinary centralization of economic control over private enterprises and production achieved by industrial concentration, cartelization, the intermarriage of banks and industry and the other contrivances of monopolistic 'finance capitalism' could also greatly facilitate the task of 'overcoming' capitalism (pp. 367–8). 'Once finance capital has brought the most important branches of production under its control, it is enough for society, through its conscious executive organ – the state conquered by the working class – to seize financial capital in order to gain immediate control of these branches of production' (p. 367). Thus in societies in the grip of monopolistic 'finance capitalism' it would suffice for the socialists to capture control of the biggest banks, because these already controlled the lion's share of large-scale industry, which in turn dominated most small producers. 'There is no need to extend the process of expropriation to the great bulk of peasant farms and small businesses because, as a result of the seizure of large-scale industry, upon which they have long been dependent, they would be indirectly socialized' (p. 368). This would allow expropriation to proceed gradually, 'precisely in those spheres of decentralized production where it would be a . . . politically dangerous process' (p. 368).

Hitherto, most Marxists had assumed that it would be necessary to wait patiently for decades to allow capitalism to complete its 'historic' task of making the economy, society and the working class wholly 'ripe' for socialism (i.e. sufficiently productive, educated, politically conscious, class-conscious and organized). However, Hilferding's 'discovery' of the new possibilities opened up by an increasingly cartelized and monopolistic 'finance capitalism' seemed to telescope the whole process into a much shorter time frame and to offer a short cut and a much quicker and easier transition to 'socialism'. Moreover, on his analysis, it was no longer necessary for Marxism to frighten and alienate the numerous small proprietors and small producers (the *petite bourgeoisie*) with threats of immediate post-revolutionary expropriation. Instead, 'since finance capital has already achieved expropriation to the extent required by socialism, it is possible to dispense with a sudden act of expropriation by the state and to substitute a gradual process of socialization through the economic benefits which ['socialist'] society will confer. While thus creating the final organizational prerequisites for socialism, finance capital also makes the transition easier in the political sense' (p. 368). At the same time 'the blatant seizure of the state by the capitalist class' in the era of monopolistic 'finance capitalism', together with the more naked use of 'the state apparatus' to serve capitalist interests, 'compels every proletarian to strive for the conquest of political power as the only means of putting an end to his own exploitation' (p. 368).

In addition, Hilferding maintained that the growth of industrial concentration, cartelization, monopoly and protectionism was intensifying the quest for captive markets, capital exports, imperialism and international tensions and conflicts. 'The old Free Traders believed in free trade not only as the best economic policy, but as the beginning of an era of peace. Finance capital abandoned this belief long ago . . . The ideal is now to secure for one's own nation the domination of the world' (p. 335). Eventually, 'as the expansion of the world market slows down, the conflicts between capitalist nations over their share in it will become more acute . . . The danger of war increases armaments and the tax burden' (p. 369). In the end, 'the policy of finance capital is bound to lead towards war, and hence to the unleashing of revolutionary storms' (p. 366).

Beginning with the largely derivative theoretical writings of Lenin and Bukharin between 1915 and 1917, Hilferding's revolutionary economic and political ideas were to furnish the essential theoretical and programmatic basis on which Marxist-Leninist communist parties subsequently proposed to seize political power, capture control of the 'commanding heights' of the economy and use them to impose 'socialism' ('from above') on countries which were in the grip of the increasingly centralized economic systems created by cartelized and monopolistic 'finance capitalism'. Thus it was that, in Marxist-Leninist terms, communist seizures of power and communist-led transitions to 'socialism' could (and indeed did) take place in the 'younger' (and in many ways 'less developed') capitalist states of central and eastern Europe, rather than in the older, more prosperous, more liberal (and in these respects more 'developed') capitalist states of north-western Europe and North America. The Habsburg Empire, Germany, Romania and Tsarist Russia were quite clearly in the grip of highly centralized, cartelized, protectionist and monopolistic forms of 'finance capitalism' by the early twentieth century (certainly more so than Britain, France and the Low Countries). In this limited sense they appeared to be 'ripe' for a rather crudely conceived 'transition' to even cruder forms of 'socialism'. Increasingly centralized industrial, financial and infrastructural systems were indeed emerging in central and eastern Europe, under the aegis of monopolistic 'finance capital' reinforced by state tutelage. It was also true that these could be (and in several cases were) captured by sufficiently ruthless, opportunistic and determined Marxist-Leninist movements, which then used their control of the 'commanding heights' of these centralized economic systems to impose ('from above') their crude, doctrinaire and rather spartan versions of 'socialism'. However, most of the inhabitants of these countries neither expressed nor secretly harboured any great wish to have coarse, doctrinaire neo-Marxist forms of 'socialism' thrust upon them or ideologically rammed down their throats. Furthermore, they were insufficiently educated and productive to attain anything remotely approaching economic 'abundance'. Therefore, all that could be achieved were mean, regimented, coercive, economically and culturally impoverished parodies of 'socialism', which were to bear some uncomfortable resemblances to Europe's more short-lived authoritarian fascist regimes.

Non-Marxists and 'orthodox' Marxist critics of Europe's communist regimes were therefore to argue that, even if cruel and perverted parodies of 'socialism' could be inflicted on largely hostile or reluctant populations using the centralized economic systems and the potentially coercive concentrations of power and control created by monopolistic 'finance capital' (alias 'monopoly capitalism'), the countries of central and eastern Europe were nevertheless far from 'ripe' for any non-coercive and more widely acceptable form of Marxist 'socialism'. Nowhere was there evident majority support for a Marxist movement, with the possible exceptions of Yugoslavia, Albania and Greece in 1944–45. Moreover, in only one of these countries, Czechoslovakia, was there a sufficiently educated, class-conscious and productive popular base on which to build a *bona fide* socialist system by consent rather than by coercion. (Indeed, if it had been allowed to do so, Czechoslovakia might well have achieved 'socialism with a human face' in the post-1945 epoch.) Furthermore, despite the growing dependence of small producers and proprietors upon bank credit and larger firms and the unhealthy degree of concentration of economic and political power and control in the hands of illiberal and undemocratic propertied oligarchies during the final decades of the Habsburg, German and Tsarist empires, Hilferding and the chief theoreticians of Marxism-Leninism greatly overestimated the extent to which it would be possible for the 'commanding heights' to exercise effective centralized control over multitudes of small producers. The loose-reined financial and commercial control wielded by banks and large firms over dependent clients and small producers under (pre-electronic) monopolistic 'finance capitalism' was of a rather lower order than the strict 'chains of command' and more comprehensive day-to-day control 'from above' necessary to the proper functioning of a command economy. Admittedly, the degree of central control exerted by the former communist regimes and planning systems was among their most oppressive and irksome characteristics. Yet in practice it fell far short of the 'total' control needed to achieve their often inappropriate, premature or even over-ambitious goals. Systems of central planning and control were indeed established. But the plans were honoured less in the observance than in the breach and the supposedly 'centrally planned' economies functioned only by courtesy of a great deal of semi-legal or downright illegal economic activity not envisaged in the plan.

HUNGARY AFTER THE 1867 'COMPROMISE'

In 1867, in the wake of the Austro-Hungarian 'compromise', the Magyar-dominated Transylvanian Diet was easily persuaded to vote itself out of existence and to allow Transylvania (whose inhabitants were 54 per cent Romanian and only 29 per cent Magyar) to be fully incorporated into a unitary Kingdom of Hungary, along with the largely South Slav Military Frontier regions. However, under an agreement concluded in 1868, Croatia was allowed to retain its own Diet and official language, 45 per cent of its tax revenue and a measure of autonomy in purely internal, religious, educational and judicial affairs, although its governor/viceroy (*ban*) was to be appointed by (and answerable to) the Hungarian government in Budapest rather than the Croatian Diet in Zagreb/Agram.

Between 1867 and 1871 Hungary was governed by a coalition of moderate pragmatic 'liberals' and paternalistic or Whiggish aristocrats, headed by Count Gyula Andrassy and sustained in office by the parliamentary 'party' of Ferenc Deak. The founding statutes of the nascent Hungarian state, particularly the 1868 Nationality Act and the 1868 Education Act, made a promising start down the road towards a unitary but relatively liberal polity based upon a broad and inclusive 'civic' conception of the emergent Hungarian nation-state (rather than a narrow, hard-edged and intolerant 'ethnic' or 'integral' conception of the ascendant Magyar nation dominating and aggressively 'Magyarizing' the numerous non-Magyars who had lived and worked for centuries on Hungarian soil). The 1868 Nationality Act, drafted by the 'progressive' writer and Minister of Religion and Education Baron Jozsef Eötvös (aided by Ferenc

Deak), declared that 'all citizens of Hungary form, politically, one nation, the indivisible unitary Hungarian nation (*nemzet*), of which every citizen of the country, whatever his personal nationality (*nemzetiseg*), is a member equal in rights' (quoted by Sked 1989: 208). Eötvös regarded the Magyars as just one *nemzetiseg* among several within the historic *nemzet* of Hungary (p. 209). In this usage, *nemzetiseg* (nationality) was an ethnic label, whereas *nemzet* (nation) referred to a broader historic territorial unit which could accommodate several distinct nationalities and linguistic communities on a formally equal footing. Thus the Magyar community, as the largest and strongest community within the historic territorial nation and state of Hungary, would merely be *primus inter pares*. This Nationality Act and the 1868 Education Act, which called for compulsory elementary schooling for all six- to twelve-year-olds, did indeed respect the diversity of peoples and cultures within the kingdom of Hungary (Jaszi 1929: 314–15). Ethnic minorities were formally entitled to conduct local government in their own language, and ethnic groups living together in considerable numbers were supposed to receive state education in their own language. Each nationality was genuinely free to develop its own national Church or Churches, while the 'emancipation' of Hungarian Jews was almost complete.

If the Magyar ruling classes had remained true to the letter and spirit of this first flush of political and cultural liberalism, Hungary could conceivably have evolved into something akin to the United Kingdom or even Switzerland. But it was not to be. In 1871 Eötvös died, while a disillusioned Deak withdrew from active politics (he died in 1876) and Andrassy was 'kicked upstairs' to the position of imperial Foreign Minister. Andrassy's successor as Prime Minister of Hungary, the former Finance Minister Menyhert Lonyay, lacked the political finesse and stature needed to hold the broad coalition together and to fend off vociferous demands from the more rowdy and nationalistic elements (mainly the Magyar 'gentry') for more aggressive 'Magyarization' of the Hungarian state, public employment and the education system. Moreover, the 1873 'crash' and the subsequent slide in international grain prices (partly in response to growing American, Russian and Romanian grain exports) inflicted additional economic and social strains on a still relatively poor, polarized multi-ethnic and largely agrarian population. The 'ruined' landed gentry raised the loudest political clamour, although they were by no means the worst-afflicted victims. They increasingly demanded a monopoly of state and professional employment for the sons of the Magyar nobility (literally 'jobs for the boys') as 'compensation' for (often exaggerated) reductions in seigneurial status and income. There was also peasant and proletarian unrest in the 1870s, but it was swiftly and firmly suppressed. Magyar governments would not tolerate the growth of either peasant or workers' movements until well into the twentieth century. Indeed, the 'ideology of [Hungarian] independence became – more or less consciously – a kind of *Verdrängungsideologie* (an ideology of repression) against all efforts which endangered the interests of the ruling classes' (Jaszi 1929: 359). The General Workers' Association, founded in 1868, was banned in 1872 (when its leaders were tried for 'treason') and was subjected to regular official harassment thereafter. Much the same fate befell the socialist Non-voters' Party (the only name the authorities would allow it to use when it was established in 1878), the General Workers' Party of Hungary (formed by a fusion of the two embryonic socialist parties in 1880) and the (Marxist) Social Democratic Party of Hungary, established in 1890. Indeed, any political or social movement which challenged the hegemonic position of the Magyar ruling classes was liable to be repressed or charged with 'treason' (including 'subversion'), 'libel' or 'incitement of national hatred'. This was to be the fate of various Slovak, South Slav, Romanian and Ruthene cultural societies and nationalist parties from 1876 onwards, as Magyar 'supremacism' intensified.

In 1875 the Magyar gentry malcontents fused with the depleted remnants of the ruling coalition to form the so-called Liberal Party. It soon became known as 'the government party', because it contrived to remain continuously in power for the next thirty years (until 1905) and because it comprised leading elements in the state bureaucracy as well as parliamentarians. From 1875 to 1890 the Liberal Party was dominated by Kalman Tisza, a prominent Calvinist landowner and a veteran of the Magyar nationalist revolution of 1848. A master of parliamentary and electoral manipulation and malpractice, Tisza ran a harsh Magyar landlords' police state behind a showy parliamentary and constitutional facade. Magyar 'liberalism', such as it was, soon 'betrayed the democratic ideas which represented the real value of 1848. Blind nationalism alone survived, narrow, stupid and corrupt' (D. Sinor, quoted by Barany 1967: 251).

The Kalman Tisza regime stepped up the creation of public service jobs for the crisis-stricken Magyar 'gentry', whose difficulties since the dissolution of serfdom were now being exacerbated by sagging international grain prices and the challenge of adapting to capitalism. Hungary's civil service had doubled from a mere 16,000 officials in 1867 to 32,000 in 1875. It was to double again by 1890 and yet again by 1914, when the total number of public employees (including the municipalities and state enterprises) reached 388,000, or 3.5 per cent of the working population (Janos 1982: 94). The Magyar gentry, who had been staunch opponents of political centralization before 1867, became its most aggressive agents after 1867, performing a complete *volte-face*.

These expanding hordes of state officials exercised inordinate central control over parliamentary elections and local government. They misused their powers of taxation, regulation, conscription and arrest to influence or intimidate voters, to forge ballot papers, to 'stuff' ballot boxes, to vet electoral registers and generally to perpetuate the Liberal Party in office. Moreover, some of the principal malefactors were allowed to stand for election in the 160 'rotten boroughs' which were safely 'in the government's pocket'. Such placemen came to constitute up to one-third of 'the government party' in the lower house of parliament, forming the nucleus of an almost unassailable parliamentary majority (Janos 1982: 95–7). Electoral manipulation and corruption were facilitated by Hungary's reliance on so-called 'open' rather than secret ballots in rural areas (enabling the local potentates to *see* that voters did as they were told), by restricting the franchise to less than 7 per cent of the adult population, and by blatant gerrymandering. Ironically, most of the 'rotten boroughs' were in areas where the Magyars were a small, privileged and vulnerable minority (dependent on government protection and favour) and the non-Magyar majority was largely disenfranchised. These areas, whose Magyar populations represented only a small fraction of the total Magyar population in Hungary, returned a relatively high proportion of the Magyar members of parliament. These were the MPs who were most in league with the government. Thus Magyars representing somewhat under half the total population of Hungary consistently 'won' over 94 per cent of the seats in the lower house of parliament, gained over 90 per cent of all official positions and held almost all the (hereditary) seats in the upper house of parliament. But this should not be allowed to overshadow or obscure the fact that not only the non-Magyar majority but also the major concentrations of Magyars (including most of the poorer ones) were grossly underrepresented in this supposedly 'representative' system of government. Conversely, through a combination of gerrymandering, vote-rigging, intimidation and a restrictive franchise, the Magyar upper classes (especially those resident in largely non-Magyar areas) were grossly overrepresented. Arguably, however, 'the new "constitutionalism" which the Compromise created . . . was only workable on the basis of a very restricted electoral law which was combined . . . in Hungary with administrative corruption and use of armed froce' (Jaszi 1929: 349). Indeed, Hungarian 'parliamentarianism' was reduced to a mere charade under a regime which disenfranchised most of the adult population and 'terrorized the minority possessing the suffrage by the system of open ballot, corruption and mobilization of the army' (p. 363).

The Kalman Tisza regime marked the beginning of much more aggressive 'Magyarization' policies in education, public administration, the legal system, the press, parliamentary representation and the promotion of cultural amenities, state enterprises (including railways) and agricultural colonization (Jaszi 1929: 318–36). These policies were to persist unremittingly until 1918 and went far beyond the haphazard 'Magyarization' stratagems of the 1840s. The Magyar ruling classes now dropped all pretence of respect for the diversity of peoples and cultures in Hungary. This sea-change came about for a variety of reasons. Under Kalman Tisza there came to power 'a new generation . . . of the "gentry" which forgot the great lessons of 1848–49' (p. 318). Indeed, they failed to understand that Hungary would 'never be capable of securing its independence from Austria as long as the Habsburgs could continue the old recipe of 1849, mobilizing the nationalities against the Magyar efforts' (p. 339).

Furthermore, the rapid growth of a Magyar state bureaucracy, the concurrent boom in Hungarian industry and infrastructure and the resultant influx of rustic Magyars into the main towns from the 1870s to the 1900s gave rise to a largely 'natural' and spontaneous 'Magyarization' of Hungary's hitherto predominantly German and Jewish urban populations. The population of Budapest rocketed from 202,000 in 1870 to 880,000 in 1910. It was in this period that the German and Jewish townspeople began to assimilate in earnest with the ascendant Magyars (from whom they had formerly remained quite separate) and to manifest the usual excessive zeal of 'new converts' (pp. 321, 324–5), while the Slovaks, South Slavs, Romanians and Ruthenes who were employed as cheap labour in urban industrial and construction work rapidly merged with their Magyar counterparts. The top-heavy concentration of 'modern' economic activity, political power, public employment and cultural amenities and patronage in booming Budapest exerted a powerful 'magnetic pull' on talent from the provinces, including the relatively few 'college-educated' Slovaks, South Slavs, Romanians and Ruthenes, and fostered a precocious yet remarkable flowering of 'modernist' cultural and scientific creativity. 'The intellectual splendour of the metropolitan city attracted into its sphere of influence all those elements of the country which were eager to embrace Western culture' (p. 325). In the process, however, the meteoric rise of Budapest imparted a major additional impetus to cultural assimilation. To stand any chance of success in Budapest, aspiring musicians, writers, academics, artists, scientists, lawyers and churchmen usually had to be or 'become' Magyars, even if that involved changing their names, beliefs and identities.

Even if the 'natural' and spontaneous economic, social and cultural processes of ethnic assimilation were not in themselves sinister or harmful, in the circumstances of Hungary after the 1867 'compromise' they did encourage and give greater weight and a sharper cutting edge to the more aggressive and oppressive 'Magyarization' policies of the

Magyar ruling classes. These were also encouraged and reinforced by the very nature of the 1867 'compromise'. Since the Magyar ruling classes had been denied a fully independent Hungarian state, they were all the more determined to achieve complete hegemony and to 'lord it' over a fully 'Magyarized' Hungary. Denied 'their own' independent armed forces, they could (by way of compensation) enlist the help of Austrian bayonets to enforce 'Magyarization' all the more ferociously, partly to vent their spleen on their 'inferiors'. Moreover, Emperor Franz Joseph and Austria's German/imperial ruling classes believed that 'the German hegemony in Austria' could be sustained only in combination with the maintenance of the hegemony of 'the Magyar feudal classes' in Hungary. At any rate, the other 'inferior' and semi-illiterate nationalities in Hungary were considered not to be suitable partners for the self-regarding Austrian Germans, who were therefore generally supportive of policies which had the appearance of buttressing Magyar mastery over the Slovak, South Slav, Romanian and Ruthene 'peasant peoples' in Hungary.

Aggressive and repressive 'Magyarization', the forceful maintenance of Magyar supremacy and all the attendant social and political evils were, in the final analysis, a bulwark for the maintenance of feudal privilege in the face of festering ethnic and class antagonisms. The Magyar ruling classes found it expedient to play up and play upon Magyar phobias, especially *vis-à-vis* the 'inferior' nationalities. 'This fear complex . . . systematically developed by press and school and by parliamentarian and social oratory paralyzed all the efforts of three generations and made any serious social and economic reform impossible' (Jaszi 1929: 326). This allowed the ruling classes to see off all political and social challenges, all demands for land reform or local autonomy or more honest, democratic and consensual government, and to preserve the political and social *status quo*.

It became axiomatic that either the ascendant Magyars would assimilate the non-Magyars or the latter would destroy the Hungarian state, that those who refused to learn the (difficult) Magyar language were traitors engaged in a conspiracy to subvert the Hungarian state, and that there existed 'only one possible culture in the country, the Magyar culture' (Jaszi 1929: 320). Indeed, the very few non-Magyars elected to the Hungarian parliament were regularly shouted down or denounced as 'traitors' if they tried to speak out against forced 'Magyarization', while writers who dared to criticize the policy in print were liable to be imprisoned either on charges of 'treason' or for 'incitement of national hatred' (pp. 327–8, 334–5, 338). However, whether out of sheer ignorance or self-delusion, 'the majority of those who applied this system and the [Magyar] bourgeois and intellectual circles were deeply convinced that in Hungary there was no nationality persecution' and that the Magyars had conferred 'unparalleled . . . liberties and privileges' on the other ('inferior') nationalities. Consequently, 'it was regarded as unheard-of ingratitude that these second-rank peoples rewarded this generosity by accusations and calumnies inciting foreign public opinion against the Magyar nation' (p. 337). (Such attitudes have prevailed in East Central Europe and the Balkans down to the present day.) Anyone who 'dared to criticize Hungarian conditions, especially the electoral and administrative systems', had to be in the service of an international conspiracy to subvert the Hungarian state and was immediately placed under 'suspicion of high treason' (as would also be the case under subsequent Hungarian regimes, whether fascist, communist or nationalist). 'Magyar domination was a command of destiny. Only a traitor could protest against it' (p. 338). Thus R.W. Seton-

Watson, the British specialist on Eastern Europe who did so much to draw international attention to the seamy Magyar methods of national oppression and electoral chicanery before the First World War, was duly denounced by the Magyar press (p. 328). Nevertheless, there did exist some genuine grounds for the Magyars' feelings of national insecurity, as they were indeed surrounded by actually or potentially expansionist Germanic, Slavic and Romanian neighbours. Jaszi was also at pains to emphasize that the Magyar ruling classes employed similar methods of subjugation against the Magyar lower classes and that 'in fairness . . . they never reached the brutality of the English against the Irish or of the Prussians against the Poles' (p. 337). The English might dispute this last remark, but we would not want this account of Magyar misdeeds to reinforce any smug feelings of Anglo-Saxon superiority!

The state employed various methods of forced 'Magyarization'. As early as 1875–76 it suppressed several Slovak secondary schools. Then, starting with the 1879 (Primary) Education Act and the 1883 (Secondary) Education Act, it made more systematic efforts to 'Magyarize' the teaching profession, to extend compulsory instruction in Magyar and to curtail the use of non-Magyar languages, in flagrant violation of the 1868 Nationality Law. By 1900 over four-fifths of all primary schools, over five-sixths of all primary school teachers, 80 per cent of all secondary school pupils and 90 per cent of all students in higher education were formally Magyar-speaking (Jaszi 1929: 328–30). Magyar was made compulsory in all schools in 1883, while the 1907 Education Act not only imposed a special 'oath of loyalty' on all teachers but also 'made them liable to dismissal if their pupils did not know Magyar' (Taylor 1976: 186). What is more, over 90 per cent of official posts were reserved for Magyars (p. 186), while 'all the cultural institutions of the country became instruments of Magyar national assimilation' (Jaszi 1929: 319). Many so-called Magyar Cultural Associations were established not so much 'for the cultural elevation of the Magyar masses' as for the harassment and intimidation of non-Magyar nationalists and cultural associations and the provision of 'sinecures for members of the privileged classes'. Other measures included the 'Magyarization' of place names (even in areas with few Magyar inhabitants) and 'Magyar agricultural colonization' (p. 336). In 1887 Lajos Mocsary, a prominent but increasingly isolated Magyar critic of aggressive 'Magyarization' policies, observed that 'the government does not regard as its proper task the checking of chauvinism in its wrong and aimless rampages but fosters it . . . This attitude gives rise to the surmise that all is allowed for the propagation of Magyarization, that the end sanctifies the means, that one can acquire by such deeds immortal merit' (quoted by Jaszi 1929: 339). 'Magyarization' engendered a cult of gratuitous violence against non-Magyars, perpetuated by upper as well as middle and lower-class thugs.

Jaszi correctly saw this whole programme as counterproductive. It used up scarce resources which could have been put to much more positive uses. For non-Magyars 'the Magyarizing drill of the elementary schools was good only for learning patriotic verses and songs by rote', with the result that 'they did not learn adequately either their mother tongue or Magyar', while the time wasted on learning Magyar 'without obtaining the desired end' reduced the time available for all subjects (p. 330). Yet the Magyar lower classes also lost out, because the state did not have sufficient resources to meet their basic educational and cultural needs and at the same time bestow/inflict Magyar education and culture upon the slightly larger non-Magyar population (pp. 328–9). Ironically, even among those non-Magyars who successfully progressed to a Magyar secondary or higher education, quite a few subsequently became ardent supporters of their own peoples' national claims (p. 330). Moreover, 'forceful assimilation demoralized the ruling nation', engendering a kind of 'moral brutalization' of the perpetrators, 'while it elevates both intellectually and morally the better elements of the oppressed nationalities'. Policies of forcible assimilation 'lower the general standard of culture' by turning schools into 'a kind of chauvinistic nursery', thereby retarding the intellectual development of their pupils. Indeed, 'real assimilation is impossible . . . All real assimilation in modern times can be based only on the spontaneous exchange of spiritual and economic values.' The possibility of such an exchange (based on the 'spontaneous' processes of urbanization, economic development and 'natural' assimilation in post-1867 Hungary) was fatally impaired 'by the policy of forcible assimilation' (pp. 340–1, 325, 321).

While the responsibility for these deeply degrading, corrosive and counterproductive 'Magyarization' policies rested mainly on the blinkered Magyar upper classes (pp. 326, 336–7), who thus strongly contributed to the incipient disintegration of the Dual Monarchy, Jaszi also contended that 'the Emperor's complete disregard of the non-Magyar nationalities of Hungary was a dominant factor in the process of dissolution' (p. 324). During the early 1880s there was even a virulent upsurge of antisemitism, fuelled by the continuing influx of Jews from Poland and their increasing prominence in trade, finance and moneylending. It culminated in the so-called Tiszaeszlar affair. In 1882, following the disappearance of a young girl from the village of Tiszaeszlar, the local Jews were accused of killing her for the purpose of ritual blood sacrifice. Their formal acquittal in 1883 unleashed a spate of anti-Jewish outrages in several counties. A new antisemitic party took off in the 1884 elections. However, many members of the Magyar 'establishment' realized that they needed the assistance of Jewish capital and commercial/financial expertise for their own solvency and that of the state, with the result that the 'party of government' soon decided to crack down on open expressions of antisemitism. Nevertheless, antisemitism simmered below the surface, especially among the lesser nobility, minor officials and sections of the peasantry and the *petite bourgeoisie*. It was again to resurface from 1919 to 1922 and from 1931 to 1956, when various social groups found it expedient to blame their own and their country's troubles on the Jews. Indeed, after the secession of Slovakia, Croatia and Transylvania in 1918, Jews replaced the Slovaks, South Slavs and Romanians as the favourite ethnic scapegoat of Hungary's 'declining' classes.

On the economic front the Kalman Tisza regime was under increasing pressure to respond to the deepening 'agrarian crisis' and, in particular, to come to the assistance of the Magyar nobility. In addition to providing more 'jobs for the boys' in the state bureaucracy, the increasingly interventionist Liberal Party inaugurated active programmes of industrial and infrastructural development, while at the same time enacting regressive and repressive rural labour legislation that was designed to assist landowners to weaken the position of rural labour, reduce rural wages, suppress agrarian unrest and impose a form of neo-serfdom.

Much has been made of the methods of state sponsorship of industrial and infrastructural development in Hungary from the 1880s to 1914. Since Hungary was prohibited from erecting tariffs against industrial imports from German Austria and the Czech Lands by the terms of the 1867 'compromise' and, what is more, could not afford to run the risk of provoking retaliatory Austrian tariffs against Hungarian agricultural exports, the Magyar government devised more roundabout means of protecting and promoting Hungarian industry. In 1881 the first of several Industry Acts offered all new factories established in Hungary tax breaks and reimbursement of customs duties paid on equipment imported from outside the empire. Additional tax exemptions for new factories were introduced in 1884, while in 1890 economic stimulation was expanded in scope to include cash grants and credits to particular industries, the manipulation of railway freight rates so as to favour Hungarian enterprises, and discrimination in favour of Hungarian companies in public procurement and in the allocation of state contracts. These policies culminated in the 1907 Industry Act, which distributed much larger subsidies on the basis of systematic studies of industrial bottlenecks and potential and more clearly formulated industrial priorities, concentrating 57 per cent of the projected subsidies on the textile industry (which offered the greatest scope for growth and import substitution right up to the 1930s).

After 1880, moreover, the state became the driving force behind infrastructural development. By 1914 Hungary had 3,500 km of waterways navigable by steam vessels, while the Hungarian State Railways diversified into water transport in the 1880s, contributing to the growth of a Hungarian fleet of 338 steam vessels and 1,500 barges by 1914. More important, Hungary's railway network expanded from 7,200 km in 1880 to 22,200 km in 1913, largely as a result of state enterprise. By 1900 the density of railway lines per inhabitant and per square kilometre in Hungary had virtually caught up with that of Austria, was not far behind that of western Europe and far exceeded that of the Balkans, Poland and European Russia. The railways and railway construction boosted economic development in general, integrating product markets, increasing labour mobility, stimulating the land and capital markets, facilitating exports and imports and providing the largest single market for Hungarian industrial products (Berend and Ranki 1974b: 37–9). Yet, however innovative or pioneering these policies were in the qualitative sense, quantitative research by Magyar economic historians has tended to downplay their relative importance. They have calculated that, at their peak, direct state subsidies to private industrial firms amounted to only 2 per cent of their total investment. 'Much more important was the fact that the state purchased 13 per cent of industrial production – indeed, in . . . machine-building it bought almost one-third of output' (p. 55). By itself, however, state intervention could not wholly compensate for the weaknesses springing from a low level of economic development and capital accumulation. In itself it could only mobilize the modest resources at Hungary's disposal. 'By and large, state activity was effective only to the degree that it created attractive conditions for foreign capital, in particular by making investments secure and profitable. Thus the unique factor in the capitalist transformation was not so much direct state intervention as the influx and collaboration of foreign capital' (pp. 69–70). By 1913 36 per cent of Hungarian industry was foreign-owned (p. 109). These are important qualifications of the influential theses put forward by Gerschenkron (1962 and 1967), which have ascribed the crucial propulsive role in the economic development of Europe's so-called 'backward economies' from the 1880s to 1914 to direct state activity and intervention in the economy.

The Hungarian strategy for attracting foreign capital involved the maintenance of political stability, 'law and order', relatively low wages, the provision of tax incentives, the repression of strikes and organized labour, and official tolerance of foreign workers, foreign personnel and a broad range of religious denominations. In practice, the thirty-year tenure of the corrupt and repressive Liberal Party probably did more to attract than to repel foreign investors and entrepreneurs, who were not too concerned with democratic niceties. Indeed, the one area in which the regime was genuinely liberal was in matters of religion. Against fierce Habsburg, aristocratic and Roman Catholic opposition (especially in the upper house of parliament), the Liberal Party fought a long and eventually successful campaign to reduce the excessive power and influence of the Roman Catholic Church in education, marriage and family affairs and to establish freedom of religion and the equal status of various faiths and denominations (including Judaism). Between 1892 and 1894 liberals, Calvinists, Lutherans, Jews, secularists and the anticlerical left united to defeat the Roman Catholic right (just as they did a century later, in the June 1994 general election). Moreover, Protestant and Jewish entrepreneurs and immigrants, including numerous engineers, managers, technicians, doctors and lawyers, were attracted by the increasing secularism, doctrinal pluralism and religious tolerance of Hungarian society (a kind of revival of or return to pre-Habsburg traditions). Thus as early as 1875 'foreigners' made up 25 per cent of the working population of Budapest (Berend and Ranki 1974b: 79).

On the agrarian front the decisive interventions of the Magyar state were intended to strengthen the economic, social and political position of the Magyar landed elite *vis-à-vis* Magyar and especially non-Magyar farm servants and labourers. The Agricultural Labour Act of 1876 curtailed the personal liberties and equality before the law of farm labour, declared the hired labourer or farm servant to be 'under his master's authority', and licensed landowners to humiliate or inflict corporal punishment upon their menials without fear of any legal 'comeback' from the victims. It also stipulated that farm servants or labourers who attempted to quit or change their jobs without their employer's consent were to be returned to their 'master' by the police or gendarmerie. The Penal Code of 1878 outlawed not only 'violent argument' and 'interference with the work of others' but any 'gatherings' in pursuit of higher wages. The Farm Servants Act of 1898 (popularly known as 'the slave law') went still further, forcing farm servants and labourers to enter into legally enforceable contracts with their employers, forbidding them either to leave their estates or to receive 'strangers' into their homes and prescribing sixty-day prison terms for incitement to strike. Finally, the 1907 Farm Servants Act banned some remnants of 'feudal' labour services and the corporal punishment of adults but retained corporal punishment for teenagers, promised landowners military assistance 'on demand' against 'disobedient' employees and prescribed severe penalties for strikers.

These were in large part economic measures, intended to strengthen agricultural employers against their employees in order to reduce the estates' wage and other production costs and thereby protect investments and grain exports, while also cushioning landowners against the effects of the late nineteenth-century fall in grain prices and the difficult transition to a wage-labour economy. The Magyar ruling classes reached a consensus 'on the need to protect the profit margin of large agricultural production units in order to maintain the country's grain exports and the accumulation of domestic capital' (Janos 1982: 131). Yet these were also socio-political measures, designed to reintroduce elements of serfdom in a more modern capitalist 'police state' guise and thereby buttress the political monopoly and rural 'social control' exercised by the Magyar landed nobility, in the face of the mounting challenges posed by the birth of socialist movements and ideas, by organized labour and, among the non-Magyars who constituted a growing proportion of the estate owners' work force as more and more Magyars migrated to the towns in search of higher wages, by the growth of nationalist movements and consciousness. In the final analysis the regime still regarded the Magyar landed estates as its main instrument of social and political control over Hungary's downtrodden but increasingly restive rural population.

In spite of all its repressive and regressive legislation, Hungary made striking economic and social progress from 1867 to 1914. Between these two dates the population of Budapest rose from 200,000 to 900,000, the railway network expanded from 2,200 km to 22,200 km, the growth of industrial output averaged 5 per cent per annum, agricultural output grew on average by 2 per cent per annum and the growth of national income averaged 3.2 per cent a year (Berend and Ranki 1974b: 73–4). The share of the work force dependent on agriculture fell from 80 per cent in 1870 to 64.5 per cent in 1910, whereas the proportion engaged in industry, trade and transport rose from 11.5 per cent to 23.6 per cent over the same period (p. 74). Gross agricultural production more than doubled between 1867–70 and 1911–13 (p. 48). The late nineteenth-century fall in international grain prices both stimulated and was more than compensated by technical and structural changes. Over the period 1873–1913 there was a 70 per cent increase in grain yields per hectare, a 30 per cent expansion of the total cultivated area, a considerable diversification out of grain crops into more intensive and remunerative livestock rearing and the cultivation of potatoes, sugar beet and other root crops, and a 60 per cent reduction in the proportion of arable land left fallow. In addition, there were major improvements in traditional farm implements. But these were later to be overshadowed by more spectacular advances in the use of both horse-drawn and steam-powered machinery on the larger estates. The number of steam threshers rose from 2,500 in 1871 to 30,000 by 1914, while the use of horse-drawn seed drills increased sevenfold between 1871 and 1895. Grain output nearly trebled between 1864–66 and 1911–13, but potato output increased sevenfold and the output of both sugar beet and turnips increased more than twentyfold over the same period, while by 1900 over 40 per cent of farm incomes came from livestock rearing (pp. 44–7). All in all, this amounted to a minor 'agricultural revolution', comparable to that which occurred in late Tsarist Russia (Bideleux 1987: 11–18; 1990).

Not surprisingly, given this rich and diversifying agricultural resource base, food-processing continued to dominate Hungarian industrial development and, as early as 1884, Manfred Weiss opened Hungary's first food canning plant ('the shape of things to come'). More remarkably, Hungary also emerged as a significant producer (and even exporter) of railway locomotives and rolling stock, flour-milling equipment, agricultural machinery and steam turbines for electricity generation (the Ganz works and Mavag). It became a European pioneer in the manufacture of electric light bulbs (of which it remains a major producer and exporter today), electric transformers, watt meters and electric locomotives. By 1914 Hungary was also a significant producer of chemicals (fertilizer and explosives), munitions and steel, and it even produced its first tractors, lorries, cars and aircraft. This technological precociousness was partly the work of enterprising foreigners such as Abraham Ganz (of Swiss origin), but it must also be credited to the promotion of scientific and technological higher education by an unusually 'developmental' Magyar state. Some of the 'leading names' (Kando, Blathy, Dery, Hevesy and Szilard) were clearly Magyars, precursors of such household names as Biro and Rubic.

It may appear even more paradoxical that the repressive (and in many ways regressive) Magyar state also presided over an 'educational revolution'. Attendance at elementary schools rose from 1.1 million in 1869 to 2.7 million in 1910 (or from 48 per cent to 89 per cent of the relevant six to twelve age group), although attendance at secondary schools increased only from 4 per cent to 5 per cent of the secondary age group. Adult literacy increased from 34 per cent in 1870 to 69 per cent in 1910 (nearly 80 per cent for males over the age of seven and 88 per cent for industrial employees). By 1914 Hungary also had 14,000 university students (Berend and Ranki 1974b: 26–8; Janos 1982: 156). The key to the apparent paradox was the fervent Magyar nationalist desire to make Hungary both 'great' and thoroughly Magyar. This involved the promotion of education as an instrument of Magyarization. Indeed, the share of the population recorded as 'Magyar' had risen from 37 per cent in 1837 to 48 per cent in 1910 in the kingdom as a whole and from 44 per cent to 52 per cent in 'Hungary proper' (i.e. excluding Croatia-Slavonia).

However, the 'educational revolution' also broadened social and political horizons, raised expectations and increased Magyar and non-Magyar discontent with the outmoded political monopoly maintained by the Magyar ruling classes. This fuelled an intensification of social and political tensions in Hungary during the 1890s and 1900s, beginning with the fall of Kalman Tisza in 1890. During 1889–90 Tisza was obliged to 'steamroller' extremely unpopular 'Germanizing' reforms of the Habsburg armed forces through the Magyar-dominated Hungarian parliament, as part of a drive to modernize and expand the empire's defences. In doing so, however, he used up all his political credit with his nationalistic Magyar 'gentry' supporters and in 1890 he felt obliged to resign. Tisza's successors, the more 'liberal' Gyula Szapary and Sandor Wekerle governments (1890–92 and 1892–95 respectively) exhausted themselves in an ultimately successful campaign for anticlerical 'secularizing' reforms. They were followed by the utterly intolerant, chauvinistic and repressive Banffy government. Baron Dezso Banffy was eventually toppled by the incipient crisis in Austrian–Hungarian relations, precipitated by the provision for decennial renewal and revision of the 1867 'compromise', as were his Liberal successors, the more emollient Kalman Szell (1899–1903) and the hard-line 'strong men' Count Karoly Khuen-Hedervary (1903) and Count Istvan Tisza (the son of Kalman Tisza; 1903–05).

In January 1905, amid increasing repression of mounting peasant, proletarian and ethnic unrest, the Liberal Party finally lost power in relatively 'free' and fiercely contested elections which were called in an unsuccessful attempt to resolve the deepening deadlock in Austrian–Hungarian relations. The tyrannical Istvan Tisza had been defeated by an unholy 'Coalition' of even more extreme Magyar nationalists, reform-minded 'liberals' and democrats and disaffected conservatives, Catholics and aristocrats, who were united only in their opposition to Tisza's compliant behaviour towards Austria and Emperor Franz Joseph. But the emperor would not allow the defiant 'Coalition' to form a government on its own terms (radical revision of the 1867 'compromise') and it was not yet ready to form a government on his terms (acceptance of the *status quo*). Amid the ensuing power vacuum peasant and proletarian unrest escalated still further, spurred on by news of the unfolding 1905 revolution in Russia. In June 1905, finally, Franz Joseph prevailed upon the 'loyalist' general (and former Defence Minister) Geza Fejevary to form a government. But this was voted down by the 'Coalition' majority in parliament, which then called for Magyar 'national resistance' in the time-honoured fashion: non-collection of taxes and non-delivery of army recruits.

Workers' protests climaxed on 'Red Friday' (15 September 1905), when 100,000 demonstrators encircled the parliament building in Budapest. But they shrank back from real revolution (entailing a transfer of political power to the streets and barricades) and eventually dispersed peacefully. Perhaps a revolutionary opportunity was missed, but it seems very unlikely that the left could have triumphed against the still well organized and disciplined forces of 'reaction'. After this hollow and inconsequential show of strength, workers' unrest rapidly lost its sense of purpose and momentum.

On 3 October 1905, in Fiume, Croat and Serb leaders issued a 'resolution' declaring their readiness to support Magyar nationalist defiance of the Habsburgs in return for Magyar recognition of the 'national rights' of Croatia and Dalmatia, including a union of these two largely Croat-inhabited provinces which had long been divided between Hungary and Austria. But this pointed show of solidarity aroused more fear than hope in the hearts of Magyar nationalists, most of whom blithely assumed that it was their manifest destiny to dominate their 'inferior' neighbours.

In early 1906, when the imperial authorities and the Fejevary government stopped paying the salaries of Magyar officials, suspended the defiant parliament, imposed military rule and threatened to introduce universal suffrage, the Magyar nationalist 'Coalition' rapidly caved in. Leading members of the 'Coalition' (including Ferenc Kossuth, son of Lajos Kossuth) joined a government headed by the former Liberal Premier Sandor Wekerle (1906–10), which secretly agreed to renew the 1867 'compromise' virtually unchanged and defend the *status quo* in Hungary. The 'Coalition' Ministers soon reneged on the position they had taken when in opposition, alienating their more radical supporters and exposing the unbridgeable divisions within their own ranks. But by passing new Farm Servants and Industry Acts, and repressing peasant, proletarian and non-Magyar nationalist unrest, they contributed to a revival of business confidence and a fresh economic boom, which helped to buoy up the government and defuse economic discontents. Moreover, taking a leaf out of Bismarck's book, they expanded and centralized a nascent system of health insurance and established a system of compulsory accident insurance for industrial workers. This move laid the foundations of a new conservative corporatism designed to defuse class antagonism and curb the popular appeal of the left.

Nevertheless, the urban working class, the peasantry and the intelligentsia had 'grown' considerably in education, consciousness, confidence and strength. During 1905 they had gained a small taste of power and a brief glimpse of freedom. It was now almost impossible to put the genie back into the bottle. The Social Democratic Party, the urban workers' movement and the Independent Socialist Peasant Party of Hungary (established in 1906) gained steadily in membership, organization, sophistication and strength, at least until the fresh waves of repression unleashed by Istvan Tisza between 1913 and 1917. The radical and liberal sections of the intelligentsia found more effective and articulate expression in the journal *Huszadik Szazad* (Twentieth Century), under the intellectual leadership of Oscar (Oszkar) Jaszi and his Citizens' Radical Party (established in 1910), and in the radicalized Independence Party, headed by Mihaly Karolyi from 1913 onward. All these movements were working out potential alternatives to conservatism, oligarchy, Magyar supremacism and repression (the key characteristics of the existing state). Although their development was to be rudely interrupted by the Istvan Tisza regime of 1913–17 and the outbreak of the First World War, they would resurface with greatly enhanced strength, acuity and popular support in 1918.

At the parliamentary and governmental levels, however, power slipped back into the hands of the former Liberal Party old guard, led by Istvan Tisza and reorganized in 1910 as the Party of National Work. It backed the government of Count Karoly Khuen-Hedervary, who returned to the premiership during 1910–11. He was toppled by united left-wing and Magyar nationalist opposition to an Army Bill in 1911. In May 1912 real power passed to Istvan Tisza, who, as speaker of the lower house, steamrollered the troublesome Bill through parliament (even evicting some opposition MPs) and faced down the mass protests and demonstrations organized by the workers' movement and the radical intelligentsia. In 1913 Tisza became Prime Minister and ruled Hungary with a rod of iron until he was forced to resign by the new, more liberal emperor Karl in May 1917.

12 War, nationalism and imperial disintegration

THE ROAD TO WAR

At the heart of the causes of the First World War lay Austria-Hungary's attempt to 'solve the South Slav problem' by subjugating (without fully incorporating) Serbia in much the same way that it had subjugated (without fully incorporating) Bosnia and Hercegovina. In doing so, it also hoped to recompense itself for its earlier losses in Italy and Germany and to prove that it was still a great power, even though that would be to run the risk of war with Serbia's more powerful patron, Russia. By contrast, Germany took (and indeed had) little interest in the subjugation of Serbia and, between 1906 and 1908, it even helped Serbia to break free from Austria-Hungary's economic stranglehold. In the end, however, Europe was to pay a colossal price for Austria-Hungary's inability to restore its prestige, prove its virility and 'solve the South Slav problem' by more peaceful means.

During the 1880s and 1890s Serbia had become in effect a political and economic 'dependency' or 'client' of the Habsburg Empire, following the discomfiture of Russia by Europe's other great powers in 1878–81. In 1882 Austria-Hungary signed a relatively liberal commercial treaty with Serbia. By 1903 60 per cent of the grain and 95 per cent of the livestock imported into the Habsburg Empire came from Serbia, which in turn obtained 87 per cent of its imports from Austria-Hungary (Jaszi 1929: 417). In 1903, however, Serbia's supine and pro-Austrian Obrenovich dynasty had been overthrown and replaced by the more assertive, pan-Slavic and pro-Russian Karageorgevich dynasty. Moreover, as part of a renewal of the Austro-Hungarian 'compromise' in 1906–07, the Magyar landed classes had secured the erection of protective tariffs against Serbia's staple exports of agricultural products (especially pork) to the Monarchy. This trade war, commonly known as 'the pig war', obliged Serbia to gain greater economic independence by exporting its agricultural produce across Greek and Ottoman territory to new markets in western Europe and Germany and to obtain loans and armaments from France in place of Austria. Nettled by the Serbs' success in these endeavours, the Habsburg Empire responded by formally annexing Bosnia and Hercegovina in October 1908, to the great fury of Serbian nationalists. So long as Bosnia and Hercegovina had remained under supposedly 'temporary' military occupation by Austria-Hungary, Serb nationalists could still entertain serious hopes that the further disintegration of the Ottoman Empire would lead to a 'Greater Serbia' encompassing Bosnia and Hercegovina as well as Macedonia, Kosovo and possibly Dalmatia, conferring unimpeded access to the sea. Formal Habsburg annexation of Bosnia and Hercegovina was intended to extinguish such hopes and to force Serbia to accept a permanently landlocked and semi-dependent status (especially as neighbouring Montenegro did not yet have a coastline to share with its Serbian 'cousins', as it does today). Serbian nationalists reacted to the Austro-Hungarian annexation of Bosnia and Hercegovina by staging angry mass meetings and by forming 'underground' nationalist associations committed to achieving 'Greater Serbia' through armed struggle: *Narodna Odbrana* (National Defence), *Ujedjenje ili Smrt* (Unification or Death; alias *Crna Ruka*, the Black Hand) and, within Bosnia, *Mlada Bosna* (Young Bosnia). However, the Russian Foreign Minister Izvolsky counselled the irate Serbian government to exercise restraint and 'do nothing which could provoke Austria and provide an opportunity for annihilating Serbia' (Malcolm 1994: 151). The Habsburg annexation of Bosnia and Hercegovina has also been regarded as a flexing of the empire's muscles to warn off any attempt by the 'Young Turks' (who had seized power in the Ottoman Empire earlier in 1908) to bring these provinces back under Ottoman rule, but there can be little doubt that by that time 'the South Slav problem' loomed larger in Habsburg fears and obsessions than did the poor old 'Sick Man of Europe'.

In 1908, as a pretext for declaring war on Serbia and putting fifty-three Serb and Croat leaders in Croatia on trial for 'treason', the Austrian imperial authorities produced forged evidence of a Serb-Croat conspiracy against the Habsburg Empire. In March 1909 the Serbian government was given an ultimatum: either it must recognize and accept the Monarchy's annexation of Bosnia-Hercegovina or the Habsburg Monarchy would declare war on Serbia. At the same time Germany told Russia that it must either give up its support for Serbia or face the risk of war with the central powers (Kann 1974: 414). Russia, which was still recovering from the disastrous consequences of the Russo-Japanese War of 1904–05 (in which Russia was defeated on both land and sea by the Japanese in the Far East) was obliged to capitulate. This forced its Serb protégé to follow suit. Thereupon the Monarchy's plans for a war against Serbia were shelved as the makers of Austro-Hungarian foreign policy belatedly woke up to the fact that such a war would solve nothing, even if it ended in military victory for their own armies. Annexation of Serbia could only people the Monarchy with even more embittered South Slavs. On the other hand, if Serbia were not annexed, she would become in reality the seething hotbed of frustrated pan-Serb ambition and South Slav discontent that Habsburg propaganda pictured her to be (Taylor 1976: 217). Moreover, Serbia could not have been incorporated into the Habsburg Empire without upsetting the precarious Austro-Hungarian 'compromise' of 1867 and the Magyar parliament would probably have vetoed any move to bring Serbia into an expanded Dual (let alone Triple) Monarchy.

Thus the empire could no more afford to acquire than to lose territory in the Balkans. Indeed, it can be argued that inter-ethnic relations within Austria-Hungary had been so tense and conflictual that the empire could have withstood major military victories no more than it could have withstood further setbacks and defeats. Major territorial gains could have had much the same disintegrating effect as a serious defeat (Kann 1950b: 288). It was in the best interests of the Habsburg Empire merely to uphold and police the territorial *status quo*. Such a conclusion was reinforced by a belated but sober recognition of the latent weaknesses of the superficially imposing Habsburg armies. Emperor Franz Joseph and Archduke Franz Ferdinand both realized that these armies had become more effective against internal than against external foes. There was a real possibility that the Serbian 'David' might inflict humiliating defeats on an invading Habsburg 'Goliath' (as indeed it did in 1914, twice, before Germany came to the Monarchy's rescue).

However, while the Habsburgs pulled back from military action against Serbia in 1909, the damage had already been done. The Serbs were convinced that Austrian aggression had merely been postponed and 'therefore began an anti-Austrian policy in earnest' (Taylor 1976: 218). Furthermore, the falsely accused Serb and Croat leaders in Croatia engaged the eminent Czech professor Tomas Masaryk to bring a libel suit against the imperial authorities in Vienna. Between them, the so-called 'Zagreb treason trial' of 1909 and Masaryk's subsequent highly publicized exposure of the official forgeries in 1910 brought the Monarchy into damaging international disrepute, by stripping away the pretence and veneer of civilized conduct which had given the Habsburg Empire a not entirely deserved aura of respectability. This seamy and mis-handled episode 'revealed the true spirit of the Habsburg Monarchy: it was not tyrannical or brutal; it was merely degenerate and moribund' (Taylor 1976: 219–20).

Since any immediate hope of 'liberating' Bosnia and Hercegovina from non-Slav rule had been temporarily doused by Austria-Hungary's formal annexation of those provinces in October 1908, Serbia and its Montenegrin 'cousins' turned their attention southwards, setting their sights on Macedonia, Albania and Kosovo. In October 1912, taking advantage of a massive crisis within the Ottoman Empire (and with the Habsburg Empire helplessly looking on), Serbia and Montenegro went to war against the Turks and, with Greek and Bulgarian assistance, rapidly drove the remaining Ottoman forces out of Kosovo, Macedonia, northern Albania and the Sandjak of Novi Pazar. This cataclysmic Balkan War, which almost doubled the territories of Serbia and Montenegro and raised South Slav nationalism to a triumphal fever pitch, posed immense problems for Austria-Hungary. 'The national principle had triumphed . . . The Balkan Wars marked the virtual end of the Habsburg Monarchy as a Great Power. The Balkans had been Austria-Hungary's "sphere of influence"; yet, in the crisis, her influence achieved nothing – even Albania was saved only with Italian assistance' (Taylor 1976: 229). Indeed, with the almost total expulsion of the Ottoman Empire from Europe, Austria-Hungary had become the new 'sick man of Europe', but it was granted a brief respite by the fact that the Balkan victors fell out among themselves in a second Balkan War in June and July 1913. During this period, significantly, 'the Germans urged a conciliatory policy towards Serbia and Romania, even if this involved an amputation of Hungary', but conciliation was as unacceptable to the Austrian Germans as it was to the Magyars (p. 230).

The best known catalyst of the outbreak of the First World War (and hence of the eventual dissolution of the Habsburg Empire) was the assassination of the Habsburg Archduke and Crown Prince Franz Ferdinand, together with his wife, by a fiercely nationalistic Bosnian Serb in Sarajevo on 28 June 1914, the anniversary of the battle of Kosovo (the most important date in the Serbian nationalist calendar). The assassin, Gavrilo Princip, had been a student in Belgrade and had received some arms and assistance from an agent of a Serbian nationalist organization (Narodna Odbrana, or National Defence) who was also working for the chief of Serbian military intelligence, Colonel Apis. On 23 July 1914, taking advantage of an international wave of revulsion against Serbian nationalist terrorism (even in Sarajevo, where the assassination of the archduke and his wife had been followed by anti-Serb demonstrations and attacks on Serbian shops and homes), Austria-Hungary gave Serbia an ultimatum comprising ten demands for various measures to suppress Serbian nationalist activity inside and outside Serbia, nine of which were in fact accepted by the Serbian government. The ultimatum did not hold Serbia *directly* responsible for the Sarajevo assassination, but it justly complained that Serbia 'had tolerated the machinations of various societies and associations directed against the Monarchy, unrestrained language on the part of the press, glorification of the perpetrators of outrages and participation of officers and officials in subversive agitation' (Malcolm 1994: 156). Serbian refusal to accept all ten of Austria's demands provided the pretext for Austria-Hungary's declaration of war on Serbia, which in turn precipitated Russian military mobilization in support of Serbia. This prompted Germany to declare war on Russia and its French ally, whereupon Britain was (ostensibly) drawn into the conflict by its treaty obligations as a guarantor of Belgian independence and neutrality, since German military strategy was premised upon an early knock-out blow against France via Belgium. However, as emphasized by the Bosnian historian Vladimir Dedijer, 'To describe the Sarajevo assassination as either an underlying or an immediate cause of the 1914–18 war is to commit an enormity. It was an incident which under more normal international circumstances could not have provoked such momentous consequences . . . It was a truly unexpected gift . . . to the Viennese war party, which had sought, ever since the annexation crisis of 1908–9, a pretext for attacking Serbia, pacifying the South Slavs and extending Habsburg power to the very gates of Salonika' (Dedijer 1966: 445).

The outbreak of the First World War was partly a consequence of the deepening division of Europe into mutually antagonistic power blocs. This inflamed international tensions, made both 'national' and international politics more intemperate and violent, accelerated the European arms race and, most pertinently, appeared to set the Germanic and the Orthodox Slavic worlds upon a collision course. Jaszi (1929: 420–1) claimed that 'a mass-psychological situation' was emerging both within the Monarchy and on its borders which was pushing the whole system 'step by step toward explosion, making the struggle between Habsburg imperialism and Russian Pan-Slavism more imminent from year to year. It became almost a political dogma that this life and death struggle was totally inevitable and . . . the leading military circles in both camps prepared feverishly for the final clash.' Even Kaiser Wilhelm referred to the approaching war as 'the last great battle between Teutons and Slavs'. But Jaszi (1929: 422–3) was also at pains to point out that the attribution of 'war guilt', in the sense of seeking out 'individual responsibility', could be misleading or inappropriate. 'No diplomatic finesses, no . . . treaties of amity, could have avoided this explosion whose real roots were in the social, economic and national structure both of Russia and of the Dual Monarchy . . . One should not forget that the natural reactionary alliance . . . among the German, the Austrian and the Russian autocrats was not dissolved by their personal rivalry but under the pressure of a widely spread national public opinion.' On the other hand, it has been asserted that 'the supposed feud between Slavs and Teutons was a Habsburg device to keep the dynasty afloat and also, of course, a Magyar device to exploit German power for their peculiar benefit' (Taylor 1976: 230). If so, they were playing with fire. The tensions between Germanic and Slavic peoples had highly combustible potential, as had already been demonstrated within Bohemia and other ethnically mixed provinces of the Habsburg Empire. But these tensions had acquired a life of their own, far exceeding the rulers' capacity to control them for their own purposes.

At the same time the existing European order was being challenged and destabilized by spatial variations in the pace and pattern of industrial development and by the consequent shifts in the distribution of power and wealth within and between states. This made European states (or their rulers) very nervous and 'jumpy', increasing their readiness to resort to 'pre-emptive' wars (regardless of whether these were perceived as defensive or aggressive in character). The growth of protectionism, cartels and monopolistic 'finance capital' was simultaneously intensifying the scramble for 'captive markets' both within Europe and in the form of extra-European 'colonies' (particularly in Africa and Asia). As emphasized by Duchêne (1965: 231), 'Conscious forces did not push the world to war in 1914. Most historians would now agree that the cause was a combination of an incapacity to work a complex system without a recognized arbiter and of the growth of anarchic forms of behaviour left unchecked until they became uncheckable. In fact, there was an inherent accelerator built into the system of aggressive competition for power and prestige.'

The mounting tensions and sources of conflict were making it increasingly difficult for the existing European states system to accommodate or cope with the severe challenges posed by the growth of nationalist movements and ideologies. In western Europe, for the most part, states had been able to harness nationalism to 'unify', strengthen and consolidate already existing or inchoate polities and allegiances. German and Italian 'national unification' harboured much greater destructive and disruptive potential, although it was at first skilfully kept under control by conservative legitimist statesmen such as Bismarck and Cavour. But in eastern Europe nationalism and national unity were, for the most part, totally at odds with the existing (mainly supranational and imperial) state structures and boundaries. The Austro-Hungarian Empire, above all, was incompatible with the emerging conception of a new European order based upon sovereign national states. Thus the rise of nationalism was conducive to violent international conflict.

However, while it is true that important elements in the European states system (along with the nationalist challenge to it) were powerfully conducive to war, it need not follow that all the states within that system were equally culpable or that no one state or group of states was particularly to 'blame' for the outbreak and rapid escalation of warfare in 1914. It has been fashionable to assign particular 'blame' or 'war guilt' to Germany. 'Historians used to write as if the war had been caused by an impersonal thing called "the international system"; but it is now widely agreed that Germany was pushing hard for a war, in order to put some decisive check on the growing power of Russia. The Austro-Hungarians were more hesitant, fearing Russia's involvement (as the protector of Serbia) as much as the Germans hoped for it' (Malcolm 1994: 157). Nevertheless, there is much to be said for the view that Austria-Hungary brought the First World War upon itself, whether out of reckless and suicidal folly or in defence of an outmoded sense of imperial honour or in pursuit of imperial aggrandizement. Indeed, it is difficult to understand (let alone accept) the frequent portrayal of Austria-Hungary as a stabilizing factor in European diplomacy if it always thought itself justified in rejecting peaceful diplomatic solutions to its problems. On the contrary, Austro-Hungarian (rather than German) ambitions, insecurities and sensitivities turned out to be the major destabilizing factors in European diplomacy between 1859 and 1914, partly because 'imperial honour demanded that no territory be surrendered without a fight' and partly because, having lost its leading position in Germany and Italy, it was determined to recoup its losses by gaining 'a predominant position in the Balkans' (Sked 1989: 181–2). As Edith Durham observed during her travels in Bosnia in 1906, 'the Austrians . . . were anxious to consolidate their position in Bosnia as far as possible, so as to be ready for a forward move. "Nach Salonik" was a favourite topic of conversation' (Durham 1920: 164).

Nevertheless, it should be emphasized that war against Serbia, whether actively expansionist or merely a pre-emptive strike, was not wholly unavoidable. The threat posed by Serbian and South Slav nationalism was wildly exaggerated. Only the Habsburg desire to avoid any further loss of imperial honour and prestige made war appear to be the only way out of the Austro-Serb confrontation, since the negative repercussions of Austro-Hungarian acquiescence in a process of South Slav unification need not have been any greater than the consequences of Austria-Hungary's grudging and belated acceptance of the processes of Italian and German unification in the 1860s. Despite a temporary loss of face, the Monarchy could have lived to fight another day (Sked 1989: 255–7). Tragically, the Monarchy deliberately risked a world war 'rather than compromise internally or externally on the South Slav question' (p. 269). In a passage which has acquired added significance in the wake of the Yugoslav conflicts in the 1990s, A.J.P. Taylor (1976: 228) similarly emphasized that Serbia did not pose an insurmountable threat to the Habsburg Empire. 'Independent Serbia, Orthodox in religion and for a long time a Turkish province, had little interest in the Habsburg lands. The Serbs aspired to liberate their brothers still under Turkish rule and to recover all the territory once historically Serb; this ambition extended to Bosnia and Hercegovina, not beyond. The Serbs certainly had no reason to feel affection for the Croats, Roman Catholic, pro-Habsburg and "western" in culture' (p. 228). Most Croats, for their part, 'despised the barbarous Serbs and their Balkan ways'. But the Serbs had already established a state of their own, which they primarily wished to extend southwards and westwards, towards the sea, to set free and unite with their Orthodox co-religionists in Macedonia, Kosovo and Bosnia, 'and they regarded the South Slav idea as no more than a secondary weapon to this end' (p. 190). Thus Serb ambitions were essentially 'limited to "Greater Serbia"', as they were as hostile to a true South Slav state as the Habsburgs themselves' (p. 237).

In 1918, and again after 1945, a broader and relatively unified South Slav state was wished upon the Serbs, but it was always made abundantly clear that few Serbs were really interested in anything more than a 'Greater Serbia'. Therefore criticism of the Serbs for not remaining 'true to the Yugoslav idea' is in a sense misplaced. The concept of a federal multinational Yugoslav state appealed mainly to cosmopolitan and intellectual idealists and to vulnerable and insecure non-Serbs with no state of their own. But Serbian nationalists (and probably most 'ordinary' Serbs) remained much more interested in an all-embracing Serbian *national* state, even when a multinational Yugoslav state was what was on offer. Arguably, the major Habsburg blunders between 1907 and 1914 stemmed from a 'mistaken analogy between the Italian and South Slav movements'. Force had seemed to be the only answer to irreconcilable Italian nationalism, so it was increasingly advocated against the South Slavs too. Yet most Croats and even most of the Serbs within the Monarchy seemed quite happy to remain Habsburg subjects (and even continued to serve quite loyally in the Habsburg armies), provided they received the 'national' recognition and rights to which they felt themselves entitled (Taylor 1976: 211).

However, even while Austria-Hungary and Serbia seemed to be set on a collision course which threatened to precipitate a larger showdown between the Central Powers and Russia (and its allies), there were also wiser heads who attempted to pull both sides back from the brink. Most notably, the Serbian Premier Vladan Georgievich placed an article in a Viennese newspaper signalling Serbia's willingness to enter the Habsburg Monarchy, 'claiming in return only such a degree of independence as was possessed by

Bavaria inside the German Empire' and, as late as 1912, another Serb Premier, Nicolai Pashich, asked Tomas Masaryk to present far-reaching proposals for an economic union (Jaszi 1929: 406–7). However, such overtures were 'contemptuously rebuffed' by Austria-Hungary (Taylor 1976: 218). As Count Polzer-Holditz, *chef de cabinet* to Emperor Karl (1916–18), recalled in 1928: 'Nobody thought of revising our Balkan policy, for this would have involved a complete change in our internal policy. The understanding that the hatred of Serbia . . . was caused by our customs policy, that the Southern Slavs did not want anything else than to unite themselves and to get an outlet to the sea, that by our Albanian policy we closed the last valve and therefore an explosion became inevitable; this understanding was never attained by the ruling elements' (quoted in Jaszi 1929: 420).

For these and other reasons there can be little doubt that 'responsibility for the war falls, in the first place, upon the Dual Monarchy' (Jaszi 1929: 423). This 'primordial responsibility' of Austria-Hungary was governed 'not by personal crimes of her statesmen, but by the social and national sins of the whole system' (p. 428). It was motivated 'by the conviction that its internal situation had become unbearable because it could no longer solve its own problems' (p. 425). Furthermore, 'leading Viennese circles . . . precipitated the war because . . . the position of Austria would have become more untenable from year to year'. They feared that 'with the completion of those military reforms which were going on in Russia and France, and with the growth of anti-Austrian irredentistic propaganda, the odds for Austria would have become practically null' (p. 428). The war party in Vienna was eager for action. 'Like an elderly man whose powers are failing, the Habsburg Monarchy sought to recover its youth by a display of virility' (Taylor 1976: 214). Declaring war on Serbia was supposed to reassert Austria-Hungary's flagging status as a great power (p. 233). Germany's fatal error, following the shock of the Sarajevo assassination, was to give Austria-Hungary *carte blanche* to respond as it wished, instead of trying to restrain its aggrieved ally. (Germany's rulers assumed, mistakenly, that Austria-Hungary would act responsibly.) Beyond that, it is just about conceivable that the ensuing conflict could have been confined to the Balkans if Germany had not also been spoiling for a fight with Russia. But it appears more likely that, amid considerable last-minute misgivings and cold feet, the German Empire felt compelled to follow its ally 'into its leap to death' (Jaszi 1929: 426).

Count Czernin, one of the last Habsburg Foreign Ministers, later wrote: 'It is, of course, impossible to say in what manner the fall of the Monarchy would have occurred had the war been averted. Certainly in a less terrible fashion than was the case through the war. Probably much more slowly, and doubtless without dragging the whole world into the whirlpool. We were bound to die. We were at liberty to choose the manner of our death, and we chose the most terrible' (Czernin 1920: 38).

JASZI'S 'CENTRIPETAL' AND 'CENTRIFUGAL' FORCES

In his seminal study of the opposing social forces involved in *The Dissolution of the Habsburg Monarchy* (1929), Oscar Jaszi identified eight supranational 'centripetal forces' which had held the empire together for centuries: 'The dynasty, the army, the aristocracy, the Roman Catholic Church, the bureaucracy, capitalism (represented in its majority by Jews), the free-trade unity and (however strange it may appear) socialism' (p. 134).

The Austrian Habsburgs saw themselves as the divinely ordained, absolutist defenders of the easternmost bulwark of Roman Catholic Christendom against heretical religious reform movements (notably Hussitism, Lutheranism and Calvinism), against the 'infidel threat' of the Ottoman Turks (who laid siege to Vienna in 1529 and 1683) and, from 1815 to 1918, against revolution (whether it be republican, nationalist, socialist or atheist). They upheld a supranational, purely dynastic conception of the state. 'The whole Empire was simply regarded as the extension of the *Hausmacht*, the patrimonial possessions of the dynasty' (p. 137). The 'most powerful pillar' of the Habsburg Empire was its unified, German-speaking supranational army, created by and solely responsible to the monarch (p. 141). As late as 1910 'at least 85 per cent of its officers were Germans' (p. 279).

The roles of the dynasty and its army were reinforced by those of the aristocracy and the Roman Catholic higher clergy as 'the chief maintaining elements of the absolutist power' (p. 220). Even after it had lost most of its legal privileges, the power of the aristocracy 'rivalled that of the monarch until the very end of the Empire' (p. 149). Some Austrian magnates owned over seventy villages and were virtual kings of their own domains, while in Hungary proper those magnates possessing more than 1,420 acres each owned 40 per cent of all land holdings. 'Though the revolution of 1848 and . . . the system of Bach destroyed feudalism from the point of view of law, and gave landed property to a part of the peasantry, the power of the leading feudal circles continued in the economic order, in the political structure, and in the moral values of society' (p. 222). About half the aristocracy lived in Vienna and moved in court circles (p. 150). They dominated the empire through their residual economic, political and administrative power and by virtue of their continuing social prestige. 'A democratic type of citizenship could not develop', because most upwardly mobile commoners still ultimately aspired to enter the lower ranks of the nobility; indeed, 'The smile of the feudal lord and the invitation into his castle were honours which few common citizens could resist' (p. 237). The aristocracy also remained 'the chief representative of the Habsburg state ideal' (p. 150). In most areas, however, the Habsburgs had 'partly tamed, partly extirpated the native nobility and replaced it with a loyal aristocracy'; and the more the empire became commercialized, industrialized and democratized, thereby enhancing the position of burghers and peasants, the more the aristocracy became 'an isolated body . . . a stranger in the soil where it was planted by the donations of the Habsburgs' (p. 151).

In 1910 the Roman Catholic Church claimed the allegiance of 91 per cent of the population in Austria and of 60 per cent of the population in Hungary proper, partly by lumping in Uniates (Ukrainian Catholics of the Orthodox rite) with Roman Catholics (p. 160). The power of the Church in the Habsburg Empire was based upon the 'backward cultural condition of the rural masses'; the vast wealth and land holdings accumulated by the Church over many centuries; the 'imposing splendour' of its art, architecture and music, which combined 'the material powers of lay feudalism with the force of spiritual culture'; its educational and charitable institutions; its supranational standing and outlook; and 'its constitutional privileges, by which it influenced, to a large extent, the legislature' (p. 155). In Austria the Church endeavoured to soothe national differences and become a protector of the underprivileged Slav majority, but in Hungary it remained 'the chief pillar' of the dynasty, feudalism and Magyar hegemony (pp. 157, 161). However, while the Roman Catholic Counter-Reformation had increased the power of both Church and state and had purged out most traces of Protestantism and Hussitism, it sometimes came close to snuffing out creativity and freethinking and it destroyed or drove into exile large numbers of valuable Protestant merchants, artisans and entrepreneurs. Moreover, the heavy, majestic 'baroque grandeur' to which the Counter-Reformation gave rise was ultimately superficial, sterile and stultifying (other than in music, which was able to flourish as part of an imposing, showy and awe-inspiring imperial facade).

The centralizing German-speaking imperial bureaucracy, with its almost mindless devotion to duty, uniformity and regulation, did its best to extirpate all forms of particularism and autonomy and to perpetuate the *Polizeistaat* of Metternich and Bach. Nevertheless, 'compared with . . . South-eastern Europe, it represented a very honourable degree of order, accuracy, honesty and humanitarianism . . . and it could seldom be accused of brutality toward the poor and the oppressed' (p. 166). In the end it even acquiesced in the growth of separate Magyar, Polish, Czech and South Slav bureaucracies (p. 167).

Another of the 'most powerful forces' holding the Empire together was the 'growing capitalistic penetration of its economic organization . . . The Empire gained through it a unity of economic life, a more complete division of labour and a more efficient credit system.' The principal 'bearer and leader' of this capitalist imperialism was the German-speaking bourgeoisie, whose interests and power radiated 'throughout the entire monarchy' (p. 170). Moreover, until Austrian capitalism was fatally disfigured and fractured by the emergence of Schönerer's antisemitic pan-Germanism (1884–1918) and the meteoric rise of Karl Lueger's antisemitic Christian Social Party (1887–1918), it had possessed a loyal ally in the Jewish community. Jewish capitalists came to control the liberal press, the textile and clothing industry and the biggest bank (the Creditanstalt), which by the 1920s had acquired control of most of Austria's industrial share capital. The 1780s 'emancipation' of the Jews had called into existence the most loyal of all Austrians, the only ethnic group that unswervingly placed imperial before national loyalties. 'The Jew was not only the chief representative of the capitalist system but also that of the Austrian state idea' (p. 173). Moreover, the Jews remained predominantly German-speaking, even though, with the development of national consciousness, they increasingly assimilated the languages and customs of the nations among whom they lived.

From 1850 to 1914 the diverse peoples of the Habsburg Empire supposedly enjoyed the benefits of free trade behind a common external tariff. This trade policy was intended to promote both imperial *Autarkie* (self-sufficiency) and complementary specialization or interdependence between the diverse peoples and territories. 'There can be no doubt that, if all the possibilities of the free-trade policy had been utilized in the right way, the centrifugal and particularist tendencies could have been checked by the growing economic solidarity of the various nations' (p. 185). Jaszi surmised that, if the various constituent territories of the empire had fully participated in sufficient levels of economic development, prosperity, mutual trade, division of labour and growing together, then the greatly enhanced interdependence might have overridden and outweighed the separatist 'centrifugal' forces, filling 'with a real content the economic framework created by the will of the Emperor'; although there remained the opposite possibility that 'industrialization would have lessened the economic interdependence among the various parts of the Empire' (pp. 189, 194).

Finally, the (Marxist) Austrian Social Democratic Party established by Viktor Adler in 1889 was a major supranational cohesive force in so far as it sought to transcend 'bourgeois' national rivalries and unite workers and labourers of all nationalities in the 'common struggle' for social justice. Its outstanding Marxist theoreticians, Karl Renner and Otto Bauer, denounced 'bourgeois' separatist aspirations and campaigned for cultural and educational autonomy and equality for ethnic groups united in a supra-national confederation or *Staatenstaat* which could eventually serve as the model or embryo for a future European socialist polity transcending national differences and conflicts. They appreciated that the 'national problems' posed the greatest threat to the realization of their socialist ambitions. Hence they 'considered the elimination or at least the mitigation of national struggles as a paramount precondition for social and cultural progress' (p. 178). In the end, paradoxically, the 'chief defenders' of imperial economic unity were *not* its rich beneficiaries, 'the German high bourgeoisie and the Magyar landed interests, but the leading theoreticians of socialism' (p. 181). This unexpected source of support against particularism and separatism contributed to Emperor Franz Joseph's bold decision to provide for proletarian representation in the Austrian parliament (*Reichsrat*) in 1897 and to impose universal male suffrage in time for the *Reichsrat* elections of 1907. The social democratic stance found favour among those (mainly German-speaking) workers who perceived the dangers of nationalist bigotry and who realized that the prosperity of Austria's major industries and the prosperity of their employees depended upon the maintenance of empire-wide markets and imperial state contracts and procurement. Hence Austrian Marxism and proletarian internationalism were driven into a tacit unholy alliance with the Habsburgs.

Jaszi argued that the 'centripetal forces' were ultimately incapable of holding the empire together, partly because 'these forces did not constitute a united front'. Only the dynasty, the army, the aristocracy and the Church were (albeit incompletely) 'united in a real political architectural scheme. The other four were conflicting with the first four and even with each other on important points' (p. 134). Moreover, some of the (erstwhile) forces of integration and cohesion became sources of imperial disintegration and dissension during the twilight years of the Habsburg Monarchy (p. 133). For example, the increasingly strident Magyar opposition to Austrian insistence on German as the sole language of command in the imperial army became a major rallying point of demands for 'total Hungarian independence' (p. 143), while the Hungarian bureaucracy 'developed into one of the chief separatist and centrifugal forces' (p. 169). Several sections of the Roman Catholic Church also abetted and sympathized with the development of national consciousness; some prominent Catholic clergy, such as Bishop Strossmayer in Croatia, Father Janez Krek in Slovenia and Fathers Hlinka and Juriga in Slovakia, 'became really the most outstanding leaders of their people in the fight for national emancipation' (pp. 157–8, 162). This, in response, encouraged the growth of the *Los von Rom* ('away from Rome') movement among Austrian pan-Germans, who increasingly saw Austrian Roman Catholicism as an obstacle to their cherished goal of union with the mainly Protestant north Germans (pp. 158–9). Yet the Habsburgs could not abandon their close link with the Roman Catholic Church because their authority and legitimacy were inextricably bound up with their position as guardians of the faith and as heirs to the former Holy Roman Empire. They benefited greatly from ecclesiastical support.

Similarly, aristocratic power and property eventually became more of a liability than a source of cohesion and strength. By impeding agrarian change 'the landed oligarchy weakened the centripetal forces of the monarchy and at the same time increased the dissolving tendencies' (p. 201). The aristocracy was becoming 'more and more a parasitic caste, performing no serious work in the interest of the state' (p. 119). Moreover, the state was ruled by 'the rigid class interest of the feudal nobility and the financial capitalism attached to it'. This 'envenomed' the empire's moral, intellectual and political atmosphere and outlook, which became a curious blend of 'feudalism, clericalism and usurious capitalism' and 'the focus of all centrifugal tendencies' (pp. 219, 234). Finally, during the First World War, 'the corrupt cruelty of the feudal administration in the backward parts of the monarchy . . . fomented despair . . . and hatred against the state and became a chief cause of dissolution' (p. 238).

Austrian Social Democracy also proved incapable of holding the ring. Despite its claim that it possessed 'the panacea of national struggles', the socialist movement was unable even to unite the various national sections of the working class in a single, supranational party. 'The truth is that national solidarity vanquished class solidarity. The centrifugal forces were victorious even in the labour movement.' Thus, starting with the Czechs, workers and socialists of the underprivileged non-metropolitan nations began to form their own separate socialist and trade union movements and organizations in 1907–10, in time to compete (successfully) with the Austrian Social Democratic Party in the 1911 *Reichsrat* elections (p. 184). Indeed, the empire's 'real problem' was not how to achieve 'the annihilation of all historical individualities . . . in the unity of a nationless superstate (as the Socialists . . . imagined), but to give fair opportunity to the nations to build up their own states . . . and to combine them as equal members of a confederation' (p. 246).

Likewise, capitalism and internal free trade failed to realize their full potential as 'the most decisive and efficient' centripetal forces (p. 171), or as 'forces tending toward cohesion and integration' (p. 208). 'Not only in the backward agrarian provinces . . . but even in upper and lower Austria and in Bohemia, where a strong manufacturing and financial organization was established, the bourgeois class always stood under the sway of the feudal and court atmosphere. What was called liberalism in the monarchy was only an artificial plant introduced by the revolutionary intellectuals of 1848 and gradually faded away.' In both Austria and Hungary 'liberalism exhausted itself' in rarified constitutional and anticlerical contests. It mouthed the rhetoric of West European liberalism 'but it was never in real contact with the popular forces of society', for whose interests and problems it displayed little sympathy or understanding (p. 171). Moreover, as capitalism and the bourgeoisie increasingly fractured and developed along ethnic lines, liberalism was eclipsed by the rise of nationalism and antisemitism (p. 172). In the end 'Austrian capitalism developed serious centrifugal tendencies by fomenting racial and national struggles' (p. 173). Indeed, 'capitalism led inevitably toward the strengthening of national feeling and consciousness' (p. 176).

Furthermore, with the emergence of predominantly German and Jewish finance capitalism and monopoly capitalism in the empire's main industrial and financial centres (Vienna, Styria and Bohemia-Moravia), 'the backward agrarian countries of the Empire played for a long time the same role as the colonies beyond the seas did for the Western states; and . . . Austrian capitalism employed very often . . . the unscrupulous methods of colonial capitalism' (p. 170). Thus the burgeoning Austrian investment banks and industrial combines and cartels successfully lobbied for higher import tariffs, behind which they were able to 'monopolize the advantages of protection' (captive markets, economic rent and monopolistic profits) at the consumers' expense (p. 205). By the same token the metropolitan industrial and financial centres profited at the expense of the poor, non-German and predominantly agrarian periphery (pp. 206–7). Thus, according to Jaszi's analysis (which itself drew heavily on the influential theses of the Austrian Marxist economist Rudolf Hilferding): 'This . . . monopolistic cartel policy of Austro-German finance capital and of certain Hungarian groups connected with it controlled almost all branches of industry. It was an economic tyranny which hindered progress in the Hungarian, Slav and Romanian territories of the monarchy . . . It is, therefore, quite natural that the working people and certain parts of the intelligentsia . . . should regard with growing dissatisfaction, even with hatred, the leading Austrian financial powers' (p. 206). The crucial point is that the non-German subjects of the Habsburg Empire felt increasingly dominated by the combined weight of Austrian and German monopolistic finance capitalism and imperialism, against which their own burgeoning capitalist ventures looked rather puny and vulnerable. This looked set to re-establish Austro-German dominance and exploitation of East Central Europe on new, more modern and much stronger foundations, to the dismay of many Slavs.

Jaszi was convinced that 'purely idealistic motives had a preponderant role in the national movements', yet he was 'equally sure that very real economic interests were unconsciously fostering them' (p 208). He was also convinced that the territorial and ethnic configuration of the empire was not conducive to the full realization of the economic benefits of capitalism and internal free trade. Industrial development was largely confined to the Czech Lands, the Vienna region and Styria. This comparatively localized industrial development failed to create enough interdependence between the manufacturing and agricultural regions 'to counterbalance the centrifugal tendencies that had arisen within the territory of the customs union'. The empire was 'not the outcome of a natural economic evolution based on economic advantage, but the artificial creation of the Habsburgs . . . Bohemia was connected with Vienna by political boundaries, whereas its natural outlet would have been the valley of the Elbe, leading toward . . . Germany and the North Sea . . . Galicia sloped toward the Baltic . . . and was separated from the bulk of the monarchy by . . . the Carpathians . . . natural obstacles made the building of railways and their operation costly . . . the various regions were not sufficiently connected by navigable waterways' (p. 189).

The ethnic diversity of the empire, in Jaszi's view, further increased the actual fragmentation (or 'segmentation') of the formally unified imperial market, because the various populations 'stood on different cultural levels and produced and consumed according to different habits and traditions'. Hence manufacturers had to produce different designs or styles of consumer products (and even tools and equipment) for each national region or market and to cope with a great diversity of cultures and languages. This assisted the survival of dispersed production by small high-cost establishments and reduced the scope for mass production, specialization and economies of scale (p. 208). Had there been greater prosperity and higher levels of consumption, Jaszi suggested, 'the geographical and national differentiation of the various regions would not have been a disadvantage but a real advantage', fostering greater inter-regional 'industrial specialization'. Given 'the low standard of life of the masses', however, the scope for inter-regional division of labour, interdependence and specialization was limited. 'The result was that the forces of dissolution were more powerful than the forces of unification. The dissolving tendency became particularly evident after 1907' (p. 209). Most controversially, Jaszi suggested that Austria-Hungary was 'already a defeated empire from the economic point of view' when it went to war in 1914 (p. 210). In these various ways, therefore, 'the most powerful centripetal forces which could have built up a real cohesion of the Empire developed more and more centrifugal tendencies' (p. 212).

In the final analysis, according to Jaszi, the Habsburg Empire foundered on its inability to solve the national problem. 'All the centrifugal forces were national' or at least assumed nationalistic forms, whether as the 'particularism' of regional landlord interests or as the struggles of rising national bourgeoisies for occupational advancement (especially into administrative positions) or as the land hunger and demands for radical land redistribution emanating from the emergent peasant nations (p. 215). 'The Empire collapsed because the historic tradition of each nation stood in a hostile and hateful way against the historical experiences of the other nations . . . The Monarchy collapsed on the psychic fact that it could not . . . establish a reciprocity among the different experiences, sentiments and ideals of the various nations' (p. 130).

From 1848 to 1918, after 'the hydra-heads of feudal particularism were already cut down', democratic nationalism was the major 'new force' which attacked the cohesion and integrity of the Habsburg Empire. Moreover, while the dynasty had defeated 'with comparative ease' feudal particularism based on oppressive and outmoded seigneurial prerogatives, the new 'democratic nationalism', which sought to reconstruct the Habsburg domains on the basis of 'popular' (alias national) sovereignty, represented 'a higher principle of political organization which the dynasty could not conquer' (pp. 246–7). The struggles of the subjugated nations were 'directed against the economic and cultural monopolies of the two hegemonic nations', the Austrian Germans and the Magyars, against whom they could triumph only by way of wholesale 'transformation' of the entire political structure (p. 282). The Habsburg Empire was torn apart by a combination of 'the blind resistance of the privileged nations against the new forces and the exaggerated claims of the formerly oppressed when they became sufficiently powerful to reverse the situation', that is, to turn the tables on their masters (p. 267). Their struggles were essentially a contest between the haves and the have-nots: between 'those in power' and 'those outside the controlling power' (p. 282). Indeed, the hegemonic nations were so convinced of their own superiority and leading role that they regarded 'the national awakening of their former bondsmen as almost a social impossibility'. For the most part the ruling groups were 'incapable of a sympathetic understanding with the national aspirations of the oppressed peoples'. The political dangers were heightened by their 'blindness concerning the nature and origin of the national movements . . . This blindness became fatal when the absolutistic state was replaced by democratic forces.' The ruling groups 'did not try to solve the problem but rather to maintain their national privileges . . . Magyar feudalism firmly opposed all efforts . . . to reform the constitution in a spirit more favourable to the Slavs' (p. 216).

Jaszi concluded that the 'outstanding groups of causes which undermined the cohesion of the old patrimonial state' were: (i) 'The growing national consciousness of the various nations which could not find a place for a true consolidation and adequate self-expression in the rigidity of the absolutist structure' (p. 453); (ii) 'The economic and social pressure of the feudal class rule, allied with a usurious kind of capitalism', which together prevented the productive potential of each of the constituent nations and territories of the empire from developing to the full; the growing indignation and exasperation of the 'weaker nations' were intensified 'by the feeling of being a kind of colony of German capitalism' as well as of 'big Viennese finance' (p. 453); (iii) 'The lack of any serious kind of civic education. All the nations lived as . . . strangers to one another. Both the dynastic epic in Austria and the feudal [one] in Hungary were incapable of creating a sufficiently strong and cohesive state idea' (p. 453).

Jaszi also concluded that the 'growing dissolution and final collapse of the Habsburg Empire' had three main causes: (i) 'The continuous growth of the various nations', whose leaders increasingly realized that their hope of a comprehensive federalization of the Empire was 'fallacious', encouraging them to turn their thoughts to 'separation or secession'; (ii) the irredentism of adjacent states which aspired to liberate their compatriots living under Habsburg 'oppression'; (iii) 'The disintegrating influence of the World War, which made the latent hatred between nations burst into flame', thereby allowing 'dissatisfied intelligentsias' to step up their struggles against the empire, while internal conflict and dissension 'gradually paralyzed the moral and economic forces of the monarchy' (p. 454); from the outset, however, Jaszi maintained that 'the World War was not the *cause*, but only the final liquidation of the deep inner crisis of the monarchy' (p. 23).

Some of Jaszi's claims and hypotheses have been challenged or even refuted. In particular, the nature and impact of nationalism in Eastern Europe and the relationship between the rise of nationalism and imperial disintegration have remained subjects of intense debate. Moreover, the quantitative historical evidence assembled by Rudolph (1975, 1976, 1983), Katus (1970), Huertas (1977), Good (1979, 1980, 1984), Eddie (1985) and Komlos (1983a, b) has demonstrated beyond all reasonable doubt that the rate of economic development achieved in both Austria and Hungary from the 1830s to 1913 compares quite favourably with that of most other parts of Europe and that inter-regional economic integration and convergence proceeded apace, despite (or perhaps because of) the emergence of monopolistic finance capitalism and the exploitation of the imperial 'peripheries' by the metropolitan 'core'. Whatever its political, social and military failings, the traditional picture of the nineteenth-century Habsburg Empire as a severe economic 'laggard' or 'failure' is ill-founded and misleading. (Admittedly, 3.5 million people 'voted with their feet' by emigrating from Austria-Hungary between 1876 and 1914. Yet this was not so very different from the concurrent mass emigration from Scandinavia, Germany, Italy, Greece, Spain and the United Kingdom. Mass emigration was more a social safety valve than clear-cut evidence of economic failure.)

But it is testimony to the ingenuity and erudition of Jaszi's theses and analytical framework that they still provide the explicit or implicit point of departure and the conceptual underpinnings of most systematic analyses of the dissolution of the Habsburg Empire (at least among Anglophone academics). More recent research may be furnishing different answers, but it is still very much indebted to Jaszi for setting the agenda and for framing the key questions with such brilliance, insight and flair.

NATIONALISM AND IMPERIAL DISINTEGRATION

The role of nationalism in the dissolution of the Habsburg Monarchy has continued to be the subject of vigorous historiographical debate. Writers in the Jaszi tradition have continued to accord the rise of nationalism pride of place, but others have argued against the notion that it was the root cause of the empire's collapse. Some have even denied that it constituted a serious threat to the empire's survival.

Fischer-Galati (1963), for example, has written that the aspirations and demands of the leaders of autonomist and separatist movements 'carried little weight', because the central authorities believed that 'they were not representative of the wishes of the population' (p. 32). Therefore, 'as long as Vienna was able to satisfy the socio-economic demands of the aristocracy and middle classes and hold out the prospect of improvement of the lot of the peasantry, all under the umbrella of *Kaisertreue*, the Empire was secure . . . These considerations emphasize the politically innocuous nature of nationalism and nationalistic manifestation as such in the Habsburg state system' (p. 33). He does concede that the integrity of the Habsburg Empire did come under serious threat in the South Slav lands and in Transylvania following the emergence of the independent states of Serbia and Romania in 1877–78. But, even so, 'the activities of Southern Slav and Romanian politicians as such did not alarm Vienna. The Monarchy's apprehension stemmed from the possibility of international, primarily Russian, support of . . . nationalistic manifestations inside and outside the Empire', i.e. the 'internationalization' of the empire's internal 'nationality problems' and the extension to Austria-Hungary of stratagems 'that had contributed to the gradual dissolution of the Ottoman Empire'. He concludes that 'only two phenomena' could have mortally threatened the Habsburg Empire: not nationalism as such, but either 'social revolution' or 'intervention by outside powers acting primarily as supporters of the nationalistic, unionistic aspirations of Romanian and Southern Slav politicians outside and inside the Empire' (p. 35). In this interpretation nationalists would have remained innocuous minor irritants had not outside powers been 'winding them up' and lending them 'muscle'. The central defects of this kind of analysis concern the implicit underestimation of the independent mobilizing power of most modern nationalist movements, which develop a life of their own that can lead in directions which are unwelcome to their supposed 'sponsors' and 'manipulators'; and, conversely, overestimation of the extent to which such movements can be 'bought off'. Even Magyar nationalism was far from assuaged or satisfied by the special privileged status granted to the kingdom of Hungary from 1867 to 1918. On the contrary, it encouraged Magyar nationalists to demand still greater independence for Hungary. Moreover, Europe has been littered with examples of nationalist movements which have thrived on their nations' economic strengths and successes (most recently Flemish, Catalan, Basque, Scottish, Croat and Slovene nationalism), as well as ones which have expressed feelings of economic frustration and relative deprivation (e.g. Slovak, Kosovo-Albanian, Macedonian and nineteenth-century Irish nationalism).

According to Sugar (1963), the examples of Switzerland and Great Britain show that the mere existence of several distinct nationalities within a single state was 'not enough to doom the Habsburg state' (p. 43); and 'once the Slav revival passed its early cultural-linguistic stage . . . the idea of Slav unity was never a serious force in the Monarchy or a serious threat to Vienna' (p. 10). Indeed, Seton-Watson (1977: 118) claims that among Western Slavs 'the only common culture was Catholicism. That there was ever a specifically "Slav" culture common to Poles, Czechs and Croats is a myth.' However, even a *united* Slav challenge need not have threatened imperial unity. On the contrary, so-called 'Austro-Slavism' could have provided a broader basis and mandate for imperial cohesion. It can be argued that the real threats to imperial unity came not from dreams of Austro-Slav unity but from the emergence of numerous separate Slav national identities and loyalties. These really did erode or curtail Czech, Slovak, Polish, Slovene and Croatian allegiance to the emperor and the empire.

The rise of nationalism was certainly a double-edged sword. In one sense it posed a serious threat to imperial cohesion and unity by creating new non-imperial foci of identity and allegiance. On the other hand, by further fragmenting the imperial polity, and by pitting the various nationalities against one another, it made it easier for the Habsburgs to pursue a 'divide and rule' strategy against their more restive subjects. The Habsburgs 'consciously played off each ethnic minority against another'; Metternich himself declared that 'if the Hungarian revolts . . . we should immediately set the Bohemian against him, for they hate each other; and after him the Pole, or the German or the Italian' (Verdery 1979: 393–4).

It has even been argued that 'there were no dominant nationalities in the Austro-Hungarian Monarchy. There were only dominant classes.' Thus the so-called 'nationality conflict' in Hungary was in reality 'a conflict between the mainly Magyar upper class and both the Magyar and the non-Magyar lower classes', while the 'nationality conflict' in the Austrian half of the empire 'consisted primarily of clashes within the multinational propertied or educated class' (Deak 1967: 303). And, objectively, to 'downtrodden' and 'exploited' workers, peasants, servants and labourers, it ought to have made little difference whether their 'oppressors' and 'exploiters' were 'aliens' or their own 'compatriots'. Some of the harshest and most blatant oppression and 'exploitation' took place within (rather than between) ethnic groups. Nevertheless, particularly in the Austro-Hungarian Empire, class conflict frequently wore a national mask. Moreover, class hatreds were often envenomed and inflamed by ethnic antagonism towards 'alien' landlords, traders, moneylenders, shopkeepers and other (often Jewish) 'middlemen' or intermediaries, who came to be seen as agents and henchmen of malign political and economic systems and an obstacle to the fulfilment of both class and national aspirations. Indeed, while most analyses of the Monarchy's 'nationality problems' have tended to focus upon the struggles and grievances of the subordinate 'underdog' nations against their 'overlords' and 'masters', it should be borne in mind that the defence of political, economic and educational dominance, supremacy and privilege probably aroused just as much heat and passion among the dominant nationalities (Austrian Germans, Magyars and Galician Poles) as did the struggles for greater equality and autonomy on the part of the underprivileged nationalities (Czechs, Slovaks, Ruthenes, South Slavs and Romanians). The attitudes and the behaviour of the Austrian Germans, Magyars and Galician Poles sometimes resembled the fervour and self-righteousness with which whites defended their privileges over blacks in the American south and in South Africa. Furthermore, 'national' and 'racial' struggles usually subsume or amalgamate with economic and social ('class') struggles. That is partly what gives them such explosive power.

It has also been argued that 'practically no one wanted to see the Monarchy break up . . . It was only defeat in war, therefore, which was to precipitate collapse; and that defeat was not certain until the early summer of 1918' (Sked 1989: 187). Thus the Habsburg Monarchy did not founder on its inability to contain or resolve its nationality problem; 'it fell because it lost a major war'. Most of its subjects dutifully supported the Monarchy's war effort 'right up until the end. Before 1914, if anything, the nationality problem seemed to be abating. [The empire's] real weaknesses in 1914 were military and financial' (p. 264). It is erroneous to assume, just because the Habsburg Empire did not survive the First World War, that it must already have been in terminal or progressive decline before the war. 'At no point between 1867 and 1914 did the Monarchy even vaguely face the sort of challenge to its existence that it faced in 1848–49. The truth is that there was no internal pressure between 1867 and 1914 for the breakup of the

Monarchy; no repudiation of the dynasty; while in some areas problems were actually being solved or compromises reached. At the same time, economic growth was continuing and the Monarchy was becoming more and more integrated in terms of living standards, infrastructure and finance' (p. 231). Thus, while commercial, industrial and agricultural integration proceeded apace (pp. 199–202), there emerged a mutually acceptable economic 'compromise' between Austria and Hungary in 1907 (pp. 232–3) and mutually acceptable linguistic and electoral accommodations in Moravia in 1905 (p. 222) and in Bukovina in 1910 (p. 225). Moreover, Romania (as an ally of Germany and Austria-Hungary) was unwilling to foment separatist tendencies in Transylvania (p. 212), while the main political forces in Croatia, Bohemia and Austrian Poland (Galicia) were still concentrating on making gains within rather than outside the imperial framework (pp. 217, 223–4). 'No major leader or party called for the destruction of the Monarchy' (Jelavich 1983b: 231).

In similar vein, and in implicit criticism of Jaszi, Kohn (1967: 256) has claimed that 'it is a mistake to stress the unsolved nationality problems of the Monarchy as the fundamental causes of its fall. The integrating or disintegrating forces were not of decisive importance for the survival of the Monarchy.' In Kohn's view it was the empire's foreign policy blunders, especially in the 1860s, the 1870s and the 1900s, 'and not the conflict of nationalities, which brought about the collapse of the Monarchy' (p. 259). In this respect, paradoxically, 'the dominant nationalities . . . contributed more to the disintegration of the Monarchy than did the Slavic or Romanian peoples . . . not so much by their resistance to timely domestic reforms as by their nefarious influence on foreign policy' (p. 256). According to Kohn, the increasingly vulnerable Habsburg Empire should have espoused 'neutrality' and the territorial *status quo*, avoiding risky foreign policy adventures and estrangements. 'The alliance with the Prussian-German Empire, promoted by the Germans and Magyars in the Monarchy, and the occupation of Bosnia-Hercegovina were the most fundamental mistakes which carried within themselves the seeds of a coming catastrophe' (pp. 262–3). He also presciently pointed out that the 'conflict of nationalities' would continue for decades after the end of the Monarchy and that, if communist rule were ever removed, 'many of the now more or less quiescent nationality conflicts may flare up again with increased bitterness' (p. 259).

However, it should be emphasized that Jaszi fully recognized the baleful consequences of the Habsburg alliance with Germany (1879–1918) and of the growth of Magyar and Austrian-German national assertion, territorial ambition and resistance to federal solutions of the empire's nationality problems. But he incorporated them into the broader framework of his analysis of 'centrifugal forces' (see Jaszi 1929: 170, 271–82, 298–311, 340–3, 349–55, 384–5). He acknowledged that the 'belief in the unalterable mission of German hegemony, which was further strengthened and developed by the example of the German Empire, made the creation of a political atmosphere propitious for the fair discussion and solution of the national problems almost impossible' (p. 289); and that 'Magyar hegemony would become the grave-digger of the Monarchy because this was the *rocher de bronze* [hard rock] on which every effort for the federalization of the Monarchy broke down' (p. 297). Moreover, Jaszi was second to none in his assertion that an increasingly vulnerable and 'defensively aggressive' Habsburg Empire embroiled Germany in foreign policy gambles and provocations in which Germany had little or no direct stake and over which it had even less control. 'Germany stood perfectly isolated in Europe, bound to Austria for life and death . . . Germany was compelled to follow its fatal ally into its leap to death' (p. 426). Starting in the 1890s, the conviction grew in official and educated circles that the Germanic and Slavic worlds were on a collision course: a situation developed which forced Austria-Hungary 'step by step toward explosion, making the struggle between Habsburg imperialism and Russian Pan-Slavism more imminent from year to year' (p. 420). The tragedy was that 'nothing serious was undertaken for the solution of a vital problem, the colossal gravity of which was keenly felt by all intelligent observers . . . as the immediate cause of the approaching catastrophe' (p. 421).

The prime responsibility for this lemming rush towards Armageddon rested not with individuals but with more deep-seated systemic and cultural factors, including the rise of nationalism and inter-ethnic tensions. The forces which were desperately and aggressively clinging to feudal, military, bureaucratic, ecclesiastical and economic privileges and monopolies in Austria-Hungary 'came into conflict with the Pan-Slavistic, militaristic currents of the Czarist autocracy' (p. 422). 'Austria fixed the date of the conflict and Germany did not stop her ally. Here lies the promordial responsibility of Austria, motivated . . . by the social and national sins of the whole system.' Germany's sin, by contrast, was one of 'omission' rather than 'commission' (p. 428).

Many British, French and 'repentant' German historians have tried to pin the blame for the outbreak of the First World War on Germany, implicitly absolving the Habsburgs on the grounds that they were passive and/or dependent junior partners of Germany in the 'Dual Alliance' (1879–1918). However, while Austria-Hungary was undoubtedly the junior partner in terms of relative economic and military might, the Habsburg Empire drew Germany into a high-risk Balkan strategy which was dictated more by Austro-Hungarian than by German interests, ambitions and anxieties. As so often happens in history, the tail wagged the dog.

The Austrian Marxist Otto Bauer, who (like Jaszi) both analysed and participated in these events, similarly emphasized the close connection between the rise of nationalism, the intensification of Austria-Hungary's nationality problems, the causes of the First World War and the dissolution of the Habsburg Monarchy. 'The accentuation of national antagonisms during the years preceding the War shook the Empire to its foundations. The Monarchy attempted to overcome its permanent crisis at home through war abroad. Consequently it plunged into the war, but this act made its existence dependent upon the outcome of the war. The terrible sacrifices of blood and treasure which the war exacted hit the Slav peoples doubly hard: they seemed to them to be sacrifices for an alien state and for a hostile cause. The longer the war lasted, the more the national revolutionary movement against Austria gathered strength' (Bauer 1925: 71–2). In this analysis, the 'immediate cause' of the First World War was 'the collision of Habsburg imperialism with the movement towards freedom and unity among the South Slav peoples', which in turn 'ushered in the national revolution to which the Habsburg Monarch succumbed' (p. 11). In Bohemia, since 1897, 'the state had been convulsed by the struggle between Czechs and Germans; since 1903 the agitation in the Slav South had assumed menacing proportions' (p. 25). The 1914–18 war against Serbia both 'antagonized' and 'fired the national aspirations of the Czechs', while on its eastern flank the Monarchy 'lost Poland without winning the Ukraine'. Before long, moreover, 'Austria-Hungary was waging war not only against external enemies but also against two-thirds of its own citizens . . . and could only force its peoples to fight the external foe by using the coercive agencies of wartime Absolutism' (pp. 14, 24, 27).

Since 1848, if not earlier, various competing economic forces and social and nationalist movements and ideologies had been stoking the boiler for another convulsive upheaval across continental Europe, comparable to the French Revolution and the Napoleonic Wars. Although it was not inevitable that it should do so, the boiler finally exploded in 1914–18. Without the Great War the Monarchy might have survived for a few more decades. However, the scale of the 1914–18 war and the additional impetus it gave to the forces of nationalism and class conflict and to the willingness of the great powers to acquiesce in the emergence of a plethora of small nation-states in the buffer zone between Germany and Russia delivered the *coup de grâce* to the Habsburg Empire, although the root causes of its disintegration ran much deeper. According to an authority on the causes of the First World War, 'the primary cause of the war was a conflict between political frontiers and the distribution of peoples, the denial of . . . the right of self-determination . . . More than any other circumstance, this conflict between existing [states] and their unhappy minorities was responsible for the catastrophe of 1914' (Schmitt 1958: 6–7).

There was indeed an international dimension to the nationality problems of the Habsburg Empire. The nineteenth-century European states required the maintenance of a strict (albeit unrealistic) distinction between internal and international affairs. Internal affairs were considered to be 'none of the business' of other states; in international affairs states were expected to speak with a single (supposedly 'national') voice, despite the existence of competing and conflicting domestic interest groups (Lafore 1971: 55–6). However, this convenient (albeit arbitrary) distinction between internal and international affairs was increasingly difficult to sustain in the context of the Habsburg Empire. 'The Habsburg Monarchy was . . . a Great Power. But it was a Great Power that *consisted*, as it were, of the very anomalies that were troublesome side-issues for other Great powers . . . The other powers were constructed upon a foundation of nationality . . . Austria-Hungary consisted entirely of minorities . . . and it was impossible for its neighbours, themselves affected by its peculiar composition, to act towards it as they could towards a national state . . . Austria-Hungary was by 1914 unique in being a Great Power in whose affairs small ones meddled. The system provided no procedure for handling such a situation . . . It was this situation that brought about the outbreak of the First World War' (pp. 56–7). In that sense the Habsburg Monarchy was destroyed by the increasing difficulty of accommodating a supranational empire within a system of nation-states (p. 82).

One of the most perspicacious assessments of the relationship between the rise of nationalism and the disintegration of the Habsburg Empire has been furnished by the Czech Academician Jiri Koralka (1967: 147–50). In his view the fundamental challenge confronting the states of East Central and South-eastern Europe since the eighteenth century has been to embrace 'the great process of *social* change from the old, privileged, feudal society to a modern industrial society based upon the active participation of all inhabitants in social and political life' (p. 147). In this perspective 'the main reason for the disintegration of the Habsburg Empire was not nationalism as such, but the failure of the monarchy to create a national concept of its own which would be in harmony with the dynamic growth of modern capitalistic society' (p. 149). 'In Western Europe very heterogeneous ethnic groups and political territories were often united by dynasties into nation-states.' The major reason why the Habsburg dynasty did not follow suit lay 'neither in the way in which the nucleus of the Austrian Empire was formed . . . nor in the strong position which its constituent parts, especially the Kingdoms of Hungary and Bohemia, enjoyed'. Rather, the Habsburgs scarcely even attempted to unify their heterogeneous domains into 'a West European-style nation-state' because they were 'overburdened for too long ... with the heritage of universalism of the Holy Roman Empire'. Until 1866 the Habsburgs' attentions 'were not exclusively, and sometimes not even primarily, concentrated on those lands which actually formed the Empire which broke to pieces in 1918' (p. 148). They were repeatedly distracted by their dynastic ambitions in Italy, in the Netherlands, in Spain and, most fatefully, in Germany. The overstretched empire ultimately fell back upon a policy of trying 'to live with all the problems without ever really attempting to solve them' (p. 149). In the end the collapse of the empire was 'a logical consequence of the inability of the monarchy to create its own concept of a modern society. Wherever a *number* of modern national societies rather than a *single* modern society have evolved within an empire it has been impossible to halt this development at the ethnic-cultural stage and prevent the formulation of political nation-state programmes' (p. 150).

This relatively undoctrinaire Marxist explanation, avoiding crude economic determinism while emphasizing broad societal changes (such as the rise of capitalism, the erosion of privilege and political mobilization of the masses) and the inability of the Habsburg dynasty to come to terms with the modern world, ought to be quite acceptable to many liberals and nationalists. The first duty of every Habsburg emperor was to defend the Habsburg patrimony, comprising a great diversity of territories and peoples, none of whom held a position of absolute predominance. Thus, even though the majority of imperial officers and officials were German-speaking (and German remained the lingua franca of administration, commerce and military command), the last four emperors could not afford to adopt German nationalism as a state ideology or to become exclusively identified with the interests and aspirations of their German-speaking subjects. With considerable justification Emperor Franz Joseph (1848–1916) in particular viewed anticlerical Austrian-German liberalism, nationalist pan-Germanism, the *Los von Rom* movement and Karl Lueger's antisemitic Christian Social Party with deep suspicion and mistrust, as implicit challenges or threats to his power, authority and position as the ruler and 'spiritual custodian' of a Roman Catholic multinational empire. (Indeed, he repeatedly annulled the election of the demagogue Karl Lueger as Mayor of Vienna.) In order to retain at least the passive allegiance of a majority of his non-German subjects (especially the propertied classes among them), Franz Joseph had to make a show of standing above narrow 'national' and 'sectional' interests; and, for a large part of his seemingly interminable reign, he ruled with the support of a predominantly Slavic, Catholic, conservative coalition (1879–93), *against* the faintly liberal, anticlerical and pan-German leanings of the Austrian-German 'chattering classes' at that time. A 'national consolidation' of monarchical absolutism was a viable stratagem for the Hohenzollerns in Germany and for the Romanovs in Russia, but it was out of the question for the Habsburgs in Austria-Hungary.

It is sometimes argued that 'the decline of the constitutional power of the monarch was even more a disintegrating force in the Habsburg Empire than nationalism. The common allegiance of the peoples under Habsburg rule was a very powerful centripetal factor in the eighteenth century. This feeling of common loyalty to the crown rapidly declined during ... the next century, precisely when [it] was more necessary than ever to offset the increasing strength of centrifugal forces' (Kann 1967: 25, 29). In similar vein, A.J.P.

Taylor (1967: 130–1) has contended that 'the Habsburg monarchy was not a multinational empire; it was a supranational empire. Nations can perhaps co-operate if they have a common loyalty to bind them together; they cannot co-operate, at any rate within a single state, merely for the sake of co-operating. The Habsburgs had once provided the common loyalty; in the nineteenth century they failed to do so any longer, and it was this Habsburg failure, not the rise of the nationalities, which doomed their Empire.'

These are important considerations, but in these instances Taylor and Kann have underplayed the crucial role of the rise of nationalism and hence of specifically *national* allegiances in diminishing and eventually replacing or superseding popular (and especially middle-class) allegiance to the supranational Habsburg Monarchy. Indeed, Kann had to concede that 'nationalism was a much greater debilitating force in Austria-Hungary than anywhere else in Europe' (Kann 1967: 25). And in one of his major works Taylor took a very different line. During the nineteenth century, he maintained, the various nations of the Habsburg Empire 'began to have their own wishes and ambitions, and these proved in the end incompatible with each other and with the survival of the dynasty' (Taylor 1976: 21). To some extent the national movements were locked in a zero sum game: the aspirations of each could be met only at the others' expense; any attempt to meet their demands also weakened the Monarchy as a whole. Thus 'the Habsburg Monarchy and nationalism were incompatible; no peace was possible between them' (p. 40).

Nationalism not only asserted the interests and aspirations of the constituent peoples and territories of the empire at the expense of the centre. It also posited a different basis for relations between the constituent peoples and territories; a different political configuration ('nation-states', whether confederated or fully independent, in place of empire); and a different principle and source of authority and legitimacy (the nation/people and national/popular sovereignty, in place of the dynasty/monarchy). The scope for resentments, rivalry and conflict between 'nationalities' was made all the greater by the pervasiveness of Habsburg 'paternalism' and the virtual absence of private and hence independent schools, universities, hospitals and railways; by 1890 they were nearly all state-owned. Consequently, 'the appointment of every school teacher, of every railway porter, of every hospital doctor, of every tax collector, was a signal for national struggle' (Taylor 1976: 173). The underdevelopment of independent, private activity ('civil society') helped to 'politicize' such appointments.

In Taylor's view the major challenge to the survival of the Habsburg Empire came not from the periphery but from Bohemia: 'When the Czechs abandoned the Habsburg Monarchy, they condemned it to death.' It could have survived the 'amputation' of territories inhabited mainly by Serbs, Romanians, Poles, Ruthenes and Italians; but an independent Bohemia would 'kill it' (Taylor 1976: 238–9). During the nineteenth century the Czechs were no longer oppressed and downtrodden *as a nation*, even if (or indeed because) more and more Czechs were oppressed and 'exploited' *as workers*, when Bohemia became the industrial heartland of the Habsburg Monarchy. The Czechs developed 'their own university and cultural life and gained an increasing share in the administration of Bohemia'. They produced a capitalist class which very successfully oppressed and 'exploited' fellow Czechs. Yet the salient struggle in Bohemia was not the class struggle but the struggle between Czechs and Germans: 'a conflict between two nations, each determined to assert its historical tradition' (p. 203). Taylor argues that 'this conflict was impossible of peaceful solution. The Czechs could not be satisfied with the use of their language . . . They claimed, and had to claim, possession of their national home' (p. 204). But, because that would 'dethrone' the hitherto dominant Bohemian German propertied classes, the latter were bound to resist tooth and nail. This bitter conflict was to have fateful consequences. Even more than Vienna, Bohemia became the crucible of Germanic 'National Socialism' before it was 'exported' to Weimar Germany in the 1920s. Second, the self-pitying plight of the 'dethroned' Bohemian (alias Sudeten) Germans in inter-war Czechoslovakia was to provide the pretext for Hitler's two-staged incorporation of Bohemia into an expanded Nazi Germany in September 1938 and March 1939 (the true beginning of the Second World War). Third, by setting dangerous precedents and giving hostages to fortune, by decimating the private sector of the Czechoslovak economy and by seriously compromising the rule of law, the summary expulsion of over 3 million Bohemian Germans in 1945–46 launched post-war Czechoslovakia down the slippery slope from (circumscribed) democracy to Stalinism. Finally, as Taylor later shrewdly observed, the experience of inter-war Czechoslovakia 'served to answer the great "if only" of Habsburg history: if only the Habsburgs had been more far-sighted and democratic'. Inter-war Czechoslovakia could not have had a more enlightened, liberal, conciliatory President than Tomas Garrigue Masaryk (1918–35), yet 'Czechs and Germans were not reconciled: instead it became clear that the two could not live within the . . . same state' (p. 254).

By 1918 every major nationality within the Habsburg Empire had its own written language, literary tradition, historians, schools and nascent or fully fledged intelligentsia, who sought preferred placements in the emergent 'national' bureaucracies, schools, universities, legal professions and newspapers. Nevertheless, in the final analysis, the nationality problem was not merely a matter of schooling and public positions. These were just the *hors d'oeuvres*. Sooner or later the emergent nations would seek or demand the power to determine their own destinies. In the final analysis 'most national groups in the Habsburg Empire, just like any others who were or felt oppressed, wanted statehood and not just national equality' (Kann 1974: 442). As a result of the defeat and disintegration of the Tsarist, Habsburg and Ottoman empires in the closing stages of the First World War, the national power-seekers of East Central Europe attained 'national independence' sooner than they had anticipated. It took them a little longer to appreciate the powerlessness of small and vulnerable nations situated in the 'marchlands' between Germany and Russia.

WAR AND DISSOLUTION

The intensification of inter-ethnic and class antagonisms in the decades preceding the First World War shook the Habsburg Empire to its foundations. In the end, the Monarchy hoped to override the permanent crisis at home through the successful prosecution of a war abroad. This well known ploy, which had been used many times before, was expected to unite everyone in support of the throne and the war effort, to divert attention from internal discontents to external objectives, to make any manifestation of social or political dissent a treasonable offence and, if successful, to restore the Monarchy's former military elan, self-confidence, prestige and *esprit de corps*. It was, nevertheless, a high-risk stratagem, a desperate 'last throw', for it made the continued existence of the Monarchy dependent upon the outcome of the war (Bauer 1925: 71).

The Monarchy's declaration of war against Serbia on 28 July 1914 triggered an international chain reaction which quickly escalated beyond the Habsburgs' control. The Habsburgs went to war in order to defend their battered imperial honour, pride and territorial integrity against the partly real, partly imagined, South Slav 'threat' and in an endeavour to prove that their empire was still a great power. These factors were to severely limit their strategic flexibility and freedom of manoeuvre during the war. The German government would have liked the Habsburgs to cede Trentino and parts of Dalmatia and Albania to Italy and at least part of Transylvania to Romania in order to induce the Italians and Romanians (who had been formally allied to Germany and Austria-Hungary since 1882–83) to enter the war on the side of the central powers against the Entente (Britain, France and Russia). However, the Habsburgs, the Austrian Germans and the Magyars were loath to accept any such deal. They had not gone to war against Serbia and its Russian protectors only to cede territory to Italy and Romania. Territorial gains in the South Slav lands would have provided meagre compensation for the loss of either Trentino or Transylvania. In any case the Magyar Prime Minister, Count Istvan Tisza, had accepted the Monarchy's declaration of war on Serbia in 1914 only on the (secret) condition that an Austro-Hungarian victory over Serbia must not result in the incorporation of additional Slavic inhabitants and territory into the Habsburg Empire, as that could only strengthen demands for a (federal) Triple Monarchy and thus destabilize the 1867 'compromise'. Indeed, since almost any territory that the Monarchy could realistically hope to gain by conquest would have been Slav-inhabited and therefore unacceptable to the Magyar leadership, Austria-Hungary in effect started the war only in order to bolster its flagging morale, honour and prestige through a show of strength and virility! There was no real possibility of major territorial gains, even if the war had ended in an Austro-Hungarian victory. Moreover, by the time a severely weakened Habsburg Monarchy finally gave in to German pressure to offer territorial blandishments to Italy in the spring of 1915, the Italian state had already decided that it could more reliably fulfil its expansionist ambitions by entering the war on the side of the Entente, which it did in May 1915. Romania followed suit in August 1916. It proved all too easy for Britain, France and Russia to promise Italy, Romania and Serbia tasty morsels of Habsburg territory if they fought on the side of the Entente. This heavily counterbalanced Bulgaria's decision to come into the war on the side of the central powers in September 1915, although the detriment was partly mitigated by their rapid conquest of Romania between September and December 1916. More generally, the precariousness of the 1867 'compromise' in effect permitted the Magyars to veto any Austrian or Habsburg attempt to mobilize more widespread and enthusiastic support for the war effort by offering to federalize and democratize the empire in a manner acceptable to the Austro-Marxists and/or the Austro-Slavs. Indeed, the Dual Monarchy system and the consequent failure to develop a highly centralized political and administrative structure (such as existed in the Russian Empire) made it harder to achieve the effective mobilization and concentration of forces and resources around the war effort.

Once the war had started, however, the goal of surviving and winning it became an end in itself. Moreover, within the Habsburg Monarchy there was at first surprisingly little overt opposition to the war. Many Austrian Germans hoped that the war would revive their waning dominance of the Austrian 'half' of the empire. Magyar nationalists relished the prospect of a latter-day German-backed 'anti-Slavic crusade', while millions of Polish Catholics welcomed a war against Orthodox Russia. Large numbers of Catholic

Croats were only too eager to fight their Orthodox Serbian cousins. 'Only the Czechs were sullenly acquiescent' (Taylor 1976: 232). Indeed, after forty-eight years of relative peace (1866–1914), most of the Monarchy's inhabitants had little idea of what all-out war would involve and those opposed to it were treated as 'traitors' (Kann 1974: 421). Everyone was taken by surprise by the impact of technological change on warfare, which allowed death and destruction on an unimaginable scale.

From the outset, however, the First World War went disastrously wrong for the Habsburg Monarchy. The Austro-Hungarian forces unleashed against Serbia and Montenegro were soon driven back, enabling the Serbs to invade southern Hungary. Only after Bulgaria had actively sided with the Monarchy and Germany in September 1915 was it possible to reinvade Serbia and Montenegro, both of which were conquered by the central powers in December 1915. The Austro-Hungarian forces launched against Russia also suffered serious defeats, with the result that the Russians were able to invade most of Galicia (Austrian Poland) in late 1914 and early 1915. The Habsburg Empire was spared further humiliations and loss of territory thanks only to Germany's stunning victories over Russia (particularly at Tannenberg in August 1914 and at Gorlice in May 1915), which obliged Russia to deploy against Germany forces which would otherwise have been used for a full-scale invasion of Hungary as well as Austria. However, the fact that Russia suffered some devastating and demoralizing defeats at the hands of a much more industrialized and well equipped German Empire (culminating in the collapse of Tsarism and of the Russian war effort in 1917) should not be allowed to obscure the fact that Austria-Hungary was, militarily, no match for Russia (or even Serbia!). Russia had been vigorously developing its heavy industries and re-equipping and reorganizing its armed forces since 1908, in the wake of its humiliating defeats in the Russo-Japanese War of 1904–05. Indeed, the central powers' military planners and strategists had preferred to make war on Russia sooner rather than later, as Russia's military strength was growing appreciably with every year that passed and its economy was booming. By 1914, in fact, Austria-Hungary was spending only a quarter as much as either Russia or Germany on defence, a third as much as either Britain or France and less even than Italy (widely regarded as the 'least of the great powers'). In comparison with 1878 German armament expenditure had quintupled by 1914, that of Russia, Britain and France had trebled, but that of Austria-Hungary had not even doubled (Taylor 1976: 229). Indeed, by 1913 Austria-Hungary was spending more than three times as much on beer, wine and tobacco as on its armed forces (Sked 1989: 262). The war strength of the Habsburg armed forces was 2.3 million men in 1914, compared with 5.3 million for Russia and 3.8 million each for Germany and France.

Decades of Austro-Hungarian wrangling over military structures and budgets had taken their toll. The Habsburgs, the Austrian *Reichsrat* and the Magyars had regularly failed to agree on the form that any military reorganization or increase in military expenditure might take, who should control it and how it should be financed. Any attempt to reorganize or expand the Austro-Hungarian armed forces engendered acrimony. Only the partial reassertion of Habsburg absolutism had averted complete deadlock on military matters in the 1890s and 1900s. Nevertheless, the still splendidly uniformed Habsburg armies became woefully under-funded and ill equipped for war, with the result that 'almost half of the regular army was killed in the campaigns of 1914' (Sked 1989: 258). Thereafter, Austria-Hungary became increasingly dependent upon and subordinate to Germany, without whom the Austro-Hungarian war effort would have collapsed. In the words of Count Czernin: 'Without knowing it, we lost our independence at the outbreak of the war. We were transformed from a subject into an object' (Czernin 1920: 38). Indeed, it is often asserted that after 1915 the Austro-Hungarian Empire remained in existence only by courtesy of Germany and, in particular, Kaiser Wilhelm II's sentimental attachment to the Habsburg dynasty. 'Austria-Hungary was "saved" by Germany; this "saving" marked the real end of the Habsburgs. They had offered a tolerable alternative to German rule [in East Central Europe]; the alternative ceased to exist when the Germans took over the military and political direction of Austria-Hungary . . . Germany was now committed to a bid for the mastery of Europe; and the Habsburgs were no more than German auxiliaries' (Taylor 1976: 233–4).

During the winter of 1914–15 Professor Tomas Masaryk, the foremost Czech leader and chief architect of the future Czechoslovak state, recognized that the hitherto sovereign Habsburg Empire had in effect been superseded by a German-controlled *Mitteleuropa* and that this threatened to obliterate permanently the limited autonomy and cultural freedoms which the Czechs and other subject peoples had acquired during the last decades of Habsburg rule (and which alone had made Habsburg dominion tolerable). The growth of Czech passive resistance to the war and the large-scale desertion of Czech soldiers (especially prisoners-of-war) to the side of the Entente demonstrated that sizeable sections of the Czech population were drawing similar conclusions. The incipient spiritual defection of the Czechs, formerly the most ardent Austro-Slavs, posed the most serious internal challenge to the continued existence of the Habsburg Empire. However, 'Masaryk did not "destroy" the Habsburg Monarchy; this was done by the Germans and the Magyars. What Masaryk did was to create an alternative' (Taylor 1976: 238–9). Even so, not until September 1918 was the Czechoslovak National Committee (led by Masaryk and Eduard Benes) recognized by the Western powers as the 'government in exile' of a Czechoslovak state that did not yet exist (Sked 1989: 260). But this decision, taken at a very late stage in the war, was nevertheless crucial because it was in effect incompatible with the preservation of Austria-Hungary (unlike the creation of a Polish or a Yugoslav state). The creation of Czechoslovakia would rip the heart out of the Habsburg Empire.

During the First World War the ever-present tensions between the Austrian Germans and the Magyars, the two 'master races' of the Austro-Hungarian Empire, escalated into 'a real frenzy' (Jaszi 1929: 365). One of the underlying reasons was that in the course of the war, both in Austria and in Hungary, agricultural output shrank to roughly half the pre-war level, mainly because about half the male agricultural work force and many (perhaps most) of the available horses had been dragooned into the armed forces, leaving behind insufficient manpower and draught animals to work the land as per normal (Berend and Ranki 1974a: 174–5, 1974b: 92). In response to this agricultural crisis, and to Magyar allegations that the predominantly Austrian-German military leadership was wantonly using Magyar conscripts as 'cannon fodder', the Hungarian government imposed severe restrictions on the usual deliveries of grain from Hungary to Austria, while the imperial authorities in turn 'accused Hungary of promoting famine in the Monarchy by its selfish policy' (Jaszi 1929: 365). However, other Hungarians have contended that 'Hungary was unable to send supplies, since she could not even take care of her own needs' (Berend and Ranki 1974a: 174). Yet the deep bitterness and venom of the mutual recriminations also reflected the fact that, at bottom, the Austro-Hungarian 'compromise' of 1867 was 'born out of' mutual mistrust (Jaszi 1929: 350).

Consequently, any massive crisis was almost certain to strain it to breaking point. Indeed, Jaszi maintained that the antagonism between the two hegemonic nations, the Austrian Germans and the Magyars, was 'even greater than the conflict between the hegemonic nations and the second rank nations' (p. 365).

The Magyar decision to restrict severely Hungary's agricultural deliveries to Austria, combined with first Russian and then German military devastation of grain-growing Galicia and the Anglo-French naval blockade against the central powers, meant that Austria suffered far greater wartime privations than did either Germany or the Western belligerents (Bauer 1925: 28). By 1918 the non-agricultural daily *per capita* consumption of flour declined from a pre-war average of 380 g to 165 g for Austria and 220 g for Hungary, while daily *per capita* meat consumption fell from a pre-war average of 82 g to 17 g in Austria and 34 g in Hungary. 'The rural population suffered from brutal requisitioning' and, taking 1914 as 100, by June 1918 the cost of living index had risen to 1,082 for the population as a whole and 1,560 for urban workers (Sked 1989: 263). Industrial production, which held up remarkably well at first, eventually declined to about half the pre-war level in both Austria (including the Czech Lands) and Hungary as a result of increasingly acute fuel, raw material and manpower shortages and transport bottlenecks during 1917 and 1918 (Berend and Ranki 1974a: 174–5, 177).

Powerful inflationary pressures were at work both on the supply side (cost push) and on the demand side (demand pull) during the war. Despite wartime rationing and wage and price controls, money wages rose about fivefold in the course of the war. However, the inflationary pressures exploded with increased force when the war and wartime controls came to an end. The war effort and the post-war reconstruction of the central powers were to a large extent financed by printing more banknotes. Thus the volume of Austrian crowns in circulation rose from about 3 billion in 1913 to 42.6 billion in 1918 and nearly 200 billion by 1921. In addition, there was widespread loss of confidence in the currencies of the defeated and dismembered powers at the end of the war. This, much more than the war-induced shortages and wartime wage rises, was what stoked up the hyperinflation that occurred over most of Central and Eastern Europe in the aftermath of the First World War, wiping out much of the private savings of the region's middle and upper-class inhabitants. Among the successor states of the Austro-Hungarian Empire, only Czechoslovakia 'contrived to avoid the harmful consequences of grave and prolonged inflation' (Berend and Ranki 1974a: 180–1). Indeed, with the exception of Czechoslovakia, all the so-called 'successor states' had succumbed to authoritarian rule by the mid-1930s. It is commonly accepted that the widespread political disenchantment resulting from the destruction of most private savings by hyperinflation after the First World War played an important part in that process (as it did in Germany as well). All the same, the stresses and strains of sustaining an overstretched Austro-Hungarian war machine were taking a heavy toll. In the course of the war 1.2 million Habsburg subjects were killed, 3.5 million were wounded and 2.2 million became prisoners-of-war, although many of the latter changed sides (Kann 1974: 483). As reported by Otto Bauer, a leading light in the Austrian Marxist opposition: 'The fearful losses of the army in the first months of the war necessitated a continuous calling up of new classes; militarism fetched children off the school benches, and old men marched with their sons. By brute force it was sought to drive the hungry workers into the war industries to work; the factories were militarized; workers were court-martialled; and military managers commanded the factories. The constitution was suspended, parliament closed, the press muzzled and the civil population made amenable to the summary justice of military courts' (Bauer 1925: 28).

Bauer also avowed that the subject peoples of the Habsburg Empire were pinning their hopes on an Entente victory. 'Austria-Hungary was waging war not only against external enemies, but also against two-thirds of its own citizens' (p. 24). 'The Habsburg Monarchy had to contend with the hostility of the Slav peoples', whom it could force to fight the external foe only 'by employing the coercive agencies of wartime absolutism' (p. 27). From the Slav standpoint, the Habsburg war effort was exacting 'terrible . . . sacrifices for an alien state and a hostile cause. The longer the war lasted, the more the national revolutionary movement against Austria gathered strength in the Slav lands' (p. 72).

The final breakdown of the Habsburg Monarchy began in the autumn of 1916. In September, amid deepening supply problems, receding hopes of an early end to the war, the evident collapse of any real danger of a Russian invasion of Austria-Hungary and mounting expectations that the United States would enter the war on the side of the Entente, serious labour unrest broke out in the war industries. Thereupon, aristocratic members of Austria's upper house requested the reinstatement of the *Reichsrat*. However, Premier Karl Stürgkh not only rejected the request but instigated a harsh new crackdown on all opposition, sedition and dissent. This intransigence prompted the anti-war socialist Friedrich Adler (son of Viktor Adler) to break the political deadlock by assassinating the Prime Minister on 24 October 1916, shortly before the death of Emperor Franz Joseph on 21 November 1916. The subsequent political 'show trial' of Friedrich Adler (18–19 May 1917) backfired on the Habsburg regime, because it gave him the perfect pulpit from which to present a detailed and heartfelt indictment of the regime and its conduct of the war. The trial helped to relight the flame of the Socialist International and turned Friedrich Adler into an Austrian and international *cause célèbre*. The almost simultaneous death of Franz Joseph, whose staid but august personage and sixty-eight-year devotion to duty had come to symbolize all that remained of the Habsburgs' battered authority, dignity and mystique, seemed to mark the end of a hallowed institution, the loss of a safe anchor and the passing of an era.

Emperor Karl (November 1916–October 1918), the great-nephew of Franz Joseph, had not been 'raised in the tradition of Austria as the presiding power in the German Confederation and of the Habsburgs as Holy Roman Emperors . . . The aim of achieving peace . . . dominated his thinking' (Kann 1974: 474). Alarmed by the Russian Revolution and the fall of Tsarism in March 1917, the young Emperor Karl and Count Stürgkh's immediate successors (Ernst Körber, Heinrich Clam-Martinic and Ernst von Seidler) relaxed labour regulations in the war industries (18 May 1917), reconvened the Austrian *Reichsrat* (30 May 1917), obtained the resignation of the reactionary and repressive Istvan Tisza government in Hungary (5 June 1917), put out peace feelers to the Western powers (March–May 1917), restored constitutional government in Austria, amnestied Austria's political prisoners (July 1917) and rescinded the death sentence on Friedrich Adler and the Czech nationalist leader Dr Karel Kramar (July 1917). The political relaxation in Austria and (to a lesser degree) Hungary during 1917 permitted a revival of party politics, trade unionism and the left, culminating in January and February 1918, when major strikes in key industries in Vienna and Budapest were followed by mutinies in Judenberg, Funfkirchen, Rumberg, Budapest and Cattaro (Kotor).

The left drew inspiration from the boldness, anti-war stance and (apparent) initial successes of the Russian Bolshevik Revolution of October 1917 (November 1917, according to the new calendar). Bolshevik influence on Austro-Hungarian workers, soldiers, sailors and intellectuals increased when, following the cessation of war with Russia in December 1917 and the conclusion of a peace treaty between Russia and the central powers in March 1918, 'ten thousand prisoners-of-war who had witnessed the revolution in Russia returned home' (Bauer 1925: 38). Still, the mutineers who hoisted red flags in early 1918 also demanded peace on the basis of US President Woodrow Wilson's famous Fourteen Points, announced in January 1918 (p. 37). This attested to the spread of American as well as Bolshevik influence. However, the left was unable to consummate its growing power and influence in Austria-Hungary at the time. As explained by Otto Bauer, the strikes and mutinies in January and February 1918 were easily suppressed by 'reliable' Habsburg forces: 'Even if Austrian militarism had no longer had at its command sufficient force to repel a revolutionary insurrection . . . an Austrian revolution could have had no other result than an invasion of Austria by the German armies . . . German imperialism was at the zenith of its power. The Russian army had melted away since the October Revolution. The gigantic armies of the German Eastern Front had become available . . . German armies would have occupied Austria in the same way as they shortly afterwards occupied an incomparably larger territory in Russia and the Ukraine . . . We realized how serious was the danger . . . We were aware that even the Czech revolutionaries feared a German invasion . . . for their tactics during the whole war were determined by the conviction that, so long as German imperialism remained undefeated, a Czech revolution could only lead to the occupation of Bohemia and Moravia by troops of the German Empire' (Bauer 1925: 34–7).

In similar vein, Hobsbawm has argued that 'in deciding to suppress revolutionary agitation and continue a lost war, the authorities of the Habsburg Monarchy made sure that there would be a Wilsonian rather than a Soviet Europe' (Hobsbawm 1992: 129). Perhaps more by accident than by design, the Habsburg imperial authorities ensured that national/ethnic aspirations and mobilization would prevail over class/socialist aspirations in East Central Europe in 1918–19. (Even so, in the eyes of many workers and peasants in the region at that time, the two would have appeared to go hand-in-hand or to be two sides of the same coin.) In the end the former subject peoples of the Habsburg Empire and Tsarist Russia, who had hitherto aspired to a combination of social and national liberation, settled for national independence without very radical social change, under the protective umbrella of the victorious Western powers (or so they thought). But for defeated Germany, Austria, Hungary and Bulgaria, Hobsbawm argues, 'there was no such fall-back position'. In their cases collapse led (at least temporarily) to social revolution, with the result that nationalism there emerged 'not only as a milder substitute for social revolution' but as the political mobilization of frustrated and deeply discontented ex-officers, officials and middle-class civilians towards counter-revolution and fascism (p. 130).

Nevertheless, the First World War had not been fought in order to create a new European order based upon the concepts of national self-determination and the nation-state. These were the consequences, not the causes, of the war. Until as late as June 1918 the Western powers were anxious to preserve the Austro-Hungarian Empire as a counterweight to Germany and Russia and thereby avoid the creation of a power vacuum in East Central Europe which would probably be filled in due course either by a resurgent

Germany or by Russia. Prior to June 1918 the dismemberment of the Habsburg Monarchy had never been on the agenda of the Western powers. They were willing to 'amputate' some of the empire's territories, but the amputations would have been more a recognition than a denial of the empire's right to exist. However, the entry of the United States into the war in April 1917 brought in its train the (seemingly) more high-minded and idealistic foreign policy of President Woodrow Wilson. He would attempt to bring peace to the world with his Fourteen Points, when Moses had already tried and failed with his Ten Commandments. This, combined with the collapse of the Russian Tsarist regime in February (March) 1917, replaced the brawl between the Entente and the central powers with an ideological contest between the 'Allies'/'democracies' and absolutism.

However, the Fourteen Points (proclaimed in January 1918) envisaged only the restructuring or federalization of the Austro-Hungarian Empire, not its complete dissolution or dismemberment into a constellation of independent 'national' states. Point Ten merely stated that 'The peoples of Austria-Hungary, whose place among the nations we wish to see safeguarded and assured, should be accorded the freest opportunity for autonomous development.' In addition, Point Thirteen stated that 'An independent Polish State should be erected which should include the territories inhabited by indisputably Polish populations, which should be assured a free and secure access to the sea and whose political and economic independence and territorial integrity should be guaranteed by international covenant.' This clearly implied that the future Polish state should be coterminous with the Polish nation and that Germany, Russia and Austria-Hungary would therefore have to cede territory to the resurrected Polish state. But the Fourteen Points did not propose the creation of any other 'national' successor states than Poland. There was no mention of a Czech or a Slovak state. Indeed, some historians, economists, politicians and publicists continued to argue that it was either inappropriate or imprudent or impossible to construct nation-states in Central and Eastern Europe. To do so would be politically and economically hazardous; it could pose a perpetual threat to European peace, prosperity and security (see, for example, Cole 1941). And in a sense such misgivings turned out to have been well founded.

By the autumn of 1918, however, three factors had finally persuaded the Western Allies that it was both necessary and safe to call into existence new 'national' states in Central and Eastern Europe: first, the continuing disintegration of Russia; second, the fatal Austro-Hungarian decision to stake everything on anticipated German victories on the western front in the spring and summer of 1918, following the imposition of a draconian peace treaty on Soviet Russia in March 1918 and the attendant German occupation of all Poland and most of Belarus, Lithuania and the Ukraine; and, third, the subsequent German military *débâcle*, caused mainly by German territorial over-extension in the East as well as the long-delayed arrival of massive, well equipped and well fed American forces in Western Europe. It became temptingly easy to pull apart and paralyse the Habsburg Empire simply by granting official recognition to putative, self-appointed Polish, Czechoslovak and Yugoslav governments-in-exile. Moreover, the concurrent military foundering of Germany and the deepening disintegration of Russia seemed to render it safe (indeed, imperative) to make 'national self-determination' the basis of a new states system in Central and Eastern Europe (if only to ward off the real or imaginary 'threat' of Bolshevism and 'red revolution'). At a single stroke, it seemed, the Western powers curtailed the war, hit upon a 'magic formula' for a supposedly just and democratic new political order, and slew the Bolshevik beast. Western leaders with a penchant for panaceas were not fully aware that, while appearing to 'put to rest' the most pressing problems, they were sowing the seeds of even bigger ones.

On 4 September 1918, in an attempt to stop the carnage, Austria-Hungary called upon all belligerents to start peace negotiations immediately, but the Western Allies rejected the appeal because they were now seeking surrender rather than negotiation. On 4 October 1918, following the capitulation of Bulgaria on 29 September 1918, the central powers proclaimed their deathbed conversion to Wilson's Fourteen Points as the basis of a non-punitive peace. A Habsburg imperial manifesto promulgated on 16 October 1918 interpreted this as meaning local national autonomy for the subject peoples within a federal Austrian Monarchy, while Hungary was to remain unchanged. But it was too late for that. Czechs, Poles and South Slavs would now be satisfied with nothing less than full national independence. On 18 October 1918, moreover, President Wilson publicly endorsed their demands.

On 27 October 1918 the last Habsburg imperial Cabinet, headed by Premier Heinrich Lammasch and Foreign Minister Gyula Andrassy, accepted the secession of the Czechs, the Poles and the South Slavs. It also sought a separate peace and armistice from the Western Allies, in a belated endeavour to detach the Monarchy from Germany's fate and salvage as much as possible. When Austria-Hungary formally surrendered on 2 November 1918, Germany's high command ordered a German invasion of Austria, but for some reason the order was not carried out (that is, not until 12 March 1938). Meanwhile, German Austria had established a socialist-led provisional government and adopted a republican constitution on 30 October 1918, although Emperor Karl and his imperial Cabinet did not abandon the pretence of a Habsburg Empire until 11 November. Karl did not formally abdicate, but simply relinquished his powers and duties to the nascent German-Austrian Republic, which sought but was not allowed union (*Anschluss*) with Germany. Hungary assumed *de facto* independence on 17 October 1918 and became a republic on 16 November 1918. Croatia and Slovakia seceded from Hungary on 29 and 30 October 1918 respectively. However, all these moves merely performed the last rites on an empire which had in reality died some months earlier. Indeed, much of its sovereignty had in effect been ceded to Germany by late 1914, while the true Habsburg spirit of tenacity and mediocrity had died with Franz Jozeph in November 1916. The First World War merely drove the final nails into the imperial coffin.

Part IV

Eastern Europe between the two world wars

Introduction: the new political order in Eastern Europe

The question of why democracy generally 'failed' in Eastern Europe between the wars is one of the most crucial issues in the history of twentieth-century Europe. The failure effectively negated the 1919–20 peace settlements, facilitating the expansion of Nazi Germany and Fascist Italy, engulfing Europe in another world war and paving the way for the mid-1940s expansion of communist power and the East–West partition of Europe. The question of why democracy generally did not take root in inter-war Eastern Europe naturally poses another question, one which has from the outset cast a shadow over the re-establishment of democracy in Eastern Europe since 1989: could history repeat itself?

In a sense Part IV is an extended answer to the pivotal first question. Some writers have argued that the entire project of basing a new political order on the concepts of national self-determination and 'national' states with borders corresponding to 'ethnic divisions' was either inherently flawed or not realizable or a recipe for disaster amid the ethnic mosaic of Eastern Europe. Others have argued that the project was basically a sound one, but that it was not applied in a sufficiently just, consistent and resolute manner. It was compromised by wartime promises, great-power ambitions, fear of Bolshevism and economic and strategic considerations. Still others have argued that the project was basically sound, that it was implemented as justly, consistently and resolutely as was possible in the circumstances and that, given two or three decades of European peace and prosperity, the new order would gradually have gained deeper and healthier roots and wider acceptance, while many of the disputes and bones of contention would eventually have been resolved either by compromise or by plebiscite or, in the last resort, by *force majeure*. What scuppered the project was the largely exogenous 1930s Depression and the (not unrelated) spread of fascism. There is much to be said for all three lines of argument. The new political order was indeed inherently flawed, but it would have produced much healthier results than it did if it had not been compromised by the factors mentioned above and deformed by the rise of fascism.

THE FALLACIOUS DOCTRINE OF NATIONAL SELF-DETERMINATION

Prior to 1918 most of Central and Eastern Europe had been ruled for centuries by supranational empires. The peace settlements of 1919–20 marked the first-ever attempt to reconstruct Eastern Europe on the basis of 'national' states and national self-determination. The Treaty of Versailles, signed by defeated Germany on 28 June 1919, settled the western frontiers of Poland and Czechoslovakia, but it left under Polish and

Czech rule large German minorities who would have preferred to be 'united' with Germany. The Treaty of Saint-Germain, signed by dismembered Austria on 10 September 1919, determined German Austria's new borders with Poland, Italy, Czechoslovakia and Yugoslavia (officially the Kingdom of Serbs, Croats and Slovenes) and prevented it from fulfilling the desire of both right and left for political and economic union (*Anschluss*) with Weimar Germany. The Treaty of Neuilly, signed by defeated Bulgaria on 27 November 1919, fixed the new frontiers between Romania, Yugoslavia, Greece and Bulgaria, in denial of Bulgarian territorial claims to Macedonia, western Thrace and southern Dobruja. The Treaty of Trianon, signed by a truncated Hungary on 4 June 1920, settled the hotly disputed frontiers of Czechoslovakia, Romania and Yugoslavia with the humbled Magyar state. However, the deeply resented loss of Slovakia, Transylvania, Banat, Vojvodina and Croatia-Slavonia left nearly 3 million Magyars outside the diminutive new Hungary, which also felt deprived of the bulk of its 'natural' economic hinterland. Lastly, on 10 August 1920, the government of the dismembered Ottoman Empire signed the Treaty of Sèvres, which awarded Greece eastern Thrace, several Aegean islands and, in effect, parts of western Anatolia (including the port of Smyrna/Izmir). However, this treaty was never ratified by the Turks, and the Greek state soon overreached itself. In 1921–22 a successful Turkish nationalist counter-offensive re-established full Turkish possession of western Anatolia and some of the Aegean islands. This gain was confirmed by the Treaty of Lausanne (24 July 1923), which also ratified Europe's only large-scale post-1918 'population exchange', whereby about 1.1 million Greek refugees (mostly from Smyrna/Izmir) were resettled in Greece and about 380,000 Moslems were expelled from Greece to Turkey (Clogg 1992: 101). Otherwise, with this one major exception, the architects of post-1918 Eastern and Central Europe mainly endeavoured to draw the new state boundaries to fit the existing (ethnic) distribution of populations, rather than to 'adjust' or relocate populations to fit the existing or predetermined state boundaries (as occurred on a massive scale, involving the relocation of about 20 million people, at the end of the Second World War).

When President Woodrow Wilson enunciated his Fourteen Points to the US Congress on 8 January 1918, he loftily declaimed that 'justice' should be done by 'all peoples and nationalities' and that political boundaries should be drawn in accordance with 'historically established lines of allegiance and nationality'. This may have sounded very fine, straightforward and reasonable to an American audience. But, perhaps because he was an American, Wilson was seemingly unaware that 'historically established lines of allegiance and nationality' simply did not exist in Europe. (Nor did they exist in Africa or Asia, for that matter.) Nations and nationalities were relatively recent mental constructs, which were not even based on uniformly applicable criteria. They were variously defined in terms of 'national' language or 'national' religion or common territory or shared history or dynastic allegiance. Therefore, far from being objectively identifiable, the extent of 'national' territories and the 'correct' positioning of national boundaries on a relatively densely populated continent were often fiercely disputed, especially in the domains of the disintegrating multinational empires of central and eastern Europe. One nation's 'justice' was often another nation's injustice. However, as President of the United States, Wilson knew that the instincts of the US Congress were essentially isolationist and that it would be almost impossible to persuade most Americans to accept a more interventionist US role in Europe unless it was conceived in terms of a moral and ideological mission to settle Europe's quarrels once and for all, by imposing a more just,

Map 4 Eastern Europe, 1923

principled and uniform 'new order' on the troubled continent. He had to appeal to the moral crusading instincts of American 'liberals' and evangelical Christians. Like the Truman Doctrine of 1947, the principle of national self-determination and the Fourteen Points were designed largely for domestic consumption. With his pious, priggish and puritanical upbringing and cast of mind, Wilson preached his doctrines with great steadfastness, certainty and quasi-religious fervour, even though they proved 'difficult to apply in any extensive or binding way' to the complex political realities of post-1917 Europe (Schultz 1972: 24–5, 85). Wilson assumed that the whole world was steadily evolving towards 'liberal' democratic nation-states and *laissez-faire* market economies. This so-called 'Wilsonian heresy' derived from nineteenth-century positivist and 'evolutionist' assumptions concerning the 'inevitability' of progress, capitalism, industrialization and the ascendancy of the bourgeoisie. These reinforced Wilson's belief that the system of sovereign 'national' states which had triumphed and prospered in most of nineteenth-century western Europe would be equally appropriate and produce similar results in twentieth-century eastern Europe.

The peace treaties of 1919–20 did indeed establish state boundaries which 'approximated more closely to ethnical divisions than any previous system in the history of Eastern Europe' (Seton-Watson 1945: 269). However, Wilson's high-flown principles could never have been fully realized in practice. They had already been compromised by the extravagant promises that Britain and France had made during the war, often in the form of binding treaty obligations and formal declarations, in order to persuade countries such as Italy, Greece and Romania to fight against (rather than for) the Central Powers. Likewise, as a result of wartime undertakings given to the Serbian government-in-exile and to Czech *émigrés* (particularly Masaryk and Benes), the Allies refused to allow Croat or Slovene or Slovak delegations a hearing at the Peace Conference in 1919. Furthermore, the Allies were concerned to ensure economic viability, easily defendable frontiers and the largest possible territories for the pro-Western 'successor states' (Poland, Czechoslovakia, Romania and Yugoslavia), in the hope that it would transform them into stronger and more dependable 'bulwarks' against any future German, Austrian, Hungarian and Bulgarian 'revanchism' and against Soviet communism. Largely as a consequence of this, they received much more favourable allocations of territory and economic resources than a stricter application of national self-determination would have allowed, while other would-be 'nations' such as Ukraine, Belorussia, Slovakia, Croatia, Slovenia and Macedonia were completely denied either national autonomy or independent statehood. (Others, notably Austria, had it thrust upon them!) Political, military and economic expediency frequently won out against Wilson's proclaimed principles, to his considerable chagrin. Indeed, particularly for Britain and France, 'The fundamental purpose of the 1919 Peace Settlement in Eastern Europe was to create a *cordon sanitaire* of new states between the two dangerous Great powers, Germany and Russia' (Seton-Watson 1945: 362).

For various reasons, therefore, the much-vaunted principle of national self-determination was not applied as rigorously as it might have been. The victorious Western powers naturally favoured those nations which had actively sided with them during the war, to the detriment of the defeated enemy nations and a 'defeatist' Soviet Russia (which had concluded a 'separate peace' with Germany with its allies at Brest-Litovsk on 3 March 1918). They also favoured those new states that partly owed their existence to Western sponsorship and were therefore expected to remain staunchly pro-

Western and actively opposed to the 'Soviet threat' and the 'revanchism' of the former enemy nations.

The victorious Western powers had seriously miscalculated, however, as soon became apparent to all sides. Instead of serving as a high moral principle that would draw no distinction between victors and vanquished and would thus be acceptable to both, the manifest inequities and inconsistencies in the application of the principle of national self-determination meant that it came to be seen as a symbol of Western perfidy, hypocrisy and duplicity, not only in the former 'enemy nations' but also in Italy, Greece and other countries which felt cheated or 'let down' by the terms of the peace settlement. This in turn intensified their angry hostility to that settlement and contributed to the rise of fascism in central and eastern Europe, as well as in Italy. Thus even those nations that had been treated most favourably by the Western powers did not always remain staunchly pro-Western, anti-Soviet and hostile to the former 'enemy nations'. Italy, which had sided with the Western Allies less out of any sense of obligation to do so than because of expectations (indeed, promises) of major territorial gains at the end of the war, felt 'cheated' by the subsequent thwarting of her imperial ambitions in the Balkans and in the Aegean. In effect, the Peace Conference awarded Italy only territories to which she could stake a plausible claim in terms of national self-determination, i.e. Trentino and Istria. During the 1920s and 1930s, therefore, Italy sided with the 'revisionist' countries, which were demanding revisions of the peace settlement in their own favour. This culminated in the emergence of the Rome–Berlin Axis in 1936. Moreover, most of the 'successor states' of central and eastern Europe sought 'accommodation' with the Axis powers and loosened their links with the Western powers, although this was mainly attributable to the failure of the West to offer the 'successor states' adequate material, moral and military support in the face of the 1930s Depression and the rise of both Fascist Italy and Nazi Germany. In the end, as the balance of power shifted in the Axis powers' favour, it even became possible for Hitler to turn the tables on the Western powers by invoking the principle of national self-determination for the Germans of Austria, Bohemia and the Baltic region as a means of overturning the peace settlement and 'destroying its keystone, Czechoslovakia', in 1938–39 (Warriner 1950: 64). Indeed, a 'liberal' German assessment of the peace treaties concludes that 'the "system of Versailles" failed not because the treaties were worthless, not because mistakes were made, but primarily because there was no timely or far-sighted attempt to revise these treaties and to continue the necessarily unfinished work of the Paris Peace Conference' (Schultz 1972: 236). This particular failure can be attributed not only to lapses and lack of imagination on the part of Britain and France, but also to the great misfortune that the 'moral author' of the peace settlement, who bore the chief responsibility for ensuring that it 'worked' and that it received adequate material, moral and military support, failed to get it ratified by the US Congress. America's refusal even to join the League of Nations, Wilson's brainchild, deprived that body of much needed power, resources and authority. The United States reverted to its former 'isolationism' in 1920 and Wilson died soon afterwards, a broken and disillusioned man.

Nevertheless, the problems which arose from weaknesses, inequities and inconsistencies in the way the principle of national self-determination was applied were not the most fundamental ones. On the whole, it has to be said, the new political order was more 'just' and more benign than the one it superseded. The number of people freed from 'alien' rule by the restructuring of central and eastern Europe was about three times greater than the number of people newly subjected to 'alien' rule (Rothschild 1974: 4). Moreover, in the main, the various anomalies and departures from the strict application of the principle of national self-determination in 1918–20 were not purely arbitrary or gratuitously offensive. They were in fact intended to accommodate legitimate and often well founded economic and security considerations and to contain potential threats and aggressors (especially Hungary, Germany and Soviet Russia), even if they were sometimes inconsistent with the proclaimed principle of national self-determination and/or conducive to the very dangers they were intended to limit or forestall. It was just unfortunate that a number of vital economic and security considerations could not be reconciled with the principle of national self-determination, which was therefore overridden. One should also set against the anger and discontent of nations which felt unjustly treated the important role of the long-delayed satisfaction of the nationalist aspirations of the Poles, the Czechs, the Romanians and the Serbs in preserving them from the violent political and social upheavals that convulsed Russia and (to a lesser degree) Hungary, Austria, Bulgaria and Germany in the wake of their defeat and territorial losses (p. 13). While it is normal to focus on the anger and discontent aroused by the peace treaties, it should be emphasized that Germany (the most voluble) was by no means the most harshly treated. (Its territorial losses and economic hardships were slight compared with those inflicted on Russia, Hungary, Austria and Bulgaria.) Some other nations for a while felt a warm glow of satisfaction, which helped to carry them through their post-war hardships.

By the 1940s it was widely believed that the principle of national self-determination was 'simply not workable'. Most of the difficulties derived from the same root cause: the attempt to impose a system of 'tidy national states on to an untidy patchwork of nationalities'. This was bound to give rise to intractable and disruptive problems because it was impossible either to draw boundaries that would create homogeneous national states or to incorporate everybody into the state 'to which by nationality they belonged' (Warriner 1950: 64; cf. Cole 1941: 63–8, 93–105).

However, the 'nationality' problems of inter-war Eastern Europe were made even more insoluble by the implicit assumptions that a 'nation-state' ought ideally to be 'ethnically homogeneous' and that people who were not members of the majority ethnic group *ipso facto* did not strictly 'belong' to or in that state, even though they and their forebears might have lived and worked there for centuries. This spurious and pernicious conception of 'ethnic homogeneity' as the ideal basis of 'national' statehood was espoused by the Western statesmen gathered at the Paris Peace Conference and accepted by the governments of most of the 'successor states', in the mistaken belief that they were merely transposing the western European pattern of 'nation-states' on to Central and Eastern Europe. In fact they were doing nothing of the sort, since such 'ethnic homogeneity' has never existed in western Europe (any more than it has in eastern Europe) and it has never been considered a basis or a requirement of 'national' statehood. Europeans are all mongrels and every western European state is a *mélange*, the product of centuries of migration, 'folk wandering', acculturation and intermarriage. In western Europe states have often defined 'nations', but 'nations' have rarely defined states. 'Nationality' has normally been conferred by citizenship of a particular state, rather than by innate 'ethnic' attributes. Therefore the endeavour after the First World War to construct 'national' states in Central and Eastern Europe on the basis of a pernicious ideal of 'ethnic homogeneity', which racists rapidly translated into concepts of (and demands for) ethnic or racial 'purity', was based on a grotesque misreading of western European history and too much reading of dangerous German 'idealist' philosophers.

This tragic error helped to create the disruptive and potentially explosive 'ethnic minority' problems which bedevilled the 'successor states'. That is to say, if genuinely western European conceptions of the nation, nationality and the 'nation-state' had been transposed to the new and reconstituted states of Central and Eastern Europe, all the people whose families had been living and working there for centuries would have been defined and treated as full citizens and 'nationals' of those states, irrespective of their ethnic affiliations. Tragically, what actually happened was that the largest 'ethnic group' in each state constituted itself as 'the nation', while the other 'ethnic groups' were classified as (implicitly 'alien' and barely tolerated) 'ethnic minorities', even though the latter had often contributed greatly to the culture and economic development of that society. Thus the narrow and exclusive manner in which East European nations were conceived and defined helped to institutionalize patterns of political and social exclusion and to foster antagonistic or adversarial relationships between the ethnic majorities and minorities. This often prevented the latter from playing the fullest possible role in the further development of the 'successor states' in which they resided and it sometimes called into question their loyalty to them. It is conceivable that the often narrow, exclusive and illiberal 'ethnic nationalisms' which had flourished in Central and Eastern Europe since the late nineteenth century predetermined these unhealthy and potentially dangerous outcomes. But Woodrow Wilson's proclamation of the principle of national self-determination placed an additional premium on 'ethnic homogeneity' because, in its absence, national self-determination would be either unworkable or a recipe for inter-ethnic conflict. Indeed, national self-determination is an extreme form of the 'winner takes all' syndrome, for whoever has a majority at the outset is likely to hold on to it indefinitely, while the ethnic minorities tend to become permanent political underdogs or at best second-class citizens.

Curiously, the Western sponsors of the new political order in Central and Eastern Europe saw only too clearly that the results of their handiwork would still leave large, vulnerable and insecure 'perpetual national minorities' in most of the 'successor states' and that this could pose major problems for a long time ahead. Above all, despite the proclamation of national self-determination, not every 'nation' would have a state of 'its own' and it would not be possible for every person to reside in his or her own 'national state'. However, instead of going back to the drawing board to reconsider the inherently flawed basis of the new order, they decided to treat the symptoms rather than the root causes of the minority problems. Under pressure from the American Jewish lobby, and advised by American 'experts', the Western powers forced each of the new or enlarged 'successor states' reluctantly to sign 'minority protection treaties', binding them to uphold certain basic laws and respect the fundamental rights of ethnic and religious minorities and granting aggrieved minorities a right of appeal to the newly established League of Nations, whose approval would have to be sought for any change in the laws governing fundamental human rights (Longworth 1994: 68). However, only the relatively liberal Czechs accepted such conditions willingly 'and even they failed to observe their undertakings. The Ruthenes . . . were never to obtain their own Diet any more than the Slovaks were to have their own assembly or law courts.' Education, law and administration in Czechoslovakia remained overwhelmingly in Czech hands, 'although the Ruthenes did secure most of the available jobs as roadmenders' (p. 69).

These treaty provisions conflicted with widespread fear, mistrust or resentment of ethnic minorities. They invited accusations of hypocrisy and double standards, since similar arrangements would not have been accepted by France or the United Kingdom for Algeria or Northern Ireland, for example. They also set a dangerous precedent which later encouraged the Nazis to champion the 'rights' of the German (*Volksdeutsche*) minorities in Poland and Czechoslovakia, the Fascists to take up the cause of the Italian minorities in Yugoslavia and Albania and the Horthy regime to fan the grievances of the Magyar minorities in Romania, Yugoslavia and Czechoslovakia as a prelude to fascist military incursions into the host countries. 'Minority protection' proved to be a double-edged sword.

The first of these 'minority protection treaties' was signed by Poland on the same day as the signing of the Versailles Treaty (28 June 1919), as a heavy hint that Poland's vital territorial gains from defeated Germany were linked with future Polish observance of the rights of the large German, Jewish, Ukrainian, Belorussian and Lithuanian minorities. Similar treaties were signed by Czechoslovakia, Greece, Yugoslavia and Romania in the autumn of 1919 and the summer of 1920, immediately after the treaties of Saint Germain, Neuilly and Trianon, dropping analogous hints (Schultz 1972: 200). Occasional appeals were made to the League of Nations under the terms of these treaties, 'but the grievances were not removed and no means was found . . . of enforcing the . . . obligations assumed. The Treaties were resented by the Successor States as limitations of their sovereignty, while the minorities complained that they were quite ineffectual as guarantees of their rights' (Seton-Watson 1945: 269).

Once the 'successor states' of Central and Eastern Europe were up and running in the 1920s, they were allowed to ignore and violate the rights of minorities with impunity. During the 1930s quite ferocious Polish oppression of Ukrainians, Belorussians and Jews, Romanian persecution of Magyars and Jews and persistent Czech and Serbian refusal to grant federal autonomy to their major 'national' minorities drew barely a protest from the Western democracies, other than from the American Jewish lobby and some Ukrainian, Belorussian, Slovak and Croatian *émigrés* operating as private citizens. The Western powers were faintly interested in these states as potential 'bulwarks' against German revanchism, Italian fascism and Soviet communism, but not in their internal policies and politics. There were no attempts to make financial or other assistance available to these states on condition that they observed minority rights or fundamental human rights. Nor was there any attempt to apply League of Nations sanctions to 'successor states' which ignored or violated such rights. This encouraged the aggrieved German, Magyar, Italian, Greek and Macedonian minorities of inter-war Eastern Europe to seek 'protection' or 'assistance' from their ethnic and cultural 'mother countries' (Germany, Hungary, Italy, Greece and Bulgaria) 'against the pressures of the "host" state' (Rothschild 1974: 12). However, even this option was unavailable to 'stateless nations' such as the Jews and Gypsies and, in a sense, Slovaks, Croats, Slovenes, Ukrainians and Belorussians.

Basing herself on an analysis of the 'national' population censuses of 1930–31, Warriner (1950: 68) estimated that the national minorities of the successor states 'numbered in all some 25 million (including 3.6 million Jews) out of a total population of some 90 million'. Besides the Jews, the major components were 6 million Germans (3.2 million in Czechoslovakia, 1 million in Poland, 0.8 million in Romania, 0.5 million in Hungary and 0.5 million in Yugoslavia), 5.4 million Ukrainians and Belorussians (4.3

million in Poland, 0.6 million in Romania and 0.5 million in Czechoslovakia) and 2.7 million Magyars (1.5 million in Romania, 0.7 million in Czechoslovakia and 0.5 million in Yugoslavia). It should be emphasized, however, that these were 'national' censuses in more senses than one. The 'national' census authorities massaged the census returns and angled the questionnaires in such a way as to understate the size of the ethnic minorities and to overstate the size of the dominant or titular 'nations' (Polonsky 1974: 157). Indeed, the census-takers in Czechoslovakia did not distinguish between Czechs and Slovaks, while those of Yugoslavia lumped together Serbs, Croats, Montenegrins, Bosnian Moslems, Macedonians and Bulgarians (pp. 160, 162). The number of Jews was understated everywhere because many Jews were to a large extent assimilated, often declaring the language of their 'host' country to be their first language or 'mother tongue'. In reality, therefore, 'national minorities' probably numbered nearly 30 million people, or about one-third of the total population. Even in defeated Bulgaria and Hungary, which were reduced to their 'ethnic core territories', national minorities made up 10 per cent of the population, while in other more populous states the proportion was over 30 per cent (Polonsky 1974: 20).

Not surprisingly, many ethnic minorities felt their plight to be much worse in the expressly 'national' successor states than it had been in the former Habsburg and Ottoman Empires, which had allowed their diverse 'nationalities' to enjoy various degrees of cultural and religious autonomy. The attainment of full 'national' independence and statehood, whether in 1878 or in 1918, gave the dominant or titular 'nation' of each of the 'successor states' the long-awaited opportunity to claim sole possession of the state apparatus and all state-funded institutions. Each one promoted its own language and culture as the 'official' language and culture of the state, while doing as little as possible (or worse) for the languages and cultures of the ethnic minorities. Indeed, the desire to 'nationalize' the language and culture of the state provided much of the driving force behind the very rapid expansion of state universities and compulsory state schooling during the inter-war years. For the nationalistic members of the dominant or titular 'nations', it was the moment of triumph. They rejoiced in their new-found 'national freedom', even if it happened to take the form of political dictatorship. For ethnic minorities, however, it raised the prospect of a permanently underprivileged status and eventual cultural 'extinction'. Little did they realize that, for some ethnic minorities, the process would actually culminate in loss of citizenship, mass expulsions or even mass extermination during the 1940s. While western European nationalism was mainly rooted in relatively liberal, inclusive 'civic' conceptions of the nation and citizenship, Central and Eastern European nationalism was predominantly based upon innately illiberal, exclusive, 'ethnic' concepts of the *Volk*, kinship, descent or, in Ignatiev's apt phrase, 'blood and belonging' (Ignatiev 1993).

In a way, indeed, President Woodrow Wilson's enunciation of the principle of national self-determination inadvertently gave the green light to ethnic chauvinism by suggesting that, if a particular ethnic group was in the majority within a specified area, that gave it the right to impose its culture and identity on all within that territory. National self-determination was interpreted in much the same way that the principle of *cuius regio, eius religio* had been in the seventeenth century. The Wilsonian 'new order' in Central and Eastern Europe was also criticized from many other angles. For example, G.D.H. Cole, an eminent British socialist, argued that 'the idea of nationality as a basis for independent statehood is obsolete . . . The independence of small states, and indeed of all states save the largest and richest in developed resources, is impractical now ... The utmost "independence" that any small state can hope for in the future is a false independence, behind which lies the reality of complete domination by a greater neighbour' (Cole 1941: 13).

Cole's strictures may not have been applicable to every small state. Sweden and Switzerland, for example, were not noted for subservience to powerful neighbours and retained considerable freedom of manoeuvre. But there is widespread agreement that the formally 'independent' successor states were in fact economically, psychologically and strategically 'dependent' on the Western powers during the 1920s and the early 1930s. Thus their formal independence was largely an illusion and, once the initial 'national euphoria' had died down, not a very comforting one. Cole also expatiated on the damaging economic consequences of the Wilsonian 'new order' in Central and Eastern Europe: 'It would be possible to enlarge at almost any length on the absurdities of the European frontiers of 1939 from the standpoint of economic convenience and well-being ... It is often suggested that these absurdities were caused by the folly of the statesmen of 1919. But in truth the cause of the trouble goes much deeper. It was utterly beyond the bounds of possibility so to draw the frontiers of Europe that each "nation" should constitute a separate state and at the same time preserve the essential units of economic co-operation. No doubt this would not have mattered if the nation-states had been prepared to treat their independence as purely "political", and to refrain from putting up any barriers in the way of the free intercourse ... But, though it was in practice impossible for the small states to be economically independent of the great, this limitation on their powers made them only the more determined to practise economic independence at one another's expense' (Cole 1941: 103–4).

Despite the fact that prudent economic considerations resulted in some significant deviations from a strict application of the principle of national self-determination, many borders were nevertheless 'drawn so as to cut right across the natural units of production and exchange' (Cole 1941: 104). Many towns and ports were detached from their former economic hinterlands, while many villages were deprived of access to their traditional grazing lands. The new frontiers frequently ruptured existing rail and trade networks, while lumping together railway systems which were previously almost unconnected (e.g. those of Slovakia and the Czech Lands, those of the disparate parts of Romania and those of the South Slav territories) or even based on different track gauges and incompatible rolling stock (the different parts of Poland). Moreover, traffic on the Danube slumped as a result of the 'Balkanization' of the Danube basin, and the river never recovered its pre-1918 role as the main economic artery of Eastern Europe. Its importance vanished along with that of the Habsburgs and the unified Danubian culture and cuisine which they had helped to foster. It was the end of an economic, cultural and culinary era, but one which might fruitfully be revived in the twenty-first century, if some desirable form of Danubian integration gets off the ground. Two eminent Hungarian Marxists have lamented that 'The creation of independent states in the place of great empires, the dissolution of large territorial and economic units, the contraction of some countries to a third of their former size and the expansion of others to twice or even three times their former extent in land and population, the economic condition of countries pieced together out of territories at different stages of economic development and taken from different states – all these circumstances created a radically new situation. Even in normal conditions, a considerable period of time, in fact an entire historical era, would have been required to complete the adjustment to new conditions, the integration into a unified economic whole, the opening up of new development possibilities and the attainment of a steady and sustained rate of economic growth. But history did not allow the problem to be presented in this fashion. The needs of the new order became apparent at a moment when the problems of the transition from a war to a peace economy were being added to the already difficult problems faced by an economy crippled by war, and all clamouring for immediate solution. The simultaneous appearance on the scene of all these problems brought about complete economic chaos' (Berend and Ranki 1969: 170).

Against this pessimistic view, the revisionist Czech economic historian Vaclav Prucha has argued that 'despite the post-war feelings of hopelessness, even the greatly reduced territories of Austria and Hungary proved viable. For the neighbours of these two countries the breakdown of the clumsy and conservative system of a multinational monarchy which involved pumping funds to Vienna and Budapest and which was linked with the privileges of the Austro-German and Hungarian landed gentry . . . and the Catholic Church, dynamized the efforts of politicians and the population to prove their capability of building up and managing the new states' (Prucha 1995: 40–1). However, without wishing to deny that the establishment of independent nation-states did have some liberating and energizing effects in the aftermath of the First World War, we are even more struck by the magnitude of the problems that inexorably weighed them down. As Aldcroft and Morewood (1993: 33) point out, not only did the new states have to deal with problems of reconstruction, 'but they literally had to create new administrations and national economies out of the motley collection of territories which they had inherited. Even worse, they were left to accomplish these tasks with little help from the West, apart from the short-lived American relief aid. Consequently, salvation was sought in restrictive trade policies, currency depreciation and inflation in a effort to achieve self-sufficiency and to promote structural change . . . Though there was an initial boost to activity and exports, once inflation got out of control it probably did more harm than good.'

'WINNERS' AND 'LOSERS': THE PEACE SETTLEMENTS OF 1919–20

The chief gainer from the 1919–20 peace settlements was Romania, which, through its acquisition of Bessarabia from Russia, southern Dobruja from Bulgaria and Transylvania and Bukovina and the Banat from Austria-Hungary, more than doubled its territory. These gains were all the more remarkable since Romania had signed a separate peace with the Central Powers in December 1917 and only re-entered the war on the Allied side on 10 November 1918, one day before the armistice! They were mainly attributable to the Allies' obsessive fear of 'Bolshevism' and their consequent willingness to maximize the size and strength of four states (Poland, Czechoslovakia, Yugoslavia and Romania) which were intended not only to guard Eastern Europe against any revival of the central powers but (more immediately) to constitute a *cordon sanitaire* against the Bolshevik 'plague'. (The original *cordon sanitaire* was a line of quarantine posts along Europe's borders with the Ottoman Empire, intended to reduce the risk of bubonic plague spreading into Europe from the more disease-prone Ottoman domains.)

The Poles also did extremely well out of the 1919–20 peace settlements. Having co-operated with and fought on both sides during the First World War, they were nevertheless treated as 'victorious Allies' at the end of it, while still keeping the gains

Pilsudski had made by working with the central powers against Tsarist Russia. Moreover, following the Polish victory in the Russo-Polish War of 1920, the Western powers allowed the Poles to hang on to large swathes of predominantly Ukrainian and Belorussian territory (amounting to half the land area of inter-war Poland), in clear breach of the principle of national self-determination.

The new order in Central and Eastern Europe was, in Otto Bauer's Austrian Marxist perspective, the combined result of 'the bourgeois national revolution of the Slav nations and the victory of Entente imperialism'. The national revolution freed the Czechs, South Slavs and Poles from alien rule and it initiated a period of democracy (albeit a short one in the cases of Poland and Yugoslavia). At the same time, however, 'the victory of Entente imperialism . . . falsified and distorted all the results of the national revolution' (p. 125). The victorious West 'has so drawn the frontiers of the new states that the national problems which disrupted the Habsburg Monarchy have again arisen in the new states'. In the case of Czechoslovakia, the Czechs 'can only rule by force the Germans, Slovaks, Magyars and Ruthenes who are included in her territory', while from the outset Yugoslavia was riven by 'the resistance of Croats and Slovenes to Great Serbian centralization' (p. 277). In Bauer's view, 'Any accentuation of the internal difficulties of the Czech and South Slav states can only favour the counter-revolutionary forces which have seized power in Italy and Hungary. Every collision between Serbia and Croatia will offer the Italian Fascisti an opportunity to realize their plans of domination over the Adriatic. The Magyar officer caste hope for much from the Magyar *irredenta* in Slovakia and Transylvania.' Thus fear of Italian imperialism and Magyar revenge 'keeps the whole area of the former Danube Monarchy in a state of latent war-like tension' (pp. 277–8). Bauer's fears were well founded, yet he failed to foresee the even greater threat that would eventually be posed by a resurgent Germany. This underestimation of the potential threat from Germany was characteristic of the 1920s (except in France) and was not just a typically Marxist (or Austrian) oversight.

Bauer believed that 'the fear of the Entente bourgeoisie at the spread of the social revolution . . . was responsible for the Czech state overflowing the boundaries of the Czech people' and that the same consideration 'also applies to Poland, which sprawls far beyond the national frontiers of the Polish people. Aggrandized at the expense of Russia and Germany, thereby incurring the enmity of both . . . Poland is forced to become a tool of French imperialism against the German Republic and the Russian Revolution' (p. 126). Indeed, Bauer suggested that the crucial roles of the Western Allies in defeating the central powers and in calling the new Slav states into existence would render the latter unduly dependent upon and 'subservient to the bourgeoisie of Western Europe' (pp. 76, 79, 126). This unhealthy psychological dependence and subservience heightened the panic and sense of betrayal when the West proved unwilling or unable to provide effective assistance to its Slav protégés during the 1930s. In similar vein, Oscar Jaszi (1929: 171) warned that none of the nations nurtured within the womb of the Habsburg Empire had produced a truly self-conscious and self-confident bourgeoisie, 'capable, as in the great Western states, of directing the evolution of the state'. In that sense the 'successor states' remained politically stunted, like many post-colonial states elsewhere in the world.

THE LATENT TRIUMPH OF GERMANY

One of the major (and often overlooked) consequences of the 1919–20 peace settlement was that, by dividing the former Habsburg territories between no less than seven small and medium-sized countries, it enhanced the strength of Germany *vis-à-vis* central and eastern Europe. The trenchant verdict of Jacques Bainville (a French nationalist) was that 'Germany was preserved but Europe was broken up' (Schultz 1972: 224). This kind of judgement tends to excite consternation and moral indignation among those who have been unduly influenced by a powerfully persuasive book by John Maynard Keynes entitled *The Economic Consequences of the Peace* (published in 1919), which forcefully argued that Germany had been too harshly treated by the victors at Versailles. Certainly Germany was disarmed, excessively burdened with 'reparations' and 'war guilt' and compelled grudgingly to relinquish Alsace-Lorraine, parts of Upper Silesia, Prussian Poland, parts of Schleswig-Holstein, its colonies and, temporarily, the Saar coal basin. Keynes correctly argued that, in view of the sheer magnitude and centrality of its economy, economic recovery in Germany was essential to the economic recovery of Europe. Furthermore, if humiliation and economic collapse were to drive the Germans to embrace Bolshevism, this great concentration of people in the centre of the continent could pull the rest of Europe towards a similar fate. There was indeed a case for reducing the astronomical 'reparations' demands, which hung like a Sword of Damocles over German economic recovery, and for a fairer apportionment of 'war guilt'. However, in his understandable desire to make his case as powerfully as possible, Keynes misled many of his readers into thinking that, as a result of the way it had been treated by the victors, Germany was now 'down and out' and no longer in a position to threaten or dominate its neighbours. He also gave powerful ammunition to the 'revisionist' cause, which was soon to include the Nazis. Many of his readers were inclined to underestimate Germany's latent or residual strengths and the degree to which the country had actually been strengthened *vis-à-vis* its eastern and south-eastern neighbours by the peace settlement, taken as a whole. This was one of the reasons why so many people were to be surprised by the apparent suddenness and speed of the revival of Germany's strength and of its capacity to dominate central and eastern Europe after 1933.

In reality the resurgence of Germany's strength was not surprising at all. It was implicitly there all along, merely awaiting a Siegfried to 'kiss' new life into the sleeping Brünnhilde. The Versailles Treaty had left Germany's major strengths (its 'high technology' and the industrial and education systems which produced it) largely intact, not least because there had been no fighting on German soil between 1914 and 1918, while the war effort had broadly accelerated the development of Germany's relatively advanced technologies and production systems. During the 1920s, despite widespread unemployment, Germany was still Europe's technological leader in the electrical, metallurgical, engineering, machine tool, chemical, petrochemical and synthetic products industries, i.e. the industries of the future and the ones that the Nazis would deploy to such devastating effect after 1933. The territories that Germany lost in 1918–19 were (in the main) relatively poor and depressed agricultural and mining areas, to most of which Germany had little or no legitimate claim in terms of the doctrine of national self-determination (which Germany professed to accept and uphold). They were mostly inhabited by non-Germans. Moreover, Germany's overseas colonies had been acquired very late in the day, after all the richest pickings had been seized by Britain and France, and were probably more of a liability than an asset. Their loss left Germany free from vainglorious extra-European 'imperial burdens' and distractions (unlike Britain and France) and allowed it to concentrate minds and resources on the further development of advanced industries and technologies which could conquer Europe economically and, under Hitler, by other means. The 'reparations' demanded under the Versailles Treaty were indeed astronomical and based on an unduly one-sided attribution of 'war guilt'. Yet during the 1920s the sums actually paid were quite modest (relative to the size and underlying strength of the German economy) and were largely offset by substantial capital inflows from America. During the 1930s Germany soon stopped paying 'reparations', initially because President Hoover of the United States pronounced a 'moratorium' and from 1933 onwards because the Nazis repudiated the whole shenanigan. The true significance of the 'reparations problem' was almost entirely political and psychological rather than economic. Indeed, in an otherwise mischievous book, A.J.P. Taylor trenchantly argued that the victorious Allies had two options in 1919. Either they could have treated Germany leniently and magnanimously, cleared it of 'war guilt' and rehabilitated it fully into the new community of nations, in order to promote full reconciliation and 'best behaviour' all round. Or, if they were bent upon holding Germany solely responsible for the war, imposing a punitive territorial settlement and 'making Germany pay', the victorious Allies should have occupied and partitioned Germany (as they did in 1945), so as to be in a position to uphold the punitive settlement and enforce 'reparations'. In the event the victors fell between two stools. They inflicted territorial losses, 'war guilt' and 'reparations' and prohibited any 'union' with German Austria and the German-inhabited parts of Bohemia, but they stopped short of partition and occupation. Thus they renounced the surest means of enforcement, while simultaneously antagonizing much (perhaps most) of the German 'nation'. First East Central Europe and later the whole of Europe were to pay the price of Allied inconsistency (Taylor 1964: 41–88).

The dangers implicit in this basic mistake, however, were compounded by the strengthening of inter-war Germany *vis-à-vis* its eastern and south-eastern neighbours. A peace settlement on the principle of national self-determination necessarily left Germany as Europe's largest country in terms of population, if one discounts truncated and devastated Soviet Russia. Indeed, 'Germany had gained through the replacement of the Habsburg Empire as a neighbour, which for all its debilities had still been a major power, by a large number of frail and mutually hostile successor states in the Danubian area . . . and through the substitution of Poland and the Baltic states in lieu of Russia as her immediate eastern neighbours' (Rothschild 1974: 5). Germany would soon find itself able to threaten and dominate an increasingly disunited Central and Eastern Europe far more effectively than it could have done before the First World War. By 1939 'Germany's economic hegemony over East Central Europe was more categorical than it could have been in 1913, demonstrating that the political advantages that accrued to her from the replacement of the Habsburg Empire by several smaller states were paralleled by economic opportunities' (p. 24). Similarly, an Austrian historian has argued that 'despite all the burdens imposed on Germany by the peace treaties, the power potential of the German Empire in 1919 remained unimpaired'. Its territorial losses were 'insignificant compared with the losses inflicted on Russia'. Moreover, Germany was fortunate that 'no plans were ever made by the Allied powers to partition the German Empire, even though the dismemberment of the *Reich* into the sovereign states in existence before 1870 . . . would have been in no way contrary to the course of modern Germany before the Franco-Prussian War' (Fellner 1968: 24–5). Indeed, it was by means of military intimidation and conquest that Bismarck had dragooned the many particularist German kingdoms and principalities into a 'unified' German Empire, which in 1918 was still of relatively recent origin. The Allies should perhaps have restored the independence of Bavaria, Saxony and Hanover in 1918–19, to match the more spontaneous break-up of the Habsburg Empire.

13 The aftermath of the First World War

The First World War precipitated the dissolution of three supranational empires: the Habsburg Monarchy, Tsarist Russia and the Ottoman Empire. A new political order in Eastern Europe was ushered in, based on the concepts of national self-determination and sovereign 'national' states. In reality, however, the so-called successor states were far from being homogeneous 'nation-states'. To be sure, powerful forces of imperial disintegration had already been at work both in East Central Europe and in the Balkans before 1914. The Austro-Hungarian Empire had suffered damaging defeats and loss of prestige in 1809, 1859 and 1866, while the Ottoman Empire had been slowly forced to retreat from south-eastern Europe between 1683 and 1912. Independent Balkan 'national' states and an autonomous Hungary had emerged in the course of the nineteenth century. But the process of imperial disintegration was greatly accelerated by the First World War, which Lenin saw as 'a tremendous historical crisis, the beginning of a new epoch. Like any crisis, the war has aggravated deep-seated antagonisms and brought them to the surface, tearing asunder all veils of hypocrisy, agitating all conventions and deflating all the corrupt or rotten authorities' (Lenin 1964: 98). Without the stresses and strains and crippling defeats engendered by the First World War, the Habsburg, Tsarist and Hohenzollern empires might well have survived for several more decades, either by making timely concessions to disaffected social and ethnic groups or, conversely, by intensifying the repression of such groups.

Like the other major wars in twentieth-century Europe, the First World War originated and had its major effects in eastern, not western, Europe. The powerful poems and images inspired by the often senseless and horrific carnage in the relatively static trench warfare on the western front have helped to distract attention from the even greater carnage and destruction inflicted by the much more mobile warfare on the eastern fronts. There were several theatres of war in eastern Europe. Poland was the major battleground between Germany and Russia and between Austria-Hungary and Russia. It was also the scene of further fighting between Soviet Russia and the resurrected Polish state in 1919 and, more seriously, in 1920. The battle lines shuttled back and forth across a prostrate Poland, causing widespread devastation and loss of life, while the Russian and Germanic protagonists escaped relatively unscathed by comparison. The eastern fronts did not get bogged down in mud, in contrast to the low-lying and easily flooded fields of Flanders. In the Balkans there were concurrent conflicts between Serbia and Austria-Hungary, between Romania and Austria-Hungary, between Bulgaria and her Balkan neighbours, and between Christians and Turks. For this segment of Europe the First World War was in a sense 'the Third Balkan War', a direct sequel to the Balkan Wars of 1912 and 1913.

In all, there were six years of almost continuous conflict, both in Poland (1914–20) and in the Balkans (1912–18).

Some idea of the enormous human and economic cost of the First World War can be gained from the following figures. Austria-Hungary suffered 1.2 million war dead (2.3 per cent of the population), 3.5 million wounded and 2.2 million prisoners-of-war (altogether 13 per cent of the population came under these categories). Other war dead totals were 335,000 for Romania (5 per cent of the population), 90,000 for Bulgaria, 45,000 for Serbia and 3,000 for Montenegro. Between 1913 and 1918–19 eastern European grain production halved. Over the period 1912–18, including the Balkan Wars of 1912 and 1913, Bulgaria suffered 300,000 dead and over 400,000 wounded. In all, 16 per cent of Bulgaria's population were killed or wounded. Romania was occupied and plundered, especially for its grain and oil (the lifeblood of the German war machine). Poland was the major battleground between Germany and Russia. By late 1920, following the Russo-Polish War of 1920, Poland had lost 18 per cent of its buildings, 55 per cent of its bridges, 48 per cent of its locomotives and nearly half its livestock.

THE REVOLUTIONS OF 1918–19

It has been argued that the dissolution of the Habsburg Empire in October 1918 was 'not a revolution but only a national and constitutional upheaval', since 'the existing social and economic order was preserved in the former provinces of the Habsburg Monarchy . . . and the administrative apparatus remained intact', albeit under 'national' rather than supranational political masters. Indeed, the dissolution of the Habsburg Empire was accomplished 'not along the lines of communist or even socialist ideology', nor 'in fulfilment of the Pan-Slav ideology which was regarded as the real danger for the multinational empire before 1914, but almost entirely in a legal manner' (Fellner 1968: 19, 23). What occurred was 'only a change of guard'. Beneath the 'superficial political changes, the social structure continued untouched; the economic system was shaken by crises but remained intact in its structure; the moral, political and practical value systems were preserved ' (pp. 97–8). In Fellner's view, the 'steps taken by the Social Democratic leaders to prevent a revolution' offer an expanation as to 'why only a political reorganization and not a social upheaval took place in 1918' and, furthermore, 'why the republicanizing of the Central European states was not followed by the democratizing of the social order' (p. 20).

This provocative line of argument is a salutary antidote to the temptation to exaggerate the scale and violence of the restructuring of East Central European society in the wake of the imperial disintegration that occurred in 1917–18. All the same, Fellner has overstated his case. Admittedly, the 'international proletarian revolution' prophesied by many Russian and East Central European Marxists (and much feared by Europe's propertied classes) failed to materialize ouside Russia (from October/November 1917 onward) and the short-lived Hungarian Soviet Republic under Bela Kun (from March to July 1919). The only other radical regime in Eastern Europe after the First World War was the 'peasantist dictatorship' established by Aleksandur Stamboliski in Bulgaria from 1919 to 1923. Both Stamboliski and Bela Kun were soon overthrown by bloody counter-revolutions. Yet this does not mean that Eastern Europe circumvented social revolution in the wake of the First World War. Rather it serves to emphasize that the social revolutions unleashed in post-1917 Eastern Europe were more akin to the French

Revolutions of 1789 and 1848 than to the Bolshevik Revolution which began in Russia in October/November 1917. The political ideas that prevailed in Eastern Europe in 1918 were those of the French Revolution, according to Seton-Watson (1945: 154). With the partial exceptions of Poland and Hungary, the post-1917 social revolutions in Eastern Europe involved significant redistribution of land from the old (often 'alien') estate owners to the peasantry, a major extension of political participation and voting rights (usually to all adult males) and the establishment of comprehensive 'national' (often fiercely nationalistic) systems of free, compulsory and (to varying degrees) secular state education. They also transferred power from the old supranational imperial aristocracies, armies and bureaucracies to the emerging peasant and bourgeois 'national' states, in which the old landed, military and bureaucratic elites certainly retained disproportionate influence and wealth but no longer monopolized political power and office. Power passed to rising 'national bourgeoisies' (the professions, the intelligentsias, managers, capitalists and non-noble officers and officials) as career structures were opened up to 'talent' and all the monied and educated classes. The old elites were rarely dispossessed, but they survived only as components of the expanding propertied and professional ruling classes.

In the words of Oscar Jaszi (1929: 454–5), 'War is sometimes a kind of revolution.' The First World War destroyed several 'petrified' political structures. 'In consequence, a great number of state embryos . . . grew into an independent life and for many millions of people the road was opened to national and social emancipation.' At the same time, however, 'war is a very crude and poor substitute for reason and morality. Like revolution, it can solve problems only in an incomplete and summary way, arousing new difficulties and injustices.'

According to Otto Bauer (the chief luminary of Austrian Marxism at the time), the final dissolution of the Habsburg Empire in October 1918 'was a national and democratic revolution' in which various national governments comprising 'the leaders of the parties of the bourgeoisie, the peasantry and the workers supplanted the dynasty, its supra-national bureaucracy, its generals and its diplomats'. However, these same events, while marking the completion of various national struggles for independent statehood, also 'awakened the Social Revolution' and let loose 'the class struggle' within each of the newly independent nations (Bauer 1925: 53). 'The Social Revolution which arose out of the war proceeded from the barracks rather than the factories . . . The four years' suppression of the dignity of the soldiers now revenged itself in a wild outburst of hatred for the officer' (p. 56). However, 'revolution in the barracks immediately provoked a revolution in the factories'. During the war industrial workers had been placed under military discipline and control, but now 'the whole authority of private enterprise and its organs crumbled with the collapse of military power', while the 'self-consciousness and the self-reliance of the workers were powerfully reinforced' (p. 60). Thus the East Central European revolutions of 1918 'inflicted a severe blow upon the capitalist mode of production'. Industry had been harnessed to the war effort. But, with the end of the fighting, 'the machines suddenly came to a stop' (p. 130). Almost immediately a whole new literature on the socialization of production appeared. 'The faith of capitalist society in itself was undermined' (p. 131), as 'shattered industry could not absorb the masses of workers returning from the Front or thrown on the streets by the idle war industries' (p. 132). The restoration of labour discipline was delayed by the workers' state of exhaustion at the end of the war, by the 'passionate excitement into which they were plunged by the revolution' and by the irregularity of fuel and raw material supplies, which rendered regular uninterrupted work impossible (p. 140). 'Many employers, discouraged by the collapse . . . made no effort to adapt their undertakings to peacetime production . . . They preferred to withdraw their capital . . . and turn it into foreign securities' (p. 133).

Like all revolutions, Bauer maintained, this one was achieved by the use of force. But the force that made the revolution possible had been expended, not in the city streets and barricades, but on the First World War battlefields on which the 'obsolete' imperial polities and armies had been 'smashed' (p. 65). The war, which began as 'a struggle of powerful imperialistic groups', became in the end 'a struggle between two political systems' (p. 70). 'The victory of the Western powers over the central powers was the victory of bourgeois democracy over the oligarchical, military monarchies. It was the greatest and bloodiest revolution in the history of the world' (p. 71). Indeed, over 8 million people had perished in the course of the conflict, not counting the additional 8 million who perished in the ensuing Russian civil war (1918–21) and Russo-Polish War (1920). Moreover, the success of the Czechs, the Poles and the South Slavs in attaining independent statehood constituted 'a bourgeois revolution' in the sense that 'it broke the power of the Habsburgs, the German-Austrian bureaucracy and the Magyar gentry', replacing it with 'the rule of the Czech, the Polish and the Jugo Slav bourgeoisies, organized in the new national states' (p. 76).

In view of the long-standing debate on the extent to which the French Revolution can properly be described as a 'bourgeois revolution', it should be emphasized that labelling a revolution 'bourgeois' does not necessarily imply (let alone require) that it was actively brokered and led by the industrial, commercial and financial bourgeoisie, or even that the revolution was perceived by them to be directly in their own interests. In the main, traders, bankers and industrialists are not noted for political daring or courage. They have tended to fear revolution and to support the *status quo*, because violent and/or cataclysmic political and social upheavals can (at least in the short term) damage property, impair business confidence and disrupt commercial networks, especially those that depend on state contracts and patronage. In the case of the Austro-Hungarian Empire, the traders, bankers and industrialists were for the most part 'risk-averse' socially and politically conservative Germans and Jews rather than political leaders of the secessionist 'nations'. In Marxist terms, nevertheless, the revolution of 1918–19 (like that of 1789) helped to weaken and 'disarm' the old ruling class and the former social hierarchy. It cleared the decks for the more 'unfettered' development of capitalism and the transfer of power to the ascendant 'national' bourgeoisies of the nascent national states of East Central Europe. As in France in 1789, the principal leaders and brokers of the revolution were not businessmen but members of the professional wing of the bourgeoisie (lawyers, teachers and journalists). Their 'historic role' was to enact a 'bourgeois democratic revolution' which would promote and consolidate the inchoate political and social ascendancy of the capitalist classes, even if at the time few of them were wholly conscious of the full significance and long-term consequences of their actions. The contours of the emerging political landscape were the outcome of a kaleidoscope of conflicting interests which, as remarked by Longworth (1994: 65), 'are difficult enough to comprehend in retrospect and were certainly not fully understood by the main protagonists'.

Indeed, any attempt to explain the revolution in terms of the pursuit of material self-interest is complicated by the fact that, between 1918 and 1923, large sections of the long-established bourgeoisie were impoverished by the unexpected severity of the economic collapse and the subsequent hyperinflation. 'Thousands who had been rich before the war could only prolong their existences by selling old furniture and jewellery and letting rooms to strangers' (Bauer 1925: 198). The real gainers were spivs, speculators and profiteers, who amassed new fortunes during the war and the subsequent hyperinflation and reconversion to a peacetime economy, while the bourgeoisies that emerged triumphant in the 1920s were by no means synonymous with the old imperial bourgeoisies. It is perhaps hardly surprising that so many downgraded and resentful Austrian and Bohemian Germans subsequently became attracted to Nazism.

REGIME CONSOLIDATION DURING THE 1920s

For Central and Eastern Europe the most immediate internal political problem bequeathed by the dissolution of Europe's 'eastern empires' was how to establish a new basis of authority, loyalty and obedience. This need was to a large extent met by 'ethnic' nationalism. The authority and legitimacy of the new states and regimes was essentially 'national'. The main motivations for loyalty and obedience among the new 'peoples of the state', i.e. the new dominant ethnic groups, were generated by 'ethnic' nationalism. As noted by Rothschild (1974: 4), however, inter-war Eastern Europe provides the classic illustration of the limitations and drawbacks as well as the strengths and advantages of nationalism as a legitimizing ideology. It may have engendered majority attachment, obedience and loyalty to each of the new states, even in the particularly difficult cases of Yugoslavia and Czechoslovakia, but it did so at the price of permanently and damagingly alienating substantial minorities. Indeed, if nationalism had been capable of contributing significantly to the dissolution of great empires, it was certainly capable of setting in motion forces which could lead to the disintegration of Czechoslovakia and Yugoslavia (as was seen between 1938 and 1941 and yet again in the early 1990s), inter-war Poland (viz. September 1939) and perhaps, at some future date, Russia, Ukraine, Macedonia, Moldova, Estonia or Latvia. Indeed, if one accepted the premises of nationalism and took them to their logical conclusion, the unravelling process seemed 'natural and legitimate and no end could be set to it' (Carr 1945: 24). Many people must by now have asked: 'Where will it all end?' In western Europe national unification and integration essentially promoted the consolidation of a large number of small political entities into a lesser number of larger 'national' states, whereas in Central and Eastern Europe nationalism and the creation of 'national' states had the very opposite effect (Rothschild 1974: 1). Between the wars, on balance, nationalism proved to be 'the curse of eastern Europe'. National grievances, whether they were real or imaginary, justified or unjustified, provided pretexts for dictatorial and oppressive rule and leverage points for Nazi and fascist influence, interference, encroachment and (eventually) domination. In the meantime, economic nationalism and 'national' tariff walls restricted regional economic integration, gains from trade and specialization and, in the long run, the whole scope for economic development (Warriner 1950: 64). Thus economic development was ultimately 'boxed in' by economic nationalism, while political nationalism rendered the region increasingly vulnerable to external interference and domination – the very opposite of what nationalism was supposed to do, in the eyes of its proponents.

During the inter-war years almost every state in Eastern Europe was governed by a rapidly expanding 'national bourgeoisie' which took over the state apparatus, gradually displaced some 'non-national' elements from the professions, commerce and finance, hi-jacked most of the political parties (including the peasant and social democratic parties) and drew in new recruits via the greatly expanded 'national' education systems (Seton-Watson 1945: 123–6). 'The task of the ruling classes of the Eastern European countries after 1918 was to attract to themselves new elements, in order to strengthen themselves against possible revolutionary forces. They needed greatly to increase the number of people interested in the preservation of the existing regimes, but had to guard against being swamped by new recruits' (p. 125). In Poland and Hungary 'national bourgeoisies' governed in partnership with the old 'national' aristocracies, which held on to power thanks to the exceptional strength of their nationalist credentials as well as their continuing control of the countryside and large parts of the professions (and, in Hungary and parts of Poland, official posts). On the economic front the Polish and Magyar aristocracies were 'placated' by the protection and subsidies accorded to the agricultural products of the big landed estates, but in most respects the policies pursued were those favoured by the 'national bourgeoisies' (p. 127).

According to Rothschild, however, the 'ruling class' in inter-war Eastern Europe 'was not, contrary to conventional assumptions, the bourgeoisie, which was quite weak and either dependent on state subsidies or else ethnically "alien" and hence vulnerable. Rather it was the bureaucracy, which was allied with and recruited from the intelligentsia' (Rothschild 1974: 17). 'Both its civilian and military components were recruited from the so-called intelligentsia, which, in turn, was simply identified by its possession of academic diplomas.' This educated class was mainly recruited from the gentry, the middle class and the peasantry. 'It might rule in association with the landed and entrepreneurial class, but it was never a mere tool of the aristocracy or the bourgeoisie' (p. 19).

In point of fact, these differing conceptions of the ruling class in inter-war Eastern Europe ('the bourgeoisie' versus 'the bureaucracy') are not as far apart as they appear to be. The dispute is mainly a matter of semantics. In its original pre-Marxist usage, which is the one employed by Seton-Watson, the term 'bourgeoisie' was not limited to the capitalist or entrepreneurial classes. The 'bourgeoisie' also comprised middle-ranking officers and officials and the liberal professions. In the agrarian or semi-agrarian states of inter-war Eastern Europe, as in late eighteenth-century France, the typical 'bourgeois' was not a capitalist entrepreneur but an office-holder, a lawyer or a doctor. Thus Rothschild's strictures mainly apply to the narrower Marxist use of the term 'bourgeoisie' to refer to the capitalist/entrepreneurial propertied classes rather than to Seton-Watson's broader use of the term. Indeed, Rothschild's claim that the ruling 'bureaucracy' was recruited from 'the intelligentsia' is even more problematic, given the mainly radical or oppositional overtones of the word 'intelligentsia' during the inter-war period.

The 'neo-mercantilist' industrialization programmes launched by the East European states during the 1920s were motivated by economic nationalism. The new regimes perceived that industrial nations were stronger than agrarian ones. Therefore, in a Europe of nation-states, each of the successor states was determined to build up industries of its own. 'A new industrial system would give the state a greater degree of international prestige, security and independence. It would offer the ruling class a means of enriching itself. It would provide employment for a considerable number of young men of the ruling class . . . Lastly, it would give employment to part of the labour overflow from the countryside' (Seton-Watson 1945: 126–7). Aside from land reform and the expansion of education and non-agricultural employment opportunities, however, the needs of the peasants were largely neglected by East European governments, which mainly 'devoted themselves to such economic activity as directly benefited the ruling class' (p. 128). Moreover, through their heavy reliance on high import duties, the profits from state monopolies of items such as salt, matches and tobacco and indirect taxes on articles of popular consumption, the taxation systems were 'calculated to make the poorer classes pay for the economic programme of the ruling class' (p. 131).

During the 1920s, with the significant exception of Czechoslovakia, the East European states were also dependent on inflows of foreign capital (mainly from western Europe) to finance their sometimes ambitious infrastructural and industrialization programmes. Indeed, by 1929 foreign ownership of industrial share capital stood at about 48 per cent in Bulgaria, 44 per cent in Yugoslavia, 40 per cent in Poland and 28 per cent in Hungary (Berend and Ranki 1974a: 236–7; 1974b: 109). Only the fiercely nationalistic Bratianu 'Liberals', who dominated Romanian politics from 1922 to 1928 under the slogan *Prin noi insine* (By ourselves alone), enacted serious obstacles to foreign investment. This was partly the result of the Bratianu brothers' unsuccessful attempt to bring about private 'national' control of Romania's largely foreign-owned oil industry, which was by 1927 the sixth largest in the world and the largest in Europe (excluding the USSR). But even Romanian industry remained to a large extent foreign-owned. Moreover, the Romanian National Peasant Party, which won a landslide victory in the 1928 elections, launched a (short-lived) 'open door' policy, in reaction to the corrupt and regressive economic nationalism of the Bratianu clientele ('capitalism in one family').

Nationalists did have substantial grounds for concern and resentment over the magnitude of Eastern Europe's dependence on foreign capital and the resulting 'political interference' by foreign creditors, although some of the grievances would not cut much ice in 'liberal' and socialist circles either then or now. Heavy dependence on foreign capital was seen as a partial negation of 'national' independence and of the nationalist goal of 'national' self-reliance. It increased Western leverage and influence on the East European states. Some foreign investors even criticized the nationalistic economic and cultural policies and the increasingly xenophobic and antisemitic attitudes and behaviour of the Polish, Hungarian and Romanian 'national bourgeoisies'. Many nationalists feared that Western investment might reinforce Western cultural influence and spread 'liberal' and secular Western values, although they actually had little to fear on that account! More seriously, the (mainly extractive) industries in which Western investors were willing to invest most heavily were not the ones which East European governments and nationalists would have favoured. Above all, partly as a result of the political instability of the region and fears that the new 'national' frontiers could eventually be challenged by Germany, Hungary, Bulgaria or the USSR (threatening the region's peace and economic stability), the East European states were able to borrow only at relatively high rates of interest and their economies became burdened by onerous debt service obligations. This was naturally seen as impairing the capacity of East European states to undertake much-needed economic and social programmes on the domestic front (Seton-Watson 1945: 130). Nevertheless, whatever its drawbacks, foreign capital helped to restore and even increase East European industrial production. By 1929, relative to 1913, real industrial output had increased by about 12 per cent in Hungary, 18 per cent in Austria, 37 per cent in Romania, 40 per cent in Bulgaria and Yugoslavia and a remarkable 72 per cent in

Czechoslovakia. (The figure for Europe as a whole was 27 per cent.) Only war-battered Poland had failed to regain its 1913 level of industrial production by 1929 (Berend and Ranki 1974a: 240).

It has been argued that a prerequisite for 'regime consolidation' in an emergent parliamentary democracy is the successful integration of a plurality of competing groups and interests with the state, which develops as a set of 'rules and structures relating to, and the personnel of a central authority exercising sovereign powers over, a defined territorial unit' (Arter 1993: 31). In the would-be parliamentary democracies of post-1918 Eastern Europe, the nascent political parties and party systems were cast in a crucial role 'as agencies of national integration', responsible for 'mobilizing, socializing and organizing mass electorates, recruiting a new class of political leaders and building a pro-system consensus'. On the other hand, less auspiciously, 'parties could serve as channels for the articulation of dissenting, anti-systemic sentiment', expressing ideological and/or territorial opposition to and challenging the legitimacy of the new states (p. 32). The newly established communist parties, the uncompromisingly separatist or autonomist ethnic minority parties, some of the peasant parties and most of the neo-fascist movements and parties of the successor states fell into the latter role, contributing to the premature death of genuine parliamentary democracy (if it was not 'stillborn') in Hungary, Bulgaria, Poland, Yugoslavia and Albania during the 1920s, as well as in Austria, Romania and finally Czechoslovakia during the 1930s.

The party systems of most of the successor states were from the outset plagued by excessive fragmentation. Thus in Poland nearly 100 political parties, including five different peasant parties, participated in elections during the first half of the 1920s and over thirty gained representation in parliament. The Czechoslovak parliament had seventeen political parties by 1920 (none with more than a quarter of the seats) and much the same was true of Yugoslavia (Longworth 1994: 72–3). Parliaments were so fractious that it was often difficult to assemble and hold together stable governing coalitions capable of taking tough decisions, decisive action and the long view. Short-term considerations were almost always uppermost. Only in Austria was there a well-defined two-party cleavage offering voters a clear choice between the sharply contrasting political, social and economic programmes of the left and the right, but the republic was riven by the violent mutual hatred between the Marxist socialism of 'Red Vienna' and the reactionary and equally doctrinaire Catholicism of the Alpine provinces. In several of the successor states most political parties were 'personal coteries united by loyalty to an individual rather than a political programme or ideology'. Political support was usually maintained 'by a system of rewards and sanctions within the elite and from the elite downwards' (Schöpflin 1993: 21). For the most part voters were looking for charismatic 'saviours' with panaceas, rather than disciplined parties offering coherent programmes. Moreover, the successor states mostly comprised territories which had previously been divided between very different states and these frequently had widely differing legal and administrative traditions, ethnic compositions, political orientations and levels of development, along with little or no experience of inter-party negotiation, compromise and parliamentary rule.

None of the states of inter-war Eastern Europe (not even Czechoslovakia) was able to integrate its ethnically and regionally diverse inhabitants into a unified all-embracing class structure and 'civil society', to make a single whole. Both the will and the means were lacking. This in turn strongly contributed to their failure to develop unified bodies of public opinion which could exercise effective control over the political sphere (Schöpflin 1993: 19). It also exacerbated the failure to promote responsible and accountable government, other than in Czechoslovakia. The various social and ethnic groups may have been 'cohesive within themselves . . . but they lacked any . . . sense of participating in the same political venture' (p. 24). Thus the state was more dominant (and autonomous actors were fewer and weaker) in inter-war Eastern Europe than in Western countries. The power of the state was occasionally challenged, but the challenges were usually emasculated or suppressed, with the result that the autonomy of social classes and other groups failed to grow. What is more, the sense of reciprocal obligation between social and ethnic groups and between rulers and ruled, while not entirely non-existent, was 'weak', as was the autonomous rule of law (p. 11). 'The state exercised a paramountcy over society that the latter could do little to modify' (p. 13), partly because East European cities lacked the high degree of civic pride and autonomy enjoyed by most Western cities (p. 17).

Under the quasi-parliamentary regimes of the early inter-war years heads of government were usually chosen from and by the political elite. The government then 'elected' a parliament to serve it. Thus governments normally determined the timing and outcome of elections, instead of elections determining who was to be in government. Rarely did an incumbent government lose an election. Elections were usually just a charade that sometimes had to be gone through in order to confirm a new government in office or to renew the existing government's 'mandate' while 'deselecting' some potentially troublesome parliamentary opponents. However, a government did not need to control the whole of the electorate, only a proportion that would give it de facto control of public affairs and policy-making. Governments mainly relied upon bribery, patronage, gerrymandering, electoral fraud, restriction of the franchise and (in the last resort) violence and intimidation to maintain themselves in office (Seton-Watson 1945: 155; Arter 1993: 45; Schöpflin 1993: 21; Longworth 1994: 73–4). Even Hungary achieved a stable quasi-parliamentary regime after 1921, but only by intimidating, disenfranchising or 'buying off' the most discontented sections of the population and restoring the use of 'open' (rather than secret) ballots in rural areas, thereby placing rural voters at the mercy of the great landowners, rural officials and the police. Only 27 per cent of the population was permitted to vote after the disenfranchising of all men under the age of twenty-four, women under the age of thirty (unless they had three children or a 'high school' education) and anyone with less than six years' schooling.

The political and economic rhetoric of post-1918 Eastern Europe often sounded quite radical, whether it was nationalist, peasantist, socialist, communist, etatist, fascist or neo-liberal. However, the principal propagators of this rhetoric were 'the educated and semi-educated class . . . whose material interests were opposed . . . to those of the peasants and workers, whom they kept in place by police terror and mulcted by taxation' (Seton-Watson 1945: 154). There were many parallels with the outcome and social/ideological contradictions of the French Revolution. Indeed, most of the political struggles in inter-war Eastern Europe took place 'between different small groups within narrow ruling classes, over the heads of the peoples'. To most of the office-holders and power brokers 'the masses' were little more than 'electoral currency, the passive objects of their policy' (p. 256).

In a vignette that could be applied with equal justice to the communist period, Seton-Watson lamented that 'the Balkan official does not like to work. He considers himself so fine a fellow that the state and the public should be proud to support him for life, and should not ask him to make efforts that will tax either his intellect or his character.' Balkan officials would happily chat over cups of Turkish coffee for hours while peasants queued, patiently awaiting various permits and receipts. After all, they had already been waiting for justice for centuries, so a few more hours would not make much difference. Indeed, Balkan bureaucracy involved 'obscure and complicated formalities and documents, the result of an accumulation of laws and taxes superimposed since the beginning of time', yielding constant sources of 'revenue to the bureaucrat and annoyance to the citizen'. Corruption was endemic. Most officials were so poorly paid that they could not support their families without taking bribes and, since the laws were 'often cumbrous, stupid, inefficient and oppressive', there was no shortage of bribe-payers. Frequently, however, official decisions were referred to a higher level and, after further days or weeks of delay, the citizen could be 'summoned to the capital, at his own expense in time and money, to settle some trifling formality' (p. 147).

Much more insidious, however, was the corruption of the upper echelons. 'In Eastern Europe the greatest fortunes are made not in industry or banking but in politics.' Petty corruption could have been cured by increasing official salaries. It was far harder to find a cure for 'upper-class corruption'. Government Ministries in most of the successor states 'possessed large "discretionary funds", of which the Ministers often embezzled part or all. Ministers of Finance enriched themselves by selling protective tariffs to industrialists.' Senior factory inspectors from Ministries of Labour also found industrialists appreciative of the omission of any mention of certain 'minor irregularities and deficiencies' in their routine inspection reports (Seton-Watson 1945: 148). In inter-war Poland, Hungary and the Balkans, moreover, taxes were often 'collected with the utmost brutality', particularly from the peasantry. There was not infrequent use of physical violence and confiscation of vital assets for non-payment of taxes and 'there was no redress against administrative abuses'. Of course there were legal rights and courts of appeal, but 'all this remained on paper'. Peasants who complained of abuses were often denounced as 'communists', beaten, hauled before military tribunals and 'sentenced either to prison or to forced labour'. Indeed, 'ruthlessness and brutality were widespread all over Eastern Europe except Czechoslovakia and even there they were not unknown' (pp. 148–9). The worst abuses occurred in recently annexed 'backward' frontier areas with mixed populations, such as Bessarabia, Bukovina, Macedonia and, in Poland, the provinces of Polesia and Volhynia, whose inhabitants 'lacked the political and cultural standards of the advanced regions and had neither material nor moral weapons with which to defend themselves'. In such areas 'officials could beat, rob and rape as they pleased'. They branded anyone who resisted or protested a 'Bolshevik' or an 'enemy of the state' and often eventually turned 'even the potentially loyal part of the population into real communists and separatists' (pp. 153–4).

With the exception of Czechoslovakia the successor states lived in constant fear of 'Bolshevism', which was one of the main motivations for their hastily conceived land reforms, largely cosmetic welfare provisions and rather more impressive educational achievements. With some justification the new regimes 'prided themselves particularly on the progress made in education'. Numerous schools were built in regions where they had previously been lacking. Systems of compulsory and universal elementary schooling were established in each state. A few regions continued to suffer illiteracy rates of over 80 per cent throughout the inter-war period (for example, parts of Bosnia and Bessarabia and much of Albania). However, Seton-Watson contended that this could not be blamed entirely on governments. 'Often children needed at home for work in the fields were not allowed by their parents to go to school' (p. 139). (A similar problem re-emerged in Albania during the early 1990s.) Moreover, even where great progress was made in educating the rising generations, there remained widespread illiteracy among older people, except in the highly educated Czech Lands. Nevertheless, during the inter-war years illiteracy rates in Eastern Europe were greatly reduced and genuine attempts were made 'to enable poor children of talent to obtain a higher education', albeit more so in Czechoslovakia, Bulgaria, Yugoslavia and Romania than in the more 'feudal' states (p. 139).

The more rapid expansion of education awoke an impressive 'appetite for knowledge', while the intellectual perhaps attained 'greater prestige in Eastern Europe than anywhere else in the world' (Seton-Watson 1945: 140). This was to be of crucial importance in the subsequent political history of Eastern Europe (right down to the fall of the communist regimes and the transition to democracy and market economies after 1989). During the inter-war years East European universities produced many distinguished intellectuals, writers and scientists and considerable sums were spent on the provision of scientific and medical facilities, particularly in Czechoslovakia and at the universities of Krakow, Budapest and Warsaw (p. 140). However, the immediate results were not always positive. Most students were of relatively humble origin and needed some financial assistance from the state to enable them to continue their studies. For such persons access to university education was seen as the gateway to individual social advancement. 'It was assumed that every student who passed his examinations had a right to a job in the state apparatus. The job might be of little importance, but it conferred great prestige on the son of a peasant or village priest . . . A university diploma was considered a claim on the state for the rest of one's life' (pp. 126, 142). (This was a foretaste of the so-called 'diploma disease' which has also afflicted many developing countries in other parts of the world.) The investments by East European states in higher education became 'disproportionately large' *vis-à-vis* their investments in primary education and 'the absorptive capacities of their still basically agrarian economies' (except in the case of the industrialized and more comprehensively educated Czech Lands). Soon more graduates were being churned out than could find gainful employment. Consequently the 'land hunger' of the peasantry was mirrored by the 'office hunger' of the intelligentsia. This strongly contributed to the 'proliferation of political parties more concerned with patronage than with policy' (i.e. 'jobs for the boys') and to the growth of swollen, nepotistic bureaucracies whose 'tenacious but essentially stagnant power' stultified the political development of the successor states (Rothschild 1974: 20). The notable exception was again the industrialized and well educated Czech Lands, which were more capable of absorbing the Czech intelligentsia into gainful employment. But, contrary to claims that 'social mobility was low to very low' in inter-war Eastern Europe (Schöpflin 1993: 24), it is clear that the growth of bloated state bureaucracies and 'bourgeois' ruling classes involved considerable upward mobility, as is emphasized by Seton-Watson (1945: 123–6).

Eastern Europe's most persistent and widespread educational problems concerned the chronic shortage of properly qualified teaching staff, rampant nepotism in educational appointments and 'grave deficiencies in the content and quality of the education provided' (Seton-Watson 1945: 140). For example, the teaching of history was often little more than crude indoctrination in narrow-minded xenophobic nationalism, with exaggerated emphasis on medieval heroics. 'The youth of each nation was taught to regard its neighbours as inferior' (p. 141). In higher education the much-needed medical, agricultural and engineering sciences remained underdeveloped. This was 'the more striking in view of the overcrowding of Law Faculties, whose students in many cases received no more than a training in chauvinism as a preparation for a bureaucratic post'. Moreover, the overproduction of law graduates was 'largely responsible' for the mounting problems of graduate unemployment, which provided 'a generous supply of "Führers" for the various fascist movements of Eastern Europe' (pp. 144–5). Especially in Poland and Romania, the universities became veritable hotbeds of fascism and antisemitism during the 1920s and 1930s, and the 'impatient and discontented idealism' of the intelligentsia was 'exploited by governments and politicians for the basest purposes' (pp. 142–3). The shock troops of the Romanian, Polish and Hungarian fascist movements were recruited from such a background, initially into the employ of corrupt governments, political parties and the police ('as toughs, agents provocateurs, strike-breakers or Jew-baiters') before graduating to careers of more blatant political criminality (pp. 143, 206–7; Longworth 1994: 84–6; Crampton 1994: 160–7).

More insidiously the arrogant, dishonest, xenophobic nationalism nurtured by most of the East European education systems 'at best encouraged chauvinism and at worst helped to destroy all conceptions of morality'. Indeed, it was 'not confined to the schools and universities, but extended to the press, publications of all sorts, the theatre, official propaganda'. Not surprisingly the ruling classes formed in such an environment 'had no sense of responsibility towards other classes, no understanding of the principle of individual liberty' (Seton-Watson 1945: 143). At the same time the 'young generation was brought up to hate and despise other nations . . . and to see in any proposal for collaboration with other states a poisonous intrigue of Reds, Jews and Freemasons', making them 'easy prey' to antisemitic, anti-democratic and fascist demagogues and agitators. Moreover, little was done to promote the study of the languages, cultures, societies and histories of neighbouring peoples. The consequent 'lack of cultural relations between the Eastern European states was one of the fundamental reasons for their failure to collaborate against common external enemies' (p. 145). This problem has persisted into the 1990s. In contrast to the major efforts to promote mutual knowledge, understanding and reconciliation between the peoples of France, Germany, Italy, the Low Countries and Scandinavia after the Second World War, the peoples of eastern Europe still know relatively little about one another. Indeed, under the so-called 'national communism' of the 1970s and 1980s they were mainly 'force-fed' fiercely nationalistic accounts of their own histories and negative stereotypes of their neighbours. Throughout the communist era it was made very difficult for inhabitants of the Balkans either to visit one another's countries or to learn each other's languages, even if they wanted to do so. (There was rather more cultural contact between the peoples of East Central Europe.) Significantly, most of the non-Romanian Balkan participants in an academic conference on the Balkan states held in Bucharest on 29–30 August 1994 informed us that they had never set foot in Romania before and that lack of mutual knowledge and understanding was still a major impediment to Balkan political co-operation and economic integration.

For all their faults, the quasi-parliamentary regimes in 1920s Eastern Europe still allowed some political and cultural pluralism, some diversity (if not always 'freedom') of expression and some (albeit limited) political and legal means of redressing certain types of individual and collective grievance. These regimes were in no sense 'totalitarian'. As emphasized by Seton-Watson (1945: 156), 'It would be a mistake to pretend that there was no difference between pseudo-parliamentarianism and open dictatorship. Under the former there were at least a few safety valves.' Gradually, however, the many failings of the pseudo-parliamentary regimes and the corrupt self-serving political parties brought so-called 'democracy' into disrepute. 'Disillusioned by the old parties, the people looked for new men', men who claimed to be able to cleanse society of corruption, chicanery, incompetence and kleptocracy. 'Extremist movements of Left and Right gained ground', promising charismatic leadership, vision, reform, moral regeneration and a new sense of common purpose, with action instead of words and strong government in place of talking-shops, trickery and drift. The onset of the 1930s Depression accelerated the growth of domestic and international tensions, popular disenchantment with 'democracy' and the groundswell of support for authoritarian panaceas, fascism and communism, but the rot had set in much earlier. In important respects the new order erected in the aftermath of the First World War was inherently flawed and sooner or later most of the successor states proved incapable of meeting the political and economic challenges posed by the twentieth century. Confronted by their own incompetence and the rising tide of popular disillusionment, deprivation and discontent, 'the ruling classes became more and more frightened'. They increasingly resorted to repression (except in relatively resilient and liberal Czechoslovakia) and, recognizing that they were no longer able to sustain pseudo-democratic facades, they allowed the last trappings of 'democracy' to be chipped away bit by bit (or even did the job themselves). Thus, except in Czechoslovakia, quasi-parliamentary rule gradually gave way to royal, nationalist, military or fascist dictatorship. If the tumultuous events of 1918–19 amounted to a real (albeit limited and flawed) 'revolution', those of the 1920s and 1930s were a creeping 'counter-revolution', accelerated by the rise of fascism and the onset of the Depression,

14 The 1930s Depression and its consequences

THE MULTIPLE CAUSES OF ECONOMIC DEPRESSION

An important cause of the economic crises which convulsed inter-war Europe was the fact that European capitalism had exhausted the dynamic technological and growth potential of the products and processes which it had developed and exploited with such spectacular success in the eighteenth and nineteenth centuries. To a large extent Europe fell victim to its own past achievements. European markets for cotton, woollen and linen textiles, processed foods and drinks, footwear, steel, coal, ships, railway construction and railway equipment were approaching saturation point and the ageing textile, coal, steel, shipbuilding and railway industries were facing problems of over-capacity which could only temporarily be assuaged by the exceptional demands generated by the two World Wars. In principle there was still considerable scope for the further development of industries such as these in Eastern Europe, except in the already industrialized regions of the Czech Lands. In practice, however, financial difficulties and constraints, the growth of Western protectionism and the relatively small size and low purchasing power of the East European 'national' markets limited their potential. Certainly it was impossible to replicate the easy profits and the largely unimpeded export-led expansion experienced by several of the Western industrial pioneers during their heyday. The once lucrative non-European markets for Europe's 'traditional' industrial products were under threat from the gathering pace of industrialization and rising levels of protectionism in Asia, Latin America and Australasia.

Many Marxists mistook the mounting crisis for the long-heralded terminal crisis of capitalism. In reality, however, a new generation of 'high technology' capitalist products and processes was already germinating in the West, particularly in the United States and Germany. But their long-term significance and dynamic potential were obscured and prevented from being fully realized (in both senses of the word), first by the severity of the 1930s Depression and later by the temporary revival of older industries under the impact of rearmament and the outbreak of the Second World War. It was not until the 1940s in the United States and the 1950s in Western Europe that the new 'high tech' industries (mainly consumer durables) became sufficiently massive to 'take up the slack' by absorbing the resources discarded or left unemployed by the older 'declining' industries. However, the latter were to be given a further lease of life by 'etatist' (state-sponsored) development of import-substituting metallurgical, engineering, shipbuilding, coal and textile industries in Eastern Europe and parts of the 'developing world' from the late 1930s onward, while the West was gradually making the transition to 'high technology' capitalism.

The 1930s Depression probably hit Eastern Europe harder than almost any other part of the world. It is commonly portrayed as an externally induced affliction, the consequence of the interplay of momentous economic forces in the dominant Western economies (primarily the United States, Britain, Germany and France), over which the puny East European states could exercise little or no influence, let alone control. The East Europeans were hapless passive victims. East European governments have thus been largely absolved of any 'blame' or responsibility for the ensuing catastrophes. Different policies and/or politicians, it is commonly assumed, could only have slightly curtailed the devastating impact of the Depression on Eastern Europe. There was indeed very little room for manoeuvre, very little that could have been done, given the weakness, fragility and highly exposed position of the East European states in the face of much larger world market forces and the magnitude of the waves that pounded these small vessels. Nevertheless, Eastern Europe was significantly involved in the causes as well as the consequences of the Depression. It was not merely passive and acted upon; it also acted.

The First World War and its immediate aftermath caused widespread disruption and some devastation of primary commodity production in both western and (especially) eastern Europe, mainly as a result of the massive mobilization of manpower, horses and transport for the war effort. This, combined with high wartime prices and inflated demand for certain categories of raw materials and fuels, stimulated large increases in agricultural and mineral production in the Americas, Africa, Asia and Australasia. Yet during the mid-1920s, particularly in the central and eastern parts of the continent, European farmers and mining companies started borrowing heavily in an all-too-successful endeavour to regain their pre-war levels of production. However, partly as a result of the massive 'population deficit' and reductions in purchasing power brought about by the war and its aftermath, Europe's effective demand for primary products either did not revive with comparable alacrity or could not become large enough to absorb both the restored European output and the increased non-European output. Therefore the markets for primary products remained relatively weak, even when European industry surpassed pre-war levels of output.

In Eastern Europe, as elsewhere in the world, over-production and cut-throat competition forced farmers and mineral producers to accept lower prices in vain attempts to increase their shares of the market. Hence, during the years immediately preceding the Wall Street Crash of October 1929, primary commodity prices weakened. Eastern Europe was most adversely affected by the sagging international prices of grain and timber (Romania, Hungary and Poland), coal (Poland and Romania), non-ferrous metals (Yugoslavia and Hungary), tobacco (Bulgaria) and even oil (Romania) during the latter half of the 1920s, as was also the case with the Soviet Union and the Baltic States. (Only industrialized Czechoslovakia was not adversely affected by the weakness of demand for and the prices of primary commodities, which helps to explain the buoyancy of the Czechoslovak economy at that time. Indeed, Czechoslovak farmers were given adequate tariff protection against cheap imports.)

The United States, as the world's largest producer and exporter of mineral and agricultural products, was also affected by the weakening of commodity prices and the consequent negative effects on land values. This was an important factor in the onset of the Depression there. Moreover, the falling real incomes and purchasing power of farmers and mineral producers, especially in Eastern Europe and the Americas, reduced their capacity to purchase west European and local manufactured goods. The Wall Street Crash sent primary commodity and real estate prices tumbling even faster, further reducing the real incomes of primary commodity producers and their effective demand for industrial products. The consequences were magnified even more by the abrupt cessation of lending to primary commodity producers, who had for a short time borrowed money in an attempt to sustain their mid-1920s expenditure levels despite the weakening of commodity prices. In Central and Eastern Europe, not only did new domestic lending cease, but so did capital inflows from the West. Thus, as in the United States (powerfully portrayed by John Steinbeck's *The Grapes of Wrath*), the central and eastern European banks were forced to start calling in existing loans from heavily mortgaged farmers. (In contrast to the United States, however, East European farmers were rarely forced off their land.) This inevitably exposed the extent to which their clients were unable to pay interest on, let alone repay, their loans, which had been secured on properties whose value was now plummeting. That in turn undermined public confidence in a number of central and east European banks, culminating in the collapse of Austria's illustrious Creditanstalt and various other central and eastern European finance houses during 1931. Like the *Krach* (crash) of 1873, the cataclysmic banking crisis of 1931 further undermined investors' confidence and business confidence and liquidity in Central and Eastern Europe, greatly deepening and prolonging the 1930s Depression in that part of the world (including, by now, Czechoslovakia, which could not isolate itself from the crises in neighbouring states).

THE COMPOUNDING OF DIFFICULTIES

This was by no means the end of Central and Eastern Europe's woes. In the West most industrialists were able to respond to declining product prices and demand by 'moth-balling' or cutting back capacity, freezing or even reducing nominal wages and laying off workers, in order to cut costs and stave off bankruptcy. Moreover, many were able to come together in quite strong and stable national and international cartels to curb competitive price-cutting and to restrict their members' output in a co-ordinated fashion, often with government backing (even in the supposedly 'liberal' United States and UK). Increased tariffs and import controls were also quite effective in protecting western European farmers, manufacturers and mineral producers (especially coal mining) against cheap imports and alleged 'dumping'. Indeed, this potent protectionism was crucial to the strength and stability of western European cartels and state farm support schemes, which might otherwise have been undercut and undermined by low-priced imports. For various reasons, however, the agricultural and mineral export economies in Eastern Europe and elsewhere were not able to defend themselves so effectively. This was partly attributable to the structural rigidities in their economies and societies, which prevented them from adjusting as quickly and flexibly as some Western economies did (e.g. Sweden and the UK). With the exception of the industrialized Czech Lands (whose recovery from the Depression was severely impeded by a menacing stand-off between the Czechs and the increasingly pro-Nazi Bohemian Germans after 1933), the countries of Eastern Europe were capable of producing only a limited range of products. It was not for want of trying. Despite the great hardships, privations and budgetary constraints, there was considerable state (and some private) investment in further education and training and in the creation of new industries (even if these were often military rather than civilian in orientation). The peoples of Eastern Europe were not deficient in would-be entrepreneurs and 'enterpreneurial spirit'. The influential claims to the contrary, especially by Gerschenkron (1962), have simply overlooked the great groundswell of private enterprise in Eastern Europe from the late nineteenth century until the tidal wave of bankruptcies and bank collapses in 1930 and 1931 (not to mention the strong revival of private enterprise in most parts of Eastern Europe after 1989, which Gerschenkron did not live to see). Even the millions of so-called 'kulaks' in Eastern Europe were essentially entrepreneurs, as were the reviled Russian middlemen and 'rich peasants' from whom they acquired their deeply derogatory name (by a Leninist legerdemain).

The peoples of Eastern Europe made valiant efforts to overcome economic adversity during the 1930s, as did many other depression-stricken societies. The real problem was that their low levels of economic development, the continued predominance of low-technology agriculture, the shortage of industrial and technical skills and the (resulting) limited versatility and purchasing power of the bulk of the population made it doubly difficult to adjust to economic shocks and setbacks by rapidly diverting financial resources and manpower into new lines of economic activity in order to change the product mix and reap higher economic returns on the investments and (often heroic) efforts that were made. Moreover, in so far as most East European farmers necessarily relied on unpaid or low-paid family labour, it was impossible for them to reduce their costs significantly by reducing wages and/or by laying off workers (in the manner of Western industrialists). Their costs were relatively fixed in the sense that they could not be reduced much further. There was no 'fat' to be trimmed. Conversely, most of the extractive industries were relatively capital-intensive and most of their capital had already been (literally) 'sunk' in mine shafts and oil wells. So they too were unable to cut their costs substantially by reducing wages and/or laying off workers, since wages were already a small part of their overall production costs. Either way, as primary commodity prices fell, primary producers desperately tried to compensate by increasing their production volume. However, while this seemed to be a rational response for each individual farmer and mine-owner, it actually worked to their collective disadvantage. Eastern Europe's primary producers were to remain locked into a vicious downward spiral of commodity prices until the rise of Nazi Germany, public works programmes, rearmament and a UK housing boom revived some of the western European economies in the late 1930s. Thus the crucial behavioural difference was that, when faced with a fall in the prices of their products, manufacturers tended to reduce their output level and industrial prices were soon stabilized at new (albeit lower) levels, whereas farmers and mine owners tended to increase their output volume and pushed the prices of their products down still further.

Furthermore, since average primary commodity prices more than halved between 1929 and 1933 (while average industrial prices fell by much less), industrialists and industrial workers reaped the benefit of a significant improvement in the terms of trade of industrial versus primary commodities. By the same token the highly industrialized West gained at the expense of primary producers everywhere. Thus a given volume of industrial products could now be exchanged for an increased volume of primary products. This, in combination with the abrupt cessation of capital inflows, greatly magnified the Depression in the primary export economies (including most of the East European countries). The latter were further disadvantaged by the fact that most primary commodity cartels and government-backed commodity price stabilization schemes were both intrinsically difficult to sustain and not very successful. This was mainly the result of the very large number of separate and widely dispersed producers involved in producing and exporting most of the principal primary commodities. The chances of producers breaking ranks rise in proportion to the number of cartel members. Products such as oil, gold, diamonds and platinum (produced by a relatively small number of companies and countries) were more amenable to cartelization, but unfortunately Eastern Europe was generally not well endowed with these.

Between 1929 and 1933, mainly as a result of the slump in primary commodity prices, the nominal value of export earnings fell by about 66 per cent for Poland, 62 per cent for Hungary, 58 per cent for Romania and Yugoslavia and 56 per cent for Bulgaria (Berend and Ranki 1974a: 248). Over the same period, for similar reasons, nominal agricultural incomes fell by about 59 per cent in Poland, 58 per cent in Romania, 52 per cent in Bulgaria and 36 per cent in Hungary (p. 245). Among the occupational groups hardest hit by the Depression were cattle exporters. Between 1929 and 1933 the nominal value of cattle exports fell by 89 per cent for Poland, 86 per cent for Bulgaria, 73 per cent for Romania and 59 per cent for Yugoslavia, as most Western and Central European states severely restricted or even prohibited cattle imports altogether in order to protect their own farmers (p. 247).

The decline in the nominal value of industrial output between 1929 and 1932 amounted to about 11 per cent in Romania, approximately 17 per cent in Yugoslavia and Bulgaria, 24 per cent in Hungary, 37 per cent in Poland and 40 per cent in Czechoslovakia (Berend and Ranki 1974a: 250–4). The fall in industrial output was less marked in the Balkans than in more industrialized countries. The reason was simply that initial industrial output was so small that the contraction in domestic demand for industrial products there was easily offset by restricting industrial imports (p. 249), while there were few industrial exports from the Balkans either before or after 1929.

There has been much less Western awareness of the impact of the 1930s Depression on the largely agrarian countries of Eastern Europe than of its impact on the industrial countries of the West and Central Europe. The main reason for this, apart from the 'closeness to home' factor, was that in the industrial countries the burden of adjustment to the Depression fell heavily on wage and employment levels, causing very visible and readily quantifiable increases in poverty and dole queues. Furthermore, these adverse effects could be quite readily alleviated through public works programmes, welfare benefits and lower interest rates on loans. The effects of the Depression on the more exposed, vulnerable and impoverished agricultural and mineral export economies of Eastern Europe were more severe, but less conspicuous, less easily quantifiable, more 'internalized' and not so readily susceptible to effective alleviation. East European countries really did have little option but to slash imports and public expenditure by imposing draconian import restrictions, foreign exchange controls and deflationary austerity programmes. The types of policies that alleviated the Depression in industrial-ized Germany, Britain and Sweden would not have achieved similarly positive results in the more rigid and constrained primary export economies. They were less able to undertake or finance anti-cyclical programmes and were more dependent on a revival of exports, even though most of them did take some significant steps down the path of 'import-substituting industrialization'. Indeed, the curtailment and increased real cost of industrial imports and the sharply contracting real returns on and scope for 'traditional' primary exports gave local entrepreneurs a major new incentive to invest in increased 'national' production of manufactured goods, irrespective of the explicit economic decisions made by the governments of agricultural and mineral exporting countries and the serious structural impediments to any major economic reorientation.

Fundamentally, especially if they were also small countries without any major industries or large urban markets of their own, the predominantly agrarian and mineral exporting countries of Eastern Europe were asymmetrically dependent on unimpeded access to the markets, finance, services and 'know-how' of the major industrial countries. When such access was curtailed during the 1920s and (to a much greater degree) the 1930s, the functioning of most East European economies was seriously impaired, but there was little they could do about it. Their own protectionism (which was inspired and guided more by strident and simplistic economic nationalism than by judicious 'selective retaliation') could secure their meagre 'national' markets, but it could not secure vital export markets. Indeed, the worldwide movement towards ever-increasing levels of protectionism placed the relatively poor, weak, small and trade-dependent states of Eastern Europe at a steadily increasing disadvantage *vis-à-vis* industrial countries with a large internal market (the United States and Germany) and those with 'captive' imperial markets (Britain and France). However, since most of the East European states were themselves built upon the pernicious doctrines of political and economic nationalism, which increasingly repressive and authoritarian rulers embraced as the whole basis of their legitimacy and of their own (often very limited) thinking, they were in no position to object 'as a matter of principle' to the growing and extremely damaging political and economic nationalism of the United States and of Europe's major industrial powers.

In international economic relations, power and control lay overwhelmingly in the hands of the 'core' industrial countries (the United States, Germany, Britain and France) rather than the agrarian and mineral-exporting 'periphery' of the capitalist system. International trade was largely conducted on terms that better suited the former, while the latter were obliged to accommodate themselves to this uncomfortable reality as best they could. Thus the inter-war years provided the clearest possible demonstration that small 'nations' can afford to be fiercely 'nationalistic' only so long as the bigger and stronger 'nations' do not follow suit. Otherwise the small 'nations' will find themselves squeezed out of the major 'national' markets and, in any ensuing battle of the titans, the small 'nations' are bound to be the main losers. Small countries, especially if they are essentially exporters of primary commodities, usually benefit from and often depend upon an open, liberal, non-nationalistic political, economic and international order, even if nationalists are sometimes too blinkered to see that. In a Europe built on concepts of political and economic nationalism (a Europe of zealously 'national' states) all lose out from the ensuing 'Balkanization' of the continent, but the smaller, weaker and most trade-dependent countries referred to here stand to lose the most. For them nationalism can be a recipe for *de facto* subordination and relative stagnation rather than 'liberation'.

POLICY RESPONSES

East European governments met in Warsaw in August 1930 in the vague hope of agreeing on a co-ordinated response to the onset of the Depression. But they were unable to agree on any framework of regional co-operation or 'collective economic security', since they were at the same time bitterly competing to sell similar products in much the same export markets and were vying for 'national' advantage, one against another. Amid a climate of intense economic and political nationalism, all proposals for regional co-operation and integration fell on deaf ears. The states of Eastern Europe were therefore doomed to embrace nationalistic beggar-my-neighbour and *sauve qui peut* responses to the Depression, including increased tariffs, import licensing, exchange controls, closed bilateral trading arrangements, competitive devaluations, debt moratoria, remission of internal debts, repudiation of external debts and the establishment of official 'national' crop procurement and marketing agencies (or 'boards'). Above all, in the wake of a persistent depression and the concurrent cessation of almost all Western investment in Eastern Europe (partly causing and partly caused by the discontinuation of East European debt service payments from 1931 onwards), the rulers of Poland, Hungary and the Balkan states embarked on etatist programmes of import-substituting industrialization (comparable to those initiated by many Latin American states in the same period). They were largely motivated by economic nationalism and a growing desire to bring many hitherto independent economic activities under increasingly extensive state control, by a xenophobic and/or antisemitic desire to eliminate 'aliens', middlemen, 'speculators', *rentiers* and potential 'fifth columnists' from the industrial, commercial and financial sectors, by the pressure to find 'jobs for the boys' (especially the sons of the 'national bourgeoisies' and the ruling oligarchies) and by 'strategic' concern to foster armaments production and potential war industries in order to enhance their illusory 'national' security. 'Governments increased their control over cartels and took over a number of industries, particularly those connected with war production' (Seton-Watson 1945: 130).

The most ambitious state-directed industrial projects were Hungary's 'Billion Pëngo Plan' (1938–40) and Poland's 'Central Industrial Region' (1936–39), both designed to build up war industries in and around their capital cities, well away from their more vulnerable frontier regions. In Yugoslavia, likewise, the Stoyadinovich government (1935–39) fostered state chemical and metallurgical enterprises. In Romania King Carol II (1930–40) and his court camarilla, who personally acquired large chunks of the armaments, textile and sugar industries, played a similar role, while lining their own pockets (Seton-Watson 1945: 131, 210). Yet in the short term (and in most cases even in the longer run) this kind of import-substituting industrialization mainly substituted inferior and more costly home-produced manufactures for cheaper and superior-quality imported ones. High tariffs, import restrictions and foreign exchange controls protected 'articles whose price was 50 to 300 per cent above that formerly paid for importing them from Western Europe. Many such "artificial" industries could not be defended on grounds of strategic necessity. They benefited the small number of persons directly interested in them and their cost was borne by the poorer section of the town population and, to a lesser degree, by the peasantry' (p. 131). In effect, increased protectionism and exchange controls encouraged 'rent-seeking' behaviour and allowed local industrial monopolists to make inflated profits by shielding them from foreign competition, to the great detriment of most local users of their products (including other industries which were more dependent on locally manufactured inputs). We see no valid objection to 'natural' or spontaneous import-substituting industrialization based on products in which the countries under consideration have actual or potential comparative cost advantages, on rational responses to shifting terms of trade and on continued exposure to the disciplines provided by foreign competition and the world market. Much could have been achieved in this direction in 1930s Eastern Europe. But excessive, indiscriminate and permanent protectionism, 'jobs for the boys' and very corrupt allocation of state contracts and subsidies encouraged 'rent-seeking', racketeering, inefficiency, waste, fraud, misallocation or misappropriation of resources and damaging distortions of the market system in general. Furthermore, the sort of import-substituting policies adopted in the 1930s, rooted as they were in economic nationalism, eventually curtailed or negated their own effectiveness by emphasizing the pursuit of autarky (self-sufficiency) and thus forgoing many potential gains from greater international trade, specialization and investment. Ironically, not until the 1950s did import-substituting industrialization attain a sufficiently large scale to transform fundamentally the income, employment and productive potential of the former primary export economies of Eastern Europe and Latin America, but by then the circumstances which had originally 'justified' the over-zealous pursuit of import-substituting industrialization had long ceased to exist and were but a distant memory!

15   The plight of the peasantry

THE AWAKENING OF 'PEASANT EUROPE'

From the 1860s to 1929, from Ireland to the Urals, peasants were on the move and on the make. As late as 1929 peasants comprised close on half the inhabitants of Europe as a whole and almost three-quarters of the population in eastern Europe. Peasants were emerging as a conscious class with specific social, economic and political interests and aspirations, although at first these were often articulated on their behalf by bourgeois politicians and intelligenti, who sometimes used peasants for their own ends. The protracted dissolution of serfdom in eastern Europe between the 1840s and the 1880s, the slowly increasing provision of rural schooling, the growing contact with the slowly expanding ranks of the rural intelligentsia (including village teachers, doctors and local government personnel) and the rural industrial proletariat (including railwaymen and miners), the eye-opening experiences provided by more universal military service and occasional employment in the towns, the widening of peasant horizons by national market integration and railway networks, and growing peasant awareness (as well as resentment) of their remaining disadvantages, all awakened peasants to the growing need to defend their interests and organize themselves politically and economically. By 1905–07 there were major peasant-based mass movements in Ireland, France, Scandinavia, Latvia, Estonia, Lithuania, Poland, Ukraine, Russia and Romania. (The great Romanian peasant revolt of 1907 was partly inspired by the peasant revolts in the Russian Empire in 1905–06.) Moreover, during 1906–14 there was a spectacular growth of peasant co-operatives in some countries, consciously modelled on the trail-blazing Danish co-operatives of the 1880s and 1890s. Thus by 1914 most Danish, Swedish, Finnish and Romanian and more than one in three Russian and Irish peasant households belonged to marketing and/or credit co-operatives.

Peasantist movements were also reaping the harvest of the momentous nineteenth-century romantic, folkloristic, ethnographic, philological, *völkisch* and Slavophil 'rediscoveries' or 'reinventions' of vernacular peasant cultures. These began to bridge the chasm which had separated elite culture from popular culture since the Enlightenment. This went hand-in-hand with the emergence of the vernacular languages and newly created literatures of long-submerged peasant nations and proto-nations (Latvian, Estonian, Lithuanian, Finnish, Ukrainian, Czech, Slovak, Croat, Serb, Bulgarian, Greek, Romanian, Albanian, Slovene, Macedonian and Irish). These linguistic–literary 'revivals' may often have been instigated initially by outsiders (e.g. Germans, Swedes and Catholic clergy), but their consequences went far beyond the original intentions, sometimes dramatically shifting the rural balance of power in favour of hitherto downtrodden peasantries and throwing alien landed elites on to the defensive, notably in Latvia, Estonia, Finland, the Ukraine, the Czech Lands, Croatia, Bulgaria and Ireland. The great groundswell of peasant radicalism and hitherto submerged peasant-national cultures in late nineteenth- and early twentieth-century Europe coincided with a growth in the relative economic strength of peasant smallholders in the course of national-revolutionary struggles to establish independent, predominantly peasant nation-states and to dispossess alien landed nobilities.

The gradual enfranchisement of peasants, the growth of peasant co-operatives, the steady extension of education and cheap transport, the rise of agricultural protectionism and even the 'progress' of industrialization, far from 'depeasantizing' the countryside (as predicted by classical Marxism), were expanding the potential for intensive small-scale livestock rearing, dairying, horticulture, viticulture and arboriculture, and granting a new lease of life to an increasingly commercialized peasant smallholder agriculture, while increasingly denying large-scale agriculture the captive pool of docile cheap labour on which its profitability had depended. The slump in international grain prices from 1874 to 1896 had hit hardest precisely those farms which employed wage labour to produce grain on a large scale for international markets, and benefited those smallholders who were net purchasers of grain. The self-employed, self-exploiting family labour of the peasant farm was also much more motivated and responsive to changing conditions than the underpaid wage labourer who only did what he was told (and no more) and who had good reason to slack when no one was watching. Agriculture based on hired hands incurred all sorts of supervision and managerial costs which simply did not arise among the more flexible and self-reliant smallholders, who could reap more fully the fruits of their own labour. This contributed to the famed 'tenacity' of peasant farmers during periods of severe economic depression, such as the early 1930s. Periods of increased hardship did not automatically result in a major exodus from the land.

The growing economic strength of peasant agriculture was reflected in generally rising levels of peasant consumption. The peasant diet became more varied (including more meat, vegetables, white bread, fruit, coffee, tea, sugar and beer) and some even took up smoking. Peasants bought increasing quantities of footwear, cheap washable clothing, matches, paraffin and paraffin lamps. Even where such goods were heavily taxed, peasant consumption of them continued to rise inexorably. Hence Europe's expanding light industries were able to count on this expanding market for their goods.

Many peasants and, more particularly, agricultural labourers largely or completely missed out on these rising rural consumption standards. The impoverished peasantry of Austrian Poland (Galicia) suffered acute Malthusian population pressure on their meagre land holdings and the Romanian peasantry were grievously exploited by rapacious 'arendasi' (middlemen). Many remote mountainous regions experienced overgrazing by sheep and goats, deforestation, soil erosion and rural depopulation, especially in the Balkans. These factors swelled the massive European emigration to the New World, although areas such as these remained the exception rather than the rule. For most of the lower-lying regions of eastern Europe it was a period of agricultural intensification and rising *per capita* crop production (Bideleux 1987: 13, 23, 250, and 1990).

The First World War produced further changes in the social consciousness and position of the peasantry, particularly in Eastern Europe. Millions of soldiers marched through or were billeted in villages, putting an end to centuries of rural isolation from events in the wider world. The war hastened the advent of rural trucking and bus services, which reached areas not served by railways. During the Great War, moreover, millions of peasant conscripts were mobilized into national and imperial armies. They participated in bloody, momentous conflicts and upheavals and, having seen how other classes and nations lived and died, they frequently decided not to return to their small, humdrum village world when the war was over. Those who did return (and many did, if only to participate in post-war land redistribution) frequently became restive and were unable to settle. In his classic study of the Romanian peasantry, Mitrany (1930: 98) observed that from the moment they entered the war 'many new truths and doubts began to work on the peasants' minds'. Everywhere they were 'extolled as heroes in speeches and articles which left a bitter taste when tested by the realities of their existence'. Indeed, as far as they could tell, 'many of their sufferings were due to the failures of their betters as leaders and administrators'.

Even before the war's end, Europe was 'changing hands'. In Western Europe, and initially in the East as well, property transfers took the form of widespread selling and letting of land by big landowners in response to war-induced shortages of labour, horses, capital and fuel, rising land values and property taxes (especially death duties), rationalization of estates and fear or anticipation of imminent peasant revolts. But where peasants began to rebel, as they increasingly did in Eastern Europe and Russia, land sales and land leasing were soon superseded both by spontaneous land seizures and by more equitable and controlled land reforms. But, by whichever means, the upshot over much of Ireland, Italy and the Baltic region as well as Russia and Eastern Europe was the final abolition or abdication of seigneurial control of the countryside. This was the *coup de grâce* against 'feudalism' and a major watershed in European agrarian history. It also challenged the structure of authority and social deference to 'superiors' who had heedlessly squandered millions of (mainly peasant) lives. Thus, according to Mitrany (1930: 101), the First World War had left the Romanian peasantry 'almost alone in the field, as undisputed masters . . . They have conquered the countryside decisively for their own class . . . The line of social contest has shifted from the village and now runs near the boundary between land and town, between agriculture and industry.' This was equally true of most other parts of Eastern Europe. Only in reactionary Hungary and Poland did landlordism survive largely intact. The lines had been drawn for the forthcoming battles between peasantries and townspeople.

Thus the proletariat was not the only class 'on the move' in post-1917 Europe. There was also a groundswell of peasant-based movements right across Europe, from Ireland and Scandinavia through Germany to the Slav world. This so-called 'Green Rising' was accelerated by the emergence of self-consciously peasant nation-states in Ireland, the Baltic region, Eastern Europe and the Ukraine, by the largely peasant revolution in Russia in 1917, by the subsequent radical land reforms in the Balkans and in the Baltic States, by the growing politicization of peasantries during and after the Great War, by electoral competition between rival political parties and by the international ideological appeal of 'blood and soil' nationalism, Gandhian ideas and Russian agrarian socialism (the latter mainly among Slavs and Romanians). Moreover, the widespread adoption of universal suffrage and compulsory elementary schooling in post-1917 Europe benefited the peasantry more than any other class, as did the continuing spread of co-operative networks. 'And what has happened in Europe since the War has been a vast victory for the peasants, and therefore a vast defeat for the communists and the capitalists,' wrote

G.K. Chesterton in 1923. 'In a sort of awful silence the peasantries have fought one vast and voiceless pitched battle with Bolshevism and its twin brother, which is Big Business, and the peasantries have won' (Chesterton 1923: 8).

THE LAND REFORMS OF THE 1920S

In 1918 the economies of Eastern Europe were mainly agricultural, with peasants and farm labourers constituting about 80 per cent of the population in Bulgaria, 78 per cent in Romania, 75 per cent in Yugoslavia, 63 per cent in Poland, 55 per cent in Hungary and 34 per cent in Czechoslovakia (Seton-Watson 1945: 75). Large landed estates dominated the agriculture of the former Austro-Hungarian Empire, Poland and Romania, while peasant smallholdings predominated in Yugoslavia and Bulgaria. After the land reforms of the 1920s. however, peasant smallholdings became dominant everywhere except Poland and Hungary.

The 1920s land reforms were not conceived as economic measures and they should not be judged as such (Seton-Watson 1945: 80). 'It should be clearly understood that the motives of the reforms were political, social and nationalist, not economic' (p. 79). They were hastily concocted pre-emptive measures, designed to defuse peasant 'land hunger' and social unrest in the wake of the First World War and to deflect the potential political 'fall out' from the Russian Revolutions of 1917. There was also a widespread feeling among the educated classes that 'as the peasantry had borne the brunt of the war, and had proved itself in the greatest crisis yet known in human history to be in fact the backbone of the nation, it deserved to be given its share of the wealth of the nation. This thought was to override all other arguments' (p. 79–80).

The land redistributions that were carried out (as distinct from the more radical ones that had been promised) involved the dispossession of thousands of 'alien' landlords. However, so long as the latter received nominal payments of compensation (in ritual obeisance to the sanctity of private property), this was seen as a price well worth paying for the sake of greater political stability and social peace. Moreover, the triumphant nationalists welcomed such expropriations as a form of so-called 'nostrification' of their nation's productive resources. Thus the redistribution of land hitherto owned by German landlords in the Czech Lands and western Poland, by Magyar landlords in Transylvania, Slovakia and the Vojvodina, and by formerly pro-Ottoman Moslem landowners in Bosnia-Hercegovina, encountered little resistance, since the interests of these dispossessed 'alien' landlords were not represented in the new or expanded 'national' states (pp. 77–8). Large landed estates remained dominant only in Poland and Hungary, whose native nobilities had played a leading role in public life and in the national movement before the First World War. They therefore managed to hang on to their great economic power and possessions after the attainment of national independence (p. 78).

RIVAL INTERPRETATIONS OF PEASANT POVERTY

Precisely because the land reforms had not been conceived as economic measures, they were widely judged to have suffered from numerous inadequacies which condemned them to economic failure. Thus, according to Seton-Watson (1945: 80–1), the owners of the new or expanded holdings lacked the requisite technical knowledge and equipment to make an economic success of them, and 'the new governments paid little attention to the improvement of agriculture or the assistance of peasant owners until the World Depression forced these tasks upon them'. Furthermore, even before the onset of the 1929–33 Depression, East European agriculture faced severe competition from grain-producing areas outside Europe. 'It was cheaper to transport grain raised on the highly capitalized farms of America by sea from New York or Buenos Aires to Hamburg than to bring the products of the less capitalized estates of Hungary (not to mention the uneconomic holdings of the Balkans) a few hundred miles. American competition more than balanced the . . . disappearance of Russian wheat from the world market.' This increased competition was felt 'more by the big and medium proprietors than by the smallholders, but it influenced directly or indirectly the whole agricultural population of Eastern Europe' (pp. 81–2). During the 'comparative prosperity' of the mid-1920s, however, 'the wealthier peasants had borrowed money . . . in order . . . to improve their lands. The poorer peasants also borrowed money in order to buy food in the critical period . . . before the harvest, when their supplies from the previous harvest had run out . . . Loans were made at a high rate of interest, particularly those made by moneylenders . . . The fall of agricultural prices enormously increased the burden of these debts, since the peasant now received half as much for his products as earlier, while . . . his debt remained the same' (p. 83). At the same time the fragmentation of land holdings was proceeding apace, because in most parts of Eastern Europe inherited land was by custom divided equally between the surviving sons. 'If the holding consisted of land of different qualities, devoted to different kinds of production, then each son must have a piece of each type . . . A holding of a few acres may consist of as many as forty small strips, separated from each other by several miles. Large acres of cultivated land are wasted in the form of paths enabling owners to walk from one strip to another. The strips are incapable of efficient production' (p. 81). Between the two world wars, according to Warriner (1950: 143), 'The average East European farm produced about one-third as much as a peasant farm in Western Europe, yet each acre had to feed and employ twice as many people.' (By 'Western Europe' it appears she meant Britain, France, Germany, the Low Countries and Denmark.)

Seton-Watson was, nevertheless, somewhat overstating his case. There were indeed serious deficiencies in East European agriculture and agrarian arrangements between the wars, but the problems need to be kept in proportion. Eastern Europe's *per capita* grain and potato output remained nearly double that of southern Europe, about 25 per cent above that of France, about 5 per cent above that of Germany and only 3 per cent below that of Denmark, while Eastern Europe's average annual grain yields per hectare remained about 17 per cent above those of southern Europe and only 22 per cent below those of north-western and west central Europe (Bideleux 1987: 250–1, tables 11 and 12). Furthermore, Eastern Europe's *per capita* holdings of livestock remained about the same as those of Europe as a whole (excluding the Soviet Union) and considerably above those of southern Europe (p. 254). In addition, Seton-Watson himself has pointed out that on balance crop yields and rural living standards were no higher in Hungary, which had a predominance of large landed estates, than in either Bulgaria or Yugoslavia, where there was a preponderance of peasant smallholdings (Seton-Watson 1945: 102). From 1934 to 1938 the average annual grain yield was 1.5 tonnes per hectare in Hungary and 1.1 tonnes per hectare in Poland (with a similar predominance of large landed estates), as against 1.7 tonnes per hectare in Czechoslovakia, 1.4 in the case of Yugoslavia, 1.2 in Bulgaria and 0.9 in Romania (Bideleux 1987: 251, table 12). The inter-war years also witnessed considerable diversification away from allegedly 'monocultural' grain production into more lucrative and labour-intensive crops and livestock products which were better suited to small-scale peasant agriculture, as noted by Rothschild (1974: 353) and Berend and Ranki (1974a: 296).

In 1934, interestingly, Henry Tiltman reported that among Bulgarians 'the word has gone forth that there is money in strawberries, peas and wine, whereas the world has too much wheat . . . In the task of transforming the country from a farm into a garden the peasants are assisted at every turn by a government awake to the vital issues at stake. Since her old markets have disappeared, Bulgaria must win new markets for her new crops. Therefore every precaution is being taken to ensure that each chicken, egg, crate of fruit and bottle of wine exported will be of a quality calculated to assist and not retard the progress of the country. To this end, a system of inspection based on the Danish model has been instituted and strict methods of grading adopted' (Tiltman 1934: 68).

On the whole, East European agricultural productivity and rural living standards were evidently much more affected by environmental factors (terrain and climatic conditions) and by levels of urbanization and industrialization, than by whether the agricultural sector was dominated by peasant smallholdings or large landed estates. Yet Seton-Watson's somewhat gloomy and exaggerated views on the allegedly negative 'parcellizing' effects of the 1920s land reforms and of peasant farming nevertheless were and continue to be widely shared, for example, by Moore (1945: 26–35, 87–94), Political and Economic Planning (PEP 1946: 26–33), Warriner (1950: xii–xiii, 142–4), Berend and Ranki (1974a: 288–95), Cochrane (1993: 851) and Crampton (1994: 35). Thus, according to Thompson (1993: 844), 'Land reform in Eastern Europe during the inter-war period did not bring prosperity to the peasantry . . . Man–land ratios in Eastern Europe changed little or [even] fell slightly by 1930 because agrarian reform did not relieve rural over-population . . . The major effect of the inter-war agrarian reforms was to hasten slightly the structural transformation of agriculture in Eastern Europe.' On the other hand, Cochrane (1993: 851) contends that the 1920s land reforms 'failed on the whole to alter significantly the structure of agriculture'. She rightly emphasizes the importance (then as now) of promoting appropriate infrastructural support for agriculture through the development of 'co-operatives, credit institutions, new marketing structures and exten-sion services' (p. 855), but she quite misleadingly claims that 'most . . . governments failed to follow up the land reforms with the institutions or infrastructure needed to support the new farmers . . . Extension services throughout the region were virtually unheard of' (p. 853). 'To the extent that the reforms of the 1920s failed to improve conditions for the rural population, it was because this necessary support was lacking' (p. 855). We shall shortly provide more evidence to the contrary. Rural infrastructure developed considerably and there were important agricultural changes.

TOWARDS A RE-EVALUATION OF THE PEASANTRY

In our view, the problems of rural poverty in inter-war Eastern Europe did not hinge upon land tenure arrangements. To think that they did is to bark up the wrong tree. One can no more blame the serious and widespread poverty simply on the legacies of the former predominance of the large landed estate than on its opposite, the effects of the 1920s land reforms and the growing preponderance of peasant smallholdings (however much either explanation might fit with one's political and economic prejudices). Nor can one simply attribute the problems to the effects of rural population growth. By this period the density of agricultural population per hectare of arable land was indeed considerably higher in Eastern Europe than in France, Germany or the United Kingdom (Moore 1945: 197–204). But there was serious and widespread rural poverty in Eastern Europe long before the emergence of problems of rural 'overpopulation'. Conversely, with higher levels of education and agricultural technology, East European landed estates and peasant agriculture would easily have been capable of sustaining such high rural population densities (comparable to those in countries as diverse as the Netherlands, Belgium, Norway and Finland). Fundamentally, rural poverty in inter-war Eastern Europe mainly resulted from (and took the form of) long-standing social and cultural deprivation and neglect. Most East European peasants and agricultural labourers still suffered from inadequate education, a deficiency of public health and sanitation provision, a lack of clean tap water and the prevalence of unhygienic housing and life styles. As observed by Seton-Watson (1945: 95), lack of education had made it difficult for peasants 'to understand the importance of hygiene or to make the best even of the scanty resources of food that are at their disposal'. Moreover, 'The majority of smallholders live in such wretched hovels that even the best hygiene experts would have difficulty in making much of them. One bed will hold six or seven persons, including children. In parts of Bosnia and other poor regions the cow or the pig sleeps in the same room as the family' (p. 92). 'The living conditions of the Hungarian rural proletariat are similar to those of the smallholder class of neighbouring countries. Families are packed into small, unhygienic rooms. Some have their own tiny houses, others are crowded together in barracks provided by the estate' (p. 102). In Bucharest one can visit a museum of traditional peasant dwellings gathered from various parts of Romania. They look very spruce and picturesque in their museum park setting, but many of them are amazingly small, dark, cramped, fire-prone and poorly insulated, while others clearly used to be little more than crudely covered 'holes in the ground'. Eastern Europe had some of Europe's lowest literacy rates (Bideleux 1987: 227, table 3), the highest rates of infant mortality (p. 225, table 2) and the highest incidence of diseases such as tuberculosis, typhoid, scarlet fever, smallpox, diptheria, whooping cough and cholera outside the Soviet Union.

If this was the essence of rural poverty in Eastern Europe, land reform *per se* could not substantially eliminate it, just as the land tenure arrangements (old and new) were not its main direct cause. Even where landed estates were expropriated and redistributed among the peasantry, most peasant smallholdings were only augmented by between 10 per cent and 35 per cent, and the short-term benefits were soon cancelled out by surging rural population growth. Thus land reforms could offer only temporary palliation of peasant 'land hunger'.

The principal consequences of the land reforms were (like the dominant motives) more political and social than economic. Indeed, by breaking (or at least diminishing) the power of the old landlord class, they did help to reduce some long-standing impediments to effective peasant organization, co-operation and self-help. (All but the most enlightened landlords and rural officials had tended to oppose anything that might tip the rural balance of power in favour of the peasantry.) More lasting solutions to rural poverty were primarily to be found in the expansion of rural education, agronomic assistance and other measures designed to enhance the capacity of the peasants to help themselves. For, other than in the Czech Lands, East European industrial sectors were not yet big enough to be capable of absorbing a large rural labour surplus (even if East European industries had developed rather more rapidly than they did), while the scope for rural emigration from Eastern Europe to North America was being severely curtailed by the introduction of ever tighter (North) American immigration quotas. As reported by Henry Tiltman (1934: 72), Bulgarians (among others) had 'discovered the vital truth that the key to the future prosperity of agrarian nations is to be found in education and then more education'.

Rather more was achieved on this front than writers such as Seton-Watson (1945), Berend and Ranki (1974a), Thompson (1993) and Cochrane (1993) have realized or cared to admit, although many of the measures adopted necessarily took time fully to bear fruit. Centuries of social and cultural deprivation could not be rectified overnight. The most important reforms lay in the establishment of free, compulsory and universal schooling in rural areas, a process which began well before the First World War. By the 1930s school enrolments as a percentage of the total population were (other than in Albania) mostly on a par with western Europe (Bideleux 1987: 22, table 3).

Of course it was still widely believed that peasants did not need much education, on the grounds that the alleged simplicity of peasant agriculture put a low premium on formal knowledge and training. Moreover, many landowners, officials and townspeople did not want the peasants to gain knowledge and skills that would help them to organize, to lobby for legislation and resources and to think for themselves. Even Mitrany was ambivalent. On the one hand he regarded 'improved education' (together with improved transport and administration) as one of the three crucial prerequisites 'if the standard of rural life is to be raised'. On the other hand, he claimed that 'hitherto such education as has been provided has on the whole rather weakened the village. It has done little to adapt the peasants to life and farming in scattered rural communities, and it has tempted the abler of the young villagers away to the towns and to the professions. This has had the additional result that most of the countries of the region were burdened with a restless intellectual proletariat' (PEP 1945: 14–15).

Nevertheless, it is an incontrovertible fact that Europe's most educated peasantries were also its most healthy, dynamic and prosperous ones (mainly to be found in Denmark, Sweden, Finland, Switzerland, the Netherlands and, more recently, in Austria and the Czech Lands). Educated peasants were increasingly receptive to new implements, technologies, cropping practices, seed varieties, building and fencing materials and ideas about sanitation and human and animal hygiene. They were also more responsive to peasant parties, agricultural co-operation and new forms of finance, marketing, food-processing and political lobbying, bringing increased access to rural services and agronomic assistance and bypassing or squeezing out the most ruthless and manipulative middlemen. By 1937 the number (and membership) of agricultural credit co-operatives was 6,080 (1,440,784) in Czechoslovakia, 3,736 (816,007) in Poland, 1,008 (421,507) in Hungary, 4,638 (905,420) in Romania, 4,283 (414,645) in Yugoslavia and 1,899 (216,538) in Bulgaria, while the number (and membership) of dairying and other agricultural marketing/processing co-operatives was 2,579 (486,385) in Czechoslovakia, 5,176 (1,082,551) in Poland, 22,435 (746,462) in Hungary, 1,906 (219,207) in Romania, 3,204 (233,939) in Yugoslavia and 1,640 (202,256) in Bulgaria (PEP 1945: 154). In addition, the (largely rural) membership of consumer co-operatives was 805,544 in Czechoslovakia, 373,516 in Poland, 127,428 in Hungary, 29,063 in Romania, 86,983 in Yugoslavia and 84,449 in Bulgaria (p. 155).

It needs to be emphasized that, until well after the Second World War, the major advances in European peasant farming were rarely based on large-scale agricultural mechanization and heavy use of chemical fertilizers. The large-scale machinery pioneered on large American and British farms during the nineteenth century was usually too expensive and in any case unsuitable for use on Europe's peasant smallholdings. The expensive chemical fertilizers pioneered in Prussia were also used much more sparingly by peasant farmers, mainly in kitchen gardens rather than for staple grain crops. Peasants usually felt that the per hectare returns on grain cultivation were too low to justify the heavy use of mineral fertilizers, and they were probably correct. Instead, the major advances in European peasant agriculture up to the Second World War were mainly based on changes in cropping patterns, including the introduction of new crops (such as root crops and legumes) and new higher-yielding seed varieties, and improvements in farm tools and other small-scale equipment. Receptivity to these forms of agricultural innovation was partly a function of farm size and wealth, but was mainly a function of the farmer's capacity to reason and to find out about newly available seed varieties, crops, tools and small-scale equipment, by reading seed and equipment catalogues, newspaper advertisements and farmers' magazines. We therefore reject Warriner's view that 'what prevented the peasant from improving their methods was not ignorance' (Warriner 1950: 144). Overcoming ignorance, in our view, was the key to overcoming poverty and 'backwardness'. The expanding peasant membership of agricultural credit and marketing co-operatives (itself closely correlated with rising levels of peasant education and consciousness) also helped to increase awareness of the new farm tools, seed varieties, crops and agricultural techniques. Just as significantly, perhaps, rising levels of education led to increased awareness of the importance of personal hygiene and of the need regularly to change and wash clothes, to boil drinking water, to clean up water supplies, to drain unsavoury, disease-ridden bogs and ditches, to develop safe ways of using or disposing of 'night soil' and to house livestock separately from humans.

Significantly, Tiltman (1934: 70–1) reported that the knowledge and skills needed to carry out the above-mentioned transformation of Bulgaria 'from a predominantly corn-growing nation to a variety of . . . more lucrative forms of cultivation have been supplied by an agricultural education system which is equal to that existing in any other European country. This system has at its apex the Faculty of Agriculture . . . of the University of Sofia and includes four agricultural high schools, fifteen practical agricultural schools (seven or eight of which are reserved for women), thirty winter schools for adult peasants and a network of agricultural continuation schools, of which in June 1933 110 had already been opened out of 800 projected. These continuation schools will, when completed, cover every large village and town throughout the country. Every child who has completed . . . primary school is obliged to attend an agricultural continuation school for two terms of four months each. During these terms, held in winter months, boys are given instruction in modern methods of farming with special reference to the type of cultivation predominating in the region where the school is situated, while girls are taught home-making, cooking, sewing, care of children and the rudiments of hygiene.'

Leaving aside the 'sexism' of these role divisions (which was none the less fully consonant with social expectations at that time), inter-war Bulgaria was laying the foundations of its subsequent agricultural prowess (1950s–1970s). Bulgarian achievements in this regard also warn us to beware of the temptation to paint too bleak a picture of inter-war Eastern Europe. There were some patches of light to relieve the gloom. Indeed, the life style of the Bulgarian peasantry was undergoing a vital transformation. 'The Bulgarian people have been "lifted off the floor" . . . The poorest Bulgarian peasant today generally has his land, his house, some pieces of furniture and his self-respect . . . And with this psychological transformation the health of the people has improved. The death rate, though still high, is falling . . . The peasantry live in modern two-roomed dwellings, often built of designs supplied by the state, and their animals are housed separately. The earth floors have been replaced by brick and wood. There are windows that open . . . Many . . . now sleep on beds and eat sitting at tables. Separate plates for each person have replaced the old communal bowl. Electric light, even, has come to some of the villages' (Tiltman 1934: 83).

In short, Bulgaria's peasants were belatedly entering the twentieth century. However, it has been forcefully argued that even the most marked intensification of agriculture would have only 'half' relieved the agrarian problems of inter-war Eastern Europe. The other 'half' of the solution (accepting that increased emigration was problematic and virtually out of the question) could have come only from faster industrialization. This was the way to increase aggregate demand for higher-value farm products, supply increased inputs of fertilizer and farm equipment and remove so-called 'surplus' population from the land (Warriner 1950: xii–xiii, 144; Seton-Watson 1945: 115–17). 'By the nineteen-thirties a large proportion of the peasant population was "surplus" – in the sense that it could have left the land without reducing agricultural production. The size of this surplus population cannot . . . be exactly estimated, since it took the form of half-employment for most of the farm population. But the various estimates that have been made agree that it was large, amounting to between one-quarter and one-third of the total population on the land . . . The pressure of population on the land meant that small farms were divided into ever smaller units. Methods of farming remained primitive, because the peasants were too poor to invest in machinery and livestock, and of necessity kept most of their land under grain . . . For this widespread poverty the only remedy would have been industrialization. But to this the obstacles were shortage of capital and the lack of an internal market due to the poverty of the peasants . . . Peasant poverty therefore created a vicious circle' (Warriner 1950: xii).

Instead of totally rejecting such arguments (which mistakenly equate agricultural advance with mechanization and increased use of chemicals supplied by industry), we would strongly emphasize the other side of the equation. More rapid, large-scale, town-centred industrialization *on its own* would only have 'half' relieved the agrarian problem of inter-war Eastern Europe (with the possible exception of Czechoslovakia). The other 'half' of the solution needed to come from the intensification of agriculture and from dispersed, small-scale, labour-intensive, rural industrialization: first, because capital and industrial skills and 'know how' were indeed in short supply; and, second, because it was therefore bound to take two or three decades for East European industrial sectors and urban infrastructures to develop sufficiently to become capable of fully absorbing the rural 'population surplus' (especially as most industries are intrinsically more capital- and skill-intensive than agriculture). In the meantime, as argued by East European peasantist parties, it would have been easier, safer and more cost effective to emphasize the development of peasant agriculture and rural industries *in situ*, rather than to transplant millions of peasants to overcrowded and undercapitalized urban industrial sectors. Indeed, a great deal hinged upon the forms of industrialization and the types of industry that were promoted. We heartily concur with the peasantist parties' contention that, in peasant societies, industrial priorities and the pattern of industrialization pursued ought primarily to have been geared to meeting the 'basic needs' of the peasantry. This was desirable not only because the latter constituted the vast majority of the population, but also because it would have fostered a harmonious and symbiotic relationship between industrial and agricultural development. The agricultural sector would have provided markets and raw materials for East European industry, which in turn would have provided markets and industrial inputs for East European agriculture, while minimizing infrastructural costs and social upheaval. Thus we fully endorse Seton-Watson's view that there was 'no need for industrialization in Eastern Europe to lead to the vast unhealthy urban agglomerations that exist in the West' (Seton-Watson 1945: 118). The lopsided emphasis on large-scale, capital-intensive, town-centred heavy industries and mining, favoured by East European dictators, economic nationalists, communist parties, military interests and some influential Western development economists (including Doreen Warriner, Maurice Dobb and Alexander Gerschenkron), has proved to be a dirty and costly mistake for which Eastern Europe is still paying a high social, economic and environmental price.

PEASANTIST MOVEMENTS IN EASTERN EUROPE

Major peasant movements emerged in almost every country in inter-war Eastern Europe, engaged in a common quest to end 'feudal' landlordism and build in its place a democratic society based on peasant proprietors united in co-operative movements. The natural constituency for peasantism was still considerably larger than that for Marxian socialism, fascism or liberalism. Only in Slovakia, Slovenia, Hungary and Poland did agrarian parties remain strongly under (Catholic) ecclesiastical influence. Only under the reactionary Sanacja regime in Poland (1926–39), under the counter-revolutionary Horthy regime in Hungary (1920–44) and under the repressive Zog regime in Albania (1924–39) did landed oligarchies survive almost intact. But even in Poland and Hungary peasant parties eventually united (in 1931 and 1939 respectively) in support of radical programmes, laying the foundations of their sweeping electoral victories in 1945.

In Czechoslovakia, however, the Agrarians were consistently the largest party in every parliament and in every government from April 1920 to September 1938. This was an impressive achievement. The Agrarian Party became 'so strongly organized, so deeply entrenched in the provincial and local government apparatus, so thoroughly involved in the co-operative and banking systems' that it became the quintessential party of government, 'indispensable to any and every Cabinet coalition', without selling out its predominantly peasant clientele (Rothschild 1974: 97). In Romania the National Peasant Party (formed by merger in 1926) won a landslide victory in the genuinely free elections of December 1928 (pp. 299–301). Its election platform promised to clean up Romania's corrupt system of government, to dismantle the protectionism that had enriched a few industrialists at the expense of consumers (mainly peasants) and to foster further expansion of rural education, health care, extension services and peasant co-operatives. Last but not least, inter-war Croatia was consistently dominated by the Croatian Peasant Party (established in 1904), first under Stjepan and Ante Radic and subsequently under Dr Vladko Macek, while Slovenia was dominated by the Catholic, peasantist and very educative Slovene People's Party and its affiliated credit and marketing co-operatives.

The major exception to the democratic and non-violent precepts and orientation of most of the peasant movements in inter-war Eastern Europe was Aleksandur Stamboliski's Peasant Union (formerly Agrarian Union, established in 1901), which ruled Bulgaria from October 1919 to June 1923. 'Regarding "the city" and its inhabitants as sinful and parasitical . . . Stamboliski's actions often degenerated into a brutal . . . externalization of hitherto frustrated peasant resentments.' His fascistic paramilitary Orange Guard became the scourge of the 'parasitic' bourgeoisie and of political opponents and rivals, and he almost appeared to be less interested in benefiting the peasants than in harassing the other classes' (Rothschild 1974: 338).

Stamboliski and many of his active supporters were wiped out in June 1923 in a very bloody military *coup* which was actively supported by a vengeful urban bourgeoisie and by nationalist extremists, while the Communists and Social Democrats gloated on the sidelines, relishing the nemesis of their major rival. Stamboliski's only lasting achievements were a very egalitarian land reform (partly reversed by his successors in 1924); a more enduring expansion of rural education, co-operatives and credit facilities; an enduring system of compulsory national labour service (in place of military service); and the displacement of private grain merchants by a state grain corporation, although this proved to be a very mixed blessing.

Stamboliski had perpetrated his excesses in the name of the peasantry, comprising about 80 per cent of the population. However, his Peasant Union had obtained only 32 per cent, 38 per cent and 53 per cent of the votes in the 1919, 1920 and 1923 elections, respectively, despite Orange Guard harassment and intimidation of rival parties in 1920 and 1923. Much of the peasantry evidently did not support him, although for a time his excesses brought the peasantry as a whole into disrepute. The whole tragedy was an object lesson in the dangers of basing a movement on violent class hatred and megalomania, rather than a reflection on peasants as such.

In Europe since the late nineteenth century large-scale industrialization and the spread of Marxian socialism had increasingly distanced urban industrial workers' movements from peasantist movements and fostered often bitter ideological divisions between them. Marxist orthodoxy was too abstract, academic and doctrinaire to elicit much support from independent peasant farmers. It failed to recognize that, in countries where peasants still constituted the bulk of the population, economic 'progress' or 'development' would be somewhat meaningless or even fraudulent if peasants did not benefit. However strongly the Marxist parties attacked and criticized specific abuses and disadvantages which weighed heavily on the peasantry, such parties could not lastingly or legitimately win the hearts and minds of a class that they had written off as hopelessly and necessarily 'doomed' to gradual extinction by large-scale capitalist or socialist industrialization, or of a class which for Marxists epitomized reactionary *petit bourgeois* attachment to private property and petty capitalism. Marxism and peasantism were worlds apart. Marxists, like capitalists, asked how the land could be made to yield a maximum return with a minimum of labour and sought to maximize economies of scale. Peasants asked how the land could be made to support the maximum number of autonomous peasant and rural industrial households organized in villages and rural co-operatives in order to preserve peasant communities, values, rituals and ways of life. Marxist orthodoxy was coldly economistic, whereas peasantism addressed wider human values and concerns (Mitrany 1951: 50, 126–7).

However much Marxist parties attacked the exploitation, abuses and alienation inherent in capitalist industrialization, they fully intended to move or 'progress' in the same direction as capitalist industrializers, only their industrial society would be under the control of socialists or communists. It would be capitalist industrialization without the capitalists. The Marxist parties supported the radical land reforms as only temporary political expedients which, by terminating the power of the oppressive and parasitic landlord class, would 'neutralize' the peasantry and clear away potential impediments to rapid large-scale industrialization (and, implicitly, the proletarianization of the peasantry). They rarely showed any interest in radical agarian reform as a means of giving a new lease of life to peasant agriculture, as they feared that this could only retard the processes of large-scale industrialization and proletarianization upon which orthodox Marxism based its vision of the future. While piously disavowing any intention of ever forcibly dispossessing the peasantry of their vital smallholdings, the Marxist parties remained wedded to the supposedly 'inevitable' and 'progressive' conversion of peasants into proletarians – that is, to a form of 'voluntary euthanasia' for the peasantry as a class!

In contrast, the peasantist movements aspired to move in an altogether different direction, inspired by a different vision of society. They envisaged a 'co-operative society', distinct from both capitalism and Marxist industrial collectivism. In their view full democracy could be achieved only if peasants were to break the political monopoly of the urban and *rentier* classes, so that society could be governed 'from below' and not 'from above'. Peasants would have to liberate and assert themselves as a class just as other classes were doing or had done.

Representatives of peasant movements in Poland, Yugoslavia, Czechoslovakia, Hungary, Bulgaria, Romania and Greece met in London in July 1942 to produce a joint statement of policies and objectives. It began thus: 'Believing, in the words of the Bible, that we are all members of one body, we maintain that the raising of the peasant's standard of life is the necessary precondition for the progress of the whole nation . . . The main basis on which a sound and progressive agricultural community can be built up is that of individual peasant-owned farms. We do not, however, believe that the peasant can live in isolation, and we recognize the desirability of voluntary co-operation in land cultivation.' They called for measures to curb land speculation and the mortgaging and distraint of farmland, in order to 'safeguard the peasant against dispossession or alienation of his land'. To overcome fragmentation, 'the holdings of each peasant must be consolidated . . . either by voluntary co-operation . . . or by machinery set up by the law'. In the peasantist view, 'The strength of the peasantry depends on the strength of their common institutions as much as on their ownership of the land . . . The peasants themselves should control marketing, credit and the supply of agricultural equipment by their own institutions, democratically organized.' Co-operative organization 'should be extended to factories for processing agricultural produce, to the markets of the products thus made, to village communities engaged in special types of production and to the promotion of agricultural education'. In areas of rural overpopulation, 'Industries, so far as possible on a co-operative basis, are required to provide the necessary employment. They should be mainly devoted to the processing of local agricultural or forest products. We are convinced that, by these measures, we can raise the standard of living of peasants and avoid excessive concentration of production in large towns.' The statement also envisaged national and international regulation of agricultural procurement prices and the development of comprehensive health care, sanitation, housing, rural banking and insurance, rural electrification, irrigation, drainage, water conservation, hydro-electric power, fertilizer and equipment supply, and seed and livestock improvement schemes. All would combine state support with local and co-operative control and initiatives by the peasants themselves. (The full text of this important document is translated in F. Gross 1945: 113–17.)

Voluntary, democratic intra-village co-operation was expected to address every need of village life, but collective agriculture on the Soviet model was rejected because of its regimentation, its subordination of peasants to the communist party, the state and central planning and its suppression of peasant autonomy, freedom, initiative, rituals and values. Vladko Macek, leader of the Croatian Peasant Party during the 1930s and 1940s, declared that peasants would not happily accept forms of rural collectivism which would 'turn the peasant into a serf of the state', especially where they had only recently freed themselves from 'feudal serfdom'. In his view 'it is possible to turn the village into an economic unit. Every peasant holding produces partly for the needs of the peasant family and partly for the market.' The former 'should remain the business of the peasant family' but the latter was evolving 'towards co-operative production as a common concern of the village as a whole. Where there is a lack of land, new possibilities of earning a livelihood must be created within the village, ranging from home industries to village factories. But the peasant's connection with the land must not be severed, he must not be driven from the soil' (quoted in Mitrany 1951: 116–17, 143).

The fortunes of peasant movements and the survival of democracy were closely intertwined in Eastern Europe. Both were under recurrent threat from the fascist and/or royalist authoritarian right and from the Marxist left, but the peasantist movements remained the highest and most authentic expression of popular and intelligentsia aspirations. The absence of large urban proletariats and Marxist parties, other than in industrialized Czechoslovakia, left the peasantist movements as the major vehicles of political mobilization and radical reform. They attracted the support of much of the radical democratic intelligentsia, who in turn provided articulate leadership and reinforced their radical democratic orientation. East European intellectuals from peasant families increasingly studied, romanticized, took pride in and wrote about their humble rustic origins, which 'formerly they had tried to leave behind them' (Mitrany 1951: 131–3, 141). During the inter-war period Eastern Europe experienced a Russian-style 'movement to the people' (almost a pilgrimage) by so-called village explorers, ethnographers, agronomists, folklorists and composers (most famously Bartok, Kodaly and Enescu). There was also a corresponding change in peasant attitudes to rural clergy, village schoolteachers and intellectuals. 'The village now wanted service, not direction, and priests and teachers could retain their influence only in so far as they helped their villagers to work out their problems in their own way' (p. 133).

Unfortunately, except in liberal Czechoslovakia, the peasantist movements did not manage to retain and expand their foothold in government. Poland's two main peasant parties played a prominent role in government between 1920 and 1926. Thus Wincenty Witos, leader of the larger party and an influential political broker, even became Prime Minister in 1920, in 1923 and again on 10 May 1926. After Marshal Pilsudski's *coup* on 12 May 1926, however, political power was monopolized by the authoritarian Sanacja (Regeneration) regime until 1939, when Poland was once more 'partitioned' between Germany and Russia. The peasantist parties of Hungary and Bulgaria took years to recover from the 'white terror' that followed the overthrow of Bela Kun's Bolshevik regime in August 1919 and from the bloodbath that accompanied the overthrow of Aleksandur Stamboliski's peasantist regime in June 1923. In Yugoslavia the strength of the peasantist movements remained heavily concentrated in areas inhabited by Croats and Slovenes, thus making few inroads into Serb dominance of central government. In practice their major function was to give the Croatian and Slovene peasantries significant degrees of *de facto* local autonomy in the face of obdurate Serbian dominance of the Yugoslav state. The peasant parties undeniably suffered from certain innate handicaps. Most peasants were still poor, uneducated, diffident and difficult to organize. Able young peasants were precisely those most likely to migrate to the towns or to the Americas, although levels of education and consciousness were rapidly rising and the rate of rural exodus was in fact decelerating. But the peasantist movements also fell victim to the singularly vicious conjuncture of world depression, fascism and neo-mercantilism (beggar-my-neighbour trading policies). In Romania, for example, the National Peasant Party government was soon riven by dissension over how to cope with the sudden collapse of export and tax revenue and with the deliberately divisive tactics of a king bent on becoming a royal fascist dictator.

In Eastern Europe, as elsewhere, the Depression and the accompanying decline in tax and export revenue scuppered schemes of democratic social reconstruction by causing public expenditure cuts, widespread financial defaults, increased ethnic tension and irredentism. This provided a fertile breeding ground for both urban and rural fascism. Furthermore, the continuing popularity of the peasantist movements and their proven ability to make effective use of the democratic rights written into most of the East European constitutions 'frightened the ruling groups as the socialist movement never had done' (Mitrany 1951: 121). It made them prime targets of the political malpractice and persecution perpetrated by monarchs, dictators, fascists and corrupt urban 'machine politicians'. Prominent peasantist politicians such as Stjepan Radic and the former Romanian Finance Minister Virgil Madgearu (1928–31) were murdered. Others, such as Wincenty Witos and the former Romanian Prime Minister Iuliu Maniu, were imprisoned.

Nevertheless, most of the East European peasantist parties endeavoured to uphold the democratic principles enshrined in their official statutes and programmes. But 'this steadfastness in conduct, this unwillingness to sully their democratic principles, also meant that the peasant parties were unable to check the spreading Reaction while reactionary forces everywhere never hesitated to wreck them by corruption or violence' (Mitrany 1951: 122, 129). Furthermore, although 'no other party or movement could by offering a basis for democratic progress provide a check alike both to fascism and Bolshevism', Western governments made little attempt to bolster the interwoven fortunes of the peasant parties and democracy in inter-war Eastern Europe (p. 129). The West failed to foresee the terrible price that Europe would pay for these 'sins of omission'. (Such shortsightedness is not entirely a thing of the past.) The Second World War was primarily unleashed by the unchecked advances of fascism in Eastern Europe, which led in turn to the post-war Soviet domination of Eastern Europe, the Cold War and the East–West division of Europe.

These political and economic setbacks forced the peasantist movements into a period of intense self-examination and self-renewal from which they were to emerge strengthened in 1945, but not before they had undergone the ordeal of fascist domination, during which millions of peasants demonstrated an extraordinary capacity for active and passive resistance. Historically, peasants have been the great passive resisters. But during the Second World War peasants also became the mainstay of the major East European resistance movements.

16 The failure of democracy

Looking back over inter-war Europe as a whole, one can see that popular expectations had been greatly raised by the consequences of the First World War, the peace settlements, the principle of national self-determination, the proclamation of democracy, the rise of mass movements and the promises of social reform. But these heightened expectations were fulfilled only to a very limited degree during the 1920s before the battered hopes were finally dashed by the 1930s Depression. On a more positive note, most states did enact significant land reforms, broaden the franchise and expand educational opportunities. But these constructive projects further raised expectations and, overall, the 1920s did not live up to the hopes held out in 1918–19. There were perhaps too many conflicting or mutually exclusive desires. Some of the dreams were impossible to fulfil. Moreover, except in Czechoslovakia, many reforms were bedevilled by corruption, incompetence and economic adversity, while the new regimes and political parties increasingly lost touch with their popular constituencies and succumbed to authoritarian, charismatic or personalistic forms of leadership. Many of the things that were done (or not done) in the name of 'democracy' merely served to bring democratic ideals into disrepute. Many people, not all of whom had innately fascist or communist leanings, became disillusioned or impatient with the East European travesties of 'democracy' and yearned for 'strong government', sometimes in order to defend the *status quo* against perceived threats from 'profiteers', 'speculators', 'aliens', Jews, Bolsheviks or 'anarchists', but in other cases to bring about 'moral' and/or 'national' regeneration and major social, political or economic changes. (There have been some disturbing parallels in post-communist Eastern Europe and in the former Soviet republics during the 1990s.)

FRUSTRATED RADICALISM

Other things being equal, the economic vicissitudes and the changes in popular mood and attitude might have been expected to result in the mushrooming of support for the communist parties. These very plausibly portrayed the rampant corruption, unrelieved economic hardship, deficiencies of the agrarian reforms, naked oppression of workers, peasants and ethnic minorities, and the growing concentration and abuse of wealth and power as the inevitable consequences of the deepening 'crisis of capitalism', the allegedly fraudulent nature of 'bourgeois democracy' and the growing recourse of capitalism to fascist or quasi-fascist methods of containing the crisis and the attendant intensification of class struggle and inter-ethnic conflict.

In the long run, ironically, nothing did more to enhance the moral and political standing of the (mostly outlawed) communist parties than the way in which conservative and authoritarian politicians, publicists and ecclesiastics habitually denounced as 'communist' anyone who campaigned for social justice or who criticized official corruption, speculation, chauvinism, oppression or the abuse and excessive concentration of power and wealth. The constant barrage of anti-communist invective (emanating from groups who were so blatantly corrupt, chauvinistic, exploitative and oppressive) encouraged many non-communists to take the communists more seriously and to accord them increased respect, if only in recognition of their apparent political courage and integrity. East European rulers thus unwittingly conferred on the communist parties a status and mystique out of all proportion to their actual strength and deeds and contributed to the communists' accession to power after the Second World War.

In the short term, however, the officially orchestrated fear of 'Bolshevism' (encouraged by France and Britain as much as by Nazi Germany and Fascist Italy) meant that the chief beneficiaries of the popular disenchantment with 'bourgeois democracy' and *laissez-faire* capitalism were the various ultra-nationalist and quasi-fascist movements that emerged in inter-war Eastern Europe and those rulers who tried to emulate Fascist and Nazi methods of popular 'mobilization' and government. However, the increasingly fascist or quasi-fascist movements and regimes of the late 1930s and the early 1940s were to prove no more capable of fulfilling popular expectations than supposedly 'democratic' parties and governments had been during the 1920s. By 1942 those East European states that had been allowed to survive had become mere pawns in the Nazi and fascist plans for Axis domination of Europe. In practice these authoritarian states, which were supposed to be the apotheosis of the 'national' principle, forfeited without a fight all but the outward trappings of national sovereignty. However, while it is all too easy to condemn the puny East European regimes for accommodating themselves to the hegemonic ambitions of Nazi Germany and Fascist Italy, it should be remembered that the leading 'appeasers' were the governments of Britain and France. Arguably, only these two states were in a position really to stand up to Mussolini and Hitler and to give a lead to others to do likewise. If strong and democratic Britain and France felt unable to face down Hitler and Mussolini before 1939, what chance or reasonable expectation was there that the smaller and more vulnerable authoritarian nationalistic states of Eastern Europe should do so?

WESTERN MYOPIA

It can be argued that, having 'called into existence' the new or expanded nation-states of inter-war Eastern Europe, and having determined that the new political order should be based upon the principle of national self-determination, the victorious Western Allies were under some obligation to assist these fledgling states to attain political stability and economic prosperity. Moreover, having rolled back Russia, it was clearly in the interests of the Western democracies to develop the East European states and economies as counterweights to Italy and a temporarily emasculated Germany. Otherwise the latter would eventually fill the resultant vacuum in the heart of Europe and again pose a potential threat to the West. Yet during the 1920s Western stabilization loans and private investment went mainly to Germany and Austria rather than to Eastern Europe. The stabilization and economic revival of Germany were, admittedly, crucial to the peace and prosperity of Europe as a whole, as John Maynard Keynes had forcefully argued in 1919. But the Western democracies made a fatal error in leaving the East European states largely to fend for themselves, aside from some small loans and modest Western investment in East European extractive and processing industries. Indeed, it has been argued that the principal weaknesses of the post-1918 peace settlements resulted not so much from intrinsic defects as from 'the failure of the Allied powers to make the necessary effort and sacrifices' to uphold and enforce them. These failings were compounded by the additional international tensions and antagonisms generated by the classification of the newly established Poland, Czechoslovakia and Yugoslavia and expanded Romania as victorious Allied states, while Austria, Hungary, Bulgaria and Germany were treated as 'enemy states' and saddled with 'war guilt' and reparations (Mamatey 1967: 234–6).

EASTERN MYOPIA

The East European states would have been more able to withstand the 1930s Depression and Italian and German blandishments, threats and encroachments if they had been able to attain some semblance of regional solidarity, economic integration and collective security. But that was precluded by 'the multiple divisions and rivalries that were born of competing territorial claims, ethnic-minority tensions, socio-economic poverty, mutually irritating psychologies and sheer political myopia' (Rothschild 1974: 8). In effect, a strong defensive union of East European states was rendered impossible by the same factor that had helped to tear the Habsburg Monarchy asunder: 'the conflict between master and subject nations' (Taylor 1976: 257).

The Little Entente established by Czechoslovakia, Yugoslavia and Romania in 1920–21 was directed primarily against Hungarian revanchism, while the Balkan Entente established by Greece, Turkey, Romania and Yugoslavia in 1934 was essentially directed against anticipated Bulgarian revanchism. But there was no provision for joint resistance to potential German, Italian or Soviet aggression. Thus the defensive regional alliances were largely directed against states that were too small on their own to pose much of a threat, rather than against the major potential external threats to Balkan and/or East Central European security. Moreover, the non-participation of Poland, which misguidedly put its faith in its bilateral links with France and non-aggression pacts with the Soviet Union (1932) and Nazi Germany (1934) and rather looked down its nose at the smaller and less aristocratic East European states, combined with the ostracizing of Hungary and Bulgaria, further reduced the efficacy of these Ententes as possible means of promoting regional unity and co-operation and protecting Eastern Europe against German, Italian or Soviet interference and aggression.

In 1936–37 the Czechoslovak Premier Milan Hodza actively canvassed the creation of an economic bloc comprising the Little Entente plus Poland, Austria, Hungary and Bulgaria, both to promote closer intra-regional ties and to counter growing German economic hegemony. But Poland, Yugoslavia, Romania and Hungary were afraid of offending Nazi Germany. Moreover, Romania and Yugoslavia were not yet ready for full reconciliation and equal partnership with Hungary and Bulgaria. Yet Hungary expected such concessions and improved treatment of the substantial minorities in Czechoslovakia, Romania and Yugoslavia, as conditions for any Magyar participation in the proposed economic union, which was also viewed 'with misgivings' by Italy and

Germany. Only the Austrian government, which was trying desperately to fend off Nazi pressure, welcomed the Czechoslovak initiatives. (Hodza's overtures and negotiations are described in Hodza 1942: 125–39.)

Rejoicing in their recently acquired national independence, the fledgling states of Eastern Europe were also extremely reluctant to accept any limitations or reductions of their sovereignty in order to secure greater regional harmony, stability, peace and prosperity. The First World War had ended in acceptance of the principles of untrammelled national sovereignty and self-determination, not supranational confederation, as the foundations on which the new political order in Eastern Europe should be built. In the economic sphere, similarly: 'The first efforts of the new states were directed towards making a clean break with their old economic ties and towards attaining as far as possible, complete economic independence. They regarded it as their main task to eliminate . . . the division of labour prevailing in the former empire[s] and to make themselves independent of even those regions which had up till then been their natural market for some goods and their main source of supply for others. The newly independent states quickly walled themselves in with import prohibitions and high protective tariffs . . . Thus the barriers which had been erected to promote self-sufficiency . . . divided the Central and East European states more deeply from each other than from those of western Europe' (Berend and Ranki 1969: 176–7). Trade between the East European states shrank to 10–15 per cent of their total foreign trade. Conversely, 75–80 per cent of their exports went to western Europe, which in return supplied 70–80 per cent of their imports (p. 178).

Furthermore, extreme political and economic nationalism in many ways impeded the resolution of East European economic problems, both by diverting precious resources into the creation of tinpot military-industrial complexes and by further fragmenting ('Balkanizing') Eastern Europe into 'national' economic units that were too small to provide adequate markets for state-sponsored import-substituting industrialization. Autarkic economic development was difficult to attain in countries as large and as diversely endowed as the Soviet Union and Nazi Germany, but it proved even more difficult, costly and inappropriate in countries as small as Hungary and Bulgaria.

ABDICATIONS OF RESPONSIBILITY

Nevertheless, despite all the debilitating intra-regional problems and conflicts in inter-war Eastern Europe, it can plausibly be argued that 'the fundamental cause of the collapse lies not in the faults of the Eastern European states, but in the policy of the Great Powers of the West' (Seton-Watson 1945: 412). Rothschild agrees that 'one must assign greater responsibility for the catastrophe of 1939–41 to the malevolence, indifference or incompetence of the Great Powers than to the admittedly costly mistakes of these states' (Rothschild 1974: 25). Moreover, in the opinion of A.J.P. Taylor (1976: 259), the Western powers 'had nothing to offer eastern Europe except protests; quite apart from military aid, they were not even prepared to assist the shifting of industrial power to Eastern Europe, which is the only solution to "the German question"'.

The US retreat into isolationism and protectionism during the 1920s and 1930s was mirrored by an Anglo-French preoccupation with empire and, in trade policy, the development of 'imperial preference' and protectionism. These inward-looking and defensive attitudes also engendered a 'bunker mentality' in the military sphere, epitomised by excessive French reliance on the notorious Maginot line. It would therefore be only a matter of time before first Fascist Italy and later Nazi Germany advanced into the resultant economic and military vacuums on the Continent, virtually unopposed as Russia had been temporarily sidelined.

Initially the rulers of the independent East European states thought that they had at last miraculously escaped Germanic hegemony without falling under Russian domination. 'The basis of this miracle was alliance with France.' However, this proved to be one of the great delusions of the inter-war system and contributed to the latter's undoing, for it encouraged the new or expanded victor states to rely on the apparent strength of post-1918 France, whereas the French state was in fact looking to its new East European allies (Poland and the Little Entente) to compensate for its own lack of strength (Taylor 1976: 259). France's Maginot mentality, combined with British and French reluctance to 'guarantee' the new international borders established in Eastern Europe between 1918 and 1921 (in contrast to their willingness to extend such guarantees to West European borders in 1925), rapidly reduced the credibility of France's alliance commitments in the east. 'That credibility was finally flushed away by her passive acceptance of Hitler's remilitarization of the Rhineland' on 7 March 1936. Thereafter Hitler could pick off his Central and East European victims one at a time, without fear of French retaliation on his western flank (Rothschild 1974: 8). This also nurtured a belief that he could attain most of his expansionist ambitions without prematurely plunging Germany into all-out war.

Furthermore, instead of reinforcing its military alliances by promoting strong commercial ties, France traded very little with its East European allies, heavily protected its own agriculture against their staple agricultural exports and obstructed some of their attempts to develop the refining or processing of their own mineral resources, many of which were owned and/or exploited by French companies. Nor did France actively encourage closer commercial ties (let alone economic co-operation and integration) between its East European allies. The members of the Little Entente maintained closer commercial ties with their 'revanchist' enemy Hungary than they did with each other, while Czechoslovakia and Yugoslavia traded more with Germany and Italy respectively than they did with their Little Entente partners.

INTO HITLER'S EMBRACE

Nazi Germany easily established its hegemony over the Balkan and Hungarian economies during the later 1930s by offering them assured markets and seemingly favourable terms for their staple agricultural and mineral exports, in return for payment in non-convertible German marks which could be held only in 'blocked' accounts in the Reichsbank and used only to purchase German products. Indeed, a leading British socialist even ventured to suggest that 'The peasants of those countries of Southern and Eastern Europe which were most subject to German economic penetration . . . were perhaps better off with Germany as a market for their produce, even on highly disadvantageous terms, than with no market at all . . . This, as well as the fear among the upper classes in these peasant states of revolutionary uprisings grounded in hunger and despair, explains the ease with which Nazism was able to penetrate their countries both economically and with its political ideas . . . The Germans were in a position to offer a market; and that, on almost any terms of exchange, was better than nothing' (Cole 1941: 73–4).

However, Hungary and the Balkan states (other than Italian-dominated Albania and British-dominated Greece) acceded to Germany's bilateral trading arrangements not just because these were the only economic lifeline that was thrown to them, but also because they fell into the then common error of underestimating the economic and military capabilities and expansionist ambitions of Nazi Germany, while overestimating those of Fascist Italy and the Soviet Union. (In practice, despite persistent Soviet hostility towards the 1919–20 peace settlements and the ensuing nationalist and anti-communist regimes, there was little evidence of serious Soviet territorial ambitions in inter-war Eastern Europe, other than in response to the German threat from 1939 onward.) Hungary and the Balkan states soon became 'utterly dependent on continuing German purchases, supplies, spare parts and infrastructure' (Rothschild 1974: 24). When the world economy and commodity prices recovered somewhat in the late 1930s, under the stimulus of international rearmament, these countries found it much harder to disentangle themselves from Germany's clutches than it had been to enter them. Moreover, they almost certainly failed to recognize the full magnitude of the threat posed by Nazism until it was too late to escape from its suffocating embrace, and even then it took time to appreciate the enormity of the consequences. Only Poland and Czechoslovakia, with their problematic German minorities, proximity to Germany, living memories of German domination, and exports that competed with (rather than complemented) those of Germany, felt directly threatened by a resurgent Germany and resisted its economic charms.

All the while British, French and American introversion and their inertia in regard to Eastern Europe encouraged *sauve qui peut* attitudes and a fateful belief that the Western powers increasingly saw the renewed German ascendancy over the region as something natural, positive and inevitable. This in turn induced most of the East European states to adapt themselves to the new facts of life as best they could. Thus the ease with which Nazi Germany won dominion over Eastern Europe arose partly from the ideological, economic, ethnic and sectarian fissures and weaknesses of the region, but also from the passivity of the other powers. Eastern Europe's ripening apples essentially fell into Hitler's lap while the Western powers stood to one side, even if they did not completely avert their gaze. As argued by Warriner (1950: xiv), 'Western Europe, so far as it was interested in eastern Europe at all, was interested in keeping it backward, as a source of cheap food and cheap labour.' If the Western powers had been able to have their way in Eastern Europe in 1945–47, 'they would have put back into power the same kind of government which [had] existed before, and whose failure led to Fascism'. During the Second World War they elaborated 'no new policy' for Eastern Europe: they supported the *émigré* governments in London, 'at best, liberal politicians of the old style, at worst, near-Fascists'. It therefore fell to the communists to break the deeply flawed moulds of the successor states. Indeed, while the Western powers had learnt little from the failure of the 1919–20 peace settlements in Eastern Europe, the Soviet Union and the communist parties of Eastern Europe had 'learnt a great deal. Their conception of the future was clear, and so also was their grasp of the strategy of gaining power' (p. xiv). (This theme is developed more fully in Chapter 18.)

Warriner astutely observed that the real significance of the East European revolutions of 1945–50 lay not only in the political transformation, including 'the destruction of the old ruling groups', but also in 'the economic dynamic' that accompanied it. 'What eastern Europe primarily needed was the industrial revolution and, without the shift in the European balance of power resulting from Soviet victory, it would never have come'

(p. xiii). There is also much to be said for her view that 'Democracy needs a middle class to make it work, and in eastern Europe as a whole there was no strong middle class, because there had never been an industrial revolution. The "bourgeois revolution" of 1919 was abortive because there was no wind to fill the sails of the new liberal constitutions. It was only in Czechoslovakia that the new pattern did work, because the country was already highly industrialized and had a strong middle class' (Warriner 1950: x–xi).

Democracy rests not only on formal rules, safeguards and procedures, but also upon the existence of a multiplicity of independent social groups who are willing and able to defend and uphold civil rights and work against excessive concentration of power and authority in too few hands, while at the same time supporting and accepting the need for viable executive, legislative and judicial institutions and the rule of law. Autonomous social groups can both curb and yet sustain authority by sharing it, i.e. acting as intermediaries who constrain one another and the state and yet help to order particular spheres of economic, social and political life. Such roles are by no means confined to the middle classes. Autonomous trade unions and peasant associations are also vital to the maintenance of democratic liberties and dispersed authority. Thus the weakness of most of the trade unions and peasant associations, as well as of the middle classes, strongly contributed to the early demise of democracy in inter-war Eastern Europe (other than in Czechoslovakia).

Nevertheless, democracy also failed to take root in inter-war Eastern Europe because 'the Western powers themselves did not support it'. The West protested hardly at all against the suppression of democracy and the violation of minority rights in Hungary and Bulgaria in the 1920s or in Poland, Yugoslavia and Romania during the 1930s. 'In reality, Britain and France were concerned with the small nations only as a *cordon sanitaire* against Russia: so long as the dictatorships were anti-Soviet it did not matter if they were also anti-democratic' (Warriner 1950: ix–x). To paraphrase Neville Chamberlain's words on his return from Munich in September 1938, these were 'faraway countries about which we know little' (and care even less). Western governments, newspapers and public opinion have only ever become concerned with the dangers to 'democracy' in Eastern Europe when the threats have come from the left rather than from the right. But both the West and Eastern Europe would pay a price for the West's long-lived double standards.

By late 1939 German economic dominance over Eastern Europe was even more complete than it had been on the eve of the First World War, indicating that the geopolitical advantages that accrued to Germany as a result of the replacement of the Habsburg Empire by several smaller states were matched in the economic sphere (Rothschild 1974: 24). Nevertheless, even though the Hungarian, Bulgarian, Yugoslav and Romanian economies were tightly bound to the German economy by late 1939, their ruling elites initially played 'hard to get' when Hitler endeavoured to translate economic ties into concrete military commitments to the Rome–Berlin Axis between 1938 and 1941. Economic dependence did not automatically engender unflinching military and political subservience (Crampton 1994: 37).

Yet, paradoxically, Eastern Europe's fate was sealed, not by the manifest weaknesses of Poland, Hungary and the Balkan states, but by the demise of the seemingly strong Czechoslovak Republic. Hitler shrewdly singled out Czechoslovakia (rather than Poland) as the weakest link in the encircling chain of potentially hostile states allied to France. On account of its major industrial resources and strategic location, the artificial creation of

Czechoslovakia (underwritten by France and Britain) was the keystone of East European security and the 1919–20 peace settlements. However, Hungary, Poland and Nazi Germany harboured implicit or explicit designs on Czechoslovak territory and, once begun, the dismemberment of Czechoslovakia would destabilize the entire region by fully exposing the fickleness of the French, British and East European ruling elites and the fragility of Europe's post-1918 frontiers, alliances and balance of power. Moreover, the extremely multinational composition of the Czechoslovak state was fundamentally at odds with the implicitly 'ethnic' principle of national self-determination around which the 1919–20 peace settlements were formally framed and legitimized. Nearly a quarter of Czechoslovakia's population was German and the eastern half of the country contained large and somewhat disaffected Slovak, Ruthene and Magyar minorities. The ascendant Czechs constituted little more than one-third of the total population, yet they tended to call the shots, dominate public employment and cultural provision and resist even the most moderate demands for a federal state. They did so partly out of fear that any substantial concession of federal autonomy to the main ethnic groups or regions would fan rather than douse the flames of ethnic separation, thus jeopardizing the security and cohesion of the state. President Tomas Masaryk (1918–35) and his 'anointed' successor Eduard Benes (1935–38) did their best to promote the ideal of a tolerant multicultural state, but they did not succeed in fostering a 'civic' Czechoslovak nation commanding the allegiance and affections of the vast majority of its putative members. Therefore, even though Foreign Minister Benes issued a diplomatic note on 20 May 1919 claiming that his government's goal was 'to make the Czecho-Slovak Republic a sort of Switzerland' (Wiskemann 1938: 92), he never believed in this sufficiently to commit either himself or his Cabinet colleagues to a Swiss-style federation. However, while the Czechs were confronted with an acute political dilemma, many Slovaks felt cheated by the persistent non-fulfilment of their demands for federal autonomy. Since Slovakia was severely lacking in higher education, large towns and modern industries, and had been under Magyar rule even longer than Wales has been ruled by England, most Slovaks felt little cultural or economic solidarity with the Czechs and primarily aspired to some sort of autonomy within a federalized state. Taken in isolation, Slovak autonomy could conceivably have done more to strengthen than to weaken the cohesion of the Czechoslovak state. The dilemma for the Czechs was that they could hardly concede federal autonomy to the Slovaks without offering the same to the larger, richer and more educated German minority, yet such a concession would have made it easier for a resurgent Germany to prise apart the constituent elements of this multinational state. It is significant that the Slovaks and the Ruthenes won their long-sought autonomy only when the Czechoslovak state was coerced into surrendering its predominantly German-inhabited territories (the so-called Sudetenland) to Germany at Munich in September 1938 and that this was but the prelude to the complete disintegration of inter-war Czechoslovakia. The security and cohesion of Czechoslovakia were indeed indivisible.

In the opinion of Milan Hodza, Premier of Czechoslovakia from 1935 to 1938, the new order established in Central and Eastern Europe in 1918–19 was not a complete failure. In his view, the region had to 'share all the pains of a new Europe which could not succeed in being created in a pacific way by diplomatic channels and which had to emerge out of blood and toil and suffering, like all great achievements and political settlements' (Hodza 1942: 5–6). During the inter-war period, Hodza contended, it was 'the noble task of many of the Slav intellectual leaders to open the windows of their peoples' cultural homes to let in the fresh air of Western civilization. The twenty years of political independence meant also cultural self-determination.' This allowed the formerly subjugated peoples of Eastern Europe to 'quench their burning spiritual thirst' and strike a new 'balance between the neighbouring German and all-European cultural influences' (p. 171). Nevertheless, the problems besetting the new order in post-1918 Eastern Europe were so severe and so numerous that the surprise is not that most of the successor states soon degenerated into authoritarian nationalist, royalist or military dictatorships, but that they nevertheless managed to maintain their sovereignty and territorial integrity for some twenty years before succumbing to Hitler's New Order. Indeed, the most enduring achievement of the successor states was that 'they legitimized their sovereign existence' in the eyes of the world, so much so that neither Hitler nor Stalin succeeded in permanently wiping them off the political map of Europe (Rothschild 1974: 24). During and after the Second World War the international community took it for granted that these states should be re-established as fully sovereign entities at the earliest opportunity, just as it had taken for granted the existence (and the right to exist) of the Habsburg and Ottoman Empires in much the same region not long before. The great powers have great powers of collective amnesia.

17 The lure of fascism

During the 1930s almost all the ruling oligarchies in Eastern Europe sought authoritarian nationalist and quasi-fascist means of resolving or containing the acute tensions, political pressures and military challenges engendered by the 1930s Depression and the growing power and territorial/hegemonic ambitions of Fascist Italy and (after 1933) Nazi Germany. The growth of protectionism, exchange controls, import and export licensing arrangements, etatist import-substituting industrialization, debt remission and agricultural price support schemes greatly increased state control over the East European economies. As if introverted and illiberal political and economic nationalism were not enough, most of these states sought additional ideological and geopolitical support and justification for such policies by developing closer economic and political relations with Italy and (from as early as 1932 onwards) Germany. They also began to emulate some of the trappings, style, rhetoric, institutions, cultural policies, political violence, intimidation and 'mass mobilization' techniques of first the Fascist and later the Nazi regimes. Indeed, these were often at least in part defensive tactics or a type of insurance policy, adopted in the (vain) hope of fending off potential external political interference, military threats and/or territorial encroachments by submitting to the economic wishes and political tutelage of the emerging fascist powers.

Nowadays, for obvious reasons, Mussolini's ambitions in this region are less well known and are usually taken less seriously than those of Adolf Hitler. At least until the mid-1930s, and possibly until 1940 or 1941, however, Mussolini's much-trumpeted military 'might' was widely overestimated and Fascist Italy was (with some justification) perceived to be posing the major immediate threat to the Balkan states, along with the rather exaggerated 'Soviet threat'. Fascist Italy harboured imperial designs upon Albania, Dalmatia and large swathes of Slovenia, Croatia, Bosnia, Macedonia and Greece, hoping to replicate the Roman dominance and 'civilization' of the Balkans in ancient times and to turn the Adriatic and the Aegean Seas into 'Italian lakes' once more. Mussolini also aspired to a domineering and protective patron–client relationship with the rulers of Austria, Hungary, Romania and Bulgaria. Fascist Italy aimed to fill the power vacuum in the Balkans, south-central Europe and the eastern Mediterranean created by the demise of the Austro-Hungarian and Ottoman Empires. To this end it aided and abetted Hungarian, Austrian and Bulgarian 'revisionism' and authoritarian-corporatist tendencies, as well as Macedonian nationalist and Croatian fascist terrorism.

The ruling oligarchies also often resorted to the creation of fascist or quasi-fascist states in the hope of heading off, undercutting or politically 'neutralizing' potential threats and challenges from the more wayward, anarchic and violent fascist and quasi-fascist movements which were emerging in most of the Balkan and East Central European states, most notably Corneliu Zelea Codreanu's violent and unruly 'Iron Guard' in Romania and Ferenc Szalasi's 'Arrow Cross' in Hungary. Concurrently, Roman Dmowski's National Democrats (who constituted Poland's main opposition party) were becoming increasingly fascist in their ideology, rhetoric, leadership cult, authoritarianism, antisemitism and use of paramilitary affiliates, youth movements and other 'mass mobilization' techniques, posing an analogous challenge to the increasingly fascist 'colonels' regime' (1935–39). Alignment with Fascist Italy also gave the small but very violent Croatian Catholic-fascist *Ustasa* movement (founded by Ante Pavelic in 1929) some hope of eventually taking Yugoslavia apart and creating an 'independent' fascist state of Croatia strong enough to incorporate large chunks of Bosnia, Hercegovina, Serbia and Montenegro. Moreover, for gym teacher Konrad Henlein's neo-Nazi Sudetendeutsche Partei (which suddenly mushroomed into the major political party of Bohemia's self-styled 'Sudeten Germans' in the mid-1930s) and for the Catholic nationalist and increasingly fascist Slovak People's Party (which became Slovakia's major political party during the inter-war years), the birth of Nazi Germany translated into a practical possibility the dream of dismembering Czechoslovakia. Likewise, for the 'revisionist' states of East Central Europe and the Balkans (Hungary, Austria and Bulgaria), political and economic alignment with the emerging fascist powers transformed the prospect of wholesale 'revision' of the hated 1919–20 peace settlements from a hopelessly unrealistic pipe dream into an imminent practical possibility and held out the promise of total subversion of the victors' 'new order' in Central and Eastern Europe.

The awesome power, dynamism, ruthlessness and successes of Italian Fascism and German National Socialism clearly encouraged the increasingly authoritarian nationalist, royalist and military regimes that were emerging in the Balkans, East Central Europe, the Baltic States, the Iberian Peninsula and Latin America to foster fascist or quasi-fascist movements, institutions and one-party systems, both in order to capitalize on fascism's apparent capacity to inspire, unite, reinvigorate and mobilize 'the nation' (alias 'the people') and in the hope of eliminating or neutralizing more violent, radical and subversive challenges 'from below'. 'States of lesser power, especially new or restored states, generally take as their model the political institutions and values of the seemingly strongest and most successful Great Power of the day' (Rothschild 1974: 21). After 1933 Western parliamentary democracy seemed increasingly effete, ineffectual and adrift, in contrast to the apparent strength, dynamism and sense of purpose of the fascist states. To the admirers of Mussolini and Hitler fascism became the *Zeitgeist*, the Spirit of the Age, the wave of the future.

However, it is often argued that the fascist or quasi-fascist parties, institutions and organizations created 'from above' by more traditional authoritarian rulers (often co-opting state officials, army officers and leaders and personnel of established and 'respectable' political parties) were fundamentally different from the more autonomous, active, radical, mobilizatory fascist movements and parties that 'conquered power' for their leaders and active supporters. 'All imitations of fascism and its style could not hide the essentially different spirit' (Linz 1979: 21). The most widely favoured explanation for this alleged fundamental difference is the contention that, although a number of eastern European states seemed to offer 'fertile ground' for fascism, they had not yet attained either the 'minimum degree of political freedom' or the requisite 'level of economic, social, cultural and political development' that would have allowed fascism to develop into an organized, disciplined 'mass movement'. Moreover, 'the urban classes that could have provided the ideological leadership of fascist-type movements were, as state bourgeoisies, too closely tied to the bureaucratic, military, professional and commercial establishment' (p. 49).

In a similar vein, Hugh Seton-Watson (1945: 257) contended that the dictatorships which emerged in inter-war Eastern Europe were 'not Fascist regimes in the proper sense of the word'. From 1938 to 1940 King Carol II of Romania 'tried to ape Fascism' through his (single-party) Front of National Rebirth, but it 'never succeeded in raising the minimum of popular enthusiasm necessary for Fascism'. At the same time 'Specifically Fascist movements, such as the Polish National Radicals, the Hungarian Arrow Cross Party and the Romanian Iron Guard, failed in their purposes. The Eastern European Dictatorships relied not even on artificially stimulated popular enthusiasm, but on police pressure . . . These regimes had no such basis of support as those of Hitler or Mussolini. They were able to survive because they had a firm grip on the bureaucratic and military machines, because the peoples were backward and apathetic, and because the bourgeoisie would always support them in case of need. Certainly a part of the bourgeois and intellectual classes suffered from these regimes . . . But if ever the regime were radically threatened from below, the great majority of bourgeois and intellectuals would rally round it' (p. 257).

These authoritarian regimes may have proclaimed national unity, moral regeneration, non-party objectivity and strong government, but in Seton-Watson's view they were 'no more than greedy, corrupt and brutal class regimes'. Their leaders were 'stupid, timorous, dishonest and pettily cunning men' who, when faced with major internal and international problems, 'could only hesitate, temporise and take the line of least resistance' (p. 156). Likewise, according to Joseph Rothschild (1974: 21), the East European dictatorships 'would not or could not emulate the totalitarian dynamism of Hitler . . . Their commitments were essentially bureaucratic and conservative, at most technocratic and oligarchical. Projecting no mass ideology, they either failed or refused to elicit mass support. Despite their sonorous rhetoric . . . they proved petty, brittle, often irresolute.'

Thus we seem to have come to a fork in the road. Either we can adhere to a narrow, uniform, 'purist' conception of fascism, which would carry the very misleading implication that fascism as such was a relatively marginal, extraneous, peripheral phenomenon in inter-war eastern Europe. Or we can uphold a broader, more variegated conception of fascism, which would allow us to include the seemingly (and often self-avowedly) fascist eastern European movements, organizations and regimes among the diverse 'national' varieties of fascism that emerged in Europe between the wars. This would make possible a greater appreciation of the multifaceted nature of European fascism, as well as the pervasive impact and significance of fascism in inter-war eastern Europe. Both approaches raise conceptual difficulties. But it will be argued that, on balance, the second approach has decisive advantages.

LIMITATIONS OF THE 'PURIST' APPROACH

The 'purist' approach starts from the premise that 'true' unadulterated Fascism (with a capital F) was a uniquely Italian phenomenon which could not be replicated outside Italy, just as 'pure' undiluted National Socialism was a uniquely Germanic response to peculiarly German and Austrian problems, preoccupations and ideological currents. This conveniently allows the 'purists' to discount or play down the significance of the increasingly fascist pretensions and proclivities of the East European dictatorships and of most of the East European political parties, movements and organizations which openly proclaimed their adherence and political indebtedness to fascism, on the (questionable) grounds that these were not 'the real McCoy'. The 'purist' approach thus makes it much easier to maintain the (not always innocent) impression that fascism was essentially an extraneous, skin-deep phenomenon in Eastern Europe and to contend that it was in essence a peculiarly Italian and Germanic malady which was 'imported' into or even 'imposed' on Eastern Europe as a result of increasing Italian and German domination of the region. Thus one of the standard texts on fascism maintains that 'the right-wing dictatorships of inter-war Europe lacked many of the essential ingredients of fascist regimes. Poland, Romania, Greece and Yugoslavia were ruled by varying forms of military dictatorships of a conservative type which, although they suppressed the left, never went as far as the totalitarian dictatorships of the fascist type.' The fascist movements of eastern Europe 'remained on the fringe of the radical right until, in some cases, such as Hungary, Croatia and Slovakia, they gained power thanks to German armies of occupation. They were thus imported regimes which did not reflect the social structure and political dynamics of the countries which they dominated' (Kitchen 1976: 88).

Such wholesale discounting of the self-avowedly fascist movements and regimes which emerged in eastern Europe during the late 1930s and early 1940s is misleading and unsound. It can be argued that, with the notable exception of Czechoslovakia, the methods, institutions and illiberal nationalist ethos of government throughout inter-war East Central Europe and the Balkans were steadily degenerating into distinctive 'eastern' forms of fascism. This process of degeneration was driven not only by circumstantial factors, such as the 1930s Depression, widespread economic misery and the rise of Fascist Italy and Nazi Germany, but also by the inherent flaws in the new order erected in Central and Eastern Europe after the First World War (see Chapters 13–16). Avowedly fascist movements and individuals were influencing and infiltrating the entire machinery and ethos of most of the East European states, which in turn increasingly sponsored and/ or adopted such movements in order to bolster their legitimacy and authority and to mobilize more active and widespread support. Thus fascism, far from being an alien, marginal or 'imported' phenomenon, was becoming an increasingly pervasive, hegemonic ideology and *Weltanschauung* in that part of the world. The notion that the fascist regimes which emerged with German support in Hungary, Croatia and Slovakia were merely 'imported regimes which did not reflect the social structure and political dynamics of the countries which they dominated' is actually quite preposterous. But it perfectly illustrates the contortions and distortions into which 'purists' are forced by their vain attempts to uphold narrow and restrictive conceptions of fascism and to 'explain away' other avowedly or seemingly fascist phenomena that fall outside their rigid definitions. As emphasized by O'Sullivan (1983: 40–1), it is necessary to reject 'the familiar procedure of first arbitrarily elevating either the Italian or the German experience of fascism to paradigmatic stature and then focusing a quest for the "essence of fascism" upon whichever movement is felt to embody this essence most completely. A method of this kind inevitably ends with results which are as arbitrary as the point from which it began.'

To be fair, Kitchen does add that, although Nazi Germany and Fascist Italy furnish 'the best examples of fascism in action', it would nevertheless be 'a serious mistake to limit a definition of fascism to these two forms', for that 'would make it impossible to analyse fascist dangers in the present day' (Kitchen 1976: 88). Yet this does not prevent him from discounting the authenticity of the fascism of *most* of the regimes established in late 1930s and early 1940s eastern Europe, including Austria, on the spurious grounds that some (but not all) of these regimes emerged 'thanks to' the presence and support of German military forces. (In the few cases where the latter really did play a crucial role, one can point to a very pertinent and instructive parallel: no one even dreams of arguing that the East European regimes which emerged partly or even mainly as a result of the presence and support of Soviet military forces in the region after the Second World War were *ipso facto* not genuinely Stalinist; and, even if they were to a large extent alien or 'imported' regimes, there is no denying that they soon succeeded in harnessing and mobilizing considerable indigenous 'activism' and support, as had also been the case with some of the partly 'imported' fascist regimes, e.g. the ruling Slovak Party of National Unity in 'independent' fascist Slovakia and the fascist *Ustasa* regime in the 'independent' state of Croatia.) In common with many 'purists', Kitchen also expressly denies the fascist credentials of Salazar's avowedly corporative *Estado Novo* in Portugal, Franco's dictatorship in Spain, the Metaxas regime in Greece, the Peronist regime in Argentina and 'the dictatorships of the underdeveloped world' (pp. 88, 91). However, while it is always correct to question whether this or that regime really was fascist, it is difficult to see what other fascist regimes he has in mind, when he has discounted all the prime candidates! Indeed, even more than Linz, Kitchen is insistent that: 'Fascism is a phenomenon of developed industrial states. If capitalism has not reached a certain level of development, the particular relationships between classes which are characteristic of fascist movements are not possible. Only in advanced capitalism can there be a powerful capitalist class, a large and organized working class with a potentially revolutionary ideology which calls for a radical restructuring of society, and a large *petite bourgeoisie* which is caught in the contradictions between capital and labour and is unable to find any way out of its social, economic and political dilemmas' (p. 83).

If these widely accepted stipulations are correct, then 'genuine' fascism was largely impossible in inter-war eastern Europe (other than in the highly industrialized Czech Lands which did indeed produce one of the most popular and impassioned fascist movements, in the form of Konrad Henlein's Sudetendeutsche Partei). However, Kitchen's rather rigid quasi-Marxist insistence on a particular 'threshold' level of capital-ist development as a condition for real fascism runs up against a number of fundamental objections. Most absurdly, it would appear to preclude the possibility of genuine fascism in the actual birthplace of fascism. Italy, the 'mother country' of fascism, was not much more industrialized, educated or capitalist than East Central Europe (and less so than either the Czech Lands or German Austria). Indeed, large-scale industrialization only got under way in Italy in the mid-nineteenth century and accelerated in the 1880s and 1890s, more or less concurrently with East Central Europe and only two to three decades ahead of the Balkan states (excluding Albania). Not until the 1930s did industry's share of Italian national income overtake that of agriculture (partly because agricultural prices fell more than industrial prices) and it was not until the 1950s that industry's share of the Italian work force surpassed that of farming. Within Italy, moreover, the main strong-holds of Fascism were not in the relatively industrialized, educated, class-conscious and capitalist north. There the relatively large and strong working class strove to remain loyal to the beleaguered left-wing parties and trade unions in the early 1920s, while big business and the bourgeoisie were strongly oriented towards Giovanni Giolitti's Liberal Party. Only the big northern landowners actively courted the Fascists, by employing them as bailiffs and bully-boys to beat up 'Bolshy' tenants, sharecroppers and farm workers. The political bastions of Fascism were in Emilia, Tuscany and central Italy, areas with a preponderance of small-scale artisanal and market towns. Here droves of young 'action hungry' ex-servicemen, unemployed persons, students, lapsed or disillusioned socialists, malcontents, blacklegs and plain thugs joined the seemingly radical and dynamic Fascist *squadri* (squads) and, with money, vehicles and weapons supplied by reactionary and apprehensive property owners and state officials, set about crushing the 'Red Peril' in the early 1920s by breaking boycotts and strikes, attacking socialist and trade union offices, print shops and meetings or hunting down and beating the life out of socialist workers and radicalized sharecroppers. In one sense, Fascism was an enormous Mafia-style protection racket which (almost inevitably) got out of control and not only terrorized its intended victims, but soon started blackmailing and intimidating its well-to-do sponsors and taking over the state. Ironically, the Fascists found it hardest to penetrate southern Italy, as the south was already 'sewn up' by long-standing local patronage, intimidation and protection racketeering networks (including, of course, the Sicilian Mafia). By their very nature, however, these patrons and protection racketeers were ready to co-operate with and 'deliver' support to whoever controlled the central government in Rome, in return for certain 'favours' and a free hand in local affairs (at least until they were 'bought off' by US money in 1942–43, to facilitate the Allied landings and advances in southern Italy).

One can in fact stand Kitchen's thesis on its head. As emphasized by William Kornhauser (1960: 197–8), 'the most highly developed capitalist societies have experienced the smallest fascist movements and the strongest commitments to democratic values on the part of the business community, and ... it has been in the less industrial countries (e.g. Italy) and in countries in which the state assumed a major responsibility for industrial development (e.g. Germany) that fascist movements have been strong and have commanded at least some business support'. Moreover, the burgeoning of extremist mass movements (whether of the right or of the left) has mainly occurred during the early stages of large-scale urbanization and industrialization (particularly if these began as eruptive rather than gradual processes), before the towns, factories and labour movements increased their capacity to absorb numerous new entrants into the urban population, work force and organizations capable of effectively defending their new class interests. These early phases of urbanization and industrialization were the ones in which the greatest social deprivation and disruption, discontinuity of community and family life, and disorientation of helpless individuals were most likely to occur (pp. 125, 145, 150–8).

Furthermore, although Kitchen's views are often couched in a pseudo-Marxist language, 'true' Marxists would be the first to insist that degrees of 'ripeness' for fascism should be judged on an international rather than a narrowly national basis, i.e. by assessing the economic, social and political conditions, trends and balance of forces in the whole or large parts of Europe rather than in each individual country separately considered.

In the final analysis the 'purist' approach is not very useful. It essentially ducks the difficult questions posed by the existence of more widespread and clearly recognizable 'fascist' or 'quasi-fascist' phenomena. Arguably it is an intellectual cop-out. For, even if it were to be generally accepted that the term 'fascism' ought to be applied only to the Italian Fascist movement and regime and possibly to the German Nazi movement and regime, it would then become much harder to come up with satisfactory labels and explanations for the 'quasi-fascist' or 'para-fascist' phenomena which are often (in a broader sense) characterized as 'fascist'. As argued in one of the most influential books on fascism: 'There is evidently an imperative need for a term for those political systems (and their corresponding strivings) which differ as much from the democratic-parliamentary type as from the communist, yet which are not merely military dictatorships or conservative regimes' (Nolte 1969: 569).

This statement is particularly pertinent to the East European dictatorships of the late 1930s and early 1940s, most of which developed into much more ferocious, far-reaching, militant, mobilizatory, activist, antisemitic and therefore 'fascistic' polities than the relatively complacent, corrupt and self-serving conservative-authoritarian military, monarchical or nationalist regimes from which they had emerged, like monstrous insects out of hairy chrysalises. Even Kitchen has to concede that after the First World War 'there were movements in almost all European states which showed distinct fascist tendencies. They rejected the idea of parliamentary democracy. They opposed the organized working class . . . they were violently nationalistic. They subscribed to a vague anti-capitalism. They preached submission to authority, discipline and an irrational sense of community' (Kitchen 1976: ix).

Labels such as 'quasi-fascism', 'para-fascism', '*ersatz* fascism' or 'pseudo-fascism' are cumbersome and unduly dismissive, often failing to do justice to either the dangers or the importance of the phenomena so described. Furthermore, narrowly restricting the use of the term 'fascism' to Italy and possibly Germany does not make the more widespread cognate phenomena 'go away'. They still have to be explained. In varying degrees, moreover, they shared or participated in the broader European trends towards increasingly illiberal and belligerent nationalism, xenophobia, anti-communism, etatism, autarky, corporativism, authoritarianism, the cult of the 'infallible' and charismatic plebeian leader, the glorification of war and conquest, the promotion of martial values, the routine use of electoral and governmental violence against actual or potential opponents and rivals (including initial coalition partners and dissident elements within fascist movements and regimes) and an 'activist' and 'mobilizatory' style of politics, which were also the principal hallmarks of 'fascism'. Hence one might as well call them 'fascist'. Accordingly, our preferred approach is to recognize not only the pertinent 'local' differences between Italy, Germany, East Central Europe, the Balkans, the Baltic States and the Iberian Peninsula, but also the existence of a widespread twentieth-century phenomenon to which the term 'fascism' has been aptly and fruitfully applied (initially by the Marxists who were its first targets, victims and consistent ideological opponents). This broad-brush approach usefully allows us to treat the avowedly fascist parties, movements and regimes that were emerging in Eastern Europe as *sui generis* national or regional variants of fascism, 'creatively' adapted to local conditions.

FASCISM VERSUS NATIONAL SOCIALISM

We maintain that in important respects Italian Fascism had more in common with kindred movements and regimes in southern and eastern Europe than it did with German National

Socialism. As remarked by one of the most influential writers on fascism and so-called 'totalitarianism': 'After the First World War, a deeply anti-democratic . . . wave of semi-totalitarian and totalitarian movements swept Europe; Fascist movements spread from Italy to nearly all Central and Eastern European countries . . . yet even Mussolini, who was so fond of the term "totalitarian state", did not attempt to establish a full-fledged totalitarian regime and contented himself with dictatorship and one-party rule. Similar non-totalitarian dictatorships sprang up in pre-war Romania, Poland, the Baltic States, Hungary, Portugal and Franco's Spain' (Arendt 1966: 308–9).

Some of the dictators (including Mussolini) would certainly have liked to have established 'totalitarian' regimes and even boasted that they were in the business of doing so. In truth, however, these countries were not sufficiently strong or populous 'to allow for total domination' on the part of their rulers. 'Without much scope for the conquest of more heavily populated territories, the tyrants in these countries were forced into a certain old-fashioned moderation lest they lose whatever people they had to rule' (p. 310). They had to husband their meagre resources. They were therefore 'tinpot' dictators who simply could not afford to take either such extreme measures or such enormous gambles as the much more powerful and ruthless Nazi regime did. The dictatorships of the smaller and less powerful states had to be more cautious, circumspect and ready to compromise, in order to preserve their more limited power. Indeed, Goebbels (the Nazi Propaganda Minister) noted in his diary in 1942 that Fascism was 'nothing like National Socialism. While the latter goes deep down to the roots, Fascism is only a superficial thing.' Similarly in 1943 a speech by Himmler (the Nazi SS leader) declared that 'there is absolutely no comparison between Fascism and National Socialism as spiritual, ideo-logical movements . . . Fascism and National Socialism are two fundamentally different things' (both quoted in Arendt 1966: 309). While Mussolini's Fascist movement was content to seize power and establish the Fascist 'elite' as the uncontested rulers of Italy, the more fanatical, formidable, 'totalitarian' Nazi movement was never content to rule by external means alone. The Nazis devised and discovered coercive, ideological and judicial techniques of 'dominating and terrorizing human beings from within', as did the Stalinist regime in Soviet Russia (pp. 323–5). This gave them much more 'total' or pervasive political, economic, social and cultural control.

The more typical goal of most fascist movements and one-party regimes, including Mussolini's Fascists and the kindred movements and regimes that emerged in 1930s and early 1940s Eastern Europe, was merely to gain control of government and fill all major and minor public offices with party members, 'to achieve a complete amalgamation of state and party'. It naturally followed that the supposedly 'ruling' party became merely 'a kind of propaganda organization for the government. The system is "total" only in a negative sense, namely in that the ruling party will tolerate no other parties, no opposition and no freedom of public opinion.' But this type of one-party dictatorship normally 'leaves the original power relationship between state and party intact; the government and the army exercise the same power as before, and the "revolution" consists only in the fact that all government positions are now occupied by party members'. Thus the ruling party's power comprises only its monopoly or near-monopoly of public office, rather than any absolute supremacy of the party over the state. By contrast, the more radical and 'totalitarian' Nazis, like their communist cousins, consciously strove 'to maintain the essential differences between state and movement and to prevent the "revolutionary" institutions of the movement from being absorbed by the government' and thereby becoming politically emasculated (Arendt 1966: 419). For Arendt, one of the distinguishing features of the more 'totalitarian' regimes is that 'all real power' and decision-making is concentrated in the higher echelons of the ruling party rather than in 'the state and military apparatuses', which become increasingly pliable instruments in the hands of the party leadership (p. 420). Therefore the frequent observation that fascist or neo-fascist parties never achieved absolute supremacy over state and military institutions in the increasingly authoritarian nationalist regimes of late 1930s and early 1940s Eastern Europe does not in itself constitute evidence that these regimes had not become fascist. On the contrary, it provides further confirmation that they were in important respects closer to the original Italian Fascist model than was Hitler's much more 'totalitarian' Nazi regime.

Fundamentally, Italian Fascism was spawned by a semi-agrarian, semi-industrial, semi-educated and strongly clientelistic society with an unchallenged monarchy, a commanding and relatively autonomous Catholic Church, powerful and aggressive propertied classes and an overweening and corrupt state bureaucracy. In the south the poorest and least educated sections of Italian society continued to be dominated by pre-Fascist potentates, such as the big landowners and the Sicilian Mafia, and remained relatively inaccessible or unresponsive to Fascism. In order to win and retain power Mussolini had to adjust to these constraining 'facts of life', which to the end remained strong enough to prevent the Fascists from attaining 'total' ascendancy over Italian society. The Fascists were therefore never able to achieve the 'total mobilization' of Italian society and resources, to Mussolini's occasional chagrin, and the human resources at his disposal always left much to be desired. This was to be the crucial 'Achilles heel' of Mussolini's regime and of the Fascist war effort during the Second World War.

This was much more like the situation in the increasingly authoritarian and fascist states of Eastern Europe than the one in Nazi Germany. Mussolini, like fascist leaders in 1930s Eastern Europe, found it necessary and/or expedient to seek an accommodation with the 'powers that be', namely the established Church, the monarchy, the military establishment and the propertied classes. More out of weakness than any innate preference for 'moderation', Mussolini had been forced into formal recognition of their continuing spheres of autonomy and their paramount influence over important aspects or sectors of national life. For example, the Catholic Church continued to enjoy ecclesiastical autonomy and exercised increased control over educational and family matters after the Lateran Treaties of 1929. Indeed, Italian Fascism always had to contend with the rival authority, influence and legitimacy of the Roman Catholic Church, which (however much it consorted with the Fascist regime or professed to be 'above politics') continued to preach its own distinct doctrines, values and codes of conduct. These were fundamentally at variance with those of Fascism. In Fascist Italy, as in several East European states (but unlike Nazi Germany), the fascist movement and the *Führerprinzip* even had to coexist or 'cohabit' with a monarchy whose legitimacy antedated and thus owed nothing to that of fascism. Constitutionally the King of Italy still out-ranked *Il Duce* and, in the last resort, Vittorio Emanuele III could dismiss the Fascist leader from Prime Ministerial office (as he eventually did, with the formal approval of the Fascist Grand Council, in July 1943).

The crucial result of all this was that in Fascist Italy, as in the increasingly authoritarian and fascist states of Eastern Europe, there remained significant elements of pluralism and spheres of relative autonomy which the fascists never managed to suppress completely. This in turn allowed the continued expression of dissent within and between the various segments of the political, military, bureaucratic, ecclesiastical and social 'establishment', as well as the emergence of a substantial wartime opposition and resistance movement which drew support from dissident members of the 'establishment' and the propertied classes. Indeed, fascism was accepted with less conviction, with less fanaticism, or in a more conditional, calculated and opportunistic manner in Italy than in Germany. The same can be said of Eastern Europe. Thus in 1943, when the Axis powers began to suffer major military reverses, key sections of the population began to turn against fascism in Italy, as in Eastern Europe and unlike Nazi Germany. The less extreme (i.e. less 'totalitarian') nature of Italian and East European fascism was what made possible the eventual emergence of widespread, open, internal opposition to fascism there (Kolinsky 1974: 59–60).

German National Socialism, by contrast, was a product of one of Europe's most advanced and highly educated industrial societies, with neither a monarchy nor a preponderant 'national' Church (the Germans being divided between Roman Catholicism and several Protestant Churches). Germany also had a somewhat discredited landed nobility, military hierarchy and state bureaucracy and a severely curtailed and restricted military establishment, as a result of its defeat in 1918 and the punitive Versailles Treaty of 1919. It was therefore relatively easy for the Nazis to 'reach' and penetrate all sectors of German society and to establish Nazi hegemony over the state apparatus and large sections of the propertied classes, the Churches and the armed forces during the 1930s. The fact that most Germans were much more educated than most Italians and East Europeans seems to have made them more (not less) susceptible to fascism. Indeed, about one-third of the (half million) officials and leaders of the Nazi Party in 1935 were teachers by profession. Support for National Socialism, extreme nationalism and pan-Germanism was particularly marked among university students and professors (Kolinsky 1974: 87–8). A quarter of the future SS elite had doctorates and in the elections to student councils in German universities during the academic year 1930–31 Nazi candidates received 40 per cent or more of the votes cast in fourteen of the eighteen universities for which such data survive and 50 per cent or more of the votes in nine of them (Kornhauser 1960: 188). It does not necessarily follow that all highly educated people were inherently susceptible to fascism. But students and university professors were strikingly over-represented within most of the major fascist movements, including those of inter-war Eastern Europe (Seton-Watson 1945: 142–5, 195, 206–7; Carsten 1967: 183; Weber 1964: 90–1, 97; Linz 1979: 26, 53). Intelligentsias had long been purveyors of extreme forms of cultural and ethnic nationalism in Germany, Austria, the Baltic States, Greece and Eastern Europe. These 'national intelligentsias', which had discovered or invented 'the nation' and propagated national myths, were the groups most likely to get excited or up in arms over nationalist issues. The less educated classes tended to be preoccupied by more mundane bread-and-butter problems, aspirations and discontents. Thus large doses of education were not in themselves likely to encourage rejection of fascism. On the contrary, the almost uniformly high standards of education and the consequent cultural unity and technological prowess of the German people helped the Nazis to achieve a more 'total' control and mobilization of German society and resources than was possible in either Italy or Eastern Europe at the time. Thus, although about 150,000 Germans died as a result of their opposition to Nazism, German resistance remained 'fragmented, individualized; it never attained the public force of an open resistance movement' (Kolinsky 1974: 59).

There were also significant doctrinal differences between Fascism and National Socialism which emphasized or reinforced the closer affinities between the Italian and East European varieties of fascism. Mussolini repeatedly put forward the goal of a 'corporative' society, conceived in ways that drew upon (but also perverted) anarcho-syndicalist as well as Catholic social doctrines. On his own admission, 'in the great river of Fascism are to be found the streams which had their source in Sorel, Péguy, in the Lagardelle of the Mouvement Socialiste and the Italian syndicalists who between 1904 and 1914 brought a note of novelty into Italian socialism' (Mussolini 1932: 168–9). Mussolini's 'corporative' doctrine did not aspire to abolish or transcend social classes. Instead, it purported to defuse class conflict by enmeshing the entire working population in a sector-by-sector network of 'syndicates' or 'corporations' (representing employers, employees, the self-employed, the major professions and the state), within which terms and conditions of work were to be negotiated and conflicts resolved by a combination of conciliation and arbitration. 'Fascism recognizes the real exigencies for which the socialist and syndicalist movement arose, but, while recognizing them, wishes to bring them under the control of the state and give them a purpose within the corporative system of interests reconciled within the unity of the state. Individuals form classes according to the similarity of their interests; they form syndicates according to differentiated economic activities within these interests' (pp. 166–7). Moreover, according to the Charter of Labour promulgated by the Fascist Grand Council in April 1927, 'only the juridically recognized syndicate which submits to the control of the state has the right to represent the entire category of employers or workers for which it is constituted, in safeguarding its interests *vis-à-vis* the state and other occupational associations, in making collective contracts of work binding on all the members of that category, in levying contributions and exercising over its members functions delegated to it in the public interest . . . The Labour Court is the organ by which the state intervenes in the settlement of labour disputes . . . after the corporative organ has first made an attempt at conciliation' (pp. 184–5).

Mussolini also eulogized the Italian 'nation' and 'race' and Italy's age-old contribution to European civilization, but he nearly always did so in cultural, historical, non-biological terms. More tellingly, he presented the Italian 'nation' and 'race' as a creature and servant of the state, rather than vice versa: 'Against individualism, the Fascist conception is for the state . . . Fascism reaffirms the state as the true reality of the individual . . . For the Fascist, therefore, everything is in the state and nothing human or spiritual exists, much less has value, outside the state. In this sense Fascism is totalitarian . . . It is not the nation that generates the state . . . Rather the nation is created by the state, which gives the people . . . a will and therefore an effective existence . . . The keystone of Fascist doctrine is the conception of the state . . . For Fascism the state is an absolute before which individuals and groups are relative . . . It is the state alone that grows in size and power. It is the state alone that can solve the dramatic contradictions of capitalism' (Mussolini 1932: 166–7, 175–7).

Thus, far from seeing the Fascist 'corporative' project as being uniquely applicable to Italy or as something only realizable by a 'master race' with markedly superior 'racial characteristics', Mussolini proclaimed it to be 'exportable' and applicable to other countries, especially those with strong 'corporative' or syndicalist traditions of their own.

Otherwise it would have been hard to sustain Mussolini's characteristically extravagant claim that 'the Corporative System is destined to become the civilization of the twentieth century'. For many the appeal of the 'corporative' model was very seductive. It purported to offer a constructive 'third way' between communism and *laissez-faire* capitalism. It conjured up visions of social unity and harmony in place of class division and strife. It facilitated and reinforced industrial and agricultural collusion, cartelization, monopolistic practices and protectionism. It seemed to offer greater long-term job security for those in work. It made it easier for fascists, nationalists, syndicalists, social Catholics, social monarchists and technocrats to work together, under the illusion that they were all united in a common cause. Some of its proponents even claimed that the 'corporative' system was a form of 'functional' or 'producers' democracy', purportedly superior to corrupt, phoney and divisive parliamentary democracy. Lastly its seemingly universalist, collaborationist, consensual rhetoric appeared to convert the naked coercive power of fascist regimes into legitimate authority, thereby conferring an aura of legitimacy and respectability on regimes which in reality rested on regimentation, repression and intimidation (O'Sullivan 1983: 132–7; Kolinsky 1974: 56–8; Kitchen 1976: 50–5). Significantly, Mussolini's 'corporative' rhetoric did indeed evoke a positive response and some emulation in Eastern Europe, Austria, Portugal, Spain, Belgium and France (especially under Marshal Pétain).

Mussolini's 'corporative' project is often glibly dismissed as 'little more than an elaborate ideological facade' (Kolinsky 1974: 56, 117) or 'merely a further enhancement of Mussolini's dictatorship' or 'only a technique for extending state control over society' or 'nothing more than the most ordinary protectionism' (O'Sullivan 1983: 136). According to Kitchen (1976: 51–2), 'The "corporative state" never existed in fact, for there was no new economic policy, no fundamental change in the structure of the economy . . . and no real authority to the *Consiglio delle Corporazioni* or to the minister of corporations . . . They remained subordinate to the traditional bureaucracy.' In Kitchen's view, Fascist 'corporativism' was merely a means of controlling labour while granting private monopolies and cartels a free hand to control prices and restrict competition to their own advantage (pp. 52–5). If that were the case it would explain part, but not all of the considerable appeal of the Fascist 'corporative' project outside Italy.

It is significant that Palmiro Togliatti, the long-serving leader of the Italian Communist Party and one of the more discerning 'fighters' against Fascism, took the Fascist 'corporative' project rather more seriously. In a series of lectures delivered in Moscow in 1935 he warned fellow communists that 'corporativism is not only a propaganda tool, a demagogic slogan fascism uses for the masses, but is also a reality: corporativism is the organizational form fascism has given and is endeavouring to give to Italian society and especially to certain aspects of the activity of the state' (Togliatti 1976: 87). 'It is no accident that the Catholic Church and the Vatican substantially accept Italian corporativism and that in Austria, where fascism is bound more closely to the Catholic Church than in Italy, fascism has immediately set about rebuilding the state apparatus on a corporative basis' (p. 91). In Togliatti's view, 'fascist corporativism' was a conservative, capitalist attempt to develop a conservative, capitalist means of 'overcoming' the inter-war 'crisis of capitalism'(p. 93). Viewed from another angle, and recalling 'the creation of the committees for industrial mobilization that organized the economy for war' during the First World War, 'the corporative structure is the groundwork for an organization of production keyed to war' (pp. 102–3). At the same time 'the corporations are an instrument for the ideological propaganda of class collaboration', for 'the destruction of every democratic liberty' and 'for suppressing any attempt by the working masses to liberate themselves' (p. 103).

The Nazis, by contrast, propounded and implemented more extreme 'totalitarian' concepts of the 'organic' state, the *Führungsprinzip* and *Gleichschaltung*, i.e. total subordination of the entire institutional complex of society to a single focus of power and authority (Kolinsky 1974: 91). Instead of belonging to various sectoral 'syndicates' or 'corporations', each of which would preserve the particularism of individual trades and professions (in the manner of medieval guilds), the entire work force was to belong to a single German Labour Front with 25 million members, controlled by a single overarching bureaucracy (pp. 92–3). As emphasized by Werner Sombart in his book *German Socialism* (1934), the Nazi goal was 'a total ordering of the German *Volk*' which would be 'uniform, born of a single spirit and extended from a single central point systematically over the entire social life' (quoted by O'Sullivan 1983: 132). In the Third Reich membership of separate social classes was (eventually) supposed to be superseded by total immersion in and subordination to an 'organic', racially 'purified' nation conceived as a single organism and *Volksgemeinschaft*. The Nazis upheld an essentially racial (*völkisch*) conception of an economy and society in which only the 'Aryan' Nordic/German 'master race' would be fully eligible to participate and 'realize itself'. For Mussolini the state was paramount and nations, social groups and individuals could have only the meaning, value and existence with which the state endowed them. But for Hitler 'the state is only a vessel and the race is what it contains. The vessel can have meaning only if it preserves and safeguards the contents. Otherwise it is worthless' (quoted by O'Sullivan 1983: 173). Thus Hitler's racial ('biological') conception of society was the very opposite of Mussolini's essentially non-racial, socio-economic, statist and almost universalist 'corporative' project.

In the Fascist conception of the state and society there were autonomous or semi-autonomous state and 'corporative' institutions which stood between the Leader and his people, mediating and constraining his purportedly absolute power and authority. By contrast, Nazi ideology posited a wholly direct unchecked, unmediated relationship between the *Führer* and his nation. In more traditional dictatorships the dictator makes no claim to be the 'tribune' or representative of the people over whom he rules. But in Nazi ideology the *Führer* was not merely the sole representative and 'tribune' of the people, but also the direct embodiment of the nation and the national 'will'. This, rather than any state office or title he might hold or the process by which he rose to pre-eminence, was the source of his legitimacy and absolute authority. State institutions derived authority and legitimacy from the *Führer*, rather than vice versa (O'Sullivan 1983: 156–8). However, the *Führer* 'depends just as much on the "will" of the masses he embodies as the masses depend on him. Without him they would lack external representation and remain an amorphous horde; without the masses the leader is a nonentity.' Hitler trenchantly expressed this relationship between the *Führer* and the nation in his speech in Berlin on 30 January 1936: 'All that you are, you are through me; all that I am, I am through you alone' (Arendt 1966: 325).

In Italy, as in Eastern Europe, fascism was also a response to the political fragmentation and weakness of the bourgeoisie. This was cogently explained by Palmiro Togliatti in an article published in *L'Internationale communiste* on 5 October 1934: 'The Italian bourgeoisie did not possess a strong political organization before the advent of fascism.' There was a multiplicity of political parties, 'but they mainly had an electoral and local character, without well-defined programmes, and from the standpoint of political organization and cadres they were insubstantial'. During the late nineteenth and early twentieth centuries Italy's leading 'bourgeois' politicians, especially Giovanni Giolitti, had been 'anxious not to create strong bourgeois parties equipped with a well-defined programme and solidly organized, but on the contrary to impede the formation of such parties. Their art of government consisted, rather, in breaking up the existing parties and forming a parliamentary majority through compromises, corruption, manoeuvres, etc.' However, when this mode of bourgeois hegemony and government was challenged by the emergence of more solid, disciplined, programmatic mass parties (such as the Socialist Party and the Catholic Partito Populare), the 'bourgeoisie's whole system of government was thrown out of kilter'. In the ensuing crisis, 'Fascism . . . set itself the task of creating a solid, united political organization of the bourgeoisie . . . Fascism has given the Italian bourgeoisie what it had always lacked, namely a strong, centralized, disciplined, *single* party equipped with its own armed force' (Togliatti 1976: 137–8). There was a gap to be filled and the Fascists set out to fill it. This almost exactly mirrored the political sitution in the fledgeling states of Eastern Europe, where the political parties of the bourgeoisie were even more fragmented, unstable, corrupt, manipulable and weak. But it was quite unlike the political situation in Weimar Germany, which had several strong, well organized, programmatic political parties of the bourgeoisie. In this respect, therefore, the rise of Fascism in Italy was more closely paralleled in Eastern Europe than in Germany. Such a contention does not rest on the banal thesis that fascism was simply created by the bourgeoisie in an endeavour to override a serious crisis in its rule and/or the capitalist system. Rather it suggests that, among other things, and with varying degrees of success, Italian and East European fascists saw (and sometimes seized) some golden opportunities to make themselves *the* party of the 'national' bourgeoisie, by thrusting themselves into the political limelight, by mobilizing new political constituencies and by viciously attacking Marxist labour movements (and/or vulnerable ethnic minorities), thereby seizing the political initiative, 'calling the shots' and violently upstaging or usurping the customary 'prerogatives' of the older 'bourgeois' parties.

Fascist ideologists and the first Italian writers and foreign commentators on the emergence of Italian Fascism initially presented it as a uniquely Italian response to peculiarly Italian problems, preoccupations and ideological currents and as a consummation of Italy's belated and incomplete national unification, industrialization and debut as a European power. Very soon, however, Italian writers, foreign observers and the Fascists themselves noticed the emergence of similar movements and manifestations in other parts of Europe and commented on their affinities with Italian Fascism (Linz 1979: 19). While claiming to have developed a uniquely Italian synthesis of Catholic, corporative, syndicalist and nationalist traditions, the Fascists were at the same time only too pleased to be seen as the pioneers and pacemakers of a major new trend in European politics. It boosted their self-importance and vanity. Thus in 1932 Mussolini boasted that, just as 'the nineteenth century has been the century of Socialism, Liberalism and Democracy', so 'this century may be that of authority, a century of the "Right", a Fascist century' (Mussolini 1932: 175). 'If every age has its own doctrine, it is apparent from a thousand signs that the doctrine of the present age is Fascism' (p. 178). 'Fascism . . . has . . . the universality of all those doctrines which, by fulfilling themselves, have significance in the history of the human spirit' (p. 179). This was indeed the form in which fascism permeated 1930s Eastern Europe. The frequent denials that the purportedly fascist movements and regimes that emerged in 1930s and early 1940s Eastern Europe were genuinely fascist rest not only on unwarranted 'purism' concerning the nature of fascism, but also on exaggeration of the affinities between Italian and German forms of fascism as well as the differences between the Italian and East European varieties of fascism. In many ways, therefore, the relationship of German National Socialism to Italian Fascism was not so much one of kinship as of rival poles of attraction; and identifying the important differences between Fascism and National Socialism helps to highlight the greater similarities between Italian Fascism and the 'lesser fascisms' that emerged in Austria, eastern Europe and the Iberian Peninsula (without which there would not be much point in employing the word 'fascism' as a generic term).

Indeed, despite the racial overtones of East European 'integral'/'ethnic' nationalism, xenophobia, antisemitism and 'ethnic purification' programmes, it seems that Mussolini's non-racial statism, activism, voluntarism and corporativism had more of an appeal among East European fascists and authoritarian rulers than did Hitler's much more dangerous racial doctrines, with their insistence on the primacy of (spurious) 'racial' characteristics and considerations, on the attainment of (bogus) 'racial purity' and 'racial hygiene', on the mass extermination of Jews, Gypsies and other alleged 'vermin' and 'degenerates', and on the Germans as the supposedly Aryan 'master race'. Eastern Europe's incumbent authoritarian-nationalist rulers obviously had more to gain from Mussolini's etatism, activism, voluntarism and corporativism, which could buttress their power and authority and mobilize the population 'from above' in support of state-sponsored projects and objectives, than they did from Hitler's potentially much more wayward, subversive and destructive racial doctrines, 'racial determinism' and 'eugenics'. Moreover, the easiest and most promising way for fascists to achieve 'hegemony' over East European states and societies was by 'infiltrating' and slowly taking over the existing ('ready made') authoritarian-nationalist regimes from within, gradually making them their own and further intensifying their increasingly fascist features and spirit: a 'top–down' strategy, leading to a form of 'fascism from above' rather than 'fascism from below'. Fascists did not need to overthrow democracy in Eastern Europe, as it was already being curtailed for them by frightened monarchs and military rulers. (The major exception was Czechoslovakia, which was surrendered to the Axis powers by the frightened British and French governments in September 1939.)

In Eastern Europe only the Croatian fascist *Ustase* enthusiastically emulated Hitler's mass extermination policies. However, *Ustasa* genocide was directed not so much against Jews and Gypsies as against Orthodox Serbs, in operations intended to achieve the 'ethnic cleansing' (using a modern term) of a Greater Croatia. The motivation derived more from vicious and fanatical 'integral' or 'ethnic' nationalism than from real racialism. Indeed, the *Ustase* found it impossible to identify consistent 'racial' or 'biological' differences between Croats and Serbs, who had been formed from much the same Balkan 'melting pot' and even used the same spoken language (Serbo-Croat). Therefore they were often able to distinguish Serbs (and Bosnians and Jews) from Croats only on the basis of religious rather than 'ethnic' affiliation or spurious 'racial characteristics'.

The pervasive stench of virulent religious, economic, political and sometimes racial antisemitism was the only major respect in which East European fascism can be said to have resembled Hitler's National Socialism more than Mussolini's Fascism. Moreover, unlike the contrived and half-hearted antisemitism adopted by Italian Fascism after 1938 (from fear of being upstaged by the Nazis), East European antisemitism was essentially 'homespun', not an alien importation. Polish, Romanian, Hungarian, Slovak, Croat and Ruthene 'integral nationalism' had become rabidly antisemitic by the mid-1930s (well before Eastern Europe fell under German domination) and the position of Polish, Romanian and Hungarian Jews in particular was increasingly insecure thereafter. Indeed, Jews were subjected to official restrictions and occasional pogroms in 1930s Poland, Romania and Hungary. By the time of the German invasion of Poland in September 1939 one in three Polish Jews had been beggared by punitive taxation and a government-backed boycott of all Jewish economic establishments (Crampton 1994: 174–6). Ironically, the enormous crimes that the Nazis perpetrated in and against Poland did much to save Poland's honour and international standing from the bestial potential of Polish nationalism and redirected Polish nationalist valour into heroic and sometimes quixotic resistance against the German occupation forces.

Nevertheless, with the exception of the Croatian *Ustase*, the East European regimes and puppet regimes that remained 'allied' to Nazi Germany did more to frustrate than to facilitate Hitler's 'Final Solution' (Crampton 1994: 187). Tsar Boris successfully resisted German pressure for mass deportation of Bulgarian Jews to Nazi death camps, while the Romanian General Antonescu did the same for the Jews of Moldavia, Wallachia and southern Transylvania, although it was beyond their power to save the Jews of Macedonia, Thrace, Bessarabia, Bukovina and northern Transylvania (p. 188). After 1938 Hungary's Jews were subjected to increasingly dangerous and life-threatening economic and military service measures, but the Regent (Admiral Horthy) endeavoured to parry growing German demands for mass deportation of Hungary's Jews to the Nazi death camps until the country came under German military occupation in March 1944 (p. 189). The Slovak puppet state similarly tried to refrain from fully enforcing the antisemitic legislation which Nazi Germany had obliged it to adopt, and it intermittently resisted German demands for mass deportation of Slovakia's Jews to the Nazi concentration camps until the country came under German military occupation in the aftermath of the Slovak uprising of August 1944 (pp. 187, 193–5). Even Ferenc Szalasi, the self-styled 'Hungarist national socialist', who was installed by the Germans as Hungary's new head of government in October 1944, baulked at Hitler's 'Final Solution' to the Jewish 'problem', as did the 'Hungarian national socialist' Gyula Gömbös during his stint as Prime Minister (1932–36). In place of genocide, Szalasi's September 1944 'plan of action' proposed that Hungary's Jews should be employed on public works projects until they could emigrate to other countries after the war (Weber 1964: 90, 95; Carsten 1967: 180). East European antisemitism was nasty and bestial, but it was also calculating and opportunistic. It was mainly inspired by envy, xenophobia, blinkered anti-capitalism and anti-communism and muddleheaded Christian vindictiveness. But, except in Croatia, it normally stopped short of Hitler's lethal, pseudo-biological, racialist fanaticism.

RIVAL CONCEPTIONS OF FASCISM: METHODS, IDEOLOGY AND 'STYLE'

There is remarkably little agreement as to which political parties, movements and regimes deserve to be labelled 'fascist', just as there has been no agreed definition of fascism and no consensus on its 'natural constituency', what it stood for or where it was located in the left–right spectrum. It cannot simply be bracketed with conservative nationalist parties and regimes committed to a stout defence of the *status quo*, as fascism was often quite radical and vociferously opposed to the established political, social and international order. Many of its most active adherents were attracted to it as a purportedly radical (or even revolutionary) movement or regime which would establish a 'new order' substantially different from the *status quo*. Yet there is no generally accepted threshold beyond which authoritarian nationalist movements or regimes can clearly be said to have become fascist. The former 'shade off' into the latter.

The form, orientation and content of fascist parties, movements and regimes were not 'predetermined' by the existence of a 'revered' common body of scriptures and doctrines, a standard constitutional template and rule book and an overarching international organization and 'papal' authority, in the way that their communist counterparts were. Unlike Stalinism, fascism was not a monolithic phenomenon. In one sense, of course, every manifestation of fascism was of necessity unique, reflecting the particular conjuncture of forces and events in each country and in the Continent as a whole at the time of its emergence and of its subsequent struggle for political power and popular support. Each exploited and drew upon its own specific national roots, traditions, preoccupations, ideologies and political, social, cultural and economic context. Fascism was, to a large extent, nationalism taken to extremes. In this respect, however, the seminal Italian and German variants were no more unique than any other form and they differed from one another just as fundamentally as they did from the other varieties. The tendency for analysts of fascism to make this self-evident and inevitable national uniqueness of the various forms of fascism a pretext for 'purism' is not only a cop-out. It is also an implicit admission that such analysts are unable to distinguish between the general and the particular or to recognize that each unique national manifestation of fascism was just one of many possible variants or expressions of a more general and deep-seated twentieth-century phenomenon, brought about by a distinctive new stage in the development of European capitalism (according to most Marxist analyses of fascism) and/or by the rise of increasingly illiberal and extreme forms of nationalism, racism, political 'activism' and 'mass' politics, tending towards (but rarely achieving) more 'totalitarian' forms of governance and 'mass mobilization' (according to many liberal analyses of fascism).

Consequently, any manageable and readily comprehensible conception or definition of something as diverse and multifaceted as fascism is inevitably partial. But that need not be an unmitigated disadvantage. One of the main functions of any coherent and illuminating definition is to 'edit' complex and variegated phenomena so as to make them more manageable and intelligible to the human brain. By considering and making use of various different definitions of fascism it is possible to draw out or focus attention on various important aspects or dimensions of the phenomenon. But it is unlikely that any single definition can ever encompass every major facet and manifestation of fascism. Indeed, attempts to construct all-inclusive composite definitions of fascism tend to become either too bland (by focusing on the lowest common denominators) or too complicated and unwieldy. Either way, the results tend not to be very enlightening. Linz (1979: 25) unwittingly illustrates the contortions and difficulties involved in any serious attempt to construct a comprehensive, composite definition of fascism: 'We define fascism as a hypernationalist, often pan-nationalist, anti-parliamentary, anti-liberal, anti-communist, populist and therefore anti-proletarian, partly anti-capitalist and anti-bourgeois, anticlerical or at least non-clerical movement, with the aim of national social integration through a single party and corporative representation not always equally emphasized; with a distinctive style and rhetoric, it always relied on activist cadres ready for violent action combined with electoral participation to gain power with totalitarian goals by a combination of legal and violent tactics. The ideology and above all the rhetoric appeals for the incorporation of a national cultural tradition selectively in the new synthesis . . . with new organizational conceptions of mobilization and participation.'

This is not only unwieldy, but also misleading, as not all these specific ingredients were present in every plausible example of a fascist movement and/or regime, while the important socio-economic aspects of fascism are not even mentioned. One can learn more about fascism by considering the implications of several more partial conceptions or definitions, taking only one or a few strands at a time, than by reaching out for more comprehensive or all-inclusive definitions of fascism. Our preferred procedure will not yield a consistent and coherent overall picture of fascism, but this faithfully reflects the fact that fascism really was a very eclectic, incoherent and contradictory phenom-enon. Indeed, it is often described as a ragbag or mish-mash of half-baked phobias, precepts and crude ideas. That is why no one is in a position to lay down the law on what did or did not constitute 'true' fascism. It is nonsensical to try to be 'purist' about something so eclectic and incoherent. It is more fruitful to consider its appalling diversity and many-sidedness.

Significantly, one of the crucial tasks of any effective fascist leader was to hold the disparate elements together by creating and sustaining the illusion that the 'ideas' he put forward and the movement he led were coherent. He did so mainly by embodying or drawing together all the potentially conflicting strands in his own person and by concentrating fascist phobias and hatreds on a single 'arch-enemy' (usually the com-munist, the Jew or the communist-Jew). In *Mein Kampf* (1925) Hitler shrewdly observed that the 'art of leadership . . . consists in consolidating the attention of people against a single adversary and taking care that nothing will divide that attention . . . The leader of genius must have the ability to make different opponents appear as if they belong to one category.' Otherwise, if 'the vacillating masses find themselves facing an opposition that is made up of different groups of enemies, their sense of objectivity will be aroused and they will ask how it is that all the others can be in the wrong and they themselves, and their movement, alone in the right' (quoted in O'Sullivan 1983: 125).

It is often emphasized that most fascist movements, including Mussolini's Fascists and Hitler's Nazis as well as those in eastern and south-western Europe, were ready 'to enter into coalitions' and 'make compromises with the Establishment, to gain access to power' (Linz 1979: 27). This was by no means peculiar to eastern Europe. 'In both Italy and Germany the old political leaders thought that they could bend the Fascist movement to their purposes' (Kolinsky 1974: 119). This would usually prove to be an awful delusion, but by the time they realized their mistake it was often impossible to turn the clock back. During their ascent to power, fascists often found themselves allied with illiberal conservatives in defending and celebrating the virtues of the nation, the family, hierarchy, order, discipline and patriotism 'against common enemies perceived as undermining these institutions and values', even though fascism was nevertheless 'bent on revolutionizing their content in ways which would eventually transform, marginalize or sweep away conservative elites' (Griffin 1993: x). Moreover, one must not underestimate the crucial importance of 'the help rendered by sections of the ruling groups and governments, or the support of the army and high-ranking officers. Without this, there would have been . . . no Mussolini government. Without the support rendered by the Bavarian government and army the National Socialists would not have become a mass party . . . in the early 1920s. Later, the ambiguous role of the Reichswehr leaders and their deep contempt of the [Weimar] Republic proved of inestimable value to Hitler, as did the financial contributions which he received from certain industrialists' (Carsten 1967: 234). The position was not fundamentally different in Eastern Europe. Thus the Romanian Garda de Fier (Iron Guard) 'would not have become a mass movement if it had not been supported for a time by King Carol and industrialist circles . . . and in Hungary the army provided invaluable help for the Fascists' (pp. 234–5). But Carsten also emphasizes that 'the Fascist movements did aim at a fundamental change of the political structure . . . and replacement of the [old] ruling groups by a new elite', even though they continued to make extensive use of 'the old experts, civil servants and generals' once in power. Nevertheless, the balance of power increasingly shifted from the old elite to 'the new leaders who often came from entirely different social groups, far below the level of the old ruling classes. The Fascist "revolution" was not fought out in the streets and on the barricades, but in the ministries and government buildings' (p. 236). In this crucial respect the differences between the increasingly fascist regimes of Eastern Europe and those of Italy and Germany were merely a matter of speed and degree. The former got off to a slower and more hesitant start and the East European fascist movements may have had less public support, resulting in a slower and more tentative displacement of power from the old elites to the fascists. Nevertheless, the basic direction and dynamics were fairly similar, and the oft-stated smallness of the base of support for fascism in Eastern Europe is open to question. In December 1937, in the last 'free' Romanian general election of the inter-war period, Corneliu Codreanu's Iron Guard officially gained 15.6 per cent of the vote, while Alexandru Cuza's antisemitic and ultra-nationalist League of National Christian Defence obtained a further 9.2 per cent, taking the 'quasi-fascist' vote to nearly 25 per cent of the total, on a 66 per cent turn-out (Rothschild 1974: 310). But it was 'conceded by contemporary political observers that the actual fascist vote was well above that percentage. In fact, the King's decision . . . to hand over the government to the right-wing coalition of Octavian Goga and A.C. Cuza was a clear reflection of his realization that the country was leaning toward the extreme right' (Fischer-Galati 1971: 117). Futhermore, in May 1939, in the first Hungarian election held under secret ballot, the votes obtained by the various 'fascist and national socialist parties' added up to about 37 per cent of the total (Barany 1971: 77). Indeed, the 250,000-member Arrow Cross (the largest of these parties) on its own gained 25 per cent of the vote and the outbreak of the Second World War strengthened 'hopes for a total fascist transformation coming from above, from the government' (Ranki 1971: 71). However, if it was true that East European 'integral nationalism' and modes of government in general were becoming increasingly fascist in the late 1930s (as we have argued), these voting statistics considerably understate the true magnitude of the base of public support for fascism in

Eastern Europe. The explicit electoral support was really just the tip of a dangerous iceberg.

Furthermore, even where fascist movements did not sweep to power, the apparent incapacity of the liberal parliamentary democracies to deal effectively with the daunting structural, economic, social, political and ethnic problems of the inter-war period left an opening for fascists to set the agenda and call the shots. To many people it appeared that the Devil had all the best tunes. The fascist parties and regimes appeared to be the ones which could get things done and put the unemployed back to work (or at least get them off the streets, whether into barracks or jails or back to the land). The fascist 'ethos of power' seemed to signify a capacity for regeneration.

In the last resort, however, just as Hitler (and, less violently, Mussolini) crushed the socially radical wing of his own movement once he had gained state power, so some East European rulers were prepared to crush the anarchic and potentially subversive autonomous fascist movements if this seemed necessary for the preservation of 'order'. Thus, faced with the mushrooming strength of Codreanu's wayward Iron Guard, in February 1938 King Carol inaugurated a one-party 'corporative' state headed by himself, with the 'hypernationalist' Orthodox Patriarch Miron Cristea as Prime Minister, while independent political parties and movements were banned and gradually suppressed. In the ensuing crackdown hundreds of Guardists were imprisoned and/or murdered. Codreanu himself was imprisoned in April 1938 and then garrotted (along with thirteen fellow Guardist prisoners) the following November, supposedly 'while trying to escape'. But many of the Guardists who survived this repression sought to avenge the death of these 'martyrs'. In September 1939, emboldened by Hitler's lightning conquest of Poland, a group of Guardists assassinated King Carol's principal 'strong man', Armand Calinescu (who as Interior Minister had spearheaded the crackdown on Guardists in 1938 and had succeeded the deceased Patriarch Cristea as Premier in March 1939). Calinescu's death was followed by further repression of the Iron Guard, with many more dead Guardists becoming revered 'martyrs' and 'saints', laid up in various Orthodox churches (Carsten 1967: 189). But in early 1940, under mounting pressure from the Axis states (which he had refrained from joining), King Carol allowed thousands of Guardists to be released from prison or to return from exile and to join his one-party regime, whereupon they began to avenge the deaths of the Guardist 'martyrs' by murdering sundry royalists, communists and Jews. The uneasy alliance between Carol and the Guard soon fell apart. The loss of Bessarabia and Bukovina to the Soviet Union in July 1940, followed by the loss of northern Transylvania to Hungary and southern Dobruja to Bulgaria on 30 August, prompted Carol to flee into exile (in fear of his life) on 6 September. His teenage son, King Michael, ceded power to the Iron Guard, now headed by Horia Sima, and pro-Guardist army officers led by General Ion Antonescu. On 14 September they proclaimed a National Legionary State in which the Iron Guard was to be the only legal party. At first the elated Iron Guard seemed to have the upper hand over the dejected military, who had been humiliated and demoralized by the unchallenged dismemberment of Greater Romania (Rothschild 1974: 315). But during the winter of 1940–41 the Guardists ran amok, indiscriminately murdering Jews, liberals, communists, royalists, prominent peasantists (including Virgil Madgearu) and even the august 'hypernationalist' historian Nicolae Iorga. With Hitler's blessing Antonescu brutally crushed the bloodthirsty Iron Guard (who were demanding his resignation) in late January 1941. He formally dissolved the National Legionary State the following month. Having finally purged the Iron Guard of its 'hooligan' element, Antonescu retained some of its less wayward members as functionaries in his military fascist dictatorship, with a more pragmatic, disciplinarian, 'corporative', technocratic orientation. Many of the surviving Legionaries and Guardists found solace and/or met 'martyrs' deaths' in the ensuing war against the Soviet Union, fighting the Antichrist. (The religious overtones of the Iron Guard and its 'spiritual vanguard', the Legion of the Archangel Michael, are taken up later.)

Like Admiral Horthy's Hungary and Admiral Tojo's Japan, General Antonescu's Romania increasingly conformed to Harold Lasswell's concept of 'the garrison state'. In 1941 Lasswell speculated that 'the trend of our time is away from the dominance of the specialist on bargaining . . . and toward the supremacy of the specialist on violence, the soldier . . . In the garrison state all organized social activity will be governmentalized; hence the role of independent associations will disappear . . . Not only will the administrative structure be centralized, but at every level it will tend to integrate authority in a few hands' (Lasswell 1941: 455, 462–3). In such a state 'at least in its introductory phases, problems of morale are destined to weigh heavily . . . It is easy to throw sand in the gears of the modern assembly line; hence there must be a deep and general sense of participation in the total enterprise of the state if collective effort is to be sustained' (p. 458). The changing nature of modern warfare (or the emergence of what came to be known as 'total war') was tending 'to abolish the distinction between civilian and military functions'. For a variety of reasons, therefore, in 'the garrison state there must be work – and the duty to work – for all. Since all work becomes public work, all who do not accept employment flout military discipline. For those who do not fit within the structure of the state there is but one alternative – to obey or die' (p. 459). Moreover, the 'rulers of the garrison state will be able to regularize the rate of production, since they will be free from many of the conventions that have stood in the way of adopting measures suitable to this purpose'. However, 'they will most assuredly prevent full utilization of modern productive capacity for non-military consumption purposes', for they will retain 'a professional interest in multipying gadgets specialized to acts of violence' (pp. 464–5). Garrison states would have to try to perpetuate a siege mentality 'as a means of maintaining popular willingness to forgo immediate consumption' and also 'in order to preserve those virtues of sturdy acquiescence in the regime which they so much admire and from which they so greatly benefit'. However, they would also tend to employ 'militaristic ritual and ceremony' as surrogates for (hazardous) real wars. 'The tendency to ceremonialize rather than to fight will be particularly prominent among the most influential elements in a garrison state' (pp. 465–6).

There were unmistakable trends towards this type of state in post-Depression Europe, Asia and Latin America. Lasswell also alluded to the need to distinguish 'the garrison state' from 'the party propaganda state, where the dominant figure is the propagandist, and the party bureaucratic state, in which the organization men of the party make the vital decisions' (p. 455). In line with this distinction it is useful to differentiate the fascist 'garrison state' from the fascist 'party state'. We can categorize Horthy's Hungary and Antonescu's Romania as fascist 'garrison states', since the military leadership managed to retain the upper hand over civilian and paramilitary fascists, who nevertheless played important mobilizing and legitimizing roles and turned these states into more than mere military dictatorships. Conversely, Mussolini's Italy and Hitler's Germany were fascist 'party states', in the sense that their fascist leaders managed to remain somewhat more important than the military hierarchy, the state bureaucracy, the old ruling classes and, in

Italy's case, the Catholic Church and the monarchy. However, these distinctions were not absolute, but mainly differences of emphasis. The active co-operation of most of the state bureaucracy, the military hierarchy, the old ruling classes and (in Italy) the Church and the monarchy was essential to the survival and to the implementation of the projects and policies of Hitler and Mussolini, just as the different arms of the political establishment needed each other's active support for the implementation of major projects and for the retention of political power in increasingly fascist Hungary and Romania (and, in different ways, in clerico-fascist Slovakia and monarcho-fascist Bulgaria). Military and paramilitary fascists could not have ruled unaided in Hungary or Romania any more than the mainly civilian fascist parties could have ruled solely by their own efforts in Italy or Germany. Extensive overlap, interpenetration and co-operation between the fascists and other elements in the political establishment was essential. Conversely, open conflict between military and paramilitary civilian fascists (of the sort that broke out in Romania in 1940–41) was potentially fatal to the survival of fascist regimes if it was not quickly brought under control.

Hitler evidently preferred to have Romania controlled by a 'reliable' military *Conducator* (Leader) who could be trusted to keep order, toe the line, enthusiastically contribute to the Axis invasion of the Soviet Union and deliver the vital Romanian oil, grain and raw materials needed by the German war machine as it prepared for the ultimate military challenge, rather than to have Romania terrorized by 'unreliable' and disruptive hooligans (Carsten 1967: 192). Antonescu subsequently became one of Hitler's most valued, decorated and respected foreign allies. (He was even allowed to disagree with the *Führer* occasionally.) Nevertheless, Hitler still took Horia Sima and other leading Guardists into asylum in Germany, in case they should be needed at a later stage. Indeed, when King Michael and some prominent anti-fascists toppled Antonescu and sided with the Allies against Hitler in August 1944, the Nazis made unsuccessful moves to establish Horia Sima as the leader of a Romanian fascist government-in-exile (Rothschild 1974: 317).

Ironically, it was often the most ardent (rather than the more circumspect and calculating) fascists who ended up as Nazi 'stooges'. Thus Ferenc Szalasi and his Arrow Cross movement were finally installed in power by Nazi Germany in October 1944 in an endeavour to ensure that Hungary would fight to the finish and fully comply with Hitler's 'Final Solution'. Szalasi was openly opposed to genocide, yet he lacked the power to stop it (Carsten 1967: 180). He had been placed in power to do Hitler's bidding, and the awful contradictions of his position contributed to his incapacity to govern effectively. Similarly in March 1939 Konrad Henlein, the founder and leader of the East European fascist party which most overwhelmingly captured the support of the community it claimed to represent, was given an exalted public office in the German *Protektorat* of Bohemia and Moravia which he had helped to bring about. But he wielded far less power than either the military governor, General Blaskowitz, or the future *Protektors*, Baron von Neurath and his dreaded successor, SS *Obergruppenführer* Reinhard Heydrich.

The Croatian fascist *Ustase*, by contrast, had a relatively free hand in the Axis-sponsored Independent State of Croatia from 1941 to 1944, partly because Croatia was incapable of contributing much to the wider Axis war effort and partly because it had never had a large Jewish population. Indeed, the *Ustase* carried out 'genocide' against the Serbs with such savagery that it even worried and sickened the local Italian and German occupation forces. (Serbia itself was ruled by an Axis-sponsored Quisling regime under

General Nedich.) Similarly, the Catholic, nationalist and increasingly fascist and antisemitic Slovak People's Party (metamorphosed into the Slovak Party of National Unity in late 1938) enjoyed a fairly free rein in the relatively insignificant Nazi-sponsored 'independent' state of Slovakia from March 1939 until the bloody suppression of the anti-fascist Slovak uprising of August 1944 by crack German army units and the SS. But the latter events confirmed that Slovakia and its ruling party had failed to attain real self-determination and sovereignty. In Slovakia, as elsewhere in Eastern Europe, fascism largely rested on nationalist self-delusions.

The fascist movements were relative 'latecomers' on the party political scene, preceded by the emergence of liberal, conservative, socialist, Christian, republican, agrarian and 'traditional' nationalist parties and the 'crystallization' of party systems and allegiances (Linz 1979: 13–14). Consequently, fascist movements were often unable to gain the support of the social groups at whom they initially targeted their appeals. Therefore they frequently found themselves obliged to champion the interests of sundry social groups who were (or felt) politically and socially neglected because they were not specifically targeted or served by the older and more established political parties. Thus in many countries the fascists remained 'minority movements with little or no electoral appeal'; and only the will to power of their core activists, the methods to which they were prepared to resort and the lengths to which they were prepared to go made them serious 'contenders for power' (p. 15). Even in Italy fascism did not gain prominence primarily through its electoral appeal (the Italian fascists remained very much a minority party on the eve of their 'seizure' of power), but rather through the lethal combination of violence, intimidation and terror with electoral participation (p. 25). Fascist parties and movements did not experience steady and continuous growth, but aimed at the acquisition of power by less orthodox means. They did not aspire to become just one party among many, each representing particular sections of the electorate, but *the* party of the whole nation (p. 14). Fascist movements tended to set themselves the 'goal of representing the whole national community, integrating all classes, overcoming class conflict and appealing to former supporters of old parties on account of common national interests in conflict with . . . groups defined as alien' (p. 19). Indeed, they did not enduringly capture distinctive class bases of support comparable to those of the socialist, communist, peasantist, liberal and conservative parties. In their doctrinal and programmatic eclecticism and their willingness to pick up potential support from almost any quarter, they were more like the 'catch-all' parties of today, with heavy dependence on support from volatile, 'footloose' floating voters (pp. 13, 16, 20). European fascism was to a considerable extent 'a conjunctural phenomenon', the product of the unique circumstances of the post-First World War crises and the 1930s Depression, 'attracting supporters from a heterogeneous social base largely on the basis of generational cleavages rather than class characteristics and allegiances' (p. 14).

This recognition that fascism was a relative latecomer on the party political scene also helps to explain why fascism was to such a large extent defined by the things it opposed: communism; the rhetoric of class struggle; materialism; (independent) organized labour; parliamentary democracy; political and economic liberalism; individualism; pacifism; cosmopolitanism; internationalism; international 'finance capital' and Jewry; 'Anglo-Saxon' imperialism; the 1919–20 peace settlements; *rentiers*, capitalist 'speculation' and 'unearned' income; and feminism, homosexuality and miscegenation (to name only the fascists' favourite bugbears!). On their own, however, these 'anti' positions were not enough, for they could alienate even more potential adherents than they attracted (pp. 29–30, 38).

Especially for veterans of the First World War and for males who entered adulthood during the turbulent 1920s, fascist movements also had a positive appeal based on their paramilitary organizations, strong-arm tactics, violent nationalist rhetoric, the promise of a 'comradely' and egalitarian yet disciplined and hierarchical 'new order', and their distinctive new styles, symbols, salutes, songs, chants, ceremonies, marches, mass rallies and eye-catching shirts. Thus the particular appeal of fascist movements to the ex-servicemen, students and young men who formed the initial nucleus of most fascist movements and the hard core of founder members who were most likely to rise to the top 'cannot be understood simply in terms of their ideology or their programmatic positions' (p. 54). For ex-servicemen who experienced acute difficulty in readjusting to civilian employment, society and attitudes after the First World War, fascist militias offered a continuation of wartime heroics, camaraderie, military values and the idealization of war and men of violence. In contrast to the more gradual and orderly demobilization of European armies after the Second World War, the demobilizations of 1918–19 were over-hasty and chaotic, contributing to the emergence of high unemployment, vigilant-ism, hooliganism and unruly paramilitary violence among ex-servicemen. Significantly, the attractions of fascist or proto-fascist militias were far greater for ex-servicemen than for serving military personnel, who normally preferred to advance their military careers through exaggerated displays of strictly 'professional' and 'apolitical' loyalty to the powers-that-be (pp. 56–61). For students and young men, on the other hand, fascism seemed to satisfy a desire for romantic gestures, heroic deeds, action rather than words, to be somebody, and involvement in daring collective exploits on behalf of 'the nation'. Fascist militias, paramilitary organizations and ceremonials substituted obedience and readiness to fight for reason and debate and offered opportunities for pseudo-military violence, excitement and camaraderie to males who had been influenced or even inspired by romanticized stories of the First World War but were too young to have served in it. For these deluded 'greenhorns', the fascists' bold coloured shirts expressed a modernist rejection of convention, individualism and humdrum, grey-suited 'bourgeois conformity' (pp. 53–60). In view of the particular appeal of fascism to young adult and adolescent males, it is significant that over half the population of Eastern Europe was under the age of thirty during the inter-war period and that in the countries with high birth rates, such as Poland and the Balkan States, that proportion was even larger (Longworth 1994: 78). In this respect the 'natural constituency' of fascism was larger in eastern than in central or north-western Europe.

The hierarchy proposed by fascism aimed to transcend class division and class conflict, to dissociate social status from accident of birth and social opportunity, to instil harmony and 'national' consensus, and slowly to redefine high social status on the basis of service to (and position in) the fascist movement. Although fascist movements invariably *failed* to carry out their promised social 'revolutions' against big landed property, big business and 'parasitic finance capitalism', active involvement in the fascist movements and in their affiliated mass organizations provided surrogate forms of social advancement for thousands of plebeian fascist officials. Most fascist movements did indeed recruit and create elites which were not limited to people of high educational, class or occupational status, but were 'open to all, irrespective of social origin, willing to devote their energies to the movement' (Linz 1979: 37).

It is sometimes argued that fascism was above all a form of nationalism. For example, Linz (1979) states that 'Nationalism was the central appeal of fascism movements' (p. 47). Thus it can be difficult to decide whether particular movements were 'fascist' or merely 'extreme nationalist' and in some instances, such as the Slovak People's Party, 'a movement that is not originally fascist becomes increasingly fascist' (p. 28). Our interpretation of East European nationalism fully concurs with his contention that 'in Eastern Europe integral nationalism would often be fascist or quasi-fascist' (p. 18). The basic reason for this was that nearly one-third of the inhabitants of the East European 'successor states' were members of so-called 'national minorities', not merely because the population was more 'mixed' than in other parts of Europe but more fundamentally because 'nations' had been defined in narrow, exclusive, 'ethnic' terms. This way of defining 'nations' fuelled nationalist preoccupations with 'ethnic purification' or 'ethnic cleansing' in order to rid 'national' territories and populations of supposedly 'alien' elements who had often been peacefully and productively living in their midst for many generations. However, we should also keep in mind the latent fascist potential within most forms of nationalism. 'Obviously, if the nation was the highest good, if it was the worldly incarnation of the divine spirit at work in history, if it was an absolute necessity for the well-being and the self-fulfilment of its citizens, then its interest must be supreme; no petty rights like property and individual liberty could be set up against it, because property, individual liberty and cultural self-expression existed only in and through the nation. The part . . . might quite properly be subordinated and sacrificed to the interests of the whole' (Weber 1964: 21). As the Jacobin leader Saint-Just observed at the height of the French Revolution, 'There is something terrible in the sacred love of the fatherland; it is so exclusive as to sacrifice everything to the public interest, without pity, without fear, without respect for humanity' (quoted by Kedourie 1960: 18).

According to Griffin (1993: xi), 'fascism is best defined as a revolutionary form of nationalism, one which sets out to be a political, social and ethical revolution, welding the "people" into a dynamic national community under new elites infused with heroic values'. He goes on to argue that the distinctiveness of fascist ideology primarily lies in 'its core *myth* of national rebirth' (p. xii). Griffin contends that it is 'the vision of a revolutionary new order which supplies the affective power of an ideology' (p. 35). In the case of fascism, the 'mobilizing vision is that of a national community rising phoenix-like after a period of encroaching decadence which all but destroyed it' (p. 38). Under certain conditions 'the fascist vision of a vigorous new nation growing out of the destruction of the old system can exert on receptive minds the almost alchemical power to transmute black despair into manic optimism'. This helps to explain the rapidity with which a fascist movement could transform the mood of a country and 'win a substantial mass following', by promising to substitute 'youth, heroism and national greatness' for 'gerontocracy, mediocrity and national weakness' and to usher in 'an exciting new world in place of the senescent, played-out one'. In Griffin's view, the critical factor was whether the fascists struck the right note and said what people wanted to hear at the time, not the feasibility or human implications of the fascists' declared goals (p. 39). Fascism reflected deep anxieties concerning 'the modern age', in particular 'fears that the nation or civilization as a whole was being undermined by the forces of decadence' (Griffin 1993: viii). That was why it promised to 'renovate', 'rejuvenate', 'remould', 'restore' or 'resurrect' the nation and to create a 'new man', a revolution of 'Youth' and a new and more fulfilling type of state and society; and it saw war as 'an intrinsically regenerating force in the life of the nation' (p. 74). Thus the Hungarian and Romanian leaderships did not need much persuading to participate in the Axis invasion of the Soviet Union in June 1941.

Indeed, it is also striking that fascism mainly developed in 'nations' which had attained 'national' unity and statehood relatively recently (to say 'late' is to imply the existence of a specious divinely ordained or natural 'timetable' against which the timing can be judged) and thus had not yet established such stable and securely anchored 'national' identities and political systems as the longer-established 'nation-states'. In 1932 Mussolini himself declared: 'Fascism is the doctrine most fitted to represent the aims, the states of mind, of a people, like the Italian people, rising again after many centuries of abandonment or slavery to foreigners' (Mussolini 1932: 178). This promise of a consummation of recently attained 'national' independence, statehood and unity was one of the fundamental features which Italian Fascism had in common with fascist and other extreme nationalist movements and regimes in Eastern Europe, the Baltic States, Finland, Greece and Germany and, in varying degrees, extreme nationalist movements and regimes in newly independent states outside Europe. But it was not a universal characteristic of fascist or quasi-fascist regimes, if Salazar's Portugal, Peronist Argentina or 1940s Spain are considered to be fascist or at least quasi-fascist. Moreover, it should be stressed that the 'decadence' against which German National Socialism and writers such as Moeller van den Bruck and Ernst Jünger were reacting in Weimar Germany was a much blacker, more profound and more desperate spiritual, philosophical and cultural crisis than the relatively superficial political and economic corruption, enervation, sterility and wheeler-dealing in relation to which fascism was partly a reaction and partly a consequence in Italy, Eastern Europe, the Baltic States, Greece and the Iberian Peninsula. This is one reason why the National Socialist reaction (including the notorious book burning and purges of 'cosmopolitan', materialist and 'degenerate' writers, artists, musicians and intellectuals) was so much more extreme or 'totalitarian'. The German national and racial rejuvenation and rebirth promised by the Nazis was supposed to be attained through racial and cultural 'purification' and a rediscovery of the 'folk community' and institutions 'which peculiarly German conditions had forged' (Weber 1964: 81).

Almost all forms of fascism relied heavily on concepts of 'rebirth', 'revival' and 'resurrection', but in Eastern Europe such concepts still had strongly religious as well as secular nationalist overtones. The Romanian, Croatian, Slovak, Polish and Hungarian manifestations of fascism had distinctly religious complexions, drew invaluable moral, personal, institutional and practical support from substantial sections of the 'national' clergy and relied heavily on religious imagery, concepts and rituals. Even where the dominant Churches did not publicly support the fascists, they seldom openly opposed them and were usually accommodating, partly because most of the East European fascist movements included the establishment of 'corporative Christian' states among their central declared objectives. Clergy were certainly far more conspicuously active participants in the Croatian, Romanian, Slovak, Hungarian and Polish fascist and ultra-nationalist movements than they were in anti-fascist movements.

The 'spiritual' core of the Romanian Iron Guard was the so-called Legion of the Archangel Michael, founded by Corneliu Codreanu in 1927. Its origins can be traced back to an Association of Christian Students (which Codreanu and his cronies had established at the University of Iasi in 1922) and to Codreanu's alleged 'visions' of the

Archangel Michael while he was in prison in 1923–24. The Legion was essentially a violently nationalistic and antisemitic Christian Brotherhood, dedicated to an ultra-nationalist form of religious revivalism. Indeed, it despatched so-called Brotherhoods of the Cross to propagate its gospel in Romanian villages, schools and universities. The Legionary elite was to be 'forged' and 'purified' through fire and struggle. Legionaries were to eschew all excess, luxury and sexual immorality, in order to lead relatively ascetic lives of practical service to others and thus win 'converts' by example. Rule No. 3 in the Legionaries' *Manual* (written by Codreanu) was the 'Rule of Silence: speak little. Say what has to be said. Speak when you need. Your oratory is the oratory of the deed. You act; let others talk' (quoted in Weber 1964: 100). But this life of asceticism and service to others was also intended to expiate sin, for Legionaries were even exhorted to kill. In the words of their *Manual*, 'When I have to choose between the death of my country and that of a thug, I prefer the thug to die; and I am a better Christian if I do not let him hurt my country and lead it to perdition' (p. 103). Moreover, every Legionary had to swear 'to work for the ever deeper popular penetration of the new spirit of Work, Honesty, Sacrifice and Justice' and to 'believe in a new Romania which we shall conquer through Jesus Christ and through integral nationalism, acting through the country's Legions' (p. 100). Codreanu also explained that Romania was 'dying for the lack of *men*, not for lack of programmes . . . It follows that the Legion of the Archangel Michael shall be more a school and an army than a political party . . . The finest souls that our minds can conceive, the proudest, tallest, straightest, strongest, cleverest, cleanest, bravest and most hardworking that our race can produce, this is what the Legionary schools must give us!' (pp. 167–8).

Consequently, the Legion has been described tentatively as 'a religiously founded movement or a rebirth or a reawakening of the Orthodox Church' (Turczynski 1971: 111) and as 'a "born again" Christian Orthodox movement' within which Codreanu's role was to be the earthly representative of the Archangel Michael' (Fischer-Galati 1984: 28). Legionary meetings were often accompanied by hymns, prayers or religious services and sometimes led to torchlit processions and 'calvary crusades' through villages. Legionary 'martyrs' were often venerated as Christian 'saints'. The Legion used the language of medieval religious chiliasm. According to Codreanu, 'The ultimate goal is not life. It is *resurrection*. The resurrection of nations in the name of Jesus Christ the Saviour . . . A time will come when all the world's nations will arise from the dead, with all their dead . . . That *final* moment, "resurrection from the dead", is the highest and most sublime goal for which a nation can strive' (quoted in Fischer-Galati 1970: 330). Utter drivel, but one can well imagine it being delivered and received with religious conviction and po-faced solemnity.

Similarly, the Croatian *Ustasa* were members of a form of militant, violent, crusading, Catholic order, a latter-day version of the Order of Teutonic Knights. Indeed, at least one organization affiliated to the *Ustasa* was called the Crusaders (*Krizari*) (Djordjevic 1971: 132). Moreover, many Croatian Catholic priests in Italy (including the Vatican) as well as in Croatia itself worked for the *Ustasa* in the belief that, if they did not do so, the Balkans would eventually fall under the thrall of atheist communism. Their ruthlessness reflected a belief that they were engaged in a fight to the death against the devil's agents, including Orthodox (i.e. pro-Russian) Serbs as well as overt communists.

Nationalist and anti-communist Catholic clergy also played a high-profile role in Slovak fascism and antisemitism, although this particular brand of antisemitism had the slight saving grace of being largely religious rather than racial (and genocidal), as was also the case in Hungary. That did not save the majority of Slovak and Hungarian Jews from the Nazi death camps. But, unlike their German counterparts, most Slovak and Hungarian fascists did not want the Jews to be exterminated, 'only' to be expelled to countries willing to receive them.

The religious fervour of East European fascism is partly to be explained by the fact that these were still mostly agrarian, provincial, Church-dominated societies with limited ideological horizons. Certainly they were much less urban, anonymous, sophisticated and secular than either Germany or north-western Europe. Inasmuch as East European fascists tailored their language and message to the audiences they addressed, they may have calculated that religious concepts and imagery would be most readily understood and absorbed by peasants, worker-peasants, rural labourers and first-generation industrial workers. What is more, East European fascists could easily exploit and draw upon living traditions of religious antisemitism. But the religious tone and 'infrastructure' of East European fascism must also be attributed to the fact that East European nationalism was already saturated with religious imagery, fervour, concepts, language and goals and was often strongly supported by 'national' Churches and nationalist clergy. West European nationalism is often described as a kind of secular religion, but most East European nationalisms were not yet secular. As in Northern Ireland, it was partly religion that gave East European nationalism its particularly sharp, bigoted, fervent, intolerant and doctrinaire edge. Orthodoxy was central to Romanian, Serb, Greek and Bulgarian nationalism and national identity, just as Roman Catholicism was central to Polish, Croatian, Slovene and Slovak national identity. (It was less so for the more secular and multi-denominational Czechs and Hungarians.) Moreover, Eastern Orthodox Christianity encouraged submergence of the individual into the collective, corporate body of the faithful and 'conciliarity', while Roman Catholicism emphasized 'corporative' social doctrines and obedience to authority and the state.

Peter Sugar has stressed that 'national' religions and the accommodating and sometimes supportive attitudes of the 'national' Churches, together with the open or tacit support given by schools, universities, state bureaucracies and the military, gave East European fascism major footholds within the main East European power structures. This helps to explain 'why the fascist movements of Eastern Europe – unlike those in the West – could operate within the existing system and could wait for their moment' (Sugar 1971a: 153). Sugar concludes that these footholds and the 'native' or homespun content of East European fascism were strong enough to have produced 'something that, without Mussolini's choice of labels for his party, we would possibly not have called fascist, but which, in their essence and numerous manifestations, would have amounted to nearly the same thing', even if Fascist Italy and Nazi Germany had never existed (p. 156).

However, precisely because of the close connections between East European fascisms and nationalisms, fascist movements never flourished among the Czechs or the Serbs during the inter-war period. There were small Czech and Serb fascist movements (Sugar 1971a: 49–51, 61–2, 129–31, 136–8). But most 'nationally minded' Czechs and Serbs had enough sense to see that fascism and their big fascist neighbours posed the greatest danger to their 'national' survival; for them fascism was simply a threat, not a salvation. Unfortunately, most East European fascists either failed to recognize or were undeterred by the fact that, by promoting fascism and collaboration with Nazi Germany and/or Fascist Italy, they were diminishing rather than strengthening their 'national' sovereignty, security and chances of survival.

One of the most useful and illuminating characterizations of fascism has been provided by O'Sullivan (1983). He presents fascism not as an aberration, but as the most extreme manifestation of one of the main currents in modern European civilization (pp. 63–4, 80). He defines fascism as 'an activist style of politics' which conceived 'the highest good for man' to be 'a life of endless self-sacrifice spent in total and highly militant devotion to the nation-state' and 'unconditional allegiance to a fascist "leader" whose arbitrary personal decree is the sole final determinant of right and wrong'. In practice this amounted to a demand for absolute obedience to the 'leader', regardless of how he had acquired or exercised his power, and a total absence of formal constitutional restraints (p. 33). It involved wholesale rejection of the 'traditional limited style of politics' and of a political order based upon states, within which political communities are governed and held together by common bodies of law and clear distinctions between the public and private domains, with strong constitutional restraints on the acquisition and use of power within specific historically determined territories and jurisdictions. An 'activist style of politics' substitutes an ideology and a sense of 'mission' (or 'shared purpose') as the basis of the new political community. It establishes an all-embracing and all-intrusive political order (abolishing the distinction between public and private domains). It dispenses with formal constitutional restraints on the acquisition and use of power. It refuses to regard existing frontiers and jurisdictions as inviolable and it endeavours to redefine frontiers in accordance with its own militant ideological mission and precepts (pp. 34–7). Fascism was 'the most extreme, ruthless and comprehensive expression of this new style of politics' (p. 41). It was revolutionary in the sense that it consciously 'set out to destroy the state concept upon which . . . limited politics had been based for the previous five centuries' and replaced it with 'a style of politics in which there was no intrinsic regard for legality; in which state and society were to be submerged into one all-pervasive movement; in which all constitutional constraints upon power were excluded, in principle at least; and in which the nation . . . was an essentially fluid entity whose territorial limits were to be determined solely by the ideological fanaticism of the fascist leaders' (p. 39). It glorified war, perpetual 'struggle', strength, youth, vigour, the heroic spirit and martial values (pp. 44, 70–4).

Fascism thus transformed politics into a millenarian crusade to build a new social and political order purged of all evil, corruption, decadence and alien elements. In the new order there were to be no laws, rules or morals other than those ordained by the leader, while 'freedom' was redefined as unconditional self-sacrifice, devotion and obedience to the 'leader', who alone embodied and expressed the 'will' of the nation (O'Sullivan 1983: 58–63). Fascism also involved the transformation of politics into spectacular public ceremonies, rituals, games, marches and singing festivals, orchestrated by the fascist regime, in order to engender more 'total' and 'active' identification with the national political community, a more complete sense of 'organic' political and social unity and more 'total' and 'active' devotion and obedience to the fascist movement and regime (pp. 94–9). Finally, O'Sullivan singles out five core ideas in the fascist *Weltanschauung*: (i) 'corporatism', in the sense of an 'all-embracing vision of an organic, spiritually unified and morally regenerated society' within which the divisions and conflicts will be defused and/or transcended in order to release citizens from petty, everyday, 'egotistical concerns' and facilitate more total devotion and service to the nation and its leaders (pp. 132–4); (ii) the need for unrelenting, perpetual 'struggle' (pp. 138–9); (iii) the 'leadership principle' (*Führerprinzip*), establishing the fascist 'Leader' as the sole, infallible embodiment and expression of the nation's destiny and will, the focus of all loyalty, self-sacrifice and solidarity and the source of all law and authority (pp. 149–53); (iv) a 'messianic mission' of conquest and domination (pp. 161, 166–7); (v) the pursuit of autarky, neo-mercantilism and etatism (pp. 170–1).

O'Sullivan concludes that 'the intellectual appeal of fascism derived principally from the skill with which it exploited the oldest and most potent of human dreams, the dream that is of creating spiritual unity and purity within societies whose institutions had come to appear divisive and corrupt' (p. 181). His stimulating essay sheds light not only on the fascist movements and regimes in Italy and Germany, but also on those that emerged in Eastern Europe. However, we consider his glib assertion that the latter were 'either copies of the two main ones or else stooge regimes created by them' (p. 34) to be a regrettable lapse, since every fascist movement and regime had its own national roots and distinctive features in addition to the common characteristics. Nevertheless, the main thrusts of his thesis are well borne out by Mussolini's pronouncements on Fascism in 1932: 'Fascism desires an active man, one engaged in activity with all his energies . . . It conceives of life as a struggle . . . Life, therefore, as conceived by the Fascist, is serious, austere . . . Fascism disdains the "comfortable" life . . . Fascism is a religious conception in which man is seen in immanent relationship with a superior law and an objective will that transcends the particular individual and raises him to conscious membership of a spiritual society . . . Above all, Fascism believes neither in the possibility nor in the utility of perpetual peace . . . War alone brings to their highest tension all human energies and puts the stamp of nobility on the peoples who have the courage to meet it . . . Thus the Fascist . . . looks upon life as duty, ascent, conquest' (Mussolini 1932: 165, 170–1).

The Fascist *Statuto* of December 1929 similarly emphasized the militant, crusading, ultra-nationalist, 'activist' character of Fascism: 'The National Fascist Party is a civil militia for all the service of the nation. Its objective: to realize the greatness of the Italian people. From its beginnings . . . the party has always thought of itself as in a state of war, at first in order to combat those who were stifling the will of the nation . . . and from henceforth to defend and increase the power of the Italian people. Fascism . . . is above all a faith . . . under the impulse of which the new Italians work as soldiers, pledged to achieve victory in the struggle between the nation and its enemies' (reprinted in Oakeshott 1940: 179).

The principal limitation of O'Sullivan's incisive characterization of fascism, as with many others which focus primarily on the distinctive methods, ideology and 'style' of fascist movements and regimes, is the relative neglect and near-dismissal of the much debated economic and class basis, dimensions and context of fascism. These other aspects are, as if by way of compensation, overemphasized by most Marxist and sociological conceptions of fascism. It is to these that we now turn our attention. We shall give special consideration to the official communist interpretations and explanations of fascism, particularly those published by the Communist International (Comintern). These not only shed important light on the pivotal relationship, competition and 'struggle' between communism and fascism in inter-war Europe, but also elucidate the basis on which Europe's communist parties aspired (and in Eastern Europe managed) to win power for themselves by (in their terms) 'leading the fight against fascism', with not a little help from their Soviet 'fatherland'.

18 Fascism and the communists' new road to power in Europe

Most of the well-known Marxist luminaries in inter-war Europe initially saw fascism as the 'death rattle' of senescent capitalism, as a 'pre-emptive strike' against the Marxist left and the proletariat, or as a drastic last-ditch response to the long-awaited (and supposedly 'terminal') crisis of 'decaying' or 'moribund' monopolistic 'finance capitalism'. This momentous crisis had begun with the First World War and its tempestuous aftermath, lifted slightly during the mid-1920s economic recovery and deepened dramatically with the onset of the 1930s Depression. The First World War had substantially expanded the size, reduced the deference and obedience, and raised the political and class conscious-ness of Europe's industrial proletariat, as the war industries drew in millions of new (usually unskilled) recruits. Millions of former soldiers and munition workers became unemployed in 1919–20. But in the turbulent wake of the First World War Europe's toiling masses were less docile and less tractable than they had been in the late nineteenth century (although the contrast with the very unsettled years between 1900 and 1914 was less marked). There was very widespread unrest in Europe's countryside as well as in urban areas, but it was more tightly orchestrated in the towns. In both town and country, none the less, there were frequent strikes, boycotts and 'sit-ins', and employers experi-enced great difficulty in restoring labour discipline, the profitability of their enterprises and 'management's right to manage' (i.e. high-handed autocratic styles of management, giving no 'say' to hired workers). Therefore employers widely resorted to lock-outs, harassment and aggressive strong-arm tactics against organized labour, often with the full backing of European governments, which since the 1890s had become increasingly vigorous and heavy-handed in the 'labour taming' methods they employed, even in the 'liberal' democracies. On the political front, old-fashioned governments and 'liberal' politicians had been accustomed to the very limited popular participation in political life before the 1914–18 war, even in the parliamentary states. They found it exceedingly difficult to cope with the recently enfranchised, increasingly educated, more and more unionized and politically 'mobilized' working class and peasant voters. Popular discontents and increasingly insistent demands accelerated the rise of the new mass parties of both the left and the illiberal-nationalist right, who in turn 'gatecrashed' many formerly sedate and patrician political institutions. Europe's 'oiks' and 'riff-raff' gained access to its gentlemen's clubs. In the face of this social upheaval, European governments all too readily resorted to repression, police harassment and other forms of aggressive suppression or dispersal of general strikes, 'sit-ins', marches and mass protests, whether in Britain, France, Sweden, Germany, Italy, Spain, Portugal, Austria or eastern Europe.

Acute labour unrest and the repressive responses it evoked from governments, industrialists and landowners were part of a Europe-wide confrontation between 'property' and 'labour', between the 'haves' and the 'have-nots'.

Despite heated and often acrimonious arguments over minor differences of interpretation, most Marxists were broadly in agreement that the frightened and crisis-stricken propertied classes were flailing out at the revolutionary left with the mad fury of a mortally wounded monster. Thus Italian Fascism was seen as merely the local Italian variant of European capitalism's desperate last counter-revolutionary offensive against organized labour and the Marxist left. Fascism was seen as a kind of protection racket in which fascist thugs interposed themselves between the propertied classes and the toiling classes and offered the former 'protection' against the latter. At first industrialists, landowners, state officials and traditional political bosses called the shots and the fascist thugs were the underlings, but the latter gradually gained the upper hand over their easily intimidated paymasters during the offensive against their proletarian and/or Marxist prey. In the words of an early 'Resolution on Fascism' passed by the Executive Committee of the Communist International (ECCI) on 23 June 1923: 'Fascism is a characteristic phenomenon of decay, a reflection of the progressive dissolution of capitalist economy . . . Its strongest root is the fact that the imperialist war and the disruption of the capitalist economy which the war intensified and accelerated meant for broad strata of the petty and middle bourgeoisie, small peasants and the "intelligentsia", instead of the hopes they cherished, the destruction of their former condition of life and especially their former security. The vague expectations which many in these social strata had of a radical social improvement have also been disappointed' (reprinted in Degras 1960: 41). This same Comintern Resolution on Fascism explicitly stated that such feelings of insecurity, disappointment, disillusionment and frustration, which often propelled dis-affected and alienated individuals towards fascism, were by no means confined to the petty and middle bourgeoisie: 'They have been joined by many proletarian elements who, looking for and demanding action, feel dissatisfied with the behaviour of all political parties. Fascism also attracts the disappointed and declassed, the rootless in every social stratum, particularly ex-officers who have lost their occupation since the end of the war' (p. 41).

The Resolution on Fascism passed by the Fifth Congress of the Comintern in July 1924 similarly affirmed that fascism 'has its roots in the middle class, doomed to decay as a result of the capitalist crisis, and in the elements (such as ex-officers) declassed as a result of the war, and partly also in the embittered proletarian elements whose revolutionary hopes were disappointed' (Degras 1960: 139).

COMINTERN-ANTICIPATED 'MASS SOCIETY' INTERPRETATIONS OF FASCISM

These Comintern resolutions strikingly foreshadowed the view, normally attributed to 'mass society' theorists such as Hannah Arendt (1966: 305–39) and William Kornhauser (1960: 14–15, 179–82 ff), that social support for fascism came not merely from one class but from disappointed, disillusioned, discontented or marginalized members of various social classes and from *déracinés*, *déclassés* or disoriented individuals who had been cut adrift from their class moorings and were thus quite likely to be seeking new affective attachments (or a new 'sense of belonging') of the sort that fascism could offer.

Since this is one of the most central and contentious themes in the whole literature on fascism, it calls for further elucidation.

The central contention of 'mass society' theorists is that modern 'totalitarian movements', i.e. movements which aspire to create 'totalitarian' regimes, 'are fundamentally mass movements rather than class movements'. That is to say, 'although fascism tends to recruit a disproportionate number of its adherents from the middle class and communism attracts more of its adherents from the working class, these movements cannot be understood merely as political expressions of the middle class and the working class respectively. For in both cases a large proportion of the movement is composed of people who possess the weakest rather than the strongest class ties. Furthermore, both movements tend to draw many adherents from all major social classes' (Kornhauser 1960: 14–15). It is partly a simple question of political arithmetic. 'Any political enterprise which aspires to power on the basis of popular support will have to command the allegiance of sizeable numbers of people from both the middle and working classes, because the size of these classes makes it a necessity. This is true even when a political group depends for primary support on only one class' (p. 194). But that is not all. The nub of the 'mass society' theory is 'the hypothesis that all social classes contributed to the social base of totalitarian movements, and that in particular it is the socially uprooted and unattached members of all classes who support these movements first and in the greatest numbers. This implies that unattached intellectuals, marginal members of the middle class, isolated industrial and farm workers have been among the major social types in totalitarian movements' (p. 182). Substitute the word 'fascist' for the word 'totalitarian' and this formulation could have been taken as one of the seminal Comintern pronouncements on fascism! These pronouncements clearly and unambiguously anticipate Kornhauser's contentions that 'fascist movements, then, are not adequately conceived as middle class phenomena' and that 'fascist movements rely on working class support for a significant portion of their following' (p. 196). Thus in 1933 42 per cent of Nazi party members were 'manual and service workers', not far below their 52 per cent share of the work force, while in 1922 43.5 per cent of Italian Fascist party members were workers (p. 219). In Hungary in 1940 workers similarly constituted 41 per cent of the membership of Ferenc Szalasi's fascist party, which by then had over 100,000 members (Barany 1971: 77). In Eastern Europe, moreover, the middle classes were far too small to constitute a mass base for fascism in the way that they did (along with many workers and peasants) in Germany, for example. In addition, most of the East European middle classes were to a considerable degree composed of Jews and other vulnerable ethnic minorities who were usually more alarmed than attracted by the rise of violent, ultra-nationalist, xenophobic, antisemitic and increasingly fascist movements and regimes (especially in Hungary, Romania and Poland). In the Czech Lands, moreover, Eastern Europe's largest and strongest 'national bourgeoisie' was similarly terrified and repulsed by the rise of fascism, which threatened both the existence and the cherished ideals of the multi-ethnic Czechoslovak state. Therefore, even if many writers have managed to get away with very misleading claims that fascism was a narrowly or specifically middle-class, 'bourgeois' phenomenon in Germany or France or Italy, such arguments are complete non-starters in the East European context, where the mass base for fascism had to come from other social classes besides the relatively small and/or predominantly anti-fascist bourgeoisies.

The 'mass society' social perspective on fascism is frequently counterposed to that of 'most' Marxists, in the mistaken belief that the latter saw fascism as simply a (middle) class phenomenon (see, for example, Kornhauser 1960: 198–207; Kolinsky 1974: 74–93, 116–20; Cohan 1975: 146–72). However, it is (and was) perfectly possible to see fascism as primarily a response to (and consequence of) a profound 'crisis of capitalism' without also seeing it as a narrowly or exclusively middle-class or 'bourgeois' phenomenon. After all, the inter-war 'crisis of capitalism' threatened the security and livelihood of workers and peasants as well as the middle classes. People of all classes lost out or felt extremely worried and insecure as a result of that crisis. It is not surprising that the Comintern identified the social basis and support for fascism in much the same way as the 'mass society' theorists did. The communist leaders had their intellectual limitations but they were not stupid, and quite a few were astute social observers and intellectuals. In this respect at least, the alleged crudity or rigidity lies less in the official Comintern view of the social basis of fascism than in the eyes of critics who either have not read and thought about the Comintern pronouncements with sufficient care or prefer to caricature the Comintern stance because it was in some other respects deeply objectionable and dangerous.

The June 1923 Comintern Resolution on Fascism also implicitly acknowledged the dangerous and disturbing political ambiguities which made fascism a direct rival as well as an opponent of communism. Communism and fascism were the two main competing forms of radical activism, purportedly dedicated to the total economic, social, political and spiritual reconstruction and cleansing (i.e. 'purging') of society in the twentieth century. Fascism was in a sense communism's *alter ego*: 'In the period of revolutionary ferment and proletarian risings, fascism to some extent flirted with proletarian revolutionary demands. The masses which followed fascism vacillated between the two camps . . . But with the consolidation of capitalist rule and the general bourgeois offensive they threw themselves definitely on to the side of the bourgeoisie . . . The bourgeoisie immediately took fascism into paid service in their fight to defeat and enslave the proletariat . . . Although fascism by its origin and its exponents also includes revolutionary tendencies, which might turn against capitalism and its state, it is nevertheless becoming a dangerous counter-revolutionary force . . . The triumph of fascism in Italy spurs the bourgeoisie of other countries to take the same course in defeating the proletariat . . . It is the task of the conscious revolutionary vanguard of the working class to take up the struggle against victorious fascism . . . The fascist forces are being organized on an international scale, and it is consequently necessary to organize the workers' struggle against fascism internationally' (reprinted in Degras 1960: 41–2).

THE HAZARDS OF INDISCRIMINATE LABELLING

The 1923 and 1924 Comintern Resolutions on Fascism saw the fascists as 'shock troops' who were not themselves exclusively bourgeois, but who were placing themselves at the service of the frightened, anti-communist bourgeoisies, even though it involved the betrayal or compromising of the more radical revolutionary elements in the fascist programme and camp following. Indeed, that was the easiest way for the fascists to win state power and gain the upper hand over their 'bourgeois' paymasters. Genuine Western liberals viewed the rise of fascism with varying degrees of horror and patrician distaste, seeing it as a negation of Western liberal norms of governance and law-abiding conduct, as indeed it was. As Mussolini himself proclaimed in 1932, 'In the face of Liberal doctrines, Fascism takes up an attitude of absolute opposition both in the field of politics and in that of economics' (Mussolini 1932: 173). Seen from a communist standpoint, however, the Fascist offensive against the Marxist parties and labour movements in 1920s Italy did not at first seem so very different from the counter-revolutionary offensive unleashed by 'capital' against 'labour' in the 'liberal' parliamentary democracies at about the same time. According to the Resolution on Fascism passed by the Fifth Congress of the Comintern in July 1924: 'Fascism is one of the classic forms of counter-revolution in the epoch when capitalist society is decaying, the epoch of proletarian revolution . . . Fascism is the bourgeoisie's instrument for fighting the proletariat, for whose defeat the legal means at the disposal of the state no longer suffice . . . As bourgeois society continues to decay, all bourgeois parties, particularly social democracy, take on a more or less fascist character . . . Fascism and social democracy are two sides of the same instrument of capitalist dictatorship. In the fight against fascism, therefore, social democracy can never be a reliable ally of the fighting proletariat' (reprinted in Degras 1960: 138–9).

It should be remembered that to the predominantly communist targets of Europe's counter-revolutionary offensives it did not initially seem to make a huge difference whether these assaults were the work of fascists, conservatives, nationalists, 'liberals', socialists or social democrats. Indeed, Europe's communist parties condemned as 'social fascists' the German, Polish and other social democratic parties that initiated or acquiesced in offensives against labour militancy and the far left in the hope of promoting the stabilization and recovery of capitalism and 'bourgeois' parliamentary rule in Western and East Central Europe. They denounced these so-called 'social fascists' as 'traitors' to the class they claimed to represent and as *de facto* allies of the overt fascists who were blatantly out to annihilate the revolutionary left and all radical proletarian and peasant movements. However, this was a fatal misrepresentation and misunderstanding of the position of social democracy *vis-à-vis* fascism (as the Comintern and its affiliated communist parties were implicitly to recognize in 1935, by performing a *volte-face* and belatedly urging co-operation with social democrats in the creation of broad 'popular fronts' against fascism).

Admittedly, Europe's socialist and social democratic parties were in full retreat from Marxism and openly proclaimed that a strong recovery of Europe's market economies and parliamentary democracies was in the best interests of their still predominantly working-class constituencies. This meant having to come to terms with the necessity and virtues of the capitalist system, which in turn involved sometimes painful acceptance of the need for relatively strict fiscal, monetary and labour discipline and for curbing the disruptive and often violent or intimidating activities of the revolutionary and anti-democratic left, to allow both capitalism and democracy to function. Therefore there were genuine disagreements and partings of minds between Europe's increasingly 'gradualist' or 'reformist' social democratic and socialist parties, on the one hand, and the revolutionary, anti-capitalist and anti-democratic left, especially the communist parties, on the other. The socialists and social democrats were inherently more committed to the defence of democracy than were the communists, who merely wanted to take advantage of democratic liberties in order to expand their own anti-democratic movements and activities in preparation for the projected establishment of communist 'dictatorships of the proletariat'. Thus the *Programme of the Communist International* (1928), which was binding on all the affiliated communist parties in Eastern and Western Europe, reaffirmed the 'historic mission of achieving the dictatorship of the proletariat' (p. 58) through 'a combination of strikes and armed demonstrations and, finally, the general strike against the state power of the bourgeoisie' (p. 61). It openly and unashamedly advocated violence and rejected peaceful constitutional methods: 'The conquest of power by the proletariat does not mean peacefully "capturing" the ready-made bourgeois state machinery by means of a parliamentary majority . . . The conquest of power by the proletariat is the violent overthrow of bourgeois power, the destruction of the capitalist state apparatus (bourgeois armies, police, bureaucratic hierarchy, the judiciary, parliaments, etc.) and the substitution in its place of new organs of proletarian power, to serve primarily as instruments for the suppression of the exploiters' (p. 23).

Europe's increasingly 'Bolshevized' communist parties began to apply the label 'fascist' to virtually all the repressive, authoritarian, anti-Marxist governments and movements that willingly promoted or participated in the propertied classes' offensives against militant labour and the revolutionary left. Thus not only Mussolini's avowedly Fascist regime, but also the authoritarian regimes established in Hungary in 1920, in Bulgaria and Spain in 1923, in Albania in 1925, in Poland and Lithuania in 1926, in Yugoslavia in 1929, in Portugal, Austria and Germany in 1933, in Latvia and Estonia in 1934, in Romania in 1938 and in Spain (for a second time) and Slovakia in 1939, came to be described as 'fascist' in many Marxist writings. Indeed, as pointed out by the Hungarian Marxist historian Gyorgy Ranki (1971: 65), in the late 1930s 'leading Hungarian politicians frequently boasted that Hungary was the first country in Europe to introduce fascism, and they even insisted that Horthy's "white terror" and the subsequent system manifested the features of the ideology and practical system that conquered Germany and Italy'. While conceding that the word 'fascism' was 'not part of the vocabulary of the Hungarian counter-revolutionaries', Ranki nevertheless affirmed that the 'white terror' of 1919–20 (and the regime it established) comprised 'several features that were also characteristic of the rising fascism in Germany and Italy', including 'a political system that mercilessly persecuted both the labour movement and, in general, democratic ideas and their proponents' while stressing 'the importance of the Hungarian "race" and the idea of a strong national state. It became the first official ideology of this sort in Europe' (p. 65). However, Ranki also recognized that Hungary's international isolation and 'total economic bankruptcy' in the early 1920s and the consequent need for Western recognition and economic assistance obliged Horthy and his new Premier, Count Bethlen, to muzzle the more wayward fascist elements headed by Gyula Gömbös and to promote a more liberal facade for the time being (p. 68), just as Mussolini did during his first two years in power.

STALIN ON THE DEEPENING 'CRISIS OF CAPITALISM'

The awesome deepening of the 'crisis of capitalism' after 1929 seemed to account for the further proliferation and hardening of fascist regimes during the 1930s. The official Soviet view was presented by Stalin in his 'political report' to the June 1930 congress of the Communist Party of the Soviet Union (CPSU). He began by emphasizing the universality of the crisis. 'The illusions about the omnipotence of capitalism are collapsing.' The crisis was 'not a mere recurrence' of previous capitalist crises. This one had 'most severely affected the principal country of capitalism, its citadel, the United States'. In addition, the 'industrial crisis in the chief capitalist countries' had become 'interwoven with the agricultural crisis in the agrarian countries', the one exacerbating and prolonging the other. Moreover, the monopolistic structure of twentieth-century capitalism encouraged 'the capitalist combines' to endeavour to maintain the 'high monopolistic prices' of their products 'in spite of over-production'. This rendered the crisis 'particularly painful and ruinous for the masses . . . who constitute the main consumers' and could only impede its resolution. 'The present crisis is developing on the basis of the *general crisis* of capitalism, which came into being already in the period of the imperialist war, and is sapping the foundations of capitalism.' The crisis 'is laying bare and intensifying the contradictions between the major imperialist countries . . . between the victor countries and the vanquished . . . between the imperialist states and the colonial and dependent countries'. Hence 'the bourgeoisie will seek a way out of the situation through further fascistization in the sphere of domestic policy', while 'in the sphere of foreign policy the bourgeoisie will seek a way out through a new imperialist war' (Stalin 1955a: 243–61).

In his report to the January 1934 congress of the CPSU, Stalin gloated that the 'continuing crisis of capitalism' was 'now in its fifth year, devastating the economy of the capitalist countries year after year and draining it of the fat accumulated in previous years'. He attributed the unprecedented duration and magnitude of the crisis to the following factors. First, 'the industrial crisis has affected every capitalist country without exception, which has made it difficult for some countries to manoeuvre at the expense of others'. Second, 'the industrial crisis has become interwoven with the agrarian crisis which has affected all the agrarian and semi-agrarian countries'. Third, 'the agrarian crisis has grown more acute' causing a technical 'retrogression of agriculture'. Fourth, 'the monopolist cartels which dominate industry strive to maintain high commodity prices, a circumstance which . . . hinders the absorption of commodity stocks'. Fifth, and most important, 'the industrial crisis broke out in the conditions of the *general* crisis of capitalism, when capitalism no longer has . . . the strength and stability it had before the war and . . . when industry has acquired, as a heritage from the war, chronic under-capacity operation of plants and . . . millions of unemployed'. Moreover, despite the resistance of 'the monopolist cartels', most commodity prices nevertheless fell, further undermining the position of debtors and 'unorganized' commodity producers ('peasants, artisans and small capitalists') *vis-à-vis* creditors and 'capitalists united in cartels'. Thus capitalism had 'succeeded in somewhat alleviating the position of industry', but mainly 'at the expense of farmers . . . and at the expense of peasants in the colonies and economically weaker countries, by further forcing down prices for the products of their labour'. In addition, the 'intensified struggle' for markets had given rise to increased dumping, protectionism and 'extreme *nationalism* in economic policy', straining international relations and sowing the seeds of 'military conflict' conducive to 'a new redivision of the world . . . in favour of the stronger states'. That was why the ruling classes of the capitalist countries were 'so zealously destroying . . . the last vestiges of parliamentarianism' and 'fascism has now become . . . fashionable . . . among war-mongering bourgeois politicians'. Hence the triumph of fascism in Germany in 1933 was to be seen 'not only as a symptom of the weakness of the working class and a result of the betrayals of the working class by social democracy' but also as further evidence that the bourgeoisie was 'no longer able to rule by the old methods of parliamentarianism and bourgeois democracy' and could 'no longer . . . find a way out of the present situation on the basis of a peaceful foreign policy'. It was 'compelled . . . to resort to terrorist methods of rule . . . and . . . a policy of war' (Stalin 1955b: 288–92, 297–300).

Few liberals, let alone Marxists, were able to foresee that within two decades capitalism and 'bourgeois democracy' would be enjoying a new lease of life in an era of unprecedented economic buoyancy, technological dynamism, welfare provision and popular participation in plural parliamentary regimes. The belief that capitalism was in 'terminal' crisis was by no means confined to the Marxist left. There were deep-seated fears for the future even among 'liberal' economists. The so-called 'under-consumptionist' school (which provided many of the theoretical underpinnings, personnel and policy prescriptions of the American 'New Deal' in the mid-1930s) feared that the increasingly monopolistic structure of American and European industry and finance was causing profits and the growth of investment and productive capacity to outstrip the growth of wages, purchasing power and hence consumption, leading to chronic problems of over-capacity or 'under-consumption'. Moreover, the so-called 'stagnationist' school headed by Alvin Hansen (and strongly influencing John Maynard Keynes) argued that European and American capitalism had lost for ever the vigour, dynamism, trade expansion, mass migration, high profits, buoyant demand and seemingly limitless opportunities generated by the European population explosion, the Industrial Revolution and the colonizing 'expansion of Europe' into the New World between the late eighteenth and early twentieth centuries. This was now perceived as a 'one-off', unrepeatable experience. Moreover, with the exhaustion of fortuitous external stimuli, the secular decline in European birth rates, the cessation of mass migration, the increasing closure of markets and the apparent saturation of demand, there seemed to be no guarantee that the American and European economies would ever again expand fast enough either to generate full employment or to avert a disastrous decline in rates of profit, with the result that investment would eventually dry up and *laissez-faire* capitalism and the profit motive would cease to be viable (let alone dynamic). Consequently, many European and American economists, politicians and intellectuals were slowly coming to the conclusion that *laissez-faire* capitalism was not only incapable of providing full employment (with all the social and political dangers that this would involve) but was almost literally 'running out of steam' and might even be 'doomed'. For many the only means of escape seemed to lie in some form of socialism or etatism or fascism.

COMINTERN'S RESPONSE TO THE RISE OF NAZI GERMANY

In December 1933, in response to Hitler's rapid and brutal consolidation of Nazi rule and his government's swift moves to reactivate the mighty German economy and rearm the German Reich, the Comintern Executive Committee promulgated new *Theses on Fascism, the War Danger and the Tasks of Communist Parties*: 'The fascist government of Germany, which is the chief instigator of war in Europe, is provoking trouble in Danzig, in Austria, in the Saar, in the Baltic countries and in Scandinavia and, on the pretext of fighting against Versailles, is trying to form a bloc for the purpose of bringing about a new bloody carving up of Europe for the benefit of German imperialism . . . Europe has become a powder-magazine which may explode at any moment' (reprinted in Degras 1965: 300). These same Comintern pronouncements anticipated that the coming conflict would culminate in an assault on the USSR. 'The bourgeoisie want to postpone the doom of capitalism by a criminal imperialist war and a counter-revolutionary campaign against the land of victorious socialism' (p. 301). The deepening world crisis and the approaching war(s) were seen as posing a mortal threat to the very survival of the Soviet Union and of Europe's communist parties, while also strengthening their chances of finally overthrowing European capitalism. Matters would soon be forced to a head. Intensified fascist repression of revolutionary forces 'cannot, in conditions when capitalism is shaken, for long frighten the advanced strata of the toilers'. Indeed, 'the indignation which this terror has aroused even among the majority of workers who followed the social democrats makes them more susceptible to communist agitation and propaganda' (p. 299). The economic crisis had sharpened all the contradictions of capitalism: 'The great task of the international proletariat is to turn this crisis of the capitalist world into the victory of the proletarian revolution . . . The great historical task of international communism is to mobilize the broad masses against war even before war has begun, and thereby hasten the doom of capitalism . . . In fighting against war, the communists must prepare even now for the transformation of the imperialist war into civil war' (reprinted in Degras 1965: 299–303).

The primacy of the contest between communism and fascism

The communists' contempt for liberalism and social democracy sprang partly from a belief that the only two forces which really counted in inter-war Europe were communism and fascism, now pitted against one another in readiness for the final showdown. There was an implicit mutual respect and understanding between communists and fascists which was largely absent from their attitudes to other political movements and ideologies. Like the fascists, most communists then believed that the liberal democracies were a spent force and that twentieth-century European liberalism and social democracy were a mere mask for the monopolistic and imperialistic 'finance capital' which had superseded nineteenth-century liberal capitalism. Thus inter-war Europe's liberals and social democrats were inherently 'soft' on fascism, which they would rather 'appease' than resist. This view was greatly reinforced when the Prime Ministers of Britain and France, Chamberlain and Daladier, virtually handed Czechoslovakia to Hitler on a plate in September 1938. In his report to the March 1939 congress Stalin wryly remarked that 'one might think that the districts of Czechoslovakia were yielded to Germany as the price of an undertaking to launch a war on the Soviet Union' (Stalin 1955c: 368). Both Hitler and the communists believed that in the approaching 'battle of the Titans' (Greater Germany and its minions versus the Soviet Union), the defeated side would probably lose everything. The stakes could not have been higher. A fascist victory would lead to the extinction of communism (not to mention European humanist civilization). On the other hand, a communist victory would hasten the downfall of European capitalism and permit a massive extension of communist rule into Central, Eastern and perhaps even Western Europe, in a different version of 'the end of history'. Therefore, whatever the cost, it came to be seen as the sacred duty of all communists to do whatever was necessary to ensure the survival of 'the socialist fatherland', without which all would be lost. Thus the Nazi–Soviet Pact of August 1939, which allowed Hitler to invade western Poland, was partly 'justified' in communist eyes as buying time for the further industrialization, rearmament and military reorganization of the Soviet Union, while keeping its powder dry for the eventual showdown.

The December 1933 Comintern *Theses* also promulgated an influential but much criticized communist definition of fascism: 'Fascism is the open, terrorist dictatorship of the most reactionary, most chauvinist and most imperialist elements of finance capital. Fascism tries to secure a mass basis for monopolist capital among the petty bourgeoisie, appealing to the peasantry, artisans, office employees and civil servants who have been thrown out of their normal course of life, and particularly to the declassed elements in the big cities, also trying to penetrate into the working class . . . Having come to power, fascism pushes aside, splits and disintegrates the other bourgeois parties (for instance Poland) or dissolves them (Germany and Italy). This striving of fascism for political monopoly intensifies the discord and conflicts in the ranks of the ruling class which follow from the internal contradictions in the position of the bourgeoisie who are becoming fascistized' (reprinted in Degras 1965: 296–7).

Guard against caricatures of the Comintern *Theses*

It should be emphasized that the Comintern *Theses* embodied a broad and far from monolithic conception of fascism (hence the references to the 'internal contradictions' of fascism, to the conflicts within the capitalist ruling classes and to Pilsudski's Poland as a form of fascist state). Moreover, the same *Theses* insisted that 'fascist dictatorship is not an inevitable stage of the dictatorship of the bourgeoisie in all countries' (p. 297) and that 'the communist parties must first of all brush aside the fatalistic, defeatist line of the inevitability of a fascist dictatorship' (p. 302). Hostile caricatures of the official communist view of fascism often overlook or wilfully ignore these important points. The communist parties saw fascism *not* as a new 'highest stage of capitalism', towards which all 'advanced' capitalist states must inevitably evolve, but rather as the most extreme ('most reactionary' and 'most chauvinistic') forms of capitalist regime, examples of which were also (not surprisingly) to be found among the fiercely nationalistic and less developed capitalist states of eastern, central and southern Europe, but not in north-western Europe (at least not before the German occupation of the Low Countries, France, Denmark and Norway in 1940). This was most clearly spelled out by the Italian communist leader Palmiro Togliatti's lectures in Moscow in 1935. He insisted that 'transition from bourgeois democracy to fascism' was not 'inevitable', since 'imperialism' (alias monopoly capitalism or finance capitalism) 'does not necessarily give birth to the fascist dictatorship . . . England, for example, is a great imperialist state in which there is a democratic parliamentary regime . . . Take France, the United States, etc. In these countries you will find tendencies toward the fascist form of society, but the parliamentary forms still exist' (Togliatti 1976: 4–5). The December 1933 Comintern *Theses* reaffirmed that 'fascist dictatorship is not an inevitable stage of the dictatorship of the bourgeoisie in all countries' (Degras 1965: 297).

This somewhat belies Kitchen's claims that the 1930s Comintern view of fascism was 'a strikingly crude example of vulgar-Marxist determinist economism', i.e. economic determinism (Kitchen 1976: 10, 29, 47, 65, 81) and O'Sullivan's similarly disparaging references to 'this crude doctrine' (O'Sullivan 1993: 17–19). Criticisms of this sort fail to understand that the communist parties were founded (even premised) upon a Leninist *rejection* of strict economic determinism in favour of an almost reckless/adventurist voluntarism. The Comintern and its affiliated communist parties quite plausibly contended that the turn to fascism was a widespread 'bourgeois' response to the profound 'crisis of capitalism' in inter-war Europe. But they did not claim that there was anything automatic, inevitable or rigidly economically determined about the passage from 'bourgeois parliamentarianism' to fascism, even though there obviously were strong economic and political forces pushing states in that direction.

Towards a 'Popular Front' against fascism, 1935–39

The Comintern saw increased support for communism as the *natural* popular reaction to the proliferation and 'hardening' of fascist regimes amid the profound (possibly terminal) 'crisis of capitalism' during the 1930s. If the communist parties played their cards right, it was believed, they could turn the situation to their own advantage. But the communist leaders did not expect Europe simply to fall into their lap. They expected to have to fight for it. As Stalin lucidly explained in an interview with H.G. Wells in July 1934: 'Capitalism is decaying, but it must not be compared with a tree which has decayed to such an extent that it must fall to the ground of its own accord. No, revolution, the substitution of one social system by another, has always been a struggle, a painful and cruel struggle, a life and death struggle. And every time the people of the new world came into power they had to defend themselves against the attempts of the old world to restore the old power by force' (Stalin 1955c: 35).

Accordingly, resolutions passed by the August 1935 Comintern congress warned 'against dangerous illusions about an automatic collapse of the fascist dictatorship', emphasized that 'only the united revolutionary struggle of the working class at the head of all toilers will bring about the overthrow of the fascist dictatorship' and reaffirmed that the transformation of the deepening crisis of capitalism into a 'victorious proletarian revolution' depended 'solely on the strength and influence of the communist parties among the broad masses of the proletariat, on the energy and self-sacrificing devotion of the communists' (reprinted in Degras 1965: 360, 355). This was extreme voluntarism, the very opposite of the economic determinism of which the communist parties have frequently been accused.

The August 1935 Comintern congress also approved a significant change of attitude towards Europe's social democratic parties, which even the March 1934 'theses' of the Comintern's Agitprop department had blamed for the latest triumphs of fascism: 'In the conditions when the last and "decisive battle" is approaching, a cleavage in the working class is the main source of its weakness . . . This cleavage is the result of the treachery of social democracy, a result of its policy of saving bourgeois rule from the proletarian revolution' (Degras 1965: 324).

In reality the communists' refusal to co-operate with so-called 'social fascists' had fatally divided the German left, scuppering all attempts to reconstruct moderate centre-left alternatives to the ultra-nationalist right, reinforcing 'bourgeois' and 'petty bourgeois' fear of 'the communist threat' and helping the Nazis to gain power in January 1933, despite having won only 33 per cent of the vote (less than the 37 per cent combined share of the communists and the socialists) in the November 1932 *Reichstag* elections (Kolinsky 1974: 77–8). Belatedly learning from their momentous mistake, the communist parties decided to foster and support broader anti-fascist coalitions known as 'Popular Fronts', although by then the Nazis were firmly entrenched in power and the German left had been crushed. Now social democrats were no longer to be denounced as 'social fascists' and cold-shouldered, but to be treated as comrades-in-arms in the struggle against fascism. However, it should be stressed that the adoption of the 'Popular Front' policy did not involve any fundamental change in the official communist conception of fascism. Georgi Dimitrov, the Bulgarian communist president of the Comintern (and future dictator of Bulgaria) simply reaffirmed the December 1933 Comintern definition of fascism (Degras 1965: 359). What is more, only the communist parties' tactics began to change, not their goals. The 1935 Comintern congress offered 'unity' between communist and social democratic parties, but only on condition that 'the necessity of the revolutionary overthrow of the bourgeoisie and the establishment of the dictatorship of the proletariat in the form of Soviets be recognized' (pp. 368–9).

The August 1935 Comintern congress passed a Resolution on the Danger of a New World War, warning that the 'frantic arming of fascist Germany' had given rise to 'a new intensified race for armaments throughout the capitalist world . . . The countries which have gone farthest in preparing for war (Germany, Japan, Italy, Poland) have already placed their national economy on a war footing.' The fear was expressed that these warmongering 'fascist governments' would endeavour to reconcile their rivalries 'at the expense of the Soviet Union. The danger of the outbreak of a new imperialist war daily threatens humanity' (reprinted in Degras 1965: 373–4). The same resolution affirmed that if such a war were to start 'the communists will strive to lead the opponents of war . . . to struggle for the transformation of the imperialist war into a civil war against the fascist instigators of war . . . for the overthrow of capitalism' (pp. 377–8). This partly contradicts claims that, as a result of the Popular Front policy, the Comintern (and the USSR) renounced its former goal of fomenting international revolution. The disavowals of revolution would no longer hold if the Popular Fronts failed to hold fascism in check. Indeed, the communist parties' undying commitment to the overthrow of capitalism was reaffirmed in an article by Georgi Dimitrov (as leader of the Comintern) in November 1939, after the outbreak of war in Europe: 'As the war goes on, the indignation of the masses will grow and the anti-war movement will become more extensive. The most furious persecution by the bourgeoisie will not hold up and stifle the struggle of the working people against the imperialist war. The historic role of the communist vanguard of the working class is at the present moment to organize and take the lead of this struggle . . . The working class is called upon to put an end to the war after its own fashion, in its own interests, in the interest of the whole of labouring mankind and thereby to destroy once and for all the fundamental causes giving rise to imperialist wars' (reprinted in Degras 1965: 458–9).

This prognosis proved to be wildly overoptimistic, from a communist standpoint. As in the First World War, most of Europe's workers loyally supported the war effort of the state they lived in. Only the substantial communist-led wartime resistance movements that developed in the Balkans and East Asia directly led to the establishment of some new communist regimes. However, the May Day manifesto issued by the Comintern Executive on 30 April 1938 demonstrated a clearer grasp of the threats hanging over both eastern and western Europe. Already German fascism, having swallowed Austria, was 'preparing an attack on Czechoslovakia. Together with Polish fascism, it strives for the occupation and partition of Lithuania.' Germany was 'crouching for a spring upon the Balkans . . . It threatens Belgium, Holland, Switzerland, and the Scandinavian countries. It surrounds France with a fascist ring and reckons to take it unawares with a sudden blow. Like a beast of prey, it scours far and wide to procure raw materials . . . and human reserves for a large-scale war against the land of socialism' (reprinted in Degras 1965: 420). This was a reasonably accurate prediction except that, instead of acting in concert with 'Polish fascism' (as suggested by the German–Polish Pact of 1934), 'German fascism' decided to devour Poland as well.

MUNICH AND THE GENESIS OF 'NATIONAL COMMUNISM'

The Anglo-French 'betrayal' of Czechoslovakia to the 'fascist camp' in September 1938 marked a major turning point in the history of communism. Indeed, it precipitated a fundamental repositioning of the Comintern and European and Asian communist parties *vis-à-vis* nationalism. There had already been some 'softening' of communist attitudes towards nationalism since 1935, under the impetus of the Popular Front policy approved in that year (and a desire to win over 'centrist' parties and opinion to more resolute resistance of the fascist powers). Until September 1938, however, communist parties continued to be seen as inherently 'internationalist' and 'anti-national'. After all, communist doctrine had repeatedly disavowed nationalism and patriotism in favour of 'proletarian internationalism', proclaiming the 'solidarity of working peoples of all nations' against 'bourgeois nationalist' trickery, duplicity and oppression of working people. Moreover, it was widely known that the world's communist parties took their 'orders' from the Comintern headquarters in Moscow. Hence there was widespread nationalist and public suspicion of communists, who were routinely regarded as 'traitors' who would readily 'betray' their countries. 'Being a communist implied being an agent of a foreign power, which to most people seemed abhorrent.' Indeed, 'the greatest deterrent to people becoming communists' was 'the feeling that communism implied disloyalty to one's country' (Hammond 1958: 282). This, along with their 'godlessness' or atheism, was certainly the communist parties' biggest electoral liability and a favourite taunt of their rivals. Public hostility to communist parties was particularly strong in countries such as Poland and Romania which not only nursed long-standing grievances against Russia but also felt that their 'territorial integrity' and 'national' security were threatened by the Soviet Union's apparent designs on their eastern marchlands and by Polish and Romanian communist parties which (in the name of 'proletarian internationalism') really were prepared to countenance (and even participate in) the imminent dismemberment of Poland and Romania by the Soviet Union. In actual fact the eastern half of Poland was inhabited mainly by Ukrainians, Belorussians and Lithuanians. Thus, by the principle of national self-determination, they did not properly 'belong' to Poland. But this highly inconvenient fact did not cut much ice with Polish nationalists, most of whom were grimly determined to hang on to the Ukrainian, Belorussian and Lithuanian territories and populations that they had conquered in 1919–20. They deeply resented all Soviet and communist intimations of the need to 'liberate' these territories from (genuine) Polish 'oppression' and implicitly to 'reunite' them with their co-nationals in the Ukrainian and Belorussian Soviet Republics and in Lithuania. Soviet designs on the Bukovina and Bessarabia (now Moldova) were not similarly underpinned by Wilsonian 'ethnic' justifications, however, since 'ethnic' Romanians were clearly in the majority and the Slavs formed minorities. Soviet 'claims' to their territories were purely 'historical' in the case of Bessarabia (which had been annexed to the Russian Empire from 1812 to 1918) and 'strategic' in the case of northern Bukovina, which had never previously tasted the blessings of Russian rule before it was annexed by the Soviet Union in June 1940. In making these annexations Stalin was to act more as a 'big power' imperialist than as a revolutionary Marxist championing world revolution.

However, the September 1938 Munich agreement between Chamberlain, Daladier, Hitler and Mussolini (to dismember Czechoslovakia) handed Europe's communist parties a golden opportunity to put themselves forward as the only 'reliable' champions of 'collective security' and as the 'true defenders' of European nations against the fascist menace and 'bourgeois liberal' trickery. After Munich, indeed, the Czechoslovak centrist parties which had misguidedly put so much faith in the Western powers suffered a severe crisis of confidence and loss of support, whereas the Czechoslovak Communist Party experienced such a strong upsurge of popularity that it took its members quite a while to get used to it! (But this was the fundamental reason why the Communist Party became Czechoslovakia's most popular party during the 1940s, winning 38 per cent of the vote in the 1946 elections.)

The Comintern was quick to capitalize on this unexpected 'gift horse' and turn of events. In a 'Manifesto' issued in November 1938 it claimed that, by reaffirming its readiness to defend Czechoslovakia against Germany (if France would do likewise), 'the Soviet government, during the Czechoslovak crisis, showed how agreements should be kept and collective security defended . . . The Munich agreement was not only a blow at Czechoslovakia. It is a conspiracy against the small nations which Britain and France are betraying to the fascist plunderers.' It was asserted that Czechoslovakia could have been saved, as Germany was not yet fully prepared for war: 'Ranged against Germany were forces on whose side was the overwhelming preponderance. Czechoslovakia possessed an excellent army and was protected by a first class system of fortresses. The British and French fleets were in a position to blockade Germany. Action by the Soviet Union would have given rise to a powerful wave of the anti-fascist movement in defence of the just cause of the peoples. Faced by such forces, German fascism would have had no alternative but to retreat. But the British bourgeoisie who dragged France in the wake of their policy did not want to permit this political defeat of the fascist gendarme of Europe. Britain and France did everything possible to compel Czechoslovakia to capitulate' (reprinted in Degras 1965: 430).

THE ESPOUSAL OF 'PROLETARIAN PATRIOTISM'

The Comintern decided to cast the communist parties and the working classes in the roles of true patriots and *bona fide* custodians of national liberty and independence in the struggle against Europe's fascists and 'false' patriots. 'The condition for a successful struggle to strengthen the cause of peace is to replace the governments of national treachery and shame in the countries menaced by fascist blows . . . A government of real national salvation cannot pursue the ruinous path of capitulation. It will conduct a ruthless struggle against capitulators and agents of foreign fascism . . . It will disarm the fascist leagues and make the working class organizations the mainstay of the country's defence. It will conduct a consistent policy of collective security and will not shrink from employing sanctions against the aggressor' (p. 432). Most tellingly of all, it declared that 'the task of the working class now is to head the liberation struggle of the enslaved nations and the defence of the peoples threatened by foreign domination. The nation is not the gang of fascists, reactionary financiers and industrial magnates who rob and betray the people. The nation is the many millions of workers, peasants and working people generally – the people that is devoted to its country, cherishes its liberty, and defends its independence . . . The working class is the backbone of the nation, the bulwark of its liberty, dignity and independence' (p. 432).

In performing this *volte-face* and embracing the nationalist and patriotic sentiments which they had eschewed for so long, the communist parties imparted a whole new significance to the Popular Front policy which they had launched in 1935. Identification with 'the people' suddenly translated into neo-populist and/or nationalist identification with the *narod*, the nation, *la patrie*, the fatherland, paving the way for the anti-fascist centre-left Patriotic or Fatherland Fronts which became the Trojan horses through which East European communist parties went on to establish so-called 'People's Democracies' in the aftermath of the Second World War. 'The workers', whom communists had hitherto held up as the historic bearers of 'proletarian internationalism' *in opposition* to reactionary 'bourgeois nationalism', were suddenly hailed as the supreme and unsullied embodiment of 'the nation' and national virtue, using much the same kind of language as fascist and extreme nationalist propagandists. With brazen inconsistency, however, communist parties continued to use the language and imagery of 'proletarian inter-nationalism' whenever it suited them, *alongside* that of the new 'patriotic' working class. Europe's more principled (internationalist) Marxists were disgusted by this unprincipled ideological 'sell-out', pandering to primitive national and patriotic pride and prejudice. Nevertheless, shedding the stigma of 'treason' and 'disloyalty' opened the way for a number of communist parties to win unprecedented 'national' followings in 1940s Czechoslovakia, Yugoslavia, Albania, Greece, Italy, France, China and Vietnam. Communists were able to turn the tables on the right by stealing their thunder (i.e. by appropriating the emotive language and imagery of patriotism for their own use) and many new or young voters unsuspectingly 'fell' for this communist stratagem. Moreover, in the course of their often bitter and heroic struggles against European and East Asian fascism and/or imperialism during the 1940s, the Yugoslav, Albanian, Italian, Chinese and Vietnamese communist parties were successfully metamorphosed into patriotic 'freedom fighters' and 'national liberation movements', vindicating and validating their new patriotic credentials by the extraordinary courage, tenacity, endurance and ferocity of their fighting.

Chalmers Johnson has argued that the major communist successes in the Balkans and East Asia during the 1940s would not have occurred if the parties in question had not abandoned their former anti-national positions and rhetoric and transformed themselves into anti-fascist and anti-imperialist 'national liberation movements', whose rapidly growing popular support and political appeal owed more to patriotism than to communism. In his view, the scale, scope and savagery of the Axis occupation of Yugoslavia and the Japanese invasion of China left the inhabitants 'little or no room for accommodation to the new order' (Johnson 1962: 157–8, 164). The persistent brutality of the subsequent 'mopping up', counter-insurgency and 'bandit extermination' operations and the reprisals against villages and towns that tried to resist raised the level of popular political and national consciousness 'in countries . . . where previous "national movements" had appealed only to educated elites' (pp. 23, 30, 172–4). The invaders unwittingly curtailed the former 'parochialism and political indifference among the peasants' and, 'mobilized by an unavoidable military challenge' yet 'bereft of their traditional foci of loyalty, the peasantry stood ready to resist the invaders but lacked effective leadership. The communist party filled the need. Possessing a valuable cadre of battle-tested and militarily competent veterans, as well as a commitment to war as a mode of social change, the communist party was not only willing but eager to lead' (pp. 156–8, 166). In the case of Yugoslavia, membership of the outlawed Communist Party had dwindled from 80,000 in 1920 to just 3,000 in 1929 and 1939 (p. 165). But about 1,200 Yugoslav communists gained combat training and experience in 'the fight against fascism' during the Spanish Civil War (1936–39) and contributed a nucleus of military commanders to the Yugoslav Partisan forces, which numbered some 800,000 members by 1945 (pp. 166, 173). Johnson concluded that 'the demands of national crisis rather than the logic of communism brought the Chinese and Yugoslav communist parties to power' (p. 180) and that 'popular communism without a basis of nationalism does not exist' (p. 179).

Johnson's thesis is very suggestive, but he was mistaken in treating 'national communism' as something that was peculiar to Yugoslavia and China during the 1940s (p. 7). By the late 1930s the Comintern was eagerly extolling patriotism (as distinct from more predatory forms of nationalism), not least because Stalin had decided to rehabilitate and make use of Great Russia nationalism within the Soviet Union in anticipation of the long-awaited fascist invasion of his own domains (the 'Great Patriotic War'). The new 'patriotic appeal' of communism was also exploited to considerable effect in 1940s Czechoslovakia, Albania, Greece, Vietnam, Bulgaria, France and Italy (despite the temporary embarrassments and confusion caused by the Nazi–Soviet Pact from August 1939 to June 1941). Moreover, Johnson's insistence that the successes of the Yugoslav Communist Party during the 1940s were based on an identification with nationalism (pp. 175, 178, 184) is misleading and problematic, as in Yugoslavia nationalism chiefly took the form of crude, fratricidal, almost racist, Croat and Serb 'ethnic' nationalism. The Partisans and the Yugoslav Communist Party did sometimes exploit or pander to these crude forms of nationalism at the local/tactical level. But the communists triumphed partly because they were the only major political force in Yugoslavia that managed (for the most part) to rise above 'ethnic' nationalism by credibly championing a supranational Yugoslavism. This was 'nationalist' only in the laudable sense of trying to persuade the various Yugoslav ethnic groups or 'nations' to stop killing each other and to unite against the external predators who had ravaged and dismembered their country. Likewise, the Czechoslovak Communist Party mainly upheld the civic Czechoslovak ideals of Masaryk and Benes, rather than the tetchy and introverted Czech and Slovak 'ethnic' nationalisms.

WHY COMMUNIST THESES ON FASCISM MERIT CONSIDERATION

Some of the mainstream Western literature on fascism seems to discount the official communist interpretations of this excrescence of European civilization simply on the basis that communist pronouncements represent the official 'party line' and must therefore be crude, simplistic, reductionist or suspect, almost by definition (see, for example, the dismissiveness of O'Sullivan 1983: 17–19; Griffin 1993: 3–4). However, while we deplore the hideous excesses perpetrated by most communist parties and regimes, we do not believe that the official communist interpretations of fascism can or should be lightly dismissed. They are no more suspect, deficient or partisan than some of the other partial or onesided conceptions or interpretations which have strongly illuminated particular facets of fascism without offering a comprehensive or rounded explanation, especially those that analyse or conceptualize fascism virtually in the abstract or with insufficient regard to its specific social and economic context and sources of social and political support, for example Nolte (1969) and O'Sullivan (1983). On the contrary, just as Nolte and O'Sullivan furnish fresh insights into the ideology, discourse, style and antecedents of fascism, so the official communist interpretations shed important and interesting light on the socio-economic dimensions of fascism, which many other approaches have tended to neglect or deliberately ignore. The communist interpretations also usefully emphasize the centrality of the titanic struggles between fascism and communism (in contrast to the weak-kneed 'appeasement' of fascism by the Western democracies) and the critical role that these played in the subsequent expansion of communist power and popular support in Eastern Europe and, for a time, in Greece, Italy and France. Indeed, until the commencement of the Nazi-sponsored genocide of the Jews in the later 1930s, the first and foremost target of fascist thuggery and persecution was 'the Bolshevik menace'. Many of Europe's leading communist analysts of fascism felt or witnessed its verbal and physical assaults at first hand and as part of a more widespread offensive by Europe's increasingly crisis-stricken, frightened and aggressive propertied classes against the Marxist left, independently organized labour and a putative 'Soviet threat', all in the wake of the Bolshevik Revolution and the massive economic disruption and social unrest bequeathed by the First World War. If only for these reasons, the communist interpretations of fascism merit serious consideration, just as one cannot and should not lightly dismiss Jewish accounts of the Holocaust. From our standpoint, the chief virtues of the official communist interpretations of fascism are that they aptly portray it as: (i) widespread, multifaceted phenomenon which was inextricably linked to the general inter-war 'crisis of capitalism' and of 'liberal'/'bourgeois' parliamentary democracy; (ii) a phenomenon which developed not only in the mind and in the realms of ideology but also in specific social and economic contexts and with specific sources of social and political support; (iii) part of a wider drift towards economic nationalism, etatism and authoritarianism; (iv) part of a 'crusade' against 'Bolshevism' and independently organized labour in most of the capitalist world, including the increasingly repressive, anti-Bolshevik, ultra-nationalist regimes of Eastern Europe.

At least in their initial stages, fascist movements usually managed to combine two potentially contradictory thrusts or manifestations of class antagonism: a 'prole-bashing' hostility to militant labour and the Marxist left; and seemingly radical hostility to 'finance capitalism', *rentiers*, 'parasites' and economic intermediaries ('middlemen'). Yet Marxists are often criticized for emphasizing the role of the former to the relative neglect of the latter. 'By assuming fascism to be an essentially anti-proletarian force, they play down its antagonism to the ethos of *laissez-faire* economics, consumerist materialism and the bourgeoisie, and are unable to take seriously its claim to be the negation of nineteenth-century liberalism rather than its perpetuation in a different guise', according to Griffin (1993: 4). However, these criticisms are hopelessly misplaced and misinformed. Marxists, including the Comintern and most communist party leaders, were among the first to recognize the important role played by the anti-capitalist rhetoric in mobilizing mass support for fascist movements, as noted above. Furthermore, Marxism not merely recognized the huge significance of the metamorphosis of nineteenth-century 'liberal capitalism' into twentieth-century 'monopoly capitalism', but also produced some of the most influential analysts of that transformation (including Hilferding, Bukharin, Lenin, Bauer, Gramsci, Togliatti and Vargas). Most Marxists directly related the emergence and historic significance of fascism to the replacement of liberal capitalism by monopolistic 'finance capitalism'. It is therefore preposterous to accuse Marxists of being 'unable to take seriously' fascism's claim that it was 'the negation of nineteenth-century liberalism rather than its perpetuation in a different guise'.

Nevertheless, Marxists were quite correct to emphasize that 'prole-bashing' anti-Bolshevism was a much more pronounced, pervasive and persistent feature of fascist ideology than its superficial and ephemeral anti-capitalism. Indeed, all successful fascist leaders (including Mussolini and Hitler) sought an accommodation with the powers that be and the propertied classes in the course of their ascent to power and depended on the active co-operation of the military, the state bureaucracy and the propertied classes once they were installed in office, even if it involved the betrayal and frequent suppression of the radical anti-capitalist elements in their own movements. 'Fascism was not the creation of capitalism since the sources of support for the former were quite varied', yet fascism could not have operated 'against the fundamental interests of big business if it wanted to achieve its aim of military conquest' (Kolinsky 1974: 84). Moreover, most industrialists in Europe's later industrializing countries not only accepted fascist economic nationalism and etatism but were 'accustomed to regarding state activity as an essential framework for economic development' (p. 85). In a well received speech to the Industrie-Klub in Düsseldorf in January 1932, Hitler declared: 'In my view it is to put the cart before the horse when today people believe that by business methods they can . . . recover Germany's power position, instead of realizing that the power position is also the condition for the improvement of the economic situation . . . There can be no flourishing economic life which has not before it and behind it the flourishing powerful state as its protection . . . There can be no economic life unless behind this . . . there stands the determined political will of the nation absolutely ready to strike – and to strike hard' (quoted by Kolinsky 1974: 84). Fascism was neither the creature nor the servant of big business, but in order to enhance its military potential it needed to protect industrial interests. It also 'deepened the interpenetration of organized business and the state' by bringing big business 'into a more bureaucratized relationship with the state' (p. 121). Fascism attracted the propertied classes into a Faustian pact by offering 'a spectacular solution to the problem of stability' (p. 119) as well as an expeditious resolution of the crisis of capitalism (p. 83).

RIVAL SOCIO-ECONOMIC EXPLANATIONS OF FASCISM

Socio-economic interpretations of fascism are by no means restricted to Marxists. For example, an influential book by James Barrington Moore Jnr has postulated the existence of 'three main historical routes from the preindustrial to the modern world', via bourgeois democratic revolution, by communist revolution and by fascism (Barrington Moore Jnr 1969: xii). He sees the fascist route as a limited 'revolution from above', occurring in industrializing societies in which the old landed ruling classes managed to avoid either losing power to or being overthrown by the bourgeoisie and/or the lower classes. In such societies the 'bourgeois impulse' was much weaker than in those that experienced bourgeois democratic revolutions. 'If it took a revolutionary form at all, the revolution was defeated. Afterwards sections of a relatively weak commercial and industrial class relied on dissident elements in the older and still dominant ruling classes, mainly recruited from the land, to put through the political and economic changes required for a modern industrial society . . . Industrial development may proceed rapidly under such auspices. But the outcome . . . has been fascism' (p. xii–xiii).

This interpretation implicitly depends upon an exceptionally broad conception of fascism. But, whatever one's reservations about that aspect of his thesis, Barrington

Moore is surely correct in his assumption that the old landed ruling classes tried to use fascism for their own purposes (pp. 450–1), not only in Italy, Germany, Japan and the Iberian Peninsula but also in parts of Eastern Europe (especially Hungary and Poland). Nevertheless, fascism was not created by the scions of the old landed ruling classes. They merely sought to manipulate and hide behind their plebeian fascist politicians, towards whom they maintained considerable aristocratic *hauteur*. Indeed, it was mostly the landed lesser nobility (rather than the magnates) who got actively involved in fascist or quasi-fascist organizations and activities and tried to infiltrate and gradually take over the conservative authoritarian-nationalist regimes that ruled these countries. Moreover, defence of the power and privileges of the old ruling class was not integral to fascist programmes and ideologies. The frequent collaboration between fascist dictatorships and the old landed classes was 'a contingent historic circumstance rather than an essential feature of the regime' (Gregor 1979: 312). Indeed, fascist regimes often found themselves irksomely constrained or even impaired by their dependence upon the collaboration of the old ruling classes, who for their part later made some attempts to throw off or escape from the fascist embrace. In any case, the collaboration of the old ruling classes was just one of several important strands in fascism. Therefore, while Barrington Moore has thrown some new light on this, he has provided a rather incomplete and one-dimensional explanation of fascism as a phenomenon.

A.J. Gregor has more provocatively portrayed Mussolini's Fascist dictatorship as a prototype of the 'mobilizing, developmental regimes that have become so prominent in the twentieth century', especially in countries experiencing 'delayed industrialization' (Gregor 1979: ix, xii, 171, 327). In contrast to the many writers who have maintained that Mussolini and his Fascist movement never developed a substantial and definitive political and economic philosophy and programme, Gregor is second to none in arguing that 'Fascism, prior to its advent to power, advertised a specific programme addressed to immediate problems that afflicted the national economy' (p. 127). 'Long before Fascism became a successful mass-mobilizing movement, it entertained ideological, doctrinal and programmatic commitments which it acted out once in power.' These were the work of 'the most aggressive and youthful revolutionary syndicalists', including Angelo Olivetti, Sergio Panunzio, Roberto Michels, Edmondo Rossoni and Massimo Rocca (p. 117). 'Fascism was the direct and documented heir of revolutionary syndicalism' (p. 97). Even though their programme was not implemented in earnest until the 1930s, 'Fascists early anticipated a corporative and revolutionary state that would displace the ineffectual parliamentary regime. That new state would undertake extensive intervention in labour relations; it would institute tariff protection (and, by implication, subventions) for selected industries . . . Fascists expected that their strong state would provide the impetus for the expansion and modernization of the entire economic infrastructure of the nation' (p. 131). Thus the Fascists fashioned 'an ideology of rapid modernization and industrialization', fostered an ethos of work, sacrifice and 'class collaboration', and promoted 'the expansion of a dynamic, interventionist and hegemonic state' under 'a charismatic and heroic leader who would incarnate the process' (p. 314). According to Gregor, 'what is essential for all mass-mobilizing, developmental regimes is not their respective class bases, but their developmental programme . . . These regimes must domesticate labour to an economy of high productivity but minimal consumption. To that end, they will try to orchestrate consensus . . . through the invocation of national myths and appeals to the providential leader' (pp. 312–13).

Gregor's critics have argued that he has underplayed the specificity and exaggerated the coherence and consistency of the Fascist ideology and economic programme. Indeed, the 'modernizing' and 'developmental' tendencies and accomplishments of the Fascist regime were not as strong as he suggests, and most authoritarian nationalist regimes have neither had such a strongly developed party base nor rested upon such charismatic leadership as that developed by Mussolini (O'Sullivan 1983: 22–3, 187–9). However, while accepting that the differences can be as important as the similarities, it seems to us that Gregor has highlighted a significant facet of the fascist and quasi-fascist regimes. Indeed, his approach yields useful insights that are even more readily transferable to the fascist and quasi-fascist regimes of inter-war Eastern Europe than they are to Nazi Germany. But they by no means exhaust the socio-economic roles and significance of such regimes. As ever, each approach and interpretation offers only an incomplete and partial explanation of fascism. This is also as true of the 'mass society' interpretations of fascism (e.g. Kornhauser 1960; Arendt 1966) as it is of the communist ones.

TOWARDS A MULTI-FACETED INTERPRETATION OF FASCISM

In his 1935 lectures on fascism Togliatti prudently warned that 'fascism must not be viewed as something which is definitively characterized; that it must be seen in its development, never as something set, never as a scheme or a model, but as the consequence of a series of real economic and political relations resulting from real factors – from the economic situation, from the struggle of the masses' (Togliatti 1976: 26). He also emphasized that fascism 'is an eclectic ideology ... Fascist ideology contains a series of heterogeneous ingredients ... It serves to solder together various factions in the struggle for dictatorship over the working masses and to create a vast movement for this scope. Fascist ideology is an instrument created to bind these elements together' (p. 9). Fascist rule had become increasingly 'totalitarian' in the course of vain attempts to cope with the heterogeneity and the inherent instability and 'contradictions' of its social support (pp. 22–3, 25–6). 'Fascism was not born totalitarian; it became so' (p. 24). However, as he pointed out in an article published in 1934, it would be a 'grave theoretical and political error to think that the setting up of the fascist dictatorship suppresses the contradictions among the various groups of the bourgeoisie' and an even graver mistake to imagine that 'by creating a fascist organization that embraces the majority of the population and all the forms of its life, fascism can ultimately suppress the fundamental antagonism that exists between the class content of the fascist dictatorship and the interests and aspirations of the working classes'. Quite the reverse: 'sheltered by this would-be "totalitarianism" and monolithic system, capitalist exploitation is increasing considerably, creating the objective conditions for an extreme sharpening of the class struggle that can be contained only for a certain period of time, exploding in the end with all the more force and impetus' (p. 140), as indeed it did in Italy, France, Greece and Eastern Europe in 1945–46. In conjunction with the (not unrelated) expansion of Soviet power, this 'action recoil' played a crucial role in the communist seizures of power in Eastern Europe at that time.

Part V

In the shadow of Yalta

Eastern Europe since the Second
World War

Introduction: the East–West partition of Europe

The victories of the Soviet Union and certain communist-led resistance movements over 'fascism' towards the end of the Second World War reduced the isolationism implicit in Soviet 'socialism in one country' by extending Soviet tutelage and communist ascendancy into Eastern Europe. By early 1945 the region had been recognized by both Britain and the United States as a legitimate Soviet 'sphere of influence', in return for Soviet acquiescence in a preponderance of British or American influence in areas such as Greece, Japan and the Arab world. Winston Churchill's war memoirs describe how, during bilateral discussions between himself and Stalin in Moscow on 9 October 1944, the British war leader had scribbled some percentages on a sheet of paper:

Romania	Russia 90 per cent
	The others 10 per cent
Greece	Great Britain 90 per cent (in accord with the USA)
	Russia 10 per cent
Yugoslavia	50–50
Hungary	50–50
Bulgaria	Russia 75 per cent
	The others 25 per cent

Churchill pushed the paper over to Stalin. 'There was a slight pause. Then he took his blue pencil and made a large tick upon it, and passed it back to us. It was all settled.' There ensued a long silence. Finally, Churchill asked, 'Might it not be thought rather cynical if it seemed we had disposed of these issues, so fateful to millions of people, in such an offhand manner? Let us burn the paper.' 'No, you keep it,' Stalin replied (Churchill 1989: 852–3). Perhaps in an attempt to allay his own sense of unease, Churchill tried to justify this extraordinary deal in a letter circulated to his 'colleagues at home'. He explained that the percentages were 'not intended to prescribe the numbers sitting on commissions for the different Balkan countries, but rather to express the interest and sentiment with which the British and Soviet governments approach the problems of these countries'. He even added that they could 'in no way' tie the hands of the United States, which had not been a party to the deal (although it seems not to have occurred to him that other *European* governments might be entitled to a say in the matter). Nevertheless, he acknowledged that 'Soviet Russia has vital interests in the countries bordering the Black Sea, by one of whom, Romania, she has been most wantonly attacked . . . and with the other of whom, Bulgaria, she has ancient ties'. In the case of Yugoslavia, 'the numerical symbol 50–50 is intended to be the foundation of joint action . . . to favour the creation of a united Yugoslavia . . . and also to produce a joint and friendly policy towards Marshal Tito'. In the case of Hungary: 'As it is the Soviet armies which are obtaining control . . . it would be natural that a major share of influence should rest with them' (pp. 855–6). Hungary and most of the Balkans were thus consigned to the communist 'sphere of influence' in late 1944. Moreover, Stalin even refrained from assisting the Greek communists in the subsequent Greek civil war; in return he expected Britain to keep its side of the bargain by allowing Tito a free hand in Yugoslavia and leaving the Russians a free hand in Bulgaria, Romania and Hungary.

Churchill later claimed that the 'informal and temporary arrangement which I had made with Stalin during my October visit to Moscow could not, and so far as I was concerned was never intended to, govern or affect the future of these wide regions once Germany was defeated' (p. 876). Nevertheless, the 'percentages agreement' proved remarkably durable, reflecting as it did the real distribution of power and influence in the region. But there is no denying that the deal was possible partly because Churchill and Stalin had similarly imperialist mindsets. At the Yalta meeting between Churchill, Stalin and Roosevelt in February 1945, moreover, it was agreed that 'Russia should advance her western frontier line into Poland as far as the Curzon Line' and that, by way of compensation, Poland 'should receive substantial accessions of German territory' (p. 943). Poland would therefore become dependent on future Soviet support against potential German revanchism and was thus very effectively caught in the Soviet net. As President of a country that still thought of itself as a former colony and as an anti-imperialist power (despite its own imperialism in Latin America and the Philippines and its commanding 'hegemonic' position in the Western world), Roosevelt may have found the old-fashioned European imperialism of his British and Soviet counterparts somewhat distasteful, but he was prepared to play along with it in order to bring the warfare against Germany and Japan to a speedier conclusion. The price would be paid by the East Europeans, who were to be left to the tender mercies of a triumphal but battle-scarred, impoverished and vindictive Soviet Union. In 1986 the Hungarian philosopher Mihaly Vajda lamented that 'Western Europe is convinced that the main condition of its freedoms is the subjection of East Central Europe. After all, if the *status quo* worked out at the end of the Second World War was once upset, anything might happen' (Vajda 1988: 336). That is one reason why the European Union has been in no hurry to agree on a firm timetable for the admission of any of Europe's post-communist states to full membership. Communist rule has collapsed and the Cold War has ended, but the institutionalized East–West partition of Europe remains largely intact. It is in this sense that East Central and South-east Europe still live in the shadow of Yalta. Many East Europeans believe that the old 'political Yalta' has merely given way to a more enduring 'economic Yalta'.

To millions of Soviet citizens who did not give a damn about communism as such, control of Eastern Europe was the *reward* for a momentous and hard-won victory over 'fascism'. There were also some who saw it as an opportunity for vengeful rape and pillage. (Thousands of East European women were sexually assaulted by their Red Army 'liberators'.) For several years Hungary, Romania, Bulgaria, Austria and Germany had been in Soviet eyes 'fascist' enemy states. Millions of East Europeans had indeed fought alongside or collaborated with Nazi Germany against the Soviet Union during the Second World War, and many had done so quite willingly or even enthusiastically. Thus the political and economic arrangements imposed on Eastern Europe after the war were in some respects quite unashamedly vengeful or punitive, as was the Soviet suppression of the Hungarian Revolution of October 1956. East European states were required to provide some of the coal, oil, industrial equipment, technology, rolling stock and other resources used in the reconstruction of the Soviet Union, which as a result of the Second World War had suffered terrible privation, devastation and the loss of 25 million to 27 million lives (estimates vary). Yet the Soviet Union levied such economic 'tribute' not only from the defeated Axis states but also from its supposed wartime allies, the Poles and the Czechs. It has been estimated that, between 1945 and Stalin's death in 1953, the Soviet Union received an unrequited transfer of resources from Eastern Europe on a scale comparable to the net transfer of resources from the United States to Western Europe under the Marshall Plan (Marrese 1986: 293). Thus former Axis states were in effect forced to pay substantial reparations to the Soviet Union, while others were similarly forced to pay a heavy price for the 'liberation' of Eastern Europe by the Red Army. Such payments were not totally unwarranted, in view of what the Soviet population had been forced to endure. But they fell exceedingly hard on the Poles, who had suffered even more than the Russians, Belorussians and Ukrainians during the war, not least through the cruel defeat of the Warsaw Rising of August 1944. However, this levying of economic 'tribute' more or less ceased after the widespread social and political unrest in East Central Europe from 1953 to 1956, and the Soviet Union later became a large-scale supplier of heavily subsidized energy and raw materials to Eastern Europe.

Historical memories tend to be long and bitter in Eastern Europe, and the West still hears a great deal about Russia's past misdeeds in the region. However, when Eastern Europe 'slipped the leash' in 1989, many Russians who had endured or fought in the Great Patriotic War against fascism felt that their country had been unjustly deprived of its legitimate and hard-won fruits of victory. Later, when Soviet forces were withdrawn from Germany and Eastern Europe, there was further resentment that there were so few reciprocal gains for Russia. To many Russians it appeared that the former fascist states had emerged as the real victors after all. This was a major reason why some ultra-nationalists and embittered 'old stagers' continued to dream of the eventual reimposition of Russian control over certain parts of Eastern Europe. Even more resentment was aroused by the 'humiliating' break-up of the Soviet Union in 1991 and the resultant loss of 'superpower' status. The rantings and ravings of the Zhirinovskys of this world have played upon feelings and beliefs that run far deeper than mere imperialism. In narrowly economic terms, control of Eastern Europe may have been more of a liability than an asset, yet it turned the Soviet Union into an imperial 'superpower'. Conversely, the Revolutions of 1989 soon 'robbed' it of that status. But Soviet domination of Eastern Europe had also satisfied a more primitive or atavistic desire for power, control and revenge. The region became, in several senses, Russia's Ireland.

The precise consequences of the recognition of a post-war Soviet 'sphere of influence' in Eastern Europe were not immediately obvious or clear-cut in 1945, however. British and American strategists mainly understood 'spheres of influence' to mean informal hegemony, in the manner of British and US capitalist imperialism in Latin America, the Arab world and Greece, whereas Stalin was prepared for something rather more far-reaching. It was relatively easy and straightforward for powerful capitalist states to achieve economic dominance over their 'dependencies' by indirect ('informal') means, conveniently avoiding most of the risks and potential drawbacks of more direct political forms of control. By contrast the innate characteristics and the war-ravaged condition of the Soviet economy after the Second World War made it much harder for Stalin to dominate his newly gained 'sphere of influence' primarily by informal economic means. In any case, the prevalence of state ownership and central planning in the Soviet Union was bound to politicize its relations with its new 'allies' and 'dependencies'. Since the 1930s, moreover, Stalin had been grooming various (often little known) communist activists to take power in sundry European states in the wake of the eventual overthrow of fascism. In Soviet eyes the liberal capitalist states of the West were inherently 'soft' on fascism, which they had often 'appeased' and always regarded as a potential ally or weapon in the 'containment' of communism. Therefore, notwithstanding the various temporary 'tactical' deals that he struck with Europe's fascist powers during the 1930s, Stalin saw the Second World War as essentially a struggle between communism and fascism, not between fascism and the supposedly effete Western democracies. Hence the comprehensive defeat of fascism in 1944–45, to a large extent at the hands of the Soviet Union and a number of communist-led resistance movements, was expected ipso facto to 'bequeath' or 'deliver' most of Europe to the victorious forces of communism. In the apt words of the celebrated Polish writer Czeslaw Milosz (1953: 221), 'The philosophy of History emanating from Moscow is not just an abstract theory. It is a material force that uses guns, tanks, planes and all the machines of war and oppression. All the crushing might of an armed state is thrown against any man who refuses to accept the new Faith.'

Nevertheless, it was possible for this extension of communist power and Soviet 'influence' to take several different forms: (i) direct incorporation of additional 'nations' into an expanded USSR as new or expanded Soviet republics, as befell the Baltic States, Bessarabia (Moldavia), western Ukraine and western Belorussia; (ii) the establishment of communist-controlled Popular Front coalition governments in formally independent People's Democracies, constitutionally responsible for managing their own economic, social and political affairs in 'indissoluble alliance' with the Soviet Union, as occurred over most of Eastern Europe; (iii) Soviet acceptance of genuinely independent communist-ruled states, as eventually transpired in relation to the Yugoslav Federation and Albania; (iv) Soviet tolerance and recognition of 'friendly' neutral states which were not permitted to join any actually or potentially anti-Soviet Western organizations but were otherwise free to determine their own destiny, as was to be the fate of post-1955 Austria and Finland.

In the long run the fourth variant proved to be the least problematic. Indeed, Finland eventually profited from its 'special relationship' with the Soviet Union, as did Austria from its 'special relation' with Eastern Europe. But hopes that so-called 'Finlandization' might also become the norm for East Europe's People's Democracies were to be thwarted by the persistence of the Cold War and by the simple calculation that, the larger the number of 'Finlandized' states, the greater the probability that they would eventually escape from the Soviet 'sphere of influence' as they became richer, stronger and more Westernized.

The third variant, autonomous revolution, was feasible only in countries where communist parties could win and retain power without direct Soviet intervention and support, namely in Yugoslavia, Albania and Czechoslovakia. That would also have been the outcome in Greece but for British and American intervention in the civil war of 1946–49. The fact that the Soviet Union exerted strong pressure on the Czechoslovak Communist Party to act in accordance with Soviet wishes should not be allowed to obscure the fact that, if Stalin had been willing to leave well alone there, the large, popular and widely respected Czechoslovak Communist Party could have led its country down a so-called 'third way' or a 'democratic road to socialism' in the late 1940s. Indeed, Czechoslovakia was one of the 'great white hopes' of democratic socialism until the Communists subverted Czechoslovak democracy in 1947–48. To the great misfortune of the Czechs and the Slovaks, democratic socialism proved as unacceptable to Moscow in 1948 as it would be in 1968.

The first variant, direct incorporation into the Soviet Union, was the tidiest and also the one most in keeping with Marxist–Leninist and Luxemburgist precepts on the need to transcend the outmoded 'bourgeois' nation-state by 'uniting' all workers (irrespective of creed, nationality or race) into a single supranational 'workers' state', for the sake of 'proletarian solidarity' against counter-revolutionaries and capitalist imperialism. But it burdened an impoverished and war-ravaged USSR with full economic and political responsibility for the peoples and territories thus absorbed and, if Stalin had tried to apply it to post-war Poland or some other East European states, he could conceivably have provoked another world war, this time between the West and the Soviet Union. The second variant (formally independent People's Democracies) prevailed partly as a result of the challenges and constraints imposed by the Cold War and the US-sponsored European Recovery Programme, commonly known as the Marshall Plan. But it soon displayed all the drawbacks consequent upon the indirect imposition of largely inappropriate and increasingly unpopular political and economic models and precepts through inherently unstable quisling regimes, against which East Europeans were likely to rebel at every opportunity (as indeed some did in 1953, 1956, 1968, 1970, 1976, 1980 and 1989). The foundation and subsequent development of Comecon (discussed below) can be seen partly as an ultimately self-defeating endeavour by the Soviet Union to counter these challenges and problems in its own 'back yard' by curtailing the East European states' links with their former markets and suppliers of machinery, equipment, capital and technology in the West and by fostering mechanisms for the closer co-ordination, synchronization and bonding of their economic plans with those of the USSR. By helping to entrench and perpetuate authoritarian and over-centralized political and economic models and by 'locking' the capital- and mineral-deficient East European states into lopsided and unduly capital- and mineral-intensive patterns of industrial development which could never become self-supporting or self-reliant, the Comecon expedient simply magnified and exacerbated the problems it was supposed to resolve or at least alleviate. Adding insult to injury, it restricted the East European states' access to the Western products, technologies and markets which really were capable of alleviating their problems, while making them increasingly dependent on subsidized Soviet energy supplies to support the inefficient and environmentally devastating patterns of industrial development foisted upon them by the Soviet Union and its client regimes. This fuelled ever-increasing resentment of Soviet tutelage, especially when East Europeans were also expected to show 'gratitude' even though they had not freely chosen the patterns of industrial development that later necessitated such large and heavily subsidized Soviet inputs.

19 The Second World War and the expansion of communist power in East Central and South-eastern Europe

THE IMPACT OF THE SECOND WORLD WAR

It is often assumed that the revolutionary changes that occurred in Eastern Europe in the aftermath of the Second World War were simply a consequence of the presence of powerful Soviet forces in the region. Stalin probably did regard Eastern Europe as a protective cordon or buffer between the Soviet Union and an increasingly hostile West. He may even have been holding it hostage against the possibility that the United States might be tempted to drop atomic bombs on Moscow, as it already had done on Hiroshima and Nagasaki. Nevertheless, reality was almost certainly more complex than such perspectives would suggest. The communist regimes were not established merely 'at the point of the bayonet', although that did play a part. There was widespread local support for radical social and economic change, if not always for communist parties as such. More generally, the enhanced status of the Soviet Union as the principal 'liberating power' in the region, as the Eastern victor over fascism and as the builder of a 'brave new world' played an important role in the expansion of communist power and Soviet influence in Eastern Europe, where both democracy (of sorts) and fascism had been tried and found wanting during the 1920s and 1930s. It should also be emphasized that Soviet forces were not actually present when communist parties seized and consolidated power in Czechoslovakia and in Albania (both of whom felt that they had been somewhat 'betrayed' by the Western powers in 1938 and 1939, respectively) and that they provided only minor and very belated assistance to Tito's Partisans in Yugoslavia. Moreover, there would probably have been an autonomous communist revolution in Greece as well, if Britain and the United States had not intervened militarily on the side of the not very popular Greek monarchists. It would be more accurate to conclude that the social and political upheavals in Eastern Europe in the second half of the 1940s and the widespread (but far from ubiquitous) presence of the Red Army were mutually reinforcing joint consequences of the Second World War.

The Second World War profoundly affected the countries of Eastern Europe. Their industrial, agricultural and mineral resources had been systematically plundered and harnessed to the Axis war machine, which had also mobilized up to 6 million forced labourers from Eastern Europe. Over 6 million Polish citizens (including 2.6 million Jews), 1.75 million Yugoslavs (including 60,000 Jews), 1.3 million Romanians (including 750,000 Jews), 700,00 Hungarians (including 200,000 Jews), 330,000 Czechoslovak citizens (including 60,000 Jews) and 60,000 Bulgarians (including 40,000 Jews) had perished during the war (Gilbert 1967: 86, 93). In the case of Yugoslavia, however, the casualties had been much more the result of internal conflict (primarily between Orthodox Serbs and Croatian Catholics and fascists) than of the activities of the German and Italian occupation forces. Material losses were equivalent to about 30 per cent of national assets or three to four years' output in Poland and Yugoslavia, about two years' output in the case of Hungary, one year's output in Czechoslovakia and about four months' output in the cases of Bulgaria and Romania (Berend and Ranki 1974a: 340–1). The massive scale of the depredations and loss of life in Poland and Yugoslavia, far exceeding anything experienced in the West and comparable only with the Soviet Union, helps to explain why these two countries produced Europe's largest resistance movements, including the pro-Western *Armia Krajowa* (Home Army) and the smaller communist-led *Armia Ludowa* (People's Army) in Poland and Tito's communist-led Partisans and Colonel Mihailovich's smaller Serbian nationalist chetniks in Yugoslavia. These fought not only against fascism but for the future control of their respective countries. Geopolitical factors and the military might of the Soviet Union ultimately tipped the scales in favour of the communist-led forces in Poland. But in Yugoslavia, as in Albania, the communists triumphed mainly through their own efforts and their capacity to transcend internal ethnic divisions and rivalries.

On the whole, Eastern Europeans had suffered far more than the Western states during the Second World War. The Nazis had not only exterminated a great many Gypsies and nearly three-quarters of Eastern Europe's 5 million Jews, but also regarded the Slavs as an inferior species, fit only to be hewers of wood and drawers of water, and treated them accordingly. Hence many Slavs joined resistance movements at least partly in order to evade possible political detention and/or seizure for forced labour. But resistance evoked barbaric German and (to a much lesser extent) Italian reprisals, including some especially notorious massacres of whole villages. This in turn polarized political and social attitudes, persuading even more people to join resistance 'cells'. The prominence of communists in the resistance movements led many people to see them no longer as 'anti-national' subversives, but as stalwart patriots untainted by collaboration with fascism. (The limited collaboration prompted by the Nazi–Soviet Pact of August 1939 seems to have been widely forgiven or perhaps simply forgotten.) Thus in post-war Czecho-slovakia, for example, the Communist Party emerged as by far the biggest political party, winning 38 per cent of the vote in the fairly free elections of May 1946. Yet, while it is quite usual to describe these elections as 'free', it should be pointed out that the Communists' electoral success was made much easier by the fact that the Agrarian Party, the most popular political party in inter-war Czechoslovakia and the natural rallying point for democratic opposition to the Marxist left, had been banned (along with the quasi-fascist Slovak People's Party) because a few Agrarians had allowed themselves to be used by Nazi Germany after 1938. Nevertheless, as mentioned above, the prestige of Europe's major communist parties had undoubtedly been enhanced by the crucial role of the Soviet Union in the defeat of Nazi Germany and in the attendant 'liberation' of Eastern Europe, although this was still somewhat mitigated by widespread fear of potential Soviet domination and by the sometimes atrocious conduct of the Soviet forces deployed in the region. By contrast, with the partial exceptions of Czechoslovakia and Poland, the old (inter-war) ruling establishments and most right-wing nationalists had been largely (if not completely) discredited by the extent to which they had succumbed to fascism.

Many (perhaps most) East Europeans were thus psychologically prepared for a thoroughgoing post-war reconstruction in which radical peasant and proletarian movements would deservedly call the shots and stoutly resist the kinds of half-measures and 'sell-outs' that had so fatally compromised and disarmed inter-war radicalism. There was a widespread determination not to repeat the mistakes of the inter-war years, not to settle for half-measures and not to allow the wily old oligarchies to retrieve their former positions. Indeed, those parts of the East European intelligentsia that had been embittered by fascist persecution and disillusioned by the failure of the inter-war regimes to solve the region's social and economic maladies were widely drawn to Marxism as an ideology which, at its best, eschewed nationalist and religious bigotry and seemed to supply the key to understanding the recent course and future direction of history. (Some British anti-fascists were similarly drawn to communism and/or espionage on behalf of the Soviet Union.) Communism promised to build a better world, and it seemed to have demonstrated its strength and viability (albeit at awesome social cost) in Stalin's Soviet Union. Furthermore, in the wake of the political and economic *débâcle* brought about by the defeat of fascism, millions of unemployed or insecure workers almost inevitably turned to communist movements that seemed capable of delivering a huge expansion of industrial employment and massive upward social mobility on the Soviet model. The peasantry, by contrast, mainly looked to the resurgent peasantist parties to enact radical land redistribution and to build up voluntary rural co-operative networks responsive to peasant needs and aspirations.

THE EMERGENCE OF NEO-STALINIST REGIMES IN EAST CENTRAL AND SOUTH-EASTERN EUROPE

Within the anti-fascist Popular Front coalitions of communists, socialists, peasantists, liberals and Christian democrats that had emerged in Eastern Europe during and after the Second World War there was broad consensus on the urgent need for radical land reform, the expropriation of German and Italian property, the expulsion of Hitler's German collaborators, planned economic reconstruction, comprehensive welfare systems and public ownership of banks, large-scale industries and public utilities. But most of Eastern Europe's major banks, large-scale industries and public utilities had already been taken into state ownership by the fascist regimes during the 1930s and early 1940s, not least through the confiscation of Jewish property. This, together with the widespread perception that the inter-war experiments with democracy had generally 'failed' and that the region's fascist and quisling regimes had culminated in defeat, disgrace and collapse, effectively prepared the ground for socialism of some sort, although it was not yet a foregone conclusion that it would take the form of Stalinist dictatorship. As testified by the Nobel Prize-winning Polish writer Czeslaw Milosz, 'To understand the course of events in Eastern and Central Europe during the first post-war years, it must be realized that the pre-war social conditions called for extensive reforms. It must further be understood that Nazi rule had occasioned a profound disintegration of the existing order of things. In these circumstances, the only hope was to set up a social order which would be new . . . so what was planned in Moscow as a stage on the road to servitude was willingly accepted in the countries concerned as though it were true progress' (Milosz 1953: x). Milosz also went on to explain why writers and intellectuals such as himself had felt that it was futile to resist the expansion of communist power in their part of the world: 'given the post-war circumstances, the Party was the only power that could guarantee peace, reconstruct the country, enable the people to earn their daily bread, and start schools and universities, ships and railroads functioning. One did not have to be a communist to reach this conclusion. It was obvious to everyone. To kill party workers, to sabotage trains carrying food, to attack labourers who were trying to build factories was to prolong the period of chaos. Only madmen could commit such fruitless and illogical acts' (p. 103).

For the most part, the centre-left Popular Front coalitions that governed Eastern Europe in the immediate aftermath of the war simply inherited already 'nationalized' banks, industries and public utilities. These assets were generally vested in the new East European states to use as they saw fit, instead of being restored to their original owners, many of whom had either emigrated or perished. The process of social transformation was greatly facilitated by the increased ethnic homogeneity of Eastern Europe after the Second World War, primarily resulting from the extermination of nearly 4 million East European Jews, the flight or expulsion of about 10 million East European Germans and the major post-war territorial adjustments (especially the westward displacement of Poland and the incorporation of almost all Ukrainians and Belorussians into an expanded Soviet Union).

The peasants confronted the increasingly communist-dominated governments of post-war Eastern Europe with their biggest initial challenge, not least because peasants were still in a majority everywhere (except for relatively industrialized Czechoslovakia and East Germany, where they respectively made up only 36 per cent and 26 per cent of the population by 1950). The discredited former rulers were summarily exiled, imprisoned or executed for their misdeeds. The middle classes, deprived of property and economic opportunities, were 'rapidly reduced to poverty and impotence' (Mitrany 1951: 171). In view of their shared Marxist heritage and working-class following, the socialist parties often felt obliged to play along with communist party policies, salami tactics (picking off opponents slice by slice), rent-a-mob demonstrations and the intimidation or liquidation of opponents, until their active or passive complicity in communist crimes or foul play made it difficult for them to resist absorption into forcibly merged communist-led parties and regimes in 1947–48. 'The peasants, however, could neither be crushed like the middle class nor cowed and absorbed like the socialists' (p. 171). Hence the communists initially conciliated the peasant parties and 'neutralized' the peasantry by backing and helping to implement radical peasantist land reforms, while surreptitiously strengthening their grip on key state institutions (especially the state security apparatus) behind the scenes.

The land reforms of 1945–47 essentially completed those of 1918–23. However, they not only redistributed many of the still surviving landed estates of Hungary, Poland and eastern Germany (the rest being turned into state farms), but also took land from many medium-sized farms (without compensation in the cases of Romania, Yugoslavia and Albania) and discriminated in favour of the poorer peasants and landless labourers. In addition, although the redistributed land was received as inheritable personal property, it could not be sold or let or mortgaged without official permission. The transitory, tactical nature of these agrarian reforms was indicated by the speed with which they were implemented (less than a month in the cases of Hungary and Romania) and the consequent lack of preparation, including the frequent absence of proper registers and surveys of the land in question. However, by discriminating in favour of poor peasants and landless labourers at the expense of so-called 'rich peasants' and by striving to affiliate poor peasants and radical peasantist groups to the proletarian parties, the communists succeeded in fomenting some dissension and conflict within the peasantry and the peasantist movements, facilitating the pursuit of 'divide and rule' tactics towards them. Communist politicians were also frequently photographed (for the media) handing out title deeds to the new landholders, in order to win political credit and gratitude in the eyes of the peasantry.

In contrast to the more firmly entrenched Stalinist regime in the Soviet Union, however, the relatively precarious and fragile communist regimes established in Eastern Europe between 1945 and 1948 simply could not afford to 'liquidate' millions of so-called 'kulaks' ('rich peasants' and village traders and moneylenders). Nor could they risk mass starvation and agricultural sabotage for the sake of rapidly achieving rural collectivization, involving the establishment of large-scale state farms and agricultural producers' co-operatives in place of independent peasant agriculture. Nor indeed was there any need for them to do so, although this raises the question of whether collectivization had really been 'necessary' in the Soviet Union. (The arguments are critically assessed in Bideleux 1987: 11, 36–7, 54–6, 62–9, 77–9, 110–13, 118–23, 194–220.) Wholesale collectivization was accomplished in stages and without widespread violence or destruction in Bulgaria, Romania, Hungary, Czechoslovakia and East Germany between 1948 and 1960 and in Albania between 1955 and 1964. Although it did involve officially acknowledged 'excesses', 'errors', 'distortions' and 'violations of the principle of voluntariness' in parts of Czechoslovakia, East Germany, Bulgaria and Hungary, such occurrences were more the exception than the rule (p. 200). Indeed, while collectivization was being carried out in each of these states, there was actually a slight increase in overall livestock numbers (with the exception of horses, which were being rapidly replaced by tractors all over Europe at that time). This was in sharp contrast to the massive destruction of livestock that had accompanied collectivization in many parts of the Soviet Union (pp. 122, 201, 205–8).

Several factors kept down the cost of collectivization in Eastern Europe. There was broader and more careful preparatory discussion and briefing on the precise forms and functions to be assumed by collectivized agriculture in each area. There was more widespread use of transitional forms and differential compensation payments, in recognition of the fact that some peasant households were contributing much more land, capital or livestock than others. Peasants were often encouraged to join co-operative farms by the offer of favours and privileges. Former landless labourers who had acquired land during the 1945–47 land reforms but lacked the means to farm it properly proved especially susceptible to official blandishments. Moreover, Czechoslovakia and the GDR were much more highly industrialized than the Soviet Union and were in a position to furnish most of the equipment and fertilizer inputs needed to make collectivized agriculture tolerably productive in these two countries and, to some extent, in the neighbouring communist states as well. In addition, the already 'tractorized' Soviet Union exported over 100,000 tractors to Eastern Europe between 1946 and 1962. Above all, whereas Stalin's regime had automatically branded all successful farmers as 'kulaks' and 'class enemies' who were to be 'liquidated' and debarred from joining collective farms, the East European communist regimes made greater efforts to utilize such farmers in the formation of successful farming co-operatives, sometimes even making them farm chairmen or managers, secure in the knowledge that they would be surrounded and closely watched by their poorer bretheren (pp. 201–2). Thus collectivized agriculture was somewhat better placed to realize at least some of its potential economic, social and technical advantages in Eastern Europe during the 1950s than it had been in the Soviet Union during the 1930s. For once, some lessons had been learned from past mistakes.

In Poland and Yugoslavia, on the other hand, fierce resistance from peasants, many of whom had actively participated in wartime resistance movements, led to the early abandonment of wholesale collectivization (Bideleux 1987: 61–3). The fact that Poland nevertheless managed to carry out large-scale centrally planned industrialization with no more difficulty or lack of success than some of its collectivized East European neighbours further calls into question the economic, social and political 'necessity' and desirability of collectivization, even from an 'orthodox' communist standpoint. Only Poland's so-called 'western territories' (the areas appropriated from Germany in 1945) were to be substantially collectivized, and here the creation of farming co-operatives was mainly a means of rapidly settling a large number of Poles on good farmland which German farmers had been forced to quit and of thus giving greater permanence to these territorial acquisitions (not unlike the use of kibbutzim to colonize Israel's 'occcupied territories'). In the final analysis, the Polish and Yugoslav communist regimes were not as ruthless, inhuman and unyielding as Stalin's had been. They knew when and how to pull back from potential human and economic disasters, instead of blundering and bludgeoning onward.

From the late 1940s to the early 1960s the East European states mobilized rapidly growing inputs of labour, capital, energy and raw materials in order to achieve rapid industrialization and impresssive rates of growth. However, it was based not so much on increased productivity or the more efficient use of resources (so-called 'intensive' growth) as on the massive mobilization of ever-increasing but inefficiently used capital, labour, energy and raw material inputs (so-called 'extensive' growth). Since this involved the prodigal exploitation of natural resources, it has also been described as a form of 'slash and burn' economy. In marked contrast to Western capitalist patterns of industrialization, priority was given to heavy rather than light industries and to the growth of 'forced savings' and investment rather than personal consumption. Thus East European economic development was propelled, not by the mass production and consumption of consumer goods, but by the production of producer goods such as steel, machinery, chemicals, coal and oil. These were mostly consumed by industry itself, with few positive effects on living standards. (This development strategy is critically assessed in Bideleux 1987: 144–60.) Moreover, overall control was exercised by means of highly centralized, comprehensive, mandatory planning and resource allocation, rather than market forces and financial discipline, although the so-called centrally planned economies were never as centrally controlled in practice as they appeared to be in principle (pp. 141–3).

Industrialization is rarely (if ever) a painless or costless process, but the social, political and economic costs of this lopsided 'extensive' development strategy were inordinately high. It involved unprecedentedly rapid urbanization, the relative neglect of consumer needs and the service sector (with the partial exceptions of education and health care), acute urban overcrowding, chronic shortages, widespread use of coercion, repression, 'show trials', purges and intimidation, massive recruitment of women into mostly menial and low-paid occupations, and major errors and waste in the over-centralized resource allocation and distribution systems. Much of what was produced never reached its intended users, while many perishable products became unfit for consumption before reaching their intended consumers. Despite (or because of) the suffocating and terrifying control of society by a monolithic state and an all-pervasive party and official ideology, these systems provided no effective mechanisms or incentives to control costs, profligacy, inefficiency and waste, no effective means of ensuring that what was produced was what users wanted and very little public accountability for what was done (or left undone).

Post-war reconstruction and Stalinist industrialization rapidly changed the nature of East European society. In 1945 most East Europeans had still lived in agrarian settings, most towns had still served as provincial market places for the surrounding rural areas, and policy debate was still centred on agrarian reform and peasant aspirations. By 1960, however, agriculture and peasants had been eclipsed by industry and workers. By then non-agricultural households constituted the following proportions of the population: 83 per cent in the GDR, 74 per cent in Czechoslovakia, 61 per cent in Hungary, 56 per cent in Poland, 46 per cent in Bulgaria and 34 per cent in Romania. Millions of young adult peasants had moved from the countryside to the towns, although many non-agricultural households continued to reside in rural areas. Thus Poland's urban population soared from 7.5 million in 1945 to 14.4 million in 1960 (rising from 32 per cent of the total population to 48 per cent), while Bulgaria's rose from 26 per cent of the total population in 1948 to 38 per cent in 1960. Between 1950 and 1960 the population of Belgrade grew from 368,000 to 585,000, that of Bucharest from 886,000 to 1,226,000, Budapest from 1,571,000 to 1,805,000, Gdansk from 170,000 to 286,000, Sofia from 435,00 to 687,000, Warsaw from 601,000 to 1,136,000, Wroclaw from 279,000 to 429,000 and Zagreb from 280,000 to 431,000 (Mitchell 1978: 12–14). In Poland urban blue-collar employment increased by 10 per cent per annum from 1947 to 1958 and new recruits from the peasantry were able to find jobs without having either to complete their schooling or improve their skills and qualifications, with the result that by 1958 42 per cent of urban workers had 'incomplete elementary education bordering on illiteracy' (Kolankiewicz and Lewis 1988: 41). Similar situations pertained in Bulgaria, Romania and Yugoslavia, but conditions were much worse in Albania.

Many East European towns became giant building sites. In both Poland and Yugoslavia over one-third of the pre-war housing stock and nearly half the factories had been destroyed during the Second World War, while serious urban devastation had also occurred in Hungary and eastern Germany during the closing stages of the war. Some cities were lovingly and sensitively restored to their former beauty, but more often than not economic austerity and the sheer magnitude of the housing and reconstruction problems resulted in the prevalence of cheap, drab, quickly dilapidated, system-built blocks of flats. (Indeed, given the scale of the problems, this might have been the outcome whatever the regime.) Urban living standards plummeted as too many resources were tied up in huge projects of long gestation, while headlong industrialization forced millions of former peasants to live in hut camps or in grim apartment blocks close to gigantic and grossly polluting industrial complexes, either in the middle of nowhere or on the outskirts of soulless new industrial towns with few amenities and even less character. Postwar food shortages also persisted as peasants reacted negatively to rural collectivization, the vilification of kulaks and the imposition of often unremunerative compulsory delivery quotas, while the low priority accorded to agricultural investment and the mass exodus of young men from the villages further depressed agricultural productivity. The suppression of 'free' (independent) trade unions and the explosive growth of the urban working classes, largely through the arrival of millions of 'new recruits' from the countryside, also resulted in widespread social fragmentation, disorientation, 'deracination' and 'atomization', further reducing their ability to resist economic oppression and exploitation in all its forms. The vulnerability of the working classes was reinforced by the fact that the potential leaders of working-class protest were frequently promoted to junior and sometimes senior managerial positions, further dissipating any residual 'proletarian solidarity'. War-weary, battered and demoralized populations quite easily fell victim to predatory authoritarian regimes once again, as they had done in the course of the two decades following the First World War.

Not surprisingly, however, the initial left-wing and working-class enthusiasm for the Stalinist development strategy soon wore off and eventually turned to bitter disillusionment. The ambivalent feelings aroused by the initial phase of communist rule were aptly described by Czeslaw Milosz: 'After the experiences of the War, none of us, not even nationalists, doubted the necessity of the reforms that were being instituted. Our nation was going to be transformed into a nation of workers and peasants and that was right. Yet the peasant was not content, even though he was given land; he was afraid. The worker had not the slightest feeling that the factories belong to him, even though he worked to mobilize them with much self-denial and even though the propaganda assured him that they were his . . . This was, indeed, a peculiar Revolution . . . it was carried out entirely by official decree' (Milosz 1953: 166–7). Sociological studies of the workers' protests which occurred in the GDR, Hungary and Czechoslovakia in the summer of 1953 and in Poland and Hungary in the summer and autumn of 1956 have emphasized that the strongest protests came precisely from those elements that had originally provided the communist parties' most enthusiastic support. Foremost among them were young workers, socialist intellectuals (many of whom had been imprisoned in 1949–53), radical journalists, peasants who had 'risen' into the industrial proletariat and young men who had volunteered to 'induct' the peasantry into the supposed benefits of Stalinist socialism and collectivized agriculture. Those who had denounced the Stalinist economic strategy from the outset could take some crumbs of satisfaction from seeing their dire predictions fulfilled, whereas those who had been indifferent or apathetic at the start often remained so. But those who had fervently believed that Stalinist industrialization and collectivization were the fast road to the 'promised land' of socialism generally felt utterly disillusioned or even 'betrayed'. Their naive fervour, idealism and courage frequently led them to open criticism and complaint, usually followed by punitive demotion to inferior jobs and housing or, in the more serious cases, to arrest, imprisonment or even execution (as was most powerfully portayed in Andrzej Wajda's film *Man of Marble*). The number of communist party members 'purged' between 1948 and 1953 was about 90,000 in Bulgaria, 200,000 in Romania, 200,000 in Hungary (which had only about a third as many inhabitants as Romania), 300,000 in East Germany, 370,000 in Poland and a colossal 550,000 in Czechoslovakia, according to Brzezinski (1967: 97). In the case of Hungary, according to other estimates, around 150,00 communists were imprisoned, 2,000 were summarily executed and 350,000 were expelled from the ruling party over the same period (Rothschild 1989: 137). In the case of Czechoslovakia about 130,000 people (over 1 per cent of the population) were sent to prisons, labour camps and mines (Sword 1991: 60). It is widely agreed that Poland, which had already suffered terrible 'purges' and bloodletting during the Second World War, was the East European country least afflicted by post-war 'purges'. Conversely, Czechoslovakia and Hungary, which had emerged from the war relatively unscathed, were the countries worst affected by the subsequent 'purges'.

The upheaval in Hungary in the autumn of 1956 was not simply an attempted 'counter-revolution' instigated by Catholic, peasant and 'bourgeois nationalist' opponents of communist rule, as Soviet interventionist propaganda maintained (and as many Western observers and commentators were equally keen to believe). It also involved a campaign for real socialism, a radical attempt by embittered and disillusioned workers and intelligenti to bring about a more authentic socialist revolution with more far-reaching gains for the working class. A network of workers' councils emerged in Hungarian factories and working-class suburbs in late October and November 1956. According to Lomax (1976: 201–3), the struggles of Hungarian workers and workers' councils were mainly directed against the monolithic control exercised by the ruling party bureaucracy over the work force and the means of production through party-appointed managerial and trade union personnel and through shop-floor party cells and informers. In November 1956 'Party-appointed managers were given the boot by the workers, Party organizers were driven out of the factories, and so were those union officials who had never given a damn for the workers' interests. The workers' councils were then set up as organizations through which the workers themselves could control their factories.' On 27 November the Central Workers' Council of Greater Budapest issued a protest against official proposals to confine workers' councils to purely economic functions and a proclamation that 'the real interests of the working class in Hungary are represented by the workers' councils' (quoted on p. 201). Indeed, the workers' councils 'did not set themselves up as a new privileged elite or a new bureaucratic caste . . . On the contrary, even the executive members of the Central Workers' Council spent the full working day on the factory floor.' Its members were expected to report back regularly to the workers and were subject to recall and replacement (p. 202). Thus the Hungarian working class 'both smashed the former state power ruled over by the Communist Party and reopened the road to that society which had been the original aim of Marxism and socialism – in which hierarchy would give way to equality, in which political institutions would be replaced by popular organs'(p. 203).

The conflicting objectives and ideologies of the rival left-wing and right-wing participants in the abortive Hungarian Revolution of 1956 facilitated its bloody suppression by the Soviet armed forces and their Hungarian collaborators, headed by Janos Kadar (party leader from October 1956 to May 1988). The casualties included over 2,000 Hungarians executed, more than 2,000 others killed and around 13,000 wounded. Meanwhile, over 15,000 Hungarians were imprisoned and more than 200,000 took refuge in the West (Molnar 1971: 240, 249). The almost complete disintegration of the ruling party, many of whose former members openly sided with the revolution and/or handed in or destroyed their party membership cards, both forced and allowed Kadar to rebuild his party almost from scratch after 1956. However, in order to crush the Hungarian Revolution, 'every independent organization of the working class had to be smashed' (Lomax 1976: 194–5). Indeed, the working class bore the brunt of the repression, partly because the 'greatest armed resistance to the Soviet forces occurred in the large iron and steel centres of Dunapentele, Ozd and Miscolc, and in the mining regions of Borsod, Dorog, Tatabanya and Pecs. In Budapest itself the Soviet military authorities had to concentrate their heaviest armoured units on the workers' suburbs, where the workers had occupied their factories and continued to defend them for several days against the Soviet tanks.' By contrast, 'the fashionable middle-class districts . . . were hardly touched' (p. 149).

A network of workers' councils similar to that in Hungary also arose in Poland in the wake of the suppression of workers' protests in Poznan in June 1956 (in which 113 people were killed by the Polish army and security police) and the campaign to restore the 'national communist' Wladislaw Gomulka to the party leadership. An official decree legalized the mushrooming workers' councils in November 1956, but confined them to dealing with a narrow range of economic and social matters at the local level. It prohibited attempts to organize a nationwide federation of workers' councils capable of bringing concerted political pressure to bear on the regime or of playing an effective role in policy-making at the national level (Brzezinski 1967: 350). By September 1957 three-quarters of the 1,936 eligible industrial enterprises had established workers' councils. But in April 1958 these were further emasculated by being subordinated to a so-called Workers' Self-government Conference in which elected representatives of workers' councils were to be outnumbered by official party and trade union appointees and the proceedings were to be chaired by the party secretary (p. 356). Polish workers' councils thus became mere 'grievance boards', serving as barometers and safety valves rather than as harbingers of authentic industrial democracy or 'workers' control'. Working-class discontent was more muzzled than assuaged, but that did not provide a lasting resolution of the recurrent conflict between the ruling party and the workers in whose name it ruled, as Gomulka and his successors were to discover to their cost during the Polish crises of 1970, 1976, 1980–82 and 1988–89.

The East European communist regimes were much more deeply affected by workers' grievances than by counter-revolutionary 'bourgeois', nationalist and religious discontents. The latter undoubtedly existed, but the combined effects of fascism, the Second World War and Stalinism had ensured that they lacked a strongly organized class base and that the communists could glibly dismiss them as 'enemies of the people' and as epigones of the former 'exploiting classes'. Their howls of pain and protest could be treated both as confirmation that the communist regimes were successfully achieving their objectives and as a pretext for the repression of 'counter-revolutionary elements' bent on overthrowing communist rule. Conversely, unrest among workers and the socialist intelligentsia, supposedly the twin pillars of communist rule, was much more threatening and embarrassing. It was nipped in the bud in 1953–58 by repression sugared with concessions to the incipient consumerism of both wage and salary earners and to the widespread desire for social and economic security, stability and upward mobility. But the price was the death of revolutionary elan and socialist idealism, which were superseded by cynical 'deals' and compromises and by pragmatic appeals to grasping and acquisitive self-interest. Buying off wage and salary earners' discontent in this way involved a far-reaching 'sell-out'. It drew most sections of society into an implicit, deeply corrupting 'social contract'. It also took a heavy toll of economic and administrative efficiency. However, the success of this political stratagem would largely depend upon the maintenance of sustained economic growth and rising consumption levels. These were objectives that none of the East European regimes could easily achieve on its own. Hence they would ultimately depend on how successfully they could escape or surmount the constraints and austerities of 'boxed in' national self-reliance by promoting trans-national and/or supranational economic co-operation, division of labour and integration within Comecon, which could also offer increased access to the vast markets and mineral resources of the Soviet Union. It is therefore vital to consider the achievements and the inherent shortcomings of Comecon, even though Western analysts have commonly regarded it as a sham and as a bureaucratic irrelevance. In reality, the long-term survival of communist rule in Eastern Europe would hinge to a significant degree on how well Comecon performed.

THE FORMATION OF COMECON

Comecon, whose official name was the Council of Mutual Economic Assistance (CMEA), was founded in 1949, at the height of the East–West division and Cold War confrontation in Europe. In parallel with the inter-party Communist Information Bureau (Cominform, founded in 1947) on the ideological front and the inter-governmental Warsaw Pact (established in 1955) on the military/political front, Comecon was intended to enhance the solidity and cohesion of the Soviet bloc. It was as much a by-product of the Second World War and of the ensuing East–West division of Europe as were the nascent supranational and intergovernmental institutions of Western Europe.

The establishment of Comecon was at least partly a consequence of Stalin's decision to veto Eastern participation in the European Recovery Programme announced by American secretary of state George Marshall in June 1947, although the precise nature and importance of the causal connections are still under debate. The United States seemingly offered so-called Marshall Aid to all the European states that were struggling to recover from the Second World War, including the Soviet Union and the young People's Democracies in Eastern Europe. Soviet representatives certainly participated in some of the preliminary discussions, but their sudden withdrawal from the July 1947 Paris conference on the European Recovery Programme contributed to 'the division of Europe into two parts' (Brabant 1989: 9). In those East European states that were not yet fully under communist control at that time, namely Czechoslovakia, Hungary and Poland, the communist parties were still formally espousing moderation, gradualism and a 'middle way' between Soviet 'socialism' and Western capitalism (for fear of frightening the numerous peasant and 'petit bourgeois' voters), and their increasingly communist-dominated coalition governments initially signalled interest in receiving Marshall Aid. They did so in spite of the fact that the conditions or 'strings' attached to it would have pledged the recipients to a restoration of market economies with convertible currencies and to multilateral integration of their economies with those of the members of the Organization of European Economic Co-operation. The OEEC was to be responsible for allocating Marshall Aid and for upholding the liberal integrationist economic conditions on which it was to be granted. The recipients would thus be drawn into the economic orbit of the richer Western capitalist economies. Presumably in order to prevent this happening in Eastern Europe, which was still supposed to be in the Soviet 'sphere of influence', in July 1947 Stalin ordered the Czechoslovak and Polish governments to reverse their earlier decision to accept Marshall Aid. The communist and socialist Ministers in these governments meekly complied, thereby precipitating serious crises in relations between them and the so-called 'bourgeois' Ministers within the ruling Popular Front coalitions. Socialists submitted to communist pressure partly out of a (misguided) commitment to left-wing and working class 'solidarity', but also from fear of losing working-class and trade union support to the communists and because of actual and potential reprisals from the increasingly communist-controlled security forces.

This was the moment of truth, the signal for the communist parties rapidly to establish more complete control of the People's Democracies during late 1947 and early 1948. The forced rejection of Marshall Aid not only foreclosed Eastern Europe's opportunity of gradual reconstruction by market methods, with Western assistance and mutual gains from liberalized multilateral trade, but also heralded East Central Europe's incipient subjection to more blatant forms of Soviet control. If Poland and Czechoslovakia had been allowed to accept Marshall Aid, other People's Democracies would almost certainly have followed suit and much of Eastern Europe could have slipped out of the still far from secure Soviet and/or communist control. Significantly, the strong revival of Czechoslovak foreign trade in 1946 had been almost entirely with its traditional Western trading partners rather than with its new Soviet 'ally' (Rothschild 1989: 93). However, once the relatively autonomous Polish and Czechoslovak governments had bowed to Stalin's will, none of the others dared to step out of line, apart from the exceptionally battle-hardened and self-reliant communist rulers of Yugoslavia. (The Yugoslav communist regime had not yet embraced the more liberal course for which it later became famous. The source of its rift with the Soviet Union in 1948 was not doctrinal heterodoxy, nor a desire to seek an accommodation with the West, but its headstrong refusal to submit to Soviet dictates, as well as Stalin's innate mistrust of communists who gave him anything less than blind and unquestioning obedience.) Thrown back on their own meagre resources, the East European states were obliged to retreat into much more autarkic and coercive methods of resource allocation and mobilization modelled on those employed in Stalin's Soviet Union and not so very different from those used by the Nazis during the Second World War.

On 25 January 1949 most communist newspapers and news agencies published a short communiqué announcing that an economic conference representing the Soviet Union, Czechoslovakia, Poland, Hungary, Romania and Bulgaria had met in Moscow on 5–8 January and, 'in order to establish still broader economic co-operation among the countries of People's Democracy and the USSR', had instituted a Council for Mutual Economic Assistance 'on the basis of equal representation, and having as its tasks the exchange of experience in the economic field, the rendering of technical assistance to one another and the rendering of mutual assistance in regard to raw materials, foodstuffs, machinery, equipment, etc.' (reprinted in Vaughan 1976: 132–3). Albania joined Comecon the following month, while the newly established GDR followed suit in 1950.

The precise motives and objectives of this unheralded announcement have long been a matter of speculation and debate, as we still have no windows on Stalin's inscrutable mind. At the time it was widely believed that the creation of Comecon was part of a slowly unfolding plan for Soviet domination of post-fascist Europe. But Western 'revisionist' historians of the Cold War have long maintained that such a plan never existed and that Stalin was merely reacting defensively to unforeseen Western challenges and provocations, improvising as he went along. The Soviet leadership correctly perceived that Marshall Aid was (among other things) an indirect attempt to subvert or renege upon the apportionment of Soviet and Western 'spheres of influence' agreed in Moscow, Yalta and Potsdam in 1944–45, since the strings attached to it were bound to enmesh the recipients firmly in the Western economic sphere. Indeed, President Truman needed to persuade Congress that the Marshall Plan was an anti-communist programme, the economic counterpart of the Truman 'doctrine' on the 'containment' of communism. (They were, in Truman's apt phrase, 'two halves of the same walnut'.) Had he not done this, the instinctively isolationist and parsimonious US legislature might well have refused to approve the requisite financial appropriations. Significantly, the above-mentioned communiqué announcing the formation of Comecon stated that the Soviet Union and the People's Democracies 'did not consider it possible to submit to the Marshall Plan dictate', because it supposedly violated their 'sovereignty' and 'the interests of their national economies'. However, having prohibited the People's Democracies from participating in the US-sponsored European Recovery Programme and the OEEC, the Soviet leadership may have felt obliged to offer them some sort of substitute, both by way of compensation for the opportunities forgone and as a means of propping up their ailing economies, which had been seriously affected by the subsequent collapse of their trade with the West. Indeed, the same communiqué noted that 'the Governments of the United States of America, Britain, and of certain other countries of Western Europe, had been, as a matter of fact, boycotting trade relations with the countries of People's Democracy and the USSR'.

Stalin's motives for allowing the establishment of Comecon are sometimes seen as 'more negative than positive'. Thus he was more 'anxious to keep other powers out of neighbouring buffer states . . . than to integrate them', and he 'envisaged Comecon as the economic counterpart of the Cominform, which he had instituted in 1947' (Wallace and Clarke 1986: 1). Indeed, Comecon was often dismissed in the West as little more than a figleaf with which to cover the nakedness of Soviet domination of Eastern Europe and as an artificial contrivance designed to confer a semblance of solidity and of economic and institutional legitimacy on the emerging Soviet bloc, to discourage East European economic links with the West and to redirect the foreign trade of the East European states towards the Soviet Union. Nevertheless, Schiavone contends that the motives for the creation of Comecon were 'not reducible to the Soviet desire to oppose to the OEEC an East European organization. The establishment of the OEEC certainly served as an incentive, but it seems to have provided no more than an occasional prompting for the establishment of a multilateral co-operation body, the need for which was already felt' (Schiavone 1981: 16). Since 1848, indeed, there had been dozens of projects and schemes for customs unions and political federations or confederations in East Central Europe and the Balkans, although quite a few of them had been expressly directed against the Russian and/or communist 'menace'.

In any case, the emergence of centrally planned economies and communist regimes obliged Eastern Europe's new rulers to place the economic and political relations between their states and between themselves and the Soviet Union on a new and more coherent footing, partly because Western economic sanctions were rapidly cutting them off from their traditional export markets and from many former Western suppliers. The new East European regimes were to be drawn together by common political systems and precepts, similar development strategies, geographical proximity and security considerations. They were also driven into each others' arms by the new international trade and payments systems that were emerging in the capitalist West. According to Brada (1988: 654), 'GATT's insistence on nondiscriminatory treatment of trade partners was at odds with the notion of socialist integration and solidarity and in any case was not observed by the industrialized West in its trade policies *vis-à-vis* planned economies.' The Western emphasis on currency convertibility was inconsistent with the conception of central planning prevalent among CMEA members. Moreover, the centrally planned economies required an international regime to mediate trade among them even more than did market economies. 'Among the latter, trade takes place between private agents at market-determined prices. States need to interact with each other only to set the rules for such transactions, to enforce contracts, and to promote the functioning of markets. Among planned economies international trade is a state monopoly. Therefore markets cannot function, since each transaction confronts a monopolist with a monopsonist. As a result . . . there is less information, transactions are much costlier to negotiate, and states must interact with each other directly as parties to each transaction rather than merely as creators and guarantors of the rules of the game' (p. 655).

The pricing formulas employed by Comecon fixed intra-CMEA prices for several years at a time. Moreover, the absence of meaningful exchange rates and of domestic prices that reflected relative costs and scarcities obliged the Comecon states to take (lagged) world market prices as a reference point. (Hence the old joke that Comecon could never have taken over the whole world, because then it would no longer have known what prices to charge.) This pricing system was particularly advantageous to centrally planned economies, in Brada's judgement. First, the maintenance of stable prices reduced 'transaction costs'. In the absence of the stable pricing formulas, the centrally planned economies would have had to undertake more frequent trade negotiations 'with no starting point for the prices at which trade would take place' and no certainty that 'prices obtained in negotiations with one country would resemble those achieved with other countries', thus making trade negotiations exceedingly costly and time-consuming. Second, the use of stable pricing formulas in international transactions helped to maintain stable contexts for central planning. Third, the systematic over-pricing of manufactured goods relative to fuels and raw materials offered the East European members of Comecon artificially high returns on their production of manufactures that were often 'not up to world standards'. This gave them considerable protection against risk and competition as well as compensation for 'the high investment costs of modernizing and developing industries to serve the Soviet market', while providing the Soviet Union with substantially larger supplies of manufactured goods from Eastern Europe than would otherwise have been the case, at overall costs that were lower than those of producing such manufactures itself (pp. 656–7). Such arrangements also economized on the Comecon members' scarce earnings of hard currency, much as the OEEC and the associated European Payments Union did in post-war Western Europe.

Some members were bound to derive greater benefit from the intensification of intra-CMEA relations and cohesion than others, just as some would incur higher costs than the rest. The main tangible and measurable costs of the collective benefit that Comecon could confer on its participants would be borne by those members who could have either sold their major exports more dearly, or purchased their import requirements more cheaply, in non-CMEA markets. Nevertheless, even if the individual balance sheet of costs and benefits varied considerably between members and over time, there was a basic presumption that all members would reap some net benefit from Comecon membership. The benefit was not just economic but also came in the form of the increased internal and external legitimacy, security, stability and room for manoeuvre procured for Eastern Europe's communist regimes, since increases in the economic strength, political stability and international stature of the Soviet Union could also enhance the standing of its client states. Members would benefit from increases in the economic strength, political stability and international standing of Comecon as a whole.

On the other hand, Vladimir Sobell has argued that the supposed benefits of Comecon membership should really be regarded as partial mitigation or compensation for some of the inherent drawbacks of the whole economic system. Indeed, co-operation and specialization within Comecon could be seen as ways of alleviating 'the disadvantages associated with participation in the grouping' or as damage-limiting responses to 'the fundamental political error' of instituting that type of economic system in the first place. Likewise, the fact that the energy-importing members of Comecon participated in investment in energy projects on Soviet territory was not a 'sign of efficient integration' but 'an expression of a fundamental disorder' in the socialist system: the importing countries were 'unable to offer the USSR goods and services of sufficient "hardness" to motivate it to invest in additional energy infrastructure'. Indeed, East European experts and officials testified that joint investment was 'not only an inefficient strategy' but a 'considerable strain on their economies' (Sobell 1984: 248–9).

However, Sobell has also pointed out that the criteria by which Comecon integration was appraised in the West were somewhat inappropriate. The CMEA was never intended to maximize integration through trade, but rather to provide a protected environment within which to maximize the power, stability and economic growth of the 'socialist' states. Therefore Comecon should be assessed primarily by the extent to which it satisfied these criteria, rather than by its failure to maximize classical gains from trade: 'When judged by the criteria operating in a market environment Comecon integration appears as a passive and wasteful process: participation in the grouping leads to losses due to undertrading with non-members which are only partially made good by intra-group trade (leaving aside the losses from sub-optimal specialization on account of the lack of a rational intra-CMEA price system). On the other hand when judged by the criteria dominating the study of economics in most of Eastern Europe the verdict would be radically different. Undertrading would be regarded as a positive measure ensuring that domestic production planning is isolated from the disruptive effects of the capitalist markets; the disproportionate trade with member countries would be seen as a sign of active integration designed to reap natural advantages stemming from countries having the same socio-political systems' (Sobell 1984: 3).

Jozef van Brabant (1989: 41) emphasizes that official East European backing for Soviet denunciations of Marshall Aid from July 1947 onward and for the 1948–49 Soviet blockade of West Berlin (following the unilateral introduction of the Deutschmark in the Western zones of occupation in June 1948) led to an escalation of Western economic sanctions against the nascent Soviet bloc. From March 1948 onwards all American exports to Eastern Europe were subject to government licensing. 'The scope of the boycott was extended on 3 April 1948 by the statutes of the Marshall Plan.' Participants in the European Recovery Programme were debarred from trading in East European goods subject to US controls. This policy was formalized by the establishment of the Co-ordinating Committee for Multilateral Trade Controls (COCOM) in 1950 (p. 17). Thus, even though the original US motivation was at least partly philanthropic, the European Recovery Programme really did become an economic weapon in the incipient Cold War. This adversely affected those East European states that were still heavily dependent on trade with the West. Ill-considered Western economic sanctions drove them deeper into the economic and political embrace of the Soviet Union. The creation of Comecon accordingly reflected the need to enhance and to demonstrate Soviet bloc 'solidarity' in the face of Western economic sanctions and provocation, which in turn 'reinforced the economic arguments for the gradual elaboration of a common regional economic policy for Eastern Europe, including the USSR' (p. 18).

It has been argued that Nikolai Voznesensky, the influential chairman of the Soviet State Planning Commission (1937–49), was keen to place Soviet economic relations with Eastern Europe on a more regular and law-governed footing. That would have removed them from the jurisdiction and interference of capricious communist politicians, at the same time enhancing the role of more 'rational' and predictable economic mechanisms and of technocrats like himself (Kaser 1967: 21–6, 32–5). However, the dismissal and arrest of Voznesensky in March 1949, not long after the death of his Leningrad 'patron' Andrei Zhdanov in August 1948, eliminated the pivotal Soviet proponent of a more 'rational' economistic conception of Comecon and facilitated its subsequent emasculation by Stalin. The continuing absence of criteria by which economic goals, performance, output, inputs, costs and demand could be adequately measured, compared, evaluated and aggregated was to become the rock on which Comecon integration would eventually founder (pp. 26, 32–8). 'The implications for Comecon of the Voznesensky approach were, it may be suggested, trade arrangements based on the analysis of comparative costs and permitting the evaluation of multilateral exchanges . . . A "law of value" operating between Comecon members would have furnished criteria for . . . rational specializations undertaken in the context of co-ordinated long-term planning' (p. 35).

Voznesensky's precise role and position in the seminal preliminary debates on the appropriate structure, powers, functioning and economic basis of Comecon will remain a matter of conjecture until the records have been investigated more fully. Nevertheless, as argued by Peter Wiles, Voznesensky 'stood for a rational economy – it is unclear whether centralized or decentralized – that made sensible use of prices'. By contrast, Stalin and Voznesensky's successors on the economic front rejected 'the use of the price mechanism, both nationally and internationally, in favour of continued physical planning'. Stalin thus 'found himself saddled with an organ he had indeed allowed to be born, but could not personally work with' (Wiles 1968: 313).

If the ideas, policies, procedures and supranational institutions and mechanisms discussed by Comecon officials, economists and technocrats in 1949–50 had actually been implemented at the time, when the new centrally planned economies were still inchoate and malleable, it is conceivable that Comecon could have developed much more advantageously and that East European industrialization and inter-state specialization could have proceeded in a less arbitrary, less autarkic and more 'rational' fashion. That would certainly have avoided a lot of wasteful duplication and would have been far more efficacious than the belated attempts to pull these processes back on to a more efficient and 'rational' path during the 1960s and 1970s, by which time the autarkic and dysfunctional features of the East European centrally planned economies were much more deeply entrenched and difficult to correct (Ausch 1972: 44; Brabant 1989: 26, 40–1). According to Sandor Ausch, Hungary's representative at Comecon headquarters in Moscow in 1949 and from 1962 to 1964, 'the concrete form of our production relations (the system of direct plan instruction) is hindering to an ever-increasing extent the unfolding of more efficient intra-regional co-operation' (Ausch 1972: 226). Indeed, each member of Comecon continued to strive for a high level of industrial and agricultural self-reliance, because each mistrusted the ability and willingness of the other members to deliver what they were supposed to deliver under the terms of Comecon's later 'specialization agreements'.

More far-reaching integration of the Eastern European economies could have been achieved either through the adoption of market principles (i.e. enterprise autonomy, prices broadly reflecting relative costs and scarcities, convertible currencies and multilateral trading) or by erecting supranational Comecon agencies with the power to plan production, control trade, direct investment and assign specializations for the Soviet bloc as a whole, from Berlin to Vladivostok. The first option, which was increasingly canvassed by liberal economic reformers, never became politically feasible, because its inherent logic pointed to the eventual abandonment of central planning and communist party control of (and interference in) the economy. Such a scenario was as unacceptable to most communist *apparatchiki*, who stood to lose power, status and control, as it was attractive to most reformers. It would have relieved the communist parties of economic responsibilities which they were ill fitted to discharge, but it would also have removed the central *raison d'être* of communist rule. The second option was taken rather more seriously. It appears that on 18 January 1949 the six founder members of CMEA signed (but never ratified) a 'protocol' on the establishment of a 'common economic organization' and a supranational economic institution which would 'formulate a common economic plan for the harmonious development of the entire region, including the USSR'. It would have been granted 'plenipotentiary economic powers' to 'dovetail the member economies', ensure 'supplies of essential inputs for the region's industrialization' and promote 'regional complementarities', specialization, standardization, transnational investment, co-ordination of national economic plans and exchange of scientific and technical information (Brabant 1989: 20). According to Milan Cizkovsky (writing in 1970), 'the prerequisites for organizing supranational unified planning were intentionally created with the decision to co-ordinate the plans, the main goal being the gradual planned elimination of all attributes of the national economies as autonomous economic units. Therefore, a supranational system should have resulted and, in consequence, the absoluteness of state sovereignty would be negated' (quoted on p. 34).

In April and August 1949 the first and second Council sessions of Comecon apparently discussed 'the co-ordination of national economic plans to foster production specialization and co-operation', the close meshing of trade plans for key commodities, the introduction of multilateral clearing and realistic exchange rates, the elaboration of 'a common economic plan for the harmonious development of the entire region', mutual aid to counteract the effects of Western economic sanctions against CMEA members, the enforcement of Comecon's analogous economic boycott of independent-minded Yugoslavia, and comprehensive scientific and technical co-operation, which would result in the sharing of know-how and the standardization of weights, measures, industrial standards and product specifications to Soviet norms (Brabant 1989: 31–6). However, while this more centralized and proactive second option seems superficially compatible with the retention of centrally planned economies and the 'guiding role' of the communist parties, in practice it would have transferred ultimate control of economic processes from *national* economic planners and industrial ministries to *supranational* planners and Comecon industrial directorates and, even more radically, from communist politicians and *apparatchiki* to economic planners and technocrats. Although the precise reasons for the early rejection of this second option have not yet been fully documented, it is clear that its long-term implications would have been as unwelcome to *national* economic planners and industrial ministries as they were to *national* communist party bosses and their henchmen, all of whom would have suffered a large loss of power, function and status. They decided to safeguard their highly prized powers and perquisites by defending the principle of national economic sovereignty. This was the formal pretext for the recurrent rejection of supranational institutions, agencies, projects and powers within Comecon. Indeed, as early as 26 January 1949, the two main Polish newspapers, *Trybuna Ludu* and *Zycie Warzawy*, proclaimed that the form assumed by the new CMEA 'would strengthen sovereignty', while the Romanian *Universul* saw it as 'protecting the rights and sovereignty of members' (quoted in Kaser 1967: 15). Moreover, it seems likely that Stalin vetoed the entire project for a thoroughgoing supranational integration of the Comecon countries (along with the more 'rational' and technocratic system of central planning that such a project would have required) not merely out of uncharacteristic regard for the interests and sensibilities of his communist acolytes in Eastern Europe, but also because it could have acquired a momentum, logic and power base of its own, outside Soviet control. Stalin evidently preferred more informal and direct methods of intervention in the affairs of the East European states through the Soviet embassies and the legions of Soviet agents attached to them. By 1950 the Soviet Union was directly supervising East European policies and 'substantial components of national economic planning were entrusted to Soviet advisers and technicians, primarily through the so-called Soviet embassy system' (Brabant 1989: 22).

Stalin's sudden emasculation of Comecon in the summer of 1950 seems to have taken its personnel by surprise. As testified by Milan Cizkovsky, 'it was certainly not known . . . that the activity of the CMEA would come to a complete standstill for the next three years' (quoted by Brabant 1989: 38). Partly as a result of the outbreak of the Korean War on 25 June 1950 and the enhanced priority for autarkic Stalinist methods of resource-mobilization and industrialization, the Soviet Union 'abruptly ceased active participation in the CMEA's Bureau' and instead relied on its 'embassy system of meddling in other countries' affairs directly'. Comecon's third Council Session was therefore delayed until November 1950 and, to the Bureau's surprise, it decided to confine Comecon to 'practical questions of facilitating mutual trade' for the time being (p. 39). Nevertheless, partly as a result of the severity of Western economic sanctions, by 1953 intra-CMEA trade accounted for nearly 80 per cent of the foreign trade of the member states, which had conducted less than 13 per cent of their trade with one another in 1938 and would transact only 54 per cent of their foreign trade with one another by 1983, following the revival of East–West trade (Robson 1987: 225–6).

If Stalin had allowed Comecon to develop in the manner envisaged by its April and August 1949 council sessions, it could have become an institutional 'buffer' mediating the East European members' relations with each other and, more important, with the Soviet Union. For the People's Democracies that would have been safer, more 'politically correct' and less unequal than direct bilateral relations with an 'overbearing' USSR. But Stalin was unwilling to countenance the emergence of any regional organization that would make it easier for them to keep the Soviet 'bear' at bay or to 'gang up' to impose a majority policy on the Soviet Union. It is conceivable that Stalin deliberately stymied Comecon in order to keep the East European states divided and powerless against him. 'The central body, the Council Session, had to reach unanimous agreement in order to respect the sovereign rights of its member states. It could not make decisions, only recommendations. These had to be ratified subsequently by all governments and, even if so ratified, still had to be translated into policy by all governments acting separately' (Wallace and Clarke 1986: 4).

Thus the Soviet Union initially limited rather than encouraged multilateral exchange and co-operation between the East European members of Comecon. It negotiated bilateral treaties with each of them, fostered direct Soviet supervision and 'guidance' of their economic development (in flagrant violation of the vaunted sovereignty which had been the pretext for prohibiting multilateral integration on a more equal footing), and forced them all to pursue relatively uniform 'closed in' patterns of development which maximized economic duplication and costly import substitution and minimized the scope for fruitful resource-saving complementarities, integration and specialization. They all tended to develop similar strengths and weaknesses, while the development of command economies concentrated economic influence and decision-making in the hands of central economic ministries and planning bureaucracies which naturally became increasingly reluctant to cede powers and functions to any supranational body. Ironically, routine Soviet violations of their political sovereignty made them cling all the more tenaciously to their formal economic sovereignty, which was their main area of limited autonomy (Brabant 1989: 4). But during the early 1950s 'Comecon was a sham. Stalin ruled Eastern Europe, as he ruled the Soviet Union, by other than constitutional means' (Wallace and Clarke 1986: 3–4). Precisely because Comecon was an organization formally based on the professed sovereignty and equal status of its members, Stalin did not have much use for it (Wiles 1968: 314). From the outset Stalin viewed his new East European 'allies' with considerable suspicion. They were too Westernized, untested and unstable for his liking. He therefore endeavoured to restrict their contacts, not only with the West, but also with each other and with the USSR. He did not trust them enough to allow Comecon to realize more than a fraction of its true potential, and it would remain permanently scarred by this early experience.

Some important initial steps were none the less taken at this time. In particular, the council session of Comecon hosted by Bulgaria in August 1949 passed a seminal resolution on the pooling or sharing of technology among member states, which came to be known as 'the Sofia principle'. Instead of setting up an elaborate patents system and scientific protectionism to safeguard the advantages of technological leaders, as has been standard Western practice, they agreed to make their technologies available to one another for a nominal charge (mainly to cover the cost of providing technical documentation). This system was much disliked by the more industrialized members of Comecon (Czechoslovakia and the GDR). The latter stood to gain little in return for the technologies they passed on to their less developed partners (especially the Soviet Union, Bulgaria, Romania and, somewhat later, Cuba, Mongolia and Vietnam). Anthony Sutton has documented (albeit with some exaggeration) the considerable extent to which Soviet economic development was based upon the systematic transference, adaptation and copying of foreign technologies, blueprints, products and processes. The seminal infusions of Western technology into the Soviet economy occurred during the late 1920s and early 1930s, when many Western firms entered into various types of management or service contract with the Soviet Union and resourceful Soviet engineers and scientists systematically copied Western prototypes, ingeniously adapting them to Soviet needs and production possibilities. The first two five-year plans, including the huge new fleets of trucks, tractors and locomotives, were in large measure based on 'pirated' Western technology. But by the mid-1940s, in spite of deriving some benefit from American wartime assistance, the increasingly isolated Soviet economy had largely exhausted the potential of its now obsolescent 1920s–1930s technologies. It stood in desperate need of large new transfusions of foreign technology in order to ward off technological stagnation. These were obtained partly through the heavy-handed removal of plant, equipment, products, prototypes, blueprints and even scientific personnel from Soviet-occupied East Germany (on a scale that gave a whole new meaning to the concept of 'technology transfer'). In addition, Czechoslovakia, Hungary and Poland were obliged to 'share' their technological know-how with the USSR and (to a lesser extent) Bulgaria and Romania under the Sofia principle (Sutton 1968–72). Similarly, some of the Western technologies acquired or 'imported' by individual East European states and enterprises during the 1960s and 1970s were passed on to their partners under Comecon's 'scientific and technical co-operation' arrangements. Arguably, this was the substantive meaning of the 'mutual economic assistance' in Comecon's official title. However, the Sofia principle was downplayed after 1968, in recognition of its implicit discouragement of original and/or expensive technological research and development (and Czech and East German grievances on this score). Moreover, as the Soviet Union itself developed more expensive and/or sophisticated military, metallurgical, aircraft and energy technologies it became less willing to share them with its Comecon partners largely free of charge.

Following Stalin's death in March 1953, there were various attempts to 'relaunch' Comecon as a new and more equitable economic partnership and to use it as a substitute for more invidious forms of Soviet hegemony over Eastern Europe. The council sessions of March and June 1954 established a permanent Comecon secretariat and a standing conference of representatives of member countries. They also initiated a series of 'specialization agreements' designed to curb costly industrial duplication and import substitution, especially in those states that lacked the appropriate resource base to sustain autarkic neo-Stalinist patterns of industrialization. In 1956 ten permanent standing commissions were established to promote specialization and co-operation in particular sectors (pp. 46–7, 52–4). Comecon was revitalized, and its scope extended, partly in response to an extension of the range of tasks and challenges confronting the Soviet Union under its frenetic new party leader, Nikita Khrushchev (1953–64). The Soviet Union increasingly relied on Eastern Europe to provide the types of machinery, equipment, manufactured consumer goods and foodstuffs that were in short supply domestically and to provide 'captive' markets for Soviet-produced plant, machinery, armaments and oil (Mellor 1971: 14). (The Soviet Union initially faced difficulties in breaking into international oil markets controlled by Western multinational oil companies.) The December 1955 and May 1956 council sessions of Comecon called for the co-ordination and synchronization of national five-year plans. In practice, however, most of the attempts at plan co-ordination at this time were limited to bilateral *ex post* harmonization of the trade implications of national economic plans and failed to achieve *ex ante* harmonization of either trade intentions or planned production (Brabant 1989: 51). In any case, the 'specialization agreements' of 1954–56 were largely nullified by the social and political upheavals of 1956 (which precipitated many hasty revisions of trade and production priorities in the hope of defusing discontent), while plan synchronization and co-ordination were derailed in 1957 by the sudden abandonment of the 1956–60 Soviet five-year plan (Brabant 1989: 47; Mellor 1971: 15).

Comecon was 'relaunched' yet again in the wake of the November 1956 invasion of Hungary. The member states hoped that, by fostering higher living standards, less costly patterns of economic growth and stronger economic bonds within Comecon, they would be spared a repetition of anything so drastic as a full-scale military invasion of one of their own 'allies', since the 1956 invasion had starkly confirmed the lack of legitimacy and popular support of Eastern Europe's communist regimes and had severely dented their confidence and international standing. The 1957 Moscow Declaration ostensibly relaunched relations between the Comecon states on a new basis of mutual respect, non-interference and equality. The June 1957 and June 1958 council sessions of Comecon initiated preparations for the introduction of multilateral clearing (including the use of the 'transferable rouble' as a unit of account in intra-CMEA clearing) and for the establishment of a CMEA clearing bank. In May 1958 a special Comecon 'economic summit' launched preparations for more far-reaching specialization of production, to be achieved by multilateral, supranational *ex ante* co-ordination of plans under the aegis of fifteen sectoral and two functional Standing Commissions. The June 1958 council session approved new rules on the pricing of goods traded within Comecon, in an attempt to promote more equitable and multilateral trading and to shield intra-CMEA trade from the vagaries of the world market, while that of December 1959 belatedly adopted a Comecon Charter, partly inspired by the 1957 Treaties of Rome (Brabant 1989: 54–60). The charter defined the status and functions of the council session ('the highest organ'), the executive committee ('the principal executive organ'), the standing commissions and the secretariat. While it proclaimed 'the sovereign equality of all member countries', it also committed them to 'the consistent implementation of the international socialist division of labour'. (The complete text is translated in Vaughan 1976: 138–44.) The supranational 'integrationist' implications of this particular formulation may not have been immediately apparent to all the signatories of the charter, but they opened a more substantive chapter in Comecon's development, while also sowing the seeds of future dissension.

20 National roads to socialism

The 1960s began as a period of rising expectations and relative optimism in Eastern Europe. At the start of the decade the ruling parties and many of their political opponents seemed to share the belief that it would be possible to work towards a *modus vivendi*. This feeling was reinforced by the optimistic assumption that (other than in recession-stricken Czechoslovakia) rapid economic development would allow the East European economies simply to grow their way out of political, social and economic difficulties. It appeared that the harsh austerity, privation, terror and coercion of the 1940s and 1950s had gone for good, allowing East Europeans to reap the fruits of an expanded infrastructural and industrial base, albeit one that had been constructed at exorbitant social and economic cost. It was now hoped that, with appropriate streamlining or reform, the centrally planned economies could be made more efficient and responsive. At the same time the rapidly increasing Soviet output of oil, coal, natural gas, iron ore and electric power enabled the Soviet Union to satisfy a growing proportion of the rapidly expanding energy and raw material requirements of Eastern Europe's increasingly mineral-intensive industries. In effect, the Soviet Union became willing to underwrite and prop up the expansion of these relatively fragile, mineral-deficient and internationally uncompetitive economies (and thus bind them more closely to itself) by forgoing payment in hard currency for its 'hard' commodity exports and by providing markets for Eastern European manufactured exports, many of which were of poor quality and/or design and could not easily have been sold elsewhere. In addition, in an endeavour to make the new economic systems less rigid and more palatable, the Soviet regime allowed the East European states greater leeway to chart their own courses towards 'socialism' and to humour and conciliate their citizens, although Moscow still laid down the overall political and economic parameters and insisted upon unswerving adherence to the Warsaw Pact and the so-called 'leading role' of the communist parties. Officially, 'national roads to socialism' were deemed necessary and permissible, but Western-style political pluralism was not. On the whole, however, the increased room for manoeuvre granted to the East European regimes enhanced public confidence in their capacity to deliver advances in social and economic welfare. So-called 'national communism' was also an attempt to cultivate specifically 'national' support and allegiances in order to remedy the general lack of legitimacy of several (some would say all) of the communist regimes, especially those that owed their existence mainly to Soviet political or military intervention and hegemony in Eastern Europe.

POLAND

During the early 1960s the Gomulka regime became the epitome of 'national communism'. Since 1956 the ruling party had forsworn forced collectivization of agriculture, relaxed travel and publishing restrictions, conciliated Poland's overwhelmingly Catholic workers, peasants and intellectuals and forged a mutually advantageous *modus vivendi* with the still powerful Roman Catholic Church, whose Polish primate Cardinal Wyszynski had been released from prison (like Gomulka himself) in 1956. Since then the state had relaxed its control of ecclesiastical appointments, religious instruction in the Catholic faith had been restored in the schools, Catholic lay organizations had been licensed to publish their own newspapers and Catholic chaplains had been appointed to state hospitals and prisons. In return, the Church implicitly undertook not to rock the boat politically and to be a force for political and social restraint and moderation. Poland's Roman Catholicism was allowed to flourish, not just as the principal focus and ingredient of national identity, but as the major legally permitted alternative set of beliefs and values which could compete with official Marxism–Leninism and atheism.

At the same time, Gomulka's grandiose industrial projects (including the development of giant steelworks, shipyards and coal mines) enhanced Poland's international standing and national self-esteem. By the mid-1960s, however, he was succumbing to delusions of Polish grandeur and to old-fashioned neo-Stalinist authoritarianism. He became increasingly out of touch with the problems and hardships experienced by ordinary citizens in an over-centralized, lopsided and severely strained economy. In the end the heavy-handed suppression of student unrest in the spring and summer of 1968 and of workers' strikes and mass protests in Poland's Baltic ports and shipyards two years later precipitated Gomulka's removal from office in December 1970.

THE GERMAN DEMOCRATIC REPUBLIC

The most paradoxical manifestations of 'national communism' occurred in the German Democratic Republic (GDR), the European state that was most conspicuously lacking in either national or international legitimacy and support. It was an entirely artificial creation, arising out of the defeat and subsequent partition of the Third Reich at the hands of the victorious Allied powers. It was sometimes portrayed as a new incarnation of the erstwhile kingdoms of Prussia and Saxony. But in reality large swathes of the former Prussian and Saxon 'homelands' had been permanently lost to Poland, Czechoslovakia and the Soviet Union. Furthermore, the East German communist regime initially dissociated itself from the rather murky and disreputable Prussian past, preferring instead to present itself as the 'new broom' that would rid or 'cleanse' the Eastern Zone of Germany of that severely tainted legacy, whereas the (West) German Federal Republic was allegedly controlled by the self-same capitalist 'monopolies' and 'cartels' that had repeatedly endeavoured to gain control of Europe, with such catastrophic results.

The Berlin Wall was built in 1961 in order to increase the GDR's seclusion from the outside world and to staunch the economically debilitating haemorrhage of (mainly young) professional and skilled manpower to the West. But the Wall was more than a monument to the deficiencies of the GDR. It also signalled the determination of the East German regime to win at least a semblance of legitimacy, popular support and public acceptance, by making a serious attempt to catch up with and surpass West Germany both economically and in terms of its social, cultural and sporting provision and achievements, by emphasizing the German provenance of Marxism, and by presenting the GDR as the most 'advanced' Marxist–Leninist state and as a custodian of Marxist 'orthodoxy'. The bid to win popularity and legitimacy by matching and overtaking West German living standards was doomed from the start, especially as large numbers of East Germans were able to make direct comparisons by watching the increasingly glamorous and glamorized images of the West projected by West German television. With more justification, however, the GDR claimed to have the most educated, competent, orderly and scientific civil bureaucracy, economic planners and industrial planners in the Soviet bloc. (Alec Nove used to remark that he could not imagine any economic system of which the Germans would not make a success!) In a belated endeavour to enhance its prestige and authority, it emphasized a conception of Marxism as 'the science of society' and of the Marxist regime as a sort of scientocracy, engaged in the 'scientific' organization and planning of the economy and society by natural and social scientists recruited on the strength of their scientific merit and credentials. This intensified the regime's efforts to draw the country's leading managers, technocrats and natural and social scientists into the ruling elite. As under the Nazi regime, the process was facilitated by the growing awareness among ambitious managers, technocrats and other professional personnel that 'loyal service' to the ruling party could bring meteoric advancement and other rewards, at the expense of those who refused to succumb to such blandishments. At least in the short term, these orientations may have enhanced the status and performance of East German industry, economic planning, science, technology, technical education, health care, sport and classical music-making, without entailing any politically risky decentralization of decision-making or relaxation of the regime's control of the economy and society. Nevertheless, the hard-line and essentially cautious leadership of the GDR inadvertently offended the equally conservative Soviet leadership in 1969–71, in the wake of the August 1968 invasion of Czechoslovakia. The Brezhnev regime took exception to the increasingly headmasterly and presumptuous sermonizing and pontification of the East German party leader, Walter Ulbricht, the (heretical) reductionism of the GDR's 'scientocratic' conceptions of Marxism and of the Marxist regime, the implicit downgrading of the importance of the working class and of non-scientific or non-technocratic party stalwarts recruited from the working class, and the corresponding dilution of orthodox Marxist–Leninist doctrine on the class basis of society and on class struggle as the prime mover of social change. According to Willy Brandt (1978: 184), 'Ulbricht rated as a persistent bore . . . German pedantry (Eastern version) reigned supreme. It can truly be said that the German bent for thoroughness received a special imprint in the GDR.' In 1971 Ulbricht was replaced by a more faceless and deferential party leader, the 'master wall-builder' Erich Honecker (who remained in power until November 1989). He subsequently attempted to cultivate a more conventional form of 'national communism' by posing as a custodian of the previously reviled heritage of Frederick the Great's Prussia and Lutheranism. Martin Luther and Richard Wagner were promoted alongside Marx as 'national' heroes, although perhaps the only traits that all three had in common were their Germanness and their antisemitism (even though Marx was a Jew and Wagner feared he might be one!).

CZECHOSLOVAKIA: SOCIALISM WITH A HUMAN FACE

The most widely applauded and appealing attempt to map out a distinct 'national road to socialism' emerged during the so-called Prague Spring. Indeed, the Czechoslovak reform movement of 1963–68 did not try to jettison either 'socialism' or the hegemonic 'leading role' of the communist party. It merely sought to establish 'socialism with a human face'. The need for reform was widely accepted (not least among members of the party appa-ratus) as an antidote to the economic and political stagnation to which Czechoslovakia had succumbed by the early 1960s. (In this respect, the Prague Spring was a direct antecedent of Gorbachev's *perestroika* in the Soviet Union.) The Czechoslovak economy had boomed during the 1950s, when it had successfully exported large quantities of engineering and metallurgical products to its rapidly industrializing Comecon partners, as well as to China, North Korea, India and Egypt. But in the early 1960s, as the industrializing communist states became less dependent on Czechoslovak producer goods, Czechoslovakia's obsolescent heavy industries went into decline. At the same time, internal economic rigidities and inappropriate neo-Stalinist methods and priorities impeded attempts to develop high-technology industries and to revive and modernize the country's once renowned light industries, which had been greatly impaired both by the post-war expulsion of 3 million Sudeten Germans and by more than a decade of under-investment. Technocratic reformist demands for economic liberalization, led by Ota Sik, began to dovetail with intelligentsia demands for political and cultural liberalization, Slovak autonomy, complete rehabilitation of victims of the 1948–52 era and the restoration of the German-speaking Czech-Jewish writer Franz Kafka (1883–1924) to a place of honour in the pantheon of great Czechoslovak writers. The Prague Spring culminated in the installation of the benign and liberal Slovak Communist Alexander Dubcek as leader of the Czechoslovak Communist Party in January 1968, the liberal 'war hero' General Svoboda as President of Czechoslovakia in March 1968 and the liberal Josef Smrkovsky as speaker of the revitalized Czechoslovak parliament in April 1968. These new leaders studiously avoided any commitment to terminate the political monopoly of the Communist Party, to withdraw from the Warsaw Pact, to decollectivize agriculture or to restore capitalism, and they bent over backwards not to rock the Soviet boat in Eastern Europe. Nevertheless, the liberal Action Programme of April 1968, the abolition of censorship, the infectious exuberance of the 'liberated' populace and the mere existence of the Dubcek regime uncomfortably exposed the hypocrisy, falsehood and coercion on which the other communist regimes still rested. On 20–1 August 1968, following a protracted war of nerves, Czechoslovakia was invaded by a million Warsaw Pact troops. Dubcek, Smrkovsky, Premier Cernik and the Popular Front chairman Frantisek Kriegel were abducted to Moscow. But President Svoboda's intercession, Moscow's initial inability to find a hard-line collaborator capable of controlling the situation and widespread Czechoslovak refusal to co-operate with the invaders secured their leaders' release, full reinstatement and a chance to prove (through initially successful appeals for self-restraint) that they alone could control Czechoslovakia at the time. However, Dubcek was unable to prevent major demonstrations against the military occupation forces, first in late October and early November 1968, then in sympathy for the self-immolation of young Jan Palach in Wenceslas Square in January 1969 and finally after Czechoslovakia beat the Soviet Union at an ice-hockey match in March 1969. This last event unleashed such uncontrollable mass jubilation in the streets of

Prague that in April 1969 Dubcek was obliged to relinquish the Communist Party leadership to the hard-line Slovak collaborator, Gustav Husak. The Husak regime soon sacked, demoted or imprisoned several hundred thousand supporters of the Prague Spring and put Czechoslovak society into a deep freeze from which it did not thaw until the miraculous autumn of 1989. In the meantime, most people withdrew into extreme privacy ('internal emigration'), consumerism, careerism, cynicism or corruption.

The Czechoslovak reform movement had been dominated by the country's relatively large and well educated intelligentsia. This was to be a source of both strength and weakness. Its leaders were articulate and commanded great moral and intellectual respect. They displayed an unusual breadth of interests and concerns. But, in contrast to the Hungarian Revolution of 1956, the Prague Spring failed to evoke large-scale peasant and working-class participation, and the Warsaw Pact invasion of Czechoslovakia in August 1968 did not meet with widespread and tenacious armed resistance from those quarters. The Prague Spring was to some extent another Revolution of the Intellectuals (like that of 1848) and it was partly for this reason that it failed. The prominence of the intelligentsia made it that much easier to denounce as a 'counter-revolution' directed against the interests of the working class and 'the workers' state', while the conspicuous role played by a few Czech-Jewish intellectuals prompted slanderous Soviet allegations that the movement was part of an international Zionist conspiracy to subvert the socialist bloc. Indeed, the Warsaw Pact invasion of Czechoslovakia was launched in the name of 'proletarian internationalism', and on 25 September 1968 *Pravda* proclaimed that the decisions of the peoples and the communist parties of the socialist countries 'must harm neither socialism in their own country nor the fundamental interests of other socialist countries'.

ALBANIA

One of the most extreme versions of 'national communism' emerged in Albania. Albania is surrounded by Serbian, Montenegrin, Greek and Italian neighbours who have not only harboured 'historic' or 'strategic' claims on Albanian-inhabited territory but have repeatedly attempted to carve the country up between them. It is therefore not surprising that Albania's local potentates have tended to look to great-power 'patrons' and 'protectors' (the Ottoman Turks, Italy, the Soviet Union and China), before subsequently discovering or deciding that each of these putative 'protectors' was really just another would-be overlord and predator. Albania had attained a fragile national independence during the inter-war years, only to find itself annexed by Fascist Italy (its erstwhile 'patron') in 1939. During the early 1940s there arose rival Albanian nationalist, royalist and communist resistance movements, which fought each other as well as the Italian occupation forces. Following the collapse of Fascist Italy in 1943, however, the country was invaded by the Nazis in order to prevent it from falling into Allied hands. Before long the Allies switched their support from the ambivalent royalist and republican nationalist resistance movements to the more consistently effective and anti-fascist communist forces led by Enver Hoxha. The latter gradually gained the upper hand and, having captured Tirana from the retreating Germans in November 1944, proceeded to establish a hard-line communist regime. Repeated Anglo-American attempts to overthrow the Hoxha regime in 1947, 1949, 1950 and 1952 were foiled with the help of the infamous British double agent Kim Philby. He not only played a pivotal role in the organization of these Albanian adventures but also disclosed the relevant details to the Soviet security services, who in turn tipped off Hoxha, with the result that hundreds of British- and American-backed insurgents were killed or captured by the Albanian authorities virtually on arrival (Jelavich 1983b: 378–9). These operations, combined with deepening resentment against Yugoslav communist tutelage and interference in Albania's internal affairs, caused a rapid deterioration in Hoxha's relations with his former British, American and Yugoslav wartime allies. They helped to transform this relatively Westernized, cosmopolitan and middle-class Marxist intellectual (who had been a student in France and Belgium in the 1930s) into Eastern Europe's most paranoid and xenophobic communist dictator, who naturally turned to and increasingly modelled himself upon Stalin. Hoxha's severance of all links with Yugoslavia in 1948 resulted in increased Albanian dependence on Soviet economic and technical assistance during the 1950s. But Khrushchev's world-famous 'secret speech' denouncing Stalin in March 1956, the Soviet invasion of Hungary in November 1956, the Soviet leader's acceptance of the need for 'peaceful coexistence with the West', the concurrent *rapprochement* between the Soviet Union and Yugoslavia and finally the Sino-Soviet schism of 1960–61 all contributed to Hoxha's decision to side with Mao's China against the Soviet Union, which he henceforth denounced as a 'revisionist' and 'social imperialist' power. In Hoxha's memoirs, significantly, Stalin is described as having been 'kindly and considerate', whereas Khrushchev is portrayed as a 'blackmailer' who wanted to turn Albania into a 'fruit-growing colony'. Not surprisingly, Soviet tutelage and assistance abruptly gave way to Chinese economic aid and technicians during the 1960s. All the while Albania continued to develop a modern education system, agriculture (including irrigation), hydro-electric power and some large-scale centrally planned extractive and processing industries, but not much else.

Under Hoxha, Albania avoided the so-called 'capitalist scourges' of unemployment, inflation, income tax, private cars, pop music, blue jeans, short skirts, pornography, foreign investment, foreign credits and external debt. Adult illiteracy rates were reduced from about 85 per cent (in 1938) to less than 10 per cent within the space of just two generations, while average life expectancy rose from thirty-eight (in 1938) to seventy-one (in 1985). But Albanian society became highly regimented and living standards remained very low. Moreover, taking his cue from Mao's China, Hoxha inaugurated an egalitarian 'proletarian cultural revolution' and radical programmes of 'workers' control' and administrative decentralization in 1966. In 1967 he proceeded to ban foreign travel, Western influences and all religious institutions and practices, having proclaimed Albania to be the world's first 'atheist state'. Over 2,000 churches and mosques were either pulled down or turned into warehouses, clinics, classrooms or so-called 'state museums of atheism and religion', while the former clergy were either 're-educated' in prison and labour camps or forced to retire. Apart from simple emulation of the egalitarian, 'proletarian', xenophobic and anti-religious features of China's Great Proletarian Cultural Revolution (1966–69), these policies were probably also intended to curb any potential threat to national unity and state security arising from the divergent Moslem, Roman Catholic and Eastern Orthodox allegiances of Albania's inhabitants and to insulate the country from foreign or transnational ideologies and cultural influences. During the 1960s and 1970s the Albanian economy, education system and health services continued to develop impressively, but Hoxha's autarkic, xenophobic, isolationist policies and excessive regulation and regimentation of society eventually engendered severe forms of economic, social and political stagnation and corruption, especially after he had severed relations with China in 1978, having accused the new post-Maoist leadership of succumbing to capitalism and 'social revisionism'. Yet many non-communist Albanians were still prepared to put up with Hoxha's oppressive and intrusive regime because, whatever his faults, he was a doughty champion of Albania's national independence. He was an ardent admirer of Stalin and Mao, but he never sold out to them completely or unconditionally. Above all, he wanted to be regarded as a latter-day Skanderbeg (Albania's fifteenth-century 'national hero'). 'In the eyes of many Albanians he succeeded', according to the former Balkan correspondent of the BBC, Misha Glenny (writing in *The Guardian*, 22 May 1990, p. 10).

ROMANIA

In the case of Romania 'national communism' developed partly as a reassertion of inter-war traditions of economic nationalism, encapsulated in the Bratianu Liberals' slogan *Prin noi insine* (By ourselves alone), and partly in reaction to the overbearing behaviour of the Soviet regime and its Romanian 'sepoys' towards Romania from 1944 to 1952, during the ascendancy of Petru Groza and the so-called 'Moscow communists', Ana Pauker, Emil Bodnaras, Vasile Luca and Teohary Georgescu. The latter were former Romanian exiles who had spent the early 1940s in Moscow, where they were groomed by the Soviet regime as potential rulers of a future communist Romania. In 1952 the so-called 'Moscow communists' were ousted by resentful (and hitherto subordinate) 'native communists', headed by the Communist Party leader, Gheorghe Gheorgiu-Dej, and his old wartime associates Chivu Stoica, Ion Gheorghe Maurer and Nicolae Ceausescu. (They had spent much of the Second World War together in various Romanian prisons, where they had forged close personal ties.) Aside from purging the widely reviled 'Moscow communists', their decisive first step was to dissolve the unpopular joint Soviet–Romanian companies (the so-called 'sovroms') that had been established in order to exploit Romania's natural wealth with the 'assistance' of Soviet capital, technology and technical personnel and, to a considerable extent, for Soviet benefit. In addition, partly as a reward for 'loyal' (even gleeful) Romanian participation in the armed suppression of the 1956 Revolution in Romania's arch-enemy Hungary, the ascendant 'native communists' secured the full withdrawal of the Soviet military forces that had been stationed in (formerly 'fascist') Romania since late 1944. Having thus been freed from the permanent presence of Soviet 'occupation forces' (with 1962 being the last year in which Warsaw Pact military exercises were held on Romanian territory), during the early 1960s Romania's new 'native' rulers angrily rejected Comecon proposals that their relatively underdeveloped country should specialize in the production and exportation of primary products and import more sophisticated manufactures from its more industrialized Comecon partners instead of attempting to produce them itself.

There was ever-increasing emphasis on autarkic ('self-reliant') development of heavy industries such as steel, oil and chemicals under Nicolae Ceausescu, who smoothly succeeded Gheorgiu-Dej as Communist Party leader in 1965. Furthermore, in contrast to other East European members of Comecon, Ceausescu refused to break off relations either with China (during the Sino-Soviet dispute) or with Israel (over the Arab–Israeli War of 1967). In a speech to 100,000 people assembled in the Piata Republici on 21 August 1968 he even condemned the Warsaw Pact invasion of Czechoslovakia (in which

Romania refused to participate): 'The penetration of the troops of five socialist countries into Czechoslovakia is a great mistake and a grave danger to peace in Europe, to the fate of socialism . . . There is no justification whatsoever and no reason can be given for admitting for even a single moment the idea of military intervention in the affairs of a fraternal socialist state . . . The problem of choosing the roads to socialism is a problem of the respective party, the respective state, the respective people. Nobody can pose as adviser, as a guide to the way in which socialism has to be built in another country. We maintain that in order to place the relations between the socialist countries, between the communist parties, on a truly Marxist–Leninist basis, an end must be put for good and all to interference in the affairs of other states, in other parties . . . We have decided to start from today forming armed patriotic detachments of workers, peasants and intellectuals, defenders of the independence of our socialist homeland . . . Here among us are many communists and anti-fascists who faced prison and death, but we have never betrayed the interests of the working class, of our people. Be sure, comrades, be sure, citizens of Romania, that we shall never betray our homeland' (quoted in Catchlove 1972: 108–9).

This was a courageous stand and, even though it initially exacerbated Romanian fears that their independent-minded and militarily vulnerable country could be invaded even more easily than either Czechoslovakia or Hungary (while evoking even fewer reprisals from the West), it considerably enhanced Ceausescu's domestic and international reputation in the immediate aftermath of 1968. There was also a temporary relaxation of the censorship of books, films and plays, an upsurge in the screening of Western films and a more enduring rehabilitation of non-communist literary classics. Consequently, Ceausescu was courted not merely by China and Israel, but also by the West, which for a time mistook his nationalism for liberalism and regarded him as a useful thorn in the Soviet Union's side. All the while, however, Romania remained essentially a hard-line Stalinist regime in terms of its domestic policies and priorities. And it was perhaps inevitable (given Romania's deep-seated traditions of corruption and nepotism) that it degenerated into a particularly venal, in-bred and incompetent 'socialism in one family', as the Ceausescu clan gradually monopolized the perquisites of office and cracked down on anyone who dared to criticize them for doing so.

BULGARIA

Like Romania, Bulgaria was ruled by so-called 'Moscow communists' (who had taken refuge in Moscow during the Second World War) from late 1944 to the early 1950s. In this case they were headed by some quite high-ranking figures in the international communist movement, most notably Georgi Dimitrov, who had won international fame as an outspoken defendant in Hitler's Reichstag fire show trial in 1934 and as president of the Communist International (Comintern) from 1935 to 1943, before serving as Prime Minister of Bulgaria from 1947 until his (natural) death in 1949. He was succeeded as Prime Minister by his brother-in-law, Vulko Chervenkov (1949–56 and 1958–60). Nevertheless, as in Romania, during the 1950s the 'Moscow communists' were gradually removed from power by a so-called 'native communist', Todor Zhivkov, who had spent the war years in Bulgaria and became leader of the Bulgarian Communist Party from 1954 until he was deposed in 1989. However, in spite of his assiduous promotion of 'native communists' and certain Bulgarian writers and musicians, his partial adoption of nationalist political and historical rhetoric and his subsequent harassment of ethnic minorities such as the Gypsies and the Turks, in his external relations Zhivkov did not emulate the nationalistic postures of Romania's 'native communists'. As a fellow Slavic and Orthodox nation with a very similar language, Bulgaria had long regarded Russia as a patron and protector. Indeed, when Comecon began to promote increased economic specialization among its member states in 1962, Bulgaria readily accepted its assigned role as a major supplier of fresh and processed Mediterranean agricultural and horticultural products to the Soviet Union and East Central Europe. (The foundations of successful production and exportation of relatively lucrative and intensive agricultural and horticultural products had already been laid during the 1930s, as mentioned in Chapter 15.) In return for this and for Zhivkov's slavish and unwavering 'loyalty' to the Soviet Union on international and doctrinal matters such as the invasion of Czechoslovakia and the curtailment of relations with China and Israel, Bulgaria received steadily increasing deliveries of subsidized Soviet fuels and raw materials, industrial equipment, nuclear power plant and technological assistance, most of which facilitated Bulgarian industrialization.

HUNGARY

'National communism' developed most successfully in Hungary under Janos Kadar, the Communist Party leader, who had participated in the Soviet invasion of his own country in November 1956 and remained in power until May 1988. From late 1961 onward, after political repression and the recollectivization of Hungarian agriculture had brutally but effectively reimposed party control and convinced the Soviet regime that its new Hungarian 'collaborators' had put their political house in order, Kadar offered an olive branch to the Hungarian intelligentsia, working class, peasantry and even Catholics by promulgating the slogan 'those who are not against us are with us'. To this end, political censorship and travel restrictions were progressively relaxed, the political police were reined in, there was increased observance of due legal process and the rule of law, the state negotiated a concordat with the Roman Catholic Church (in 1964) and most of Hungary's political prisoners were gradually amnestied, released and rehabilitated. In effect, Kadar offered Hungarians increased economic and cultural freeedom as a substitute for more radical changes in the country's political system. This 'pact with the devil' particularly appealed to those who were weary of revolutionary upheaval, repression, privation and anxiety about the future. In addition, non-party luminaries were increasingly encouraged to play a prominent role in intellectual and cultural life, in public administration and in programmes of economic reform. In their eagerness to expand and to take full advantage of the new freedoms, Hungarian writers, film-makers and musicians did much to repair and restore their country's international standing. Ironically, the unsavoury origins of the Kadar regime also gave it a latent advantage. Over 85 per cent of the 800,000 people who were members of the ruling party in the autumn of 1956 had left it by 1958 (Molnar 1971: 251). Thus the need and the opportunity to rebuild the ruling party in his own image helped Kadar to retain full control of the pace, direction and extent of his liberalization and reform programmes. This enabled him largely to avoid (or at least contain within safe limits) potentially hazardous in-fighting between hard-line 'dogmatists' and reforming 'revisionists' within the governing elite. (Nevertheless, conflicts of this sort did contribute to a temporary setback in the reform process during the 1970s and to the regime's final downfall in

1988–89.) Furthermore, the fact that Kadar was so clearly the master of his own house made him invaluable, perhaps even indispensable, to the Soviet leadership, which therefore gave him a relatively free hand to pursue liberalization and reform in accordance with his own judgement of what was politically acceptable and sustainable.

In the rural sector, which still accounted for about half of Hungary's population in the 1960s, the new collective farms were granted unprecedented commercial and managerial autonomy in recognition of their (hitherto ignored) formal legal status as autonomous self-managed agricultural producers' co-operatives. Peasant hostility to collectivization, evinced by a mass exodus from collective farms in 1956, was also mollified by official encouragement of private sidelines or by-employment within the re-collectivized sector, by the resultant proliferation of rural industrial co-operatives and by a rapid expansion of rural services and amenities. The collective farmers responded by vigorously expanding Hungary's agricultural production and exports, especially food and wine exports to Western markets, thus reinforcing the revival in Hungary's international visibility and standing. During the 1960s food and drinks production provided one-third of Hungarian employment and gross material product and nearly half the country's hard currency earnings (Bideleux 1987: 188). Agriculture was in fact the seedbed of Hungary's so-called 'market socialism', as the new commercial and managerial freedoms which produced such successful results in this sector were gradually extended to the food-processing, catering, retailing, personal services and handicrafts sectors. Then in January 1968, while Soviet and Western attention was nervously fixed upon the more dramatic political and economic changes that were being introduced in neighbouring Czechoslovakia, the Kadar regime quietly inaugurated a comprehensive and carefully prepared New Economic Mechanism in Hungary. Henceforth industrial productivity growth, innovation and responsiveness were to be promoted by encouraging industrial enterprises to establish direct contractual relations with one another and with their final customers at home and abroad, to become self-financing, and to use repayable interest-bearing credits in place of outright grants from the state budget. State subsidies were sharply reduced and mandatory central directives and the centralized allocation of supplies were largely superseded by indirect economic regulators, such as fiscal and monetary instruments, credit policy, wage and price controls, foreign trade licences and multiple exchange rates. Consequently, by 1971 manufacturing enterprises were funding two-thirds of their fixed investment, mandatory output targets had been largely abandoned, only 3–4 per cent of the 'intermediate' (producer) goods used by industry were centrally allocated and Hungary had ceased to be a command economy, even though large-scale industry remained state-owned (Granick 1975: 242–82). As a counterweight to the increased commercial and financial autonomy and powers of enterprise managers, the still party-controlled trade unions were exhorted to become more active in defending and representing workers' interests. Indeed, the 1967 labour code gave them a regularly used right to veto some management decisions, and unions retained a major role in national policy-making, in the maintenance of labour discipline and in the administration of holidays, sick leave and social welfare benefits. Enterprise managers were neither empowered nor permitted to dismiss workers at will, and industrial over-manning and inefficiency were supposed to be reduced mainly through mergers and redeployment rather than through socially disruptive and politically hazardous plant closures and dismissals. Nevertheless, in spite of fears that the new system would be plagued by labour immobility, labour turnover averaged 32–36 per cent per annum from 1968 to 1971 (pp.

245–7). Moreover, the worker's lot was far from being a bed of roses. The sheer size of Hungarian industrial enterprises was more conducive to hierarchy, inequality and workers' alienation than to the growth of workers' participation, control and contentment, as emphasized by Miklos Haraszti in his famous report on the soulless work regime at the Red Star tractor factory (Haraszti 1977). By 1973 Hungary had, on average, 1,070 employees per industrial enterprise, which was more than ten times the average for many Western states (Bideleux 1987: 147).

All the same, many Hungarians prospered under Kadar's reforming rule. For some people, Kadarism signified a purely materialistic 'refrigerator communism': better food, consumer durables, fashion goods, weekend cottages in the countryside and foreign travel. Yet for others it also held out the promise of a spiritual release from the grim repressiveness and restrictions of Stalinism and the initial post-1956 regime. Within the limits dictated by prudence and by memories of 1956, it allowed the natural energy, ebullience and creativity of the Hungarian people to effervesce into economic and cultural achievement. The Kadarist social contract was nevertheless highly vulnerable, and it is perhaps remarkable that it survived for so long. There was an ever-present danger that the economic and cultural fermentation which it both required and evoked could bubble out of control, outgrowing the political limits set by Kadar and by Hungary's Soviet overlords. Most Hungarians realized that their country was constantly 'on probation', at least during the 1960s and 1970s, and this was a source of deep-seated resentment which eventually burst into the open in the late 1980s. Furthermore, in owing its origin to Soviet military intervention, and in being unable to admit the truth about the course of events from October 1956 up to the execution of Imre Nagy on 16 June 1959, the Kadar regime always lacked political legitimacy. Its survival therefore depended upon qualified and pragmatic popular acceptance of its promise of limited and conditional liberalization and sustained increases in economic prosperity. This made the regime and its small, mineral-deficient economy exceptionally vulnerable to external factors which were beyond Kadar's control, especially to international economic fluctuations.

YUGOSLAVIA

The circumstances of its birth gave Marshal Tito's Yugoslav communist regime the freedom and authority to define its own distinctive 'Yugoslav road to socialism'. Yugoslavia had been liberated from fascism by the often heroic resistance of a million communist-led Partisans, with meagre assistance from the West, the Soviet Union and the Serbian nationalist chetniks. The communists created the one Yugoslav movement that succeeded in transcending the country's perilous religious and ethnic divisions and drawing substantial support from each of its constituent ethnic groups. At first, however, their hard-won 'liberation' of Yugoslavia transformed the leading Yugoslav communists into headstrong, unremitting ultra-Stalinists. Against Stalin's wishes, they actively supported the communist side in the Greek civil war (1945–49), lorded it over Hoxha's Albania and talked of creating a communist-ruled Balkan Federation strong enough to stand up to Soviet hegemonism. In 1947, contrary to Soviet advice, they launched a premature and over-ambitious five-year plan for rapid state-directed development of heavy industry and mechanized large-scale collective agriculture, for which they expected the Soviet Union to provide a large part of the requisite resources (especially fuels, equipment, capital and technical assistance). This Stalinist development strategy was singularly inappropriate for Yugoslavia, which lacked a suitable human and natural resource base. The mainly mountainous terrain did not readily lend itself to large-scale mechanized cultivation, the requisite economic and political centralization could only revive inter-war resentment of Serbian domination, and it was highly unlikely that peasants who had successfully resisted fascism would now meekly submit to forced collectivization. When Tito's regime refused to come to heel, Yugoslavia was 'excommunicated' from the Soviet bloc in 1948 – not as the result of any developmental or ideological heterodoxy, but for getting 'too big for its boots' and trying to be even more Stalinist than Stalin. Deprived of crucial imports and technical assistance from the Soviet Union and Czechoslovakia, the Yugoslav economy was plunged into crisis. Initial headstrong attempts to persevere with ultra-Stalinism unaided from 1948 to 1950 actually deepened the crisis still further, and Tito's regime probably survived only because it was unexpectedly bailed out by massive Western aid (amounting to over US$2 billion at 1950s prices) during the 1950s. (By way of comparison, American Marshall Aid to the whole of Western Europe came to US$13 billion at early 1950s prices.)

Consequently, the quest for a distinctively Yugoslav road to socialism did not really begin until after the ignominious collapse of Tito's initial over-ambitious ultra-Stalinism in 1950. Henceforth, to have any real chance of success, the communist regime would have to build on its vaunted capacity to transcend Yugoslavia's religious and ethnic divisions. Since no ethnic group constituted an absolute majority of the population, a Soviet-style federation dominated by the largest ethnic group would have been neither acceptable nor workable in a country which had been riven by inter-ethnic and interdenominational strife as recently as the Second World War. That made it all the more vital to move towards a system that could devolve decision-making to local or regional institutions, in the hope that this would assist and encourage the diverse nations within the Yugoslav Federation to live and work together peacefully and constructively. However, since mere regional devolution could just as easily have reinforced the strong centrifugal tendencies in Yugoslav society, there was an even stronger case for devolving power to the lowest possible level, i.e. to individual enterprises and local communes. This came to be seen as the framework most capable of peaceably holding Yugoslavia together. An embryonic system of 'workers' self-management' emerged in 1950, when elected workers' councils with a key role in enterprise management were established in almost all industrial enterprises employing more than thirty workers each. By 1952 there were workers' councils in 8,800 industrial enterprises, including 4,187 enterprises with less than thirty workers apiece. Between them these employed over a million workers. According to the June 1950 Basic Law on workers' councils, 'state economic enterprises, as the property of the people, shall be managed by working collectives on behalf of the social community, within the framework of the state economic plan . . . Working collectives will exercise this right of management through the workers' councils' (quoted in Singleton 1976: 126).

The development of Western and Algerian ideas on workers' participation and industrial democracy and Tito's central role in the launching of the Non-aligned Movement in 1955 provided additional motives for distancing his own communist regime doctrinally from those of the Soviet bloc. The 1958 Programme of the League of Communists of Yugoslavia (as the party was renamed in 1953) warned that managing the economy and society 'exclusively through the state apparatus inevitably leads to greater centralization of power' and thence to 'bureaucratic-etatist deformities' and the betrayal of socialism. The preferred 'way out' of the cul-de-sac of state socialism was to instigate forms of direct participatory democracy and direct producers' control of the means of production. Thus the state was expected gradually to 'wither away' as socialist consciousness and new autonomous forms of collectivism developed. The state was intended to become 'less an instrument of coercion and more and more an instrument of social self-government, based on the consciousness of the common material interests of working people and on the concrete needs of their producing organizations'. The League of Communists of Yugoslavia (the SKJ) was still expected 'to give ideological guidance in the process of socialist development . . . But this does not confer any special prerogatives or privileges on members of the League' (quoted in Singleton 1976: 135–6). To these ends, compulsory deliveries of farm produce to the state were discontinued in 1950, enterprise managers ceased to be central government appointees after 1951, rural collectivization and command planning were finally abandoned in 1952, and public administration was largely devolved to local communes and the constituent Republics of the Yugoslav Federation in 1953, leaving only five Ministries (employing less than 4 per cent of public officials) in the hands of central government. The 1963 constitution extended the principle of 'self-management' to education, health and social administration, introduced 'rotation' of all elective offices (other than Tito's 'presidency for life') and prohibited individuals from simultaneously holding office in the state apparatus and in the SKJ or in both Federal and Republican bodies. But until 1965, for the most part, Yugoslavia continued to be managed from the centre and in accordance with political rather than economic criteria, while in practice decentralization was mainly to Republics and local communes rather than to enterprises. Most prices were still regulated by central or Republican authorities and banks, credit, foreign trade and most investment remained centrally controlled. Most enterprise directors continued to be political appointees, chosen through elaborate systems of patronage and clientelism, rather than freely elected representatives of the work force. Indeed, so long as enterprises had little political or commercial autonomy, there was not much scope for genuine workers' self-management.

During 1965 and 1966, however, the champions of full decentralization and enterprise autonomy decisively outmanoeuvred and defeated the centralizers (who were headed by the Serb security chief Alexander Rankovich) and breathed new life into the hitherto cosmetic or even moribund system of self-management. Yet critics claimed that full-blown self-management (lasting from 1965 to 1974) gave insufficiently accountable and often monopolistic enterprises undue licence to do as they pleased, with highly inflationary, inegalitarian and anti-social consequences, even when enterprise directors took decisions in consultation with their workers. Therefore, from 1974 onwards, enterprises were to varying degrees circumscribed by various investment and price controls, planning agreements, 'social contracts' and macro-economic stabilization programmes, in (often vain) endeavours to limit the resultant over-investment, wage inflation, excess demand, over-expansion of the money supply, trade deficits and mounting foreign indebtedness, while registered unemployment rose from an average of 7 per cent of the work force in the 1960s to an average of 10 per cent in the 1970s and 13 per cent in the 1980s.

In spite of these problems, however, during the 1960s and 1970s Tito's increasingly decentralized and confederal Yugoslavia managed to achieve rapid economic growth, which was buoyed up by booming tourism earnings and emigrants' remittances, yet managed to contain the demands for even greater autonomy which erupted in (largely Albanian) Kosovo in 1968 (and again in 1981) and in Croatia from 1970 to 1972. At least until Tito's death in 1980, it seemed that rampant consumerism, judicious federalism and the Marshal's firm hand and 'divide and rule' tactics were keeping the upper hand over potentially fractious and fratricidal sectarianism and 'ethnic' nationalism. There was widespread peaceful coexistence, intermarriage and mutual reconciliation between diverse ethnic and religious communities, most notably in Bosnia-Hercegovina, and there were some genuine grounds for hope that inter-ethnic hatreds were being assuaged by constructive achievement and that secularization was at last taking the sting out of age-old religious tensions. Beneath the seemingly calm surface, however, local communist potentates were cultivating and consolidating increasingly 'national' clienteles and fiefdoms within the constituent Republics and within Serbia's autonomous regions. These developments, in combination with the concurrent Catholic, Orthodox and Muslim religious revivals in Croatia, Serbia and Bosnia-Hercegovina, reinforced the centrifugal ethnic and confessional allegiances and aspirations that were finally to tear Yugoslavia apart during the early 1990s (almost as brutally as they had done during the early 1940s). The violent break-up of the Yugoslav Federation might have been avoided if its communist rulers (particularly at the Republican level) had not stirred up and used 'ethnic' nationalism for their own purposes, especially in order to cling to power by fomenting 'states of emergency' which served to prolong their authoritarian rule. This metamorphosis of Yugoslavia's Republican communist politicians into authoritarian-nationalist rulers was accomplished with consummate Machiavellian skill, but at a terrible human and economic cost. It left poisonous legacies which could take decades to overcome.

THE DARK SIDE OF 'NATIONAL COMMUNISM'

Thus the evolution of the East European communist regimes towards 'national communism' was, in varying degrees, a retrograde rather than a progressive trend. It was naively welcomed by many myopic Western commentators as a retreat from the rigours of communist internationalism and as an attempt to gain greater political legitimacy by pandering to deep-rooted (and mostly brutish) nationalist traditions and aspirations. But it naturally paved the way for increased discrimination and fulmination against ethnic and religious minorities, be they Jews, Gypsies, Turks, Magyars, Albanians or whatever, and it made the eventual transitions to 'post-communism' much nastier and more fraught with dangers of intolerance, authoritarianism, demagogy and inter-communal violence. As Godfrey Hodgson remarked in 1991, 'Everywhere reconstruction is hindered by the revival of nationalism; not only the jealousies of nation states, but the ancient aspirations and resentments of the buried nations and provinces that were treated as so many estates to be exploited by the Russian, German, Austro-Hungarian, Turkish, Nazi and Stalinist empires' (*The Independent on Sunday*, 13 October 1991). The greatest bounties that communism could have offered the region were rooted in its formal 'internationalist' commitment to the goal of transcending inter-ethnic and interdenominational jealousies and conflicts, which have been the bane of twentieth-century Eastern Europe. Communist rule did initially suppress, contain or restrain the destructive nationalist and religious aspirations of the inter-war period and the early 1940s. But, even before the gradual abandonment of 'internationalism' in favour of 'national communism', the Stalinist purges of 1948–52 were strongly influenced by crude 'ethnic' stereotyping, hatreds and vendettas. In succumbing to nationalist demagogy and mind sets, the communist regimes muffed their main chance to do something creditable in this fatally riven region.

THE INTERNATIONAL SOCIALIST DIVISION OF LABOUR, 1960–68

During the 1960s East European economists and reformers increasingly looked to the development of foreign trade and other external economic relations as an important way of increasing economic specialization, economies of scale, factor productivity and the returns on investment. This was seen as a basis for more 'intensive' patterns of economic growth, making more productive use of more slowly growing resource inputs, now that the previous potential and scope for 'extensive' economic growth had been largely exhausted. They were also prodded in this direction by the example of Western Europe (which was achieving impressive increases in output and factor productivity partly on the basis of increased economic integration) as well as by fears that East European access to West European markets might in time be curtailed by the 'group preferences' of the European Community (Brabant 1989: 65).

Mainly for these reasons, the December 1961 council session of Comecon approved the Basic Principles of the International Socialist Division of Labour. These proclaimed that each socialist country would draw up its own economic development plan on the basis of 'the concrete conditions in the given country, the political and economic goals set out by the Communist and Workers' Parties, and the needs and potentialities of all the socialist countries', thus combining 'the development of each national economy with the development and consolidation of the world economic system of socialism as a whole'. The explicit objectives of this International Socialist Division of Labour were 'more efficient social production, a higher rate of economic growth, higher living standards . . . industrialization and gradual removal of historical differences in economic development levels of the socialist countries, and the creation of a material basis for their more-or-less simultaneous transition to communism'. (Most of the text is reproduced in Kaser 1967: 249–54.) The planned International Socialist Division of Labour would contribute to 'the maximum utilization of the advantages of the socialist world system . . . the determination of correct proportions in the national economy of each country . . . the rational location of production . . . the effective utilization of labour and material resources, and . . the strengthening of the defensive power of the socialist camp' (quoted in Brabant 1989: 67). While the 'principal means' of realizing these objectives would continue to be the 'co-ordination of economic plans', this would have to be 'strong and stable', since 'any deviation, even by a single country, would inevitably lead to disturbances in the economic cycle in the other socialist countries' (Kaser 1967: 251). More controversially, the Basic Principles talked of 'concentrating production of similar products in one or several socialist countries', exploring 'the possibilities for further specialization in agricultural production' and 'resultant recommendations for specialization and co-operation' (pp. 252–4). This appeared to imply that some states could be asked to concentrate on agriculture while others would specialize in industry. In November 1962, moreover, Khrushchev proclaimed the need for 'a common single planning organ . . . composed of representatives of all countries coming to CMEA' (quoted in Smith 1983: 183).

In practice, however, the Comecon states did little to implement the Basic Principles, whose implicit supranationalism was resisted by Czechoslovakia, Hungary, Poland and, most volubly, Romania (Brabant 1989: 69–70). They generated more vituperation than integration. Romania's increasingly nationalistic communist elite was committed to autarkic forced industrialization and indignantly denied that Comecon had any right to 'recommend' a self-respecting sovereign state to specialize in agriculture. In April 1964 the Central Committee of the Romanian Communist Party issued a public declaration that industry, not agriculture, held the key to the 'harmonious, balanced and ever-ascending . . . growth of the whole national economy' and that the proposed transfer of some economic responsibilities 'from the competence of the respective state' to supranational bodies was unacceptable, for two main reasons: (i) 'The planned management of the national economy is one of the fundamental, essential, inalienable attributes of the sovereignty of the socialist state' and the chief means by which it 'achieves its political and socio-economic objectives'; and (ii) 'The state plan is one and indivisible', since centrally planned 'management of the national economy as a whole is not possible if the questions of managing some branches or enterprises are . . . transferred to extra-state bodies'. (The full text is reproduced in Vaughan 1976: 148–50.) In a sense, this was a new unilateral declaration of Romanian independence.

Beyond the nationalist claptrap there lurked serious operational considerations. Comprehensive *national* economic planning really did depend upon untrammelled *national* economic sovereignty. It was becoming increasingly clear to East European economists that the proposed surrender of various planning and co-ordinating functions to Comecon agencies would not only further impair national economic planning, but also reproduce at the supranational level (and in greatly magnified forms) most of the rigidities, diseconomies, disincentives and malfunctions that already bedevilled central planning at the national level (Brabant 1989: 70). Politically, it would have increased the preponderance of Soviet predilections over those of its much smaller East European 'vassals'.

Ironically, the Soviet Union had declined to impose supranational planning and a thoroughgoing international socialist division of labour in the early 1950s, when it still had the power to do just that, whereas by the early 1960s the Soviet leadership had acquired the will but forfeited the power to do so (Wiles 1968: 311). Furthermore, the emergence of major East European reform movements between 1961 and 1968, along with the more enduring expansion of East–West trade and 'co-operation', somewhat reduced the pressure to develop intra-CMEA 'co-operation' and integration, which could indeed have restricted Eastern Europe's room for manoeuvre (both in the pursuit of domestic economic restructuring and in the cultivation of West European economic partners). Conversely, the significant 1960s expansion of East–West economic relations (including subcontracting and the importation of 'turnkey' installations) seemed to reduce 'the need to adapt the CMEA economic structures to the fundamental requirements of more ambitious economic reforms' (Brabant 1989: 77). It was in many ways easier and more immediately rewarding for the centrally planned economies to expand their links with the West than with each other. This was not merely the line of least resistance, but also the avenue of maximum advantage, as East–West trade offered increased access to much-needed Western products, equipment, technology, finance, design and more modern production, management and marketing systems.

Intra-CMEA co-operation, specialization and integration did none the less make some headway during the 1960s, mainly by sidestepping the resistance of 'national' vested interests. There were expanded roles for Comecon's sectoral and functional standing commissions, mirroring sectoral and 'neo-functionalist' approaches to West European integration. Six new standing commissions were established, including ones to deal with standardization, scientific and technical co-operation, statistics and currency and finance. This was supplemented by increased reliance on bilateral and trilateral joint ventures and the exchange of East European manufactures, equipment and foodstuffs for Soviet oil, gas, coal, metal ores and nuclear technology. Comecon's physical cohesion was considerably enhanced by the construction of the *Druzhba* (Friendship) oil pipeline, in order to increase East European reliance on imported Soviet oil (and on re-exports of refined oil products to earn precious hard currency), and the *Mir* (Peace) electricity grid, in order to 'even out' power supplies. An International Bank for Economic Co-operation was founded in 1963, in an unsuccessful attempt to facilitate multilateral intra-CMEA 'clearing' via the new 'transferable rouble'. In 1967, moreover, Comecon adopted the so-called 'interested party principle'. This allowed individual member states simply to opt out of any Comecon project they did not like, permitting the rest to go ahead unencumbered by awkward or reluctant participants. In the last resort, a member state could veto a Comecon project or policy which was deemed to threaten its vital national interests, since Comecon's joint decision-making still rested ultimately on unanimity or consensus between 'equal' and 'sovereign' member states.

As mentioned before, the tenacious predominance of bilateralism over multilateralism could have been overcome only by supranational central planning of Comecon as a single economy or by the adoption of market mechanisms (including convertible currencies and realistic pricing). But the first option would have increased Soviet dominance and was therefore resisted by both the more market-oriented and the more nationalistic member states, while the second option would have allowed the more commercially-minded members (Hungary, Czechoslovakia and Poland) to draw away from Comecon towards the West and was therefore unacceptable to the USSR and its 'hard-line' allies. In the long run, therefore, Comecon was destined to fall between two stools.

21 From the crisis of 1968 to the Revolutions of 1989

REPRESSION, ANTI-ZIONISM AND EAST–WEST *DÉTENTE*

The optimism of the 1960s was seriously deflated by a crackdown on mounting student unrest and on the radical-liberal intelligentsia in Poland in March 1968 and by the Warsaw Pact invasion of Czechoslovakia in August 1968. These acts of repression were accompanied by a barrage of virulent 'anti-Zionist' propaganda orchestrated by the Soviet Union. In the wake of the defeat of the Soviet Union's Arab allies during the six-day Arab–Israeli War of June 1967, it was alleged that 'Zionist' Jews in Israel, the United States and the Soviet bloc were acting as agents of American imperialism in a three-pronged international conspiracy to subvert communist rule in Eastern Europe, to deny the Palestinians an independent homeland and to provide pretexts for the US presence and US intervention in the Middle East. Accordingly the Soviet media and other 'anti-Zionist' publications highlighted and wilfully exaggerated the important (but far from hegemonic) role played by a few Jewish intellectuals, dissidents and 'refuseniks' (Jews who had been refused permission to emigrate) in the Soviet and East European dissident and reform movements. There was a very thin line separating Soviet 'anti-Zionism' from more traditional forms of antisemitism and anti-intellectualism. Official 'anti-Zionism' stirred the embers of a residual popular antisemitism and anti-intellectualism within the Soviet bloc (especially in Poland), thereby helping to alienate the radical-liberal intelligentsia from potential proletarian and peasant support. Indeed, 'anti-Zionism' was not just a diversionary tactic that damagingly isolated and vilified Jews, but also a means of isolating and discrediting the radical-liberal intelligentsia and dissidents in general, although Jews obviously bore the brunt of this latter-day 'counter-reformation'. This inevitably fuelled Jewish fears and anxieties, with the result that many Jews who had hitherto been 'loyal' Soviet or East European citizens (often as doctors, scientists, lawyers, academics and journalists) or even members of the ruling communist parties were harassed, blocked in their careers, demoralized, disillusioned and driven to seek permission to emigrate either to the West or to Israel.

Despite the widespread climate of repression, 'anti-Zionism', anti-intellectualism and demoralization in Eastern Europe at the end of the 1960s, a more subdued and pragmatic optimism was rekindled in the early 1970s by the continuing reforms in Kadar's Hungary, by the initial two- or three-year 'honeymoon' period of political relaxation and social reconciliation which followed the accession of Eduard Gierek in Poland in December 1970 and Erich Honecker in the GDR in May 1971 and, above all, by the process of East–West *détente* initiated by Willy Brandt's *Ostpolitik* in 1969 (reinforced by US President Nixon's path-breaking visit to Moscow in 1972). West Germany's non-aggression treaties with the Soviet Union and Poland in 1970 and its state treaty with the GDR in 1972 paved the way for greatly increased East–West commerce, contacts, credit and technology transfers, as the West gradually followed Willy Brandt's lead.

As early as 1968 the West German Foreign Minister, Willy Brandt, declared his 'clear conviction that reconciliation of Poles and Germans will someday have the same historical importance as the friendship between Germany and France' (Brandt 1968: 272), although he had already formed this view long before that (Brandt 1978: 183). He also seized the opportunity presented by the Prague Spring to normalize West German relations with Czechoslovakia in 1968. But the principal thrust of his *Ostpolitik* was towards German–Polish reconciliation. On 7 December 1970, the day that he signed the treaty normalizing relations between the Federal Republic and Poland and ratifying the Oder–Neisse frontier between the two states, Brandt went down on his knees in front of the memorial to those who had died in the Warsaw Ghetto. 'This gesture, which attracted worldwide attention, was not "planned", though I had certainly debated earlier that morning how best to convey the special nature of this act of remembrance at the Ghetto monument . . . Oppressed by memories of Germany's recent history, I simply did what people do when words fail them . . . My gesture was intelligible to those willing to understand it' (p. 399). As one unnamed reporter wrote afterwards: 'Then he knelt, he who has no need to, on behalf of all those who ought to kneel but don't' (p. 399). This visit opened the way to a similar thaw in West German relations with other East European states, including the GDR. Another (unanticipated) effect was to deprive the Polish communist regime and its Soviet overlord of the claim that they were defending Poland's post-1945 frontier against pent-up German revanchism.

The high point of East–West *détente* was the 1975 Helsinki Final Act, which established the Conference on European Security and Co-operation (CSCE). At the time it was condemned by many Western conservatives and Cold Warriors as an abject act of 'appeasement' towards the communist regimes of the Soviet bloc (or as another Yalta), because it ostensibly involved general acceptance of the territorial *status quo* in Europe. Certainly, the Soviet Union had long advocated the holding of a major international conference to bestow international recognition on the GDR and on the post-1945 borders of Poland, and that was what it obtained at Helsinki in 1975. But the so-called third 'basket' of the Helsinki accords also committed all signatories to respect 'civil, economic, social, cultural and other rights and freedoms, all of which derive from the inherent dignity of the human person' (Stokes 1993: 24). They spelled out these rights and freedoms in great detail, giving East European dissidents a legal basis on which they could challenge their governments, through Helsinki Watch Committees established to monitor East European observance of the provisions of the Final Act. This threw the communist regimes on to the defensive. Instead of endorsing the *status quo*, the Final Act was 'a charter for change. Instead of legitimizing the Soviet sphere of influence, it legitimized Western intrusion into it . . . Instead of confining itself to interstate relations, it reinforced the principle that peace depends also on how states treat their people' (Davy 1992: 19). Indeed, 'without the Final Act and the Western interest it aroused, opposition in Eastern Europe would have been weaker, less coherent, easier to suppress' (p. 251). Conversely, 'by helping to support the development of civil societies in Eastern Europe, *détente* paved the way for a *smoother* transition to democracy when the [communist] regimes crumbled because it had fostered alternative structures and authorities to take their place' (p. 263).

SOCIALIST ECONOMIC INTEGRATION IN THE 1970s AND 1980s

Until the late 1960s the term 'integration' remained taboo in communist circles. It had carried connotations of 'monopoly capitalist' collusion against workers and consumers (in the hope of postponing the elusive but long predicted 'terminal crisis of capitalism'). Consequently, the intra-regional projects and policies of the European members of Comecon were largely confined to 'fraternal' inter-party and intergovernmental co-operation, modest 'mutual economic asssistance' and minimal *ex post facto* harmonization of national economic plans (Brabant 1989: xxi). Economic integration became Comecon's formal goal only after the 'special' council session of April 1969, at which communist leaders discussed ways and means of keeping member states 'in line' and 'on side' in the aftermath of the August 1968 Warsaw Pact invasion of Czechoslovakia. Subsequent progress toward greater integration between the European members of Comecon from 1969 to 1989 was limited, not by a lack of official blueprints and declarations, but by the existence of deep-seated barriers or impediments to integration between sovereign centrally planned economies. It was possible to attain 'hyper-integration' between Soviet republics, as these were components of a single supranational state, tightly controlled by a single centre of power. By the same token, however, inter-state integration was virtually a contradiction in terms for the centrally planned economies. Their development strategies were neither conceived nor implemented with wide-ranging economic co-operation as a central or paramount concern. Nor was Comecon ever endowed 'with the power to promote desirable or expedient dependences among its members' (Brabant 1980: 9–10). Integration within Comecon was also hindered by the extremely disparate nature of its membership, exacerbated by the admission of underdeveloped and non-European Mongolia in 1962, Cuba in 1972 and Vietnam in 1978 (as a matter of political expediency), and by the overwhelming asymmetry between the Soviet Union (a real 'superstate') and the motley assortment of small and medium-sized members. Some of these became in a sense merely extra-territorial 'appendages' or 'extensions' of the USSR. Thus Bulgaria was often described as the sixteenth Soviet republic, and there was a well known Soviet ditty: *Kuritsa ne ptitsa, Bolgaria ne za granitsa* (A hen is not a bird, Bulgaria is not abroad). Indeed, for many purposes, it was more meaningful to think of Comecon as an imposed monolith and (from 1955 onwards) as the economic arm of the Warsaw Pact (the only 'defensive alliance' that repeatedly invaded its own member states!), rather than as the vehicle of voluntary co-operation, mutual assistance and (belatedly) integration between 'equal' and 'sovereign' member states that it always professed to be. In 1983 the Soviet Union accounted for 88 per cent of Comecon's territory and 60 per cent of its population (Comecon 1984: 7). Soviet priorities and preferences naturally predominated, and the vast disparities between the Soviet Union and the other member states inevitably fostered more suspicion and animosity than mutual trust. Intra-CMEA co-operation and integration inevitably became 'a contest in which each participant endeavoured to extract the maximum advantage at the minimum price' (Brabant 1980: 3). Hence the Soviet bloc was never quite as monolithic as its leaders (as well as many Western commentators) would have liked us to believe. Indeed, Comecon's persistent emphasis on inter-state 'co-operation' and 'mutual assistance' and on the co-ordination of national economic plans did more to reinforce than to reduce the primacy of individual member states over the collectivity, while post-Stalinist 'national assertion' placed additional obstacles in the path of any far-reaching integration within Comecon. To a far greater degree than the European Community, Comecon was a *Europe des patries* or, better still (in the words that de Gaulle actually used), a *Europe des états*.

In 1989 the East European members of Comecon accounted for no more than 4 per cent of world trade. East European states and enterprises endeavoured to minimize their dependence on potentially unreliable external suppliers. Comprehensive, mandatory economic planning was found to be less difficult in relatively self-sufficient and secluded economies than in ones heavily dependent on foreign trade, whose volume and composition lay largely outside the control of national economic planners. Indeed, 'planners do not see foreign trade as a desirable pursuit in its own right but merely as an additional source of supplies, the volume and composition of which is contingent on the requirements of the production plan' (Sobell 1984: 4). In most centrally planned economies, foreign trade was legally a state monopoly, in order to safeguard state control of the economy and of the terms and extent of any foreign involvement, and it had to be channelled through cumbersome and often corrupt state agencies and foreign trade corporations. Thus it was limited to what these were willing and able to handle. This extreme institutional separation of domestic producers from foreign customers also increased the unresponsiveness of the former to the needs and desires of the latter. In addition, the use of arbitrary, overvalued multiple exchange rates typically resulted in formal accounting 'losses' on exports and 'profits' on imports. This effectively ruled out any meaningful calculation of relative costs, economic returns and gains from trade. Endemic shortages of 'hard' currency, the inability of most state enterprises to penetrate and hold their own in internationally competitive markets and the failure to develop convertible currencies and rational price mechanisms that could have facilitated multilateral trading brought about a predominance of bilateral trading. The volume of trade was limited to the quantities and types of products that the weaker partner could manage to export. Each partner was discouraged from running a trade surplus, and this acted as a further disincentive to increase exports. Indeed, most of the better products were reserved for particular domestic projects, since producers and planners were essentially judged and rewarded in accordance with the domestic performance of high-priority or high-profile industries and projects, especially those of strategic importance. Consequently, with exceptions such as Soviet oil and gas, the products available for export were to a large extent unwanted 'left-overs'. The centrally planned economies thus found it difficult to trade with one another. Economic integration became even harder to achieve as the centrally planned economies became more highly industrialized and produced a wider range of products. That was a principal reason why dependence on intra-CMEA trade peaked in the early 1950s and then slowly declined until Comecon's collapse in the early 1990s.

The scope for intra-CMEA trade and integration could have been increased by stronger moves towards market mechanisms, multilateralism and currency convertibility, which would have increased the latitude for autonomous integrative forces. However, such moves were strongly resisted by most of the communist party and central planning hierarchies, not least because they would have downgraded the overriding priority given to defence and heavy industry (the military-industrial complex), thereby increasing the consumer orientation of these economies and allowing the more successful and market-oriented members of Comecon to reduce their economic dependence on the Soviet Union. There would also have been a loss of 'captive' markets and suppliers, while the increased exposure to international competition and market forces would have threatened the solvency and survival of many obsolete, inefficient or feather-bedded industries and enterprises, as indeed came to pass after 1989. Yet, while it was obvious to all that the so-called 'full market solution' to Comecon integration would depend on currency convertibility, multilateralism and prices reflecting relative costs, returns and scarcities, it was insufficiently appreciated that supranational central planning, specialization and division of labour within Comecon as a whole had remarkably similar prerequisites. For, in the absence of convertible currencies, multilateral payments systems and realistic prices and exchange rates, supranational central planners would not have been able to make rational decisions, calculations or comparisons.

However, except in the cases of Hungary and Yugoslavia, East European moves towards 'market socialism' were unceremoniously halted by the August 1968 Warsaw Pact invasion of Czechoslovakia and the subsequent suppression and/or emasculation of the reform movements. For a time even the Hungarians had to tread carefully, referring merely to a New Economic Mechanism (inaugurated in January 1968), rather than to 'reform' or to 'market socialism' as such. Yet, even if the 'reform' movements were emasculated politically, the communist regimes still had to try to surmount the tightening resource constraints and the deteriorating economic performance which had contributed to the emergence of 'reform' movements in the first place. Therefore, despite (or even because of) the resultant setbacks to fundamental systemic change and to East–West trade, it seemed all the more necessary to foster increased trade, assistance, co-operation and cohesion between members of Comecon, in the hope of enhancing economic performance, 'buying off' economic and social discontent and reducing the likelihood of another blatant and traumatic Warsaw Pact invasion of a 'fraternal' state in the near future. The 1968 invasion has even been described as 'a watershed in CMEA relations' (Brabant 1989: 78). It was certainly the major impetus behind the convocation of a 'special' council session of Comecon in April 1969, ostensibly to celebrate the organization's twentieth anniversary, and the proclamation of a new panacea: Socialist Economic Integration (SEI). However, it was one thing to proclaim this and another to agree on what it meant and how to achieve it. During the late 1950s and the early 1960s it had been agreed that each communist regime would have to chart its own 'national road to socialism', although the Soviet regime arrogantly reserved the right to prescribe the destination (and, if necessary, change the driver!). But by 1969 the various economic systems and policy preferences of the communist regimes had become too diverse, entrenched and mutually incompatible to lend themselves to a common conception and mode of integration. The Complex Programme for the Further Extension and Improvement of Co-operation and the Development of Economic Integration by the CMEA Countries, published by Comecon in 1971, was therefore an incoherent hotchpotch of disparate ingredients cooked up by seventeen different committees. 'No attempt was ever made to weave these propositions into anything remotely resembling a coherent, let alone comprehensive, concept of SEI and how it should or could be fostered' (Brabant 1989: 86). However, Sobell (1984: 16) has offered a more positive interpretation, arguing that 'the document is significant in that it imbued the organization with an unprecedented spirit of pragmatism: the fundamental issues were left unresolved but co-operation schemes went ahead regardless; Romanian opposition was bypassed by *de facto* abandonment of the single-member veto in favour of the "interested party" principle'. In effect, Comecon fell back on rather British methods of 'muddling through'.

It may be objected that the European Community never had a coherent, clear-cut, comprehensive and generally accepted concept of integration either, and yet Western Europe has made significant progress towards 'ever closer union' since the 1950s. The crucial difference is that, once 'national' barriers to the free movement of goods, capital, labour and services have been largely eliminated and a permissive framework of institutions and ground rules has been established, integration between market economies will normally proceed automatically, even while the politicians and bureaucrats are asleep. To set in motion the economic integration of the six founder members of the European Economic Community, all that was really required was a limited 'compact of abstention': an agreement to remove all restrictions on trade between the Six and subsequently to refrain from impeding cross-border flows of goods, capital and labour within the resultant 'common market'. As emphasized by Shonfield (1973: 14), 'agreeing on a number of specific things that governments will not do is much easier than arriving at a positive agreement on a line of action to be taken in common'. Integration within Comecon, by contrast, was much more dependent on continuous active intervention by economic planners and politicians and a consensus on what they were trying to achieve, if they were not to cancel each other out by pulling in different directions. In practice, it was limited to what could be agreed in advance between mutually mistrustful communist states and incorporated into their current and prospective five-year plans. Unless they ceased to be centrally planned economies, they could not easily generate or accommodate spontaneous, decentralized, cross-border or transnational trade, investment, migration or joint ventures.

Integration between the Comecon states was also restricted by their historic rivalries, frictions and animosities and by the additional tensions and mutual suspicion and mistrust generated by the very unequal, oppressive, hegemonic and intrusive relationship between the Soviet Union and its East European 'allies'. Indeed, whereas 'capitalist' integration helped Western Europeans to sidestep and surmount the bitter legacies of their recent past, East Europeans had the opposite experience. They came out of the Second World War at least as disunited, aggrieved, suspicious and resentful as they went into it. The Soviet Union was able to muzzle or suppress many of the mutual enmities and suspicions between its East European 'vassals', but it did little to dissipate or defuse the underlying sentiments. There was no comprehensive post-war settlement and reconciliation between former belligerents in Eastern Europe, comparable to that achieved by the Marshall Plan, the Organization of European Economic Co-operation and the European Coal and Steel Community in Western Europe. Nor did the East Europeans ever achieve the levels of prosperity and hedonistic consumerism and oblivion that helped to soothe, dissipate and divert attention from inherited enmities and resentments in post-1940s Western Europe.

In view of all these impediments, Socialist Economic Integration had to assume roundabout and limited forms, rather than 'head-on' and comprehensive ones. Since it was impossible to agree on a common approach to pricing, economic reform, multilateralism, currency convertibility and intra-CMEA capital and labour mobility, Comecon had to settle for sub-optimal or second-best solutions. It had to limit itself to whichever half-measures and sector-specific programmes its disparate membership would accept and in which not everyone would have to participate. This was consistent with the 1967 'interested party' principle, which appears to have been reaffirmed as part of the price paid by the Soviet Union for East European 'fraternal assistance' in the invasion of Czechoslovakia. Thus in 1971 an International Investment Bank was established to finance and facilitate intra-CMEA co-operation on transnational investment projects, especially in energy production, power grids, pipelines, mining, transport, chemicals, metallurgy and machine-building. In 1975, 1980 and 1985, moreover, the Comecon states cobbled together a series of five-year 'concerted plans for multilateral integration measures', which were intended to synchronize with their national five-year plans and to resource and co-ordinate transnational projects in key sectors such as the energy and extractive industries. These projects were pushed by the Soviet Union as a way of getting its East European 'partners' to bear part of the increasing investment and production costs of the fuels and other minerals which they consistently imported from the Soviet Union at considerably less than world market prices (and sometimes re-exported to the West to make a nice hard-currency profit) in return for supplies of 'soft' East European manufactured goods. However, from their own very different standpoint, most East Europeans resented having to defray some of the costs of developing the economy of their hated overlord and oppressor. It is possible to see both points of view. In 1975 it was also proposed that Comecon members should adopt a cluster of binding, collective 'target programmes' to relieve bottlenecks in the production and transportation of energy, raw materials, foodstuffs, industrial consumer goods and transport and to increase inter-state specialization in the various branches of engineering. However, these did not become operational until the 1980s, when the trade flows covered by these 'specialization agreements' do not seem to have exceeded 25 per cent of all intra-CMEA trade in engineering products or 10 per cent of total intra-CMEA trade (Robson 1987: 225; Brabant 1989: 91–3).

From the early 1970s onward, the Soviet Union and most East European members of Comecon began to devolve some of their economic planning, allocation and decision-making tasks to giant industrial combines and/or 'industrial associations'. This was done partly with the aim of reducing the so-called 'operational and informational overload' on central planners in increasingly complex and industrialized centrally planned economies by establishing intermediate tiers of economic decision-making and partly in the hope of replicating the dynamic roles of huge, highly integrated and increasingly science-based industrial combines and conglomerates in the Western and East Asian capitalist economies. The new industrial associations and combines were expected to develop strong research, development, design and supply capabilities, to reap increased economies of scale and to 'internalize' the more detailed planning and allocation functions, by transforming these into managerial tasks performable within giant enterprises or groups of enterprises. In theory, this would free the overloaded central economic organs to concentrate on their overarching macroeconomic roles. It was also hoped that these industrial associations and/or combines would foster decentralized 'horizontal' contractual links with one another to supplement (and partly supplant) the 'vertical' chains of command extending from the central planning and supply agencies and Industry Ministries to the myriad industrial enterprises. All this was expected to have a major impact on intra-CMEA integration, by facilitating the autonomous development of direct transnational links, investment, joint ventures and scientific and technical co-operation between industrial associations and/or combines in different Comecon economies.

In practice, however, the new conglomerations or groupings of enterprises were often unwieldy, conservative, risk-averse and bureaucratic. They tended to reproduce most of the deficiencies, errors and rigidities of the central planning and supply organs and

Industry Ministries, which they were supposed to ameliorate. They were often little more than additional intermediate links in essentially unchanged 'vertical' chains of command. Indeed, it was never clearly explained how the 'horizontal' links which the industrial associations and combines were supposed to foster would intermesh with the 'vertical' chains of command radiating from the central planning and supply organs and Economic Ministries. It can be argued that, in order to have any chance of functioning in accordance with some idealized (or nightmarish) cybernetic vision, a command economy needs to have clearly defined and free-standing chains of command. Any cross-currents are more likely to generate disorganization and chaos than increased efficiency and productivity. In any case, the 'really existing' centrally planned economies lacked most of the financial, commercial, legal and distributive infrastructure that sustains or facilitates autonomous 'horizontal' links between industrial enterprises in developed market economies. Industrial associations and combines were therefore unable to foster many direct 'horizontal' links within (let alone between) the centrally planned economies. As Leslie Collit once remarked, 'In the absence of market economies there is nothing to propel companies inside Comecon into co-operating across national borders as in the West. Prices do not reflect real costs and artificial exchange rates between Comecon currencies and the absence of a convertible currency mean it is virtually impossible to determine whether direct ties are profitable (*FT*, 22 July 1987, p. 2).

THE ROAD TO 1989

From 1973 to 1978, while the Western world went into economic recession in the wake of the quadrupling of OPEC oil prices in 1973–74, the East European economies continued to grow, in some cases even faster than they had done during the 1960s. This superficially impressive feat was made possible by several special factors. The East European economies became increasingly dependent on the Soviet market and on imports of underpriced Soviet oil and gas, which were largely to be paid for by stepping up exports of agricultural and (mostly 'soft') manufactured products to the Soviet Union. In addition, the Soviet Union provided Eastern Europe with considerable amounts of power-generating equipment and technology (including nuclear power plants) on concessionary terms. These forms of Soviet 'assistance' helped not only to cushion most of the East European economies against adverse trends in their terms of trade and in their access to Western markets, but also to continue to grow (albeit at diminishing rates) through most of the 1970s. However, while increased dependence upon the Soviet Union helped to shield the East European economies from the potentially damaging effects of recession and higher oil prices in the capitalist world, in the longer term it further impaired their capacity to export successfully to the West. (At the same time, the increasingly nationalistic and independent-minded Romanian and Albanian communist regimes were increasingly denied such Soviet 'assistance'. However, they had significant, albeit rapidly diminishing, mineral resources of their own. Albania, which had ceased to be an active member of Comecon since 1960, also received considerable Chinese economic assistance in return for supporting China in the Sino-Soviet disputes of the 1960s and the early 1970s.)

There has been a major Western debate about the scale, direction and significance of the (implicit) transnational subsidies resulting from the trade patterns that developed within Comecon. These have raised complex and emotive issues to which we cannot fully do justice here. But, in view of the importance of the debate, it is necessary to highlight the main issues. Notwithstanding the substantial economic and technical assistance rendered to Cuba, Vietnam and Mongolia between 1960 and 1990, Comecon never undertook any large-scale fiscal transfers between its European member states analogous to those engendered by the Common Agricultural Policy and the so-called 'structural' and 'cohesion' funds within the European Community.

Debate has mainly centred on the implicit transfers (so-called 'trade subsidies') generated by the systematic deviations of intra-CMEA prices from world market prices, especially the fact that from 1973 to 1990 large quantities of Soviet oil and natural gas were supplied to East European states at prices that were substantially below those paid in the capitalist world. The most influential Western view has been that this implicit Soviet subsidization of the East European states represented a politically motivated endeavour to 'underwrite' the further development of these rather shaky centrally planned economies, to defuse East European economic discontents, to encourage and reward East European compliance with Soviet wishes and security arrangements, to give preferential treatment to the states that most loyally toed the line and to maintain (or even enhance) the cohesion of the Soviet bloc without periodic recourse to military invasion (Marrese and Vanous 1983; Marrese 1986; Reisinger 1992). But some analysts, particularly Holzman (1986a, b), Desai (1986) and Brada (1985, 1988), have favoured more narrowly economic explanations of the implicit subsidies. They have argued that within any trade bloc whose internal prices systematically deviate from those on the world market, some members will benefit and others will lose out; and that, in the case of Comecon, this was not necessarily the result of concerted Soviet attempts to reward loyalists and penalize recalcitrants. Thus the vagaries of the Common Agricultural Policy have similarly given rise to gainers (most notably the Netherlands, Ireland and Denmark) and losers (especially Britain) within western Europe. Brada has argued that 'such subsidies are far from unique and arise whenever a number of countries engage in preferential trade among themselves'. Indeed, the magnitude of the Soviet subsidies to its CMEA partners was 'not at all unusual' and their existence depended 'neither on the planned nature of these economies nor on Soviet hegemony over Eastern Europe'. Instead, they arose because intra-CMEA trade, like intra-EC trade, was 'not carried out at world market prices' (Brada 1988: 641–3). Moreover, the growth of implicit Soviet subsidies to East European states after 1973 was a largely fortuitous consequence of factors beyond Soviet control, primarily the large rises in world oil prices in 1973–74 and in 1979–80 (pp. 646, 657). 'Soviet subsidies to Eastern Europe were basically related to a slow adjustment of CMEA oil and gas prices to the two "energy shocks" of the 1970s' (Poznanski 1993: 923).

Rather than exaggerating the role of political considerations (in the manner of Marrese and Vanous), the distribution of implicit gains and losses between Comecon members could be just as plausibly explained by the fact that within Comecon as a whole mineral resources were relatively abundant, whereas capital was perennially scarce. Consequently, viewed purely in terms of relative factor endowments, the more capital-rich member states (the GDR, Czechoslovakia and, to a lesser extent, Hungary) were most likely to benefit at the expense of the relatively mineral-rich ones (the Soviet Union and, to a lesser extent, Romania) (Brada 1988: 652–3). Nevertheless, most East Central Europeans indignantly dismiss any suggestion that they were therefore being subsidized by the Soviet Union or that they were in some way benefiting from Soviet largesse. They have retained a strong belief that they were underpaid for their own exports to the Soviet Union. In their eyes the magnitude of the implicit 'subsidies' has been greatly exaggerated (as a result of excessive attention to the easily quantifiable trade in oil and gas, to the relative neglect of the less easily evaluated trade in manufactures). If they existed at all, such subsidies were meagre compensation for the coercive imposition of economic systems and development strategies that were utterly inappropriate to Eastern Europe's particular economic needs and factor endowments, keeping them much poorer than they would have been if they had been allowed to adopt economic systems and strategies of their own choosing (Koves 1983; Poznanski 1993).

There is broader agreement that, at least in the short term, the 1970s East–West *détente* facilitated increased inflows of Western capital and technology into the still expanding East European economies. There was an uncontrolled proliferation of East–West joint ventures, production licensing agreements and imported 'turnkey' installations, many of which were financed by recycled 'petro-dollars', as Western banks often incautiously re-lent to Eastern Europe some of the oil 'windfalls' deposited in them by the newly rich oil states. The East European regimes eagerly accepted Western loans, investments, joint ventures, industrial installations and 'technology transfers' as a substitute for more fundamental reforms in their socio-economic systems. Admittedly, in the absence of far-reaching systemic reforms to increase their economic efficiency, they were unable to reap in full the potential benefits or 'pay-off' that could have been obtained from such transfers. Nevertheless, in the wake of the ill-fated Prague Spring, most of the East European regimes perceived radical reforms to be socially and politically dangerous. (The exceptions were Kadar's Hungary and Tito's Yugoslavia.) 'Technology transfer' and import-led growth, largely financed by foreign loans, seemed to offer politically safer means of modernizing the East European economies, both by raising productivity and by expanding the range of products and equipment available.

All the same, increased reliance on Western capital, technology and firms had unanticipated political and social repercussions. Increased contact with Western visitors (both tourists and businessmen), together with the proliferation of amenities catering to their needs, helped to diffuse Western values, consumerism and pop culture, especially among the young. The resultant Westernization of East European attitudes, values, dress and leisure activities was, in the end, just as corrosive of communist influence on the minds of the young as any radical systemic reform. Moreover, through their clumsy attempts to curb the growing influence of rock concerts, Western pop music, blue jeans and consumerism, the ageing dictators made themselves seem increasingly old-fashioned, puritanical, out-of-touch and ridiculous, especially in the eyes of the young.

Excessive reliance upon Western capital and technology transfers posed equally serious economic hazards. Production licensing agreements, such as that between the Polish Ursus tractor plant and Massey-Ferguson-Perkins, often incurred great expense for relatively little benefit to the East European side (Stokes 1993: 19). Debt service payments became very burdensome, absorbing resources which could have been spent on much-needed infrastructure or imports, and by the late 1970s they had begun to exceed any fresh inflows of Western capital. The latter quickly dried up as East European credit ratings fell. Some East European states even had difficulty in completing existing projects involving Western capital or equipment and in obtaining Western spare parts. This further impaired their capacity to increase exports on the scale anticipated or required. Indeed, the East European states found themselves under increasing pressure to expand their exports to the West to service their uncomfortably large hard-currency debts at the very moment when the further doubling of OPEC oil prices in 1979 plunged the West into another economic recession, which in turn further depressed demand for (and raised trade barriers against) Western imports from Eastern Europe. This time, moreover, the Soviet Union was less able to come to Eastern Europe's rescue. The 1979–82 world recession coincided with the nadir of the Brezhnev 'years of stagnation', during which Soviet economic growth sharply decelerated and crucial sectors such as oil, coal, iron and steel stopped growing altogether. The Soviet Union's inability to continue supplying ever-increasing quantities of fuel and raw materials to Eastern Europe on preferential terms also reduced its willingness and capacity to absorb (in return) ever-increasing quantities of obsolete and/or poor-quality East European industrial products, some of which must have contributed to the deterioration in Soviet economic performance. Eastern Europe was therefore caught in a 'two-way squeeze' between a stagnating Soviet economy and a recession-stricken West. The crisis was compounded by the simultaneous termination of East–West *détente* and the start of the 'new Cold War', precipitated by a dramatic escalation of the nuclear arms race (1978–84), the Soviet invasion of Afghanistan (December 1979), the accession of Ronald Reagan to the US presidency (1980–88) and the imposition of martial law in Poland (December 1981).

From 1979 to 1983, therefore, the East European economies were plunged into acute economic recessions from which they still had not fully recovered in 1989, when the 'iron curtain' finally lifted. Between 1979 and 1989, with the possible exceptions of the GDR and Bulgaria, the East European economies hardly grew at all in real *per capita* terms and, in the extreme cases of Romania and Poland, experienced severe economic contractions and drastic reductions in living standards. Moreover, it was later revealed that the relative success of the GDR and Bulgaria during the 1980s was more apparent than real and that the full magnitude of their economic crises, infrastructural decay and mounting external indebtedness had been obscured by the selective suppression and falsification of economic and social statistics and partial concealment of the sheer scale of the costly environmental damage incurred through the reckless development of their chemical, metallurgical, lignite and power-generating industries (social, economic and environmental costs that would continue for years to come). In the early 1990s it became clear just how much of the Western capital and equipment imported during the 1970s had been wasted on 'white elephants' or diverted into luxurious accommodation and social amenities for the political, managerial and military elites (the 'edifice complex'), instead of being used for the originally intended modernization of East European industry and physical infrastructure. The worst affected countries were Poland and Romania.

From crisis to crisis in Poland

In Poland the resultant shortages, hardships, sporadic repression of student and labour unrest and official attempts to conceal the full dimensions of the mismanagement of the economy, the misappropriation of funds and the ensuing economic and social crisis aroused more open and politically active opposition to the Gierek regime. A belated attempt to restore market equilibrium in Poland in 1976 by decreeing large rises in retail food prices sparked off widespread and sometimes violently suppressed strikes and protests, forced Gierek to rescind the decreed price increases and precipitated the formation of a prominent Committee for Workers' Defence (KOR) in 1976, partly in order to promote increased solidarity between intelligentsia and working-class opponents of the regime. Led by Adam Michnik, Jacek Kuron, Jan Lipski and Edward Lipinski, KOR began to circulate an illegal fortnightly news-sheet called *Robotnik* (The Worker), which publicized oppression and abuses and provided guidance to workers' protests from 1977 to 1980. The movement also had the tacit support of the Catholic Church. KOR was not suppressed by Edward Gierek, perhaps because he had lived in the West and was anxious to safeguard his international reputation as the builder of a new Poland. He seemed to accept that it was more prudent to allow intellectuals to criticize and let off steam than to try to repress them (Stokes 1993: 28–9).

Then, out of the blue, the election of Cardinal Karel Wojtyla to the papacy in 1978 and his fully televised triumphal return to Poland as Pope John-Paul II in 1979 gave an enormous uplift to Polish Catholic nationalism and national self-confidence at a critical juncture in the country's history. In the words of an outstanding Western reporter on Polish affairs, it was an awakening. 'The Pope did nothing so crude as to attack the regime openly or urge the people to rise. Instead, he spoke straight past the government to the real feelings, the real memories of the Poles' and he 'evoked an ancient Christian nation, as if Communist rule was a transient phenomenon of little importance'. The upshot was that 'Poles felt a surge of returning confidence. Given freedom, the people could organize Polish life for itself, true to its own sense of what was just and appropriate.' The visit was both a catharsis and an exorcism. In public attitudes towards the ruling communists, hatred gave way to 'something even more ominous: a contemptuous indifference'. It also became increasingly apparent that 'the Polish nation was mature and strong enough to make its own choices', without the irksome tutelage of either the party or the state (Ascherson 1988: 192).

In this highly charged situation, the new Prime Minister, Edward Babiuch, made another abortive attempt to raise retail food prices and introduce measures to boost exports of foods that were in short supply in Polish shops in June 1980. These ill-judged actions triggered a growing wave of peaceful strikes and sit-ins in the big Baltic shipyards and in the vast Silesian steelworks and coal mines during July and August 1980. To everyone's surprise, the Polish authorities allowed KOR to act as an 'information exchange' and pass reports on the strikes and sit-ins to foreign news agencies and radio stations, which in turn broadcast much of this information back to Poland. A major strike and sit-in at the Lenin shipyard in Gdansk brought to prominence a (hitherto little known) dissident marine electrician, Lech Walesa, who began to negotiate with government representatives on behalf of his fellow workers, closely advised by Jacek Kuron, Adam Michnik and Catholic Church leaders. The negotiations were soon being televised to the outside world, making it virtually impossible for the government to extricate itself from this clever political trap without losing face. Walesa's team negotiated the following far-reaching concessions, which were embodied in the so-called Gdansk Agreement of 31 August 1980: the right to strike and to form independent trade unions; increased wages; public broadcasts of Sunday Mass; a relaxation of censorship; reform of welfare provision; the selection of enterprise managers on the basis of ability rather than party affiliation; and a commitment to a thorough overhaul of the entire economic system in consultation with the new independent trade unions. 'Not since the revolutions of the nineteenth century had a European people forced such a treaty on its own rulers. In a communist system . . . the agreements were almost unimaginable. They were possible only because in Poland . . . the party's "leading role" had become an official sham. The reality was a sort of crude pluralism' (Ascherson 1988: 198). Thus KOR was even permitted to play a crucial role in brokering the agreement, partly because its most prominent intellectuals and the government negotiators, divided though they were politically, 'sprang from the same Warsaw milieu and spoke the same language' (p. 196). (Much the same was true of the metropolitan intelligentsias and bureaucrats of Prague, Budapest, Belgrade and even Sofia, Tirana and Bucharest.)

These mass protests and the Gdansk Agreement soon resulted in the rapid emergence of *Solidarnosc* (Solidarity), an independent trade union claiming 10 million members (in a country with 35 million inhabitants). Indeed, 'as one strike committee after another all over Poland adopted the outline of the Gdansk Agreement, adding local points of their own, Solidarity swelled into a nationwide organization' (Ascherson 1988: 198). Gierek was obliged to resign in September 1980. Yet his successor, the rather colourless communist apparatchik Stanislaw Kania, soon proved incapable of dealing with the deepening crisis. The situation was not helped by the way in which Solidarity encouraged its members to believe that they could enjoy the benefits of political and economic liberalization without forgoing job-security, over-manning and fixed prices and to refuse to recognize any link between remuneration and productivity. At grass-roots level, Solidarity also encouraged strikes, wage demands and a ban on weekend work for miners, thereby exacerbating shortages and inflation and further depressing production, real incomes and exports. National income contracted by about a quarter between 1980 and 1982, while the annual inflation rate jumped to 18 per cent in 1981 and 109 per cent in 1982. During 1981 Solidarity wielded power without responsibility. It did not make a bid for formal governmental responsibility, partly because it still saw itself as 'only a trade union' and partly because it feared that any such move might have precipitated Warsaw Pact intervention. Yet many people on both sides came to believe that if the communist authorities did not destroy Solidarity, then Solidarity would finish off the party. At heart, the fiercely Catholic members of Solidarity detested materialist and atheist communism. Conversely, with the notable exceptions of those who 'defected' to Solidarity (as a more authentically working-class organization than the Polish United Workers' Party), many communists saw Solidarity as a reactionary and national-chauvinist 'God squad', bent on suppressing Marxist-Leninist materialism and atheism. Such attitudes precluded any real possibility of a lasting or stable truce, accommodation or *modus vivendi* between the two sides. At the same time, however, neither was really capable of completely vanquishing the other. They were condemned to live and slug it out together, in a mutually debilitating political stalemate.

General Wojciech Jaruzelski (Defence Minister since 1968) became Prime Minister in February 1981 and leader of the ruling party in October 1981, in successive attempts to restore 'discipline', halt the downward spiral of production and consumption and avert Soviet military intervention. At first it was widely hoped that the army would act as a 'non-political patriotic force', placing the national interest above divisive ideology, and that Jaruzelski would emerge as a patriotic authoritarian nationalist ruler in the Pilsudski mould. Yet, even after Jaruzelski's declaration of martial law in December 1981, the military found it exceedingly difficult to arrest the economy's downward slide (Ascherson 1988: 211–13). Under martial law, key industries were placed under military discipline and thousands of Solidarity and KOR activists were interned or beaten up or killed (mainly by the hated ZOMO security police). Solidarity was outlawed in 1982, driving it underground. Industrial production nevertheless continued to contract in 1982 and it remained below the (already falling) 1979 level throughout the 1980s. Moreover, despite the lack of fresh infusions of Western capital during the 1980s, the continually accumulating arrears on debt-service payments jacked up Poland's onerous (hard-currency) foreign debt from $25 billion in 1981 to $43 billion in 1989, while its average annual inflation rate merely fell to about 15 per cent in the mid-1980s before climbing back up to 60 per cent in 1988 and 244 per cent in 1989. Military rule, communism's last recourse, was deemed a failure, even if it had pre-empted a potential Warsaw Pact invasion of Poland in 1981–82. The military regime missed its chance to carry out a radical reform of the economy in 1982–83, while its opponents were in disarray and in retreat. Poland was locked into a treadmill from which it would have been very hard to escape without a fundamental change of regime.

Their painful experience since the late eighteenth century had taught the Poles that they could hasten their own destruction as a nation if they were to resort to unchecked conflict among themselves. This hard lesson made the nation and its leaders reluctant to push any confrontation to its logical extreme. This had helped to restrain Poland's first communist leaders from indulging in full-blown Stalinist purges and show trials in the late 1940s and early 1950s. It had also contributed to the avoidance of a bloody outcome to the Polish crisis of 1956 (in contrast to the Hungarian Revolution of 1956 and the resultant Soviet invasion of Hungary in November that year). 'This inner tolerance, which has made Poland such a mature society in comparison to Germany or Russia, had led to a history of half-measures, of belligerent words and symbols accompanied by only hesitant deeds. The nation had suffered for this, but because of this it had also survived' (Ascherson 1988: 207). The martial law regime was indeed a characteristically Polish half-measure, carried out with a brutality that 'appalled and alienated the nation', yet 'not brutal enough to terrorize the Poles into passivity' (p. 215). Most of the regime's opponents concluded that 'the price of all-out resistance was too high', while the regime concluded that 'the price of reducing Poland to conformity and obedience was also too high' (p. 218). Thus Jaruzelski was unable to achieve his main political aim of a 'national reconciliation' that marginalized Solidarity. Nor was he able to broaden his power base. His Patriotic Front of National Rebirth (PRON), established in 1982, 'never acquired a convincing life of its own'. After July 1983, when the army formally returned to barracks, 'his only tool of government was the state, which often meant the security police'. Furthermore, his regime was neither able nor willing to destroy the distinctive pluralism of Polish society. Even though the press was strictly censored, Poles continued to speak out and, with Solidarity driven underground, 'the influence of the Catholic Church increased enormously' (pp. 216–17).

Church mediation and Jaruzelski's evident desire to propitiate Poland's Western creditors by introducing a small dose of much-needed economic liberalization and by refraining from an unrestrained reign of terror also helped Solidarity to survive. Indeed, Solidarity continued to pose an ever-present threat to communist rule because it had successfully exposed the lack of legitimacy and 'proletarian' credentials of the ruling party, with the result that from 1980 onwards the East European communist regimes were increasingly on the defensive. Whether they resorted to repression or concession, they could not credibly claim to be the true representatives and custodians of the working class. Thus the emergence of Solidarity in 1980 marked the beginning of the end of communist rule in Eastern Europe, even though Poland and (less overtly) Romania and

Albania constituted the only cases in which the main challenges to communist rule came overwhelmingly 'from below', from the working class.

In 1983, in a vain endeavour to win international respectability and 'national reconciliation', Pope John Paul II was again allowed to visit Poland, martial law was formally rescinded (in return for the lifting of US trade sanctions), censorship was relaxed, most political detainees were released and a programme of economic reform was announced (although it did not go very far in practice). But in 1984 overt opposition to the regime was reignited by the shockingly brutal murder of the popular priest Jerzy Popieluszko by members of the security police. This barbaric act helped to derail Jaruzelski's 'controlled liberalization' strategy, as its perpetrators presumably intended. Consequently, the political and economic stalemate and war of attrition continued until August 1988, when the hated Interior Minister, General Czeslaw Kiszczak, broke the deadlock by proposing 'round-table talks' between the principal elements in Polish society, including the Catholic Church and Solidarity. In addition the hitherto passive lower house of parliament (the Sejm) unprecedentedly voted down the government in September 1988, clearing the way for the formation of a new administration headed by the 'reform communist' Mieczyslaw Rakowski, in consultation with Church leaders. The remarkably open and constructive 'round-table talks' of February and March 1989 resulted in a formal agreement on extensive political and economic reforms (including the re-legalization of Solidarity) on 5 April 1989. It paved the way for the holding of contested multi-party elections to the Sejm and a new upper house (the senate) in June 1989, although sixty-five of the 100 seats in the Sejm were reserved for the communists and their allies. Solidarity candidates duly won ninety-nine of the 100 senate seats and all thirty-five of the freely contested seats in the Sejm. Meeting in joint session, the two houses narrowly elected General Jaruzelski President of the republic, but the communists were largely deserted by their hitherto passive coalition partners and were thus thwarted in their attempts to form a government under General Kiszczak. In August 1989, finally, a Solidarity-dominated government was formed under Tadeuz Mazowiecki, a widely respected Catholic intellectual who was at that time close to Lech Walesa. In Poland the communist abdication of power was mercifully non-violent and in that respect the Polish communists did perform a valuable last service to their country. Yet communist rule had ended in total failure, amid incipient economic and social collapse and runaway inflation.

'Socialism in one family' in Romania

In Romania, not altogether dissimilarly, the economic miscalculations of the 1970s (such as the over-expansion of oil-refining and the petrochemical industry, when Romania's proven oil reserves were being rapidly depleted), the mounting shortages, the large-scale corruption and misappropriation of funds by the Ceausescu kleptocracy, the bloodily suppressed Jiu Valley coal miners' strike in July 1977 and the spectre of *Solidarnosc* all induced the communist regime to tighten its grip. The Western capital borrowed during the 1970s had helped to expand the country's inefficient and capital-intensive heavy industries far beyond Romania's capacity either to meet their voracious energy requirements or to feed its fast-growing non-agricultural population. Western capital and technology transfers had served as a substitute rather than as a catalyst for the radical reforms needed to make Romania's economy more efficient.

By 1977 this long-standing net exporter of oil and foodstuffs had become a net importer of such products. As a result, without in any way curbing the excesses of the extended ruling family, from late 1981 to late 1989 Ceausescu put Romanians through the most draconian austerity programme of any state in the Soviet bloc. It even included power cuts and the rationing of food and petrol. In 1987 a state of emergency was declared in the energy sector, which was gradually subjected to military discipline and control from 1985 onwards.

The various economic reforms announced by the Ceausescu regime were largely cosmetic exercises. Moreover, as a result of the austerity drive, the country's $10 billion foreign debt (which had had to be rescheduled in 1981) was almost entirely repaid by 1989, so as to deny Romania's increasingly critical Western creditors any handle on the Romanian state. But the human and economic costs of these policies were enormous. They included the widespread neglect and rapid decay of Romania's social infrastructure (hospitals, schools, housing, services) and severe strains on the social fabric, as was to be revealed to the world by lurid photographs of the shocking conditions in Romanian orphanages and homes for the mentally retarded after the fall of Ceausescu at the end of 1989. Despite sporadic social unrest among peasants, workers (notably in the city of Brasov in November 1987) and the large Magyar minority in Transylvania, there was no let-up, only brutal repression.

The more he sullied his international reputation, the greater was Ceausescu's determination to repay the foreign debt and root out potential 'subversion' (the hated state security police, the *Securitate*, allegedly recruited one in five adult males) and the more he played up crude 'ethnic' nationalism, xenophobia and persecution of the country's sizeable Gypsy and Hungarian minorities. In 1988 he started to implement his infamous 'systematization' programme. This aimed to erase over 7,000 villages (those with fewer than 3,000 inhabitants) and to resettle their former inhabitants in 550 'agro-industrial centres' by the year 2000, ostensibly in order to increase the cultivable area, modernize rural infrastructure and reduce the differences between town and country. Viewed from another angle, however, millions of Romanian, Hungarian and Romany villagers were to be bulldozed out of the relatively safe havens provided by their traditional close-knit small communities and herded into soulless 'bugged' apartment blocks, within which their opinions and activities could be more easily monitored by networks of police 'spies' and informers. This aroused fears particularly among Romania's increasingly victimized ethnic minorities. Fortunately, for lack of time and money, the programme had not got very far before Ceausescu was overthrown. But it contributed significantly to the growth of inter-ethnic tensions in Transylvania, where the concurrent official persecution of the Hungarian Lutheran pastor Lazlo Tokes in the relatively liberal university city of Timisoara evoked mass protests from Romanians as well as Hungarians and became the catalyst of the widespread confrontations between the *Securitate* and ordinary citizens (especially students) and the mainly conscript army, which precipitated the violent overthrow of the Ceausescu cabal in December 1989.

It is not yet clear just how 'spontaneous' the Romanian Revolution of 1989 really was. There were numerous indications that some of Ceausescu's former henchmen had had a hand in his overthrow and execution and that they were all too ready step into the dead man's shoes. The indecent haste with which Ceausescu and his wife were put to death (without due process of law) on Christmas Day 1989 may well have been intended (in some quarters at least) to stop the dictator making any damaging revelations concerning the new regime's senior personnel, many of whom had been Ceausescu's cronies at one time or another. Nevertheless, there is little doubt that the acute social and economic crises and inter-ethnic tensions of the 1980s created the flammable materials which the leaders of the new National Salvation Front were able to exploit for their own ends.

Albania's economic collapse

The even more severe social and economic crisis that developed in Albania during the late 1980s was primarily a result of the country's growing international isolation rather than the problems afflicting the Comecon states. Following the death of Mao Zedong in 1976 and the subsequent retreat from Maoism in China, Hoxha soon fell out with China's new leaders, whom he denounced as 'revisionists'. After Hoxha's death in 1985 power passed to Ramiz Alia, whose daughter was married to Hoxha's son. But Hoxha's widow Nexhmije continued to wield considerable (hard-line) back-door influence in an endeavour to keep power 'within the family', and President Alia initially ruled out any attempt at an Albanian *perestroika*. That left Albania completely bereft of friends and benefactors, with the result that its hitherto dynamic economy stagnated during the 1980s (although its population was growing by over 2 per cent per annum, the fastest rate of population growth in Europe). According to the *Statistical Yearbooks* published by the communist regime, Albania's officially recorded gross national income increased only 1.5 per cent per annum from 1980 to 1985 and contracted by 1.1 per cent per annum from 1985 to 1990, after growing by 4.6 per cent per annum during the 1970s, 7.4 per cent per annum during the 1960s and 9.1 per cent per annum during the 1950s (Pashko 1996: 95). By 1989 10.7 per cent of the work force was unemployed (Jeffries 1996: 388) and nearly 40 per cent of Albanian children were suffering from malnutrition (according to World Health Organization data, cited in the *FT*, 14 December 1991, p. xx). The economy of communist-ruled Albania finally collapsed between 1990 and 1992, when (according to early estimates) net agricultural output more than halved, industrial output fell to about a quarter of its 1989 level and GDP fell by more than a third. Officially recorded unemployment peaked at 39 per cent of the work force in 1992, while the average rate of inflation rocketed to 36 per cent in 1991 and 226 per cent in 1992. Food rationing had to be introduced in 1991 and there was also a mass exodus from the countryside (where the collective farm system was rapidly crumbling), in addition to the much-publicized emigration of thousands of Albanian 'boat people', desperate to escape from the collapsing urban sector and a restrictive and politically bankrupt communist regime. By 1992 Albanians were heavily dependent on emergency aid from the West (including food aid) for their survival.

The system in crisis

Conditions may have been less grim in other parts of Eastern Europe. Nevertheless, there was widespread revulsion against the pervasive corruption, 'kleptocracy', police brutality, surveillance, irksome restrictions, baronial power and perversion or concealment of truth that characterized Eastern Europe's communist regimes. Citizens increasingly resented the perennial shortages and the time spent queuing or 'fruitlessly' searching for goods in short or highly erratic supply. Even in relatively well-stocked East Germany, Czechoslovakia and Hungary, the spread of Western comparators (aided by growing access to Western visitors, cultural goods and radio and television broadcasts) produced a threatening escalation of expectations and discontent. It became natural for East Europeans to compare their own plight with that of their relatively prosperous Western neighbours, rather than with even worse-off Eastern ones.

At the same time, various ecological and peace movements and some of the Protestant Churches intensified public environmental concern during the 1980s as increasing numbers of Soviet nuclear weapons and nuclear power plants were installed in Eastern Europe. The nuclear disaster at Chernobyl (in the Ukraine) in April 1986 was especially important. The environmental damage caused by neo-Stalinist economic development, with its heavy reliance and emphasis on old-fashioned ('smokestack') metallurgical, power-generating and chemical industries which were poisoning and acidifying the air and water supplies, was also a source of mounting concern. Thus 'Ecoglasnost', an environmental group demanding greater openness and veracity about the environmental costs of neo-Stalinist patterns of industrialization, was to play a prominent role in the toppling of the Zhivkov regime in Bulgaria in November 1989. By then, however, the economic and social programmes of Eastern Europe's communist regimes had lost all credibility, and after a decade of stagnation and retrogression even the ruling parties were losing faith in their capacity to lead their countries out of the deepening economic and social impasse in which they found themselves. This loss of faith, capacity and credibility seems rather more calamitous than the often alleged 'loss of legitimacy', given that most of these regimes had never had much legitimacy in the first place! Loss of legitimacy was mainly a problem for the Albanian and Yugoslav communist regimes, which had always been heavily dependent upon autonomous internal support

COMECON'S LAST GASPS

There were some last-ditch attempts to breathe new life into Comecon during the 1980s, in a vain attempt to revitalize the increasingly moribund centrally planned economies. A major Comecon 'economic summit' held in Moscow in June 1984 called for an accelerated transition to 'intensive growth', through a more 'rational' use of Comecon's resources, closer co-ordination of national economic plans, a strengthening of bilateral ties between Comecon states and 'active utilization of commodity–money relations' in addition to co-operation and plan co-ordination. Moreover, the Soviet leaders served notice that low-priced deliveries of fuel and raw materials to the East European states would be increased (to make good unilateral reductions imposed on them in 1982) only in so far as they upgraded their shoddy exports to the Soviet Union (Brabant 1989: 114–16). However, instead of having the intended effect, this further encouraged the East European states to expand their economic relations with the West, the more so since the Soviet Union was doing the same.

Much was expected of Mikhail Gorbachev, however, when he became Soviet leader in March 1985 and caught the world's attention with his programmes of *perestroika* (restructuring), *uskorenie* (acceleration), *demokratizatsiya* (democratization) and *glasnost* (openness). The December 1985 council session of Comecon approved a Comprehensive Programme to Promote the Scientific and Technological Progress of the Member Countries of the CMEA up to the Year 2000, calling for increased scientific and technical co-operation in the fields of electronics, information technology, automation, robotics, nuclear energy, new materials and biotechnology, with the declared aim of doubling output per worker by 2000. As a substitute for more fundamental systemic change, which could have aroused formidable opposition from powerful vested interests, Gorbachev and his chief economic mentor, Abel Aganbegyan, basically gambled on finding a quick technological fix for the problems of the Soviet economy and Comecon: 'Especially important is the preferential development of external economic ties within the framework of the CMEA . . . Of key significance here is the implementation of programmes of scientific technological progress with these countries . . . Since we must overcome the current trends and achieve a qualitative breakthrough in the development of the forces of production, we can no longer rely on the evolutionary form of scientific and technological progress. It cannot guarantee radical increases in economic efficiency. Such radical increase can only be assured by *revolutionary changes* in scientific and technological progress, with the transition from the old generation of technology to fundamentally new technological systems . . . Science will increasingly become a "direct productive force", as Marx foresaw, and a fundamental integration of science with production will take place as large scientific and production associations will become the bases of scientific and technological progress . . . By the year 2000 . . . the renewal of plant and machinery . . . will be running at 6 per cent or more per year. Virtually no machinery that is now in use will then remain . . . This is to be assured by trebling machine-building output over the fifteen years' (Aganbegyan 1988: 38, 84, 220).

Comecon's new scientific and technical co-operation programme reflected Gorbachev's essentially voluntarist and directive approach to the acceleration of economic growth, involving the imposition of new priorities and technologies 'from above' on a largely unchanged economic system. The programme failed, however, because it grossly underestimated both the extent and the negative consequences of the institutional isolation of the centrally planned economies (and their scientific communities) from each other and from the outside world and the (not unrelated) inability of centrally planned economies to match the continuous and all-pervasive pressures on capitalist economies to innovate in order to survive in increasingly competitive environments (Bideleux 1987: 151–55). The Gorbachev regime made too many commitments on too many fronts, thereby overstretching and overheating the Soviet economy. Bottlenecks and shortages were not relieved but exacerbated, while the East European members of Comecon resented being asked to contribute scarce capital to projects that were chiefly of interest to the Soviet Union and were always placed under the overall direction of Soviet scientific institutions. In any case, the hastily cobbled together scientific and technical co-operation programme emerged slightly too late to get incorporated into the new 1986–90 five-year plans (Brabant 1989: 117–21).

In 1985 the Soviet regime also launched an initiative that unwittingly hastened Comecon's demise. (If the likely consequences had been fully understood, it would surely have acted differently.) In June that year the secretary-general of Comecon, Vyacheslav Sychov, sent a letter and a draft joint declaration to the new president of the EC Commission, Jacques Delors, proposing reciprocal diplomatic recognition and relations between the European Community and Comecon, within the parameters of 'their respective competences' (Pinder 1991: 24). This signalled tacit acceptance that the European Community could directly negotiate trade agreements with individual Comecon members. (Unlike the European Community, Comecon had never been recognized as a legal person and its members had never empowered it to negotiate trade treaties on their behalf.) In October 1985 the EC commissioner for external relations,

Willy De Clercq, informed the European Parliament that the draft joint declaration could be accepted in principle, provided that mutual recognition and relations were accompanied by the normalization of bilateral relations between the European Community and Comecon's individual member states, which would then accredit diplomatic representatives to the European Community, negotiate trade agreements with it and cease to oppose EC representation on other international bodies. De Clercq sent Comecon and each of its members a letter to this effect in February 1986. By May all had formally accepted this twin-track approach to 'normal relations' between the two groups and their individual member states, paving the way for formal negotiations between Comecon and the European Community to commence in September 1986 (p. 25). The negotiations were prolonged by a dispute over the status of West Berlin, but the much-needed joint declaration of mutual recognition, reciprocal relations and co-operation on matters of joint interest was finally signed on 25 June 1988. This enabled the European Community to conclude trade and co-operation agreements with each of the European members of Comecon, starting with Hungary in December 1988, Poland in December 1989 and the Soviet Union, Czecho-Slovakia (as it became known), Romania and Bulgaria in 1990. These were soon superseded by so-called 'Europe Agreements' (beefed-up treaties of association), which were concluded with Poland, Hungary and Czecho-Slovakia in December 1991 and with Romania and Bulgaria in late 1992.

In July 1989, moreover, on the eve of the revolutions that ended communist rule, Mikhail Gorbachev made a major declaration at the Council of Europe: 'The political order of one country or another changed in the past and may change in the future. This change is the exclusive affair and choice of that country. Any interference in domestic affairs and any attempt to restrict the sovereignty of states, both friends and allies or any others, is inadmissible' (quoted in Arter 1993: 237). The so-called 'Sinatra doctrine' (that they could 'do it their way') reversed the previous 'Brezhnev doctrine' concerning the alleged 'limited sovereignty' of the 'fraternal' East European states (by which Brezhnev had tried to justify the Warsaw Pact invasion of Czechoslovakia in 1968) and gave the green light to sweeping reforms in Eastern Europe. In December 1989 the Soviet Union also proposed that from January 1991 onwards intra-CMEA trade should be conducted in hard currencies and at current world market prices, signalling the end of Soviet willingness (and even ability) to meet on concessional terms Eastern Europe's ever-increasing energy needs. The East European states were being allowed to go their own ways. But, by the same token, that was seen as absolving the Soviet Union of any further obligation towards them. Henceforth they would have to 'stand on their own feet', unconstrained but also unsupported by the Soviet Union. In January 1990 Czecho-Slovakia threatened to secede from Comecon if the other members did not agree to put it into liquidation. In the event a commission was established to assess the options and a Comecon meeting held in Prague in March 1990 proposed a rapid switch from multilateral to bilateral co-operation and plan co-ordination. In reality, however, there were no longer any plans to co-ordinate, since the new five-year plans for 1991–95 never left the drawing board.

Unfortunately, the trials and tribulations of the East European transition to market systems and untrammelled national sovereignty were seriously exacerbated by this over-hasty abandonment of the modest economic interdependences that had been so laboriously nurtured during Comecon's forty-one-year life span. From 1 January 1991 all intra-CMEA trade was officially to be conducted in hard currencies and at current world market prices (though the switch was already under way in 1990). The effects were earth-shaking. According to OECD estimates, the cost of the implicit shifts in Eastern Europe's terms of trade was, as a percentage of GNP, 4 per cent for Bulgaria, 2 per cent each for Hungary and Czechoslovakia, 1.5 per cent for Romania and slightly below 1 per cent for Poland (*FT*, 21 December 1990, p. 6). The volume of intra-CMEA trade fell by about 15 per cent in 1990 and more than halved in 1991. The OECD estimated that this, combined with the costs of the switch to trading in hard currencies and at current world prices, accounted for as much as two-thirds of that year's 10–15 per cent decline in Eastern European output (*Economic Outlook*, June 1992, p. 43).

Partly as a result of the collapse of intra-CMEA trade in 1990–91, trade with the European Community rose to about 50 per cent of the foreign trade of the East European states by 1992, from a mere 25 per cent in 1989. Nevertheless, trade with Eastern Europe (excluding the Commonwealth of Independent States) still accounted for only 1.7 per cent of the European Community's foreign trade in that year, i.e. less than the value of EC trade with countries such as Austria or Sweden at that time (David Marsh and Lionel Barber, *FT*, 7 June 1993, p. 13). Conversely, the share of other former members of Comecon in the foreign trade of the East European states had fallen to less than 25 per cent by 1993, from an average of just over 50 per cent in 1988. Thus Eastern Europe had merely exchanged asymmetrical trade dependence on the Soviet Union for an equally asymmetrical commercial dependence on the European Community. The final council session of Comecon was held in Budapest on 28 June 1991. The organization was to be disbanded within ninety days (i.e. by 28 September 1991). It is an exaggeration to claim, as Jonathan Eyal does, that Comecon amounted to 'little more than a medieval bazaar in which second-rate economies transacted barter deals and cheated each other' (*The Independent*, 22 February 1995, p. 15), but few mourned its demise. It may have been beyond redemption, but the manner of its passing would have inflicted less pain if it had been more dignified and gradual. The export niches which members had carved for themselves as suppliers of highly specific products to the former Soviet republics were incautiously thrown to the wind.

Unfortunately, the somewhat unhappy experience of externally imposed 'mutual economic assistance' and co-operation within Comecon has not helped to prepare either the peoples or the new rulers of Eastern Europe to work closely together in pursuit of further integration with the European Union and for the construction of interim arrangements to promote the requisite economic integration within Eastern Europe, both in order to salvage some of the fruitful interdependences that emerged in the communist era and to overcome Western doubts as to whether East European states are really capable of sinking their differences and becoming worthy partners in a wider Europe. Writing on the eve of the Revolutions of 1989, the Czechoslovak dissident Miroslav Kusy remarked that 'economic integration within the Soviet bloc has essentially taken place at such exalted levels that it does not affect daily life in the countries involved in such a way as to make all inhabitants directly aware of it . . . and generate in them a feeling of belonging to the bloc, a shared sense of East Europeanness' (Kusy 1989: 95).

THE REVOLUTIONS OF 1989–91

The collapse of the communist regimes of Eastern Europe in 1989 or, in the cases of Yugoslavia and Albania, 1990 and 1991, should not be attributed simply to the severity of the economic, social and environmental crises over which they presided during the 1980s. Measured in terms of telephones, televisions, washing machines, refrigerators, teachers, doctors, nurses, hospital beds or housing space per thousand inhabitants, East European living standards had been considerably lower during the 1950s and 1960s than they were in the late 1980s. The major difference was that the communist parties could still put forward plausible 'socialist' solutions to the problems of the 1950s and 1960s and hold out credible 'socialist' visions and hopes for the future, whereas they could see no 'socialist' way out of the economic, social and environmental crises of the 1980s. By then even 'market socialism' had fallen into disrepute, partly because the experiments in economic liberalization and decentralization in Hungary and Yugoslavia had run into seemingly insoluble difficulties. In addition, partly as a result of the neo-liberal counter-revolution in Western economics, market socialism and other so-called 'middle ways' between full-blown socialism and capitalism had ceased to be intellectually fashionable, in sharp contrast to the 1950s and 1960s. Few people, in either East or West, believed in them any longer. Reformist half-measures were ceasing to be acceptable. There seemed to be a straight choice between various viable forms of capitalism and several discredited variants of 'socialism'. Furthermore, even though the communist regimes managed to conceal the full magnitude of the 1980s crises from the public, and even from Western specialists on eastern Europe, the key figures within those regimes knew that their time was running out and gradually gave up the search for 'socialist' solutions. There was growing cynicism, a crisis of belief and a loss of vision at all levels. Indeed, Poznanski, Kolakowski and others have argued that the masses would not have undermined communist rule on their own. The communist parties themselves were, paradoxically, 'an equal or more essential force in the collapse'; and 'this self-destruction was in response not so much to the frustrated masses' as to the communists' own appreciation of 'the grim future that lay ahead'. Party leaders 'stopped believing', while the party faithful 'lost faith in what used to be perceived as the historic mission of the apparatus' (Poznanski 1992: 204). Many were at a complete loss as to what to do. In 1989 they lost control of a situation in which they should never have found themselves. The only obvious way out of the general crisis of Marxist-Leninist regimes was 'to relax the political structures and change property rights so that strong social groups interested in economizing on resources were reintroduced' (p. 93).

Significantly, Marxists have long argued that revolutions usually occur (i) when there is a fatal split within a ruling class which has lost faith in its own capacity to govern and to resolve crises, (ii) when the prevailing mode of production and social relations of production have reached the limits of their productive potential and have become a brake on any further development of society's productive forces, (iii) when a large section of the educated classes no longer support the *status quo* and (iv) when there is growing demoralization and discontent among the toiling classes. All these insights were clearly applicable to 1980s Eastern Europe. The ruling parties were manifestly losing faith in their own doctrines and competence to govern, there were paralysing splits between hard-line 'dogmatists' and more liberal 'reformers', the East European economies were visibly stagnating or contracting, there was a widespread 'defection' of the intelligentsia, and most workers felt badly let down (or even betrayed) by these self-proclaimed workers' states. There was widespread moral revulsion of the ruled against the mendacity, mediocrity, sleaze and corruption of the communist rulers, who had long ceased to command any respect. Their continuing claims to a monopoly of truth, wisdom and virtue became all the more derisory or repugnant. As argued by Ernest Gellner, 'the sleazy but . . . relatively mild squalor of the Brezhnev years proved far more corrosive for the image of the faith than the total, pervasive, random and massively destructive terror of Stalinism. That terror could at least be seen as the fearful but appropriately dramatic heralding of a totally new social order, the coming of a new man . . . The squalor, on the other hand, heralded nothing at all except, perhaps more squalor' (Gellner 1996: 3). In other words, 'When the *nomenklatura* killed each other and accompanied the murderous rampage with blatantly mendacious political theatre, belief survived; but when the *nomenklatura* switched from shooting each other to bribing each other, faith evaporated' (p. 41). Consequently, these regimes were unable to achieve any re-legitimation or self-renewal through competitive, pluralistic elections.

Not surprisingly, therefore, 'revisionist' and reform-minded Marxists played a seminal role in the gradual breakdown of communist rule and in the struggles for freedom in Eastern Europe, especially in Poland, Hungary, Czechoslovakia and Yugoslavia (Michnik 1985: 135–48). In the words of Adam Michnik, the doyen of Polish dissent (and like Lezlek Kolakowski and Jacek Kuron, himself a lapsed Marxist), critical Marxism left official communism 'with its teeth kicked in'. Critical Marxists pioneered the recreation of an 'independent space' for philosophical discourse and the revival of political engagement and activism in place of apathetic acceptance of the apparent unassailability of the communist regimes (Taras 1992: 3–12). By producing the most damaging critiques of 'actually existing socialism', by having the courage and the capacity to challenge it on its own terms and from within, and by exposing intrinsic failings which tended to get overlooked by right-wing critics attuned to a very different agenda and discourse, dissident Marxism hit the communist regimes where it hurt most. It was second to none in undermining Marxism as an official ideology and reducing it to a hollow shell.

The social and political upheavals of 1989–91, which ended communist rule in Eastern Europe, were in large measure a 'revolution from above' stage-managed by the white-collar intelligentsia, reform communists and 'closet reformers' within the Soviet KGB. Even the apparently spontaneous demonstrations of popular hostility to the dying communist dictatorships were to a considerable extent prepared and informed by 'passive revolutions' (in the Gramscian sense), i.e. by significant shifts in the balance of power, values, aspirations and ideas which established the cultural and political leadership and hegemony of the white-collar intelligentsia in East European societies. Through their growing dominance of the media and information services, the white-collar intelligentsia and reform communists committed to political and economic liberalization were able to manipulate the symbols and ideology of the incipient East European revolutions and indicate to the population at large what was taking place, how and when popular pressure ('people power') could most effectively be applied and where mass demonstrations should assemble or converge.

The communist dictatorships had sown the seeds of their own destruction. The future ruling class was being nurtured, as always, within the womb of the old system. East European industrialization, mass education and the vaunted 'scientific-technological revolution', vigorously promoted by communist regimes, had elevated both the so-called 'creative intelligentsia' and the white-collar professional, managerial and technical intelligentsia to 'leading' (guiding) roles in East European societies. By the 1980s such groups constituted 20–30 per cent of the work force, according to official classifications and calculations. Since the 1960s, conversely, the old 'blue collar' working class had steadily shrunk as a proportion of the work force and had become increasingly differentiated, heterogeneous and, in its upper echelons, 'embourgeoised'. As in the West and in the Soviet Union, increased mechanization, complex control systems and the 'scientific-technological revolution' had progressively reduced the importance of manual labour and enhanced that of technical, professional and managerial skills, expertise and training. Moreover, the ruling parties and so-called 'techno-bureaucratic personnel' were increasingly recruited from the ranks of the intelligentsia rather than the shrinking 'blue collar' working class. Indeed, while it remained fashionable to dwell on antagonisms between the intelligentsia at large and the narrower party-state bureaucracy, in reality the intelligentsia was not sharply separated from but increasingly overlapped with the party-state bureaucracy. As the Hungarian sociologist Ivan Szelenyi pointed out in 1979, the borderline between the intelligentsia and the party-state bureaucracy was 'a very shaky one in terms of personal career patterns. Many university graduates with high academic ambitions enter the party bureaucracy' and, 'from the point of view of material privilege, it is practically impossible to distinguish between the techno-bureaucracy and the intelligentsia. Their living standard is practically identical' (Szelenyi 1979: 59). He also argued that the all-pervasive roles of central planning under the highly 'teleological' (goal-oriented) and 'redistributive' communist regimes had enhanced the ideological and managerial roles and social status of the intelligentsia far above that attained under capitalism, placing the intelligentsia rather than capitalists in the driving seat and transforming the intelligentsia into a type of secular priesthood that not only managed social resources but also arrogated the exclusive right to prescribe society's goals and values. This virtually 'integrates the whole intelligentsia into a dominating class' (pp. 65–6). Furthermore, by the mid-1950s in Poland and Hungary, by the 1960s in Czechoslovakia, Yugoslavia and the GDR, and by the 1980s elsewhere in the rest of Eastern Europe, the growing 'creative' and 'technical' intelligentsias fostered by the communist regimes were chafing against the crudities, the narrow-mindedness, the excesses and the irksome tutelage of one-party rule. However, in contrast to the archetypal nineteenth-century radical/oppositional intelligentsias (which characteristically led a precarious existence on the margins of society and of the economy and were essentially independent of the state), the new intelligentsias fostered by the communist states mainly consisted of state employees whose power, aspirations, special status, privileges and sense of importance and vocation were largely determined by their position and role as servants and functionaries of hegemonic state institutions, even after the collapse of communist rule. They have remained very dependent on somewhat humbled and impoverished but still dominant states to protect and provide for them and to give them a continuing status and sense of importance in the new post-communist societies, despite (or even because of) the fact that many of their former functions have become redundant or superfluous as a result of the dismantling of command economies and communist regimes. Many have found themselves in an extremely vulnerable, impoverished and wholly unenviable position. Not surprisingly, therefore, their enthusiasm for political and economic liberalism has been tempered by acute awareness of their continuing dependence on the state and by prudent reluctance to bite the hand that has not only fed them but has also given them some sense of usefulness and public worth. The initial predominance of the intelligentsia was reinforced by the fact that an entrepreneurial business class was only just beginning to emerge and was not yet politically effective at the time of the East European Revolutions of 1989–91. This and the continuing preponderance of the state sector, which could not be privatized overnight, left the 'hegemonic' leading roles of the intelligentsia and state functionaries almost unchallenged for the time being.

Poland and, to a much lesser extent, Romania and (in 1991) Albania provided the only clear-cut examples of worker-led rejection of communist rule. But even the Solidarity government formed in June 1989 was completely dominated by the liberal-minded intelligentsia, to the disgust of many of Solidarity's 'blue collar' grass-roots supporters, thousands of whom were to be made redundant or dismissed from their jobs by agents and official receivers appointed by the Solidarity government as a result of the economic 'shock therapy' administered in 1990. The major problem for most of Eastern Europe's 'blue collar' workers was that, except in Poland (where Solidarity was indeed in a position to provide genuinely independent grass-roots union representation and defence of the interests of workers, but was placed in an invidious position when Solidarity intellectuals took up the principal reins of government), the capacity of workers to represent and defend their interests during the transition from communist rule and command economies was limited by the fact that the existing official trade unions were greatly weakened and discredited by their close links with and subservience to the now defunct communist parties and regimes. Moreover, the fact that many of Eastern Europe's heavy industries were grossly over-manned, inefficient, struggling to survive and, in effect, surplus to requirements (especially after the communist regimes collapsed and the Cold War ended) placed most of Eastern Europe's 'blue collar' workers in an extremely weak bargaining position.

The peasantry played even less of a role in the East European Revolutions of 1989–91. Although East European peasants had received a raw deal during the 1950s, their plight had on the whole improved significantly during the 1960s and 1970s. The basic reason for this reversal of fortune was, paradoxically, that agriculture had come to be seen as a problem sector. During the Stalinist era, when the still mainly agricultural East European economies were able to maintain basic self-sufficiency in agricultural products despite the rapid growth of urban industrial sectors, the remuneration and resource requirements of East European agriculture had been been given a relatively low priority. But by the 1960s and 1970s, as the growth of urban industrial sectors, incomes and effective demand for agricultural products began to outstrip the growth of domestic agricultural output, agricultural remuneration, resource requirements and state subsidies were gradually accorded a higher priority, in an endeavour to minimize urban food shortages, workers' discontent and the expenditure of scarce foreign exchange on imports of agricultural products. Nevertheless, the communist regimes' persistent reluctance to raise official retail food prices (partly for fear of provoking urban unrest), combined with an accelerating growth of disposable money incomes in the towns, meant that aggregate demand for agricultural products continued to outstrip the more moderate growth of farm output. Indeed, it was in the interest of the farm population to make only modest increases in agricultural deliveries to the state distribution networks. For, so long as agriculture remained a 'problem' in the eyes of the state, farmers could expect to receive increased farm subsidies, remuneration and investment from the state and to be allowed increasingly to engage in lucrative sidelines, private enterprise and petty pilfering, to which farm officials increasingly turned a blind eye because they were either in on the game or fearful of alienating a still somewhat resentful peasant population. Conversely, if farmers had delivered enough agricultural produce to satisfy rapidly growing demand, agriculture would have ceased to be seen as such a serious problem and the state would have treated them less generously, while farm officials could have become stricter. It therefore paid the farm populations to fulfil their obligations to the state and to the collective farms as perfunctorily as they could and increasingly to concentrate on their private 'home improvements' and increased private production not only of food but of clothing, footwear, jewellery and drinks for their own consumption and for the relatively high-priced 'free' markets and the black market. These private activities increasingly diverted resources from the collective and state farms, both legally and illicitly, but that was the state's problem, not the peasantry's. Even during the relative stagnation of the 1980s, the real incomes and assets of the farm populations continued to increase as states desperately pumped in more and more resources in a vain endeavour to reinvigorate collective and state farming, while persistent urban food shortages perpetuated the opportunities for private profiteering and black-marketeering. In effect, farmers got their own back for the hardships and privations to which they had been subjected during the 1940s and 1950s. In the process, however, they became less interested in radical change. Like their West European counterparts, East European farmers had much to fear from the freer trade, price reforms, withdrawal of subsidies, runaway inflation and loss of captive markets that could result from a change of political and economic regime.

During 1990 it gradually came to light that 'closet reformers' in the Soviet KGB (state security police) had also played a significant role in the subversion of the hard-line communist regimes in East Germany and Czechoslovakia in November 1989 and possibly in Romania the following month. The aim was not to end but to prolong communist rule by replacing embarrassingly hard-line rulers with more palatable and pragmatic 'reform communists' in the Gorbachev mould, who could be relied upon to initiate a managed transition to more market-oriented and pluralistic regimes in keeping with the liberal image projected by Soviet *perestroika* and *glasnost* and the 'reform communism' of neighbouring Hungary. These manoeuvres misfired, however, triggering changes which rapidly went beyond what reform communists and the KGB had intended. The KGB-backed reform communists lost out because of a complete loss of faith in and rejection of the ruling communist parties, other than in their new 'socialist', National Salvation Front and Serbian nationalist incarnations in Bulgaria, Romania and Serbia, respectively. In most cases, moreover, reform communists still had the cautious mind sets of enlightened and paternalistic planners, aiming at limited reforms 'from above' rather than more radical initiatives 'from below'. They were afraid of the working classes and of any real spontaneity and, as soon as large numbers of East Europeans displayed a will to move beyond the limited agenda of reform communism in late 1989, the reform communists lost their political power base almost overnight. They suddenly became 'yesterday's men' as they were quickly overtaken by events.

The Revolutions of 1989–91 took Western specialists on Eastern Europe (among others) by surprise because their underlying assumptions about communist regimes overestimated their resilience and staying power and underestimated the extent to which East European civil society was able to foster alternative political cultures which could erode the increasingly threadbare political legitimacy of communist rule. The revolutions were the result of a prolonged systemic crisis allied to the unwillingness of the Soviet leader, Mikhail Gorbachev, to emulate his predecessors by employing force to keep Eastern Europe's communist leaders in power. Command economies could function only so long as commands were generally obeyed. As the ruling elites became increasingly divided as to how to react to the systemic crisis, civil society lost some of its former fear of the seemingly formidable apparatus of repression, while the diminution of fear decreased the disposition to obey. Nevertheless, the East European revolutions probably would not have succeeded if Gorbachev had not unilaterally renounced old habits of Soviet military-political intervention in Eastern Europe's internal affairs. The emergence of the Gorbachev regime was therefore a necessary (though not a sufficient) condition for the democratization of Eastern Europe.

Gorbachev's team may have decided as early as autumn 1986 to renounce the use of force in Eastern Europe and had an ideal opportunity to inform the East European communist party leaders of this at the CMEA summit held in Moscow on 10–11 November 1986 (*Pravda* 1992: 17–18, 70). 'Gorbachev realized that the Europeanization of the Soviet Union could not proceed without the de-Sovietization of Eastern Europe' (Dawisha 1990: 198). Conversely, Gorbachev's concept of a 'common European home' dovetailed with the East European intelligentsias' undying belief in the oneness of Europe and it reinforced their efforts to deepen or renew their emotional and cultural ties with the West, implicitly turning away from Russia. At the same time, paradoxically, Gorbachev's programme of *perestroika* profoundly influenced Eastern Europe by providing a potent model and symbol of reform from above and of liberalization, by licensing or igniting a ferment of ideas, debate and demands for reform in other communist states and by encouraging East European communist leaders to ape Gorbachev (pp. 208–10). Thus the imperatives of Soviet *perestroika* destabilized Eastern Europe in the late 1980s, much as Khrushchev's 'de-Stalinization' programme had done in 1956. Furthermore, by abandoning the customary requirement of Soviet approval of successors to East European communist party leaders after 1985, Gorbachev ended a direct channel of Soviet supervision of its East European 'allies' (Light 1994: 154–5), although the KGB continued to operate behind the scenes from Soviet embassies in Eastern Europe at least until the end of 1989. Gorbachev's announcement in 1988 that Soviet troops would be withdrawn from Afghanistan was widely seen not just as a blow to the aura of Soviet invincibility and to Soviet military morale, but also as tangible confirmation of his renunciation of Soviet military interference in the affairs of 'fraternal socialist states'. This helped to lift the veil of fear which had hitherto kept East European hostility to communist rule in check.

Gorbachev's marked reluctance to express approval of the Berlin Wall, let alone the Soviet invasions of Hungary in 1956 or of Czechoslovakia in 1968, reduced the security and legitimacy of the Honecker, Kadar and Husak regimes, because Honecker had risen to power as the man who oversaw the building of the Berlin Wall in 1961 and the GDR's role in the 1968 invasion of Czechoslovakia, while both Kadar and Husak headed quisling regimes initiated by Soviet invasions. Without his having to issue explicit disavowals or condemnations, the distaste with which Gorbachev regarded the unsavoury hard-line rulers of the GDR, Czechoslovakia, Bulgaria and Romania became plainly visible to millions of television viewers who watched the official television coverage of his public meetings with and visits to East European communist leaders. It was also difficult to disguise the pointed contrast between the spontaneous enthusiasm of the crowds that greeted Gorbachev during his visits to Eastern Europe and their sullen indifference to their own rulers. Eastern Europe's hard-line communist regimes were further undermined when there was no public Soviet protest either against the opening of Hungary's border with Austria in May 1989 or against Hungary's decision officially to allow East German 'holiday-makers' to escape through that bolthole to the West on 10 September 1989. This and Gorbachev's refusal to sanction a military crackdown on mounting East German popular demands for freedom in October 1989 increased the pressure on the regime to allow East Germans freely to cross the Berlin Wall on 9 November 1989, thereby imparting an unstoppable momentum to German unification and to further popular challenges to brittle communist authority throughout Eastern Europe. As Havel remarked on 9 April 1990, 'We all know how much harder our road to freedom would have been if the great work of renewal in our society had not been linked with the name of President Gorbachev' (Havel 1994a: 63).

Nevertheless, Gorbachev was mainly 'reacting to events rather than initiating them' (Light 1994: 154). There is no suggestion that he was acting out a master plan for the dismantling of communist rule in Eastern Europe. Rather, he hoped to ensure its survival by encouraging the deposition of hard-liners in favour of reformers in his own image. However, the undermining of hard-liners unleashed forces which also dethroned the reform communists.

In the final analysis, Gorbachev precipitated the democratization of Eastern Europe not so much by what he consciously did as by what he *was*, namely a tonic, a beacon of hope, a humane voice of reason and an opponent of falsehood, intimidation, sleaze and hypocrisy. In some ways, curiously, he was quite out of tune with the darker forces that were unleashed by the democratization of the Soviet bloc and the long retreat from communist 'proletarian internationalism'. For example, when he visited the victims of the devastating earthquake which struck Armenia in 1988, he was understandably shocked and angered to discover that some Armenians were much more interested in the line he would take in Armenia's territorial dispute with the neighbouring Soviet Republic of Azerbaijan than in what was to be done to assist the earthquake victims lying on the ground all around them (Roxburgh 1991: 122–3). Gorbachev avoided military invasions and crackdowns, other than in Georgia and the Baltic Soviet Republics, where Soviet forces may conceivably have defied his wishes, although the evidence is ambiguous. (Most Georgians and nationalists of the Baltic States are convinced of Gorbachev's complicity, but we are not.) Gorbachev thus contributed to the remarkably low levels of violence employed by either side (other than in Romania and Yugoslavia) during the collapse of communist rule in Eastern Europe. Moreover, by adopting a new foreign policy and continuing it even though it cost the Soviet Union its external sphere of influence, Gorbachev 'created the conditions in which democratic forces within Eastern Europe could come to the fore, and Western democratic and market forces could penetrate the region'. However, 'only the East Europeans themselves were in a position to ensure that the outcome was democracy' (Light 1994: 163–4).

22 Eastern Europe since 1989: the 'triple transition'

1989 IN HISTORICAL PERSPECTIVE

In 1989 most of Eastern Europe embarked on an arduous 'triple transition': from communist dictatorship to pluralistic democracy; from centrally administered to market economies; and from Soviet imperial hegemony to fully independent nation-statehood. It was the third time that Eastern Europe had embarked on a transition of such magnitude. After the First World War much of the region underwent an analogous triple transition: from semi-absolutist monarchies to ostensibly democratic regimes; from a supranational imperial order to an order based on fully independent nation-states; and from a social order dominated by imperial bureaucracies and armies and large landed estates to societies with a preponderance of peasant farmers, dominated by national bureaucracies, national armies and ascendant national bourgeoisies. After the Second World War, Eastern Europe attempted yet another triple transition: from fascist imperial domination to independent national statehood; from fascist dictatorship to pluralistic democracy; and from fascist (autarkic) administered economies to more open, semi-planned market economies. The post-1918 transition came to grief on the rocks of illiberal 'ethnic' or 'integral' nationalism, irredentism, revanchism, beggar-my-neighbour protectionism and increasing 'asymmetrical' commercial dependence on a resurgent German Reich and, to a lesser extent, Fascist Italy. The post-1945 transition succumbed to an extension of Soviet imperial hegemony over the East European states and the imposition of neo-Stalinist regimes and programmes of coercive, centrally planned industrialization and rural collectivization, whose limited positive appeal rested in part on their alleged capacity to transcend the ethnic, irredentist and economic problems that had plagued Eastern Europe from 1918 to 1947.

These woeful outcomes raised fundamental doubts concerning the intrinsic viability and applicability of the Wilsonian ideals of the sovereign nation-state and national self-determination in Eastern Europe. The sceptics argued that the small and weak East European states could at best hope for an illusory national independence (camouflaging actual dependence upon or domination by either the Soviet Union or Germany) and that the inextricably intermingled ethnic patchwork of Eastern Europe made it virtually impossible to draw frontiers that would allow nations to occupy discrete and contiguous territories capable of completely satisfying all conflicting ethnic claims and national aspirations while maintaining viable economic units and the necessary levels of inter-national trade and co-operation. No amount of redrawing of frontiers and subdivision of territorial units could accommodate all ethnic claims and thereby eliminate all substantial ethnic minorities and irredentism. The implication was that the peoples of Eastern Europe required some kind of supranational order, policed by an external overlord or arbiter capable of standing above their endemic quarrels, or that all-round peace and prosperity could not be attained on the basis of fully independent nation-states. For some East European political movements, notably the Austro-Marxists and the federalist elements in the peasantist movements, the ideal route to a prosperous and harmonious new order was through some sort of supranational federation, uniting East Europeans on an equal footing in a single economically integrated state large enough and therefore strong enough to withstand external pressures and encroachments. However, doubts as to whether such an arrangement would have been capable of withstanding the internal inter-ethnic tensions and rivalries of Eastern Europe and their potentially paralysing effects on structural reform and collective decision-making were rather borne out by the near-paralysis and gradual disintegration of the multinational Yugoslav federation during the 1980s and by the more rapid disintegration of post-communist Czechoslovakia in 1991–92.

The previous attempts to build a 'new order' in Eastern Europe on the basis of fully independent nation-states coincided with crises arising from the concurrent social and economic transitions and the attendant disruption of natural or long-established trade patterns. These crises fostered extreme nationalism, labour unrest and the rise of neo-fascist and communist movements, curbed popular support for liberal democracy and 'free market' economics, and invited external intervention in East European affairs. Unfortunately, the post-1989 transitions recreated similar conditions and opportunities in former Yugoslavia during the first half of the 1990s and came close to doing so elsewhere. Although the communist regimes were officially atheist and internationalist, and frequently persecuted clergy, active 'believers' and outspoken independent-minded nationalists, they nevertheless fostered or revived 'official nationalism' and tolerated the dominant 'national' religions, in a vain and ultimately self-destructive attempt to compensate for deficiencies in their own political legitimacy and popular support from the 1960s through the 1980s. This left nationalism and 'national' religions as the only available value and belief systems that were immediately capable of filling the spiritual and ideological vacuum exposed by the decline and eventual fall of the moribund communist dictatorships. The initial national euphoria unleashed by the collapse of communist rule enhanced the influence of exclusive and potentially intolerant 'ethnic' nationalism and national religions and aroused expectations which could not rapidly be fulfilled. The initial frenzied hopes of instant prosperity soon dissolved into realization that the market too can be a ruthless and tyrannical master.

The situation was exacerbated by the fact that there had never been much of a politically and economically independent middle-class constituency for either political or economic liberalism in eastern Europe. It was going to be as difficult to create liberal democracy and capitalism with insufficient capital and without highly developed bourgeoisies as it had been to create 'proletarian dictatorships' and centrally planned economies with insufficient capital and without highly developed industrial proletariats. Admittedly, the eighteenth and nineteenth centuries had seen the emergence of auton-omous mercantile, professional and industrial activities in parts of Eastern Europe. That and the expansion of education, journalism, publishing and political activities also gave rise to autonomous 'national intelligentsias' who came to see themselves as the champions and apostles of the emerging East European nations during the ensuing struggles for 'national liberation' from supposedly 'alien' Habsburg, Ottoman and Tsarist imperial rule. Once the East European nations attained independent statehood, however, these emergent 'national bourgeoisies' and 'national intelligentsias' became, for the most part, servitors, clients or protégés of the new 'national' states, in which they naturally gained an exalted status as key constituents of the ruling 'nations'. They thus tended to be less independent of the state than the professional, intellectual and entrepreneurial segments of certain ethnic minorities, especially the widespread German and Jewish minorities, the Hungarians of Transylvania, Slovakia and Vojvodina, the Italians of Croatia and Slovenia and the Greeks of southern Albania, Bulgaria and Romania. Moreover, the major institutions of most of the newly independent East European states were largely controlled by 'national' leaderships which upheld increasingly narrow, exclusive and illiberal 'integral' or 'ethnic' conceptions of the nation, in contrast to the more inclusive 'civic' definitions of the nation which prevailed in western Europe (excluding Germany). They favoured their own 'national' entrepreneurs, professionals and intellectuals, who became increasingly dependent on state patronage and nepotism and endeavoured gradually to marginalize the more autonomous, prosperous, educated, cosmopolitan, entrepreneurial and independent-minded ethnic minorities. Czecho-slovakia was a partial exception to the rule, in that the relatively large, educated and successful Czech middle class and intelligentsia remained much more liberal than their counterparts in other East European states. Yet even the Czechs tended to keep a disproportionate share of political and economic power (including state employment, funding and contracts) in their own hands and resisted even the most reasonable demands for a reorganization of this multinational state along federal lines.

Having belatedly won independent 'national' statehood, after what the triumphant nationalists and 'national' historians now saw as centuries of national oppression at the hands of 'alien' imperial overlords, the new dominant ethnic groups felt quite justified in taking the lion's share of any political, economic or cultural 'spoils'. (This mentality was still very much alive in Eastern Europe in the 1990s. Soon after Slovakia became independent at the beginning of 1993, its nationalistic ex-communist Prime Minister, Vladimir Meciar, declared: 'We have waited 1,000 years for this opportunity, 1,000 years of oppression and discord. I want to tell all those who wish to take revenge on the government for 1 January 1993, all adventurers who do not understand the way history works, that should we lose this state, then the waves of European development will swallow us, just as they swallowed the Lusatian Sorbs': quoted in *The Independent*, 18 May 1993, p. 9. In truth, far from dreaming of a Slovak national state for a thousand years, hardly anyone had seriously entertained such an idea before the twentieth century.) A major consequence of the triumphalism of exclusive, intolerant and messianic 'ethnic' nationalism was that there came to be no possibility of a politically and ethnically impartial state, one that dispensed justice and upheld and applied the law without ethnic, racial, religious or clannish bias. Increasingly, there was one law for ethnic minorities and another (very bendable) law for the ruling clientele. Patronage, nepotism and clientelism prospered at the expense of (generally weak) civil institutions, social underdogs and vulnerable/marginalized ethnic minorities, particularly as chronic political and economic instability, the rise of fascism, growing threats to 'national' security and the 1930s Depression reinforced the underlying trend towards intolerant 'integral' or 'ethnic' nationalism and illiberal, introverted etatism and economic nationalism.

The still comparatively small independent entrepreneurial and professional middle classes were drastically reduced in size by the mass extermination of most East European

Jews during the Second World War, the subsequent emigration of most of those who survived and the hasty departure or expulsion of some 10 million Germans from Eastern Europe at the end of the war. Besides horrific suffering and loss of human life, this also inflicted enormous economic and political costs, since Jews and Germans had (between them) made up at least half of Eastern Europe's independent urban professional and entrepreneurial middle classes up to the Second World War. The Stalinist regimes established in Eastern Europe in the later 1940s quickly completed the work begun by illiberal nationalists and fascists, by bringing all public institutions and activities under communist control and destroying the last vestiges of 'civil society' and of the legal, administrative, educational and cultural impartiality of the state. Indeed, East European politics remained very violent during the late 1940s and early 1950s, as the post-war (anti-fascist) Popular Front coalitions sought retribution against thousands of known or suspected fascists and their wartime collaborators, even before the ascendant communist parties instituted large-scale 'purges' against tens of thousands of actual or potential opponents. The survivors of the decimated pre-war intelligentsia and the professional and entrepreneurial middle classes were either 'liquidated' by these purges and the attendant suppression of almost all independent activity or 'swamped' by the large, malleable and subservient 'technical' and 'creative' intelligentsias fostered by the Stalinist regimes. These new intelligentsias were to a large extent recruited from the educated upper layers of the working class and the peasantry, thus 'buying off' or 'creaming off' the potential spokesmen or ringleaders of proletarian and peasant opposition and discontent, while also creating a new privileged class which consciously owed its position and perquisites to communist favours and patronage. Thus one of the major initial impediments to the maturation of democracy in Eastern Europe states since 1989 has been the fact that, other than in the Czech Lands, independent and impartial political and civil institutions have hardly existed before and those that did emerge were largely destroyed by the combined effects of intolerant 'ethnic' nationalism and authoritarianism, the 1930s Depression, fascism, the Second World War, the Holocaust and neo-Stalinist dictatorship, all of which had helped to decimate or drive abroad the ethnic and social groups that were most capable of producing or recreating autonomous, pluralistic and liberal-minded 'civil societies'.

THE POST-1989 'DEMOCRATIC TRANSITIONS' IN COMPARATIVE PERSPECTIVE

Sudden or rapid transitions from authoritarian to at least outwardly democratic government in societies that have lacked strong liberal-democratic and constitutionalist traditions inherently involve major discontinuities in political legitimacy and authority and raise great dangers of anarchy, rampant criminality, social/economic insecurity, and chronic political paralysis and/or instability. Democratic rights and institutions which are suddenly won, granted or ceded 'from on high', from authoritarian associations, networks or power structures that are still to a large extent intact tend to be relatively easy to revoke. Conversely, when liberal democracy is established via the sudden collapse of an authoritarian regime, the new rulers cannot readily lean on pre-existing procedures, institutions or principles of legitimacy to stabilize their authority. Successful transitions to liberal democracy have usually been underpinned by a prior or concurrent burgeoning of social forces that have 'constrained pre-existing ruling groups progressively to share their power and privileges with wider and wider sections of society', especially by the emergence of 'a plurality of independent groups jealously guarding their autonomy' (Kornhauser 1960: 135, 141). The survival of liberal democracy normally depends upon the existence of a rich diversity of responsible and autonomous social groups. It requires 'limitations on the use of power by majorities as well as minorities', involving not only 'constitutional checks and balances (e.g. separation of powers), but also a system of social checks and balances', typically in the form of a multiplicity of autonomous competing 'interest groups'. Otherwise, in the absence of 'constitutional rule, backed by a system of social checks and balances', there are insufficient safeguards against the potential tyranny of majorities and/or the state (pp. 130–1). In the absence of autonomous, articulate and effectively organized pressure 'from below', it is easier for ruling elites to abuse their powers and privileges, to stonewall or to get away with murder, and policies are less likely to be thrashed out and debated as much as they should be. Conversely, a plurality of independent social groups not only works against excessive concentration of power and authority in too few hands, but also supports and sustains authority by sharing it. Autonomous social groups act as 'intermediate authorities capable of ordering limited spheres of social life' and simultaneously support and enlarge 'the sphere of liberty' by constraining each other and the state to seek mutual accommodation within a framework of rights of free association, freedom of expression, the rule of law, etc. (p. 136).

The strength and vigour of democracies and market economies depend even more on the size, health and vitality of these intermediate layers, networks and associations, which stand and mediate between the state and individuals, than on having the requisite formal political and economic institutions. In this respect, economics and politics go hand-in-hand, for the most dynamic economies are those with the most vigorous networks of intermediate associations, viz. the East Asian 'tigers' as well as the most successful Western economies (Ian Davidson, *FT*, 1 February 1995, p. 14). Crude neo-liberal free-marketeers in the Thatcherite mould mistakenly equate civil society with the market and individuals and overlook the extent to which both democracy and market systems rest on the autonomous intermediate institutions, associations, ties and networks and standards of probity which neo-liberal policies did so much to weaken, emasculate, undermine or erode in Britain and the United States during the 1980s and, in the absence of which, the state stands omnipotent over isolated and unprotected individuals.

The increasingly voluminous (but often opaque) political science literature on democratic 'transition' and 'consolidation' has generated some useful distinctions and conceptual taxonomies. Democratic transition is widely seen as 'a process of regime change commencing at the point when the previous authoritarian regime begins to be dismantled, abruptly or gradually'. During this phase 'democratic rules of procedure have to be negotiated and accepted; institutions have to be restructured; and political competition has to be channelled along democratic lines'. Democratic consolidation, by contrast, is normally a lengthier process involving 'the removal of the uncertainties that invariably surround transition and the full institutionalization of the new systems, the internalization of its rules and procedures and the dissemination of democratic values' (Pridham *et al.* 1994: 2). In addition to contingent economic and social circumstances, various studies of democratic consolidation in southern Europe and Latin America have sought to emphasize the crucial importance of so-called 'elite settlements' and 'elite convergence', i.e. processes which encourage elites to engage in 'politics as bargaining' rather than 'politics as war'. Elite settlements involve formal pacts, under the terms of which 'previously disunified and warring elites suddenly and deliberately reorganize their relations by negotiating compromises on their most basic disagreements, thereby achieving consensual unity and laying the basis for a stable democratic regime'. Elite convergence, by contrast, involves 'a series of deliberate, tactical decisions by rival elites that have the cumulative effect . . . of creating elite consensual unity', perhaps over the space of a generation. Elite convergence often occurs in two stages. In the first, 'some of the warring factions in a disunified national elite enter into sustained, peaceful collaboration in order to mobilize a reliable electoral majority, win elections repeatedly, and thereby dominate government'. In the second stage, 'the major elite factions opposing this coalition tire of continuous government by their ideological and programmatic opponents'. However, instead of resorting to violent conflict, 'they conclude that there is no way to challenge their rivals' hegemonic position except . . . by forming an electoral coalition . . . to compete according to the regime's rules, implicitly or explicitly acknowledging the legitimacy of its institutions'. In the main 'this is accompanied by a reduction of ideological and programmatic polarization in the party system' (Higley and Gunther 1992: xi–xii).

The recent 'democratic transition' literature is an advance on the old 'modernization' theories (which naively saw democracy as an inevitable concomitant of economic and educational development). It takes some account of circumstantial and volitional factors. It also acknowledges that democracy is not an automatic accompaniment of economic and educational advance, and that processes of democratization can suffer reverses and/or impediments even in quite educated and economically developed societies. Nevertheless, despite the usefulness of some of its terminology and insights, much of the 1980s and 1990s 'democratic transition' literature is fundamentally flawed or misleading. It often appears to assume that 'democratic transitions' involve movement from broadly comparable starting points towards broadly comparable destinations, that elites are free to choose whatever political arrangements they fancy, and that democracy can be established and consolidated from the top downwards.

In reality, however, the points of departure can vary enormously, as can the 'democratic' destinations. The word 'democracy' is an umbrella term covering many different forms of democratic polity and governance. Moreover, political systems are not simply the fruits of the wishes of their participants. They are to a large degree socially constrained, even socially determined: 'Men are born into and live within the institutions and culture of their society, which they often take for granted . . . A culture is a system of prejudgement. Social institutions and cultures are seldom chosen: they are our fate, not our choice . . . But, generally speaking, the democratic model ignores the fact that institutions and cultures *precede* decisions rather than *follow* them' (Gellner 1996: 185). In rejecting the cruder versions of Marxist economic determinism, which insisted that the socio-economic 'base' rigidly determines a society's political and ideological 'superstructure', Eastern Europeans must beware of falling into the opposite error of assuming that the superstructure operates autonomously. Much of 'democratic transition' (and comparative government) literature misleadingly abstracts political systems and institutions from their social and cultural context and therefore ignores the extent to which they are socially and culturally conditioned and constrained. Political institutions are dependent rather than independent variables. Democracy can become firmly established only if it is undergirded by the emergence (even prior existence) of horizontal social networks and groupings and widespread adherence to impartial and civil codes of law and conduct. A constitutional democratic regime becomes secure only when 'its ways have become engrained in the habits and instinctive reactions – *dans les moeurs* – of the political nation: it safeguards civilized life, but it presupposes agreement and stability as much as it secures them' (Namier 1946: 31). In this regard it is especially unfortunate that the Balkan nations have always been ruled by people, not laws.

Quite apart from these fundamental objections, it is also necessary to qualify or take issue with particular arguments put forward by the recent 'democratic transitions' literature.

It is widely held that the range and magnitude of the problems and challenges faced and posed by democratic transitions and consolidation have been far greater in post-1989 Eastern Europe than they were in Greece, Portugal, Spain and most parts of Latin America during the 1970s and 1980s (Higley and Gunther 1992: 344–7 ff.; Pridham *et al.* 1994: 7–9, 52–3, 168–71). With the significant exception of Cuba, which as yet has neither democracy nor a market economy, the newly democratized states of southern Europe and Latin America already had long-standing market economies (even if some of them contained many very poor people), whereas the East European states have changed their economic systems at the same time as moving from one-party dictatorships to democracy. In post-communist Eastern Europe, it is argued, democratization has been associated with greatly increased economic and social disruption, insecurity and hardship. Second, it is usually argued that, with the possible exception of Castro's Cuba, the authoritarian regimes of twentieth-century southern Europe and Latin America have never suppressed the plurality and autonomy of social and economic groups to anything like the degree that the communist regimes of Eastern Europe did. Most of the post-communist states of Eastern Europe are having to recreate a plurality of autonomous social and economic groups, whereas it is generally maintained that the new democratic regimes of Latin America and southern Europe have been able to take for granted the prior existence of such groups and that this has facilitated economic change and responsiveness as well as democratization. Third, it is widely assumed that democratic transitions and consolidation in southern Europe and Latin America have not had to contend with problems of irredentism and/or inter-ethnic antagonism on anything like the scale that most East European states have done, not only in recent years but also at earlier points in the twentieth century. This is not to deny that most southern European and Latin American states contain some unreconciled ethnic or racial minorities, but rather to point out that they are generally smaller and less of a threat to the territorial integrity of existing states than is the case in most of the East European states. Only Poland, Hungary, Slovenia and, since 1993, the Czech Republic are largely free from such problems, but even there this is not the full picture. Many Czechs have become increasingly hostile to their Gypsy minority during the 1990s, and many Poles continue to harbour resentment against their German minority and/or their almost non-existent Jewish minority, while some Hungarians still nurture strong irredentist claims against Romania, Serbia and Slovakia and/or resentments against their large Gypsy minority.

However, while they are not without substance, such contrasts have been somewhat glib or overdrawn. Thus, while democratization has clearly been taking place in even less favourable circumstances and to the accompaniment of even more painful and funda- mental changes of economic system in post-communist Eastern Europe than was the case in post-authoritarian Chile, Uruguay, Argentina, Venezuela and southern Europe, it is by no means clear that democratization has been taking place in conditions that are more difficult than those in other Latin American states which are variously afflicted by endemic criminal, social and political violence, grinding poverty, widespread drugs-related problems, very low standards of education, extensive slums and shanty towns, minimal health and social welfare provision, chronic mass unemployment, exceptionally unequal distributions of wealth, income and power, and the enduring legacies of racial oppression and slavery. In spite of all its transitional problems, post-communist Eastern Europe has for the most part inherited industrialized economies with a very run-down but still substantial physical and social infrastructure and well educated, largely urban populations possessing considerable occupational experience and skills. Indeed, while the states of southern Europe and Latin America have never experienced forms of authoritarian rule as doctrinaire, systematic, party-based, all-pervasive and 'total' as those created by Stalinism, communist rule did attach great importance to education, skills, social protection, full employment and (in its official propaganda) the work ethic. Moreover, after the dark years of Stalinism, a limited plurality of autonomous social groups did re-emerge, especially in Yugoslavia, Poland, Hungary and, to a lesser degree, Czechoslovakia and East Germany. These countervailing advantages need to be offset against the ways in which the democratization of Eastern Europe is perceived to have been beset by difficulties which have not loomed so large in other regions.

The new elites of post-communist Eastern Europe are still far from united. Nevertheless, the moderate centrist parties in the region have in most cases achieved a broad consensus on the new 'rules of the game', the desirability of EU and NATO membership and the reforms required to make them more eligible for full membership of the European Union and, if they have their way, NATO. Yet in many parts of Eastern Europe there are significant numbers of aggrieved or overwrought nationalists and a few unreconstructed neo-Stalinists who are not greatly enamoured of the new democratic polities and who do not relish the painful implications and stringent requirements of either the market system or candidacy for EU and NATO membership. Indeed, it is not always clear that they fully appreciate either the need for or the magnitude of the adjustments that will have to be made in order to strengthen and safeguard minority rights, individual liberties, civil society and the rule of law, partly as entry tickets into the world of civic nations, inter-ethnic tolerance and level 'playing fields'. East European politics still hinges on non-negotiable values and absolutes (such as religion, ethnic nationalism, irredentism and demands for retribution). It is rather more uncompromising than the materialism and the politics of negotiable social and economic interests prevalent in the West. Nevertheless, elections in most East European states are increasingly being fought on policy choices, rather than on the nature of the new political systems. That in itself suggests that a broad measure of democratic consolidation has taken place (other than in Serbia, Croatia, Bosnia, Albania and Slovakia).

Influential contributors to the comparative democratic transition literature have also maintained that democratization has taken place within largely autonomous states in southern Europe and Latin America, whereas most of the formerly communist-ruled states in Eastern Europe lived under Soviet domination and therefore had to regain their full sovereignty before they could consummate the transition to democracy. Higley and Gunther (1992: 347) have claimed that 'in no case is the impact of foreign powers on political developments as great as in Eastern Europe. Indeed, before the Soviet proclamation of the "Sinatra Doctrine" . . . the wave of democratization that swept across

Eastern Europe in 1989 was virtually unimaginable.' In Latin America and southern Europe, according to Whitehead (1986: 5), 'Local political forces operated with an untypically high degree of autonomy. The international setting . . . seldom intruded too conspicuously on an essentially domestic drama.' In East Central Europe, by contrast, 'the communist parties . . . were turned into accomplices of foreign imposition, and of the suppression of popular rights and aspirations. This is the fundamental reason why all later attempts to stabilize communist rule through liberalizing it were doomed to failure' (Whitehead 1994: 55). 'By 1989 "democracy" in East Central Europe was universally equated with the dismantling of an externally imposed system of communist rule' (p. 34). Nowhere have the international dimensions of regime change been as important as in the democratization process in Eastern Europe, according to Pridham (1994: 7–8). Such claims have been endorsed by Judy Batt, a leading British specialist in contemporary East European politics, who has argued that most of the communist-ruled states of Eastern Europe were 'characterized by a uniquely *low* degree of autonomy. The "penetratedness" of East European politics was of a qualitatively different order than that identified by scholars pursuing the theme of "linkage" of domestic and international politics elsewhere.' The Kadar and Husak regimes were even installed by 'Soviet military intervention, replacing reformist regimes which had overstepped the limits set by Moscow. These limits were subsequently codified in the so-called "Brezhnev Doctrine" which attempted to define a set of ideological principles to be observed by all communist regimes.' But Soviet dominance went beyond that. It was 'institutionalized in "the leading role of the communist party", whose leaders were appointed by Moscow and subject to close supervision. A back-up chain of control was also maintained through the security forces, which were run directly by the Soviet KGB and which, in times of crisis, clearly . . . were answerable primarily to Moscow.' Indeed, 'the military structures were fused in the Warsaw Treaty Organization, and were unable to operate independently'. What is more, 'the East European economies . . . were tied into the Soviet-dominated trading bloc . . . which greatly limited room for manoeuvre in economic policy'. This was reinforced by 'the imposition throughout the bloc of a "model" of economic management derived from Soviet experience but held to embody universally valid principles'. This 'fusion' of the domestic and international dimensions of East European politics, security and economic matters was 'a constant source of tension and crisis'. When East European regimes sought to enhance their stability and legitimacy by making 'concessions to domestic popular aspirations, they ran into conflict with their Soviet masters . . . The transition to democracy was only possible once the entire international structure of the Soviet system collapsed' (Batt 1994b: 168–9).

These contrasts are not without foundation, but they are again somewhat overstated. Major Western powers have long been prepared to accept (and not infrequently assist) authoritarian regimes in southern Europe and Latin America. Indeed, during the Cold War, almost any dictatorship that opposed an actual or imagined 'communist' threat was applauded by the United States as a 'defender of freedom' and was often amply rewarded for doing so. ('They may be bastards, but at least they're our bastards!') Moreover, while there was obviously extensive formal and informal Soviet penetration of communist-ruled East European states (other than post-1950s Albania and Yugoslavia), one should not overlook the extent and significance of informal American penetration of most of the states of twentieth-century southern Europe and Latin America, not least through the activities and 'influence' of American multinational companies. American attitudes have often had a bearing on whether Latin American and southern European states are ruled by dictators or democrats (even if the difference has sometimes seemed to be merely cosmetic). The Soviet Union under Gorbachev helped to create the conditions in which democratic forces came to the fore in Eastern Europe. Yet this was not so very different from the ways in which the policies and even the mere existence of the European Community (as it then was) helped to create the conditions in which democratic forces could come to prevail in Spain, Portugal and, to a lesser degree, Greece (or in which the West during Jimmy Carter's presidency belatedly started pressing for greater democracy and observance of human rights in Latin America, Iran, Taiwan, South Korea and the Philippines in the late 1970s). Similarly, the European Union is strongly supporting the consolidation of democratic and market systems in post-communist Eastern Europe. Yet even as the European Union attempts to develop a common foreign and security policy, the inability of the armed forces of most of the former communist-ruled states of Eastern Europe to operate independently of the former Soviet command-and-control system is still mirrored by the continuing inability of the EU states to project large amounts of military power outside their own borders without American assistance. It is not just Eastern Europe that has been seeking to reassert its autonomy. Almost all states have been chasing the mirage of national autonomy in an increasingly interdependent world.

There is no denying the importance of external influences and constraints on the democratization of Eastern Europe. But one must beware of the temptation to exaggerate the extent to which Eastern Europe has differed in this respect from southern Europe, Latin America (or, for that matter, countries such as South Africa, Taiwan, South Korea and the Philippines). Democratic transition analysts ('transitologists') have been on much stronger ground in emphasizing the exceptionally large *international consequences* (more than the international context) of the East European Revolutions of 1989–91. Whereas the transition to democracy in Latin America, southern Europe, the Philippines, South Korea and Taiwan caused a few small ripples in the international states system, the democratization of Eastern Europe abruptly ended the bipolar East–West division of the world into mutually antagonistic power blocs which had prevailed from 1945 to 1989. The East European Revolutions of 1989–91 were in that sense events of global and epochal significance, like the French Revolution of 1789 (which changed the face of Europe and Latin America) or the Russian Revolutions of 1917 (which soon divided the world into two ideologically opposed armed camps) or even the East European Revolutions of 1918 (which marked the beginning of the era of national self-determination, not just in Eastern Europe, but on a world scale). Moreover, as a consequence of the East European Revolutions of 1989–91, the era in which Europe was divided into three rival regional groupings (the EC, EFTA and Comecon) came to an end. There re-emerged the possibility of constructing one Europe, which the European Union hopes will be centred on itself. A few Western liberal ideologues also proclaimed, somewhat prematurely, that the East European Revolutions of 1989–91 marked the final triumph of Western liberal democracy and liberal capitalism over all rival ideologies and economic systems and thus 'the end of history'. But the turbulent course of events in Russia and Eastern Europe since 1989 has demonstrated that the future still hangs in the balance. Outcomes are never preordained, even though the battle lines are sometimes radically redrawn. The unexpected often happens.

THE REORIENTATION OF EASTERN EUROPE SINCE 1989

Since the Revolutions of 1848, and even more markedly since the collapse of the Eastern empires in 1917–18, Eastern Europe has been struggling to replace the dynastic authority and legitimacy, the (relative) military and legal security, the economic union and the (relative) political stability and autonomy that were previously provided by the multinational Austro-Hungarian Empire and, to a lesser extent, by the Tsarist and Ottoman Empires. The military defeat and collapse of the Austro-Hungarian Empire in 1918 left a major ideological and power vacuum in the true heart of Europe. This vacuum was more readily filled by illiberal 'integral' or 'ethnic' and economic nationalism, by native and Italo-German fascism, and by Soviet communism than by liberal democracy. That in itself did not bode well for the 1990s. When, in addition, the (re)establishment of democratic rule is not buttressed by a prior or concurrent emergence of a multiplicity of autonomous social groups committed to fighting for the maintenance of individual and minority rights, while at the same time supporting and accepting the need for a viable framework of executive, legislative and judicial authority, fledgling democracies can all too easily succumb to new forms of authoritarianism (especially when 'democratization' has been accompanied by economic collapse, mass impoverishment, unbridled corruption and organized crime). When we diffidently expressed a fear that we might have been exaggerating the threat to democracy posed by the persistence or revival of 'ethnic' nationalism and the continuing weakness of civil society and of civic conceptions of the state in the Balkans at a conference on the Balkan states held in Bucharest in July 1994, the Balkan participants urged us to regard the vaunted constitutional guarantees of individual and minority rights in the 1990s Balkan states merely as 'pieces of paper which anybody can write' and to realize that what matters is the capacity and willingness of civil society to defend those rights and uphold an impartial 'civic' conception of the state and the nation. On that score, however, they were rather more pessimistic than we were.

While the first priority of the post-communist states of Eastern Europe has rightly been to create or restore formal democratic institutions, rights and procedures, the formal provisions to that effect will still have to be reinforced by a vigorous development of civil societies with liberal and multicultural 'civic' conceptions of the nation-state, if they really wish to become fully democratic, peaceful, prosperous and eligible for membership of the European Union. All citizens of the Union, regardless of nationality, have equal rights under Article 7 of the Treaty of Rome, in contrast to the invidious ethnic exclusion and discrimination which still operates over much of Eastern Europe. East European states ought not to be admitted to the European Union until they have fully accepted its rules and cosmopolitan ethos. The European Council in Copenhagen in June 1993 belatedly laid down more explicit conditions of entry. 'Membership requires that the candidate country has achieved stability of institutions guaranteeing democracy, the rule of law, human rights and respect for and protection of minorities, the existence of a functioning market economy as well as the capacity to cope with competitive pressures and market forces within the Union. Membership presupposes the candidate's ability to take on the obligations of membership, including adherence to the aim of political, economic and monetary union' (quoted in Baldwin 1994: 155). In order to avoid accusations of double standards and hypocrisy, however, the European Union should fully enforce these same rules in all the existing member states by imposing penalties (including, if necessary, suspension of structural funds and/or membership rights) on those who do not fully abide by them.

The reorientation necessary to meet such conditions is bound to take time, however, as it involves fundamental changes in political and cultural values, in attitudes, in the structures of ownership and power and in the ways that East European nations and states have been accustomed to seeing and defining themselves and each other. The 'accession strategies' championed by Sir Leon Brittan, Hans van den Broek and Henning Christophersen in 1994–95 recognized the tactical advantages of producing a European Union White Paper setting out a list of concrete steps that East European states should take in order to make themselves 'eligible' for EU membership. This more positive, prescriptive approach, seeking to repeat the successful strategy behind the 1985 White Paper on the creation of a Single European Market, represented a major advance on the European Union's former passivity towards Eastern Europe. Nevertheless, this approach placed undue emphasis on technical economic and commercial preparations, to the relative neglect of the much more difficult and fundamental changes or reorientations required in the political and cultural spheres, especially in matters of national self-definition. The creation or restoration of strong and healthy 'civil societies', as prerequisites for 'civil economies' as well as secure democracies, is bound to be equally difficult and protracted (Rose 1992: 13–26).

By definition 'civil societies' cannot be created or recreated 'from above'. Creatures of the state tend to remain dependent upon and subservient to the state. But the penury, retrenchment and atrophy of the post-communist states has vacated many 'social spaces' which will have to be filled or taken over by autonomous civil associations and individuals, if they are not to remain under the control of the former communist *nomenklatura* and/or criminal elements. Above and beyond any private motives and ambitions that they may cherish, East European professionals, legitimate entrepreneurs, writers, journalists, broadcasters, trade unions and farmers' organizations are facing an historic opportunity and responsibility to maximize their autonomy and self-reliance and to minimize their dependence on the state, in order to secure the conditions in which the post-1989 transition to pluralist democracies and market economies can be consummated and consolidated. Their degrees of success in this regard will be even more important in determining their countries' fortunes than either the crumbs of assistance received from the West or the more technical tasks of managing the transition to competitive capitalism. If they flunk or pass up this historic opportunity and responsibility they will be among the first to suffer, and they will have no one else to blame, for the creation or recreation of vibrant, autonomous and plural 'civil societies' is not something that can be done for them by the state or politicians or foreign assistance. Indeed, the post-communist states lack the capacity to direct a vast panoply of social and economic activities, and any lingering insistence that they should attempt to do so in an endeavour to provide universal economic and social security will only lead back to forms of authoritarian paternalism and corporatism that have already been tried and found wanting. We are not so much advocating a minimalist role for the state as warning of the dangers posed by expecting too much of it, especially when so much of the existing state apparatus has been inherited from a rather murky past and the rule of law is not firmly entrenched. Once again, state tutelage can be only as effective as the state that exercises it!

Unfortunately, outside the relatively developed Czech Republic, Slovenia and, to a lesser extent, Hungary and Poland, social and economic conditions during the first half of the 1990s were not very conducive to a healthy resurgence of 'civil society'. For instance, the formal institutions of post-communist Bulgaria became democratic and 'civic', but the ex-communist *nomenklatura*, mafia-type gangsters and so-called 'wrestlers' (toughs) gained informal control over much of the economy and hence public life. In Bulgaria the *nomenklatura* 'have become fabulously rich running private trading companies that buy from and sell to Bulgaria's state-run factories, creating a bizarre economic subsystem in which production is state-run but profits are private . . . Essentially, private trading companies control everything sold to the factories and market their production too. Such enterprises can be lucrative through kickbacks or the manipulation of antiquated accounting methods. The private trading companies can make windfall profits selling raw materials at market prices, buying finished products at low prices and then selling them at a profit. As the state-run enterprises slip deeply into debt, the private trading companies reap huge profits' (John Pomfret, *IHT*, 14 May 1994, p. 11). Indeed, 'Bulgaria's state enterprises are being comprehensively asset-stripped by managers and private businessmen with close ties to the former communists' (Julian Borger, *The Guardian*, 17 December 1994, p. 9). Problems such as these contributed to the collapse of the Bulgarian economy in 1996. Incompletely 'reconstructed' ex-communists also continued to run Romania, Croatia, Serbia and Slovakia, at least until 1996. Such problems have not been entirely absent from Poland or Hungary either, while large areas of Serbia and Bosnia have been controlled by gangsters, black-marketeers, paramilitary thugs and local 'war lords'.

Regrettably, the 'national' euphoria which initially greeted the ending of communist dictatorship in Eastern Europe also unleashed potentially intolerant, bigoted and xenophobic nationalist and religious revivals and fostered hopes of welfare gains which the embattled, inexperienced and cash-strapped new regimes were unable to fulfil, at least in the short term. The high hopes aroused in late 1989 and early 1990 were soon dashed by the grim realities of falling output, soaring inflation, mounting unemployment, fiscal retrenchment, continuing infrastructural decay, an intractable environmental crisis and simmering inter-ethnic tensions (particularly in the Balkans and Slovakia). This did not surprise many Western specialists on Eastern Europe, but it did wrong-foot those exultant Western politicians and pundits who had subscribed to the naive belief that the ending of communist rule would automatically usher in secure democracy, vigorous market economies, vibrant civil societies and a new era of sweetness and harmony. Most Western specialists on Eastern Europe took the gloomier view that the 'natural' reaction or backlash against over forty years of communist rule was more likely to assume the form of resurgent 'ethnic' nationalism and illiberal religious revivalism than of profound and enduring support for and commitment to political and economic liberalism. Nationalist and religious bigots aimed merely to replace one form of authoritarianism with another. In the West, 'freedom' is normally taken to mean absence of oppressive government. But in the East, for the most part, 'freedom' has normally been taken to mean something much more limited and rudimentary: national self-determination and 'self-realization', absence of alien rule or freedom from foreign domination.

The generous and optimistic sentiments that were widely expressed during the initial jubilation were bound to evaporate when varying degrees of political and economic 'liberalization' not only failed to deliver the commonly anticipated rapid improvements in living standards, but also plunged most people into extremes of economic and social hardship for which they were almost totally unprepared and for which there were inadequate 'social safety-nets'. Indeed, a major report released by UNICEF in early 1994 claimed that the collapse of Europe's command economies and communist regimes had precipitated a slump in birth rates, a great surge in poverty, death rates, morbidity rates, malnutrition, truancy, family breakdowns and violent crime and that by 1993 conditions in eastern Europe were even worse than those in Latin America during the 'lost decade' of the 1980s or in western Europe during the 1930s Depression (*The Independent*, 28 January 1994, p. 10). Any circumspect and liberal-minded observer was bound to harbour doubts about the durability of political and economic liberalism in conditions of severe economic contraction, retrenchment, high inflation, acute social hardship, environmental crisis and widespread dilapidation and infrastructural decay, which were the immediate legacies of communist rule.

However, Sachs (1996: 131) has argued that 'changes in life expectancy vary widely across countries and appear to be inversely correlated with the speed and depth of reforms . . . In the Czech Republic, Poland and Slovakia life expectancy rates continued to rise during the post-1989 transition period; in Hungary life expectancy fell, continuing a downward trend from the pre-1989 period. In Russia and Ukraine life expectancy has plummeted.' According to the World Bank (1996: 127), 'Rapid reform is not necessarily detrimental to health indicators, but slow reform does little to impede a long-run deterioration.' In many of the former Soviet republics 'the long-run trend toward worsening mortality has accelerated since transition began, particularly for men . . . By contrast, infant mortality and life expectancy improved in the advanced reformers.' The jury are still 'out' and are not yet in a position to reach a definite verdict on this complex issue.

There has been a restoration of free elections, to be sure, but secure democracy involves much more than the holding of free elections, just as the restoration of market economies entails far more than the mere 'freeing' of prices. 'The new political systems are still in their early infancy . . . Politicians and parties are unsure of their roles. The accumulated experience of the West is of little use, for politics still centres on personalities rather than programmes or parties' (Patricia Clough, *The Independent*, 24 April 1992, p. 19). Universal suffrage could still usher in 'the counter-revolution', as Proudhon had always feared it would. Free elections and price liberalization unleashed irrational and unruly forces which, paradoxically, have made it all the more difficult to consummate perilous transitions to pluralistic parliamentary democracy and thriving private-enterprise economies. The problems have been compounded by the continuing prevalence of 'ethnic' nationalism and religious dogmatism and the attendant failure of liberal values, concepts of limited government and the rule of law to put down deep roots in Balkan and (to a lesser extent) East Central European societies and cultures. Unfortunately, Eastern Orthodox Christianity and East European Roman Catholicism have nurtured and sustained Manichean dichotomies between Good and Evil (between God and the Devil) which all too easily resurfaced in various forms within East European nationalist, fascist and communist propaganda and rhetoric, notably as exaggerated contrasts between 'them' and 'us', between capitalists and workers and between 'socialist' states and the West. The new populist politicians and demagogues of post-communist Eastern Europe similarly counterpose their valiant but impoverished nations against a rich, powerful, materialistic and perfidious West, victorious outsiders against victimized locals, 'rootless cosmopolitans' against 'true patriots'.

Furthermore, those who led the Revolutions of 1989 were not necessarily the most suitable people to provide leadership and direction during the consolidation of democracy and market economies. Indeed, by early 1995 parties with roots in the communist past were back in power in almost all the East European states, with the notable exception of the Czech Republic, where President Vaclav Havel and Premier Vaclav Klaus managed to rise above the popular hardships, disillusionments and resentments which had by then unseated most of the revolutionary leaders of 1989. But the 'new look' ex-communists were, for the most part, almost as strongly committed to liberal democracy and market systems as the anti-communists, intellectuals and former dissidents whom they had unseated. In the minds of many voters, perhaps, the reconstructed ex-communists held out the prospect of a more modest pace of change and the provision of stronger social safety-nets for the victims of macroeconomic stabilization and microeconomic restructuring, but they also promised to bring greater experience of governing and of 'getting things done'. To varying degrees, they have embraced or resuscitated long-dormant social democratic traditions which are more in tune with the economic and social philosophies that prevail in the European Union than are those of their more clerical, sectarian and nationalistic rivals, many of whom were more intemperate, xenophobic, anti-Western or etatist than the ex-communists. The qualities and outlooks that had brought many former dissidents national and international acclaim and respect as dogged and unyielding opponents of the communist regimes were not normally the ones that were needed in government, especially when the major issues and choices were no longer as black-and-white as they used to be. Thus we fully concur with the following judgement on ex-President Lech Walesa: 'His undoubted qualities of courage and cunning and his intuitive understanding of ordinary peoples' desires and fears made him an effective saboteur of communist rule ... With all his accumulated prestige, Mr Walesa could have been a great president, taking the lead in strengthening the institutional base to underpin post-communist rule. Instead he has shown himself incapable of understanding that democracy is based on the rule of law and respect for democratic institutions. His declared role model is Marshal Pilsudski, the inter-war military dictator; his political style, ironically, is that of the all-powerful communist party first secretary, hectoring and intriguing behind the scenes' (*FT*, editorial, 7 February 1995, p. 19). During periods of very difficult and often painful adjustment, there is a higher premium on conciliation, the healing of old wounds, clarity of vision, political acumen and sound judgement.

In December 1994 President Havel lamented that 'the birth of a new and genuinely stable European order is taking place more slowly and with greater difficulty and pain than most of us had expected five years ago. Many countries that shook off their totalitarian regimes still feel insufficiently anchored in the community of democratic states. They are often disappointed by the reluctance with which that community has opened its arms to them. The demons we thought had been driven for ever from the minds of people and nations are dangerously rousing themselves again, and are surreptitiously but systematically undoing the principles upon which we began to build the peaceful future of Europe' (Vaclav Havel, *The New York Review of Books*, 2 March 1995, p. 43).

Fears of this sort were by no means confined to the Czech President. In October 1993 Hungary's Foreign Minister Geza Jeszenszky wrote: 'Three times in recent history Western powers have promised liberation to the peoples of Eastern Europe, but the East European nations finally won freedom for themselves. Today, however, a crisis of confidence is emerging on both sides: the West is questioning Eastern Europe's ability to make good use of freedom, while East Europeans are voicing doubts about the seriousness of Western helpfulness. In my region people feel disoriented and increasingly unhappy. They find themselves in a polluted environment wasted away by redundant industries. The attractions of consumer society beckon but prove unobtainable, except to the old political bosses, who profit in commercial business. The spirit of compassion and tolerance was not cultivated under communism. This social environment creates space for the demagoguery of onetime Communists now donning national colours, as well as for the resurgence of extremist (neo-Stalinist and/or neo-Nazi) tendencies.' In Jeszenszky's view, East European democrats are determined to persevere with political reform and economic transformation and to overcome extremism, 'but they need stronger and better-directed support from the developed democracies. Carrot and stick policies do not seem to work in Eastern Europe . . . We in Eastern Europe are not asking for miracles. However, as new members of the community of democratic nations, we believe that we are within our rights when asking for strong leadership, clearly articulated priorities and decisive action by those with the resources and the moral responsibility to prevent the backsliding of Eastern Europe' (Geza Jeszenszky, *IHT*, 22 October 1993, p. 8).

THIRD TIME LUCKY?

In some ways the post-1989 transitions to the market and multi-party democracy have been even more fraught with difficulties than the post-1918 and post-1945 attempts. Much of the industrial capacity inherited from the communist regimes was either technologically obsolete or environmentally hazardous or produced goods for which there was no longer a market. If stringent commercial and health and safety criteria had been ruthlessly applied, large parts of Eastern Europe's industrial capacity (including most of its power stations) would have had to be closed down, with massive loss of employment. This view is consistent with the slump in total output and employment which took place in East Germany (the most industrialized of the former command economies) during the early 1990s. Between 1989 and 1993 the total number of jobs in East Germany shrank from 9.3 million to 6.2 million, manufacturing employment fell from 3.2 million to 1.3 million (i.e. by 60 per cent) and the number of people working on the land dropped from over 920,000 to 210,000 (i.e. by 70 per cent), while the size of the population available for work declined from 10.8 million to 8.2 million, mainly as a result of emigration to the West. By March 1994, 1.3 million people (16.8 per cent of the work force) were registered as unemployed, but in reality 37 per cent of the diminished work force were without employment in March 1994 and, if the absolute size of the available work force had not shrunk by 2.6 million, this percentage would have been even higher (Judy Dempsey and Quentin Peel, *FT*, Survey, 4 May 1994, pp. ii, iv). Moreover, between 1989 and 1991 East German GDP fell by 45 per cent, while the total number of hours worked plummeted from 8.9 billion to 4.0 billion (Martin Wolf, *FT*, 17 July 1992, p.16, and David Goodhart and Andrew Fisher, *FT*, 13 September 1991, p. 17). This devastating contraction occurred because, in addition to the loss or collapse of captive Comecon markets which had previously taken over 65 per cent of East German exports, the somewhat precipitate incorporation of East Germany into the German Federal Republic and the West European economy in 1990 prematurely exposed it to the full blast of market forces and competition from much more advanced Western products and producers. Admittedly, East Germany gained much-publicized advantages from massive eastward fiscal transfers within reunified Germany, which provided various forms of 'life support' for redundant East Germans and helped to conceal the true magnitude of the job losses. In 1993, for example, financial transfers from Western to Eastern Germany amounted to DM 170 billion ($100 billion) or 5 per cent of West Germany's GDP, with the result that total East German expenditure that year was almost twice the value of its output (Judy Dempsey, *FT*, 14 October 1993, p.15). But these advantages were offset by the immediate loss of the political and economic autonomy, leverage, insulation and self-defence mechanisms which would have been furnished by the retention of a separate East German state, currency and trading system with the power to preserve some of the more positive social, scientific and cultural features of the former East German regime and to set its own tariffs, excise duties, import quotas and exchange rates at levels that would have allowed most enterprises to survive in the face of fierce Western competition, as was the case in post-communist Poland, Hungary and the Czech Republic. Instead, the exchange rate at which East German Marks (and hence prices and production costs) were converted into Deutschmarks at the time of the German economic and monetary union in mid-1990 was set too high to allow large swathes of East German industry to have any real chance of holding its own against Western products, especially as unit labour costs also rose rapidly.

In 1945 and in 1918, by contrast, the East European economies were much less industrialized. They were damaged and dislocated by war, but they did not have to contend with such extensive closures of industrial capacity. Even if they were still subject to wartime controls, they were already market economies. Therefore, they were not required to undergo a profound change of economic system at the same time as they embarked on economic reconstruction and stabilization programmes. Furthermore, when the East European states embarked on the post-1989 transition, most of them were burdened by large foreign debts and heavy debt-service payments inherited from the foregoing communist regimes. In 1918 and in 1945, by contrast, the newly independent states started with a relatively clean slate, although they incurred considerable foreign debts during the 1920s.

In other ways, however, the post-1989 transitions to independent national market economies and plural liberal democracy initially appeared much easier and more hopeful than the post-1918 and post-1945 attempts. This time round, Eastern Europe was not having to recover from the devastating effects of a world war. Second, it was widely assumed that, because of the redrawing of East European state boundaries and the elimination of most of the former Jewish and German communities of Eastern Europe and many of its Gypsies during the 1940s, the scope for renewed inter-ethnic conflict in Eastern Europe had been greatly reduced. Third, Eastern Europe no longer appeared to be menaced by dangerous or potentially dangerous neighbours. Fourth, the West appeared to be much more willing and able to assist the economic recovery and reconstruction of Eastern Europe in the early 1990s than it had been after 1918 or after 1945. Finally, the existence of a peaceful, prosperous and highly integrated European Community appeared to hold out the prospect of much more propitious political and economic frameworks and mechanisms through which Eastern Europe could gradually be integrated into the mainstream of European development than was the case in the past. Certainly, the new post-communist East European governments entertained high hopes of a rapid 'return to Europe', starting with the bilateral trade and co-operation agreements between the European Community and East European states signed in 1988–90, continuing with the bilateral 'Europe' (Association) Agreements which the European Community concluded with Hungary, Poland and Czecho-Slovakia in December 1991 and with Romania and Bulgaria in late 1992. These provided for a phased reciprocal reduction and removal of trade barriers over a ten-year period and held out the possibility (but no firm promise) of East European accessions to the European Union as Europe entered the new millennium.

Unfortunately, the supposed advantages of the post-1989 transitions have been much weaker than they appear at first glance. Although Eastern Europe has not been recovering from a world war this time, it is struggling to recover from a state of economic collapse, high levels of inflation, severe infrastructural neglect and decay, acute social strains, the draining effects of the Cold War, the lopsided economic priorities of communist rule, life-threatening environmental crises and long-suppressed inter-ethnic tensions, which soon boiled over into catastrophic fratricidal conflicts in the case of the former Yugoslav Federation. On the economic front, the tasks that Eastern Europe has confronted have turned out not to be so very different from those involved in the reconversion of a ravaged and run-down war economy to civilian production. Furthermore, even though the ethnic map of Eastern Europe has been subjected to drastic surgery since 1918, a considerable potential for violent inter-ethnic conflict has still survived, sadly vindicating the view that no (acceptable) amount of resettlement and/or redrawing of East European state boundaries can either satisfy all conflicting territorial claims or allow all peoples to occupy discrete territories (or even cantons, in cases such as Bosnia-Hercegovina and Macedonia), because many are still inextricably intermingled. Indeed, the ingenious territorial expedients and stratagems that Marshall Tito had adopted in his attempts to 'cut Serbia down to size' and thereby allay non-Serb fears of potential Serbian dominance of Yugoslavia backfired disastrously during the early 1990s, when the Serbs brutally reversed some of the territorial losses inflicted on them by the 1946 and 1974 federal constitutions. Moreover, in the mid-1990s there were still sizeable aggrieved and vulnerable ethnic minorities in Serbia, Croatia, Macedonia, Bulgaria, Romania, Albania, Greece, Slovakia and the shattered remains of Bosnia-Hercegovina. Poland has dormant territorial disputes with Lithuania and the Czech Republic, as does Italy with Slovenia and Germany with Poland. In addition, Greece temporarily revived old territorial disputes with Albania and the Macedonian Slavs, while Hungary has had understandable anxieties concerning the plight of the 3 million Hungarians in neighbouring Romania, Slovakia and Serbia. Perhaps in part because the East European states have no longer felt themselves to be under any immediate external military threat from Russia or Germany or Italy, they have faced greater dangers of destructive internal and intra-regional armed conflict than at any time since the end of the Second World War. External threats and patronage and policing have had their uses, even though they have been deeply resented. After all, fear of the external threats posed by Italy, Hungary and Germany was the main factor that had brought Serbs, Croats and Slovenes and the Czechs and Slovaks together to form the multinational states of Yugoslavia and Czechoslovakia, respectively, in 1918/19.

It is sometimes suggested that, where populations have become ethnically homogeneous (by whatever means), the problems formerly associated with ethnicity and ethnic nationalism will automatically cease or 'go away'. But this is to miss the point that the illiberal and introverted attitudes, conduct and values associated with ethnic nationalism and exclusivism can persist (and can be less subject to healthy scrutiny and challenge) even when ethnic minorities have been largely eliminated. For example, antisemitism has survived long after the almost complete elimination of the former Jewish minorities in East Central Europe.

23 The new East European economies: what is to be done?

EASTERN PROMISE, WESTERN PARSIMONY

Western politicians, economists and political commentators have said and written a great deal about the need for a new 'Marshall Plan' to assist the transitions to the market and parliamentary democracy in Eastern Europe and have recognized that it is in the self-interest of the West (especially Western Europe) to provide such assistance. Thus Richard Gephardt, then majority leader in the US House of Representatives, wrote after the abortive *coup* by Soviet hard-liners in August 1991: 'The United States and its allies cannot escape the consequences of economic and political collapse in the countries of the former Soviet bloc. Not only will Washington face the potential of new military threats if strife and turmoil intensify, but it will also miss the chance to create new jobs and investment in its own economy by taking advantage of expanding markets in the East . . . It is crucial to show the people who have fought for freedom that their courage will be rewarded' (*IHT*, 1 September 1991, p. 6). On 27 December 1991 an editorial in *The Independent* gave expression to a similar belief in 'virtuous circles': 'There can hardly be a higher interest for the West than that democracy should take root in the former Soviet bloc. If it does so, Russia will cease to pose a military threat for the first time in centuries. With the Russian lands pacified, Central Europe, too, might no longer generate the tensions and rivalries that have dragged the Continent into so many wars . . . Then, as market economies spread eastward and new members are drawn into the European Community, an area of huge economic potential will emerge, spreading its benefits far beyond Europe.'

However, Western annual aid commitments to Eastern Europe (excluding East Germany and the former USSR) amounted to only $20 billion to $25 billion in 1991 and 1992 (Stephen Fidler, *FT*, 17 April 1991, p. 2). This was equivalent to less than 0.3 per cent of the European Community's annual GDP. Compared with Eastern Europe's external financing needs or the $70 billion to $90 billion annual transfer payments from Western to Eastern Germany or the $500 billion that the Group of Seven (G7) leading industrial economies spent on defence in 1990, Western aid commitments to Eastern Europe were niggardly. William Pfaff remarked that 'more money is being paid annually to the West from the East in loan interest and loan repayments, than the East European countries have yet received from the West' (*IHT*, 14 September 1991, p. 6). It is perverse that the West has been willing to spend vastly more on winning the Cold War than on securing the subsequent peace. In 1995, despite the recession of the former Soviet threat, defence expenditure still stood at $263 billion in the United States, $56 billion in Japan,

$37 billion in France and $34 billion in Britain (Bernard Gray, *FT*, 11 October 1995). According to the World Bank (1996: 138), aid under the Marshall Plan after the Second World War averaged 2.5 per cent of the incomes of the recipient countries at the time. Total official disbursements to the Central and Eastern European countries accounted on average for about 2.7 per cent of their combined GDP in 1991–93. Under-recording of GDP in these economies may bias this ratio upward, but on this measure Marshall Plan disbursements were not materially larger than official flows to Central and Eastern Europe. But the Marshall Plan was much more generous relative to the donor economy's income, at 1.5 per cent of US GDP. Moreover, whereas 80 per cent of Marshall Aid had been in the form of non-repayable grants, most of the Western 'aid' to Eastern Europe in the early 1990s took the form either of loans (which would eventually increase the recipients' already massive indebtedness and heavy burden of debt service, just when they were supposed fully to open up their economies to EU exports) or of trade credits and guarantees to Western firms in order to promote Western exports to the region.

PROBLEMS OF TRANSITION

The great danger is that the traumas of transition and painful disappointment at the parsimony, protectionism and pusillanimity of the West will more or less quickly translate into further disillusionment with democracy and the market system. There is a very difficult interval between the abandonment of a centrally administered economic system and the emergence of a fully functioning market economy. The guarantees, subsidies and certainties of the former centrally planned economy are forfeited some considerable time before the new market system is up and running. During the transition life for many people gets considerably tougher, facing increased hardships, greater job insecurity and unaccustomed levels of inflation. The transition has been made even harder by the rapid collapse of the patterns of trade and specialization established within Comecon and by the fact that Eastern Europe (like the former Soviet Republics) has to a large extent 'missed the boat' in the information technology, electronics and bio-technology revolutions. It is not just lagging far behind Japan and the West. It is also far behind many of the 'new industrial countries'. To the end, the Soviet and East European communist regimes remained wedded to old-fashioned 'smokestack' industries which had only limited export and growth potential. The replacement of these ossified, moribund industries is a painfully protracted process.

If market systems are to work effectively in Eastern Europe, one must establish the necessary legal, financial and telecommunications infrastructure and bring about extensive industrial deconcentration (to foster economic pluralism and inter-enterprise competition) and effective regulation of monopolies (to curb abuse of monopolistic powers). Indeed, there is no such thing as 'a free market'. Markets are governed by rules, institutions and laws. The transitions from command planning towards more decentralized, market-oriented economic systems that enhance lower-level account-ability and decision-making require 'not only ... proper macroeconomic policies and institutions but also well-defined behavioural rules for integrating the decisions of decentralized agents ... Perhaps of utmost importance is rule certainty for all economic agents' (Brabant 1989: 404–5). 'Only a fool would have expected a successful capitalism to emerge from the ashes in a couple of years. The fact that a carefully nurtured system of law, legislation, customs and habits – and of course infrastructure – is required should surprise no one except a few equilibrium economists' (Samuel Brittan, *FT*, 9 November 1992, p.10). Moreover, the effective functioning of market economies also depends on the existence of an 'enterprise culture' that goes far beyond the 'hucksterism' of black-marketeers, brokers, speculators and gangsters. The 'hucksters' who are often quoted as evidence of the existence of 'enterprise cultures' in Eastern Europe mainly know about so-called 'dealing' and corruption, how to buy and sell in captive or monopolistic 'sellers' markets', how to corner scarce supplies, how to misappropriate public property and funds, and how to obtain 'favours' and 'protection' from corrupt government agencies and officials, often in league with so-called 'mafias' or networks of gangsters. They have had little experience of large-scale corporate manufacturing and provision of services in sophisticated and fiercely competitive product markets, as these economies have long been highly monopolistic and sealed off from the outside world. As argued by Robert Heilbroner, 'hucksterism does not develop the attitudes of innovation and management that modern corporate life requires, much less the skills of accountancy or finance' (*IHT*, 17 September 1991, p. 8). It should be pointed out, however, that areas like foreign trade in the former command economies provided a more useful training ground for entrepreneurs, since direct dealings with overseas customers were involved. 'Many of Central Europe's budding conglomerates are former foreign trade organizations . . . One reason is that, of all command economy sectors, foreign trade was the closest thing to real-world business' (*Business Central Europe*, June 1994, p. 7).

The implementation of radical marketizing reforms and 'structural adjustment', including the promotion of small businesses and the restructuring of state enterprises to make them fit for privatization, was bound to require considerable initial inputs of capital, much of which could only come either from the West or from native black-marketeers, embezzlers and other criminal elements. It was therefore greatly in the West's interests that much of the 'pump priming' or 'seed' capital should come from the West, which could help develop Eastern Europe into a successful low-cost, export-oriented production base and help Europe as a whole meet the formidable challenges posed by the rise of the dynamic industrial export economies of East Asia. Some (perhaps most) of the East European states could become Europe's future 'tiger economies', if they play their cards right. Europe's post-communist states possess considerable reserves of cheap, underemployed, skilled and educated labour with a will to prosper. On the other hand, if the West fails to come forward with sufficient short-term assistance, know-how and long-term venture capital, it could find itself having to 'do business' with lacklustre East European states and economies run by seasoned gangsters or criminal elements or the old *nomenklatura*.

If only for these reasons, we therefore support aid to the transitional economies of Eastern Europe on a Marshall Plan scale, rejecting the arguments that they are incapable of absorbing such aid and that it would act as a deterrent to the taking of painful measures, thus transforming them into permanent 'basket cases'. Aid on appropriate conditions would cushion responsible but 'fragile' governments during the painful early period, while large-scale technical aid would (as under the Marshall Plan) increase the absorptive capacity of the economy by helping to create the institutions of a market economy (as well as helping to set up the political institutions of a political democracy free from the rampant corruption and organized crime so common in Eastern Europe today). As argued by Jeffrey Sachs, who was economic adviser to Poland (1989–91) and Russia (1991–92), Western aid could 'help sustain political support for the reforms long enough for them to take hold. The Marshall Plan did not provide Europe with the funds for economic recovery. It provided governments with enough financial backing to achieve economic and political stability, give hope to the population and thus make economic recovery possible' (Jeffrey Sachs, *IHT*, 16 May 1991, p. 6). Western aid could buy time, which may not otherwise be available. 'In the absence of a generous and visionary approach by the West . . . it will prove impossible to achieve success in the reforms – no matter how resolute Eastern Europe is with its actions' (Sachs 1994: 6). Schemes such as the widely praised UK 'Know-how Fund' have been useful as far as they go, but they are just peanuts in comparison with Eastern Europe's actual needs.

It has been interesting to witness Jeffrey Sachs rail against some of the advice offered and some of the conditions laid down for aid by the IMF: 'Rather than concentrating nearly all its efforts on budget-cutting, as it does now, the IMF should aim to combine fiscal restraint with ample foreign loans, exchange rate stabilization, increasing central bank independence and debt relief, all designed to restore confidence in the currency and in the government's ability to honour its (restructured) debts.' The package should mobilize sufficient support to enable the government to continue providing essential services. The IMF should help governments mobilize international financing of budget deficits early in the reform process and so minimize the risk that a 'fragile' government might be brought down by hostile reaction to heavy spending cuts and tax increases (Jeffrey Sachs, *The Economist*, 1 October 1994, p. 28).

We concur wholeheartedly with Sachs's advocacy of generous international aid to the post-communist states. It is also vital not to take for granted the very things that they most lack, including the rule of law, a modern commercial banking system, ethnically impartial states, efficient tax collection and effective bankruptcy and redundancy laws.

THE CASE FOR 'BIG BANG'/'SHOCK THERAPY'

This is not the place to unravel all the twists and turns of a debate in which there is often disagreement about terms, let alone more substantive issues. Our own feeling is that the virulence of the debate often hides substantial areas of agreement. Although we shall explore in the follow-up volume the complexities of the transition to the market since 1989 in the various countries of Eastern Europe, it seems appropriate to outline our own views here as a way of concluding our excursion through time. Part of the problem is the attempt by economic theorists to impose neat categories on a messy world, especially in an essentially new area of study. The term 'shock therapy' is more often than not used in a broad sense to cover both (i) severe austerity measures and (ii) a rapid and comprehensive change in the economic system. But at other times the term has been used in a narrower sense, referring only to (i). In our opinion it would be preferable to reserve 'shock therapy' for (i) and 'big bang' for (ii), but current usage obliges us to apply the composite term 'big bang'/'shock therapy' to this school of thought.

Two of the leading proponents of 'big bang'/'shock therapy' have been Leszek Balcerowicz (who was Poland's Finance Minister 1989–92) and the Harvard economist Jeffrey Sachs, who was his chief economic adviser from 1989 to 1991. Balcerowicz has argued that it is a fallacy to believe that a gradualist approach is milder in terms of its social consequences when one is dealing with hyperinflation. 'What is crucial in such circumstances is to change the basic monetary conditions and to eliminate or at least reduce inflationary expectations. In such a situation a consistent and credible radical stabilization is much more likely to succeed and could be far less costly than a gradualist approach.' In his view, 'tough stabilization and comprehensive liberalization seem to be the necessary conditions for any meaningful structural change'. Such an environment 'encourages many state enterprises to restructure, transferring their resources to the private sector, and/or to change their sphere of operations' (Balcerowicz 1994: 38–40). Balcerowicz has put forward a number of arguments in favour of the comprehensive liberalization of most prices: (i) one should make use of the political 'honeymoon' period; (ii) it is a necessary (and largely sufficient) means of removing widespread shortages quickly, which is in turn necessary for consumers' well-being and for the more efficient operation of enterprises; and (iii) slow price liberalization would prolong the existence of distorted prices: the performance of enterprises cannot be judged reliably and the soft budget constraint is likely to persist if loss-makers are able to blame distorted prices (Balcerowicz 1994: 42). The actual choice in Eastern Europe 'was between maintaining widespread price controls with the corresponding shortages and distortions, or liberalizing prices within initially very imperfect market structures'. In his opinion, 'comprehensive price liberalization should be complemented by comprehensive liberalization of foreign trade' (p. 28). Foreign trade liberalization was necessary to provide the competition lacking in a domestic economy dominated by state monopolies.

Sachs has emphasized the need to take full advantage of the 'unique opportunity to make an economic breakthrough to the market and a political breakthrough to democracy', the necessity to compensate for the 'lack of experienced personnel in the ministries' through maximum reliance on market forces and the belief that 'tinkering with the old system would produce no results' (Sachs 1994: 43). 'The key idea was to break decisively with the communist system, to end halfway reform . . . Balcerowicz understood extremely well from the experience of Latin America that to break the back of a hyperinflation, half measures cannot work. The stabilization measures must be extraordinarily tough' (p. 45). The five main prongs of the strategy were (i) macroeconomic stabilization (ii) microeconomic liberalization (iii) privatization (controls on the private sector can be very quickly removed, but the privatization of large enterprises takes much longer than the privatization of small ones) (iv) the establishment of a 'social security net' (especially an unemployment compensation scheme) and (v) the mobilization of international financial assistance (pp. 45–7). In the Polish case, 'First, to eliminate shortages and to allow markets to function, virtually all prices were decontrolled . . . Second, to cut the budget deficit and eliminate hyperinflationary pressures, most subsidies to households . . . and industry were slashed or eliminated . . . Overall budget spending was restrained, through sharp cuts in public investment and subsidies. Monetary policy was also tightened substantially. Cheap credits to industry were discontinued, and the central bank rediscount rate . . . was raised sharply, even brutally . . . To establish a free-trade regime, the currency was sharply devalued and made convertible from the start . . . Existing restrictions on international trade were almost entirely lifted . . . and tariffs were kept low' (pp. 48–9). Indeed, the highly monopolistic or oligopolistic structure and behaviour of the existing industrial structure prompted maximum reliance on international competition to discourage giant enterprises from simply responding by raising prices (pp. 49–50).

THE CASE FOR GRADUALISM

Brabant (1993: 94–5) has argued that outside advisers have 'obfuscated the tasks of the transformation by focusing too much on pitting the potential virtues of shock therapy [in the broad sense of the term] against the potential drawbacks of gradualism. All too often many of the participants in these debates have ignored that any substantial transformation programme must embody elements of both. Not only that, these elements can only be tailored relative to the specific conditions of time and place . . . rather than in terms of a preset technocratic blueprint.' A 'big bang' approach may be accused of largely avoiding the issue of choosing the proper sequence of reforms in each particular case. (It has always been recognized, of course, that restructuring and large privatization take a long time to accomplish.) The proponents of 'big bang'/'shock therapy' seem to underestimate the time needed to accomplish the transition (e.g. the time needed for behaviour patterns, attitudes and institutions to change). The cost of making a mistake is likely to be large. The general lack of personnel qualified to deal with the changed political, administrative and economic conditions also hinders the transition substantially. It may be unwise to release prices in 'big bang' fashion when the authorities do not possess effective instruments of monetary control. McKinnon (1994: 462) believes that 'the big bang argument for total price decontrol is flawed if the important actors bidding for scarce resources have soft budget constraints'. Indeed, 'until budget constraints are hardened, uncontrolled bidding by state enterprises will cause the producer price level to increase indefinitely'. Murrell (1993: 113) is similarly critical of 'big bang' advocates such as Sachs: 'Their discussion does not examine existing institutional structures and how to change them to reach the goal [the creation of a Western-type economic system], but rather focuses on ways, the methods, and the strategies to replace these structures entirely. There is complete disdain for all that exists.' Murrell (1992b) has argued that an understanding of the success of capitalism requires primary emphasis to be placed on mechanisms that produce growth and change, as opposed to equilibrium processes. In Schumpeterian fashion, he thus focuses on the role played by innovation rather than on allocative efficiency. The evolutionary approach stresses 'the existence of rigidities in organizational behaviour and the importance of entry and exit processes to the dynamism of capitalism' (p. 52). For example, during the transition privatization should be given a lower priority than policies encouraging the growth of new private firms (pp. 36, 46). Murrell also argues that some of the existing structures could be used. Thus 'during the transition there might be a case for direct controls on state enterprises to promote macroeconomic stability, rather than relying upon solely market-based measures' (p. 47).

Neuber has criticized the 'big bang' approach on the grounds that 'Although the creation of market-enhancing institutions figures in the transition blueprints, their lagged creation is not seen as an indispensable condition for the initial stages. Underlying that faithful leap into a market setting characterized by a hybrid institutional environment is the neoclassical assumption that markets operate in a frictionless world, the institutions of which do not play any instrumental role' (Neuber 1993: 514). 'The erroneous belief in the automaticity of market-based incentives and signals, especially when coupled with the advocacy of wholesale import of institutions that neglects the existence of surviving institutions (however much disliked) has led to a vast underestimation of the difficulties and subtleties involved' (p. 527).

Jackman has pointed out that, even in pacemakers such as Poland and the Czech Republic, East European governments have tended to support most of their enterprises. Bankruptcies and closures have been rare, and implicit and explicit subsidies have continued. Even so, unemployment has risen and has placed heavy burdens on budgets. 'In these circumstances, arguments for a "gradualist" approach, not to the restructuring programme as a whole but to the rate of run-down of production and employment in state firms, are gaining ground. It will often be less costly in both social and fiscal terms to maintain employment than [to] close down an enterprise, and there is no reason to think the growth of new private firms will be impeded as a result' (Jackman 1994: 344). (Growing private firms tend to recruit their workers primarily from those employed in the state sector rather than from among the ranks of the unemployed: p. 334.)

China since 1978 has been the classic example of a gradualist approach to economic reform. Its fast-growing economy cannot help but impress, and it has presented advocates of 'big bang'/'shock therapy' with quite a challenge. Woo (1994: 306) has gone so far as to argue that 'gradual reform in China was not the optimal reform for China'. But the usual response is to say that economic circumstances in China were different. (We shall explore the debate about the role of a one-party state in the transition in the companion volume.) In 1978 China did not face severe inflationary pressures, its foreign debt was low and it was still basically an agrarian country. Abundant, cheap labour was readily available to supply the fast-growing non-state sector of the economy, and China has thus been able to postpone fundamental reform of its relatively small state-run industrial sector. The more industrialized Eastern European countries, in contrast, have been less able to delay the process of restructuring and privatizing their large, generally inefficient state-run industrial sectors. It is also argued that China's highly successful township-village enterprises (which can perform well even in the absence of conventional property rights) flourish only in a culture such as China's. (See, for example, Sachs and Woo 1994; Layard 1993; Weitzman 1993; Weitzman and Xu 1993, 1994.)

A major report by the World Bank (1996) concluded that 'Differences between countries are very important, both in setting the feasible range of policy choice and in determining the response to reforms. Which works best, rapid or gradual reform? This question has no single or simple answer. Nevertheless, for the bulk of these economies the answer is now clear: fast and more consistent reform is better' (p. 143). 'A country's starting circumstances, both economic and political, greatly affect the range of reform policies and outcomes open to it. Within this range, however, the clear lesson of the past few years' reforms is that, regardless of the starting point, decisive and consistent reform pays off' (p. 9). 'In every case what matters is the breadth of the policy reforms attempted and the consistency with which they are maintained' (p. 21). 'Consistent policies, combining liberalization of markets, trade and new business entry with reasonable price stability, can achieve a great deal – even in countries lacking clear property rights and strong market institutions' (p. 142).

THE CASE FOR CIRCUMSPECTION AND PRAGMATISM

No one has ever suggested that 'everything' can be done 'at once', so the question essentially revolves around how much can or should be attempted all at the same time. We have always been sceptical about the wisdom and feasiblity of a 'big bang' solution, but we are equally aware that doing next to nothing brings about economic catastrophe.

(In the early years of Ukrainian independence there was hyperinflation and collapsing output at the same time; hence the pejorative term 'Ukrainianization'.) Consequently, we see merit in the idea of (i) a 'critical mass' of co-ordinated measures on a sufficient scale to provide an irreversible and on-going momentum to the reform process and (ii) a credible programme for which a democratically elected government must seek and maintain popular approval (as stressed by the UN Economic Commission for Europe 1994: 9). Choosing the appropriate blend and scale of measures best suited to individual countries is a political art rather than an economic 'science'. The initial circumstances vary between countries, such as the size of the private sector, the extent of previous reforms, the burden of foreign debt and the availability of aid. Clearly, chronic inflation has to be tackled as a matter of urgency. But in general any adverse effects on output and employment must be taken into account, and care should be taken to ensure that the magnitude of the stabilization measures is proportional to the scale of the inflationary problem.

The debate seems to us to boil down to what is politically and economically feasible. Anders Åslund, himself an eminent advocate of 'big bang'/'shock therapy', who has advised both the Russian and the Ukrainian governments, has concluded that 'the interesting limitation is what is practically and politically possible, and nothing else' (Åslund 1994: 37). It is also worth bearing in mind that in reality 'the range of sensible strategies is limited and there may be little margin for choice' (Portes 1994: 1180). Many of the alleged protagonists in the debate would probably agree that as much as possible should be done as quickly as possible. But the snag is that this begs all sorts of questions. There is no room for arrogance and dogmatism here. Pragmatism should be the order of the day, and the policies of Vaclav Klaus, the Prime Minister of the Czech Republic, are well worth studying in this regard. This free-marketeering but pragmatic politician has engineered a generally successful transition while using subsidies to avoid sudden, large-scale bankruptcies and lay-offs.

Klaus has cogently argued that the creation of a 'normally functioning' society and economy requires a comprehensive and painful transformation. 'Such a change takes years to complete; it cannot be accomplished merely with some sort of overnight shock therapy.' Nevertheless, the transition is proving successful. 'For the countries of Central and Eastern Europe, the important thing now is to push ahead with the process of self-transformation, and to resist any temptation to settle for half measures or to make useless political and social concessions.' The reforming politician must beware of 'reform fatigue'. He must be able to formulate a clear vision of a future which is both attractive and achievable. He must explain this vision to his citizens and defend it against populists. He must implement a consistent reform strategy and introduce unpopular and painful measures as and when they are needed. He must not defer to 'rent-seekers' and lobbyists who pursue their own short-term advantage to the detriment of society as a whole. 'The reforming politician must take into account the fact that radical transformation of any society is a complex and dynamic process, not merely an exercise in applied economics or political science.' The people that such changes affect are not passive objects, but are human beings who must be offered a fair deal politically as well as economically. A system of political parties has to be created as the means of achieving a basic political and social consensus. 'To privatize, deregulate and liberalize, and yet to retain an appropriate degree of macroeconomic stability; such is the essential aim.' Although most of Europe's post-communist countries have already introduced a first set of reform measures, 'some have done so hesistantly or inconsistently, falling short of the critical mass of reforms needed to change the basic system and so deliver some tangible results'. Where that is so, initial euphoria has evaporated and with it the early mood of national unity. In some cases there is a high degree of political instability. It is not easy to find 'an optimal equilibrium point in the real world between the freedom of individuals and the need for regulation by the state – not to mention by supranational institutions' (Vaclav Klaus, *The Economist*, 10 September 1994, pp. 45–6).

The UN Economic Commission for Europe has emphasized that 'many of the achievements so far are more likely to impress professional economists and international officials than the long-suffering electorates of the countries concerned'. Indeed, 'with the possible exception of the Czech Republic, there is still widespread disillusionment with the transition process and dissatisfaction with the fall in living standards: the essentially political task of organizing and maintaining popular support for the ultimate objectives of market-based economies and democratic institutions remains as urgent as ever' (UN Economic Commission for Europe 1994: 1). It concedes that official economic data may overstate the depth of the initial falls in East European output. However, 'Even though the overall reliability and accuracy of macroeconomic statistics may legitimately be questioned because of difficulties connected with measuring changes in real output and demand levels under conditions of high inflation and rapidly growing unregistered private sector activities, it is very unlikely that even more elaborate and accurate estimates would yield a fundamentally different picture of the macroeconomic perform-ance of transition countries' (p. 58). 'The persistence over many years of a harsh macroeconomic environment runs the risk of tipping the balance of the economy from a situation in which the majority of enterprise managers perceive a reasonable likelihood of viability in the market economy to a situation in which viability appears improbable. If the enterprise is thought to have "no chance" under market conditions, management and employees will be prone to seek survival strategies for the "enterprise community" which may not be market-conforming . . . If loss-making becomes prevalent there is a danger that the incentive for managers to push forward with restructuring is dulled' (p. 160).

The late Alec Nove (1994) argued in favour of a government-co-ordinated investment programme because of the decline of investment. 'The danger is not of "creative destruction" as envisaged by Schumpeter, but just of destruction, de-industrialization, with nothing creative taking its place. Here, in my view is *the* Achilles heel of the transition models. The necessary adjustments on the supply side . . . require investment' (p. 865). The chances of success would be higher if 'the government, instead of giving sole emphasis to macroeconomic stabilization, launched and publicized a recovery programme, and mobilized opinion and private (and foreign) capital to that end' (p. 869). Indeed, there is increasing recognition that the transition to the market is too important to be left to the market, e.g. state control is needed to ensure that the privatization process is not abused by the *nomenklatura* (the importance of high ethical standards in government is crucial, of course) and to protect the most vulnerable sections of society. In addition, Richard Portes (*Transition*, 1994, vol. 5, no. 8, p. 13) has pointed out that even 'if immediate stabilization is not feasible, there may still be very useful things that can be done, which by constructing parts of the microfoundations may also make stabilization that much easier when it does become feasible'.

We accept that severe inflationary pressure has to be combated. If the malady is not quickly brought under control it can lead to hyperinflation, total loss of confidence in the currency, a flight from production (into hoarding and speculation) and total economic collapse. In such cases delay is dangerous and there are no soft options. Poland's first Solidarity government grasped this particular nettle in 1990, and, after experiencing a large contraction in recorded output between 1989 and 1991, Poland became the first East European state to achieve positive growth (in 1992) thanks to factors such as exports and a rapidly expanding private sector. But internal dissension over the enormous pain and hardship inflicted on its mainly blue- and white-collar supporters helped to tear Solidarity apart as a movement and to return Poland's ex-Communists to power at the head of 'new look' socialist and peasant parties in 1993. In the case of the increasingly centrifugal Yugoslav Federation, the power, authority and collective decision-making of the federal government had become so weakened that it was unable to persevere with remedial measures of sufficient strength and duration to bring the inflationary pressures under control (despite Premier Markovic's brave attempt to do so in 1990). The subsequent descent into hyperinflation contributed to the accelerating disintegration of both the economy and the federation in 1991.

Other less dire situations allow more leeway. The former communist states with still viable economies were able to embark on more gradual and cautious transitions to the market. But the zealots of 'big bang'/'shock therapy' have argued that their approach is always necessary in order to get the pain over with the more quickly (rather than prolonging the agony), for a variety of reasons. First, once reformers started dismantling the old system, its malfunctions would increase exponentially (with very negative effects on output, employment, prices, distribution and living standards), and it was therefore vital to get the new system up and running as rapidly as possible, in order to arrest the contraction and initiate new growth at the earliest opportunity. Second, as a result of the complementarity and interdependence of macroeconomic stabilization, structural (or systemic) change and the various components of a market system (all of which would need to be put in place simultaneously in order to attain optimal results), a gradual or piecemeal transition would most probably yield damagingly 'sub-optimal' economic results and would therefore risk alienating parliamentary and popular support for the government of the day and for the transition to the market. Similarly, the more one prolonged the agony of transition (by proceeding cautiously and gradually), the greater would be the risks of a neo-communist or neo-fascist backlash against the entire reform programme, including democracy itself and/or market economics. It was generally assumed that there was a unique 'window of opportunity' for systemic change which had to be seized while the going was good. If that opportunity was missed, or if the change was implemented too cautiously and gradually, the entire momentum of reform could be lost or, worse still, the systemic malfunctions and loss of output and employment resulting from the incomplete or piecemeal introduction of the various components of the new system could precipitate a reactionary political backlash, whether from ex-communists, extreme nationalists or neo-fascists. Politically the 'big bang'/'shock therapy' approach to systemic change meant striking while the iron was still hot.

Looked at purely in the abstract, as the most direct means of getting from A to B, the economic and political arguments for 'big bang'/'shock therapy' seem very plausible. However, too much 'shock' can be counterproductive and lead to a backlash against the market reform process, particularly as the 'pain' is largely here and now, while many of the benefits take time to appear and are dependent on the success of the reforms. Yet 'big bang'/'shock therapists' reply that, if one proceeds more cautiously, the pain will still be immediate but the benefits will take even longer to materialize and there will still be the increased risk of a backlash, and that it is therefore safer and more advantageous to proceed as fast as possible. Nevertheless, what is 'possible' is more a matter of politics than of economics. In the words of Marshall Goldman, 'As economists we can draw up any reform plan that we want; but in a democracy . . . the leaders can only push so far' (*IHT*, 23 February 1995).

In several post-communist states that had embarked on programmes of macro-economic stabilization, enterprise managers (among others) soon decided that they could not (or would not) tolerate any further financial stringency and started creating their own forms of credit by ceasing to pay their bills and taxes or delaying payment long enough for galloping inflation drastically to reduce the amounts they would have to pay (in real terms). However, this mushrooming growth of inter-enterprise credit (or debts) and corporate tax arrears merely added fuel to the fires of inflation by undermining monetary policy. That made it still more advantageous to defer payments. This is a phenomenon long familiar in Latin America. Once it takes hold of a country, it makes any kind of macroeconomic stabilization exceedingly difficult to achieve, especially when the authority and credibility of the government are weak (and any 'non-payment' crisis does a lot to reduce them still further).

In the less liberal East European states the most likely outcome is that the transitions to democracy and the market will 'get stuck half-way': they will have many of the outward trappings but little of the substance or, worse still, most of the pain with few of the benefits. It will be easy for them to get caught in the so-called 'transition trap' or even to succumb to a 'creeping' counter-revolution. The initial window of opportunity for a clean break with the past was, for a variety of reasons, evidently missed in countries such as Serbia and Bulgaria. Their long-suffering citizens have subsequently had to settle for the long haul. However, it becomes much more difficult to push forward programmes of political and economic reform and fundamental structural change in countries that are already mired in mounting unemployment, inflation, poverty, crime, gangsterism, apathy and cynicism, and after the former communist *nomenklatura* have had time to regroup, change their outward appearance and capture (or acquire) large chunks of the new semi-marketized and quasi-democratic systems. All the East European states have embarked on the transition to a market economy, but some are still wavering between different types of market economy, between ones that are relatively open, law-governed and free from excessive state interference and ones that are closed, corrupt and 'dominated by insiders fighting for government-allocated privileges' (Chrystia Freeland, *FT*, 3 September 1995, p. 16).

Creating capitalism amid a shortage of legitimate capitalists and capital has been proving at least as difficult as consolidating democracy without sizeable middle classes. On the political front, one can improvise substitutes for 'the missing bourgeoisie'. On the economic front, finding effective substitutes for the missing capitalists and capital which do not lead back to etatism and excessive concentration of power in the hands of easily corrupted state functionaries is rather more difficult. The task of privatization is an altogether more difficult one in transitional than in Western economies. In the West 'privatization' merely involves relatively modest transfers of assets from the state into private hands within flourishing and well established market economies with highly developed capital market institutions. In the post-communist East, by contrast, it involves the wholesale transformation of the very nature of the economic system and the creation of the institutions of a market economy (including a sophisticated capital market) virtually from scratch (Clague and Rausser 1992: 18).

The post-communist states of East Central Europe and (to a lesser extent) the Balkans have made considerable headway towards the establishment of viable market economies, and by 1997 most were achieving significant economic growth. However, the EBRD *Transition Report* for 1996 rightly emphasized that 'While great strides have been made in most countries in the region, the challenges that remain are persistent and difficult' (EBRD 1996b: 2). We would stress that, just as democracy is not secure until it has taken deep root in the political habits and conduct of the general public (*dans les moeurs*), a capitalist system is not secure until it is similarly rooted in the economic habits and behaviour of the population as a whole. It is in this regard that the 1990s 'Europe Agreements' and eventual membership of the EU could do most to assist and to consolidate the transition to market economies (and, in a more general way, to democracy) in East Central and South-eastern Europe. For the EU is above all a 'rules regime' or a 'regulatory federation' (Majone 1992: 299) based upon the acceptance and implementation of common rules, regulations and policies within a single (supranational) legal framework. Membership of the EU confers greater certainty and clarity concerning the rules that must govern economic and political behaviour.

24 Conclusion

A tentative 'return to Europe'

The European Union's 'founding fathers' never intended their brainchild to remain an exclusively Western European club. In a speech delivered on 15 January 1959 the West German Foreign Minister, Heinrich von Brentano, declared that 'just as the European economic communities we have created are not intended to be restrictive, nor would a European political community be. It would be open to any European country prepared to accept the necessary political conditions in the interests of all' (Brentano 1964: 161). On 9 December 1989, amid the excitement and optimism generated by the revolutions in East Central Europe, the European Council affirmed that the European Community and its member states were 'fully conscious of the common responsibility that devolves upon them in this decisive phase in the history of Europe'. Conversely, the first post-communist governments of Eastern Europe attached great importance to the so-called 'return to Europe', a slogan that embodied a whole web of aspirations: to fast-track entry into the European Union; to the rapid adoption of Western-style laws, institutions and market systems (which some people thought would soon result in Western-style living standards); to freer travel and migration; to major cultural, economic and geo-political reorientations; and to international acceptance as 'normal' countries. All European states are now greatly influenced by their relationship to the European Union and, with the notable exceptions of Russia, Belarus, Ukraine, Serbia, Norway and Switzerland, almost all are either members or prospective candidates for membership. It is significant (indeed, reassuring) that in Eastern Europe, in contrast to Russia, few political parties have made major electoral gains by adopting a cool attitude towards the West. (Meciar's Movement for a Democratic Slovakia has been an exception to the rule.) Identification with Europe runs much deeper in Eastern Europe than it does among the more ambivalent Russians. Thus Bosnian Moslems get justifiably angry when the West tries to bracket them with the Moslems of the Middle East, instead of fully accepting them as Europeans who just happen to adhere to a Moslem faith which shares its Middle Eastern origins with Christianity and Judaism. Moreover, in spite of the fact that western Europe openly sided with the Croats, Slovenes and Bosnian Moslems against the Serbs during the 1991–95 Yugoslav conflict, in the end even Serbia sought to ingratiate itself with the West.

Contrary to expectations, however, the European Union has been slow to integrate Eastern Europe into the mainstream of European development. The 'Europe Agreements' concluded in late 1991 and late 1992 with Poland, Hungary, Czechoslovakia, Romania and Bulgaria seemed, in the words of Jacques Attali, to have been designed to 'restrict their access to key western markets rather than to integrate them' (quoted in *FT*, 29

October 1992, p. 19). They did so mainly by maintaining various 'safeguard' and 'anti-dumping' provisions (so-called 'contingent protection', which could and would be invoked against any 'disruptive' exports from Eastern Europe) and stringent EC restrictions on imports of agricultural products, processed foods, drinks, steel, chemicals, textiles, footwear, clothing and other so-called 'sensitive goods'. These happened to be Eastern Europe's main exports to the West. Such restrictions were to be maintained for at least the next ten years (after which further restrictions could be written into prolonged 'transitional arrangements' for any East European states that might be granted 'full' membership of the European Union). The European Community adopted a restrictive and defensive attitude despite the fact that these East European exports posed little threat to EC producers, since they amounted to less than 1 per cent of EC output (and less than 4 per cent of EC imports of each of the products in question) and were being more than offset by increased EC exports to Eastern Europe (Edward Balls, *FT*, 19 October 1992, p. 6, David Marsh and Lionel Barber, *FT*, 7 June 1993, and Jim Rollo, *FT*, 18 June 1993, p. 15). However, the development of common regional, social, industrial and agricultural policies and the veto powers of individual member states had left the Community hostage to producer interests which were much stronger, more effectively organized and better placed to apply pressure on national governments and EC institutions than were the West European consumers who would have been net beneficiaries of unrestricted access to East European products. The European Union was also slow to commit itself to a firm timetable for East European negotiations for full membership, although it made provision for regular 'structured dialogue' with the states concerned.

East European governments were soon offended by the EC's defensive, niggardly and patronizing language and attitudes. In the words of the former Polish Finance Minister Leszek Balcerowicz: 'Western governments do not seem to realize their own potential to damage or increase the chance for successful economic reform in the former socialist countries through actions that appear to be quite marginal to them . . . What for Western countries is a marginal restriction of access to their markets may cause great harm to countries undergoing radical economic reform, reducing their chances of success' (cited by Reginal Dale, *IHT*, 7 December 1993, p. 9). What was really needed was 'a reappraisal of the European idea which would allow them to participate in framing an enlarged Community . . . in which Germany's size and power would be counterbalanced on the east as well as the west' and which 'could create a better framework for dealing with the resurgence of nationalist feeling all over Europe' (*FT*, editorial, 22 September 1992, p. 18). Admittedly, premature admission of East European states to the EC could have been as damaging as it had been in the case of East Germany (via German reunification) in 1990. But the EC initially failed to spell out the steps that the East European states would have to take in order to become eligible for EC membership in due course, to give the East European states potent inducements to pursue an economic union of their own in the interim or to provide a clear and generous timetable for the removal of EC barriers against East European exports. A more positive action programme was needed in order to encourage the East Europeans to 'stay the course' of painful and politically costly economic liberalization, to persuade more Western firms to invest in Eastern Europe (secure in the knowledge that their products would be assured of unimpeded access to the EU market before long), and to help sustain East European export-led recoveries. Export markets were needed, partly because their domestic markets were in most cases small (and levels of domestic purchasing power were low) as a result of the declines in their (already meagre) real incomes during the late 1980s and early 1990s (caused in large part by the collapse of their former economic systems and of 'captive' Comecon markets for their main exports) and partly because they would have to earn enough hard currency to service their often extremely burdensome foreign debts and also pay for their reviving fuel requirements, most of which would have to be imported, as Eastern Europe was becoming increasingly deficient in domestic fuel resources. By retarding the growth of East European exports to Western Europe, EU import restrictions would not only retard East European economic recovery and long-term economic growth (and hinder West European exports to Eastern Europe in the long run), but would also (by the same token) substantially delay their potential eventual accession to the EU on the grounds that their economies were still too weak to withstand EU membership.

Why has so little Western support been forthcoming? In the first place, there is no longer a 'communist bogy', a fear of 'the Soviet threat'. This had undoubtedly been a major determinant of the scale of American Marshall Aid to Western Europe at the start of the Cold War. During the early 1990s, the West's new bogies were predominantly Islamic, whether in the shape of Saddam Hussein, Iranian Ayatollahs, Islamic fundamentalism in Algeria, Tunisia, Egypt and Turkey, or millions of North African, Kurdish and Turkish migrants fleeing civil strife, mass unemployment and actual or potential political and religious persecution. Far from encouraging Western generosity toward Eastern Europe, these new bogies have prompted French and southern European calls for a major reallocation of EU resources away from eastern Europe towards a strengthening of Europe's 'southern flank'. Beyond these xenophobic anxieties lie 'Latin' fears that the accession of Austria, Sweden and Finland to the European Union in January 1995 and intensified efforts to strengthen EU links with East European states during the late 1990s could increasingly shift the European Union's centre of gravity towards a resurgent *Mitteleuropa*. Thus in November 1994 the French Premier Edouard Balladur wrote: 'To avoid being . . . marginalized by the enlargement of the EU to the north and east, France must set itself several objectives: to deepen further the Franco-German relationship, to develop co-operation with the UK particularly in defence, and to tighten its links with Italy and Spain' (quoted in *FT*, 30 November 1994, p. 2). Moreover, in December 1995 Franklin Dehousse, Belgium's representative in the EU 'reflection group' charged with preparing the agenda for the intergovernmental conference to review the Maastricht Treaty, wrote that 'by deciding to enlarge the European Union with just about all the countries of Central and Eastern Europe, the EU leaders have signed a death warrant for the European Community as conceived by Jean Monnet, Robert Schuman and Walter Hallstein . . . Most of the new candidates are very different from the current member states. They are much less rich. They have only limited experience in democratic government (and even less in negotiating in supranational institutions)' (*IHT*, 29 December 1995, p. 6).

Furthermore, for most of the 1990s Western European states have been preoccupied with their own internal problems, including the effects of prolonged economic recession, high unemployment and sometimes sizeable budget deficits. Indeed, it was extremely unfortunate that the mammoth tasks of building liberal, plural parliamentary democracies and market economies in Eastern Europe coincided with the onset of severe economic recession in the West and with politically problematic and divisive moves towards deeper integration within the EC, including the fraught negotiation, ratification and implementation of an increasingly unpopular and possibly non-viable Maastricht Treaty.

But there was also a grave failure of political leadership. As Edward Mortimer pointed out in November 1992, 'No European leader has set out clearly for his electorate the nature of the opportunities and dangers which events in the east have produced for western Europe. As a result, it seems that none now has the authority to demand the sacrifices required from domestic vested interests, notably the farming and other producer lobbies which oppose the opening of the west European market to the most competitive east European products' (*FT*, 18 November 1992, p. 19). In his memoirs the first West German Chancellor, Konrad Adenauer, remarked that after the Second World War 'the former Europe, the Europe of contending nations, no longer had a future. The only future for Europe lay in unification and integration . . . Europe had a great future; but this could be realized only by great men capable of great deeds. The world was fortunate that at this critical moment, when its fate was in the balance, Europe had produced a number of wise and vigorous men who were equal to this great historic task' (Adenauer 1966: 434). The sad fact is that, during Eastern Europe's hour of need in the early 1990s, there was a dearth of West European leaders of comparable vision and vigour to mount a massive reconstruction and integration effort in Eastern Europe.

Western governments, parliaments, economists and political commentators have become increasingly aware of the scale of support required by Eastern Europe. But each Western state (with the notable exception of Germany) has hoped that other Western states will provide it, while still hoping to cash in on the opportunities that others have created. In an interview in *The Guardian* (Supplement, 26 January 1994, p. 7), Jacques Attali (the former president of the EBRD) stated: 'I have always said that they will need at least twenty years to get out of the mire and sufficient resources from Western institutions. Otherwise, the desperate populations of these countries will start to think a return to military dictatorship is a small price to pay for a return to employment, social protection and accessible consumer goods. Western Europe has no global vision of a continental union. Everybody is fixated with their own national problems. We really need a new generation of visionary statesmen.' In October 1993, moreover, President Havel warned that 'Twice in this century Europe has paid a terrible price for the narrowmindedness and lack of vision of its democracies . . . Democratic Europe cannot afford a third failure' (Havel 1994a: 242–3). The stakes are very high not merely for Eastern Europeans but for Europe as a whole. Yet most of the existing members of the EU have continued to expect most of the hardships, sacrifices and burdens of adjustment to be borne almost entirely by Eastern Europe. There has been little willingness to face up to the *reciprocal* adjustments and sacrifices which have to be made by and within the EU. It takes two to tango!

On the joint initiative of Jacques Delors and US President George Bush, the lead role in mobilizing and co-ordinating Western assistance to Eastern Europe was entrusted to the Commission of the EC. As a French Catholic socialist with a trade union background, and as president of the EC Commission (1985–95), Delors was seen as the ideal person to empathize and develop Western ties with the new Catholic/Solidarity government in Poland and the new Catholic/nationalist Democratic Forum government in Hungary. Moreover, the hard-pressed President of an overburdened United States was only too eager to relinquish the main responsibility for mobilizing and co-ordinating Western efforts in the post-communist east to the European Community, and this arrangement seemed to accord with the professed Western preference for multilateral rather than bilateral relations with eastern Europe, in order to ensure that the burdens and the potential benefits would both be distributed more equitably and in a manner that would encourage rather than discourage multilateral integration with and between the intended beneficiaries. The principal outcomes of the July 1989 G7 summit were, first, the setting up of a 'Group of Twenty-four' aid donors (the G24) comprising all the large and medium-sized Western states (including Japan) and, second, an initial EC-sponsored programme of aid for Poland and Hungary which was given the acronym Phare (*Pologne, Hongrie: activité pour la restructuration économique*; the word *phare* means 'light-house' or 'beacon of light' in French). This name became something of a misnomer, however, when Phare was extended to include Czechoslovakia, Romania, Bulgaria and Yugoslavia in May 1990, Albania, Lithuania, Latvia and Estonia in December 1991 (when the shattered Yugoslav Federation was dropped) and Slovenia in 1992. The main emphases were on microeconomic and technical assistance for agriculture, food aid, the distribution and processing of food, restructuring of industrial enterprises and banking, urgent projects to raise energy efficiency and safety, retraining, the encouragement of (small-scale) private enterprise, the provision of rudimentary social 'safety-nets' and the promotion of democratic procedures, legal reform, minority rights and civil society (Phare 1994: 7). Phare has tried not to involve itself in programmes of macroeconomic stabilization, which were seen as a task for the IMF, nor in large-scale programmes of structural adjustment, which were to be left to the World Bank and the International Finance Corporation. In May 1990 the EC also launched the Trans-European Mobility Scheme for University Studies (TEMPUS). It was designed to promote links, co-operation and student and staff exchanges between East European and EC institutions of higher education, mainly to help East European universities to change the structure and content of their higher education and research and to upgrade their books and equipment.

Furthermore, despite US misgivings, the EC summit held in Strasbourg in December 1989 approved President Mitterrand's proposal for the establishment of a European Bank for Reconstruction and Development. The EBRD was formally inaugurated on 15 April 1991. Situated in London, its twenty-three-strong board of directors was headed by Jacques Attali. There were thirty-nine participating countries and two institutional shareholders. Shareholding was as follows: EC countries, the EC Commission and the European Investment Bank, 53.7 per cent; the seven (former) Warsaw Pact members plus Yugoslavia, 13.5 per cent (the Soviet Union had a 6 per cent shareholding, but its eligibility for loans was limited to the stipulated one-third paid-in capital for at least a three-year period); the United States, 10 per cent; Japan, 8.5 per cent; the EFTA countries, 10.7 per cent; the other members were Malta, Cyprus, Mexico, Egypt, Morocco, Lichtenstein and Israel. The EBRD was capitalized at Ecu 10 billion, one-third of the capital being paid in and the remainder on call. The aim was 'to promote private and entrepreneurial initiative in the Central and Eastern European countries committed to and applying the principles of multi-party democracy, pluralism and market economics'. Funds could be used for loans at market rates of interest, investment in equity capital, joint ventures, underwriting guarantees and technical assistance grants. Sixty per cent of funding was to be devoted to the development of the private sector, although state enterprises in the process of being privatized were eligible (recipients in the private sector were to be commercially viable but unable to attract private capital). The remaining 40 per cent was to be used for infrastructure investments such as transport and communications. In February 1992 it was decided that 60 per cent of its funds were to be allocated to Eastern Europe and the three Baltic Republics and the remaining 40 per cent was to go to eleven of the remaining ex-Soviet republics (the one missing was Georgia). The former Soviet Union's 6 per cent shareholding was reallocated among the successor states.

According to Jacques Attali, the EBRD's first president, 'The vision was and is to build the first pan-European institution, in order to make totally irreversible the end of the split of the European continent in two . . . We could have thought about a confederation, about political institutions. But today the main problem is finance . . . The EC was not built up through the ideas of European political union – although that was useful – but through the first institutions having money.' He expressed the hope that, in helping to transform the post-communist states into democracies and market economies, the EBRD would metamorphose into a truly 'pan-European institution', much as the European Coal and Steel Community had mutated into the Common Market (*FT* interview, 15 April 1991, p. 25). Unfortunately the EBRD soon gained a reputation for lavishing more money on itself than on its intended clients, and Attali resigned on 25 June 1993 (and left his desk on 16 July 1993) after a highly critical audit committee report. Yet the low disbursements were not entirely the fault of either Attali or the EBRD. Attali had attempted to secure a relaxation of the restrictions placed upon the EBRD. He had also suggested that a soft-loan facility should be set up to help convert defence to civilian production and to restructure sectors such as nuclear power. But resistance came in particular from the United States and its Treasury Secretary Nicholas Brady, partly as the result of the well-known US aversion to public enterprise as well as its misgivings about setting up the EBRD in the first place. In some eyes, especially American ones, the EBRD involved an expensive and unnecessary European duplication of functions that were already being performed to US satisfaction by institutions such as the World Bank. Attali's protest that 'The bank has more money than it has projects' had fallen on deaf ears (*FT*, 13 April 1992, p. 2). Richard Portes, a Western expert on European East–West economic relations, strongly defended Attali 'because he brought excellent people to the bank and because he was an eloquent public voice for eastern Europe and the right Western policies for dealing with the region . . . Those who saw no need for the bank ignored the historic importance of its mission and the unique profile of its activities' (letter to *FT*, 29 June 1993, p. 14). By the time of Attali's dismissal, ironically, the expansion of private enterprise in Eastern Europe was rapidly increasing the number of potential borrowers who fell within the EBRD's narrow remit, causing most of the problems that had bedevilled the Attali presidency to evaporate. Meanwhile the EBRD had lost a leader with vision.

Jacques de Larosière, the new president of the EBRD, was appointed on 19 August 1993. (A former managing director of the IMF, he became governor of the Bank of France in 1987.) On 8 November 1993 a radical reorganization of the EBRD was approved. The division into the development banking department (responsible for infrastructure projects) and the merchant banking department (responsible for encouraging the private sector) was scrapped. Two new departments were established, covering the more northerly and the more southerly of the twenty-five countries catered for (most of the countries in the latter group are less developed and therefore need more attention to infrastructure). Sectoral specialists were to be attached either to each of the departments or to a separate support group. There was to be greater concentration on increasing operations and personnel in the receiving countries themselves.

The EBRD's record for net disbursements rose from Ecu 127 million in 1992 to Ecu 409 million in 1993, Ecu 591 million in 1994 and Ecu 988 million in 1995. On 15 April 1996 the EBRD gained unanimous approval from its sixty shareholders to double its capital base to Ecu 20 billion. (The member countries now total fifty-eight, Bosnia being the latest to be accepted, on 11 April 1996.) The new capital contribution was to be spread over twelve years. Only 22.5 per cent was to be made in a combination of cash and promissory notes, with the remainder being 'callable shares' (effectively government guarantees to allow the EBRD to borrow on international capital markets). The EBRD agreed that it should start preparing for an eventual 'gradation' away from the more advanced countries of East Central Europe and towards the less advanced countries of the former Soviet Union. Some commentators argue that attention should shift 'from the question of whether the bank should exist – to how long . . . Its new goal must be to run out of clients before it runs out of money' (*FT*, editorial, 16 April 1996, p. 19). However, we believe that the EBRD (like the Asian Development Bank) may have a longer-term role to play in the future development of its region.

Programmes such as Phare, TEMPUS, the European Training Foundation (ETF) and Technical Assistance to the CIS (TACIS) have assisted the post-communist transitions. *The Economist* (10 April 1993, p. 21) reported that TACIS and Phare, managed by the EU, were supplying about 70 per cent of the West's technical aid. By the end of 1992 Ecu 2.3 billion ($2.6 billion) had been committed by Phare, although only Ecu 888.8 million had actually been paid out. The respective figures for TACIS were Ecu 815.4 million and Ecu 32.6 million (*Business Central Europe*, December 1993/January 1994, p. 18). By the end of 1994 Ecu 3.784 billion had been committed by Phare and Ecu 1.747 billion by TACIS. However, these programmes have been criticized for being over-centralized, unwieldy, constrained by short-term budgets, possessing weak monitoring systems and duplicating the work of other organizations. As a result changes have been made, for example a shift from technical assistance into investment support and the direct financing of projects. In addition, multi-annual budgeting has been approved, co-financing with other multilaterals has been initiated, and Phare's small and medium-size enterprise programme is considered a success (*Business Central Europe*, April 1995, pp. 37, 44–8).

Nevertheless, the sum total of EU-co-ordinated Western assistance to Eastern Europe has been minute, not only in comparison with the needs of the recipients and the magnitude of the stakes for the whole of Europe, but also in relation to the vast sums that the West has continued to spend on defence despite the demise of the Warsaw Pact. Furthermore, this assistance was initially rendered within an essentially unaltered structure of East–West relations. There was little attempt to change or challenge long-established frameworks. Timorous Western governments were only too happy to abdicate responsibility to the EC Commission, which, in the words of Heinz Kramer, 'resorted mainly to well-established means and procedures in EC foreign relations'. These have had two main prongs, 'one concentrating on aid measures in various forms and the other emphasizing the establishment of a long-term trade regime to which are added measures of economic and political co-operation'. The *Leitmotif* of the former was 'help for the promotion of self-help', whereas the latter essentially relied on 'integration by organized free trade' (Kramer 1993: 222). EC aid and trade commitments to Eastern Europe were developed in ways that would do more to reinforce than to recast the existing bilateral structural relationships with East European states. Increased aid and trade were simply to be 'added on' to existing structures, keeping the East Europeans in the position of economically 'dependent' foreign states or supplicant 'orphans at the gate'. This was a civil servants' strategy for preserving as much as possible of the *status quo*. The grafting of increased EC aid to and trade with Eastern Europe on to the existing EC structure minimized disturbance to the current members, institutions and procedures and avoided any fundamental reconsideration of Europe's architecture. It also dampened the quest for new structures more capable of bridging the East–West divide. Thus the more ambitious proposals for a (pan) European Confederation put forward by President Mitterrand in 1990 and by President Havel in 1991 were almost immediately kicked into touch. Yet such a European Confederation, dealing primarily with matters of European security and high politics, could have avoided some of the dilemmas which the EU and NATO later confronted over how to deal with Russia and Ukraine and could have provided a more appropriate and effective forum for handling border disputes and threats to minority rights of the sort that reignited long dormant inter-ethnic conflicts in the Caucasus region, former Yugoslavia and, on a smaller scale, Moldova, Transylvania and Slovakia. Another advantage of the European Confederation proposals was that they could have embraced the former Soviet Republics as well as Eastern Europe and the 'Little Europe' of the EC. A European Confederation would also have found it easier to offer viable security guarantees to East European states and the smaller ex-Soviet Republics within an overarching framework that need not have excluded or antagonized Russia.

We should be in the business of genuinely uniting Europe rather than erecting new divisions and barriers. As emphasized by Vaclav Havel in Aachen in May 1991, 'no future European order is thinkable without the European nations of the Soviet Union, who are an inseparable part of Europe' (Havel 1994a: 128). In his speech to the US Congress in July 1991, on the eve of the abortive *coup* by Soviet hard-liners, Havel declared that it was essentially 'in the interests of my country, of Europe and of the whole world to make the Soviet Union a more free, more democratic and more stable place . . . You can help us most of all if you help the Soviet Union on its irreversible but immensely complicated road to democracy' (*IHT*, 15 July 1991, p. 6). It seems unlikely that Russia will ever become a full member of the EU, notwithstanding President Yeltsin's pronouncements to the contrary. As an Asian and Pacific power, Russia has other fish to fry. But even if Russia and Ukraine are too large and problematic to be accommodated in NATO and the EU, the West should not freeze them out of the 'common European home'. Such a move would be a new Yalta. We should be moving towards a barrier-free 'single European space', linking together several regional sub-groupings with varying commitments to deeper integration. There can be no lasting security for Eastern Europe so long as Russia remains a 'loose cannon'. If the main justification for binding Germany ever more closely into the European Union is that we cannot afford to have a German loose cannon rolling around on the European deck, then surely this reasoning applies even more strongly to Russia. Any eastward enlargement of NATO in a form that isolates and antagonizes Russia will diminish rather than enhance East European security (although some Russophobes are too blinkered to see this). In such circumstances, any NATO security 'guarantees' to Eastern Europe would be about as effective as the undertakings that Britain and France gave to Poland and Greece in 1939. So long as Russia remains 'out in the cold', NATO can offer East European states only illusory forms of security, and by now East European politicians ought to know better than again to put their faith in Western 'protectors' in the way that the Czechs and the Poles did (to their enormous cost) during the 1930s. The preference of the Russian government and the Russian military has been for a strengthened Organization for Security and Co-operation in Europe (OSCE) to replace NATO. Moreover, NATO 'insiders' are understandably wary of importing into NATO Eastern Europe's debilitating local disputes and quarrels (which are not unlike those that have bedevilled relations between two existing members of NATO, Greece and Turkey, which in February 1996 nearly went to war over some tiny islands inhabited by goats), while the conflict in former Yugoslavia from 1991 to 1995 demonstrated (among other things) NATO's great reluctance to overextend itself or to get involved in policing such disputes. NATO is ill-equipped to deal with the new security problems confronting post-Cold War Europe, which do not lend themselves to military solutions. They have more to do with inter-ethnic tension, political and economic instability, environmental hazards, drugs, terrorism and crime than with Russian (or other peoples') tanks, aircraft and missiles.

In 1996, however, the Russian government began to adopt a more sophisticated stance. Instead of expressing outright hostility to any form of eastward enlargement of NATO, Foreign Minister Yevgeny Primakov starting talking in public of conditions under which NATO expansion might be accommodated by Russia. These conditions involved NATO not stationing foreign troops or nuclear weapons in its new East Central European members (steps that NATO would not expect to undertake in peacetime in any event). Primakov also raised the idea that the East Central European members should keep their shrinking military forces out of NATO's integrated military planning. That was more problematic (Jim Hoagland, *IHT*, 11 April 1996, p. 8). Primakov has long cultivated close links with the Russian military and hard-liners. In contrast to his predecessor, Andrei Kozyrev, he has always been seen as giving priority to Russian geopolitical interests and he has studiously avoided Kozyrev's reputation among many Russians as being too sycophantic and ingratiating towards the West. Instead, he has usually waited for Western statesmen to come to Moscow. This has granted Primakov greater room for manoeuvre in his dealings with the West. He has displayed degrees of flexibility which were unavailable to Kozyrev, who was increasingly detested and mistrusted by Russian 'patriots' fearful of further 'capitulations' or 'sell-outs' to the West.

The emergence of Primakov has been matched by increased circumspection and sophistication on the Western side. For example, the EU Commissioner and Vice-president Sir Leon Brittan warned in 1994: 'The collapse of the Soviet empire has altered the entire European landscape, burying the simple if dangerous certainties based on nuclear deterrence and forcing us to contemplate a less polarized, more unstable world ... Today, a poor, disintegrating Russia is a far greater threat than a confident, stable and prosperous one' (Brittan 1994: 2, 137). Similarly, in *Foreign Affairs* in May 1996, the last American ambassador to the Soviet Union (1987–91), Jack Matlock Jnr, warned that 'Much of recent Russian recalcitrance can be traced to a feeling that their country is being left out of the European security club. As a loner, Russia will always be a problem. Washington must reassure Moscow that it places a high priority on creating a European security structure to which Russia is a party. Whether that is done through a treaty relationship between Russia and NATO, an augmentation of the authority of the Organization for Security and Co-operation in Europe, or some other mechanism is less important than the commitment to include Russia. NATO expansion to the east should be deferred while these arrangements are under active negotiation, provided Russia does not threaten other countries or violate its OSCE obligations' (Matlock 1996: 49). We fully concur with this stance. It is not in the interests of either the West or East Central and South-eastern Europe to marginalize, antagonize or humiliate Russia. The economic crises, power vacuums and inter-ethnic conflicts in the territory of the former Soviet Union are potentially even more dangerous than those of Eastern Europe. 'To many former Soviet citizens it now seems that the ethnic and criminal violence which has wracked their fallen superpower is the result not of excessive state power, but of the very opposite – a collapse of all authority, leaving a vacuum which ruthless warlords and mobsters can exploit' (*FT*, editorial, 19 July 1996, p. 15). (Indeed, although there is still a widespread stereotyped perception of an 'oversized' and excessively powerful Russian state, the actual problem is that this state is in many ways too weak and under-resourced to cope very effectively with the enormous problems of transition to some sort of market economy and of holding the country together, especially as the always underdeveloped civil arm of the state is no longer backed up by an effective 'parallel administration' in the form of the Soviet Communist Party, while the superficially imposing military arm of the Russian state is now demoralized, under-resourced and atrophied. The dangers confronting or emanating from Russia stem from the weakness rather than from the strength of the Russian state.) The emphasis ought to be on the creation of a pan-European security structure and a barrier-free 'single European space', in which all who are willing and able to abide by a set of common rules, norms and values should be allowed to participate on an equal basis.

On 21 October 1993 NATO decided to adopt a US proposal that non-aligned and former communist countries should be offered a Partnership for Peace rather than immediate membership. The idea was formally accepted at the NATO summit held in Brussels on 10–11 January 1994 as a way of reconciling conflicting pressures: (i) the eagerness of the East European and Baltic states in particular to join in order to benefit from NATO's security guarantees (especially after the December 1993 general election in Russia and the failure of the West to deal with the crisis in Bosnia); (ii) the desire to avoid a security vacuum in Eastern Europe; (iii) the danger of stirring nationalist passions in a Russia perceiving potential isolation (on 10 January 1994 Vladimir Zhirinovsky warned that the incorporation of Eastern Europe 'would mean NATO took the path of preparing for World War Three'); (iv) the fear of involving NATO in a still unstable region and drawing new lines of division in Europe; (v) the fear of weakening NATO if countries not yet ready for membership were to be admitted.

A NATO communiqué issued on 11 January 1994 stated: 'We expect and would welcome NATO expansion that would reach to democratic states to our east, as part of an evolutionary process, taking into account political and security developments in the whole of Europe.' No former communist country and member of the North Atlantic Co-operation Council would be excluded from *consideration* as a future member. But there was no *guarantee* of membership, no timetable was laid out and no detailed and specific eligibility criteria were listed (as opposed to the general requirement to be, for example, a democracy accepting existing national borders and ensuring democratic civilian control of the military). What was promised was closer co-operation with NATO on a bilateral, individually tailored basis, which might lead to membership in the fullness of time. The idea was to sign a standard framework; individual deals could be worked out in detail later. The forms of co-operation include information exchange, transparency in defence planning and budgeting, joint planning, exercises and training (including preparation for peacekeeping duties), and consultation with any country that faced 'a direct threat to its territorial integrity, political independence or security'. On 9 May 1994 the Western European Union offered 'associate partner' status to Bulgaria, the Czech Republic, Hungary, Poland, Romania, Slovakia, Estonia, Latvia and Lithuania. On 31 May 1995 Russia joined the Partnership for Peace (as the twenty-sixth country to do so) and a NATO report on the expansion of full membership was published in late summer 1995, in time for consideration at the NATO meeting in December that year. As of mid-1996 there were twenty-seven participants in the Partnership for Peace programme: Albania, Armenia, Austria, Azerbaijan, Belarus, Bulgaria, the Czech Republic, Estonia, Finland, Georgia, Hungary, Kazakhstan, Kyrgyzstan, Latvia, Lithuania, Macedonia, Malta, Moldova, Poland, Romania, Russia, Slovakia, Slovenia, Sweden, Turkmenistan, Ukraine and Uzbekistan (*The Economist*, 1 June 1996, p. 22).

In parallel with these developments, the French government hosted a conference on stability in Europe in Paris on 26–7 May 1994, with the express purpose of promoting a so-called Stability Pact designed to constrain, forestall and defuse border and ethnic minority problems of the sort that have devastated much of the former Yugoslavia. A necessary (but not sufficient) condition of entry to the European Union and NATO was to be the signing of 'good neighbour' accords, with guarantees of borders and minority rights. Two regional round tables were set up, one for the Baltic region and one for Central and Eastern Europe. Bilateral agreements were to be signed within one year. Together with existing friendship agreements, these were to form part of the Stability Pact. The countries taking part were Bulgaria, the Czech Republic, Hungary, Poland, Romania, Slovakia, Estonia, Latvia and Lithuania. Slovenia was debarred from participating as a full member by Italy, which was demanding compensation for property allegedly seized by Yugoslavia after the Second World War. An important breakthrough occurred on 16 September 1996 when the Prime Ministers of Hungary and Romania signed a 'basic treaty' (i.e. a treaty of 'reconciliation and friendship'). Country borders were deemed inviolable. Although ethnic Hungarians in Romania were granted human rights, the treaty did not recognize their 'collective rights' or grant autonomy along ethnic lines. Yet the treaty required both countries to protect the civil liberties and cultural identity of national minorities. Education at all levels was guaranteed by the state in the minority's native tongue, as was the right to use one's historic language in administrative and judicial proceedings in areas of minority concentration. The same went for road signs, print and broadcast media and virtually every other aspect of communal life. Each country committed itself in the treaty to support NATO and EU membership for the other (Donald M. Blinken and Alfred H. Moses, US ambassadors to Hungary and Romania respectively, *IHT*, 19 September 1996, p. 8). It was hoped that this treaty, concluded in the face of virulent protests from intransigent nationalists on both sides, would become an exemplar encouraging and facilitating the settlement of similar disputes elsewhere in the region.

A non-binding set of principles to 'render irreversible the advance of democracy and institute durable good-neighbourliness in Europe' was agreed at a meeting held in Paris on 20–1 March 1995. All the individual deals were to be monitored by OSCE, e.g. the one signed by Hungary and Slovakia on 19 March 1995. All fifty-two countries present were in the OSCE, but some of its members were not represented, e.g. Croatia, Slovenia and the Federal Republic of Yugoslavia. However, while Europe's post-communist states have generally been ready to participate in initiatives of this sort, they retain sneaking suspicions that such arrangements are in reality intended, not to accelerate their own integration into Europe's major political, economic and security structures, but rather to slow down the process and to keep them at arm's length.

Fundamentally, the EU has been ill equipped to play the roles assigned to it (which may of course be a principal reason why it was given them in the first place!). Composed of twelve (now fifteen) quarrelsome, cantankerous and mutually competitive national states, it remains a somewhat introverted organization, increasingly preoccupied with its own internal problems, disputes and objectives. With nominal control over a mere 1.2 per cent of the European Union's GDP (roughly half of it in the rigid form of 'compulsory expenditure' on the CAP), the supranational institutions of the EU have had neither the wherewithal nor the political muscle and strength of resolve to break the mould of the East–West division of Europe. Moreover, the EU has lacked well developed institutions, procedures and competences for dealing with external relations, as was demonstrated by its divided and ineffective handling of the 1990/91 Gulf crisis and the conflicts in former Yugoslavia between 1991 and 1995.

It may well be that the European Community and its successor, the European Union, have been hostage to too many vested interests which could all too easily block any radical overtures to Eastern Europe, whether in terms of economic assistance or trade liberalization or in terms of fundamental changes in Europe's overall 'architecture'. In 1992 Professor Richard Baldwin argued that, in the final analysis, a combination of southern European and farming interests would probably veto East European member-ship of the EU for at least another twenty years (*FT*, 9 November 1992, p. 4). However, this view has been countered by arguments that the particular economic profile and technological level of the southern European economies will cause them to have the most both to offer and to gain from future East European membership of the EU. A study conducted by National Economic Research Associates on behalf of the EC Com-mission in 1993 concluded that, if EC trade with Eastern Europe were to be liberalized, that would initially reduce total EC output by 0.2 per cent, but by 2010 the subsequent increase in East European imports of EC products would (on balance) raise EC industrial output by 1.2 per cent and total EC output by 0.8 per cent, with the largest increases (2.2 per cent for industry and 1.0 per cent for total output) occurring in Spain, Portugal and Greece, because their industries and products are best suited to the import needs of Eastern Europe and because Greece is so advantageously located (Edward Balls, *FT*, 13 September 1993, p. 6). Interestingly, opinion polls conducted in May 1994 on behalf of eight West European newspapers found that popular opposition to East European membership of the EU was lowest in Southern Europe. Asked 'Do you favour EU enlargement to [include] the Czech Republic, Hungary, Poland and Slovakia ?', the percentage of negative replies was 13 in Spain, 14 in Italy, 17 in Portugal, 24 in the Netherlands, 28 in Eastern Germany, 29 in Greece, 31 in Belgium and Ireland, 38 in the UK and Luxembourg, 40 in France, 43 in Western Germany and 46 in Denmark (*FT*, 1 June 1994, p. 4). Unfortunately, the decisive questions pertaining to Eastward enlargement will probably be answered by politicians (who tend to be unduly influenced by sectional producer lobbies), while the electorates of existing EU member states will continue to have as little say in this as in previous EU enlargements. All the same, there was a glimmer of hope in the very positive attitude towards Eastward enlargement adopted by the Spanish presidency of the EU during the second half of 1995.

It has been widely assumed that East European entrants into the EU would automatically expect to become major net recipients of EU 'structural funds' and that such expectations would evoke strong resistance from major current recipients of EU 'structural transfers' and from the EU's principal 'paymasters' (the richer 'northern' members, especially Germany). However, in the context of steadily increasing fiscal and monetary stringency in an increasingly competitive market environment (and in the run-up to monetary union), there is no guarantee that the EU states will agree to continue with the present levels of 'structural funding' beyond the current quinquennium (1994–99). Indeed, with Spain and Ireland rapidly raising their levels of *per capita* GDP, these two countries should soon cease to qualify for substantial net receipts of EU 'structural funds', and similar considerations should apply to the rapidly developing Portuguese economy (and perhaps even to Greece) in due course. Moreover, although Greece, Spain, Portugal, Ireland and the EU have attached considerable importance to these 'structural funds' as a means of 'topping up' infrastructural expenditure and provision in the poorer members of the EU, such receipts have in fact been rather less important than the large net inflows of private foreign capital which have contributed so strongly to the recent economic and social transformation of Spain, Portugal and Ireland. Conversely, the member state most heavily dependent on EU 'structural' transfers (Greece) has fared markedly less well. These contrasting experiences have crucial implications for prospective East European entrants. EU membership is likely to be far more remunerative as an additional means of attracting foreign private investment (which can import valuable technologies and managerial, technical and marketing expertise) than as a 'golden road' to EU 'structural funds' (whose importance may well diminish in the future).

There has been much discussion of the effects that a major eastward enlargement of the European Union might have on the Common Agricultural Policy (CAP). Many agricultural economists claim (or even hope!) that the admission of countries such as Poland, Romania and Hungary would wreck the CAP (and the present structure of EU finances) by greatly increasing the cost of farm subsidies and the agricultural surpluses which the EU would have to absorb, dump or destroy. If the wailing Cassandras (and Pollyannas!) are correct, some of the current members of the EU would almost certainly veto the offending enlargement rather than acquiesce in the destruction of the CAP. Those who hope to use EU enlargement as a means of wrecking the CAP are therefore barking up the wrong tree. However, it is not difficult to demonstrate that the likely effects of eastward enlargement on the CAP have been greatly exaggerated (probably for political motives). In our view, the problems posed would be more political than economic, but they are not insurmountable and it is conceivable that they could diminish quite rapidly.

Taking 1990 as a base year, it would appear that the admission of all the East European states would nearly double the EU's cultivated area and more than double its agricultural population. Therefore, in the doomsday scenarios, the total financial claims on the CAP could roughly double and, if offered CAP prices and full access to West European markets, East European agriculture could vastly expand the EU's farm surpluses, thereby bankrupting the EU. On any realistic scenario, however, it is very unlikely that the East European states would be admitted to the EU all at the same time. They will probably be admitted singly or in pairs. In any event, the Czech Republic, Slovenia, Slovakia and Albania would not pose any major challenge to the CAP, in view of their smallness and/or infertile terrain and, in the case of the Czech Republic and Slovenia, their relatively high levels of industrialization and urbanization. Like Portugal and Greece, these four countries could even be net importers of temperate farm products, thereby helping to relieve pressures on the CAP. Thus admitting them need not pose major difficulties in this respect. The real problems concern the admission of Poland and Romania, because their relatively unproductive farmers are so numerous, and Hungary and Bulgaria, because their farms are relatively productive and export-oriented. But, if the 70 per cent reduction in East Germany's farm work force between 1989 and 1993 is at all indicative, one can expect the East European agricultural population to slump as and when opportunities for leaving the land (including emigration) open up. This in turn should lead to some reductions in cultivated area, restraining potential increases in agricultural output. As in the West, not many young East Europeans want to remain on the land for ever more. Few can resist the lure of the cities, with their wider range of occupations and amenities. Furthermore, prolonged 'transitional arrangements' could blunt the Polish, Hungarian, Bulgarian and Romanian challenges to the CAP long enough for domestic and Western investment in East European industrial regeneration to reduce Eastern Europe's agricultural sectors to more manageable proportions. Thus the potential threat has been somewhat exaggerated by the alarmists, many of whom want either to scrap or to 'repatriate' EU farm support (which they regard as little more than a costly and corrupt system of 'outdoor relief' for ne'er-do-well farmers). The more blinkered critics fail to grasp that the CAP was an essential component of the political contract that created the EEC and that the motives for its creation were not merely to placate rural political constituencies and anxious Frenchmen, but also in order to banish the *national* agricultural protectionism, which, if it were to return in the guise of 'renationalization' of farm support, would soon prompt tit-for-tat *national* protectionism in other sectors and quickly unravel the invaluable achievements of the Common Market (not to mention its sequel, the Single European Market). Indeed, it needs to be more widely understood that the CAP is not merely a system of farm support but a system of food security and a fee that we all pay for the prevention of any repetition of the beggar-my-neighbour trade wars that bedevilled inter-war Europe, politically as well as economically. During the early 1990s it cost less than 0.7 per cent of the European Union's GDP. It should also be pointed out that between 1993 and 1995 there was a dramatic reduction in the size of world food surpluses and the EU 'food mountains', as well as a sharp rise in world food prices. This was mainly a result of rapid industrial development and greatly increased food imports in East Asia, where rapidly rising personal incomes have been causing big increases in the consumption of livestock products and in imports of the feedstuffs needed to fatten livestock. By 1995 EU grain prices were actually below those on the world market. If such trends were to persist, as seems quite possible, the cost of the CAP and of a major Eastward enlargement of the EU could tumble, while EU consumers and governments may even be only too glad to establish preferential access to relatively cheap East European farm surpluses.

Even on the most optimistic assumptions, however, there was not going to be any immediate accession of East European states to the European Union. Confronted by seemingly intractable wrangles and problems of their own, most of the EU states have been in no hurry to admit them, even though the states with which the EU has signed Treaties of Association have been led to believe that they will become full members in due course. Even if enlargement negotiations were to get under way as planned in the late

1990s, it should be remembered that it took six years to negotiate mutually acceptable terms of Spanish and Portuguese entry (and most East European applicants pose greater problems), while Greece had to wait nearly twenty years for its Treaty of Association to 'ripen' into full membership of the EC. In the long run, however, even if East–West economic disparities and the problems of the CAP are capable of being surmounted, it is by no means certain that a European Union with a further expanded and increasingly disparate membership would remain politically and institutionally viable. It is almost unworkable and incapable of acting very decisively with just fifteen member states. This is not just a trumped-up pretext for delay, but a serious and genuine problem which would have to be surmounted prior to any significant further enlargement. The EU's first duty is to maintain its own viability and survival (as is NATO's). No one would benefit from an Eastward enlargement of the EU which either wrecked it or rendered it largely unworkable. Yet even the most modest proposals for institutional and procedural changes that could make the EU more viable evoke howls of protest from vested interests with the power to veto any major departure from the *status quo*. This problem is compounded by the fact that most of the prospective entrants are small states whose accession would further exacerbate the tensions between large and small states within the EU. Small member states are loath to accept any reductions in their disproportionate influence and representation in EU institutions, policy-making and decision-making. Yet the larger member states are very reluctant to accept any further increases in the collective capacity of the small states (comprising a minority of the EU's population) to outvote the larger states (containing the vast majority of EU citizens). There is also a problematic discrepancy between the East European states' desire for EU membership in order to consolidate their fledgling democracies and market economies, and EU insistence that they must achieve consolidated democracy and market systems as prerequisites of membership. If no rapid further enlargement of the EU really seems feasible, for these or other reasons, the sooner the East Europeans are told so the better, because they can then concentrate on alternative arrangements without being distracted by the chimera of imminent EU membership. Nor is it a foregone conclusion that East European peoples and governments will be willing and able to make the requisite cultural reorientations. After all, Article 7 of the EEC Treaty of Rome clearly states that: 'Within the scope of this Treaty . . . any discrimination on grounds of nationality shall be prohibited.' This rule is not fully observed in Western Europe, but it is much harder to uphold in states whose legitimacy and *raison d'être* has rested on narrow ethnic nationalism.

The prospect of eventual East European accessions to the EU could still turn out to have been a mirage or even a grand deception. The prospects for entry to the EU in the foreseeable future vary substantially. Normally the Czech Republic, Hungary and Poland are put well in the lead and the year 2000 has been seen as the earliest conceivable entry date even for those countries. However, a study by the European Commission has suggested that the Czech Republic and Slovenia may be the only countries economically strong enough to be admitted by the end of the 1990s. The scope for obstruction is considerable. Slovenia already has a higher *per capita* income than either Greece or Portugal (John Palmer, *The Guardian*, 24 September 1994, p. 14), but Greece has threatened to veto Eastward enlargement of the EU if it were either to precede the admission of Cyprus to the EU or to involve formal EU consultations and negotiations with the Turkish Cypriots.

Yet the longer any major Eastward enlargement of the EU is delayed, the greater the potential geopolitical hazards – for Eastern Europe, for Germany and for the EU. These risks have been most clearly spelled out in a position paper on Europe written by senior members of Germany's ruling Christian Democratic Union, Karl Lamers and Wolfgang Schäuble (Chancellor Kohl's second-in-command and heir apparent): 'Now that the East–West conflict has come to an end, a stable order must be found for the eastern half of the continent . . . This is in the interests of Germany in particular since, owing to its position, it would suffer the effects of instability in the East more quickly and directly than others. The only solution which will prevent a return to the unstable pre-war system, with Germany once again caught in the middle between East and West, is to integrate Germany's central and eastern European neighbours into the (west) European post-war system and to establish a wide-ranging partnership between this system and Russia. Never again must there be a destabilizing vacuum of power in Central Europe. If (west) European integration were not to progress, Germany might be called upon, or be tempted by its own security constraints, to try to effect the stabilization of Eastern Europe on its own and in the traditional way . . . memories are still very much alive that a German policy towards the East historically has concentrated on closer co-operation with Russia at the expense of the countries in between. Hence Germany has a fundamental interest both in widening the Union to the East and in strengthening it through further deepening. Indeed, deepening is a precondition for widening. Without such further internal strengthening, the Union would be unable to meet the enormous challenge of eastward expansion. It might fall apart and once again become no more than a loose grouping of states unable to guarantee stability. Only if the new system set up after 1945 to regulate conflicts, to effect a balancing of interests, to promote mutual development and to ensure Europe's self-assertion in its external relations can be further developed and expanded to take in Germany's neighbours in Central and Eastern Europe, will Germany have a chance of becoming a centre of stability in the heart of Europe. This German interest in stability is essentially identical with that of Europe' (translated as 'Reflections on European policy', *European Access*, October 1994, no. 5, pp. 11–12). Hence Chancellor Kohl's determination to bring East Central Europe into the EU as soon as feasible has been driven 'not by economics but politics, just as it was when he made his expensive dash for German unification. He no more wants Germany's eastern neighbours left languishing in a no man's land between Europe and Russia than he wants its eastern border exposed to instability. So neither cost nor Russia should be allowed to dictate the terms of the EU's eastward expansion' (*The Economist*, 15 July 1995, pp. 35–6).

Nevertheless, the German strategy is similarly fraught with risks. Powerful vested interests could feel seriously threatened (not least within Germany itself), the economic and social costs could be considerable and the EU could become increasingly unworkable and/or riven by conflicting agendas. A modest or cautious Eastward enlargement of the EU would, regrettably, further increase the real or perceived marginalization and isolation of any Eastern states left outside it, especially if (in an attempt to placate the opponents of enlargement) the EU were to announce a line beyond which it resolved not to expand. This would indeed be a new Yalta. At the same time, the existing EU members whose interests are least likely to be served (and could conceivably be harmed) by any significant Eastward enlargement may well be tempted to exercise their still considerable powers of procrastination, obstruction and veto.

Unfortunately, however, the total fixation of the first post-communist East European governments on eventual accession to the European Union has discouraged serious consideration of adequate interim alternatives to EU membership. An interim scheme to foster political and economic integration and supranational institutions within Eastern Europe, going far beyond the minimalist commitments to East Central European free trade and inter-governmental co-operation agreed at Visegrad in February 1991 and the Central European Free Trade Area (CEFTA) inaugurated in March 1993, would help to prepare East European states for eventual membership of a wider European Union by developing and demonstrating their capacity for constructive participation in joint institutions, for resolving bitter intra-regional disputes and for promoting 'national reconciliation' between former foes. 'If these countries want to open up to the new Europe, they must first open up to each other' (Havel 1994a: 86). That in turn could help to convince West European opponents of an Eastward enlargement that it would not simply import into the EU (and conceivably NATO) all the conflicts that have for so long beset relations between East European nations and states. Conversely, those same opponents would be handed an almost unassailable objection to any Eastward enlargement of the EU (beyond perhaps Slovenia and the Czech Republic) if East Europeans prove incapable of integrating among themselves as a first step towards integration between Eastern and Western Europe. As President Havel argued when the East Europeans were first stepping out on their perilous post-communist journey, 'The former communist countries must find a way into the wider economic and market system of Europe. We should not try to overtake each other. We have to co-ordinate our progress in this field, and it is possible we will find some intermediate steps and institutional arrangements.' But for 'the economically more advanced western European states to welcome us into their midst as returning members, they will have to transform them-selves into institutions which will be truly European and not just Western European' (*FT*, 19 March 1990, p. 34).

Unfortunately, the European Union still sees itself as an expressly Western European club to which some especially favoured East European states may be admitted in due course and it prefers to negotiate with East European states individually rather than as a group, while the Czech government headed by Vaclav Klaus has chosen to ignore Havel's wise advice and to seek the best possible deal for itself rather than act in unison with its Visegrad partners (least of all Slovakia). Indeed, instead of co-ordinating their relations with the EU, each of the East Central European states is seeking to steal a march on its neighbours. This, together with the abrupt disintegration of Czecho-Slovakia during 1992, has dealt a severe blow to the concept of 'Central Europe' as a distinct and cohesive region and to the credibility of the projects of East Central European and pan-European integration. Inotai (1994), for example, is a stern critic of the idea of any kind of Central (and/or Eastern) European payments union. In his view the European Payments Union (EPU) set up after the Second World War 'rested on altogether different conditions. The participating countries had a strong interest in mutual trade, and had historically developed complementary trade patterns . . . Intra-regional trade amounted to 60–70 per cent of total trade, or ten times the current proportion of trade among the Visegrad countries' (p. 38). In present-day East Central Europe, by contrast, 'intra-regional trade is a very modest fraction of total trade – less than 5 per cent for Hungary and Poland, and less than 10 per cent for the Czech Republic and Slovakia' (p. 37) and 'there is little interest in reviving any Comecon-like co-operation' (p. 38).

More generally, intergovernmental co-operation and confederal integration are still greatly impeded by the long-standing jealousies, rivalries and mutual suspicions that have bedevilled relations between the states and nations of Eastern Europe and by a shared loathing of the phoney co-operation and mutual assistance imposed in the communist era by Comecon. This is another reason why leadership will probably continue to have to come at least partly from outside the region if progress is to be made, even though the European Union is in no rush to provide it. It would be safer and more efficacious for that leadership to come at least partly from the EU as a whole than from one or more medium-sized powers each acting separately, divisively and vying for individual advantage or, worse still, from the United States. (That would be a pathetic abdication of European responsibility and an implicit admission that Europe is still incapable of putting its 'common home' in order by its own efforts and in accordance with its own priorities and values.)

By any standard, however, the European Community and its successor, the European Union, have done too little to counteract the unhelpful effects that its own successes and powers of attraction have had on neighbouring countries and regions. As Edward Mortimer warned in 1993, 'The EC congratulates itself on its powers of integration internally and the "magnetic attraction" it exercises on those around it. What has not been sufficiently noted is that this powerful magnetic pull tends to provoke the disintegration of other federal or co-operative structures in the neighbourhood. The EC may preach local and regional co-operation, but the audience is not interested. What the audience sees is a rich and powerful club, membership of which eclipses the value of any local association. Every nation or potential nation . . . starts to think how it could get in and how, above all, it must not be held back by association with less wholesome or less fortunate neighbours' (*FT*, 7 July 1993, p. 16). In Mortimer's view, one could not blame the EC for feeling flattered by its own attractiveness and the growing queue of prospective candidates for membership, but it should have made more effort to limit the resultant disintegrative effects on neighbouring countries and regions by stipulating that they must pursue integration among themselves as a condition of closer links with and assistance from the EC, instead of dealing with each of them separately on a divisive and hegemonic 'hub and spoke' basis. He has repeatedly quoted the apt precedent of the Marshall Plan, which astutely made the receipt of Marshall Aid conditional upon the recipients sinking their differences and coming together in an Organization of European Economic Co-operation, designed to promote a joint European Recovery Programme and market integration between its members. No one has yet come up with a more appropriate model for the integration of post-communist Eastern Europe, either within itself or with Western Europe.

Nevertheless, East Central European governments are dragging their feet with regard to intra-regional integration, not only because they find it very difficult to work together, but also because they fear that the European Union might come to regard a successful Visegrad grouping and CEFTA as a substitute for (rather than an antechamber to) membership of an expanded EU. (Visegrad, as mentioned in Chapters 5 and 6, had also been the venue for a famous meeting and pact between the kings of Hungary, Poland and Bohemia in 1335.) Not surprisingly, moreover, many East Europeans have become somewhat disenchanted or even embittered by the sufferings and hardships induced by their rush to the market, by the delayed appearance of many compensating benefits (most of which are beyond the reach of the poorer sections of the population) and by the

European Union's stand-offishness, delaying tactics and prevarication on anything relating to increased access to EU markets and/or a timetable for Eastward enlargement. This has resulted in a certain cooling of popular enthusiasm for the 'return to Europe'. In early 1994 a Eurobarometer opinion poll found that positive evaluation of the EU had declined to 37 per cent, on average, in the four Visegrad states (Kolankiewicz 1994: 478). Nevertheless, this has not dissuaded a growing number of East European governments from formally applying for full membership of the EU, starting with Hungary and Poland in April 1994. Indeed, in most cases there has been (or would be) almost unanimous parliamentary approval for such a step, even though there is no immediate prospect of these applications either being taken seriously by the EU or making any tangible difference to the pace and direction of the enlargement process.

At the very least, in our view, the European Union owes it to Eastern Europe to be more open and honest about what it considers to be possible or impossible within a given time frame, if only to concentrate East European minds on the construction of more substantial interim schemes of intra-regional integration and co-operation because that is all that is immediately on offer. Portes (1994: 1188–9) contends that the 'hub-and-spoke pattern of trade relations marginalizes the individual Eastern countries' and 'discourages economic relations among them . . . All this argues for mapping out a clearer path to accession that would multilateralize the Europe agreements so as to create a comprehensive free trade area, then deepen integration in an approach to something like the EU–EFTA "European Economic Area".'

The EU's major (but unlauded) achievement in relation to Eastern Europe during the first half of the 1990s has been a purely negative one. The institutionalized political and economic interdependence of west European states has 'largely prevented the re-emergence of classic balance of power politics between the main European actors', thereby helping to avert an escalation of the local wars in former Yugoslavia and Moldavia into major European conflicts (Kramer 1993: 218). West European states have jostled for 'national' economic advantage in Eastern Europe, but they have largely refrained from jockeying for geopolitical dominance over the region in the manner of nineteenth- and early twentieth-century great powers. On the whole, with exceptions such as Germany's premature pushing for EC recognition of Croatian and Slovenian independence, the larger EU states have attempted to pursue concerted policies towards Eastern Europe. These concerted policies, Russia's laudably restrained conduct in the Balkans from 1991 to 1995 and the fact that Britain, France, Germany and Italy rarely broke ranks (by trying to 'go it alone') were little short of miraculous by past standards. However, this negative achievement has been eclipsed by the inevitable public denunciations and criticisms of Europe's calamitous failure either to maintain or to restore peace in former Yugoslavia before 1995.

Since the First World War, or since the late eighteenth century in the case of Poland, East Europeans seem to have laboured under persistent illusions concerning the scale of the economic, military or political assistance or support which West European states might be willing to provide, whether in support of national self-determination or democracy or 'free-market' economies or against a common foe (usually Germany or Russia). East Europeans repeatedly deluded themselves that, when the West avowedly shared or supported their concerns or aspirations, significant practical support would be forthcoming. But Poles looked in vain for West European assistance against the 'partitioning powers' in 1791–95, in 1831 and in 1863, as did Hungarian nationalists during their revolution against the Habsburgs in 1848–49. The Western Allies did re-establish or 'call into existence' independent East European states in the wake of the First World War. During the 1920s and 1930s, however, these East European states looked in vain for substantial Western financial, commercial, technical or even moral support for their faltering, crisis-torn democracies and fragile, trade-dependent economies. The 'appeasers' who governed Britain and France did little to discourage Hitler's dismemberment of Czechoslovakia in 1938–39 or Mussolini's occupation of Albania in 1939. Many East Europeans also felt betrayed by the agreements reached by Churchill and Stalin in Moscow in October 1944 and by the Allied leaders at Yalta and Potsdam in 1945, which effectively surrendered Eastern Europe to the post-war Soviet 'sphere of influence'. However, as Professor Doreen Warriner remarked in 1950, 'Western Europe, so far as it was interested in eastern Europe at all, was interested in keeping it backward, as a source of cheap food and cheap labour'. In her view, if the Western powers had been able to have their way in post-1944 Eastern Europe, 'they would have put back into power the same kind of governments which had existed before, and whose failure led to Fascism . . . During the war the Western powers had evolved no new policy for eastern Europe: they supported the *émigré* governments in London, at best, liberal politicians of the old style, at worst, near-Fascists.' The West 'learnt nothing' from the failure of the 1919–20 peace settlements in inter-war Eastern Europe (Warriner 1950: xiv). She had a point, even if she overstated it.

Undeterred by the West's unwillingness to come to the assistance of the Hungarian Revolution of October 1956, the Prague Spring in August 1968 or Poland's Solidarity movement in 1981, East Europeans still expected Western Europe and the United States to underwrite their post-1989 transition to liberal, plural democracy and market economies. To some extent, such delusions have been a consequence of centuries of subjugation by powerful Russian, Austrian, German and Turkish neighbours and the resultant belief that Eastern Europe could be liberated and economically developed only with external assistance. This fostered a damaging psychological dependence upon the West. Western Europe, for its part, has regularly raised and disappointed East European hopes, and this cycle has been repeated yet again during the 1990s. For the EC, however, the emergence of Eastern Europe from its communist cocoon in 1989 was rather inconvenient, for the EC had partly relied on the Cold War partition of Europe for much of its cohesion, self-discipline, sense of purpose and stability. The new post-Cold War Europe will take time to find new sources of cohesion and a new sense of direction.

Ever since the collapse of the Austro-Hungarian Empire in 1918, Eastern Europe has been an economic and power vacuum waiting to be filled, formerly by Germany and/or Russia, but since 1989 by Germany and/or the EU. This is almost a law of physics. Nature abhors a vacuum. The most likely outcome is German domination under EU auspices. There certainly are benefits to be gained by the host country in attracting direct foreign investment and wider ones in terms of capital flows helping to unite Europe. But there is also the danger that Eastern Europe could become an informal colony or a 'captive' market for the EU states, simply a provider of very cheap labour to EU subcontractors and subsidiaries that helps EU economies to withstand growing competition from outside Europe. West European investors could be primarily interested in 'saving' (i.e. buying) the plums or potential competitors among East European enterprises while leaving the rest to founder, pocketing any available subsidies or investment grants, spiriting away key East European personnel and their technological know-how, or simply making 'a quick killing', before turning their attention elsewhere. West European entrepreneurs may be less interested in sustainable long-term development for the benefit of East Europeans than in 'rent-seeking', cornering markets, capturing booty and subjugating the East European economies to West European industrial and finance capitalism. They are primarily there to make money (although it is worth bearing in mind Joan Robinson's legendary remark that, if there is anything worse than being exploited by foreign capital, it is *not* being exploited by foreign capital!). This may be too cynical a picture, but it is a necessary antidote to any idea that capitalist Western Europe and the EU are engaged in a great philanthropic venture. One must not be hoodwinked by the hypocritical language of 'aid'. The Western Allies handed the East Europeans over to Soviet domination in 1945 and this should now put the West 'under a serious obligation to help these countries' (William Pfaff, *IHT*, 14 September 1991, p. 6). Yet, in matters involving sacrifice or risk, Western attitudes towards these 'faraway countries about which we know little' have not changed all that much since 1938 or 1945. Formally the Yalta agreement no longer applies, but in practice it will take a long time fully to undo it.

CONCLUSIONS

In the medium term the success of macroeconomic stabilization and microeconomic reforms in post-communist Eastern Europe will primarily depend on the maintenance of parliamentary and popular support for such measures and on the degree to which the European Union opens up its markets to East European exports, as well as on appropriate domestic supply-side responses to the new conditions. In the longer term, however, even more difficult requirements will have to be met. The prevailing approaches to democratization and marketization in Eastern Europe misleadingly assume that these projects can and should be contained within the existing national states. But in reality these supposedly 'national' units and processes will have to be supplemented in various ways if they are to be capable of retaining the semblance of national autonomy on which they depend. Most of the purportedly 'national' states that have been established in Eastern Europe since the late nineteenth century have not been 'self-made' states on the British and French models, but have owed their legitimacy and existence to international recognition (primarily from the Western powers, but also from Russia, Germany, Turkey and Italy). Therefore, they have always found it difficult to sustain the claims that states usually make to exclusive jurisdiction over what they consider to be 'their own internal affairs' and to fend off external scrutiny of (and often interference in) their conduct of those affairs. Moreover, in an increasingly global and interdependent world, the locus of policy-making and decision-making is gradually shifting back from nation-states to international institutions such as the World Trade Organization (successor to GATT), the IMF, the World Bank and NATO and to regulatory confederations such as the EU. As yet, however, there is not a great deal of democratic accountability in the workings of such international organizations. They remain essentially 'cartels of governments', which sidestep democratic processes and take decisions over the heads of elected parliaments. Yet, since their policy-making and decision-making roles largely deal with matters that transcend national boundaries, it would not be very helpful or constructive to bring them within the jurisdiction of national parliaments. That would just be a recipe for chronic international or interparliamentary bickering, deadlock and immobilism. Effective democratic accountability in international or supranational matters can be secured only by enhancing the roles of, and democratic participation in, supranational fora, even though that may mean that existing confederal and intergovernmental organizations will have to take on a more federal character. The role played by the EU and EU member states in the 1986–93 Uruguay Round of GATT negotiations suggests one way in which this might conceivably work. But it will not be either smooth or easy.

Increased national assertion can at best achieve only an illusion of increased democratic control of supranational policies, processes and organizations. Chasing such chimeras could reinforce the belief that 'democracy does not work' and reduce public support for the democratic institutions on which post-communist Eastern Europe has initially pinned its hopes. Durable and far-reaching democratization cannot focus exclusively on the formal structures, procedures and activities of the nation-state. Enduring democratization has also to engage and address sub-state (subnational) and supra-state (supranational) groups, issues and institutions, instead of being excessively or almost exclusively focused on the project of 'national' state-building, as has been the case thus far in post-communist Eastern Europe. There is also a need for increased emphasis on the rights of 'people' rather than 'peoples', on individual and local (as distinct from national) self-determination. The rights of individuals and local communities need greater recognition and attention, but this need not be achieved in the ways that national self-determination has been attained and upheld, for these have posed some of the main dangers to individual, local and regional interests and rights. Instead, there will probably have to be greater emphasis on a binding international framework of rules and law, i.e. an international 'civil association' of states and market economies.

In the twentieth century the collapse of multinational empires has often resulted in the fragmentation of their former territories into a profusion of small successor states animated by an upsurge of liberated nationalism. This was certainly the outcome in Eastern Europe after the collapse of the Ottoman, Habsburg, Tsarist empires, and as it has been since the collapse of the Soviet empire. Even if the collapse of such empires was inevitable, it does not necessarily follow that what replaced them was an improvement. The decisive challenge facing East Europe politicians has been to find ways of accommodating ethnic loyalties and nationalism consistent with raising incomes and maintaining peace and security. The post-communist governments of Eastern Europe have wished to sidestep this challenge by gaining rapid accession to the EU and NATO. But, even if they were eventually to achieve these objectives, it would not occur soon enough to see them through the 1990s. In the interim, therefore, they 'need to construct voluntary supranational organizations of their own that are strong enough to referee quarrels, to keep borders open to trade and to protect the human rights of minorities. They need to build a moral equivalent of the old empires' (*IHT*, editorial, 10 June 1992, p. 8). In other words, the basis of East European polities needs to be moved away from the building of rather exclusive, intolerant and egotistic 'ethnic' nation-states towards the construction of more open, inclusive and tolerant societies embedded in a supranational confederal structure or structures, if the region is to escape endemic conflict, instability, national messianism and the attendant dangers of a return to various possible forms of authoritarianism. The region must escape from the tyranny of ethnic collectivism. Undoubtedly, such a fundamental reorientation will take time and will need strong external encouragement and generous support if it is not to founder yet again on the rocks of inter-ethnic and inter-state jealousies, rivalry and conflict.

With regard to the historical significance of the end of communist dictatorship in Eastern Europe, we do not consider that this in any sense marked 'the end of history' or the final irreversible triumph of liberal democracy. The 'demons' of nationalist and religious exclusiveness, intolerance and bigotry are still very much alive, and it may be premature to write the 'final obituaries' on communism. (After all, when China's Premier Zhou En Lai was asked what was the significance of the French Revolution of 1789, he famously replied that it was 'too early to say'.) Instead, we concur with the view that the collapse of communist rule in Eastern Europe marked the termination of one of the most extreme expressions of the various 'modernist projects' set in motion by the Renaissance and the Enlightenment. As eloquently stated by President Vaclav Havel at the World Economic Forum in Davos in February 1992, 'The modern era has been dominated by the belief, expressed in different forms, that the world – and Being as such – is a wholly knowable system governed by a finite number of universal Laws that man can group and rationally direct for his own benefit. This era, beginning in the Renaissance and developing from the Enlightenment to socialism, from positivism to scientism, from the Industrial Revolution to the information revolution, was characterized by rapid advances in rational, cognitive thinking. This, in turn, gave rise to the proud belief that Man, as the pinnacle of everything that exists, was capable of objectively describing, explaining and controlling everything that exists, and of possessing the one and only truth about the world. It was an era . . . of belief in automatic progress brokered by the scientific method. It was an era of systems . . . It was an era of ideologies, doctrines, interpretations of reality, an era when the goal was to find a universal theory of the world and thus a universal key to unlock its prosperity. Communism was the perverse extreme of this trend' (Havel 1994a: 177). Marx and Engels fondly believed that 'the rational order dreamt of by the Enlightenment, based on consent and truth, not only *could* come about, but in the end inevitably *would* come about' (Gellner 1996: 35). The communist parties and regimes saw themselves as the ultimate secular scientocracies of the new age, the culmination of the drive to place Man (eventually, just one man!) in control of everything. The collapse of Europe's communist regimes dramatically exposed the hollowness, the fraudulence and the self-delusions behind such claims, and delivered a powerful warning to those who would otherwise rush to follow in the communists' footsteps. Yet it is still too soon to proclaim the death of the modernist project. For example, those who dogmatically believe that secular *laissez-faire* capitalism (rather than communism or fascism) holds the key that will unlock the secrets of prosperity, peace and social as well as scientific and technological progess are still in its thrall, as are the latter-day champions of unilinear modernization theories. It cannot be assumed either that *laissez-faire* capitalism will always carry all before it or has 'all the answers'. The moral is *caveat emptor*. Beware of doctrines claiming to have found the universal cognitive keys and panaceas. They are most likely to lead to tyranny and to endanger both Man and Nature.

Bibliography

Adenauer, K. (1966) *Memoirs, 1945–53*, London: Weidenfeld and Nicolson.

Aganbegyan, A. (1988) *The Challenge: Economics of Perestroika*, London: Hutchinson.

Aldcroft, D. and Morewood, S. (1993) 'Eastern Europe since Versailles', *Economic Review*, vol. 10, no. 3.

—— (1995) *Economic Change in Eastern Europe since 1918*, Cheltenham: Edward Elgar.

Ali, R. and Lifschultz, L. (1994) 'Why Bosnia?', *Third World Quarterly*, vol. 15, no. 3.

Alter, P. (1989) *Nationalism*, London: Edward Arnold.

Anderson, P. (1979) *Lineages of the Absolute State*, London: Verso.

Andreades, A. (1948) 'The economic life of the Byzantine Empire' in Baynes and Moss (1948).

Arendt, H. (1966) *The Origins of Totalitarianism*, third edition, New York: Harcourt Brace.

Arnakis, G. (1963) 'The role of religion in the development of Balkan nationalism' in Jelavich and Jelavich (1963).

Arter, D. (1993) *The Politics of European Integration in the Twentieth Century*, Aldershot: Dartmouth Publishing.

Ascherson, N. (1988) *The Struggles for Poland*, London: Pan Books.

Åslund, A. (1994) 'Lessons of the first four years of systemic change in Eastern Europe', *Journal of Comparative Economics*, vol. 19, no. 1.

Ausch, S. (1972) *Theory and Practice of CMEA Co-operation*, Budapest: Akademiai Kiado.

Avakumic. I. (1971) 'Yugoslavia's fascist movements' in Sugar (1971a).

Balcerowicz, L. (1989) 'Polish economic reform, 1981–88: an overview' in Economic Commission for Europe, *Economic Reform in the European Centrally Planned Economies*, Economic Studies No. 1, New York: United Nations.

—— (1993) 'Transition to market economy: Central and East European countries in comparative perspective', *British Review of Economic Issues*, vol. 15, no. 37.

—— (1994) 'Common fallacies in the debate on the transition to a market economy', *Economic Policy*, no. 19 (supplement).

Baldwin, R. (1994) *Towards an Integrated Europe*, London: CEPR.

Barany, G. (1967) 'Hungary: the uncompromising compromise', in Austrian History Yearbook, vol. III, Part 1.

—— (1971) 'The dragon's teeth: the roots of Hungarian fascism' in Sugar (1971a).

Barrington Moore Jnr, J. (1969) *Social Origins of Dictatorship and Democracy*, Harmondsworth: Penguin.

Bartha, I. (1975) 'The development of the bourgeois national reform movement' and 'Towards bourgeois transformation, revolution and war of independence, 1790–1849' in Pamlenyi (1975).

Bartlett, W. (1996) 'From reform to crisis: economic impacts of secession, war and sanctions in the former Yugoslavia' in Jeffries (1996b).

Basch, A. (1944) *The Danube Basin and the German Economic Sphere*, London: Kegan Paul.

Batt, J. (1988) *Economic Reform and Political Change in Eastern Europe: a Comparison of the Czechoslovak and Hungarian Experiences*, London: Macmillan.

—— (1991) *East Central Europe from Reform to Transformation*, London: Pinter (Chatham House Papers: the Royal Institute of International Affairs).

—— (1994a) 'The political transformation of East Central Europe' in Miall (1994).

—— (1994b) 'The international dimension of democratization in Czechoslovakia and Hungary' in Pridham *et al.* (1994).

Bauer, O. (1925) *The Austrian Revolution*, London (reprinted by Burt Franklin, New York, 1970).

Bauer, T. (1988) 'Economic reforms within and beyond the state sector', *American Economic Review*, Papers and Proceedings, May.

Baynes, N. and Moss, H. (1948) *Byzantium: an Introduction to East Roman Civilization*, Oxford: Clarendon Press.

Benes, V. and Pounds, N. (1970) *Poland*, London: Benn.

Berend, I. (1986) 'The historical evolution of Eastern Europe as a region', *International Organization*, vol. 40.

Berend, I. and Ranki, G. (1969) 'Economic problems of the Danube region after the break-up of the Austro-Hungarian Monarchy', *Journal of Contemporary History*, vol. 4.

—— (1974a) *Economic Development in East-Central Europe in the Nineteenth and Twentieth Centuries*, New York: Columbia University Press.

—— (1974b) *Hungary: a Century of Economic Development*, Newton Abbot: David and Charles.

Betts, R. (1931) 'The *Regulae Veteris et Novi Testamenti* of Matej z Janova', *Journal of Theological Studies*, vol. 32.

—— (1947) 'The place of the Czech Reformation in the history of Europe', *Slavonic and East European Review*, vol. 25.

—— (1970) 'The central monarchies' in Hay (1970).

Bialostocki, J. (1985) 'Borrowing and originality in the East-Central European Renaissance' in Maczak *et al.* (1985).

Bicanic, I. (1996) 'The economic divergence of Yugoslavia's successor states' in Jeffries (1996b).

Bideleux, R. (1987) *Communism and Development*, London: Methuen.

—— (1990) 'Agricultural advance under the Russian village commune system' in Bartlett, R. (ed.) *Land Commune and Peasant Community in Russia*, London: Macmillan.

—— (1994) 'Alexander II and the emancipation of the serfs' in Catterall, P. and Vine, R. (eds) *Europe 1870–1914*, London: Heinemann.

—— (1996) 'The southern enlargement of the EC: Spain, Portugal and Greece' in Bideleux, R. and Taylor, R. (eds) *European Integration and Disintegration: East and West*, London: Routledge.

Bizzell, W. (1926) *The Green Rising*, New York: Macmillan.

Black, C. (1963) 'Russia and the modernization of the Balkans' in Jelavich and Jelavich (1963).

Blum, J. (1957) 'The rise of serfdom in Eastern Europe', *American Historical Review*, vol. 62.

—— (1978) *The End of the Old Order in Rural Europe*, Princeton, N.J.: Princeton University Press.

Bogucka, M. (1982) 'Polish towns between the sixteenth and eighteenth centuries' in Fedorowicz (1982).

Bourne, K. (1990) *The Foreign Policy of Victorian England, 1830–1902*, Oxford: Clarendon Press.

Brabant, J. Van (1980) *Socialist Economic Integration*, Cambridge: Cambridge University Press.

—— (1989) *Economic Integration in Eastern Europe*, London: Harvester Wheatsheaf.

—— (1991) 'Renewal of co-operation and economic transition in Eastern Europe', *Studies in Comparative Communism*, vol. XXIV, no. 2.

—— (1993) 'Lessons from the wholesale transformations in the East', *Comparative Economic Studies*, vol. XXXV, no. 4.

—— (1994) 'Trade, integration and transformation in Eastern Europe', *Journal of International Affairs*, vol. 48, no. 1.

Brada, J. (1985) 'Soviet subsidization of Eastern Europe: the primacy of politics over economics', *Journal of Comparative Economics*, vol. 9, no. 1.

—— (1988) 'Intepreting Soviet subsidization of Eastern Europe', *International Organization*, vol. 42.

Bradley, J. (1971) *Czechoslovakia: a Short History*, Edinburgh: Edinburgh University Press.

Brandt, W. (1968) 'A peace policy for Europe' in Harprecht, K. (ed.) *Willy Brandt: Portrait and Self-portrait*, London: Abelard-Schuman (1972).

—— (1978) *People and Politics: the Years 1960–1975*, London: Collins.

Brenner, R. (1989) 'Economic backwardness in Eastern Europe in the light of developments in the West' in Chirot (1989a).

Brittain, L. (1994) *Europe: the Europe we Need*, London: Hamish Hamilton.

Brock, P. (1957) *The Political and Social Doctrines of the Unity of Brethren*, Gravenhage: Mouton.

Brown, J. (1970) *Bulgaria under Communist Rule*, New York: Praeger.

—— (1991) *Surge to Freedom: the End of Communist rule in Eastern Europe*, London: Adamantine Press.

Brown, P. (1971) *The World of Late Antiquity*, London: Thames and Hudson.

Bryant, C. and Mokrzycki, E. (1994) *The New Great Transformation: Change and Continuity in East-Central Europe*, London: Routledge.

Brzezinski, Z. (1967) *The Soviet Bloc*, Cambridge, Mass.: Harvard University Press.

Bugajski, J. (1995) *Nations in Turmoil: Conflict and Co-operation in Eastern Europe*, Boulder, Colo.: Westview Press.

Burke, U.P. (1985) 'Introduction: a note on the historiography of East Central Europe', in A. Maczak, H. Samsonowicz and U.P. Burke (eds) *East Central Europe in Transition*, Cambridge: Cambridge University Press.

Callinicos, A. (1991) *The Revenge of History*, Cambridge: Polity Press.

Cameron, R. (1966) *Banking in the Early Stages of Industrialization*, London: Oxford University Press.

Campbell, J. (1963) 'The Balkans: heritage and continuity' in Jelavich and Jelavich (1963).

Carabott, P. (ed.) (1995) *Greece and Europe in the Modern Period: Aspects of a Troubled Relationship*, London: Centre for Hellenic Studies, King's College.

Carr, E. (1945) *Nationalism and After*, London: Macmillan.

Carsten, F. (1967) *The Rise of Fascism*, London: Batsford.

Catchlove, D. (1972) *Romania's Ceausescu*, Tunbridge Wells: Abacus Press.

Chesterton, G.K. (1923) 'Introduction' in H.D. Irvine, *The Making of Rural Europe*, London: Allen and Unwin.

Childs, D. (1987) *East Germany to the 1990s: Can it Resist Glasnost?*, London: EIU.

—— (1988) *The GDR: Moscow's German Ally*, second edition, London: Unwin Hyman.

Chirot, D. (ed.) (1989a) *The Origins of Backwardness in Eastern Europe: Economics and Politics from the Middle Ages until the Early Twentieth Century*, Berkeley: University of California Press.

—— (1989b) 'Causes and consequences of backwardness' in Chirot (1989a).

Churchill, W. (1989) *The Second World War*, Harmondsworth: Penguin.

Cipolla, C. (1970) *European Culture and Overseas Expansion*, Harmondsworth: Penguin.

Clague, C. and Rausser, G. (eds) (1992) *The Emergence of Market Economies in Eastern Europe*, Oxford: Blackwell.

Clissold, S. (ed.) *A Short History of Yugoslavia*, Cambridge: Cambridge University Press.

Clogg, R. (1992) *A Concise History of Modern Greece*, Cambridge: Cambridge University Press.

Cochrane, N. (1988) 'The private sector in East European agriculture', *Problems of Communism*, March–April.

—— (1990a) 'Reforming agricultural prices in Eastern Europe', *Problems of Communism*, January–February.

—— (1990b) 'Reforming socialist agriculture: Bulgarian and Hungarian experience and implications for the USSR' in Wädekin (1990).

—— (1993) 'Central European agrarian reforms in a historical perspective', *American Journal of Agricultural Economics*, vol. 75, no. 3.

Cohan, A. (1975) *Theories of Revolution*, London: Nelson.

Cole, G.D.H. (1941) *Europe, Russia and the Future*, London: Gollancz.

Coles, P. (1968) *The Ottoman Impact on Europe*, London: Thames and Hudson.

Collingwood, R. (1946) *The Idea of History*, Oxford: Clarendon Press (revised edition 1994, Oxford University Press).

—— (1994) *The Idea of History*, revised edition (with lectures, 1926–28), Oxford: Oxford University Press.

Comecon (1984) *Statisticheski ezhegodnik stran-chlenov Soveta ekonomicheskoi vzaimopomoshchi*, Moscow: Comecon Secretariat, Finansi i statistika.

Comintern (1929) *The Programme of the Communist International*, London: Modern Books (Moscow edition 1928).

Connor, W. (1979) *Socialism, Politics and Equality: Hierarchy and Change in Eastern Europe and the USSR*, New York: Columbia University Press.

Coudenhove-Kalergi, R. (1926) *Pan Europe*, New York: Knopf.

Crampton, R. (1994) *Eastern Europe in the Twentieth Century*, London: Routledge.

Croan, M. (1989) 'Lands-in-between: the politics and cultural identity in contemporary Eastern Europe', *East European Politics and Societies*, vol. 3.

Czernin, Count Ottaker (1920) *In the World War*, New York: Harper.

Darby, H., Woodhouse, C., Crawley, C. and Heurtley, W. (1965) *A Short History of Greece*, Cambridge: Cambridge University Press.

Davies, N. (1981) *God's Playground: a History of Poland*, vol. I, *The Origins to 1795*, Oxford: Clarendon Press.

—— (1982) *God's Playground: a History of Poland*, vol. 2, *1795 to the Present*, Oxford: Clarendon Press.

—— (1986) *Heart of Europe: a Short History of Europe*, Oxford: Oxford University Press.

Davy, R. (ed.) (1992) *European Détente: a Reappraisal*, London: Sage/RIIA.

Dawisha, K. (1990) *Eastern Europe, Gorbachev and Reform*, Cambridge: Cambridge University Press.

Deak, I. (1967) 'Comment' in *Austrian History Yearbook*, vol. III, Part 1.

—— (1979) *The Lawful Revolution: Lajos Kossuth and the Hungarians, 1848–49*, New York: Columbia University Press.

Dedijer, V. (1967) *The Road to Sarajevo*, London: Macgibbon and Kee.

Degras, J. (ed.) (1956) *The Communist International, 1919–1943*, Documents, vol. I, *1919–22*, London: Oxford University Press.

—— (ed.) (1960) *The Communist International, 1919–1943*, Documents, vol. 2, *1923–28*, London: Oxford University Press.

—— (ed.) (1965) *The Communist International, 1919–1943*, Documents, vol. 3, *1929–43*, London: Oxford University Press.

Desai, P. (1986) 'Is the Soviet Union subsidizing Eastern Europe?', *European Economic Review*, vol. I.

Deutsch, K. (1969) *Nationalism and its Alternatives*, New York: Knopf.

Diehl, C. (1948) 'From AD 1204 to AD 1453' in Baynes, N. and Moss, H. (eds) *Byzantium: an Introduction to East Roman Civilization*, Oxford: Oxford University Press.

Djordjevic, D. (1971) 'Fascism in Yugoslavia, 1918–1941' in Sugar (1971a).

Dobb, M. (1963) *On Economic Growth and Underdeveloped Countries*, London: Lawrence and Wishart.

—— (1967) *Papers on Capitalism, Development and Planning*, London: Routledge.

Donia, R. and Fine, J. (1994) *Bosnia and Hercegovina: a Tradition Betrayed*, London: Hurst.

Drage, G. (1909) *Austria-Hungary*, London: Murray.

Duby, G. (1974) *The Early Growth of the European Economy*, Ithaca, N.Y.: Cornell University Press.

Duchêne, F. (1965) 'Britain in a harder world', *Journal of Common Market Studies*, vol. 3.

Duray, M. (1989) 'The European ideal: reality or wishful thinking in Eastern Europe' in Schöpflin and Wood (1989).

Durham, E. (1920) *Twenty Years of Balkan Tangle*, New York: Putnam.

Dvornik, F. (1949) *The Making of Central and Eastern Europe*, London: Polish Research Centre.

—— (1962) *The Slavs in European History and Civilization*, New Brunswick, N.J.: Rutgers University Press.

EBRD (1994) *Transition Report*, London: European Bank for Reconstruction and Development.

—— (1995a) *Transition Report Update* (April), London: European Bank for Reconstruction and Development.

—— (1995b) *Transition Report*, London: European Bank for Reconstruction and Development.

—— (1996a) *Transition Report Update* (April), London: European Bank for Reconstruction and Development.

—— (1996b) *Transition Report*, London: European Bank for Reconstruction and Development.

Eddie, S. (1985) 'Economic policy and economic development in Austria-Hungary, 1867–1913', in *The Cambridge Economic History of Europe*, vol. 8, Cambridge: Cambridge University Press.

Estrin, S. (1983) *Self-management: Economic Theory and Yugoslav Practice*, Cambridge: Cambridge University Press.

—— (1991) 'Yugoslavia: the case of self-managing market socialism', *Journal of Economic Perspectives*, vol. 5, no. 4.

Evans, R. (1973) *Rudolph II and his World*, Oxford: Oxford University Press.

—— (1979) *The Making of the Habsburg Monarchy, 1550–1700*, Oxford; Oxford University Press.

Fedorowicz, J. (ed.) (1982) *A Republic of Nobles: Studies in Polish History to 1864*, Cambridge: Cambridge University Press.

Feher, F. (1988) 'Eastern Europe's long revolution against Yalta', *Eastern European Politics and Societies*, vol. 2.

—— (1989) 'On making Central Europe', *Eastern European Politics and Societies*, vol. 3.

Fejto, F. (ed.) (1974) *A History of the People's Democracies*, London: Pelican.

Fellner, F. (1967) 'Comment' in *Austrian History Yearbook*, vol. III, Part 2.

—— (1968) 'The dissolution of the Habsburg Monarchy and its significanace for the new order in Central Europe: a reappraisal' in *Austrian History Yearbook*, vol. IV.

Fine, J. (1976) *The Bosnian Church: a New Interpretation*, Boulder, Colo.: Westview Press.

—— (1987) *The Late Medieval Balkans: a Critical Survey from the Late Twelfth Century to the Ottoman Conquest*, Ann Arbor: University of Michigan Press.

—— (1991) *The Early Medieval Balkans: a Critical Survey from the Sixth to the Late Twelfth Century*, Ann Arbor: University of Michigan Press.

Fischer-Galati, S. (1963) 'Nationalism and *Kaisertreue*', *Slavic Review*, vol. 22.

—— (ed.) (1970) *Man, State and Society in East European History*, New York: Praeger.

—— (1971) 'Fascism in Romania' in Sugar (1971a).

—— (1984) 'Autocracy, orthodoxy and nationality in the twentieth century: the Romanian case', *East European Quarterly*, vol. 18, no. 1.

Freudenberger, H. (1967) 'State intervention as an obstacle to economic growth in the Habsburg Monarchy', *Journal of Economic History*, vol. 27.

Garton Ash, T. (1986) 'Does Central Europe exist?' in Schöpflin and Wood (1989).

Gati, C. (1990) *The Bloc that Failed*, Bloomington: Indiana University Press.

Gellner, E. (1996) *Conditions of Liberty: Civil Society and its Rivals*, Harmondsworth: Penguin.

Geremek, B. (1982) 'Poland and the cultural geography of medieval Europe' in Fedorowicz (1982).

Gerschenkron, A. (1962) *Economic Backwardness in Historical Perspective*, Cambridge, Mass.: Harvard University Press.

—— (1968) *Continuity in History and other Essays*, Cambridge, Mass.: Harvard University Press.

Gierowski, J. (1982) 'The international position of Poland in the seventeenth and eighteenth centuries' in Fedorowicz (1982).

Gilbert, M. (1967) *Recent History Atlas*, London: Weidenfeld and Nicolson.

Glenny, M. (1990) *The Rebirth of History: Eastern Europe in the Age of Democracy*, Harmondsworth: Penguin.

—— (1992) *The Fall of Yugoslavia*, Harmondsworth: Penguin.

Good, D. (1979) 'Issues in the study of Habsburg economic development', *East-Central Europe*, vol. 6, Part I.

—— (1980) 'Modern economic growth in the Habsburg Monarchy', *East-Central Europe*, vol. 7, Part 2.

—— (1984) *The Economic Rise of the Habsburg Empire, 1850–1914*, Berkeley: University of California Press.

—— (1994) *Economic Transformation in Central and Eastern Europe*, London: Routledge.

Gorbachev, M. (1987) *Perestroika: New Thinking for our Country and the World*, London: Collins; New York: Harper and Row.

Gramsci, A. (1971) *Selections from the Prison Notebooks*, London: Lawrence and Wishart.

Granick, D. (1975) *Enterprise Guidance in Eastern Europe*, Princeton, N.J.: Princeton University Press.

Grant, M. (1978) *A History of Rome*, London: Book Club Associates.

Gregor, A. (1969) *The Ideology of Fascism*, London: Collier-Macmillan.

—— (1979) *Italian Fascism and Developmental Dictatorship*, Princeton, N.J.: Princeton University Press.

Grell, O. (1994) 'Scandinavia' in Scribner *et al.* (1994).

Griffin, R. (1993) *The Nature of Fascism*, London: Routledge.

Grochulska, B. (1982) 'The place of the Enlightenment in Polish social history' in Fedorowicz (1982).

Gross, F. (1945) *Crossroads of Two Continents*, London.

Gross, N. (1973) 'The Habsburg Monarchy, 1750–1914' in Cipolla, C. (ed.) *The Fontana Economic History of Europe, 1750–1914*, vol. 4 (1), Glasgow: Collins–Fontana.

Gunst, P. (1989) 'Agrarian systems of Central and Eastern Europe' in Chirot (1989a).

Halasz, Z. (ed.) (1960) *Hungary*, Budapest: Corvina.

Hale, J. (1971) *Ceausescu's Romania*, London: Harrap.

Halecki, O. (1942) *The History of Poland*, London: Dent.

—— (1950) *The Limits and Divisions of European History*, New York: Columbia University Press.

—— (ed.) (1957) *Poland*, Praeger: New York.

Hammond, T. (1958) 'The origins of national communism', *Virginia Quarterly Review*, vol. 34.

—— (1975) *The Anatomy of Communist Takeovers*, New Haven: Yale University Press.

Hanak, P. (1975a) 'Economics, society and sociopolitical thought in Hungary during the age of capitalism' in *Austrian History Yearbook*, vol. XI.

—— (1975b) 'The period of neo-absolutism, 1849–1867' in Pamlenyi (1975).

—— (1975c) 'The Dual Monarchy, 1867–1914' in Pamlenyi (1975).

—— (1989) 'Central Europe: a historical region in modern times' in Schöpflin and Wood (1989).

Haraszti, M. (1977) *A Worker in a Workers' State*, Harmondsworth: Penguin.

Hare, P., Radice, H. and Swain, N. (1981) *Hungary: a Decade of Reform*, London: Allen and Unwin.

Haussig, H. (1971) *A History of Byzantine Civilization*, London: Thames and Hudson.

Havel, V. (1994a) *Towards a Civil Society: Selective Speeches and Writings, 1990–1994*, Prague: Lidove Noviny Publishing House.

—— (1994b) 'A call for sacrifice: the co-responsibility of the West', *Foreign Affairs*, vol. 73, no. 2.

Hay, D. (1970) *Europe in the Fourteenth and Fifteenth Centuries*, London: Longman.

Heinrich, H-G. (1986) *Hungary: Politics, Economics and Society*, London: Pinter.

Higley, J. and Gunther, R. (1992) *Elites and Democratic Consolidation in Latin America and Southern Europe*, Cambridge: Cambridge University Press.

Hilferding, R. (1910) *Das Finanzkapital*, Vienna. (Published by Routledge in 1981 as *Finance Capital*, ed. Tom Bottomore.)

Hinsley, F. (1973) *Nationalism and the International System*, London: Hodder and Stoughton.

Hobsbawm, E. (1992) *Nations and Nationalism since 1870*, Cambridge: Cambridge University Press.

Hodza, M. (1942) *Federation in Central Europe: Reflections and Reminiscences*, London: Jarrold.

Hoffman, G. (1967) 'The political bases of the Austrian nationality problem' in *Austrian History Yearbook*, vol. III, Part 1.

Holborn, H. (1967) 'The final disintegration of the Habsburg Monarchy' in *Austrian History Yearbook*, vol. III, Part 2.

Holzman, F. (1976) *International Trade under Communism*, New York: Basic Books.

—— (1986a) 'The significance of Soviet subsidies to Eastern Europe', *Comparative Economic Studies*, vol. 28, no. 1.

—— (1986b) 'Further thoughts on the significance of Soviet subsidies to Eastern Europe', *Comparative Economic Studies*, vol. 28, no. 3.

—— (1987) *The Economics of Soviet Bloc Trade and Finance*, Boulder, Colo., and London: Westview Press.

Hristov, H. (1985) *A History of Bulgaria*, Sofia: Sofia Press.

Huertas, T. (1977) *Economic Growth and Economic Policy in a Multinational Setting: the Habsburg Monarchy, 1841–1865*, New York: Arno Press.

Hus, J. (1972) *The Letters of John Hus*, Manchester: Manchester University Press.

Ignatiev, M. (1993) *Blood and Belonging: Journeys into the New Nationalism*, London: Chatto and Windus/BBC Books.

Ignotus, P. (1972) *Hungary*, London: Benn.

Inotai, A. (1994) 'Transforming the East: Western illusions and strategies', *Hungarian Quarterly*, vol. 35, no. 133.

Irvine, H. (1923) *The Making of Rural Europe*, London: Allen and Unwin.

Issawi, C. (1989) 'The Middle East in the world context' in Sabagh, G. (ed.) *The Modern Economic and Social History of the Middle East in its World Context*, Cambridge: Cambridge University Press.

Jackman, R. (1994) 'Economic policy and employment in the transition economies of Central and Eastern Europe: what have we learned?', *International Labour Review*, vol. 133, no. 3.

Jackson, G. (1966) *Comintern and Peasant in Eastern Europe, 1919–1930*, New York: Columbia University Press.

Janos, A. (1982) *The Politics of Backwardness in Hungary, 1825–1945*, Princeton, N.J.: Princeton University Press.

Jaszi, O. (1929) *The Dissolution of the Habsburg Monarchy*, Chicago: University of Chicago Press.

Jeffries, I. (ed.) (1981) *The Industrial Enterprise in Eastern Europe*, New York: Praeger.

—— (1990) *A Guide to the Socialist Economies*, London: Routledge.

——— (1992a) 'The impact of reunification on the East German economy' in Osmond (1992).

——— (ed.) (1992b) *Industrial Reform in Socialist Countries: from Restructuring to Revolution*, Aldershot: Edward Elgar.

——— (1993) *Socialist Economies and the Transition to the Market: a Guide*, London: Routledge.

——— (1996a) *A Guide to the Economies in Transition*, London: Routledge.

——— (ed.) (1996b) *Problems of Economic and Political Transformation in the Balkans*, London: Pinter.

Jeffries, I., Melzer, M. (eds), and Breuning, E. (advisory ed.) (1987) *The East German Economy*, London: Croom Helm.

Jelavich, B. (1983a) *A History of the Balkans*, vol. I, Cambridge: Cambridge University Press.

——— (1983b) *A History of the Balkans*, vol. II, Cambridge: Cambridge University Press.

Jelavich, C. and Jelavich, B. (eds) (1963) *The Balkans in Transition*, Berkeley: University of California Press.

——— (1977) *The Establishment of the Balkan National States, 1804–1920*, Seattle: University of Washington Press.

Jelavich, C. and Rath, R. (eds) (1967) *Austrian History Yearbook*, vol. III, Parts 1 and 2.

Jenks, W.A. (1967) 'Economics, constitutionalism, administration and class structure in the Monarchy', in *Austrian History Yearbook*, vol. III, Part I.

Johnson, C. (1962) *Peasant Nationalism and Communist Power*, Stanford, Calif.: Stanford University Press.

Joll, J. (1977) *Gramsci*, Glasgow: Collins–Fortuna.

Jones, E. (1981) *The European Miracle*, Cambridge: Cambridge University Press.

Kaminski, A. (1975) 'Neo-serfdom in Poland-Lithuania', *Slavic Review*, vol. XXXIV.

Kaminsky, H. (1967) *A History of the Hussite Revolution*, Berkeley: University of California Press.

Kann, R. (1950a) *The Multinational Empire*, vol. I, New York: Columbia University Press.

——— (1950b) *The Multinational Empire*, vol. II, New York: Columbia University Press.

——— (1967) 'The dynasty and imperial idea' in *Austrian History Yearbook*, vol. III, Part 1.

——— (1974) *A History of the Habsburg Empire, 1526–1918*, Berkeley: University of California Press.

Karpat, K. (1972) 'The transformation of the Ottoman state, 1789–1908', *International Journal of Middle East Studies*, vol. 3.

Kaser, M. (1967) *Comecon: Integration Problems of Planned Economies*, London: Oxford University Press.

——— (1981) 'The industrial enterprise in Bulgaria' in Jeffries (1981).

——— (1986) 'Albania under and after Enver Hoxha', US Congress, Joint Economic Committee, Washington, D.C.: Government Printing Office.

Kaser, M. and Radice, E. (eds) (1986) *The Economic History of Eastern Europe*, vols I and II, Oxford: Oxford University Press.

Katus, L. (1970) 'Economic growth in Hungary during the age of dualism, 1867–1913: a quantitative analysis', in Pamlenyi, E. (ed.) *Social-Economic Researches on the History of East-Central Europe*, Budapest: Akademiai Kiado.

Kaufmann, T. (1995) *Court, Cloister and City: the Art and Culture of Central Europe, 1450–1800*, London: Weidenfeld and Nicolson.

Kavka, F. (1960) *An Outline of Czechoslovak History*, Prague: Orbis.

——— (1994) 'Bohemia' in Scribner *et al.* (1994).

Keane, J. (ed.) (1993) *Civil Society and the State: New European Perspectives*, London: Verso.

Kedourie, E. (1960) *Nationalism*, London: Hutchinson, fourth edition (1993).

Keens-Soper, M. (1989) 'The liberal state and nationalism in postwar Europe', *History of European Ideas*, vol. 10, no. 6.

Kennan, G. (1979) *The Decline of Bismarck's European Order: Franco-Russian Relations, 1875–1890*, Princeton, N.J.: Princeton University Press.

Kennedy, P. (1989) *The Rise and Fall of the Great Powers*, London: Harper-Collins Fontana.

Kidd, M., Malinovsky, W. and Wittlin, J. (eds) (1943) *For Your Freedom and Ours: Polish Progressive Spirit through the Centuries*, New York: Frederic Ungar.

Kiraly, B. (1975) 'Neo-serfdom in Hungary', *Slavic Review*, vol. 34.

Kiss, C. (1987) 'Central European writers about Central Europe' in Schöpflin and Wood (1989).

Kitchen, M. (1976) *Fascism*, London: Macmillan.

Kitromiledes, P. (1995) 'Europe and the dilemmas of modern Greek conscience' in Carabott (1995).

Klaniczay, T. (1992) 'Hungary' in Porter and Teich (1992).

Klaus, V. (1992a) 'Policy dilemmas of Eastern European reforms: notes of an insider' in A. Prindle (ed.) *Banking and Finance in Eastern Europe*, London: Woodhead-Faulkner.

—— (1992b) 'Transition: an insider's view', *Problems of Communism*, January–April.

Kleinwächter, F. (1883) *Die Kartelle. Ein Beitrag zur Frage der Organisation der Volkswirtschaft*, Innsbruck.

Klima, A. (1957) 'Industrial development in Bohemia, 1648–1781', *Past and Present*, no. 11.

Kochanowicz, J. (1989) 'The Polish economy and the evolution of democracy' in Chirot (1989a).

Kohn, H. (1944) *The Idea of Nationalism: a Study in the Origins of Background*, New York: Macmillan (second edition 1961).

—— (1967) 'Was the collapse inevitable?' in *Austrian History Yearbook*, vol. III, Part 2.

Kolankiewicz, G. (1994) 'Consensus and competition in the eastern enlargement of the EU', *International Affairs*, vol. 70.

Kolankiewicz, G. and Lewis, P. (1988) *Poland: Politics, Economics and Society*, London: Pinter.

Kolinsky, M. (1974) *Continuity and Change in European Society*, London: Croom Helm.

Komlos, J. (1981) 'Economic growth and industrialization in Hungary, 1830–1913', *Journal of European Economic History*, vol. 10, no. 1.

—— (1983a) *The Habsburg Monarchy as a Customs Union: Economic Development in Austria-Hungary in the Nineteenth Century*, Princeton, N.J.: Princeton University Press.

—— (ed.) (1983b) *Economic Development in the Habsburg Monarchy in the Nineteenth Century*, New York: Columbia University Press.

Konrad, G. (1984) *Antipolitics: an Essay*, London: Harcourt Brace.

—— (1986) 'Is the dream of Central Europe still alive?' in *Cross Currents: a Yearbook of Central Europe Culture*, vol. 5.

Konrad, G. and Szelenyi, I. (1979) *The Intellectuals on the Road to Class Power*, New York: Harcourt Brace.

Koralka, J. (1967) 'Comment' in *Austrian History Yearbook*, vol. III, Part 1.

Korbonski, A. (1990) 'CMEA, economic integration, and *perestroika*, 1949–89', *Studies in Comparative Communism*, vol. XXIII, no. 1.

Kornhauser, W. (1960) *The Politics of Totalitarianism*, third edition, London: Routledge.

Kornai, J. (1986) 'The Hungarian reform process: visions, hopes and reality', *Journal of Economic Literature*, vol. XXIX (December).

—— (1990) *The Road to a Free Economy*, New York: W.W. Norton.

—— (1992) *The Socialist System: the Political Economy of Communism*, Oxford: Oxford University Press.

Kostanick, H. (1963) 'The geopolitics of the Balkans' in Jelavich and Jelavich (1963).

Koves, A. (1983) 'Implicit subsidies and some issues of economic relations within Comecon', in *Aeta Oeconomica*, vol. 13.

—— (1992) *Central and East European Economies in Transition: the International Dimension*, Boulder, Colo.: Westview Press.

Kramer, H. (1993) 'The European Community's response to the "new Eastern Europe"', *Journal of Common Market Studies*, vol. 31, no. 2.

Krofta, K. (1932) 'Bohemia in the Fourteenth Century' in Bury, J. (ed.) *The Cambridge Medieval History*, vol. VII, Cambridge: Cambridge University Press.

—— (1936) 'Bohemia in the Fifteenth Century' in *The Cambridge Medieval History*, vol. VIII, Cambridge: Cambridge University Press.

Kukiel, M. (1955) *Czartoryski and European Unity*, Princeton, N.J.: Princeton University Press.

Kumar, K. (1992) 'The 1989 revolutions and the idea of Europe', *Political Studies*, vol. XL (September).

Kundera, M. (1984) 'The tragedy of Central Europe', *New York Review of Books*, 26 April 1994.

Kusy, M. (1989) 'We, Central European East Europeans' in Schöpflin and Wood (1989).

Lafore, L. (1971) *The Long Fuse: an Interpretation of the Origins of World War I*, Philadelphia: Lippincott.

Lampe, J. (1975) 'Varieties of unsuccessful industrialization: the Balkan states before 1914', *Journal of Economic History*, vol. 35.

—— (1986) *The Bulgarian Economy in the Twentieth Century*, London: Croom Helm.

—— (1989) 'Imperial borderlands or capitalist periphery? Redefining Balkan backwardness, 1520–1914' in Chirot (1989a).

Lampe, J. and Jackson, M. (1982) *Balkan Economic History 1550–1950*, Bloomington: Indiana University Press.

Lasswell, H. (1941) 'The garrison state', *American Journal of Sociology*, vol. 46.

Layard, R. (1993) Comment in *Transition*, vol. 1, no. 3.

Lenin, V. (1964) *Collected Works*, vol. 21, Moscow: Progress Publishers.

Leslie, R. (1971) *The Polish Question*, London: Historical Association.

—— (ed.) (1980) *The History of Poland since 1863*, Cambridge: Cambridge University Press.

Lewis, B. (1961) *The Emergence of Modern Turkey*, London: Oxford University Press.

Light, M. (1994) 'The USSR/CIS and democratization in Eastern Europe' in Pridham *et al.* (1994).

Linz, J. (1979) 'Some notes toward a comparative study of fascism in sociological historical perspective' in Laqueur, W. (ed.) *Fascism: a Reader's Guide*, Harmondsworth: Penguin.

Lomax, B. (1976) *Hungary, 1956*, London: Allison and Busby.

Longworth, P. (1994) *The Making of Eastern Europe*, London: Macmillan.

Lydall, H. (1989) *Yugoslavia in Crisis*, Oxford: Clarendon Press.

Macartney, C. (1969) *The Habsburg Empire, 1790–1918*, London: Weidenfeld and Nicolson.

Macartney, C. and Palmer, A. (1962) *Independent Eastern Europe*, London: Macmillan.

Macek, J. (1958) *The Hussite Movement in Bohemia*, second edition, Prague: Orbis.

—— (1992) 'Bohemia and Moravia' in Porter and Teich (1992).

McFarlane, B. (1988) *Yugoslavia: Politics, Economics and Society*, London: Pinter.

McKinnon, R. (1994) 'Financial growth and macroeconomic stability in China, 1978–92: implications for Russia and other transitional economies', *Journal of Comparative Economics*, vol. 18, no. 3.

Macurek, J. (1948) 'The achievements of the Slavonic Congress', *Slavonic Review*, vol. XXVI.

Maczak, A. (1982) 'The structure of power in the Commonwealth of the sixteenth and seventeenth centuries' in Fedorowicz (1982).

—— (1992) 'Poland' in Porter and Teich (1992).

Maczak, A., Samsonowicz, H. and Burke, U. (eds) (1985) *East-Central Europe in Transition: from the Fourteenth to the Seventeenth centuries*, Cambridge: Cambridge University Press.

Majewski, W. (1982) 'The Polish art of war in the sixteenth and seventeenth centuries' in Fedorowicz (1982).

Majone, G. (1992) 'Regulatory federalism in the European Community', *Government and Policy*, vol. 10.

Makkai, L. (1975a) 'The origins of the Hungarian people and state' in Pamlenyi (1975).

—— (1975b) 'The independent Hungarian feudal monarchy to the battle of Mohacs (1000–1526)' in Pamlenyi (1975).

—— (1975c) 'From the battle of Mohacs to 1711' in Pamlenyi (1975).

—— (1975d) 'Neo-serfdom: its origins and nature in East-Central Europe', *Slavic Review*, vol. 34.

Malcolm, N. (1994) *Bosnia: a Short History*, London: Macmillan.

Malowist, M. (1959) 'The economic and social development of the Baltic countries from the fifteenth to the seventeenth centuries', *Economic History Review*, vol. XII.

—— (1974) 'Problems of the growth of the national economy of Central Eastern Europe in the late Middle Ages', *Journal of European Economic History*, vol. 2.

Mamatey, V. (1967) 'Legalizing the collapse of Austria-Hungary at the Paris Peace Conference', *Austrian History Yearbook*, vol. 3, Part 2.

Mansfield, P. (1992) *A History of the Middle East*, Harmondsworth: Penguin.

Marer, P. (1974) 'Soviet economic policy in Eastern Europe' in US Congress Joint Economic Committee, *Reorientation and Commercial Relations of the Economies of Eastern Europe*, Washington, D.C.: Government Printing Office.

Marrese, M. (1986) 'CMEA: effective but cumbersome political economy', *International Organisation*, vol. 40, no. 2.

Marrese, M. and Vanous, J. (1983) *Soviet Subsidization of Trade with Eastern Europe*, Berkeley: Institute of International Studies.

März, E. (1953) 'Some economic aspects of the nationality conflict in the Habsburg Empire', *Journal of Central European Affairs*, vol. 13.

Matlock, J. (1996) 'Dealing with a Russia in turmoil', *Foreign Affairs*, vol. 75, no. 3.

Matvejevic, P. (1989) 'Central Europe seen from the east of Europe' in Schöpflin and Wood (1989).

May, A. (1951) *The Hapsburg Monarchy, 1867–1914*, Cambridge, Mass.: Harvard University Press.

Mellor, R. (1971) *Comecon: Challenge to the West*, New York: Van Nostrand.

Merritt, G. (1991) *Eastern Europe and the USSR: the Challenge of Freedom*, London: Kogan Page.

Miall, H. (ed.) (1994) *Redefining Europe*, London: Pinter.

Michnik, A. (1985) *Letters from Prison and other Essays*, Berkeley: University of California Press.

Mikus, J. (1977) *Slovakia and the Slovaks*, Washington, D.C.: Three Continents Press.

Milosz, C. (1953) *The Captive Mind*, London: Secker and Warburg.

—— (1986) 'Central European attitudes' in Schöpflin and Wood (1989).

Mitchell, B. (1978) *European Historical Statistics, 1750-1970*, London: Macmillan.

Mitrany, D. (1930) *The Land and the Peasant in Romania*, London: Oxford University Press.

—— (1945) 'Introduction', in PEP (1945).

—— (1951) *Marx against the Peasant: a Study in Social Dogmatism*, Chapel Hill: University of North Carolina Press.

Molnar, M. (1971) *Budapest 1956*, London: Allen and Unwin.

Moore, B. (1977) *Social Origins of Dictatorship and Democracy*, Harmondsworth: Penguin.

Moore, W. (1945) *Economic Demography of Southern and Eastern Europe*, Geneva: League of Nations.

Murrell, P. (1992a) 'Evolutionary and radical approaches to economic reform', *Economics of Planning*, vol. 25, no. 1.

—— (1992b) 'Evolution in economics and in the economic reform of the centrally planned economies' in Clague and Rausser (1992).

—— (1993) 'What is shock therapy? What did it do in Poland and Russia?', *Post-Soviet Affairs*, vol. 9, no. 2.

Mussolini, B. (1932) 'The doctrine of fascism' in *Enciclopedia Italiana*, reprinted in Oakeshott (1940).

Myant, M. (1989) *The Czechoslovak Economy 1948–88: the Battle for Economic Reform*, Cambridge: Cambridge University Press.

Namier, L. (1946) *1848: the Revolution of the Intellectuals*, Cambridge: Cambridge University Press.

Nelson, G. (1993) 'Agricultural policy reform in Eastern Europe', *American Journal of Agricultural Economics*, vol. 75, no. 3.

Neuber, A. (1993) 'Towards a political economy of transition in Eastern Europe', *Journal of International Development*, vol. 5, no. 5.

Nolte, E. (1969) *Three Faces of Fascism*, New York: Mentor.

Nove, A. (1994) 'A gap in transition models? A comment on Gomulka', *Europe–Asia Studies*, vol. 46, no. 5.

Oakeshott, M. (ed.) (1940) *The Social and Political Doctrines of Contemporary Europe*, London: Basic Books.

—— (1975) *On Human Conduct*, Oxford: Clarendon Press.

Obolensky, D. (1974) *The Byzantine Commonwealth: Eastern Europe, 500–1453*, London: Weidenfeld and Nicolson.

Okey, R. (1982) *Eastern Europe, 1740–1980: Feudalism to Communism*, London: Hutchinson.

Osmond, J. (ed.) (1992) *German Unification*, London: Longman.

O'Sullivan, N. (1983) *Fascism*, London: Dent.

Owen, D. (1996) *Balkan Odyssey*, London: Indigo-Cassell.

Palacky, F. (1948) 'Letter sent by Frantisek Palacky to Frankfurt', *Slavonic Review*, vol. XXVI.

Palmer, A. (1970) *The Lands between: a History of East Central Europe since the Congress of Vienna*, London: Weidenfeld and Nicolson.

Pamlenyi, E. (ed.) (1975) *A History of Hungary*, London: Collet.

Pashko, G. (1991) 'The Albanian economy at the beginning of the 1990s' in Sjöberg and Wyzan (1991).

—— (1993) 'Obstacles to economic reform in Albania', *Europe–Asia Studies*, vol. 45, no. 5.

—— (1996) 'Problems of the transition in Albania, 1990–94' in Jeffries (1996b).

Pearson, R. (1983) *National Minorities in Eastern Europe, 1848–1945*, London: Macmillan.

Peter, K. (1994) 'Hungary' in Scribner *et al.* (1994).

Phare (1994) *Operational Programmes 1994*, Update no. 4, Brussels: Phare Information Office, European Commission.

Pinder, J. (1991) *The European Community and Eastern Europe*, London: Pinter.

Polisensky, J. (1974) *The Thirty Years' War*, London: New English Library.

PEP (Political and Economic Planning) (1945) *Economic Development in South-east Europe*, London: Oxford University Press.

Polonsky, A. (1974) *The Little Dictators*, London: Routledge.

Porter, R. and Teich, M. (eds) (1992) *The Renaissance in National Context*, Cambridge: Cambridge University Press.

Portes, R. (1994) 'Transformation traps', *Economic Journal*, vol. 104, no. 426.

Poznanski, K. (ed.) (1992) *Constructing Capitalism: the Reemergence of Civil Society and Liberal Economy*, Boulder, Colo.: Westview Press.

—— (1993) 'Pricing practices in the CMEA trade regime: a reappraisal', *Europe–Asia Studies*, vol. 45.

Pridham, G., Herring, E. and Sandford, G. (eds) (1994) *Building Democracy? The International Dimension of Democratization in Eastern Europe*, London: Leicester University Press.

Prout, C. (1985) *Market Socialism in Yugoslavia*, London: Oxford University Press.

Prucha, V. (1995) 'Economic development and relations, 1918–89' in Musil, J. (ed.) *The End of Czechoslovakia*, Budapest: Central European Press.

Pryor, F. (1963) *The Communist Foreign Trade System: the other Common Market*, London: Allen and Unwin.

Purs, J. (1960) 'The Industrial Revolution in the Czech Lands', *Historica*, vol. 2.

Ranki, G. (1971) 'The problem of fascism in Hungary' in Sugar (1971a).

Rath, J. (1957) *The Viennese Revolution of 1848*, Austin: University of Texas Press (reprinted in 1969 by Greenwood Press, New York).

Rau, Z. (1991) *The Reemergence of Civil Society in Eastern Europe and the Soviet Union*, Boulder, Colo.: Westview Press.

Raupach, H. (1969) 'The impact of the Great Depression on Eastern Europe', *Journal of Contemporary History*, vol. 4.

Reddaway, W., Penson, J., Halecki, O. and Dyboski, R. (eds) (1941) *The Cambridge History of Poland, 1697–1935*, Cambridge: Cambridge University Press.

—— (1950) *The Cambridge History of Poland to 1696*, Cambridge: Cambridge University Press.

Reisinger, W. (1992) *Energy and the Soviet Bloc: Alliance Politics after Stalin*, Ithaca, N.Y.: Cornell University Press.

Robson, P. (1987) *The Economics of International Integration*, London: Unwin Hyman.

Rollo, J. and Smith, A. (1992) *The Political Economy of Central Europe Trade with the European Community: Why so Sensitive?*, London: Royal Institute of International Affairs.

—— (1993) 'The political economy of Eastern European trade with the European Community', *Economic Policy*, no. 16.

Rollo, J., Batt, J., Granville, B. and Malcolm, N. (1990) *The New Eastern Europe: Western Responses*, London: Royal Institute of International Affairs (Chatham House Papers).

Ronnas, P. (1996) 'Romania: transition to underdevelopment' in Jeffries (1996b).

Rosati, D. (1992) 'The CMEA demise, trade restructuring, and trade destruction in Central and Eastern Europe', *Oxford Review of Economic Policy*, vol. 8, no. 1.

—— (1994) 'Output declines during the transition from plan to market: a consideration', *Economics of Transition*, vol. 2, no. 4.

Rose, R. (1992) 'Toward a civil economy', *Journal of Democracy*, vol. 3.

Rothschild, J. (1974) *East-Central Europe between the Two World Wars*, Seattle: University of Washington Press.

—— (1989) *Return to Diversity: a Political History of East-Central Europe since World War II*, London: Oxford University Press, second edition (1994).

Roxburgh, A. (1991) *The Second Russian Revolution*, London: BBC Books.

Rudolph, R. (1975) 'The pattern of Austrian industrial growth from the eighteenth to the early twentieth century' in *Austrian History Yearbook*, vol. II.

—— (1976) *Banking and Industrialization in Austria-Hungary, 1873–1914*, Cambridge: Cambridge University Press.

—— (1983) 'Economic revolution in Austria? The meaning of 1848 in Austrian economic history' in Komlos (1983b).

Rupnik, J. (1990) 'Central Europe or Mitteleuropa?', *Daedalus*, winter.

—— (1995) 'The international context' in Musil, J. (ed.) *The End of Czechoslovakia*, Budapest: Central European University Press.

Sachs, J. (1994) *Poland's Jump to the Market Economy*, Cambridge, Mass.: MIT Press.

—— (1995) 'Consolidating capitalism', *Foreign Policy*, no. 98.

—— (1996)'The transition at mid-decade', *American Economic Review*, Papers and Proceedings (May).

Sachs, J. and Woo, W. (1994) 'Structural factors in the economic reforms of China, Eastern Europe and the former Soviet Union', *Economic Policy*, no. 18.

Samsonowicz, H. (1982) 'Polish politics and society under the Jagiellon monarchy' in Fedorowicz (1982).

Schiavone, G. (1981) *The Institutions of Comecon*, London: Macmillan.

Schmitt, B. (1958) *The Origins of the First World War*, London: Historical Association.

Schnytzer, A. (1982) *Stalinist Economic Strategy in Practice: the Case of Albania*, London: Oxford University Press.

—— (1992) 'Albania: the purge of Stalinist economic ideology' in Jeffries (1992b).

Schonfield, A. (1973) *Europe: Journey to an Unknown Destination*, Harmondsworth: Penguin.

Schöpflin, G. (1993) *Politics in Eastern Europe*, Oxford: Blackwell.

—— (1994) 'The rise of anti-democratic movements in post-communist societies' in Miall (1994).

Schöpflin, G. and Wood, N. (eds) (1989) *In Search of Central Europe*, Totowa, N.J.: Barnes and Noble.

Schultz, G. (1972) *Revolutions and Peace Treaties 1917–1920*, London: Methuen.

Schwartz, E. (1989) 'Central Europe: what it is and what it is not' in Schöpflin and Wood (1989).

Scribner, R. (1994) 'A comparative overview' in Scribner *et al.* (1994).

Scribner, R., Porter, R. and Teich, M. (eds) (1994) *The Reformation in National Context*, Cambridge: Cambridge University Press.

Seton-Watson, H. (1945) *Eastern Europe between the Wars*, Cambridge: Cambridge University Press.

—— (1977) *Nations and States*, London: Methuen.

—— (1985) 'What is Europe, where is Europe? From mystique to politique', *Encounter*, vol. 65, no. 2.

Shafir, M. (1985) *Romania: Politics, Economics and Society*, London: Pinter.

Shaw, S. (1962) 'The aims and achievements of Ottoman rule in the Balkans', *Slavic Review*, vol. 21.

—— (1963) 'The Ottoman view of the Balkans' in Jelavich and Jelavich (1963).

Shaw, S. and Shaw, E. (1977) *A History of the Ottoman Empire and Modern Turkey*, Cambridge: Cambridge University Press.

Simecka, M. (1987) 'Which way back to Europe?' in Schöpflin and Wood (1989).

—— (1985) 'Another civilization? An other civilization?' in Schöpflin and Wood (1989).

Singleton, F. (1976) *Twentieth Century Yugoslavia*, London: Macmillan.

Sirc, L. (1979) *The Yugoslav Economy under Self-management*, London: Macmillan.

Sjöberg, Ö. and Wyzan, M. (eds) (1991) *Economic Change in the Balkan States: Albania, Bulgaria, Romania and Yugoslavia*, London: Pinter.

Sked, A. (1989) *The Decline and Fall of the Habsburg Empire, 1815–1918*, London: Longman.

Skowronek, J. (1982) 'The direction of political change in the era of national insurrection, 1795–1864' in Fedorowicz (1982).

Skwarczynski, P. (1956) 'The problem of feudalism in Poland up to the beginning of the sixteenth century', *Slavonic and East European Review*, vol. XXXIV.

Smith, A. (1991) *National Identity*, Harmondsworth: Penguin.

Smith, A. H. (1983) *The Planned Economies of Eastern Europe*, London: Croom Helm.

Smith, G. (1994) 'Can liberal democracy span the European divide?' in Miall (1994).

Sobell, V. (1984) *The Red Market*, Aldershot: Gower.

Soisson, P. (1977) *The World of Byzantium*, Geneva: Minerva.

Spinka, M. (1968) *John Hus: a Biography*, Princeton, N.J.: Princeton University Press.

—— (1972) *The Letters of John Hus*, Manchester: Manchester University Press.

Spulber, N. (ed.) (1963) 'Changes in the economic structure of the Balkans, 1860–1960' in Jelavich and Jelavich (1963).

Stalin, J. (1955a) *Works*, vol. 12, Moscow: Foreign Languages Publishing House.

—— (1955b) *Works*, vol. 13, Moscow: Foreign Languages Publishing House.

—— (1955c) *Works*, vol. 14, Moscow: Foreign Languages Publishing House.

Stavrianos, L. (1958) *The Balkans since 1453*, New York: Holt Rinehart and Winston.

—— (1963) 'The influence of the West on the Balkans' in Jelavich and Jelavich (1963).

Steams, P. (1975) *European Society in Upheaval*, New York: Macmillan.

Stoianovich, T. (1960) 'The conquering Balkan Orthodox merchant', *Journal of Economic History*, vol. 20, no. 2.

—— (1962) 'Factors in the decline of Ottoman society in the Balkans', *Slavic Review*, vol. 21.

—— (1963) 'The social foundations of Balkan politics, 1750–1941', in Jelavich and Jelavich (1963).

—— (1967) *A History of Balkan Civilization*, New York: Knopf.

Stokes, G. (1991) *From Stalinism to Pluralism: a Documentary History of Eastern Europe since 1945*, Oxford: Oxford University Press.

—— (1993) *The Walls came Tumbling Down: the Collapse of Communism in Eastern Europe*, Oxford: Oxford University Press.

Sugar, P. (1963) 'The nature of non-Germanic societies under Habsburg rule', *Slavic Review*, vol. 22.

—— (1967) 'The rise of nationalism in the Habsburg Empire' in *Austrian History Yearbook*, vol. III, Part 1.

—— (ed.) (1971a) *Native Fascism in the Successor States, 1918–1945*, Santa Barbara, Calif.: ABC-Clio Press.

—— (1971b) 'External and domestic roots of East European nationalism' in Sugar and Lederer (eds).

—— (1977) *Southeastern Europe under Ottoman Rule, 1354–1804*, Seattle: University of Washington Press.

—— (1995) (ed.) *Eastern European Nationalism in the Twentieth Century*, Washington D.C.: American University Press.

Sugar, P. and Lederer, I. (eds) (1971) *Nationalism in Eastern Europe*, Seattle: University of Washington Press.

Sutton, A. (1968–72) *Western Technology and Soviet Economic Development*, vols I, II and III, Stanford, Calif.: Stanford University Press.

Sword, K. (ed.) (1991) *The Times Guide to Eastern Europe*, second edition, London: Times Books.

Szelenyi, I. (1979) 'The position of the intelligentsia in the class structure of state socialist societies', *Critique*, nos 10–11.

Szucs, J. (1988) 'Three historical regions of Europe' in Keane (1988).

Tampke, J. (1983) *The People's Republics of Eastern Europe*, London: Croom Helm.

Taras, R. (ed.) (1992) *The Road to Disillusion: from Critical Marxism to Postcommunism in Eastern Europe*, Armonk, N.Y.: M.E. Sharpe.

Tarr, D. (1994) 'The terms-of-trade effects of moving to world prices on the countries of the former Soviet Union', *Journal of Comparative Economics*, vol. 18, no. 1.

Taylor, A.J.P. (1940) *The Habsburg Monarchy*, vols I and II, London: Macmillan.

—— (1964) *The Origins of the Second World War*, Harmondsworth: Penguin.

—— (1967) *Europe: Grandeur and Decline*, Harmondsworth: Penguin.

—— (1976) *The Habsburg Monarchy, 1809–1918*, Chicago: University of Chicago Press.

Tazbir, J. (1982) 'The fate of Polish Protestantism in the seventeenth century' in Fedorowicz (1982).

—— (1994) 'Poland' in Scribner *et al.* (1994).

Thompson, S. (1993) 'Agrarian reform in Eastern Europe following World War I: motives and outcomes', *American Journal of Agricultural Economics*, vol. 75, no. 3.

Thompson, S.H. (1933) 'Pre-Hussite heresy in Bohemia', *English Historical Review*, vol. 48.

Tiltman, H. (1934) *Peasant Europe*, London: Jarrold.

Togliatti, P. (1976) *Lectures on Fascism*, New York: International Publishers.

Topolski, J. (1981) 'Continuity and discontinuity in the development of the feudal system in Eastern Europe', *Journal of European Economic History*, vol. 10, no. 2.

—— (1982) 'Sixteenth century Poland and the turning point in European economic development' in Fedorowicz (1982).

Toynbee, A. (1954) *A Study of History*, vol. VIII, London: Oxford University Press.

Turczynski, E. (1971) 'The background of Romanian fascism' in Sugar (1971a).

Turnock, D. (1986) *The Romanian Economy in the Twentieth Century*, London: Croom Helm.

United Nations Economic Commission for Europe (1994) *Economic Survey of Europe in 1993–94*, New York: United Nations.

Vajda, M. (1986) 'Who excluded Russia from Europe?' in Schöpflin and Wood (1989).

—— (1988) 'East Central European perspectives' in Keane (1988).

Vaughan, R. (ed.) (1976) *Postwar Integration in Europe*, London: Edward Arnold.

Verdery, K. (1979) 'Internal colonialism in Austria-Hungary', *Ethnic and Racial Studies*, vol. 22.

Vlasto, A. (1970) *The Entry of the Slavs into Christendom: an Introduction to the Medieval History of the Slavs*, Cambridge: Cambridge University Press.

Vucinich, W. (1962) 'The nature of Balkan society under Ottoman rule', *Slavic Review*, vol. 21.

—— (1963) 'Some aspects of the Ottoman legacy' in Jelavich and Jelavich (1963).

—— (1965) *The Ottoman Empire: its Record and Legacy*, Princeton, N.J.: Van Nostrand.

Wädekin, K-E. (ed.) (1990) *Communist Agriculture: Farming in the Soviet Union and Eastern Europe*, London: Routledge.

Wallace, W. (1976) *Czechoslovakia*, Boulder, Colo.: Westview Press.

Wallace, W. and Clarke, R. (1986) *Comecon, Trade and the West*, London: Pinter.

Wallerstein, I. (1974a) *The Modern World System: Capitalist Agriculture and the Origins of the European World Economy*, New York: Academic Press.

—— (1974b) 'The rise and future demise of the world capitalist system', *Comparative Studies in Society and History*, vol. 16.

Wandycz, P. (1974) *The Lands of Partitional Poland, 1795–1918*, Seattle: University of Washington Press.

—— (1992) *The Price of Freedom: a History of East-Central Europe from the Middle Ages to the Present*, London: Routledge.

Warriner, D. (1950) *Revolution in Eastern Europe*, London: Turnstile Press.

Weber, E. (1964) *Varieties of Fascism*, New York: Van Nostrand.

Weitzman, M. (1993) 'Economic transition: can theory help?', *European Economic Review*, vol. 37, nos 2/3.

Weitzman, M. and Xu, C. (1993) *Chinese Township Village Enterprises as Vaguely Defined Co-operatives*, London: LSE CP no. 26.

—— (1994) 'Chinese township-village enterprises as vaguely defined co-operatives', *Journal of Comparative Economics*, vol. 18, no. 2.

Wheatcroft, A. (1995) *The Habsburgs*, London: Viking.

Whitehead, L. (1986) 'International aspects of democratization' in O'Donnell, G., Schmitter, P. and Whitehead, L. (1986) *Transitions from Authoritarian Rule*, vol. III, Baltimore: Johns Hopkins University Press.

—— (1994) 'East-Central Europe in comparative perspective' in Pridham *et al.* (1994).

Whiteside, A. (1967) 'The Germans as an integrating force in imperial Austria' in *Austrian History Yearbook*, vol. III, Part 1.

Wiener, R. (1994) *Change in Eastern Europe*, New York: Praeger.

Wiles, P. (1968) *Communist International Economics*, Oxford: Blackwell.

Williams, A. (ed.) (1994) *Reorganizing Eastern Europe*, Aldershot: Dartmouth Publishing.

Wiskemann, E. (1938) *Czechs and Germans*, London: Oxford University Press.

Woo, W. (1994) 'The art of reforming centrally planned economies: comparing China, Poland and Russia', *Journal of Comparative Economics*, vol. 18, no. 3.

Woodhouse, C. (1977) *Modern Greece: a Short History*, London: Faber.

Woods, W. (1972) *Poland: Phoenix in the East*, Harmondsworth: Penguin.

World Bank (1996) *World Development Report: from Plan to Market*, New York: Oxford University Press.

Wright, W. (1975) 'Neo-serfdom in Bohemia', *Slavic Review*, vol. 34.

Wyczanski, A. (1982) 'The problem of authority in sixteenth-century Poland' in Fedorowicz (1982).

—— (1985) 'The system of power in Poland, 1370–1648' in Fedorowicz (1985).

Wyrobisz, A. (1982) 'The arts and social prestige in Poland between the sixteenth and eighteenth centuries' in Fedorowicz (1982).

Zamoyski, A. (1987) *The Polish Way: a One Thousand Year History of the Poles and their Culture*, London: Murray.

Zeman, J. (1977) *The Hussite Movement and the Reformation in Bohemia, Moravia and Slovakia, 1350–1650*, Ann Arbor: University of Michigan Press.

Zientara, B. (1982) '*Melioratio terrae*: the thirteenth-century breakthrough in Polish history' in Fedorowicz (1982).

Zollner, E. (1967) 'The Germans as a disintegrating force', in *Austrian History Yearbook*, vol. III, Part 1.

Index

DATE DUE